S0-BSI-183

HARLEM RENAISSANCE

A Gale Critical Companion

HARLEM RENAISSANCE

A Gale Critical Companion

Volume 2: Authors A-H

Foreword by *Trudier Harris-Lopez, Ph.D.*
University of North Carolina at Chapel Hill

Janet Witalec, *Project Editor*

Detroit • New York • San Diego • San Francisco • Cleveland • New Haven, Conn. • Waterville, Maine • London • Munich

Harlem Renaissance, Vol. 2

Project Editor
Janet Witalec

Editorial
Tom Burns, Kathy D. Darrow, Lisa Gellert, Madeline S. Harris, Edna M. Hedblad, Michelle Kazensky, Jelena Krstović, Allison Marion, Ellen McGeagh, Jessica Menzo, Thomas J. Schoenberg, Lawrence J. Trudeau, Russel Whitaker

Research
Nicodemus Ford, Sarah Genik, Tamara C. Nott, Tracie A. Richardson

Permissions
Kim Davis, Susan Rudolph

Imaging and Multimedia
Leitha Etheridge-Sims, Lezlie Light, Christine O'Bryan, Kelly A. Quin

Product Design
Pamela Galbreath, Michael Logusz

Composition and Electronic Capture
Carolyn Roney

Manufacturing
Stacy L. Melson

For more information, contact
The Gale Group, Inc.
27500 Drake Rd.
Farmington Hills, MI 48331-3535
Or you can visit our internet site at
http://www.gale.com

LIBRARY OF CONGRESS CATALOGING-IN-PUBLICATION DATA

The Harlem Renaissance : a Gale critical companion / Janet Witalec, project editor.
p. cm. -- (Gale critical companion collection)
Includes bibliographical references and index.
ISBN 0-7876-6618-1 (set hardcover) -- ISBN 0-7876-6619-X (v. 1) --
ISBN 0-7876-6620-3 (v. 2) -- ISBN 0-7876-6621-1 (v. 3)
1. American literature--African American authors--History and criticism--Handbooks, manuals, etc. 2. American literature--New York (State)--New York--History and criticism--Handbooks, manuals, etc. 3. American literature--20th century--History and criticism--Handbooks, manuals, etc. 4. Harlem (New York, N.Y.)--Intellectual life--20th century--Handbooks, manuals, etc. 5. African Americans--Intellectual life--Handbooks, manuals, etc. 6. African Americans in literature--Handbooks, manuals, etc. 7. Harlem Renaissance--Handbooks, manuals, etc. I. Witalec, Janet, 1965- II. Series.
PS153.N5 H245 2003
810.9'89607307471--dc21

2002010076

Printed in the United States of America
10 9 8 7 6 5 4 3

CONTENTS

VOLUME 1

VOLUME 2

VOLUME 3

FOREWORD

In 1950, Alain Locke offered several reflective comments on the significance of the Harlem Renaissance. He considered it a movement that never surpassed the "gawky" and "pimply" stage of adolescence, one that had essentially failed in its attempt to achieve universal, objective approaches in its creations. Overall, he concluded that perhaps he and others had "expected too much of the Negro Renaissance" (*Phylon* 11 : 391). Locke, who had been one of the key supporters of and inspirational figures in the lives of several of the writers who came to prominence during that period, was perhaps more critical of what the movement had achieved than his contemporaries during the Renaissance or in the 1950s. He was certainly more disparaging than literary evaluations have proven to be in the past five decades. The period of the1920s has become one of the most written about in African American literary history and one in which numerous scholars specialize. And not undeservedly so. By most standards of measurement, especially ones that might take into consideration a before and after effect, the Harlem Renaissance, or the New Negro Movement as some prefer to call it, is arguably *the* defining moment in African American literary creativity.

That moment occurred because of the confluence of historical and social forces. The devastation the boll weevil wrought on southern crops and the ensuing economic chaos led many Blacks to migrate from the South to northern cities as a part of what became known as the Great Migration, a mass movement that noted artist Jacob Lawrence captures vividly and colorfully in his Migration Series. Economic opportunity the North represented was appealing not only because of the decline in the southern farm economy but because the mythical presentations by relatives of Black people who had migrated north made it equally glamorous. The legendary promise of the North and particularly New York City, as Rudolph Fisher depicts in "The City of Refuge" (1925) and about which Langston Hughes rhapsodizes in several poems as well as his autobiographies, drew Black people from the southern United States, the Caribbean, and Africa. Harlem thus more than tripled its Black population between 1900 and 1930. Word of mouth was powerful, but determined efforts to gather a critical mass of young Black creative artists were also factors in bringing about the literary production known as the Harlem Renaissance. Charles Spurgeon Johnson, who became editor of *Opportunity,* the official organ of the National Urban League, directed his secretary, Ethel Nance, to write to aspiring young writers and artists and encourage their migration to New York. While many responded eagerly, it was only with repeated coaxing that Aaron Douglas, who became the foremost artist of the period, was persuaded to leave his position as an art teacher in Kansas and head to

New York. Of the writers who are now prominently identified with the movement, Hughes came from Kansas and Ohio, Zora Neale Hurston from Florida, Wallace Thurman from Idaho, Claude McKay from Jamaica, Eric Walrond from British Guiana, Jean Toomer from Washington, D.C., Dorothy West from Boston, and Countee Cullen from Kentucky (although he always claimed New York as his point of origin).

From its beginnings, therefore, the Harlem Renaissance was spawned by a mixture of happenstance and deliberate planning. This was the first time in African American literary history that editors and writers saw the possibilities of collaborative creative efforts—or at least creative efforts expended in the midst of others who were also about literary production. Such concerted effort distinguished the 1920s from what had gone before, distinguished the New Negro with a self-directed cultural purpose from the Old Negro who was often driven by circumstance. Awareness of themselves as artists in a variety of media was one of the distinguishing characteristics of the editors, writers, visual artists, and musicians who became the most well-known figures of the Harlem Renaissance and about whom Hughes wrote in his first autobiography, *The Big Sea* (1940), and whom Thurman fictionalized in *Infants of the Spring* (1932).

The movement thus marks the period in African American literary development during which Black writers could *claim* their creativity in ways that were not previously available to them. The tradition of slave—or *freedom*—narratives was the most productive group effort prior to the Harlem Renaissance (the grouping, however, was not something the writers themselves orchestrated); the productivity was frequently cast in a white envelope/Black message mold. Abolitionists and other persons who identified potential writers as well as those who published their works often had their own agendas for what Black narrators could or should put forth in their own so-called individualized works. Black writers did not control the means of production of their words or the editorial prerogatives that sometimes shaped their final form. Black literary dependency on white cultural philanthropy was the order of the day. While it would be rash to suggest that such limitations completely disappeared during the 1920s, it is nonetheless reasonable to argue that persons of African descent had a stronger say in what they published, where, and under what circumstances. Of course we are familiar with the stories of how Carl Van Vechten, guru and midwife extraordinaire of the Renaissance, read, revised, and suggested further revisions to *The Weary Blues* (1926), Hughes's first volume of poetry. And the tales of Mrs. Charlotte Osgood Mason's attempts to interfere in the creativity of Hughes and Hurston are equally well known. More to the point, however, are the instances in which African American writers were mostly in charge of what they produced and the manner of its production.

Two significant outlets for "in charge" production were *Opportunity* magazine and its counterpart, the *Crisis,* the official publication of the National Association for the Advancement of Colored People (NAACP). The latter was developed by the eminent W. E. B. Du Bois, who served as general editor; Jessie Fauset served as literary editor, a position from which she would encourage many of the younger writers. For these two publications, Black writers did not go, hat in hand, to white editors requesting publication of their work. As African Americans, both Charles S. Johnson and Du Bois were acutely aware of the need for as much African American control of publishing outlets as possible. This position, combined with their general notions of mission and service, led both editors to sponsor contests to encourage Black writing even as they regularly published what came to them voluntarily. By establishing the outlets for publication, determining the criteria, and passing judgment on the works, these editors and their staffs moved dramatically away from the censorship that had defined cross-racial publication by writers such as Paul Laurence Dunbar and Charles W. Chesnutt prior to this period. Again, an assessment of the Harlem Renaissance in this area is not to suggest that all was sweetness and light, for both Johnson and Du Bois had rather specific notions of what they believed should be published. The point is that African Americans, whatever their criteria, were making the decisions that they had not previously made except for newspapers, white-owned/Black-edited small magazines (*Voice of the Negro*), and denominational outlets (the *Christian Recorder,* the *A.M.E. Church Review*).

The claiming of creativity was even history-making in the anthologies that appeared during this period. Two of the most important were *The Book of American Negro Poetry,* edited and published by James Weldon Johnson in 1922, and *The New Negro,* edited and published by Alain Locke in 1925 (expanded from a special issue of *Survey Graphic*). Black writers had appeared in yearbooks such as William Stanley Braithwaite's *Anthology of Magazine Verse* (beginning in 1913), but Johnson's and Locke's were volumes devoted almost exclusively to African American writers. Johnson was careful to include as many up-and-coming poets as he could locate, and he expanded his original inclusions when the volume was revised and republished in 1931. Locke's volume, of course, served as the defining statement for the Renaissance, just as Hughes's "The Negro Artist and the Racial Mountain" (1926) served as the defining manifesto for younger Black writers. Locke wanted to assure his readers that the Old Negro was dead, that this was an age of unparalleled creativity by African American writers. While it has become clear that Locke, even in his seeming expansiveness, gave preferential treatment to certain kinds of writers and subjects, it is nonetheless more significant that he was doing the choosing, that an African American scholar, researcher, and writer was in charge of shaping a volume that showcased the richness of African American cultural creativity. The bountifulness of that creativity could not be constrained by the mind that offered it for public consumption. Thus the legacy of the Renaissance was measurable from even that single volume of claimed creativity.

An even more proper appreciation of the claiming of African American creativity during the Harlem Renaissance might begin in the middle of the 1920s, with the publication of the little magazine called *Fire!!* (1926). The work of Hughes, Hurston, Thurman, Richard Bruce Nugent, Gwendolyn Bennett, and a few others, it represented the efforts of younger African American writers to claim their creativity from their elders, all members of Du Bois's "talented tenth" of well-educated Blacks with leadership potential (and often "high yaller"), as well as from potential white exploiters. *Fire!!* was in bas relief against the backdrop of prevailing elder wisdom represented by the likes of Du Bois, James Weldon Johnson, and Braithwaite, all of whom espoused best-foot-forward, universalized portrayals of Black experience that could serve to bridge the gaps between Blacks and whites. *Fire!!* represented the first time a group of young African American writers consciously sought to define themselves against a larger tradition, which means that it was the first time that there were measurable *layerings* of African American literary creativity. When Nugent and Thurman flipped a coin to see who would write a story on prostitution and who on drugs, they were claiming their creativity as young writers breaking away from their elders: "If black people are pleased, it doesn't matter."

The fact that *Fire!!* exists would be reason enough to label the 1920s a noteworthy period of African American creativity. Here were several young Black writers bent upon cultural production at a time when it was not yet historically established that they indeed had a culture. That independence of spirit is no less remarkable than that exhibited by Frederick Douglass and others who escaped from slavery in the South and went on to produce narratives about their experiences. The difference is one of orchestration, not one of kind. Whereas Douglass was manipulated—though his genius nonetheless showed through that manipulation—these young writers made their own decisions about who and what to publish. They may have failed to sustain the magazine, but what they sought to accomplish is the guiding motivation for scholarly focus on the Harlem Renaissance: the documentation of African American creative genius as widespread, diverse, and ever evolving.

A careful look at Johnson's *Book of Negro Poetry* will reveal that several of the figures Johnson singled out for greatness did not make it. Of those who did, Countee Cullen, Langston Hughes, and Claude McKay have garnered critical attention worthy of their talent, and that attention continues. In 2002, when the Academy of American Poets conducted a survey to determine who was the most well-known American poet, Langston Hughes won by a landslide. It would have been difficult in the 1920s, however, for literary observers to conclude that Hughes's reputation would exceed Cullen's, for Cullen was the darling of critics and critical readers. His imitation of Keatsian poetic forms undoubtedly informed those judgments, whereas Hughes's focus on the Black masses was a bit more to the left than some elitists in the "talented tenth" tradition might have wished. Ensuing decades, especially the Black-centered 1960s, coupled with Hughes's own longevity and interaction with later writers, probably influenced ultimate scholarly and popular preference for Hughes.

Hughes and McKay, whose strong emotional sentiments overshadowed his Shakespearean sonnets, make clear the importance of audience as an ongoing, shaping force in Harlem Renaissance successes. The increase in Black audiences during the 1920s, which found their parallels in the 1960s, spurred acceptance by some of sentiments that were slightly more militant than many of Cullen's sugar-coated creations. Publication in outlets aimed primarily at Black people during the 1920s was a marked contrast to the outlets in which Dunbar and Chesnutt had published their early works, such as the *Atlantic Monthly*. Talented poets such as Hughes and McKay, along with a host of other writers during the 1920s, thus facilitated the institutionalization of African American literary arts within Black communities.

The anthologies, volumes of poetry, novels, dramas, and newspaper columns that the Harlem Renaissance has yielded make the claim more than anything else for the period having been substantive and of greater import than Locke allowed. We can certainly measure individual accomplishment, as with Hughes's focus on the blues as a source for literary creativity in *The Weary Blues,* or Jean Toomer's experimentation in *Cane* (1923), or Hurston's concern with colorphobia in *Color Struck* (1926). Of greater import is the stage-setting or path-breaking that these accomplishments pointed toward. *Fire!!* easily leads to *Black World/Negro Digest* and on to *Callaloo. Cane* anticipates works such as Ntozake Shange's *Sassafras, Cypress and Indigo* (1982), Alice Walker's *The Color Purple* (1982), and practically all of Toni Morrison's novels. Hurston is godmother to a host of African American women writers, including Walker, Tina McElroy Ansa, and Gloria Naylor. Thus institution-building and midwifing a literary tradition were functions Harlem Renaissance writers served for ensuing generations as assuredly as Alain Locke and Jessie Fauset midwifed them.

Godmothering, however, is not always altruistic, as was the case with Mrs. Mason's impact on Hurston as well as on Hughes. The issue of patronage for African American writers remains a central concern in the twenty-first century. What does a writer owe to the providers of fellowships and leisure time to write? At what point does a writer who receives such aid give up his or her autonomy to his or her work? The issue is relevant not only to isolated writers trying to find the funds for a semester's leave from teaching, but also to the choreographer or the dramatist or the musician whose creative space can be provided by funders who may or may not be sympathetic to the total direction of the project. The Harlem Renaissance gave us models for thinking through these crucial issues and for weighing the shackles as well as the opportunities of patronage across racial lines. That continues to be a source of exploration in contemporary scholars' understanding of the factors that influenced how successful some of the most important writers of the Harlem Renaissance were —or were not—in claiming their creativity.

In the early years of the twenty-first century, the Harlem Renaissance is a scholarly industry. It became institutionalized with the advent of Black studies courses and programs in American academies in the 1960s and 1970s. No scholar of African American literary studies could be taken seriously without in-depth knowledge of the Harlem Renaissance. No doctoral candidate studying for written and oral examinations could expect to be taken seriously without detailed knowledge of the Harlem Renaissance. In contrast to the 1960s, when a single survey course might have sufficed to introduce students to African American literature, today there are two and three courses designed to provide that coverage. Specialized courses focusing exclusively on the Harlem Renaissance are offered routinely. Equally as significant, graduate students in African American literary studies remain engrossed enough by the Renaissance to select writers and topics relevant to it for the subjects of their masters theses and doctoral dissertations. Their interest, in turn, has been guided in large part by the numerous scholarly studies of the Harlem Renaissance that have been published in the past thirty years. In striking contrast to Alain Locke's assessment, the Harlem Renaissance is alive and well in every college and university in the United States where students explore the multi-faceted meanings and ramifications of the literature, its producers, and its production. These three volumes are welcome additions to those ongoing dialogues and will undoubtedly provide invaluable insights that will continue to illustrate the undying significance of the Harlem Renaissance.

—Trudier Harris-Lopez, Ph.D.
J. Carlyle Sitterson Professor of English
University of North Carolina at Chapel Hill

The Gale Critical Companion Collection

In response to a growing demand for relevant criticism and interpretation of perennial topics and important literary movements throughout history, the Gale Critical Companion Collection (GCCC) was designed to meet the research needs of upper high school and undergraduate students. Each edition of GCCC focuses on a different literary movement or topic of broad interest to students of literature, history, multicultural studies, humanities, foreign language studies, and other subject areas. Topics covered are based on feedback from a standing advisory board consisting of reference librarians and subject specialists from public, academic, and school library systems.

The GCCC is designed to complement Gale's existing Literary Criticism Series (LCS) , which includes such award-winning and distinguished titles as *Nineteenth-Century Literature Criticism* (NCLC), *Twentieth-Century Literary Criticism* (TCLC), and *Contemporary Literary Criticism* (CLC). Like the LCS titles, the GCCC editions provide selected reprinted essays that offer an inclusive range of critical and scholarly response to authors and topics widely studied in high school and undergraduate classes; however, the GCCC also includes primary source documents, chronologies, sidebars, supplemental photographs, and other material not included in the LCS products. The graphic and supplemental material is designed to extend the usefulness of the critical essays and provide students with historical and cultural context on a topic or author's work. GCCC titles will benefit larger institutions with ongoing subscriptions to Gale's LCS products as well as smaller libraries and school systems with less extensive reference collections. Each edition of the GCCC is created as a stand- alone set providing a wealth of information on the topic or movement. Importantly, the overlap between the GCCC and LCS titles is 15% or less, ensuring that LCS subscribers will not duplicate resources in their collection.

Editions within the GCCC are either single-volume or multi-volume sets, depending on the nature and scope of the topic being covered. Topic entries and author entries are treated separately, with entries on related topics appearing first, followed by author entries in an A-Z arrangement. Each volume is approximately 500 pages in length and includes approximately 50 images and sidebar graphics. These sidebars include summaries of important historical events, newspaper clippings, brief biographies of important non-literary figures, complete poems or passages of fiction written by the author, descriptions of events in the related arts (music, visual arts, and dance), and so on.

The reprinted essays in each GCCC edition explicate the major themes and literary techniques of the authors and literary works. It is important to note that approximately 85% of the essays reprinted in GCCC editions are full-text, meaning that they are reprinted in their entirety, including footnotes and lists of abbreviations. Essays are selected based on their coverage of the seminal works and themes of an author, and based on the importance of those essays to an appreciation of the author's contribution to the movement and to literature in general. Gale's editors select those essays of most value to upper high school and undergraduate students, avoiding narrow and highly pedantic interpretations of individual works or of an author's canon.

Scope of Harlem Renaissance

Harlem Renaissance, the inaugural set in the Gale Critical Companion Collection, consists of three volumes. Each volume includes a detailed table of contents, a foreword on the Harlem Renaissance written by noted scholar Trudier Harris-Lopez, and a descriptive chronology of key events of the movement. The main body of volume 1 consists of entries on five topics relevant to the Harlem Renaissance, including 1) Overviews and General Studies; 2) Social, Economic, and Political Factors that Influenced the Harlem Renaissance; 3) Publishing and Periodicals during the Harlem Renaissance; 4) Performing Arts during the Harlem Renaissance; and 5) Visual Arts during the Harlem Renaissance. Volumes 2 and 3 include entries on thirty-three authors and literary figures associated with the movement, including such notables as Countee Cullen, W. E. B. Du Bois, Jessie Redmon Fauset, Langston Hughes, Zora Neale Hurston, Claude McKay, and Jean Toomer, as well as entries on individuals who have garnered less attention, but whose contributions to the Harlem Renaissance are noteworthy, such as Alice Dunbar-Nelson, Angelina Weld Grimké, Georgia Douglas Johnson, Richard Bruce Nugent, and Willis Richardson.

Organization of the Harlem Renaissance

A *Harlem Renaissance* topic entry consists of the following elements:

- The **Introduction** defines the subject of the entry and provides social and historical information important to understanding the criticism.
- The list of **Representative Works** identifies writings and works by authors and figures associated with the subject. The list is divided into alphabetical sections by name; works listed under each name appear in chronological order. The genre and publication date of each work is given. Unless otherwise indicated, dramas are dated by first performance, not first publication.
- Entries generally begin with a section of **Primary Sources**, which includes essays, speeches, social history, newspaper accounts and other materials that were produced during the time of the Harlem Renaissance.
- Reprinted **Criticism** in topic entries is arranged thematically. Topic entries commonly begin with general surveys of the subject or essays providing historical or background information, followed by essays that develop particular aspects of the topic. For example, the Publishing and Periodicals topic entry in volume 1 of *Harlem Renaissance* begins with a section providing an overview of the topic. This is followed by three other sections: African American Writers and Mainstream Publishers; Anthologies: *The New Negro* and Others; and African American Periodicals and the Harlem Renaissance. Each section has a separate title heading and is identified with a page number in the table of contents. The critic's name and the date of composition or publication of the critical work are given at the beginning of each piece of criticism. Unsigned criticism is preceded by the title of the source in which it appeared. Footnotes are reprinted at the end of each essay or excerpt. In the case of excerpted criticism, only those footnotes that pertain to the excerpted texts are included.
- A complete **Bibliographical Citation** of the original essay or book precedes each piece of criticism.
- Critical essays are prefaced by brief **Annotations** explicating each piece. Unless the descriptor "excerpt" is used in the annotation, the essay is being reprinted in its entirety.
- An annotated bibliography of **Further Reading** appears at the end of each entry and suggests resources for additional study. In some cases, significant essays for which the editors could not obtain reprint rights are included here.

A *Harlem Renaissance* author entry consists of the following elements:

- The **Author Heading** cites the name under which the author most commonly wrote, followed by birth and death dates. Also located here are any name variations under which an author wrote. If the author wrote consistently under a pseudonym, the pseudonym will be listed in the author heading and the author's actual name given in parentheses on the first line of the biographical and critical information. Uncertain birth or death dates are indicated by question marks.

- A **Portrait of the Author** is included when available.
- The **Introduction** contains background information that introduces the reader to the author that is the subject of the entry.
- The list of **Principal Works** is ordered chronologically by date of first publication and lists the most important works by the author. The genre and publication date of each work is given. Unless otherwise indicated, dramas are dated by first performance, not first publication.
- Author entries are arranged into three sections: **Primary Sources, General Commentary**, and **Title Commentary.** The Primary Sources section includes letters, poems, short stories, journal entries, and essays written by the featured author. General Commentary includes overviews of the author's career and general studies; Title Commentary includes in-depth analyses of seminal works by the author. Within the Title Commentary section, the reprinted criticism is further organized by title, then by date of publication. The critic's name and the date of composition or publication of the critical work are given at the beginning of each piece of criticism. Unsigned criticism is preceded by the title of the source in which it appeared. All titles by the author featured in the text are printed in boldface type. However, not all boldfaced titles are included in the author and subject indexes; only substantial discussions of works are indexed. Footnotes are reprinted at the end of each essay or excerpt. In the case of excerpted criticism, only those footnotes that pertain to the excerpted texts are included.
- A complete **Bibliographical Citation** of the original essay or book precedes each piece of criticism.
- Critical essays are prefaced by brief **Annotations** explicating each piece. Unless the descriptor "excerpt" is used in the annotation, the essay is being reprinted in its entirety.
- An annotated bibliography of **Further Reading** appears at the end of each entry and suggests resources for additional study. In some cases, significant essays for which the editors could not obtain reprint rights are included here. A list of **Other Sources from Gale** follows the further reading section and provides references to other biographical and critical sources on the author in series published by Gale.

Indexes

The **Author Index** lists all of the authors featured in the *Harlem Renaissance* set, with references to the main author entries in volumes 2 and 3 as well as commentary on the featured author in other author entries and in the topic volume. Page references to substantial discussions of the authors appear in boldface. The Author Index also includes birth and death dates and cross references between pseudonyms and actual names, and cross references to other Gale series in which the authors have appeared. A complete list of these sources is found facing the first page of the Author Index.

The **Title Index** alphabetically lists the titles of works written by the authors featured in volumes 2 and 3 and provides page numbers or page ranges where commentary on these titles can be found. Page references to substantial discussions of the titles appear in boldface. English translations of foreign titles and variations of titles are cross-referenced to the title under which a work was originally published. Titles of novels, dramas, nonfiction books, and poetry, short story, or essay collections are printed in italics, while individual poems, short stories, and essays are printed in body type within quotation marks.

The **Subject Index** includes the authors and titles that appear in the Author Index and the Title Index as well as the names of other authors and figures that are discussed in the set. The Subject Index also lists hundreds of literary terms and topics covered in the criticism. The index provides page numbers or page ranges where subjects are discussed and is fully cross referenced.

Citing Harlem Renaissance

When writing papers, students who quote directly from the *Harlem Renaissance* set may use the following general format to footnote reprinted criticism. The first example pertains to material drawn from periodicals, the second to material reprinted from books.

> Alvarez, Joseph A., "The Lonesome Boy Theme as Emblem for Arna Bontemps's Children's Literature," *African American Review* 32, no. 1 (spring 1998): 23-31; reprinted in *Harlem Renaissance: A Gale Critical Companion,* vol. 2, ed. Janet Witalec (Farmington Hills, Mich: The Gale Group, 2003), 72-8.

> Helbling, Mark, introduction to *The Harlem Renaissance: The One and the Many* (Westport, Conn.: Greenwood Press, 1999), 1-18; reprinted in *Harlem Renaissance: A Gale Critical Companion,* vol. 1, ed. Janet Witalec (Farmington Hills, Mich: The Gale Group, 2003), 27-38.

Harlem Renaissance *Advisory Board*

The members of the *Harlem Renaissance* Advisory Board—reference librarians and subject specialists from public, academic, and school library systems—offered a variety of informed perspectives on both the presentation and content of the *Harlem Renaissance* set. Advisory board members assessed and defined such quality issues as the relevance, currency, and usefulness of the author coverage, critical content, and topics included in our product; evaluated the layout, presentation, and general quality of our product; provided feedback on the criteria used for selecting authors and topics covered in our product; identified any gaps in our coverage of authors or topics, recommending authors or topics for inclusion; and analyzed the appropriateness of our content and presentation for various user audiences, such as high school students, undergraduates, graduate students, librarians, and educators. We wish to thank the advisors for their advice during the development of *Harlem Renaissance.*

Suggestions are Welcome

Readers who wish to suggest new features, topics, or authors to appear in future volumes of the Gale Critical Companion Collection, or who have other suggestions or comments are cordially invited to call, write, or fax the Project Editor:

Project Editor, Gale Critical Companion Collection
The Gale Group
27500 Drake Road
Farmington Hills, MI 48331-3535
1-800-347-4253 (GALE)
Fax: 248-699-8054

ACKNOWLEDGMENTS

The editors wish to thank the copyright holders of the criticism included in this volume and the permissions managers of many book and magazine publishing companies for assisting us in securing reproduction rights. We are also grateful to the staffs of the Detroit Public Library, the Library of Congress, the University of Detroit Mercy Library, Wayne State University Purdy/Kresge Library Complex, and the University of Michigan Libraries for making their resources available to us. Following is a list of the copyright holders who have granted us permission to reproduce material in this edition of *Harlem Renaissance.* Every effort has been made to trace copyright, but if omissions have been made, please let us know.

Copyrighted material in Harlem Renaissance *was reproduced from the following periodicals:*

African American Review, v. 26, Fall, 1992; v. 27, Fall, 1993; v. 31, Autumn, 1997. All reproduced by permission of the *African American Review,* formerly the *Black American Literature Forum.*/v. 32, Spring, 1998 for "The Lonesome Boy Theme as Emblem for Arna Bontemps' Children's Literature," by Joseph A. Alvarez. Copyright © 1998 by the author. Reproduced by permission of the publisher and the author./v. 32, Winter, 1998 for "Countee Cullen's *Medea,*" by Lillian Corti. Reproduced by permission of the author./v. 32, Winter, 1998 for "The World Would Do Better to Ask Why Is Frimbo Sherlock Holmes?: Investigating Liminality in Rudolph Fisher's *The Conjure-Man Dies,*" by Adrienne Johnson Gosselin. Reproduced by permission of the author./v. 33, Fall, 1999 for "And Yet They Paused and A Bill to be Passed: Newly Recovered Lynching Dramas by Georgia Douglas Johnson," by Judith Stephens. Reproduced by permission of the author.—***Afro-Americans in New York Life and History,*** v. 10, 1986. Reproduced by permission.—***American Drama,*** v. 5, 1996. Reproduced by permission.—***American Literary History,*** v. 3, 1991 for "Community and Cultural Crisis: The 'Transfiguring Imagination' of Alain Locke," by Everett Akam. Reproduced by permission of Oxford University Press and the author.—***American Literature,*** v. 43, March, 1971; v. 44, 1972; v. 47, 1975; v. 51, March, 1979. Copyright © 1971, 1972, 1975, 1979 by Duke University Press, Durham, NC. All reproduced by permission.—***American Quarterly,*** v. 17, Summer, 1965; v. 32, Winter, 1980; v. 48, March, 1996; v. 50, September, 1998; v. 51, 1999. © The Johns Hopkins University Press. All reproduced by permission.—***American Studies,*** v. 18, Spring, 1977 for "Combatting Racism with Art: Charles S. Johnson and the Harlem Renaissance," by Ralph L. Pearson. Copyright Mid-America American Studies Association Reproduced by permission.—***ANQ: A Quarterly Journal of Short Ar-***

ticles, Notes, and Reviews, v. 8, Summer, 1995. Copyright © 1985 Helen Dwight Reid Educational Foundation. Reproduced with permission of the Helen Dwight Reid Educational Foundation, published by Heldref Publications, 1319 18th Street, NW, Washington, DC 20036-1802.—***Arizona Quarterly,*** v. 39, Fall, 1983 for "Jean Toomer's *Cane*: The Search for Identity through Form," by Alan Golding. Copyright © 1983 by the Regents of the University of Arizona. Reproduced by permission of the publisher and the author.—***Black American Literature Forum,*** v. 12, Autumn, 1978; v. 14, 1980; v. 19, 1985; v. 21, Fall, 1987; v. 21, Spring-Summer, 1987. All reproduced by permission of the *Black American Literature Forum,* currently the *African American Review.*—***Black World,*** v. 20, November, 1970 for "Alain Locke," by Richard A. Long. Reproduced by permission of the author./v. 20, November, 1970 for "Voice for the Jazz Age, Great Migration, or Black Bourgeoisie," by Faith Berry. Reproduced by permission of the Gail Berry for the author./v. 21, April, 1972 for "Alain Locke & Black Drama," by Samuel A. Hay. Reproduced by permission of the author./v. 25, February, 1976 for "Renaissance 'Renegade'? Wallace Thurman," by Huel D. Perkins. Reproduced by permission of the author./v. 25, February, 1976 for "The Genesis of Locke's *The New Negro,*" by Richard A. Long. Reproduced by permission of the author./v. 25, February, 1976 for "Toward a Sociological Analysis of the Renaissance: Why Harlem?" by Jabulani Kamau Makalani. Reproduced by permission of the author.—***Callaloo,*** v. 9, 1986; v. 21, Fall, 1998. Both reproduced by permission.—***CLA Journal,*** v. 15, March, 1972; v. 16, March, 1973; v. 16, June, 1973; v. 17, September, 1973; v. 18, 1974; v. 19, 1976; v. 26, December, 1982; v. 29, September, 1985; v. 32, December, 1988; v. 32, March, 1989; v. 32, June, 1989; v. 34, March, 1991; v. 35, June, 1992; v. 37, March, 1994; v. 38, September, 1994; v. 39, December, 1995; v. 41, June, 1998; v. 42 September 1998; 42, June 1999. Copyright, 1972, 1973, 1974, 1976, 1982, 1985, 1988, 1989, 1991, 1992, 1994, 1995, 1998, 1999 by The College Language Association. All reproduced by permission.—***The Crisis,*** v. 76, March, 1969; v. 78, July, 1971; v. 90, June/July, 1983. All reproduced by permission.—***Federal Writers' Project,*** August 23, 1938; December 1, 1938; January 17, 1939; January 19, 1939; April 19, 1939. All courtesy of The Library of Congress. All reproduced by permission.—***Georgia Historical Quarterly,*** v. 80, Winter, 1996. Courtesy of the Georgia Historical Society. Reproduced by permission.—***Georgia Review,*** v. 5, Fall, 1951, renewed 1979 by the *Georgia Review.* Reproduced by permission.—***International Review of African American Art,*** v. 4, 1995. Reproduced by permission.—***Journal of Black Studies,*** v. 12, September, 1981. Copyright © 1981 by Sage Publications, Inc. Reproduced by permissions of Sage Publications, Inc.—***Journal of Negro History,*** v. 52, 1967; v. 57, 1972. Both reproduced by permission.—***Langston Hughes Review,*** v. 1, Fall, 1982. Reproduced by permission.—***Legacy: A Journal of American Women Writers,*** v. 18, 2001. Reproduced by permission.—***Markham Review,*** v. 5, Summer, 1976. Reproduced by permission.—***The Massachusetts Review,*** v. 24, Autumn, 1983; v. 28, Winter, 1987. © 1983, 1987. Both reproduced from The Massachusetts Review, Inc. by permission.—***The Modern Schoolmen,*** v. 74, May, 1997. Reproduced by permission.—***MELUS,*** v. 23, 1998. Copyright, MELUS: The Society for the Study of Multi-Ethnic Literature of the United States, 1998. Reproduced by permission.—***The Midwest Quarterly,*** v. 24, Winter, 1983. Reproduced by permission.—***Narrative,*** v. 7, May, 1999. Reproduced by permission.—***Negro American Literature Forum,*** v. 14, January, 1965; v. 6, Summer, 1972. Both reproduced by permission of the *African American Review.*/v. 5, Spring, 1971 for "The Vagabond Motif in the Writings of Claude McKay," by Mary Conroy. Copyright © 1971 by the author. Reproduced by permission of the publisher and the author./v. 10, 1976 for "Carl Van Vechten and the Harlem Renaissance" by Mark Helbling. Reproduced by permission of the author.—***New England Quarterly,*** v. 74, March, 2001 for "Encouraging Verse: William S. Braithwaite and the Poetics of Race," by Lisa Szefel. Copyright held by *The New England Quarterly.* Reproduced by permission of the publisher and the author.—***New Orleans Review,*** v. 15, 1989. Copyright © 1989 by Loyola University. Reproduced by permission.—***New York Herald Tribune Books,*** January 10, 1926. Reproduced by permission.—***The New York Times,*** February 29, 1932. Copyright 1932 by The New York Times Company. Reproduced by permission.—***The New York Times Book Review,*** August 21, 1927; March 4, 1945; Copyright © 1945, renewed 1972 by The New York Times Company; September 20, 1992 Copyright © 1992 by The New York Times Company; January 3, 1999. Copyright © 1999 by The New York Times Company. All reproduced by permission.—***The New Yorker,*** v. 74, September 27, 1998 for "Beyond the Color Line," by Henry Louis Gates, Jr. © 1998 by the author. All rights reserved. Reproduced by permission of the author.—***Novel,*** v. 30, Winter, 1997. Copyright NOVEL Corp. © 1997 Reproduced with permission.—***Pacific Coast Philology,*** v. 15, December, 1980. Reproduced by permission.—***Phylon: The Atlanta University of Race and Culture,*** v.6, 1945; v. 9, 1948; v. 11, 1950; v. 17, 1956; v. 18, 1957; v. 21, 1960;v. 25, 1964; v. 32, 1971; v. 39, 1978; v. 40, 1979; v. 57, 1996. Copyright 1945, 1948, 1950, 1956, 1957, 1960, 1964, 1971, 1978, 1979, 1996 by Atlanta University. All reproduced by permission.—***PMLA,*** v. 105, January, 1990. Copyright © 1990 by the Modern Language Association of America. Reproduced by permission of the Modern Language Association of America.—***Poetry,*** v. 24, February, 1930. Reproduced by permission.—***South Carolina Review,*** v. 2, May, 1970. Reproduced by permission.—***Studies in American Fiction,*** v. 19, Spring, 1991. Copyright © 1991 Northeastern University. Reproduced by permission.—***Studies in Black Literature,*** v. 3, Summer, 1972; v. 5, Winter, 1974. Copyright 1972, 1974 by the editor. Both reproduced by permission.—***Studies in Short Fiction,*** v. 2, 1965. Reproduced by permission.—***Studies in the Literary Imagination,*** v. 7, Fall, 1974. Reproduced by permission.—***Susquehanna University Studies,*** v. 7, June, 1963. Reproduced by permission.—***Theatre Annual,*** 1985. Reproduced by permission.—***Virginia Cavalcade,*** v. 27, 1978. Reproduced by permission.—***Western American Literature,*** v. 6, Spring, 1971. Copyright 1971, by the Western American Literature Association. Reproduced by permission.—***Western Journal of Black Studies,*** v. 22, 1998. Reproduced by permission.

Copyrighted material in Harlem Renaissance *was reproduced from the following books:*

Anderson, Paul A. From "'My Lord, What a Morning': The 'Sorrow Songs' in Harlem Renaissance Thought," in ***Symbolic Loss: The Ambiguity of Mourning and Memory at Century's End.*** Edited by Peter Homans. University Press of Virginia, 2000. Copyright © 2000 by University Press of Virginia. All rights reserved. Reproduced by permission.—Baker, Houston A., Jr. From ***Modernism and the Harlem Renaissance.*** University of Chicago Press, 1987. Copyright © 1987 by University of Chicago Press. All rights reserved. Reproduced by permission.—Balshaw, Maria. From ***Looking for Harlem: Urban Aesthetics in African American Literature.*** Pluto Press, 2000. Copyright © 2000 by Pluto Press. All rights reserved. Reproduced by permission.—Barfoot, C. C., et al. From "The New Negro in Context," in ***Wallace Thurman's Harlem Renaissance.*** Editions Rodopi B.V., 1994. Copyright © 1994 by Editions Rodopi B.V. All rights reserved. Reproduced by permission.—Barksdale, Richard K. From "Langston Hughes and the Blues He Couldn't Lose," in ***The Harlem Renaissance: Revaluations.*** Edited by Amritjit Singh, William S. Shiver, and Stanley Brodwin. Garland Publishing, Inc., 1989. © 1989 Amritjit Singh, William S. Shiver, and Stanley Brodwin. All rights reserved. Reproduced by permission of the editors.—Bearden, Romare and Harry Henderson. From ***A History of African-American Artists From 1792 to the Present.*** Pantheon Books, 1993. Copyright © 1993 by Pantheon Books. All rights reserved. Reproduced by permission.—Bone, Robert. From ***The Negro Novel in America.*** Yale University Press, 1958. Copyright © 1958 by Yale University Press. Revised edition © 1965 by Yale University. Copyright © renewed 1985 by Robert Bone. Reproduced by permission of the author.—Bontemps, Arna. From ***Personals.*** P. Breman, 1973. Reproduced by permission of Harold Ober Associates, Inc. for the Literary Estate of Arna Bontemps.—Booker, Peter. From "Modernism Deferred: Langston Hughes, Harlem and Jazz Montage," in ***Locations of Liberty Modernism: Region and Nation in British and American Modernist Poetry.*** Edited by Alex Davis and Lee M. Jenkins. Cambridge University Press, 2000. Copyright © 2000 by Cambridge University Press. All rights reserved. Reprinted with permission of Cambridge University Press and the author.—Brown-Guillory, Elizabeth. From "Disrupted Motherlines: Mothers and Daughters in a Genderized, Sexualized, and Racialized World," in ***Women of Color: Mother-Daughter Relationships in 20th-Century Literature.*** Edited by Elizabeth Brown-Guillory. University of Texas Press, 1996. Copyright © 1996 by University of Texas Press. All rights reserved. Reproduced by permission.—Byrd, Rudolph P. From "Jean Toomer and the Writers of the Harlem Renaissance: Was He There with Them?" in ***The Harlem Renaissance: Revaluations.*** Edited by Amritjit Singh, William S. Shiver, and Stanley Brodwin. Garland Publishing, Inc., 1989. © 1989 Amritjit Singh, William S. Shiver, and Stanley Brodwin. All rights reserved. Reproduced by permission of the editors.—Champion, Laurie. From "Dorothy West (1907-1998)," in ***American Women Writers, 1900-1945: A Bio- Bibliographical Critical Sourcebook.*** Edited by Laurie Champion. Greenwood Press, 2000. Copyright © 2000 by Greenwood Press, Greenwood Publishing Group, Inc., Westport, CT. All rights reserved. Reproduced by permission of Greenwood Publishing Group, Inc., Westport, CT.—Clum, John M. From ***Ridgely Torrence.*** Twayne Publishers, 1972. Copyright © 1972 by Twayne Publishers. All rights reserved. The Gale Group.—Coleman, Leon. From ***Carl Van Vechten and the Harlem Renaissance: A Critical Assessment.*** Garland Publishing, Inc., 1989. Copyright © 1989 by Garland Publishing, Inc. All rights reserved. Reproduced by permission.—Collier, Eugenia. From "Message to the Generations: The Mythic Hero in Sterling Brown's Poetry," in ***The Furious Flowering of African American Poetry.*** Edited by Joanne V. Gabbin. University of Virginia, 1999. Copyright © 1999 by University of Virginia. All rights reserved. Reproduced by permission.—Cripps, Thomas. From "Introduction: A Monument to Lost Innocence," in ***The Green Pastures.*** Edited by Thomas Cripps. University of Wisconsin Press, 1979. Copyright © 1979 The Board of Regents of the University of Wisconsin System. All rights reserved. Reproduced by permission.—Cullen, Countee. From ***Caroling Dusk: An Anthology of Verse by Negro Poets.*** Edited by Countee Cullen. Harper & Row, 1974. Copyright © 1974 by Harper & Row. All rights reserved. Reproduced by permission of Thompson and Thompson for the Estate of Countee Cullen.—Cullen, Countee. From ***Copper Sun.*** Harper, 1927. Copyright 1927 by Harper. Renewed 1954 by Ida M. Cullen. All rights reserved. Reproduced by permission of Thompson and Thompson for the Estate of Countee Cullen.—Davis, Thadious M. From "Nella Larsen's Harlem Aesthetic," in ***The Harlem Renaissance: Revaluations.*** Edited by Amritjit Singh, William S. Shiver, and Stanley Brodwin. Garland Publishing, Inc., 1989. © 1989 Amritjit Singh, William S. Shiver, and Stanley Brodwin. All rights reserved. Reproduced by permission of the editors.—Douglas, Aaron with L. M. Collins. From "Aaron Douglas Chats about the Harlem Renaissance," in ***The Portable Harlem Renaissance Reader.*** Edited by David Levering Lewis. Viking, 1994. Copyright © 1994 by Viking. All rights reserved. Reproduced by permission.—Doyle, Don H. From the introduction to ***Mamba's Daughters: A Novel of Charleston,*** by DuBose Heyward. University of South Carolina Press, 1995. Copyright © 1995 by University of South Carolina Press. All rights reserved. Reproduced by permission.—Driskell, David. ***From Harlem Renaissance: Art of Black America.*** Harry N. Abrams, Inc., 1987. Copyright © 1987 by Harry N. Abrams, Inc. All rights reserved. Reproduced by permission.—Du Bois, W. E. B. "Editing The Crisis," in ***Black Titan: W. E. B. Du Bois: An Anthology by the Editors of "Freedomways."*** Edited by John Henrik Clarke, et al. Beacon Press, 1970. Copyright © 1970 by Beacon Press. All rights reserved. Reproduced by permission.—Durham, Frank. From ***DuBose Heyward: The Man Who Wrote Porgy.*** University of South Carolina Press, 1954. Copyright © 1954 by University of South Carolina Press. Renewed 1982 by Kathleen C. Durham. All rights reserved. Reproduced by permission.—Early, Gerald. From ***My Soul's High Song.*** Doubleday, 1991. Copyright © 1991 by Doubleday. All rights reserved. Reproduced by permission.—Ellington, Duke. From ***Music is My Mistress.*** Doubleday, 1973. Copyright © 1973 by Doubleday. All rights reserved. Reproduced by permission.—Fabre, Michel. From ***From Harlem to Paris: Black American Writers in France, 1840-1980.*** University of Illinois Press, 1991. Copyright 1991 by Board of Trustees. Used with permission of the University of Illinois Press.—Flamming, Douglas. From "A Westerner in Search of 'Negroness': Region and Race in the Writing of Arna Bontemps," in ***Over the Edge: Remapping the American West.*** Edited by Valerie J. Matsumoto and Blake Allmendinger. University of California Press, 1999. Copyright © 1999 by University of California Press. All rights reserved. Reproduced by permission.—Flynn, Joyce. From the introduction to ***Frye Street & Environs: The Collected Works of Marita Bonner.*** Edited by Joyce Flynn and Joyce Occomy Stricklin. Beacon Press, 1987. Copyright © 1987 by Beacon Press. All rights reserved. Reproduced by permission.—Garber, Eric. From "Richard Bruce Nugent," in ***Dictionary of Literary Biography, Volume 51: Afro-American Writers from the Harlem Renaissance to 1940.*** Edited by Trudier Harris and Thadious M. Davis. Gale Research, Inc., 1987. Copyright © 1987 by Gale Research, Inc. All rights reserved.—Govan, Sandra Y. From "A Blend of Voices: Composite Narrative Strategies in Biographical Reconstruction," in ***Recovered Writers/Recovered Texts: Race, Class, and Gender in Black Women's Literature.*** Edited by Dolan Hubbard. University of Tennessee Press, 1997. Copyright © 1997 by University of Tennessee Press. All rights reserved. Reproduced by permission.—Gray, Christine Rauchfuss. From ***Willis Richardson: Forgotten Pioneer of African-American Drama.*** Greenwood Press, 1999. Copyright © 1999 by Greenwood Press. All rights reserved. Reproduced by permission of Greenwood Publishing Group, Inc., Westport, CT.—Greene, J. Lee. From "Anne Spencer," in ***Dictionary of Literary Biography, Volume 51: Afro-American Writers from the Harlem Renaissance to 1940.*** Edited by Trudier Harris and Thadious M. Davis. Gale Research, Inc., 1987. Copyright © 1987 by Gale Research, Inc. All rights reserved.—Greene, J. Lee. From ***Time's Unfading Garden: Anne Spencer's Life and Poetry.*** Louisiana State University, 1977. Copyright © 1977 by Louisiana State University. All rights reserved. Reproduced by permission of the author.—Hayden, Robert. From the preface to ***The New Negro.*** Edited by Alain Locke. Atheneum, 1968. Copyright © 1968 by Atheneum. All rights reserved. Reproduced by permission.—Helbling, Mark. From the introduction to ***The Harlem Renaissance: The One and the Many.*** Greenwood Press, 1999. Copyright © 1999 by Greenwood Press, Inc., Westport, CT. All rights reserved. Reproduced by permission of Greenwood Publishing Group, Inc., Westport, CT.—Hemenway, Robert E. From "Zora Neale Hurston and the Eatonville Anthropology," in ***Harlem Renaissance Remembered.*** Edited by Arna Bontemps. Dodd, Mead, 1972. Copyright © 1972 by Dodd, Mead. All rights reserved. Reproduced by permission.—Henderson, Mae Gwendolyn. From "Portrait of Wallace Thurman," in ***The Harlem Renaissance Remembered.*** Edited by Arna Bontemps. Dodd, Mead & Company, 1972. Copyright © 1972 by Dodd, Mead & Company. All rights reserved. Reproduced by permission.—Herron, Carolivia. From the introduction to ***Selected Works of Angelina Weld Grimké.*** Edited by Carolivia Herron. Oxford University Press, 1991. Copyright © 1991 by Oxford University Press. All rights reserved. Reproduced by permission.—Hill, Robert A. From the introduction to ***Marcus Garvey: Life and Lessons.*** University of California Press, 1987. Copyright © 1987 by University of California Press. All rights reserved. Reproduced by permission.—Howard, Elizabeth F. From "Arna Bontemps," in ***The Scribner Writers Series.*** Gale Group, 2002. Copyright © 2002 by Gale Group. All rights reserved.—Huggins, Nathan Irvin. From "Alain Locke: Aesthetic Value-System and Afro-American Art," in ***Revelation: American History, American Myths.*** Edited by Brenda Smith Huggins. Oxford University Press, 1995. Copyright © 1995 by Oxford University Press. All rights reserved. Reproduced by permission.—Hughes, Langston. From "The Negro and the Racial Mountain," in ***African American Literary Criticism.*** Edited by Hazel Arnett Ervin. Twayne Publishers, 1999. Copyright © 1999 by Twayne Publishers. All rights reserved. Reproduced by permission of Harold Ober Associates for the Estate of Langston Hughes.—Hull, Gloria T. From "Black Women Poets from Wheatley to Walker," in ***Sturdy Black Bridges: Visions of Black Women in Literature.*** Edited by Roseann P. Bell, Bettye J. Parker, and Beverly Guy-Sheftall. Anchor Books, 1979. Copyright © 1979 by Anchor Books. All rights reserved. Reproduced by permission of the author.—Hull, Gloria T. From the introduction to ***Give Us Each Day: The Diary of Alice Dunbar-Nelson.*** W.W. Norton, 1984. Copyright © 1984 by W.W. Norton. All rights reserved. Reproduced by permission of the author.—Hurston, Zora Neale. From "What White Publishers Won't Print," in ***I Love Myself When I Am Laughing ... And Then again When I Am Looking Mean and Impressive: A Zora Neale Hurston Reader.*** Edited by Alice Walker. The Feminist Press, 1979. Copyright © 1979 by The Feminist Press. All rights reserved. Reproduced by permission of the Victoria Sanders Literary Agency for the Estate of Zora Neale Hurston.—Hutchinson, George. ***The Harlem Renaissance in Black and White.*** The Belknap Press of Harvard University Press, 1995. Copyright © 1995 by The Belknap Press of Harvard University Press. Reprinted by permission of the publisher.—Hutson, Jean Blackwell. From ***Black Bibliophiles and Collectors: Preservers of Black History.*** Howard University Press, 1990. Copyright © 1990 by Howard University Press. All rights reserved. Reproduced by permission.—Ikonne, Chidi. From ***From Du Bois to Van Vechten: The Early New Negro Literature, 1903-1926.*** Greenwood Press, 1981. Copyright © 1981 by Greenwood Press. All rights reserved. Reproduced by permission of Greenwood Publishing Group, Inc., Westport, CT.—Jimoh, A. Yemisi. From "Dorothy West (1907-1998)," in ***Contemporary African American Novelists: A Bio-Bibliographical Critical Sourcebook.*** Edited by Emmanuel S. Nelson. Greenwood Press, 1999. Copyright © 1999 by Greenwood Press. All rights reserved. Reproduced by permission of Greenwood Publishing Group, Inc., Westport, CT.—Johnson, Abby Arthur and Ronald Maberry Johnson. From ***Propaganda and Aesthetics: The Literary Politics of Afro-American Magazines in the Twentieth Century.*** University of Massachusetts Press, 1979. Copyright © 1979 by University of Massachusetts Press. All rights reserved. Reproduced by permission.—Johnson, Charles S. From "The Negro Renaissance and Its Significance," in ***The Portable Harlem Renaissance Reader.*** Edited by David Levering Lewis. Viking, 1994. Copyright © 1994 by Viking. All rights reserved. Reproduced by permission.—Johnson, Eloise. From ***Rediscovering the Harlem Renaissance: The Politics of Exclusion.*** Garland Publishing, Inc., 1997. Copyright © 1997 by Garland Publishing, Inc. All rights reserved. Reproduced by permission.—Kellner, Bruce. From "Carl Van Vechten's Black Renaissance," in ***The Harlem Renaissance: Revalua-***

tions. Edited by Amritjit Singh, William S. Shiver, and Stanley Brodwin. Garland Publishing, Inc., 1989. © 1989 Amritjit Singh, William S. Shiver, and Stanley Brodwin. All rights reserved. Reproduced by permission of the editors.—Kostelanetz, Richard. From ***Politics in the African American Novel: James Weldon Johnson, W. E. B. Du Bois, Richard Wright, and Ralph Ellison.*** Greenwood Press, 1991. Copyright © 1991 by Greenwood Press. All rights reserved. Reproduced by permission of Greenwood Publishing Group, Inc., Westport, CT.—Lang, Robert. From "'The Birth of a Nation': History, Ideology, Narrative Form" in ***The Birth of a Nation: D.W. Griffith, Director.*** Edited by Robert Lang. Rutgers University Press, 1994. Copyright © 1994 by Rutgers University Press. All rights reserved. Reproduced by permission.—LeSeur, Geta. From "Claude McKay's Marxism," in ***The Harlem Renaissance: Revaluations.*** Edited by Amritjit Singh, William S. Shiver, and Stanley Brodwin. Garland Publishing, Inc., 1989. © 1989 Amritjit Singh, William S. Shiver, and Stanley Brodwin. All rights reserved. Reproduced by permission of the editors.—Lewis, David Levering. From the introduction to ***The Portable Harlem Renaissance Reader.*** Edited by David Levering Lewis. Viking, 1994. Copyright © 1994 by Viking. All rights reserved. Reproduced by permission of Brandt & Hochman for the editor.—Locke, Alain. From "Art or Propaganda," in ***The Critical Temper of Alain Locke: A Selection of His Essays on Art and Culture.*** Edited by Jeffrey C. Stewart. Garland Publishing, Inc., 1983. Copyright © 1983 by Garland Publishing, Inc. All rights reserved. Reproduced by permission.—Locke, Alain. From "The Negro Takes His Place in American Art," in ***The Portable Harlem Renaissance Reader.*** Edited by David Levering Lewis. Viking, 1994. Copyright © 1994 by Viking. All rights reserved. Publisher, 1994. © info from verso. Reproduced by permission of the author.—Lutz, Tom. From "Claude McKay: Music, Sexuality, and Literary Cosmopolitanism," in ***Black Orpheus: Music in African American Fiction from the Harlem Renaissance to Toni Morrison.*** Edited by Saadi A. Simawe. Garland Publishing, Inc., 2000. Copyright © 2000 by Garland Publishing, Inc. All rights reserved. Reproduced by permission.—Martin, Tony. From ***Literary Garveyism: Garvey, Black Arts, and the Harlem Renaissance.*** Majority Press, 1983. Copyright © 1983 by Majority Press. All rights reserved. Reproduced by permission.—McDonald, C. Ann. From "James Weldon Johnson," in ***American Women Writers, 1900-1945: A Bio-Bibliographical Critical Sourcebook.*** Edited by Laurie Champion. Greenwood Press, 2000. Copyright © 2000. Reproduced by permission of Greenwood Publishing Group, Inc., Westport, CT.—McKay, Nellie. From "Jean Toomer in his Time: An Introduction," in ***Jean Toomer: A Critical Evaluation.*** Edited by Therman B. O'Daniel. Howard University Press, 1988. Copyright © 1988 by Howard University Press. All rights reserved. Reproduced by permission.—McLaren, Joseph M. From "Early Recognitions: Duke Ellington and Langston Hughes in New York, 1920-1930," in ***The Harlem Renaissance: Revaluations.*** Edited by Amritjit Singh, William S. Shiver, and Stanley Brodwin. Garland Publishing, Inc., 1989. © 1989 Amritjit Singh, William S. Shiver, and Stanley Brodwin. All rights reserved. Reproduced by permission of the editors.—Meche, Jude R. From "Marita Bonner," in ***Dictionary of Literary Biography, Volume 228: Twentieth-Century American Dramatists.*** Edited by Christopher J. Wheatley. The Gale Group, 2000. Copyright © 2000 by The Gale Group. Reproduced by permission.—Miller, Nina. From "'Our Younger Negro (Women) Artists': Gwendolyn Bennett and Helene Johnson," in ***Making Love Modern: The Intimate Public Worlds of New York's Literary Women.*** Oxford University Press, 1998. Copyright © 1998 by Oxford University Press. All rights reserved. Reproduced by permission.—Miller, R. Baxter. From "'Some Mark to Make': the Lyrical Imagination of Langston Hughes," in ***Critical Essays on Langston Hughes.*** G.K. Hall, 1986. Copyright © 1986 by G.K. Hall. All rights reserved. The Gale Group.—Mitchell, Verner D. From the introduction to ***This Waiting for Love: Helene Johnson, Poet of the Harlem Renaissance.*** University of Massachusetts Press, 2000. Copyright © 2000 by University of Massachusetts Press. All rights reserved. Reproduced by permission.—Parascandola, Louis J. From ***An Eric Walrond Reader.*** Wayne State University Press, 1998. Copyright © 1998 by Wayne State University Press. All rights reserved. Reproduced by permission.—Peplow, Michael W. From ***George S. Schuyler.*** Twayne Publishers, 1980. Copyright © 1980 by Twayne Publishers. The Gale Group.—Perry, Patsy B. From "Willis Richardson," in ***Dictionary of Literary Biography, Volume 51: Afro-Ameican Writers from the Harlem Renaissance to 1940.*** Edited by Trudier Harris and Thadious M. Davis. The Gale Group, 1987. Copyright © 1987 Gale Research Company.—Rampersad, Arnold. From "Langston Hughes and Approaches to Modernism in the Harlem Renaissance," in ***The Harlem Renaissance: Revaluations.*** Edited by Amritjit Singh, William S. Shiver, and Stanley Brodwin. Garland Publishing, Inc., 1989. © 1989 Amritjit Singh, William S. Shiver, and Stanley

Brodwin. All rights reserved. Reproduced by permission of the editors.—Robinson, William H. From ***Black New England Letters: The Uses of Writings in Black New England.*** Trustees of the Public Library of the City of Boston, 1977. Copyright © 1977 by Trustees of the Public Library of the City of Boston. All rights reserved. Reproduced by permission.—Sanders, Mark A. From "The Ballad, the Hero, and the Ride: A Reading of Sterling Brown's 'The Last Ride of Wild Bill,'" in ***The Furious Flowering of African American Poetry.*** Edited by Joanne V. Gabbin. University of Virginia, 1999. Copyright © 1999 by University of Virginia. All rights reserved. Reproduced by permission.—Sinnette, Elinor Des Verney. From ***Arthur Alfonso Schomburg: Black Bibliophile & Collector.*** The New York Public Library & Wayne State University Press, 1989. Copyright © 1989 by The New York Public Library & Wayne State University Press. All rights reserved. Reproduced by permission of the author.—Slavick, William H. From "Going to School to DuBose Heyward," in ***The Harlem Renaissance Re-Examined.*** Edited by Victor A. Kramer. AMS, 1987. Copyright © 1987 by AMS. All rights reserved. Reproduced by permission.—Slavick, William H. From ***DuBose Heyward.*** Twayne Publishers, 1981. Copyright © 1981 by Twayne Publishers. The Gale Group.—Stewart, Jeffrey C. From ***Rhapsodies in Black: Art of the Harlem Renaissance.*** University of California Press, 1997. Copyright © 1997 by University of California Press. All rights reserved. Reproduced by permission.—Stoff, Michael B. From "Claude McKay and the Cult of Primitivism," in ***The Harlem Renaissance Remembered.*** Edited by Arna Bontemps. Dodd, Mead & Company, 1972. Copyright © 1972 by Dodd, Mead & Company. All rights reserved. Reproduced by permission.—Sundquist, Eric J. From the introduction to ***The Oxford W. E. B. Du Bois Reader.*** Oxford University Press, 1996. Copyright © 1996 by Oxford University Press. All rights reserved. Reproduced by permission.—Tate, Claudia. From ***The Selected Works of Georgia Douglas Johnson.*** G.K. Hall & Co., 1997. Copyright © 1997 by G.K. Hall & Co. All rights reserved. The Gale Group.—Tracy, Steven C. From "To the Tune of Those Weary Blues," in ***Langston Hughes: Critical Perspectives Past and Present.*** Edited by Henry Louis Gates, Jr., and K.A. Appiah. Amistad Press, 1993. Copyright © 1993 by Amistad Press. Reproduced by permission of Henry Louis Gates, Jr.—Turner, Deborah. From ***Gay and Lesbian Literature,*** Volume 2. St. James Press, 1998. Copyright © 1998 by St. James Press. All rights reserved. The Gale Group.—Tuttleton, James W. From "Countee Cullen at 'The Heights,'" in ***The Harlem Renaissance: Revaluations.*** Edited by Amritjit Singh, William S. Shiver, and Stanley Brodwin. Garland Publishing, Inc., 1989. © 1989 Amritjit Singh, William S. Shiver, and Stanley Brodwin. All rights reserved. Reproduced by permission of the editors.—Tyler, Bruce M. From ***From Harlem to Hollywood: The Struggle for Racial and Cultural Democracy, 1920-1943.*** Garland Publishing, Inc., 1992. Copyright © 1992 by Garland Publishing, Inc. All rights reserved. Reproduced by permission.—van Notten, Eleonor. From ***Wallace Thurman's Harlem Renaissance.*** Rodopi, 1994. Copyright © 1994 by Rodopi. All rights reserved. Reproduced by permission.—Walden, Daniel. From "'The Canker Galls … ,' or, the Short Promising Life of Wallace Thurman," in ***The Harlem Renaissance Re-Examined.*** Edited by Victor A. Kramer. AMS Press, 1987. Copyright © 1987 by AMS Press. All rights reserved. Reproduced by permission.—Walker, Alice. From "Dedication," in ***I Love Myself When I am Laughing … And Then again When I am Looking Mean and Impressive: A Zora Neale Hurston Reader.*** Edited by Alice Walker. The Feminist Press, 1979. Copyright © 1979 by The Feminist Press. All rights reserved. Reproduced by permission.—Wall, Cheryl A. From "Zora Neal Hurston: Changing Her Own Words," in ***American Novelists Revisited: Essays in Feminist Criticism.*** Edited by Friz Fleischmann. G.K. Hall, 1982. Copyright © 1982 by G.K. Hall. All rights reserved. Reproduced by permission.—Wall, Cheryl A. From "Whose Sweet Angel Child? Blues Women, Langston Hughes, and Writing during the Harlem Renaissance," in ***Langston Hughes: The Man, His Art, and His Continuing Influence.*** Edited by C. James Trotman. Garland Publishing, Inc., 1995. Copyright © 1995 by Garland Publishing, Inc. All rights reserved. Reproduced by permission.—Wall, Cheryl A. From the foreword to ***This Waiting for Love: Helene Johnson, Poet of the Harlem Renaissance.*** Edited by Verner D. Mitchell. University of Massachusetts Press, 2000. Copyright © 2000 by University of Massachusetts Press. All rights reserved. Reproduced by permission.—Wall, Cheryl A. From ***Women of the Harlem Renaissance.*** Indiana University Press, 1995. Copyright © 1995 by Indiana University Press. All rights reserved. Reproduced by permission.—Washington, Mary Helen. From "'I Love the Way Janie Crawford Left Her Husbands': Hurston's Emergent Female Hero," in ***Zora Neale Hurston: Critical Perspectives Past and Present.*** Edited by Henry Louis Gates, Jr. and K.A. Appiah. Amistad Press, 1993. Copyright © 1993 by Amistad Press. Reproduced by permission of Henry Louis Gates, Jr.—

Washington, Sarah M. From "Frank S. Horne," in ***Dictionary of Literary Biography, Volume 51: Afro- American Writers from the Harlem Renaissance to 1940.*** Edited by Trudier Harris. Gale Research, Inc., 1987. Copyright © 1987 by Gale Research, Inc. All rights reserved. Reproduced by permission.—Willis-Braithwaite, Deborah. From ***James Van DerZee: Photographer 1886-1983.*** Harry N. Abrams, Inc., 1987. Copyright © 1987 by Harry N. Abrams, Inc. All rights reserved. Reproduced by permission.—Wintz, Cary D. From "Booker T. Washington, W. E. B. Du Bois, and the 'New Negro' in Black America," in ***Black Culture and the Harlem Renaissance.*** Rice University Press, 1988. Copyright © 1996 by Texas A&M University Press. Reproduced by permission.—Wolseley, Roland E. From ***The Black Press, U.S.A.*** Iowa State University Press, 1990. Copyright © 1990 by Iowa State University Press. All rights reserved. Reproduced by permission. Copyright to all editions of the Black Press, U.S.A. is owned by Alice A. Tait.—Woodson, Jon. From ***To Make a New Race: Gurdjieff, Toomer, and the Harlem Renaissance.*** University of Mississippi Press, 1999. Copyright © 1998 by University of Mississippi Press. All rights reserved. Reproduced by permission.—Zamir, Shamoon. From ***Dark Voices: W. E. B. Du Bois and American Thought, 1888-1903.*** University of Chicago Press, 1995. Copyright © 1995 by University of Chicago Press. All rights reserved. Reproduced by permission.

Photographs and illustrations in Harlem Renaissance *were received from the following sources:*

African American soldiers of the 368 Infantry, photograph. Corbis. Reproduced by permission.—Apollo Theater marquee, "See You Soon," photograph. AP/Wide World Photos. Reproduced by permission.—"Aspects of Negro Life: The Negro in an African Setting," painting by Aaron Douglas, photograph by Manu Sassoonian. Schomburg Center for Research in Black Culture, The New York Public Library, Art Resource, NY. Reproduced by permission.—"Ethiopia Awakening," sculpture by Meta Warrick Fuller, photograph. Schomburg Center for Research in Black Culture, The New York Public Library/Art Resource, NY. Reproduced by permission. Bailey, Pearl, photograph by Carl Van Vechten. Reproduced by permission of the Estate of Carl Van Vechten.—Baker, Josephine, in a scene from the 1934 film Zou Zou, directed by Marc Allegret, photograph. The Kobal Collection. Reproduced by permission.—Bennett, Gwendolyn, photograph. Reproduced by permission of Helaine Victoria Press and the Moorland-Spingarn Research Center, Howard University.—Black Cross nurses, parading down a street in Harlem during the opening of the Universal Negro Improvement Association convention, photograph. © Underwood & Underwood/Corbis. Reproduced by permission.—Bonner, Marita, sitting with her husband, William Occomy, photograph. Radcliffe Archives, Radcliffe Institute, Harvard University. Reproduced by permission.—Bontemps, Arna, photograph. Fisk University Library. Reproduced by permission.—Braithwaite, William Stanley, photograph. Fisk University Library. Reproduced by permission.—Brown, Sterling, photograph. Fisk University Library. Reproduced by permission.—Calloway, Cab, photograph by Carl Van Vechten. The Estate of Carl Van Vechten. Reproduced by permission.—Circular diagram showing difference between speech and silence (Figure A), compared with circular diagram showing the linearity of silence and speech by marking the trajectory as a circuit (Figure B). The Gale Group.—Cotton Club, Harlem, New York City, ca. 1920-1940, photograph. Corbis Corporation. Reproduced by permission.—Cover from *Black Thunder,* by Arna Bontemps. Beacon Press, 1992. Copyright 1936 by The Macmillan Company, renewed 1963 by Arna Bontemps. Reproduced by permission.—Cover from *The Crisis: A Record of the Darker Races,* edited by W. E. B. Du Bois, 1910, print.—Cover of the program for DuBose Heyward and Ira Gershwin's libretto *Porgy and Bess,* photograph. Hulton/Archive. Reproduced by permission.—Cullen, Countee, photograph. The Bettmann Archive/Corbis-Bettmann. Reproduced by permission.—Diagram showing the word fixed in the middle of a diagrammatically circumscribed cross becoming a vehicle for the attempted transcendence of silent difference and the aspiration to silent non-difference. The Gale Group.—Douglas, Aaron (oil on canvas painting), photograph. Gibbs Museum of Art/CAA. Reproduced by permission.—Du Bois, W. E. B., photograph. Fisk University Library. Reproduced by permission.—Du Bois, W. E. B (top right), and others working in the offices of the NAACP's *Crisis* magazine, photograph. © Underwood & Underwood/Corbis. Reproduced by permission.—Ellington, Duke, and Louis Armstrong (performing), 1946, photograph. AP/Wide World Photos Inc. Reproduced by permission.—Exterior view of Abyssinian Baptist Church, New York City, c. 1923, photograph. Corbis Corporation. Reproduced by permission.—Exterior view of Lafayette Theatre in Harlem, 7th Avenue between 131st and 132nd Streets, photograph. Corbis. Reproduced by permission.—"Ezekiel Saw the

Wheels," painting by William H. Johnson. The Library of Congress.—Fauset, Jesse Redmon, photograph. The Library of Congress.—Fauset, Jessie, Langston Hughes and Zora Neale Hurston, photograph. Schomburg Center for Research in Black Culture, The New York Public Library/Art Resource, NY. Reproduced by permission.—Fisher, Rudolph, photograph. The Beinecke Rare Book and Manuscript Library. Reproduced by permission.—Frontispiece, caricature drawing by Miguel Covarrubias, from "Keep A-Inchin' along," written by Carl Van Vechten, (left to right), Carl Van Vechten, Fania Marinoff, and Taylor Gordon. Special Collections Library, University of Michigan. Reproduced by permission.—Garvey, Marcus (center), handcuffed to a deputy after he is escorted from a courtroom after being sentenced to five years in Atlanta Penitentiary for mail fraud, photograph. © Bettmann/Corbis. Reproduced by permission.—Garvey, Marcus, photograph. Consulate General of Jamaica. Reproduced by permission.—Garvey, Marcus, standing in front of a UNIA club in New York, photograph. Hulton/Archive. Reproduced by permission.—Grimké, Angelina Weld, photograph. Reproduced by permission of Helaine Victoria Press and the Moorland-Spingarn Research Center, Howard University.—Harlem bookstore known as the "House of Common Sense and the Home of Proper Propaganda" hosting the registration for the Back-to-Africa movement, photograph. © Bettmann/Corbis. Reproduced by permission.—Heyward, DuBose, photograph. The Library of Congress.—Horne, Frank, photograph. AP/Wide World Photos. Reproduced by permission.—Hughes, Langston, photograph. The Bettmann Archive/Newsphotos, Inc./Corbis- Bettmann. Reproduced by permission.—Hurston, Zora Neale, photograph. Yale Collection of American Literature, Beinecke Rare Book and Manuscript Library. Reproduced by permission of Carl Van Vechten Papers.—Jacket of *The Souls of Black Folk,* by W. E. B. Du Bois. Random House, 1996. Jacket portrait courtesy of the Bettman Archive.—The January, 1991 PLAYBILL for Langston Hughes and Zora Neale Hurston's *Mule Bone,* directed by Michael Schultz by the Ethel Barrymore Theatre, at Lincoln Center Theater, some men and one woman are sitting on a porch listening to a man playing a guitar, photograph. PLAYBILL ® is a registered trademark of Playbill Incorperated, N.Y.C. All rights reserved. Reproduced by permission.—Johnson, Charles S., photograph. Fisk University Library. Reproduced by permission.—Johnson, William H., self portrait painting. The Library of Congress.—Johnson, James Weldon, photograph. The Library of Congress.—Larsen, Nella (1891-1964), photograph. The Beinecke Rare Book and Manuscript Library. Reproduced by permission.—Larsen, Nella (shaking hands, four men to her left), photograph. UPI/Corbis-Bettmann. Reproduced by permission.—Leibowitz, Sam, Patterson, Heywood (Scottsboro boys), phototgraph. UPI/Corbis-Bettmann. Reproduced by permission.—Locke, Dr. Alain, photograph. The Library of Congress.—McKay, Claude, photograph. The Granger Collection, New York. Reproduced by permission.—Members of the NAACP New York City Youth Council holding signs and picketing for anti-lynching legislation in front of the Strand Theatre in Times Square, photograph. Courtesy of The Library of Congress. Reproduced by permission.—NAACP anti-lynching poster, photograph. Archive Photos. Reproduced by permission.—Nelson, Alice Ruth Moore Dunbar, photograph. Reproduced by permission of Helaine Victoria Press and the Ohio Historical Society.—Original typewritten manuscript from *Harlem/Good Morning, Daddy,* written by Langston Hughes. Reproduced by permission of Harold Ober Associates Incorporated for the Estate of Langston Hughes.—Parade of men, opening of the annual convention of the Provisional Republic of Africa in Harlem, carrying banners and a paintng of the "Ethiopian Christ," banner above street: "Summer Chatauqua of the Abyssinian Baptist Church," New York, photograph by George Rinhart. Corbis Corporation. Reproduced by permission.—Pedestrians walking on East 112th Street in Harlem, New York, photograph. © Bettmann/Corbis. Reproduced by permission.—Rex, Ingram, photograph. The Kobal Collection. Reproduced by permission.—Robeson, Paul, as Brutus Jones, throwing his hands up, surrounded by ghosts, scene from the 1933 film *The Emperor Jones,* photograph. ©Underwood & Underwood/Corbis. Reproduced by permission.—Robinson, Bill (with Shirley Temple), photograph. AP/Wide World Photos. Reproduced by permission.—Scene from the movie *Birth of A Nation,* 1915, photograph. The Kobal Collection. Reproduced by permission.—Schuyler, George S., photograph by Carl Van Vechten. Reproduced by permission of the Estate of Carl Van Vechten.—Smith, Bessie, photograph. New York Public Library.—Spencer, Anne, photograph. Reproduced by permission of Helaine Victoria Press and the Literary Estate of Anne Spencer.—Thurman, Wallace, photograph. Reproduced by permission of the Beinecke Rare Book and Manuscript Library.—Title page from *Anthology of Magazine Verse for 1920,* edited by William Stanley Braithwaite, all text. Courtesy of the Graduate Library, University of Michigan. Reproduced by permission.—Title page from *The Book of American Negro Poetry,* written by James Weldon Johnson, all text. Courtesy of the Graduate Library, University of Michigan. Reproduced by permission.—Title page from *Caroling Dusk,* edited by Countee Cullen, all text. Special Collections Library, University of Michigan. Reproduced by permission.—Title page from *Frye Street & Environs: The Collected Works of Marita Bonner,* by Joyce Flynn and Joyce Occomy Stricklin. Copyright © 1987 by Joyce Flynn and Joyce Occomy Stricklin. Reproduced by permission of Beacon Press, Boston.—Title page from *The Weary Blues,* written by Langston Hughes. Special Collections Library, University of Michigan. Reproduced by permission.—Toomer, Jean (foreground), sitting in front of typewriter while his wife, Marjory Latimer, stands next to him looking over his shoulder, photograph. © Bettmann/Corbis. Reproduced by permission.—Toomer, Jean, photograph. Beinecke Library, Yale University. Reproduced by permission.—Two women walking with two girls, photograph. Corbis. Reproduced by permission.—Unemployed black men talking together, 1935, Lennox Avenue, Harlem, photograph. Corbis-Bettmann. Reproduced by permission.—VanDerZee, James, photograph. AP/Wide World Photos. Reproduced by permission.—Van Vechten, Carl, photograph. AP/Wide World Photos. Reproduced by permission.—View of Lenox Avenue in Harlem, photograph. Corbis. Reproduced by permission.—Walrond, Eric, a drawing. Winold Reiss Collecection/Fisk University Library. Reproduced by permission.—West, Dorothy, Martha's Vineyard, Massachusetts, 1995, photograph. AP/Wide World Photos. Reproduced by permission.—White, Walter, photograph. Library of Congress.

● = historical event

■ = literary event

1890

● Between 1890 and 1920, about two million African Americans migrate from the rural southern states to the northern cities, where they hope to find better opportunities and less discrimination.

1908

● The Frogs, a group of African American theatrical professionals including George Walker, James Reese Europe, and Bert Williams, is founded.

● Reverend Adam Clayton Powell is named pastor of Harlem's Abyssinian Baptist Church.

1909

● The National Negro Committee holds its first meeting. The organization will evolve into the National Association for the Advancement of Colored People (NAACP) the next year.

1910

● The NAACP is founded, and prominent Black leader W. E. B. Du Bois becomes editor of the group's monthly magazine, *Crisis,* which publishes its first issue.

● The National Urban League, a merger of the Committee for Improving the Industrial Conditions of Negroes in New York, the Committee on Urban Conditions, and the National League for the Protection of Colored Women is founded under the direction of Dr. George E. Haynes.

1912

■ James Weldon Johnson's influential novel *The Autobiography of an Ex-Colored Man* is published.

1914

● Madame C. J. Walker, the first African American woman to become a self-made millionaire, moves to New York City with her daughter L'Alelia. The family moves to Harlem in 1916. The founder of a line of hair and cosmetic products for Black women, Madame Walker's fortune will finance her daughter's foray into the nightclub and literary salon business.

1917

● Jamaican-born Marcus Garvey arrives in Harlem and founds the Universal Negro Improvement Association (UNIA), an organization that urges Blacks to unite and form their own nation.

- Between 10,000 and 15,000 African Americans join the Silent Protest Parade, marching down Fifth Avenue in complete silence to protest violence against Blacks.
- The politically radical Black publication *The Messenger* is founded.
- Two of Claude McKay's poems, "Invocation" and "The Harlem Dancer," are published in the white literary journal *Seven Arts.*

1918

- Garvey's UNIA begins publishing *Negro World,* the organization's weekly newspaper.

1919

- The 369th Infantry Regiment, a highly decorated unit made up entirely of African American soldiers, returns from World War I to a heroes' welcome in Harlem.
- During the "Red Summer of Hate," African Americans react angrily to widespread lynchings and other violence directed against them, with race riots occurring in Chicago, Washington, D.C., and two dozen other American cities. The NAACP holds a conference on lynching and publishes *Thirty Years of Lynching in the United States 1889-1918.*
- Jessie Redmon Fauset becomes literary editor of *Crisis.*
- McKay publishes "If We Must Die" in the *Liberator.*

1920

- James Weldon Johnson becomes the first African American executive secretary of the NAACP.
- Garvey's UNIA holds the First International Convention of the Negro Peoples of the World in New York
- The NAACP awards the Springarn Medal to W. E. B. Du Bois for "the founding and the calling of the Pan African Congress."
- Acclaimed American playwright Eugene O'Neil's drama *The Emperor Jones* opens at the Provincetown Playhouse with Black actor Charles Gilpin in the lead role.

1921

- Harry Pace founds the Black Swan Phonograph Corporation and begins production of the "race records" that will help to bring jazz and blues music to a wider audience.
- The musical revue *Shuffle Along* opens on Broadway, delighting audiences with its high-energy singing and dancing and, many believe, providing the spark that ignites the Harlem Renaissance.
- An exhibition of works by such African American artists as Henry Tanner and Meta Vaux Warrick Fuller is held at Harlem's 135th Street branch of the New York Public Library.
- Langston Hughes's great poem "The Negro Speaks of Rivers" is published in *Crisis.*

1922

- Marian Anderson performs at New York's Town Hall, launching her career as a classical singer.
- Warrick Fuller's sculpture *Ethiopia Awakening* is shown at the "Making of America" exhibition in New York.
- The first major book of the Harlem Renaissance appears when Claude McKay's novel *Harlem Shadows* is published by Harcourt, Brace.
- James Weldon Johnson's *The Book of American Negro Poetry* is published by Harcourt, Brace.

1923

- Bessie Smith records "Downhearted Blues" and "Gulf Coast Blues," soon becoming the most famous blues singer in both the northern and southern states.
- Roland Hayes makes his New York debut, singing a program of classical music as well as African American spirituals.
- Marcus Garvey is arrested for mail fraud and imprisoned for three months.
- Joe "King" Oliver's Creole Jazz Band makes a series of thirty- seven recordings with trumpet player Louis Armstrong.
- Pianist, composer, and band leader Duke Ellington arrives in New York with his band, the Washingtonians.
- Louis Armstrong joins Fletcher Henderson's orchestra, which— performing at the famed Roseland Ballroom— becomes the most popular dance band in New York.
- Kansas City-born artist Aaron Douglas arrives in New York and begins developing a new style that will make him the official artist of the Harlem Renaissance.

- Harlem's largest and most famous cabaret, the Cotton Club, opens.
- Josephine Baker appears in *Chocolate Dandies* on Broadway.
- Roland Hayes performs at Carnegie Hall.
- The Harlem Renaissance Basketball Club is formed to provide Black athletes who have been unable to play on white teams with a league of their own.
- The National Urban League establishes *Opportunity* magazine, which will not only publish the work of Harlem Renaissance writers and artists but will help to support them through an annual contest.
- The National Ethiopian Art Players produce Willis Richardson's *The Chip Woman's Fortune,* the first drama by a Black playwright to appear on the Broadway stage.
- Jean Toomer's innovative novel *Cane* is published and Toomer is hailed as one of the most promising young authors of the Harlem Renaissance.
- The Ethiopian Art Players perform Eugene O'Neill's play *All God's Chillun Got Wings* in Washington, D.C., while in Cleveland the Gilpin Players at Karamu Theatre present *In Abraham's Bosom* by Paul Green.
- Poems by Harlem Renaissance star Countee Cullen appear in four major white publications.

1924

- James VanDerZee begins a series of photographs chronicling Marcus Garvey and the activities of UNIA.
- Filmmaker Oscar Micheaux completes *Birthright* and *Body and Soul,* the latter starring Paul Robeson.
- At the Civic Club dinner hosted by *Opportunity*'s Charles S. Johnson, promising young writers meet the influential editors and publishers who can boost their careers.
- *The Fire in the Flint,* a novel by NAACP leader Walter White, is published.
- ...e publication of Jessie Redmon Fauset's ...*e Is Confusion* marks the first Harlem Re-...nce book by a woman writer.

- ...musical form known as jazz ... "First American Jazz Con-...l in New York.

- Small's Paradise nightclub opens in Harlem; the club will prove to be a one of the city's most popular jazz destinations.
- Marcus Garvey is convicted of mail fraud and imprisoned in the Atlanta Penitentiary.
- Marian Anderson wins a singing competition sponsored by the New York Philharmonic Orchestra.
- Artist Sargent Johnson exhibits his paintings at the San Francisco Art Association, and Archibald Motley wins a medal from the Art Institute of Chicago for his painting "A Mulatress."
- James Weldon Johnson is awarded the NAACP's Springarn Medal for his work as an author, diplomat, and leader.
- *Survey Graphic* magazine publishes *Harlem: The Mecca of the New Negro,* an issue devoted entirely to the work of Harlem Renaissance writers and artists.
- Zora Neale Hurston publishes her short story "Spunk" in *Opportunity.*
- Countee Cullen's first volume of poetry, *Color,* is published.
- Wallace Thurman moves from Los Angeles to New York and soon becomes a leader of the younger generation of Harlem Renaissance writers and artists.
- Zora Neale Hurston enters Barnard College on a scholarship, studying anthropology.
- Well-known white poet Vachel Lindsay reads the poems of the Langston Hughes, then working as a restaurant busboy, to the audience at his own poetry reading, announcing that he has discovered a bright new talent.
- The *New Negro* anthology, edited by Alain Locke, introduces the work and ideas of the Harlem Renaissance.

1926

- W.C. Handy's *Blues: An Anthology* is published, bringing wider attention to this unique African American musical form.
- Another jazz hotspot, the Savoy Ballroom, opens in Harlem with Fletcher Henderson and his orchestra established as the house band.
- The Harmon Foundation holds its first annual art exhibition of works by African American artists, and Palmer Hayden and Hale Woodruff win top awards.

- The Carnegie Corporation buys Arthur Schomburg's African American collection and donates it to the newly established Negro Reference Library at the Harlem branch of the New York Public Library.
- The NAACP-sponsored theatrical group the Krigwa Players stages three plays.
- White author Carl Van Vechten's controversial novel *Nigger Heaven* is published.
- Langston Hughes's first volume of poetry, *The Weary Blues,* is published.
- *Crisis* awards its first prizes in literature and art. Winnners include Arna Bontemps, Countee Cullen, Aaron Douglas, and Hale Woodruff.
- A daring new (but short-lived) literary journal called *Fire!!* is launched by Langston Hughes, Wallace Thurman, Zora Neale Hurston, Aaron Douglas, and Richard Bruce Nugent, with artwork by Douglas and Nugent.

1927

- Duke Ellington begins a three-year stint at the Cotton Club, gaining fame and praise for his innovative style and compositions.
- Ordered to leave the United States, Marcus Garvey returns to Jamaica.
- Wealthy African American L'Alelia Walker, whose mother founded a successful Black hair and skin care business, opens a nightclub and literary salon called the Dark Tower.
- *Caroling Dusk: An Anthology of Verse by Negro Poets,* edited by Countee Cullen, is published by Harper.
- Charles S. Johnson publishes *Ebony and Topaz: A Collectanea,* an anthology of writings that originally appeared in *Opportunity.*
- Dorothy and DuBose Heyward's *Porgy,* a musical play with Black characters and themes, opens on Broadway; the work is adapted from DuBose's novel of the same name.
- James Weldon Johnson's *God's Trombones,* a book of poems modeled after sermons by Black preachers and illustrated by Aaron Douglas, is published.
- Several young Harlem Renaissance writers and artists—notably Zora Neale Hurston and Langston Hughes— accept money and other help from wealthy patron Charlotte Osgood Mason, who insists that those under her patronage call her "Godmother."
- Langston Hughes's second poetry collection, *Fine Clothes to the Jew,* features blues rhythms and Harlem-inspired imagery.

1928

- Palmer Hayden's work is featured in a one-man exhibition at a Paris art gallery, and Archibald Motley exhibits his paintings at the New Galleries in New York
- Aaron Douglas is awarded a fellowship to study at the Barnes Foundation in Pennsylvania.
- A number of important Harlem Renaissance works are published, including Rudolph Fisher's *Walls of Jericho,* Nella Larsen's *Quicksand,* Jessie Redmon Fauset's *Plum Bun,* W. E. B. Du Bois's *Dark Princess,* and Claude McKay's *Home to Harlem* (which becomes the first bestseller by a Black author).
- Poet Countee Cullen marries Yolande Du Bois, daughter of the great Black leader, in an extravagant wedding that is one of the most memorable social events of the Harlem Renaissance.
- Wallace Thurman edits another literary journal, *Harlem,* that is—like its predecessor, *Fire!!*— destined to appear only once.

1929

- The Harmon Foundation sponsors the exhibition *Paintings and Sculptures by American Negro Artists* at the National Gallery in Washington, D.C.
- The Negro Experimental Theater is founded.
- Films showcasing African American musicians debut, including *Black and Tan,* featuring Duke Ellington and his orchestra, and *St. Louis Blues,* which features Bessie Smith.
- The Broadway show *Ain't Misbehavin'* features music by piano player Fats Waller.
- The stock market crashes, ending the Jazz Age and ushering in the Great Depression.
- Wallace Thurman's play *Harlem,* writte[illegible] William Jourdan Rapp, opens on Br[illegible] becoming the most successful su[illegible] tion by a Black author.
- Novels by Wallace Thurman[illegible] *Berry*) and Claude M[illegible] lished, as is Countee [illegible] *and Other Poems.*

1930

- Aaron Douglas is commissioned to create a series of murals for the campus library at Fisk University in Nashville.
- James V. Herring creates the Howard University Gallery of Art. It is the first gallery in the United States to be autonomously curated and directed by African Americans.
- Marc Connelly's play *The Green Pastures,* notable for its African American characters and content, opens to great acclaim on Broadway.
- Langston Hughes's novel *Not without Laughter* is published.
- James Weldon Johnson's historical account of Harlem, *Black Manhattan,* is published by Knopf.
- Willis Richardson's *Plays and Pageants from the Life of the Negro* is published by Associated Publishers.

1931

- Artist August Savage opens the Savage School of Arts and Crafts in Harlem. It is the first of several art schools she will open in Harlem.

1932

- Louis Armstrong stars in the musical film short *A Rhapsody in Black and Blue.*

1933

- A number of Harlem Renaissance writers and artists find employment with the Works Project Administration (WPA), a government-sponsored program designed to put Americans back to work.
- Aaron Douglas paints murals for the YMCA in Harlem.
- The film adaptation of Eugene O'Neill's *The Emperor Jones,* starring Paul Robeson, is released. The screenplay is written by DuBose Heyward.

1934

- Aaron Douglas is commissioned to create a series of murals, which will be entitled *Aspects of Negro Life,* for the 135th Street (Harlem) Branch of the New York Public Library.

- Th
Ther
naissa.

1925

- The exciting new r
is showcased in the
cert" at Aeolian Hal

- The NAACP and the American Fund for Public Service plan a coordinated legal campaign, directed by Howard University Law School vice-dean Charles H. Houston, against segregation and discrimination.
- Oscar Michaux releases his film *Harlem After Midnight.*
- Wallace Thurman's death in the charity ward of a New York hospital stuns and sobers his Harlem Renaissance friends.
- Zora Neale Hurston's first novel, *Jonah's Gourd Wine,* is published by Lippincott.
- Nancy Cunard, a British socialite, assembles and edits the *Negro Anthology,* a sprawling 855 page work that features photographs and scores for African music as well as articles on ethnography, linguistics, poetry, and political commentary. Contributors include Sterling Brown, Langston Hughes, and Zora Neale Hurston.

1935

- Harlem is the scene of a major riot sparked by anger over discrimination by white-owned businesses.
- The exhibition *African Negro Art* opens at the Museum of Modern Art in New York City.
- Carl Van Vechten debuts his first collection of photographs in *The Leica Exhibition* at the Bergdorf Goodman in New York City.
- Lippincott publishes Hurston's ethnographic study *Mules and Men,* with illustrations by Miguel Covarrubias.

1936

- African American actors Paul Robeson and Hattie McDaniel appear in director James Whales's film adaptation of Kern and Hammerstein's musical *Show Boat.*

1937

- *Their Eyes Were Watching God* by Zora Neale Hurston is published by Lippincott.

GWENDOLYN BENNETT

(1902 - 1981)

"It was fun to be alive and to be part of this . . . like nothing else I've ever been a part of."

—Gwendolyn Bennett

American poet, short story writer, journalist, and artist.

A literary figure and artist of the Harlem Renaissance, Bennett wrote poetry and provided illustrations for African American journals of the 1920s. Her poetry and short stories have never been collected in a single volume, although several individual works have appeared in anthologies.

BIOGRAPHICAL INFORMATION

Born on July 8, 1902, in Giddings, Texas, Bennett was the only child of Joshua Bennett and Maime Abernathy Bennett. Shortly after she was born, the family moved to Nevada, where her parents taught school on an Indian reservation, and then to Washington, D. C., where her parents divorced. Although custody of Bennett was granted to her mother, her father kidnapped her when she was seven years old; she was not reunited with her mother until 1924, when she was twenty-two years old. Father and daughter lived in several small towns in Pennsylvania and eventually settled in Brooklyn, New York, after Joshua's marriage to Marechel Neil. Bennett was an honor student in Harrisburg, Pennsylvania, and at the Brooklyn Girls' High School, where she displayed a talent for both art and literature and became the first Black member of both the literary society and the drama society. After her graduation in 1921, Bennett attended the Pratt Institute and Columbia University, taught in the fine arts department of Howard University, and studied art in Paris for a year on a scholarship.

In 1923 Bennett's poem "Heritage" was published in the African American journal *Opportunity,* and that same year she provided the cover illustration for the NAACP's journal *Crisis.* Encouraged by such older writers of the Harlem Renaissance as W. E. B. Du Bois and Charles S. Johnson, Bennett joined the informal Harlem Writers Guild along with such other young authors as Langston Hughes, Countee Cullen, and Helene Johnson. She continued contributing poetry and book reviews to various periodicals, and in 1926 began writing "The Ebony Flute," a regular column of "literary chit-chat" for *Opportunity.* In 1927 Bennett married Alfred Joseph Jackson, a doctor, and a year later moved with him to Florida. In 1930, the couple settled on Long Island, and when Jackson died shortly thereafter, Bennett returned to New York City, where she took positions with the Works Progress Administration's Federal Writers Project and Federal Arts Project. She served as assistant director of the Harlem Community Art Center and in 1937 succeeded sculptor Augusta Savage as its director; however, she was suspended from that post in 1941 because of her political views. She then accepted positions with the Jefferson School for

Democracy and the George Washington Carver School, both considered fronts for Communist organizations and both investigated by the House Committee on Un-American Activities. Driven from public life, Bennett retired to Kutztown, Pennsylvania, where she and her second husband, Richard Crosscup, collected and sold antiques. Bennett died on May 30, 1981, of congestive heart failure.

MAJOR WORKS

Bennett's poetry appeared in the leading African American journals of the 1920s and in anthologies such as James Weldon Johnson's *The Book of American Negro Poetry* (1922) and Countee Cullen's *Caroling Dusk: An Anthology of Verse by Negro Poets* (1927). Her poems were never collected into a single volume. Much of her work expresses the racial pride and militant spirit associated with the Harlem Renaissance. "To a Dark Girl" (1927) is a tribute to the beauty of African American women, and "To Usward," written for the 1924 National Urban League dinner, celebrates the youthful spirit and diverse aesthetic visions of artists of the Harlem Renaissance; it was subsequently published in both *Crisis* and *Opportunity.* At the same time her poetry could be highly personal and lyrical; "Hatred" (1926), for example, involves a seemingly unmotivated hatred for an unspecified individual target.

Bennett produced two short stories, both written while she was in France, and both set in the Rue Pigalle in Paris. "Wedding Day" (1926) features a Black American soldier who remains in France after the war in an attempt to avoid racial discrimination in America, only to find himself the victim of racism in Paris. He falls in love with a white American woman who abandons him on their wedding day, explaining in a note that it would simply be inappropriate for a white woman to marry a Black man—even in France. "Tokens" (1927) also involves an American expatriate, a musician dying of tuberculosis who recalls his life with bitterness and regret. In addition to her poetry and stories, Bennett also produced book reviews, social commentary, and her monthly column of literary news, "The Ebony Flute," which appeared for almost two years in the journal *Opportunity.*

CRITICAL RECEPTION

Reaction to Bennett's work by her contemporaries was quite positive. Her writing was regularly featured in the journals and anthologies edited by the more famous writers and editors of the Harlem Renaissance. Her biographer, Sandra Y. Govan (1997) reports that Bennett "was considered a skillful and evocative lyric poet who also made use of such recurring New Negro themes as pride *in* and celebration *of* racial heritage, the importance of cultural icons, recognizing Black folk experience, and commemorating the exuberance and camaraderie of youth on the move." After her retirement from public life in the early 1940s, however, Bennett's work was largely neglected until the resurgence of interest in African American women writers in the late twentieth century, and even then, according to Govan, Bennett's work did not receive the recognition that other women writers of the Harlem Renaissance—particularly Zora Neale Hurston and Nella Larsen—earned.

Bennett's talent as a visual artist and illustrator has been recognized as an important factor in her poetry. Nina Miller (1998) claims that the poem "Fantasy" (1927) is "an apparently direct translation of Bennett's art deco drawing" and constitutes a "verbal tapestry." According to Miller, "Bennett carried her fine arts sensibility forward into her high renaissance work as one of its major foundations and an important instrument of ideological critique." Miller also considers Bennett's work within the context of the women's lyric tradition and the avant-garde movement of the Harlem Renaissance, suggesting that the poem "To Usward" fuses the "feminine selfhood" of the former "into the very definition of renaissance artistry" of the latter.

PRINCIPAL WORKS

*"Nocturn" (poem) 1922

"Heritage" (poem) 1923

"To Usward" (poem) 1924

"Wind" (poem) 1924

"Purgation" (poem) 1925

"Hatred" (poem) 1926

"Lines Written at the Grave of Alexander Dumas" (poem) 1926

"Moon Tonight" (poem) 1926

"Song" (poem) 1926

"Street Lamps in Early Spring" (poem) 1926

"Wedding Day" [published in journal *Fire!!*] (short story) 1926

"Fantasy" (poem) 1927

"To a Dark Girl" (poem) 1927

"Tokens" (short story) 1927

* All of Bennett's poems were published in periodicals (most often *Opportunity*) and in anthologies. No collection of her writings exists.

GENERAL COMMENTARY

MICHEL FABRE (ESSAY DATE 1991)

SOURCE: Fabre, Michel. "Jessie Fauset and Gwendolyn Bennett." In *From Harlem to Paris: Black American Writers in France, 1840-1980,* pp. 114-28. Urbana: University of Illinois Press, 1991.

In the following excerpt, Fabre examines Bennett's year in Paris during which she studied art and wrote poetry and short stories.

Although Gwendolyn Bennett was not a major writer, her account of her stay in France when she was twenty-three is of special interest, not only because she was both an artist and a writer, but because her loneliness rendered her particularly sensitive to the atmosphere of Paris and to its impingement on her sense of personal and national identity. A poet published in *Opportunity* and the *Crisis,* a fine-arts teacher at Howard University, she was awarded a $1,000 scholarship by the Delta Sigma Theta sorority in December 1924 and chose to study in Paris for a full year. Although she hardly knew the language, she was well versed in modern French fiction from Flaubert to Anatole France and, like Countee Cullen, she wrote poetry under the influence of the symbolists.

She sailed for Cherbourg on June 15, 1925, with great expectations: having exciting encounters with artists and writers, going on merry sprees with friends from home, discovering art treasures in exhibitions and museums, sharing chic Parisian life. After visiting one of the art salons, riding all around the city in a taxi with her friend Alston Burleigh, son of the well-known black singer and composer Harry T. Burleigh, and seeing the Luxembourg Museum, she remarked: "There never was a more beautiful city than Paris. . . . There couldn't be! On every hand are works of art and beautiful vistas. One has the impression of looking through at fairy-worlds as one sees gorgeous buildings, arches and towers rising from among the mounds of trees from afar. And there are flowers, too, in Paris, oh, just billions of them. . . . And if it did not make me sad it would make me glad to be privileged to enjoy its beauty."[1]

Thrilled to find the Pantheon and Notre-Dame as magnificent as the stories she had read about them, she shared her enthusiasm with friends at home on illustrated postcards of the Paris monuments. But why should this beauty make her sad instead of glad? Apparently the reason was being away from home, all by herself, far from her beloved Gene, hence incapable of sharing her romantic discoveries and overly sensitive to the slightest difficulty. Missing an appointment with an art professor, being talked to as though she were a little girl, could bring her to the verge of tears. And imagine her panic on the night when, after seeing a movie with a French girl, she lost her way in the Latin Quarter and walked the streets frantically, clutching the medal Gene had given her like a talisman!

Always dreading to be alone, Gwendolyn did not, in fact, lack company. On June 27, 1925, by sheer chance she ran across Langston Hughes's sweetheart of the previous year, Anne Coussey, as she was going down the Boulevard Saint-Michel. Anne took her to Gwen Sinclair, who was studying fashion drawing, and she joined in Sinclair's quest for a studio, but in vain. They visited many museums, and Bennett loved to go shopping with Alston Burleigh and his father, but as shortage of money was her perpetual affiction, she bought only a pair of inexpensive and much-needed gloves. However, she enjoyed the congenial simplicity of the great singer when he took them to the English tearoom on the Rue de Rivoli or when he attempted, in broken French, to buy a pair of corduroys at the Louvre department store. And there were breathtaking cultural highs, as when, in the Musée des Arts Décoratifs, she could admire dozens of Monets and Manets or catch a glimpse of Corot's palette and hat and Delacroix's brush and pipe at the nineteenth-century French retrospective exhibition.

On the Fourth of July loneliness filled her with a new, strange patriotism, and she confided to her journal: "There are times I'd give half my remaining years to hear the 'Star-Spangled Banner.' And yet when I feel that way, I know it has nothing to do with the same 'home' feeling I have when I see crowds of American white people jostling each other about the American Express." Clearly, being away from home enabled her to see America in a rosier light, even though the presence of her fellow citizens reminded her from time to time of race prejudice. She had been taken with black musician Louis Jones to a tea dance at the fashionable Les Acacias in the Bois de Boulogne. There she felt like a dream girl in a dreamland until a remark nettled her: "It must have galled the Americans to death to see us there on a par with them. As Louis and I danced together, I heard a group of them saying among themselves: 'They dance nicely, don't they? You know, they have that native rhythm. Whoa!'"[2]

This was already on August 2. Gwendolyn had just returned from a trip to Marseilles when Dr. Owen Waller, a friend fresh from the United States, hauled her out of bed to help him find a room. But she was rewarded with a fine lunch, and then a shopping spree with three girlfriends, before being taken to the Bois de Boulogne with the party. At the beginning of her stay, Bennett enjoyed quite a lot of socializing. On Bastille Day the Wests, Mercer and Vashti Cook, Harold Jackman, Edwin Morgan, and a few others took her to the Moulin Rouge, the Rat Mort, and Bricktop's cabaret. On August 6, some of them repeated the round with Mr. Jenkins. After dinner at a Chinese restaurant, they repaired at 2 A.M. to dance and drink champagne at the Royal Montmartre, where Louis Jones, who had briefly left Chez Florence, where he was then performing, danced with Gwendolyn. Then, finding the Grand Duc too crowded with black Americans, they went to Bricktop's: at Brick's, Lottie Gee on her first night in town was singing her hit from *Shuffle Along,* "I'm Just Wild about Harry." Bricktop herself sang her favorite, "Insufficient Sweetie." After hot cakes and sausages, *de rigueur* at the Grand Duc, the party stepped out into the lovely grey morning light at 6:30 A.M., the young lady proudly recorded. And there were more dances at Les Acacias, and nights at the Opera. On August 2, 1925, she was taken to a performance of *Thaïs,* "beautiful music and shades of Anatole France," and in that world of glitter and beauty, enjoyment and ease, she only regretted that lack of money kept her from so much.[3] The next day she attended Wagner's *Lohengrin,* thinking the French were perfect asses to have translated the opera from the German on the strength, she strangely figured, that they had been at war. This paradoxically led her to regret both the hatred between the two countries in the name of New World liberalism and the lack of such fierce patriotism in America!

Indeed, to many Gwendolyn Bennett's first months in Paris would have been paradise, yet by the end of August she was not sure whether she liked the place or not, as she wrote Countee Cullen: "My first impressions were of extreme loneliness and intense homesickness—this and incessant rain—now through the hazy veil of memories I see Paris is a very beautiful city and that people here are basically different from those I have always known. I feel I shall like being here bye and bye."[4]

For lack of contact with cultured French people rather than out of choice, Bennett kept very much in the company of Americans. One of her favorite companions was Harold Jackman, who did not write much himself but was refined and wonderfully able to enjoy high society life. At that time Jackman himself was discovering Paris for the first time. Staying at the Hotel Marignan on the Rue du Sommerard in the Latin Quarter, he wrote Langston Hughes: "Paris lives up to its name and I am not at all disappointed. . . . These days it is so lovely with its gaiety and there is so much of it. Love here in the springtime must be next to divine for in the summer it is a lovely sight to view two lovers on the boulevard just cooing to each other as it were. I tell you, rather I should ask you, what other place under the sun is like Paris, except somewhere in the tropics under the soft moonlight? I could stay there for ever."[5]

Jackman did not allude to Bennett, but she later reported spending wonderful hours in his company, trotting around the city making discoveries. She joined the private lending library run by Sylvia Beach and Adrienne Monnier on the Rue de l'Odéon, which featured the latest writers in English: "Harold and I have already ordered *Ulysses* from them. . . . Those of us who are akin to Croesus can also get a copy of Frank Harris's *Life and Loves* for 300 francs or 15 dollars. The *Ulysses* only cost 60 francs. I should love to have them both to add to my library of pornography."[6] At Shakespeare and Company she also enjoyed a few literary teas, timidly mixing with Joyce, Arthur Moss, Lewis Galantière, Ernest Hemingway, and composer George Antheil, and Sylvia Beach later invited her to a Thanksgiving dinner at her home. Bennett was also invited to tea at Gertrude Stein's and at Matisse's and even at a millionaire's place near the Bois de Boulogne. During the last week of August, she was glad to have the company of the Robesons: Paul had enjoyed a warm reception in London, and they were heading for the Riviera. She visited them nearly every day at their hotel, going around with them a lot before they curtailed their stay on account of the rainy weather.

In the fall she still entertained conflicting opinions about her stay. She could understand, she wrote Hughes, why he had not "got on" in Paris: "I know of no one place on earth where people are as joyous and gaiety-filled with the doing of a number of things and yet where one can be so unutterably alone. I spent during the first two weeks I was here the most miserable time imaginable. Too many times it seemed I had no right to be here." She had become somewhat reconciled to the cruel, cold rains that seemed to pierce her to the marrow of her bones, but she felt that "the authors who babble about 'sunny France' are damned fools."[7]

Bennett, who was no beginner in art, was angry when confronted with the impossibility of taking evening classes in Paris and at having everybody advise her to attend the New York School of Fine and Applied Arts, and she had not succeeded in finding a studio to share with Gwendolyn Lewis. As a *pis aller* she registered at the Académie de la Grande Chaumière, where she was working hard on her first nude in early August. She also registered at the Collège de la Guilde for French courses, but weary of learning so much and understanding so little, she gave them up so as not to waste three precious hours each morning. Later she attended the Académie Julian, the Académie Colarossi, and the École du Panthéon—all for art courses. Through artist Konrad Bercovici she met Franz Masereel, an imaginative Belgian painter and probably the boldest engraver of the time. She gave him English lessons, and the hospitality of the Masereels, who welcomed her into their home and introduced her to their friends, did much to alleviate her loneliness.

Before the end of September, however, her scholarship checks failed to arrive, and she was in financial difficulty. She decided to move to the northwest of the city and stay in a small pension in Pontoise, with Madame Raffalli. She loved the place: with the smell of grass and trees, the murmur of the river nearby, the quaint beauty of the little town, she felt she was retreating into the calm, impersonal heart of the countryside. She could go cycling, feeling the fresh invigorating air in the early morning. As she was the only guest at that time of the year, she became part of the family, and when her landlady's relatives came for the weekend, she would play tag or blindman's buff on the lawn with the aunts and uncles, listen to the children's laughter, and eat piles of food. One night she awoke full of fear, startled by the sound of people snoring in the nearby room, but as she saw the great, pale disc of the moon rising, she was nearly moved to write poetry, she confided to her journal on September 29, 1925.

On several occasions her sensitivity to a new way of life indeed brought her to the verge of creative writing. As she entered Saint-Sulpice during mass on August 23, she was surprised to find that the Chapelle de la Vierge was no ordinary altar but a grandiose niche with the madonna carved in marble between the heavens and the earth. Although by no means a Catholic, she knelt to pray with the worshipers, filled with awe by the pealing bells and majestic chords of the organ. Her eyes brimming with tears, she sat there, enveloped in the waves of music, feeling protected by the huge pillars. She summed up her experience in literary as well as religious terms: "Saint-Sulpice with its marvellous organ is a veritable stage for romance, set as it is in the very heart of the quarters of Dumas's 'Three Musketeers' and scene as it is for Massenet's 'Manon.' Surely one must be worse than stone not to thrill at the neighborhood itself! If there is one store selling church furniture—crosses, madonnas and altar ornaments—in the neighborhood, there must be a hundred! True, there is a gilded look to their displays but there is also the thought behind it all that devout, God-fearing people believe in and worship the 'something' of God, Truth that these things represent."[8] She came even closer to creative writing when, after a night in the Montmartre cabarets, she caught sight of the Sacré-Coeur at dawn: "I shall never forget the shock of beauty as we stepped out into the early morning streets. . . . up rue Pigalle, there stood the Sacred Heart . . . beautiful, pearly Sacré-Coeur, as though its silent loveliness were pointing a white finger at our night's debauchery. I wished then that so worthy an emotion as I felt might have been forever caught in a poem but somehow my muse refuses to work these days."[9]

She did write poetry, though. In contrast to her generally subdued, reflective, melancholy verse, her tribute to the author of *The Three Musketeers,* **"Lines Written on the Grave of Alexandre Dumas,"** sounds unexpectedly solemn and grandiloquent:

> Thou, great spirit, wouldst shiver in thy granite
> shroud
> Should idle mirth or empty talk
> Disturb thy tranquil sleeping.
> A cemetery is a place for shattered loves
> And broken hearts . . .[10]

After the mad whirl at Christmas time and the ensuing nostalgia, Gwendolyn Bennett settled in at last, having found a suitable studio. Paris had finally gotten hold of her, and it did inspire two of her stories, both about exiled black Americans with broken hearts.

Paul Watson, the protagonist of **"Wedding Day,"** comes to the city around 1910, giving boxing lessons and performing in special bouts arranged for him. Later he plays the banjo with the first colored jazz bands in small cafés patronized mostly by French people. He hates his white compatriots, and one day, when a drunken Kentuckian calls him first "bruther" and then "nigger," he beats up all the American customers, earning the reputation of a "black terror." After shooting and wounding two U.S. soldiers, he serves a long prison term but is pardoned to fight in the French army, where he behaves like a true hero.

Bennett's knowledge of the area allowed her to have her character shamble down the Rue Pigalle, which "in the early morning has a sombre beauty—gray as are most Paris streets and other worldish. To those who know the district it is the Harlem of Paris and rue Pigalle is its dusty Seventh Avenue. . . . He reached the corner of rue de la Bruyère and with sure instinct his feet stopped. Without thinking he turned into the Pit." Indeed, the Flea Pit bistro has a telephone, which Paul desperately wants to use, and, the narrator intervenes, "French telephones are such human faults."[11]

In a brand-new, pearl-gray suit, Paul is about to get married. Indeed, some time before, he has met on the street a white American girl without a sou to her name. His racial hatred has turned to compassion, and soon, to the astonishment of the Negro musicians, he is taking her to Gavarni's every night for supper. But on this their wedding day she has failed to come. Frantically, Paul rides the Métro to her place, lost in his anguished musings, but "the shrill whistle that is typical of the French subway pierced a way into his thoughts." With a bitter sense of irony, he realizes that he is traveling second class with a first-class ticket: "funny how these French said 'descend' when they meant 'get off'; funny how, after living here for all those years, he couldn't pick up French properly." Where did he really belong? Certainly not in "white" America, the story makes clear, since when he reaches the future bride's hotel, Paul finds only a note: Mary just could not go through with it—"white women don't marry colored men," she had written—and she only a street woman![12]

Baffled love is again the theme of **"Tokens,"** a vignette about the sad fate of a black musician. Jenks Barnett had first arrived in Europe with the jazz orchestra of Will Marion Cook. In Paris he falls in love with Tollie Saunders, a Negro entertainer, and when she leaves him, he starts on the headlong road downward: he becomes a drunkard; he spends two weeks in jail with a terrible pain in his back until his friends rescue him. After "endless days of splashing through the Paris rain in search of a job . . . then night upon night of blowing a trombone in a stuffy little *boîte de nuit,*" he is sent to the American Hospital.[13] Finally, sick with tuberculosis, he ends up in the Saint-Cloud sanitorium. Just before dying, Jenks, faithful to the last, asks his friend Bill to send Tollie his silver picture frame and give his radium clock to a tubercular French kid who used to visit him. Bennett thus weaves her poetic dirge of the loveless black jazzman into a kind of Paris blues, framed by the ominous lines of the landscape: "High on the bluff of Saint-Cloud stands the Merlin Hospital, immaculate sentinel of Seraigne . . . Seraigne with its crazy houses and aimless streets, scrambling at the foot of Saint-Cloud's immense immutability. Row on row the bricks of the hospital take dispassionate account of lives lost and found." As a refrain, the "wanton unconcern of the Seine" (is this an echo of Apollinaire's "Pont Mirabeau"?) slowly flows past the rustic stupor of the suburban town: "The Seine . . . mute river of sorrows . . . grim concealer of forgotten secrets . . . endlessly flowing . . . touching the edges of life . . . moving purposefully along with great disdain for the empty, foolish gaiety of Seraigne or the benign dignity of the Merlin Hospital, high on the warm cliffs of Saint-Cloud."[14]

In June 1926 Bennett returned home to resume teaching design and water color at Howard University while acting as an associate editor for *Opportunity.* Later she was an educator in several states, a supervisor for the Federal Arts Teaching Project, and the initiator of a progressive school for Harlem children. Until her left-wing sympathies nearly brought her to face the Committee on Un-American Activities, she had an active and committed career. In comparison, the echoes of her French experience in her journal and in her writing seem strangely romantic. Was this due to an extraordinary sensitivity or simply to her youth? After all, after riding a bicycle over the soft earth along the Oise, with her lips whistling, "for hours on hours of heaven," or after relishing Van Vechten's *Blind Boy* or Alfred Kreymborg's *Troubadour,* was she not the girl who had wondered "if all people who are twenty-three and have loved are this melancholy?"[15]

Notes

1. Gwendolyn Bennett, unpublished journal, June 28, 1925, 8, Schomburg Collection.
2. Bennett, journal, 15-16, 20.
3. Bennett, journal, 20.
4. Bennett to Cullen, August 23, 1925, Amistad.

5. Harold Jackman to Langston Hughes, August 13, 1925, Yale.
6. Bennett to Cullen, August 23, 1925, Amistad.
7. Bennett to Hughes, September 1925, Yale.
8. Bennett, journal, 31.
9. Bennett, journal, 27.
10. Bennett, "Lines Written on the Grave of Alexandre Dumas," *Opportunity*, June 1926, 136-37.
11. Bennett, "Wedding Day," *Fire!* (November 1926), 26-27.
12. Ibid., 28.
13. Bennett, "Tokens," in *Ebony and Topaz*, ed. Charles S. Johnson (Freeport, N.Y.: Books for Libraries Press, 1971), 148.
14. Ibid., 149.
15. Bennett, journal, 38.

SANDRA Y. GOVAN (ESSAY DATE 1997)

SOURCE: Govan, Sandra Y. "A Blend of Voices: Composite Narrative Strategies in Biographical Reconstruction." In *Recovered Writers/Recovered Texts: Race, Class, and Gender in Black Women's Literature,* edited by Dolan Hubbard, pp. 90-104. Knoxville: University of Tennessee Press, 1997.

In the following essay, Govan recounts her attempt to reconstruct the life and career of Bennett, whose critically acclaimed poetry of the Harlem Renaissance has been neglected until recently.

In a 1991 Harlem interview, author, scholar, and social and cultural historian John Henrik Clarke jocularly posed the paradigm of the biographer as God. "Like God," Clarke said, "biographers engage in the act of Creation." However, before they can fulfill the mandate of a godhead, particularly in the matter of black women whose lives may well be given over to public service (largely service in the capacity of behind-the-scenes nurturer and service too soon forgotten), all too often biographers must first recover and rediscover the essence of those lives. Then they may proceed to the more artistic acts of re-creation and reconstruction.

It is after the figure has first been partially restored that biographers may then begin the task of fitting together the puzzle pieces, the bits and fragments of a subject's life from a variety of sources to aesthetically re-create and reconstruct some semblance of the life/lives of their protagonist for the biography. If the writer is "good" at what he/she does, an animated person moves again. If the writer only "slickly manipulates the facts," then only a shadow, not the substance, of a figure people knew flits fitfully across the printed page.

Apart from the deity model, biographers do have other strategic aims undergirding the construction of a vital and informative text. Some, for instance, may search for the "life-myth" that has served the subject. Others attend closely to a subject's work "for clues to the life," recognizing that "public lives are not lived in isolation." Still another concern is the treatment of "amorous details"; should these be omitted for reasons of propriety or decorum, the biographer is still obligated to "probe beneath [the] public polished self." Indeed, what must be included in any honest and thoroughly grounded biographical treatment are the "doubts and vulnerabilities, the meannesses, ambitions, and private satisfactions that are hidden within a social personality" of the subject, for these "yield [the] greatest insights" (Pachter 3-15). Stretching beyond the acquisition and presentation of facts, the biographer must learn to interpret these facts, be it artistically or scientifically, in the context of all that has been learned.

In his penetrating article "Biography and Afro-American Culture," Arnold Rampersad makes several valuable observations. By far the most momentous is that for too long black biography has ignored or shunned "the role of psychology in the structure of Afro-American biographical writing" (194). Rampersad argues that while countless scholars have cited W. E. B. Du Bois's paradigm of the divided soul, the "two warring ideals in one dark body" first posited in 1903 in *The Souls of Black Folk* (215), black biography has not moved beyond this conception of black psychology. Confronted by the psychological or psychoanalytical imperative, the texts retreat, their authors withdrawing from rather than engaging in or taking "into account, the insights, discoveries, and methods of the psychologists" (198). Having surveyed the field, it is Rampersad's judgment that rather than tackling the challenge posed by psychology or admitting the utility and conceivable power of psychology as a tool, "black biography has kept a vast distance between itself and that discipline" (198).

While the stance of biographer, whether friendly, neutral, or antagonistic remains the operative guide behind the entire enterprise, this pattern is being altered to allow the participation of other voices in the project. No longer must the black biographer be *either* advocate and propagandist (often "for the race" in the case of older biographical portraits about African Americans) *or* vilifier and muckraker, castigating the subject. Like biographers of old, contemporary biographers must still rummage—through trash cans, letters, news clippings, and so on. Now, however, in addition to these traditional resources, the modern biographer can inform the work by blending these customary or typical methods more actively with voices or perspectives from other locales.

Such a composite narrative strategy encourages autobiographical testimony—from diaries, scrapbooks, letters—in an active rather than passive manner. Such a narrative blending could grant, upon verification, more privilege to oral testimony by giving peers, colleagues, friends, and associates a larger role. Their input would be neither categorically dismissed as idle gossip nor relegated to footnote status. A truly composite narrative structure seeks space not only for the voices of the literary or social and cultural historian, but, as Rampersad argues, it could also seek insights from a psychoanalytic perspective; welcome the acumen of a feminist perspective (which can have crucial applications when examining the life story of a woman); and/or encourage the artistic vision of the fictionist or filmmaker. Spike Lee's film biography of Malcolm X, for instance, attests to the rich and bold possibilities of this kind of composite structural approach.

In sum, a creative blending of the narrative format possibilities from different disciplines, from different genres, and from different modes of approaching the craft/art/science of biography can create a truly engaging "speakerly text," leading, we can hope, to a more engaging and more accurate biographical reconstruction. This, at least, is the model in mind, informing my own biographical enterprise on the life of Gwendolyn Bennett. The working title of that ongoing project is "Tapestry: The Lives of Gwendolyn Bennett." And while I quite concur with Rampersad's injunction that "remarks about biography should be made only with caution" (194), in order that readers obtain some sense of the color and complexity of that "tapestry" I will indicate a part of the trail already traversed in the struggle to recover Gwendolyn Bennett and some of the steps taken to recover her and reclaim for her a more suitable place within the canon.

Bennett's life story captured my attention during the early seventies, when as a master's candidate at Bowling Green State University, I first read several of her poems in concert with the work of other women writers from the Harlem Renaissance. Several of those we studied then, most notably Zora Neale Hurston and Nella Larsen, have since been recovered and reclaimed. Yet for Gwendolyn Bennett, deemed by Harold Cruse to be one of the "most outstanding personalities of the Harlem Renaissance," recognition has been slow in coming (23). In her day, however, Bennett's poetry was well received, even heralded. She was considered a skillful and evocative lyric poet who also made use of such recurring New Negro themes as pride *in* and celebration *of* racial heritage, the importance of cultural icons, recognizing black folk experience, and commemorating the exuberance and camaraderie of youth on the move.

Like Langston Hughes, with whom she shared a poetic sensibility, Bennett could play the race card, but she could also evoke the delicate image or sound the poignant, or angry, note. Her **"To Usward,"** which appeared simultaneously in the May 1924 issues of *The Crisis* and *Opportunity,* was dedicated to Jessie Fauset at the integrated literary gala sponsored by Charles S. Johnson to mark the "debut" of Harlem's writers and artists. The poem celebrates the moment and illustrates the unity within diversity of the spirited younger New Negroes with whom she found a bond:

> If any have a song to sing
> That's different from the rest
> Oh let them sing before the urgency of youth's
> behest!

Her **"Quatrains,"** which was published in Countee Cullen's 1927 anthology *Caroling Dusk,* paints the mood of the contemplative artist struggling with a divided artistic consciousness:

> Brushes and paints are all I have
> To speak the music in my soul
> While silently there laughs at me
> A copper jar besides a pale green bowl.
>
> (155)

Yet **"Hatred"** demonstrates Bennett's capacity to reveal more stark emotion. Her speaker declares in no uncertain terms:

> I shall hate you
> like a dart of stinging steel
> shot through thin air at eventide.
> Hating you shall be a game. . . .

Although her poetry was never collected into a volume, her work nonetheless received favorable attention and comment from leading critics and scholars of her day. Sterling Brown placed her work squarely within the "New Negro school" and found it "generally race conscious" (Brown 74). While he appreciated Bennett's verse in the "freer forms," James Weldon Johnson believed that she was at her best with the "delicate poignant lyric" (*Negro Poetry* 243). Alain Locke thought enough of her work to include it in *The New Negro,* and Countee Cullen asked her for contributions not only to his *Caroling Dusk* anthology but also to the little poetry magazine he guest edited, *Palms*. Clearly, in her own time Bennett was respected as the peer of and was celebrated along with Langston Hughes and Countee Cullen as a promising New Negro poet. Yet Bennett could acknowledge that poetry was not the only facet of the arts that held her interest, especially during the heady moments of the Harlem Renaissance. Reflecting upon the mood of the era years later, she fondly recalled its endless possibilities: "There was more of a freedom of one person doing several things. This was the first time I wrote prose. I also did journalistic work on *Opportunity*. And the same with anybody who felt like doing something. You didn't have to be labeled as a poet and stay right with poetry" (interview).

Despite the obvious intrinsic worth attached to a thoroughgoing study of her poetry, it was not her poetry alone, nor the fiction nor the journalism nor the illustrations, that kept bringing my attention back to Bennett despite interventing projects. Rather, it was the peculiarly elusive quality about Bennett's life, the sense of mystery connected to the information available in the 1970s about her which I found intriguing. Here was a woman who was clearly "there" and involved, and yet so little was known about her. The biographical data which appeared always recited essentially the same facts: born in Giddings, Texas, in 1902; graduated from Girls High in Brooklyn; went to Pratt Institute, graduating in 1924; and took some course work at Columbia. It was not just her work but her life which called for recovery and reclamation.

And oddly enough, in the years since Gwendolyn Bennett first caught my attention, both her career and her presence as a participant, a shaper, and a contributor to the arts community, have attracted the attention of sundry other scholars. Indeed, Bennett's status as a marginalized so-called minor figure situated within what Ronald Primeau designated as the "second echelon" of Renaissance poets, has evolved from virtual dismissals or casual mentions in texts such as Wilson Record's *Negro in the Communist Party* (1971), Nathan Huggins's *Harlem Renaissance* (1971), and Jervis Anderson's *This Was Harlem 1900-1950* (1981) to more than passing attention in more recent reexaminations of the period. Gloria Hull's *Color, Sex, and Poetry* (1987) alludes to Bennett several times and features a Bennett illustration on its cover. Other more careful, critical comments have come in the several entries composed for various biographical and critical dictionaries,

FROM THE AUTHOR

EXCERPT FROM "TO A DARK GIRL"

Oh, little brown girl, born for sorrow's
  mate,
Keep all you have of queenliness,
Forgetting that you once were slave
And let your full lips laugh at Fate!

SOURCE: Gwendolyn Bennett, "To a Dark Girl," in *Caroling Dusk: An Anthology of Verse by Negro Poets,* edited by Countee Cullen, Harper, 1927.

including the *Dictionary of Literary Biography, The Herlem Renaissance Reexamined, Afro-American Women Writers 1746-1933* (1988), and *Notable Black American Women* (1992). Indeed, in the 1990s, Bennett's literary stock has seen some real appreciation. For the first time she has been included in a major "mainstream" college textbook, the *Heath Anthology of American Literature,* volume 2 (1990), and she finally achieved chapter status (actually, Bennett and Jessie Fauset share a chapter) with the publication of Michel Fabre's *From Harlem to Paris: Black American Writers in France, 1840-1980* (1991).

My Ph.D. dissertation, entitled "Gwendolyn Bennett: Portrait of an Artist Lost" (1980), was the first extensive treatment of Bennett. It focused on her life as an eager and willing New Negro. Following the completion of that dissertation and the recognition of its gaps, I continued my search for more about Bennett, albeit fitfully. Through the succeeding years, I had available to me limited blocks of time, derived from summer grants, spring breaks, and a research fellowship, with which to further the task of amassing facts, compiling details, tracing leads and sifting through scattered bits of data to collect and store the raw material which will eventually shape the projected "Tapestry."[1]

There have been several phases to this project, of necessity undertaken at different times and with varying degrees of skill and success. The initial step, what can be called Phase I or the "published papers phase," geared to secondary sources, was largely captured in the dissertation. This phase noted and recorded all publications by Bennett, all references to her work in literature or in art as these appeared in contemporaneous publications. All of the allusions to Bennett or to her accomplishments which repeatedly occurred in the pages of the NAACP's *Crisis* and the Urban League's *Opportunity* were tracked. I collected all of the poems, fiction, essays, and reviews by Bennett appearing in both the black and white media, including various New York newspapers and *Fire, Palms, Black Opals, Southern Workman, Ebony,* and *Topaz,* in addition to the small literary magazines or journals associated with the New Negro era. In the case of *Fire,* Bennett not only contributed a story but with Hughes, Wallace Thurman, and Bruce Nugent, among others, Bennett served on the editorial board. The highly influential Alain Locke not only included some of her poetry in the *New Negro* but subsequently placed a photograph of one of her paintings in his later work, *Negro in Art* (1940). In fact, Bennett has been included in nearly all the major anthologies edited by the leading figures of the period. Additionally, Hughes mentions Bennett favorably several times in his 1940 autobiography, *The Big Sea.*

During this phase of the research, while copying the two years of "Ebony Flute" columns which Bennett wrote for *Opportunity,* columns that served the purpose of carrying "informal literary intelligence" throughout the black arts community, thus circulating a variety or "arts" news concerning personalities or events—who had published what, who was talking to a particular publisher, who was traveling where—I chanced to look at the actual cover of a bound copy (rather than a microfilm text only version) of an *Opportunity* issue. That was the first confirmation I found that Bennett was also an artist-illustrator. Acting on the supposition that if there was one cover illustration there may be others, I subsequently discovered that during this era, Bennett had drawn five cover illustrations for both *The Crisis* and *Opportunity.* The concerted effort, then, of this initial phase was to obtain all Bennett's publications records. The next step was to locate Bennett herself. At the time Phase II of the research began I was still a student, working toward my doctorate, and Gwendolyn B. Bennett was very much alive.

Although she was not in hiding, when she retired from the hectic pace of life in New York, Gwendolyn Bennett had seemingly dropped so completely from public view that no one I contacted initially knew how to find her. She was using her married name, Mrs. Richard Crosscup, and I had been looking for "Gwendolyn Bennett." Eventually, through persistence, the right contacts, some detective work and sheer dumb luck, I found her trading in antiques, using her Kutztown, Pennsylvania, home as her base.[2] And while she was surprised by the thought of becoming the subject of a doctoral dissertation, she actually did not mind being "discovered." In fact, she seemed glad she had been "found," because the process of being recorded for posterity gave her the opportunity to share her impressions and voice her thoughts about the twenties and New Negro era, a period she clearly considered the best part of her life. Thus, in May of 1979, we held a three-day marathon interview session. During our conversations Bennett proved warm and cordial, completely willing to help a novice scholar further the doctoral process.

One of Bennett's more incisive comments about the artists of the era turned on a personal note: "It was fun to be alive and to be part of this . . . like nothing else I've ever been a part of . . . there's been nothing exactly like this . . . nothing like this particular life in which you saw the same group of people over and over again. And you were always glad to see them. You always had an exciting time with them." In a later portion of the same interview, commenting on both the supportive nature of the group and on a singular lack of envy, she argued that during the Renaissance, "the idea that you had to get an inspiration to write or paint never existed because your peers were your inspiration. Nobody was ever sorry [about] anyone's success."

Yet even as she was speaking, lending her voice to the chorus of tales told about the Renaissance, I soon recognized that what Bennett committed so graciously to the oral record would need to be verified, then supplemented or corroborated by other available secondary sources. While not gifted with second sight, I also anticipated some future backtracking, seeing the need to visit every place in which Bennett mentioned having lived during the interview, anticipating the recreation of the "sense of atmosphere" and place for the big book down the road.

It did not take a particularly keen insight to recognize Bennett as a living repository or to understand that, somehow, we had established a sympathetic relationship. I realized early on that it was advisable to conduct another extensive interview as soon as was feasible, given the vagaries of health and age. Then, too, I harbored the dream of being Gwendolyn Bennett's George Bass—of being, despite my youth and inexperience, her literary executor.[3] We had spoken of this in the months preceding our next interview, scheduled for June 1981. But sadly, tragedy struck before those plans were finalized. Richard Crosscup, Bennett's husband, suffered a heart attack in January 1979; embittered and stricken by her loss, Gwendolyn Bennett passed on 31 May 1981, a mere eighteen months later.

As might be imagined, the sudden and unexpected death of both Bennett and her husband almost derailed the projected text. The loss of her voice, the loss of the recollective tone and the rich colors that came with it, was dispiriting. Too, the absence of a second detailed interview also meant starting not quite anew but certainly charting a new plan. Thus began the second paper chase, Phase III. This time the target was Bennett's private papers, the uncollected and unpublished material, the memorabilia or "stuff" of her past, the personal mementos of every day life that had been formerly saved, quite literally, in the attic. That this sensitive material had been stored in her home was no secret because she had agreed to let me peruse it on my next visit. Fortunately, following her death the bulk of her papers were removed from her home and given unto the care of her stepdaughter, Martha Tanner, in Foster, Rhode Island. In 1982, an American Council of Learned Societies (ACLS) Summer Grant provided funding to visit Tanner, who graciously permitted me to examine, copy, and catalog all Bennett's papers before they were deposited in the archives of the Schomburg Center for Research in Black Culture, New York Public Library.

While there were some intermittent research forays during the mid-1980s (I did, for instance, go to Giddings, Bennett's birthplace), a full-time teaching load and commitments to other projects forced delays on the Bennett project until the summer of 1990. The summer began with a university research travel award to visit almost all the places where Bennett had lived and worked, and saw the paper chase begin again in earnest. A special feature of this phase was that I also met and interviewed people who had known Bennett when she lived with her first husband, Dr. Alfred Jackson, for a brief period in Eustis, Florida. This phase of the process then stretched through 1991 with the aid of a Schomburg Center Fellowship. It is not possible to describe here all of nearly twelve months' work. Suffice it to say that archival collections housed at Atlanta University and at Howard, Yale, and New York University; educational records located in various schools; the unique arts and artist oral history archive at the Hatch-Billops Collection; and of course the Schomburg's own massive files were all carefully examined. In pursuit of the details, I traveled from Florida to Washington to Pennsylvania. On my second and third trips to D.C., I worked with crucial materials in the Martin Luther King Library, the National Archives, and the Archive of American Art. In addition, upon returning to New York, the personal papers of artist Norman Lewis, held by his widow, Ouida Lewis, were graciously made available for examination. From one locale to the next, I checked newspaper accounts, clipping files, reports, letters, bills, contracts, journals, diaries, ledgers, bulletins, catalogs, yearbooks, legal proceedings, court records, interview tape transcriptions, scribbled notes on the back of envelopes—the stuff of written record, or "the facts."

While all this material is neither concentrated nor voluminous, it does offer the careful reader insights into the ethos suffusing the twenties and the shifting emphasis clearly apparent in the far more politically radicalized decades that followed. In the twenties Bennett could agonize over her writing. "I feel as though that if I don't write this year, my mouth must remain sealed forever," she wrote in a 1925 letter to Langston Hughes. This was a prophetic comment, for by the forties, the bulk of her writing was geared to generating reports for the Federal Art Project agency she directed, The Harlem Community Art Center, or toward bulletins and curriculum guides for various "left-wing" community schools. Every attempt to be thorough was made; yet, I know something was overlooked.

Beyond chasing documents, being in New York, living in Harlem, had distinct advantages, enabling me to launch Phase IV of the process: locating and interviewing colleagues, co-workers, peers, and friends of Bennett's, people who knew her after the Renaissance years, during the more politically turbulent 1930s-1940s. These interviews were vital because while repositories have been cited, by no imaginative stretch can Bennett's papers be deemed extensive; materials about her in other collections are fragmentary at best. Some respondents, Jean Blackwell Hutson and Elton Fax, were interviewed at the Schomburg; others, such as artist Ernest Crichlow or playwright Loften Mitchell, or former Harlem politico Doxey Wilkerson, spoke to me in their Brooklyn homes or in Queens or Connecticut. One informant suggested I had come "ten years too late"; that I should have tried to find people earlier when perhaps their recollections were better.

Actually, most of my informants came to light at just the right time. They still had good recall and, most important, their sense was that the of the political tenor of the country had sufficiently changed so that they no longer felt uncomfortable or threatened by disclosing and sharing their memories. People were not silenced by "sensitive" topics any longer. They were not daunted by the specter of formerly taboo subjects such as speculation about possible membership in the Communist Party nor concerned with having been politically progressive in that era and thus attuned to the Party's program for the arts and education. In this context, my informants could address questions of professionalism, of sexuality, of political activism, of jealousy and pettiness, of personality conflicts between prominent persons. They spoke about work habits or personal habits, about attitudes toward students or colleagues and about dress and personal appearance; about struggles within the community; about issues of concern to the community; about mentoring by and reactions and responses to Gwendolyn Bennett. Their various testimonies, while not scientific, added tint and shadings to the segments of her lives where before there was merely an outline. Even areas which were gray to them began to show more color for me when a pattern could be discerned from the very consistency of testimony from very different witnesses. For instance, from Bennett's own testimony I knew she tended to gain weight under stress; more than one informant commented on her love of food and the fact that she was a gourmet cook who enjoyed cooking. Couple that knowledge to information that Bennett was constantly trying to diet and a clear indication of a woman in conflict emerges.

Unquestionably, eliciting some of this information from informants was often challenging. To help them and to prepare myself for the interview process, I first constructed a letter wherein, without recourse to pedagogical theories about the genre, I attempted to define my thinking about biography as craft and then share these perceptions of the genre's function. This was a deliberate strategy embarked upon to gain trust; these people were keepers of memory and guardians of an individual's reputation—they needed to respect and trust the person to whom they confided "Gwen's" story. Interestingly, they all felt her story should be told. Only one person had reservations about issues best described as "decorum," manifested in the idea that the best biography is still hagiography and therefore anything which might diminish image should be suppressed. But those who spoke candidly and on the record to me, who responded to my letter, were very generous indeed. I include some portions of that letter here because it is an amalgam of internalized critical directives and shows my first attempts to define or shape biographical narrative.

"Any good biography," I wrote to potential contacts, "conveys to readers, in a detailed, thorough, yet lively and engaging narrative, the life of the person examined. Good biography strives to report fairly the context of the times in which the person lived, analyzing the person against the setting of his or her particular milieu. Thus, good biography is also good social and cultural history." Next, anticipating hesitations regarding intentionality I wrote: "Biography is not vicious gossip; nor is it a witch-hunt or a crusade. Its concern is neither 'bashing' old villains nor pedestal building for the 'heroic' or 'oppressed.' Its aim is not to rake open old wounds for the sake of causing pain but to bring significant parts of the past back to life so that the full story, as completely as possible, can come to life."

The largest issue indicated in the letter was cast as a quest for truth: "The intent of any true scholar's project is to enable readers to see not a cardboard figure, all one dimensional, so good and virtuous as to be saintly—but a real human being, a flesh and blood individual who encompassed, sometimes simply endured, the normal range of human emotions. That is to say, the subject laughed as well as cried—cried as well as laughed; was cheerful and pleasant—was angry and unhappy; was moody—with blue moods and red moods, and sun moods, and ice moods and the full range between. The subject fussed, loved only certain colors but hated others, was a perfectionist, craved power, was callow, showed ambition, displayed peculiar habits, said outlandish things, was a terrible organizer and worse procrastinator, loved sesame seed bagels with cream cheese or fresh fried fish and greens."

This last element was an attempt to get beyond the mask informants often donned. In guarding the reputation of the subject, I had already learned that some informants wanted either to build pedestals or present a draped figure; I was determined to shake the stand and pull the drape. The letter concluded with this plea: "I am trying to touch base and get the testimony of as many of Bennett's peers as I can. For this book to work best, to present the life story of Gwendolyn Bennett best, it needs the testimony of other voices. Take a moment, collect your thoughts, then, lend your voice so that the story of Gwen Bennett can be told in more than casual mentions."

Yet even as the database was rising, subconsciously my thoughts on crafting drifted more toward voice in biography, with blending various voices rather than the straightforward factual recitation. I am not concerned with imaginary reconstructions of dialogue or with the "art of the inferred hypotheses" as demonstrated by Joe McGinniss's *The Last Brother,* an apparently specious 1993 biography of Ted Kennedy attacked by reviewers because of its many problems. Nor am I planning to impose scarcely credible interpretations on diary or journal notations. (One recent biography turned a diary comment about the frustration of being lost in a foreign city into fear of rape and murder.) What is important to me is that the person people knew appear on the page, not flit fitfully across it as shadow rather than substance.

The best way to do that right now seems to be to use the resonance in different voices as an active part of the narrative strategy. Whether we call it "storytelling" or "individual history," when biographers fit together the puzzle pieces, the bits and fragments of a life, when we re-create and animate some semblance of that life wherein the crafting becomes so skillful that the subject functions as protagonist in her or his own story, then the biographer has found an effective narrative strategy. And I believe that treating voice will prove a highly useful tactic.

Having said that, it also seems clear that specifying the various ways we hear voice, or the ways that issues may be voiced, or that a voice may conceal issues, is a legitimate concern. Most often, both with older works and with fuller biographical portraits, the choices made by the biographer can filter and control the volume of other voices participating in the storytelling. In an interview for Gail Mandell's *Life into Art,* Arnold Rampersad privileges Hughes's autobiographical voice, the authentic voice that emerged not so much from Langston's two atypical autobiographies but from his early poems and early letters, before he became aware of posterity (60). By contrast, Rampersad concedes he has "little or no regard for the interview process" because too many people without real knowledge really want to "help" and thus are inclined to "invent" the helpful detail. Rightly, Rampersad warns of the possibility of "deep inaccuracies" (59-60).

I agree that autobiographical voice as heard in the unguarded poem or story, the lonesome or cheery voice present in "unguarded moments" heard in a diary or letter, is highly prized. And when there is a significant collection of such material, so much the better. I disagree, however, about the value assigned interviews. "Trust and verify" has been my motto; and, thus far, the additional witnesses called to testify about Gwen Bennett have been honest, if sometimes reluctant, speakers. Impressions or vaguely recalled details were often confirmed by independent verification from other sources. Where memory was thought to be unreliable, these informants conscientiously sought to cross-check their recollections with others who also knew her; thus "invention," in Rampersad's context, has yet to become an issue. Indeed there was a desire to be useful, to help with the project; my informants, however, seemed less willing to speculate or volunteer "help" when they were unsure. Almost all were forthright individuals who once led public lives themselves. This contributed to a tacit understanding of need and of task. Rather than taking refuge in created fact, during the course of free-flowing conversation is when some forgotten fragment emerged; some long buried nugget about a feature or aspect of Bennett's life when they knew her came to light, then surfaced, without fanfare, in the proverbial "unguarded" moment. It seems that not only was Bennett a gourmet cook, she was also very attentive to her clothing and she loved browsing New York shops for antiques. During the several rambling and convoluted conversations held with informants where memory eddied and swirled, my function was to listen acutely for tone, for nuance of delivery to try to detect any variance conscientiously given for my benefit. To my knowledge then, no one "invented" facts for me. Their voices spoke to a truth as each recalled it.

And again, in addition to calling upon witnesses, I am inclined to use Bennett's voice as it resonates through her scrapbooks, her Paris diary, her letters to Howard University, her reports for the Federal Art Project, and her creative work in an active rather than passive manner. This will be especially critical when the focus of my study turns to Bennett's life during the WPA years and shortly thereafter. In a way, there is some anticipation of something akin to a dialectical approach using the three voices of Bennett available to me: the youthful, wistful, encouraging and courageous voice that comes through her 1920s letters to Cullen and Hughes or her Paris diary ("There was never a more beautiful city than Paris. . . . There couldn't be!" [June 28, 1925]);[4] the bitterness, fear, capability, and adeptness reflected in written documents from the late thirties and forties; the reflectiveness present in the late oral testimony. Without question, for these reasons and others Bennett should be able to carry much of the weight of her own story. Certainly, the autobiographical impulse was one she possessed.

At one point in her life, she even outlined the life history she planned to tell; she had planned to call her uncompleted project "Rubbing Shoulders." If she followed the Hughes model, and it was likely that she would have as the two were kindred spirits in many ways, she may well have muted her voice, in the self-effacing manner she frequently adopted, painting only the image of a charming and colorful childhood of which she spoke in an interview, or seeking to evoke the bright, witty, remarkable or interesting people she came into contact with during her varied career in the arts. She might well have omitted the darker aspects of that period in her life, the fact, for instance, that her father had kidnapped her from her mother when she was only eight years old (interview).

Parenthetically, given the roseate quality of the times Bennett recalled most fondly, it is rather doubtful that she would have found in her projected volume the necessary psychic space to do any true introspection. What James Olney called the "individual's special peculiar psychic configuration" would remain masked by Bennett; what Olney judged the "moral tenor" of her being might show itself, but only in bits and snippets (20). There were many silences in Bennett's life, periods when she remained silent by choice or social circumstance and periods when silences were imposed by political constraints. Yet each of these silences is in itself telling; each one says something about the woman within. To illustrate with two brief examples: seldom did an informant report that he or she ever saw Bennett angry. Consistently, all of them often recalled a gracious, charming, warm, and generous person. But how could Bennett have avoided anger when driven from a job she loved as director of the Harlem Community Art Center and hounded, repeatedly, by the specter of the "red menace" at wherever she next worked?

In *Writing a Woman's Life,* Carolyn Heilburn maintains that for women, anger is an emotion virtually denied. Heilburn's thesis posits that anger is as discomforting as an "open admission of the desire for power and control over one's life," and thus something women dared not show (13). Did Bennett deny or mask her anger; or did others merely fail to see it? Certainly, Bennett was adept at masking her past; people who knew her in one context knew little about her life in another. Intriguingly, Heilburn also maintains that "nostalgia, particularly for childhood, is likely to be a mask for unrecognized anger" (15). I'm speculating here, but it seems credible to assume that "unrecognized anger" may well be manifested in raging emotion turned inward, thus producing a silence that speaks for itself.

More than likely, Gwendolyn Bennett would concur with Arnold Rampersad's premise in the Mandell interview that in "the second half of our lives, we're not as interesting" (57). Despite her own protestations and not withstanding the dearth of published texts to analyze, the changes that occurred in the course of Bennett's life—her movement from New Negro to mentor and facilitator in the progressive arts struggle of the thirties to forgotten woman by the fifties and antiques dealer in the seventies—nonetheless conspire to make her life very "interesting" to anyone looking to tell a complete story about a woman of mystery. Although she clearly no longer had the energy to engage in the host of multiple exciting activities as she had in her youth, others who knew her also found her as interesting, although perhaps somewhat enigmatic and puzzling, at the midpoint of her life. These were the people who worked with her in the Federal Arts Project of the 1930s and early 1940s, or with her in the Negro Artist Guild, or at the community based and government targeted community schools in the late 1940s, or at Consumer Union during the 1950s and early 1960s. These are the people who had something to say about Bennett and about her life in the context of those times.

I believe there is an obligation to listen. These voices are both subjective and objective. And perhaps because Bennett is still regarded as a "minor" figure, not a public legend, there is no vested interest in inflating her memory. Hence, because of all these circumstances, I think respondents to my inquires have offered careful, deliberate, and thoughtful reflections, commenting upon the actions of a black woman artist as they observed them, in a particular social and cultural milieu, a particular time and place.

Postscript: Apart from juggling the various voices Bennett employed and those of the witnesses taking the stand to tell the story or speak the truth as they saw it, there still remains the question of authorial voice in the narrative process. According to some injunctions, despite an author's sense of commitment and concern for "narrative power," the biographer "must avoid center stage" (Pachter 8). Yet, customarily certain stylistic trademarks stamp my prose. For instance, I prefer the active voice; I have an affection for the alliterative mode; I'm fond of the parenthetical sentence. Given these traits, my voice may intrude too pervasively into the narrative. Mine is an oral style and, typically, those perusing my prose pronounce that it "sounds" just like me. Yet as sound sense and the striking visual image are also the tools of the good creative writer, perhaps these traits can be muted, subordinated, or bent to the service of crafting dramatic moments. Recalling that the purpose of any good biographical narrative is not only the recovery, reclamation, and revelation of a life but the telling of a good story, I shall endeavor to contain my voice by shifting focus to setting, character, chronology, or evocation of mood in the recreation of circumstance rather than by calling attention to an omniscient presence.

While the procedures being contemplated are not fully operational, trying to formulate some form of composite narrative strategy or structure seems the better part of wisdom. Such a structure should create space for multiple voices, providing a place for the comment from several different resources: individuals, texts, and academic disciplines—history, sociology, psychology, art. My theory is that listening to Gwen Bennett's interior voice will be every bit as essential to the biography as is our ability as readers of Zora Hurston's narrative to hear Janie Crawford's interior voice. The trick, or rather the art, will come from a creative blending of the narrative format possibilities, using different modes, perhaps different genres, to re-create the life of Gwen Bennett inside a "speakers text." When the subject gives you the mantle and entrusts you with her story, there is an obligation to allow her to speak for herself and then to speak up and speak for her. Implicitly, when recovery and restoration is a part of the charge, some advocacy seems inherent whether the trumpet or a muffled drum roll is the instrument.

At this juncture, it looks like treating "voice" is where I have planted my flag. Regardless of whatever other "angle of consistency" seems suitable for the final text, blending the different voices raised in concert should help pull together the disparate threads of Gwendolyn Bennett's lives. Both as artist using differing media and highly regarded community figure Bennett merits more from our cultural historians. By incorporating and blending a host of voices, the intent is to make the shadowy figure of the woman embedded in the warp of the fabric more pronounced. The hues and multiple tones in the tapestry I hope one day to hang should take on a richer texture. That, at least, is the theory; bear with me; I'm working on it.

Notes

1. My research on Gwendolyn Bennett has been supported, at various times, by an American Council of Learned Societies summer grant; several summer grants from the University of North Carolina-Charlotte, and a New York Public Library Schomburg Scholar in Residence award funded by the National Endowment for the Humanities for 1990-91. This allowed me to live in Harlem for nine months and conduct my research in a more sustained manner.
2. Margaret Burroughs, director, DuSable African-American History Museum, Chicago, was an instrumental early contact whose help led me to Bennett.
3. Founder of Rites and Reason Theatre at Brown University, the late George Houston Bass formerly served as secretary to Langston Hughes and eventually became the executor of the Hughes estate.
4. See her 1920s letters to Cullen and Hughes or her Paris diary ("There was never a more beautiful city than Paris. . . . There couldn't be!" [28 June 1925]) Her letters are in the Beinecke Rare Book and Manuscript Library at Yale University in the James Weldon Johnson Collection. Her diary is in the New Public Library in the Schomburg Center for Research in Black Culture.

Works Cited

Bennett, Gwendolyn. Personal interview with Sandra Y. Govan. Mar. 1979.

Benstock, Sheri. "Authorizing the Autobiographical." *The Private Self: Theory and Practice of Women's Autobiographical Writings.* Ed. Sheri Benstock. Chapel Hill: U of North Carolina P, 1988. 10-33.

Brown, Sterling A. *The Negro in American Fiction and Negro Poetry and Drama.* 1937. New York: Arno/New York Times, 1969.

Clark, John Henrik. Interview with Sandra Y. Govan. 9 May 1991.

Cruse, Harold. *The Crisis of the Negro Intellectual.* New York: William Morrow, 1967.

Cullen, Countee, ed. *Caroling Dusk.* New York: Harper, 1927.

Govan, Sandra Yvonne. "Gwendolyn Bennett: Portrait of an Artist Lost." Diss. Emory U, 1981.

Heilburn, Carolyn. *Writing a Woman's Life.* New York: Norton, 1988.

Huggins, Nathan. *Harlem Renaissance.* New York: Oxford UP, 1971.

Hull, Gloria T. *Color, Sex, and Poetry: Three Women Writers of the Harlem Renaissance.* Bloomington: U of Indiana P, 1987.

Olney, James. "Some Versions of Memory/Some Versions of *Bios*." Ed. James Olney. *Autobiography: Essays Theoretical and Critical.* Princeton, NJ: Princeton UP, 1980. 236-67.

Pachter, Marc. "The Biographer Himself: An Introduction." *Telling Lives: The Biographer's Art.* Ed. Marc Pachter. Philadelphia: U of Pennsylvania P, 1981. 3-15.

Primeau, Ronald. "Frank Horne and the Second Echelon Poets." *The Harlem Renaissance Remembered.* Ed. Arna Bontemps. New York: Dodd, 1972. 247-67.

Rampersad, Arnold. "Biography and Afro-American Culture." *Afro-American Literary Studies in the 1990s.* Ed. Houston A. Baker Jr. and Patricia Redmond. Chicago: U of Chicago P, 1989. 194-230.

———. "A Conversation with Arnold Rampersad." *Life into Art.* Ed. Gail Porter Mandell. Fayetteville: U of Arkansas P, 1991. 44-67.

Record, Wilson. *The Negro and the Communist Party.* New York: Atheneum, 1971.

NINA MILLER (ESSAY DATE 1998)

SOURCE: Miller, Nina. "'Our Younger Negro (Women) Artists': Gwendolyn Bennett and Helene Johnson." In *Making Love Modern: The Intimate Public Worlds of New York's Literary Women,* pp. 209-41. New York: Oxford University Press, 1998.

In the following excerpt, Miller discusses the ways in which Bennett and Johnson worked within the conventions of Romantic lyric poetry as well as within the avant-garde aesthetic of the Harlem Renaissance.

Women's Lyric Poetry

The notion of the "lyric moment" has potentially profound implications for the speaking self the poem projects. Seeming to escape time and the social contract, suffused with the emotion of a single consciousness, the lyric poem echoes the perfect self-sufficiency of pre-Oedipal subjectivity, that state before the fall into "lack"—of maternal nurturance, of personal wholeness, of an unmediated relation to the universe—a state characterized by the utopian fullness of plenitude. I make this point not to characterize the practice of lyric poetry as infantile regression but rather to illuminate the way that a variety of lyric modes might tend toward the production of a speaker whose psyche was underwritten by a primordial experience of self-worth. If the context of Harlem subcultural imperatives made escape from a certain kind of performative femininity occasionally desirable, it also created the positive need for a feminine identity that was fundamentally noncontingent. In sharp contrast to the palpable presence of the Other in, for example, Parker's complex rhetorical dynamics, much of renaissance lyric principally concerned itself with the projection of an unassailable and free-standing feminine self.

Marion Grace Conover's "Comment" from 1928 is a straightforward use of lyric to establish an inviolable black femininity.

> Perhaps you have forgotten
> That a lotus flower
> Pure, fragile, white,
> May blossom in foul places
> Far from the sun's pale light.[1]

We might be inclined to dismiss Conover's conventional association of whiteness with purity and fragility as false consciousness, yet, when the lotus expresses its inherent virtue despite adverse circumstances, it creates an imagistic space in which the same possibility exists for the speaker as a black woman. Two points from Houston A. Baker Jr.'s *Workings of the Spirit: The Poetics of Afro-American Women's Writing* are relevant here. The first is the importance of the larger historical context from which, according to Baker, any interpretation of African American women's writing must proceed. The foundational experience in this history is the massive and systematic rape that characterized the Middle Passage:

> A rejection of the assumptions, if not the conditions, of violation—an obstinate insistence on a deeper intimacy, as it were, provided conditions of possibility for the very existence of [an] Afro-American [cultural] system. The unmediated, above-deck world [where the rape takes place] reduces the scope of concern from a desire for possession of the Western machine to a psychic quest for an achieved and ordering intimacy of women's *self*-consciousness. The shift is something like that between world historic forces and embedded ancestral energies of survival and even poetic consciousness.
>
> (136; emphasis in original)

Baker's second point concerns the primacy of *space* as a set of luminous sites which gather meaning over the course of cultural generations—as against the white-Western pursuit of progress through *time* (which Baker associates with the writings of key male African American writers like Ralph Ellison and Richard Wright). Space "is a function of images," and though Baker has in mind a more or less constant "imagistic field" which constitutes the African American women's literary tradition, the general argument seems clarifying in the present case as well: images and the spaces they create provide black women writers with alternative values and meanings in a world whose given terms render black women's existence precarious.[2] When the speaker of "Comment" spins out a vision of a lotus fully and deliberately *being* a lotus regardless of the "foul[ness]" it confronts, she creates not merely an allegory of black womanhood for the benefit of the "you" she addresses but an imagistic space for her own habitation, a place in which the embedded logic of biological essence unfolds in space, escaping the temporal dimension in which any "foul" eventuality is possible.

An important source of the self-sufficiency we see in play in "Comment" may well derive from the black church. Explicitly Christian poems are fairly common among renaissance writers generally, nearly always figuring an analogy between the crucifixion and ostensibly nongendered Negro suffering, especially lynching.[3] But Christian experience may make itself felt at a more pervasive level and have particular significance for women. One dimension of this significance is more or less spelled out in Alice Dunbar-Nelson's "Of Old St. Augustine."

> Of old, St. Augustine wrote wise
> And curious lore, within his book.
> I read and meditate, my eyes
> See words of comforting, I look
> Again, and thrill with radiant hope.
> "They did not sin, those white-souled nuns of
> old,
> Pent up in leaguered city, and despoiled
> By knights, who battered at the peaceful fold,
> And stole their bodies. Yet the fiends were foiled,
> They could not harm their stainless, cloistered
> souls."[4]

What the speaker articulates here is the final preserve Christianity provides for noncontingent feminine selfhood: the soul, standing as bulwark against the bodily denigration of rape. Yet the radical split of soul and body expressed in this poem, while a commonplace of Anglo-European epistemology, is actually quite rare in renaissance women's poetry as a whole. Pervasive, by contrast, is the implicit notion that to believe in God is to be personally suffused with God's spirit. In her study *Conversions and Visions in the Writings of African-American Women,* Kimberly Rae Connor states that black women confront "a dominant culture that not only devalues but often-times erases their identity. . . . Conversion for these women yields to creation—creation of a self and of a story." More specifically, "for African Americans conversion is an experience . . . where women and men ask not for God's forgiveness but for God's *recognition.*"[5] Connor offers a definition of conversion itself that bears a strong similarity to what I am arguing is the cultural function of lyric for renaissance women.

> Bearing qualities of both transcendence and immanence, the goal of conversion is to create: where there was absence to create presence; where there was no self a self emerges; where God was a transcendent listener on high, there is an immanent god participating in the lives of black women.
>
> (12)[6]

Lending significant force to the self called into being by lyric, this black Christian experiential framework also converges powerfully with the romantic sense of a world saturated with spiritual meaning.

Dora Lawrence Houston's "Preference," published in the June 1925 issue of *Opportunity,* projects the sense of overdetermined plenitude resulting from this convergence of generic and spiritual registers—and brings out another of its dimensions.

> I love all quiet places—
> Low prairies, placid seas,
> The heart of woods in winter
> When no wind shakes the trees.
> People are much like places:
> Oh I could travel far
> With one who loves to ponder
> The tip of a burning star.
>
> (164)[7]

Sexual love (along with religious feeling) is the classic approximation of plenitude, and as "Preference" finally suggests, the point of such love is not the lover or togetherness but the being loved, the enhancement of self that love provides. The speaker conjures places of perfect symmetry and stillness: the "low prairies" in balance with the "placid seas," the "heart of woods" where not even "wind shakes the trees." The completeness of the natural world she "loves" extends to the speaker herself, not just explicitly ("People are much like places") but in the unmistakable sense that the lover she invokes is nearly redundant to the psychical state she values. The exquisite rapture suggested by mutually "ponder[ing] / The tip of a burning star" is merely an intensification of the "quiet places" that precede it—an immanent, white-hot center to all that perfection and stillness. The shift from solitude to sexual love, then, is merely one of degree. In contrast to the compulsion we have seen for white women poets of the period to generate literary selfhood strictly within the confines of heterosexuality (or, at least, to appear to do so), black women poets had almost the reverse imperative: to present a womanly self luminous with "the desire of the other" yet extricated from the degrading implication that that self is sexually derived. The African American woman lover must be the product, not of her human lover, but of God, poetry, and, as we shall see, nature.

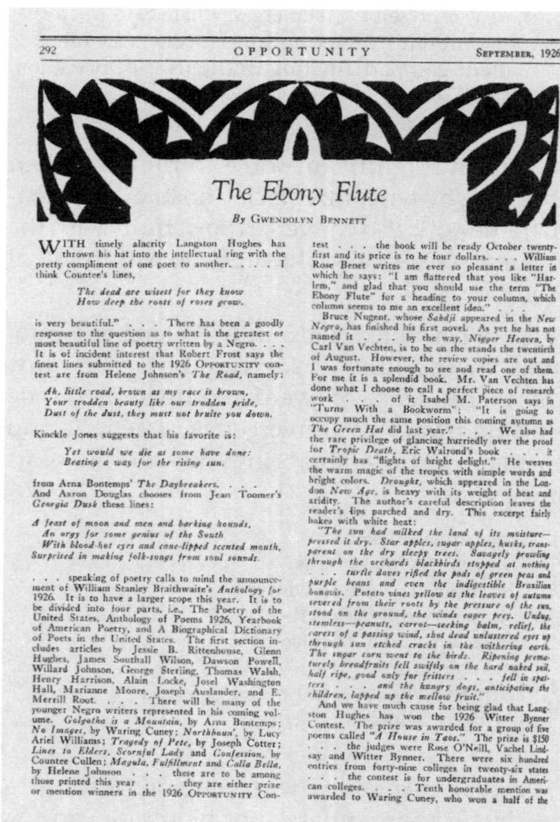

292 OPPORTUNITY SEPTEMBER, 1926

The Ebony Flute

By GWENDOLYN BENNETT

WITH timely alacrity Langston Hughes has thrown his hat into the intellectual ring with the pretty compliment of one poet to another. . . . I think Countee's lines,

The dead are wisest for they know
How deep the roots of roses grow.

is very beautiful." . . . There has been a goodly response to the question as to what is the greatest or most beautiful line of poetry written by a Negro. . . . It is of incident interest that Robert Frost says the finest lines submitted to the 1926 OPPORTUNITY contest are from Helene Johnson's *The Road*, namely:

Ah, little road, brown as my race is brown,
Your trodden beauty like our trodden pride,
Dust of the dust, they must not bruise you down.

Kinckle Jones suggests that his favorite is:

Yet would we die as some have done:
Beating a way for the rising sun.

from Arna Bontemps' *The Daybreakers*. . . . And Aaron Douglas chooses from Jean Toomer's *Georgia Dusk* these lines:

A feast of moon and men and barking hounds,
An orgy for some genius of the South
With blood-hot eyes and cane-lipped scented mouth,
Surprised in making folk-songs from soul sounds.

. . . speaking of poetry calls to mind the announcement of William Stanley Braithwaite's *Anthology for 1926*. It is to have a larger scope this year. It is to be divided into four parts, i.e., The Poetry of the United States, Anthology of Poems 1926, Yearbook of American Poetry, and A Biographical Dictionary of Poets in the United States. The first section includes articles by Jessie B. Rittenhouse, Glenn Hughes, James Southall Wilson, Dawson Powell, Willard Johnson, George Sterling, Thomas Walsh, Henry Harrison, Alain Locke, Josel Washington Hall, Marianne Moore, Joseph Auslander, and E. Merrill Root. . . . There will be many of the younger Negro writers represented in his coming volume. *Golgotha is a Mountain*, by Arna Bontemps; *No Images*, by Waring Cuney; *Northboun'*, by Lucy Ariel Williams; *Tragedy of Pete*, by Joseph Cotter; *Lines to Elders, Scornful Lady* and *Confession*, by Countee Cullen; *Magula, Fulfillment* and *Calla Bella*, by Helene Johnson . . . these are to be among those printed this year . . . they are either prize or mention winners in the 1926 OPPORTUNITY Contest . . . the book will be ready October twenty-first and its price is to be four dollars. . . . William Rose Benet writes me ever so pleasant a letter in which he says: "I am flattered that you like "Harlem," and glad that you should use the term "The Ebony Flute" for a heading to your column, which column seems to me an excellent idea." . . .

Bruce Nugent, whose *Sahdji* appeared in the *New Negro*, has finished his first novel. As yet he has not named it . . . by the way, *Nigger Heaven*, by Carl Van Vechten, is to be on the stands the twentieth of August. However, the review copies are out and I was fortunate enough to see and read one of them. For me it is a splendid book. Mr. Van Vechten has done what I choose to call a perfect piece of research work . . . of it Isabel M. Paterson says in "Turns With a Bookworm"; "It is going to occupy much the same position this coming autumn as *The Green Hat* did last year." . . . We also had the rare privilege of glancing hurriedly over the proof for *Tropic Death*, Eric Walrond's book . . . it certainly has "flights of bright delight." He weaves the warm magic of the tropics with simple words and bright colors. *Drought*, which appeared in the London *New Age*, is heavy with its weight of heat and aridity. The author's careful description leaves the reader's lips parched and dry. This excerpt fairly bakes with white heat:

"The sun had milked the land of its moisture—pressed it dry. Star apples, sugar apples, husks, transparent on the dry sleepy trees. Savagely prowling through the orchards blackbirds stopped at nothing . . . turtle doves rifled the pods of green peas and purple beans and even the indigestible Brazilian bonavis. Potato vines yellow as the leaves of autumn severed from their roots by the pressure of the sun, stood on the ground, the winds eager prey. Undug, stemless—peanuts, carrot—seeking balm, relief, the caress of a passing wind, shot dead unlustered eyes up through sun etched cracks in the withering earth. The sugar corn went to the birds. Ripening prematurely breadfruits fell swiftly on the hard naked soil, half ripe, good only for fritters . . . fell in spatters . . . and the hungry dogs, anticipating the children, lapped up the mellow fruit."

And we have much cause for being glad that Langston Hughes has won the 1926 Witter Bynner Contest. The prize was awarded for a group of five poems called *"A House in Taos."* The prize is $150 . . . the judges were Rose O'Neill, Vachel Lindsay and Witter Bynner. There were six hundred entries from forty-nine colleges in twenty-six states . . . the contest is for undergraduates in American colleges. . . . Tenth honorable mention was awarded to Waring Cuney, who won a half of the

"The Ebony Flute," from the August 1926 edition of *Opportunity*. This literary criticism column, written by Bennett, appeared in *Opportunity* for two years.

Honey argues that, for renaissance women poets, "Nature offered an Edenesque alternative to the corrupted, artificial environment created by 'progress'" (7). These writers "saw the cityscape as manmade," whereas "nature, like them, had been objectified, invaded and used by men seeking power and wealth" (8). Indeed, the evidence of African American women's strong identification with nature runs all through the period. Starting from this central observation, we soon see what a flexible tool the trope of nature provides in the literary construction of renaissance women's subjectivity. Jessie Redmon Fauset's "Rain Fugue" is exemplary in important respects: its feminine speaker's negotiations with desire are played out through nature, while nature functions not merely to reflect her emotions but, as an ontologically distinct entity, to actively engage them. The result is a dynamic process of self-construction.

The speaker traces four seasons of rain and eros—without the implicit denigration of either personal embodiment or the presence of a lover. The first season is summer:

Slanting, driving, Summer rain
How you wash my heart of pain!
Ships and gulls and flashing seas!
In your furious, tearing wind,
Swells a chant that heals my mind;
And your passion high and proud,
Makes me shout and laugh aloud![8]

The sheer excess of the summer storm produces in the speaker an intense present-orientation. "Wash[ed]" of her "pain"—freed of her past—the speaker gives herself over to the "swell[ing] chant" of an insistent "passion[,] high and proud," which she matches with her own "shout[ing] and laugh[ter]." Only abstractly figured by her "heart" and "mind," she is yet concretely performative (though, indeed, her very willingness to shout and laugh in forgetfulness of her own pain serves ironically to underscore her physical elusiveness).

The rain of autumn is calmer, but more disturbing for all that:

Blotting, blurring out the Past,
In a dream you hold me fast;
Calling, coaxing to forget
Things that are, for things not yet.

Forcing her out of the full present of the summer, the autumn rain instigates desire in the speaker for that which she lacks (the "things not yet") but keeps her from pursuing them in the world by "hold[ing her] fast" in the "dream" of a still, pre-Oedipal suspension. The speaker resists such manipulation, however, with nature's own help, as intensity returns with the winter.

Winter tempest, winter rain,
Hurtling down with might and main,
You but make me hug my heart,
Laughing, sheltered from your wrath.
Now I woo my dancing fire,
Piling, piling drift-wood higher.
Books, and friends and pictures old,
Hearten while you pound and scold!

Though autumn gave her a coaxing whiff of "lack," winter is its very essence and here attempts to drive her forward into the cruel teleogically driven (narrative) world. She scornfully resists: "You but make me hug my heart, / Laughing." Ironically, in taking "shelter . . . from [its] wrath," she escapes winter's specific intentions without violating the larger natural order, which is, of course, to go indoors in a tempest. In typical fashion, this woman struggles with nature while staying always in harmony with it.

This is the specific meaning of her identification with nature: the two are autonomous and yet coextensive as a poetic space apart from worldly imperatives. In contrast to the unity of passion we saw in "summer," winter is the site of the speaker's differentiation from nature and development of her own desire. The domestic space we are conventionally given to see as bourgeois confinement here springs from the feminine speaker's own need as the very shape of her desire. Forced by winter to grapple with lack, she refuses the (futile) narrative pursuit of wholeness in the world and instead directs her grappling inward to the creation of her own domain. Ensconced in her hearth and thus defended against the world, the speaker's erotic self emerges with witchy abandon: "Now I woo my dancing fire, / Piling, piling drift-wood higher." The seemingly incongruous "Books, and friends and pictures old" of the subsequent line (assuming that she is not actually throwing these items in the fire) signal a crucial difference from the incipient erotics of the first two stanzas: having come into her own, the feminine speaker seeks not a particular, heterosexual locus of desire, but the multiple sites—and hence, the multiply grounded self—that domesticity affords.

Spring mirrors the muted power of autumn, but given a now-articulated feminine subject, its force all flows to her greater autonomy:

Pattering, wistful showers of Spring
Set me to remembering
Far-off times and lovers too,
Gentle joys and heart-break rue,—
Memories I'd as lief forget,
Were not oblivion sadder yet.
Ah! you twist my mind with pain,
Wistful, whispering April rain!

The poem now concludes by concretizing the difference of spring:

Summer, Autumn, Winter rain,
How you ease my heart of pain!
Whispering, wistful showers of Spring,
How I love the hurt you bring!

Having successfully resisted the "things not yet" held out to her by autumn, the speaker allows herself to be lured by spring into contemplation of the past. The past brings "hurt" that she "loves"—as against the pain of stanza one, which she was happy to lose. Whence the shift to pleasure in pain? The seasonal ordeal of autumn and winter has given the speaker a core self, whose boundaries are only enhanced by the look backward. Memory by definition pulls life into the orbit of a controlling consciousness. Pain under these circumstances is likewise an intensity lending itself to an even greater sense of the speaker's emotional world as subject only to her own control and as intrinsically, autonomously meaningful. (Indeed, numerous poems from the period suggest that literary masochism may have had this specific function for women writers.)[9]

In a subcultural context that renders the woman's love poem per se as an oblique genre—more explicitly about selfhood than body, less interested in the relationship than in the person it produces—the line between the love poem and the lyric tends to blur. "Love" finally becomes something about voice and eros—finding, directing and keeping them despite the cultural conspiracy to render one silent, asexual, or animalistic.

Bennett and Johnson in the Lyric Context

Though Gwendolyn Bennett and Helene Johnson both found their strongest literary identity in relation to avant-garde aesthetics, they came to write poetry within the matrix of this emergent women's lyric tradition. Moreover, they did so not by struggling against its "feminine constraints" but by exploiting to the fullest its significant potentials. The best testimony to that potential is the variety of lyric resources Bennett and Johnson drew on to forge their very distinct avant-garde voices. The subsequent discussion describes the central modes of each poet's participation in the women's lyric tradition while developing further dimensions of the tradition itself. Following the trajectory of Bennett's and Johnson's own uses of lyric, the analysis of their conventional lyricism slides inevitably into the unconventional appropriations that lead them to identifiably avant-garde expression.

Like many of their female contemporaries, both Bennett and Johnson were drawn to what might be called the "nightwoman" poem—simply, a poem in which night and woman are rendered in terms of each other. Bennett's **"Street Lamps in Early Spring"** suggests the genre's appeal for the Harlem Renaissance woman poet.

Night wears a garment
All velvet soft, all violet blue . . .
And over her face she draws a veil
As shimmering fine as floating dew . . .
And here and there
In the black of her hair
The subtle hands of Night
Move slowly with their gem-starred light.[10]

The first, most important characteristic of the nightwoman is her sheer scale. Larger than life, the center of her world, even the matrix of that world itself, her position bears certain key resemblances to that of the bourgeois Negro Woman—but without the strains of "exaltedness." Their differences are built into the particular cultural register that each inhabits: iconic status can provide the Negro Woman with only the protections and power attendant on the commodification she has undergone; by contrast, metaphoric status lends the Night Woman the magnificence and the imperturbable stillness of poetry—as well as the greater remove of metaphor itself.

Intrinsic to the figure of night is, of course, the elevation of darkness to a world on its own terms; indeed, the night has a persistent presence in renaissance poetry as a point of reference for black legitimacy, as in Langston Hughes's "Proem": "I am a Negro: / Black as the night is black, / Black like the depths of my Africa."[11] But the autonomous night has a special felicity for women writers, one which Bennett here exploits fully. The night is larger than life, metaphorically magnificent, but simultaneously *veiled;* prominent, powerful, yet unavailable to prying eyes; ubiquitously "public" yet private unto herself. Even beyond resolving what is a central contradiction of bourgeois Negro womanhood, the nightwoman eradicates a second, culturally imposed contradiction between black skin and genteel womanhood: in the metaphoric context of the nightwoman poem, *darkness* is intrinsic to (modest, demure—i.e., bourgeois) *femininity.* Johnson's "Night," from the same year, wraps the metaphoric woman in the additional mantel of Christian selfhood:

> The moon flung down the bower of her hair,
> A sacred cloister while she knelt at prayer.
> She crossed pale bosom, breathed a sad amen—
> Then bound her hair about her head again.[12]

Again, femininity is inextricable from the dark. The woman herself has become the "pale-bosomed" moon, but the darkness of night remains in her hair—emblem of femininity and the means of her "cloistered" modesty.

Johnson's "What Do I Care for Morning" explores the potential of the nightwoman metaphor within a more ambitious ideological framework. Contrary to convention, night is here explicitly contrasted with day, as the title suggests, while day itself is rejected as the disorderly realm of aggressive and disjointed activity.

> What do I care for morning,
> For a shivering aspen tree,
> For sun flowers and sumac
> Opening greedily?
> What do I care for morning,
> For the glare of the rising sun,
> For a sparrow's noisy prating,
> For another day begun?[13]

When the speaker chooses night, as she inevitably must, it is for the calm unity that emanates from that domain's central organizing presence, the moon.

> Give me the beauty of evening,
> The cool consummation of night,
> And the moon like a love-sick lady,
> Listless and wan and white.
> Give me a little valley
> Huddled beside a hill,
> Like a monk in a monastery,
> Safe and contented and still,
> Give me the white road glistening,
> A strand of the pale moon's hair,
> And the tall hemlocks towering
> Dark as the moon is fair.

In drawing day into the comparative shadow of night, Johnson invites certain oppositions: between industry and love, drive and contentment, desire and satiety. We can hear in this structure of values strong echoes of the (by 1926) long-standing argument among black and, increasingly, white intellectuals that African America had soulful qualities badly needed by the grasping, frenetic world of white capitalism.[14] The poem's final lines feed into this contrast of the ancient race with the hard, youthful one.

> Oh what do I care for morning,
> Naked and newly born—
> Night is here, yielding and tender—
> What do I care for dawn![15]

To the extent that the night is, indeed, identified with African America, the function of the metaphoric woman is significant. At the center of her world, she provides the magnetic charge from which comes order—and eros. Here the affective positioning of the speaker is significant, for whereas more or less straightforward identification is implied by the nightwoman lyric in its simpler forms, in this instance the speaker claims a place for herself as a woman distinct from the metaphor. She accomplishes this through a declaration of her desire. Having begun by asserting in broad terms the superior attractions of the night over the day, she finishes with a fairly precise articulation of the possibilities for intimacy each offers her. The "naked and newly born" morning asks her to be mother to the child who goes forth to strive with the rest of the striving world. This scenario leaves her behind and redundant, as, indeed, the dominant culture traditionally relegates the African American woman to its forgotten domestic and psychological spaces to do its drudgery. The "yielding and tender" night, by contrast, is the omnipotent mother of pre-Oedipal plenitude, the mother who *is* the world, and the invitation is to the "cool consummation" of "safe[ty]," "content[ment]," and "still[ness]." This language of adult sexuality signals the speaker's choice as a conscious return to a culturally sanctioned state: though premised on infant pleasure, this is the world of courtly love and monastic life, as well as the beauty and allusiveness of poetry itself. Indeed, morning has no trace of culture to its credit, only raw nature untouched by poetry. Johnson's poem thus extends the reach of the nightwoman metaphor to encompass culture itself, newly defined as feminine and African American.

Bennett's 1926 **"Moon Tonight"** situates the feminine speaker and her lover within the terms of a world emanating from the Nightwoman, granting this figure yet another province of meaning, that of the lover's psychology:

> Moon tonight,
> Beloved. . . .
> When twilight
> Has gathered together
> The ends
> Of her soft robe,
> And the last bird-call
> Has died.
> Moon tonight—
> Cool as a forgotten dream,
> Dearer than lost twilights
> Among trees where birds sing
> No more.[16]

With the opening address, the speaker ushers her beloved into the night-world, asserting in the process her control over its meaning. First comes the twilight, and with the imagistic brevity to which she was so frequently drawn, Bennett evokes the privacy we have seen as typical for the nightwoman, modestly "gather[ing] together / The ends / Of her soft robe." Having thus established the inviolable feminine space as the very matrix of their love, the speaker introduces the moon, traditional catalyst for romantic passion. Yet this moon brings only displacements of emotion—"cool," "forgotten," and a "dream"; "lost twilights" and birds who "sing / No more"—images signaling that this is an affair of the past (or the soon-to-be past). The felicity of the moon in this love scenario lies in the aesthetic residue it retains after the affair itself has burned away; left behind in the twilight and the nostalgia is a metaphorically and artistically enhanced self.

The imagist aesthetic of **"Moon Tonight"** suggests both Bennett's significant avant-garde affiliation with international modernism and her strong roots in graphic art. Though Bennett is remarkable for the variety of her renaissance pursuits (not only poetry and cultural commentary but also cover illustrations for *Crisis* and *Opportunity*), graphic art provided the principal educational and vocational structure to her career. First studying art at Pratt and Columbia and in Paris, Bennett then taught at Howard and Tennessee State College and, much later, directed the Harlem Community Art Center. Not surprisingly, then, graphic art also served her as a powerful resource in the poetic problems of love, self, and African American womanhood under conditions of compulsory publicity.

In **"Purgation,"** Bennett uses the notion of aesthetic process and value as the basis for a love not in conflict with the complexities of her selfhood; like so many other Harlem Renaissance women writers, she strives for disembodiment as a context for love. This ascetic impulse is evident from the beginning of the poem.

> You lived
>   and your body
> Clothed the flames of earth.
>
> Now that the fires have burned away
> And left your body cold,
> I tremble as I stand
> Before the chiseled marble
> Of your dust-freed soul.[17]

The speaker of **"Purgation"** makes no appearance in the first stanza and thus avoids any proximity to the lover and his body while they "live." Once "the fires" have put an irrevocable distance between them, however, the speaker appears, passionately embodied in her "trembling"—but trembling in response to the work of art the lover has left in his place. Indeed, his worthiness to be loved at all seems to reside in the implication that his soul, or essence, is "chiseled marble." The purgation of the title, most obviously a reference to the lover's transition into death, more importantly describes the process by which the affair itself achieves the purity of art—and lends the woman speaker a comparably timeless and exalted self.

Bennett also rallied her visual artistry to tackle a more pervasive dilemma of artistic subjectivity in the renaissance and thereby extended her purview to critique of both establishment and avant-garde practice. Several of Bennett's poems implicitly target the tendency of bourgeois artists to render the racial subject they celebrate in the exoticizing terms of an alien Other. Drawing on a conception of nature implicit to the art deco aesthetic of her drawings, Bennett derives a poetics that is finally democratic in its implications. In the context of the renaissance, Bennett's "fairy sketches"—pagan fantasies of animistic nature—displace exotic Africa as the terrain in which to establish artistic positionality. Though its subject and tone are "light," the poem **"Wind"** suggests the contours of a world that neatly sidesteps the ruling, racially freighted dichotomies both of Christian good and evil and of awed artist and "aweful" primitive.

The wind was a care-free soul
That broke the chains of earth,
And strode for a moment across the land
With the wild halloo of his mirth.
He little cared that he ripped up trees,
That houses fell at his hand,
That his step broke calm on the breast of seas,
That his feet stirred clouds of sand.

But when he had had his little joke,
Had shouted and laughed and sung
When the trees were scarred, their branches
broke,
And their foliage aching hung,
He crept to his cave with a stealthy tread,
With rain-filled eyes and low-bowed head.[18]

The casual destruction that follows from the exuberant expression of "a care-free soul" highlights the poem's refusal to impose a sense of evil or mystery on the natural world. The compunction that creeps over the wind at the close of the poem arises from a natural moral sense and demands neither redemption nor restitution. Or perhaps the "rain-filled eyes and low-bowed head" are only the tail end of a mood that has spent itself.

"Fantasy" is continuous with the amoral, animistic world of **"Wind"** and builds in an apparently direct translation of Bennett's art deco drawing into a verbal tapestry:

I sailed in my dreams to the Land of Night
Where you were the dusk-eyed queen,
And there in the pallor of moon-veiled light
The loveliest things were seen . . .

A slim-necked peacock sauntered there
In a garden of lavender hues,
And you were strange with your purple hair
As you sat in your amethyst chair
With your feet in your hyacinth shoes.

Oh, the moon gave a bluish light
Through the trees in the land of dreams and
night.
I stood behind a bush of yellow-green
And whistled a song to the dark-haired
queen . . .[19]

The scene Bennett puts before us is highly visual and echoes the drawing she made for the March 1924 cover of *Crisis:* fauns and nymphs dance and play pipes while a slight young black man reclines among them (Figure 8.1). In both representational worlds, subjectivity—including artistic subjectivity—is manifested and contained within its boundaries; no outside gaze exists to impose an exoticizing regime on the natural world. In the drawing, the young man—figure for the African American artist—is off-center and asleep. The nymphs, meanwhile, are distinctly separated from him in the background and are clearly pursuing their own ends, as indeed are the fauns, intent on playing their pipes. This visual decenteredness carries over to **"Fantasy."** The speaker of the poem begins explicitly as the controlling consciousness of the fantastic world depicted, which is, after all, her or his dream or **"Fantasy."** But, though "dusk-eyed" and "dark-haired," the queen is a fantasy of fairy aesthetics, not the racial phantasm dredged up from the bourgeois artistic unconscious. However, in the final lines, the speaker abdicates the voyeuristic control his or her position "behind a bush" affords to offer up a "whistl[ing] song." This gesture initiates an interaction that is born of the speaker's own, acknowledged desire and pitched at the register of social intercourse—flirtation, a not-too-invested game of equals.

Bennett carried her fine arts sensibility forward into her high renaissance work as one of its major foundations and an important instrument of ideological critique. Together with the resulting aesthetic of chiseled modernist control, the "art" poetry we have thus far examined suggests the direction of Bennett's full-blown claim to subcultural entitlement—her avant-garde voice—discussed later in this chapter. In stark contrast is the aesthetic of abandon to which Helene Johnson was drawn. Establishing lyric selfhood through lyric rapture, Johnson was pulled immediately into serious engagement with the explicit poetics of race; accordingly, her progress toward avant-garde expression occurs over an explicitly racial terrain from its very beginnings.

"My Race," from 1925, the first year of Johnson's published career, testifies in an odd way to the appeal of a rapturous voice for a renaissance woman poet who would speak directly of race.

Ah my race,
Hungry race,
Throbbing and young—
Ah, my race,
Wonder race,
Sobbing with song—
Ah, my race,
Laughing race,
Careless in mirth—

Ah, my veiled
Unformed race,
Fumbling in birth.[20]

At this early stage, Johnson would seem to have only her abstract desire to speak to and for the race, without a clear subject position from which to do it. The result can only be a string of "Ahs"; the passionate/rapturous impulse expressed "from nowhere." By the time of "The Road," published the following year, Johnson has given her rapturous feeling the lyric medium of sustained metaphor and thereby begun the process of finding for herself a concrete positionality. On its face a more attenuated treatment of "her race," **"The Road"** actually goes much further (its vestigial "Ahs" notwithstanding) to bringing the race into focus than the abstract paean could do.

Ah, little road all whirry in the breeze,
A leaping clay hill lost among the trees,
The bleeding note of rapture streaming thrush
Caught in a drowsy hush
And stretched out in a single singing line of
dusky song.
Ah little road, brown as my race is brown,
Your trodden beauty like our trodden pride,
Dust of the dust, they must not bruise you down.
Rise to one brimming golden, spilling cry![21]

As the race takes on concreteness, so does the speaker. Held to a definite metaphor, the race comes through as "like a road"—and by the same token, as defying our expectations for a road. Principally at issue is the idea that a road is the means to a destination, that it implies forward motion and future orientation. To the contrary, Johnson's poem conspicuously insists that we view the road as a stationary convergence of directionless, even ludic activity: a road "whirry in the breeze," "leaping" and "lost" in a "drowsy hush." The road has, in effect, been brought within the terms of lyric time; accordingly, the life of the race has been rendered a synchronic, lyric moment ("a single singing line of dusky song") in which all movement tends toward overflow ("bleeding," "brimming," and "spilling"). The exhortation of the final line brings this redefinition into full visibility in the same moment that the speaker herself comes into view. In the passionate call to passionate expression—"Rise to one brimming golden, spilling cry!"—we see the identification of the lyric woman poet and the race in their mutual rapture. Even more to the point, we see the way that rapture—a lyric "I"—has been implicit from the first line, calling our woman speaker into being.

"Fulfillment" builds on this dynamic with a more ambitious and particularized evocation of race and self. The opening stanza suggests the romantic voice associated with Edna St. Vincent Millay and (closer to home) Georgia Douglas Johnson:

To climb a hill that hungers for the sky,
To dig my hands wrist deep in pregnant
earth,
To watch a young bird, veering, learn to fly,
To give a still, stark poem shining birth.[22]

The distinctiveness of "Fulfillment" starts to emerge in the subsequent stanza, as the Harlem topos of the street insinuates itself into the poem's giddy romantic vista:

To hear the rain drool, dimpling, down the drain
And splash with a wet giggle in the street,
To ramble in the twilight after supper,
And to count the pretty faces that you
meet.

Johnson now hits her stride, giving her romantic rapture over entirely to the celebration of street life:

To ride to town on trolleys, crowded, teeming
With joy and hurry and laughter and push
and sweat—
Squeezed next a patent-leathered Negro dream-
ing
Of a wrinkled river and a minnow net.

To buy a paper from a breathless boy,
And read of kings and queens in foreign
lands,
Hyperbole of romance and adventure,
All for a penny the color of my hand.

At the center of Johnson's synthesis of Harlem and the romantic is a clear consciousness that, while the latter demands and cultivates an individualistic (if expansive) self, the former has a fundamentally collective structure—Harlem *is* its "pretty faces," the uniquely multicultural, rainbow-colored population of African Americans. On the face of it, Johnson has made the not insignificant gesture of "elevating" Harlem to the status of a traditionally "inspiring" subject for poetry. But as a woman of the renaissance, she has also begun the process by which she will finally achieve full access to the subculture she rightly feels is her own.

Taking herself away from the supper table and down to the street, there to be agent and not object, requires a sense of female self not built into Harlem poetics, which typically feature flaneurs like *Home to Harlem*'s Jake, visually sweeping the street for "sweet browns." Neither Jake nor "brown," Johnson's speaker hits the street armed with a selfhood derived from her stanza in nature, her romantic subjectivity. By the time she contemplates "a penny the color of [her] hand," she has achieved a truly remarkable identification of self with the world she would claim. Within the transaction this fourth stanza describes, this woman has gone beyond even the prerogative of observer-chronicler. In a final distancing of the commodity status her presence as a woman on the street raises, she asserts herself as a *buyer* in the marketplace—and not a buyer of fashion (the paradoxical buying of one's own self) but of a newspaper, vehicle of public discourse, her purchase "from a breathless boy" underscoring her potential power in this sphere. If the contents of the paper sound better than a women's novel ("hyperbole of romance and adventure"), that only serves to naturalize further the public entitlement of the female speaker, whose very skin, after all, is the color of currency.

Yet taken from another angle, "a penny the color of my hand" signals the imminent dissolution of self into the larger racial, urban body—just as did the collective human cloud of "joy and hurry and laughter and push and sweat." However desirable the Harlem matrix, the renaissance identity of the bourgeois female speaker is too fragile and hard-won to allow itself to disappear without a trace, hence the abrupt reversion to nature in the poem's final two stanzas, where we find a romantic subjectivity dialectically heightened by the journey to Harlem.

To lean against a strong tree's bosom, sentient
 And hushed before the silent prayer it breathes,
To melt the still snow with my seething body
 And kiss the warm earth tremulous underneath.

Ah, life, to let your stabbing beauty pierce me
 And wound me like we did the studded Christ,
To grapple with you, loving you too fiercely,
 And to die bleeding—consummate with Life.

The culminating crucifixion lacks any obvious preparation in the foregoing stanzas, except in the (rather trivial) sense that being "pierced" by "stabbing beauty" offers a "climax" to the experience of "Life." But if we attend to the drama of subjectivity the poem has unfolded until now, the advent of Christian masochism serves nicely to negotiate the impasse between the (bourgeois) bounded self and the (Harlem) collective self. As the extension of romantic subjectivity Johnson clearly intends it to be, crucifixion annihilates the boundaries of self by way of an apotheosis of self. And in its powerful presence within the poetics of African American rhetoric generally and renaissance women's poetry in particular, Christianity lets this speaker's selfhood come to rest within black tradition—if not quite yet on the streets of Harlem.

Bennett and Johnson in the Avant-Garde

Feminine identity and male prerogative were key categories in the development of both Bennett's and Johnson's poetic subcultural entitlement—their sense of a place in the avant-garde. Johnson rode the rhetorical passion peculiarly available to feminine speakers to finally touch down square in the middle of an urban space and poetics more or less cordoned off as male territory. Bennett effectively shored up a genteel femininity with the distance and delicacy of her specifically imagist aesthetic and her generally modernist aestheticism. But she also took quickly to the masculine liberty of directing culture, in her own way orchestrating the renaissance as consciously as Wallace Thurman himself.

Bennett's relation to the avant-garde needs to be seen in the context of her renaissance activities as a whole, which involve her equally in establishment and fringe cultural circles. Bennett produced several signature cover illustrations for *Crisis* in the high renaissance years, and one of her first poems, **"To Usward,"** officially served to honor Jessie Redmon Fauset at the famous Civic Club dinner that launched the renaissance. Less well known is the fact that Bennett was one of the two or three people to suggest the idea of the dinner itself to Charles Johnson.[23] Bennett was among the editorial collective that produced the de facto manifesto of the Harlem avant-garde, *FIRE!!;* she also served as guest editor for the second issue (of a total of three) of *Black Opals,* the ambitious art journal of the Philadelphia New Negroes. The invitation was testimony to her prestige: her editorial staff included Jessie Redmon Fauset, and contributors (aside from the young Philadelphians the journal was intended to showcase) included Alain Locke and Langston Hughes.[24] Thus, *Black Opals* was conspicuously a cross-generational venture, and the choice of Bennett as guest editor may well reflect specifically on the ability she cultivated to orchestrate the divergent voices of the renaissance. In fact, Bennett made a public renaissance ideal of such orchestration in her role as *Opportunity* columnist.

Through **"The Ebony Flute,"** a literary news column that ran in *Opportunity* from August 1926 through May 1928, Bennett created for herself a truly singular subcultural voice. The only column of its kind in the renaissance public sphere, **"Ebony Flute"** was a miscellaneous collection of publication announcements, marriages, journeys, works in progress, and so forth. Its coherence derived from the voice of Bennett herself. Though she took no part in the cultivation of high-profile "personality" characteristic of self-consciously "modern" writers like those of *The Messenger,* Bennett made her presence felt through the paradoxically self-effacing role of speaking the renaissance. The renaissance took Harlem as its symbolic, affective locus, but the majority of people for whom the movement was a matter of active and intense interest lived elsewhere, as evidenced by the many New Negro "little magazines" scattered around the country, and the national readership of the New York-based journals. As an identifiable and ongoing cultural event, the renaissance had to be visibly and explicitly constructed—not simply interpreted but built up out of social and cultural bits gathered from around the United States and the world. Under these circumstances, a column of the "lighter side" of literary life takes on the status of cultural exoskeleton to lend shape and ontological status to what would otherwise be amorphous or invisible. Presiding over this subcultural materialization of the renaissance was the unobtrusive but distinctly enthusiastic voice of Bennett. It was Bennett's occasionally whimsical, deliberately inclusive voice that brought the renaissance into being for her readers, her stream of associations that served as its connecting tissue—quite explicitly so, her favorite segue being "which reminds me that. . . ." Moreover, the fact of the column as an identifiable center to renaissance life had the self-perpetuating effect of prompting newsy letters from itinerant renaissance celebrities, which, when they appeared in print addressed to her, testified to Bennett's personal force.

Just months after the first installment of **"The Ebony Flute,"** *Opportunity* presented a second column, "The Dark Tower," written by Countee Cullen. Their mirror relation was reflected in their distinctive, identical graphics; not surprisingly, there is evidence that the two were intended to be complementary.[25] In this light, Bennett's inclusivity seems even more pointed: while Cullen chose just two or three topics each month and subjected them to close critical analysis and, often, ringing judgments, Bennett went out of her way to channel local political-aesthetic debates into a greater vision of racial progress, in a manner clearly suggesting the weight of real "race work." The pointedness of this strategy is evident in the comparison between Cullen's review and Bennett's counterreview of *Meek Mose,* a "Comedy of Negro Life" from 1928. Cullen pans it as "a wooden, amateurish play in which at intervals, apparently mathematically conceived, spirituals are indulged in for no good reason whatever, except that the action is on the wane."[26] In the subsequent month's "Ebony Flute," Bennett brings *Meek Mose* back before the public in order to refocus their attention.

> to us the play in itself and its success or failure was unimportant. We were more concerned with the fact that here had arrived the day when the theatre goers of Broadway were willing to attend seriously to the things that Negroes had to say about their own lives.[27]

Having made her point, Bennett goes on to specifically invert Cullen's complaint that the veteran actors of *Meek Mose* "do not fit a new day and time and, more to the point, a new play." Bennett celebrates the fact that actors "who were in essence the spirit of the old school in Negro acting . . . were taking a leading part in the new movement towards true Negro expression upon the American stage." Her next line is surely to be taken as a mischievous parting shot: "So . . . de sun do move. . . ." [original ellipses].

Not a mushy avoidance of conflict, Bennett's vision of racial progress seems more an assertion of faith in the force of her own enthusiastic chronicling to hold together all manner of contradictory things. The role of renaissance columnist and the Bennett persona as it had developed by 1926 dialectically produced in each other a certain subcultural ideal, for which Bennett took personal responsibility: one of inclusivity, with the obligation to orchestrate inclusivity's inevitible plurality.

Like "Ebony Flute" itself, Bennett's best-known poems take the renaissance as their subject, and with the same strong drive to bring it into being in its greatest possible multiplicity. This is evident from the early days of the commemorative poem she wrote for the historic Civic Club dinner. But as this text reveals, the "us" of **"To Usward"** is first and foremost the younger Negro artists and the ideal of inclusivity, Bennett's positioned response to her perception of antagonism (or, at least, interference) from the elder Negro leadership. **"To Usward"** includes a direct plea for tolerance:

If any have a song to sing
That's different from the rest,
Oh let them sing
Before the urgency of Youth's behest!
For some of us have songs to sing
Of jungle heat and fires,
And some of us are solemn grown
With pitiful desires,
And there are those who feel the pull
Of seas beneath the skies,
And some there be who want to croon
Of Negro lullabies.[28]

In the context of the politicized aesthetic debates of even these early days of the renaissance, Bennett seems here quite pointedly to defend artistic youth against appropriation to any preexisting racial agendas.

Yet the interest of this poem lies less in its call for artistic freedom and tolerance than in the strategies of Bennett's self-designation—from the very start of her career and the renaissance—as the voice of unity. The explicit imperative to transcendence—directed to herself *and* the movement—weaves itself into the rhetorical traces of her situatedness as a woman poet and her impulse toward avant-garde identity. The central metaphor, which frames the poem at beginning and end, draws directly on the lyric structure we have seen as core to public feminine self-construction in the renaissance. **"To Usward"** begins,

Let us be still
As ginger jars are still
Upon a Chinese shelf.
And let us be contained
By entities of Self. . . .

Having invoked the self-sufficiency, protective privacy, and fullness out of time so fundamental to contemporaneous African American women's poetry, Bennett goes on to merge this feminine selfhood into the very definition of renaissance artistry.

Not still with lethargy and sloth,
But quiet with the pushing of our growth.
Not self-contained with smug identity
But conscious of the strength in entity.

But if the ginger jars serve to root the new generation's art in the feminine tradition out of which Bennett herself emerges, they likewise gesture forward to Bennett's own avant-garde telos. To begin with, they echo a key trope of international modernism: Imagism's dense and luminous "oriental" object. But in the discursive context of a well-developed and ideologically purposive Africanist poetics, we might well ask, Why "ginger jars . . . / Upon a Chinese shelf"? Why not a metaphor of Africa to articulate the call "to usward," not least because Africa was as rich a vein of modernist meaning as China?[29]

In fact, Bennett's ginger jars displace not just Africa but China itself, substituting for the essential exoticism of the non-Western "homeland" (one's own or another's) the mediated encounter with heritage that city life provides: not the diffuse mystery of China, then, but the dusty shelf in Chinatown; not a soul-threatening encounter with the Other but a foray into the quietly receptive downtown herb shop. The struggle to locate and define African heritage and African American identity, particularly intense in this first flowering of a racially distinct aesthetic (as the Harlem renaissance understood itself), takes on particular contours for those who embrace the urban context in which the struggle takes place—that is, those of an avant-garde renaissance sensibility. In Bennett's poem, urban life provides access to concretely situated and embodied sites of culture into whose mystery transcendent, peripatetic urban subjects—modern artists—enter voluntarily, as an act of will (*Let us be* like ginger jars).[30] "Us"—we—are, of course, African American artists, but in the context of Bennett's displacement of African for Chinese exoticism, necessity goes out of the racial marking. However paradoxical this outcome, given the occasion of the poem, it captures the peculiar felicity of life in Harlem, where the norm is black and, wandering the streets free from the gaze that fixes one's otherness, the black artist glimpses the (flaneurial) promise of modern urban transcendence. For Harlemite urban artists, exoticism, Chinese or African, is (or might be) a matter of voluntary association. Importantly, Bennett invokes an artistic community who do choose such association; just as importantly, they do so as moderns whose aesthetic appropriations proceed from the freedom in identity conferred upon them by the urban space of Harlem. Bennett's ginger jars isolate the utopian moment of modernity and aesthetic endeavor as such, channeling the poem toward avant-garde affiliation even as they implicate the avant-garde in the feminine literary selfhood of lyric plenitude.

Written one year after **"To Usward," "Song"** takes Bennett significantly further in the development of her aesthetic politics. Aside from its titular self-designation, **"Song"**'s highly focused sense of actively orchestrating African American art may explain why Alain Locke placed it in the "Music" rather than the "Poetry" section of his landmark 1925 anthology, *The New Negro: Voices of the Harlem Renaissance.* The poem foregrounds its status as a performative act

I am weaving a song of waters,
Shaken from firm, brown limbs,
Or heads thrown back in irreverent mirth.
My song has the lush sweetness
Of moist, dark lips
Where hymns keep company
With old forgotten banjo songs.
Abandon tells you
That I sing the heart of a race
While sadness whispers
That I am the cry of a soul. . . .[31]

Even as she takes the "weaving" function to herself, the speaker renders the impulse an intrinsic part of African American cultural life: "moist dark lips" are home to modern Christian "hymns" as well as secular, antebellum "old forgotten banjo songs." Weaving, or orchestrating, racial culture puts her not so much above as immersed within the race, and the test of her cultural authenticity is in the African American reader's weaving response, in which the feeling of "Abandon tells you / That I sing the heart of a race / While [the feeling of] sadness whispers / That I am the cry of a soul." As the second stanza shifts to dialect, the speaker recedes behind a vernacular vision seemingly conjured up by the first stanza interactions of speaker and audience.

A-shoutin' in de ole camp-meetin' place,
A-strummin' o' de ole banjo.
Singin' in de moonlight,
Sobbin' in de dark.
Singin', sobbin', strummin' slow . . .
Singin' slow; sobbin' low.
Strummin', strummin', strummin' slow . . .

When the speaker returns to the fore in stanza three, it is to assert the power of Art to orchestrate culture in a more inclusive mode than folk expression could do:

Words are bright bugles
That make the shining for my song,
And mothers hold brown babes
To dark, warm breasts
To make my singing sad.

In clearly distinguishing between her song and the human life it celebrates, the speaker gives mothers and words their full due. At the same time, she reminds us of her own integrative task, performed with the sanction of the people, but out of her own power as an artist.

The concluding stanza is devoted to the general power of art with a specific focus on its effects within African American cultural life. Bennett wrests the Brown Girl, icon of renaissance artistry, from the disembodied gaze of her usual bourgeois viewer and sets her before a woman of the street: "A dancing girl with swaying hips / Sets mad the queen in a harlot's eye." What happens when contemporary art is not just for artists? The short answer for what we see here is racial—and feminine—pride. At the more complicated level of aesthetic politics, Bennett has effectively revealed what the bourgeois context of reception manages more or less successfully to obscure: the dangerous proximity to the harlot—and not just to the queen—of African American artistry's central icon. Given a viewer of her own class, the Brown Girl loses much of her transhistorical aura, but for a good cause, as we see the (African) queen take hold of the "lost" and generally unspeakable woman. More precisely, we see this woman gain access to what art has to offer. Bennett thus displays a supreme faith in art's redemptive power, a utopian dimension of modernism not often acknowledged in the (ostensibly) cynical renaissance avant-garde. And perhaps she forces an even more important avant-garde contradiction by actually crossing class lines to stage the redemption.

In the high renaissance year of 1927, Bennett circled back on the Brown Girl in what we might well see as an obligatory paean to this most essential figure of renaissance aesthetics. **"To a Dark Girl"** seems more or less to conform to its generic type, rendering the historical body of the race through the admiring scrutiny of her bourgeois explainer.

I love you for your brownness,
And the rounded darkness of your breast;
I love you for the breaking sadness in your voice
And shadows where your wayward eyelids rest.

Something of old forgotten queens
Lurks in the lithe abandon of your walk,
And something of the shackled slave
Sobs in the rhythm of your talk.

But if this speaker engages in the usual projections, she also manages finally to suggest that the "dark girl" might herself be the subject of history:

Oh, little brown girl, born for sorrow's mate,
Keep all you have of queenliness,
Forgetting that you once were slave,
And let your full lips laugh at Fate!

In thus granting the Brown Girl an unmediated relation to fate here in this most critical context of bourgeois African American self-understanding, Bennett gestures toward the sort of democratic decentering that constitutes her chief contribution to renaissance poetry.

A mere seventeen at the official launch of the Renaissance, Helene Johnson came of age in the Harlem milieu and even more than Gwendolyn Bennett, wrestled fully with the avant-garde speech she perhaps misrecognized as her birthright. Moreover, she came closest to creating within it a space for feminine subjectivity and cultural authority. Precursor to "A Missionary Brings a Young Native to America" (chapter 6) is the exemplary **"Magalu,"** in which Johnson deliberately overrides the conventional boundaries of primitivist femininity. **"Magalu,"** an individual person with a name, has neither the fetishized body nor the "barbaric dance" of Brown Girl convention; hence, no voyeuristic thrill drives the poem. Indeed, we are fully halfway through its twenty-four free verse lines before Magalu herself appears. Preceding her entrance is a lush but finally not exoticized junglescape.

> Summer comes.
> The ziczac hovers
> 'Round the greedy-mouthed crocodile.
> A vulture bears away a foolish jackal.
> The flamingo is a dash of pink
> Against dark green mangroves,
> Her slender legs rivaling her slim neck.
> The laughing lake gurgles delicious music in its throat
> And lulls to sleep the lazy lizard,
> A nebulous being on a sun-scorched rock.[32]

The busy calm of this scene derives as much as anything from the particularity with which it is rendered; Africa is not a psychological state or a phantasm but a place, with seasons and inhabitants. When we finally encounter Magalu, we understand her, too, to be an inhabitant, distinguished by her darkness and pursuing her own individual purposes.

> In such a place,
> In this pulsing riotous gasp of color,
> I met Magalu, dark as a tree at night,
> Eager-lipped, listening to a man with a white collar
> And a small black book with a cross on it.

Dangerously close to losing herself to this missionary, Magalu is yet tempted at the level of her own "eager" intellect. The speaker addresses her accordingly:

> Oh Magalu, come! Take my hand and I will read you poetry,
> Chromatic words,
> Seraphic symphonies,
> Fill up your throat with laughter and your heart with song.
> Do not let him lure you from your laughing waters,
> Lulling lakes, lissome winds.
> Would you sell the colors of your sunset and the fragrance
> Of your flowers, and the passionate wonder of your forest
> For a creed that will not let you dance?

The speaker engages in a struggle with the missionary for the heart and mind of Magalu by pitting her book of poems against his book of pieties. Once unleashed, her "chromatic words" and "seraphic symphonies" infiltrate the meaning of the jungle, bringing it into an articulate aesthetic order to present to Magalu—in the "*colors* of your sunset" and the "*lulling* lakes, *lissome* winds." The poem assumes Magalu's sentience, her susceptibility to cognitive appeals (whether of an aesthetic or theological nature). But perhaps more fundamentally disruptive of her conventional Brown Girl status is Magalu's very separateness from the jungle she inhabits: not the embodiment of African culture (and hardly embodied at all), not the feminized symbol of the passive land, "Magalu" pulls the Brown Girl free from the heavily freighted meanings that typically subsume her. The revised Brown Girl who emerges is likewise distinct from the ideological dichotomy of ascetic white religion and lush black poetry. Magalu has the prerogative to choose between them—and embedded in that choice is the power to "sell," and even to "sell out." Johnson here extends to this most objectified figure of renaissance femininity, the African native, the redemptive possibility which she (like Bennett, in her own way) finds native to the city street: atomistic modern identity, the boundaries of which provide—or, at least, promise—an empowering distance from gender, race, and history itself.

Central to Johnson's work was the performance of this kind of rescue—from objectification, as in the case of the Brown Girl, or from obscurity, as in the several poems she devoted to celebrating the man in the (Harlem) street in her high-renaissance years of 1926 and 1927. And somewhere in the variety of speaking positions these poems afforded her, Johnson came into an identity which was feminine, urban, and quintessentially avant-garde.

"Bottled" is Johnson's best-known poem, published first in the premier journal of urbanity, *Vanity Fair,* for which it got considerable attention in literary circles both inside and outside Harlem.[33] It is the only one of Johnson's poems to utilize an explicitly male voice, but one imagines that its success stems not from the gender of the speaker per se, but from the exuberant sense of urban mastery his gender affords him. Having once captured that sense "as a man," Johnson will work to appropriate it to feminine terms.

"Bottled" may be seen as an extended encounter with racial heritage against the backdrop of urban Harlem, with which the speaker is strongly identified. In its central focus, "Bottled" turns the redemptive light of African heritage on an unappreciated man on the street, while giving considerable space to its speaker, whose vernacular voice renders him a full-blown character and whose musing, peripatetic relation to the city provides the structure of the poem. Strikingly, for a poem of the renaissance, the continuity of Harlem and Africa is never assumed; in fact, their disjunction constitutes the poem's central tension. Such skepticism regarding Africa is at least as common among the avant-garde as the converse embrace of primitivism. Not just ornery refusal to glorify the ancestry, the distanced relation to Africa was necessary to a certain avant-garde investment in modern identity, however ambivalent. Hence, Africa appears in the very first stanza of "Bottled," but as an anthropological oddity.

> Upstairs on the third floor
> Of the 135th Street library
> In Harlem, I saw a little
> Bottle of sand, brown sand
> Just like the kids make pies
> Out of down at the beach.
> But the label said: "This
> Sand was taken from the Sahara desert."
> Imagine that! The Sahara desert!
> Some bozo's been all the way to Africa to get
>   some sand.

The speaker's diction ("some bozo") ensures his identity as a city dweller, just as the fact that Africa is contained in a remote ("third floor") library exhibit ensures that Harlem is a space separable, at some level, from racial heritage.

When, in the next stanza, we come to the man who constitutes the visual focus of the poem, the spectacle he creates on the street enters the poem as intentionally analogous to the bottle of sand—arcane, remote, not of Harlem, but for Harlem's amusement.

> And yesterday on Seventh Avenue
> I saw a darky dressed fit to kill
> In yellow gloves and swallow tail coat
> And swirling a cane. And everyone
> Was laughing at him. Me too,
> At first, till I saw his face
> When he stopped to hear a
> Organ grinder grind out some jazz.
> Boy! You should a seen that darky's face!
> It just shone. Gee he was happy!
> And he began to dance. No
> Charleston or Black Bottom for him.
> No sir. He danced just as dignified
> And slow. No, not slow either.
> Dignified and *proud*! You couldn't
> Call it slow, not with all the
> Cuttin' up he did. You would a died to see him.

As the stanza progresses, the generational difference that has seemed to define this man—unaware of contemporary popular dances, happy in dandy's clothes, his very happiness seemingly anachronistic and minstrel-like—is replaced by a historical difference going beyond the space of a generation to racial ancestry. His dance, when it comes, is "dignified / And slow. No, not slow either. / Dignified and *proud*!" At this point, the speaker has become the privileged audience for the man's essential self, as well as its articulator—at the same time that he must insist on his own character and generational distance from what he sees. In the clash of these two aims, we are confronted with the possibility that what he "sees" is, in fact, a youthful urban fantasy of Africa projected onto the old man. In the next stanza,

> The crowd kept yellin' but he didn't hear,
> Just kept on dancin' and twirlin' that cane
> And yellin' out loud every once in a while.
> I know the crowd thought he was coo-coo.
> But say, I was where I could see his face,
> And somehow, I could see him dancin' in a
>   jungle,
> A real honest-to-cripe jungle, and he wouldn't
>   have on them
> Trick clothes—those yaller shoes and yaller
>   gloves
> And swallow-tail coat. He wouldn't have on
>   nothing.
> And he wouldn't be carrying no cane.
> He'd be carrying a spear with a sharp fine point
> Like the bayonets we had "over there."
> And the end of it would be dipped in some kind
>   of
> Hoo-doo poison. And he'd be dancin' black and
>   naked and gleaming.
> And he'd have rings in his ears and on his nose
> And bracelets and necklaces of elephants' teeth.

As the fantasy becomes increasingly visual and ornate, a series of primitivist clichés, we get a glimpse of what motivates it.

> Gee, I bet he'd be beautiful then all right.
> No one would laugh at him then, I bet.
> Say! That man that took that sand from the
>   Sahara desert
> And put it in a little bottle on a shelf in the
>   library,
> That's what they done to this shine, ain't it?
>   Bottled him.
> Trick shoes, trick coat, trick cane, trick
>   everything—all glass—
> But inside—
> Gee, that poor shine!

Even as it seems to establish his perfect sympathy, the conclusion deliberately asserts the young speaker's impassable distance from the problems of "that poor shine."

A second poem from the same year imagines the same scenario, but with a feminine speaker/observer—and somewhere in the gender transition the rich, variegated terrain of Harlem fades away, leaving only speaker and object where there was a whole world. Given the centrality of the world of Harlem to Johnson's poetics, its disappearance warrants the suspicion that critical stakes are afoot in this poem. "Sonnet to a Negro in Harlem" attempts to embed a feminine presence on the street through an implicitly heterosexual framework. But adopting heterosexuality as a framework within which to speak as a subcultural bard apparently problematizes the value of the street itself.

"Sonnet to a Negro in Harlem," as its title suggests, makes a declaration of love to an anonymous and, perhaps more important, a generalized man of the race. More accurately termed a protolove poem, **"Sonnet"** channels its submerged love through the purest expression of appreciation. The subject of this paean is an exotic, but, unlike the Brown Girl, whose links to primitivism arise unbidden—and largely unnoticed—by her for the benefit of her bourgeois spectator, this "Negro" wears his primitivism as a self-conscious mantle of defiance:

> You are disdainful and magnificent—
> Your perfect body and your pompous gait,
> Your dark eyes flashing solemnly with hate,
> Small wonder that you are incompetent
> To imitate those whom you so despise—
> Your shoulders towering high above the throng,
> Your head thrown back in rich, barbaric song,
> Palm trees and mangoes stretched before your
> eyes.[34]

Most obviously, gender accounts for the man's difference, specifically, the masculine burden of exclusion from the white capitalist enterprise. Johnson deploys the long-standing African American critique of white capitalist greed in service to the imperative of masculine self-worth, as the poem concludes.

> Let others toil and sweat for labor's sake
> And wring from grasping hands their meed of
> gold.
> Why urge ahead your supercilious feet?
> Scorn will efface each footprint that you make.
> I love your laughter arrogant and bold
> You are too splendid for this city street!

Registered through her empathy with the disenfranchised black man, the speaker sees the city as the degraded territory of capitalist strife—a striking contrast to the celebration with which we have seen her female personae take to the very same turf. This divide would seem to reflect the classic gender dichotomy of male production, here prohibited, and female consumption, presumed to be easy. But in fact, the class difference between speaker and "Negro" overrides the gender difference in this case, perhaps willfully so: her privilege as a bourgeois intellectual (including the fact that *her* exoticism *makes* her money) affords her modern transcendence. By contrast, his greater economic vulnerability keeps him tied to regimented wage work, which, in fact, he *cannot* afford to despise, and for which his exoticism is a hindrance. But this celebration of the man's class defiance—this assertion of class empathy—functions implicitly to shore up the speaker's precarious claim to the street as a woman. The "Negro" is lordly, king of the street but not a part of it, and the street itself fails to offer him refuge, either as a general site of pleasure and variety or as a special black world standing between the individual African American and the capitalism of downtown (as epitomized by McKay's *Home to Harlem*). With no hint of a larger racial community, this man is isolated as no other figures we have seen in Johnson's poetry.

The key to so significant a departure from her usual depiction of Harlem life lies not in the man himself, however, but in the ontological needs of the speaker who addresses him. In isolating the male, the speaker comes into being as the one to recognize the true worth of this princely exotic, scorned by the world. Her identity—and his—are thus anchored in her necessary perception. In their intimate mutual interdependence, they are like lovers, but in her singularity and disembodiment (for the "Negro" of her admiring gaze does not physicalize her as a mere woman by gazing back) the speaker emerges as transcendent and authoritative poet of the race. This gendered dynamic of identification and desire crystallizes around the issue of urban alienation. The man's entitlement to ease on the street, as a man, is as much assumed as the female speaker's awkwardness. In letting this "magnificent" African bear the burden of alienation for both of them—and in particular for the alienation displaced from her to him—she transforms alienation itself from a mark of outsiderhood to a core component of racial authenticity *and* racially specific masculinity. To the extent that her displacement of alienation is successful, she is free of it; to the extent that her femininity inevitably draws alienation back to her, it returns dialectically transformed as a mark of inclusivity.

In their identification and difference, in their mutual need, the speaker and object of **"Sonnet"** are protolovers. **"Poem,"** Johnson's most ambitious claim to avant-garde identity, is also grounded within this heterosexual framework. But the work of making a place for herself really begins in earnest when she melds heterosexual identity—by itself, a potentially hazardous basis for artistic authority—with vernacular diction. Contrary to what we might expect, Johnson's vernacular did not function to identify her with a specific—more racially "authentic"—class. Just the reverse, vernacular diction tapped into the potential for class transcendence implicit in modernity. With the voice of a slangy urbanite, Johnson could glide lightly across femininity *and* the street, heterosexuality *and* autonomy. Most significant for her contribution to avant-garde representation, she (like Bennett in her own way) could close the gap between racial authenticity and artistic authority.

Published alongside **"Sonnet"** in Countee Cullen's landmark anthology, *Caroling Dusk,* **"Poem"** emanates from the extraordinary rhetorical situation of a female modern watching a male vaudeville performer in a popular Harlem theater.

Little brown boy,
Slim, dark, big-eyed,
Crooning love songs to your banjo
Down at the Lafayette—
Gee, boy, I love the way you hold your head,
High sort of and a bit to one side,
Like a prince, a jazz prince. And I love
Your eyes flashing, and your hands,
And your patent-leathered feet,
And your shoulders jerking the jig-wa.
And I love your teeth flashing,
And the way your hair shines in the spotlight
Like it was the real stuff.
Gee, brown boy, I loves you all over.
I'm glad I'm a jig. I'm glad I can
Understand your dancin' and your
Singin', and feel all the happiness
And joy and don't care in you.
Gee, boy, when you sing, I can close my ears
And hear tom toms just as plain.
Listen to me, will you, what do I know
About tom toms? But I like the word, sort of,
Don't you? It belongs to us.
Gee, boy, I love the way you hold your head,
And the way you sing, and dance,
And everything.
Say, I think you're wonderful. You're
Allright with me,
You are.[35]

Johnson has, in effect, seized the means of avant-garde cultural production: her female speaker claims the right of the public space, the right of the specularizing gaze, and the power of cultural/racial definition. But what this appropriation entails is the transformation of the discursive apparatus itself, a transformation that points the way out of the impasse facing the avant-garde Harlem intellectual (delineated in chapter 6): his class distance, which slips easily into modernist exoticization or self-irony, and his generational embattlement, which necessitates modernist iconoclasm targeted at women. **"Poem"** radically restructures the Brown Girl paradigm: the "girl," first of all, has become a "boy"; the "barbaric dance," a theatrical number; the distant bourgeois viewer, a concretely situated, social equal (the Lafayette being the popular nightspot for ordinary Harlemites); and the "essential" race itself, a race under construction.

After briefly introducing us to the "little brown boy," the poem's speaker intrudes herself fully upon the space of the poem by force of her speech. The voice that says "Gee, boy," "the real stuff," "Listen to me, will you," "Say," and "You're / Allright with me" emanates from a modern girl, a "sheba,"[36] even. At this point, vernacular speech comes into focus as a marker that specifically overrides the class (and the race) of the speaker in favor of an identity that is generational only. We feel strongly her modernness and her youth without having much sense of the very vexed question of her class (vexed, since indeed she *is* a woman in a public place). According to historian Paula Fass, classlessness was the whole point of the American youth culture that emerged in the 1920s: the slanginess of self-conscious youth let nation and generation subsume the situatedness of class and race beneath a democratizing (and consumable) style.[37] Faced with the challenge of putting an African American woman into the public terrain of Harlem, Johnson avails herself of this national modernness to transcend the unsatisfying choice between degradation (for the working-class woman) and the threat of degradation (for the bourgeois woman). Socially situated, Johnson's sheba yet escapes such sexual definition and, from her seat in the darkened theatre, even bypasses embodiment.

As possessor of the gaze, **"Poem"**'s speaker takes no liberties outside her contractual relationship of audience to performer; having paid the price of a ticket, she has public sanction to look appraisingly at a man, as well as the tacit invitation of this man in particular. While the immediate benefit of this situation may be the protection it affords the female viewer, it also stands as a critique of the artist/viewer who helps himself voyeuristically to the fortuitous siting of his object, whether in a cabaret, in a forest glade, or through the window of a church.

But the theatrical context also authorizes the speaker's racial pronouncements. Whereas the image of a woman—and the Brown Girl in particular—is always already saturated with publicness by virtue of being in public circulation, this man needs to be literally placed on a theatrical stage to carry the same charge and thereby underwrite the speaker's cultural authority to ponder the meaning of race through his performance. But since their encounter is thus staged across a vaudevillian space, still strongly tied to minstrelsy, that performance is forcibly seen in light of a theatrical tradition that calls the very idea of racial authenticity into question. The speaker finds her brown boy "crooning . . . to [his] banjo" but simultaneously holding his head "Like a prince, a jazz prince." His teeth and eyes "flash," as do his "patent-leathered feet"; his shoulders "jerk," while his "hair shines in the spotlight / Like it was the real stuff." But she can "close [her] ears / And hear tom toms" in his singing. Rather than let even this trope of "Africa" stand, she topples its essentialist implications—and restores the tom toms to their rightful importance.

> Listen to me, will you, what do I know
> About tom toms? But I like the word, sort of,
> Don't you? It belongs to us.

Far from an unconscious cultural reservoir manifested in the more "primitive" members of the race, the true meaning of "Africa" is the possibility it offers for social solidarity and the collective construction of an enabling culture.

As this last point suggests, the theatrical context also makes African American culture-building the business of ordinary African Americans—not merely an elite literary exercise of translating the unspoiled peasant to the world. Using the "African-ness" of a vaguely minstrel performance as the starting point for a construction of race puts the African American quest for racial self-definition squarely in mainstream culture, a suggestion buoyed by the mainstream modernness of the speaker herself. Moreover, the mainstream context preserves the possibility of a claim to American identity, an explicitly held value of Harlem discourse generally.

But what of the fact that this avant-garde paean to the race is also a suppressed love poem? The speaker says "I love" no less than five times, in an insistent chorus that holds its own against the racial message. In fact, the two are closely tied in their dynamics and finally inextricable in the ideological visions they project. Sitting in the audience, the speaker is part of a cultural collective—a remarkable female participant in the life of Harlem—and also unique in her recognition of the boy. Buried in her description is the strong implication that she sees something through the very ordinariness of his performance, something that makes her "glad [she's] a jig." That something is, in fact, the complex racial identity we have been examining. Her ability to "understand [his] dancin' and [his] / Singin', and [to] feel all the happiness / And joy and don't care in [him]" is both cause and effect of her love. Though attenuated, the "love" in this poem provides a structuring relation of mutually constituting uniqueness for the players: she sees the prince in him, and that very vision sets *her* apart. Conventional love and the theatrical context save both boy and girl from objectification and essentialism, paradoxically rescuing them for individuality. Through her privileged articulation of the boy's individual essence, the girl gains cultural authority. But the essence she articulates is clearly her own as well as his; they have in common this complex, urban, African, American way of being—and becoming. The avant-garde project of establishing independent racial self-definition emerges here as necessarily a function of self-implication and even affect. Love, not as a private indulgence but as a public embrace of an embodied cultural ethos, is finally the enabling condition for Johnson's feminization of the Harlem Renaissance avant-garde.

At this point, we seem ironically to have come full circle to Jessie Redmon Fauset and the values driving ***There Is Confusion*** (chapter 7). That "public love" (or, "love in public") could signify both discursive extremes, of women's constraint and women's freedom within renaissance subcultural identity, suggests the tremendous creativity with which women writers responded to their cultural imperatives, as well as the sobering power of the imperatives themselves.

Notes

1. Marion Grace Conover, "Comments," *Saturday Evening Quill* (June 1928): 64. The *Saturday Evening Quill* was the journal of a literary club by the same name, which comprised the Boston outpost of the renaissance. Helene Johnson got her start there, as did Dorothy West (Abby Arthur Johnson and Ronald Maberry Johnson, *Propaganda and Aesthetics: The Literary Politics of Afro-American Magazines in the Twentieth Century* [Amherst: University of Massachusetts Press, 1979] 92-93).

2. In the interest of avoiding misappropriation of Baker's argument, I must note that *Workings of the Spirit* (and Baker's work generally) very explicitly takes those works that engage what Baker calls vernacular modes as the true African American cultural tradition. Bourgeois identity and style, under discussion here, fall distinctly outside Baker's purview. My implicit contention, however, is that bourgeois writers do participate in the African American literary tradition, even to the point of engaging many of the same issues and with similar strategies as their vernacular counterparts.
3. Not even Hagar, the slave whose enforced surrogate motherhood made her a primary and enduring figure of African American women's Christian experience, is a presence in the poetry of the time. On Hagar and the history of black women's experience in the church generally, see Delores S. Williams. *Sisters in the Wilderness: The Challenge of Womanist God-Talk* (Maryknoll, N.Y.: Orbis Books, 1993).
4. Alice Dunbar-Nelson, "Of Old St. Augustine," *Opportunity* (June 1925): 216.
5. Kimberly Rae Connor, *Conversions and Visions in the Writings of African-American Women* (Knoxville: University of Tennessee Press, 1994) 14; my italics.
6. Connor's argument is consistent with Lawrence W. Levine's landmark 1977 study *Black Culture and Black Consciousness: Afro-American Folk Thought from Slavery to Freedom,* in which, discussing the earlier spirituals, he argues, "The religious music of the slaves is almost devoid of feelings of depravity or unworthiness, but is rather, as I have tried to show, pervaded by a sense of change, transcendence, ultimate justice, and personal worth" ([New York: Oxford University Press] 39).
7. Dora Lawrence Houston, "Preference," *Opportunity* (June 1925): 164.
8. Jessie Redmon Fauset, "Rain Fugue," Crisis (August 1924): 155.
9. Most prominent in this mode are Georgia Douglas Johnson's poems for *The Crisis.* See "Armageddon" (March 1925): 231; "Escape" (May 1925): 15; "Companion" (August 1925): 180; and "Finality" (September 1926): 247.
10. Gwendolyn Bennett, "Street Lamps in Early Spring," *Opportunity* (May 1926): 152.
11. Langston Hughes, *The Weary Blues* (New York: Knopf, 1926) 19.
12. Helene Johnson, "Night," *Opportunity* (January 1926): 23.
13. Helene Johnson, "What Do I Care for Morning," in *Caroling Dusk: An Anthology of Verse by Negro Poets,* ed. Countee Cullen (New York: Harper Brothers, 1927) 216.
14. This intellectual tradition includes such major works as W. E. B. Du Bois, *Souls of Black Folk* (1903) and Pauline Hopkins, *Of One Blood* (1901).
15. Importantly, as the renaissance wore on, the equation of African American race with youth reversed the terms of the earlier rhetoric, all the while keeping the values intact but adding the crucial emphasis on color and pleasure.
16. Gwendolyn Bennett, "Moon Tonight," in *Gypsy* (Cincinnati: October 1926): 13.
17. Gwendolyn Bennett, "Purgation," *Opportunity* (February 1925): 56.
18. Gwendolyn Bennett, "Wind," *Opportunity* (November 1924): 335.
19. Gwendolyn Bennett, "Fantasy," in *Caroling Dusk,* 158.
20. Helene Johnson, "My Race," in *Caroling Dusk,* 221.
21. Helene Johnson, "The Road," *Opportunity* (July 1926): 221.
22. Helene Johnson, "Fulfillment," *Opportunity* (June 1926): 194.
23. Hull, *Color, Sex, and Poetry,* 6.
24. Johnson and Johnson, *Propaganda and Aesthetics,* 89-90.
25. For example, they divided the labor of eulogizing Florence Mills and Clarissa Scott Delaney, who both died in the fall of 1927. My characterization of the columns refers mostly to their first year or so of existence, after which they lose their prominent graphics and much of their column space (especially "Ebony Flute").
26. Countee Cullan, "The Dark Tower," *Opportunity* (March 1928): 90.
27. Gwendolyn Bennett, "The Ebony Flute," *Opportunity* (April 1928): 122.
28. Gwendolyn Bennett, "To Usward," *Crisis* (May 1924): 19.
29. Michael North's *The Dialect of Modernism: Race, Language and Twentieth Century Literature* (New York: Oxford University Press, 1994) thoroughly explores the largely buried function of Africa (and African America) for the high modernists.
30. I allude here to the flaneurial tradition inaugurated by Charles Baudelaire ("The Painter of Modern Life" [1845]) and theorized by Walter Benjamin (*Charles Baudelaire or the Lyric Poet of High Capitalism* [London: New Left Books, 1969). For state-of-the-art flaneurial scholarship, see Keith Tester, ed., *The Flaneur* (New York: Routledge, 1994).
31. Gwendolyn Bennett, "Song," in *The New Negro,* ed. Alain Locke (1925; New York: Atheneum, 1992) 225.
32. Helene Johnson, "Magalu," in *Caroling Dusk,* 223-224.
33. Helene Johnson, "Bottled," *Vanity Fair* (May 1927):76.
34. Helene Johnson, "Sonnet to a Negro in Harlem," in *Caroling Dusk,* 217.
35. Helene Johnson, "Poem," in *Caroling Dusk,* 218-219.
36. See n. 59, chapter 6.
37. Paula Fass, *The Damned and the Beautiful: American Youth in the 1920s* (New York: Oxford University Press, 1977).

FURTHER READING

Criticism

Chambers, Veronica. "Renaissance Women." In *The Harlem Renaissance,* pp. 61-82. Philadelphia: Chelsea House, 1998.

Discussion of the African American women associated with the Harlem Renaissance, including the claim that Bennett was one of the writers who suggested the 1924 Civic Club dinner to Charles Johnson.

Honey, Maureen. Introduction. In *Shadowed Dreams: Women's Poetry of the Harlem Renaissance,* pp. 1-42. New Brunswick: Rutgers University Press, 1989.

Includes a brief discussion of night imagery in Bennett's "Street Lamps in Early Spring."

Hull, Gloria T. "Black Women Poets from Wheatley to Walker." *Negro American Literature Forum* 9, no. 3 (fall 1975): 91-96.

A survey of African American female poets from colonial times to the present, including a brief mention of Bennett, whom Hull praises for the painterly quality of her poetry.

Johnson, Abby Arthur and Ronald Maberry Johnson. "Toward the Renaissance: *Crisis, Opportunity,* and *Messenger,* 1910-1928." In *Propaganda and Aesthetics: The Literary Politics of Afro-American Magazines in the Twentieth Century,* pp. 31-64. Amherst: University of Massachusetts Press, 1979.

A description of two of the regular columns in the journal Opportunity: *Countee Cullen's "Dark Tower" and Gwendolyn Bennett's "Ebony Flute."*

Lewis, David Levering. "Enter the New Negro." In *When Harlem Was in Vogue,* pp. 89-118. New York: Oxford University Press, 1979.

Includes a brief description of Bennett's recitation of her poem "To Usward" at the Civic Club dinner in 1924.

OTHER SOURCES FROM GALE:

Additional coverage of Bennett's life and career is contained in the following sources published by the Gale Group: *Black Writers,* Ed. 1; *Contemporary Authors,* Vol. 125; *Dictionary of Literary Biography,* Vol. 51; *World Poets.*

MARITA BONNER

(1898 - 1971)

(Full name Marita Odette Bonner Occomy) American short story writer, playwright, and essayist.

Although she is more closely associated with the literary salon known as the Round Table in Washington, D.C., than with Harlem of the 1920s and 1930s, Bonner is credited with contributing a unique perspective to this vital period in the history of African American literature. Her primary influences were her experiences at Radcliffe College and life in the cities of Washington, D.C., and Chicago. Set in the fictional locale of Frye Street, a multiethnic Chicago neighborhood, Bonner's stories and plays explore what it meant to be a Black woman struggling with familial and community problems during the years between World War I and World War II.

BIOGRAPHICAL INFORMATION

One of four children born to Joseph Andrew, a machinist, and Mary Anne Bonner, Bonner received the best schooling then available. Her father had attended but not graduated from the Boston Latin School for boys, and he worked hard through his adult life to ensure that his children completed their educations. Bonner grew up in the Boston area. While in high school, she contributed regularly to the student magazine *The Sagamore,* whose faculty sponsor encouraged Bonner to apply to Radcliffe. After graduating from Brookline High School, she entered Radcliffe College in 1918. She lived at home with her family and commuted to classes, since neither Radcliffe nor Harvard allowed Blacks to live in the dormitories. For the next four years, she studied English and comparative literature. She also earned admission to Charles T. Copeland's prestigious writing seminar. In 1922, Bonner graduated with a B.A. in English and went on to teach in the Washington, D.C., area, where she became involved in Georgia Douglas Johnson's cultural and literary salon, the Round Table—a group whose aim was the development and recognition of African American art. Through her association with the Round Table, Bonner came in contact with notable Harlem Renaissance writers including Langston Hughes, Jessie Fauset, and Zora Neale Hurston. It was also during this time that Bonner published her first works. In 1925, *The Crisis,* a journal devoted to African American literature and culture, published Bonner's essay "On Being Young—A Woman—And Colored," and the journal *Opportunity* awarded an honorable mention to and published her short story "The Hands." Bonner continued to participate in the Round Table as she taught and composed short stories about the Black working class. In addition, she wrote and published three one-act plays, all of which are strongly allegorical and, despite meticulous directions, were intended primarily to be read. The best known of these plays, *The Purple Flower* (1928), is an allegory of race relations with the flavor of a morality play. In 1930 Bonner married William Almay Occomy, a graduate of Brown University with an M.B.A. from Boston University. The newlyweds moved to a multiethnic Chicago neighborhood that same year. Bonner took a three-year hiatus from publishing as she began raising their growing family. In 1933, Bonner, now using her married name, began publishing stories based on her Chicago neighborhood. Fictional Frye Street became the center of Bonner's focus for the rest of her writing career. In these stories, she examines urban life in a community comprised of segregated whites and Blacks as well as immigrants from around the world. Typically centering on female characters, the plots involve inter-racial relations, romantic intrigue, the economic hardships of the Depression, violence, and hopefulness. In 1941, Bonner published her last short story. That same year she became involved in the First Church of Christ Scientist, although it is not known whether her involvement with the Church is tied to her abandonment of literary pursuits. When the youngest of her three children was ready for school, Bonner returned to teaching, to which she devoted herself until she retired in the 1960s. She died in 1971 following a fire in her apartment.

MAJOR WORKS

Bonner's first published story, "The Hands," is a short piece in which the first-person narrator, while riding a bus, becomes fascinated with the work-worn and rough hands of an older male passenger. The narrator creates an imaginary history of the man whose life had so roughened his hands. This imaginary life reveals class consciousness and comments on the unjust treatment of African Americans. Bonner's first of three one-act plays, *The Purple Flower,* which some scholars consider her masterpiece, is an allegory of African Americans' struggle for freedom and pursuit of happiness. In the play, the "Us's" are situated on a plain between the hill "Somewhere" and the distant border of "Nowhere." The Us's want to climb to Somewhere's summit to reach the desirable purple Flower-of-Life-At-Its-Fullest. The hill, however, is defended by quick-moving, grotesque people called White Devils. The Us's devise strategies to move past the White Devils by blending Black experience and blood in a magical cauldron. While the play was never produced in Bonner's lifetime, it shares some of the characteristics of the Black pageant movement and elements of the morality play. Another of her published short stories, "A Sealed-Pod" (published in *Opportunity* in 1936), is set in Bonner's Frye Street and examines the destructive power of gossip. The story revolves around the murder of a young Black girl named Viollette Aurora Davis. Suspicion and street justice lead the neighborhood—and Viollette's own mother—to point to married African American Dave Jones as the murderer. The actual perpetrator is a white, unmarried Italian American man named Joe Tamona, who avoids suspicion and goes free when gossip leads to the arrest and false conviction of Jones. The community ousts Jones's wife in an attempt to rid themselves of the scandal. The community believes the lies about the perpetrator of Viollette's violent murder because it is the story they want to believe. In one of Bonner's posthumously published stories, "On the Altar," originally written in 1938, Bonner examines women's duty to sacrifice personal and sexual fulfillment for the betterment of their families. In this story, Beth, who has happily married a working-class, dark-skinned African American man named Jerry, is forced by her Grandmother Breastwood to leave the man whom she loves for a second unfulfilling but socially advantageous marriage. Grandmother Breastwood forces Beth to abort her unborn child, then removes Beth from her first husband, and finally takes her away to Europe. Despite his attempts, Jerry cannot find Beth, whose letters from Europe never reach him because the city has renumbered the apartments in Jerry's tenement and the post office is unable to locate him. Jerry learns of his wife's activity in the local newspaper's society column. Beth is eventually remarried to a well-off doctor whom she does not love. Through her grandmother's machinations, Beth learns that marriage is not about love or passion but instead signals economic dependency for the wife as it preserves and advances the class and social rank of her family.

CRITICAL RECEPTION

Bonner's short stories, plays, and essays were not collected in book form until the publication in 1987 of *Frye Street & Environs: The Collected Works of Marita Bonner.* Consequently, there has been little critical commentary on Bonner's writing until recent years. Of all her works, *The Purple Flower* has gained the most attention for its allegorical portrayal of African American struggles for personal and artistic equality. "On The Altar" has also earned notice for its commentary on the constraints placed on African American women by family and marriage and the subversion of their own sexual and romantic desires by their responsibility to others. Central to all discussion of Bonner's work is her fictional Frye Street locale, which critics have ultimately judged a positive and creative place. Here, as Carol Allen argues, Bonner exposes the neighborhood's dehumanizing and debilitating aspects, while at the same time celebrating pockets of African American resistance to these forces.

PRINCIPAL WORKS

"The Hands" [published in journal *The Crisis*] (short story) 1925

"On Being Young—A Woman—And Colored" [published in journal *The Crisis*] (essay) 1925

"Drab Rambles" [published in journal *The Crisis*] (short story) 1927

"One Boy's Story" [published in journal *The Crisis*] (short story) 1927

The Pot-Maker: A Play to Be Read [published in journal *The Crisis*] (play) 1927

Exit—An Illusion [published in journal *The Crisis*] (play) 1928

The Purple Flower [published in journal *The Crisis*] (play) 1928

"Young Blood Hungers" [published in journal *The Crisis*] (essay) 1928

"A Possible Triad on Black Notes" [published in journal *Opportunity*] (short story) 1933

"Tin Can" [published in journal *Opportunity*] (essay) 1933

"A Sealed Pod" [published in journal *Opportunity*] (short story) 1936

**Frye Street & Environs: The Collected Works of Marita Bonner* (short stories, plays, and essays) 1987

* This volume contains five stories unpublished during Bonner's lifetime: "On the Altar," "High Stepper," "Stones for Bread," "Reap It as You Sow It," and "Light in Dark Places."

GENERAL COMMENTARY

JOYCE FLYNN (ESSAY DATE 1987)

SOURCE: Flynn, Joyce. Introduction to *Frye Street & Environs: The Collected Works of Marita Bonner,* edited by Joyce Flynn and Joyce Occomy Stricklin, pp. xi-xxvii. Boston: Beacon Press, 1987.

In the following essay, Flynn provides an overview of Bonner's life and works, commenting on many of her short stories and her three one-act plays.

> *Now, walking along Frye Street, you sniff first the rusty tangy odor that comes from a river too near a city; walk aside so that Jewish babies will not trip you up; you pause to flatten your nose against discreet windows of Chinese merchants; marvel at the beauty and tragic old age in the faces of the young Italian women; puzzle whether the muscular blond people are Swedes or Danes or both; pronounce odd consonant names in Greek characters on shops; wonder whether Russians are Jews, or Jews, Russians—and finally you will wonder how the Negroes there manage to look like all men of every other race and then have something left over for their own distinctive black-browns.*
>
> *There is only one Frye Street. It runs from the river to Grand Avenue where the El is.*
>
> *All the World is there.*
>
> From the Foreword to **"A Possible Triad on Black Notes"**

The Frye Street that anchored a fictional universe in Chicago functioned as a daring symbol of the diversity, novelty, and opportunity available in cities like Chicago and Detroit, meccas for black migration from the South in the decades surrounding World War I. The architect of Frye Street, Marita Bonner (1899-1971), was one of the most versatile early twentieth-century black writers. Her contributions to *The Crisis* and *Opportunity* between the two world wars include essays, reviews, plays, short stories, and fictional narratives published in several parts. The focus of much of her work—urban life in the interwar period—probably stemmed from her residence in three urban centers: Boston, where she was born and educated; Washington, D.C., where she worked for eight years; and Chicago, where she moved after her marriage to William Almy Occomy in 1930 and lived for forty-one years, raising her three children, William Almy, Jr., Warwick Gale, and Marita Joyce Occomy.

Bonner's works offer the perspective of an educated black female consciousness on a rapidly changing America between the two world wars. She focuses on black Chicagoans and their neighbors, internal immigrants from the South or immigrants from Europe, as they deal with discrimination and the brutalized exhaustion of the working poor. Bonner's vision of Chicago contrasts sharply with that of Theodore Dreiser or of her own contemporaries James T. Farrell and Richard Wright. In her evocation of the cramped apartments in which mothers attempt to protect their children from the streets, she anticipates the heroine and architectural focus of Ann Petry's *The Street* (1946). Bonner's cityscapes capture the terrible cost of life on the northern urban frontier.

On the multi-ethnic Frye Street of Bonner's Depression fiction, black residents mingle with immigrants but watch the newcomers obtain better jobs and their children better futures. But "Frye Street (black)" saw no promise equal to the possibilities offered "Frye Street (white)." The black working mothers of Bonner's Chicago stories battle against poverty, gangs, and prejudice, but too often find that their children are destroyed while the parents are absent, working the long hours at low wages that are the share allotted them by prejudice in the new city.

Bonner's preparation for writing included the finest schooling then available, and that opportunity inspired her lifelong commitment to those less fortunate. She was one of four children born to Jospeh Andrew and Mary Anne (Noel) Bonner. She was raised in the Boston area and educated locally, attending Brookline High School, where she acquired musical training and the beginnings of her fluency in German. Upon entering Radcliffe College in 1918, she concentrated in English and comparative literature, winning admission to Charles T. Copeland's exclusive writing seminar. During Bonner's college years, black students at Harvard and Radcliffe were not allowed dormitory accommodations, but like the majority of women students enrolled, Bonner commuted from home. While still a college student, Bonner taught at a nearby Cambridge high school; after her graduation in 1922, she continued her teaching career, first in the Washington, D.C., area and later in Chicago. At Radcliffe, Bonner was active in campus activities such as the Radcliffe song competitions, which she won in 1918 and 1922. She continued her studies in musical composition and in German literature, which would be important influences on her later literary career.[1]

Literary Apprenticeship: The Early Sketches and Stories

Though Bonner had shared some of her writing with Radcliffe colleagues through the Copeland writing seminar and the Radcliffe songwriting competition, her first published works—**"The Hands"** and the autobiographical essay **"On Being Young—a Woman—and Colored"**—appeared in the black journal *The Crisis* in 1925, when she was living and working in Washington, D.C., and a member of Georgia Douglas Johnson's "S" Street salon. A poet, playwright, and composer thirteen years Bonner's senior, Johnson forged a lifelong friendship with the new arrival from Boston and involved her in regular Saturday night gatherings that included over the years such authors as Langston Hughes, Countee Cullen, Alain Locke, Jessie Fauset, S. Randolph Edmonds, Willis Richardson, May Miller, and Jean Toomer.[2]

These early pieces, as well as others published in the 1920s, are notable for their brevity, their original perspective on the unfolding action, and their striking imagery that unites theme and tone. In addition, they demonstrate Bonner's early interest in telling the stories of the black working class, stories largely neglected in the writings of her Afro-American contemporaries such as Jessie Fauset and Nella Larsen. Bonner's attempts to find the genre and narrative techniques most suited to her work proceeded unevenly through stories and sketches published between 1925 and 1928. During the twenties, she tended to shape essays, fiction, and even plays as personal meditations, making it difficult to classify her work generically. Bonner characteristically employed the second-person pronoun "you" in the narration that frames her stories and plays.

"The Hands: A Story" and **"On Being Young—a Woman—and Colored"** provide the sensitive perspectives of black female narrators. Observing the lives of the black masses, both women try to bridge the gap, if only in imagination. A very brief story, **"The Hands,"** is framed by the opening meditation of a narrator who boards a bus and becomes fascinated by the work-roughened hands of an older male rider. She creates a whole imaginary world of work, love, and family served by those hands, described in terms of alligator scales and nodes on a branch. The narrator imagines the man's simple hard work, devout religion, and family life. The ending of this touching vignette of the worker repeats the narrator's dual fantasies: one about "snakes, peopling the forest" (likened to a jungle in the story); the other about "Christ-in-all-men."

These fantasies comment obliquely on the two-dimensional treatment of blacks in American literature. One aspect of this treatment was an exoticism with hints of the jungle or the tropics as exemplified in a number of early twentieth-century works, including Vachel Lindsay's "The Congo" (1914), Eugene O'Neill's *The Emperor Jones* (1920), and Countee Cullen's "Heritage" (1925). Another was the portrayal of dutiful, religious, excessively humble characters, a tradition dating back to nineteenth-century fiction and abolitionist tracts and updated in Bonner's day in O'Neill's *All God's Chillun Got Wings* (1924).[3] In **"The Hands"** Bonner seems to be expressing skepticism about romantic racialism of either kind.

Though less technically skilled than Bonner's later work, **"The Hands"** shows the same consciousness of class differences represented in **"On Being Young—a Woman—and Colored."** This autobiographical piece conveys skillfully and openly its author's sense of comparative privilege and obligation as well as her ambivalence about living in segregated Washington, "flung together . . . in a bundle" with other blacks "because of color and with no more in common." She feels obligated to identify with the black poor, even though that identification leads to entanglement in what she calls "the seaweed of a Black Ghetto."

The essay also explores a dichotomy seen in many works by Afro-American writers: the dichotomy between inner reality and socially sanctioned racial and gender roles. Bonner laments the fact that, like all black women, she is seen primarily as "a gross collection of uncontrolled desires." Viewing her own situation, she is determined to wait, with Buddha-like composure, until "time is ripe" for her to rise to her full stature.

The breadth of Bonner's reading and her tendency to present new angles on old subjects are evident in the two pieces from the 1920s that focus on male artist-heroes. **"Nothing New"** (1926) is Bonner's first story with an explicitly Chicago setting. The story's account of would-be painter Denny Jackson's collision with the society around him touches on a number of themes that the author would continue to develop: ties between white and black, thwarted youthful aspiration, and the complexities of racial intermixture. In **"Nothing New"** Bonner introduces her key symbol of the Frye Street neighborhood as multiethnic cosmos, an urban universe shared by Irish, Chinese, Russian, Jewish, French, German, Swedish, and Danish immigrants, as well as blacks, many themselves recent arrivals from the South. In introducing Frye Street, Bonner uses the familiar second-person narration of her early work:

> You have been down on Frye Street. You know how it runs . . . from freckled-faced tow heads to yellow Orientals; from broad Italy to broad Georgia; from hooked nose to square black noses. How it lisps in French, how it babbles in Italian, how it gurgles in German, how it drawls and crawls through Black Belt dialects. Frye Street flows nicely together. It is like muddy water.

But this image of Frye Street's ethnic groups "flowing nicely together" is marred by two violent episodes that divide the neighborhood into black and white. The protagonist Denny has two collisions with the racially unjust society that surrounds the comfortable ethnic cocoon of integrated Frye Street. The first of these involves his crossing an imaginary racial divide in a public park; the second, and more dangerous, involves his choice of a white lover. He defends his right to love Pauline, a white art student. In both these encounters, Denny refuses to heed repeated warnings to stay on his own side of an invisible color line. (Bonner's inspiration for the story of Denny's life and death may have derived from accounts of the much-publicized 1919 Chicago race riots. The days of violence were precipitated by the drowning of young Eugene Williams. While swimming, he had strayed from the unofficially black Twenty-seventh Street beach to the unofficially white Twenty-ninth Street beach, but could not approach the shore because of stone-throwing whites.)[4]

FROM THE AUTHOR

"ON BEING YOUNG—A WOMAN—AND COLORED"

You wonder and you wonder until
you wander out into Infinity,
where—if it is to be found
anywhere—Truth really exists

SOURCE: Marita Bonner, excerpt from "On Being Young—A Woman—and Colored," in the *Crisis,* December 1925.

Bonner's Chicago stories of the thirties and forties would assume the background of episodes such as those experienced by Denny in **"Nothing New."** They would deal with Chicago as a fallen world both in terms of race relations and the doomed aspirations of the city's black immigrants from the South. Her last two stories published in the twenties—**"One Boy's Story"** and **"Drab Rambles"**—anticipate this development.

In **"One Boy's Story"** (1927), her only short story with a male narrator, Bonner continues the exploration of color issues. Told by a young black boy, the story treats the classic theme of the identity crisis that mixed racial origins create. (Bonner shared this interest in mulatto characters with such contemporaries as Nella Larsen, Jessie Fauset, Georgia Douglas Johnson, Paul Green, and Langston Hughes.) Donald, the young narrator—illegitimate child of a southern black woman and a white father—comes to a tragic awakening concerning his illegitimacy and the identity of his white father. Through Donald's absorption in a book of legends, Bonner evokes not only the biblical tale of David and Goliath, but the classical tragedies of father-son conflicts in the myths of Oedipus and Orestes.[5] The story's denouement is a paradigm of literary silencing and the dangerous truth that cannot be spoken: Donald, having unknowingly killed his real father, is wounded by his mother in a strange accident that results in the amputation of his tongue. Donald's recollections become blurred with the tales he has read:

> a forked whip . . . I am Orestes with the Furies' whips in my mouth . . . I am Oedipus and . . . I cut [my tongue] out for killing my own father.

The maiming of the story's child narrator (and the fact that Bonner chose to publish this story under a pseudonym)[6] suggests both the pain and the forbidden quality of such distorted family relations.

One month later Bonner published **"Drab Rambles"** in *The Crisis*. The narrative frames two portraits, one male and one female, of black city dwellers in the final stages of being crushed by the economic slavery and racism they have encountered. The exact location of their city is unspecified, although there are similarities between Peter Jackson of Sawyer Avenue and the Georgia-born Chicago parents of Denny Jackson in **"Nothing New."** Both protagonists in **"Drab Rambles"** face destruction from a power structure that gives them few opportunities for employment: the man in the first sketch faces death from overwork, and the young woman in the second confronts either dismissal from her job or an unwanted liaison with her white employer that could produce a second yellow child for her to support. (The young mother's first child takes her name from her mother and is called Madie Frye.) The narrator of **"Drab Rambles"** elevates such mixed-race children to mythic status, asserting the black Everyman through the figure of the mulatto: "I am all men tinged in brown. I am all men with a touch of black. I am you and I am myself."

Other early pieces were less focused and less successful. **"The Prison-Bound"** (1926) is interesting as an early treatment of Chicago's impact on a simple black woman from the South, a situation later explored in **"The Whipping"** (1939) and **"Reap It As You Sow It"** (1940-41). A short essay, **"The Young Blood Hungers"** (1928), lacks a concrete central image, and its repeated phrases fall short of what was apparently intended to be a haunting refrain effect. But the essay's militant content and apocalyptic tone link it to the early stories and sketches and to Bonner's 1928 dramatic masterpiece ***The Purple Flower.***

Experimental Plays

In Washington, influenced by Georgia Douglas Johnson and other playwriting members of the "S" Street salon,[7] Bonner attempted three plays: ***The Pot Maker: A Play to be Read*** (1927), ***The Purple Flower*** (1928), and ***Exit, an Illusion*** (1928). All three dramas feature elaborate stage directions couched in Bonner's second-person narration and innovative structures built around a central metaphor. ***The Purple Flower*** is generally regarded as Bonner's masterpiece and has been hailed by Margaret Wilkerson as "perhaps the most provocative play" written by a black woman during the first half of the twentieth century.[8] Bonner had deplored the lack of a theater for black Washington residents in her 1925 autobiographical essay. Theater historian Addell Austin has established that Bonner was a member of the Krigwa Players in Washington,[9] but Bonner's own dramas may have been intended for reading rather than performance. The plays were not produced in Bonner's lifetime.[10] All three dramas continue her exploration of the black American as Everyman/Everywoman and are structured as morality plays: the protagonists undergo a testing experience on an imagined stage whose fourth wall is the territory of death, a force personified as the mysterious lover Exit in Bonner's final play.

The test to determine true worth is explicit in the parable of the silver, brass, and tin pots preached by Elias in ***Pot Maker. The Pot Maker***'s cottage setting suggests its affiliation with the folk-drama vogue in the American theater,[11] but it shares the premise of the urban ***Exit, an Illusion:*** in both plays the black male protagonist must decide whether to act with love and compassion toward a light-skinned black woman. His personal salvation depends upon his ability to love and, when necessary, forgive others. Both plays are short and suspenseful: in ***The Pot Maker*** the audience waits for the preacher to discover the flaw in his own wife; in ***Exit, an Illusion,*** for the arrival of Dot's white lover, who turns out to be Death.

Bonner's allegory of the black quest for freedom and happiness in post-Emancipation America, ***The Purple Flower,*** combines first- and second-person perspectives to define the "Us's," and sympathetic communal protagonist of the play. The "Us's" are situated on a plain that lies between a looming hill called Somewhere and a distant border called Nowhere, but they wish to climb the hill to reach the purple Flower-of-Life-At-Its-Fullest bloom at the summit. However, small, grotesque, and quick-moving White Devils defend the hill, which bears some relation to the "racial mountain" that Langston Hughes saw as an obstacle to the black artist.[12]

The Purple Flower is set at the time of the most powerful challenge to the White Devils ever mounted, a time of new strategies for the "Us's." The play begins in the "Middle-of-Things-as-They-Are," though this time is interpreted differently by the two groups. It spells the "End-of-Things for some of the characters and the Beginning-of-Things for others." On the surface, the play shares some characteristics with the black pageant movement that began with W. E. B. Du Bois's *The Star of Ethiopia* and continued with the work of such playwrights as Maud Cuney Hare and May Miller.[13] But Bonner explicitly orients the play toward the future rather than the past.[14] While symbolically rejecting the compromise course of Booker T. Washington,[15] ***The Purple Flower*** may also suggest the struggles of the third world against white colonialism.[16] E. Quita Craig in *Black Drama of the Federal Theatre Era* argues that Bonner's inclusion of drum music seems a deliberate Africanism,[17] an interpretation that lends itself to an international reading of the struggle of the "Us's" to gain the mountain with the purple flower.

The new plan to attain the flower involves the rejection of past strategies and a new blending of black experiences in a cauldron that may be magical. The concoction requires blood, either black or white, "blood for birth so the New Man can live." On one level, the ascent of the "Us's" deals with black aspiration in America and the possible relevance of the myth of the melting-pot, in which all ethnic groups are combined and transformed. On another level, the drama seems to assume a less optimistic solution, the inevitability of violent racial revolution, a theme echoed in **"The Young Blood Hungers,"** published four months later.

Measuring the Black Metropolis: Chicago

When Bonner next examined the melting-pot, it was an on-site inspection of an urban crucible in the North. After moving to Chicago as a bride in 1930, she took a short break from writing and then began to write and publish fiction exclusively. The subject of her new direction was the variety of black Chicago, its class and color demarcations, its interaction with European and to a lesser extent Asian immigrants, its strained relations between parents and children, and its vulnerability to crushing economic and social forces. She resumed publishing in 1933 under her married name and noted in the introduction to a three-part story called **"A Possible Triad on Black Notes"** that the piece was part of "'Black Map,' a book entirely unwritten." Her eldest son believes he heard Bonner refer to the work-in-progress as "Frye Street Trilogy."[18]

During the thirties, Bonner made significant changes in her narrative technique to better convey the complexity of her subjects. The most notable was her new tendency to compose stories in several separately published parts, which allowed her to juxtapose different characters as well as outer and inner impressions of the same character. Her new narrative organization had been anticipated by the double narrative in **"Drab Rambles,"** but Bonner intended a work much larger in scope than pairs or triplets of stories: her "Black Map" was planned on a scale comparable to James Joyce's mapping of the Irish capital in *Dubliners.*

The first of the new narratives of Chicago life, **"A Possible Triad on Black Notes,"** was published as three parts in the July, August, and September issues of *Opportunity* 11 (1933). (With the exception of the early **"Drab Rambles,"** published in *The Crisis* in 1927, all of Bonner's multipart narratives appeared in *Opportunity.* As the cultural arm of the Urban League, the magazine's emphasis was sociological and urban, making it especially appropriate for pieces of the cycle.)

Each of the three stories in **"A Possible Triad"** contains an internal juxtaposition of Chicago lives to supplement the larger juxtaposition of the triple framing. **"There Were Three"** (July 1933) describes the events that eventually destroy a light-skinned family of three and leaves open the surviving daughter's choice of social streams—black, white, or yellow. The author's foreword speaks of Frye Street as the ultimate ethnic intersection ("All the World is there") and serves as an advance introduction to the second and third stories, which deal with more "respectable" protagonists. In **"Of Jimmy Harris"** (August 1933), Jimmy, a hard-working and successful immigrant from Virginia, dies of a stroke as his wife Louise stalks his doctor for her next husband. By the final paragraph, the story's opening line, "Jimmy Harris was dying," has come to mean that the protagonist has been dying for the fifteen years since he left love and Luray, Virginia, for Chicago's prosperity. (Bonner steadfastly refused to romanticize the rural Southern pasts of her black Chicago characters, however. The near-starvation of the sharecropping family in **"The**

Whipping," the inhuman adherence to the rules of the color caste by a prominent light-skinned family in **"On the Altar,"** and the family violence of **"One Boy's Story"** and **"Patch Quilt"** seem to allow little happiness for blacks rich or poor in the early twentieth-century South.)

In the third story, **"Corner Store"** (September 1933), Bonner's sole white protagonist, Esther Steinberg, painfully misses her lost German-Jewish ghetto, remembering it as a place with more feeling than the comfortable but joyless life behind her husband's grocery store on Frye Street. Like **"Of Jimmy Harris," "Corner Store"** deals with marital betrayal and family strife. Esther's husband Anton, long involved with a woman of black and Jewish ancestry, is being blackmailed by his own daughter. Esther is prostrate and sobbing at the story's end, the fabric of her family having been irrevocably torn.

The two-part story **"Tin Can"** won the *Opportunity* literary prize for fiction in 1933 and was published in that magazine in July and August of 1934. With a more developed plot than most of Bonner's stories, **"Tin Can"** chronicles the transformation of a high-spirited seventeen-year-old con artist and high school student named Jimmie Joe into an inadvertent murderer. The other members of Jimmie Joe's family have only generic names—"Ma," "Little Brother," and "Pa"—but "Ma" in particular is drawn in detail. A hard-working and religious parent, Ma loses control over her elder son through overwork and fatigue. Images of hollowness reverberate throughout the story: the opening image of the tin can with pebbles, the near-emptiness of Ma's purse, the coffin that Jimmie Joe's twisted corpse cannot properly fill, and the ending's speeding, rattling patrol wagon that carries Ma off to the station house instead of the hospital because she collapses in grief but is thought to be drunk. The hollowness is also metaphorical in its applications: both representatives of authority in the black community, "Black Bass Drum," the principal, and the Reverend Brown, are hypocrites who preach to their impoverished charges virtues that they themselves flout. Jimmie Joe and his friends repudiate these male role models and turn to gangs instead. Like Richard Wright's *Native Son* (1940), **"Tin Can"** traces the effects of poverty, low expectations, and peer pressure on the development of personality.

"A Sealed Pod," with its image of peas close together but not touching, a metaphor of Frye Street, was published in 1936. It presents further portrayals of Frye Street families in trouble, and focuses on young Viollette Harris, "warmed with an odd mixture of uncontrolled passions and bloods" until she is murdered by the only man she has ever loved, an Italian immigrant named Joe Tamona. Three 1939 stories, **"The Makin's," "The Whipping,"** and **"Hongry Fire,"** also show the city's destruction of children virtually before their parents' eyes. In **"A Sealed Pod,"** Ma Harris comes home from her all-night cleaning job to find Viollette with her throat cut. In the three 1939 stories, David Brown's parents in **"The Makin's"** are too preoccupied with their own self-destructive habits to do anything but applaud their son's decision to write numbers when he grows up; in **"The Whipping,"** Lizabeth's son dies in a fluke fall when his mother slaps him for repeating a hurtful lie; and in **"Hongry Fire"** a mother seeing her children on the verge of ruin resorts to poisoning the daughter-in-law who is corrupting them. The innocent suffer more often than the guilty: the innocent Ma Harris returns every morning to an empty house and the wrong man is hanged for her daughter's death. Nothing happens to the irresponsible parents in **"The Makin's,"** but the pathetic Lizabeth in **"The Whipping"** is accused of murdering her child and is too ignorant to defend or even explain herself. Like Lutie Johnson in Petry's *The Street,* she is ultimately overwhelmed.

Bonner's Chicago fiction does not present the middle-class element of black Chicago as a source of strength or hope for the black working class. In the pseudonymously written **"Hate Is Nothing"** (1938), Bonner, herself the target of prejudice on the part of Chicago's predominantly light-skinned middle-class matrons, awards a daughter-in-law victory over a mother-in-law whose notion of respectability is based on color rather than behavior. **"Black Fronts,"** published the same year, presents three sketches of the lives of black married women in different strata of Chicago society. The most affluent of the three protagonists, the illegitimate daughter of a washerwoman by a white doctor, is viciously snobbish and color-conscious. Bonner's character Aunt Margaret in **"Stones for Bread"** (1940) is similarly pretentious, dismissing her less-educated and darker brother with contempt. The grandmother of the heroine in **"On the Altar"** is the most destructive of Bonner's enforcers of the color code. Mrs. Breastwood annuls her granddaughter Beth's marriage to a darker school classmate without Beth's knowledge. She even goes so far as to hire an obstetrician who will assure that the baby of the match is born dead: "Never can tell about colored babies. . . . Next one might have been a tar-kettle." While Mrs. Breastwood keeps Beth out of town and away from Jerry, she sends back social notices that serve as a bitter satire on color obsession within the black community:

> Mrs. Blanche Kingsman Breastwood and her granddaughter, the lovely Elizabeth Grey, dainty blonde replica of her mother, Mrs. Louise Grey—are circling the states.

Even some of the names (Blanche, Grey) underscore the persistent use of color as a gauge of human worth. Other upper-middle-class practices, including parties, weddings, and card playing, are also satirized.

Fully drawn examples of males in black middle- and upper-middle-class society are rare in Bonner; her caricatures of the principal and the minister in **"Tin Can"** have already been noted. Similarly, the protagonist of **"High Stepper"** has earned wealth but not respectability through his gambling house, and thus is scarcely an admirable figure in the community. For positive ideals, Bonner turns to the thrifty working class: the laborer/church deacon who helps others in **"Drab Rambles,"** for example, or unpretentious Dan and Mary, building cleaners in **"Stones for Bread,"** who, in contrast to the rest of the family, seem to represent a positive ideal of tolerance and economic self-reliance.

In her last published story, **"One True Love"** (1941), Bonner returned to some of the problems of black female aspiration to which she alluded in **"On Being Young—a Woman—and Colored."** Her heroine Nora changes overnight from "just a butter-colored maid with hair on the 'riney' side" to a determined young woman with a dream. Nora's dedication to studying the law is finally thwarted by exhausting full-time employment combined with color and class prejudice, obstacles Bonner had explored in the earlier autobiographical essay. The love that develops between Nora and Sam, "a runty, bow-legged, dark brown janitor's helper," suggests a *rapprochement* between light-skinned and dark, between the black intelligentsia and their working-class allies. However, this alliance is never tested because the story ends with Nora's death as she struggles to tell Sam that she loves him.

The last story in the Chicago cycle was **"Light in Dark Places,"** completed in 1941. Conveying Bonner's deepening pessimism concerning the fate of young black Chicagoans, the story presents a new worry of growing up black and female in a city: the possibility of rape by a school classmate. Though the protagonist Tina is saved by the blind but quick-thinking grandmother, the reader senses that Tina will be radically altered by the experience. Bonner speculates mid-story on the reasons why black Chicago shapes so many young males like Luke, whose indifference to Tina's well-being is total and whose only motto is "Anything that gives Luke a good time!" She decides that the problems start with the excesses that characterize crowded Chicago:

> Too many young people: too few houses: too many things to long for and too little money to spend freely: too many women: too few men: too many men weak enough to make profit of the fact that they happen to be men: too few women with something in them to make them strong enough to walk over weak men: too much liquor: too many dives: too much street life: too few lovely homes: life from the start—too many people—too few houses.
>
> Too many peasants lured out of cotton and corn fields. . . . Too many neon signs winking promises. . . .
>
> All this slaps a woman—loose.
>
> All this slaps a man loose from every decent bit of manliness.

After 1941 Bonner wrote rarely, raised her three children, and taught. Her interest in writing, however, was lifelong: at the edge of sixty-eight, she mentioned on a Radcliffe alumna questionnaire that she was currently enrolled in a correspondence course from the Famous Writers School, an ironically amateur affiliation given her talent and past record of publication and prizes. She never completed to her satisfaction her planned charting of black Chicago. One reason for this was a busy work and family life; but her increased intellectual involvement with Christian Science and her growing despair concerning the city's effect on the individual may have been factors in her goodbye to Frye Street.

Marita Bonner died in 1971 of injuries she suffered in a fire in her Chicago apartment—a city accident of the type she understood so well. But her writing has kept alive an entire world—the stories and feelings of the black universe coming to consciousness in northern cities in the decades that separated the world wars. For that act of imaginative deliverance, future generations will be grateful.

Notes

1. All information about Marita Bonner's college years was supplied by Radcliffe archivist Jane Knowles, Radcliffe College. On Bonner's later career see Joyce Flynn, "Marita Bonner Occomy (1899-1971)" in *Afro-American Writers from the Harlem Renaissance to 1940, Dictionary of Literary Biography* 51 (Detroit: Gale Re-

search, 1987), 222-28, and Diane Isaacs, "Marita Bonner," in *Dictionary of the Harlem Renaissance* (Westport: Greenwood Press, 1984).

2. For an account of Georgia Douglas Johnson's life and work, see Winona Fletcher, "Georgia Douglas Johnson (1886-1956)," *Dictionary of Literary Biography 51: Afro-American Writers from the Harlem Renaissance to 1940* (Detroit: Gale Research, 1987), 153-64.

3. Some of Bonner's work seems particularly framed to suggest alternatives to O'Neill's plays *The Emperor Jones, The Hairy Ape,* and *All God's Chillun Got Wings.* O'Neill left Harvard one year before Bonner entered Radcliffe.

4. *The Negro in Chicago* was prepared by the Chicago Commission on Race Relations, on which Johnson served in the capacity of associate executive secretary. For background on early twentieth-century black Chicago, see Emmett J. Scott, *Negro Migration during the War* (Carnegie Endowment for Peace, 1920; rpt. New York: Arno Press and the New York Times, 1969), and Allan H. Spear, *Black Chicago: The Making of a Negro Ghetto, 1890-1920* (Chicago: University of Chicago Press, 1967). St. Clair Drake and Horace Cayton's *Black Metropolis: A Study of Negro Life in a Northern City* (New York: Harcourt, Brace, 1945) provides a rich study of a period closer to Marita Bonner Occomy's Chicago cycle.

5. For a discussion of the American mulatto and themes from classical tragedy, see Werner Sollors, "The Mulatto, An American Tragedy?," *Massachusetts Review: A Quarterly of Literature, the Arts, and Public Affairs* 27 (1986):293-316.

6. The pen name used by Bonner here is an amalgam of her own nickname and the first names of her brothers, Joseph and Andrew. She may have felt that a male name was more appropriate to the story's claim to be a boy's autobiographical narrative. On one other occasion, while dealing with in-law stresses, Bonner published a story about conflict between mother and daughter-in-law ("Hate Is Nothing") under a pen name, presumably for reasons of privacy.

7. See Fletcher, "Georgia Douglas Johnson," 154, 158.

8. Margaret Wilkerson, "Introduction" to *Nine Plays by Black Women* (New York: New American Library, 1986), xvii.

9. Addell Austin in conversation, September 1986. Professor Austin interviewed Willis Richardson before his death in 1977 and has amassed considerable information concerning the black theater scene in Washington, D.C., and New York City during the years of the Harlem Renaissance. For background on the Howard University Players and the Krigwa Players, see Austin's "Pioneering Black Authored Dramas," Ph.D. dissertation, Michigan State University, 1986, and Fannie Ella Frazier Hicklin, "The American Negro Playwright, 1920-1964," Ph.D. dissertation, University of Wisconsin, 1965, 34, 178.

10. Errol Hill and I concur on this point. See his discussion of *The Purple Flower* in "The Revolutionary Tradition in Black Drama," *Theatre Journal* 38 (December 1986):419-21.

11. Black and white playwrights were attracted to the folk play. Literary creators of American folk drama included Paul Green, Georgia Douglas Johnson, Lula Vollmer, Willis Richardson, and S. Randolph Edmonds, among others.

12. Langston Hughes, "The Negro Artist and the Racial Mountain," *Nation* 23 (June 1926); reprinted in *The Ideology of Blackness,* ed. Raymond Betts (Lexington: D.C. Heath, 1971), 82-86.

13. An anthology *Plays and Pageants from the Life of the Negro,* ed. Willis Richardson (Washington, D.C.: The Associated Publishers, 1930) presents a sampler of these dramas, which were often the work of black women authors.

14. Hill, "The Revolutionary Tradition in Black Drama," 419.

15. James V. Hatch, "The Purple Flower" in *Black Theater U.S.A.: Forty-Five Plays by Black Americans, 1847-1974,* ed. Hatch and Ted Shine (New York: The Free Press, 1974), 201.

16. Nellie McKay, "What Were They Saying? Black Women Playwrights of the Harlem Renaissance," forthcoming in *The Harlem Renaissance Re-Examined,* ed. Victor Kramer (New York: AMS Press, 1988).

17. E. Quita Craig, *Black Drama of the Federal Theatre Era* (Amherst: University of Massachusetts Press, 1980), 88.

18. Letter from William Almy Occomy, Jr., to Joyce Flynn, October 1986.

LORRAINE ELENA ROSES AND RUTH ELIZABETH RANDOLPH (ESSAY DATE 1987)

SOURCE: Roses, Lorraine Elena, and Ruth Elizabeth Randolph. "Marita Bonner: In Search of Other Mothers' Gardens." *Black American Literature Forum* 21, nos. 1-2 (spring-summer 1987): 165-83.

In the following essay, Roses and Randolph provide recollections of Bonner by her children and discuss her six posthumously published stories written between 1937 and 1941.

Bibliographies of black writers of the twentieth century list the name Marita Odette Bonner Occomy and the titles of some twenty of her short stories and plays. Little else is told about this Bostonian writer, aside from the "fact" that she was born in 1899 (actually it was 1898) and died in 1971.[1] This essay presents the results of our preliminary research on Bonner's life and offers a thematic analysis of a group of her unpublished stories. With it, we hope to open the way for more scholarship on Bonner and to expand the perspectives on black women writers of the Harlem Renaissance.[2] We offer this contribution at a time when, according to Mary Dearborn, the tradition of black female authorship "has become solidified and therefore explicable" and when "a second black literary Renaissance in which women are taking significant part, seems well under way" (61).

I

Our search for the story of Marita Bonner led us to a Chicago address corresponding to her married name, Occomy, and on August 4, 1985, we made contact with a son, Warwick Gale Occomy, who confirmed his kinship with Marita. He informed us that he and Marita's other two children, William and Marita Joyce, had pertinent documents, notebooks, and photographs that we could examine, and we agreed, in return, to send him copies of those of his mother's published works which we found. We also spoke with Marita Joyce, who agreed to correspond with us through cassette tapes and/or letters.

On Saturday, October 26, 1985, we met in Wellesley, Massachusetts, with Warwick Gale, his wife Donna, their sons Noel and Todd, and Donna's mother, Mrs. Glover. What follows is an outline, based on our interviews with the Occomy family and documents provided by them,[3] for a biography of a sophisticated artist and intellectual who should be placed in the company of such Harlem Renaissance figures as Nella Larsen, Jessie Fauset, and Zora Neale Hurston, and recognized as a forerunner of such current-day luminaries as Alice Walker, Toni Morrison, Gloria Naylor, Toni Cade Bambara, and Gayl Jones. Had Bonner published her many stories and other works as a volume, her recognition would perhaps not have been so long in coming.

Marita Bonner with her husband, William Occomy.

Marita's mother, Mary A. Nowell, was from Petersburg, Virginia, her mother's having been a free woman who married a slave. The marriage made the groom a free man and obliged him to adopt his wife's surname. Marita's New England roots stem from her father's family. Marita's father, Joseph Bonner, a native Bostonian born in 1872, attended the Boston Latin School for boys, but did not finish high school. On his children's birth certificates, his occupation is identified as "laborer" and "machinist." Bonner worked long and hard to support his growing family—Joseph, Jr. (born in 1893), Bernice Annette (born in 1895), Marita (born on June 16, 1898), and Andrew, who died in babyhood—and to provide them with the education that he had not had.

Marita attended school in Brookline, Massachusetts, a predominantly middle-class community. She was a student at the Cabot School from kindergarten through third grade, the Edward Devotion School (a public grammar school) through eighth, and graduated from Brookline High School in 1918. Marita was a gifted pianist who vied with her sister Bernice, and sometimes surpassed her, in performing skill. But she always felt that Bernice, the more beautiful sister, with her "classic" features and violet eyes, was the favored child. Their mother counseled Marita to "always be sweet and that way people will like you." This Marita found difficult to do, and she continued to feel deeply envious of Bernice, to the point where relations between them became strained; the adult Marita had face-to-face contact with her sister only once, during a family trip east in 1940. When Bernice died in 1957, Marita flew to Boston for her funeral (Occomy children audiotape).

At Brookline High School, Marita contributed regularly to *The Sagamore,* a student magazine. The faculty sponsor of the magazine, Alice Howard Spaulding, urged her to apply to Radcliffe, where she could take writing with Charles Townsend Copeland, known at Harvard and Radcliffe as "Copey."

Joseph Bonner, Sr.'s steady livelihood, as well as probable scholarship assistance from their church,[4] enabled Bernice to graduate from the New England Conservatory of Music and Marita to finish Radcliffe with the class of 1922. Blacks were not permitted to live on campus and had either to commute, as Marita did, or, in the case of out-of-town students, live in a house set aside for black women.

At Radcliffe, Marita majored in English and comparative literature, was a member of a number of musical clubs, and twice won the Radcliffe song competition (Kellner 45). One of a small number of black students, Marita founded the Radcliffe chapter of Delta Sigma Theta, a black sorority. Evidence of her desire to become a writer is that she applied and was accepted to Professor Copeland's writing class, limited on a competitive basis to sixteen students. Copeland praised Marita but qualified his recognition with a caveat. According to Marita, "He urged me to write—but not to be 'bitter'—a cliché to colored people who write" (**"Extra Notes"**). We do not know if Marita wrote for any magazines while at Radcliffe, but she went on, in 1925, to publish her first piece, the essay **"On Being Young, a Woman and Colored"** in *The Crisis,* at the zenith of what would come to be known as the Harlem Renaissance.

Marita's mother died suddenly, of a brain hemorrhage, in 1924. Joseph, Sr., died two years after his wife, having seen Marita complete her education at Radcliffe. Marita Joyce tells that Marita never ceased to recall her parents' premature deaths (they were fifty-three and fifty-five, respectively) and viewed herself as having been "left alone and struggling" (Occomy children audiotape). The lasting impression of that experience also brought about Marita's recognition of her own strength in adversity. After her graduation from Radcliffe, Bonner taught at the Bluefield Colored Institute in Bluefield, Virginia, between 1922 and 1924 and, between 1924 and 1930, at Armstrong High School in Washington, D.C. (Kellner 45). While in Washington she was a participant in the literary salon called "The Round Table," held at the home of Georgia Douglas Johnson (Sullivan interview).[5]

Bonner subsequently wed William Almy Occomy, who would later tell his children how impressed he was with his wife's literary background. When he was courting her, he marveled at the size of the Bonner library. To their own household in Chicago, Marita brought a set of Harvard Classics. Occomy, a graduate of Brown University with an M.B.A. from Boston University,[6] further cluttered the house with business and accounting books. The Occomys lived in a multi-ethnic neighborhood in Chicago, where Bonner would frequently surprise her neighbors by using her fluent German.[7] The Occomy children remember their house as one in which education was taken seriously, and there was no question but that they would go to college. During the early Chicago years, Marita's short stories and plays appeared regularly in *The Crisis* and in *Opportunity;* the last was published in 1941. In that year, Marita and William Occomy became members of the First Church of Christ Scientist (or Mother Church, in Boston) and of a local branch of the Church in Chicago.[8] The reason that Marita's joining the Church coincides with the cessation of her literary activity as a publishing author is unclear, since there is no conflict between writing and Church tenets.

When her youngest child was almost school age, Marita decided to return to teaching. However, the Board of Education, perhaps doubting the reality of the Radcliffe degree she showed them and discounting her previous experience in Washington, still required her to take education courses, which she sometimes literally slept through and in which she drew A's. She taught at Phillips High School between 1944 and 1949 and at the Dolittle School, where she taught educationally and mentally handicapped children between 1950 and 1963. In her own offspring she instilled the New England values of self-discipline and perfectability, saying, "The best is not too good for you, but everything must be done with poise" (Occomy children audiotape).

Marita died in 1971 after a sparking lamp caught fire in her apartment. She apparently attempted to smother the flames with a blanket and then, in fear, barricaded herself in the bathroom. Firemen found her unconscious and rushed her to the hospital, where she began to recover. When her son Gale called one morning, he received a report of her improved condition. But when he arrived, he was told that his mother had just expired. It is probable that the death resulted from complications due to smoke inhalation. Marita Bonner was seventy-three at the time of her death. She had lived to see the flowering of the Civil Rights Movement and the airing of the issues of racism and sexism that she had explored decades earlier in her work.

Much research still remains to be done on the life of Marita Bonner, especially on the question of how her creative genius was absorbed during the period from 1941, the year of her last known story, to December 6, 1971, the day of her death.

II

A notebook[9] left by Marita Bonner at the time of her death in 1971 contains six completed short stories, handwritten in fountain pen and dated from 1937 to 1941. It is imperative that these stories be considered as part of Marita Bonner's opus, which is more extensive than what has been published, and be analyzed in the light of new studies on the tradition of black women's writing. If we are, like Alice Walker, "in search of our mother's gardens," this writer's patch has been too long choked with the weeds of oblivion, waiting to be tended and its fruits harvested. It is fitting that our article, probably the first to deal with Bonner's stories, should begin by introducing the unpublished stories.

The notebook has a coarse, brown, imitation leather cardboard cover, with minimal yellowing of its pages and a little fraying around the edges. Held together by a metal spiral binder, it is in very good condition for a notebook almost fifty years old. Approximately half of its two hundred pages are blank, perhaps so that ink would not smudge or leak onto the backs of the pages. The page size is 9 by 7.5 inches, and the writing is usually contained on the front and not the back side of each one. The paper is heavy, with rag content, and is smooth to the touch. Bonner used both black- and blue-ink fountain pens, with cramped hand strokes' rendering small, tight markings. Sometimes this lettering gives way to more generous and loose strokes, slanting rightward. The variations in handwriting could be due to the fact that, as a child, the writer coerced herself to change from left- to right-handedness (Occomy children audiotape).

The six completed stories contained in the notebook are **"On the Altar"** (29 ⅓ pages), **"High Stepper"** (11 ½ pages), **"One True Love"** (almost 13 pages), **"Stones for Bread"** (slightly over 18 ½ pages), **"Reap It as You Sow It"** (17 ½ pages), and **"Light in Dark Places"** (11 ½ pages). On page 6, there is a hastily scrawled, unfinished story draft called **"White Man's War"** and on pages 195 and 200 are other fragments. There is also a loose leaf of legal-sized, lined paper entitled **"Lesson 103A."** Each story is preceded and followed by dates—presumably those of composition.

Words inked into the margins appear to be clarifications, where the ink was smudged or the handwriting was unclear. In the story **"High Stepper,"** there are red-penciled insertions and comments such as "weak." In **"Light in Dark Places"** are black-penciled and black-inked comments such as "too repetitious," "banal," and "rewrite" as well as a running word count, as if the author were testing the story for conformity to length specifications of some magazine or newspaper. All corrections appear to have been done by the author herself.

A definite order of the stories is apparent in this "final copy" notebook, but there is evidence of hurried activity on the final leaf pasted into the notebook, which contains notations that appear to be preparations for submitting stories or songs to various contests. Scrawled on it are the names [Elmer A.] Carter, [?] Wilkins, [W. E. B.] Du Bois, and Alain Leroy Locke.

III

Barbara Smith has enunciated a black feminist approach to literature that takes into consideration that "thematically, stylistically, aesthetically and conceptually Black women writers manifest common approaches to the act of creating literature as a direct result of the specific political, social and economic experience they have been obliged to share" (32). To this awareness, Gloria Wade-Gayles adds a vivid description of black women as being "confined to both the narrow space of race and the dark enclosure of sex" and subject not only to a "double jeopardy" resulting from their race and gender, but a tertiary jeopardy of the lesser, though not negligible, element of class (4). In her stories, Bonner repeatedly distinguishes among these kinds of oppression and elaborates many subtle variations thereof. As early as 1925 she enumerated the trials she faced as a woman, separate from those she experienced as a black (**"On Being Young,"** 63-65). In four of the six notebook stories, Bonner presents situations in which black women and their vulnerability are sensitively portrayed: **"On the Altar," "High Stepper," "One True Love,"** and **"Reap It as You Sow It."** In analyzing these works, we will identify, within the categories of race, sex, and class, specific areas in which conflict arises as a result of the black female's double jeopardy. These areas can be expressed in a series of dualities in black and white that emanate from a feminist perspective: black female versus black male, black female versus white female, and black female versus black female. In exploring these dualities that recur in Bonner's stories, we will search out synchronic parallels with other female texts of the Harlem Renaissance era.

IV

The first of the completed stories in the notebook is **"On the Altar"** (1937-Oct. 1940), the tale of a young black girl's romance, thwarted by the manipulations of her socially ambitious grandmother and complicitous mother. Like the novel of manners of the nineteenth century, this piece revolves around marital matchmaking, but Marita Bonner infuses subtle observations of the black experience into her story. Her images of black middle-class matriarchy and intergenerational conflict are dimensions that must be explored further in the work of Bonner and other writers of the period. The story's strengths lie in the portrait of the grandmother and the depiction of a female black bourgeoisie, with its bridge parties, social affairs, gossip, and considerable power over the family, even to the point of driving a son-in-law from the marital home or separating newlyweds. Beth, a girl with "curly light brown hair," just graduated from high school, has eloped and married Jerry Johnson, a black classmate much darker skinned and of lower social class than she. Her mother and grandmother succeed in separating her from her new husband, annulling the marriage, and ultimately marrying her off to a prestigious but unsavory doctor.

The story's structure is methodical, with discrete segments dedicated to the discovery of the elopement and the plan to undo it; a cross-country trip; Beth's confinement and the stillbirth of her child; and finally the achievement of a new marriage, which also suggests the beginning of a life of unhappiness and escape through alcohol for Beth.

The grandmother, with her black taffeta garments, "Queen Victoria" style, and peremptory manner, is the evil genius who seals the girl's future, in flagrant contradiction with Beth's own wishes: "Out in the country had been Jerry, a hired room, and all the heaven on earth that Beth was ever to know in all the years she would live" (5). The two older women are bent on achieving a middle-class, monied marriage for Beth at any cost. Like Janie's grandmother in Zora Neale Hurston's *Their Eyes Were Watching God,* they believe that tangible assets will avoid a life of toil for their daughter and also secure privilege. It is noteworthy that both Hurston and Bonner create strong but overbearing mother figures whom their daughters must elude or else be crushed by.

Parental and grandparental control over Beth is depicted as unyielding and geared to creating a façade in harmony with black bourgeois expectations. The grandmother artfully camouflages Beth's elopement with excuses to friends and circumvention of the rumors that travel rapidly "in any corner of any colored town" (5). With her two tones of voice, one a "backbone tenor" used to give orders and the other a "chirruping soprano" (10) used in social phone conversations, she exemplifies the determination to hide behind the fortress of their manufactured pride.

Jerry, "a tall slim black boy, the handsomest boy in the class according to even its most prejudiced member" (4), is rejected by Beth's family because of his color and the fear that his offspring are likely to be "tar kettles" (27). Ironically, these black women adhere to prejudices very much like those of the white society that has oppressed and subordinated them for centuries. Jerry is also rejected because he comes from a part of the town where "most Negroes had no telephone"(9). As such, he is a threat to their endeavor to maintain and increase social status. The mother and grandmother see themselves as superior, though they are not wealthy and must re-mortgage their home to accomplish the divorce and outfitting of Beth for another alliance. Their obsession with pigmentation and status leads to tragic personal consequences.

They display themselves in the society column "of the colored newspaper" (13), announcing the trip around the United States that will separate Beth from her chosen husband as if it were a debutante's coming out: "Mrs. Blanche Kingsman Breastwood and her granddaughter, the lovely Elizabeth Grey, dainty blonde replica of her beautiful mother, Mrs. Louise Grey—are circling the States" (15). The destruction of Beth's relationship with Jerry and the abortion of her full-term pregnancy are events which later haunt Beth as she enters into her subsequent arranged marriage and which contribute to her ruin.

The constrictions of social and familial pressure are underscored by such telling details as the tiny shoes, a size too small, and the bone corset in which Beth is made to dress during her U.S. tour. These images, as well as that of the aborted baby, motionless on its white receiving blanket, mirror the repression that bespeaks woman's struggle against overwhelming odds. After the death of Beth's grandmother, her mother Louise perpetuates her control by implanting guilt: "It's all your fault! . . . Killing my mother this way" (29). Though this story predates Dorothy West's *The Living is Easy* (1948), Beth's grandmother is very similar to Cleo in her manipulation of others' destinies.

The mother and grandmother here separate themselves from the black community on the basis of their light skin color and their enthrallment to white upper-class standards. Rather than make a choice between the "black black" community and crossing over into white society, they have created a third alternative—a fair-skinned, but still segregated from whites, bourgeoisie. In so doing, they unwittingly contribute to the creation of a hierarchical system that intensifies the problems of subordination and oppression in the larger society in which they live.

The story takes place in none of the cities in which Bonner herself resided but in a mythical construct called "Chestershire," which can be taken to indicate the ubiquitous nature of the problem Bonner exposes. The issues raised transcend time and can be read in 1987 as well or better than in 1940. The de-emphasis on time and place also allows the reader to focus on theme. Bonner delivers a sharp critique of the values of almost all her characters, with their passion for "things, things, things" (39), and couples her rage against the materialism of the older women with sympathy for the young woman whose future is being sacrificed on such an altar.

A cry for freedom of choice, the story is laced with bitter ironies. The letter Beth entrusts to a porter is forgotten and sent two months late; subsequent letters are destroyed by Jerry's suspicious mother. The story ends with the supremely ironic comment "So long as pride and the old order had been held in place, I guess it does not matter if an unborn life, a girl's life, a boy's life have been tossed on the altar, consumed in the flames of vanity" (55).

If in **"On the Altar"** a woman was treated as a pawn in the game of social advancement, female vulnerability is again a prominent theme in **"High Stepper"** (26 May 1938-14 Nov. 1940). The system of double jeopardy, with an axis of conflict centered on the black male/black female relationship, is more obvious here than in Bonner's other stories. The protagonist, Sadie Allen, is the victim of a sexual disease transmitted to her by her unfaithful husband Jim. As the story opens, Sadie has become mentally as well as physically impaired as a result of this illness. Yet in the course of the story Sadie gathers the strength and the sanity necessary to both voice her pain and express her anger at Jim.

Three characters—Sadie, Jim, and Sadie's mother—are sharply delineated and skillfully balanced against each other. The author pleads each one's case through a third-person narrator but also through indirect discourse, interior monologues, and stream of consciousness. However, it is Sadie's emotions that are most crucial to the story's dynamic. The mother's thoughts, mirroring Sadie's own, are the vehicle that conveys the injustice of Sadie's situation and feelings of hatred for Jim, "a man who has brought dirty disease . . . to the baby girl you bore" (65). Through the mother, Bonner sways the reader to sympathy for Sadie. The mother rarely confronts Jim openly for fear Sadie will be sent to an asylum "where the colored patients ate the leavings from other folks' plates and slop-pails stood un-emptied for days on end beneath beds. She did not want Sadie there!" (63). Therefore, the tragedy Jim has brought on Sadie and the rage of the two women remain unspoken. Both Jim and the mother use language not as a tool of communication but as a means of evading the truth; for Sadie, too, silence is the means of evasion. But her outward silence conceals a feverish meditation on the potency of language as a signifier of intense emotion and a struggle to become rational:

> Sometimes words are merely a fountain, flooding from the soul—shaping-twisting-gesturing in the Winds of Hate. Sadie once heard this within herself: Words are a fountain—shaping-twisting-gesturing in the Winds of Hate. Shaping in the Winds of Hate that sleep all day in a cave of ugliness and bitterness and wait until Night to whip out to shape and make gesture of words that are fountains for more hate. Shaping—now a sword—now a tongue—now a needle—always thrusting, thrusting, thrusting through the Dark—shaping, gesturing and thrusting in the winds of Hate.
>
> (71)

Sadie's hallucination that rats will swarm over her (69) is a sexual metaphor evoked by the stimulus of loud men in the streets and part of a realization that she is a victim at the hands of her husband. The men's guffaws are confused with the cries of rats, thus bringing out the anti-male connotations of her dilemma. So, too, is the phallic reference implicit in her obsession with words of hate "always thrusting, thrusting, thrusting." These images reinforce the idea of sexual oppression and the duality of black female and black male.

Just as the theme of illness and disease was used by women writers of the nineteenth century "to represent (and parody) the sort of intellectual incapacity patriarchal culture has traditionally required of women" (Gilbert and Gubar 58), Bonner shows her protagonist to be suffering as a result of the passive role imposed on her and in which she finds herself imprisoned. Her illness is not only a physical state, but a mental and spiritual fragmentation born of pain and loss. From this abject state the character ascends in search of wholeness.

It is a sensorial impression, the smell of another woman's perfume, that awakens Sadie to her situation and triggers her action. When Sadie recognizes that scent, the past telescopes into the present to create a bridge of lucidity and logical connection for Sadie: ". . . she had been plunged backwards over the precipice of a mind degenerating—carrying with her three straws of memory:

the name of a woman—Dora: the scent of some perfume a woman might use and the dazzle of a diamond set knife that Jim had once boasted that this Dora had given him" (73). This three-part symbolism is later repeated in inverse order, following the stirring of her mind: "the dazzle of the diamonds, the scent of the perfume, the woman's name—Dora" (75). It reinforces the three aspects of Sadie's suffering—physical, spiritual, and mental. The three blades in the knife suggest the damage to Sadie's spirit, soul, and body, and the tripartite violation of her person. That the knife, a gift from Dora to Jim, becomes the instrument of poetic justice is the final irony in this tale.

The causal connection between past and present enables Sadie to cast off her passivity and alienation. As the story ends, Sadie plunges the knife, with its three switchblades, into Jim's side: "Then three blades, as slender as a blade of grass, as sharp as flint and steel could make them—sprang out, all on one side of the handle" (74).

The act of violence committed by Sadie is unusual in the work of women writers of Bonner's generation. In Charlotte Perkins Gilman's turn-of-the-century text "The Yellow Wallpaper," for example, a woman destroys the imprisoning wallpaper and escapes from the room in which her doctor/husband has enclosed her, but she does not strike out at the husband. In the writing of black women, violence is even more rare, Ann Petry's *The Street* being one notable exception, until Alice Walker's Sophia strikes the mayor's wife in *The Color Purple* (1982).[10] Perhaps Bonner was suggesting that, for the oppressed, the only means of regaining integrity and strength is violence.[11] No advocate of violence, she saw it as an inevitable consequence when other channels of expression are blocked.

Does Sadie's attack on Jim imply that she escapes the bondage of her illness or her marriage? Does her act of violence result in freedom or further victimization? The author prefers that we not know. Her focus, instead, is on the destruction of spirit, body, and soul that is the consequence of the black woman's double jeopardy. The ambiguities that remain are an indication that woman's future is full of uncertainty.

Gloria Wade-Gayles concludes, in her examination of more recent black women writers, that "the most distinguishing feature of black women's fiction (since the 1960s) is the thesis that black men, unwittingly or deliberately, participate in the victimization of black women" (223). It is clear that, in **"High Stepper,"** Bonner anticipated the issue of "the sometimes bitter antagonism between black men and women" that has, in Mel Watkins' words, recently become "a volatile social and political [one] for many blacks" (1). That Bonner was ahead of her time could have been the cause of the story's remaining unpublished. Frances E. W. Harper's dictum that "the lesser question of sex must go," for "being black is more precarious and demanding than being a woman" (Chafe 54), can be said to have denied access to the question of the black woman's perspective until very recently.

Though color is not the central issue in Bonner's story, she ties the exploitation of woman as mere sex objects or chattel to black oppression, thus signaling as a coupling theme double oppression. Sadie would be treated as inferior if she were institutionalized, because of her color.

Bonner also reintroduces the question of social façades, so prominent in **"On the Altar,"** thus incorporating the class issue. Jim "keeps" his wife and mother-in-law rather than to send them away (an idea with which he toys from time to time) not out of loyalty or love but out of fear for his reputation. He values his status as owner of a pool room and club on Frye Street that gives black men the illusion of belonging to an exclusive club. Dressed in "spats, fawn-colored vests, flowers in his button hole, diamonds in his ties—in his watch—and on his hands" (59), Jim reflects a concern with money, ostentation, and "stepping high." The desire to elevate himself, rooted in the oppression experienced by the black male, has repercussions for the female as well. Yet Jim's shabby treatment of Sadie is camouflaged by his solicitousness for her physical maintenance. In the eyes of society he is respectable, but the roots of marital strife run deep in his own disenfranchisement as a black in white America.

Marriage, then, is the institution that protects Sadie economically, yet subjects her to other perils and acts as the agency of her subjugation to her husband's caprice. Marriage becomes another state of limbo, like the one that occupies the inert space between Jim and Sadie's mother.

Sadie's stabbing of Jim is not presented as the act of a crazed person but is shown as a moment of logical connection and lucidity. Her attack, preceded as it is by a speech act ("He is hurting me" [75]) is symbolic of the need of the black woman to speak out against the injustice done her. Unlike Jim, who never contemplates the pattern of relationships in which he is enmeshed,

Sadie sees herself as part of a web of relatedness—to Dora, to Jim, to her mother. The essence of the story is an act of resistance carried out by a long-silenced women.[12]

In **"One True Love,"**[13] Bonner, extending the range of her vision across class boundaries, presents a working-class world of domestics and custodians. Nora, a maid who once was startled to discover that the attorney expected as a dinner guest in the household of her white employers was a woman, seizes upon the idea of becoming an attorney herself. Unaware that her race as well as her sex pose obstacles to this goal, she enrolls in courses at City College. As a light-skinned, "riney-haired" woman, she is supposed to have a better chance. Her boyfriend Sam Smith, a janitor's helper, points out that love, not education, is the most important thing in life. Nora's naïve belief is that education is the answer to happiness ("If you're educated you know how to do everything just right all the time"), to which Sam gives the very reasonable retort "Edjucation aint everything! You've got to love folks more than books!" (87). Nora, who repeatedly reproaches Sam for "ignorance," fails to realize that education doesn't prevent her white employers from quarreling and continues to desire what they have. She also does not realize the pathos implicit in her attempting to model herself on a white woman. It is Nora who is ignorant, more so than Sam, of the obstacles posed by her race, class, and sex.

Nora's failure in her exams and the onset of illness from overwork put an end to her dreams. What precludes her success is not male oppression but the lack of an educational foundation that would aid her in understanding torts and estates and in locating the access routes to the lofty things she desires.

The story is a comment on the American Dream that upholds the myth of unlimited opportunity and advancement. Black leaders of the early twentieth century believed in education as a stepping stone and a liberating force to further the race. W. E. B. Du Bois, for example, propounded the theory that a black "talented tenth" should be educated to excel in all areas of American life in order to help eradicate racial prejudice. **"One True Love"** is a critique of the idealistic nature of those beliefs.

Nora is a striking example of a strong, aspiring female, determined "to make herself" (92), to use a phrase that Toni Morrison would put in the mouth of *Sula* several decades later. Nora's extraordinary ambition is an attempt to penetrate the invisible race, class, and sex barriers that surround her: "Nora had a touch of this something that made her struggle to get beyond a store, a sink, a broom, and a dust mop and someone else's kitchen" (91). The story deals, too, with the issue of whether a woman with high aspirations must forgo finding a loving mate. But this set of choices is not the greatest obstacle, for Sam ultimately "wishes he had been elegant and wonderful enough to match the wonder in Nora" (101) and tearfully begs her to recover. "Just get well! I'll help you get that law!" (99). It is not any antagonism between black male and black female that jettisons Nora's dream, but the convergence of race, class, and sex prejudices in American society. Nora has the desire and the means to enroll in law courses but neither adequate academic preparation nor the acceptance of white male society necessary to make a success of herself. "City College . . . endured a few colored students there but they had always been men—men whose background of preparation made professors and students of the lesser type keep their sneers under cover" (89).

Nora's progress from City College to her death in a public ward of the City Hospital offers a poignant comment on the implacability of the oppressors. Bonner, in this story, recognized the systemic biases that must be countered before black women may be free.

The last story we will examine, **"Reap It as You Sow It"** (3 Feb. 1940-15 Dec. 1940), evinces a moralistic and religious dimension present elsewhere in Bonner's work, but never so saliently as here. As a result, the story eludes the categories of analysis that we have been employing. It does not speak so directly of the problems of sex, color, and class as the other stories we have discussed. The story transcends external factors in order to emphasize spiritual being, which is the essence of human commonality.

The story begins with a reference to the Ten Commandments and the implication that retribution awaits transgressors. This potentially intimidating and moralistic discourse is tempered by the tongue-in-cheek tone used to describe the central character, Nola, as one who knows the Scriptures but "thought it said: Go ahead! Do what you want to do! You won't have to pay! Never! No one keeps the books that balance your account of living" (139). The metaphor of God as an accountant balancing the books at the end is used to intensify the story's ironic effect.

James, newly arrived in Chicago from the South with his wife Mollie, "brown and stout, wide-eyed and clean country" (143), is quickly seduced by the "tawny, easy-limbed" (141) Nola, who frequents every tavern on Frye Street and Grand Avenue. Mollie, broken-hearted and abandoned, dies in childbirth, while Nola goes on to marry James and to become a fervent Pentecostal churchwoman who shouts and dances on the pews. She gives birth to a little girl named after her whom she "worships." When that child's life is imperiled, Nola freezes, unable to save her daughter, "for a hand—woman's hand—brown, stubby, plump—with cracked worn fingernails and an old gold-wedding like Mollie's old fashioned ring—held her. A woman's hand locked in a steel grasp in the window . . ." (169). In introducing that supernatural hand of retribution, Bonner audaciously goes beyond the confines of the realistic tradition.

The initial allusion to Old Testament Scripture is followed by abundant Garden of Eden imagery. If James first eats "forbidden fruit" (beer) at a party in Nola's flat, Nola is the serpent that brings about the fall of James' idyllic marriage to Mollie. She goes on to lure James away from his wife, and in so doing violates the Commandments against coveting and adultery. Like the Biblical serpent, condemned to crawl on its belly forever, Nola sinks "lower and deeper" (171). She is punished for her wickedness.

Nola is further developed as the anti-heroine of the story when she marries James and has a little daughter whom she "idolizes." James too is punished: At the end, "sorrow [lies] darkly on him" (171).

In the sequence of the stories we have been examining, it is clear that Bonner first examines race prejudice, then class prejudice, then sexual oppression, and ultimately a convergence of all three. In **"Reap It as You Sow it,"** one black woman is pitted against another black woman in a dialectic that undermines marital harmony. Since the female protagonist and antagonist have in common their race, their class, and their sex, the issue between them is a moral one that transcends the categories we have been examining. Bonner seems to be exploring the deeper causes for racial, class, and gender conflict.

Bonner places her characters in a setting of ethnic confusion, a patchwork neighborhood in Chicago in which European immigrants live cheek by jowl with black migrants from the South. The resulting melange of values and linguistic confusion creates a backdrop that evidences how easily James and Mollie are lost and Nola comes to naught. This backdrop suggests that Nola's actions can perhaps be attributed to the crisis of values that ensues when people of different origins, who feel no responsibility toward each other, are crowded together and resources are few. But Bonner, in punishing Nola and James so severely, makes it clear that they as individuals are responsible for their choices and the harm they do.

Toward a Conclusion

Although Bonner did not during her lifetime adopt a vocal political stance, she appears to have held views that were in the forefront of her time. Her fictional portrayals of the conflicts motivated by differences of race, class, and gender anticipate authors of a later generation, such as Alice Walker. Bonner shows that, while conflicts often arise from the black female's triple jeopardy, to define them as such is to ignore the deeper problem, which lies within. Moreover, she separates the struggle of the black woman from that of the struggle for racial equality. We present as a question for future speculation that her education at a women's college, Radcliffe, especially as a black among whites, may have contributed to a heightened awareness of gender. As a woman writer, and especially as a black woman writer, she is several decades in advance of her time. In adding a fourth conflict, an internal and moral one that can arise even when race, class, and sex are shared, Bonner shows that human conflict cannot be explained only by external differences or what she called "the skin of civilization" (**"Black Fronts"** 210).

In the four stories we have examined, Bonner moves from the sociological to the moral and existential realms by steps that imply a developmental link and a broadening vision. She shows women, impeded by race, class, and sex prejudices, both racial and intraracial, who seek self-realization. Through marriage, children, education, religion, and sexual expression, they aspire to give birth to themselves, a dream that is elusive and perhaps impossible because of the odds they face. Bonner's vision may seem naturalistic or deterministic, yet she holds out the possibility that women can find their own voices and achieve wholeness.

It is striking that Bonner's many stories appeared exclusively in *The Crisis* and *Opportunity*, the organs of the NAACP and the National Urban League, respectively. It is within the narrow space of race, then, that she found her audience. A step beyond this success would have brought her across the color line, before a white audience. This did not occur, for black authors have not frequently commanded a biracial audience. To reach such an audience, Bonner might have had to speak in another voice. Mary Dearborn, in exploring the strategies of authorship available to ethnic women writers, asks, "If the ethnic woman sets out to mediate between her culture and the one that seems to her oppositional, what does she gain and what does she give up?" (9-10). The mediator is often exposed to attack for unorthodox presentations or compromises and overlooked afterward—the case of Nella Larsen and Jessie Fauset. How much more would this have been true of Marita Bonner, less accommodationist, more trenchant in her social criticism?

The unpublished stories, left languishing in their cardboard notebook for some thirty years in a musty attic in Chicago, are testimony to her unwillingness to relinquish control of her voice and her vision. Marita Bonner tended her garden as lovingly and as long as she could—it now remains for younger generations to reap its fruits.

Notes

1. Rush, Myers, and Arata list three plays and ten short stories by Bonner; "A Sealed Pod," listed as a poem, is a short story. Fairbanks and Engeldinger name thirteen short stories. Weiner shows nine items under Bonner's name and one under her pseudonym, Joseph Maree Andrews. Diane Isaacs has done the first bio-bibliographical paragraph on Bonner (see Kellner 45). As far as we know, there has been virtually no criticism on Bonner's work, save Doris E. Abramson's article "Angelina Weld Grimké, Mary T. Burrill, Georgia Douglas Johnson, and Marita O. Bonner: An Analysis of Their Plays."

2. For time limits on the Harlem Renaissance phenomenon, we follow Bruce Kellner in defining 1917-1935 as dates for the era. Geographically, we include an area that encompasses such cities as Philadelphia, Washington, D.C., Boston, and others that had substantial black populations. Participants and critics whom we have interviewed (e.g., May Miller Sullivan and Arthur P. Davis) also think of the Renaissance as the "New Negro" movement, not confined to Harlem.

3. Birth dates, death dates, and occupational facts, however, are taken from records held by the City of Boston Registry of Records and Vital Statistics.

4. Interview with Wilhelmina Crosson, educator and Bonner family friend, Boston, November 1985. Ms. Crosson reports that the Bonners were members of the Ebenezer Baptist Church in Boston.

5. Bonner published a review of Georgia Douglas Johnson's *Autumn Love Cycle* in *Opportunity* in 1929.

6. Photocopies of William's degree from Boston University and Marita's degree from Radcliffe were furnished us by Warwick Gale Occomy.

7. The speech patterns of the characters, newly urbanized migrants to Chicago, serve to accentuate their race and class identities. Here Bonner uses Negro dialect, miming black folk culture in order to create a vibrant and organic ensemble of characters. Many women writers of Bonner's generation shunned "Black English" (see Wall 79).

8. Archives, First Church of Christ Scientist, Boston.

9. Grateful acknowledgment is made to William, Warwick Gale, and Marita Joyce Occomy for allowing us to examine their mother's notebook.

10. Far more extreme is the example of Gayl Jones's novel *Eva's Man,* in which the female protagonist retaliates by poisoning her lover, then castrating him with her teeth.

11. That violence is inevitable if equality is to be attained is suggested, too, in Bonner's 1928 play "The Purple Flower," in which only the shedding of blood wins access to the top of the mountain.

12. It is interesting to contrast Sadie, whose act of speaking out against her oppressor becomes her deliverance, with Jimmy, a character in an earlier story by Bonner described as being "fastened inside his body by a tongue that could not speak" (243). Jimmy, a victim of brain hemorrhage from overwork, dies without voicing his pain in "Of Jimmy Harris."

13. "One True Love" is the only one of the notebook stories that has been published, as far as we know.

Works Cited

Abramson, Doris. "Angelina Weld Grimké, Mary T. Burrill, Georgia Douglas Johnson, and Marita O. Bonner: An Analysis of Their Plays." *Sage* 2.1 (1985): 9-13.

Bonner, Marita. "Black Fronts." *Opportunity* 16.7 (July 1938): 210.

———. "Extra Notes" to her children. © 1965. [Copy furnished by Warwick Gale Occomy.]

———. "High Stepper." Ms. 55-77.

———. "Light in Dark Places." Ms. 173-95.

———. "Of Jimmy Harris." *Opportunity* 11 (Aug. 1933): 242-44.

———. "On Being Young, a Woman and Colored." *Crisis* 31 (Dec. 1925): 63-65.

———. "On the Altar." Ms. 3-55.

———. "One True Love." Ms. 77-101. Also in *Crisis* 48 (Feb. 1941): 46, 47, 58, 59.

———. "The Purple Flower." *Crisis* 34 (Jan. 1928): 9-11, 28, 30.

———. "Reap It as You Sow It." Ms. 139-73.

———. Rev. of *Autumn Love Cycle,* by Georgia Douglas Johnson. *Opportunity* 7 (Apr. 1929): 130

———. "Stones for Bread." Ms. 101-39.

———. "White Man's War." Ms. 6.

Chafe, William H. *Women and Equality: Changing Patterns in American Culture.* New York: Oxford UP, 1977.

Crosson, Wilhelmina. Personal interview. October 1985.

Dearborn, Mary V. *Pocahontas's Daughters: Gender and Ethnicity in American Culture.* New York: Oxford UP, 1986.

Fairbanks, Carol, and Eugene A. Engeldinger. *Black American Fiction: A Bibliography.* Metuchen: Scarecrow P, 1978.

Gilbert, Sandra, and Susan Gubar. *The Madwoman in the Attic: The Woman Writer and the Nineteenth Century Imagination.* New Haven: Yale UP, 1979.

Kellner, Bruce, ed. *The Harlem Renaissance: A Historical Dictionary for the Era.* Westport: Greenwood P, 1984.

Morrison, Toni. *Sula.* New York: Knopf, 1974.

Occomy children audiotape. May 1986. [A recorded response to a questionnaire designed by Roses and Randolph and sent in Sept. 1985 to the children of Marita Bonner. The respondents were William Occomy, Warwick Gale Occomy, and Marita Joyce Occomy Strickland. Tape in possession of Randolph and Roses.]

Rush, Theresa Gunnels, Carol Fairbanks Myers, and Esther Spring Arata. *Black American Writers Past and Present: A Biographical and Bibliographical Dictionary.* 2 vols. Metuchen: Scarecrow P, 1975.

Smith, Barbara. "Toward a Black Feminist Criticism." *Conditions: Two* 1977: 25-44.

Sullivan, May Miller. Personal interview. 20 April 1986.

Wade-Gayles, Gloria. *No Crystal Stair: Visions of Race and Sex in Black Women's Fiction.* New York: Pilgrim P, 1984.

Wall, Cheryl. "Poets and Versifiers, Singers and Signifiers: Women of the Harlem Renaissance." *Women, the Arts, and the 1920s in Paris and New York.* Ed. Kenneth W. Wheeler and Virginia Lee Lussier. New Brunswick: Transaction Books, 1982. 74-98.

Watkins, Mel. "Sexism, Racism and Black Women Writers." *New York Times Book Review* 15 June 1986: 1, 35.

Weiner, Thomas, ed. *Analytical Guide and Index to* The Crisis *1910-1960.* Westport: Greenwood P, 1975.

JUDE R. MECHE (ESSAY DATE 2000)

SOURCE: Meche, Jude R. "Marita Bonner." In *Dictionary of Literary Biography, Vol. 228: Twentieth-Century American Dramatists,* second series, edited by Christopher J. Wheatley, pp. 35-39. Detroit, Mich.: The Gale Group, 2000.

In the following essay, Meche presents an overview of Bonner's life and dramatic works, emphasizing her "reformist spirit" in regard to problems faced by African Americans.

Marita Bonner is perhaps the most unorthodox playwright of the early part of the century to turn her attention toward the concerns of the African American community. Yet, despite an unusual, nonrealistic approach to her subject, Bonner won a great deal of praise for her dramatic work—as well as for her short fiction—in the black magazines *Crisis* and *Opportunity.* Her three one-act plays—***The Pot Maker: A Play to Be Read*** (1927), ***The Purple Flower*** (1928), and ***Exit, An Illusion*** (1929)—remained unstaged during her lifetime, probably because of the nationwide economic difficulties following 1929 and the subsequent neglect and dismissal of her work as that of a minor author; but each play nevertheless offers a compelling glimpse into the realities of being an African American during the first half of the twentieth century. Beyond merely presenting a portrait of black life in America, as she does in her short stories and essays, Bonner seemed to envision the dramatic space as one of more freedom and possibility than the fictional sphere in which she most often worked.

While Bonner's short stories almost inevitably have a tragic outcome, and while race and class always play a contributing role in these conclusions, her plays—particularly her best-known work, ***The Purple Flower***—offer a possibility of change for her protagonists. And while strife among the generations is inevitable in Bonner's fiction, ***The Purple Flower*** shows cooperation between young and old. Perhaps most significantly, Bonner's use of questions directly addressed to her predominantly black audience suggests that the potential for change lies with them rather than with those who would oppress them. However, despite such hints of promise, these plays are not fantasies; they are grounded in the African American's actual situation in the American landscape, and they guarantee neither salvation nor freedom but merely the possibility of both. In the end, this mixture of unfriendly reality and potential future redemption makes her plays compelling and still worthy of attention.

Bonner's birthdate is a subject of debate; while the date is generally held to be 16 June 1899, scholars Lorraine Elena Roses and Ruth Elizabeth Randolph assert that her actual birthdate was 16 June of the previous year. Bonner was the third of four children born to Joseph Andrew and Mary Anne Noel Bonner. She was educated in Brookline, Massachusetts, where she attended the Cabot School until third grade. After the Cabot School, she attended the Edward Devotion School and Brookline High School, from which she graduated in 1918. In high school Bonner contributed to the student magazine, *The Sagamore,* and gained the attention of its faculty sponsor, Alice Howard Spaulding, who urged Bonner to apply to Radcliffe. Bonner did so and was accepted, graduating in 1922. Despite regulations prohibiting blacks from residing on campus, Bonner was active in the university community, joining several musical clubs (she was an accomplished pianist) and founding the Radcliffe chapter of the black sorority Delta Sigma Theta. She majored in English and comparative literature and studied creative writing in Charles Townsend Copeland's exclusive writing seminar. Bonner also continued her study of German, which she had begun in high school. Toward the end of her career at Radcliffe, Bonner began teaching at the nearby Cambridge High School, perhaps for financial reasons.

In 1924 Bonner's mother died of a brain hemorrhage. Her father died two years later. After her graduation and during these years of hardship, Bonner again obtained teaching positions to support herself. She taught at the Bluefield Colored Institute in Bluefield, Virginia, from 1922 until 1924 and at the Armstrong High School in Washington, D.C., from 1924 until 1930. During her time in Washington, Bonner joined "The Round Table," Georgia Douglas Johnson's literary salon; she also began to seriously pursue writing and publishing her work. Her first published story, **"The Hands,"** appeared in 1925 in *Opportunity*. In the same year, she published her essay **"On Being Young—A Woman—and Colored"** in *Crisis*.

Bonner married William Almy Occomy in 1930. Occomy was a graduate of Brown University and held an M.B.A. from Boston University. Following their marriage, the couple moved to Chicago, where they raised three children: William Almy Jr., Warwick Gale Noel, and Marita Joyce. In 1941, the same year in which she ceased publishing her work, Bonner and Occomy joined the First Church of Christ Scientist. Around the same time, Bonner also decided to return to teaching and, after satisfying Board of Education questions concerning her qualifications, taught at Philips High School from 1944 until 1949. From 1950 until 1963 Bonner taught at the Dolittle School, working with mentally handicapped students.

Prior to 1941, however, Bonner's move to Chicago had a momentous impact upon her writing, because there she found and developed the microcosm of Frye Street. This fictional location became the setting for much of her subsequent fiction and became, for Bonner, a universal landscape representing all the varieties of life for the urban-living African American as well as for the other ethnic minorities of the city. She describes the street, in a foreword to **"A Possible Triad on Black Notes,"** in the following terms:

> *Now, walking along Frye Street, you sniff first the rusty tangy odor that comes from a river too near a city; walk aside so Jewish babies will not trip you up; you pause to flatten your nose against discreet windows of Chinese merchants; marvel at the beauty and tragic old age in the faces of the young Italian women; puzzle whether the muscular blond people are Swedes or Danes or both; pronounce odd consonant names in Greek characters on shops; wonder whether Russians are Jews, or Jews, Russians—and finally you will wonder how the Negroes there manage to look like all men of every other race and then have something left over for their own distinctive black-browns. . . .*
>
> *All the World is there.*

The Purple Flower

TIME:

The Middle-of-Things-as-They-are. (Which means the End-of-Things for some of the characters and the Beginning-of-Things for others.)

PLACE:

Might be here, there or anywhere—or even nowhere.

CHARACTERS:

Sundry White Devils (They must be artful little things with soft wide eyes such as you would expect to find in an angel. Soft hair that flops around their horns. Their horns glow red all the time—now with blood—now with eternal fire—now with deceit—now with unholy desire. They have bones tied carefully across their tails to make them seem less like tails and more like mere decorations. They are artful little things full of artful movements and artful tricks. They are artful dancers too. You are amazed at their adroitness. Their steps are intricate. You almost lose your head following them. Sometimes they dance as if they were men—with dignity—erect. Sometimes they dance as if they were snakes. They are artful dancers on the Thin-Skin-of-Civilization.)

The Us's (They can be as white as the White Devils, as brown as the earth, as black as the center of a poppy. They may look as if they were something or nothing.)

SETTING:

The stage is divided horizontally into two sections, upper and lower, by a thin board. The main action takes place on the upper stage.

30

Title page of *The Purple Flower,* from *Frye Street & Environs: The Collected Works of Marita Bonner* (1987).

Frye Street challenges the then-current idea of the American "melting pot" in which all races merge into a single identity. The Frye Street of Bonner's fiction, rather, serves as a refuge for those who are unable to achieve the ideal homogeneity of the American, and it is a place where the residents' race, ethnicity, and otherness are never to be forgotten.

Bonner's plays have frequently been labeled allegories, but though there is some truth to this labeling—each play contains at least a few allegorical elements—Bonner's works function in ways entirely different from the medieval morality plays to which they have been compared. Unlike these earlier works that each carry a specific, clear didactic message, Bonner's plays allow an ambiguity to enter into their allegoric structures.

The final actions of each play do not ring with the unswerving optimism of a work such as *Everyman,* and even allegorical characters such as the White Devils in ***The Purple Flower*** do not perform only acts of deviltry; in addition to their trickery, Bonner attributes to them a grace, an "adroitness," and an artfulness that are not essentially negative. Through this ambivalence, Bonner seems intent not upon forcing a view upon her audience but upon forcing her audience to arrive at a decision of their own.

Bonner's use of second-person narration in her stage directions and descriptions of sets and characters further emphasizes the necessity for audience participation in any effort to extract a meaning from her plays. Particularly, Bonner's use of queries directed to her audience makes clear the viewer's need to answer fundamental questions before any understanding can be gained. Additionally, Esther Beth Sullivan observes that the use of second-person narration implicates the viewer in those social issues that Bonner presents through her plays, further compelling her audience to work toward their own understandings of the actions on the stage since—finally—those actions are inextricably related to their own actions offstage.

In her first play, ***The Pot Maker,*** Bonner begins with her characteristic use of the second-person point of view to draw her audience into the setting and then the action of the play. The setting is a room in which Elias Jackson, who has been "called of God," is preparing to rehearse his first sermon before his father and mother; his wife Lucinda; and her lover, Lew Fox. Bonner offers descriptions of each person, calling for the audience to recognize each of them for what they are: Lew as a ridiculous, foolish, facetious swaggerer; Lucinda as the "base fool" who is the only one capable of loving him; the mother as guardian of the family's pride and propriety; the father as quietly proud; and Elias as "ruggedly ugly" though "You want to give both hands to him." Elias's calling has not allowed him time to go to a theological school: "God summoned him on Monday. This is Wednesday. He is going to preach at the meeting-house on Sunday."

As the curtain rises, Elias busily seats his audience so that they simulate the audience he expects for his first sermon. Immediately after, he attempts to begin his sermon only to be cut off by his mother's objection that his opening, "Brothers and sisters," has been overused. Beginning again, he attempts to launch into his parable of a pot maker and his pots only to be interrupted by Lucinda and then again by his mother. Throughout Elias's attempts to launch into his sermon, Lucinda and Lew are exchanging amorous glances while Elias's mother casts venomous looks toward her daughter-in-law.

After these repeated false starts, Elias is finally able to relate his parable of a pot maker who promises his pots that if they are able to stand through the long night and hold all of their contents, they will then be transformed from earthenware into higher metal: "Tin pots, iron pots, brass pots, silver pots. Even gold." After he offers this promise, one pot cries out that it is cracked, and the pot maker bends over it and seals it. The pot maker then leaves, and several of the pots tip over from fear of the dark or of noises. When the pot maker returns, he points to those pots that are still standing, and they realize that they have turned into gold. Those pots that "kinder had hung their heads but was still settin' up" were transformed into silver, and those pots on the ground that "snuk up and tried to stand up and hol' up their heads" were turned into brass. Those that simply lay on the ground turned to tin. Elias then points to his congregation and tells them that if they are able to hold the truth as the pot maker's pots held their contents that they would then be transformed by God, and urges any member of his congregation with a crack to call out, as did the pot, and be healed by God.

Elias's sermon has little impact on his listeners, all of whom are too preoccupied with the actions of others. In fact, the only member of Elias's audience who reacts favorably to the sermon is his father. Lew makes a quick exit after the sermon, and Lucinda escorts him under the ruse of getting a drink of water. When she returns, she decides to go out "where folks got some sense" and fights with Elias's mother over a good pair of shoes, eventually giving them up to their rightful owner. Elias's mother and father then leave, and Elias confronts Lucinda. Lucinda accuses Elias of being unmanly since he is unable to provide her with a home of her own and since they must live with his parents. While she berates Elias, they hear Lew whistle. Lucinda tries to join Lew, but Elias holds her back. Then Lew, stumbling around in the dark outside the house, falls into the well. Lucinda breaks free from Elias, and she too falls in the well. As their struggles are heard offstage, Elias berates both as "tin," but then he cries out *"God, God, I got a crack in me too!"* and runs out to the well only to fall in as he tries to rescue his wife. The play ends with Bonner's stage directions: *"A crack has been healed. A pot has spilled over the ground. Some wisps have twisted out."*

This ending, comprised of both a healing and a falling over, offers little in the way of a clear meaning for Bonner's audience and allows the play to move beyond the didacticism of the morality play from which it borrows many elements. Indeed, while the son who is "called of God" is clearly suggestive of Christ, his death in the well is not the kind of sacrifice for the sins of others that one might expect from a Christ figure. Bonner does suggest that Elias's death might be redemptive with the observation that a crack was healed, but her final stage directions simultaneously suggest that even he is unable to hold God's truth.

The Pot Maker also offers interesting commentary on the role that the African American community plays in the formation of both the Christian leader and—since Elias is also involved in the fashioning of a story—of the artist. In the presence of both, the family becomes more of an obstruction than an aid. Elias's mother attempts to shape both Elias's Christianity and his artistic production through her criticism of his unorthodox parable. Similarly, Lew and Lucinda draw the attention of Elias and the rest of his small congregation away from his message and art and down to their own base level. Finally, Lucinda's attacks upon Elias's manhood, implying that his new, nonpaying vocation is less manly than his previous employment in the cornfields, suggest that religious and artistic inclinations are incompatible with the community's vision of masculinity.

Bonner's next play, ***The Purple Flower,*** also examines the role of community in the progress of a people toward a goal. In this play, perhaps Bonner's most allegorical, the protagonists, the Us's, are prevented by the White Devils from climbing the hill to reach the purple Flower-of-Life-at-Its-Fullest. Bonner describes the White Devils as thoroughly artful creatures and ones who are skilled at deceit. She gives no definite requirements for the Us's color or appearance.

The play is set during the Middle-of-Things-as-They-Are and focuses on a group of Us's discussing their fate in the valley at the foot of the White Devils' hill. This valley lies between Nowhere and Somewhere. Bonner also divides the set horizontally, with an upper stage where the action takes place and an underlit lower stage. She notes that the division between upper and lowers stages is The Skin-of-Civilization—a boundary so thin that a thought "can drop you through it."

As the curtain rises, the Us's bemoan their situation. Some of the Us's describe the way that they have worked for the White Devils all day, only to be pushed off the hill at nightfall. Most of the Us's agree that work is not a viable means of winning the White Devils' respect or of reaching the Flower. Next, and Old Man among the Us's calls for a Young Man who has been reading books to tell them what he has learned about getting up the hill. The Young Man, however, throws his books down in disgust. These books, written by the White Devils, have no information of use to the Us's. The Us's then turn to another Us, who carries bags of money, and they question him about his unhappiness. This Us replies in turn that his money does him no good in reaching the top of the hill. Meanwhile, during the course of this conversation, a young Us named Sweet comes running onstage crying because a White Devil hiding in the bushes pinched her as she walked by.

Finally, one Old Lady tells the others of her dream in which "I saw a White Devil cut in pieces—head here *(pointing),* body here—one leg here—one there—an arm here—an arm there." Upon hearing this, an Old Man proclaims that "It's time then!" and calls for an iron pot. He then calls for a handful of dust, one from "the depths of the things you have made," to put into the pot. The Old Man then asks for books, which the Young Man supplies, and gold, which the Us with money readily provides. Only the Old Man's call for blood makes the Us's pause. They deliberate over whose blood should be taken, objecting to the offer by an Us named Finest Blood to use his own blood. Other Us's suggest that they ambush the White Devil hiding in the bushes, but the Old Man tells them "An Old Us will never tell you to play the White Devil's games!" Instead, the Old Man instructs Finest Blood to lure the White Devil out of the bushes and then issue a challenge, saying to him:

> White Devil, God is using me for His instrument. . . . He says it is almost day, White Devil. The night is far gone. A New Man must be born for the New Day. Blood is needed for birth. Blood is needed for the birth. Come out, White Devil. It may be your blood—it may be mine—but blood must be taken during the night to be given at the birth. . . . You have taken blood. You must give blood. Come out. Give it.

After receiving these instructions, Finest Blood asks if there is another way, but the Old Man tells him that there is none. The play ends as the Us's listen to Finest Blood's voice offstage as he issues the challenge to the White Devil. Bonner calls for the curtain to close *"leaving all the Us, the White Devils . . . listening, listening. Is it time?"*

With this final question directed toward her audience, Bonner again prevents her work from slipping into the didacticism of a medieval morality play and also underscores the importance of the events in her play to those who are witnessing these actions. The play is clearly a call to violent resistance and leaves little question about what actions Bonner advocates as a means of achieving equality between whites and blacks, but this final question does place the responsibility for choosing the appropriate time for this violence squarely upon the viewer. Indeed, the action that Bonner advocates must be one agreed upon by the entire community just as, for the Us's, the formation of the New Man required contributions from all members of the Us community.

Bonner's final play steps away from race relations to examine the effects of racism within the black community. Particularly, ***Exit, An Illusion*** focuses upon the ways in which racial concerns interfere in the relationship between protagonists Dot and Buddy. Dot is of mixed blood and is the victim of rumors that she is trying to pass for white. The play opens with stage directions that immediately bring the main issue to the forefront: *"The room you are in is mixed. It is mixed."* This statement refers not only to gender but also to racial mixing, as Dot is described as almost as "pale as the sheets" while Buddy is "blackly brown," and the emphasis on passing and mixing continues as Dot applies white powder to her face through much of the play.

When the curtain rises, Dot is sprawled in bed, and Buddy lies asleep on the floor beside the bed. Dot awakens with a start, waking Buddy in the process, and begins rushing around in preparation for a date. Buddy objects to her plans to go out, because she is clearly ill. However, as he questions Dot about her upcoming date, he finds even more reason to object. Dot admits that she has "been knowing the guy all my life" and tells Buddy that her date's name is Exit Mann. Buddy mocks the name but grows suspicious as he sees Dot applying heavy amounts of powder to her face.

His questions are about whether she plans to go out passing are quickly dismissed by Dot, but Buddy becomes increasingly suspicious and begins to connect this date to the white man that rumor has linked to her name. Despite Dot's protests, Buddy becomes increasingly certain that Exit Mann is that white man, and he vows that he will kill both Dot and her date. Dot tells Buddy that, if he loves her, her date will not be able to come; however, Buddy is so enraged that he denies his love for Dot. When Exit suddenly appears behind Buddy, Dot begins to panic and begs Buddy to tell her that he loves her before it is too late. Buddy instead commands Dot to join her lover; when she does she falls limp, and Buddy realizes that Exit Mann is, in reality, Death.

At this moment, suddenly, the lights flare, and the room and its occupants again appear as they did at the opening curtain. Dot cries for Buddy to say he loves her before she goes, but he does not hear her. The stage directions note, however, that "You think you hear the rattling" of her throat. Immediately after Dot's cries cease, Buddy awakens, still shouting that he does not love her. Upon realizing that he was dreaming, he turns to Dot, touches her, "begins to cry like a small boy" and finally admits, "Oh Dot! I love you! I love you!" As the curtain falls, it is by no means certain that Dot hears Buddy's declarations of love for her. What is clear, though, is that Buddy's concerns with race obscure all else from his view. Indeed, he cannot associate Dot's paleness with anything other than whiteness and does not realize until too late that her skin color is no longer a signifier of race but of declining physical health.

Exit, An Illusion is Bonner's least ambiguous play. Unlike ***The Pot Maker*** or ***The Purple Flower,*** Bonner's final play does not leave a great deal for the audience to interpret for themselves. She offers no question for her viewers to ponder as they leave the theater. In fact, this play—though not the most allegorical of her dramatic pieces—is her most didactic work. In her fiction Bonner also criticizes black prejudices against other blacks because of skin color, opposing this behavior in no uncertain terms.

Bonner died on 6 December 1971 from smoke inhalation after a lamp in her apartment caught fire. After trying to smother the flames, Bonner barricaded herself in a bathroom, where she was found by firefighters. She was rushed to the hospital, where she later died. Her literary output consisted, finally, of twenty short stories, three plays, and two essays.

Despite her tendency toward a more didactic drama in ***Exit, An Illusion,*** Bonner's willingness to initiate racial and political discussions dominates her dramatic style. And though there is no evidence—nor even the suggestion—that Bonner's style was influenced by her German contemporary, Bertolt Brecht, her drama shares with Brecht's the intent of reforming humankind. Certainly Bonner merits comparison with Brecht, despite her relative anonymity and her geographical distance from the German playwright. Both were adept at forcing social issues into the consciences of their audiences. And like Brecht—and her other contemporaries in the Harlem Renaissance—Bonner was undoubtedly aware of the discussions of class inspired by Karl Marx's treatises on the bourgeosie's abuses of the proletariat. Bonner's drama took up this reformist spirit and turned the viewer's attention to the problems of the African American.

FURTHER READING

Biography

Kellner, Bruce, ed. "Marita Bonner." In *The Harlem Renaissance: A Historical Dictionary for the Era,* pp. 18-23. Westport, Conn: Greenwood Press, 1984.

Overview of Bonner's life and works.

Criticism

Allen, Carol. "Urban Problems, Urban Answers: Segregation and the Subject in the Work of Marita Bonner." In *Black Women Intellectuals: Strategies of Nation, Family, and Neighborhood in the Works of Pauline Hopkins, Jessie Fauset, and Marita Bonner,* edited by Graham Russell Hodges, pp. 77–120. New York: Garland Publishing, 1998.

Examines Bonner's works for their representation of urban neighborhoods of the 1920s and 1930s.

Sullivan, Esther Beth. Introduction to *The Purple Flower.* In *Modern Drama by Women 1880s-1930s: An International Anthology,* edited by Katherine E. Kelly, pp. 309-11. London: Routledge, 1996.

Introduces Bonner's dramatic works and considers her one-act play The Purple Flower *as an allegory.*

OTHER SOURCES FROM GALE:

Additional coverage of Bonner's life and career is contained in the following sources published by the Gale Group: *Black Writers,* Ed. 2; *Contemporary Authors,* Vol. 142; *Dictionary of Literary Biography,* Vols. 51, 228; *Drama for Students,* Vol. 13.

ARNA BONTEMPS

(1902 - 1973)

(Full name Arnaud Wendell Bontemps) American novelist, poet, essayist, short story writer, children's writer, young adult writer, biographer, playwright, historian, literary critic, and editor.

A pioneering and significant figure in the Harlem Renaissance, Bontemps brought the empowered and creative spirit of that period to the American reading public, particularly its young readers. His poetry, novels, essays, and short stories for adults center on the need for a Black American identity embracing the myriad of African American experiences. His children's and young adult literature strives to provide positive images of Black children—images that didn't exist in the literature of his own childhood. Bontemps also brought to light the stories and life experiences of slaves and freedmen in his anthologies of slave narratives, folklore, poetry, and in his biographies for young readers. In a career that spanned fifty years, Bontemps's work gracefully straddles genres, offering Americans—especially children—a richer canvas of literature, history, and biography.

BIOGRAPHICAL INFORMATION

Bontemps was born in 1902 in Alexandria, Louisiana, to Marie Caroline Pembrooke, a school teacher, and Paul Bismark Bontemps, a brick mason. As a result of several racially motivated incidents, when Bontemps was four, his father decided to move the family from the dangers of the deep south to Los Angeles, California. When Bontemps was twelve, his mother died, leaving Paul to raise Arna and his little sister Ruby. He took their education very seriously and hoped for better lives for his children through integrated schooling and a self-conscious break from their ethnic culture. However, Bontemps became captivated with southern Black folk culture, as personified in his Uncle Buddy. Bontemps thus grew up with two very different male role models—his father, a new minister in the Seventh-Day Adventist church, advocating "colorlessness" as the path to success, and Uncle Buddy, a hard-drinking, penniless man who embraced the minstrel shows, folk stories, dialect, and culture of the South. Bontemps attended the San Fernando Academy, a white boarding school, from 1917 to 1920, where he was appalled that there were no realistic or positive literary images of Blacks and that African American history was relegated to brief—or nonexistent—discussions full of stereotypes, misinformation, and blatant omissions. After high school, Bontemps attended Pacific Union College in the early 1920s, while he worked at the local post office. In 1924, Bontemps published his first work, a poem called "Hope" in the journal *Crisis.* Intrigued by the literary activity occurring in Harlem during this period, Bontemps decided to head East and join the other writers of the Harlem Renaissance, where he had a teaching job waiting for him at the Harlem Academy, an Adventist high school.

The Harlem of the early 1920s offered Bontemps a vision of a Black community where art, music, literature, and opportunity were not only possible, but essential. He was accepted in literary circles, befriending several important figures including Langston Hughes, Claude McKay, and Countee Cullen, as well as other writers including Willa Cather, Sinclair Lewis, and Ernest Hemingway. In 1926 Bontemps married Alberta Johnson, one of his students. In 1931, Bontemps's first novel, *God Sends Sunday,* was published and met with generally positive reviews. The Depression of the 1930s, however, challenged the positive spirit of the Harlem Renaissance as many artists embarked on a search for employment elsewhere. Funding for Bontemps's position at the Harlem Academy was cut, so he took a position at Oakwood Junior College in Hunstville, Alabama. This position brought him back to the South, which he romanticized from his Uncle Buddy's stories, but now Bontemps found that life in Alabama was often oppressive for a Black. Bontemps had collaborated with Langston Hughes on a children's book, *Popo and Fifina* (1932), and from this point forward spent a considerable amount of his literary effort on creating realistic and positive images of Blacks for young readers. While his writing continued in the vein inspired by the Harlem Renaissance, Bontemps found the South less tolerant of those ideals. Freedom of thought was not welcome at Oakwood, and despite being an all-Black institution, the college discouraged its students from developing racial awareness. In 1934, after being ordered to burn his books, which according to the administration contained subversive content, Bontemps resigned his position. He packed his growing family into the car and drove to Los Angeles, just as his own father had done before him. Although his family had financial troubles and he was forced to move in with his father and stepmother, Bontemps continued to write. In 1936, he published *Black Thunder,* a novel with decidedly adult themes, centered on the historical events surrounding a failed slave rebellion in 1800. Between working steadily to support his wife and their six children and writing, Bontemps earned a master's degree in library science from the University of Chicago in 1943. He was soon thereafter appointed head librarian at Fisk University in Nashville, Tennessee, where he worked until 1965. This period was one of great activity for Bontemps as he collected, edited, and published works of African American history, biography, literature, poetry, folklore, and slave narratives. In 1969 Bontemps taught at the University of Illinois at Chicago Circle. That same year, he became Yale University's James Weldon Johnson Memorial Collection curator, where he was responsible for a significant collection of original materials from the Harlem Renaissance. In 1971, Bontemps returned to Fisk University as writer-in-residence, where he remained until his death on June 4, 1973.

MAJOR WORKS

While Bontemps's literary contribution is sizeable, his novels and children's literature are of particular interest. His first novel, *God Sends Sunday,* a celebration of southern folk culture, focuses on Little Augie, a successful Black jockey in St. Louis. Modeled on Bontemps's Uncle Buddy, Little Augie is a flashy, hard-drinking, gambling man who lives for good times and instant gratification. In the early 1890s Augie meets with success, but when his luck turns and he loses his money, he heads to California to find his sister. In California he also finds communities that have transplanted southern culture to the west. With the help of his sister and her grandson, Terry, who closely resembles Bontemps, and his grandmother, Little Augie tries to reform his lifestyle. Unfortunately, his restlessness and lust lead him into a violent knife fight over a woman, and Augie flees to Mexico. The novel met with mixed critical reaction because of the frankness of Bontemps's portrayal of dialect and southern folk culture. While some critics considered the novel a rich and realistic portrayal of the Black southern experience, others, including W. E. B. Du Bois, felt it was a hateful, stereotypical presentation of everything the Harlem Renaissance was struggling against. In his next novel, *Black Thunder,* Bontemps utilizes historical events as the backdrop as he explores the Black revolutionary spirit and the battle for freedom. He recounts the thwarted conspiracy of 1800, popularly known as "Gabriel's Defeat," wherein Gabriel Prousser, a "trouble-making" slave was harshly punished, and in reaction, planned a rebellion to take over the Richmond weapons arsenal and seize the town. He gained considerable support from fellow slaves, freedmen, and some sympathetic whites. The conspiracy, however, was thwarted by a torrential rainstorm and last minute betrayals, causing the revolutionaries to be hunted down and executed.

Bontemps's most celebrated novel, *Black Thunder,* is the first Black historical novel.

While he wrote and collaborated on many children's and young adult books, Bontemps's first endeavor, a collaboration with Langston Hughes, was the critically acclaimed *Popo and Fifina.* It is the story of two Haitian children living in a seacoast town with their parents and follows the children through their adventures and daily chores in a lush tropical locale. *Sad-Faced Boy* (1937) focuses on Slumber and his two brothers who run away to Harlem to visit their uncle. Musically inclined, the boys start a band and meet with some success, but when winter comes, the boys miss their warm cabin in Alabama. They soon leave behind excitements of Harlem for the familiar comforts of home. This was the first of Bontemps's children's books to employ the lonesome boy theme; it is a recurring theme throughout much of his work and one he revisited in his story *Lonesome Boy* (1955). Written for adults, but deemed by some more appropriate for younger readers, it tells of Bubba, a boy who constantly plays his silver trumpet. Bubba's grandfather warns him about caring only for his trumpet, which he says might get Bubba into "devilment." Bubba doesn't heed his grandfather's warning, and when he grows up, he plays his trumpet in jazz clubs in New Orleans. One night, things get out of control and Bubba learns what his grandfather meant when he warned about "devilment." In addition to children's literature, Bontemps also composed histories and biographies of Black Americans, including *Story of the Negro* (1948), a comprehensive examination of the history of slavery. Bontemps's poetry, mostly written and published after the Harlem Renaissance, includes *Personals* (1963) and *I Too Sing America* (1964), the latter written with Langston Hughes. Hughes also collaborated with Bontemps on the anthology *The Poetry of the Negro, 1746–1949,* published in 1949 and enlarged in 1970.

CRITICAL RECEPTION

Lauded for his determination to create a body of literature documenting the Black experience, Bontemps has met with consistently favorable critical reaction. Some critics felt that in his early work his use of southern dialect and his portrayal of folk culture was crass and self-defeating, but others praised his realism and sensitivity as he attempted to recreate genuine experiences. His poetry has received much critical notice, winning him numerous awards and contests in his early days in Harlem. Kirkland C. Jones, a preeminent Bontemps biographer, emphasizes the significance of location and environment as influences on Bontemps's conception of Black American identity. Critics such as Joseph A. Alvarez and Elizabeth F. Howard have examined the significance of Bontemps's children's literature, histories, biographies, and collections, acknowledging that it is Bontemps's determination to help create and enrich young people's understanding of the Black experience that makes his work so important to American literature. Many critics regard *Black Thunder* as Bontemps's most important creative work for its presentation of Black history as legitimate literary material. The historical basis of the novel and his creative choices in his fictionalized retelling captured critical interest, as did the stark difference in tone and style between this work and his earlier novel. A torchbearer for preserving and enriching Black heritage, Bontemps stands amongst the leaders of the Harlem Renaissance.

PRINCIPAL WORKS

God Sends Sunday (novel) 1931

Popo and Fifina, Children of Haiti [with Langston Hughes] (juvenilia) 1932

Black Thunder (novel) 1936

You Can't Pet a Possum (juvenilia) 1936

Sad-Faced Boy (juvenilia) 1937

Drums at Dusk (novel) 1940

Father of the Blues: An Autobiography by W. C. Handy [editor] (autobiography) 1941

Golden Slippers: An Anthology of Negro Poetry for Young Readers [editor] (poetry) 1941

The Fast Sooner Hound [with Jack Conroy] (juvenilia) 1942

They Seek a City [with Jack Conroy] (juvenilia) 1945; revised and enlarged as *Anyplace But Here,* 1966

We Have Tomorrow (juvenilia) 1945

St. Louis Woman [with Countee Cullen] (play) 1946

Slappy Hooper, The Wonderful Sign Painter [with Jack Conroy] (juvenilia) 1946

Story of the Negro (history) 1948; enlarged 1955

Free and Easy (play) 1949

The Poetry of the Negro, 1746-1949 [editor; with Langston Hughes] (poetry) 1949; revised and enlarged as *The Poetry of the Negro, 1746-1970,* 1970

George Washington Carver (biography) 1950

Chariot in the Sky: A Story of the Jubilee Singers (novel) 1951

Sam Patch, the High, Wide, and Handsome Jumper [with Jack Conroy] (juvenilia) 1951

The Story of George Washington Carver (biography) 1951

Lonesome Boy (novel) 1955

The Book of Negro Folklore [editor; with Langston Hughes] (folklore) 1958

Frederick Douglass: Slave, Fighter, Freeman (biography) 1959

100 Years of Negro Freedom (history) 1961

American Negro Poetry [editor] (poetry) 1963; revised 1974

Personals (poetry) 1963

Famous Negro Athletes (biography) 1964

I Too Sing America [with Langston Hughes] (poetry) 1964

Great Slave Narratives [editor] (prose) 1969

Hold Fast to Dreams: Poems Old and New [editor] (poetry) 1969

Mr. Kelso's Lion (juvenilia) 1970

Free at Last: The Life of Frederick Douglass (biography) 1971

The Harlem Renaissance Remembered: Essays [editor] (essays and memoirs) 1972

Young Booker: Booker T. Washington's Early Days (biography) 1972

The Old South; "A Summer Tragedy," and Other Stories of the Thirties (short stories) 1973

PRIMARY SOURCES

ARNA BONTEMPS (POEMS DATE 1920S)

SOURCE: Bontemps, Arna. "A Black Man Talks of Reaping" and "Southern Mansion." In *Personals.* 1963. 2nd ed., pp. 16, 36. London: Paul Breman, 1973.

Originally written in the 1920s, these two poems are considered among Bontemps's finest, valued for conveying the sense of possibility and wonder that the author felt toward Harlem.

"A BLACK MAN TALKS OF REAPING"

I have sown beside all waters in my day.
I planted deep, within my heart the fear
that wind or fowl would take the grain away.
I planted safe against this stark, lean year.

I scattered seed enough to plant the land
in rows from Canada to Mexico
but for my reaping only what the hand
can hold at once is all that I can show.

Yet what I sowed and what the orchard yields
my brother's sons are gathering stalk and root;
small wonder then my children glean in fields
they have not sown, and feed on bitter fruit.

"SOUTHERN MANSION"

Poplars are standing there still as death
And ghosts of dead men
Meet their ladies walking
Two by two beneath the shade
And standing on the marble steps.

There is a sound of music echoing
Through the open door
And in the field there is
Another sound tinkling in the cotton:
Chains of bondmen dragging on the ground.

The years go back with an iron clank,
A hand is on the gate,
A dry leaf trembles on the wall.
Ghosts are walking.
They have broken roses down
And poplars stand there still as death.

ARNA BONTEMPS (ESSAY DATE 1965)

SOURCE: Bontemps, Arna. "Harlem: The 'Beautiful' Years." *Negro Digest* 14, no. 3 (January 1965): 62-69.

The following essay is a memoir of the Harlem Renaissance in its heyday, with Bontemps recalling the vibrant music, literature, and culture that thrived in the city.

In some places the autumn of 1924 may have been an unremarkable season. In Harlem it was like a foretaste of paradise. A blue haze descended at night and with it strings of fairy lights on the broad avenues. From the window of a small room in an apartment on Fifth Avenue and 129th Street I looked over the rooftops of Negrodom and tried to believe my eyes. What a city! What a world!

And what a year for a colored boy to be leaving home for the first time! Twenty-one, sixteen months out of college, full of golden hopes and romantic dreams. I had come all the way from Los Angeles to find the job I wanted, to hear the music of my taste, to see serious plays and, God willing, to become a writer.

It did not take long to discover that I was just one of many young Negroes arriving in Harlem for the first time and with many of the same thoughts and intentions. Within a year or two we began to recognize ourselves as a "group" and to become a little self-conscious about our "significance." When we were not too busy having fun, we were shown off and exhibited and presented in scores of places, to all kinds of people. And we heard the sighs of wonder, amazement and sometimes admiration when it was whispered or announced that here was one of the "New Negroes."

Nothing could have been sweeter to young people who only a few weeks or months earlier had been regarded as anything but remarkable in Topeka and Cleveland and Eatonville and Salt Lake City—young people who, more often than otherwise, had seemed a trifle whacky to the home folks. In Harlem we were seen in a beautiful light. We were heralds of a dawning day. We were the first-born of the dark renaissance. We were not just struggling artists trying to find ourselves.

No, there was something special about being young and a poet in Harlem in the middle 'Twenties. We couldn't quite explain it, but one of our advocates on Park Avenue made an interesting suggestion. Primitive man, she said, had contacts with the infinite which civilization has broken. Primitive man was sharper, more acute in his intuition. Relying always on logic and reason, civilized man has lost the one thing most essential. In America the Indian and the Negro are nearer to the unspoiled primitive than are other people. The Indian's spirit is crushed. The Negro—well, see for yourself!

Up and down the streets of Harlem untamed youngsters were doing a wild dance called the Charleston. They were flitting over the sidewalks like mad while their companions, squatting nearby, beat out tom-tom rhythms on kitchenware. The unsuspecting stranger who paused to observe the performance was in danger of being surrounded, shoved into their circle and compelled to attempt a Camel Walk.

At parties, in ballrooms and on neighboring stages the older people proved that age, or lack of it, had nothing to do with this joy, this abandon, this . . . *primitivism.* They proved it, too, at house-rent parties where they drank bathtub gin ate pig's knuckles and danced with the lights off.

> Darkness brings the jungle
>   to our room . . .
> darkness hangs our room
>   with pendulums
> of vine . . .

The link with the jungle was obvious. In the little house-front churches there was swaying and moaning and shouting. Wasn't that proof? On a voodoo island such behavior would be called "possession." Would it be any more real or complete than this? No, the American Negro, our friend insisted, was not quite civilized—*fortunately.* In his play and in his worship his wildness was still apparent. In his work and his art it had almost disappeared.

The "New Negro" was to recapture this definite, though sometimes dim, quality in poetry, painting and song. By this means he must transmit it to all America. Through us, no less, America would regain a certain value that civilization had destroyed.

The idea intoxicated us. We went to work zealously, and some Americans saw the things we did. And the miracle of the whole notion was that it came so near taking root. Our group came within an inch of giving America, if not as much as our friend from Park Avenue had hoped, at least a certain new aesthetic value. It came close to repeating in the United States, say, what the Pre-Raphaelite Brotherhood had done in England two generations or so earlier.

The gusto and flavor of Zora Neale Hurston's story-telling, for example, long before the yarns were published in *Mules and Men* and other books, became a local legend which might easily have spread further under different conditions. A tiny shift in the center of gravity could have made the books bestsellers. And it is easy to see how the startled surprise that greeted the poems of Countee Cullen and the wonderment that followed discovery of Langston Hughes' completely effortless lyrics might have taken other directions and given the young poets an even wider vogue than they enjoyed at first. The same, or more, could have happened to the stylized figures in Aaron Douglas' drawings. His bookjackets and illustrations were followed by household decorations, furniture designs, public murals. These might have started a trend had they gone into other rooms, different hotel lobbies, more strategically situated university libraries.

Even so, the reception which the "New Negroes" received was warmly gratifying. Never before in America, never since, and perhaps not for much time to come, has it been or will it be possible for a Negro poet to say with feeling, speaking of Harlem.

> Let us roam the night together
>   singing.
> In those days it was said and
>   meant.

But there were moments when the "New Negroes" betrayed a strange uneasiness. Of course, none went so far as to suggest that there might be something wrong with Harlem or that the romantic concept that our group had the link with the primitive, the key to joy and intuitive understanding, might be a little far-fetched—but now and then one of us would say a shocking thing, almost beyond understanding then. I remember, for example, hearing Countee Cullen say that he thought it fitting that a creative artist should die young. He himself wanted all his work crowded into the next few years. He wouldn't care to live a day beyond the age of forty. Langston Hughes, less inclined toward self-analysis but sharper in his intuitions than most of the group, sometimes imagined that he would have his fill much sooner.

> Be kind to me,
> oh, great dark city . . .
> I will not come
> to you again.

But why—why this note in the music of the "New Negro"?

Something was wrong. When The Depression came and artists of every kind began to feel the pinch, the Harlem group was not excluded. "New Negroes" were scattered from Boston to Florida, from Pleasantville to Carmel-by-the-Sea, from Alabama to the pearly gates. A decade passed; twelve years, perhaps. Then some of us thought we could safely return to see what had happened to the city that had once filled us with song.

The Harlem we found in 1942 and 1943 was another place. One of the first things to shock us was the revelation that the people by whom Harlem was favorably known, did not live there any more. Paul Robeson and Marian Anderson were less familiar figures in Harlem in the early forties than were Mrs. Roosevelt and Mayor La Guardia. Richard Wright and Countee Cullen lived within shooting distance, more or less, but they were safely removed from the sounds of the streets. It took an hour's journey for either of them to see the rooftops of Negrodom. E. Simms Campbell and W. C. Handy lived on quiet hillsides, surrounded by trees and lawns. There was still a hill in Harlem, a fine, proud one, to be sure, but it was not the same as theirs, and the trees and lawns were not in people's yards. Hazel Scott and Cab Calloway and Jimmie Lunceford and the rest would certainly not have been moved by a poem which invited them to "roam the night together" in Harlem. They lived in Westchester.

At least one reason for avoiding the Harlem night streets in 1942 would have been the fear of muggers. Where poets went about singing in the days of the new awakening, angry, frustrated boys now prowled. Where "primitive" children had danced on the sidewalks, hungry, evil-eyed little criminals lurked in doorways. The rent party was a forgotten legend. Outlandish cults were meeting in some of the housefront churches where the moaning and shouting had formerly been spontaneous and filled with joy. What, in God's name, had happened?

To me there seemed only one explanation. No matter what else one might see there, Harlem remained what it had always been, in essence: a black ghetto and slum, a clot in the American bloodstream. And the fruit it was bearing was the fruit of the ghetto and the slum—the fruit of compulsory group segregation based on race. The children born there in the beautiful years of the middle 'Twenties had grown up to be muggers and cultists.

When Harlem rioted, somewhat later, a fuller answer emerged. It is now known that a Negro soldier was shot and wounded slightly when he attempted to take the part of a Harlem *poulet* in an altercation with a white policeman in the lobby of a small hotel. The soldier's mother happened to be nearby. Word of mouth reports of the incident were brief, intense, untrue: a colored soldier had been shot and killed by white policemen in the presence of the soldier's mother.

At first it seemed that the mad rage which followed this incident in Harlem was a protest and a reaction against the true reports of the kicking around, sometimes the killing, of colored soldiers in the South. It suggested to me a story I had once planned to write about a gang of tough, slum-hardened black kids in Chicago who, hearing about a lynching in Mississippi, went out and overturned the fruit cart of an Italian peddler and beat him up in a South Side alley.

This early tendency to see the riot simply as an extension of the conflict in the South seemed good enough at first. To me it seemed to sweep away the claim that the South had a special right to deal with the problem of race relations in America as it sees fit, irrespective of the interests of the nation as a whole—to maintain its caste mores, as a leading editor asserted during World War II, in defiance, if necessary of all the Allied and Axis armies. It confirmed a belief (which, incidentally, I still hold), namely, that the trouble with Harlem is Birmingham. The trouble with Los Angeles is New Orleans. The trouble with Illinois is Mississippi.

The only flaw in that first impression, as it related to Harlem, is that Harlem did not riot against white people. Harlem rioted against Harlem. True, it ravaged the shops and businesses of owners who get their living in Harlem but do not live there. Likewise beyond dispute is the fact that the mob went for the symbols of exploitation and oppression, but that was not its deepest impulse. Harlem was trying to commit suicide. It was sick of muggers and cultists and zoot suits. It was horrified and disgusted by the fruit of the beautiful years, and in a moment of confusion and frustration it rioted against itself and tried to wipe the slate clean.

The young intellectuals who came to Harlem in the middle 'twenties made a wonderful discovery. They found that it is fun to be a Negro under some conditions. Those who, like myself, had grown up in mixed or predominantly white communities even found that some segregation can be fun, when it's completely voluntary. But the "New Negroes" had lived long enough to learn that it is never fun to be alien. It is neither pleasant nor wholesome to be deprived of the freedom of movement or of friendship or of participation in the essential life of one's country.

Harlem must go. The American bloodstream cannot manage hard clots of such size and density. And all the other little Harlems must change. Otherwise America will be balkanized into a nation of mutually incompatible minorities. For the ideas and plans and the vigilance and distrust necessary to hem Harlem in and to keep it there, will create or maintain other Harlems, and all of them will not be black.

GENERAL COMMENTARY

ELIZABETH F. HOWARD (ESSAY DATE 1988)

SOURCE: Howard, Elizabeth F. "Arna Bontemps." In *The Scribner Writers Series,* pp. 77-83. Farmington Hills, Michigan: Gale Group, 2002.

In the following essay, originally published in 1988, Howard examines Bontemps's children's literature about the African American experience as a fulfillment of the Harlem Renaissance mission to awaken Americans to the value and significance of African American culture.

In Writing Fiction depicting the black experience for young people, Arna Bontemps (pronounced BON-tomp) was a trailblazer. As Arthur P. Davis remarked in *From the Dark Tower,* "Few, if any, books by Negro writers produced expressly for children were in existence in 1932." Bontemps was also a pioneer in writing black history and biography for young people. He led the way in informing not only blacks about themselves but also whites about Afro-Americans. His publications in the middle third of this century formed the necessary foundation for the award-winning black children's authors of the 1970's and beyond. In the words of his own poem, **"The Daybreakers,"** Bontemps was "beating a way for the rising sun."

Any consideration of Arna Bontemps as a writer, specifically a children's writer, must acknowledge his part in creating and being created by the Harlem Renaissance, that great blossoming of black culture in the 1920's. Bontemps's importance as a writer for children is rooted in the underlying concern of this group of black writers and artists using various media to present the black experience to all America. It is just this preoccupation that sets Bontemps apart from other black writers of the period and certainly from other, nonblack children's writers. Bontemps was unique and an innovator.

Bontemps was among the black artists, musicians, and writers who converged upon Harlem in the 1920's, offering their own talents and aspirations, and, through the support of their peers, finding new inspiration. In a real sense, then, they were creating the Renaissance even as they were being brought to life by the movement. As Nathan Huggins wrote in *Harlem Renaissance*:

> . . . to presume to be an actor and creator in the special occurrence of a people's birth (or rebirth) requires a singular self-consciousness. The era produced a phenomenal race consciousness and race assertion, as well as unprecedented numbers of poems, stories, and works of art by black people. Harlem was making it all happen, because black men were coming together there, some intending to build a cultural capital of the black world.
>
> (pp. 3, 83)

For the first time in American history, white intellectuals were "discovering" the Negro; black writers were being regarded seriously by publishers, reviewers, and readers. The publishers Alfred A. Knopf, Boni and Liveright, and Harper and Brothers helped to bring black authors into the public's awareness. In particular, author and critic Carl Van Vechten, in his writing and friendships with black intellectuals acted as a missionary in focusing attention on their work. And although some have said that the Renaissance flourished largely because of the white intelligentsia's patronage, their hungering for the exotic, and their penchant for the primitive, yet this cultural explosion forced American and world literati to recognize and to appreciate the creative genius of the Afro-American. As Huggins notes:

> After a history of struggle, of being an outcast, of being viewed with contempt or pity, the Negro

> was now courted and cultivated by cultured whites. How grand it was to be valued not for what one might become—the benevolent view of uplift—but for what was thought to be one's essential self, one's Negro-ness.
>
> (p. 118)

The Harlem Renaissance was Truly a Celebration of Blackness

Otey Scruggs, professor of American history at Syracuse University and specialist in Afro-American history, has suggested that perhaps Bontemps, because he was less flamboyant than some of the Renaissance leaders, has had the greatest staying power and influence. Of course, Bontemps had the advantage of outliving all of the other major figures in the movement, and in later years developed as a highly respected critic and commentator. But it is the thesis of this essay that Bontemps's writing for young people about the black experience provided an excellent medium for carrying out an essential concern of the Harlem Renaissance—the awakening of the American people to a recognition of the Negro and of Negro culture as a dynamic force in American arts and letters.

For children's literature, it is important to note that of all of the writers of the Harlem Renaissance only Bontemps and Langston Hughes produced works for children. Certainly it is Bontemps who deserves continuing credit for having recognized the dearth of young people's materials on black culture and history and for endeavoring throughout his life to fill this gap. As Professor Scruggs notes, his historic and biographical writings for young people and his efforts on behalf of black history have earned him enduring respect among historians and librarians.

Arna Bontemps was a Renaissance man both in the time-honored definition of that term and in the sense of the many-sided nature of black cultural expression in Harlem. A man of many talents, he published in virtually every literary genre. Bontemps was poet, novelist, short-story writer, anthologist, critic, essayist, playwright, historian, folklorist, biographer, and children's author.

Family, geography, education, and tradition all affected Bontemps' formation as a writer. Some of the personal influences important to his development were his father's rejection of things southern and "colored," a stance against which young Bontemps felt impelled to rebel; the robust, devil-may-care life-style of his colorful great-uncle Buddy, an anomaly in Bontemps's middle-class-conscious family; his education in Seventh-Day Adventist schools; the fever and fervor of life in Harlem in the 1920's amid other creative young blacks; The Great Depression, which forced Bontemps to leave Harlem for a teaching post in an Adventist school in Alabama; his welcome immersion in the "down home" culture of the rural South; another immersion in a Chicago ghetto where he worked on the WPA Writers' Project; his "oasis" at Fisk University in Nashville, where he settled and which for twenty-two years provided him with the opportunity to become well versed in Negro folklore as he built up the university library's Afro-American collection; his lifelong friendship with Langston Hughes, beginning with their days in Harlem; and his close relationship with his wife and six children.

Arna Bontemps was born in Alexandria, Louisiana, in 1902 and died in Nashville, Tennessee, in 1973. His father, Paul Bontemps, a bricklayer and sometime trombonist, made a good living for his wife, Marie, and their two children. According to family lore, one racial incident too many—the night two white men forced Paul Bontemps off the sidewalk—was the "straw that broke the camel's back," and Paul precipitously moved his family to Los Angeles.

Growing up in Los Angeles young Bontemps became aware of the conflicting strains of "twoness," first described by noted black social critic, writer, and civil-rights leader W. E. B. Du Bois. The Afro-American, Du Bois had written, is caught in two cultures, and in attempting to become part of the dominant culture he often must deny his African roots. Bontemps's father had been determined to separate himself and his family as far as possible from his unpleasant memories of being regarded as colored and inferior in the South. That meant Bontemps had to play down African-ness, to avoid black speech patterns, to be restrained in order to "fit in." Bontemps mentions that his father's attitude was reflected in his disapproval of Uncle Buddy, Bontemps's great-uncle, a happy-go-lucky character whose relaxed manner and tendency to imbibe definitely ran counter to family values. [But these parental admonitions produced an opposite reaction. Uncle Buddy so impressed young Bontemps as being "real folk"—unpretentious, unthreatened by whites, and refusing to imitate the dominant culture—that he later appears in some of his short stories and as the hero of his first novel, ***God Sends Sunday*** (1931).]

While growing up in Los Angeles, Bontemps began to sense something missing from the history he learned at school and from the books he devoured in the public library children's room. Were there no Negroes in American history? And why were there no stories about Negro children? These early pressures to suppress one side of his heritage had a lasting effect on Bontemps. Finding and expressing the Negro past were to become his lifelong obsession. His works for young people reveal this deep concern.

Bontemps graduated from Pacific Union College in 1923 and went to work as a mail clerk at the Los Angeles post office. In the summer of 1924 his first poem, **"Hope,"** was published in the NAACP's *Crisis Magazine.* At last he was a published writer, but for bread and butter he accepted a teaching post in the largest Adventist high school, Harlem Academy. And so Arna Bontemps went to Harlem.

It was the best of times and the best of places to be young, gifted, and black. Bontemps found himself the midst of the whirl of the Renaissance, part of that legendary circle which included, among others, Langston Hughes, Wallace Thurman, Claude McKay, Countee Cullen, Jean Toomer, Charles S. Johnson, Aaron Douglas, Dorothy West, and Zora Neale Hurston. During the next several years Bontemps taught and wrote poetry. But he became dissatisfied with poetry as a medium for expressing the black experience and turned to writing prose fiction. ***God Sends Sunday,*** the story of a picaresque jockey, was well reviewed, but 1931 was no time for a black writer to earn a living by writing. The Depression had dried up enthusiasm for new writers by shriveling the funds of patrons and stifling publishers' willingness and ability to take risks. The primitive and exotic ways of the Negro seemed no longer to be the stuff needed to sell books. Some called Bontemps's novel the last creative contribution of the Harlem Renaissance.

The Harlem Academy could no longer afford to pay Bontemps, so in 1931 he accepted a post at another church school, Oakwood Junior College in Huntsville, Alabama. This new setting promised new inspiration. Bontemps later wrote rhapsodically about his feelings of being plunged into the black folk culture of the Deep South. Absorbing the verdant, somnolent milieu of rural Alabama; listening to the old folks; and going to the country churches fed his longing to know and be part of southern Negro life.

It was during his Alabama sojourn that Bontemps first began to write for children. The impetus came from his friend Langston Hughes, who had visited Haiti and asked Bontemps to collaborate with him on a children's book about the island. ***Popo and Fifina: Children of Haiti*** (1932) was immediately successful. Eight-year-old Popo and his ten-year-old sister, Fifina, are described taking part in the everyday life of a small fishing village: gathering soap-weed, catching crabs, washing dishes at the community fountain, persuading Papa to make a red kite, learning to carve wood at Uncle's cabinetmaking shop. Warm words convey the lushness of this tropical island. Black-and-white illustrations by black artist E. Simms Campbell complete this glimpse into rural life in Haiti. Children's book critic Anne Thaxter Eaton, writing in the *New York Times* in October 1932, stated, "Popo and Fifina prompt us to wish that all our travel books for children might be written by poets." Bontemps, a poet, novelist, and short-story writer, was launched as a writer for young people.

Children in his Alabama neighborhood, barefoot and irrepressible, provided him with more story ideas. ***You Can't Pet a Possum*** (1934) describes Shine Boy's efforts to convince his grandmother to let him keep Butch, a vagrant hound. The story received favorable reviews in the *New York Times* and in the *Saturday Review.* Published after Bontemps had left Alabama but based on the actual escapades of three young farm boy neighbors, ***Sad-Faced Boy*** (1937) recounts the adventures of Slumber, Rags, and Willie, who run away to get a look at Harlem. Hiding aboard freight trains and hitching a ride in a truck these three budding street musicians make their way to the many-splendored city, and find a warm welcome from their uncle, a custodian in a high-rent Harlem apartment building. Through their dancing and singing they earn a fair amount of change, but eventually homesickness and the thought of ripe persimmons bring them back to Alabama.

Lonesome Boy, originally written while Bontemps was in Alabama, but published as a children's book 1955, is a hauntingly mysterious story of a boy struggling to grow up, confronting authority, but unsure of himself. Bubba plays a silver trumpet but ignores his grandfather's warning: "You better mind where you blow that horn, boy!" One night he wanders off to New Orleans and finds lots of jobs playing his horn for fancy parties and riverboat excursions. In a nightmare a faceless chauffeur drives him off to play for a frantic all-night dance, which has been interpreted as a Devil's ball. Bubba wakes up in the morning, apparently realizing that he cannot run from responsibility. The traditional values represented by his grandfather are the essential truths

FROM THE AUTHOR

THE LONGEVITY OF LITERATURE

Survival qualities are not necessarily synonymous with excellence. Some good books live and some don't. Most bad books die, but now and then one survives. Another thing to remember is that literary tastes change. The popularity of a writer of the past is likely to rise and fall with these changes in public taste . . .

SOURCE: Arna Bontemps, excerpted from a letter to Jean Blackwell, curator of the Schomberg Collection, May 25, 1951.

of life, comments Sandra Alexander in her Ph.D. work on Bontemps. Bubba returns home, trumpet now *under* his arm, to find out that his grampa had had the same experience when he was a horn-blowing youngster.

Another story written out of the Alabama experience but not published as a children's book until 1970 was ***Mr. Kelso's Lion.*** Again the protagonist is a young boy who faces a crisis. Percy goes to Alabama with his grandfather to visit his Aunt Clothilde. It is Percy who must confront the lion in Mr. Kelso's yard. The theme of a child attaining a measure of maturity through coming to terms with obstacles, within or without, real or psychological, occurs in several of Bontemps's works, both fictional and biographical. His belief that young blacks must strive for a sense of self flows through his writings for children and young adults.

The use of dialect in these stories is realistic and tasteful, reflecting southern black speech patterns of the 1930's. The stories are rich in their depiction of important black values such as family closeness, respect for elders and for hard work, rewards for being good, and the conviction that the good old-fashioned virtues of home and family are best. Bontemps's belief in the viability of black culture is revealed in his creative use of black dialect and folklore. He used cadenced, bantering dialogue laced with colloquialisms, folk motifs, and folk speech to create recognizable black characters in his short stories and children's books written out of this southern experience.

Before long Bontemps recognized that Alabama was not the Eden he had first believed. Racial tension reached a frightening peak during the trial in nearby Scottsboro of nine black youths who had ridden a freight train with two young white women who later accused them of rape. And then the directors of the Adventist school began to question his friendship with black writers, and even wanted him to get rid of the black books in his library. Bontemps decided to leave Alabama. In 1934 he moved with his wife and three children to one room in his father's house in Los Angeles.

There he concentrated on writing for adults. He wrote what some critics have called his best work. ***Black Thunder*** (1936), the first black-authored book of historical fiction with a black theme, is the powerful story of the slave Gabriel Prosser, who was the leader of an abortive insurrection in Virginia in 1808. This book was greatly informed by Bontemps's exploration into the Fisk University collection of "slave narratives," stories told by escaped slaves and written down by abolitionists, or stories collected in more recent times from former slaves. This was a rich source of black folklore and history hitherto untapped. Bontemps made extensive use of black folklore motifs in making Gabriel Prosser an archetypal hero. The book was well received. "If one were looking for a sort of prose spiritual on the Negroes themselves, quite aside from the universal dream that they bear in this story, one could not find it more movingly sung," cheered the *New York Times.* Although originally published for the adult market, this work provided young adults with valuable insights into the history of the protest against slavery.

In 1935 Bontemps moved to Chicago as principal of another Adventist school. However, after three years and increasing disinclination to live under the denomination's constraints, he permanently severed his connection with the Adventists. But the Chicago years were productive for his writing and for his future career. With the help of Rosenwald Fund scholarships he was able to obtain a master's degree in library science at the University of Chicago, and was also able to travel to the Caribbean to substantiate his research on another historical novel, ***Drums at Dusk*** (1939). He published his first anthology of poetry, ***Golden Slippers,*** in 1941. The book was promoted as the "first collection of Negro poetry suited to young as well as adult readers." Represented in it are such well-known poets as Paul Laurence Dunbar, Langston Hughes, James Weldon

Johnson, Claude McKay, Countee Cullen, and Bontemps himself; some lesser known poets; and traditional folk songs and spirituals. This selection provides a valuable introduction to poetry by blacks written before the mid-twentieth century.

Another important outgrowth of his years in Chicago was the development of a mutually fruitful friendship with the white writer Jack Conroy, whom he met while working on the WPA Writers' Project. Together they wrote several books, among them three books for children: ***The Fast Sooner Hound*** (1942), ***Slappy Hooper, the Wonderful Sign Painter*** (1946), and ***Sam Patch, the High, Wide and Handsome Jumper*** (1951). These three books have the timeless quality of the tall tale. Slappy Hooper's signs were painted so realistically that even the birds were fooled and tried to fly into the painted trees. Sam Patch learned to jump farther and farther until he could beat Hurricane Harry, the Kaskaskia snapping turtle. ***Sam Patch*** "is all very funny, and ever so well written," wrote L. S. Bechtel in the *New York Times.* ***The Fast Sooner Hound*** was the most successful and the most enduring story. An oddjobs railroad man wagers with his prospective boss that his dog, Sooner, can outrun any train. Sooner even passes up the Wabash Cannon Ball. In reflecting on Bontemps's career as a writer, his collaboration with Conroy undoubtedly enabled him to reach a wider audience of children. Perhaps this was due to Convoy's contacts in the publishing world. Indeed the fact that Convoy was white probably increased the possibility that the books would be noticed by editors.

In 1943 Bontemps left Chicago to become chief librarian at Fisk University in Nashville. He wrote that this was the oasis he had been seeking. The best of all possible worlds for Negroes in the 1940's, the Negro college offered financial security, a congenial community, and professional flexibility to continue his writing while building up the library's collection of works on Negroes. While he tried his hand at playwriting, his primary commitment was to literature for young people, and particularly for adolescents, who he felt had been ignored. Some of his works aimed at this age group are excellent; others suffer from didacticism. But at the time, there was virtually nothing in print on the history and biography of blacks. Bontemps was able to respond to a critical need.

In ***Story of the Negro*** (1948), which received the Jane Addams Children's Book Award, Bontemps introduces young readers to the drama of black history. The prologue notes the arrival of a Dutch ship a Virginia port in 1619 with a cargo of twenty black men. Bontemps then provides glimpses of the ancient kingdoms of Africa, including Ethiopia, Timbuctoo, and the Sudanic empires. This book is chiefly about people, black men and women, whose stories, unknown or half forgotten, needed to be told to all young readers. Blacks who played a role in American history are highlighted, as are events from the time of slavery, the slave revolts, the Civil War, the disillusion after Emancipation, the growth of Jim Crow laws, and the continuing struggle for civil rights. ***Story of the Negro*** is written anecdotally and is often dramatic and suspenseful—reminiscent of Hendrik Van Loon's *Story of Mankind* (1921). The book was hailed in all of the leading review periodicals. "A primer for white folks, young and old," remarked the *Saturday Review of Literature.*

Shortly thereafter Bontemps published a work of historical fiction for young people about the Jubilee Singers from Fisk University, who for over a hundred years have traveled widely, singing spirituals an raising money for the college. ***Chariot in the Sky*** (1951) is primarily the story of the beginning of the Fisk Jubilee Singers, and how the original little group of eleven students (several former slaves) introduced to captivated audiences in America and Europe a "new" type of music—the slave song, or spiritual. The Jubilee Singers assured the permanent recognition of the spiritual as basic American folk music. But this is also the story of Caleb, a slave, who is trained to be a tailor, later teaches himself to read, and eventually finds his way to Fisk. Bontemps undoubtedly used some of the materials in the slave narratives to give detail to the story. He incorporated black folklore, excerpts from spirituals, and bits of folk legend, such as the story of the flying Africans. "Freedom is a powerful word, children. Make you fly like a bird sometimes."

During the 1940's blacks believed that World War II would be a turning point, and that the Negro would at last become truly part of American society. Bontemps exemplified this hope in his historical and biographical writing. He published books on George Washington Carver, *Frederick Douglass,* and Booker T. Washington. He wrote two collective biographies describing living people. ***We Have Tomorrow*** (1945) introduces to young readers twelve young blacks who had begun to excel in their careers. That they are not all of national significance was Bontemps's point: ordinary people do have a chance. (Among the more well-known blacks in this volume are E.

Simms Campbell, cartoonist; Dean Dixon, violinist; Hazel Scott, pianist; and Benjamin Davis, Jr., West Point graduate and later general.) In his note for the eighth printing (1960) Bontemps states: "If deciding on a career and making a start in an unfamiliar field is still hard for some young people today, perhaps the success of these brave ones will still be encouraging." ***Famous Negro Athletes*** (1964) presents lively sketches of nine towering figures: Joe Louis, Sugar Ray Robinson, Jackie Robinson, Satchel Paige, Willie Mays, Wilt Chamberlain, James Brown, and Althea Gibson. Another largely biographical work, ***100 Years of Negro Freedom*** (1961), was written on the eve of the centenary of the Emancipation Proclamation, marking the struggles and achievements of known and lesser-known figures who tried to make real the promise of the proclamation. Frederick Douglass, Booker T. Washington, and W. E. B. Du Bois are treated in detail. Among the many others included are B. P. S. Pinchback, lieutenant governor of Louisiana; Paul Laurence Dunbar, poet; Ralph Bunche, United Nations mediator and Nobel Prize recipient; A. Philip Randolph, head of the Brotherhood of Sleeping Car Porters; and Rosa Parks, heroine of the Montgomery bus boycott. Bontemps is truly perceptive in his short statement on Martin Luther King, Jr., who had just come into the limelight: "His influence is beyond words, deriving from the wisdom of folk who have long recognized the power of the symbol."

What then is the significance of Arna Bontemps for children's literature? The key to his importance lies in his conviction, demonstrated throughout his writing, that black history is important for all young Americans. As Charles Nichols notes in the preface to his compilation of the letters of Bontemps and Langston Hughes: "Perhaps more consistently than many better known black leaders, he [Bontemps] was the 'keeper of the flame.'" Bontemps was a genteel yet adamant crusader, promoting awareness of black history and life for young readers. Early in his career he stated that his own generation was probably beyond saving, but that in young people lay the hope for a better world. Therefore, it was essential to communicate to young people the history and folklore of black America. This conviction was the foundation of his life and his art.

Bontemps's children's books cannot be seen apart from his total literary output. He promoted the cause of black history and culture through his historical novels, his folklore interpretations, his histories and biographies, his anthologies of poetry, and his children's stories. He wanted blacks to know who they were and whence they came in order to better envision where they might go. But Bontemps had more than black readers in mind. Although he believed deeply in the necessity of books on black themes for black readers, he was also committed to bringing about an awareness of the Afro-American to all young readers. As the Harlem Renaissance had aroused interest in the Negro among white literati, so Arna Bontemps saw his children's books, legacy of his experience of the Harlem Renaissance, as reaching white as well as black readers. As the literary parent of such prominent black children's authors as Virginia Hamilton, Mildred Taylor, Walter Dean Myers, Ashley Bryan, and Rosa Guy, Bontemps cleared a path for acceptance of black themes in the wider world of children's literature. Through his more than twenty-five books he "heightened our sense of the range, the peril, the promise of American life in our pluralistic society," declared Charles Nichols. For children's literature on the black experience in the mid- and late twentieth century, Arna Bontemps was truly a trailblazer, "beating a way for the rising sun."

JOSEPH A. ALVAREZ (ESSAY DATE 1998)

SOURCE: Alvarez, Joseph A. "The *Lonesome Boy* Theme as Emblem for Arna Bontemps's Children's Literature." *African American Review* 32, no. 1 (spring 1998): 23-31.

In the following essay, Alvarez considers Bontemps's children's literature and his motivations for turning from literature for adults to stories, novels, and histories for children and adolescents. The critic also examines Bontemps's novel Lonesome Boy *and the autobiographical nature of the recurring theme of a lonesome boy as it permeates his work.*

In a letter dated March 2, 1955, Langston Hughes wrote his longtime friend Arna Bontemps to congratulate him on the publication of Bontemps's latest children's book: "***Lonesome Boy*** is a perfectly charming and unusual book. I read it right off[;] it came in the mail today. I LOVE books that short and easy and pretty to read. It ought to make a wonderful gift book" (Nichols 330). Bontemps himself had written Hughes about the book a little more than a year earlier (on December 10, 1953): "This is the book I *enjoyed* writing, perhaps because I did it impulsively for myself, while editors hounded me for my misdeeds and threatened me if I did not deliver manuscripts I had contracted for. So I closed the door for two days and had myself a time" (Nichols 319). Another, perhaps more valid, reason he wrote this particular story about Bubber, a boy so lonesome he plays his trumpet whenever and wherever he can—ending up, as his grandfather subsequently explains, at a devil's ball—stems from Bontemps's own nostalgic feelings about his Louisiana heritage and, more specifically, about his own sense of being a lonesome boy.

A careful look at Bontemps's work shows the lonesome boy theme appearing over several years and in different forms. For example, Bontemps wrote a version of the story, **"Lonesome Boy, Silver Trumpet,"** in the 1930s, but it was not published until his collection of short fiction ***The Old South: "A Summer Tragedy" and Other Stories of the Thirties*** appeared a few weeks after his death in 1973. And on May 5, 1966, he delivered a speech at the New York Public Library which was published in December of that year as "The ***Lonesome Boy*** Theme" in *The Horn Book* magazine. There, he states that he has often used the theme, particularly to reflect on himself, since he began writing fiction:

> With me the lonesome-boy theme has persisted. Consciously or unconsciously, it too reflects influences. I used to avoid the first[-]person[-]singular in my writing; for some reason or other it embarrassed me. But despite my efforts—despite careful stratagems—I am afraid I did not always avoid autobiography. Born in Louisiana, carried by my parents to California at a very early age, I suspect that it is myself I see as I look back in each of the guises in which the lonesome boy has appeared since I introduced him in ***God Sends Sunday,*** my first book.
>
> (674)

Bontemps's use of the lonesome boy theme applies mainly to his children's literature, even though he clearly wrote ***God Sends Sunday*** for adult audiences.

While it would be facile to claim that all of his works—either for adults or children—reveal this autobiographical theme, his use of the theme suggests a reason behind the author's interest in writing for the young. A close examination of Bontemps's ***Lonesome Boy,*** therefore; can help explain his motivation to become one of the first authors of the twentieth century to write books for young African Americans. It can also explain some of his disillusionment with adult books and with the economics of the publishing world, which was still dominated by white publishers and white readers during the 1930s, even though the Harlem Renaissance would usher in permanent change.

Bontemps, at least temporarily, was shown to a bad seat during the 1930s. All three of his adult novels—***God Sends Sunday*** (1931), ***Black Thunder*** (1936), and ***Drums at Dusk*** (1939)—appeared during the Great Depression; none sold well. And even though he proposed several other novels and wrote at least one full-length, unpublished novel between 1939 and 1973, when he died, he did not publish an adult novel after ***Drums at Dusk. Chariot in the Sky*** (1951), Bontemps's semi-fictional account of the famous Fisk University Jubilee Singers, straddles the line between adolescent and adult material, although it was published as a book for older adolescents. As we shall see, economics as well as politics and autobiographical impulses motivated Bontemps to write for juvenile readers.

For public consumption, Bontemps justified his turn to juvenile writing from poetry and adult fiction with the claim that his novels were falling on blind eyes. Consider, for example, his "Introduction to the 1968 edition of ***Black Thunder,***" made more timely because of the Civil Rights Movement and the riotous explosions of anger in many American cities, including Watts, where Bontemps had lived as a child. Referring to the 1930s, he writes, "I began to suspect it was fruitless for a Negro in the United States to address serious writing to my generation, and I began to consider the alternative of trying to reach young readers not yet hardened or grown insensitive to man's inhumanity to man, as it is called" (xxiv).

In a 1970 interview with Margaret Perry, Bontemps claimed that he started writing children's literature because, when he was coming of age, he couldn't find images of black people) in his junior and senior high school reading experiences. Bontemps repeated this theme when he answered a question about his turn to writing children's books in a 1972 interview with John O'Brien:

> I was in no mood merely to write entertaining novels. The fact that *Gone With the Wind* was so popular at the time was a dramatic truth to me of what the country was willing to read. And I felt that black children had nothing with which they could identify.
>
> (13)

Carolyn Taylor provides another dimension to Bontemps's decision to write for children: ". . . he wanted young black people to be provided with carefully researched and documented facts about the richness of their historical past in Africa and America. He believed that only through knowledge of this complicated past could black youngsters direct and understand their identities and chart their own personal growth" (14). Kirkland Jones's biography of Bontemps, *Renaissance Man from Louisiana,* adds a slight variation before echoing Taylor: "He hoped to add a few stories that would help counteract the unpleasant traditions and associations of such stories as *Little Black Sambo* and *Epaminandos.* He was convinced that he had something better to offer America's children . . ." (83).

Finally, Bontemps revealed, albeit indirectly, another variation on these themes of his motivation for writing literature for African American children in his 1969 essay **"The Slave Narrative: An American Genre,"** printed as an introduction to his selected ***Great Slave Narratives.*** These comments reflect Bontemps's unusual scholastic history of being one of a very few African Americans educated in the predominantly white, religiously conservative, Seventh-Day Adventist San Fernando Academy. Paradoxically, the comments also reflect both a powerful and deeply felt sense of injustice and an equally heartfelt nostalgic longing coalescing around his plans in the 1960s to write his autobiography (titled ***A Man's Name***), but left unfinished at his death:

> When I was growing up, my teachers, as well as others unaware of what they were doing, gave me to understand that the only meaningful history of the Negro in the United States (possibly even in the world) began with the Emancipation Proclamation of 1863. In the half[-]century since my school days, I have had a chance to observe the tenacity of this assumption. As evidence to the contrary is disclosed, I begin to suspect that the colossal omissions they perpetuated were more than inadvertent. They were deliberate. Many may have been vindictive.
>
> (vii)

No wonder Bontemps wrote novels for adults about slave rebellions (***Black Thunder*** and ***Drums at Dusk***), as well as nonfiction history like ***The Story of the Negro*** and ***One Hundred Years of Negro Freedom.*** No wonder he wrote ***Chariot in the Sky*** and edited ***Golden Slippers*** and ***Hold Fast to Dreams*** (poetry anthologies for young people). No wonder he wrote about Bubber, the lonesome boy; Slumber, the sad-faced boy; and several other young African American males in their callow youth or in their adolescent curiosity learning about life as African Americans, learning of both their heritage and their status in a predominantly white society. Earlier, he had publicly bemoaned the lack of diversity in his scholastic reading assignments and the effect on him as a minority student when he accepted the Jane Addams Award in 1956 (for the enlarged 1955 edition of ***The Story of the Negro***): "These things I would like to have known as a school boy and as a college student in the integrated schools of California are also things I wish my classmates had learned on the same days when we were given the small fragments of generally uncomplimentary information about Negro Americans that was found in the texts and references then in use" (1). In other words, we see Bontemps, over and over again, addressing the lack of stories, nonfiction and fiction, about African Americans. We also see Bontemps's recognition that all students suffer when schools socialize students in a monocultural context. He set about remedying that no-longer-acceptable situation through his own literary production.

In her 1990 essay on Bontemps's children's literature published in *The Lion and The Unicorn,* Violet J. Harris asserted that his work in this field is oppositional. That is, its "author, consciously or unconsciously, creates a text that contradicts traditional portrayals of an ethnic, religious, linguistic, or gender group" (110). Harris credits Bontemps with "forging an oppositional tradition in children's literature," in part by creating "authentic images" (111), and she contends that Bontemps "is omitted from current editions of children's literature texts" and that his children's literature has not received the critical attention it deserves, even though he "almost single-handedly created a 'canon' of children's literature that focused, primarily, on the African-American experience" (110). As Harris also asserts, in spite of these oversights, some of Bontemps's books remain in print, and others have been reissued (110), most notably ***Lonesome Boy,*** which was reissued in both 1967 and 1988 but is currently out of print. (Oxford University Press recently republished Bontemps's and Hughes's ***Popo and Fifina: Children of Haiti*** in 1993, which helps to support Harris's contention.)

Although Bontemps publicly stated his political (that is, social and racial) motives for writing, especially for writing children's literature, the economic aspect remains submerged in his unpublished letters and papers. The most concise of his declarations that children's books were more economically feasible to produce than adult books occurs in a letter to John B. Turner (formerly John J. Trounstine), Bontemps's literary agent in the late 1930s and the 1940s. In a letter dated April 9, 1945, he takes pleasure in the fact that he is still receiving royalties from his 1934 juvenile ***You Can't Pet a Possum***: "Juveniles are wonderful. Every new one sells better than the rest, and all stay in print and keep moving. Would that the same could be said for novels." Unfortunately, some of the books stayed in print as long as they did because Bontemps agreed to reduced royalties as a condition of their longevity. A 1949 letter he wrote to Thayer Hobson of Morrow publishers illustrates this kind of agreement: "Of course I want to see You Can't Pet a Possum stay in print, and I'll agree to a limited royalty cut if that's the only possible way." At the same time, he tried to keep the percentage as high as possible, as his last paragraph indicates: "But I do not admire 9 [percent] as a figure. 10 is prettier."

As a writer, Bontemps constantly juggled many projects at the same time, often falling far behind projected deadlines. With its talk of being "hounded" and "threatened" by editors (Nichols 319), the letter to Hughes about ***Lonesome Boy*** quoted at the beginning of this essay alerts us to the pressures to complete work Bontemps often felt. In part, his production imperative stemmed from a relentless sense of providing an income for his family of eight (by 1945): himself, his six children, and Alberta, his wife. Not only did he have the writing projects, but also he tried—largely successfully—to keep a full-time job as either a teacher or a librarian, with interim work on the Illinois Writers' Project, a Work Projects Administration initiative to employ writers during the Depression years. He taught for three Seventh-Day Adventist schools early in his career: Harlem Academy in the 1920s, Oakwood Junior College (Huntsville, Alabama) in the early 1930s, and Shiloh Academy (Chicago) in the middle to late 1930s. The restrictive atmosphere—at both Oakwood and Shiloh, school officials suggested he burn his offending books, many by fellow Harlem Renaissance writers—finally forced him to cut off his association with the Church. According to Alex Bontemps, one of Arna's children, this action caused a rift in Arna Bontemps's relationship with his father, Paul Bismark Bontemps, who had become the top-ranking African American Adventist church official in California, but Arna held on as long as he did because he needed the income to support his family. Even when he found relative security in the library at Fisk University, where he worked for nearly thirty years, he still found it necessary to write for extra income, as well as to satisfy his creative drive.

Bontemps's family legacy (on both the paternal and maternal sides) embodied a strong work ethic and an even stronger sense of family responsibility, which leads us back to ***Lonesome Boy*** and its autobiographical elements. The relationship between the story's two main characters—Bubber, the prodigious boy trumpeter of the title, and his grandfather—resembles Bontemps's relationships with his father and, oddly, with his favorite family member, Joseph "Uncle Buddy" Ward, his maternal grandmother's brother. Paul Bismark Bontemps had himself been an itinerant trombone player in Claiborne Williams's jazz band, but he gave that up for a more stable job as a bricklayer-stone mason after study at Straight University in New Orleans (Jones 14-15). In the story, Bubber's grandfather admonishes him to watch how and where he plays his trumpet to avoid trouble. However, Bubber is so lonesome that blowing his trumpet hard, loud, and fast relieves his lonesomeness, even though it also causes him to be careless about his surroundings. He disregards his grandfather's warnings, goes to New Orleans, becomes a famous musician, and, finally, summoned by the devil himself, plays at the devil's ball, not realizing what has happened until he finds himself playing his trumpet in a pecan tree. Sheepishly, he returns to his grandfather's home and is welcomed with what we now call comfort food and an understanding grandfather who also played at a devil's ball when he was young. The authority figure of the grandfather resembles Paul Bontemps, who became an Adventist minister in California. But he also resembles Joseph Ward, an alcoholic labeled by Paul Bontemps as "don't care folks" (qtd. in Jones 39), in his knowledge of the folk tradition. That Bontemps combined elements of these significant figures in his life suggests he yearned for a parental figure with a mixture of seriousness and carelessness about life.

One could argue, in fact, that the story signifies Arna Bontemps's early career, with its rapid rise in Harlem during the Renaissance, as an equivalent to Bubber's New Orleans success. Bontemps's sojourn in Alabama could be signified by the devil's ball in the story, and Bubber's return home could signify Arna Bontemps's return to his father's home in California to finish writing ***Black Thunder,*** away from the scornful gaze of the Oakwood elders. As Charles James points out, however, the roles could be taken back a generation, with Bubber signifying Paul Bismark Bontemps as a youthful musician who learned the major lesson of the book (115n): "When you're lonesome, that's the time to go out and find somebody to talk to" (Bontemps, ***Lonesome*** 28). The elder Bontemps "was born in 1872 near Marksville[, the locale of Bubber's grandfather's house in the story,] at a small site known as Barbin's Landing" (James 115). In the story, Bubber catches a river boat headed toward New Orleans at Barbin's Landing, and he is known in New Orleans as the boy from Marksville. At least the caller who summons him to play at the devil's ball identifies him as "the boy from Marksville, the one who plays the trumpet" (***Lonesome*** 13).

Other evidence that the story has autobiographical elements includes Bontemps's comments in letters to his editors that the dedication should read "To Constance" (his youngest daughter) and that the location should be Louisiana, with the use of Robert Flaherty's documentary *Louisiana Story* as a good source for exterior illustrations. Kirkland Jones maintains that the story's autobiographical base lies in

> an episode the author during his boyhood heard a preacher tell in church. It was a narrative about a young man who liked jazz. He awoke one morning to find himself up high in an apple tree and announced he had been celebrating the devil's ball. . . . Actually, the book is about Bontemps's own conception of "waltziness": a person hearing faraway music within himself is so pleased with it, so engrossed in seeking self-satisfaction, that the end result is negative.

Jones deduces a substantial concept about Bontemps's philosophy from this story: "Hedonistic self-gratification" isolates a person "within his own heart," creating a kind of self-violation and "shutting out all the rest of experience" (132).

In addition to his declaration that the lonesome boy theme fits his own experiences, Bontemps seemed to treat this story differently from most of his other work. For example, its singular status as a story Bontemps published twice during his life (as ***Lonesome Boy,*** separately, 1955, and in ***The Book of Negro Folklore,*** edited by Bontemps and Hughes, 1958) and once posthumously in the collection of stories titled ***The Old South: "A Summer Tragedy" and Other Stories of the Thirties*** (as **"Lonesome Boy, Silver Trumpet"**) suggests his affinity for it. The other two stories—both published in the 1930s and in ***The Old South*****—"A Summer Tragedy"** and **"Saturday Night"** (published with two different subtitles), do not quite rival Bontemps's publication frequency of ***Lonesome Boy*** and do not involve parent-child relationships. (Neither space nor affinity allows a discussion of either **"A Summer Tragedy"** or **"Saturday Night"** within the context of Bontemps's children's literature.) And apparently Bontemps identified himself as the **"Sad-Faced Author,"** the title of another *Horn Book* magazine article about his children's literature published in 1939. Aside from the title, however, he did not strongly identify himself with the sad-faced type. Instead he traced the origin of his ***Sad-Faced Boy*** characters (Slumber, Rags, and Willie) to J. P. Morgan and two of his three cousins, real children in Alabama who sang for Bontemps and his family. After hearing stories about Harlem from Bontemps, they journeyed north to Harlem to enjoy moderate success as street musicians, only to return to their home relieved to be back after their urban adventure turned sour when Morgan had his new shoes stolen while wearing them (Bontemps, **"Sad"** 11-12). As Bontemps indicates near the end of this article, the story of J. P. Morgan and his cousins became, with the basics intact but with authorial embellishment, his 1937 children's book ***Sad-Faced Boy.***

The three publications of the "Lonesome Boy" story differ, but not by much, mainly at the very end of the story (and in the titles, of course). In fact, the galley pages of the 1955 edition more closely resemble the version published in ***The Old South*** than they resemble the 1955 separate publication of the story. The Table of Contents galley page from ***The Old South*** contains this note written by Bontemps:

> "***Lonesome Boy*** and ***Mr. Kelso's Lion,*** both written originally as adult short stories, have been published as juveniles by Houghton Mifflin and J. B. Lippincott, respectively" (v).

The differences speak to Bontemps's sense of adult as opposed to children's literature. The children's version has a longer reconciliation scene between Bubber and his grandfather, part of it repeating dialogue from the beginning of the story.

Trying to distinguish between adult and children's literature can prove difficult with this story since Bontemps himself commented about its ambiguity. Both the Houghton Mifflin editor and some reviewers also stated that it didn't seem to separate its audiences cleanly. In a letter dated December 9, 1952, Houghton Mifflin's Editor of Children's Books, Mary Silva Cosgrave, wrote to Bontemps, "Some of our readers feel that it is too old in theme for the young and too slight for the old. . . . I have been toying with the idea of a book for the 11-13 age group. . . ." Bontemps responded on December 12, 1952, in part by speculating about audience differentiation: "I have dared to think that, given a little luck, this might become the kind of story that certain adults might also pick up and chuckle over, especially repentant hep cats and be-boppers. Perhaps after an evening in a night club." A little over a year later, in a letter dated February 26, 1954, Bontemps expressed a similar sentiment about the manuscript to Cosgrave in a postscript, "Are you hoping, as I am, that ***Lonesome Boy*** will have some appeal for the adult audience that reads the juveniles of, say Thurber and E. B. White? Is there a way to point up this other dimension?"

Reviewers, too, initially noticed this apparent audience ambiguity. For example, Augusta Baker's *Saturday Review* comments describe a "most unusual story . . . for the sensitive, perceptive child and adult" (40). Writing in *The New York Times Book Review,* Ellen Lewis Buell suggests that the story can be read as a cautionary tale against investing too much in a private world to the neglect of meaningful relationships with other people, a warning valid for both youth and adult. Violet Harris discusses the story using the archetypal quest as the governing motif, a motif found universally in literature written for all ages, while claiming it as "arguably his best for children" and declaring it an unacknowledged "classic in children's literature" (123).

Examining the five different variations on the ending reproduced in the Appendix shows that Bontemps worked closely with his editor at Houghton Mifflin to tailor the story to reach the early adolescent reading audience. Such an analysis might also help to support Harris's claim to classic status for ***Lonesome Boy.*** The variation published as an adult story and comprising Drafts A and B, as well as the 1973 published version (written earlier, ostensibly in the 1930s), leaves the most to the imagination and to the creative reading and interpretive skills of adults. It emphasizes reconciliation and a return home over morals or messages. The longer version published as the children's book elaborates but simplifies the ending and repeats some of Grandpa's admonitory dialogue from earlier in the story. The Galleys version adds only one sentence to the adult version: a sentence suggested by Bontemps in response to his editor's request to clarify the aftereffects of Bubber's experience playing for the devil (or dreaming about it, at least). The addition of the line "'A little bit of trumpet playing is all right, but too much is enough'" suggests Grandpa's willingness to encourage Bubber to continue to blow his trumpet—but only in moderation and awareness, not with abandonment. That seems fair enough, but the final published version goes much further in this direction. It takes Grandpa into the realm of morality, like a priest at confession—stern, but forgiving. It also reiterates the message, almost to a fault, at least for adult readers. The sentence "'Raising a boy like you ain't easy'" fits this description.

Quoting at length from Bontemps's Houghton Mifflin editor provides a fitting end to this essay about the importance of the "Lonesome Boy" theme, as well as the story itself, in Bontemps's children's literature. Mary Silva Cosgrave's initial response of December 9, 1942 (eighteen days after her marriage), speaks for itself: "Thank you for introducing us to Bubber. We have all enjoyed the story tremendously. It has the wonderful free quality of 'pouring itself out' with a tremendous sweep and feeling. The writing is beautiful." Not only is it beautiful, but it signifies the range of ambition Bontemps set for himself to serve as a catalyst for and to produce authentic African American children's literature comprising real characters confronting real problems, with a healthy dollop of folklore thrown in as lagniappe, of course, to remind us of its author's Louisiana heritage and to point to its autobiographical possibilities.

Works Cited

Baker, Augusta. Rev. of *Lonesome Boy. Saturday Review* 19 Mar. 1955: 40.

Bontemps, Alex. Interview. Hanover, NH. 5, 9 Aug. 1994.

Bontemps, Arna W. "Introduction to the 1968 Edition." *Black Thunder.* Boston: Beacon, 1992, xxi-xxix.

———. Letters to Mary Silva Cosgrave. 12 Dec. 1952, 8 Dec. 1953, 14 Dec. 1953, 29 Jan. 1954, 26 Feb. 1954. Arna W. Bontemps Collection, Syracuse U Library, Syracuse, NY.

———. Letter to Thayer Hobson. 29 Mar. 1949. Arna W. Bontemps Collection. Syracuse U Library, Syracuse, NY.

———. Letter to John B. Turner. 9 Apr. 1945. Arna W. Bontemps Collection, Syracuse U Library, Syracuse, NY.

———. *Lonesome Boy.* Boston: Houghton, 1955.

———. "Lonesome Boy, Silver Trumpet." Draft A ts.; Draft B ts.; Galleys. Arna W. Bontemps Collection, Syracuse U Library, Syracuse, NY.

———. "Lonesome Boy, Silver Trumpet." *The Old South: "A Summer Tragedy" and Other Stories of the Thirties.* New York: Dodd, 1973. 57-70.

———. "The *Lonesome Boy* Theme." *Horn Book* 42 (1966): 672-80.

———. "On Receiving the Jane Addams Book Award." Ts. of speech delivered 20 Nov. 1956. Arna W. Bontemps Collection, Syracuse U Library, Syracuse, NY.

———. "Sad-Faced Author." *Horn Book* 15 (1939): 7-12.

———. "The Slave Narrative: An American Genre." *Great Slave Narratives.* Ed. Bontemps. Boston: Beacon, 1969. vii-xix.

Buell, Ellen Lewis. "The Silver Trumpet." Rev. of *Lonesome Boy. New York Times Book Review* 1 May 1955: 28.

Cosgrave, Mary Silva. Letter to Arna W. Bontemps. 9 Dec. 1952. Arna W. Bontemps Collection, Syracuse U Library, Syracuse, NY.

Harris, Violet J. "From *Little Black Sambo* to *Popo and Fifina*: Arna Bontemps and the Creation of African-American Children's Literature." *Lion and the Unicorn* 14 (1990): 108-27.

James, Charles L. "Arna Bontemps's Creole Heritage." *Syracuse University Library Courier* 30 (1995): 91-115.

Jones, Kirkland C. *Renaissance Man from Louisiana: A Biography of Arna Wendell Bontemps.* Westport: Greenwood, 1992.

Nichols, Charles H., ed. *Arna Bontemps-Langston Hughes Letters: 1925-1967.* 1980. New York: Paragon, 1990.

O'Brien, John. "Arna Bontemps." *Interviews with Black Authors.* Ed. O'Brien. New York: Liveright, 1973. 2-11.

Perry, Margaret. Interview with Bontemps. 11 Dec. 1970. New Haven, CT. Tape in Arna W. Bontemps Collection, Syracuse U Library, Syracuse, NY.

Taylor, Carolyn. Discussion Guide. *Profiles of Black Achievement: Arna Bontemps/Aaron Douglas.* Sound Filmstrip. New York: Guidance Associates, 1973.

DOUGLAS FLAMMING (ESSAY DATE 1999)

SOURCE: Flamming, Douglas. "A Westerner in Search of 'Negro-ness:' Region and Race in the Writing of Arna Bontemps." In *Over the Edge: Remapping the American West,* edited by Valerie J. Matsumoto and Blake Allmendinger, pp. 85-104. Berkeley: University of California Press, 1999.

In the following essay, Flamming examines Bontemps's life, the conflicting male role models offered by his father and his Uncle Buddy, and his determination to find a Black American identity—a search that compelled him to leave behind the Californian west of his childhood to head first to the East (the center of the Harlem Renaissance), and then to the South, the land of his ancestors.

In 1917, Paul Bontemps of Watts, California, sent his only son, Arna, to a boarding school in nearby Los Angeles. Arna Bontemps, destined to become one of the most prolific and versatile African American writers of the twentieth century, was not quite fifteen at the time. Before parting, the father advised his son: "'Now don't go up there acting colored.'" These were words Arna Bontemps never forgot and, in a sense, never forgave. Fifty years later he recalled his father's admonition and answered: "How dare anyone—parent, schoolteacher, or merely literary critic—tell me not to act *colored.*"[1]

What did it mean to act "colored" in the early twentieth-century West? Bontemps's own answer, negotiated during his young adulthood in California and subsequently represented in his literature, suggests the complex relationship between region and racial identity. Bontemps saw his father as a manifestation of the West, as one who had forsaken his Afro-southern roots in an effort to become colorless. He saw his great uncle, Buddy Ward, as a manifestation of the South, as one who had reluctantly migrated West and refused to surrender his Afro-southern folkways. Growing up largely isolated from the small black community in Los Angeles, Arna gradually began to question his father's view and to envy Uncle Buddy's sense of heritage. He developed a longing for what he later called "Negro-ness," which he saw as a southern, not western, quality. Throughout his high-school and college years, he grappled with the conflict between his father and Buddy. ultimately concluding that he must re-establish ties with the African American culture he felt he had lost in the West. That was why, in 1924, at the age of twenty-one, he left Los Angeles for New York's Harlem and the "New Negro" Renaissance, hoping not only to establish himself as a writer but also to discover his own identity as a black American.

Later in life, Bontemps published several autobiographical essays that examined his childhood in California and the tensions between his father and Uncle Buddy.[2] In these self-reflective pieces, Bontemps reduced the complex personalities of Paul and Buddy to their least common denominators; the two men functioned as simple metaphors for complicated realities. The autobiographies themselves were thus something akin to fiction, as Bontemps probably realized. But in the question of identity—Bontemps's identity and everyone else's—personal constructions intersect with empirical context in fascinating and instructive ways. The cultural conflict between Paul and Buddy, and more particularly Arna's understanding and reaction to that conflict, opens a window on a much-neglected topic of Afro-western history—the issue of black identity:

A recent biography of Arna Bontemps by Kirkland C. Jones bears the curious title, *Renaissance Man from Louisiana.* Bontemps was born in Louisiana, but he was not really *from* there. The only "Southland" he really knew in the 1920s was southern California; his family brought him to Los Angeles County when he was four years old and, except for his college years in northern California, he remained there until he moved to Harlem in 1924. In a symbolic sense, though, Jones's title hits the mark. It reflects Bontemps's yearning for his Louisiana "home," a longing that profoundly influenced his life and literature.[3]

Arna was born in the small town of Alexandria in 1902, the first child of Paul and Maria (Pembrooke) Bontemps. Both of his parents were from mulatto families with long, mostly free-black histories in the heavily French Creole region of central Louisiana. Maria was a schoolteacher who prized learning, purged her voice of southern accent, and longed for her children to receive good educations outside of the South. Arna's father had received formal vocational training in New Orleans and, like so many Creole men in Louisiana, had become a skilled brick mason. In his youth, Paul Bontemps was also a musician, occasionally blowing horn for Louisiana ragtime bands. Thinking back on his life in a 1965 autobiographical essay, Arna Bontemps reflected that "mine had not been a varmint-infested childhood so often the hallmark of Negro American autobiography. My parents and grandparents had been well-fed, well-clothed, and well-housed."[4]

His parents nonetheless felt compelled to leave the South in 1906, when Arna was only four. The education they wanted for Arna and his sister, Ruby, could not be had in Louisiana. And there were more immediate concerns. The Atlanta race riot of 1906 stirred racial animosities across the South and rippled through Alexandria. Paul Bontemps did not want to leave the South, but his safety and that of his family seemed increasingly imperiled.[5]

He therefore moved his own family and Maria's parents to southern California, settling just south of Los Angeles city. Paul and Maria bought a house in the small settlement of Watts. "We moved into a house in a neighborhood where we were the only colored family," Arna remembered. "The people next door and up and down the block were friendly and talkative, the weather was perfect, there wasn't a mud puddle anywhere, and my mother seemed to float about on the clean air." Maria's parents, preferring a more rural environment, bought several acres of farmland between Watts and Los Angeles, in what local residents called the "Furlough Track," where they built a substantial house and a barn.[6]

Watts and the Furlough Track were scarcely developed when the Bontemps and Pembrooke families arrived in 1906. What growth there was resulted from Henry E. Huntington's Pacific Electric streetcar line, completed in 1902, which stretched from Los Angeles to Long Beach and ran north-south through the area. Watts became an incorporated municipality not long after the Bontempses arrived, but even by 1910 the population of the town had not reached two thousand, with fewer than forty blacks. Slightly to the north of Watts, the Furlough Track was an eclectic, diverse area. A scattering of black families had settled amidst the Anglo farmers, along with a small community of Mexican families who had moved there to construct the interurban railway and then put down roots.[7]

Los Angeles city boomed in the early twentieth century, and its black population grew rapidly as well—from about 100 in 1880 to nearly 7,600 by 1910. By 1920, African Americans in Los Angeles numbered at least 15,579; ten years later the figure rose to nearly 39,000, which now included the blacks who lived in Watts, which was annexed by Los Angeles in the mid-1920s. Still, the concomitant growth of the European, Japanese, and Mexican-heritage communities meant that blacks made up only a small percentage of the local population, usually between 2 or 3 percent. The African American community in Watts, like that in nearby Pasadena, was a smaller version of the black community in Los Angeles. Throughout the towns and cities of Los Angeles county, black communities represented small minority populations that were predominantly middle class, with high rates of home ownership and political activism. In this regard, they had much in common with other African American communities that emerged in the principal Pacific Coast cities.[8]

As more blacks moved to Los Angeles and surrounding communities, Anglo resistance to blacks in "white" residential districts forced most African Americans to live in certain areas, which amounted to embryonic ghettos. But the key word is embryonic, for the Los Angeles neighborhoods "open" to people of color remained predominantly white through the 1920s, with blacks, Mexicans, Russian Jews, Japanese, and Filipinos occupying loosely defined ethnic enclaves therein. For blacks in southern California during Arna Bontemps's childhood and young adulthood, the West offered a more open and diverse society than the Jim Crow South, whose viciously discriminatory racial system had driven Paul Bontemps westward.

For Arna's father, the move to California was more than a relocation. It was a conscious break from the past, from the South, and even, to some degree, from his race. He gave up playing jazz and committed himself to masonry and construction work. More important, he gave up the Catholicism of Creole Louisiana and led his entire family into the Seventh-Day Adventist Church, a decision that profoundly influenced Arna's life. Shortly after joining the Adventist fold, Paul Bontemps became the first black Adventist minister in the West. Eventually, he would abandon the masonry trade and devote himself full-time to the church.[9]

Paul Bontemps gave himself to the standard American vision of the West—to the idea of starting over, to the creed of a better future. His was not a frivolous undertaking. He made hard, disciplined decisions. He committed himself to his children's future. Reminiscing about Louisiana with relatives, he said: "Sometimes I miss all that. If I was just thinking about myself, I might want to go back and try it again. But I've got the children to think about—their education.'" When Maria died of illness in 1914, leaving Arna motherless at twelve, Paul's parental duties weighed heavier and his commitment to the children's education deepened. Arna later recalled that his own education and that of his sister was "one of the things [my father] took pride in and devoted himself to."[10]

For Paul Bontemps education was one means of becoming fully American, or perhaps as he saw it, fully western. In southern California, he strove not to be a successful "black" man, but a successful man. Success, as he saw it, required a certain colorlessness, a conscious abandonment of ethnic culture. Not that he misunderstood the power of race. His masonry work in Los Angeles was curtailed in part by racist white trade unions, and the churches he pastored were all-black (by custom as much as by Adventist polity). But he saw his racial identity as something to rise above. For him, acting "colored" meant a way of thinking and behaving that kept individuals down. For him, "colored" meant aspects of Afro-southern folk culture that he and other middle-class blacks thought of as checks on middle-class respectability and economic success: loud talk, dialect speech, ostentatious dress, belief in superstition. He hoped Arna's integrated upbringing and schooling would shield him from such influences, and he sought to set an example for Arna to follow. Or so Arna perceived his father's views.

But there were other examples for Arna's observation, in particular his great-uncle, John Ward, known to the family as Buddy. In his youth, Buddy had been an urbane ladies' man with style and flash. But it was hard to maintain Creole pride in Jim Crow Louisiana, and Buddy's life eventually sank deep into a bottle. Ruined and penniless, he was institutionalized in New Orleans until he dried out. Then he moved West, joining the family (his sister was Arna's grandmother) in southern California. His arrival caused a stir. Young Arna, expecting the "young mulatto dandy with an elegant cravat and jeweled stickpin" that he has seen in a family photograph, was shocked when a terribly disheveled Buddy stumbled through the door: "he entered wearing a detachable collar without a tie and did not remove his hat. His clothes did not fit. They had been slept in for nearly a week on the train. His shoes had come unlaced. His face was pocked marked. Nothing in his appearance resembled the picture in the living room."[11]

But Uncle Buddy had an ace up his sleeve, or rather in his suitcase, which contained no clothes at all but was filled with treats and gifts from Louisiana—"jars of syrup, bags of candy my grandmother had said in her letters that she missed, pecans, plus filé for making gumbo." He talked about the South and held the family's rapt attention. As Buddy brought the Californians up-to-date on the news from back home, young Arna "became entranced" with Buddy and the South. It was a feeling he never quite lost, reinforced as it was by Buddy's ongoing presence. From 1908, when Arna's grandfather Pembrooke died, until 1917, when Arna went to boarding school, the Bontempses lived at the Pembrooke farmhouse. Buddy lived there, too, during Arna's most impressionable years.[12]

Living at the Pembrooke house, Buddy turned out to be everything Paul Bontemps sought to avoid. Buddy used the word "nigger" with a casual ease that Paul openly condemned, and he brought loud, drunken friends to the house. In Arna's estimation, "they were not bad people." But they were "what my father described as don't-care folk." And, to make matters worse for Paul, "Buddy was still crazy about the minstrel shows and minstrel talk that had been the joy of his young manhood. He loved dialect stories, preacher stories, ghost stories, slave and master stories. He half-believed in signs and charms and mumbo-jumbo, and he believed whole-heartedly in ghosts." Paul Bontemps had a word for such a person, and that word was "colored." To his distress, Buddy and Arna spent long hours together; his son loved the old man and was fascinated by his stories of the South.[13]

The conflict between Paul Bontemps and Uncle Buddy was nothing less than a struggle for young Arna's soul. It was one man's West against another man's South; it was disciplined practicality against joyful folkways. It was hope for an integrated future versus love of a racial past. And as the years passed, Arna began to understand the dynamics of that struggle. When his father sent him to the Adventist academy in the San Fernando Valley, Arna "took it that my father was still endeavoring to counter Buddy's baneful influence." There was more to it than that: Paul needed to take a well-paying masonry job outside the city, and the San Fernando Academy offered an excellent academic environment for his smart son. No doubt, though, Paul Bontemps hoped the distance between Arna and Buddy would be advantageous. Hence, his admonition to Arna: "'don't go up there acting colored.'"[14]

Through high school and college the son respected his father's wishes. Arna thrived in the Adventist schools and followed Paul Bontemps's disciplined, intellectual path. He did not act like Uncle Buddy. He worked hard, watched his manners, and excelled in his studies. Throughout his entire life, Bontemps would remain an efficient, disciplined worker. In actual fact, there was nothing "colorless" about such behavior, but Arna had come to define his world and his race in the diametrically opposed examples of Paul and Buddy. Arna mildly defied his father during his college years (at Pacific Union, an Adventist school some fifty miles northeast of San Francisco), when he abandoned the pre-med studies Paul had recommended, changed his major to English, and announced his intention of becoming a writer. Paul Bontemps voiced his disapproval but nonetheless took pride in Arna's educational achievements.[15]

Ironically, the academic world that Paul Bontemps assumed would keep Arna's Negro-ness at bay had just the opposite effect. With the exception of one colored girl in his second grade class, Arna was always the only black person in his class, from first grade through his college graduation. "I was just a lone wolf," he recalled. Despite his generally positive school experiences, and his friendships with classmates and teachers, color obviously set him apart. "Teachers always assumed that I was going to be at the bottom of the class, and when they found out I wasn't, this sort of shook 'em up a little bit." Arna laughed it off, but deep down those racial assumptions began to grate. So did the absence of black people in his history books. As early as age twelve he was frequenting the public libraries in Watts and Los Angeles looking for books about Negro life. "I was seeking a recognizable reflection of myself and my world in the collections of books available to a boy reader," he recalled. "What I found was cold comfort, to say the least."[16]

Gradually, he concluded that his schoolteachers were shielding him from a proper understanding of the African American past. Some did not know any better, he thought, but others probably did. "I began to suspect," he later wrote, "that the colossal omissions they perpetuated were more than inadvertent. They were deliberate. Many may have been vindictive." Thus, a young and bookish Arna Bontemps, surrounded in school by whites who knew nothing of black history and cared less, developed an intense longing for a meaningful racial heritage and began what his biographer has aptly called a "journey into blackness."[17]

Buddy was more than happy to help Arna make that journey, and, as a result, Arna's definition of Negro-ness would always bear a close resemblance to Buddy and his stories of the South. Buddy had said "I'd a heap rather be down home than [in California], if it wasn't for the *conditions.*" Even his father, in more relaxed moments, longingly recalled Louisiana. For Arna, that only underscored the lure of the South and made the West seem increasingly colorless.[18]

One curious point here—and Bontemps himself, introspective and insightful as he was, never quite registered it—was that Los Angeles was in no way devoid of Negro-ness, however it might be defined. The vast majority of blacks in southern California were southern-born and southern-raised, and Arna had relatives from Alexandria living in Los Angeles, including his close friend and cousin, Benny.

Consider, too, Arna's experiences when he came home summers from college (usually staying in the city with cousin Benny). In 1922, while taking summer school courses at UCLA, he discovered a copy of *Harlem Shadows,* a collection of poems by the Jamaican-born writer Claude McKay. Bontemps devoured it several times over, and "then began telling everybody I knew about it." When he read McKay's poems to his black friends, Bontemps was struck by their reactions. "Nearly all of them stopped to listen," he later wrote. "There was no doubt that their blood came to a boil when they heard 'If We Must Die.' 'Harlem Dancer' brought worldly-wise looks from their eyes. McKay's poems of longing for his home island melted them visibly, and I think these responses told me something about black people and poetry that remains true."[19]

That same summer he discovered Jelly Roll Morton and jazz. Morton, from New Orleans via Chicago, would play in town until the midnight curfew, then move south of the city limits, beyond Watts to Leak's Lake pavilion and play some more. Bontemps and his cousin Benny, who played trumpet with a band at Leak's Lake, would go "and listen closely to the haunting music throughout the night." About that time, too, the messianic Back-to-Africa leader, Marcus Garvey, visited Los Angeles and packed the Trinity Auditorium, Bontemps being one in attendance.[20]

FROM THE AUTHOR

BONTEMPS ON BEING COLORED

How dare anyone, parent, schoolteacher, or merely literary critic, tell me not to act colored.

SOURCE: Arna Bontemps quoted in *Colored People: A Memoir,* by Henry Louis Gates, Knopf, 1994.

Despite the richness of these experiences and the increasing vitality of the local black community, Arna Bontemps felt that he could not truly find himself or his heritage in Los Angeles. Other observers were more impressed with the black West. Chandler Owen of Harlem, editor of the national black journal *The Messenger,* visited southern California on a speaking tour in 1922. Owen gazed upon Central Avenue and called it "a veritable little Harlem, in Los Angeles." And yet, for Bontemps, Los Angeles could never be what Harlem was, a Mecca for the black world of the twenties.[21]

"Before I finished college," he wrote, "I had begun to feel that in some large and important areas I was being miseducated, and that perhaps I should have rebelled." The Adventist schools he attended in California were academically excellent, and some of his teachers actively promoted his writing talents; in that sense, his western upbringing had given him permission to dream of being a writer. But at the same time, he felt that the West had somehow robbed him of his birthright—a personal connection to Negro life. His father's coldness for things "colored" clashed with Arna's love for Buddy and his curiosity about black history.[22]

The result was Arna's sharply bifurcated view of heritage, region, and identity. "In their opposing attitudes toward roots my father and my great uncle made me aware of a conflict in which every educated American Negro, and some who are not educated, must somehow take sides," Arna wrote in the last decade of his life. "By implication at least, one group advocates embracing the riches of the folk heritage; their opposites demand a clean break with the past and all it represents." By the time he graduated from Pacific Union, there was no possibility that he would choose the latter.[23]

"So," asked Arna Bontemps, "what did one do after concluding that for him a break with the past and the shedding of his Negro-ness were not only impossible but unthinkable?" His own answer was to go to Harlem: where the "Negro Art Renaissance," as W. E. B. Du Bois called it, was blooming; where Claude McKay had written his poems; where Langston Hughes (another young heritage-starved westerner) and other black writers were publishing verse and fiction. In 1924 Bontemps left a post-office job in Los Angeles to become a writer in the Harlem Renaissance.[24]

It was a cautious rebellion. His father was at the station to see him off. Arna already had the promise of a teaching job at the Harlem Academy, an Adventist high school. He had also received some affirmation of his talent on a national scale. Early in the summer of 1924 he received word that *Crisis* would publish one of his poems, appropriately titled **"Hope."** That was all the incentive he needed. His train pulled into New York in August 1924, he caught the subway to Harlem, got off at 125th Street, and walked up into what was for Arna Bontemps the most beautiful world he had ever seen.[25]

As he later described it, Harlem in 1924 "was like a foretaste of paradise. A blue haze descended at night and with it strings of fairy lights on the broad avenues. From the window of a small room in an apartment on Fifth and 129th Street I looked over the rooftops of Negrodom and tried to believe my eyes. What a city! What a world!" He went to the Harlem public library and found young black women employed at the front desk, a sight unknown back home. Better yet, the young woman who accepted his application for a library card recognized his name from his recently published poem in *Crisis.* It was a sweet beginning, and things only got better as he quickly became an accepted figure in Renaissance circles. By day, he taught at Harlem Academy. By night, he roamed with the poets. Before long he married and roamed less, but he continued to love Harlem and to write about the heritage of race.[26]

Arna Bontemps went to Harlem to explore the South or, as he might have said it, southern *Negroness.* The irony was that he was a westerner seeking Dixie's soul in a northern ghetto. It would be years, in fact, before he actually experienced the South first hand. In Harlem, Bontemps became part of a young generation of western writers and artists who were energizing the New Negro Renaissance. Although Harlem attracted blacks from all across the United States and from the Caribbean, most of the young mavericks of the Renaissance's explosive years—from the publication of ***The***

New Negro in 1925 to Wallace Thurman's *Infants of Spring* in 1932—were from the West. Besides Bontemps, blacks from the West included the well-known Langston Hughes (from Lawrence, Kansas), Aaron Douglas (from Topeka, Kansas, with a B.A. in Fine Arts from the University of Nebraska), and Wallace Thurman (from Salt Lake City, Utah, with some time spent at the University of Southern California). Like Bontemps these young people were educated in predominantly white schools. They shared his emotional need to explore black culture (especially the lower-class black culture that seemed to them unquestionably "Negro") and to express that culture in their art.[27]

Bontemps's career in Harlem evolved differently from that of the other black westerners. His work was less dramatic than that of Hughes or Douglas, and it was never explosively controversial, like that of Thurman. But he began producing award-winning poetry and short stories immediately, establishing the disciplined work habits that would mark his astonishingly productive career of nearly fifty years as a writer of novels, short stories, poetry, children's literature, memoirs, and history, and as an editor of historical and literary anthologies. Largely ignored in the standard accounts of the Renaissance, and inaccurately described by one scholar as a poet who was "struggling in Harlem," Bontemps found a comfortable niche in Harlem early on.[28]

A good day job and his marriage in 1926 to one of his students, Alberta Johnson, set him apart as an unusually settled member of the young Renaissance crowd. He was one of the few black artists of the Renaissance to marry, settle down, and have children. Family life curtailed Bontemps's appearances on Harlem's night-club circuit, but he gave no indication that he missed the bohemian scene. If his soul found comfort in Uncle Buddy's world, Arna nonetheless maintained a substantial share of his father's discipline and responsibility.

Bontemps accepted the prevailing worldview of the young generation of New Negro artists and the wealthy whites who underwrote much of their work. The basic goal was to restore "primitivism" to a soulless world. Broadly put, the new ethic ran as follows: the modern world was on the verge of disaster because the European pursuit of civilization had crushed the primitive and natural aspects of life that were critical to humanity's well being; Negroes—African and American alike—had preserved at least some of their primitivism; by presenting that primitivism in their art and letters, New Negroes might save modern civilization from its drought of soul. A resurgence of primitivism (and a romanticization of it) was not Du Bois's idea of Renaissance, but it *was* what Hughes, Douglas, and Bontemps had in mind. In giving voice to primitivism—to what they considered the authentic and almost-extinct voice of African Americans—the black westerners sought at last to find their own true selves, to save Negro Americans from their ongoing loss of Negro-ness, and perhaps to save the soul of the nation. "The idea," Bontemps recalled, "intoxicated us."[29]

Acting colored, or rather the self-expression of "color" in literature and art, was largely the aim of Bontemps and the western contingent of the Renaissance crowd. Before long, this trend prompted a struggle between some of the "old guard" Harlem writers (led by Du Bois) and the western newcomers, a struggle that paralleled the rift between Paul Bontemps and Uncle Buddy, and a cultural schism that might best be understood as a regional fault line.

For Du Bois, black art had a specific political purpose. White racist stereotypes of black Americans seized upon promiscuous, dialect-speaking, lower-class caricatures to discredit all blacks. Respectable art by educated blacks, Du Bois reasoned, offered the best way to undermine white racist stereotypes. This dominant assumption among leading black intellectuals rendered some subjects taboo, including black promiscuity, drunkenness, and southern-style primitivism in general.

But the western blacks who dominated the post-1925 Renaissance had no desire to distance their art from the earthier aspects of African American culture. Indeed, they had moved to Harlem to close the gap between themselves and Afro-southern folk culture. Artistically, they loved jungle scenes, jazz rhythms, blues sensibilities, sensuality, thick dialect—all the things Paul Bontemps saw as "colored."

The trend could be seen in a series of works by the black western writers. Langston Hughes's first book of poems, *The Weary Blues* (1926), set the tone by plunging his verse into the world of the black masses, explicitly linking African jungle moons and tribal dances with Harlem cabarets and jazz-filled nights. That same year, Wallace Thurman's ill-fated journal *Fire!!* (it lasted only one issue) received the ire of New York's established black intellectuals for showcasing the very subjects considered inappropriate by the old guard. (Subsequently, Thurman's two successes in 1929—the Broadway hit *Harlem* and his first novel, *The Blacker the Berry . . .*—would also emphasize the bawdier aspects of black life in Harlem.) The debate over "racial" art boiled up in New York's intellectual circles, but Arna Bontemps never wavered in his belief that "colored" representations (as he and his friends defined them) were much-needed in literature.[30]

Bontemps's first novel ***God Sends Sunday*** (1931) underscored his commitment to racial art by presenting as its main theme the Afro-southern misadventures of Uncle Buddy.[31] Bontemps did not care to write about a westerner who moved to Harlem, as did Wallace Thurman in *The Blacker the Berry . . .*[32] Nor did he use the black West as his setting, as Langston Hughes did in his novel, *Not Without Laughter* (1930).[33] Bontemps wanted to write about the South, the region he once called "that vast everglade of black life."[34]

God Sends Sunday is all about Afro-southern folk culture. The protagonist is Buddy incarnate, thinly veiled as a jockey named Little Augie. Virtually all of the characters in the book are what Bontemps's father would have called "don't-care" folks. They are sporting men and painted women, whose earthy dialect and violent behavior flow like the Mississippi in full flood as they wander up and down between New Orleans and St. Louis. And they do not, in fact, care about anything but good times and immediate gratification. Little Augie race horses, chases women, gambles, and fights, his luck with horses and women running hot and cold until he finally hits rock bottom. Then he goes West to find his sister.

At last Augie arrives in Los Angeles, or rather in Mudtown, "the Negro neighborhood" outside of Watts. Mudtown, he discovers, "was like a tiny section of the deep south literally transplanted." With his sister, Leah, and her grandson Terry (close representations of Arna's grandmother and Arna himself), Augie plans to settle down at last—but he cannot. His restless, volatile personality leads him once again into drunkenness and trouble. In a fight over a young woman, he cuts up a neighbor—perhaps mortally—with a beet knife. Facing nothing but trouble in Mudtown, Augie flees to Mexico, hitching a ride to the border with his only possession—freedom of movement.[35]

The curious thing about ***God Sends Sunday*** is that it is not about the black West, which Bontemps knew best, or about the northern ghetto, which surrounded him as he wrote, but about the black South, which he had never seen. Even the part of the novel situated in southern California is really about the South, not the West. The novel's "Mudtown" is obviously based on the Furlough Track where Arna had lived for a time with his grandmother and Buddy; but the real Furlough Track, as later described by Arna himself, was nothing like a transplanted section of the Deep South.[36] Except for the different landscape and a few Mexicans in the background, Little Augie's West proves no different than his South. In an aside in the novel, Bontemps mentions that most blacks in the West live in the large metropolitan areas; but those blacks never appear in Bontemp's book. His story is about a very southernized "Mudtown," a virtually all-black, rural world, filled mostly with "don't-care" Negroes.

The novel received mixed, sometimes heated, reviews. Some critics praised it as an authentic, sensitive portrayal of Afro-southern culture. Others judged it a crude, uninspiring portrayal of the same. Uncle Buddy received a copy from Arna, celebrated with his friends, and wandered drunk onto a road where a car ran him down. Paul Bontemps, reading his copy in Watts, had less to celebrate and lived to question his son's chosen vocation.[37]

A shocked W. E. B. Du Bois hated the book. The *Crisis* editor, who had bestowed prizes on Bontemps's early poetry, now turned a sharp pen against the author. "A profound disappointment," he fumed.

> There is a certain pathetic touch to the painting of his poor little jockey hero, but nearly all else is sordid crime, drinking, gambling, whoremongering, and murder. There is not a decent intelligent woman; not a single man with the slightest ambition or real education, scarcely more than one human child in the whole book. . . . In the "Blues" alone Bontemps sees beauty. But in brown skins, frizzled hair and full contoured faces, they are to him nothing but ugly, tawdry, hateful things, which he describes with evident caricature.[38]

Du Bois called Bontemps a race hater, but nothing could be further from the truth. Du Bois mistook Bontemps's joyful representation for hateful misrepresentation. Bontemps later said: "Du Bois did not fail to express pained displeasure—in much the same terms as my own upright father used when he read it—and I, in my exhilaration, was convinced that neither quite understood."[39] In fact they did not understand. Bontemps wrote what he did in ***God Sends Sunday*** not because he despised poor southern blacks but because he loved them, even envied them. He felt they still possessed what he had lost growing up out West—a culture linked to primitivism, an enduring tie to an African past, an undeniable sense of self.[40]

But Bontemps soon discovered the South first hand, and the experience affected his work. Shortly after the publication of ***God Sends Sunday,*** the Great Depression undercut Bontemps's job at the Harlem Academy, and he accepted a position at Oakwood College, an all-black Adventist school (with a white president) in northern Alabama. Bontemps loved the rural landscape and the ordinary black southerners he found there, but he quickly came to hate the South's suffocating racism and intolerance. "We had fled here to escape our fears in the city," Bontemps wrote, "but the terrors we encountered here were even more upsetting than the ones we had left behind." Bontemps began at last to realize what prompted his father to leave Alexandria for Los Angeles. Now it was Arna's turn to be a young black father with a family's safety and future to consider.[41]

Bontemps's Alabama years gave rise to his second novel, ***Black Thunder*** (1936), which offered a fundamentally different vision of Afro-southern culture. Troubled by the racism that surrounded him in northern Alabama, Arna journeyed briefly to Fisk University in Nashville, Tennessee, where some of his friends from the Harlem Renaissance had established a haven for black education and art.[42] There, Bontemps found a treasure of slave narratives and read them "almost frantically" and "began to ponder the stricken slave's will to freedom." He found the slave rebellions—"efforts at self-emancipation," he called them—especially compelling, and he decided to write his next novel on Gabriel Prosser, whose 1800 rebellion ended in failure and his execution. To Bontemps, Prosser's desire for freedom seemed like an "unmistakable equivalent of the yearning I felt and which I imagined to be general."[43]

Back at Oakwood, tensions became unbearable. Bontemps fell under suspicion, and he did not even feel free enough to tell his black colleagues about the Gabriel Prosser project. Meantime, friends from the Renaissance, including the increasingly radical Langston Hughes, kept stopping by Oakwood to visit the Bontemps family, thereby rousing more suspicions about the young black intellectual. Bontemps stayed through spring 1935, when the school's president horrified him by stating that Arna could save his position on the faculty only by publicly burning his books by Renaissance writers.[44]

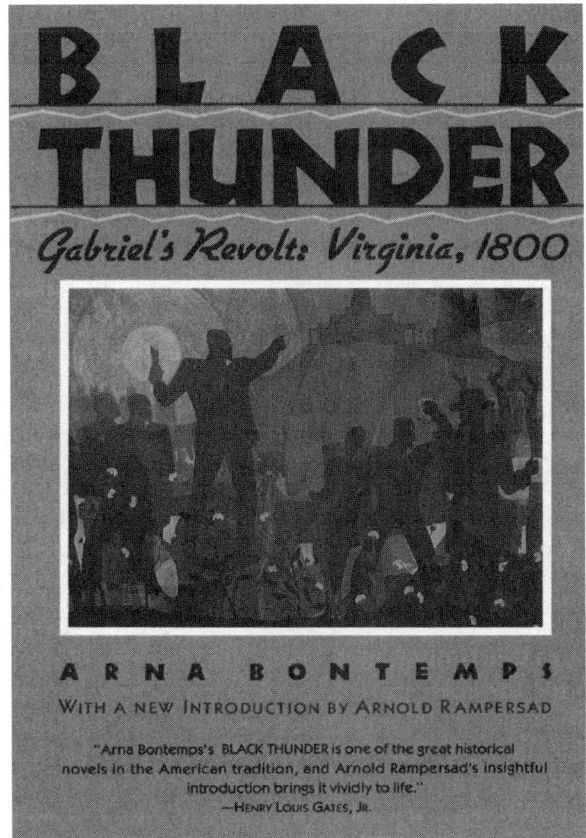

Book cover of *Black Thunder,* written by Arna Bontemps.

Arna Bontemps kept his books and returned to the West. At the time, he perceived this move as the great failure of his early manhood.[45] In 1935, driving his family across the Southwest and marveling at the caravans of Okies, he knew his homecoming would be less than pleasant. He was broke, Alberta was expecting their third child, and all five of them would have to live with Paul Bontemps and his second wife in their small house in Watts. Upon arrival Arna sold the Ford "in the hope that what we had received for the car would buy food till I could write my book."[46]

Back in Watts, Bontemps spent half a year writing one of the strongest (yet least-appreciated) novels of the Renaissance era. Circumstances were rather strained. His father accepted the imposition with stiff politeness and once openly criticized his son for arriving at such straits. With no space for a typewriter or even a writing table, Arna "wrote the book in longhand on the top of a folded-down sewing machine." Compared to Alabama, though, southern California seemed tranquil. In the mid-1930s, class and race tensions were actually running high in Great-Depression

Los Angeles; but from his writing window, Bontemps looked out on a landscape of peaceful ethnic diversity. "A Japanese truck farmer's asparagus field was just outside our back door," he recalled. And "in the vacant lot across from us on Wiegand [Avenue] a friendly Mexican neighbor grazed his milk goat." Bontemps loved the climate. "We could smell eucalyptus trees when my writing window was open and when we walked outside," he said, "and nearly always the air was like transparent gold in those days." Despite Arna's sense of failure, his family had survived the South and made it safely to the West—just as Paul Bontemps's family had done in 1906.[47]

Having now fled Dixie himself, Arna wrote about the South differently. ***Black Thunder*** was not about preserving folk life. It was about getting free, about harnessing the revolutionary potential of Afro-southern culture. In ***Black Thunder,*** the slave Gabriel can no longer abide bondage. He seizes upon Old Testament promises of God's vengeance against evil and rallies his fellow slaves for freedom. They plot to kill the white people in Richmond in hopes of fostering a general black uprising. For Gabriel, the only choice was freedom or death. And in the end a betrayed Gabriel dies calmly on the gallows, "excellent in strength, the first for freedom of the blacks, savage and baffled, perplexed but unafraid, waiting for the dignity of death."[48]

From the vantage point of Little Augie's flippant escape to Mexico in ***God Sends Sunday,*** Bontemps had moved a very long way. His early longing for "Negro-ness" in what he perceived to be a "Negro-*less*" West had led him to Harlem and, by twists of fate, to Alabama. Profoundly disturbed by the Deep South, he returned to the relative safety of the West to write a novel whose basic theme, as Bontemps himself described it, was the "self-assertion by black men whose endurance was strained to the breaking point."[49]

Oddly, Bontemps would ultimately move back to the South and remain there until his death in 1973. With a small advance for ***Black Thunder,*** he moved to Chicago and remained there several years, attending graduate school and working for the federal writers program. But the northern ghetto disturbed him. Blacks were confined to the South Side, which Bontemps viewed as a hellish cauldron of poverty and crime. Nor could he return to Harlem, where the Renaissance had been devastated by the Great Depression and the riot of 1935. So, in the early 1940s, when Fisk University asked him to join the faculty and serve as Head Librarian, he accepted.[50]

Arna Bontemps thus returned to the South at the very time that hundreds of thousands of southern blacks were moving to Los Angeles to work in the war industries. The South he moved to was not quite the Alabama he had fled. Fisk University, along with the black middle-class community that surrounded it in the upper-South city of Nashville, offered his family a less threatening form of Jim Crow than they had found in Alabama and a safer middle-class environment than they had found in Chicago. And although Arna occasionally accepted visiting appointments at Yale and other universities, he would remain in Nashville until the end. But in a final testament to the power of region in shaping Bontemps's life and art, his last book of essays, published posthumously and titled ***The Old South,*** includes three autobiographical stories. Those stories are not about the Old South, of course, but about his coming-of-age—and his quest for identity—in the twentieth-century West.

The issue of African American identity was a matter of concern and debate among blacks throughout the United States in the first three decades of the twentieth century. The question of "acting colored" was never an exclusively "western" matter. It rattled through black middle-class households everywhere, as concerned parents pointed out local variants of Uncle Buddy and warned their children that "loud" and "lazy" were tickets to poverty. But for Arna Bontemps in California—and for the other black westerners who made their way to the Harlem Renaissance—the question of "acting colored" would always be a matter of culture that transcended class. And it was a matter of region as well.

Indeed, whenever the issue of "acting colored" arose, it reflected a regional context. In the South, where the vast majority of blacks still lived, a crushing apartheid-like system circumscribed the issue by forcing all blacks into a tightly restricted subservient caste.[51] In northern cities the African American population soared (especially beginning with the Great Black Migration of World War I), prompting a conflict between northern-born blacks and southern-born newcomers and also sparking a white backlash that resulted in the widespread ghettoization of all blacks.[52]

The West, by comparison, had the smallest black population to begin with and received fewer Afro-southerners than the North during the Great Migration. Most black western migrants moved to the growing coastal cities, which, prior to the 1890s, had only the tiniest of black communities.

For that reason, it was not clear where blacks would fit into the rapidly changing society of the West Coast. Despite pervasive discrimination by whites against all people of color, black residential patterns in the West were less concentrated than in the South or North. By the 1930s, blacks would find themselves locked into highly restricted residential areas. But in the formative years of the century, there was more flux and uncertainty—all the more so because the West was a decidedly multiracial environment, and it was not clear where blacks would stand in the regional hierarchy of ethnic status and power. African Americans therefore found relatively more openness in the West than elsewhere (at least for a while), and that openness complicated the issue of black identity.[53]

Bontemps understood the power of place in shaping racial identity. For him, the openness of western society felt strangely like a severance of heritage and created in him a longing for the identifiably black aspects of African American culture. He found black culture first in the stories of Uncle Buddy, then in Harlem, and finally in the South itself. But he seems never to have found it in the West. It is not too much to say that the early-twentieth-century West turned Arna Bontemps into a cultural nationalist, albeit a soft-spoken one.[54] A disciplined, religious, hard-working family man, he lived his life much in accordance with his father's example. But his art remained close to the soul of Uncle Buddy.

From the summer of 1922, when he read African American poetry to his young friends in Los Angeles, Arna Bontemps expressed his love for black culture—for "Negro-ness." He never saw any contradiction between racial appreciation and racial integration. In matters of civil rights, he was staunchly integrationist, citing Charles S. Johnson's injunction to be engaged in "intensive minority living."[55] But Bontemps's idea of integration never included the abandonment of what he saw as black culture. He desired to be a full citizen of society *and* to celebrate the richness of his racial heritage. Bontemps's cultural journey thus presaged what remains today an important and recurrent tension in the singularly diverse society of the American West.

Notes

The author wishes to thank Blake Allmendinger, Bill Deverell, Valerie Matsumoto, Marlon Ross, and Bryant Simon for their thoughtful and timely critiques of this essay as it moved from one draft to another. Special appreciation also to Peter Reill and all the good people at the Clark Library for the wonderful "American Dreams, Western Images" program, which offered an exceptional opportunity to think long and hard about region and race.

1. Arna Bontemps, "Why I Returned," in Arna Bontemps, *The Old South: 'A Summer Tragedy' and Other Stories of the Thirties* (New York: Dodd, Mead, and Co., 1973), p. 10.

2. See especially Bontemps, "Why I Returned"; and Arna Bontemps, "The Awakening: A Memoir," in Arna Bontemps, ed., *The Harlem Renaissance Remembered* (New York: Dodd, Mead, and Co., 1972).

3. Kirkland C. Jones, *Renaissance Man from Louisiana: A Biography of Arna Wendell Bontemps* (Westport, CT: Greenwood Press, 1992). This paragraph represents my own reading, not necessarily Jones's view, of the book's title.

4. Ibid., chs. 1-2; Bontemps, "Why I Returned," p. 1.

5. Bontemps, "Why I Returned," pp. 3-5; Jones, *Renaissance Man,* pp. 26-28.

6. Bontemps, "Why I Returned," pp. 5-6; what Bontemps and other residents called the Furlough Track was officially designated by the county as the Furlong Tract; see Patricia Rae Adler, "Watts: From Suburb to Black Ghetto" (Ph.D. diss., University of Southern California, 1977), p. 280, n. 24.

7. Adler, "Watts," pp. 49-50, 101, table V.6, and ch. 4 generally.

8. Pacific Coast African American history during the early twentieth century is examined in Albert S. Broussard, *Black San Francisco: The Struggle for Racial Equality in the West, 1900-1954* (Lawrence, KA: University of Kansas Press, 1993); Lawrence P. Crouchett, et al., *The History of the East Bay Afro-American Community, 1852-1977* (Oakland: Northern California Center for Afro-American History and Life, 1989); Douglas Henry Daniels, *Pioneer Urbanites: A Social and Cultural History of Black San Francisco* (Berkeley: University of California Press, 1990); Rudolph M. Lapp, *Afro-Americans in California,* 2nd ed. (San Francisco: Boyd and Fraser Publishing, 1987); and several works by Quintard Taylor: *The Forging of a Black Community: Seattle's Central District from 1870 through the Civil Rights Era* (Seattle: University of Washington Press, 1994); "Black Communities in the Pacific Northwest," *Journal of Negro History* 64 (Fall 1979): 342-54; "Black Urban Development—Another View: Seattle's Central District, 1910-1940," *Pacific Historical Review* 58 (November 1989): 429-48; and "Blacks and Asians in a White City: Japanese Americans and African Americans in Seattle, 1890-1940," *Western Historical Quarterly* 22 (November 1991): 401-29.

   Principal works on African Americans in Los Angeles include: Adler, "Watts"; J. Max Bond, "The Negro in Los Angeles" (Ph.D. diss., University of Southern California, 1936), with population figures, p. 55, table 8; Lawrence B. de Graff, "City of Black Angels: Emergence of the Los Angeles Ghetto, 1890-1930," *Pacific Historical Review* 39 (1970): 323-52; Emory J. Tolbert, *The UNIA and Black Los Angeles* (Los Angeles: Center for Afro-American Studies, 1980); and Douglas Flamming, "African American Politics in Progressive-Era Los Angeles," in William Deverell and Tom Sitton, eds., *California Progressivism Revisited* (Berkeley: University of California Press, 1994), pp. 203-28. The author of this essay is currently at work on a book entitled *A World to Gain: African Americans and the Making of Los Angeles, 1890-1940.*

9. Arna Bontemps, *Black Thunder* (New York, 1936; reprint, with a new introduction by the author, Boston: Beacon Press, 1968), p. xxiii; Jones, *Renaissance Man,* p. 36.

10. Bontemps, "Why I Returned," p. 8; Ann Allen Shockley, interview with Arna Bontemps, July 14, 1972, Arna Bontemps Collection, Fisk University, Special Collections Library.

11. Bontemps, "Why I Returned," p. 6.

12. Ibid., pp. 6-7.

13. Ibid., p. 9.

14. Ibid., p. 10; for Arna's softer version of why he was sent to the Academy (which does not present Buddy's baneful influence as a factor in his father's decision), see his story, "3 Pennies for Luck," in Bontemps, *The Old South,* pp. 233-35.

15. Bontemps, "Why I Returned," pp. 10-12.

16. Shockley interview with Bontemps; Jones, *Renaissance Man,* p. 45.

17. Arna Bontemps, "Introduction," *Great Slave Narratives* (Boston: Beacon Press, 1969), vii, quoted in Jones, *Renaissance Man,* pp. 44-46.

18. Bontemps, "Why I Returned," pp. 8-9.

19. Bontemps, "The Awakening," p. 7.

20. Ibid., pp. 7-8.

21. Chandler Owen, "From Coast to Coast," *The Messenger* (May 1922): 409.

22. Bontemps, "Why I Returned," p. 10.

23. Ibid., p. 11.

24. Ibid., p. 12. Du Bois explained the meaning of the "Negro Art Renaissance" to Angelenos in the *Los Angeles Times* (June 14, 1925, p. 1 of the Sunday Literary section); the article also promoted his theatrical pageant, "Star of Ethiopia," which was presented in two performances at the Hollywood Bowl. By the time Du Bois's article and pageant appeared in Los Angeles, Bontemps had been in Harlem for nearly a year.

25. Jones, *Renaissance Man,* pp. 51-53.

26. Arna Bontemps, *Personals* (London: Paul Breman Limited, 1973), pp. 4-5. *Personals* is a collection of Bontemps's poetry, which includes an introduction in which he discusses the Renaissance.

27. Studies of the Harlem Renaissance, which include many excellent works, have largely ignored the western-ness of the young Renaissance crowd. Fundamental works on the Renaissance include, Nathan Irvin Huggins, *Harlem Renaissance* (New York: Oxford, 1971); David L. Lewis, *When Harlem Was In Vogue* (New York: Knopf, 1981), and Lewis's introduction to his edited anthology, *The Portable Harlem Renaissance Reader* (New York: Viking, 1994), pp. xv-xliii; Arnold Rampersad, *The Life of Langston Hughes, Vol. I: 1902-1941, "I, Too, Sing America"* (New York: Oxford University Press, 1986), and Ann Douglas, *Terrible Honesty: Mongrel Manhattan in the 1920s* (New York: Farrar, Straus and Giroux, 1995). There were other westerners (not mentioned in the text paragraph) involved in the Renaissance: Louise Thompson, a minor Renaissance player who became an important New York Communist in the 1930s, had lived in various towns in the mountain West but grew up mainly in Sacramento, California, and received her B.A. from Berkeley; Sargent Johnson moved to San Francisco as a young adult, decided to become an artist, and emerged as one of the finest sculptors of the period (he won prizes in Harlem, but continued to live in San Francisco); finally, Carl Van Vechten, the leading white supporter of the young black writers, was, despite his cosmopolitanism and world travels, the product of Cedar Rapids, Iowa.

28. "Struggling" quote in Lewis, *Portable Harlem Renaissance Reader,* p. xxx. For Bontemps's own pleasant recollection of his early years in Harlem, see his "3 Pennies for Luck," p. 236; and "The Awakening," p. 24.

29. Bontemps, *Personals,* p. 5. The relationship between primitive Africa and modern black life is a theme in two of Bontemps's early poems: "Nocturne at Bethesda," winner of the *Crisis* poetry award for 1926; and "Golgotha is a Mountain," winner of the *Opportunity* poetry prize the same year. "Nocturne" is reprinted in *Personals,* pp. 28-29. "Golgotha" is reprinted in Lewis, *Portable Harlem Renaissance Reader,* pp. 225-26, and, with slightly different punctuation, in Bontemps, *Personals,* pp. 18-20.

30. The westerners' emphasis on "colored" art sparked a backlash. George Schuvler, a New Yorker by upbringing, debunked the racial-ness of his peers' work in "The Negro-Art Hokum," an essay appearing in *The Nation* (June 16, 1926). Langston Hughes shot back immediately with his powerful "The Negro Artist and the Racial Mountain," which appeared in the following issue of the same journal (June 23, 1926) and quickly became the New Negro manifesto, cheered by Bontemps and the other western-raised blacks. Both essays are reprinted in Lewis, *Portable Harlem Renaissance Reader,* pp. 91-99; and see Rampersad, *Life of Langston Hughes,* vol. 1, pp. 130-31, 134, 137-38. Wallace Thurman issued a powerful defense of "colored" art in his 1927 essay "Negro Artists and the Negro," *The New Republic* (August 31, 1927): 37-38. Thurman's journal has been reprinted: *Fire!! A Quarterly Devoted to the Younger Negro Artists* (Metuchen, NJ: Fire!! Press, 1982).

31. Arna Bontemps, *God Sends Sunday* (New York, 1931; reprint, New York: AMS Press Inc., 1972).

32. Wallace Thurman, *The Blacker the Berry . . . : A Novel of Negro Life* (New York, 1929; reprint, New York: Macmillan, 1970).

33. Langston Hughes, *Not Without Laughter* (New York, 1930; reprint, New York: Alfred A. Knopf, 1969). Hughes's novel (set in the small town of "Stanton" Kansas) is not so much about the black West he knew in Lawrence, Kansas, but about the black West he *wished* he had experienced there.

34. Bontemps, "The Awakening," p. 1. Bontemps even tried at first to write "autobiographically" about a southern boy and his adventures in the South, a project doomed to fail, one might say, because Bontemps had no real experience living in the South and only the fewest childhood memories of the place.

35. Bontemps, *God Sends Sunday,* pp. 116, 119, 197.

36. See Bontemps's introduction to Arna Bontemps and Jack Conroy, *Any Place but Here* (New York: Hill and Wang, 1966).

37. See Robert E. Fleming, *James Weldon Johnson and Arna Wendell Bontemps: A Reference Guide* (New York: Macmillan, 1978), pp. 72-73, 79-81.

38. Du Bois quoted in James P. Draper, ed., *Black Literature Criticism: Excerpts from Criticism of the Most Significant Works of Black Authors over the Past 200 Years* (Detroit: Gale Research Inc., 1991), vol. 1, pp. 209-10, citing *Crisis* 40 (September 1931): 304. See also Bontemps, "The Awakening," pp. 25-26.

39. Bontemps, "The Awakening," p. 26.

40. Marlon Ross of the University of Michigan's English Department, whose book on the Harlem Renaissance is forthcoming, has suggested that my reading of Bontemps's "love" of Afro-southern folk culture is too simple. His alternative suggestion, oversimplified here, deserves consideration: Bontemps's "love" was tinged with self-hatred, for ultimately Lil' Augie is an impotent and pathetic character. *God Sends Sunday* is thus a novel about the death of the South and southern types; it leaves unanswered the question of what will replace these types precisely because it is a book about a past life passing into an unknown future.

41. Bontemps, *Black Thunder,* p. x. See also Rampersad, *Life of Langston Hughes,* vol. 1, pp. 227-28; and John O'Brien interview with Arna Bontemps, reprinted in Draper, ed., *Black Literature Criticism,* vol. 1, p. 222.

42. James Weldon Johnson, Charles S. Johnson, and Arthur Schomburg, all of whom Bontemps had known in Harlem, had settled in at Fisk. "All, in a sense, could have been considered as refugees living in exile," Bontemps wrote, "and the three, privately could have been dreaming of planting an oasis at Fisk where, surrounded by bleak hostility in the area, the region, and the nation, if not indeed the world, they might not only stay alive but, conceivably, keep alive a flicker of the impulse they had detected and helped to encourage in the black awakening in Renaissance Harlem." Bontemps, *Black Thunder,* p. xi.

43. Ibid., pp. xi, xii, xiii.

44. Ibid., p. xiv. Bontemps thought he might be removed from the faculty earlier than 1935. In about 1932, he wrote Hughes, "I was . . . pointed out as being favorable to the revolution and, as a result, may not be rehired. I am not really bumped, but the faculty is to be cut in half (due to depression) and I may not be on the new slate." Bontemps to Hughes c. 1932, in Charles H. Nichols, ed., *Arna Bontemps-Langston Hughes Letters, 1925-1967* (New York: Dodd, Mead and Co., 1980), pp. 18-19.

45. Bontemps had not always been so reluctant to return. In his first year at Oakwood, he wrote to Langston Hughes that if he should leave Alabama, he would "come to California and go to U.S.C. next winter—that is really what I want to do." Once back in Los Angeles, he speculated, "I could spend time in Mexico, write more children's books, finish a long delayed novel, etc. etc." Bontemps to Hughes, c. 1932, in Nichols, *Arna Bontemps-Langston Hughes Letters,* pp. 18-19.

46. Bontemps, *Black Thunder,* p. xiv.

47. Ibid., p. viii; Rampersad, *Life of Langston Hughes,* vol. 1, p. 306.

48. *Black Thunder,* pp. 69, 222. The novel won widely favorable reviews. In words that must have validated Bontemps's search for racial authenticity, the reviewer for the *New York Times* wrote: "If one were looking for a sort of prose spiritual on the Negroes themselves, quite aside from the universal dream that they bear in this story, one could not find it more movingly sung." Another reviewer stated that Bontemps had "written of the Virginia countryside as one who knows it and loves it." Quotes from *Book Review Digest, 1936,* p. 105 (all five reviews listed were graded as positive). Sales lagged far behind the reviews, however, and Bontemps made almost no money for his best work until *Black Thunder* was revived amidst the black power movement of the late 1960s. Appreciation of *Black Thunder* has now reached a high point; in 1992, Beacon Press issued a new edition of the novel with an introduction by Arnold Rampersad.

49. Bontemps, *Black Thunder,* p. xv.

50. "We had fled from the jungle of Alabama's Scottsboro era to the jungle of Chicago's crime-ridden South Side," Bontemps wrote, "and one was as terrifying as the other." Bontemps, "Why I Returned," p. 18. On his move to Fisk and his decision to remain in the South, see ibid., pp. 19-25.

51. Basic works in the enormous literature on southern race relations in the late nineteenth and early twentieth century include: J. Morgan Kousser, *The Shaping of Southern Politics: Suffrage Restriction and the Establishment of the One-Party South* (New Haven, CT: Yale University Press, 1974); Earl Lewis, *In Their Own Interests: Race, Class, and Power in Twentieth-Century Norfolk, Virginia* (Berkeley: University of California Press, 1991); Howard N. Rabinowitz, *Race Relations in the Urban South, 1865-1890* (New York: Oxford University Press, 1978); and C. Vann Woodward, *The Strange Career of Jim Crow,* 3rd rev. ed. (New York: Oxford University Press, 1974).

52. In the rapidly growing field of Great Migration studies, basic works include: Kenneth L. Kusmer, *A Ghetto Takes Shape: Black Cleveland, 1870-1930* (Urbana: University of Illinois Press, 1978); Peter Gottlieb, *Making Their Own Way: Southern Blacks' Migration to Pittsburgh, 1916-1930* (Urbana: University of Illinois Press, 1987); James Grossman, *Land of Hope: Chicago, Black Southerners, and the Great Migration* (Chicago: University of Chicago Press, 1989); Alan H. Spear, *Black Chicago: The Making of a Negro Ghetto* (Chicago: University of Chicago Press, 1967); Joe William Trotter, Jr., *Black Milwaukee: The Making of an Industrial Proletariat, 1915-1945* (Urbana: University of Illinois, 1985); Joe William Trotter, Jr., ed., *The Great Migration in Historical Perspective: New Dimensions of Race, Class, and Gender* (Bloomington: Indiana University Press, 1991).

53. On the black West, particularly the Pacific Coast, during this period, see note 8.

54. See especially Bontemps's discussion of things "colored" in "Why I Returned," pp. 10-11.

55. Ibid., p. 22.

TITLE COMMENTARY

Black Thunder

SANDRA CARLTON-ALEXANDER (ESSAY DATE 1991)

SOURCE: Carlton-Alexander, Sandra. "Arna Bontemps: the Novelist Revisited." *CLA Journal* 34, no. 3 (March 1991): 317-30.

In the following essay, Carlton-Alexander examines Black Thunder, *the first historical novel by an African American author, noting its characterizations, narrative technique, and mythic qualities.*

At the height of his literary career, Arna Wendell Bontemps, poet, essayist, and short fiction writer, produced the little-known historical novel ***Black Thunder.*** Though never popularly acclaimed, the novel once enjoyed high regard in literary circles. However, the spirit of the present age may well work in favor of the once respected fictional work. With the growing interest in genealogical study and the ever increasing concern with the search for personal historical truth, ushered in by Alex Haley's *Roots,* revisiting this penetrating novel of the early thirties seems both timely and especially meaningful.

Bontemps got the urge to write ***Black Thunder*** in 1933 when he made a trip to Fisk University to visit some friends. Still emotionally shattered by the horror of the Scottsboro trial, then in progress not too far from Huntsville, Alabama, where he lived and taught at Oakwood Academy, Bontemps writes that he discovered on the shelves of that university's library an extensive collection of slave narratives and began to read them almost "frantically."[1] With the gloom of the darkening Depression settling around him, he began pondering the slaves' will to freedom or, as he writes on another occasion, began "brooding over a matter so depressing that he would find no relief until it resolved itself in ***Black Thunder.***"[2]

The novel deals with the famous Gabriel Prosser slave insurrection, which occurred in and around Richmond, Virginia, in 1800. In his introductory remarks to the 1968 reprint of the novel, Bontemps explains why he selected Gabriel's rebellion in preference to those of Denmark Vesey and Nat Turner:

> Vesey's effort I dismissed first. It was too elaborately planned for its own good. . . . Nat Turner's Confession . . . bothered me on two counts. I felt uneasy about the amanuensis to whom his account was related and the conditions under which he confessed. Then there was the business of Nat's "visions" and "dreams." Gabriel's attempt seemed to reflect more accurately for me what I felt then and feel now might have motivated slaves capable of such boldness and inspired daring.[3]

The novel represents a unique contribution to the American literary tradition. Before the publication of ***Black Thunder,*** no large recognizable body of black novelists subscribed to the historical method. Richard Barksdale and Keneth Kinnamon voice the opinions of most literary historians when they cite Bontemps' work as "a significant 'first' in this particular genre of black literature."[4]

According to critic John O. Young, Bontemps spent "three years" in "painstaking" research for his novel[5] in an effort to increase the accuracy and authenticity of his final product. In point of fact, Bontemps drew his materials from actual Virginia court records. But the beauty and magical quality of the novel rest entirely on the skill with which the novelist shapes and molds these details into a powerful and gripping drama.

The author's intention to depart from the traditional narrative method becomes apparent almost immediately. In the first paragraph of the novel, Bontemps plunges his reader into an atmosphere of suspense, urgency, and tension. He depicts with near cinematic accuracy a series of seemingly unconnected events occurring on the day of Gabriel Prosser's famous trial:

> Virginia Court records for September 15, 1800, mention a certain Mr. Moseley Sheppard who came quietly to the witness stand in Richmond and produced testimony that caused half the State to shudder. The disclosures, disturbing as they were, preceded rumors that would positively let no Virginian sleep. A Troop of United States cavalry was urgently dispatched, and Governor James Monroe, himself an old soldier, paced the halls of Ash Lawn with quaking knees and appointed for his estate three special aides-de-camp.[6]

With this opening passage, Bontemps captures his reader's interest and secures his trust by grounding the novel in historical reality. Analyzing Bontemps' style in this paragraph, Roger Whitlow found that the novel "opens with a statement, detached and journalistic, yet descriptive of a seething social unrest."[7] In the paragraphs that follow, it becomes apparent that Bontemps is employing a familiar strategy, for the remainder of the novel is presented in one long flashback which provides us with the concrete experience which led up to that trial.

The plot line in the main body of the novel is fairly simple. Touched off by a white master's vicious beating of a harmless oldster called Bundy, eleven hundred slaves led by a young Negro named Gabriel plan to take the city of Richmond and thereby secure their freedom. Further encouraged by faint rumors concerning the exploits of Toussaint L'Overture in Haiti and also by the revolutionary theories of French Jacobins in the vicinity, the slaves have determined the armed strength of the city, accumulated their own weapons and ammunition, and plotted to capture the city arsenal. The well-devised plan is eventually subverted by a torrential rainstorm and by the eleventh-hour betrayal of two fellow slave conspirators.

But a bare plot summary of ***Black Thunder*** rings hollow to anyone who has experienced the world of the novel. As is true of any artistic creation, the whole can best be appreciated by examining the skillful interworkings of its parts. At the core of the work is a familiar theme: the irrepressible longing for freedom that lies within the hearts of all men.

Bontemps relies on skillfully drawn characterizations to carry much of the thematic burden. It is through this vivid portrayal of tortured souls at the most poignant juncture in their existence that the larger meaning of the novel begins to emerge. In the words of George Schuyler, "Here we have unforgettable pictures of slavery at its best and its worst; pictures of the mentality alike of slave and masters."[8]

Gabriel, the gigantic, keen-minded young coachman, is the hero. Our opinion of Gabriel as a man of persuasion and personal magnetism begins to form even before he makes his first appearance. In Chapter One, Bundy, while attempting to persuade a doubtful Ben to join the slave fraternity, expresses his confidence in the rebel leader: "I just want you to talk to Gabriel; I ain't asking you to j'ine no mo,. . . . You just wait'll Gabriel 'splains it. . . . Don't say a word. Just you wait'll you talks to Gabriel" (p. 13). We, like the slaves he leads, are drawn to Gabriel by his intelligence and by his inherent capacity for leadership, which the following passage dramatizes:

> This what *you* got to remember, Pharaoh: You's leaving for Carline County with Ben next Sad-dy evening. You can send word up by the boys going that a-way so everything'll be in shape. We going to write up something like that what Mingo read from Toussaint, soon's we get our power, and you ain't got to do nothing up there but spread the news. Them's all our brothers. I bound you they'll come when they hears the proclamation.
>
> (p. 67)

In this passage, Gabriel demonstrates the forcefulness and sense of direction that we commonly associate with men who possess the ability to control human destinies. In a perceptive analysis of Gabriel's major characteristics, Arthur P. Davis writes, "Bontemps does not make Gabriel too brave or too clever. . . . He describes him as a powerful black man with a gift for organization and leadership. He has no visions, is not unusually superstitious, and is not particularly religious. His driving force is a deep conviction that 'anything what's equal to a grey squirrel wants to be free'" (p. 91). Stubbornly loyal to his followers, he refuses to inform on them. To his executioner, he says merely: "Let the rope talk, suh" (p. 223).[9]

The personalities of the other central characters are drawn with an equal dedication to psychological truth. Juba, the voluptuous, "tempestuous brown wench" (p. 29) who gives the signal for the revolt to begin, is portrayed as incapable of understanding her lover's deepest convictions about freedom and more concerned about being by his side than about the goals of the conspiracy. The dialogue between Juba and Gabriel in the following passage aptly illustrates her mental limitations:

> "What you thinking about, big sugar?" [Juba]
>
> "Thinking about I don't know my mind and I ain't satisfied no mo." [Gabriel]
>
> "Stop it, boy; stop thinking like that. It ain't good. . . .
>
> Yo' head is on my breast; there. . . . Yo' arms; there. Stop thinking." [Juba]
>
> "Thinking about how I'd like to be free." [Gabriel]
>
> (p. 30)

Similarly, Bontemps pictures with penetration and pity the soul of the subservient traitor Old Ben. Portraying Ben as torn between a superstitious fear of being haunted by the ghost of Buddy if he doesn't participate in the rebellion and by a sense of having betrayed his loyalty to a kindly old master if he does, Bontemps neither praises nor condemns, but maintains restraint and detachment throughout. In the following passage he dramatizes the psychological dilemma that plagued the old slave shortly before he divulged all to the whites:

> He [Ben] could even feel the warmth and security that came to Mr. Moseley Sheppard's supper table. . . . There, without warning, the devil spoke to his mind.
>
> What cause I got feeling sorry for a rich old white man that God don't even love. You ought to know them kind by now. They oppress the stranger, and they oppresses the poor.
>
> (pp. 71-72)

Likewise Pharoah, the ignorant field hand, is adequately motivated for his part in the betrayal by his jealousy of Gabriel and his thwarted endeavors to induce the leader to let him "lead a line into Richmond" (p. 71).

Davis contends that Gabriel is so well developed in the work that we tend to forget the other characters.[10] To be sure, the two slave masters, Thomas Prosser and Moseley Sheppard, one kindly, the other a Simon Legree, are the least realized in the novel. However, the two Jacobins are well developed. Cruezot, the French printer, who merely sympathizes with the rebel cause, is portrayed as a helpless victim caught up in the web of events not of his own making. On the other hand, the idealistic lawyer, Alexander Biddenhurst, actively participates in the underground-railroad movement. His philosophical musings about the Henrico County, Virginia, rebellion and its relationship to other liberation movements of history lend scope and universality to the novel. Generally, Bontemps' characterizations are condensed but very well drawn.

Bontemps must have sensed that short but rounded characterization was imperative given the demands of the unusual narrative technique he chose to employ. In brief, Bontemps plays the role of the self-effacing author relating history with apparent objectivity through the shifting consciousnesses of a series of narrators. Robert H. Bone states that the action of the story is conveyed "by a progressive treatment of the participants" and sees the technique as reminiscent of the one employed in the novels of John Dos Passos.[11] As Bontemps shifts his emphasis from character to character (and setting to setting) in the chapters or parts of chapters which open with the name of the particular individual being treated, we are forced to piece together the narrative from the reactions of these individuals. These scenic divisions, which may be compared to development scenes in a drama, form the basic structural units of the novel and have a clearly identifiable internal pattern as well: there is (1) a brief introductory statement about the character under consideration; (2) a short description of setting; (3) next, a brief presentation of the character's interior state, which is followed by (4) action and conversation presented directly; and (5) a conclusion consisting of a series of interior responses which interpret the character's thoughts about the preceding action and dialogue. The following section on Mingo, the free black, serves to illustrate Bontemps' technique. Note that here, the action/conversation segment is rendered through the use of stream-of-consciousness:

> Mingo, the freed Negro, locked the door of his shop [introductory statement] and said farewell to the stimulating odors of new saddles and leather trimmings [setting]. The whole adventure was going to be a plunge into the dark, he reasoned, but at least one thing was certain—nothing would be the same thereafter. The saddle-shop, if he returned to it again, would hold a new experience. His slave wife and children [would remain] out on Marse Prosser's place . . . [interior dialogue]. Anything would be better than sight of his own woman stripped and bleeding at a whipping post. Lordy, anything. He raised a hand to cover his eyes from the punishing recollection, but he failed to put by the memory of the woman's cries.
>
> "Pray, massa; pray, massa—I'll do better next time. Oh, pray, massa" [direct action and conversation].
>
> Mingo locked his shop with a three-ounce key, turned away from the familiar door and hurried down the tree-shaded street. Nothing was going to be the same in the future, but anything would be better than Julie stripped and bleeding at a whipping post and the two little girls with white dresses and little wiry braids growing up to the same thing. Lord Jesus, anything would be better than that, anything [interior response to preceding action].
>
> (p. 78)

Stream-of-consciousness and interior monologue, as they are employed here, are not the exclusive methods of Bontemps' entire novel, but they are skillfully and selectively used in the presentation of character in depth.

The narrative technique gives the novel an immediacy perhaps unattainable through traditional narrative methods. No doubt, as Bone maintains, the shifts in point of view are "especially suited to the presentation of complex historical events."[12] But Lewis Gannett's comments in a *New York Herald Tribune* review more accurately express the illusion that Bontemps must have intended to create. Gannett finds that this technique enables the author to capture "the atmosphere of the days of wondering and whispering which must have preceded that outbreak"[13] and which must have followed in the agonizing days of white retribution. His gradual disclosure of the plot serves to heighten the drama. Abrupt shifts from one character to the next require total absorption on the part of the reader and give the novel both the urgency and presence of a powerful drama. Through the use of selective detail, Bontemps make the subjective reference of character the medium of presentation. By combining sharp characterization with shifting points of view to illuminate the inner worlds of the slaves, he succeeds in recreating a momentous incident in the Negro's past with nearly three-dimensional clarity.

The author's adept handling of metaphor helps to further reinforce meaning. Critic Robert H. Bone discovered in the novel a leitmotif that runs throughout. "As the novel unfolds," he writes, "the idea of freedom becomes linked with death." To support his contention, he quotes Gabriel's speech: "A wild bird what's in a cage will die anyhow, sooner or later. . . . He'll pine himself to death. He just as well to break his neck trying to get out." By creating a tension between freedom and death, Bone states, the author suggests that "the determination to be free is itself a kind of bondage."[14]

Likewise, Bone recognizes the sexual overtones that color parts of the novel, for they do loom largely. But he arrives at his conclusion that the novel is "above all an assertion of manhood" from mere surface association. He fails to acknowledge the folk details which give texture to the novel and help to develop a metaphorical link between sex and rebellion. Bone sees the link established in Juba's challenge to the men, and he selects the following passage to support his claim: "Always big-talking about what booming bedmen you is. . . . Well, let's see what you is good for, sure 'nough. Let's see if you knows how to go free; let's see if you knows how to die" (p. 81).[15] He seeks to buttress his argument with even more speculative surface detail. Juba's "flashing things," he says, are the signal for the rebellion to begin.

An examination of a more complete passage excerpted from the novel illustrates that Bone is oblivious to an important folk allusion that Bontemps uses to establish the sexual metaphor in no uncertain terms:

> Dust around now, you old big-foot boys. Get a move on. Remember how Gabriel say it: you got to go on cat feet. You got to get around like the wind. Quick. On'erstand? Always big-talking about what booming bed-men you is. Always trying to turn the gals' heads like that. Well, let's see what you is good for sure 'nough. Let's see if you knows how to go free; let's see if you knows how to die, you big-footses, you.
>
> (p. 81)

Through the details which he overlooks, Bone reveals the source of his critical ineptitude. Unmindful of the folk material that colors the novel (here the reference to "bigfoot") and thus incapable of understanding its function, Bone simply denies its existence through omission. According to Richard M. Dorson, Juba's epithet, "you big-foot," alludes to a contest/ritual that had its roots in slavery, the purpose of which was to determine by foot measurements whose slaves could rightfully boast of superior physical strength.[16] What Bone has failed to point out is that in many folk cultures the size of the feet is often related to the size of the genitals. Freud, for example, writes that "the foot, for instance, is an age old sexual symbol."[17] Bone's interpretation of the passage, made without consideration of Bontemps' folk allusions, thus seems weak and unsubstantiated. As a critic, Bone fails to take into account the technical means by which Bontemps firmly establishes the metaphorical relationship between sex and rebellion.

Folk materials, in the form of lore, rituals, legend, and song, are everywhere present in the novel; and in many instances they figure prominently in the author's artistic achievement. The author integrates usable relics from the Negro past into the fabric of his fictional world so smoothly that they never seem obtrusive or merely grafted on.

Dorothy Weil, in her article "Folklore Motifs in ***Black Thunder,***" explains the function of folk motifs in Bontemps' novel. The only critic who has traced in-depth Bontemps' achievement as folklorist/novelist, Weil finds that the major function fulfilled by folk materials in the novel is to "sustain interest in the action."[18] We find ourselves, for instance, totally absorbed by the drama surrounding Bundy's funeral as the slaves take great pains to perform rituals and observe customs that will insure them against being haunted by the restless spirit of the corpse. For example, the custom of putting a preferred food or drink on the grave of the deceased is followed faithfully: "Down, down, down: old Bundy's long gone now. Put a jug of rum at his feet. . . . Roast a hog and put it on his grave" (p. 52). Secondly, Bontemps uses folk tradition to "characterize individual personalities" and "to provide them with credible psychologies,"[19] in Weil's estimation. For example, the tortured souls of Ben and Pharoah are filled with haunts, signs, spirits, and potions, and in light of this, their erratic and eventually neurotic behavior seems consistent with their superstitious nature. Finally, the ritual and myth testify to the deep understanding of black folk traditions; events such as deaths and funerals are related to larger patterns of human experience.

Folk materials also provide an appropriate vehicle for foreshadowing. When the first dew drops of the ensuing torrential rain fall, the slave Martin sets a tone of foreboding and prepares us for the part it plays in subverting the rebellion: "Yet and still it might be a sign," he says. "Bad hand or something like that" (p. 84). In the days following the thwarted revolt, Juba, sensing that Gabriel failed because he neglected the signs, seeks out a good luck charm for him. Also, the incident in which Pharoah goes insane from fear of being conjured is adumbrated earlier by the intrusion of a frightened bird into the Sheppard house (p. 94), a sign of bad luck in black folklore.

Many aspects of Bontemps' folk method have yet to be explored. For example, to what extent does he employ agricultural ritual to add dimension, as he does so movingly in the sketch on Criddle, the stable boy? Here he defines the boy's eager anticipation of the insurrection with imagery from the hog-killing ritual:

> It was like hog-killing day to Criddle. He knew the feel of warm blood, and he knew his own mind. He knew, as well, that his scythe-sword was ready to drink. He could feel the thing getting stiffer and stiffer in his hand. . . . Criddle knew what blood was like. He remembered hog-killing day.
>
> (pp. 106-07)

The descriptive language surrounding the sword has Freudian sexual overtones. The phallic symbol combines with the imagery of the hog-killing ritual to strengthen the basic tension on which the novel pivots: life/freedom/sexual potency vs death/slavery/sexual impotency.

Beneath the surface of the novel lies an even deeper beauty that warrants exploration. It echoes something so elusive and so indigenous to the Negro's tortured history and tragic tradition that only those who have shared in that tradition are capable of grasping it and of seeing its universal significance. It thus seems fitting that Richard Wright, a man whose life Bontemps once described as "a total exposure to the callousness and cruelty of a closed society,"[20] has come closer to articulating it than any other. He writes that ***Black Thunder*** is something besides "a thumping story well told." It is, Wright feels, a "revelation of the very origin and source of folk values in literature," that "transcends the limits of immediate consciousness." Wright concludes that his illusive "deathless quality" can adequately be classified only as "myth-like."[21] But he stops short of any clearer explanation, and we are forced to make speculations of our own.

Analyzing the mythic qualities of the novel brings the reader closer to its deeper truth. At the outset, Bontemps establishes Gabriel firmly in the tradition of the hero through a related pattern of imagery. Initially, he uses physical description and allusions to set him apart and to establish his kinship with classical archetypes. He is described as being "almost a giant for size" (p. 16) with legs of "extraordinary length" (p. 16) and features "straight as a Roman's" (p. 16). Through implication, Bontemps suggests that Gabriel has a timeless, ageless quality, being "too old for joy" (p. 16) and "too young for despair" (p. 16). His fight with Ditcher represents a rite of passage, of a sort, in the tradition of Oedipus, who engages in a similar struggle at the place where three roads meet. Just as Oedipus kills Laius and replaces him as King of Thebes, so Gabriel defeats Ditcher and thereby establishes himself as the rightful leader of the plantation slaves. The fact that the blacks consider him "a man of destiny (p. 17) places him squarely in mythic tradition and affirms him as the archetypal hero.

Likewise, Bontemps' narrative technique helps to establish the mythic quality of the novel. His psychologically penetrating characterizations and shifting point of view put us in touch with the inner world of the slave, which is alive with magic, music, ritual, and lore accumulated through the ages. This created world, which recalls centuries of the African past, is both limitless and enduring.

Similarly, the author chooses the choral-response pattern of the spiritual, not only to link the novel to the enduring tradition of the folk but to give it a structural base in the larger thematic sense as well. In tone and mood, the novel achieves the level of a prose spiritual as Gabriel voices in solo his deep desire for freedom and as his fellow slaves echo these sentiments in kind, while affecting subtle variations on the refrain. Linking his novel with the spiritual tradition establishes it as a classical expression of primordial longings that are both fundamental and everlasting.

In short, Bontemps re-creates the conscience of his race and renders it in mythic proportions. Through these efforts, he establishes his novel as one of universal importance and transforms his main character into a symbol of the irrepressible, indomitable spirit of the black race, the soul, if you will, that physical bondage can never crush. In a sense, Bontemps has produced an epic of black consciousness. In ***Black Thunder*** he has given us not only a poetic folk history which captures the essence of the black experience but also, in the words of one reviewer, "one of the most brilliant and dramatic pieces" of fiction ever to come from the pen of a black writer.[22]

Notes

1. Arna Bontemps, *Black Thunder* (1936; rpt. Boston: Beacon Press, 1968), p. xii.
2. Arna Bontemps, "The Awakening: A Memoir," in *The Harlem Renaissance Remembered,* ed. Arna Bontemps (New York: Dodd, 1972), p. 2.
3. Arna Bontemps, *Black Thunder,* p. xii. Subsequent quotations from the novel will be cited parenthetically by page number in the text.
4. Richard Barksdale and Keneth Kinnamon, eds., *Black Writers of America* (New York: Macmillan, 1972), p. 629.
5. John O. Young, *Black Writers of the Thirties* (Baton Rouge, La.: State Univ. Press, 1973), p. 224.
6. C. W. E. Bigsby, "The Black American Writer," in *The Black American Writer,* ed. C. W. E. Bigsby (Deland, Fla.: Everett/Edwards, 1969), p. 5.
7. Roger Whitlow, *Black American Literature* (Chicago: Nelson Hall, 1973), p. 73.
8. George Schuyler, rev. of *Black Thunder,* by Arna Bontemps, *The Pittsburgh Courier,* n.d., n. pag., in the Bontemps Papers.
9. Arthur P. Davis, *From the Dark Tower: Afro-American Writers 1900-1960* (Washington, D.C.: Howard Univ. Press, 1974), pp. 87-88.
10. Ibid.
11. Robert H. Bone, *The Negro Novel in America* (New Haven, Conn.: Yale Univ. Press, 1963), p. 121.
12. Ibid.
13. Lewis Gannett, review of *Black Thunder,* by Arna Bontemps, *New York Herald Tribune,* 5 February 1936, n. pag.
14. Bone, p. 122.
15. Ibid.
16. Richard Dorson, *Negro Tales from Pine Bluff* (Bloomington: Indiana Univ. Folklore Series No. 12, 1958), p. 55.
17. Sigmund Freud, *Three Essays on the Theory of Sexuality* (New York: Basic Books, 1962), pp. 19, 21.
18. Dorothy Weil, "Folklore Motifs in *Black Thunder,*" *Southern Folklore Quarterly,* 35 (March 1971), 1.
19. Ibid., p. 13.
20. "Reflections on Richard Wright: A Symposium on an Exiled Native Son," in *Anger and Beyond,* ed. Herbert Hill (New York: Harper, 1966), p. 208.
21. Richard Wright, "A Tale of Folk Courage," *Partisan Review and Anvil,* 3 (April 1936), 31.
22. *Liberty,* 15 (February 1936), n. pag.

DANIEL REAGAN (ESSAY DATE 1991)

SOURCE: Reagan, Daniel. "Voices of Silence: The Representation of Orality in Arna Bontemps's *Black Thunder.*" *Studies in American Fiction* 19, no. 1 (spring 1991): 71-83.

In the following essay, Reagan examines Black Thunder *for its representation of the nature of orality, arguing that the failure of the written word to capture orality consequently makes the medium fall short as a tool for revolutionary change.*

Many recent studies of African-American literature assume that the foundations of black cultural identity rest in vernacular traditions. John F. Callahan states this assumption succinctly when he claims that the characteristic African-American literary voice is defined by "the attempt to conjure the spoken word into symbolic existence on the page."[1] Arna Bontemps' novel ***Black Thunder: Gabriel's Revolt: Virginia: 1800*** (1936) makes a crucial contribution to this oxymoronic literary-vernacular tradition by exploring the significance and limitations of writing the spoken word. Through a variety of voices and points of view, the novel tells the story of an actual slave rebellion, led by Gabriel Prosser, which almost succeeded in capturing Richmond, Virginia. In this work, Bontemps juxtaposes written and oral cultures by depicting the white community as the literate producers and consumers of printed texts and the slave community as illiterate generators of oral discourse. The slaves' orality, Bontemps suggests, differs from the printed word because it is pneumatological, that is, it originates in nature and is both alive and life-giving. An anonymous refugee from the San Domingo slave revolt who watches Gabriel's hanging identifies the pneumatological nature of speech when he mutters, "words like *freedom* and *liberty* drip blood—always, everywhere there is blood on such words."[2] This compelling statement suggests that only when spoken aloud do such words as "freedom" and "liberty" come alive. Bontemps' interest in the animating power of orality leads him to undertake what Callahan has more recently defined as the "sacred political purpose involved in many African-American writers' use of voice: the pursuit of freedom, equality, and diversity as American first principles."[3]

Most critical readings of ***Black Thunder*** center on this political purpose. Bernard W. Bell, for example, argues that "Bontemps uses history to express his imaginative vision of the nature and function of revolution . . . [and to reveal] the timeless problems man has in overpowering color and class oppression to achieve freedom and social equality."[4] Certainly the observations of Bell and others accurately describe Bontemps' political motivation, but they provide only abbreviated discussions of the narrative techniques with which he achieves this vision.

On the other hand, those critics who have expressed so much recent interest in the oral and folk sources of Afro-American literature strangely overlook ***Black Thunder,*** even though it is one of the first black novels to examine the nature of orality. In fact, these studies elide the issue that Bontemps would say is critical in the movement from oral expression to written word, the fundamental difference between the act of speaking and the printed text as social forces. Instead of highlighting the differences between writing and orality as racial and cultural markers, recent commentators have attempted to articulate the similarities between written texts and spoken words. Callahan, for example, claims that a residue of orality resides in printed texts. Because readers hear as well as see words, he argues, writing keeps oral expression alive.[5] Bontemps, on the other hand, suggests that although orality itself binds speaker and audience, the written reduplication of orality necessarily distances the reader from the spoken voice. As a result, his book does not affirm Callahan's model of Afro-American literary history as a progressive movement toward the principles of freedom, equality, and diversity. Instead, Bontemps' narrative posits that the black literary tradition is defined by an alternation between the progressive demand for freedom and the suppression of liberty through the very act of writing itself.

As sources for this novel, Bontemps relied on court records reprinted in the *Calender of Virginia State Papers,* contemporary newspaper accounts, and letters describing the insurrection.[6] These second-hand accounts provide the only surviving evidence about the nature of this slave revolt. Gabriel's own voice has disappeared from history since he left no personal account of the incidents in which he was so crucially involved. The existing records present Gabriel and his followers not only as imposing and frightening but also as "the tools of foreign agitators" (p. 210), suggesting that they had been inspired by such revolutionary texts as the *Dictionnaire Philosophique* and Thomas Jefferson's essays. Bontemps challenges this written interpretation of the revolt, and the texts which inspired it, by juxtaposing the slave community's songs, whispered conversations, and interior monologues against these documents. By insisting on the priority of oral rather than written texts, he restores Gabriel's voice to the record of history, challenges the power of writing to define reality, and ultimately argues that black literary history is shaped by a dialectic between the liberating force of speech and the repressive force of writing.

A peripheral yet pivotal character through whom Bontemps examines the repressive force of texts is the American Revolutionary War pamphleteer Thomas Callender. Throughout the duration of the novel, Callender has been imprisoned in Richmond under the Alien and Sedition Act for writing a scurrilous attack on John Quincy Adams and the Federalists. He is, according to the narrator, a man driven by a "fire [that] demanded prose. So prose it had been, pages and pages of it, the biting, acid prose of a man sick with the need of liberty" (p. 124). Ironically, his very "need of liberty" causes his incarceration. Even before the book begins, his demands for revolutionary change and his support of the French Revolution have provoked reactions that have driven him first from England, then from Philadelphia, and finally to prison. Virginia Federalists, willfully misreading his pamphlets, identify Callender "with hated atheistic propaganda and with the French *Amis des Noirs* and their encouragement to the slaves to free themselves by armed insurrection" (p. 146). In short, he is accused of inciting Gabriel's revolt through his writing. Callender's fate illustrates that the printed text becomes a free agent, available for use or misuse by the most powerful bidder. As a result, writers frequently become victims of their own words, and texts oppress the very people they are intended to inspire.

A pamphlet Callender did not write, however, reveals most clearly the power of texts to distance authors from word and from audience. After Gabriel's revolt fails, Federalists accuse Callender of writing "Slavery and the Rights of Man" to link him and his patron, Thomas Jefferson, to the Jacobin call for world revolution. Their motive is to weaken Jefferson's chances in the 1800 presidential campaign. To prevent this plot from succeeding, Callender writes to the Norfolk *Epitome of the Times* disowning the pamphlet even though, ironically, it was one with which he would agree. This incident reveals the dangerous pliability of written texts. Bontemps suggests through Callender's dilemma that in the hands of hostile readers, the written word can become a tool of oppression rather than a voice of liberation.

Texts are no less dangerous in the hands of sympathetic readers, however. In his creation of the myopic, white abolitionist Alexander Biddenhurst, Bontemps illustrates that readers as well as writers are distanced from the world by the written word. Biddenhurst is steeped in the literature of the French Revolution and even carries the *Dictionnaire Philosophique* under his arm wherever he goes. He reads "Rousseau and Voltaire with conviction [and is] intrigued by the *Amis des Noirs* [and approves] the Jacobin ideal of utter equality for all men" (p. 205). Nevertheless, Biddenhurst's reading does not move him to act. Rather, it breeds in him "a romantic love of liberty" and allows him to feel "a rather special burden for abused minority groups" (p. 205). He writes in his journal about revolution as the joining of hands around the globe or, alternatively, as the drip of water on stone. Biddenhurst's encounter with the written word leads him to see revolution as an object of contemplation rather than an action, and when he realizes he may actually have incited Gabriel to revolt by spouting revolutionary rhetoric, he decides that "the prudent act for a stranger who had quoted Rousseau quite freely on the equality of man was to secure passage on the first public conveyance headed north" (p. 74).

The printed text, then, oppresses in two ways. If it finds a hostile audience, it makes its author a victim of his or her own words, as Callender's experience illustrates. If it finds a friendly audience, it represses the reader's impulse to act in the world by diverting attention from action to word, as Biddenhurst's passivity shows. Indeed, whether white characters in the novel are hostile to the revolt, like Governor James Monroe, or sympathetic, like Biddenhurst and the French immigrant printer Creuzot, texts define and limit their understanding of Gabriel's motives. These characters all feel they can explain the rebellion only by insisting that the rebels must have been inspired by texts such as "Slavery and the Rights of Man" despite knowing that the slaves could have no knowledge of such works. As Creuzot observes, "the proletariat is innocent of letters" (p. 36). No white character in the novel confronts the implications of this contradiction because none can conceive of action that is not inspired by the written word. As Gabriel himself observes, "them white folks . . . is sure got great heads for figuring out something what ain't. . . . Nothing going to do them now but to make somebody say white mens was telling us to rise up" (p. 219). For white society, the world must be viewed through the opaque filter of writing; the text therefore ultimately separates both writer and audience from reality itself. Even those like Creuzot who are sympathetic to the Jacobin call for world revolution assume that, because slaves are illiterate, they are not "capable of that divine discontent that turns the mill of destiny" for they are "without the necessary faculties" (p. 63). This belief that literacy is fundamental to the generation of social action leads both to the assumption that slaves are not fully human and to a misunderstanding of the nature of freedom.

Because the white community in ***Black Thunder*** lives by the fictions writing creates, the written word divorces them from what Bontemps defines as "nature." The slave community's orality, on the other hand, reconnects language to its roots in the natural world. Bontemps establishes the "naturalness" of orality through a series of formulaic tropes. At the simplest level, he develops a series of similes that compare slaves individually and collectively with birds. The rural crowd Gabriel expects to amass in his support will "rise up like a flock of sparrows in a wheat field" (p. 71). The power of flight, of escape from bondage, is one potent element of this comparison, and Bontemps exploits it when Gabriel compares himself to "a wild bird what's in a cage" (p. 69) and later to a "bird in the air" (p. 104). The comparison has a more complex resonance, however, when it is presented as a metaphor. Bontemps describes the early morning on a plantation by presenting a provocative juxtaposition: "The handsome great house was dark as death inside, but in the fields thousands of gleaming birds were crowing up the sun" (p. 11). The house, where the master lives, is both prison and tomb; its inhabitants cannot communicate with life or nature. But the fields, already populated by slaves in the early morning, are alive with the language of nature itself. Moreover, the crows in the fields devouring the profits that support the great house reflect in their action the slaves' revolutionary impulse. The language of white culture in this metaphor is bound within a construction of its own making (the great house) and thus is both separated from and dead to the natural world. The language of slaves, on the other hand, like the language of birds, crows up the sun. Orality thus is embedded in nature for, as this metaphor suggests, the speech of slaves and the sounds of the natural world are often indistinguishable. In ***Black Thunder,*** the act of speaking, rather than the meaning of words, is the salient feature of orality.

Early in the novel Bontemps writes that "somewhere the thrashers called. The Negroes cupped their hands, whispered through the tall corn" (p. 14). Frequently slave conversation is represented simply by the act of whispering, rather than the words whispered. The import of the slaves' words is no more comprehensible than the thrasher's call, but as the novel progresses, the two sounds merge. Often Bontemps intimates that what sounds like the thrasher's call may in fact be the voice of a slave mimicking the sound. Thus when the "incredibly sweet . . . voice of a brown thrasher" (p. 164) draws Gabriel into the swamp in his effort to escape, he could either be "reading" this text of nature or responding to the secret call of a slave. For Gabriel, the two forms of language are one.

The thrasher's call suggests that oral discourse is most potent when it leaves words behind altogether and becomes, through its sound, an expression embedded in nature. Such wordless communication occurs most often in ***Black Thunder*** when the slave community's identity is at stake. For example, at the critical moment when the conspirators agree to Gabriel's plan for the rebellion, an ill-defined third-person narrative voice says "they all murmured. Their assent, so near the ground, seemed to rise from the earth itself. H'm. There was something warm and musical in the sound, a deep tremor. It was the earth that spoke" (p. 61). The wordless "H'm," which is the language of nature itself, not only bonds the conspirators to their enterprise, it also bonds the enterprise to nature. The rebellion is sanctified both as a natural and a communal act at this moment.

White characters frequently note the whispering of slaves in the novel; however, they have no access to the words whispered so they cannot interpret the significance of the act. In fact, the white community in ***Black Thunder*** never comprehends the nature or significance of orality, as two encounters between slave culture and white culture demonstrate. In the first, Gabriel overhears Biddenhurst expounding upon "liberty, equality, fraternity" as abstract concepts that can "awaken the masses" (p. 21). If Biddenhurst is paralyzed by his own words and the slogan of the French Revolution remains a sterile concept to him, for Gabriel these same totemic words have a physical and sensuous potency. He feels the words, "they put gooseflesh on . . . [his] arms and shoulders," and he is inspired more by their sound than their sense, for the words make "a strange music" (p. 21). The words themselves do not provoke Gabriel's revolt, however, for they are simply "words for things that had been in his mind, things that he didn't know had names" (p. 21). The white community cannot accept the idea that a mind can house concepts for which it has no words; therefore, it cannot understand the real impetus behind this slave revolt. Despite the claim of one conspirator that "we didn't read no pamphlets. Them pamphlets didn't have nothing to do with us" (p. 200), the white characters insist, even at Gabriel's trial, that he and his followers must have been inspired by the written word. Therefore, they miss the most socially radical fact about this rebellion, that it is prompted by forces outside literate society itself. Gabriel attempts to explain the source of his inspiration by saying "something keep telling me that anything what's equal to a gray squirrel wants to be free. That's how it all come about" (p. 210). This statement is echoed as a formula by various slaves throughout the novel, becoming a communal justification and motto for the rebellion. Gabriel's phrase suggests that freedom is not dependent for its meaning on literate articulation; rather, it is embedded in all nature and thus is a consistent part of all living identity. To deny a being freedom in this sense is to commit an unnatural act. By extension, writing, when used as a tool for oppression, becomes unnatural.

Because Bontemps' white community cannot accept the existence of unarticulated thought, it cannot understand the potent moments of discourse without words in which the slave community affirms its most revolutionary commitments. In a scene that echoes the natural sanctification of the rebellion, the slave community buries Bundy, who has been beaten to death by his master, Thomas Prosser. At Bundy's funeral, the slaves "raised a song without words. They were kneeling with their faces to the sun. Their hands were in the air, the fingers apart, and they bowed and rose together as they sang. Up came the song like a wave, and down went their faces in the dirt" (p. 52). The paradox presented by the song rising like a wet wave out of the dry earth suggests the further paradox that, although the song has no words, it has a communal meaning. Bontemps injects a lyrical passage just after this description, told through an unattributable, communal, narrative voice, that explains the revolutionary intent of the song. Prosser, the interlude explains, "don't even know a tree got a soul same as a man, and . . . [he] act like he done forgot smoke get in his eyes and make him blink" (p. 53). Bundy, who the song claims will become "a *real* smoke man" after his death, will "be in . . . [Prosser's] eyes and in his throat too" (p. 53). Through this curious narrative strategy, the song is depicted for the reader as a wordless communal language, but its import is uninterpretable to those, like Prosser, who depend upon written words to make meaning. As Prosser approaches the mourners, they again break into song as an act of safe but profound rebellion.

The identity and language of slave culture in ***Black Thunder*** is deeply embedded in the natural world, and the white community of the novel has no understanding of or access to the significance of the slaves' acts of speech. This distance, however, is not reciprocal. Significantly, slave culture is not immune to the corrupting influence of the written word. Gabriel's visceral reaction to the phrase "liberty, equality, fraternity" hints at the strange attraction the words of white society have for slaves. Bontemps presents this attraction as the fundamental reason for the failure of Gabriel's revolt, for Gabriel does not rely solely on an appeal to "natural rights" to inspire his followers or establish his authority to lead the revolt. He also appeals to the dangerous authority of Scripture.

When Gabriel first introduces the idea of rebellion to the central group of conspirators, he justifies both the act and his claim to leadership by invoking passages from the Bible. Mingo, a free man and the only literate member of the group, reads passages that describe the punishments God will mete out to those who oppress and enslave the poor, and Gabriel interprets the passages for the group: "God's aiming to give them in the hands of they enemies and all like that. He say he just need a man to make up the hedge and stand in the gap. He's going to cut them down his own self" (p. 47). Gabriel claims to be God's man, and the Scripture he invokes mesmerizes his audience into accepting the rebellion as a fulfillment of the written word.

However, Scripture eventually proves as deceptive and oppressive as other writing in ***Black Thunder.*** Gabriel may claim that God's help is assured because "it says so in the book, and it's plain as day" (p. 47), but on the night the rebellion is to occur, nature offers a different sign, one which Gabriel refuses to read. The worst storm in any character's memory begins on that night, and some of the rebels read the rain as a warning to suspend the revolt. Gabriel, however, rejects this reading of nature by saying:

> They ain't a lasting man nowheres ever heard tell of rain being a sign of a bad hand. . . . I'm going to give the word directly, and them what's coming can come, and them what ain't can talk about signs. Thunder and lightning ain't nothing neither. If it is I invites it to try me a barrel. . . . Touch me if you's so bad, Big Man.
>
> (p. 86)

In this oral challenge to nature's power reminiscent of Ahab's, Gabriel rejects the very source out of which his language and community have been formed. Here he privileges the scriptural word over the language of nature.

The opinion of an anonymous slave woman, told and repeated among the community, asserts that Gabriel's dependence on Scripture is the reason for the rebellion's failure. She complains that there was "too much listening to Mingo read a white man's book. They ain't paid attention to the signs" (p. 166). Gabriel echoes her interpretation: "Maybe we should paid attention to the signs" (p. 214). In this interesting turn on the romantic formula that equates the signs of nature and the words of the Bible as two languages of one author, Bontemps asserts the fundamental difference between the book of nature and Scripture. The call of the thrasher, the warning storm, the "H'm" rising from the ground, all collapse the distinctions between speaker, word, and referent. At its most potent, orality recreates a prelapsarian relation between people and their world. As long as it reads and heeds the signs of nature, the slave community is empowered to act.

Scripture, on the other hand, creates a duplicitous and distancing relationship between people and their world. Because the authority of Scripture preempts the authority of nature's language, it drives a wedge between Gabriel and the source of his identity. It becomes, therefore, another tool of oppression. Like Callender and Biddenhurst before him, Gabriel becomes a victim of the written word, a point Bontemps reinforces by the insistent repetition of the word "Scripture," which means, literally, the written word.

Even if Gabriel had not turned to Scripture for inspiration, however, writing would inevitably have betrayed his cause. He knows that his revolt could be sustained and expanded only by the written word rather than through word of mouth. He vows as soon as the attack on Richmond is complete to send "to all the black folks in all the States" (p. 116) a note similar to the one Toussaint L'Ouverture sent to American slaves encouraging them to expand the slave revolt he had just led in San Domingo. Mingo realizes what Gabriel does not, that Toussaint's note ultimately carries an ironic echo of oppression. Bontemps describes Mingo lying in prison listening for the noise of the gallows and thinking: "What was it Toussaint said? *Brothers, come and unite with me.* Suddenly Mingo awakened to a meaning he had not previously seen in the words. Toussaint was in jail now, maybe dead. *Brothers, come and unite with me*" (p. 169). In this shifting and treacherous phrase lies the paradox that informs Bontemps' view of Afro-American literary history. Orality, despite its direct connection to lived experience, is ephemeral. Because speaking produces no permanent and ineffaceable residue, it only exists at the moment of enactment. The power of orality rests in its capacity to bind speaker, word, and audience together. This power is also a weakness, however, for it is limited temporally and spatially to the moment of action. Only the written word can transcend time and space and thus make permanent the potent but ephemeral declarations of revolution first developed out of the characteristic orality of African-American experience. But writing is an enterprise controlled by the oppressive forces of white society. Because books are free agents subject to the use of all readers, they inevitably function as conservative rather than liberating objects in the world. Therefore, the effort to write revolutionary words will ultimately backfire. To the extent that Gabriel must depend upon the written word to inspire and sustain his revolt, he employs the very mechanisms by which it will be suppressed.

The silencing of "black thunder" lies at the heart of this novel, and the dynamics of suppression, so complexly detailed in this text, lie at the heart of Bontemps' concept of African-American literary history. African-American voice, he claims in his introduction to the 1968 reprint of ***Black Thunder,*** swings between utterance and enforced silence: "Time is not a river," he writes; "Time is a pendulum" (p. vii). The swing of the pendulum is evident not only in the experience of individual writers like Frederick Douglass and Bontemps himself but also in the publishing history of books by American blacks, a history that is punctuated by long periods of public silence like the one which occurred in the wake of Gabriel's revolt.

While conducting research for ***Black Thunder*** during the early 1930s, Bontemps became aware of the "intricate patterns of recurrence, in . . . [his] own experience and in the history . . . [he] had been exploring" (p. vii). He taught at a small Alabama school while he was working on the novel, and his activities, from receiving library books through the mail to discussing the project with outspoken activists like Langston Hughes, aroused the "quaint hostilities" (p. xiii) of his headmaster. The headmaster, perhaps fearing retribution at the hands of whites for employing a black political activist, insisted that Bontemps "make a clean break with the unrest in the world" (p. xiv) if he wished to keep his job. The way to make this break was "by burning most of the books in . . . [his] small library, a number of which were trash in . . . [the headmaster's] estimation anyway, the rest, race-conscious and provocative" (p. xiv). This suggestion taught Bontemps at least three things. First, he learned that books like Frederick Douglass' *My Bondage and My Freedom,* W. E. B. Du Bois' *The Souls of Black Folk,* and Claude McKay's *Harlem Shadows* were considered dangerous in the hands of black Americans because they asserted an independent black voice and identity. Second, he learned that, for the African-American of the 1930s, reading and writing were considered subversive activities. Finally, he encountered directly the power of society to eradicate voices from history. The demand that he burn his library was, by extension, a demand that he reject those voices that most directly spoke to his experience.

Not only do these lessons become the shaping force of Bontemps' rendering of Gabriel's revolt, but he also considers them to be the laws that shape and limit African-American literary history. He finds in the history of Frederick Douglass' autobiography a paradigm for the problem all black writers face in America. In his essay **"The Slave Narrative: An American Genre,"** Bontemps explains that Douglass wrote his autobiography to refute two contradictory accusations leveled against him by Northern whites—either that he was an imposter, or that his accomplishments were proof of the beneficial effects of slavery. Ironically, the book "inadvertently disclosed his new name and whereabouts to . . . [Douglass'] former owner; and he was obliged to flee the country to avoid being apprehended and returned to slavery."[7] Douglass' experience mirrors the situation all African-American writers face, Bontemps argues. Black Americans must write to assert the validity of their own identities in the face of white disbelief, yet the very audience to whom they are writing uses that writing to suppress and silence them.

The fate of ***Black Thunder*** itself provides evidence of the pattern of African-American literary history it proposes. Bontemps wrote it in the wake of the 1929 stock market crash, and he saw the critically acclaimed novel fail commercially because, he claims, "the theme of self-assertion by black men whose endurance was strained to the breaking point was not one that readers of fiction were prepared to contemplate at the time" (p. xv). He viewed its reprinting in 1968, during a period of resurgence in the public recovery of African-American voices, with very guarded hopes: "Now that ***Black Thunder*** is published again," he wrote in the introduction, ". . . I cannot help wondering if its story will be better understood by Americans, both black and white" (p. xv).

Given the absence of ***Black Thunder*** from critical studies of the uses of vernacular traditions in African-American literature, Bontemps' caution appears to be justified. The past decade has been a period of what Bontemps would call "resurgence." During such a period, it is natural to focus on those voices that have been heard and recovered, rather than those voices that have been silenced. This novel, however, attempts, by recreating a voice that has been silenced, to compel its readers to consider the role and consequences of silence in African-American literary history. Bontemps' sense of history as a pendulum informs the narrative structure of ***Black Thunder*** and allows him to define and challenge the silence that history has imposed on black Americans. Gabriel's execution and the subsequent suppression of any inside narrative of the revolt reveals to Bontemps a pattern of systematic elimination of black voices by white society. Martin Luther King's assassination is one example of this pattern; the periodic suppression of slave narratives and the periodic absence of black writers from the lists of major publishers are more subtle but also more pernicious examples.[8] ***Black Thunder*** conquers this aspect of silence by recreating Gabriel's voice and thus posing, as Hazel Carby argues, a "challenge to dominant interpretations of American history."[9] Bontemps' narrative bears a more problematic relationship with a second aspect of silence, however.

The various tropes Bontemps employs to portray oral folk culture suggest that both the individual and communal identities of slaves are forged in a wordless discourse that excludes outsiders and depends for its vitality on its ephemeral and situational nature. The most provocative and significant statements of African-American cultural identity in ***Black Thunder*** occur not in writing but in oral discourse. Further, the printed text radically distorts the social and communal nature of oral expression. Bontemps' assertion that the written word fails both rhetorically and sociologically to be a tool for revolutionary change therefore renders paradoxical his effort to write the spoken word. He acknowledges this limit of writing when he observes that "I never felt that the kind of change a novel could bring would be instantaneous or explosive; nor did I want it to have an explosive effect."[10] If, as Callahan contends, the African-American literary voice transforms orality into the written word, Bontemps examines the limits and difficulties inherent in that transformation. His attempt to give voice to the silence surrounding orality may only be a shadowed success; nonetheless, the whispered yet powerful voices he evokes reveal the complex dynamics of suppression that shape African-American literary history and suggest that the resulting silence is as meaningful as the song of the thrasher.

Notes

1. John F. Callahan, *In the African-American Grain: The Pursuit of Voice in Twentieth-Century Black Fiction* (Urbana: Univ. of Illinois Press, 1988), p. 14. During the past five years alone, books with such diverse critical approaches as Houston A. Baker, Jr., *Blues, Ideology, and Afro-American Literature: A Vernacular Theory* (Chicago: Univ. of Chicago Press, 1984), which studies the relationship of blues and Afro-American literature; Keith E. Byerman, *Fingering the Jagged Grain: Tradition and Form in Recent Black Fiction* (Athens: Univ. of Georgia Press, 1985), which examines the yoking of "methods of modern fiction making with the materials of folk culture" (p. 1) in contemporary black fiction; Henry Louis Gates, Jr., *The Signifying Monkey: A Theory of Afro-American Literary Criticism* (New York: Oxford Univ. Press, 1988), which posits a theory of Afro-American literary criticism based on a cross-cultural study of signifying; and Callahan's study of voice all explore the relation of Afro-American identity and vernacular traditions. Interestingly, this shared assumption is widespread enough to have prompted Hazel Y. Carby, in "Ideologies of Black Folk: The Historical Novel of Slavery," *Slavery and the Literary Imagination,* ed. Deborah E. McDowell and Arnold Rampersad (Baltimore: Johns Hopkins Univ. Press, 1989), pp. 125-43, to observe that "contemporary critical theory . . . has . . . produced a discourse that romanticizes the folk roots of Afro-American culture and denies the transformative power of both historical and urban consciousness" (p. 140).

2. Arna Bontemps, *Black Thunder: Gabriel's Revolt: Virginia: 1800* (Boston: Beacon Press, 1968), p. 196. Subsequent citations will be given in the text.

3. Callahan, p. 15. Bontemps articulates his abiding interest in the link between orality and nature in John O'Brien, ed., *Interviews With Black Writers* (New York: Liveright, 1973), pp. 3-15. He argues that "spontaneity seems quite important in black culture. The person who can act with spontaneity is the one favored by nature." Bontemps then links spontaneity and Primitivism, a topic he "talked about a great deal when . . . [he] taught at Yale." Primitivism, he argues,

    > is often thought of as having no rationale to it. In fact, oftentimes it was actually the result of a long development that had been experimented with. . . . Some African tribes that had no written language—tribes we would take to be the more primitive ones—sometimes had the most sophisticated art. . . . A tribe in Eastern Africa which has given so many collections of proverbs to us had no written language either until very recently. I have deduced from this that they had some reason for not writing down their language, not that they were incapable. . . . They must have very carefully considered the disadvantages of writing. . . . The "book" is something they knew all about, talked about, and rejected.
    >
    > (pp. 14-15)

4. Bernard W. Bell, *The Afro-American Novel and Its Tradition* (Amherst: Univ, of Massachusetts Press, 1987), p. 104. See also Jane Campbell, *Mythic Black Fiction: The Transformation of History* (Knoxville: Univ. of Tennessee Press, 1986), who argues that *Black Thunder* "hinges on the notion that the unschooled common

folk are more likely to initiate and sustain revolt against oppression than are the 'favored' blacks" (p. 8), which leads her to define the novel as "a romance augmented by the oral narrative tradition" (p. 14). Even John M. Reilly, in "History-Making Literature," *Belief vs. Theory in Black American Literary Criticism,* Studies in Black American Literature 2, ed. Joe Weixlmann and Chester Fontenot (Greenwood: Penkevill Publishing Co., 1986), who warns against considering the success of literature to lie "in its utility as social documentation" (p. 89), argues that "the maintenance of cultural continuity" (p. 98) is Bontemps' purpose.

5. Callahan, p. 18. He follows Walter Ong's argument in *Orality and Literacy: The Technologizing of the Word* (New York: Routledge, 1982) when he makes this assertion. Callahan does not, however, acknowledge the ineradicable differences between orality and literacy that Ong carefully traces. Bontemps' novel to some extent anticipates those differences. Campbell notes some of the characteristics of orality Bontemps embeds in his text: the "use of demotic rather than formal language," the use of black English, simile, and formulaic expressions (p. 15).

6. Bell, p. 104, observes that Bontemps depends upon "court records, newspapers, journals, and letters . . . as documentary sources." William Palmer, P. S. McRae, H. W. Flourney, eds., *Calender of Virginia State Papers and other Manuscripts Preserved in the Capitol at Richmond,* 11 vols. (Richmond, 1875-1893), *ix,* 140-73, was Bontemps' source for the transcripts of Gabriel's trial.

7. Arna Bontemps, "The Slave Narrative: An American Genre, *Great Slave Narratives,* ed. Arna Bontemps (Boston: Beacon Press, 1969), p. xvii.

8. In "The Slave Narrative" (p. xvi), Bontemps argues that the backlash from Gabriel's revolt "was responsible for a changed attitude in dealing with the will to freedom by blacks. . . . An intensive effort to obscure, if not to blot out, the names and deeds of black people from the records of time ensued." He then goes on to explore other such moments of silencing in American history.

9. Carby, p. 129.

10. O'Brien, p. 12.

FURTHER READING

Bibliography

Flemming, Robert E. *James Weldon Johnson and Arna Wendell Bontemps: A Reference Guide.* Boston: G. K. Hall & Co., 1978, 149 p.

A comprehensive annotated bibliography on both Bontemps and Johnson, with introductions and indexes for each author.

Biographies

Conroy, Jack. "Memories of Arna Bontemps, Friend and Collaborator." *American Libraries* 15, no. 11 (December 1974): 602-06.

Conroy reminisces about his numerous collaborations with Bontemps on children's literature, and offers commentary on some of Bontemps's other works.

Jones, Kirkland C. *Renaissance Man from Louisiana: A Biography of Arna Wendell Bontemps.* Westport, Conn: Greenwood Press, 1992,

Seminal biography of Bontemps's life and works.

Criticism

Bishop, Rudine Sims. "Heaven is . . . Three African-American Literary Folktales." *The Horn Book Magazine* 75, no. 2 (March-April 1999): 176-81.

Reviews Bontemps's Bubber Goes to Heaven, *along with two other works of children's fiction by African American writers.*

Davis, Mary Kemp. "From Death unto Life: The Rhetorical Function of Funeral Rites in Arna Bontemps's *Black Thunder.*" *Journal of Ritual Studies* 1, no. 1 (winter 1987): 85-101.

Examines Black Thunder *for its use of funeral rites as its central metaphor in its inversion of the typical presentation of death as transition from the world of the living to the world of the dead in the retelling of the Gabriel Prosser conspiracy.*

———. "Arna Bontemps's *Black Thunder*: The Creation of an Authoritative Text of 'Gabriel's Defeat.'" *Black American Literature Forum* 23, no. 1 (spring 1989): 17-36.

Considers Bontemps's novel Black Thunder *in light of the four historical versions of "Gabriel's Defeat"—the thwarted African American conspiracy against white oppressors in 1800—and examines the significance of Bontemps's research into the subject and his literary license with his retelling.*

Gray-Rosendale, Laura. "Geographies of Resistance: Rhetorics of Race and Mobility in Arna Bontemps's *Sad-Faced Boy.*" In *Alternative Rhetorics: Challenges to the Rhetorical Tradition,* edited by Laura Gray-Rosendale and Sibylle Gruber, pp. 149-65. Albany: State University of New York Press, 2001.

Reads Bontemps's children's novel Sad-Faced Boy *from a rhetorical criticism perspective for its presentation of mobility—both physical and psychological.*

Jones, Kirkland C. "Bontemps and the Old South." *African American Review* 27, no. 2 (summer 1993): 179–85.

Traces Bontemps's fondness for and characterizations of the Old South in his work, providing brief discussions of several of Bontemps's novels, short stories, and children's works.

Krzemienski, Ed. "Bontemps's *Black Thunder.*" *The Explicator* 60, no. 1 (fall 2001): 42-44.

Examines the novel Black Thunder *as the first work of fiction to treat slavery as a literary topic.*

Nichols, Charles H., editor. *Arna Bontemps-Langston Hughes Letters, 1925-1967.* New York: Dodd, Mead, 1980, 529 p.

Collection of letters between Harlem Renaissance greats and collaborators Bontemps and Hughes.

OTHER SOURCES FROM GALE:

Additional coverage of Bontemps's life and career is contained in the following sources published by the Gale Group: *Black Literature Criticism,* Vol. 1; *Black Writers,* Ed. 1; *Children's Literature Review,* Vol. 6; *Contemporary Authors,* Vols. 1-4R; *Contemporary Authors New Revision Series* Vols. 4, 35;*Contemporary Authors-Obituary,* Vols. 41-44R; *Contemporary Literary Criticism,* Vols. 1, 18; *Dictionary of Literary Biography,* Vols. 48, 51; *DISCovering Authors Modules: Multicultural, Novelists,* and *Poets*; *DISCovering Authors 3.0*; *Junior DISCovering Authors*; *Major Authors and Illustrators for Children and Young Adults,* Vol. 1; *Major 20th-Century Writers,* Ed. 1, 2; *St. James Guide to Children's Writers,* Vol. 5; *Something about the Author,* Vols. 2, 44; *Something about the Author-Obituary,* Vol. 24; *World Poets*; and *Writers for Children.*

WILLIAM STANLEY BRAITHWAITE

(1878 - 1962)

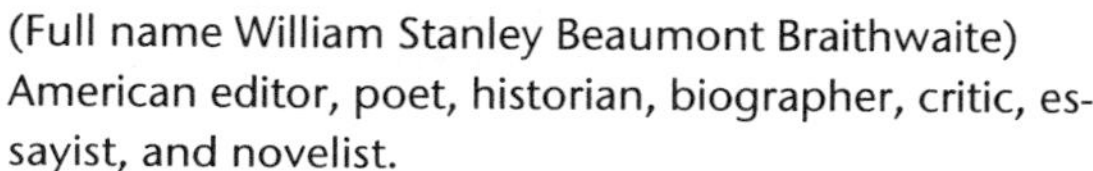

(Full name William Stanley Beaumont Braithwaite) American editor, poet, historian, biographer, critic, essayist, and novelist.

While he was active as a poet and fiction writer throughout the first half of the twentieth century, including the period of the Harlem Renaissance, Braithwaite is considered more significant as an editor whose contribution to American literature took the form of the numerous anthologies of poetry he compiled from various periodicals. He scoured the journals and literary magazines of the first decades of the twentieth century for poetry that he felt deserved greater recognition. In doing so, he helped popularize American poetry and gave many poets, including Robert Frost, significant exposure. Often criticized for his disinterest in using his position as one of the most recognized African American literary figures of his time to help further the New Negro movement, he chose instead to devote himself to nurturing poetry in the United States. As an editor, lecturer, and essayist Braithwaite helped generate a wider appreciation for poetry and in doing so he influenced popular tastes as well as the careers of many American poets.

BIOGRAPHICAL INFORMATION

Braithwaite was the second of five children born to William and Emma Braithwaite. Braithwaite's father, a descendent of European aristocracy and West Indian nobility, was a brilliant man with English ideals who had studied first in Georgetown and then in England. Braithwaite, Sr., was six months away from receiving his medical degree when he returned to Boston; it was always a source of much regret to him that he never completed his degree and instead worked as a nurse. Braithwaite's mother, who married his father when she was sixteen, was the daughter of a light-skinned ex-slave who had been taken advantage of by her master, and who bore several of his children. Braithwaite and his siblings were home-schooled because of his father's belief that neither public nor private schools were good enough for his children. They nevertheless enjoyed middle-class advantages such as summer vacations and a well-stocked library. When Braithwaite was eight, his father died, leaving the family without financial resources. Not long before Braithwaite turned twelve years old, he left his family home in Boston to find full-time employment to help support his mother and his siblings. He found work at a print house, Ginn and Company, where he started as an errand boy and quickly gained the favor of his employers. They let him proofread the galleys and later apprenticed him as a compositor. As he was setting type for an anthology of poetry, he read for the first time the work of John Keats. This experience ignited a passion for writing poetry in the young man. However, as an African American in turn-of-the-century Boston, his opportunities were extremely limited. After moving to New York City, he found his prospects there to be even worse than they had been in Boston. The racism he faced as he looked for work led Braithwaite to determine to work towards fostering a cultural understanding that African Americans were equal to whites in their pursuit and creation of literature. He felt that the best way to do this was to avoid the backlash of a double standard by refusing to treat racial experience and Black culture in his work until that cultural understanding had been acknowledged and accepted. This philosophy came in direct conflict with the tenets of the Harlem Renaissance writers and thinkers, who felt it was only by assertion of those racial experiences and Black culture that any advance could be made towards equality.

In 1903 Braithwaite married Emma Kelly and returned to Boston, where he felt racial discrimination was less of an impediment to his pursuit of a literary career. His poetry began appearing in Boston newspapers, and in 1904 his first collection of poetry, *Lyrics of Life and Love,* was published. It had not been an easy task for Braithwaite to secure a publisher, as they agreed to publish his work only if he could obtain 200 advance subscriptions. Braithwaite was able to obtain the subscriptions, but the process left him angry and disheartened. Braithwaite would publish another slender collection of his own verse, but he soon found his greater interest and aptitude lay in collecting, editing, and anthologizing the works of other poets. Always enamored of English poetry from earlier centuries, in 1906 he published the anthology *The Book of Elizabethan Verse,* which he followed with *The Book of Georgian Verse* (1908) and *The Book of Restoration Verse* (1909). Braithwaite, who had not received even an eighth-grade diploma, was now positioned as a scholar whose editions were being used in college classrooms. W. E. B. Du Bois, who would become a lifelong friend, selected Braithwaite to serve as a member of the editorial board on his revolutionary literary magazine *The Crisis,* which Du Bois founded in 1910. Braithwaite's increasing passion for American poetry led him to collect the first of his anthologies of magazine verse. Unable to find a publisher who supported his vision for an anthology of the best magazine verse of a given year, Braithwaite issued the first and second of these annual anthologies at his own expense. He chose poetry that he felt was universal, upheld his beliefs in beauty and life, and was color-blind in its message and intent. He met with popular success and seventeen successive annual collections were published. His choices for inclusion often met with criticism from those who felt his selections were too traditional and by personal resentment from poet friends who were angered by his exclusion of their work. The growing momentum of the Harlem Renaissance found no great advocate in Braithwaite or his anthologies, as he generally excluded works that were overtly ethnic, racial, political, modernist, or revolutionary. This is not to say that Braithwaite turned his back on his African American heritage. Long before his first annual anthology appeared, he had put together a collection of writings by African Americans that he had planned to publish as *The Anthology of Negro Authors: Prose and Verse.* This collection was never accepted by any publisher, and what could have been a significant contribution to African American letters never saw the light of day. Braithwaite also contributed essays to periodicals and wrote historical studies, including *The Story of the Great War* (1919). With the onset of the economic hardship of the Depression, Braithwaite was forced to cease publishing his annual anthologies. He moved south to Atlanta, where he accepted a position as a professor of English and American Literature at Atlanta University. There he taught for ten years, along with his friend Du Bois. In 1945 Braithwaite retired from Atlanta University and moved back to New York. He continued to contribute essays to magazines and searched in vain for a publisher for his anthology of African American writers. He published one last collection of magazine verse, the *Anthology of Magazine Verse for 1958.* As his eyesight was failing, Braithwaite made himself personally available to a new generation of poets and students looking to interview him in search of a connection to the formative years of the new African American identity born out of the Harlem Renaissance. He died in 1962.

MAJOR WORKS

While the bulk of Braithwaite's work was editorial in nature, his two volumes of poetry, *Lyrics of Life and Love* and *The House of Falling Leaves* (1908), offer verses Pre-Raphaelite in spirit and traditionally Romantic in technique. *The House of Falling Leaves* is generally thought to be the stronger of the two collections, with pieces such as "La Belle de Demerara," which concerns his great-grandmother, who was the daughter of a French nobleman and fled her native Martinique with her lover, an Englishman. His poetry does not contain racial themes or touch on African American culture; instead, Braithwaite's poems largely imitate the Romantic writers he loved. In addition to his poetry, Braithwaite contributed essays to periodicals, including his "Some Contemporary Poets of the Negro Race" (published in *Crisis* in 1919), in which he considers the contributions of Paul Lawrence Dunbar, William Wells Brown, and W. E. B. Du Bois, among others. In this same essay, he discusses his belief that African American writers did not need to think or write on racial subjects to be considered great artists, and that by doing so they were separating themselves from white writers and thus upholding the cultural assumption that Blacks and whites are different. His annual anthologies, which came to be known as "The Braithwaites," were the source of his fame. Inclusion of Robert Frost in his anthology helped further the then struggling poet's career. However, Braithwaite also included works by many poets who quickly fell back into obscurity. Likewise, he did not favor Modernism and excluded works that have since become recognized as masterpieces of the time, including T. S. Eliot's "Love Song of J. Alfred Prufrock." Considered by some critics mediocre and undiscriminating in taste, Braithwaite's anthologies are nevertheless significant because of the attention they brought to American poetry and for the subtle but sure influence Braithwaite's editorial taste had on shaping the tastes of readers and poets alike.

CRITICAL RECEPTION

Much of the critical attention devoted to Braithwaite is centered on his conscious opposition to the New Negro movement. Called by some contemporaries an Uncle Tom, his belief in assimilation as the best route towards equality caused contemporaries such as Langston Hughes to criticize the poet-editor and invited the scorn of many Black figures involved in the 1960s civil rights movement. Critics today are interested in where Braithwaite's social and literary stance places him in the history of Black letters, and Lisa Szefel has argued that Braithwaite was in fact a positive, if often unassuming, influence on Black identity in the first half of the twentieth century. Others concern themselves with the breadth of influence Braithwaite had on the development of early twentieth century poetics. In his role as popularizer of poetry, he is often compared to Harriet Monroe, founder of *Poetry* magazine, for they had similar goals in the same time period. While his own creative output is relatively small and arguably of minor significance, his personal and editorial influence, as well as his controversial belief in assimilation as a means to gaining eventual equality, continue to spark modest critical and scholarly interest in Braithwaite and his work.

PRINCIPAL WORKS

The Canadian (novel) 1901

Lyrics of Life and Love (poetry) 1904

The Book of Elizabethan Verse [editor] (poetry) 1906

The Book of Georgian Verse [editor] (poetry) 1908

The House of Falling Leaves (poetry) 1908

The Book of Restoration Verse [editor] (poetry) 1909

**Anthology of Magazine Verse* [editor] (poetry) 1913-29

Year Book of American Poetry [editor] (poetry) 1914

The Poetic Year for 1916 [editor] (poetry) 1917

The Book of Modern British Verse [editor] (poetry) 1919

The Golden Treasury of Magazine Verse [editor] (poetry) 1919

"Some Contemporary Poets of the Negro Race" [published in the journal *Crisis*] (essay) 1919

The Story of the Great War (history) 1919

Victory: Celebrated by Thirty-Eight American Poets [editor] (poetry) 1919

Going Over Tindel (novel) 1924

Our Lady's Choir: A Contemporary Anthology of Verse by Catholic Sisters [editor] (poetry) 1931

Selected Poems (poetry) 1948

The Bewitched Parsonage: The Story of the Brontës (biography) 1950

Anthology of Magazine Verse for 1958 [editor] (poetry) 1958

The William Stanley Braithwaite Reader (criticism, reminiscences, autobiography, and letters) 1972

* This anthology of poetry from American periodicals was edited by Braithwaite and published annually for sixteen years between 1913 and 1929.

GENERAL COMMENTARY

BENJAMIN BRAWLEY (ESSAY DATE 1930)

SOURCE: Brawley, Benjamin. "William Stanley Braithwaite." In *The Negro in Literature and Art in the United States*, pp. 89-96. New York: Duffield & Company, 1930.

In the following excerpt, Brawley provides an overview of Braithwaite's poetry.

Prominent for some years, first as poet and then as critic, has been William Stanley Braithwaite, of Boston. The work of this author belongs not so much to Negro literature as to American literature in the large, and he has encouraged and inspired a host of other writers. With singleness of purpose he has given himself to books and the book world, and it is by this devotion that he has won the distinct success that he has achieved.

In 1904 Mr. Braithwaite published a small volume of poems entitled ***Lyrics of Life and Love.*** This was followed four years later by ***The House of Falling Leaves.*** Within recent years, however, he has given little time to his own verse, becoming more and more distinguished as a critic of American poetry. For several years he has been a valued contributor to *The Boston Evening Transcript,* and he has had verse or critical essays in *The Forum,* the *Century, Scribner's,* and the *Atlantic.* He has collected and edited ***The Book of Elizabethan Verse, The Book of Georgian Verse,*** and ***The Book of Restoration Verse;*** he has published the ***Anthology of Magazine Verse*** for each year since 1913, also ***The Golden Treasury of Magazine Verse;*** and, while editor of the *Poetry Review* in 1916, he projected a series of Contemporary American Poets. In 1917 he brought together in a volume, ***The Poetic Year,*** a special series of articles which he had contributed to the *Transcript.* The aim of this was, in the form of conversations among a small group of friends, to whom fanciful and suggestive Greek names had been given, to discuss the poetry that had appeared in 1916. After the war appeared ***Victory: Celebrated by Thirty-eight American Poets*** and ***The Story of the Great War*** for young people. In 1918 Mr. Braithwaite was awarded the Spingarn Medal.

In a review of this writer's poetry we have to consider especially the two collections, ***Lyrics of Life and Love,*** and ***The House of Falling Leaves,*** and the poems that have more recently appeared in the *Atlantic, Scribner's,* and other magazines. It is to be hoped that before very long he will publish a new edition of his poems. The earlier volumes are out of print, and a new book could contain the best of them, as well as what has appeared more recently. ***Lyrics of Life and Love*** embodied the best of the poet's early work. The little book contains eighty pages, and no one of the lyrics takes up more than two pages, twenty in fact being exactly eight lines in length. This appearance of fragility, however, is a little deceptive. While Keats and Shelley are constantly evident as the models in technique, the yearning of more than one lyric reflects the deeper romantic temper. The bravado and the tenderness of the old poets are evident again in the two Christmas pieces, **"Holly Bery and Mistletoe,"** and **"Yule-Song: A Memory":**

The trees are bare, wild flies the snow,
  Hearths are glowing, hearts are merry—
High in the air is the Mistletoe,
  Over the door is the Holly Berry.
Never have care how the winds may blow,
  Never confess the revel grows weary—
Yule is the time of the Mistletoe,
  Yule is the time of the Holly Berry.

. . . . .

December comes, snows come,
  Comes the wintry weather;
Faces from away come—
  Hearts must be together.
    Down the stair-steps of the hours
    Yule leaps the hills and towers—
  Fill the bowl and hang the holly,
  Let the times be jolly.

"The Watchers" is in the spirit of Kingsley's "The Three Fishers":

Two women on the lone wet strand—
  (*The wind's out with a will to roam*)
The waves wage war on rocks and sand,
  (*And a ship is long due home.*)

The sea sprays in the women's eyes—
  (*Hearts can writhe like the sea's wild foam*)
Lower descend the tempestuous skies,
  (*For the wind's out with a will to roam.*)

"O daughter, thine eyes be better than mine,"
  (*The waves ascend high on yonder dome*)
"North or South is there never a sign?"
  (*And a ship is long due home.*)

They watched there all the long night through—
  (*The wind's out with a will to roam*)
Wind and rain and sorrow for two—
  (*And heaven on the long reach home.*)

The second volume marked a decided advance in technique. When we remember also the Pre-Raphaelite spirit, with its love of rhythm and imagery, we are not surprised to find here an appreciation **"To Dante Gabriel Rossetti."** Especially has the poet made progress in the handling of the sonnet, as may be seen in the following:

My thoughts go marching like an armèd host
  Out of the city of silence, guns and cars;
Troop after troop across my dreams they post
  To the invasion of the wind and stars.
O brave array of youth's untamed desire!
  With thy bold, dauntless captain Hope to lead
His raw recruits to Fate's opposing fire,
  And up the walls of Circumstance to bleed.
How fares the expedition in the end?

When this may heart shall have old age for
king
And to the wars no further troop can send,
What final message will the arm'stice bring?
The host gone forth in youth the world to meet,
In age returns—in victory or defeat?

Then there is the epilogue with its heart-cry:

Lord of the mystic star-blown gleams
Whose sweet compassion lifts my dreams;
Lord of life in the lips of the rose
That kiss desire; whence Beauty grows;
Lord of the power inviolate
That keeps immune thy seas from fate,

. . . . .

Lord, Very God of these works of thine,
Hear me, I beseech thee, most divine!

Within very recent years Mr. Braithwaite has attracted unusual attention among the discerning by a new note of mysticism that has crept into his verse. This was first observed in **"Sandy Star,"** that appeared in the *Atlantic* (July, 1909):

No more from out the sunset,
No more across the foam,
No more across the windy hills
Will Sandy Star come home.

He went away to search it,
With a curse upon his tongue,
And in his hands the staff of life
Made music as it swung.

I wonder if he found it,
And knows the mystery now:
Our Sandy Star who went away
With the secret on his brow.

The same note is in **"The Mystery"** (or **"The Way,"** as the poet prefers to call it) that appeared in *Scribner's* (October, 1915):

He could not tell the way he came
Because his chart was lost:
Yet all his way was paved with flame
From the bourne he crossed.

He did not know the way to go,
Because he had no map:
He followed where the winds blow,—
And the April sap.

He never knew upon his brow
The secret that he bore—
And laughs away the mystery now
The dark's at his door.

Mr. Braithwaite has done well. He has consistently kept before him his vision, and after years of hard work his position is now one of unique distinction. A few years ago a special reception was accorded him in New York by the authors of America, and in an editorial of November 30, 1915, the *Transcript* said: "He has helped poetry to readers as well as to poets. One is guilty of no extravagance in saying that the poets we have—and they may take their place with their peers in any country—and the gathering deference we pay them, are created largely out of the stubborn, self-effacing enthusiasm of this one man. In a sense their distinction is his own. In a sense he has himself written their poetry. Very much by his toil they may write and be read. Not one of them will ever write a finer poem than Braithwaite himself has lived already."

GLENN CLAIRMONTE (ESSAY DATE 1973)

SOURCE: Clairmonte, Glenn. "The Cup-Bearer: William Stanley Braithwaite of Boston." *College Language Association Journal* 17, no. 1 (September 1973): 101-6.

In the following essay, Clairmonte offers an account of the influences on Braithwaite's early life and his apprenticeship to a printer.

When it was known that a certain Bostonian was for fifteen years a college professor of English literature and was awarded an honorary doctorate although he had not attended school long enough to receive the eighth-grade diploma, many people shook their heads in wonder, not being able to divine the reason for his extraordinary erudition. But the secret lay in a childhood occurrence that could scarcely have been an accident. Arthur Koestler's recent book, *The Roots of Coincidence,* encourages me to realize that the golden thread connects many of the mysterious incidents in history.

William Stanley Braithwaite was the native Bostonian who during twenty years as contributing editor of the Boston *Evening Transcript* became the cup-bearer to countless striving poets as well as the means of their recognition.

I made his acquaintance in the fall of 1915 when the death of my mother left me isolated from the world of beautiful language, with which my mother had been my only contact. Without her I was devastated, to say the least. As usually happens in this life, the void had to be filled. It was William Stanley Braithwaite who attracted me like a magnet—for, when reading his essay on the rhythm of April I cried, "And he's alive, not dead like Byron and Shelley!"

I wrote him a letter, not knowing that hundreds of other hungry young souls were doing the same. He not only replied but actually published the poem I had enclosed in my letter. But, especially, he called on me the next time he was in New York. Although I was shy enough to treat him with the dignity of my ignorant youth, my emotional life fed upon his friendship, you may be sure. Then, in 1916, when the country was convulsed with the eerie madness of a presidential campaign, I fled to Boston to get the balance I needed. Years afterward, when I recalled how he had allowed me to visit in his studio for several days while he sonorously read poetry to me, I said, "Why didn't you get rid of me? I'm always so busy these days that I get rid of callers." He replied, "I did get rid of many, but not you." By that time I was grown-up enough to savor the compliment.

Now that he has slipped over the ridge to inhabit a less physical area of the universe, I have been reading Dr. Philip Butcher's selection of his literary effusions and want to make my own comments in his memory.

He was born in 1878 to a colored family emigrated from British Guiana, where they had become prominent while installing democratic reforms during two generations of effort. When his father died the year he was seven, Braithwaite might have seemed saddled with enough misfortune to preclude his later fame. He had been kept out of school because his proud father tried to improve upon the public school system by teaching his children at home and thus giving them a touch of the Oxford accent that lifted them as with a touch of aristocracy. Later the boy volunteered to quit school for the sake of his widowed mother. Whenever he watched her going down the walk toward the home of strangers for her day's work, tears gushed with anguish not only at his own loneliness during her absence but more pointedly at the waste of her youth in scarcely remunerative labor among people who failed to gauge her beautiful humanity. He wanted to undertake man's estate in order to relieve her of the family responsibility.

Although in later years his friends called him Stanley, his mother called him Willie as she buttoned his coat before letting him start out. To her he must have seemed too frail to make any impact upon a hostile world. There was certainly anguish of her own when she saw him square his bony shoulders without half guessing how steep was the road before him.

"I recall the early September day in 1890," said Braithwaite years later, "three months before I had reached my thirteenth birthday, when I rode up to the East Boston terminal of the Boston Revere Beach and Lynn Railroad, and took the ferry across the harbor to Boston in quest of my first job."

This lanky light-colored boy was aware that he was sacrificing school, and surely he believed there was no possibility of his ever acquiring an education. His sadness, he said, "must have pierced the future and tasted the mood and temper of regret and struggle which denial of an opportunity for schooling was to impose. A gentle depression pursued me all the way to Boston."

But even then the mellow sunlight beguiled him, and he admired the ochre-colored marsh grasses that edged the muddy flats. The gleam of the ocean far off encouraged him as he left his boyhood behind and accepted the fact that his destiny had to be shaped out of confusion and the unknown. He said afterward, "While I crossed the harbor on the ferryboat the future was tumbling through my heart, my spirit absorbing the foams of fate." He could see the gray shaft of the Ames Building not far from the domed State Capitol in the city where he meant to demand the right to operate as a man.

"There was the city I loved, veined with memories of happy hours playing hockey on the Common and shadows of childhood disappointments."

In that final hour of childhood William Stanley Braithwaite could not even have hoped that he would become the confidant of three generations of English and American poets. He was to spend his whole life in supplying them with the refreshment of appreciation, using a dearly earned education to evaluate their production. The most noticeable symbol of his assistance to making poetry a force was his dogged publication for seventeen years of an annual anthology of the best among verses that appeared in magazines. Editors who had not previously been inclined to spare space for unknown versifiers took a new attitude when there was a possibility that their journals would be honored by inclusion of their chosen poems in the anthology each year.

Many elements contrived to bring Braithwaite to his fullest usefulness, and his original necessity to earn a living turned out to be not an isolated incident. Was his way already prepared before that dreamer-going-on-thirteen set out on his frightened attack upon the practical world? Or was it an accident that he obtained a position with Ginn and Company, the textbook publishers at the corner of Pearl and Purchase Streets? In this job it was his duty to deliver proofs from the press to the publisher's offices on Tremont Street, returning with authors' corrected proofs.

Between his four-a-day trips to the editorial offices he had nothing to do, but as he sat at a little table outside the manager's office he watched the nimble fingers of compositors selecting type and setting it for the printing of books. He learned that the textbooks emanating from this center were going out for use by students in public schools and colleges, those places forever closed to him. The manager had the impulse to ask if he would like to read during the waiting periods, offering him a chance at any books on the office shelves. The first title the boy selected was Church's *Greek Gods and Heroes.* Suddenly he was engulfed in a grand new universe, and many other books on those shelves contained oil for the lamp of his imagination. This casual upliftment was to catapult him into his profession.

The manager himself must have had an imagination for, after observing "the new boy" several days, he asked, "Would you like to learn the trade of compositor?"

No doubt he had noticed the poise and courtesy that the boy's father had taught him as a carry-over from the days under English rule in the Caribbean.

It was necessary for Mrs. Braithwaite to give her consent to her son's apprenticeship, and she must have been pleased that her thin child was beginning to carve a niche for himself. How much could she have supposed of the importance this step was toward his eventual contribution to literature?

While learning to distribute type from the page-forms returned from the foundry after the plates were made, he was given a "case," a square hollow box three feet by two, containing racks of unequal width that held the lead letters of the alphabet. The racks were arranged so that the letters most frequently used were nearer the compositor's hand for a rapid pick-up. When he began to show dexterity the manager gave him a text to set up.

In his autobiography he said, "I have never lost the savor of this triumph, for the mechanical skill which won it was glorified by the acquaintance I made with the story of England's greatest naval hero."

He found himself setting the type for the publication of *Life of Lord Nelson,* by the Poet Laureate of England, Robert Southey. Imagine having the pleasure of reading while earning a living!

Early in January of the following year the Ginn press was moved to its newly built home on First Street in Cambridge. That location was then but a river road along the banks of the Charles River basin between the old Longfellow and East Cambridge bridges. This building was the first of the many large structures that gradually evolved into an industrial center in that marshy region. Henceforth it was Braithwaite's duty to print the galley proofs of the reading materials, and there was no objection to his making an extra impression for himself. Reading had already become his passion, and at home he collected the galleys into a personal library that consisted of the best subjects taught in the colleges. He pored over them for many a fleeting hour. As his taste developed, his fascination with the intricacies of beautiful language represented his rebirth.

In the new building, with a linotype and other new equipment, he was stationed beside a top-floor window that over-looked the Charles River, and across it he could see the terraced houses of Beacon Hill as well as the gilded dome of the State House. That outlook seemed gift enough.

"I did not know it was a day of annunciation," said he, "and that my spirit would magnify the Lord for making me a chosen vessel."

But that was the day when the manager handed him a sheaf of printed pages and instructed him as to the character of type and size of type pages that he was to prepare. He fixed the pages to the copy-holder, seized the stick, and began to pick the type-letters from the case. Innocently enough he found himself setting the line:

Thou still unravish'd bride of quietness

and the rhythm in those words captivated him, hurtling him into the abyss of love. By the time he had reached the further lines:

"Beauty is truth, truth beauty"—that is all
Ye know on earth, and all ye need to know,

he had become inflamed, lost forever in magic. Moving from Keats to the other poets in the textbook, he felt new revelations erupting in his mind and heart. The contagion was too virulent to be disregarded. His thoughts burned into words of his own, which in turn took on an orchestration within his helpless cranium.

His first book of original poems appeared in 1904, but he had already explored the wide field of English poetry. In 1906 he edited ***The Book of Elizabethan Verse,*** and in 1908 that was followed by ***The Book of Georgian Verse,*** the same year that his own second volume reached the public. By that time he was more a scholar than a poet, and he collected ***The Book of Restoration Verse*** in 1909. What a comfort to know that his own work was being used in college teaching!

At an Episcopal revival in Rhode Island he met his future wife, whose name was Emma as his revered mother's had been. They raised seven handsome sons and daughters, most of them named after poets, and several grandchildren who enriched their lives. For many years they lived in Arlington Heights, in a large frame house surrounded by an immense garden.

Braithwaite was now aware of the value of unsung poets, and he determined to give them as much audience as he could attract to them. It was for this reason that in 1913 his first ***Anthology of Magazine Verse*** went on the market, and in 1914 he added to a similar collection the ***Year Book of American Poetry.*** This combination he continued to give yearly to his ever growing number of readers.

"The West must be a wonderful place to live," he said to me. "Bookstores there order many copies of the anthology every year. People there must love poetry."

Of course he inserted in the list of his accomplishments various other titles: in 1917 ***The Poetic Year for 1916;*** in 1918 ***The Golden Treasury of Magazine verse;*** and the following year ***The Book of Modern British Verse*** as well as ***Victory: Celebrated by Thirty-Eight American Poets.*** He wrote ***The Story of the Great War*** that same year. In 1931 he presented ***Our Lady's Choir: A Contemporary Anthology of Verse by Catholic Sisters.*** In 1948 his own ***Selected Poems*** appeared, and in 1950 ***The Bewitched Parsonage: The Story of the Brontës.***

Braithwaite's wide acquaintance among editors and writers continued over all the years, mostly by correspondence because he never had the means for far traveling. His phenomenal memory made it possible for him constantly to address poets with detailed comments on their best works and to congratulate those who won honors. He always lived the lives of others, not only in the reading and loving of the great works and the contemporary expressions but actually in the satisfaction that others garnered from their own works. Perhaps for this very reason his experience was many faceted, bulging with satisfaction of his own in recognition of all others who carried literature on to the next and the next generation. He might have called that process "carrying the torch," for he had many of the old-time similes in his thoughts.

Braithwaite had been self-reliant for so many years that he had a surprise on one of the days when he was in a busy section of the city. Too proud to appeal for funds to his rather affluent grown-up sons, he had gone to "the Harvard yard" in order to dispose at the Library of some letters he owned that had been signed by famous writers. On his way home, as he was about to step off the curb in order to cross the street, a Boy Scout stepped up and took his elbow, eager to see him safely through the traffic. With his most courteous suavity he thanked the Boy Scout and yet, as he told me, "I realized for the first time that I was nothing but an old man." Even as he said this his eyes were twinkling and he was clearly not at all judging himself as old.

But he did want to wind up his years of lauding the poets of America with one more splurge, and he was fortunate in winning the without-compensation assistance of the Virginia poet, Margaret Haley Carpenter. She backed the project with faith and hard work, in order to make possible his 1959 publication of the ***Anthology of Magazine Verse for 1958,*** with insertion of many poems that had been included in his previously published collections. Although he continued to write away up into 1962, there were no further publications under his name.

On his eightieth birthday the American Poetry Society honored him with a dinner at New York, and the photograph taken of him on that occasion shows that his charm and goodlooks were prolonged.

At about this time he wrote a friend, "I am reconciled to the fact that some day I must be blind, but Oh, I shall be grateful for all the Seasons I have known, the multi-colored flowers, the curving hills, the roll and dash of the sea upon rocks and sands."

When he succumbed at the home of his librarian daughter, Katherine Keats (so-named in remembrance of the English poet), there were generous obituaries, and hundreds mourned throughout the country when the news of his death was flashed by television. Even in England many poets whose works had been praised in Braithwaite's reviews realized their loss. His unique position as one loved by both whites and Negroes without discrimination, throughout his four-score years, may have been one of the basic reasons for the current bond between the races. He had consciously aimed all his attention upon literature regardless of racial origin, and in that way he forged a bridge permanent though not easily defined.

The latest evidence of Braithwaite's significance has been the 1972 publication by the University of Michigan Press of *The William Stanley Braithwaite Reader,* compiled by Philip Butcher,

Dean at Morgan State College. It has been suggested that Braithwaite's range gave him a perspective that can improve the output of every embryonic author; that everyone preparing to publish should first read this book in order to appraise his work as to whether it can add to the past history of literature.

WILLIAM H. ROBINSON (ESSAY DATE 1977)

SOURCE: Robinson, William H. "William Stanley Beaumont Braithwaite." In *Black New England Letters: The Uses of Writings in Black New England,* pp. 89-111. Boston: Trustees of the Public Library of the City of Boston, 1977.

In the following essay, Robinson considers Braithwaite's literary relationship with notable African American writers of the 1920s through the 1940s and refutes claims that the poet-editor was removed from the canon of Black literature.

On the Black Heights of Parnassus

In his 1937 autobiography, *A Long Way From Home,* poet and novelist Claude McKay wrote,

> I had sent some poems to William Stanley Braithwaite, who was highly placed as a critic on the *Boston Evening Transcript.* Mr. Braithwaite was distinguished for his literary dialogues in the Literary Supplement of the *Transcript,* in which the characters were intellectual Bostonians with Greek names and conversed in lofty accents that were all Greek to me.
>
> In Mr. Braithwaite's writings there was not the slightest indication of what sort of American he might be. And I was surprised to read in the Negro magazine, *The Crisis,* that he was a colored man. He said that my poems were good, but that, barring two, any reader could tell the author was a Negro. And because of almost insurmountable prejudice against all things Negro, he said, he would advise me to write and send to magazines only such poems as did not betray my racial identity. . . . So, I thought, that was what Boston made of a colored intellectual. . . .[1]

In 1973 appeared Jean Wagner's *Black Poets in the United States,* and there is no sampling therein of Braithwaite's poetry. By way of explanation, Wagner said,

> Braithwaite's persistent silence certainly amounts to the rejection of his blackness, for it is extremely difficult to accept the polite but specious explanation offered by James Weldon Johnson, also of West Indian background. "He has written no poetry motivated or colored by race. This has not been a matter of intention on his part; it is simply that race has not impinged upon him as it has upon other Negro poets." . . . Even if Johnson's supposition could be considered valid for Braithwaite's own poetry, it would fail to account for the biased tendency that also marks his activity as an anthologist. Setting aside the anthologies of magazine poetry that he published almost every year from 1913 on, we find it strange that he could bring out in succession ***The Book of Elizabethan Verse*** (1906), ***The Book of Georgian Verse*** (1909), ***The Book of Restoration Verse*** (1910), ***Modern British Verse*** (1919), an ***Anthology of Massachusetts Verse*** (1922), and even a ***Contemporary Anthology of Verse by Catholic Sisters*** (1931), but not a single anthology of Negro Poetry. We cannot be convinced that it just so happened that he felt a greater kinship with poetry written by Catholic nuns than that of Negro writers! The facts impose on us the conclusion that Braithwaite had not the least desire to be identified with the black world and what it stands for. There is, consequently, no need to examine him here.[2]

Something very like these uninformed and misinformed opinions has for too long clouded the real career of Braithwaite; as a result he is today not as widely known and/or reprinted as he ought to be. Both McKay and Wagner badly misunderstand the realities involved. No person with William Stanley Braithwaite's background or history could hope to be neglectful of black concerns.

He was born December 6, 1878, on Osborne Street in Boston, of a distinguished, mixed family from Europe and the West Indies. He was that sickly a child that his British-minded father, from the Crown colony of Guiana on the northern coast of South America, was prompted to take him back to Georgetown, where for a year the baby was nursed and loved back into good health by Aunt Hester, an English nursemaid of the family. Braithwaite's great-grandfather was a shoe merchant in Barbados, where he enjoyed a reputation for being the best Latin scholar thereabouts. His great-grandmother was the daughter of a French nobleman, educated in Paris, who eloped with an Englishman named Smith to Georgetown, Demerara, British Guiana (today's independent Guyana) and they had two children, Henrietta and William. William went on to become Sir William Haynes Smith, then Lord High Commissioner of Cyprus, when that Turkish island was transferred to English authority in 1882; upon retirement he became next chairman of the Naval Strategy Board, which office was recorded to his credit in Burke's Peerage as late as 1910. "My grandfather migrated from Barbados to Georgetown where he met and married the remarkably beautiful Henrietta Smith; both of them were well provided for by a legacy upon the death of my great-grandmother. With the money my grandfather bought and edited a newspaper, *The Creole,* which championed the rights of the colonists." Worn out from his tireless crusading on behalf of the colonists, he was urged to rest back in Barbados, where he died in 1874, insolvent but fulfilled. Grateful residents of Demerara erected in Georgetown a bronze monument in recognition of his unselfish services. His maternal grandmother was a beautiful slave who, he suspected, was taken advantage of by some "lustful master" by whom she bore three girls, one of whom, Emma, was his mother, born in 1860. Neither his mother nor her sisters looked notably black and when their mother took them to Boston, where she found work as a cook, resentful, bad-mouthing blacks attacked them unmercifully. His father, who had interrupted his medical studies at Oxford to migrate to Boston, was only twenty-three when he married Emma, who was only sixteen. From their union came five children, of whom William Stanley was the second.

With his lofty notions of selfhood, Braithwaite's father did not believe that any children were good enough to associate with his own. He refused to allow neighborhood English, Scotch, and Irish children to play with his; and, not believing in the American school system, he kept young Braithwaite (and his older sister) out of the public schools, instructing them at home. It was not until he was eight years old, when his imperious father died insolvent, that the children were allowed to attend public schools. Poor, the mother finding whatever work she could—"I used to watch her going down the walk banked with snow on bitterly cold winter mornings, the tears gushed from my eyes with sympathy"—young Braithwaite had to quit school at age twelve to get work and help support the family. There was a string of menial jobs, errand boy in a barber supply house at a weekly salary of $2.50; a door opener at a ladies cloak house—"my duties . . . were reserved for a colored boy. . . ." Managing to squeeze in some hockey play on the Boston Common, he finally got a job with Ginn and Company, school and textbook publishers, his job being to deliver proofs to the firm's printing house, located elsewhere, and returning them, corrected, in the afternoons. He became a compositor at this firm and quickly took to setting type. It was while so doing that he read before him some lines from a poem by John Keats—*"Thou still unravish'd bride of quietness"*—that he was hypnotized by a love for poetry that would remain with him throughout the rest of his long life. He even began composing and setting his original verses until he soon had an entire manuscript, which, his mother moving to New York in 1900, he took to William Dean Howells, who, as a rule, did not read the poems, but became Braithwaite's friend for life. He was rejected from newspaper after newspaper in New York where he sought work, and where he was forever asked the same question: "You don't mind if I ask you your nationality?" To which he always replied that he was an American Negro. This persistent racism was what helped young Braithwaite to resolve his ambitions.

> I had a taste that winter in New York of what the difficulties and injustices were for one of color who wanted to be accepted at his worth and on terms of equality in the vocation of his choosing. I was forced to face problems which somehow I had deluded myself would solve themselves upon the higher, the universal, the spiritual plane of art. It was my belief that Beauty and Art were the leveller of all distinctions. . . .
>
> The racial conditions which closed the doors to opportunities for employment of the kind I sought in New York that winter convinced me that whatever may be the quality and distinction of achievement in literature, if that literature was confined to racial materials and experiences, it would be appraised and judged by a different standard than the literature of American writers in general. For the good of the artistic sincerity, for the cultural values, which must be purified and sustained in a country so much below the standard of European achievements, this double standard of criticism must be destroyed. This purpose became the dominating influence upon my efforts in the career I dreamed for the future. . . .[3]

Other realities would soon impinge upon him and he would modify these notions, but he was on his way toward an understanding of the peculiarities of American aesthetics; he was on his way toward a lifelong dedication toward making a literary point for himself, his fellow black Americans, and, in his own way, for all American culture.

> The resolution I formed . . . was to express myself on the common ground of American authorship, to demonstrate, in however humble a degree, that a man of color was the equal of any other man in possession of the attributes that produced a literature of human thought and experience, and to force a recognition of the reading public and the authority of critical opinion. And I resolved with equal determination, not to treat in any phase, in any form, for any purpose, racial materials or racial experiences, *until* this recognition had been won, recorded, and universally confirmed.[4]

With such daring stance, he left New York in April of 1901 and returned to Newport to work but really to realize a book of poems that would physically document his resolve. He had already, by then, published a few pieces in the old Boston *Courant* and the Boston *Journal.* His greatest good luck came when the Boston *Transcript* began to publish his poems. He met Emma Kelley, a black woman, in Newport in 1901, married her in 1903, and set to work to establish himself as "a poet among poets." He and his wife returned to Boston, where eventually the Herbert B. Turner & Company publishers consented to publish his manuscript, but only at his expense. He was to secure the promise of two hundred persons to buy a copy of the book in advance of publication, thus guaranteeing at least its expense. For seven months, Braithwaite walked the streets of Boston, Cambridge, and Roxbury getting prominent newspaper and literary people to agree to buy a copy of his poems. He secured the names of people like Colonel Thomas Wentworth Higginson, then in his eighties, Julia Ward Howe, Thomas Bailey Aldrich, Arlo Bates, Mark A. DeWolfe Howe, and Edward Everett Hale. The volume of poems finally appeared in 1904 as ***Lyrics of Life and Love*** and displayed his picture as a frontispiece.

To charge that "Braithwaite's persistent silence certainly amounts to the rejection of his blackness" and that "Braithwaite had not the least desire to be identified with the black world and what it stands for" is to know the man embarrassingly little. One of his very first published essays, **"A Grave Wrong to the Negro,"** published in the Boston *Globe* of 1906, excoriates white caricatures and stereotypes of blacks:

> There was never in real life a prototype of the negro [*sic*] of the execrable "coon song," the vaudeville stage, the musical comedy, or the pages of the comic weeklies; yet this exotic individual has been so long and so persistently exploited that the world believes in these "fundamentals" of his character and has become callous to the difference between the "chicken-stealing preacher" and a bishop of the [African Methodist Episcopal] Church. . . . Now it were better if this country were a nation of chicken-stealers than one of money-thieves, soul-murderers and homedestroyers who are bank and insurance presidents, for a surfeit of chicken meat can only at worst beget indigestion, much more easily cured than the decay of bad morals and ethics whose decomposition no power but the resurrection day or revolution can restore to the salvation of clean social and civil life. . . .[5]

And there are numerous other such pieces written by Braithwaite. But it is his career with the Boston *Transcript* that is more widely known. Beginning in 1904, he began publishing in that distinguished and powerful newspaper critical reviews and essays and book notes that would rank him at the top of Bostonian critical circles. Few Boston critics of his day were as widely read in major English and European and American poets. Among the poets he first reviewed favorably were Robert Frost, Amy Lowell, Edwin Arlington Robinson, James Weldon Johnson, and Countée Cullen. In fact, he was personally friendly with many of the talented staff of the *Transcript* and several of the poets whom he reviewed. With Edwin Arlington Robinson, Braithwaite was especially close for many years after he had favorably reviewed Robinson's fourth book, *The Town Down the River,* 1908. On his way to a Harvard-Dartmouth football game, Robinson stopped by the *Transcript* offices to thank Braithwaite and to promise to meet again soon for dinner in New York, a dinner which they did enjoy; but they enjoyed boozing until 2 A.M. in the Village even more. Robinson would dine often with Braithwaite when he was in Boston for summer vacation. In New York, later, Robinson showed Braithwaite the manuscripts for a new volume and when Braithwaite promised to typewrite the manuscript of the long monologue, "Ben Jonson Entertains a Man from Stratford," Robinson gave him the manuscript. Later, in a financial emergency, Braithwaite sold it for $12.00 and was embarrassed to have to confess to Robinson, who asked for the manuscript, that he had sold it. Robinson was not upset, "Oh, that's all right. I think anybody has a right to dispose of anything they want to, and I'm not at all offended. But if you had it, I could get $500 for you, for it. $500! I know a man who wants it very, very badly!" Despite Braithwaite's searches, he could not ever again find it.

It was Braithwaite who arranged for Robert Frost, newly hailed American poet, to meet Robinson; and it was Braithwaite who again found himself involved in some embarrassment: in front of Sylvester Baxter, Commissioner of Parks, Braithwaite, by way of introducing Robinson to Frost, said to Frost, "Frost, when anybody thinks of poetry in America, he always thinks of Robinson as our greatest poet." So Braithwaite introduced them, but was nagged by the suspicion that Frost would never forgive him that statement. It was, compensatorily, Braithwaite who urged Robinson to bring out a collection of his works in 1921. Robinson obeyed the promptings and "with the publication of that first collected volume in 1921, his fame skyrocketed. It had a very large sale and in 1922 it won him the Pulitzer Prize."

Braithwaite, established as a valued critic, met Amy Lowell at a meeting of the Twentieth Century Club in Boston, where he and others were invited speakers. She invited him to dinner at her place; he went, the "following Tuesday evening," and thereafter practically every two weeks for two years, from early fall until spring, when she went up to Dublin, her summer place; "with occasional breaks now and then, she was quite insistent upon it." This was at a time when, new from London where she had learned about "Imagism" from Ezra Pound and John Gould Fletcher, Lowell was in Boston to propagate this "new school." Braithwaite could get only so excited about it, for he knew, if Pound and Amy Lowell did not, that "Stephen Crane and Emily Dickinson had practised it without conscious intention." Her enormously overweight body notwithstanding, she made it blatantly clear to Braithwaite and to anyone else who would listen to her that she wanted to be the greatest woman poet that this country had ever produced, and a match for the great women poets of England. She often would say that God may have made her an excellent businesswoman, but she made herself a great poet.

Her chief rival for such poetic eminence was the fragile Josephine Preston Peabody (Mrs. Lionel Marks), who, knowing Braithwaite had preempted the pages of the *Transcript* for reviews of books of poems, wrote a favorable review of Amy Lowell's volume, *Sword Blades and Poppy Seed,* for the Boston *Herald.* But readers of her review, especially the knowledgeable Braithwaite, knew that Peabody was not temperamentally suited for Lowell's robust experimentation and that she had written favorably only in the hopes that Amy Lowell would influence her brother, Amos Lawrence Lowell, president of Harvard University, to promote her husband, Lionel Marks, from his position of assistant professor, from which position he had not been promoted in "twenty years or more." Amy Lowell took mean delight in saying, "I never make any recommendations to my brother. I do not attempt to influence him in any way—." Josephine Peabody became angry. "Amy told me one day that she called her up about something and Josephine was so furious she hung up on her."

When Lowell learned that, at nomination time, she was not likely to be elected president of the newly formed New England Poetry Club and that Josephine Peabody likely would have been elected, she stormed out of the meeting held on Dartmouth Street; "she dashed out of the room, out into the courtyard, into and down Dartmouth Street. Can you imagine her as a woman? Can you imagine her size—what a huge woman she was?" Along with Edward O'Brien and Conrad Aiken, Braithwaite hurried after Lowell, but she stormed into the Copley Plaza Hotel. "And then, what a tirade! If she couldn't be president she didn't want to have anything to do with the club, and so forth and so on." Braithwaite and other friends resolved the issue by promising Lowell that she would be their president and that Josephine Peabody would be elected honorary president—this seemed especially tactful in the light of the fact that Josephine Peabody was too ill for the position anyway. Lowell once tried to commandeer Braithwaite into accompanying her to the home of Josephine Peabody, where she ordered, "you're going to do that article about her." But, himself somewhat individualistic, Braithwaite left Amy Lowell huffing up the front stairs to Peabody's apartment. "When she turned around and didn't see me there she was furious! . . . She caught up with me. 'Get in,' she said, 'I'll take you home.' 'Thank you,' I said. Then she took me home, and she was furious all the way home."

Amy Lowell was jealous of any woman who showed talent in verse, and talent is what Braithwaite saw in a poem written by Leonora Speyer. She was once Mrs. Howard and then married the wealthy philanthropist, Sir Edgar Speyer, before the two of them, refusing to subscribe to the loyalty oath of the English government, migrated to Boston. Immediately, Amy Lowell suspected Speyer of being concerned with espionage on behalf of the German government. "To think of her marrying that dirty little Jew for his money!" Amy Lowell said once. At another time, Braithwaite published Leonora Speyer's picture to accompany her poem, which he had reprinted in the *Transcript.*

> The next time I visited with Miss Lowell we had, as usual, a very pleasant dinner after which we went into the library and lit our cigars. . . . She reclined on the couch and lit her cigar and blew a great puff of smoke into the air, and then rising to a sitting posture, pointing her finger at me and said, "Why did you print Leonora Speyer's picture in the Boston *Transcript,* Saturday?"
>
> I'm afraid I was very rude. My response was, "It's none of your damned business."
>
> Well, we had it. . . . We went through the night, with her maintaining sovereignty, as it were, over the poetic women of America, or England for that matter, or any where. . . . I missed [the 11:45 train] that night because when I was leaving she came out of the house with me and walked a good eighth of a mile from her house door to the gate. She walked all the way down there with me, begging that I would not let this quarrel break up our friendship, and saying that much had been said on both sides that was in anger, thoughtless and unkind. . . . I never saw her after that night. I never saw her. She telephoned. She telegraphed. She sent emisarries. . . .[6]

Locating and, if warranted, praising Amy Lowell's poetic values—he allowed her to use his name in getting her poems published in magazines and he helped her publish "Patterns," her most famous poem—was one thing, but toadying to her domineering was something else, something that he, a fellow New England literary aristocrat, would abide just so long.

Since 1913, Braithwaite had been editing and publishing annual anthologies of magazine verse, and in these volumes, which would continue through 1929, he went on to popularize once obscure and now famous American poets like Carl Sandburg, Edgar Lee Masters, Vachel Lindsay, James Weldon Johnson, and Claude McKay. It was an important matter for these and other poets to have their pieces reprinted from various magazines and selected for inclusion in one of Braithwaite's annual anthologies and yearbooks. The work that went into their preparations was backbreaking, for Braithwaite was obliged to read through as many magazines as he could lay his eyes and hands on, secure reprint permissions from original publishers, and then tend to the editing of the anthologies and the compilations of the yearbook sections. No man with less ambition and sense of service could have done his mighty chores, and he was a man possessed with the critical value of poetry. He wrote Amy Lowell in 1915:

> Two more features I am adding to the "Year Book" this year: one is to give a complete list of all the essays, criticisms, and important reviews of poets and poetry that have appeared in the magazines, weeklies and quarterly reviews, and such literary papers as *The Transcript, N.Y. Evening Post, Times* and *Chicago Evening Post.* You would be surprised how interesting this would be to the poets and the students of poetry. Another is, I shall try and induce readers to begin the building of a private library of modern American verse. And so I am giving a list of fifteen or twenty of the volumes that every one ought to have which have been published since 1900. In conjunction with this I am going to see if the publishers won't agree to have these volumes bound uniformly and sold as a set. . . .[7]

His other literary labors included the selection and assembling and editing of four anthologies of English period poetry: ***The Book of Elizabethan Verse*** (1906); ***The Book of Georgian Verse*** (1908); ***The Book of Restoration Verse*** (1909); and ***The Book of Modern British Verse*** (1919). (Reprint rights for several major English Victorian poets were impossible to secure and Braithwaite was unable to publish a book of Victorian verse.) There were four special collections: ***The Poetic Year for 1916; A Critical Anthology*** (1917); ***The Golden Treasury of Magazine Verse*** (1918); ***Victory! Celebrated by Thirty-Eight American Poets*** (1919); and ***Our Lady's Choir: A Contemporary Anthology of Verse by Catholic Sisters*** (1931). In addition to a full-length study, ***The Bewitched Parsonage: The Story of the Brontës*** (1959), there were two novels, ***The Canadian: A Novel*** (1901) and ***Going Over Tindel, a Novel*** (1924). Braithwaite also wrote uncounted introductions to volumes of verse by friends and poets, obscure and well known. He published poems in magazines like *The Century, Book News Monthly, The Christian Endeavor World, The Voice, The New England Magazine, The American Magazine, New York Times, Saturday Review of Books, National Magazine, Howard Spectator,* and *The Colored American Magazine.*

FROM THE AUTHOR

THE NEGRO IN LITERATURE

True to his origin on this continent, the Negro was projected into literature by his neighbor. He was *in* American literature long before he was part of it as a creator.

SOURCE: William Stanley Braithwaite, excerpt from "The Negro in Literature," in *Crisis* 28, September 1924.

Braithwaite's unflagging interest in the literature of his fellow blacks was lifelong. Even "before he edited the collection of Elizabethan poetry (1906) he did his best to find a publisher for quite a different project, ***The Anthology of Negro Authors: Prose and Verse,*** that he never succeeded in getting into print. Like every author who must live by his pen, Braithwaite was at the mercy of the publishing world and the reading public. His literary career did not begin in a period hospitable to black writers unwilling to use the approved formulas, dialect pathos, and minstrel comedy." His failure to find a publisher for his anthology of black literature did not alienate him from his several prominent black friends, James Weldon Johnson, Alain Locke, W. E. B. DuBois, and others. Instead, he contributed single pieces, critical reviews, full-length essays, and poems about his friends to both white and black periodicals. For instance, in the pages of the Boston *Transcript,* he published a review of Johnson's *Fifty*

Years and Other Poems in 1917; in 1921, he reviewed Claude McKay's *London,* published *Spring in New Hampshire* and also *Wings of Oppression* by Leslie B. Pinckney. In several of his annual anthologies of magazine verse, he reprinted poems by Jessie Fauset ("Christmas Eve in France," 1918) and Claude McKay ("The Harlem Dancer," 1918; "The Little Peoples," 1919; "Subway Wind" and "La Paloma in London," 1922). He included Fenton Johnson's "The New Day" among the pieces published in ***Victory! Celebrated by Thirty-Eight American Poets*** (with an introduction by Theodore Roosevelt).

One could easily assemble a good-sized anthology from the collection of pieces he published in black periodicals. Some of his observations made in his essay, **"Some Contemporary Poets of the Negro Race,"** in *The Crisis* for April, 1919, are as clear today as when he first defined them:

> When Mr. Howells said that Dunbar was the first poet of his race to express and interpret the life of his people lyrically, he told only a half-truth; what survives and attracts us in the poetry of Dunbar is the life of the Negro in the limited experience of a transitional period. . . .
>
> [T]he fact is as solid as the earth itself, that Dr. DuBois in "The Souls of Black Folk" began a poetic tradition. This book has more profoundly affected the spiritual nature of the race than any other written in this country; and has more clearly revealed to the nation at large the true idealism and high aspiration of the American Negro. . . .[8]

Along the way, incidentally, Braithwaite asserts his own aesthetic position:

> I am not one who believes that a Negro writer of verse—or fiction, for that matter—must think, feel, or write racially to be a great artist; nor can he be distinctively labeled by the material he uses. This is a fallacy too often expressed by the critics to confirm the desired hypothesis that the Negro is humanly different in the scale of mankind, that even after some centuries of civilizing process in America he is still nearer in his most cultivated class to the instincts of his ancestral forebears than any other of the conglomerate races who compose the citizenry of the Republic. In every race and nation there are primitives who retain the impulses of barbarism. . . . But the Negro has absorbed in his advanced class, just as in the advanced class of any other people, the culture of the best civilizations in the world today, and in his imaginative and artistic expression he is universal. . . .
>
> In Georgia Douglas Johnson we have the foremost woman poet of the race. . . . But I do not mean, and I do not wish it to be understood, that I limit her horizons when I characterize her as the foremost woman poet of the race. She expands beyond into the universal, and as the title of her volume, "The Heart of a Woman," indicates, she renders and interprets the mysterious and inexplicable secrets of femininity. . . .[9]

For Alain Locke's celebrated anthology, *The New Negro* (1925), Braithwaite wrote an essay, **"The Negro in American Literature,"** whose basic challenges to white or black American writers have not been met to this day:

> True to his origin on this continent, the Negro was projected into literature by an overmastering and exploiting hand. In the generations that he has been so voluminously written and talked about he has been accorded as little artistic justice as social justice.
>
> Controversy and moral appeal gave us *Uncle Tom's Cabin*. . . . Here was sentimentalized sympathy for a downtrodden race . . . but the moral gain and historical effect of Uncle Tom have been an artistic loss and setback. The treatment of Negro life and character, overlaid with these forceful stereotypes, could not develop into artistically satisfactory portraiture. . . . Between the Civil War and the end of the century, the subject of the Negro in literature is one that will some day inspire the literary historian with a magnificent theme . . . because of the immense paradox of racial life which came up thunderingly against the principles and doctrines of democracy, and put them to the severest test they had known. . . . The writers who dealt with him for the most part refused to see more than skin-deep. . . . For more than artistic reasons, indeed against them, these writers refused to see the tragedy of the Negro and capitalized his comedy. . . .[10]

It would seem perfectly predictable that Braithwaite, himself of mixed background, would be critically compatible with the novels of Jessie Fauset (1882-1961), *There Is Confusion* (1924), *Plum Bun* (1928), *The Chinaberry Tree* (1931), and *Comedy American Style* (1933), all of which depict fair-skinned black people and their strivings for happiness, which sometimes involves "passing" for white. But he sees these characters as something more: in **"The Novels of Jessie Fauset,"** published in *Opportunity* for January of 1934, he would view these books as novelized case histories documenting the inability or unwillingness of America to fulfill its highest democratic ideals. He points out that black novelists up to his time—Chesnutt, DuBois, McKay, Nella Larsen, Walter White, Rudolph Fisher, Wallace Thurman, Langston Hughes, Countée Cullen, and Arna Bontemps—have all "described and interpreted Negro life and experience with an art built, with two or three exceptions, to the same pattern. There has not been much variation to the theme nor to the *milieu.*" As much can be said for white writers, especially white American writers: "Miss [Sarah Orne] Jewett's Maine folk in her 'country of the pointed firs,' are fundamentally of the same dramatic substance in motive and experience as Miss [Willa] Cather's Nebraska pioneers; Miss [Edith] Wharton's Knickerbocker aristocrats are essentially one with the same pride and mellow grace of mind and habit as Miss [Ellen] Glasgow's Virginia 'first families.' . . . Many of these novelists, in spite of their reputations and the authoritative praise given them, are scarcely more than deft craftsmen, manipulating the profoundest emotions of humanity for the sake of capturing their readers' attention and interest."

Not so with Miss Fauset, argues Braithwaite. Not since Hawthorne do we find a similar and singular devotion to the philosophy of *rebuke* to an inhuman principle, elevated to an institution and safeguarded by both law and public opinion. For Hawthorne's novels were the vehicle for, and presented types of human lives as, a brooding, passionate rebuke to the hard, callous Puritan spirit, which denied earthly happiness and fulfillment, the sense of joy and beauty, to the people. So, Braithwaite goes on, with Miss Fauset can be found this same philosophy of rebuke, brooding and passionate also, against the contemporary spirit of the American people, who have elevated prejudice into an institution, safeguarded also by law and public sentiment, denying the freedom of development, of the inherent right to wellbeing, and the pursuit of happiness:

> These people want, most of all, to be themselves. To satisfy the same yearnings and instincts which God has given them in the same measure bestowed upon other people. When some of their members "cross over" into the white world, to enjoy the advantages and privileges for which they are fitted and worthy . . . it was not because they desire to be "white," but because a cruel, blind, and despising tradition had taught them it was wiser and more profitable "not to be colored."[11]

All persons interested in the literary life of late nineteenth-and early twentieth-century black Boston will be indebted to Braithwaite's brief but informed essay, **"Negro America's First Magazine,"** published in *Negro Digest* in December of 1947. Because he contributed to the magazine himself, Braithwaite knew much of the intimate goings on among the other personnel, including the delicate ego of novelist Pauline E. Hopkins, who edited the publication briefly before it was moved to New York where in 1909 it concluded. Other pieces Braithwaite contributed to black publications include **"A Tribute to W. E. Burghardt DuBois, First Editor of *Phylon*,"** a sketch that presents no unknown information about DuBois; a short piece on **"The First Negro Novelist,"** concerning William Wells Brown and his novel, *Clotel; or, The President's Daughter*, published in London in 1853; two pieces on his friend of "over forty years," Alain Leroy Locke (1886-1954), Harvard Ph.D. and Rhodes Scholar to Oxford University, critic and editor of the milestone anthology, *The New Negro* (1925), both pieces appearing in *Phylon:* **"The Passing of Alain Leroy Locke,"** 1954, and **"Alain Locke's Relationship to the Negro in American Literature,"** 1957.

Braithwaite had also given much of his personal time to black causes, such as serving as president of the national advisory council of Delta Phi Delta, an intercollegiate society founded at Morehouse College in Atlanta. In 1917 he accepted honorary membership in the Boston chapter of Alpha Phi Alpha fraternity. He was on the first board of DuBois's newly founded magazine, *The Crisis*, in 1910; and he served as literary judge for black-written materials. In 1918, several important honors were bestowed on him: he was awarded an honorary M.A. degree from Atlanta University; Talladega awarded him the LL.D.; and he won the coveted Spingarn Medal as "the American citizen of African descent who made last year the highest achievement in any field of elevated human endeavour."

Using the money from his publisher's advance for his ***Story of the Great War*** (1919), he moved into a newly bought house at 243 Park Avenue in Arlington Heights, just outside of Boston. While "the reviews and essays he published in the Boston *Transcript* were a major source of income for him for twenty years . . . he never was a salaried member of that staff." And although for years after buying his beloved home, "Arcturus," he was visited by ranking poets, little was done to provide for his growing family, which became seven. With the Depression, he was without a regular income and so accepted, a few years later, a position as a professor of English and American literature at Atlanta University. He would remain at Atlanta University for ten years, until 1945, all the while delaying the ultimate foreclosure on his Massachusetts home.

He recalled his years at Atlanta University with some misgivings, as he felt his pedigreed colleagues were degree conscious, which feeling registered deeply within Braithwaite, who had no earned degrees at all, not even a high school diploma. Still, he knew his literary value, his experiences, personal and professional, with several major American poets, black and white, and, so feeling, he is said to have refused "the command of his department chairman to attend a staff meeting to prepare an examination on fundamentals, reminding her that he had come to the university in 1935 to teach literature to English majors and to direct the research of graduate students." He was happy, however, to be a participant in the second annual meeting of the Association of Teachers of English in Negro Colleges in 1938, largely because he was advised that compatible spirits would also be speaking, persons like James Weldon Johnson and W. E. B. DuBois, also of Atlanta University. No doubt he was dismayed to see later that neither Johnson nor DuBois showed up, but he is reported to have spoken "extemporaneously and at length" anyhow.

When he retired from teaching at Atlanta University in 1945, it would be at 409 Edgecombe Avenue in New York, and not 243 Park Avenue in Arlington Heights, where he would live, across the hall from his old friend, DuBois, who had also taught at Atlanta since 1934 and retired in 1944. After a career with such prolific output, Braithwaite would not easily take to a rocking chair and do nothing for the rest of his dedicated life: he would still look for publishers to bring out his collection of black writers. As late as 1952 he wrote to the editor of Viking Press, who was once on the old Boston *Transcript* staff, and outlined his hopes for an anthology, *A Century of the Negro Novelist:*

> Thirty years ago I conceived the idea of summing up the Negro's contributions to American poetry in an anthology. It was a work that needed to be done, but I could not at the time undertake it, and so told James Weldon Johnson about it and urged him to do it. He produced "The Book of American Negro Poetry," which was very successful, and was the first of some half dozen anthologies of the kind successfully published. It seems strange that poetry, which is acknowledged to have none of the commercial appeal of fiction, should have given the Negro author his day in the critical literary court while the novelist has been denied. This lack was what prompted me to propose the work outlined in the draft submitted to you. . . .[12]

But in 1953, he wrote the black newspaper, the *Pittsburgh Courier Magazine,* and, thanking them for paying him for his article on William Wells Brown, the first American black novelist, he went on to solicit commissions for other articles that would be drawn from his vast autobiographical material:

> Appearing in your magazine they would have twofold significance. First, I think, presented by our leading racial newspaper, they would reveal our literary integration into American literature at a time when a double-standard of criticism was prevalent; and secondly, establish for our younger generation a historical note of importance in the early years of our broadening literary progress.[13]

The characters he proposed writing about were Colonel Thomas Wentworth Higginson, Amy Lowell, Professor Charles T. Copeland—"the famous 'Copey'—of Harvard, whose influence upon American letters has been exerted through the young men who, taking his courses—Broun, Benchley, Perkins, etc.—went on to achieve distinction." He would have also included Edward J. O'Brien, "author of 'The Best Short Stories' and many other books," and James Gould Cozzens, whom Braithwaite first published years ago, before Cozzens went on to win a Pulitzer prize. The *Pittsburgh Courier Magazine* did not commission him to do these articles, not surprisingly: Braithwaite and the black masses were still some distance apart. Nonplussed, Braithwaite persisted, and, as late as February 24, 1962, he was trying to sell "two Vignettes on the Civil War. They were suggested by the recollection of my boyhood association with two women around whom the stories evolve, who gave me a vivid sense of the conflict which raged a hundred years ago. . . ." One of these vignettes was entitled **"Mrs. Washburn,"** about a colored woman who came with her family to Boston, after the Civil War. It was never sold. And a few months later, he was dead.

There is little doubt that William Stanley Beaumont Braithwaite, on his own terms, died an uncommonly fulfilled man; there is little doubt, too, that he died an unusually misunderstood man, especially by black readers who would dismiss his poetry as obscure, esoteric, and racially irrelevant. J. Saunders Redding declared that Braithwaite was "the most outstanding example of perverted energy that the period from 1903 to 1917 produced." Even his bibliography has come down to us somewhat confused. *Webster's Biographical Dictionary,* first edition, 1943, credits him with *Our Essayists and Critics of Today* (1920), *Sandy Star* (1926), and *Frost on the Green Leaf* (short stories) (1928). Besides *Lyrics of Life and Love* (1904) and *The House of Falling Leaves* (1908), *Black American Writers Past and Present* credits him with a third volume, *A Tale of a Walled Town and Other Verses* (Philadelphia, J. B. Lippincott, 1920). Dr. Philip Butcher, editor of *The William Stanley Braithwaite Reader* (Ann Arbor, 1972), on whom most of my remarks here are based, is authoritative and does not list any of the volumes noted in *Webster's Biographical Dictionary,* nor does he list *A Tale of a Walled Town and Other Verses.*

Because he was a man of amazing literary output, it is perhaps understandable that his yet incomplete bibliography might yield some confusions, but his aesthetic position does not seem to have been all that difficult to comprehend. He was a totally dedicated, firmly convinced disciple of pure beauty, which he found in disciplined literary expression. He never, thereby, denied the worth of black literature but felt that too often it dissipated its own best creative energy as it became preoccupied with only racial matters. As he could write of Richard Wright's powerful book *Black Boy*, "I am afraid there is an overemphasis, much as I admire the book, on the kind of philosophy intensified in 'Black Boy.' The truth is that Jews, Italians, Poles, and the Irish themselves, as my Boston nativity is aware of, have all suffered indignities and injustices in *democratic* America. . . . Nature has kept the secret for all the solutions in her keeping—and always in the end she is triumphant." Even before he had published ***The House of Falling Leaves*** (1908), he had made his position on his raceless poetry clear to a white writer on the race question who was curious about Braithwaite's stance:

> The question you ask concerning a racial note in my verse is one that I have often had pointed out to me. I confess that in my earliest days of poetic expression I had a great ambition to do that sort of thing—and tried it to a realization of failure. I discovered limitations in my temperament, as well as a certain undeveloped material in the race's history that prevented in me . . . spontaneous expression. There has been only one way—and this method will hold priority yet for half a century or more to come—to express the Negro in verse, and that is the manner in which Dunbar made his appeal. . . .
>
> Now, as I grew in artistic conscience in those days, I found that this sort of thing was not in me, but something which seemed to me higher in the universality of human nature, something in the vision of the soul, in the aspirations of the heart toward God, toward nature . . . and I dedicated what power I possessed in poetic expression to this service. This was something I discovered to be holier than patriotism and race—the perfect goodness, the absolute beauty, the divine evolutions of spiritual and physical growth towards the perfection of God's conception of man. . . .[14]

It is obvious from these remarks that Braithwaite never forgot the impact of a lecture by the famous English Platonist, G. Lowes Dickinson, who gave the Ingersoll Lecture at Harvard on the immortality of the soul, beginning by saying there was no difference between men: "nor race, nor wealth, nor social position, makes any difference; it is only in the *growth of the soul.*" Understand Platonic idealism and you understand much of William Stanley Braithwaite.

In his ***Lyrics of Life and Love*** is displayed an array of the usual romanticist's concerns, delight in surrounding nature, romantic love, nostalgia, heroism, and metaphysical meditation in sixty-three fragile, delicately poised verses. Some of the seeming mysticism of Platonic idealism can be seen in several poems:

> Up and down the beach I wander
> Here to-night beside the sea,
> In my ears the ocean-thunder,
> In my heart the dreams of thee.
> The sea, the sea is high, love,
> Dark, dark, O dark, the sky, love,
> And sad is my heart.
>
> In the outward journey passing
> Through the narrow gates of night,
> Was there travail in the massing
> Of the waters void of light?
> O the sea, the sea is high, love,
> Swift surge the waters by, love,
> And sad is my heart.
>
> **"Song"**

And such philosophical notions are clearer in **"Voice of the Sea":**

> Voice of the sea that calls to me,
> Heart of the woods my own heart loves,
> I am part of your mystery—
> Moved by the soul your own soul moves.
>
> Dream of the stars in the night-sea's dome,
> Somewhere in your infinite space
> After the years I will come home,
> Back to your halls to claim my place.

Not all of these early pieces succeed; too few contain lastingly memorable lines, but there are some, in this volume and in ***The House of Falling Leaves,*** that deserve more anthologizing. In autobiographical celebration, **"Sic Vita"** displays some of the strengths and weaknesses:

> Heart free, hand free,
> Blue above, brown under,
> All the world to me
> Is a place of wonder.
>
> Sun shine, moon shine,
> Stars, and winds a-blowing,
> All into this heart of mine
> Flowing, flowing, flowing!
>
> Mind free, step free,
> Days to follow after,
> Joys of life sold to me
> For the price of laughter.
>
> Girl's love, Man's love,
> Love of work and duty,
> Just a will of God's to prove
> Beauty, beauty, beauty!

"My father's grandmother," Braithwaite wrote in his incomplete autobiography, was "the daughter of a French nobleman in the island of Martinique, who had been educated in Paris, possessed that indefinable charm and passion of the Parisian temperament as an urgency in her blood, and had eloped with her lover, an Englishman by the name of Smith, to Georgetown, Demerara." Braithwaite, in a rare contradiction of his poetic creed, turned to his great-grandmother in aristocratic verse flourish:

> Her face was a fair olive hue;
> Eyes like a tropic night when dew
> Makes the air heavy to the sea's rim;
> Figure like a willow, subtle, slim,
> That had the grace of a young queen;
> Hair, as the Empress Josephine
> Fashioned, when Paris bowed to her:
> —La belle de Demerara.
>
> I see it all as in a dream:
> Georgetown's seawall, where the stream
> Of Quality flows; among them moves
> She, whom the city's pride approves,
> What beauty gave and virtue crowned
> When music charmed their lips to sound
> This name their hearts bestowed on her,
> —La belle de Demerara.
>
> Sir Francis Hincks, at Government House
> On a gala night before her bows;
> Out from England on duty sent
> The Colonel of the regiment
> Glides with her in the stately dance;
> And in her soft vivacious glance
> Chief Justice Beaumont bends to her:
> —La belle de Demerara.
>
> O Poet who sang of Dorothy Q.;
> I have a Great-Grandmother too,
> Born in a British colonial place,
> Sent to learn Parisian grace;
> Who won all hearts in her demesne
> By the Caribbean's warm blue sheen:
> And large is the debt I owe to her,
> —La belle de Demerara.
>
> **"La belle de Demerara"**

Elsewhere he includes pieces to his daughter, "Fiona," but no "racial details" are evident; nor would readers realize that Dr. Marcus F. Wheatland, to whom is dedicated **"A Song of the Living,"** was a black man; and he likens "E. A. B.," his wife, Emma, **"To A Persian Rose,"** who "was more than fair! / Thou Rose of Paradise—/ In lips, and cheeks, and hair,—/ All beauty wonderwise / 'Neath those hot skies." Other pieces remember Dante Gabriel Rossetti, William Morris, William Dean Howells, and William Blake, all poets he much admired. There is no poem in either volume dedicated to John Donne, but **"The Book of Love"** tries and fails to use a typical John Donne "Metaphysical conceit":

> I hold the book of life in my hands
> When I hold your face, and press your lips
> To my lips in a kiss, and touch all lands
> In a thousand dreams that sail as ships,
> Out of my soul across your soul
> To the ends of the world you keep.
> Between each shadowy golden goal
> Of your eyes where the kingdoms sleep.
> Shall I ever read the history through,
> And learn the dates of wars and kings—
> How nations fell and rose and grew?
> Ah, life's too short for smaller things
> When your face is mine—the world itself,
> Of past and future and present in one;
> A book God wrote for my own heart's shelf,
> And bound in the bindery of the sun.

Braithwaite spent his latter years contending with failing eye-sight, arthritis, but a no less diminished poetic heart; he enjoyed researching for his projected but never published life of Alain Locke, reading and writing about Erasmus, and he was always helpful to students of earlier poets whom he knew personally and could supply intimate biographical or literary information about. And he was a prodigious writer of letters; Professor Butcher points out that "the Index of Names for correspondence in the William Stanley Braithwaite Papers at Harvard University runs to more than thirteen typed pages, single-spaced and double column." It is clear enough from a selection of these letters that Braithwaite fully realized that he had lived a rich, rewarding, and extraordinarily useful life, and he had done it his own way. As he wrote to Nella Larsen, author of two novels, *Quicksand* (1928) and *Passing* (1929):

> For twenty-five years I gave my best for the poets and poetry of America; it was a labor of love that cost me dearly; at the same time I proved something that no other man of the race dared even so much as to attempt; I won something precious for the future hope and aspiration of the artistic and creative youth of the Negro. . . .[15]

That says things best; and surely in the future, scholars, black and white, and students, black and white, will realize the enormous legacy created and passed on by a most unusual, determined, and believing black man of American letters.

Notes

1. Claude McKay, *A Long Way From Home* (New York, 1931), pp. 26-27.
2. Jean Wagner, *Black Poets in the United States* (Chicago, 1973), p. 128.
3. Philip Butcher, ed., *The William Stanley Braithwaite Reader,* p. 177.
4. Ibid., p. 179.
5. Ibid., p. 13.
6. Ibid., pp. 229-230.
7. Ibid., p. 255.
8. Ibid., pp. 52-53.

9. Ibid., pp. 53-58.
10. Ibid., pp. 68-70.
11. Ibid., p. 99.
12. Ibid., p. 301.
13. Ibid., p. 302.
14. Ibid., pp. 246-247.
15. Ibid., p. 284.

CRAIG S. ABBOTT (ESSAY DATE 1994)

SOURCE: Abbott, Craig S. "Magazine Verse and Modernism: Braithwaite's Anthologies." *Journal of Modern Literature* 19, no. 1 (summer 1994): 152-59.

In the following essay, Abbott considers Braithwaite's anthologies as reflective of his desire to appeal to a wide audience and his anti-modernist and largely unsympathetic stance towards the racially conscious work of the Harlem Renaissance.

William Stanley Braithwaite has been credited with "bullying and cajoling American readers into accepting modern and unconventional writings," largely through the annual collections of magazine verse which he edited from 1913 through 1929.[1] Yet that was neither his intention nor his role. As his introduction to the 1913 ***Anthology of Magazine Verse*** makes clear, Braithwaite had in mind no poetic revolution. He wanted to counter the public's (and the poets') "disparaging opinion" of conventional magazine verse (p. ix), the kind used at the time as filler in such wide circulation magazines as *Century* and *Harper's*.[2] While his anthologies did generate interest in poetry during the 1910s, they became by the end of the decade primarily a continuing assertion of the qualities against which Modernism was defining itself. Moreover, although he himself was an African-American, his critical predilections left him unsympathetic to the racially conscious poetry of the Harlem Renaissance. Thus, although he regretted the narrowing canon of Modernism, he was also opposed to a significant body of work that challenged it. Instead, he continued to favor poetry that he believed could appeal to a wide audience, even though such an audience existed more in his hopes than in reality.

Braithwaite's view of poetry was pre-modern, and it underwent no substantial revision, despite the developments that his anthologies imperfectly recorded. He was more poetry-lover than critic. In his autobiography, he traced his unbounded enthusiasm for poetry to an epiphanic moment. In 1893, at the age of fifteen, he began a typesetting apprenticeship with a book that included Keats's "Ode on a Grecian Urn." This poem, he recalled, "broke upon both my sense and spirit with the flush of a sunrise." Continuing his work, he came upon poems by Wordsworth and Burns, from which he "received communications, impressions, and revelations" that remade his world "in terms of poignant imaginative desires." He was transported, it was "a day of annunciation," and he settled on a "poetic and literary career."[3] Poetry remained for him a means of transportation, a vehicle to empyreal destinations. His own was remarkably genteel and conventional, a product of the twilight era of American poetry; it was magazine verse. His criticism was guided by a Romantic idealism, tinged with mystical impressionism, that discounted both theme and technique. Introducing his 1914 anthology, he argued that poetry is concerned with the ideal and that "all which is seen with the physical eye, and touched with the fleshly hand, is illusion" (p. x). Again, in 1915, he contended that the form of poetry "has everything to do with expression and nothing whatever with substance"

ANTHOLOGY
OF
MAGAZINE VERSE
FOR 1920

AND YEAR BOOK OF
AMERICAN POETRY

EDITED BY
WILLIAM STANLEY BRAITHWAITE

BOSTON
SMALL, MAYNARD & COMPANY
PUBLISHERS

Title page from *Anthology of Magazine Verse for 1920*, edited by William Stanley Braithwaite.

(p. xv). And, in 1918: "Poetry begins and ends in feeling, moves from the heart of the creator to the heart of the reader in a vehicle of dream whose motive power is a mystical intelligence" (p. xviii). On the one hand, Braithwaite's locating the essence of poetry somewhere outside theme and technique did allow him to appreciate some of the early efforts at poetic experimentation associated with what David Perkins has called "popular modernism."[4] These efforts, after all, sought to remove traditional techniques that were thought to stand between reader and creator, and they introduced subject matter thought closer to the lives of readers. On the other hand, Braithwaite's critical views also prevented his sympathy with any theme or technique that might call attention to itself or foreground the poem as a verbal artifact.

These views guided him as a poet, as a regular contributor of poetry reviews to the *Boston Evening Transcript* beginning in 1905, as an editor of *Poetry Journal* from December 1912 through July 1913 and of *Poetry Review* from May 1916 through February 1917, and as the editor or editor-publisher of his annual ***Anthology of Magazine Verse*** from 1913 through 1929. In the anthology, he sought to cull from an annually increasing number of magazines the best poems of each year, after submitting them "to an impartial critical test." This test was, it seems, his own fairly catholic although conventional taste, which allowed into the anthology a poetic output wide in both variety and quality. Like the celebrated 1912 anthology *The Lyric Year,* for which Braithwaite had served as a judge and which may have suggested to him his own anthology, and like Harriet Monroe's early volumes of *Poetry* magazine, his first several volumes of magazine verse served to convince poets and public alike that a renaissance was in progress.[5] Gathered from wide circulation magazines such as *Century* and from little magazines such as *Poetry,* the output of each year took on, at the least, an impressive bulk. Reviewing the 1913 anthology, Joyce Kilmer was at a loss to say "which of the selections is best," but he was certain that Braithwaite had "triumphantly refuted the charge that this is a prosaic land in a prosaic age." The following year, another reviewer saw the anthology as evidence that "America is awakening to its poets."[6]

Braithwaite himself explicitly announced such an awakening as a goal. Like Monroe, who had adopted as the motto for *Poetry* Whitman's "To have great poets there must be great audiences too," Braithwaite often repeated his sense of need for reciprocity between poets and public. In his 1914 anthology, for example, he asserted that "a period or epoch of the highest achievement" in poetry "has always been one of popular appreciation" (p. xii), and in a review three years later, he argued that "fine poetry is encouraged by public patronage and appreciation."[7] This belief in reciprocity and a conviction that Braithwaite was promoting it were frequent themes in the reviews of his early volumes. Thus, in 1915, an anonymous reviewer in the *New York Times Book Review* saw evidence that the anthology had imposed upon the public the conviction that America was producing great poetry, and the reviewer supposed that "when a continent of people accept it as fact that they are producing or about to produce great poetry, good if not great poetry is very apt to result."[8]

The 1915 anthology, like the others, suggests both Braithwaite's more or less catholic taste and the diversity that characterized the early years of the poetry renaissance. One finds in it poets conservative (Hermann Hagedorn, George Edward Woodberry), socially if not poetically revolutionary (James Oppenheim, Louis Untermeyer), mildly modern (Witter Bynner, Charles Hanson Towne), imagistic (H.D., Amy Lowell), nativist (Frost, Lindsay), lyrical (Amelia Josephine Burr, Sara Teasdale), and so on. The arrangement of the 1915 anthology and of all the others prior to 1921 implies the promotion of Poetry, not of individual poets or poems. Although its basis is never indicated, the arrangement is thematic. Braithwaite was transforming magazine verse not only into book verse but into a book, one in which divergent schools and voices would join in one large poem, with Braithwaite as its editorial author. Thus the son who has left Odell Shepard's "The Adventurer" to follow "unquestioning after joy" in effect becomes, on the next page, Flammonde in Robinson's Tilbury Town and then the defeated artist in Dana Burnet's "Gayheart." There were, however, works that Braithwaite's "impartial critical test" evidently would exclude from his grand anthological poem. Listed in the yearbook section of the 1915 anthology were, for example, Eliot's "Portrait of a Lady" and "The Love Song of J. Alfred Prufrock," Moore's four poems from *Poetry,* and Williams' poems from *Poetry* and *Others.* Braithwaite chose neither to reprint them nor to mark them with an asterisk as among the many "poems of distinction" for that year.

Nonetheless, the 1915 anthology seems in retrospect the highpoint of the series, just as the year itself was a highpoint for the early stage of the poetry renaissance. Among the anthology's

101 poems selected from about fifteen hundred works by 530 poets appearing in twenty-five magazines (according to Braithwaite's count) are H.D.'s "Sea Iris," John Gould Fletcher's "Green Symphony," Frost's "Birches," "The Road Not Taken," and "Death of the Hired Man," Vachel Lindsay's "The Chinese Nightingale," Amy Lowell's "Patterns," Robinson's "Flammonde" and "Cassandra," and Stevens' "Peter Quince at the Clavier." Along with them, however, were such poems as those by Mahlon Leonard Fisher, whom Braithwaite calls "one of the very best sonnet-writers in the entire history of American poetry" (p. xix). Earlier, in the 1913 anthology, he had also singled out Fisher's work for special praise. Fisher's "November," he said, must "rank with Lizette Woodworth Reese's 'Tears' and Longfellow's 'Nature' as the best sonnets" by American poets. The poem "cannot be too highly estimated" (p. vii):

> Hark you such sounds as quivers? Kings will hear,
> As kings have heard, and tremble on their thrones;
> The old will feel the weight of mossy stones;
> The young alone will laugh and scoff at fear.
> It is the tread of armies marching near,
> From scarlet lands to lands forever pale;
> It is the bugle dying down the gale;
> It is the sudden gushing of a tear.
> And it is hands that grope at ghostly doors;
> And romp of spirit children on the pave;
> It is the tender sighing of the brave
> Who fell, ah! long ago, in futile wars;
> It is such sound as death; and, after all,
> 'Tis but the forest letting dead leaves fall.

While such poets as Frost and Lowell were testing the consensus regarding poetic value that was assumed by Braithwaite's critical test, those like Fisher were feeding his appetite for the conventionally (even if unskillfully) poetic.

If the early reviews of the anthologies praised Braithwaite for generating public interest in poetry, those after 1917 became especially harsh, questioning his abundance of praise, his lack of discrimination, his precariously lofty critical pronouncements, and his command of English. In that year O. W. Firkins, writing in the *Nation,* found Braithwaite's criticism "more impalpable that the poetry itself," complained that he kept "his praise in a *tank,*" and supposed that he had severed his relationship with standard English. In 1918, Jessie Rittenhouse, herself a conservative and popular anthologist, called for a "campaign of suppression" in response to the proliferation of verse represented by the previous year's anthology. Pointing out Braithwaite's inflated praise of Fisher, she wondered whether "the poet who feeds on sugared encomiums is already on the way to fatty degeneration." "Democracy," she said "may be the hope of Society, but discrimination is the hope of Art." In 1921, a reviewer in the *Double Dealer* concluded that the anthologies had "failed miserably" because of Braithwaite's "aptitude for the selection of the non-essential" and consequent anthologizing of "depressing drivel." Reviewing the 1925 anthology, Allen Tate reckoned that Braithwaite must have reprinted "about six poems out of every hundred" published that year. Tate doubted whether that many should find their way out of magazines and into further circulation. In 1926, Genevieve Taggard complained that Braithwaite "has always managed to shock our taste and hurt our feelings even when he included a good many of our poems." The anthologies, she said, included poetry "so palpably bad that we squirmed to be between the same covers with it." Also that year, Louis Untermeyer called the anthologies "Braithwaite's yearly blunder" and a "monument of mediocrity" in which a few good poets consent to appear because of his early "service to the cause" and because "they feel sorry for him."[9]

Braithwaite's most persistent critic was Conrad Aiken. The feud that developed between them was, in a larger sense, a clash between a canon open to great variety and one closed around the emerging major poets, between an indiscriminate critical impressionism on the one hand and the early stirrings of New Criticism on the other. In "Prizes and Anthologies," in 1915, Aiken attacked Braithwaite's anthologies, claiming to be "smitten with cold nausea" by their "preening and attitudinizing . . . over so much sentimental and vulgar mediocrity." He particularly objected to Braithwaite's generous lists of "poems of distinction."[10] In the 1913 anthology, Braithwaite had found distinctive 211 poems among the 506 he had read in seven magazines; in 1915 he had found 310 poems among the 772 in thirteen magazines. Aiken charged that Braithwaite's practice, like Monroe's in awarding prizes in *Poetry,* was "creating not a poetry, but a *market* for poetry," with the result that mediocrity was flourishing and crowding out the "genuine poet." Good poetry, he said, cannot "be made essentially popular, in this time and place."[11]

The feud continued in the pages of the *Poetry Journal,* with Braithwaite arguing that his activities had "immeasurably advanced" American poetry and that the introduction of criticism would be "fatal to its further progress" because it would stand between poets and public and thus poison "the art at its root" and with Aiken contending that "the prime necessity" was "an enforcement of high and severe critical standards."[12] Then, in the 1918 anthology, Braithwaite sought to counter Aiken's essay "The Mechanism of Poetic Inspiration," which saw poetry as neither "mysterious" nor "translunar" but as an object for critical analysis.[13] Braithwaite offered in contrast his view that "the reality of poetry lies wholly in the abstract, and to reach that reality, comprehend and interpret it, is completely a matter of sentiment and not science" (p. x).

It is testimony to the prevalence of the views held by Braithwaite and to the influence of Braithwaite himself in the first decade of the poetry renaissance that Aiken's *Scepticisms,* published in 1919, is written in opposition to Braithwaite. This book, which anticipates the New Criticism in insisting that poetry is an object open to analysis, attacks Braithwaite not only implicitly, through its arguments for critical analysis and discrimination, but also quite explicitly, even engaging in frequent Braithwaite bashing: Braithwaite is "not by endowment a critic," is "incredibly undiscriminating," possesses "a very decided intellectual limitation," has "a singular incapacity for perceiving the real meaning of words," writes with "a cloudy inaccuracy of style," and, again, has "an extraordinary lack of discrimination."[14]

In his anthology for 1923, Braithwaite himself came to admit the rising tide of mediocrity that Aiken and other reviewers had deplored, but he placed the blame for it not on his own activities but on Aiken's. He supposed that the "countless fledglings who make loud the air with tinkling song" had been encouraged by "the insistent statement of a contemporary that there is nothing 'mysterious' about this matter of poetry, and that it is made, as well as explained, by scientific standards" (p. xiv). If he complained about the minor fowl, however, he also persisted in filling his anthologies with their songs. Indeed, he continued to increase the number of poets in each, from forty in 1913 to 319 in 1929. There was, of course, a financial reason for the increase. As Allen Tate observed in 1926, the anthologized poets became the market for their own work. Minor and fledgling poets were more likely than major ones to buy their work bound in Braithwaite's covers, just as they were more likely to accept his invitation to buy their way into the biographical dictionary appended to the 1926 anthology.[15] The major poets who emerged during the renaissance no longer needed his anthological or promotional mediation.

But there were other reasons as well for the progressive swelling of the volumes. Braithwaite had been generally (though not enthusiastically) sympathetic to the Modernism represented by Lindsay, Lowell, Masters, Sandburg, and others. By 1922, however, he recognized their decline. "Only Robinson," he said, "kept steadily progressive towards a consistently high achievement" (p. xi). And in 1927 he observed that "an era in American poetry had come to fullness and decline" (p. x). After the period of Robinson and Frost, Sandburg and Masters, Lowell and Teasdale, no new poets had "risen so high nor kept for any length of time popular attention" (p. xiii). What Braithwaite does not admit is that these poets had been displaced, in critical if not popular attention, by the poets whom he disparaged in 1922 as "the so-called 'intellectualists'" who make "a fetich [*sic*] of technique" (p. x). His anthologies ignored the publication of Eliot's *The Waste Land* in 1922, and when Moore's *Observations* won for her the *Dial* award in 1925, Braithwaite mentioned the volume only to dismiss it as demonstrating "to what pitch irony and allegory may be pushed if one gives perfect freedom to a strong intellectual arrogance" (p. xvi). In 1927 he cited Wallace Stevens as proof that critical praise cannot establish popular appreciation (p. ix).

One recent critic has claimed on Braithwaite's behalf that he "reconstructed and redefined the American poetic canon by broadening the base of authors to be considered."[16] "Reconstructed" and "redefined" are inaccurate terms here, of course, since Braithwaite's anthologies were appearing simultaneously with the construction of the canon. It could be argued, though, that their catholicity of content stood in opposition to the narrowing of the canon. If so, that opposition was largely ineffectual. Braithwaite's critical predilections made him unsympathetic not only to the major poets of a developing High Modernism but also to other poets who might have claimed a place in the canon, such as those of the Harlem Renaissance. It may be an exaggeration to say, as Cary Wintz has, that Braithwaite was "an unequivocal critic of the Renaissance," but he was certainly no champion of it.[17] Although his anthologies of the 1920s continued to include the work of Black poets, Braithwaite would exclude or apologize for any that struck him as too "racial." Noting that Braithwaite himself wrote "nonracial," that is, white, poetry, J. Saunders Redding called him "the most outstanding example of perverted energy that the period 1903 to 1917 produced.[18]

Braithwaite attempted to guide other black poets down the same road that he had taken. In his autobiography, which appeared serially in *Phylon* (1941-1942), Braithwaite offered an apologia for his avoidance of and discrimination against "racial materials and interests." Searching for employment had demonstrated, he recalled, the "difficulties and injustices . . . for one of color who wanted to be accepted at his worth" and the vanity of believing that these difficulties "would solve themselves on the higher, the universal, the spiritual plane of art." Closing himself in a darkened room, he engaged in a "birthday meditation"—it was his twenty-first birthday—from which he emerged with the resolution to avoid racial material in his work and to express himself "on the common ground of American authorship." He resolved to prove that "a man of color" could produce work that would force recognition from the public and critics—and not a recognition based on "the sentiment and sympathy" that he might win in literature, if not in employment, as a result of his race.[19] It is a curious defense. Although it begins with acknowledging the vanity of believing that the higher, universal plane of art offered a solution, it ends by embracing just this belief. Whatever contradictions it contained (originally or when recalled years later as an apology), Braithwaite's meditation would prove just as determinative as his earlier, more epiphanic encounter with Keats.

One sees its results in his poetry, of course, but also in his response to work by other black poets. In reviewing James Weldon Johnson's *Fifty Years and Other Poems* (1917), for example, he finds that "from an artistic point of view," the poet's most felicitous work is that which strikes "a universal note" rather than a racial one.[20] The evolution from the racial to the universal similarly informs his article **"Some Contemporary Poets of the Negro Race,"** which appeared in *Crisis* in April 1919. In this article, Braithwaite argues that Negroes have lacked art but not its substance, which has found crude expression in folk ballads, communal songs, and the like. Now, he says, "the Negro has absorbed in his advanced class . . . the culture of the best civilizations in the world today, and in his imaginative and artistic expression he is universal"[21] In his view, a concern with race or an attempt to develop a Negro poetic would be atavistic; and to incorporate the black folk tradition would violate "the glorious and perfect instrument of English poetic art, which we know as the common possession of Chaucer, Shakespeare, Milton, Wordsworth, Keats, Shelley, Swinburne, Browning, Longfellow, Poe, and Lowell" (p. 51). In the introduction to his 1925 ***Anthology of Magazine Verse,*** Braithwaite grants that Countee Cullen is "undoubtedly a gifted poet of brilliant ability" but also regrets that he is "an intensely racial singer," a "limitation, which may negative, by narrowing, the powers he possesses" (p. xvii). In the same introduction, the praise of the Fugitives for having achieved "a result that has more spirit and verve than is to be found in any other group-expression in the country" (p. xii) stands as an implied criticism of the Harlem Renaissance.

As Wintz has said, Braithwaite was simply "not in tune with the New Negro movement or the resurgence of racial pride that defined much of the intellectual content of the Renaissance,"[22] and he attempted, with some success, "to divert black literature into channels he felt more appropriate and more beneficial to blacks as a whole."[23] Braithwaite's resistance to both Modernism and the Renaissance—or rather the predilections and prejudices motivating that resistance—come together in his review of Eliot's 1920 *Poems.* He charges Eliot with being an "exotic" poet and turns on him an epithet from the lexicon of white racism: he calls him a "monkey."[24]

In opposition to the emerging canon, Braithwaite scoured the country for poets more to his liking. In the 1920s, as general circulation magazines such as the *Nation, New Republic,* and *Vanity Fair* became receptive to the products of Modernism, there arose little magazines not avant-garde but reactionary. Appearing as early as 1918, *The Country Bard* contained frequent editorials denouncing "esoteric stuff" and calling for a return to the simplicity of "the older poetry." The mid-1920s saw a proliferation of such magazines: *The Lariat* (1923-1929), defending "pure and wholesome literature"; *The Mesa* (1925), announcing only "a sincere devotion to Beauty"; *Pan, Poetry and Youth* (1925-1926), seeking "to prove that there are young people today who can write poems as beautiful as dusk-tinted clouds"; *The American Parade* (1926), taking art as "the expression of an ecstasy . . . the spirit's overflow of emotion"; The *Journal of American Poetry* (1927-1928), insisting on verse in the "exalted mood" expressing "noble truths"; and so on.[25]

Here Braithwaite could find verse reminiscent of that which he had set out to redeem in the public mind. In the same anthology in which he dismissed Moore and regretted Cullen's racial singing, he announced that the "most impressive" of the new poets that year, 1925, was Milton

FROM THE AUTHOR

BRAITHWAITE ON POETIC EXPRESSION

Poetry is one of the realities that persist. The façade and dome of palace and temple, the monuments of heroes and saints, crumble before the ruining breath of time, while the Psalms last. So when another year passes and we sum up our achievements, there is no achievement more vital in registering the soul of a people than its poetry. But in all things that men do, their relationship is objective except those things in which art, religion, love, and nature express their influence through the private thoughts and feelings of men. These four things are the realities, all the others are symbols. And the essence of art, as well as religion and love and nature, is a conscious and mysterious thing, called Poetry. And men will find, if they will only stop to look, that at the bottom of all this poetry, no matter what the theme or the particular artistic shaping, there is something with which they are familiar, because in their own souls there has been an unceasing mystery which they find named in the magic utterance of some lonely and neglected maker of verses.

SOURCE: William Stanley Braithwaite, excerpt from the introduction to *Anthology of Magazine Verse for 1913*, W.S.B., 1918.

Rose of Colorado Springs, "who possesses a clear visual power, which lifts significant symbols out of common objects and invests them with suggestive meaning that is of singular quality." He reprinted from *The Mesa* three poems by Rose. Two were sonnets displaying the cobbled up poetic diction and sentiment for which Braithwaite had an unfailing weakness. The first, addressed to a blind father, began:

> A stroke of darkness cuts thy life in twain
> And stains with chaos all thy nights and days;
> It walls with emptiness thy earthly ways;
> It drops thy past, like a dumb, spacious pain
> About thy spirit. . . .
>
> (p. 270)

Between the sonnets Braithwaite placed something by Rose in a more modern vein, a poem beginning with a confession—"Green passions rise in me like monstrous frogs, / Jutting broad sensual noses through the mind"—and ending with the consoling thought that these frogs "breathe air, and may one day be birds" (pp. 270-71).

In this year Braithwaite also found Margaret Perkins Briggs, who was awarded the Kansas Author's Club First Prize, and Whitelaw Saunders, who won second prize. He noted that Portland, Oregon, "can now take pride in the fast growing reputation of such poets as Ethel Romig Fuller, Ellinor L. Norcross, Ada Hastings Hedges, and Howard McKinley Corning," all of whom had sprung from the soil to replace "the lamented Hazel Hall" (p. xiv). So too, in 1929, the search continued: "Two poets who have made exceptional progress in their work the past year, are Benjamin Musser and Ernest Hartsock. Both have written and published a great deal. In power of emotion and verbal subtlety they seem to have arrived at a maturity which should advance them rapidly to a place among the most important of the younger American Poets" (p. xxxix). He included four poems by Hartsock—all in somewhat the same manner as the first, "April Mile," consisting of couplets recounting a walk in which the poet attempts, as he says, to extricate "a harebell hanging in my mind" but is dissuaded or distracted by nature, as when "A poplar full of juice and jolly / Slapped me soundly for my folly." It has been asserted that "poets regarded an invitation to reprint their lines in 'Braithwaite' as tantamount to an award of merit."[26] Hartsock may well have regarded it so; some who shared the anthology with him, including Hart Crane, Frost, Robinson, and Williams, may not have. Nor, evidently, would Aiken, Sandburg, and Tate, three poets who refused him permission to reprint their work.[27]

In 1959, thirty years after his series had died as a victim of the Depression and of its own marginality, it returned once more as the ***Anthology of Magazine Verse for 1958 and Anthology of Poems from Seventeen Previously Published Braithwaite Anthologies,*** with the first section edited by Braithwaite and the second by Margaret Haley Carpenter.[28] Carpenter's foreword praises Braithwaite as a gifted and astute critic and for "making the recent work of America's most accomplished poets available to a large audience" (p. xxvii). Carpenter's concern for the "large audience" provides the link between her taste and Braithwaite's. Looking over the past anthologies, she observes that there was a time when poets spoke not to "private audiences" but to a great audience—and to it "clearly and compellingly" (p. xxxv). Similarly, in his introduction, Braithwaite regrets the fact that modern poetry is "no longer the embodiment of an intensified mood spontaneously revealed in the melodious simplicities of speech." Instead, he says, the "lyric impulse" has come to be "adulterated with an excess of intellectuality before it can manifest itself in the image or metaphor of joy or beauty, hope or aspiration" (p. lxiv). He thus repudiates the developments in poetry that had taken place during his years of anthological labor. He had set out in 1913 to redeem magazine verse in the eyes of the American public, seeking to convince it that what he had found in *The Bellman, Century, Harper's, Forum, Lippincott's, Scribner's,* and *Smart Set* was of "a general high standard" (p. v). Yet it was this magazine verse against which the Modernist poets would strive to define their own work. And it was in the little magazines that these poets found space in which to develop their art in isolation from a wide public. Even before the demise of his annual anthology, the gap between the mass and elite audiences had widened, and Braithwaite was out of touch with both.

Notes

1. William H. Robinson, "William Stanley Braithwaite," *Dictionary of Literary Biography,* LIV (Gale, 1987), p. 4.
2. The yearly anthologies were published under various imprints but largely at Braithwaite's own expense: W.S.B. (Braithwaite), Cambridge, Mass., 1913-1914; Gomme & Marshall, New York, 1915; Laurence J. Gomme, New York, 1916; Small, Maynard & Company, Boston, 1917-1922; B.J. Brimmer (Braithwaite's own vanity house), Boston, 1923-1927; Harold Vinal, New York, 1928; and George Scully and Company, New York, 1929. As reflected by an expansion of the title in 1914 to include the words *and Year Book of American Poetry,* the volumes also provided an annual index to poetry and magazines and, irregularly, indices to articles and reviews, lists of poetry volumes, brief reviews by Braithwaite, addresses of poetry societies, and so forth.
3. Braithwaite, "The House under Arcturus: An Autobiography" (1941-42), rpt. *The William Stanley Braithwaite Reader,* ed. Philip Butcher (University of Michigan Press, 1972), pp. 173-74.
4. David Perkins, *A History of Modern Poetry from the 1890s to the High Modernist Mode* (Harvard University Press, 1976), 294-97.
5. See G. Thomas Tanselle, "*The Lyric Year:* A Bibliographical Study," *Papers of the Bibliographical Society of America,* LVI (1962), pp. 454-71, and Ellen Williams, *Harriet Monroe and the Poetry Renaissance: The First Ten Years of* Poetry, *1912-22* (University of Illinois Press, 1977).
6. Joyce Kilmer, "Last Year's Verse," *New York Times Book Review,* 18 January 1914, p. 21; Dorothea Lawrence Mann, "American Poetry," *Forum,* LIII (1915), p. 232.
7. "The Year in Poetry," *Bookman,* XLV (1917), p. 278.
8. "Anthology of Magazine Verse for 1915," *New York Times Book Review,* 9 January 1916, p. 11.
9. O.W. Firkins, "The Irrepressible Anthology," *Nation,* CV (1917), p. 596; Jessie Rittenhouse, "Contemporary Poetry," *Bookman,* XLVI (1918), p. 679; F.X.B, "Anthology of Magazine Verse for 1920," *Double Dealer,* I (1921), p. 124; Allen Tate, "Mr. Braithwaite's Anthology," *New York Herald Tribune Books,* 14 February 1926, p. 48; Genevieve Taggard, "Thunder in the Index," *New York Herald Tribune Books,* 12 December 1926, p. 3; Louis Untermeyer, "Current Poetry," *Saturday Review of Literature,* 7 May 1927, p. 804.
10. Conrad Aiken, "Prizes and Anthologies," *Poetry Journal,* IV (1915), p. 96.
11. Aiken, p. 99.
12. Braithwaite, "Poetry and the Public," *Poetry Journal,* IV (1915), p. 154; Aiken, "Looking Pegasus in the Mouth," *Poetry Journal,* 5 (1916), p. 22.
13. "The Mechanism of Poetic Inspiration" (1917), rpt. in his *Scepticisms: Notes on Contemporary Poetry* (Knopf, 1919), pp. 32-47.
14. Aiken, *Scepticisms,* pp. 53, 56, 129, 130, 131. Reviewing this book in the *Boston Evening Transcript* (11 February 1920, p. 6), Braithwaite accused Aiken of a "critical charlatanry" that has "befogged and perverted" what it "makes an intellectual flourish of judging." In his anthology *Modern American Poets* (Martin Secker, 1922; Modern Library, 1927), which was limited to fifteen poets, Aiken exhibited his sense of discrimination.
15. Allen Tate, "Mr. Braithwaite's Anthology"; Taggard, "Thunder in the Index."
16. Kenny J. Williams, "An Invisible Partnership and an Unlikely Relationship: William Stanley Braithwaite and Harriet Monroe," *Callaloo,* X (1987), p. 516.
17. Wintz, *Black Culture and the Harlem Renaissance* (Rice University Press, 1988), p. 130.
18. J. Saunders Redding, *To Make a Poet Black,* (University of North Carolina Press, 1939), pp. 89-91. Redding's judgment is echoed in Blyden Jackson and Louis Rubin's *Black Poetry in America: Two Essays in Historical Interpretation* (Louisiana State University Press, 1974), pp. 31-33. For Braithwaite's poetry, see his *Lyrics of Life and Love* (Herbert B. Turner, 1904), *The House of Falling Leaves with Other Poems* (John W. Luce, 1908), and *Selected Poems* (Coward-McCann, 1948).
19. *William Stanley Braithwaite Reader,* pp. 177-79.
20. *Boston Transcript,* 12 December 1917, rpt. *William Stanley Braithwaite Reader,* p. 46.
21. Rpt. *William Stanley Braithwaite Reader,* p. 54.
22. Wintz, p. 131.
23. Wintz, p. 133.
24. "A Scorner of the Ordinary Substance of Human Nature," *Boston Evening Transcript,* 14 April 1920, II, p. 6.
25. These and others are listed in Frederick J. Hoffman, *et al., The Little Magazine: A History and Bibliography* (Princeton University Press, 1946).
26. Butcher, Introduction, *The William Stanley Braithwaite Reader,* p. 4. See also Kenny Williams' assertion:

"To be recognized by Braithwaite was to receive a significant imprimatur" (p. 520).

27. Braithwaite, Introduction, *Anthology of Magazine Verse for 1929,* p. xxxvi.

28. Published in New York by the Schulte Publishing Company, 1959.

LISA SZEFEL (ESSAY DATE 2001)

SOURCE: Szefel, Lisa. "Encouraging Verse: William S. Braithwaite and the Poetics of Race." *New England Quarterly* 74, no. 1 (March 2001): 32-61.

In the following essay, Szefel examines Braithwaite's criticism for the light it sheds on the development of both modern poetry and Black identity in the first half of the twentieth century.

By the first years of the twentieth century, America boasted international leadership in industry, finance, and corporate organization. The country could not, however, brag about its literary prowess. In the decades following the Civil War, no poet arose to rival Whitman, nor did any endowments, prizes, or professional forums exist to promote verse. Magazines sometimes printed poems to fill space, but only if they conformed to genteel guidelines. As Edgar Lee Masters lamented about the era, "There was no market for anything."[1] In a society that venerated businessmen and a Protestant work ethic, pursuing a career in poetry seemed precious, and so aspiring bards such as Ezra Pound, T. S. Eliot, and Robert Frost sought more cordial prospects overseas.

The situation for African-American men and women of letters was even more dismal. Between 1880 and 1910, a series of state laws and Supreme Court decisions had produced a segregated society. Although racism certainly existed in the North, it was more habitual than systematic; in the South, on the other hand, states embarked on an aggressive strategy of molesting African Americans' rights. In response to this alarming onslaught of bigotry, calamity, and disenfranchisement, black spokesman Booker T. Washington proposed a policy of compliance. African Americans would forego claims to civil and political equality; they would focus instead on creating material prosperity, on tilling fields rather than writing poems.

It is remarkable, then, that one person responsible for resuscitating America's moribund literary life was an African American, poet and critic William Stanley Braithwaite. While other authors fled the country or shrugged their shoulders, Braithwaite, a journalist for the *Evening Transcript* in Boston, Massachusetts, determined to revise the rules of poetic decorum and reverse the public's disregard for native verse. Six years before the establishment of the Poetry Society of America and eight years before the founding of Harriet Monroe's *Poetry: A Magazine of Verse,* Braithwaite single-handedly promoted the cause of American poetry. Still, Braithwaite's campaign perturbed many African Americans, who chafed at his romance of high culture and refusal to address racial issues. They accused him of ignoring his people to further his career, of selling out his birthright, Esau-like, for a pot of beans. Like W. E. B. Du Bois, Alain Locke, James Baldwin, and Richard Wright, Braithwaite endured taunts concerning his "authenticity": to his black peers he was not "black" enough; later, to the New Critics, whose masculinist ethos and methodology would become institutionalized in the universities, this writer of lyrics was not manly enough. Yet his influence on the history of American and African-American culture looms. An examination of his published criticism and private encouragement will bring the development of modern poetry as well as black identity into bolder relief.[2] Braithwaite presents a revealing case study for observing racial making and the diversity of anti-modern values in a newly modern America.

. . . . .

In the late nineteenth century, America's upper class became intrigued with medieval heraldry.[3] From an early age, William Stanley Braithwaite set out to prove that he had a right to joust with the best of them. In mapping his genealogy, he laid claim to participation in Boston's upper-class literary community. Born in Boston in 1878 to middle-class parents, his paternal lineage traced back to Barbados, where a black newspaper publisher had married the white daughter of a French nobleman. The mixed marriage was socially recognized in the racially fluid island of Demerara, British Guiana. Braithwaite conspicuously chronicled his claims to gentility: a great-grandfather was "the best Latin scholar in the Colony"; a great-uncle was knighted and listed in Burke's Peerage as late as 1910; his grandfather won the rights of colonists to participate in their government; his paternal grandmother was "the belle of the Capital," renowned for her "beauty, charm and wit." Yet Braithwaite crossed this latitude of refinement with the longitude of race:

> If my paternal grandmother was by birth and breeding a lady, my maternal grandmother, whose origin was in the dark and tragic house of bondage, whose motherhood was the result of a vicious system of rape, and whose life was spent

in the humble ranks of service, was also a lady, because of her personal integrity and through training in the holy Episcopal faith.[4]

Braithwaite's father, William, as his son remembered him, was a "leader of men," "brilliant of mind, magnificent in physique," who was saddled with "the arrogance of the aristocrat, the passion of the radical, and the somber fatalism of the thwarted conqueror." In 1875, he married Emma DeWolfe, a light-skinned daughter of a mulatto ex-slave. Poor, but beautiful, she comfortably traveled with her husband in circles that included Harvard President Charles W. Eliot, Bishop Phillips Brooks, and the Irish patriot and poet John Boyle O'Reilly. Convinced of his children's superiority, William did not allow them to play with neighboring children or attend school. The Boston household at 199 Pleasant Street, modeling itself on an English country manor home, observed Victorian mores and required "Fauntleroyish" attire. Family sermons were straight out of Carlyle: "Always . . . [William] spoke of the greatness of men. Without their examples life would be a more discouraging affair than it is" (2.1:21).

Braithwaite's father had a deep sense of personal failure. He had studied medicine first in Georgetown, then England, but he left the country six months shy of receiving his medical degree. Although President Eliot encouraged him to complete his degree at Harvard, William desisted. Instead, he served as a nurse for a Back Bay physician, Doctor George Shattuck, Jr. He earned enough for the family to summer in the countryside of either New York or New Jersey, but he did not set aside money for savings or insurance (2.1:23). In Dickensian fashion, he died insolvent at the age of forty-two, leaving his impassive wife in charge of a destitute family. Eight-year-old Braithwaite's prospects narrowed from a secure future reading law at Harvard to a precarious present hawking newspapers at Park Square. He attended school for the first time but had to leave four years later to support his mother and siblings. Nevertheless, he did not relinquish his dreams. Although time or maturity may have eroded memories of confusion, anger, and self-doubt, in his memoirs Braithwaite concentrated on the series of aesthetic, religious, and racial epiphanies that gave him the confidence to pursue his ambition despite immense obstacles.

In 1890, at the age of twelve, Braithwaite, the second eldest of five children (two of whom died in childhood), secured full-time employment to support his family. Each summer, he and his mother traveled to New York or Newport to find more lucrative work. After successive jobs as a doorman, errand boy, and barber shop "brush boy," he apprenticed as a compositor at Ginn and Company, where his life would radically change. On a day he would later refer to as "annunciation day," he "wandered into a world of magical beauty" while setting type for the lines "'Beauty is truth, truth beauty,'—that is all / Ye know on earth, and all ye need to know." Keats's words kindled in young Braithwaite a passion for poetry that would soon flame into "a fanatical determination" after he read Wordsworth and Burns (2.2:258-59).

Like poetry, High Church rituals fed Braithwaite's need for intense, vital experience. Years later, he recalled the "spirals of exotic incense, sweetening, with a mad, burning ecstasy, the too sensitive and responsive flesh" where he "began to feel the mounting exhilaration of ritual and incense, the sharpening yearnings of the ceremonial mysteries" (2.3:34). Braithwaite vowed to serve Christ ("essentially a man of sorrows, as all great poets must be") by preaching the gospel of "Truth and Beauty." Aware that his resolve would engender ridicule and resistance, he began an ascetic regimen of reading: "When it became known among the colored people in Boston that I had literary ambitions, they laughed at me."[5]

Nor was Braithwaite accepted by white folks. Several months of searching for employment as a book clerk in New York City had forced him to confront bigotry as never before. At the end of each interview, the twenty-one-year-old was told that his knowledge of literature exceeded that of any other candidate. But the inevitable question always followed: "You don't mind if I ask you your nationality, not that it makes any difference?" The answer, "I am an American Negro," invariably lost him the job. His Whitmanesque dreams about the democracy of culture evaporated: "I was forced to face problems which somehow, I had deluded myself would solve themselves upon the higher, the universal, the spiritual plane of art. It was my belief that Beauty and Art were the leveler of all distinctions" (3.2:186).

In the midst of his experiences, Braithwaite made two resolutions: to force a recognition that in the realm of literature African Americans were equal and able; and to avoid a double standard by refusing to treat racial materials and racial experiences "*until* this recognition had been won, recorded, and universally confirmed." He theorized that a de-politicized poetry would win respect that, in turn, would open a space to address issues of race. In response to criticism accusing him of a retreat from, and discrimination against, racial materials and interests, Braithwaite defended his controversial strategy: "I was taking a way unique, and single-handed to help solve their problems, which were essentially my own personal problems as well, and which were insidious and perplexing" (3.2:187).

Braithwaite had good reason to pursue an assimilationist plan. Shortly after marrying Emma Kelly in 1903, he returned to Boston because he believed he would face less racial discrimination there. He and his wife settled into an apartment near Harvard Square but eventually purchased a house in Arlington Heights to accommodate their growing family. As journalist Ray Stannard Baker documented at the time, African Americans who lived in the North enjoyed a greater degree of freedom. Although one would not want to overstate the case, Boston, in particular, seemed amenable to racial integration. Blacks could freely ride streetcars and railroads and attend the theater and other public gatherings. They worked as policemen, firemen, and office holders, and they sent their children to free, racially mixed schools. An African-American woman, Maria Baldwin, served as principal of the Agassiz School in Cambridge, which had an all-white enrollment of six hundred schoolchildren. Alain Locke had recently graduated from Harvard, after receiving one of the three prestigious Bowdoin prizes awarded as well as a Rhodes scholarship to Oxford.[6]

The extent to which Braithwaite penetrated Boston's elite literary community is striking. By the age of twenty-four, he began to enjoy success as a published poet. From 1902 to 1904, his work appeared in Boston newspapers. In 1904, after compiling his work into a book titled ***Lyrics of Life and Love,*** he secured a contract with Herbert B. Turner and Company. The firm agreed to publish the volume if Braithwaite could obtain two hundred advance subscriptions, an arrangement common among publishers of the time. Boston luminaries including Julia Ward Howe, Louise Chandler Moulton, Thomas Bailey Aldrich, Bliss Perry, and Arthur O'Shaughnessy pledged their support. The most enthusiastic endorsement came from Colonel Thomas Wentworth Higginson, the abolitionist, soldier, man of letters, and commander of the 55th Massachusetts, a regiment of Negro troops who fought bravely in the Civil War (3.2:190-92).

Still, Braithwaite walked away from many residences not only empty handed but full of ire. A visit to Edward Everett Hale, then chaplain of the United States Senate and president of The Lend-A-Hand Society, particularly angered him. Dr. Hale reluctantly added his name to the booklet of signatures, then remarked, "Young man, it is no disgrace to hoe potatoes" (3.2:193). In this one sentence, Hale encapsulated the debate between adherents of Booker T. Washington and those of W. E. B. Du Bois, a debate about whether the African-American cause could best be advanced by focusing on technical education or on a liberal arts education.

. . . . .

In his autobiography, Booker T. Washington recorded that he thought it tomfoolery for ambitious blacks to study Greek while working in the fields.[7] W. E. B. Du Bois, on the other hand, savored the image. The classics, he believed, would have a salubrious effect on any reader's character. Raised in Great Barrington, Massachusetts, Du Bois was steeped in the traditional New England ethos of discipline, industry, restraint, and culture. The only black boy in an all-white school, he experienced little interference while absorbing the writings of Calvin, Carlyle, Emerson, and Arnold.[8] In a famous passage from *The Souls of Black Folk,* Du Bois laid claim to the whole of western tradition:

> I sit with Shakespeare and he winces not. Across the color line I move arm and arm with Balzac and Dumas, where smiling men and welcoming women glide in gilded halls. . . . I summon Aristotle and Aurelius and what soul I will, and they come all graciously with no scorn nor condescension. So, wed with Truth, I dwell above the veil.[9]

Braithwaite, too, had referred to "the common possession of Chaucer, Shakespeare, Milton, Wordsworth, Keats, Shelley, Swinburne, Browning, Longfellow, Poe, and Lowell."[10] Appreciating that writing occupies an elite space where important cultural capital accumulates, both Braithwaite and Du Bois were committed to drawing African-American authors into that coveted territory. Du Bois evidently understood that he and Braithwaite shared a philosophical point of view as well as a strategy for effecting it, for he selected Braithwaite to serve as a member of the first editorial board of *Crisis,* the monthly magazine Du Bois founded in 1910.

Like Braithwaite, Du Bois believed that race could be transcended in universality. He argued against racial essentialism by insisting that oppressive surroundings fringed with hatred, not defective biological characteristics, cultivated undesirable traits such as laziness, ignorance, and crime. Far from a locus of immorality, as lynchers and supremacists would have it, the black household sheltered white middle-class values; pigmentation did not produce promiscuity or penury. He objected to Washington's unnecessarily narrow focus on money making and practical trades because it occluded spiritual values: "To make men, we must have ideals, broad, pure, and inspiring ends of living, not sordid money-getting, not sapples of gold." In his paean to the virtues of his race—poised, as it was, in the midst of a modern, capitalist society—Du Bois sounded like a Knight of Labor or a back-up speaker for William Jennings Bryan: "Our black men seem the sole oasis of simple faith and reverence in a dusty desert of dollars and smartness."[11]

As editor of an Atlanta University series of sociological studies, Du Bois met whites' fears with dismay. "The Negro's ignorance, superstition, vice and poverty do not disturb and unnerve his enemies," reported one commentator, "so much as his rapid strides upward and onward." A Northern black correspondent lamented, "I sometimes think it is the progress rather than our lack of progress that is causing the continued friction between the races."[12] In his landmark *The Souls of Black Folk,* Du Bois identified the African Americans' struggle to merge their racial with their national identity, that is, "to make it possible for a man to be both a Negro and an American, without being cursed and spit upon by his fellows, without having the doors of Opportunity closed roughly in his face."[13]

Insofar as it affected the "spiritual nation of the race" and revealed "the true idealism and high aspiration of the American Negro," *The Souls of Black Folk,* Braithwaite believed, had launched the modern poetic tradition for African Americans. He objected to the imposition of racial categories and notions of authenticity. Race, he argued, was simply a construct designed to stabilize privilege and status. No grand ontological divide separated the races. "We believe the Negro writer must think, feel, or write racially to be a great artist. This is a fallacy too often expressed by critics to confirm the desired hypothesis that the Negro is humanly different in the scale of mankind." Race was an inherited tradition that could be donned or discarded, a performance that could expand or constrict the parameters of black identity. All great artists, Braithwaite insisted, were "interracial" or "co-racial."[14]

Along with poet James Weldon Johnson, Braithwaite was convinced that "a people that has produced great art and literature has never been looked upon as distinctly inferior."[15] Still, his preferred method for achieving that end was gradual, not confrontational. He could not bring himself to shed his patrician legacy and desire for racial accord; any form of discord unnerved him. By composing in the lyric form and by masking, at least in print, his racial identity, he hoped to elevate the image of blacks. Braithwaite's first volume sang of nature, myths, dreams, beauty, and love rather than slavery or racism. He consciously avoided free verse and poems with a social message so as not to appear irreverent. Black dialect, a style all the rage after the publication of Paul Dunbar's 1895 *Majors and Minors,* was also to be avoided because, according to Braithwaite, it made African Americans sound exotic and inferior. Braithwaite found fault with Dunbar for lacking subtlety of expression, rhythm, and "haunting forms of expression."[16]

African-American female poets also took to the lyric out of similar political and aesthetic concerns. Whites stereotyped the black woman as a licentious temptress, uneducated breeder, or a sexless Aunt Jemima. Poets such as Helene Johnson and Gwendolyn Bennett appropriated romantic poetry as a means to contest such representations. In the 1989 anthology *Shadowed Dreams: Women's Poetry of the Harlem Renaissance,* Maureen Honey argued that the poets she studied had chosen to embrace a white-encoded aesthetic dealing with apolitical topics of love and nature in order to refute notions of black inferiority.[17] Their verse honored spiritual values in a materialistic world controlled by whites. Love's passion was depicted as inspiring, rather than denigrating, and emotional bonds between blacks could be celebrated. An exploration of the lyric, then, was also an inquiry into selfhood, the body, and eroticism in an environment that sought to render African-American women writing about such matters "silent, asexual, or animalistic."[18] And for the black women to whom the poems were directed, the act of reading literature served as a catalyst to promote a "sense of coalition" and social change.[19] Poetry thus provided a necessary psychological space and performed important cultural work.

In 1906, Braithwaite followed his first book with an anthology, ***The Book of Elizabethan Verse,*** which prompted Colonel T. W. Higginson to nominate him for membership in the Boston Authors' Club. In due course, Braithwaite received official notification from the club's treasurer. The man he refers to only as a Southern gentleman kindly adjured Braithwaite to decline the offer of membership lest he suffer the racial discrimination that would undoubtedly be his lot. Braithwaite, though, did not need instruction on Yankee racism, and he refused to bow to such faintly veiled bigotry. When he informed club Vice-President Colonel Higginson and President Julia Ward Howe about the treasurer's recommendation, they vowed to withdraw and organize another club if anyone discriminated against the club's newest member.[20]

Having successfully negotiated his authorial debut, Braithwaite turned his attention to aiding fellow poets. Editorial policies prevented a good deal of verse from seeing print, he believed, and so he proposed to act as a cultural mediator between poets and their public. He viewed his mission in ministerial terms: to raise the "standard" and advance "the crusade in behalf of the recognition and appreciation for American poets and poetry."[21] However, his 1904 proposal to review the best examples of magazine verse in the *Boston Evening Transcript* met with gales of laughter from the paper's editors.

At the turn of the century, many Americans viewed poetry as a female vocation not worthy of serious attention. As Ann Douglas has demonstrated, the connections among literature, religion, sentimentalism, and women forged in the nineteenth century led to a real or perceived "feminization" of American literature. The esteemed literary critic and patron Edmund Clarence Stedman, for example, readily deemed the artistic temperament "androgynous" and the poet's composition transgendered: "The woman's intuition, sensitiveness, nervous refinement join with the reserved power and creative vigor of the man to form the poet."[22] At the same time, cultural configurations of manhood were shifting. The exemplary man now had to prove his mettle not in intellectual or religious pursuits but on some more vigorous field such as sport, business, or industry. Women's suffrage, as well as the growing force of immigrant votes and labor strikes, threatened middle-class male dominance in the political sphere. New categorizations of homosexuality and neurasthenia further distilled fears of class and gender disintegration.[23] A redesigned discourse about race, class, and gender, a discourse that highlighted virile, white manhood, met its challenges head on and asserted primary claims to an authority that had been rapidly dispersing.

The power of this reactionary discourse was evident in the general public's derisive view of poetry. More poems were being produced than ever before. In the 1890s, 1,900 men and women produced more than 2,400 volumes of verse.[24] The British romantic tradition lived on in local Browning and Tennyson societies. In Boston, New York, Chicago, and San Francisco, versifiers and critics gathered at salons to discuss the latest artistic offerings. Newspapers published jingoistic verse, while magazines such as *Harper's, Century,* and *Scribner's* showcased more stately stanzas. But such riches, because they were encoded as feminine, proved an embarrassment. While on an extended train journey, Robert Frost later enjoyed telling audiences, he fell into a long and pleasant conversation with a man he had just met. The next morning, the man asked Frost what he did for a living. When he responded that he wrote poetry, the man exclaimed, "My god! My wife writes that stuff!"[25]

To receive the kind of respect that accrued to other professions, poetry could no longer parade in drag; it had to be decked out in businessmen's attire. A younger generation, not to the manor born, appropriated the discourse on manliness to justify making a living from writing poetry rather than merely dabbling in it as a hobby. Edwin Arlington Robinson was among the first of the young poets to "Put these little sonnetmen to flight" and pursue a more consciously masculine, American verse. After he self-published his first volume, *The Torrent and the Night Before,* in 1896, he bragged to friends, "There is not a red-bellied robin in the whole collection."[26] Wallace Stevens winced at the association of verse with effeminacy. He sidestepped the opprobrium by succeeding as an insurance executive in Hartford and choosing to specialize in epic poems, which, unlike the lyric, offered a "masculine" cast of characters and legendary heroes.[27]

In such a hyper-masculine environment, the African-American male occupied a particularly ambivalent position. Whites tended to view black men as oversexed savages who raped white women (a scurrilous logic that justified lynching and the denial of full political and civil rights). Even such an esteemed enterprise as the *Encyclopedia Britannica* propagated phrenological canards about stunted cranial growth and the resulting obsession with sex.[28] Given the prevalence of such notions in the media, it is not surprising that Braithwaite chose the lyric, an apparently non-threatening form, to subvert the despicable, and ultimately untenable, ideas he encountered.

Nonetheless, one surefire way to insult an enemy was to hint that he versified for the magazines. In response, Braithwaite titled his first *Boston Evening Transcript* article on magazine verse as if it were a story out of Ripley's Believe It or Not:

"Forty-Five Lines of *Actual* Poetry in the Magazines of 1906."[29] The report, an instant sensation, elicited hundreds of letters from enthusiastic poets, editors, publishers, and readers. The same editors at the *Transcript* who had derided Braithwaite for wanting to review magazine verse in 1904 now hired him to contribute a bi-weekly column. His fame grew so great that in 1910, when a group of poets led by the eccentric German-American bard George Sylvester Viereck organized the Poetry Society of America, they invited him to be a charter member and to attend the first dinner. Braithwaite sympathized with the PSA's goal of building the public's appreciation for American poetry, and so he gladly joined the organization. In the *Transcript,* he described the group's first dinner meeting. Members were praised for their "virtue and honor" in an era "when materialism had seemed to smother it."[30] Advocating poetry as a means to counter capitalist consumerism and cupidity was a motivating creed for many early PSA members. Five years later, along with Conrad Aiken, Amy Lowell, and Edward O'Brien, Braithwaite organized a similar organization in Boston, the New England Poetry Club.

. . . . .

Braithwaite broadened his involvement in the poetic cause by launching an annual anthology, a project that grew naturally out of a 1911 review in which he listed twenty poems worthy of such notice. Hundreds of inquiries requesting the phantom book poured in to Braithwaite's office at the newspaper. Encouraged, Braithwaite decided to meet public demand, and in 1913 he published his first anthology of poetry. Because he could not find a publisher who would support the endeavor, he issued the first two annuals at his own expense.

As with his writing for the *Transcript,* the *Poetry Journal* (which he edited from December 1912 through July 1913), and the *Poetry Review* (from May 1916 through February 1917), in the anthologies Braithwaite aimed to create a forum for poets that appealed to a wide audience: "The poets are doing satisfying and vitally excellent work, and it only remains for the American public to do its duty by showing a substantial appreciation." Poetry belonged to the people; it "sprang from the folk." The appeal, Braithwaite believed, lay in its universality: "the deepest and truest expression of the human spirit, the one art through which the profoundest mysteries and the highest ideals of life could be interpreted and communicated."[31] And that one art was color blind.

Braithwaite praised and encouraged others who shared his poetic philosophy. He assisted Sara Teasdale in the compilation of her anthology *The Answering Voice* because she judiciously "gave praise where it was due. Where it was not due, she was inclined to be rather silent." In her follow-up collection, *Rainbow Gold: An Anthology of Poems Old and New for the Young,* she answered the critic's calling to "please as well as instruct."[32]

In this first, critical stage of a poetic resurgence, from 1910 to 1916, Braithwaite believed that unity and applause, not divisiveness and discouragement, were key to the movement's ongoing success. He appreciated the poem's evocative power, glad simply to admire without having to analyze. Being in the presence of beauty, touching its trailing garments, was a benediction: "The first test was the sense of pleasure the poem communicated; then to discover the secret or the meaning of the pleasure felt; and in doing so to realize how much richer I became in the knowledge of the purpose of life." Poetry resembled sorcery more than science: "The final test of poetry is its magic. . . . This is the haunting quality in poetry, a thing that has no web of reasoning and whose elements are so unaccountably mixed that no man has yet learned its secret."[33] Critics were well advised to forsake the antiseptic methodology of the scientist because, ultimately, the power of poetry remained inscrutable. While scientists could explain a prism, poets, with their superior powers, could refract its splendors.

The "Braithwaites," as the anthologies came to be known, extended the poet-editor's celebrity. "You have no idea how the trail of William Stanley Braithwaite lies all over the growth of poetry here in the East," Amy Lowell wrote conspiratorially to Braithwaite's rival, *Poetry* editor Harriet Monroe. "It never occurred to me that the man had any standing, with his Magazine anthology, until the other day in New York, when Edwin Arlington Robinson and Louis Ledoux [*sic*] informed me that they thought his opinion carried a great deal of weight."[34] William Dean Howells deemed Braithwaite "the most intelligent historian of contemporary poetry I know."[35] *Boston Evening Transcript* editor Burton Kline attributed the surge in the number and stature of poets soliciting publication in his paper to his employee's selfless efforts: "At every cost to himself, by years of labor that should have gone to himself, he has taken a joke and made it a literature."[36] In 1915 the *éminence grise* of the poetry community, Edwin Markham, along with Edwin Arlington Robinson and Louis LeDoux, held a special dinner in Braithwaite's honor. The next year, he was inducted into the exclusive Boston chapter of the honor society Alpha Phi Alpha.[37]

Poets and publishers courted Braithwaite hoping for notice either in his column or his yearly collection. Robert Frost was one poet who benefited from the attention. *Poetry* and *Atlantic Monthly* had rejected Frost's initial submissions. In 1915, his British publisher had sent only two copies of his first book, *A Boy's Will,* to America for review. Chagrined that his work was being neglected, Frost desperately sought recognition. He invited Braithwaite and his family to visit in New Hampshire (Braithwaite declined), wrote long letters, and sent copies of his books.[38] Braithwaite composed three highly favorable reviews and included Frost's poems in his annual anthologies.[39] Despite the endorsement, Frost's animosity for Braithwaite was cutting, even if, to forward his purposes, covert. When Frost discovered that the 1918 anthology contained none of his poems, he flew into a rage:

> Breathweight had no choice in the matter of taking or leaving any poetry of mine for his anthology. There was none. Nary a drop. I have shown not a poem to an editor since I gave The Ax Helve to The Atlantic summer before last. So that lets the nigger out. . . . Not that I've absolutely stopped writing. I do a little and let it lie around where I can enjoy it for its own sake and not for what some nigger may think of it.[40]

Likewise, Arthur Inman, a white Southerner and recipient of Braithwaite's personal praise and editorial benevolence, maintained a friendly rapport in public but lobbed racial epithets in private. Indeed, his personal correspondence shows Inman to be baldly opportunistic: "I would get down on my belly and go through the motions of making obeisance to a pink-eyed worm if by so doing I were sure I could further my work. In this case I think I can. Therefore I associate with a nigger."[41]

By 1916, most commentators would have agreed, the country was in the midst of a poetic renaissance. Various "schools" had arisen, and they gave voice to imagists, lyricists, conservatives, and radicals. The anthologies reflected this polyphony. Robert Frost, Vachel Lindsay, Amy Lowell, Edgar Lee Masters, Edna St. Vincent Millay, Edward Arlington Robinson, Wallace Stevens, and Sara Teasdale, despite their various styles, each received citations as "distinctive" poets. Braithwaite particularly enjoyed Imagists, not because of their experiments in exactitude but for their approach, which approximated his own belief that "All poetry comes out of feeling."[42]

Yet, because of his conservative taste, Braithwaite overlooked or dismissed significant compositions. Poets listed in the 1915 yearbook but not anthologized included, for example, William Carlos Williams and (for what became the modernist classic, "The Love Song of J. Alfred Prufrock") T. S. Eliot. These mentions did not even garner an asterisk denoting "poems of distinction," while other works that quickly sank into obscurity (such as those by Lizette Woodworth Reese) received effusive praise.[43]

In the anthologies' initial years, Braithwaite's success in building a public responsive to poetry overshadowed such unfortunate gaffes. In time, though, detractors stepped forward to question his critical acumen. Secretary of the Poetry Society of America, Jessie B. Rittenhouse, derided Braithwaite's overly generous pronouncements. "Democracy may be the hope of Society," she argued, but "discrimination is the hope of Art." The *Double Dealer* bemoaned the anthologizing of "depressing drivel." Louis Untermeyer, Frost booster and editor of anthologies himself, deemed the yearly editions "Braithwaite's yearly blunder" as well as a "monument to mediocrity." Poets allow their work to appear, Untermeyer contended, because "they feel sorry for him."[44]

Braithwaite's most obdurate critic was Harvard-educated Conrad Aiken, the transplanted Southerner from Savannah, Georgia. Aiken maintained that "the real business of the poet" was to "consciously or unconsciously give the lowdown on himself, and through himself on humanity." Aiken's offensive began mildly enough with a 1915 letter to the *New York Times Book Review* editor in which he denounced all magazine verse as "not worth a fig." His vitriol became more pronounced as he greeted each new anthology with an attack in the *Dial.* Aiken deemed Braithwaite "incredibly undiscriminating," "insular in outlook," "intolerant," and "limited intellectually." His selections betrayed an "inane falsifying and posturing" and an "infantile lack of humor or ordinary intelligence." Along with an overly generous spirit, Aiken found a bounty of "inaccuracies," "hasty superficialities," "the hog-trot of mediocrity . . . mawkishness, dullness, artificiality, and utter emptiness." Missing was "anything like a profound approach to the problems of our lives, or a serene and proportioned understanding of them, or a passionate rebellion at them."[45]

Aiken's nascent modernism anticipated New Criticism in its proposal that critics look at poems "with more of the scientist's eye, and less of the lover's." Poetic inspiration had nothing "mysterious and translunar about it" that "escapes human analysis, which it would be almost sacrilege for analysis to touch." Poetry must be demystified and professionalized: "Our criticism is still a rather primitive parade of likes and dislikes," Aiken complained. American critics and poets were "a sentimental lot" who needed to develop precise skills in discernment. Approaches such as Braithwaite's "quaint notion of the holiness of poetry" led to verse that consisted of "all marshmallows and tears."[46]

Chafing at sentimentalism, modernists defined themselves against people like Braithwaite. They looked to such theorists as T. E. Hulme, who campaigned against the opiate effects of reading Swinburne, searching for "truth," and equating poetry with religion. Such pursuits gave poetry the legitimacy of patent medicine. Detached interest, accurate description, and "dry, hard, classical verse" would move the practice of poetry into the modern wards of science.[47] While Braithwaite and others remained content to stand in awe of poetry's mysteries, modernists embarked on a kind of poetic genome project, in which they relentlessly borrowed scientific methods in their quest for precision and knowledge about poetry's origins.[48]

Taking the attacks to heart, Braithwaite mounted his own offensive. In the anthology's next installment, he insisted that poetry "is not as Conrad Aiken thinks, anatomy to be dissected in the laboratory." Rather, "Poetry begins and ends in feelings, moves from the heart of the creator to the heart of the reader in a vehicle of dream whose motive power is mystical intelligence." The reality of poetry, Braithwaite argued, "lies wholly in the abstract and to reach that reality, comprehend and interpret it, is completely a matter of sentiment and not science." In his view, a formalist approach overlooked a poem's deeper meaning. He chastised "the so-called 'intellectualists' from Bodenheim to Aiken whose intellectualism made a fetich [*sic*] of technique, and like the priest and Levite, led them to pass on the other side of the street where Life lay stricken."[49]

Moreover, in Braithwaite's estimation, a fragile, reciprocal relationship existed between the critic and the general audience. The renaissance in poetry was a direct result of those who had fostered an appreciation for the art and established an audience that, in turn, "quickened the creative impulse of the poets." Contentious or detached criticism could have a ruinous effect: "If the public heeds such criticism, audiences will diminish, and the consequent discouragement of the poets themselves will produce a decline in creativeness." Criticism accrued value insofar as it provided insight: "Criticism is not a judgment of literary styles and materials, but an interpretation of life . . . not the form, but the substance is the main thing."[50]

Braithwaite's insistence on substance over form constituted the literary equivalent of his conviction that character mattered more than color. Likewise, his preference for Imagists over "intellectualists" reflected his own position; he did not want others who, like himself, had little formal education to be barred from active participation in the poetic community. If harmony and egalitarianism could be achieved in poetry, perhaps they could then be achieved in reality.

. . . . .

By 1920, Braithwaite's reality certainly needed a boost. Despite his critical success, his finances had steadily deteriorated. His work as a freelance writer barely supported his wife and their seven children. As he sorted through piles of unpaid bills, foreclosure notices, and collection agency warning letters, it is a wonder he could concentrate on literary pursuits at all. Each year, even though the anthologies were tremendously popular, Braithwaite lost thousands of dollars. None of the large publishing houses would do business with him, and the smaller companies with which he dealt required substantial retainers and, he thought, had cheated him out of his royalties. Many were not long active, and when the companies failed, he had no way of recouping his losses.[51]

In hope of turning a profit, Braithwaite launched his own publishing firm with Winifred Jackson, president of the North Carolina College for Women. Soon, though, the firm was forced into bankruptcy by individuals—Braithwaite refers to them as speculators—who wanted to secure a proposed manuscript from a noted Harvard professor, Charles Copeland.[52] Swindled out of his hard-earned money, Braithwaite suspected racism and wondered if he would have faced as much adversity if he were white.

To ease his financial burdens, Braithwaite devised a plan to sell his critical expertise, an asset he had given away freely for years. In a time before the proliferation of M.F.A. programs, his fee of thirty-five cents per line for general criticism and fifty cents per line for more detailed analysis was a bargain. The majority of solicitations arrived from women who had no formal education beyond high school. Although his remarks could be stringent, Braithwaite developed life-long friendships with some of his correspondents.[53]

Several students in particular may have wished that he had ignored their pleas for more rigorous commentary. About the submissions of Miss Ada Norrington, of Rochester, New York, he wrote: "Poetry is a heart-breaking art to master and in your case seems more heart-breaking than ever." After suggesting a course of reading, he predicted that she would soon realize "how far short" of the mark her efforts fell.[54] To Susie A. Jordan he recommended further education prior to more poetic attempts: "one must not merely rely upon the wish to write poetry." As it stood, her poem was "an entirely sentimental one" (7 February 1922).

At times, Braithwaite exhibited even less diplomacy, particularly toward those who composed in free verse. Elizabeth E. Lowe must have laid her pen to rest after she read her letter of 15 March 1922:

> It is very evident that your desire to write verse immeasurably exceeds your ability to write it. You are lacking in a command of the very fundamental elements of verse structure. . . . Your verse, then, lacks the ordinary rudiments of metrical form; you apparently have not the ear for rhythmical expression. . . . There is not, as far as I have been able to discover, a single stanza nor even a single line of these manuscripts that can be scanned.

Poor James G. Conner, an American living in Paris, received the verdict that "there is no great body of natural poetic gifts under your command. . . . I am afraid poetry is lacking in your work" (14 March 1922). Even after receiving such discouraging remarks, many expectant writers continued to solicit Braithwaite's criticism. Responding to his counsel that she keep her day job, Shirley Dillan Waite insisted that "My innate love of the rhythmic line is so deep and my desire to write so overpowering that I dare not turn back. I am willing to work and work hard in order to improve my technique" (4 June 1930).

As Braithwaite's economic status suffered, so too did his standing in the African-American community. His reputation reached its apex in 1918, when he received the Spingarn Medal, awarded annually to "the American citizen of African descent who made last year the highest achievement in any field of elevated human endeavor."[55] Teachers at all educational levels, from grammar to graduate school, requested photographs and biographical information. Black instructors held up his success to inspire their students; white teachers did so to enlighten theirs about racial issues. As a final accolade, Atlanta University invited Braithwaite to deliver the commencement address in 1918, after which they granted him an honorary degree.

Despite the recognition he received as an African American, as well as a poet and editor, Braithwaite continued to forswear race as a topic for his writing. Black acquaintances regularly stopped him on the street and requested that he use his platform at the *Transcript* to address racial issues. Braithwaite simply replied that that was not his role.[56] For the same reason, he declined invitations to speak on such issues as the "Negro Problem."

Braithwaite continued to champion African-American authors who shared his point of view. He particularly revered the work of his close friend James Weldon Johnson, author of the highly acclaimed novel *The Autobiography of an Ex-Colored Man.* In a review of Johnson's autobiography, *Along This Way,* Braithwaite opened with an admonition: "One should not in the least be interested in the fact of Mr. Johnson being a colored man." Johnson's opus, "based upon a broader contemplation of life," took up universal concerns that extended beyond the limits of racial experience. In those few instances in which Johnson did pursue racial themes, he did so with tact: "He gives an intellectual virility to the treatment of racial problems and subjects hitherto unapproached."[57] Even though Countee Cullen could be "an intensely racial singer," he generally eschewed racial polemics. Cullen reciprocated the esteem, dedicating his 1927 anthology *Caroling Dusk* to his mentor.[58] Braithwaite also admired Georgia Douglas Johnson, whose work focused on "feminine" issues. He wrote the introduction to her 1918 debut, *The Heart of a Woman,* and several of her poems appeared in his 1918 anthology (Braithwaite did not indicate her race). In 1922, B. J. Brimmer issued her second collection, *Bronze: A Book of Verse,* for which Braithwaite wrote the foreword.

While these African-American writers whom Braithwaite admired shared a veneration for the romantic and pre-Raphaelite traditions, they all publicly pursued the cause of racial advancement. In addition to writing poems dedicated to Keats, Cullen explored the liminality of black citizenship in poems such as "Heritage," "Tableaux," "Incident," and "Yet Do I Marvel." Georgia Johnson wrote pamphlets against lynching as well as poems and plays about it. Du Bois devoted his life to asserting and valorizing black identity. As a journalist, James Weldon Johnson often wrote on issues surrounding African-American life, and he served as a field secretary in the NAACP.

While others strode to the barricades, Braithwaite felt confident that his contribution to the cause lay in tending to the façades. One of his closest literary predecessors, the writer Charles Chesnutt, made the same choice. Chesnutt decided that "the subtle almost indefinable feeling of repulsion toward the Negro, which is common to most Americans . . . cannot be stormed and taken by assault; the garrison will not capitulate." He believed that "the province of literature" would grant African Americans the "social recognition" and "equality" they deserved.[59] Braithwaite expressed similar views in various magazines, including: *The Colored American; Crisis: A Record of the Darker Races; Opportunity: A Journal of Negro Life;* and *Phylon.* Eugene O'Neill, usually praised for his depiction of black life in such plays as "Emperor Jones," "All God's Chillun Got Wings," and "Goat Alley," received nothing but rebuke from Braithwaite, who objected to the dramatization of only "sordid aspects of life and undesirable types of character" rather than the "best and highest class of racial life."[60]

Braithwaite joined Du Bois in objecting to Vachel Lindsay, also accused of objectifying African Americans. Although praised by men of such eminence as Professor William Lyon Phelps and Professor Nelson Crawford, Lindsay, Braithwaite wrote, "neither understands nor represents" blacks. Having attended one of Lindsay's famous readings of "The Congo," Braithwaite concluded that he regarded blacks purely as spectacle: "he drew little difference between the emotionalism of the aboriginal and the individual so interfused with other bloods and environments who was as far removed from the 'big, black bucks' as the poet himself."[61]

Uplift, universality, and transcendence did not sit well with activists, particularly in the 1920s era of "The New Negro." Renaissance figures in Harlem no longer paid obeisance to cautious commentators of the century's first decades. Langston Hughes's "The Negro Artist and the Racial Mountain" took on the character of a manifesto calling all African-American writers to unite behind the banner of black advancement. The "urge within the race toward whiteness," which Hughes observed in poets such as Countee Cullen, blocked the emergence of "true Negro art" in America.[62] Jean Toomer's *Cane,* in which the author insisted that he had to embrace his black racial identity in order to discover his writing, became the totemic Renaissance text.[63] Traveling to the South and experiencing "the folk" became a rite of passage or mark of legitimacy for authors claiming to speak for their brethren. Du Bois did a tour of teaching below the Mason-Dixon line. Inside his Pullman car, life-long Northerner Countee Cullen made his Southern journey with trembling and fear. James Weldon Johnson gave up a scholarship to Harvard Medical School to become principal of a Southern school where he could work with the folk, "the basic material for race building."[64]

Among this younger generation, Braithwaite was tagged the "Old Negro." Early in his career, Claude McKay sought out Braithwaite's encouragement and inclusion in the anthologies. Encounters with racism, the wave of lynching in 1919, and travel to the Soviet Union radicalized the Jamaican-born writer.[65] He joined the Communist party and shed ties to gentility, viewing his association with the conservative Bostonian as an embarrassment. In the same month that Braithwaite gave generous praise (and genial criticism) to McKay, McKay wrote to Langston Hughes lambasting Braithwaite's labors. His former mentor's work was "both bad and worthless." He added, "Braithwaite is the Booker T. Washington of American literature—a bread-in-the-bone sycophant."[66]

. . . . .

When William Stanley Braithwaite eventually traveled to the South, he at long last turned his attention to issues affecting the black community. After the 1929 stock market crash, the fifteen-year run of anthologies came to a halt and his finances went into a free fall as creditors, long patient, called in loans. When Braithwaite received an offer from Atlanta University to join the faculty as professor of English and Creative Writing, Braithwaite readily accepted. His Southern sojourn, a phenomenal consciousness-raising experience, left him no room to doubt the standing of a black man in Dixie. In letters to James Johnson, who remained solvent with his work as professor of literature at Fisk University, in Nashville, Tennessee, Braithwaite discussed plans for a lecture tour on the theme of race. "Jim, we have got to build a great Racial Soul, to win this conflict and controversy with America."[67] Four years before the College Language Association urged courses on the "Negro in American literature," Braithwaite taught such a class and encouraged graduate theses on black writers.[68] He also served on various committees with his colleague and old friend Du Bois. After retiring in 1945, he moved to the famous residence building on 490 Edgecomb Street in Harlem where his neighbors included Du Bois as well as Thurgood Marshall.

Braithwaite could take pride in the robust state of American letters. He knew that culture and representation mattered in redefining reality and ideology; poetic melodies could help orchestrate perceptions. His encouragement and unflagging devotion to the cause of poetry had helped create a vital community. Clubs, prizes, publications, and university positions abounded. Few histories or anthologies, however, acknowledge his efforts. When African-American studies arose out of the black arts movement of the 1960s, Braithwaite was viewed forlornly. Instead of admiration for his integrity, this new generation viewed his contribution with vexation. They bridled at his moderation and at his insistence on succeeding by any standard, except a racial standard. Privileging solidarity and liberation over complexity and diversity, Harold Cruse echoed Langston Hughes by writing that "The American Negro cannot be understood culturally unless he is seen as a member of a detached ethnic bloc of people of African descent reared for three hundred years in the unmotherly bosom of Western civilization." Ignoring the sometimes invented character of identity (or "ethnic fictions," as Locke deemed races), Cruse assailed "Caucasian idolatry in the arts, abandonment of true identity, and immature childlike mimicry of white aesthetics."[69]

Braithwaite's detractors believed that his conservative views blinded him to radical, innovative developments in poetry and to the destructive qualities of subtle racism. His disavowal of the vernacular verse of Paul Dunbar and the jazzy riffs of Langston Hughes were viewed as a negation of his racial heritage. Although his work in the first two decades of the century courageously sought to transcend racial categories, to imagine a community founded on devotion to beauty and creativity rather than bigotry and color, his critics believed otherwise. To them, he never understood that while the content of our character may be measured by adherence to beauty and truth, in life, as in poetry, form matters.

Yet Braithwaite's career is not a tale of noble failure or over-looked success. His literary criticism and determination reflected a world view that crossed racial and class borders. Preserving the ideal of the heroic, romantic poet promised some hope for authenticity and the regeneration of selfhood in an industrial, bureaucratic society that venerated the bottom line. Without regard for monetary gain, Braithwaite worked to establish a space where beauty and harmony could thrive and where all Americans, regardless of color, could nurture their hearts and souls. His life demonstrated that African Americans could appreciate and partake in a high culture of gentility and formal verse. In black schools and colleges across the country, teachers extolled him as an exemplar of their race, as evidence that African Americans could choose any profession they desired. The vehemence with which modernists and Renaissance artists attacked him suggests the degree of Braithwaite's influence. His convictions reshaped cultural attitudes regarding the significance of poetry and redefined the boundaries of race. Like Du Bois, Braithwaite created opportunities for black expression never before available. By establishing his own legitimacy, he created a foothold in the history of American culture, one that deserves more than a footnote, and on which others could stand and move forward.

Notes

1. Quoted by Ellen Williams, in *Harriet Monroe and the Poetry Renaissance: The First Ten Years of Poetry, 1912-1922* (Chicago: University of Illinois Press, 1977), p. 9.

2. Poet James Weldon Johnson was one of the few black authors who approved of Braithwaite: "He [Braithwaite] has written no poetry motivated or colored by race. This has not been a matter of intention on his part; it is simply that race has not impinged upon him as it has upon other Negro poets" (*Book of American Negro Poetry* [New York: Harcourt, Brace and Company, 1922], p. 99). Less charitable accounts issued from Jean Wagner, who angrily dismissed Braithwaite in *Black Poets of the United States: From Laurence Dunbar to Langston Hughes* (Chicago: University of Illinois Press, 1973), p. 128, and Southern University professor Saunders Redding, who decried Braithwaite as "the most outstanding example of perverted energy" in *To Make a Poet Black* (Chapel Hill: University of North Carolina Press, 1939), p. 89. See also Sterling Brown, *Negro Poetry and Drama* (Washington, D.C.: Associates in Negro Folk Education, 1937), p. 49, and Blyden Jackson and Louis Rubin, *Black Poetry in America: Two Essays in Historical Interpretation* (Baton Rouge: Louisiana State University Press, 1974), pp. 31-33.

3. T. J. Jackson Lears, *No Place of Grace: Anti-Modernism and the Transformation of American Culture, 1880-1920* (1981; reprinted, Chicago: University of Chicago Press, 1994), p. 188.

4. Braithwaite, "The House under Arcturus," *Phylon,* vol. 2, no. 1 (1941): 16. Further citations will appear in my text by volume, issue, and page.

5. "The Reminiscences of William Stanley Braithwaite," May-June 1956, p. 78, in the Columbia University Oral History Research Office Collection. Permission to quote from this oral history kindly provided by the Oral History Research Office, Columbia University.

6. Ray Stannard Baker, *Following the Color Line: An Account of Negro Citizenship in the American Democracy* (New York: Doubleday, Page & Co., 1908), pp. 119, 123.

7. Booker T. Washington, *Up from Slavery: An Autobiography* (1900; reprinted, New York: Doubleday and Co., Inc., 1953), pp. 88, 125-28, 154-55.

8. Arnold Rampersad, *The Art and Imagination of W. E. B. Du Bois* (1976; reprinted, New York: Schocken Books, 1990), pp. 1-3.

9. W. E. B. Du Bois, *The Souls of Black Folk* (1903), ed. Eric Sundquist (New York: Oxford University Press, 1973), p. 109.

10. W. S. Braithwaite, "Some Contemporary Poets of the Negro Race," *Crisis,* April 1919, reprinted in the *The William Stanley Braithwaite Reader,* ed. Philip Butcher (Ann Arbor: University of Michigan Press, 1972), pp. 49-61.

11. Du Bois, *Souls of Black Folk,* pp. 142-43, 87, 11.

12. See Grace Hale, *Making Whiteness: The Culture of Segregation in the South, 1890-1914* (New York: Pantheon Books, 1998), p. 36.

13. Du Bois, *Souls of Black Folk,* p. 4.

14. Braithwaite, "Some Contemporary Poets," pp. 53-54.

15. See Hale, *Making Whiteness,* p. 37.

16. Braithwaite, "Some Contemporary Poets," pp. 49-61.

17. *Shadowed Dreams: Women's Poetry of the Harlem Renaissance,* ed. Maureen Honey (New Brunswick: Rutgers University Press, 1989), pp. 2-3, 6-7, 20-21.

18. Nina Miller, *Making Love Modern: The Intimate Public Worlds of New York's Literary Women* (New York: Oxford University Press, 1999), pp. 210-11, 216.

19. Elizabeth McHenry discusses reading and other literary activities among black women at the turn of the century in "African-American Literary Societies," in *Print Culture in a Diverse America,* ed. James Danky and Wayne Wiegand (Urbana: University of Illinois Press, 1998), pp. 149-72.

20. Braithwaite, "Reminiscences," pp. 71-72.

21. Braithwaite, "Arcturus," 3.2:183, and "Reminiscences," p. 6.

22. Edmund Clarence Stedman, *Nature and Elements of Poetry* (1893; reprinted, Boston: Houghton Mifflin Co., 1930), p. 127.

23. For an analysis of the fin-de-siècle discourse on masculinity, see Gail Bederman, *Manliness and Civilization: A Cultural History of Gender and Race in the United States, 1880-1917* (Chicago: University of Chicago Press, 1995), pp. 12-15.

24. Carlin Kindilien, *American Poetry in the 1890s* (Providence: Brown University Press, 1956), p. ix.

25. *Poetry Society of America Newsletter,* April 1937, p. 4. PSA newsletters can be found at the Poetry Society of America Archives, Gramercy Park, New York City.

26. Edwin Arlington Robinson, quoted by Donald Stauffer, in *A Short History of American Poetry* (New York: E. P. Dutton & Co., Inc., 1974), p. 221.

27. Kim Townsend, *Manhood at Harvard: William James and Others* (New York: W. W. Norton & Co., 1996), pp. 142-46, and Helen Vendler, "Wallace Stevens," in *The Columbia History of American Poetry,* ed. Jay Parini (New York: Columbia University Press, 1993), p. 380.

28. Thomas Athol Joyce, an ethnologist associated with the British Museum, and Cornell Professor Walter F. Willcox composed the Britannica's entry "Negro" for the eleventh edition, published in 1910-11.

29. W. S. Braithwaite, "Forty-Five Lines of *Actual* Poetry in the Magazines of 1906," *Boston Evening Transcript,* 14 February 1906.

30. W. S. Braithwaite, "The Feast of the Poets," *Boston Evening Transcript,* 31 December 1910. Other organizers were Edward J. Wheeler, Edwin Markham, Jessie B. Rittenhouse, and Robert Sterling.

31. W. S. Braithwaite, *Anthology of Magazine Verse for 1913* (Boston: William S. Braithwaite, 1913); *The Poetic Year for 1916: A Critical Anthology* (Boston: Small, Maynard and Co., 1917), p. xviii; "Another Year of American Poetry in Review," *Boston Evening Transcript,* 11 December 1912.

32. Braithwaite, *Reminiscences,* p. 153; and review of "Rainbow Gold," *Boston Evening Transcript,* 14 October 1922.

33. W. S. Braithwaite, "Another Year of American Poetry in Review," *Boston Evening Transcript,* 11 December 1912; and *Anthology of Magazine Verse for 1915 and Yearbook of American Poetry* (New York: Gomme and Marshall, 1915), p. xxiii.

34. Amy Lowell, quoted by Kenny J. Williams, in "An Invisible Partnership and an Unlikely Relationship: William Stanley Braithwaite and Harriet Monroe," *Callaloo* 10 (Summer 1987): 520.

35. William Dean Howells, quoted in *Braithwaite Reader,* p. 1.

36. Burton Kline, "William Stanley Braithwaite," *Boston Evening Transcript,* 30 November 1915.

37. See the exchange of letters and telegrams between Edwin Markham and William Braithwaite, January 1915, and the notice of induction, in the William Stanley Braithwaite Collection (#6787), Clifton Waller Barrett Library, Special Collections Department, University of Virginia Library, Charlottesville.

38. *Selected Letters of Robert Frost,* ed. Lawrance Thompson (New York: Holt, Rinehart and Winston, 1964), pp. 158-60, 164, 187, 200.

39. W. S. Braithwaite, "A Poet of New England," *Boston Evening Transcript,* 28 April 1915 (review of *A Boy's Will*); "Robert Frost: New American Poet," 8 May 1915; "A Poetic Chronicle of New Hampshire," 2 December 1916 (review of *Mountain Interval*).

40. Robert Frost to John Bartlett, 7 April 1919, Robert Frost Collection (#6261), Clifton Waller Barrett Library, Special Collections Department, University of Virginia Library. Quoted by permission of the Estate of Robert Lee Frost and the Barrett Library.

41. Arthur Inman, quoted by George Hutchinson, in *The Harlem Renaissance in Black and White* (Cambridge: Harvard University Press, 1994), pp. 513-14.

42. Braithwaite, *Anthology . . . for 1915,* p. xxi.

43. Williams's poems listed were: "A Confidence," "Appeal," "Metric Figures," "Pastoral," "The Ogre," "The Shadow," and "Slow Movement, Sub Terra." Despite certain lapses in judgment, Braithwaite did, to his credit, include in his anthologies poems that soon formed part of an enduring canon: Robert Frost's "Birches," "The Road Not Taken," "Death of the Hired Man"; E. A. Robinson's "Flammonde"; Amy Lowell's "Patterns"; Wallace Stevens's "Peter Quince at the Clavier."

44. Louis Untermeyer, quoted by Craig S. Abbott, in "Magazine Verse and Modernism: Braithwaite's Anthologies," *Journal of Modern Literature* 19 (Summer 1994); 154.

45. Conrad Aiken to the Editor, *New York Times Book Review,* 17 January 1915, *Selected Letters of Conrad Aiken,* ed. Joseph Killorin (New Haven: Yale University Press, 1978), pp. xiii, 40; "Poetry in America," review of Braithwaite's *Anthology of Magazine Verse for 1916, Dial,* 8 March 1917, pp. 179-182.

46. Aiken, "Poetry in America," p. 181, and *Skepticisms: Notes on Contemporary Poetry* (New York: Alfred A. Knopf, 1919), pp. 32, 128-29.

47. T. E. Hulme, "Romanticism and Classicism" (1911) and "A Lecture on Modern Poetry" (1908), in *The Collected Writings of T. E. Hulme,* ed. Karen Csengeri (New York: Oxford University Press, 1994).

48. Daniel Albright investigates the modernist ardor for science in *Quantum Poetics: Yeats, Pound, Eliot, and the Science of Modernism* (New York: Cambridge University Press, 1997).

49. W. S. Braithwaite, *Anthology of Magazine Verse for 1918 and Yearbook of American Poetry* (Boston: Small, Maynard and Co., Publishers, 1918), pp. xvi, xviii, x; *Anthology of Magazine Verse for 1922 and Yearbook of American Poetry* (Boston: Small, Maynard and Co., Publishers, 1922), p. x.

50. W. S. Braithwaite, "The Year in Poetry," *The Bookman,* March 1917, p. 36; and *Anthology of Magazine Verse for 1917 and Yearbook of American Poetry* (Boston: Small, Maynard and Co., Publishers, 1917), pp. xi-xiv.

51. W. S. Braithwaite to Miss Robinson, 3 January 1930, quoted in *Braithwaite Reader,* pp. 279-80.

52. Braithwaite related the details of this affair in "Reminiscences," pp. 168-72.

53. Some of the women wrote heartfelt letters in response to Braithwaite's descriptions of his woeful economic situation. Edith Mirick, editor of *Star-Dust* magazine, organized a nationwide campaign to raise money for him. She received contributions ranging from one to ten dollars. She had less success among Southerners, who "can wrap their bombs so delicately in lace handkerchiefs." And Harriet Monroe sent "an ACID letter" refusing to contribute. Edith Mirick to Braithwaite, 1930, Braithwaite Collection (#6787). Quoted by permission of the Barrett Library.

54. Braithwaite to Miss Ada Norrington, 10 May 1921, Braithwaite Collection (#6787). Further quotations from this correspondence are from this collection and will be identified in the text by recipient and date. All quotations are by permission of the Barrett Library.

55. Braithwaite was the fourth recipient of the award, founded in 1915 by philanthropist Joel Spingarn. See *Braithwatie Reader,* p. 1. The award is still given out each year.

56. Braithwaite, "Reminiscences," pp. 76-77.

57. W. S. Braithwaite, "The Poems of James Weldon Johnson," *Boston Evening Transcript,* 12 December 1917, p. 43, and "The Negro in Literature," *Crisis,* September 1924, p. 208.

58. W. S. Braithwaite, *Anthology of Magazine Verse for 1925 and Yearbook of American Poetry* (Boston: B. J. Brimmer Co., 1925), p. xvii.

59. Charles Chesnutt, quoted by Ross Posnock, in *Color and Culture: Black Writers and the Making of the Modern Intellectual* (Cambridge: Harvard University Press, 1998), p. 8.

60. Braithwaite, "Negro in Literature," p. 206. In a 1928 *Opportunity* article, "The Dark Tower," Countee Cullen also adjured African Americans to write with discretion: "Decency demands that some things be kept secret." Such an approach "might improve race relations more than the wholesale betrayal of racial idiosyncrasies and shortcomings which seem so rampant." Quoted by Miller, in *Making Love Modern,* p. 154. Between February and November 1926, W. E. B. Du Bois published responses in *Crisis* to a questionnaire asking, among other questions, "What are Negroes to do when they are continually painted at their worst and judged by the public as they are painted?" Almost all the esteemed contributors advocated putting forward more favorable images.

61. Braithwaite, *Anthology . . . 1918,* p. 253.

62. Langston Hughes, "The Negro Artist and the Racial Mountain," reprinted in *The Politics and Aesthetics of "New Negro" Literature,* ed. Cary Wintz (New York: Garland Publishing, Inc., 1996), p. 166.

63. Jean Toomer, *Cane* (New York: Harper and Row, 1925). In the 1930s Toomer repudiated *Cane,* calling it his swan song, and refused to reproduce it. He adopted instead a transcendent, meta-American identity that he expressed in such poems as "Brown River, Smile" and "Blue Meridian."

64. James Weldon Johnson, quoted by J. Martin Favor, in *Authentic Blackness: The Folk in the New Negro Renaissance* (Durham: Duke University Press, 1999), p. 27. Johnson and Braithwaite shared much in common. Both were mulattoes who grew up in "puritan," middle-class households, were shocked to experience discrimination in grammar school, and believed great literature provided one of the master keys to advancement. Both also saw language as a tool for assimilation and respectability and as a matter of gaining cultural fluency. In a flattering review of Johnson's *Along This Way,* Braithwaite rhapsodized over the passage in which Johnson describes how being in France freed him from the "Man-Negro dualism" he incessantly faced in America (*Opportunity,* December 1933, pp. 376-78).

65. Rupert Lewis, "Claude McKay's Political Views," *Jamaica Journal* 19 (1986): 39-45.

66. Braithwaite reviewed McKay's work in the September 1924 issue of *Crisis,* p. 208; Claude McKay to Langston Hughes, 22 September 1924, quoted by Hutchinson, in *Harlem Renaissance,* pp. 353-54.

67. W. S. Braithwaite to James Johnson, 12 August 1934, quoted by Philip Butcher, in "W. S. Braithwaite's Southern Exposure: Rescue and Revelation," *Southern Literary Journal* 3 (1971): 56.

68. Philip Butcher. "W. S. Braithwaite and the College Language Association," *College Language Association Journal* 15 (December 1971): 124.

69. Harold Cruse, "An Afro-American's Cultural Views," in *Rebellion or Revolution?* (New York: Morrow, 1967), pp. 49, 53, 56.

FURTHER READING

Criticism

Thomas, Lorenzo. "W. S. Braithwaite vs. Harriet Monroe: The Heavyweight Poetry Championship, 1917." In *Reading Race in American Poetry,* edited by Aldon Lynn Nielsen, pp. 84-106. Urbana: University of Illinois Press, 2000.

Examines the work of Braithwaite and Monroe as foregrounding the 1920s issues surrounding artistic innovation, literary politics, editorial influence, and the mechanisms of cultural exchange.

Wattles, Willard. "On Reading the Braithwaite Anthology for 1916." *Poetry: A Magazine of Verse* 10 (1917): 52-4.

Review of Braithwaite's Anthology of Magazine Verse for 1916.

Williams, Kenny J. "An Invisible Partnership and an Unlikely Relationship: William Stanley Braithwaite and Harriet Monroe." *Callaloo* 10, no. 3 (summer 1987): 516-50.

Considers Braithwaite and Monroe's influence on the development of an American poetic renaissance despite their professional differences.

OTHER SOURCES FROM GALE:

Additional coverage of Braithwaite's life and career is contained in the following sources published by the Gale Group: *Black Literature Criticism,* Vol. 1; *Black Writers,* Ed. 2; *Contemporary Authors,* Vol. 125; *Dictionary of Literary Biography,* Vols. 50, 54; *DISCovering Authors Modules: Multicultural Authors.*

STERLING ALLEN BROWN

(1901 - 1989)

American poet, literary critic, essayist, and folklorist.

Poet, critic, scholar, teacher, and teller of tall-tales, Sterling Allen Brown is a significant twentieth-century African American literary figure. While the Harlem Renaissance blossomed in the Northeast, Brown found his inspiration in African American folklore, blues, and ballads found within the Southern culture that was rapidly disappearing as the Great Migration changed the American landscape. Credited with preserving and celebrating the Black Southern folk culture, Brown's criticism and poetry employs familiar legends, heroes, and myths in an often musical style. Over a long and distinguished career Brown helped legitimize African American cultural history and the ethnic rural experience.

BIOGRAPHICAL INFORMATION

Brown was born in Washington, D.C., on May 1, 1901, to Rev. Sterling Nelson Brown, a minister and professor of religion at Howard University, and Adelaide Allen Brown, who graduated valedictorian of her class at Fisk University. The youngest of six children, Brown received an excellent education, gaining his academic interests from his father and a love of poetry from his mother. In high school Brown edited the Dunbar High School newspaper and began writing poetry. After graduation he was awarded a scholarship to Williams College, and in 1921 his scholastic achievements led to his being elected to the prestigious Phi Beta Kappa honor society. In 1922, he graduated with a B.A. and was awarded a scholarship to Harvard, where he received a master's degree in 1923. His own education concluded, Brown went on to a long and illustrious teaching career, with his first position at Virginia Theological Seminary and College at Lynchburg. At this time he married Daisy Turnbull, and the couple later adopted a son. From Virginia, Brown transferred to Fisk University in Nashville, and then to Lincoln University in Missouri. In 1929, Brown received a position as professor of American literature at Howard University, the same institution where his father taught. During his tenure at Howard, Brown also served as a visiting professor to several other universities. In 1932, after the Harlem Renaissance had flourished and then faded, Brown's first book of poetry, *Southern Road,* was published and received considerable acclaim. The young author began to be categorized with Harlem Renaissance luminaries such as Langston Hughes, Jean Toomer, and Zora Neale Hurston. Renowned critic Alain Locke called Brown "The New Negro Folk Poet," a characterization that stuck despite Brown's reluctance to be grouped with the Harlem movement. Brown had published extensively in the great Harlem journals of the day, including *Crisis, Opportunity,* and *Contempo,* but the author would later deny that a literary movement ever arose out of Harlem and called the label a "publisher's gimmick." Brown wrote a second volume of poetry, which he called *No Hiding Place* and had planned on debuting it in 1937, but this work was rejected by publishers for reasons that are unclear, leaving Brown bitter. It would be many years before Brown would again attempt to publish his poetry.

From 1936-1939 Brown was involved in the Federal Writers' Project as Editor of Negro Affairs, an office from which he oversaw all the Project's studies by and about Blacks. He also produced essays on African American literature and culture, including the highly regarded essay "The Negro in Washington" (1937). He was awarded a Guggenheim Fellowship for 1937-38, and he continued to study and critique African American literature, with two important works of criticism, *The Negro in American Fiction* and *Negro Poetry and Drama,* appearing in 1937. He also, along with Arthur P. Davis and Ulysses Lee, edited an important anthology of African American literature from 1760-1941—*The Negro Caravan* (1941)—which enjoyed many years of preeminence as an invaluable resource. During his forty-year tenure as professor at Howard University (1929-1969), Brown contributed essays on folklore, jazz, sociology, history, and education to leading periodicals, contributed introductions and essays on Black literature, and published short stories, sketches, and tall tales. Although he retired in 1969, by 1973 he was back in front of the classroom on a part-time basis until 1975. The Black Consciousness movement of the 1960s and 1970s found an enthusiastic new audience for Brown's poetry, and he was persuaded in 1975 to publish a second book of poetry, *The Last Ride of Wild Bill and Eleven Narrative Poems.* In 1980, *The Collected Poems of Sterling A. Brown* appeared, which included pieces from his never published *No Hiding Place.* With this collection, the steadily growing interest in this formidable scholar, cultural commentator, folklorist, and poet exploded, and the latter half of the twentieth century has seen much critical activity regarding his work. In addition, Brown has received honorary degrees from an impressive list of universities, including Boston University, Harvard, Brown, Vassar, and Howard University—with which he had been associated nearly all of his life. He was also elected to the Academy of American Poets and was proclaimed the poet laureate of the District of Columbia. Brown died in 1989.

MAJOR WORKS

Southern Road is divided into four parts, with the first three sections employing dialect and folk culture and the fourth section, commonly called "The Vestiges," including more traditional literary forms such as the sonnet. In "The Odyssey of Big Boy," the first poem in the collection, Brown portrayed itinerant Calvin "Big Boy" Davis, an acquaintance from his days in Lynchburg, Virginia. The poem, a ballad sung by Big Boy himself, celebrates Davis's travels and sexual conquests with boisterous musicality. Big Boy is also the central figure in such poems as "Long Gone" and "When De Saint Go Ma'chin Home." In another poem, "Ma Rainey," Brown captures the blues and jazz music born in African American Southern culture and the reverence felt for the musical tradition. Ma Rainey, the real-life Mother of the Blues, becomes a healer, consoler, and priestess to an enraptured crowd of poor working people who have flocked from far and wide to watch her perform. She recounts all that she has seen and suffered, sharing the strength she gained from these hard experiences. The poem captures both the music that she sang and her status as a cultural icon. In Brown's 1975 collection of poetry *The Last Ride of Wild Bill and Eleven Narrative Poems,* the central piece is the long poem about Wild Bill, which is composed with a rhythmic and witty rush of verse. Employing mythic conventions and themes of heroism and endurance, Wild Bill, a hero to the people, is a numbers operator set in opposition to an insidious police chief. After a series of mock heroic clashes, Bill is defeated by the police chief and winds up in hell where he is met with enthusiasm by the damned throng that has gathered to greet him. Brown's critical work collects and preserves the folk traditions of the South and upholds a sense of Black identity and heritage by encouraging people to embrace and revere the culture. He contributed to scholarship on the African American literary audience, the Black writer's place within a white American literary environment, and contributed to criticism on African American poetry, drama, prose, politics, and culture.

CRITICAL RECEPTION

Brown's work has generated much scholarly interest. The mythic conventions employed in his poetry have led to investigation into his reliance on universal themes such as ritual and the hero as well as more localized themes unique to African American folk culture. His work has also been considered in terms of its ethnographic importance, while critics such as David Anderson argue that Brown goes beyond preserving oral traditions by attempting to adapt the transplanted Black urban communities of the North to a new cultural paradigm that still contains elements of the tradition that was in many ways left behind with the Northern migrations. The musicality of Brown's verse is another source of interest for scholars seeking to draw connections between the jazz and blues music traditions and the rhythms, lyrics, and themes in his poetry. Throughout most criticism on Brown there is a respect for his efforts to validate the African American experience by celebrating dialect, folk beliefs, and an oppressed heritage when others were dismissing them as painful reminders of an ugly past or misappropriating them as validation of a separate and lesser Black culture. Browns's frank and masterful portrayal of folk culture, his ethnographic contributions to the study of American cultures, his inspiring work as a teacher and mentor, and his rich, musical poetry stand in testament to his considerable influence on and significance to twentieth-century American literary and cultural studies.

PRINCIPAL WORKS

Outline for the Study of the Poetry of American Negroes (criticism) 1931

Southern Road (poetry) 1932

The Negro in American Fiction (criticism) 1937

Negro Poetry and Drama (criticism) 1937

*"The Negro in Washington" (essay) 1937

The Negro Caravan [editor with Arthur P. Davis and Ulysses Lee] (poetry) 1941

The Last Ride of Wild Bill and Eleven Narrative Poems (poetry) 1975

The Collected Poems of Sterling A. Brown (poetry) 1980

* Published in *Washington: City and Capital.*

PRIMARY SOURCES

STERLING ALLEN BROWN (POEM DATE 1932)

SOURCE: Brown, Sterling Allen. "Southern Road." In *The Collected Poems of Sterling A. Brown,* edited by Michael S. Harper, pp. 52-53. New York: Harper & Row, Publishers, 1980.

The following poem, first published in Brown's 1932 collection of the same name, is considered a prime example of the poet's facility with imagery as well as his mastery of the Negro dialect.

"SOUTHERN ROAD"

Swing dat hammer—hunh—
Steady, bo';
Swing dat hammer—hunh—
Steady, bo';
Ain't no rush, bebby,
Long ways to go.

Burner tore his—hunh—
Black heart away;
Burner tore his—hunh—
Black heart away;
Got me life, bebby,
An' a day.

Gal's on Fifth Street—hunh—
Son done gone;
Gal's on Fifth Street—hunh—
Son done gone;
Wife's in de ward, bebby,
Babe's not bo'n.

My ole man died—hunh—
Cussin' me;
My ole man died—hunh—
Cussin' me;
Ole lady rocks, bebby,
Huh misery.

Doubleshackled—hunh—
Guard behin';
Doubleshackled—hunh—
Guard behin';
Ball an' chain, bebby,
On my min'.

White man tells me—hunh—
Damn yo' soul;
White man tells me—hunh—
Damn yo' soul;
Got no need, bebby,
To be tole.

Chain gang nevah—hunh—
Let me go;
Chain gang nevah—hunh—
Let me go;
Po' los' boy, bebby,
Evahmo' . . .

GENERAL COMMENTARY

ROBERT G. O'MEALLY (ESSAY DATE 1983)

SOURCE: O'Meally, Robert G. "Sterling Brown's Literary Essays: The Black Reader in the Text." *Callaloo* 21, no. 4 (fall 1998): 1013-22.

In the following essay, originally published in 1983, O'Meally considers the Black audience of the American 1920s and 1930s, and examines Brown's call for realism in literary portrayals of African Americans.

> "All poetry is the reproduction of the sounds of actual speech."
>
> —Robert Frost

> "Whenever I feel uneasy about my writing, I think: what would be the response of the people in the book if they read the book? That's my way of staying on track."
>
> —Toni Morrison

> "You can read my letter, baby, But you sure can't read my mind."
>
> —Blues lyric

A realist not only by artistic and critical persuasion, but by temperament, Sterling A. Brown has shown concern throughout his career with poetry as an art of communication—not just among airy Muses and free spirits, but among real people in this world, actual writers and their readers. Publishers, editors, reviewers, and "blurbists" shape this communication process, as do those persons whose lives are depicted in literature. Brown's critical writings deal mainly with the literary portrayal of Afro-Americans. The question sounding through virtually every critical piece he writes is this one: How true is this work to the lives of the people portrayed, as their real-life counterparts themselves see it? Here literary virtuosity is just *one* test for value: Granted a given work about black life is well-made and "interesting" (to use Henry James's key term); but would the blacks put in the book recognize their own speech and actions, their own sense of life? Or are these more stick and stock "Negro Characters as Seen by White Authors"?[1]

Complicating these questions is the issue that Sterling A. Brown laments in several critical pieces of the 1930s and 1940s: Afro-American, for the most part, "are not yet a reading people."[2] When blacks did read works about themselves, too many reacted with insecurity or "bourgeois" diffidence. Why was this true of a group for whom, as many authors of slave narratives made clear, writing and reading were deemed near magic gifts, ones for which 19th-century blacks prayed, stole, tricked, studied in secret, and sometimes paid with lashings and other dire punishments? And what are the literary implications of the black audience's neglect and misperception? What are the costs for black writers who, observes Brown, are the only ones really called upon and able to give a comprehensive "insider's" look at Afro-American life?[3] Finally how, considering the tastes and distastes of black readers and potential readers, might the black writer reach them?

In many of his early essays and reviews, Brown turns his attention to the vagaries of the Afro-American audience. One reason blacks did not read was that to do so seemed frivolous for a group beset by the crushing economic pressures of the Depression. "What help in books for an increasing breadline?" they asked.[4] "Why should poor people needing their money for necessities such as bread and shoes, rent and coal, pay from two dollars to five dollars for a book?"[5] But even those not under the threat of economic collapse usually did not read: "Our practical man, often self made, and often admirably so, distrusts mere book learning as a useless appendage." When the black college graduate picked up a book, he tended, Brown says, to shun books by or about blacks:

> Some of this is based upon an understandable desire to escape the perplexities and pressures of the race situation in America. Some of it is based upon the ineptitude of immature authors dealing with difficult subject matter. Quite as much is based upon a cast-ridden disdain of Negro life and character, and anguish at being identified with an ignorant and exploited people to whom many "upper class" Negroes are completely unsympathetic.[6]

In a key essay, **"Our Literary Audience,"** Brown declares that "there is a great harm that we can do our incipient literature. With a few noteworthy exceptions, we are doing that harm, most effectively."[7] The short answer to the essay's topic question—Why aren't black readers good readers?—is quoted from Brown's "young friend" whose survey reported: "Too much bridge."

Charging that many blacks who read are put off by realistic literature about Afro-American life, Brown cites four fallacies that distract black readers:

> . . . We look upon Negro books, regardless of the author's intention, as representative of all Negroes, i.e. as sociological documents.

. . . We insist that Negro books must be idealistic, optimistic tracts for race advertisement.

. . . We are afraid of truth telling, of satire.

. . . We criticize from the point of view of bourgeois America, of racial apologists.[8]

Each of these categories is rife with complexities. As for the fallacy of "representativeness," it is suffered by the reader who sees any realistic black character in literature as "a blanket charge against the race." For this super-sensitive reader "the syllogism follows: Mr. A. shows a Negro who steals; he means by this that all Negroes steal; all Negroes do not steal; Q.E.D. Mr. A. is a liar and his book is another libel on the race."[9] Made defensive by attacks by propagandists like Thomas Dixon and Thomas Nelson Page, this part of the black audience "cannot enjoy 'Green Pastures' for fear that the play will be considered typical of all Negroes."[10] Nor can they really approve of *Cane, Their Eyes Were Watching God,* or the fiction of Richard Wright. We are not all like the characters in these books, they complain. Here of course the problem involves overconcern among the black audience with what the white audience is thinking.

These "best-foot-forward" readers want books as "race advertisements," with pictures not of Hurston's fresh Janie or Wright's bumptious Big Boy, but of the "best" Negroes. And "by the 'best' Negroes these idealists mean generally the upper reaches of society, i.e. those with money." By this standard, says Brown, "a book about a Negro with a mule would be, because of the mule, a better book than one about a muleless Negro; about a Negro with a horse and buggy a better book than about the mule owner; about a Negro and a Ford, better than about the buggy rider; and a book about a Negro and a Rolls Royce better than the one about a Negro and a Ford. All that it seems our writers need to do, to guarantee a perfect book and deathless reputation is to write about a Negro and an aeroplane." This Negro with an "aeroplane" would be too refined to indulge in satire. Nor would he speak dialect, because "Negroes of my class don't use dialect anyway," quoth our highbrown reader. "Which mought be so," taunts Brown, "and then again it moughtn't."[11]

This yearning for self glorification in art, says Brown, typifies the "racial" audience member who, "after the fashion of minorities, is on a strict defensive when any aspects of its life are presented." The same "minority" reaction beset Lady Gregory, Synge, and Yeats, pioneers in modern Irish theatre whose work challenged the British stereotype of the "simple" Irishman, "smiling through his tears," with true-to-life portraits. To their dismay these writers found their works "misunderstood by the people whose true character they wanted to show, and whose latent geniuses they wished to arouse and sustain. Riots were frequent when in contradistinction to the stereotype of the vaudeville stage they refused to set up plaster-of-paris saints."[12]

Typical, too, of other oppressed minorities, blacks generally misunderstood the new drama of the 1930s—by O'Neill, Paul Green, and Langston Hughes—because of sheer *inexperience.* Rather than sad and shocking plays set on the wrong side of the tracks, such audiences desired either "complete escape" or what they called "worth-while" books and "elevating" shows. In Brown's words, "They are pleading, one has reason to suspect, for musical comedy which may have scenes in cabarets, and wouldn't be confined to Catfish Row. With beautiful girls in gorgeous 'costumes'; rather than Negroes in . . . tattered clothing."[13] Elsewhere, Brown writes that "the typical audience of our small towns has a confused idea of drama as compounded of a church pageant, a fashion show, and an object lesson in etiquette, and that of our larger towns is sold to Hollywood. Neither furnishes much sustaining interest for our aspirant Ibsen."[14]

Well-cropped black youngsters, "with some Little Theatre Movements the honorable exceptions, want to be English dukes and duchesses, and wear tuxedoes and evening gowns. Our 'best' society leaders want to be mannequins."[15] And too often black colleges failed to modernize and broaden students' literary tastes by failing to offer them good courses in writing. "Within the not too distant past," wrote Brown in 1932, "the chronicler has known educators whose idea of literature was a concoction of Emily Post, the Boy Scouts handbook, and somebody's cyclopedia of quotations, and who knew that the only authors were dead authors and since his students were alive, authorship (for them) was out of the question."[16]

Like other critical realists Brown not only analyzes the mind-set and class adhesions of the audience, he makes moral assessments of them, too. His most cutting charge against the black audience is that they are worse than "typically bourgeois": too many lack the "mental bravery" and family loyalty to face the unvarnished truth about themselves and their ethnic brethren. These are the Negro Babbitts whose "deities are pocketbooks and fine cars and what they misname 'Kultchoor'": those who cannot respond to lowly Porgy or Teacake or Big Boy because of class prejudice, those guilty of "a cowardly denial of our own." In Brown's words:

> . . . It seems to acute observers that many of us, who have leisure for reading, are ashamed of being Negroes. This shame makes us harsher to the shortcomings of some perhaps not so fortunate economically. There seems to be among us a . . . fundamental lack of sympathy with the Negro farthest down.[17]

This shallow grasper after "Kultchoor" "preferred Spanish folksongs to Negro"; he called "the song of the Volga boatman a classic whereas 'Water-Boy' was beneath contempt. He was so far removed from the Water-Boy, he said."[18]

Miseducated, riddled with class prejudices, conservative, escapist—"our literary audience" is depicted by Sterling A. Brown in his early criticism. He quotes Whitman's cryptic complaint and warning: "To have great literature, there must be great audiences, too."[19] But in these essays Brown goes far beyond mere scoring against inept black audiences. He not only pointed out their failings, but he put these failings into perspective, analyzed them (E. Franklin Frazier called Brown "my favorite literary sociologist"),[20] and persuaded against them with great force. In so doing he presented a rigorous defense of literature as more than a social phenomenon but as "equipment for living." "There is more to lowliness than 'lowness'," he wrote. "If we have eyes to see, and willingness to see, we might be able to find in Mamba, an astute heroism, in Hagar a heartbreaking courage, in Porgy, a nobility, and in E. C. L. Adams' Scip and Tad, a shrewd philosophical irony. And all of these qualities we need, just now, to see in our own group."[21] "A vigorous literary movement," wrote Brown, "is part and parcel of social change."[22]

Brown also presented in his early essays an excellent course in how to read a modern book. He dealt with questions like these: When does tragedy give way to mere sentimentality? When does comedy yield to farce? What is the significance of "point of view"? What is the relation of realism and melodrama? How might the use of folklore in art provide more than "local color"? In his companion booklet to James Weldon Johnson's *Book of American Negro Poetry,* Brown defined literary realism with succinctness. He termed it:

> . . . the attempt to create the illusion of life, generally by the use of contemporary material. It deals with the familiar and the usual. The so-called "new poetry," dating from 1912, is in the main realistic in tendency. It was a reaction to sentimentality, to didacticism, to Pollyanna optimism, to exotic escapes from modern conditions by dreaming. It aimed instead at reflecting contemporary life . . . Social protest took the place of optimistic complacence; and unflinching acceptance of the realities of life as subject matter, a greater objectivity instead of an all-consuming subjectivity, these are a few of the changes that came in with the new poetry. The influence . . . is to be seen in what James Weldon Johnson calls the "younger group" of Negro poets.[23]

Beyond offering to readers that rarest of commodities, intelligent criticism, Brown also addressed black *writers,* and called on them to add their voices to the "new poetry." He even suggests ways in which black authors might reach through the briar patch of their audience's flaws and command their attention. Despite everything the potential audience was there, witness the success of Atlanta University's Summer Theatre and, on a national scale, Richard Wright's fiction. Of the Atlanta Players' 1934 season, which included not only stagey items like "Lady Windemere's Fan" but Shaw and some contemporary American works, Brown wrote: "In a city known for a full round of social activities, the intruding summer theatre was nevertheless received with hospitality."[24] And though many white and black readers spurned Wright's *Uncle Tom's Children* as "propaganda"—for certain readers labelled as such all fiction about blacks refusing to show "Harlem to be a round of cabarets and parties or the South to be a sunny pastoral"—Wright's success nonetheless proved that "social protest fiction, even about Negro experience, can sell widely . . . Wright is a craftsman who can tell a story with the best of them today; he can reach out and hold an audience. He is a publisher's find."[25] *Native Son,* Brown reported with enthusiasm, was "a literary phenomenon . . . discussed by literary critics, scholars, social workers, journalists, writers to the editor, preachers, students, and the man in the street." The book inspired debates "in grills and 'juke joints' as well as at 'literary' parties, in the deep South as well as in Chicago, among people who have not bothered much to read novels since *Ivanhoe* was assigned in high school English."[26]

In calling for realistic literature about Negro life, Brown invited not special pleas or exaggerations, quite the contrary: he called for books containing the unprettied truth of Negro life, just the facts well-rendered. The point here is not that dubious whites could read the real truth of life among the black lowly and, at last, Give a Damn. Though interested in all readers, whatever their background, Brown most urgently desired the creation of a community of *black* readers who received from literature images expressing the meanings of their lives, and strategies for coping with them. Brown seemed to have had in mind something like what Robert Stepto has termed a call-and-response[27] (or call-and-recall) pattern between black writers and their readers, an enriched exchange between "implied writers" and "implied readers" (both, according to one terminology, "embedded in the text")[28] and *actual* readers recognizing their experiences transformed in literature. For this literary "conversation" or "group creation" (to maintain the black church or blues metaphor, for call-and-recall sermons and songs are *communally* created) to be fully realized—for a book to be a success—the reader must read well. And, to be sure, the writer must create image and action well enough to invoke in the reader a *déjà vue* so irresistibly vivid that in his heart (if not out loud) he says, "Amen."

In his criticism Brown taught several ways for black writers to win black readers' attention. Crucial here, of course, is the matter of *form*. "Form," writes Kenneth Burke, may be defined as "the psychology of the audience" and "the creation of an appetite in the mind of the audience, and adequate satisfying of that appetite."[29] Effective literary form involves meeting the audience—as the vernacular has it—"part way down the road." The black audience was sold on the sudden turns of plot and the coincidences of melodrama, so black writers could capture their attention using some of these same techniques. "Melodrama," wrote Brown, "can be expert and inexpert in its cogency."[30] Moreover, "a critic would have to be blind," he wrote in 1938, "to deny that . . . melodrama and tragedy abound [in] southern Negro life."[31] The trick here, as critics from Aristotle to Booth have written, involves preserving verisimilitude while keeping the audience interested.

Controlling the point of view was another key aspect of Brown's poetics of effective communication in literature. Seen from the peanut gallery, a razor-toting badman laying to cut his women can be a tiresome minstrel cliché, a hackneyed stage joke. But told from the viewpoint of the women whose terror, in Faulkner's "That Evening Sun," is real, the old story comes frighteningly to life.[32] Likewise the comic Negro is a stock stage figure; but shift the point of view, and the reader laughs not just at the figure of fun but *with* him: even the "rough and ribald" humor of Caldwell's *Kneel to the Rising Sun* does not descend to mere burlesque.[33] Hurston's characters are often comic, but they are not cartoons.[34] And as Brown points out, blacks laugh not *only* "to keep from crying," they sometimes laugh because they are *tickled.*[35]

Brown's main point here is that of the realist: To reach the reader, the writer presents the reader with "the familiar and the usual" aspects of a world he already knows. Thus middle- and upper-class black life should not be treated with the worn conventions of "copybook gentility" comedy, but with modern techniques revealing first-hand, lived experience.[36] Like most realists, Brown wrote with greatest force about the portraits of poor blacks—not, in Brown's case, because they are "simpler" and thus easier to get on paper;[37] this pastoral and prejudiced stance is challenged in virtually everything Brown writes. He considered the "dominance of the lowly as subject matter" in modern literature to be "a natural concomitant to the progress of democracy."[38] And anyway most blacks *were* poor, especially during the depression. Brown felt that if black middle and upper classes became comfortable in their evasiveness about the terrors and trials of being poor, they themselves would be dragged down, both morally and economically, or their children would be.[39] If literary realism could shock the reader out of his dreaminess and blindness, that, too, was one of its saving features. Brown's realism reflected the artistic movement in Europe and America which claimed as proper subjects for serious treatment the forgotten men and women at the bottom of the social hierarchy: migrants, workers, roustabouts, dwellers on the outskirts of town. In one essay Brown quotes Thomas Hardy's words, which might be taken as a credo of Brown's realism:

> That if way to the Better there be,
> it exacts a full look at the worst.[40]

To view the world from the stand-point of the black masses themselves, several writers of the 1930s and 1940s tapped the rich source of black folklore: that other crucial element informing the tastes of Afro-American audiences, highborn and lowly. This use of black lore was natural enough, for, as Brown says, through the 19th century there was no written black poetry to compare with the spirituals or with the "sly and sardonic" couplets of secular folk verse. In the folktales and the blues, the worksongs and the ballads, lay a goldmine of material: here were figures of speech, characters, themes, and narrative and lyric shapes created by black Americans themselves—obviously from their own point of view—and tempered with centuries of New World living. Nor was folklore merely a localizing ingredient: Melville, Mark Twain, Faulkner—creators of American masterpieces—had taken a page from "the *fabliaux,* Boccacio, Chaucer, Rabelais, and Muchausen and like them had drawn artistic strength from the speech and the folkways of people around them, and from their tales and songs."[41] These writers had found the passage to the universal "through the narrow door of the particular." In America, wrote Brown quoting Constance Rourke "this (vernacular) tradition is 'subtle, sinewy, scant at times, but not poor'"; it "is the new thing prophetically seen by Emerson over a century ago . . . a new literature that sought the meaning of 'the milk in the firkin, the meal in the pan, the ballad in the street'," and explored "the familiar and the low."[42] Chesnutt; Johnson, Hughes, Hurston, and, of course, Brown himself, had continued, often with magnificence, to work this folk vein as it ran through black America.

Like black folk, black lore had been much abused, to be sure. Roark Bradford's *John Henry* "presents certain features of the lives of roustabouts and migrant workers along the Mississippi, the 'back' of such towns as New Orleans and Memphis, gris-gris, coonjining, and folk-songs."[43] Thus his writing had many of the elements of realism. But even so the book is "more of a study in local color . . . than the showing of a folk hero . . . John Henry just isn't there." Here again the issue involves point of view:

> *John Henry* poses the interesting problem of how many liberties an artist may take with folk material. That is, between mere recording and alteration that leaves the folkstuff unrecognizable, where is the place of genuine artistry, of the Burns or of the Hardy? . . . *Certain it is that the artist must look at the material in as nearly as possible the manner of the ultimate creators of it.* One has the feeling that Mr. Bradford's attitude is still one of sophisticated condescension.[44]
>
> (Italics mine)

Julia Peterkin, on the other hand, uses black folklore more realistically, and thereby sets an example for black writers:

> One thing might be suggested to our writers by this woman. She has shown in our day the truth of Wordsworth's belief in rural as significant, suggestive of truth. She is with Hamsun; Anderson, Powys, Hardy. From her we might get a hint of the need of going back to the soil; of digging our roots deeply therein.—There is strength there, and coolness for draught.[45]

Sad to say, some of "our writers" were afflicted by the same disease that plagued "our literary audience": Brown termed it "an aristocratic disdain of our masses." Straightshooting Brown brings this high-falutin writer down from his perch: "Though it may be *lése majesté* to say so, our elite is only one remove—even our 'ritziest' only one and a half removes—from our masses . . . Our folklore and songs are being assiduously collected by white editors . . . Material in abundance exists; do our artists believe it to be so far beneath their notice? Has it been so easy, then, for school and society to fix in us a savage contempt for the rock whence we were born?"[46] There are significant exceptions: Bontemps's novel *God Sends Sunday* has some of the quick turns and refrains one hears in Negro ballads; Hurston's *Their Eyes Were Watching God* has characters with some of the "unabashed shrewdness of the Blues."[47] At a conference on folklore, Brown said: "I became interested in folklore because of my desire to write poetry and prose fiction. I was first attracted by certain qualities that I thought the speech of the people had, and I wanted to get for my own writing a flavor, a color, a pungency of speech. Then later I came to something more important—I wanted to get an understanding of people, to acquire an accuracy in the portrayal of their lives."[48]

The lasting power of Brown's poetry derives not only from its technically accurate capturing of folk speech—at times Roark Bradford could manage that—it derives too from his deceptively straightforward ability to portray, in vigorous American language—sometimes country, sometimes city, sometimes in folk language, sometimes not—the complex drama and richness of what it meant to be Sister Lou, Sporting Beasley, or Old Lem. The durability of Brown's poetry comes too from his perspective as a realist in a world with no hiding place. Certainly his poems show that

Brown is not the "outsider" or the blind escapist he wrote about in this passage from ***The Negro in Washington*** (1937):

> . . . When the outsider stands upon U Street in the early hours of the evening and watches the crowds go by, togged out in finery, with jests upon their lips—this one rushing to the pool-room, this one seeking escape with Hoot Gibson, another to lose herself to Hollywood glamor, another in one of the many dance halls—he is likely to be unaware, as these people momentarily are, of aspects of life in Washington of graver import to the darker one-fourth. This vivacity, this gayety, may mask for a while, but the more drastic realities are omnipresent. Around the corner there may be a squalid slum with people jobless and desperate; the alert youngster, capable and well trained, may find on the morrow all employment closed to him. The Negro of Washington has no voice in government, is economically proscribed, and segregated nearly as rigidly as in the southern cities he contemns. He may blind himself with pleasure seeking, with a specious self-sufficiency, he may point with pride to the record of achievement over grave odds. But just as the past is not without its honor, so the present is not without bitterness.[49]

As a critic, too, Brown is a realist. Part of what is so durable in Brown's criticism is the compelling drive to see the complete picture of literature, its makers, their sources, the effects on readers. As we have seen, he is particularly concerned with bringing together black readers and black writers (not only them, but especially them). The way to do it, aside from somehow getting both writers and readers to give up the false gods of Babbitry, was for the writers to put the readers and potential readers right between the covers of books: to capture on the page real people, full of anguish and beauty, frailty and roguishness, and the love to lie. The trick was to do so as Sterling Brown had done in his poetry: to portray black characters with so much vividness that not only will a conference of writers and teachers say of the poem, "How realistic!" "How mythic in reference!" "How well structured!" "How well-deconstructed!" But in the backrow, or in the Amen Corner, even Wild Bill or Joe Meek or Ma Rainey or Big Boy Davis or Jack Johnson or Sporting Beasley Daniels might hear Sterling Brown's poetry and say, "*Ouch,* I do believe this man Brown, he is talking about *me!*"

Notes

1. Sterling A. Brown, "Negro Characters as Seen by White Authors," *The Journal of Negro Education* 2 (April 1933): 179-203.
2. Brown, "The Literary Scene," *Opportunity* 9 (February 1931): 53-54.
3. Brown, "More Odds," *Opportunity* 10 (June 1932): 188.
4. Brown, "The Literary Scene," p. 53.
5. Brown, "The Negro Writer and His Publisher," *The Quarterly Review of Higher Education Among Negroes* 9 (July 1941): 143.
6. Brown, "The Negro Writer and His Publisher," p. 143.
7. Brown, "Our Literary Audience," *Opportunity* 8 (February 1930): 42.
8. Brown, "Our Literary Audience," p. 42.
9. Brown, "Our Literary Audience," p. 42.
10. Brown, "Poor Whites," *Opportunity* 9 (October 1931): 320.
11. Brown, "Our Literary Audience," p. 42.
12. Brown, "A Literary Parallel," *Opportunity* 10 (May 1932): 153.
13. Brown, "Our Literary Audience," p. 43.
14. Brown, "Concerning Negro Drama," *Opportunity* 9 (September 1931): 284.
15. Brown, "Our Literary Audience," p. 43.
16. Brown, "Signs of Promise," *Opportunity* 10 (September 1932): 287.
17. Brown, "Our Literary Audience," p. 46.
18. Brown, "More Odds," p. 188.
19. See Walt Whitman, "Ventures on an Old Theme," *Prose Works* (Philadelphia: David McKay, 1924), 324: quoted by Sterling A. Brown in "Our Literary Audience" (p. 42) and in "The Negro Author and His Publisher" (p. 146).
20. Inscribed in Sterling A. Brown's personal copy of E. Franklin Frazier's *The Negro Family in the United States* (Chicago: University of Chicago Press, 1939).
21. Brown, "Our Literary Audience," p. 46.
22. Brown, "More Odds," p. 188.
23. Brown, *Outline for the Study of the Poetry of American Negroes* (New York: Harcourt, Brace, 1931), 49-50.
24. Brown, "The Atlanta Summer Theatre," *Opportunity* 12 (October 1934): 309.
25. Brown, "The Negro Author and His Publisher," p. 144.
26. Brown, "Insight, Courage, and Craftsmanship," *Opportunity* 18 (June 1940): 185.
27. See Robert B. Stepto, *From Behind the Veil* (Urbana: University of Illinois Press, 1979).
28. See Susan R. Suleiman, "Introduction: Varieties of Audience-Oriented Criticism," *The Reader in the Text,* ed. Susan R. Suleiman and Inge Crosman (Princeton: Princeton University Press, 1980), 3-45; see also Jane P. Thompkins, *Reader-Response Criticism* (Baltimore: John Hopkins, 1980).

29. Burke's definition is quoted by Stanley Edgar Hyman in *The Armed Vision,* revised edition (New York: Vintage, 1955), 375.

30. Brown, "Six Plays for a Negro Theatre," *Opportunity* 12 (September 1934): 280.

31. Brown, "From the Inside," *The Nation* 166 (April 16, 1938): 448.

32. Brown, "The Point of View," *Opportunity* 9 (November 1931): 347.

33. Brown, "Realism in the South," *Opportunity* 12 (October 1935): 311.

34. Brown, "'Luck is a Fortune'," *The Nation* 166 (April 16, 1938): 448.

35. Quoted from a conversation with Brown, November 22, 1977.

36. See Brown, "Biography," *Opportunity* 15 (September 1937): 216; also see Brown, "Not Without Laughter," *Opportunity* 8 (September 1930): 311-12.

37. See George Becker, *Documents of Modern Literary Realism* (Princeton: Princeton University Press, 1963), 24.

38. Brown, "Our Literary Audience," p. 44.

39. Brown, "Our Literary Audience," p. 44.

40. Brown, "Never No More," *Opportunity* 10 (February 1932): 56.

41. Brown, "In the American Grain," *Vassar Alumnae Magazine* 36 (February 1951): 8.

42. Brown, "In the American Grain," p. 8.

43. "Never No Steel Driving Man," *Opportunity* 9 (December 1931): 382.

44. "Never No Steel Driving Man," p. 382.

45. Brown, "The New Secession—a Review," *Opportunity* 5 (May 1927): 148.

46. Brown, "More Odds," p. 189.

47. Brown, "'Luck is a Fortune'," p. 410.

48. Brown, "Remarks at a Conference on the Character and State of Studies in Folklore," *Journal of American Folklore* 59 (October 1946): 506.

49. Brown, "The Negro in Washington," *Washington: City and Capital* (Washington: Government Printing Office, 1937), 89.

GARY SMITH (ESSAY DATE 1989)

SOURCE: Smith, Gary. "The Literary Ballads of Sterling A. Brown." *CLA Journal* 32, no. 4 (June 1989): 393-409.

In the following essay, Smith considers Brown as the foremost figure of the Harlem Renaissance due to his restoration of African American ethnic identity through his use and promotion of Black American folk literature. Smith also lauds Brown's perceptive portrayal of the tension between the traditional representation of Black Americans and the figure of the New Negro.

> *Sterling Brown, more reflective, a closer student of folk-life, and above all a bolder and more detached observer, has gone deeper still, and has found certain basic, more sober and more persistent qualities of Negro thought and feeling; and so has reached a sort of common denominator between the old and the new Negro. Underneath the particularities of one generation are hidden universalities which only deeply penetrating genius can fathom and bring to the surface. Too many of the articulate intellects of the Negro group—including sadly enough the younger poets—themselves children of opportunity, have been unaware of these deep resources of the past.*
>
> —Alaine Locke[1]

Although one might now quibble with the limitations of Alaine Locke's perceptive review of Sterling Brown's poetry—especially in light of the 1980 publication of Brown's ***Collected Poems***[2] and the numerous reconsiderations[3] that have placed Brown's poetry within the mainstream of both American and Afro-American literature—Locke nonetheless touches upon what is still Brown's major achievement as a poet: his restoration and recreation of black American folk literature. In retrospect, Brown's achievement clearly over-shadows his contemporaries, Jean Toomer, Countee Cullen, Langston Hughes, and Claude McKay, all of whom, in their poetry, were important architects of the New Negro but who did considerably less than Brown to restore the ethnic identity of black Americans.[4] The vitality of Brown's poetry is the constant tension between the old and new, between what is ostensibly a traditional way of viewing black Americans and a radical reconstruction. While New Negro poetry generally portrayed black Americans as militantly determined to participate in America's democratic processes, Brown's poetry first assumes that black Americans are as inherently complex and diverse as white Americans; hence, the essential and perhaps more meaningful dialogue is not between new and newer representations of black Americans but rather between what is old and new.

This dialogue leads, in part, to Locke's second insight into Brown's poetry: its detached observation. Brown neither idealizes the past nor romanticizes the present. As the title of his first published work, ***Southern Road,***[5] indicates, he creates a dynamic, almost seamless, relationship or quest between the past and present; the road that leads away from the South also leads back.[6] His characters, in such poems as **"The Ballad of Joe Meek"** and **"The Odyssey of Big Boy,"** are not in conflict with the past as much as they are with the inherent paradoxes of the human heart. Joe, for example, is both an old and new Negro. He is self-effacing and deferential to white authority; however, when provoked by what he considers a gross miscarriage of justice, he becomes militantly self-assertive. The odyssey of Big Boy is also a circuitous journey from self-discovery to self-recovery; he finds his presence in his past.[7] In his characterizations, Brown does not overlook the particular issues of poverty, racism, and social injustice, but these issues, however important, are interwoven with the universals that underscore his characters' lives. These universals include not only love and brotherhood but also their antitheses, hate and cruelty. Indeed, his best poetry engages the energetic hope and idealism of the New Negro as well as the resigned pessimism and realism of the old Negro.

FROM THE AUTHOR

BROWN ON NEGRO CHARACTER

The sincere, sensitive artist, willing to go beneath the cliches of popular belief to get at an underlying reality, will be wary of confining a race's entire characters to a half-dozen narrow grooves.

SOURCE: Sterling Allen Brown, "Negro Character as Seen by White Authors," in *The Journal of Negro Education,* April 1933.

The complexity of Brown's artistic vision is nowhere better illustrated than in his choice of poetic forms. While trained academically at Williams College and Harvard in traditional English and Anglo-American literature, he wrote the bulk of his poetry in ballads and blues poems.[8] His rejection of Modernism—what he termed the "puzzle poetry" of T. S. Eliot and Ezra Pound—was not, however, prompted by his search for an idealized folk past. The hallmarks of Modernist poetry, socio-psychological fragmentation and displacement of human values, are also important themes in Brown's poetry. However, these themes do not replace the need for social and aesthetic continuities within black American literature. For Eliot and, to a lesser degree, Pound, the past constitutes an idealized order, although the poet's relationship with this order is often antithetical.[9] For Brown, though, the past is not a static, idealized order; the poet is as responsible for the past as he is responsive to it. Indeed, his choice of ballads and blues, as poetic forms, is reflective of his need to invoke continuities between the past and present.

Stylistically, ballads and blues are more dynamic and open than closed poetic forms such as the Petrarchan sonnet. While the latter, traditionally written in syllogistic form, offers the poet discursive possibilities, ballads and blues are primarily performative. The blues singer/poet is more directly or intimately engaged with his audience, and his performances/poems often occur as spontaneous creative exchanges with his audience. Similarly, the traditional ballad is a communal art form that originates in rhythmic group action.[10] The balladist is thus an inextricable part of his folk community. Indeed, in poems such as **"Ma Rainey"** (***CP*** **[*Collected Poems*]**, pp. 62-63) and **"When de Saints Go Ma'ching Home"** (***CP,*** pp. 26-30), Brown explores the relationship between the singer, song, and folk community. The famous blues singer, Ma Rainey, is both the poem's subject and its performer:

O Ma Rainey,
Sing you' song;
Now you's back
Whah you belong,
Git way inside us,
Keep us strong. . . .

Similarly, Big Boy Davis, as a "saint," provides subject and style in his song, **"When de Saints Go Ma'ching Home"**:[11]

He'd play, after the bawdy songs and blues,
After the weary plaints
Of "Trouble, Trouble deep down in muh soul,"
Always one song in which he'd lose the role
Of entertainer to the boys. He'd say,
"My mother's favorite." And we knew
that what was coming was his chant of saints,
"When de saints go ma'chin' home. . . ."
And that would end his concert for the day.

With ballads and blues, Brown was also able to personalize his otherwise tragically ironic and objectively detached artistic vision. This dynamic viewpoint permits him to focus objectively and ironically upon the individual plight of blacks within American society, yet underscore the paradoxical relationship of blacks to America's democratic ideals and harsh realities. The ballad, historically, has always been a vehicle by which the folk masses could realize a measure of poetic understanding in an unjust world.[12] And the blues, an art form that originates in the slave seculars and work songs, invokes the human injustice of slavery as well as the universal plight of the underclass. This poetic strategy juxtaposes personal, deep-seated longings for socio-economic justice with public performances.

While Brown found certain continuities between the past and present within black American life and literature, he also found discontinuities. He is acutely aware of how, in spite of their dynamic interrelationship, the past differs from the present in style and substance. **"Children's Children"** (***CP,*** p. 94) and **"Cabaret"** (***CP,*** p. 101) are poems that portray black Americans who, while they have definite affinities with the past, are essentially at odds with it. "They have forgotten / What had to be endured," or they are simply apathetic to the past:

I've been away a year today
To wander and roam
I don't care if it's muddy there

Therefore, Brown is interested in both the continuities and discontinuities that underscore his generation. His poems are paradoxical bridges and sometimes gaps between traditional rural and contemporary urban representations of black Americans. He is as mindful of what makes the new Negro old as he is of what makes the old Negro new. This poetry of paradox is nowhere better illustrated than in Brown's literary ballads. In them, Brown has freely adopted the traditional features of black folk ballads, while radically altering their themes and styles. In ballads such as **"Frankie and Johnny," "A Bad, Bad Man,"** and **"Break of Day,"** Brown portrays traditional folk characters restored and recreated within his dynamic perception of the continuities and discontinuities of black American literature.

"Frankie and Johnny"[13] is arguably one of the oldest and best known black folk ballads. Although its title often varies, its narrative usually tells the story of Frankie and her unfaithful lover, Johnny, whom she kills after finding him in bed with another woman. Structurally, the folk ballad leaps from one moment to another in the ill-fated romance. The first three stanzas quickly establish the basic plot: Frankie and Johnny are lovers who have sworn to be true to each other, but Johnny's infidelity leads to Frankie's murderous revenge:

Frankie went down to the hotel
Looked over the transom so high,
There she saw her lovin' Johnnie
Making love to Nelly Bly
He was her man; he was doing her wrong.

Frankie threw back her kimono,
Pulled out her big forty-four;
Rooty-toot-toot: three times she shot
Right through that hotel door,
She shot her man, who was doing her wrong.

The final three stanzas turn upon Johnny's confession of infidelity, "I was your man, but I done you wrong." The *noncupative testament* that follows includes the sheriff's sentence, "It's the 'lectric chair for you," and Frankie's remorseless testimony:

Frankie says to the sheriff,
"What are they going to do?"
The sheriff he said to Frankie,
"It's the 'lectric chair for you.
He was your man, and he done you wrong."
"Put me in that dungeon,
Put me in that cell,
Put me where the northeast wind
Blows from the southeast corner of hell,
I shot my man, 'cause he done me wrong."

As a black folk ballad, **"Frankie and Johnny"** is distinguishable from "Fuller and Warren" and "The Jealous Lover," American folk ballads of similar romantic crimes, by the fulsome details in which Frankie's actions are described and the precise nature of her punishment.[14] The incremental refrain clearly establishes that the narrator's and, presumably, the reader's sympathies are with Frankie's plight; yet, in spite of the mitigating circumstances, she, as well as Johnny, dies.

This rather simple tragic irony informs the larger complexities of Brown's **"Frankie and Johnny"** (***CP,*** p. 44). Structurally, he shortens his version of the folk ballad by three stanzas and eliminates the incremental refrain and testament. The burden of the narrative is thus more forcefully rendered, and the reader plays a larger role in determining the motivation of Frankie and Johnny. In the case of Frankie, her innocence is based upon her demented psychology and equally demented "cracker" father:

Frankie was a halfwit, Johnny was a nigger,
Frankie liked to pain poor creatures as a little 'un,
Kept a crazy love of torment when she got bigger,
Johnny had to slave it and never had much fun.

Frankie liked to pull wings off of living butterflies,
Frankie liked to cut long angleworms in half,
Frankie liked to whip curs and listen to their drawn out cries,
Frankie liked to shy stones at the brindle calf.

Frankie took her pappy's lunch week-days to the sawmill,

Her pappy, red-faced cracker, with a cracker's
thirst,
Beat her skinny body and reviled the hateful
imbecile,
She screamed at every blow he struck, but tit-
tered when he
curst.

In spite of their racial differences, Johnny is at least Frankie's equal as a victim. As a "nigger," he is as much a social outcast as she is though not as depressed. Their romance is thus a macabre parody of the folk ballad.[15] In this regard, the mismatched lovers are a reversal of our expectations for love and fidelity; their romance is not reflective of communal norms, but rather of its abnormalities.

In the next three stanzas of his version, Brown shifts his focus from Frankie to Johnny. His tone also changes from melodramatic to tragic:

Frankie had to cut through Johnny's field of
sugar corn
Used to wave at Johnny, who didn't *'pay no
min'*—
*Had had to work like fifty from the day that he was
born,*
*And wan't no cracker hussy gonna put his work
behind*—.

But everyday Frankie swung along the cornfield
lane,
And one day Johnny helped her partly through
the wood,
Once he had dropped his plow lines, he dropped
them many
times again—
Though his mother didn't know it, else she'd
have whipped him
good

Frankie and Johnny were lovers; oh Lordy how
they did love!
But one day Frankie's pappy by a big log laid him
low,
To find out what his crazy Frankie had been
speaking of;
He found that what his gal had muttered was
exactly so.

Brown transforms Johnny from social outcast to victim. Unlike Frankie, his relationship with nature and his mother is wholesome, and his dedication to hard work and self-discipline is admirable. Ironically, the moral edge Johnny has over Frankie and her father lies in his simple determination to work within an unjust socio-economic system. His tragic fate, then, seems doubly cruel. He is a victim not only of racism and socio-economic injustice, but also his own emotional vulnerability. His fidelity to hard work, of course, does not mitigate his fate but instead leads to his death. In Brown's version, then, the final stanza does not conclude the poem in the usual way as much as it circles back to the initial dilemma of injustice and victimization:

Frankie, she was spindly limbed with corn silk
on her crazy
head,
Johnny was a nigger, who never had much fun—
They swung up Johnny on a tree, and filled his
swinging hide
with lead,
And Frankie yowled hilariously when the thing
was done.

Here, Johnny becomes one of the "poor creatures" victimized by Frankie's dementia. In this, he is a part of the natural order in the poem—butterflies, angleworms, curs and brindle calf—subject to Frankie's cruelty. The ballad is thus still an indictment of racism and, more importantly, the psychological disorders that racism often precipitates in human beings, but by reversing the traditional roles of Frankie and Johnny, Brown changes the narrative from simple melodrama to complex tragedy. Its complexity lies in the gross miscarriage of justice that leads to Johnny's lynching: the reader must decide whether he is a victim of his own vulnerability to racism or Frankie's wanton pathology.

Brown's ballad **"A Bad, Bad Man"** (***CP,*** pp. 144-45), is based, in part, on the folk ballad "Bad Man Ballad."[16] As with his version of **"Frankie and Johnny,"** Brown made substantial changes in theme and style. In the original folk ballad, Lee Brown, a bad man, kills his "woman" for no apparent reason:

Late las' night I was a-makin' my rounds,
Met my woman an' I blowed her down,
Went on home an' I went to bed,
Put my hand cannon right under my head.

His escape from justice is cut short in Mexico, where another bad man, "Bad Texas Bill," takes him into custody:

"Yes, oh, yes" says. "This is him.
If you got a warrant, jes' read it to me."
He says: "You look like a fellow that knows
what's bes'.
Come 'long wid me—you're under arres'."

When I was arrested, I was dressed in black;
Dey put me on a train, an' dey brought me back.
Dey boun' me down in de county jail;
Couldn' get a human for to go my bail.

As a traditional black folk ballad, "Bad Man Ballad" emphasizes the vulnerability of the black criminal who is often victimized by the justice system.[17] Lee Brown's trial lasts only five minutes, and he is sentenced to "Ninety-nine years on de hard, hard groun'."

The testament that closes the ballad again highlights Lee Brown's ironic vulnerability and the price he has to pay for his crime:

Here I is, bowed down in shame,
I got a number instead of a name.
Here for de res' of my nachul life,
An' all I ever done is kill my wife. . . .

Lee Brown's simple, remorseless testimony reinforces his reputation as a "bad man." Ironically, he is more concerned about his loss of identity and freedom than his dead wife. Moreover, his testimony does not reveal why he murdered his wife. On one level, his motiveless malignancy substantiates the moral rigidity of the poem; good and evil are inherent, often inexplicable human qualities. On another level, though, the poem indicts America's judicial system. Lee Brown's misfortune, however justly deserved, is compounded by the mistreatment he receives during his trial.

By its title alone, Brown's **"A Bad, Bad Man"** is suggestive of the farcical nature of his ballad. He has transformed the tragedy of Lee Brown's misfortune into comic burlesque. The narrative remains basically the same, but the indictment is rendered in terms that belie its seriousness; **"A Bad, Bad Man"** is actually a parody of "Bad Man Ballad." This parody begins with an epic invocation:

Forget about your Jesse James,
And Billy the Kid;
I'll tell you instead what
A black boy did.

Here, Brown invokes the legendary outlaws from American folklore as company for his character. In so doing, he not only places John Bias, "a black boy," within the American folk tradition of outlaws and bad men, but he also debunks the prevalent myth that black bad men somehow exist apart from this tradition. That Jesse James and Billy the Kid are celebrated as heroes is yet another way of illustrating the double standards of American socio-history and justice.

The character sketch that follows the invocation, however, places John Bias in opposition to the outlaw tradition. He is a "squinchy runt, / Four foot two" and married to a "strapping broad. / Big-legged Sue." The grotesque humor that informs his character also informs the plot. The narrative begins with the misadventures of another "black boy," Sam Johnson:

Another boy, Sam Johnson,
Was getting lynched because
His black mule had bust
A white man's jaws.

The crackers gathered in the woods
Early that night.
Corn liquor in pop bottles
Got 'em right.

They tied Sam Johnson to a tree.
Threw liquor on the fire.
Like coal oil it made the flames
Shoot higher.

The tragic possibilities of this scene are undermined, however, by the appearance of John Bias, who rushes to Sam Johnson's rescue. "Waving a great big / Forty-four." The caliber of his gun is, of course, larger than John Bias' physical size, but, more to the point, his disruption of the lynching places him on the side of the good man. His character thus changes from a bad man to a seriocomic Robin Hood. Ironically, John Bias' legendary stature, as a bad man, then grows in reverse proportion to his physical size:

The crackers spoke, from then on,
Of the giant nigger,
Every day he grew a
Little bigger.

The testament, in part, provides a psychological motive for John Bias' actions that, in the folk ballad, is missing:

Johnnie was told the next day
What he had done for Sam,
Scratched his head and said, "Well
I be dam!

"Never had no notion
To save nobody's life,
I was only jes a-lookin'
For my wife."

Here, again, tragedy is transformed into comedy. John Bias is not simply a hero or antihero: he is a complex mixture of both. As his name changes—from the serious John Bias to the playful Johnnie—he is a would-be sinner as well as a reluctant saint. He thus straddles several important traditions in the black folk ballad.

Big Jess, in Brown's ballad **"Break of Day"** (***CP***, p. 146) is also a complex mixture of personality traits. His story is actually a conflation of several versions of the folk ballad "Casey Jones."[18] In the first, Joseph Mica, a railroad engineer, represents the heroic ideal of a faithful worker, whose dedication to his job transcends his own personal safety:

Joseph Mica was good engineer,
Told his fireman not to fear,
All he want is water'n coal,
Poke his head out, see drivers roll.

Early one mornin' look like rain,
'Round de curve come passenger train,
On powers lie ole Jim Jones,
Good ole engineer, but daid an' gone.

Another version generally repeats this simple narrative of the engineer's ill-fated train ride, but adds three stanzas that further develop the engineer's heroism in contrast to the fireman's cowardice:

Casey Jones, I know him well,
Tole de fireman to ring de bell;
Fireman jump an' say good-by,
Casey Jones, you're bound to die.

Went on down to de depot track,
Beggin' my honey to take me back,
She turn 'round some two or three times,
"Take you back when you learn to grind."

Womens in Kansas all dressed in red,
Got de news dat Casey was dead;
De womens in Jackson all dressed in black,
Said, in fact, he was a cracker-jack.

Here, the testament reinforces the difference between the engineer and the fireman. The engineer is mourned by women dressed symbolically in red and black for his reckless courage, whereas the fireman is suspected of impotent cowardice: "Take you back when you learn to grind."

Within the conventional moral code of the ballad, the fireman's censure is justly deserved. Outside this code, however, the fireman's misdeed presents the same problem of interpretation as John Bias' crime; in both instances, the key element of motive is missing. The poem never makes clear whether the fireman abandons the train because he is a coward or, perhaps, wiser than the engineer.

The final three stanzas of a third version of "Casey Jones" substantially alters the nature of the fireman's cowardice and the engineer's heroism:

Just as he got in a mile of the place,
He spied number Thirty-five right in his face.
Said to the fireman, "You'd better jump!
For these locomotives are bound to bump."

When Casey's family heard of his death,
Casey's daughter fell on her knees,
"Mamma! mamma! how can it be,
Papa got killed on the old I. C.?"

"Hush your mouth, don't draw a breath;
We'll draw a pension from Casey's death!"

Here, the engineer's command prompts the fireman's actions; he "jumps" the train under orders from the engineer. On the other hand, the testament does not affirm the engineer's tragic heroism. Although his daughter mourns his death, his wife quickly sees economic advantage in his misfortune: "We'll draw a pension from Casey's death!" The wife thus not only trivializes the engineer's heroism; she also raises doubts about his wisdom in remaining aboard the ill-fated train. Indeed, her greed undermines the engineer's reckless courage.

In his ballad **"Break of Day,"** Brown further alters the folk ballad by reversing the dramatic roles of the fireman and engineer. The fireman, Big Jess, is presented as the main character, whereas the engineer, Mister Murphy, is his foil. More importantly, Brown increases the racial tension in the poem by making Jess a black man whose heroic ideals of hard work, fair play, and devotion to his family are jeopardized by white racism. The plot, therefore, develops in a melodramatic fashion, but with the forces of good and evil clearly identified:

Big Jess fired on the Alabama Central,
Man in full, babe, man in full.
Been throwing on coal for Mister Murphy
From times way back, baby, times way back.

Big Jess had a pleasing woman, name of Mamie,
Sweet-hipted Mama, sweet-hipted Mame;
Had a boy growing up for to be a fireman,
Just like his pa, baby, like his pa.

Out by the roundhouse Jess had his cabin,
Longside the tracks, babe, long the tracks,
Jess pulled the whistle when they high-balled
    past it
"I'm on my way, baby, on my way."

Crackers craved the job what Jess was holding,
Times right tough, babe, times right tough,
Warned Jess to quite his job for a white man,
Jess he laughed, baby, he jes' laughed.

Structurally, the incremental refrain, absent from the folk ballad, underscores the realities of Jess' heroism: his fidelity to his job and family as well as his single-minded, rugged individualism. The refrain also slows the pace of the narrative. Rather than leap from one select moment to another in the story, the forward thrust of each stanza is slowed by the counterweight of the repetitive refrain. On another level, the refrain, with its insistent repetition of "baby," forces the tone of the melodramatic ballad toward a tragic-comic blues poem. In this, it invokes the themes of tragic fate and personal loss that characterize the traditional blues song.

Indeed, the next two stanzas further close the aesthetic distance between the poem's melodramatic plot and its tragic theme. Big Jess becomes more of a doomed figure whose ritualized actions do not create suspense within the narrative as much as they foretell his doom:

He picked up his lunch-box, kissed his sweet
woman,
Sweet-hipted Mama, sweet-hipted Mame,
His son walked with him to the white-washed
palings,
"Be seeing you soon, son, see you soon."

Mister Murphy let Big Jess talk on the whistle
"So long sugar baby, so long babe";
Train due back in the early morning
Breakfast time, baby, breakfast time.

The final two stanzas, therefore, do not close the poem as much as they conclude the simple rituals of Jess' work day:

Mob stopped the train crossing Black Bear
Mountain
Shot rang out, babe, shot rang out.
They left Big Jess on the Black Bear Mountain,
Break of day, baby, break of day.

Sweet Mame sits rocking, waiting for the whistle
Long past due, babe, long past due.
The grits are cold, and the coffee's boiled over,
But Jess done gone, baby he done gone.

Here, Brown has omitted the testament that, in the folk ballad, usually resolves the conflict between good and evil. The mob prevails against Jess' rugged individualism, and the values that inform Jess' character are undermined by the mob's racism and vengeful terror. As the poem's title suggests, the circle of Jess' work day as well as the self-sustaining rituals within his family are now hollow: "Sweet Mame sits rocking, waiting for the whistle."

Brown's literary ballads reinforce his achievement and importance within the black American literary tradition. His ballads successfully bridge the gap between rural and urban representations of black Americans and underscore the essential continuities between these representations. In this, Brown's ballads underscore the persistent themes of black American literature: the need for freedom and socio-economic justice. His relationship with the ballad tradition, however, is not simply that of a restorer. As his complex literary ballads suggest, he has effectively recreated the folk ballad in terms that reflect the complexity of our modern age. In this, too, his ballads are radical reconstructions of the past that demythologize the present. His poetry of paradox recreates and restores the universals that belie the particularities of our generation.

Notes

1. Alaine Locke, "Sterling Brown: The New Negro Folk-Poet," in *Negro Anthology,* ed. Nancy Cunard (New York: Negro Universities Press, 1969), p. 115.
2. Sterling A. Brown, *Collected Poems* (New York: Harper, 1980). Subsequent references to this source will be cited parenthetically in the text as *CP.*
3. See Robert G. O'Meally, "Reconsideration: Sterling A. Brown," *The New Republic,* 11 February 1978, pp. 33-36; Stephen E. Henderson, "Sterling Brown: The Giant Unbowed," *The Black Collegian,* April/May 1981, pp. 138-40; Philip Levine, "A Poet of Stunning Artistry," *Saturday Review,* October 1981, pp. 42, 47; and John F. Callahan, "Sterling Brown: In the Afro-American Grain," *The New Republic,* 20 December 1982, pp. 25-28.
4. It should be further noted that Brown, along with Zora N. Hurston, were unique among the writers of the Harlem Renaissance, since they conducted actual fieldwork in the South to substantiate their artistic visions. See Clyde Taylor, "The Human Image in Sterling Brown's Poetry," *The Black Scholar,* March/April 1981, p. 13.
5. Sterling Brown, *Southern Road* (New York: Harcourt, 1932).
6. See Vera M. Kutzinski, "The Distant Closeness of Dancing Doubles: Sterling Brown and William Carlos Williams," *Black American Literature Forum,* 16 (1982), 21.
7. See Kimberly W. Benston, "Sterling Brown's After-Song: 'When De Saints Go Ma'ching Home' and the Performances of Afro-American Voice,' *Callaloo,* 5 (1982), 34.
8. See Sterling Brown, "A Son's Return: 'Oh, Didn't He Ramble'," *Chant of Saints,* ed. Michael S. Harper and Robert B. Stepto (Urbana: Univ. of Illinois Press, 1979), pp. 3-22.
9. T. S. Eliot, *The Sacred Wood: Essays on Poetry and Criticism* (London: Methuen, 1920), pp. 49-53.
10. See Robert Graves, *The English Ballad: A Short Critical Survey* (London: Ernest Benn Ltd., 1927), p. 8.
11. Benston, "Sterling Brown's After-Song," p. 39.
12. See Alan Bold, *The Ballad* (London: Methuen, 1979), p. 49.
13. "Frankie and Johnny," *The Negro Caravan,* ed. Sterling A. Brown, Arthur P. Davis, and Ulysses Lee (New York: Dryden, 1941), pp. 461-62. For other variants of this folk ballad, see *Folk Ballads of the English Speaking World,* ed. Albert B. Friedman (New York: Viking, 1956), pp. 211-17.
14. See G. Malcolm Laws, Jr., *Native American Balladry* (Philadelphia: The American Folklore Society, 1964), 86-87.
15. For two other interesting interpretations of this poem, see Charles H. Rowell, "Sterling A. Brown and the Afro-American Folk Tradition," *Studies in the Literary Imagination,* 7 (1974), 148-49, and Jean Wagner, *Black Poets of the United States* (Urbana: Univ. of Illinois Press, 1973), p. 489.
16. "Bad Man Ballad," *Negro Caravan,* pp. 455-56.

17. For a general study of the bad man in black folklore, see Lawrence W. Levine, *Black Culture and Black Consciousness* (Oxford: Oxford Univ. Press, 1977), pp. 404-20, and for a specific discussion of the bad man in Brown's poetry, see Robert G. O'Meally, "'Game to the Heart': Sterling Brown and the Bad Man," *Callaloo*, 5 (1982), 43-54.

18. For several variants of this folk ballad, see *Folk Ballads of the English Speaking World*, pp. 309-17.

JOANNE V. GABBIN (ESSAY DATE 1997)

SOURCE: Gabbin, Joanne V. "Sterling Brown's Poetic Voice: A Living Legacy." *African American Review* 31, no. 3 (autumn 1997): 423-31.

In the following essay, Gabbin, an acquaintance of Brown, offers an appreciation and appraisal of his career and legacy, focusing on his powerful recitals and the objective balance he achieved in his work.

When I first heard Sterling Brown reciting **"Long Gone,"** I knew that I was in the presence of a large and vibrant soul. The deep resonance of his voice, with its rumbling bass, brought me willingly into his world of stoic heroes and Southern roads:

I don't know which way I'm travelin'—
  Far or near,
All I know fo' certain is
  I cain't stay here.

Ain't no call at all, sweet woman,
  Fo' to carry on—
Jes' my name and jes' my habit
  To be Long Gone. . . .

(***Poems*** [***The Collected Poems of Sterling A. Brown***] 23)

Sterling A. Brown—poet, critic, legendary teacher, irreverent raconteur—whose life spanned the first eighty-eight years of the twentieth century, is gone, but fortunately his voice remains. His is the voice of the poet that captures the blues moan of lost and long-gone loves, the chant of saints who pray to be in the number, the tragicomic cry in the face of injustice and violence, and the jubilee songs of endurance and perseverance.

The man who would capture the authentic nuances of black people was born in Washington, D.C., on May 1, 1901, in a house at Sixth and Fairmount. He was the last of six children and the only son born to Reverend Sterling Nelson Brown and Adelaide Allen Brown. The young Sterling grew up on the campus of Howard University, where his father had taught in the School of Religion since 1892. A preacher's kid, Sterling was brought up hearing the hymns and spirituals sung at Lincoln Temple Congregational Church, where his father pastored. Later in life, when he became a devotee of blues and jazz, he had no difficulty combining and synthesizing these forms, generally considered antithetical, in his work. Though Brown's fun-loving personality rejected his father's penchant toward sobriety and reserve, the Reverend Brown's standards of integrity and spiritual strength made an indelible mark on his son's character. In the poem **"After Winter,"** Brown tenderly remembers the days with his father on a farm near Laurel, Maryland:

He snuggles his fingers
In the blacker loam
The lean months are done with,
The fat to come.

His eyes are set
On a brushwood-fire
But his heart is soaring
Higher and higher.

Though he stands ragged
An old scarecrow,
This is the way
His swift thoughts go,

"Butter beans fo' Clara
Sugar corn fo' Grace
An' fo' de little feller
Runnin' space."

(***Poems*** 74)

Brown is the "little feller" who remembers his father as hopeful, loving, and bound to the soil. The depth of feeling in the poem serves to suggest the extent of his father's impression on him.

From his mother, Adelaide Allen Brown, the young Sterling inherited a love for poetry and books. On May 14, 1973, Brown recalled for me that she read widely and had a great facility with reading poetry:

> My mother read . . . Longfellow, she read Burns; and she read Dunbar—grew up on Dunbar—"'Lias! 'Lias! Bless de Lawd!" "The Party," and "Lay me down beneaf de willers in de grass." . . . I remember even now her stopping her sweeping . . . now standing over the broom and reading poetry to me, and she was a good reader, great sense of rhythm.

It is this inherited sense of rhythm, unmistakably sure, that we hear in Brown's poetry.

Through his poetry we also come to know ourselves in all our beauty and ugliness, truth and treachery, confidence and insecurity, humor and pathos. Brown created portraits of the blues-singing roustabout Calvin "Big Boy" Davis, the phlegmatic Old Lem, the flamboyant Sporting Beasley, Ma Rainey, and the irrepressible Slim Greer, whose images parade before us as convincing portraits of ourselves. He took our speech with the rich cadences of backwater blues and field hollers and transformed it into poetry that touches our soul.

Brown's most significant achievement was his subtle adaptation of song forms, especially the blues, to his poetry. Experimenting with the blues, spirituals, work songs, and ballads, he invented combinations that, at their best, retain the ethos of folk forms and intensify the literary quality of the poetry. Because these folk forms were conceived and developed in the matrix of the folk community, they were products of folk aesthetics. In his introduction to the "Folk Literature" section in ***The Negro Caravan*** (1941), Brown gave a convincing view of how the folk, for instance, pulled from a common storehouse in producing the spirituals. He explained that individuals "with poetic ingenuity, a rhyming gift, or a good memory" (414) composed or remembered lines out of the folk tradition and—in conjunction with the group, and with its approval—shaped the stanzas. As these songs were passed from one generation to the next, the songs were changed, updated, and sometimes lost. The folk artists who created the blues created in solitude, yet their blues messages intimately touched their listeners. Blues singers conveyed their listeners' preoccupation with love (in all its varieties), their misfortunes and losses, their wisdom and resilience.

In the hauntingly melancholic **"Long Track Blues,"** Brown becomes the blues singer with a poetic intensity that allows us to understand more than the railroad lore of the early twentieth century, more than lost or unrequited love. We hear in his words something about permanent loss, death, and an end that may not round into a beginning:

> Red light is my block,
> Green light down the line;
> Lawdy, let yo' green light
> Shine down on that babe o' mine.
>
> (***Poems*** 253)

Stepping up the tempo in **"Puttin' on Dog,"** Brown cleverly alternates stanzas that echo the rhythms and rhyme of a children's game song with ballad stanzas. The poem tells of old Scrappy, a flamboyant showoff, who runs up against badman Buck:

> Look at old Scrappy puttin' on dog,
> Puttin' on dog, puttin' on dog,
> Look at old Scrappy puttin' on dog,
> Callin' for the bad man Buck.
>
> (***Poems*** 240)

Or consider the sorrowful line of **"Sharecroppers."** Here Brown is successful in suggesting several of the qualities, themes, and idioms we associate with the spirituals. In the poem the victimization of the steadfast sharecropper is punctuated by his "wife's weak moans" and his "children's wails":

> Then his landlord shot him in the side.
> He toppled, and the blood gushed out.
> But he didn't mumble even a word,
> And cursing, they left him there for
> dead.

Clothed with sacrifice and hope, the sharecropper gives up no secret but one:

> "We gonna clean out dis brushwood
> round here soon,
> Plant de white-oak and de black-oak
> side by side."
>
> (***Poems*** 182)

What black folk expressed in story, proverb, and song, Brown considered and absorbed in his poetic imagination and infused in his poems. Besides the song forms themselves, he adopted themes and symbols from the folk storehouse; catastrophe, hardship, superstition, religion, poverty, murder, death, loneliness, travel, and courage are among the ideas that Brown handles with originality. In **"Break of Day,"** Brown tells the tragic story of Big Jess, who "fired on the Alabama Central." Big Jess "had a pleasing woman, name of Mame," and "Had a boy growing up to be a fireman, / Just like his pa." Yet Jess was denied his full man's right to life and happiness when he was ambushed and killed by "crackers" who "craved his job":

> Mob stopped the train crossing Black
> Bear Mountain
> Shot rang out, babe, shot rang out.
> They left Big Jess on the Black Bear
> Mountain,
> Break of day, baby, break of day.
>
> Sweet Mame sits rocking, waiting for
> the whistle
> Long past due, babe, long past due.
> The grits are cold, and the coffee's
> boiled over,
> But Jess done gone, baby he done
> gone.
>
> (***Poems*** 156)

In presenting Big Jess's story, Brown avoids a sentimental and melodramatic treatment by conveying the tale in the form of a ballad/work song. Written in an idiom that is direct, terse, and brimming with the vernacular of the railroad song, the poem is marked by a series of caesuras that punctuate the lines. Through repetition and well-placed emphasis, Brown intensifies the tragic circumstances of Big Jess's bid for a decent life. Jess's refusal to quit his job and his laugh in the face of intimidation were, for Brown, badges of courage.

With a remarkable ear for the idiom, cadence, and the tones of folk speech, Brown absorbed its vibrant qualities in his poetry. Brown naturalizes his black dialect, softens and elides the sounds, and captures the inflection, the timbre, the racial sound of the vernacular. Brown effectively creates the accent of the Creole patois in **"Uncle Joe,"** the twangy drawl of the sheriff in **"The Ballad of Joe Meek,"** and the edgy crackle of the old woman's voice in **"Remembering Nat Turner."** All of these accents add to the expressiveness of his reading/performance.

Part of Sterling Brown's effectiveness as a poet lies in his ability to reproduce the dialect of black rural folk. When Brown began writing poetry in the 1920s, there was a tendency among many writers to discard dialect and indict it because of the spurious, often demeaning conventions that had come to be associated with it. In 1922, James Weldon Johnson, writing in the preface to *The Book of American Negro Poetry,* recognized that black writers were breaking away from the use of conventionalized dialect and called for originality and authenticity in racial expression that would not limit the poet's emotional and intellectual response to life. Ten years later, Brown, with the publication of ***Southern Road,*** came as close to achieving Johnson's ideal of original racial expression as any American poet had before. Johnson, introducing Brown's poetry to the American public, said that Brown "infused his poetry with genuine characteristic flavor by adopting as his medium the common racy, living speech" of black life (***Poems*** 17). What Johnson applauded in 1932, we treasure today as we hear Brown exploring with uncompromising honesty the range of folk responses.

If we are fortunate to hear a recording of Brown reading his poetry, the genius of his achievement is amplified. The poems assume an added dimension because of his voice. I will never forget the first time I heard Sterling Brown read **"Old Lem."** It was in the spring of 1972 when I met Sterling and Daisy Brown. I felt at once in the presence of two people who carried the mantle of the past as gossamer. Their brilliance, infectious humor, and great depth of feeling and understanding endeared them to me. They shared with me their stories, anecdotes, and personal legends in the cozy setting of their home at 1222 Kearney Street on the northeast side of Washington. I still remember their eyes, with one telling, the other listening, and both remembering so many unspoken things. That is the way I first experienced **"Old Lem."** Brown's voice intones:

> I talked to Old Lem
> and Old Lem said:
> "They weigh the cotton
> They store the corn
>   We only good enough
>   To work the rows;
> They run the commissary
> They keep the books
>   We gotta be grateful
>   For being cheated. . . ."

(***Poems*** 180)

I saw Daisy Brown, Sterling's wife since 1927, respond to his reading with fresh and genuine emotion. As he read, they both seemed to remember the man who was lynched in a county south of Atlanta in 1935 and their own anger and feeling of powerlessness as they recalled other lynchings, too many to remember decently. It was one of those special moments when we became one in our understanding.

During the next seven years, until Daisy's death in 1979, they brought me into the circle of their special memories. On several occasions, they would talk about the luminaries of Howard University where Brown taught for more than fifty years, or tell me stories about Calvin "Big Boy" Davis or Leadbelly, or invite me to the basement to hear an old recording of Bessie Smith's "Backwater Blues" from their marvelous record collection. They would always brighten as they talked about the Virginia Seminary days when they first met. Brown, often with a rakish twinkle in his eyes, would tell how he was attracted to the auburn-haired beauty, Daisy Turnbull. In his poem **"Conjured,"** Brown captures the lasting magic that she held over him:

> "She done put huh little hands
> On the back uh my head;
> I cain't git away from her
> Twill I'm dead."

(***Poems*** 252)

It was also in the rural communities surrounding Lynchburg that Brown met the people who would open up his poetic sensibility to black folk culture and unstop the wellsprings of his literary power. The people as steeped in the traditions of the spirituals, blues, aphorisms, old lies, and superstition of folk life as they were in the rich soil of the foothills of the Blue Ridge mountains taught the young seminary professor something of folk humor, irony, fortitude, and shrewdness.

The poetry that came out of these experiences vibrates with nuances and depth. We hear in **"Sam Smiley,"** the first ballad that Brown wrote, his masterful use of irony. Sam, a black soldier returning from the war in France, finds that his sweetheart is in jail. He soon learns the full circumstances of her tragic fall; however, he cannot save her from her shame and from the "narrow gaping hole" that eases it. Sam—whom "the whites have taught . . . to rip / A Nordic belly with a thrust / Of bayonet"—"sent a rich white man / His woman's company to keep." The ubiquitous mob completes the scenario. Brown has the man who had danced to cheer the steerage on his return home buckdance "on the midnight air" (***Poems*** 45-46).

This same ironic tone can be heard in **"Transfer."** However, in this poem Brown's irony is edged with a steely rage as he recounts the tale of a man who broke the Jim Crow law because "he didn't say sir" on Atlanta's Peachtree trolley line:

And then the motorman brained him
with his crank,
And the conductor clubbed him with
his gun,
But before they could place the nickels
on his eyes,
The cops rushed up to see justice done.

(***Poems*** 190)

The ballad ends with the man's message hard won in the street and prisons of the land:

"I stayed in my place, and my place
stayed wid me,
Took what was dished, said I liked it
fine:
Figgered they would see that I warn't
no trouble,
Figgered this must be the onliest line.
"But this is the wrong line we been
ridin',
This route doan git us where we got to
go.
Got to git transferred to a new direction.
We can stand so much, then doan stan
no mo'."

(191)

The intensity that we hear filtered through the character's voice emanates from Brown's own familiarity with an integrity that demanded militance. In the 1930s, as the national editor of Negro affairs in the Federal Writers' Project, he battled racist state directors who were determined to keep blacks off their payrolls and to keep libelous and stereotypical treatment of black images in their publications. In the 1940s, often with resistance from his own colleagues, he struggled to gain acceptance for courses in black literature at Howard University, where there was still an overzealous attempt to imitate white institutions. During the McCarthy period in the 1950s, Brown, along with several of his colleagues, was interrogated by the Federal Bureau of Investigation for alleged subversive activities, and refused to back down from a radical adherence to the principle of academic freedom. By the 1960s, when Howard University students were testing their own militance, they discovered Sterling Brown. Students would crowd into his basement, lined with shelves of books and phonograph records, and talk well into the night about Marxism, Pan Africanism, Civil Rights, Malcolm X, Martin Luther King, Jr., and non-violence versus direct action.

Sometimes the discussions would give way to an impromptu reading by the "Prof," and Brown would invariably read **"The Ballad of Joe Meek."** The poem outlines the exploits of a "fighting fool" who started out as a mild-mannered man curious about the rough treatment of a black woman. The ballad ends with Joe talking in a different way:

"Ef my bullets weren't gone,
An' my strength all spent—
I'd send the chief something
With a compliment.

"An we'd race to hell.
And I'd best him there,
Like I would of done here
Ef he'd played me fair."

(***Poems*** 162)

In this poem and others, Brown becomes the African voice, the eloquent griot who makes the past merge into the present by dint of his virtuoso skill. Those who heard Brown read his poems, tell his remarkable "lies," or give his irreverent toasts are convinced of the power of this man whom Sonia Sanchez calls in her tribute poem "griot of the wind/glorifying red gums smiling tom-tom teeth" (92).

Perhaps nowhere is his power more evident than in his signature poem **"Strong Men."** Taking the leitmotif from Carl Sandburg's line "The strong men keep coming on," Brown celebrates the indomitable spirit of black people in the face of racism and economic and political exploitation. As Brown recounts the horrors of the Middle Passage, the scourges of slavery, and the humiliation of economic peonage and social segregation, his message is not merely one of unrelieved suffering and victimization but one of stoicism. Evoking the sound of spirituals and seculars, Brown allows these songs with all of their remembered stoicism and irony to transport the listener from the past to the present:

They dragged you from homeland,
They chained you in coffles,
They huddled you spoon-fashion in
filthy hatches,
They sold you to give a few gentlemen
ease.

They broke you in like oxen,
They scourged you,
They branded you,
They made your women breeders,
They swelled your numbers with bas-
tards. . . .
They taught you the religion they dis-
graced.

You sang:
Keep a-inchin' along
Lak a po' inch worm. . . .

You sang:
Bye and bye
I'm gonna lay down dis heaby load,

You sang:
Walk togedder, chillen,
Dontcha git weary. . . .
The strong men keep a-comin' on
The strong men git stronger.

(***Poems*** 56)

Much of the force of the poem may be attributed to syntax. Brown launches most of his lines with heavily stressed verbs that are preceded by the contrasting pronouns *they* or *you,* which also must be stressed strongly. The cadence of the poem suggests the rhythm of a martial approach, which quickens and becomes more pronounced as the poem reaches its conclusion:

What, from the slums
Where they have hemmed you,
What, from the tiny huts
They could not keep from you. . . .

One thing they cannot prohibit—
The strong men . . . coming on
The strong men gittin' stronger.
Strong men. . . .
Stronger. . . .

(57-58)

Brown also becomes the African American voice, the elegant trickster, the bodacious badman, the heroic strong man, as he juggles wit, understatement, irony, and humor with his inimitable style. Perhaps nowhere does Brown take humor more as his metier than in the Slim Greer tales. A favorite of many generations, the character is based on a virtuoso tall-tale teller whom Brown met waiting tables at the Hotel Jefferson in Jefferson City, Missouri. In the Slim Greer tales, we find the hero in humorous situations that obliquely comment on the absurdity of Southern racism. In **"Slim in Hell,"** the joke exposes Southern racism and oppression with a kind of laughter out of hell. Brown's unsuspecting hero makes a discovery on his visit to hell:

St. Peter said, "Well,
You got back quick.
How's de devil? An' what's
His latest trick?"

An' Slim say, "Peter,
I really cain't tell,
De place was Dixie
Dat I took for hell."

Then Peter say, "You must
Be crazy, I vow,
Where'n hell dja think Hell *was,*
Anyhow?"

(***Poems*** 92)

Informing this poem are not only the familiar images found in hell-and-brimstone sermons of the folk tradition but also subtle allusions to the Orpheus and Eurydice story in classical Greek mythology. Slim, like the favored Orpheus, is allowed to go to and leave the underworld. Here also is Cerberus, the terrible dog that guards the entrance to the infernal regions, now transformed to a "Big bloodhound . . . bayin' / Some po' devil's track" (90). By a synthesis of two viable traditions, Brown created this ballad through "cross-pollination." He linked the early stirrings of expression with present literary development, affirming the breadth of the black creative experience in America. He made the necessary connections between folk culture and self-conscious literature, identifying in his own poetry his debt to the folk. Significantly, he also managed to eliminate the much-touted gulf between particular racial experiences and the so-called "universal" experience.

Because Brown's poetry succeeds in expressing the universality of human experience, in bridging the experience of one generation with the next, it has a timeless quality. Poems that appeared in ***Southern Road*** in 1932 have a strong sense of contemporaneity when heard today. In **"Remembering Nat Turner,"** Brown retells in eloquent free verse the historic story of the fiercest of the black insurrectionists. As we figuratively follow the path that Nat Turner took from Cross Keys to Jerusalem, we get his story from blacks who "had only the faintest recollections" of who he was, and from an old white woman whose memory of Nat's deeds had been made concomitantly more vivid by an inherited sense of hysteria or dulled by present-day inconsequence:

"Ain't no slavery no more, things is
going all right,
Pervided thar's a good goober market
this year.
We had a sign post here with printing
on it,
But it rotted in the hole, and thar it
lays,
And the nigger tenants split the mark-
er for kindling.
Things is all right, now, ain't no trou-
ble with the niggers
Why they make this big to-do over
Nat?"

(***Poems*** 209)

Another reason for the lasting appeal of his poetry is his ability to draw some of the most memorable portraits in American literature. In his poems we meet Sporting Beasley, Slim Greer, Old Lem, and Joe Meek, characters that are now considered national treasures. Brown directs us:

Good glory, give a look at Sporting
Beasley
Strutting, oh my Lord.

Tophat cocked one side his bulldog
head,
Striped four-in-hand, and in his but-
tonhole
A red carnation; Prince Albert coat
Form-fitting, corset-like; vest snugly
filled,
Gray morning trousers, spotless and
full-flowing,
White spats and a cane.

Step it, Mr. Beasley, oh step it till the
sun goes down.

(***Poems*** 109)

With a measured irony and equally measured hyperbolic humor, Brown acquaints us with a man for whom exaggeration is small compensation for all that Sam Beasley has lost or never had. Sporting Beasley is allowed to forget the insults and drabness of his inconsequential life as he, resplendent with Prince Albert coat, white spats, and cane, struts it "till the sun goes down." In a tone that is decidedly mock-epical, the speaker describes the bon vivant at a concert as he strides down the aisle to his seat in row A and majestically pulls out his opera glasses amid the laughter of the crowd. One of Brown's folk transplanted in the city, Sporting Beasley is a character based on a hero from Brown's youth named Sporting Daniels "who used to walk up and down in front of the Howard Theater in Washington, D.C., in all his sartorial excellence." In actuality, Sporting Daniels did strut into a huge auditorium about twenty minutes late, walked slowly down the aisle to give those seated ample time to admire his clothes and cane, and, once at his seat in the very front of the auditorium, pulled out opera glasses in order to see the gigantic Paul Robeson in concert (14 May 1973 interview).

Brown achieves in these portraits truth in representation because of his willingness to refrain from idealizing his subjects and his insistence on an approach that eschews sentimentality and special pleading. For example, Brown's masterful portrait of Uncle Joe may be attributed to his keen observation and his excellent ear for dialect. We hear Unc' Joe, the garrulous old Creole, in a one-sided dialogue with the narrator, expounding on educating his children and standing up to the gratuitous threats and intimidation of the whites and Cajuns in the parish. With a penchant for humor and under-statement, Unc' Joe smiles at the narrator and says, "'You know, I gret big liar, me . . . / But still I kin do what I gots to do. / And dats no lie.'" When the narrator concludes "Unc' Joe, *c'est drole,*" we agree (***Poems*** 230).

Invariably Brown's poetry reveals an exploration of selfhood, a celebration of the strength and stoicism of Black people, and an abiding faith in the possibilities of their lives. Brown becomes the myth-maker, keeper of the images, preserver of values and definitions. As was the case in his life, Brown does not glorify or belittle race in his poetry. His quest is to explore the wellsprings of the racial strength and endurance that he so often celebrates. In **"Children's Children,"** Brown chastises those who would deny their heritage and identity:

They have forgotten
What had to be endured—

That they, babbling young ones,
With their paled faces, coppered lips,
And sleek hair cajoled to Caucasian
straightness,
Might drown the quiet voice of beauty
With sensuous stridency;

And might, on hearing those memoirs
of their sires,
Giggle,
And nudge each other's satin clad
Sleek sides. . . .

(***Poems*** 104)

Brown's message is conveyed in language that is "simple, sensuous, and impassioned" (Gabbin 38). As vivid and vibrant as a Romare Bearden collage, Brown's poetry displays strikingly imaginative, metaphoric language somehow akin to that of the unknown bards. Whether Brown is describing the beautiful fallen woman whose life has been twisted by the corruption of Rampart Street in **"Cloteel"** or the young healer in **"Parish Doctor"** who tells the parishioners that "he's the best conjuh doctor . . . / North of New Orleans" (***Poems*** 227), we sense in Brown's characterizations his intimacy with their humanity.

Brown's poetic sensibility experiments with diverse elements in literature and culture, amplifies understanding through performance, confronts the tragic-comic conditions of life, and attests to the continuity of black creativity. In **"Ma Rainey,"** one of Brown's finest poems, he skillfully brings together the ballad and blues forms and, demonstrating his inventive genius, creates the blues ballad. In this brilliant portrait of Gertrude "Ma" Rainey, the husky-voiced mother of the blues, Brown allows us to see her make her entrance on stage with a sequined grown hugging her short, stocky frame; an elaborate gold necklace encircling her cleavage; tasseled earrings; and a brilliant, gold-toothed grin. But even more than giving us a vivid portrait of the venerated blues singer, he draws an emotional portrait of the people who flocked to hear "Ma do her stuff."

> An' some jokers keep deir laughs a-
> goin' in de crowded aisles,
> An' some folks sits dere waitin' wid
> deir aches an' miseries. . . .
>
> (***Poems*** 62)

Brown effectively frames these portraits with a performance. Ma Rainey is on stage articulating the pain and suffering of her people. She sings "'bout de hard luck / Roun' our do' / . . . 'bout de lonesome road / We mus' go. . . ." Her power over her audience emanates from her ability to translate the chaos and uncertainty of their lives into terms that can be understood and confronted. When she sings "Backwater Blues," she catches "'hold of us, somekindaway'" (63).

In the final analysis Brown's poetry, too, has the effect of getting "hold of us dataway" (63). Through his poetry, Brown offers us a kind of clairvoyance, a sure vision, that gives guidance, warning, admonishment, and encouragement. When we flounder in confusion, fear, and divisiveness, Brown offers us in **"Sharecroppers"** the images of blacks and whites who became comrades in mutual struggle. When our children cast their heads down in collective shame upon first learning that their ancestors were slaves, Brown's **"Strong Men"** speaks to them of endurance, resilience, and strength of character. When we find it comfortable to forget our past and expedient to deny who we are, Brown shows in **"Children's Children"** the tragic emptiness and falseness of the "babbling young ones" who "have forgotten / What had to be endured" (104). Even when we take ourselves too seriously and view life as through a veil of tears, Brown sends us Ole Slim Greer:

> Talkinges' guy
> An' biggest liar,
> With always a new lie
> On the fire.
>
> (***Poems*** 77)

Remarkably balanced in his approach, Brown brought to American literature a voice rich in racial memory and resonant with messages of struggle and strength. When he died on January 13, 1989, I lost a dear friend and mentor, and the literary world lost a champion. Now what remains is his voice resonating with dignity and truth. His poetry is his legacy to all of us.

Works Cited

Brown, Sterling A. *The Collected Poems of Sterling A. Brown.* 1980. Chicago: TriQuarterly P, 1989.

———. "Folk Literature." *The Negro Caravan.* Ed. Brown, Arthur P. Davis, and Ulysses Lee. 1941. New York: Arno, 1970. 412-34.

Gabbin, Joanne. *Sterling A. Brown: Building the Black Aesthetic Tradition.* 1985. Charlottesville: UP of Virginia, 1994.

Sanchez, Sonia. *I've Been A Woman: New and Selected Poems.* Sausalito: Black Scholar P, 1978.

TITLE COMMENTARY

Southern Road

NICOLE L. B. FURLONGE (ESSAY DATE 1998)

SOURCE: Furlonge, Nicole L. B. "An Instrument Blues-Tinged: Listening, Language and the Everyday in Sterling Brown's 'Ma Rainey.'" *Callaloo* 21, no. 4 (fall 1998): 969-84.

In the following essay, Furlonge examines Brown's work—and his poem "Ma Rainey," which appeared in Southern Road*—for its depiction of everyday folk and dialect, and uses this conception to illuminate the poetics of the New Negro Renaissance.*

> I am everyday people.
>
> —Sly and the Family Stone

> I do not doubt that the ultimate art coming from black folk is going to be just as beautiful, and beautiful largely in the same ways, as the art that

> comes from white folk, or yellow, or red; but the point today is that until the art of the black folk compels recognition they will not be rated as human. And when through art they compel recognition then let the world discover if it will that their art is as new as it is old and old as it is new.
>
> —W. E. B. DuBois, "Criteria of Negro Art"

> Without great audiences we cannot have great literature.
>
> —Sterling A. Brown, **"Our Literary Audience"**

> The issue in art is regeneration.
>
> —Duke Ellington

I

The first published illustration of Aaron Douglas, one of the most renowned visual artists of the New Negro Renaissance, appeared in the September 1925 issue of *Opportunity*. This drawing of an African-American runner serves as an illustration to Georgia Douglas Johnson's "The Black Runner," a poem extolling the honor of energetically pursuing goals. Douglas portrays a loin-cloth clad black male, running with his eyes toward the heavens, whose well-defined musculature recalls ancient Greek sculptures of athletes.

Drawn in mid-stride, the runner emerges from a miniature, natural landscape, holding a scroll in his right hand. A large dust cloud rises from the road into the sky, suggesting that his eyes, mind, and action are focused on lofty aims. The road, winding from the foreground into the background of the illustration, suggests that the runner has emerged from the past, and is now planted firmly in the present with his right foot on the ground. His left foot is suspended, anticipating its entry into the future. By combining symbols of intelligence, perseverance, power, and the heroic, Douglas' "Black Runner" reaches beyond the boundaries of its pairing with Douglas Johnson's poem to represent the determined and conscious construction of the New Negro.[1]

This conscious construction is central to the New Negro Renaissance, a cultural and political movement largely propelled by a concern with "how the black writer represented and what he/she represented" (Gates, *Signifying* 177). This concern extended beyond literature to music and art, and influenced the explicitly interdisciplinary nature of this cultural movement. As was language, visual art and music during this period were seen as national possessions. The issue surrounding the spirituals, for instance, was whether they were "merely" folk music or could be seen as a musical tradition as high and celebrated as the German national music of, for example, Mozart and Wagner.[2] In terms of visual art, Alain Locke envisions the development of African-American art as a national endeavor, one that parallels "the development of a national character in the American art of our time" ("The Negro Takes" 136-37). The majority of cultural "treatises" written, however, focused on the central role language played in representing and authenticating the New Negro.

The focus on language by New Negro Renaissance spokespersons was, in part, reflective of American modernist writers and their obsession with creating and reflecting a distinct national literary language. Representative of this moment is H. L. Mencken's *The American Language,* a text "concerned with the omnivorous and ever-forming language of American peoples, and of the effect that language might have on literature" (Hutchinson 321). Mencken stresses the importance of learning the speech of common folk (vulgus), and of distinguishing American speech and culture from that of England.

Language was also viewed as an important means to proving the intellectual and creative capacity of the African American in modernity. The Enlightenment notion that written and spoken language is the concrete proof of reason was espoused by Alexander Crummell. In "The English Language in Liberia" (1860), Crummell argues that mastering the English language is the only means to civilization for the Negro, noting that "[l]anguage, in connection with reason . . . raises man above the lower orders of animals, and in proportion as it is polished and refined, contributes greatly . . . to exalt one nation above another, in the scale of civilization and intellectual dignity" (8). He further asserts that dialect carries "definite marks of inferiority . . . plac [ing it] then at the widest distances from civilized languages" (19). By emphasizing language and its role in representing the New Negro, New Negro Renaissance spokespersons also focused on the necessity of negotiating the claiming of a "standard" English on the one hand and, on the other, the creation of a unique African-American expressivity based on the vernacular.

Not only is language a national possession, but also the central means by which a nation comes into being. As Houston Baker suggests, just as "the codes, statues, declarations, articles, amendments, and constitution of colonial America" create an "American nation . . . [that] is an edifice and enterprise of distinctive and distinguishing words," so too does language serve as a mode of expression in African-American literature, particularly during the New Negro Renaissance (71-72). In this verbal "edifice," words work as bricks, or units, which the writer uses to *sound* a nation into existence. Through this race-specific sounding, African Americans form a cultural nation of their own by placing their selves—displaced within the context of a larger America—in a claimed space. Sounding allows for a transformation of the African-American image from displaced to placed, from dispossessed to possessed, from being a "problem" to becoming a nation.[3]

While I agree that sounding creates a cultural nation that allows for the exercise of various levels of power, what interests me most are the dynamics of vocal transformation within the space of sounding. What exactly is being sounded and by whom? Aaron Douglas' comments on the New Negro Renaissance are telling in this regard:

> [T]he man in the street actually had no thoughts upon [the New Negro Renaissance] as being a matter . . . of cultural importance. But he was a part of it, although . . . he did not actually, consciously make a contribution; he made his contribution in an unconscious way. He was the thing on which and around which this whole idea was developed. And from that standpoint it seems to me his contribution is greater than if he had attempted consciously to make a contribution . . . He didn't mold anything, excepting the thing . . . coming out of him which the various artists responded to, could get hold of and make something that was later known as the Harlem Renaissance.
>
> (119-20)

In the process of "getting hold of" what the folk were emitting and creating a cultural movement from and around it meant essentially that the folk were being "remade" into forms of artistic expression. This transformation of the folk into art was propelled by the desire to prove that the Negro was indeed intelligent and talented. For poets such as Countee Cullen and James Weldon Johnson, of great importance was the establishment of a literary tradition that would reconstruct and situate the African American, thereby gaining acceptance for members of the race in the American literary canon. Their underlying assumption was that discrimination would cease when blacks presented their cultural achievements to the world, since "[n]o people that has produced great literature and art had ever been looked upon by the world as instinctly inferior" (Johnson, *The Book* 9).

But the project of claiming a standard language while simultaneously sounding the folk, the site of the vernacular, or a non-standard language, creates an interesting paradox. For if, as Michel de Certeau suggests, "a body is itself defined, delimited, and articulated by what writes it" (139), how can the folk serve as the foundation of a cultural nation which locates uplift in a language that inherently "unwrites" the folk? In other words, if Locke and other cultural leaders of the New Negro Renaissance were sounding the masses into and as a nation, how do we reconcile their simultaneous discomfort with the language generally associated with the folk? What does "the folk" become in this sounding? How do artists of the period engage with, react to, and enact this sounding?

This essay is an examination of the ways in which the folk—occupying the site of the everyday—and dialect are deployed by poet and cultural critic Sterling A. Brown. Brown is very self-conscious in his making the folk as audience central to the creation and reception of his work and in his relationship to the images he deploys. He also reacts directly to New Negro Renaissance debates concerning the place of the everyday and dialect in representing the New Negro. Because of Brown's self-consciousness and his role as a direct descendant of New Negro Renaissance poets, this discussion will help to illuminate New Negro Renaissance poetics in general, and Brown's poetics in particular.

II

Although the folk was central to the refashioning of African-American images, and served as a source of creative and spiritual inspiration, dialect was often viewed as limiting and underdeveloped during the New Negro Renaissance. Responding to the New Negro Renaissance concern about the limited expressivity of the vernacular, or dialect, Sterling A. Brown remarks that:

> Dialect, or the speech of the people, is capable of expressing whatever the people are. And the folk Negro is a great deal more than a buffoon or a plaintive minstrel. Poets more intent upon learning the ways of the folk, their speech, and their character, that is to say, better poets, could have smashed the mold. But first they would have to believe in what they were doing. And this was difficult in a period of conciliation and middle class striving for recognition and respectability.[4]

As Brown suggests here, the perception of the vernacular's poetic limitations stemmed not from the mode of language itself but from the stereotyped contexts with which dialect was often associated. While James Weldon Johnson argues that "for poetry the dialect has only two main stops, humor and pathos," he recognizes that these expressive and representative limitations are "due to conventions that have been fixed upon the dialect and the conformity to them by individual writers" (*The Book* 4). Although many contemporary critics read Johnson as disdaining the use of dialect whole-heartedly, I agree with Richard Carroll's view that "[i]n Johnson's opinion, there was not so much wrong with dialect in itself. The trouble was that it had been cast in the mold of a stereotyped tradition, and this tradition did not reflect the spirit of the black man himself but what the white man thought him to be" (359). If Carroll is correct, Johnson is calling not for a rejection but a redefinition of dialect and a folk poet with the ability to thoroughly accomplish the task.

Such a task, however, was and is wrought with tension, particularly at the height of the New Negro Renaissance. In his insightful study *The Dialect of Modernism,* Michael North notes that

> For African-American poets of this generation . . . dialect is a 'chain.' In the version created by the white minstrel tradition, it is a constant reminder of the literal unfreedom of slavery and the political and cultural repression that followed emancipation. Both symbol and actuality, it stands for a most intimate invasion whereby the dominant actually attempts to create the thoughts of the subordinate by providing it speech.
>
> (11)

Couched within minstrel traditions and marking the site of the primitive and uncivilized, the use of dialect by an African-American writer hindered the process of claiming, placing, and sounding one's self as modern subject.

While dialect as the linguistic sign of ultimate difference functioned as a "chain" for African-American writers, dialect became a means to freedom and self-creation for the "mainstream" modernist writer. Generally, the 1920s was a time when writers were rebelling against the rising tide of language standardization, most notably marked by the first publication of the *OED* in the 1880s (North 11-12). For writers like T.S. Eliot, Gertrude Stein, and H. D., dialect, particularly that of the African American, became an essential means to breaking through a stable and "normal" English language to a space of self-realization ironically formed by the language of the Other. Consequently, as North argues, "[l]inguistic imitation and racial masquerade are so important to transatlantic modernism because they allow the writer to play at self-fashioning" (11). These poets, however, are also attempting to estrange the reader from this language (at least when the reader is presumed to be white). It seems, then, that in addition to allowing for self-fashioning, they also see dialect as fragmented and self-alienating.

The tension between dialect and its limiting contexts presents a problem not only to the African-American writer/producers of the New Negro, but to the notion of producing the New Negro itself. The New Negro Renaissance project pivots on what I term an anxiety of production, which affects both the production of an African-American nation in modernity, or "body politic," and the fixed and embodied image as figured in the New Negro. This tension between the disembodied and embodied reenacts the problem in what Karen Sanchez-Eppler refers to as "the incorporeal national ideal of a free and equal American citizenry" (3). American citizens are disembodied through codification, thus contrasting the "body politic" with the bodies that comprise the nation. As Sanchez-Eppler explains:

> The relation of the social and political structures of the "body politic" to the fleshy specificity of embodied identities has generally been masked behind the constitutional language of abstracted and implicitly bodiless "persons," so that, for example, it did not seem absurd for the founding fathers to reckon slaves as "three-fifths of a person."
>
> (1)

While the New Negro Renaissance seeks to remedy this exclusionary representation of nationhood by placing the New Negro within a claimed and reconstructed space, this project takes on characteristics of American nation building. In other words, the sounding of a nation, while disrupting the hegemony of an American nation, then deploys similar acts of bodily masking in order to position a reconstituted black nation. It is in this complicated paradoxical space that the issue of production—the product referred to as "the New Negro" and the larger project termed the "New Negro Renaissance"—becomes problematic.

III

In "Popular Culture," John Fiske examines the differences between "popular" and "mass" culture. The "popular," while referencing the majority's desires, also signifies the interests of "the people," "a shifting set of social interests and positions defined by a subordinate relationship to dominant society" (322). Mass culture, on the other hand, is an amalgamation of high and popular culture, and appears in industrial societies, where technology allows for the mass or widespread (re)production of cultural materials. While popular and mass culture, then, are always connected, the former functions by appropriating the products of the latter: "Popular culture [then] is more a culture of process than of products" (323, my emphasis). Thus, popular culture has the ability to disrupt mass culture for "[it] is performed not by universal aesthetic criteria of quality, but by socially located criteria of relevance" (327).

It is the folk and dialect—spaces of the everyday—that problematize the products termed "New Negro Renaissance" and "New Negro." The folk, as represented in the everyday by writers such as Sterling Brown and Langston Hughes, disrupt any mass image produced by New Negro Renaissance spokespersons. Hughes' autobiography *The Big Sea,* for instance, embodies an anti-production stance. His discussions of writing poetry in particular stress process over product:

> [T]here are seldom many changes in my poems, once they're down. Generally, the first two or three lines come to me from something I'm thinking about, or looking at, or doing, and the rest of the poem (if there is to be a poem) flows from those first few lines, usually right away. If there is a chance to put the poem down then, I write it down. If not, I try to remember it until I get to a pencil and paper; for poems are like rainbows: they escape you quickly.
>
> (56)

In addition, Hughes insists on the New Negro Renaissance's failure, thereby undermining any power it may contain as a cultural product.

While Hughes declares the Renaissance's end, Brown insists on the movement's continuation well beyond the Depression. He views this cultural movement as a project that could be referred to in terms of Duke Ellington's notion of regeneration, the constant evolution of artistic expression, or with regards to Zora Neale Hurston's definition of "originality."[5] While both Brown and Hughes operate against the grain of production, Hughes attempts to negotiate production by adopting a common modernist notion of "words magically appearing on the page," while Brown reconceptualizes the Renaissance and folk poetry as a movement, as a continual becoming.[6]

As evidenced by his comment on dialect which I referenced earlier, Brown has more room to maneuver as a "poet of the folk" than does Hughes. His ability to critique the use or lack thereof of dialect by earlier New Negro Renaissance writers in this manner has much to do with the time at which he published his first volume of poetry. ***Southern Road*** was published in 1932, near the end of general notions of the New Negro Renaissance. Because Brown's literary precursors constructed a space in which black writers could situate themselves, Brown was able to further expand the boundaries of black poetic expression.

IV

Along with this chronological "advantage," Brown possessed the understanding needed to write folk poetry; he knew the importance of listening. His status as a "better poet," a poet who heard and expressed the range of the folk in his poetry, won him acclaim from James Weldon Johnson:

> [Brown] infused his poetry with genuine characteristic flavor by adopting as his medium the common, racy, living speech of the Negro in certain phases of real life . . . He has made more than mere transcriptions of folk poetry, and he has done more than bring it to mere artistry; he has deepened its meanings and multiplied its implications . . . In a word, he has taken this raw material and worked it into original and authentic poetry.
>
> ("Introduction" 16-17)

This introductory remark to Brown's ***Southern Road*** is a coming full-circle of the New Negro Renaissance. Johnson had found a poet who could write the multiple possibilities of folk language onto the page and into poetic form.

Brown's ability to deepen the meanings of folk poetry has much to do with his role as what I term a *listening poet.* That is, Brown saw the role of the audience as central to the creation and reception of his poetry. His aesthetic is informed by his notion that "[w]ithout great audiences we cannot have great literature" (**"Our Literary"** 122). He was concerned with both creating that audience and writing the great literature which that audience could both receive and assist in making. Brown writes: "I have . . . a deep concern with the development of a literature worthy of our past, and of our destiny; without which literature certainly, we can never come to much. I have a deep concern with the development of an audience worthy of such a literature" (114).

What is interesting is Brown's complex and fluid conception of a literary audience. His audience includes readers/listeners of literature (who will both consume and assist in creating literature) and the poet. In this move, Brown makes listening an important figure in literary and cultural expressivity and emphasizes the importance of individualization. Listening becomes a central means of gathering information and knowledge about the folk and folkways of which he writes. Writing poetry, then, is transmission of that knowledge gained through the sensual experience of listening. In his poetic positionality as audience member and simultaneous insistence on the seamless connection between poet and audience member, Brown works to narrow the gap between oral and written, between poet and the folk.[7] Overall, Brown's poetics are a movement from the notion of spokespersons sounding the folk to a writing of a discourse that allows the folk to sound like themselves.

Brown demonstrates the ability to negotiate the limits of what de Certeau terms the "scriptural economies" through which his work appears. This negotiation entails blurring the often stiffly drawn lines between the oral and written. Brown accomplishes this by keying into the sites of orality that are embedded within written forms. As de Certeau observes, the voices of oral traditions "can no longer be heard except within the interior of the scriptural systems where they recur. They move about like dancers, passing lightly through the field of the other" (131).

But, while de Certeau locates bourgeois power in the scriptural, I would argue that Brown contests this notion by illustrating poetic power in his ability to engage with both oral and scriptural economies without making sharp distinctions between the two. Such negotiation, as well as the positing of a complex, fluid audience, is evident in Brown's **"Ma Rainey,"** a poem that in part explores listening as an important figure in African-American poetic expressivity.

V

Although **"Ma Rainey"** is not technically a blues poem, Brown suffuses it with various blues elements.[8] For example, the poem presents a reflection on the dynamic relationship between performer and audience. It also records a traumatic group experience through the individual utterance of that experience with the use of graphic imagery.

Every aspect of "Backwater Blues"—the song itself and as record of the disastrous Floods of 1927, and the singer who performs it—provides the main framework for this poem. Paul Oliver offers a poignant and concise account of the natural disaster. Since it so vividly captures the scene, I shall quote it here at length:

> No one had anticipated the full horror of the 1927 floods. Houses were washed away with their terrified occupants still clinging to the roof-tops; the carcasses of cattle and mules floated in the swirling, deep brown water; isolated figures whom none could rescue were last seen crying for help as they hung in the gaunt branches of shattered trees. Dressers and table-tops, clothes and toys were caught in the driftwood and floating timber, to twist madly in a sudden whirlpool, and then sweep out of sight in the surging, eddying, boiling waters which extended as far as the eye could see.
>
> (Henderson 36)

After this natural disaster, blacks suffered even more because of corrupt landlords overseeing federal relief programs. Both "Backwater Blues" and Brown's poem act as a historical record, musically and literally recording this disaster. This song is also a communal memory of the floods and of Ma Rainey as performer, so Brown chooses to focus on a piece of history and of Rainey's career that is readily recognizable by the folk.

Brown's poem opens with a panoramic description of the frenzy invoked upon Ma Rainey's arrival to town:

> When Ma Rainey
> Comes to town,
> Folks from anyplace
> Miles aroun',
> From Cape Girardeau,
> Poplar Bluff,
> Flocks in to hear
> Ma do her stuff.
>
> (ll. 1-8)

The tone here is celebratory, as expressed through the high level of physical movement and the short, staccato-like lines, which quicken the pace of the verse. Within this compressed space, Brown captures the excitement of Ma Rainey's arrival. Note that Ma Rainey is an aural attraction (the folk come "to hear / Ma do her stuff").[9]

Note also that the subject of this first verse is the people who travel to listen. In writing the poem from the perspective of the people who will constitute the audience, Brown emphasizes the importance of reception in the making of poetry. As Paul Zumthor notes in his discussion of oral poetry,

> Audience members 'take part' in the performance. The roles they play contribute no less than that of the interpreter. Poetry, therefore, is what is [received]; but its reception is a unique, fleeting, irreversible act, and an individual one.
>
> (183)

While the audience comes together in a common space and for a common event, thereby creating a temporary community, the role of the individual listener within that community is crucial. This will become more evident throughout this discussion, but Brown multiplies the implications of audience participation by focusing on the group as comprised of individual listeners. Thus, the response to Ma Rainey's performance is not one of a homogeneous group, but of listeners speaking from the authority of their own experience.

Brown complicates the notion of audience further by including himself as poet within it. As I discussed earlier, Brown viewed the poet's role as an audience member, listening and transmitting what is heard onto the page. The poet, then, functions not only as a mediator but also as a part of the listening public. In the second stanza, for instance, the perspective becomes more particular and focused as the poem's persona surmises the audience's emotional state:

> An' some jokers keeps deir laughs a-goin' in de crowded aisles,
> An' some folks sits dere waitin' wid deir aches an' miseries,
> Till Ma comes out before dem, a-smilin' gold-toofed smiles
> An' Long Boy ripples minors on de black an' yellow keys.
>
> (ll. 23-26)

In contrast to the first verse, the lines of the second verse are longer, and have a slower rhythm. The longer line reflects the diminished movement of the folk. It also suggests that the wait for this performance seems long to those who wait for relief through the song. The presence of the narrator / poet in the poem in no way interrupts the poem's prioritizing of the audience's perspective, nor does it interfere with the reader's ability to grasp the scene, for "[i]n the [spoken] the physical presence of the speaker is more or less attenuated; it tends to blend into the circumstances" (Zumthor 142). In this blending with the event, the speaker's ability to draw us into the scene, making us feel as if we are present at this event, is heightened.

In this verse in particular, Brown employs very vivid imagery which demonstrates his locating African-American expressive possibilities in the folk. As Stephen Henderson notes in his insightful essay on the blues energies in Brown's poetry, "Sterling Brown consciously deepened the meanings and multiplied the implications of a Black American folk base . . . by his skillful selection and synthesis of the imagery" (34). First, in the lines quoted above, Brown conflates the piano and Ma Rainey, describing the ebony and ivory keys as "black an' yellow." While it is possible that the ivory keys were discolored because the piano was aged, I think that the yellow also refers to Rainey's "gold toofed" smile. In this move, Brown emphasizes Rainey's voice as the instrument to be listened to. Her voice, not the piano, is the true blues instrument.

Even more poignant is Brown's conspicuous insertion of flood imagery:

> Dey stumble in de hall, jes a-laughin' an' a-cacklin',
> Cheerin' lak roarin' water, lak wind in river swamps.
>
> (ll. 21-22)

Brown creatively references the disaster in describing the movement of the crowd, conflating audience and disaster just like he conflates Rainey and the piano. In doing so, he suggests that they are a more true record than he or anyone else who did not live through the experience could provide. These folk carry the memory of the flood within them.

The fourth verse introduces a communal voice into the poem. The pronouns progress from "you" to "us" to "we," suggesting that Ma Rainey and her listeners are a community. Rainey is not an outsider; she is singing from within. The lines act as a response to Rainey's musical call in the preceding verse. They also act to prompt Rainey along, and to inform her that her listeners are aware of (and in need of hearing) her musical message:

> O Ma Rainey
> Sing yo' song;
> Now you's back
> Whah you belong,
> Git way inside us,
> Keep us strong. . . .
> O Ma Rainey,
> Li'l an' low;
> Sing us 'bout de hard luck
> Roun' our do';
> Sing us 'bout de lonesome road
> We mus' go. . . .
>
> (ll. 27-38)

Although these lines are truncated like those of the first verse, their rhythm slows. Brown employs assonance in effect to clog the poetic line, making it difficult to speak them quickly. In using this device, Brown emphasizes aurality, for assonance essentially is an aural device. The punctuation—repeated ellipses, multiple use of semicolons and commas, and the absence of end-stopped lines—indicates a dragging, burdened, continuing rhythm.

Ma Rainey takes on the persona of a lay minister testifying, possessing the sermonic message that will speak of the congregation's pains and move toward a hopeful view. The listeners and Ma Rainey both possess this song. Her audience tells her to "sing yo' song," which is also its song, for it is the song (read: situation) they know. And it is the song that gives Rainey access to their pained hearts in order to make them strong enough to cope with the trying times ahead. Her voice works like the balm in Gilead, healing the souls of these flood ravaged folk.

Brown switches the perspective and voice of the poem once again in the fourth and final verse. The voice moves from the communal "we" of the previous stanza to that of one man who is of the audience. He recounts Ma Rainey's performance of "Backwater Blues," noting that "She jes' catch hold of us, somekindaway" (l. 52). It is interesting that the folk gets voiced individually rather than as a collective utterance. Part of the problem with dialect was exactly the tendency for it to represent the sameness of black-ness, a collective comprised of individually nuanced voices so that they all point back to a single reduced stereotype. In this move from the collective to the individual, it is evident that Brown learned from Paul Laurence Dunbar's poetry and Charles Chestnutt's fiction that individualization in the use of the vernacular was crucial.

Instead of describing the way the crowd felt after the performance, Brown allows one of the folk to express his response to the performance and, in that, the sentiments of the communal "whole." Then Brown allows the blues, in the same way, to speak for themselves:

> *'It rained fo' days an' de skies was dark as night,*
> *Trouble taken place in de lowlands at night.*
>
> *'Thundered an' lightened an' the storm begin to roll*
> *Thousan's of people ain't got no place to go.*
>
> *'Den I went an' stood upon some high ol' lonesome hill,*
> *An' looked down on the place where I used to live.'*
>
> (ll 42-47)

Just as he places the fellow's comment in quotation marks, he places the poetically adapted lyrics in quotes to stress their orality. The words are not transcribed exactly from Ma Rainey's performance. Instead, Brown captures the main point of each three line stanza in the song in two summarizing lines each, all the while maintaining the blues flavor of the piece.

What is so masterful about this poem is Brown's maintenance of oral qualities even within this necessarily fixed literary medium of expression (i.e., a poem in print). Part of his ability to accomplish this fluidity despite the limitations of print media lies in his allowing the blues, and in particular the "Backwater Blues," to speak for themselves. But even before that pointed moment in the poem, the piece feels full of orality. The poem is obviously influenced by its suffusion of the blues. The level of voice/listener is constantly changing from one verse to another, using these verses as individual "musical" movements, carrying the poem along. These changing levels allow the poem to exist as a "fluidly printed" text. Although the words of the song do not appear until the last stanza of the poem, the listener/reader knows the song is there, hovering behind the words of the poem, resonating in this literary form. The melody lies behind the text, propelling it along.

The song resonates so much in the fabric of the poem that it literally moves into the voice of the fellow commenting on the event. After the song is sung in the poem, the fellow goes on to say:

> An' den de folks, dey natchally bowed dey heads an' cried,
> Bowed dey heavy heads, shet dey moufs up tight an' cried,
> An' Ma lef' de stage, an' followed some de folks outside.
>
> (ll. 48-50)

Brown renders this portion of the fellow's commentary in the traditional blues form, suggesting the major impact Ma Rainey's blues has on the listener. His response is improvised in that it is "made on the spot," but is informed and inscribed by what the commentator heard and felt during the performance.[10] The parallel change Brown makes in adverbs from "somekindaway" (l. 40) to "dataway" (l. 52) reflects this improvisation. The poem ends with the folk's observation: "She jes' gits hold of us dataway" (l. 52). The adverbs move from the nonspecific to the specific. The fellow cannot specifically define how Ma Rainey gets inside the audience until she actually sings her song, which occurs in the italicized space of this last verse.

This centrality of the performer to the production of emotional response is central to oral poetry and its reception/production. Zumthor notes that

> In every exercise of oral poetry, the role of the performer counts more than that of the composer(s). Not that it eclipses it entirely, but it is apparent in the performance that it contributes all the more to determining auditory, corporeal, emotive reactions of the audience, the nature and the intensity of its pleasure
>
> (168)

While the speaker or narrator of the event previously and quite vividly relates the scene to the reader, it is by and through the actual performance and the witnessing of that performance that emotional expression and healing takes place. The last line of the poem points back to

"Backwater Blues" as a direct illustration of what the man means, and also allows the folk to have the last word, thereby emphasizing the central role the folk play in Brown's poetry.

By employing the song's "lyrics," Brown also notes that the blues cannot be fixed. They are an oral/aural form that emerges during their performance, so that the speaker lets the performance take place before he ventures to explain how the blues "gits inside" the listener. At this point in the poem, he can gesture back to how the blues work. Brown cannot and will not describe the blues; they must describe themselves.

While Brown functions as mediator of oral and written forms, a role which complicates the notion of his full inclusion in Ma Rainey's audience, the poem seems to insist on the inseparable nature of artist and audience. Like the audience, Brown is meditating on his reaction to Ma Rainey upon seeing her perform. He, in effect, acts as a spectator, a role fundamental to poetic reception, while transmitting the experience. In this role, Brown

> recreat[es] for his own use . . . the signifying universe that is being transmitted to him. The traces that this re-creation impress on him belong to his intimate life and do not necessarily and immediately appear outside. But it may happen that they are exteriorized in a new performance: the spectator becomes, in turn, interpreter, and on his lips, in his gesture, the poem is modified perhaps radically. Hence, in part, traditions are enriched and transformed.
>
> (Zumthor 183-84)

Brown, then, enacts a kind of doubling as both listener and coauthor of the event. Like Ma Rainey's audience, he listens—to the audience, the singer, the accompanying music, and the raging waters of the floods—and lays it down for us to hear.

Standing on the edge of the New Negro Renaissance and at the threshold of a generally more overtly political African-American literature of the 1940s, Sterling Brown listened and wrote the blues music form into poetry. He believed in "the validity, the power, the beauty of folk culture," and left us believing as well.

Notes

1. Although Alain Locke was the first to apply the term "New Negro" to this movement, Henry Louis Gates, Jr. notes that the term was defined in the 1745 edition of *London Magazine* as the phrase enslaved blacks used to describe those "newly brought from Africa." Gates notes that, even at this early point, the term conjured notions of "a temporal order of succession and the ahistorical dimensions of the American experience . . . [it] also denotes a direct spatial association with Africa, implying a state of consciousness that is perhaps a form of racial dignity or integrity, an 'organic community.'" See Henry Louis Gates, Jr., "The Faces and Voice of Blackness" (xxxv).
2. W. E. B. DuBois suggests that spirituals, "the sole American music," are "the single spiritual heritage of the nation and the greatest gift of the Negro people." See *The Souls of Black Folk* (378).
3. Alain Locke suggests in *The New Negro: An Interpretation* that this creation of a cultural nation is integral to forging alternative bonds between and among African-American people:

    > The chief bond between [American Negroes] has been that of a common condition rather than a common consciousness; a problem in common rather than a life in common. In Harlem, Negro life is seizing upon its first chances for group expression and self-determination. It is—or promises at least to be—a race capital . . . Without pretense to their political significance, Harlem has the same role to play for the New Negro as Dublin has had for the New Ireland or Prague for the New Czechoslovakia.
    >
    > (7)
4. See Brown's introduction to *The Negro Caravan.*
5. Hurston writes, "What we really mean by originality is the modification of ideas" (58).
6. In this constant emphasis on process, Brown negotiates the gap between the folk that he seeks to represent in his poetry and the "high form" in which he writes. In other words, he creates an in-between, a poetry that is neither "high" nor "low."
7. Langston Hughes is also a listening poet. As Arnold Rampersad argues, "[I]n his willingness to stand back and record, with minimal intervention as a craftsman, aspects of the drama of black religion or black music, Hughes had clearly shown already that he saw his own art as inferior to that of either black musicians or religionists . . . At the heart of his sense of inferiority . . . was the knowledge that he stood to a great extent outside the culture he worshipped" (64). But, unlike Hughes, Brown insists on his belonging to the folk. Thus, the anxiety that is apparent in Hughes' poetry is not present explicitly in Brown's and, I would argue, allows him in part to expand the expressive possibilities of folk poetry.
8. "Ma Rainey" is not written in traditional blues form—aa'b—where the first line introduces a theme, the second line repeats that theme with a difference, and the third line resolves the verse. Brown's "New St. Louis Blues," for instance, is a poem in traditional blues form:

    > Market Street woman is known fuh to have dark days,
    > Market Street woman noted fuh to have dark days,
    > Life do her dirty in a hundred onery ways.
    >
    > (ll. 1-3)
9. In these lines, Brown also manages to record the general geography of the Backwater region. See Henderson's "The Heavy Blues of Sterling Brown" (37).
10. Duke Ellington's comments on improvisation are suggestive here:

> [t]he word "improvisation" has great limitations, because when musicians are given solo responsibility they already have a suggestion of a melody written for them . . . Anyone who plays anything worth hearing knows what he's going to play, no matter whether he prepares a day ahead or a beat ahead. It has to be with intent.
>
> (Ellington 465)

Works Cited

Baker, Houston A., Jr. *Modernism and the Harlem Renaissance.* Chicago: University of Chicago Press, 1987.

Brown, Sterling A. *The Collected Poems of Sterling A. Brown.* Ed. Michael Harper. New York: Harper & Row, 1989.

———. "Our Literary Audience." *Speech and Power: The African-American Essay and its Cultural Content from Polemics to Pulpit.* Vol. 2. Ed. Gerald Early. Hopewell, NJ: The Echo Press, 1993.

———, ed. *The Negro Caravan.* New York: Arno Press, 1969.

Carroll, Richard. "James Weldon Johnson Spiritual Blackness." *Black American Literature Journal* 4 (Spring 1982).

Crummell, Alexander. *The Future of Africa.* New York: Charles Scribner, 1862.

de Certeau, Michel. *The Practice of Everyday Life.* Berkeley: University of California Press, 1984.

Douglas, Aaron. "Aaron Douglas Chats about the Harlem Renaissance." *The Harlem Renaissance Reader.* Ed. David Levering Lewis. New York: Penguin Books, 1994.

DuBois, W. E. B. "Criteria of Negro Art."

———. *The Souls of Black Folk. Three Negro Classics.* Ed. John Hope Franklin. New York: Avon Books, 1965.

Ellington, Duke. *Music is My Mistress.* New York: DaCapo Press, Inc., 1973.

Fiske, John. "Popular Culture." *Critical Terms for Literary Study.* Ed. Frank Lentricchia and Thomas McLaughlin. Chicago: University of Chicago Press, 1995.

Gates, Henry Louis, Jr. "The Faces and Voice of Blackness." *Facing History: The Black Image in American Art 1710-1940.* Ed. Guy C. McElroy. San Francisco: Bedford Arts, 1990.

———. *The Signifying Monkey: A Theory of African-American Literary Criticism.* New York: Oxford University Press, 1988.

Henderson, Stephen. "The Heavy Blues of Sterling Brown: A Study of Craft and Tradition." *Black American Literature Forum* 14 (Spring 1980).

Hughes, Langston. *The Big Sea.* New York: Hill and Wang, 1995.

Hurston, Zora Neale. *The Sanctified Church: The Folklore Writings of Zora Neale Hurston.* Berkeley: Turtle Island, 1981.

Hutchinson, George. *The Harlem Renaissance in Black and White.* Cambridge, MA: Harvard University Press, 1995.

Johnson, James Weldon. *The Book of American Negro Poetry.* New York: Harcourt, Brace, and World, 1931.

———. "Introduction to *Southern Road.*" *The Collected Poems of Sterling A. Brown.* Ed. Michael Harper. New York: Harper & Row Publishers, 1989.

Locke, Alain. "The Negro Takes His Place in American Art." *The Harlem Renaissance Reader.* Ed. David Levering Lewis. New York: Penguin Books, 1994.

———, ed. *The New Negro: An Interpretation.* New York: Arno Press, 1968.

North, Michael. *The Dialect of Modernism: Race, Language, and Twentieth-Century Literature.* New York: Oxford University Press, 1994.

Rampersad, Arnold. *The Life of Langston Hughes.* New York: Oxford University Press, 1986-1988.

Sanchez-Eppler, Karen. *Touching Liberty: Abolition, Feminism, and the Politics of the Body.* Berkeley: University of California Press, 1993.

Zumthor, Paul. *Oral Poetry: An Introduction.* Minneapolis: University of Minnesota Press, 1990.

DAVID ANDERSON (ESSAY DATE 1998)

SOURCE: Anderson, David. "Sterling Brown's Southern Strategy: Poetry as Cultural Evolution in *Southern Road.*" *Callaloo* 21, no. 4 (fall 1998): 1023-37.

In the following essay, Anderson considers Brown's Southern Road *to be more than an attempt to preserve African American Southern oral traditions, characterizing the work as an effort to adapt the Black urban communities to a new cultural production of art. Anderson also provides close readings of several poems.*

With the publication of ***Southern Road*** in 1932, Sterling Brown portrayed, and sought to address, what he perceived to be a profound cultural crisis facing African Americans: the gradual disappearance of their rural cultures as they entered the urban, industrialized economies of the North and South, and their consequent loss of autonomous art. Brown especially feared the loss of folklore, which he believed helped African-American culture renew itself, not only by preserving and strengthening traditions and social practices, but also by serving as a conduit through which individuals devised and communicated new strategies for surviving racial oppression. Once African Americans moved to urban areas, Brown believed that they would no longer produce songs and stories reflecting their communities' needs and interests and, accordingly, would no longer devise and communicate new strategies for survival. Instead, he feared they would passively consume a bigoted popular culture, or worse yet, be coopted into producing art that pandered to the economic demands and stereotypes of the dominant culture.

In response, ***Southern Road*** was not merely an attempt to preserve oral traditions on the printed page, but to adapt the cultural production of art in black communities to an urban, capitalist society. In a close reading of **"Strong Men,"** I examine Brown's portrayal of folklore as an evolving cultural process that adapts and preserves traditions despite external changes and threats. In addition, with readings of **"Children's Children"** and **"Cabaret,"** I discuss Brown's portrayal of mass culture and commercialism as threats both to folk traditions and to artistic creation. Finally, I examine Brown's attempt to write poetry that, despite the distance between writer and audience, could perform many of the social functions traditionally performed by folklore.

Although numerous scholars praise Brown's poetry for its realism, cultural authenticity, and portrayal of folklore's social usefulness, they do not analyze Brown's ideas concerning folklore's role in cultural evolution—specifically, art's role in adapting cultural practices to social or environmental changes or threats. For instance, such scholars as Stephen Henderson, Charles Rowell, and Joanne Gabbin have written extensively on Brown's reliance on vernacular traditions, and both John Wright and Gabbin discuss Brown's portrayal of folklore's functions within the black community, such as maintaining group values, identities, traditions, and loyalties. Nevertheless, these studies do not emphasize Brown's conception of culture as a process and folklore's important role within that process, so that black culture and consciousness in these works often seems unitary and static, even transhistorical—that is, exempt, to quote Ronald Radano, from "the circumstances of political, cultural, and social change" (73). Even when Houston Baker notes the "self-conscious evolutionism" of the final "Vestiges" section of ***Southern Road,*** in which Brown cordons off his early Romantic poetry as an aesthetic dead end, Baker reads the section only as Brown's comment about his artistic development, not as a broader comment about the relationship between African-American art and culture (Baker 100; see Brown, ***Collected Poems*** 115).[1]

Nevertheless, Brown's criticism and poetry overtly link artistic production to cultural evolution and group survival. For instance, in arguing for realistic portrayals of all elements of black life, not merely of the educated and middle class, Brown wrote:

> We are cowed. We have become typically bourgeois. Natural though such an evolution is, if we are *all* content with evasion of life, with personal complacency, we as a group are doomed.
> (**"Our Literary Audience"** 46)

Brown presented this threat in **"Tin Roof Blues,"** the penultimate section in ***Southern Road*** which documents the social problems wrought by the Great Migration. Some recent migrants suffer from social alienation:

> Gang of dicties here, an' de rest want to git dat
> way,
> Dudes an' dicties, others strive to git dat way,
> Put pennies on de numbers from now unto de
> jedgement day.
> (***Collected Poems*** 102.10-12)

Others experience personal and sexual insecurity (**"Effie"**), cultural alienation (**"Children's Children"**), conspicuous consumption (**"Mecca," "Sporting Beasley"**), sexual exploitation (**"Chillen Get Shoes," "Harlem Street Walkers"**), and cultural co-optation (**"Cabaret"**).

The ten "Vestiges" poems which follow **"Tin Roof Blues"** in ***Southern Road*** are an evolutionary dead end because they ignore social problems for the sake of literariness—ostentatious titles (**"Nous n'irons plus au bois . . ."**), apostrophe, hyphenated adjectives, inverted word order, and literary allusions:

> . . . gone
> Is all your arrant nimble grace,
> And worms preposterous feed upon
> The sweet flesh of your lovely face . . .
> (**"Against That Day,"** ***Collected Poems*** 125.5-8)

As Maureen Honey has noted, most African-American poets in the 1920s and early 1930s used British Romantic poetry as models for their own writings and favored such forms or elements as "[t]he sonnet, the ode, the elegy, and classical allusion" (6). Accordingly, these "Vestiges" poems reflect the forms, themes, and diction common among such well-published New Negro poets as Claude McKay, Countee Cullen, and Georgia Douglas Johnson, including six sonnets, an ode to the poet Anne Spencer (**"To a Certain Lady, in Her Garden"**), a blank verse meditation (**"Mill Mountain"**), and even imagistic free verse (**"Thoughts of Death"**). Their themes are well-worn, ranging from the racial protest sonnet (**"Salutamus"**), to pastoral (**"Return," "Nous n'irons plus au bois . . ."**), to death and the fleetingness of beauty and love (**"Thoughts of Death," "Challenge," "Telling Fortunes," "Against That Day"**). Absent from these poems are any attempts to portray everyday rural life, dialect, and expressive conventions that characterize much of his mature work—for instance, the earthy humor of a tall-tale teller in **"Slim in Atlanta"**:

Down in Atlanta,
De whitefolks got laws
For to keep all de niggers
From laughin' outdoors.

Hope to Gawd I may die
If I ain't speakin' truth
Make de niggers do deir laughin'
In a telefoam booth.

(***Collected Poems*** 81.1-8)

Indeed, these Vestiges poems exemplify the aesthetic equivalent of the social alienation, breakdown, and vulnerability cataloged in **"Tin Roof Blues,"** particularly since they illustrate a gulf separating poetic creation from community interest, to the detriment of both. By contrast, Brown desired that literature, similar to folklore, participate in the cultural process of constructing, communicating, negotiating, and re-constructing social practices and beliefs—notions of heroism, appropriate behaviors, world-views, the meanings and values of rituals, and so on.

For instance, Brown portrays folklore's dynamic role in cultural evolution in his poem **"Strong Men."** Charles Rowell has aptly described this poem as a portrayal of "black people's strength to survive in the face of racism and economic exploitation" (326). Yet the poem portrays not only a static "stoicism" (326), but also African-American folk culture as a kind of Darwinian juggernaut—a process that selects adaptive responses to an oppressive environment and leads to a stronger people and culture. As the speaker says at the end of the poem, "*One thing they [whites] cannot prohibit—*/ The strong men . . . coming on / The strong men gittin' stronger" (***Collected Poems*** 57-58.62-64).

The poem enacts this process of cultural development through its rhetorical structure, presenting catalogues of racial oppression followed by excerpts from folk songs, culminating in the refrain "The strong men git stronger" (Rowell 326):

They broke you in like oxen,
They scourged you,
They branded you,
They made your women breeders,
They swelled your numbers with bastards. . . .
They taught you the religion they disgraced.

You sang:
Keep a-inchin' along
Lak a po' inch worm. . . .

You sang:
Bye and bye
I'm gonna lay down dis heaby load. . . .

You sang:
Walk togedder, chillen,
Dontcha git weary. . . .
The strong men keep a-comin' on
The strong men git stronger.

(***Collected Poems*** 56.5-21)

As the poem unfolds as a pattern of abuse and cultural response, we witness the folk devising and communicating strategies for action (*"Keep a-inchin' along," "Walk togedder, chillen, / Dontcha git weary"*) and constructing a world-view (*"Bye and bye / I'm gonna lay down dis heaby load"*) (ll. 12, 18-19, 15-16). Additionally, we witness a folk tradition taking form, and with it the reinforcement of group identity and solidarity (with the constant juxtaposition of "they" and "you") and the growth of political sophistication and power as the community moves from stoicism (*"Keep a-inchin' along / Lak a po' inch worm. . . ."*) to group effort (*"Walk togedder, chillen, / Dontcha git weary"*) to pride (*"Ain't no hammah / In dis lan', / Strikes lak mine, bebby, / Strikes lak mine"*) to political reflection (*"They bought off some of your leaders / . . . / You followed a way. / Then laughed as usual"*) and ultimately to the point of contemporary revolutionary action (ll. 12-13, 18-19, 27-30, 41, 43-45).

Yet Brown did not usually portray African-American life as inevitable evolutionary progress, but rather as a series of necessary adaptations in the grim, Malthusian struggle for subsistence.[2] For instance, farmers and sharecroppers in the section entitled **"On Restless River"** often fight against storms, floods, and other natural disasters that threaten to annihilate them and their ways of life. In **"Old King Cotton,"** the economic precariousness of sharecroppers renders them all the more vulnerable to the vicissitudes of nature:

Buy one rusty mule
To git ahead—
We stays in debt
Until we'se dead;

Ef flood don't git us
It's de damn bo' weevil
Crap grass in de drought,
Or somp'n else evil;

Ef we gits de bales
When de hard luck's gone,
Bill at de commissary
Goes right on.

(***Collected Poems*** 64.17-28)

Similarly, the flooding Missouri River in **"Foreclosure"** is described as a senile "treacherous skinflint" (***Collected Poems*** 70.19) who "gratuitously" loans out rich farmland (l.3), then seizes it and whatever prized possessions the farmers place upon it. Even in the "Tornado Blues" portion of the triptych **"New St. Louis Blues,"** natural and economic calamity occur hand in hand:

Dey got some ofays, but dey mostly got de Jews
an' us,
Got some ofays, but mostly got de Jews an' us,
Many po' boys castle done settled to a heap o'
dus'.

. . . . .

Foun' de moggidge unpaid, foun' de insurance
long past due,
Moggidge unpaid, de insurance very long past
due,
All de homes we wukked so hard for goes back to
de Fay and Jew.

(***Collected Poems*** 68-69.22-24, 28-30)

Despite adverse natural and social conditions, African Americans in Brown's poems are determined to survive and embody that determination in their folk culture and folklore. For instance, the first section of the poem **"Memphis Blues"** stresses African Americans' ability to outlast power and oppression, comparing Memphis, Tennessee, to fallen ancient empires and thus hinting at the natural or divine destruction that awaits the segregated American South:

Nineveh, Tyre,
Babylon,
Not much lef'
Of either one.
All dese cities
Ashes and rust,
De win' sing sperrichals
Through deir dus' . . .

. . . . .

Dis here Memphis
It may go;
Floods may drown it;
Tornado blow;
Mississippi wash it
Down to sea—
Like de other Memphis in
History.

(***Collected Poems*** 60.1-8, 13-20)

It does not matter whether Providence or nature destroys these cities—more fundamental than causation is the conviction that African Americans must and will survive, a point stressed in the second section of the poem. Far from being upset about the end of the United States, the disparate members of the black community share a comic lack of concern, as well as a mode of expression (call and response) to relate their plans for survival:

Watcha gonna do when Memphis on fire,
Memphis on fire, Mistah Preachin' Man?
Gonna pray to Jesus and nebber tire,
Gonna pray to Jesus, loud as I can,
Gonna pray to my Jesus, oh, my Lawd!

Watcha gonna do when de tall flames roar,
Tall flames roar, Mistah Lovin' Man?
Gonna love my brownskin better'n before—
Gonna love my baby lak a do right man,
Gonna love my brown baby, oh, my Lawd!

Watcha gonna do when Memphis falls down,
Memphis falls down, Mistah Music Man?
Gonna plunk on dat box as long as it soun',
Gonna plunk dat box fo' to beat de ban',
Gonna tickle dem ivories, oh, my Lawd!

(60-61. 21-35)

With his poem **"Ma Rainey,"** Brown illustrates how folk culture sustains such resolve—indeed, how Rainey's concerts are not merely a single person's performance but a communal event during which people share experiences, reaffirm values, and renew bonds of loyalty and support. First, Ma Rainey's presence draws black audiences together from all over the South:

When Ma Rainey
Comes to town,
Folks from anyplace
Miles aroun',
From Cape Girardeau,
Poplar Bluff,
Flocks in to hear
Ma do her stuff. . . .

(***Collected Poems*** 62.1-8)

Each concert brings together working-class people from different areas and livelihoods, enabling them to become acquainted or reacquainted, to talk, joke, and commiserate:

Dey comes to hear Ma Rainey from de little river
settlements,
From blackbottom cornrows and from lumber
camps;
Dey stumble in de hall, jes a-laughin' an'
a-cacklin',
Cheerin' lak roarin' water, lak wind in river
swamps.

An' some jokers keeps deir laughs a-goin' in de
crowded aisles,
An' some folks sits dere waitin' wid deir aches an'
miseries,
Till Ma comes out before dem, a-smilin' gold-
toofed smiles
An' Long Boy ripples minors on de black an' yellow keys.

(ll. 19-26)

Besides strengthening a sense of community, the blues, as Sherley Anne Williams notes, also gives audiences an opportunity to reflect upon their experiences. Williams argues that "the blues singer strives to create an atmosphere in which analysis can take place," helping audiences put "analytic distance" between themselves and traumatic experiences (125). Ma Rainey's rendition of "Backwater Blues" in part four of the poem exemplifies the blues' capacity to help listeners comprehend chaotic experiences. "Backwater Blues" was composed by Bessie Smith from folk materials after the disastrous Mississippi river floods of 1927 and is peculiarly apt, since the towns and cities listed in the poem are on or near floodplains:

> *'It rained fo' days an' de skies was dark as night,*
> *Trouble taken place in de lowlands at night.*
>
> *'Thundered an' lightened an' the storm begin to roll*
> *Thousan's of people ain't got no place to go.*
>
> *'Den I went an' stood upon some high ol' lonesome*
> *hill,*
> *An' looked down on the place where I used to live.*
>
> (63. 42-47)

The crowd experiences an emotional catharsis ("An' den de folks, dey natchally bowed dey heads an' cried" [l. 48]), partly because the song brings a broad tragedy and blur of events into a tight, personal focus that people can comprehend. The song shifts from the havoc wreaked upon an entire community by the river to individual experience (from *"Thousan's of people"* to *"I"),* and from the midst of chaos to a detached perspective, high on a hill, to assay the personal damage from the flood (*"looked down on the place where I used to live").* As the speaker notes, the power of this music on the audience is profound, almost ineffable: "Dere wasn't much more de fellow say: / She jes' gits hold of us dataway" (ll. 51-52). By portraying the social impact of Rainey's performance, Brown was insisting upon the ability of folklore to sustain old values while creating opportunities for communication of new ideas and strategies, thus contributing to cultural evolution.

Not surprisingly, Brown's linking of folklore and cultural evolution mirrors the work of recent folklorists, who describe folklore as a social process for creating and selecting new, adaptive strategies for survival. For instance, John Roberts notes in his book *From Trickster to Badman: The Black Folk Hero in Slavery and Freedom* that cultures endure through individuals "endlessly devising solutions to both old and new problems of how to live under ever-changing social, political, and economic conditions" (11). Individuals, not groups as a whole, develop these adaptive strategies and communicate them to others:

> Just as a species does not "struggle to survive" as a collective entity, but survives or not as a consequence of the adaptive changes of individual organisms, so too do sociocultural systems survive or not as a consequence of the adaptive changes in the thought and activities of individual men and women who respond opportunistically to cost-benefit options.
>
> (Harris 61)

Folklorists have long insisted that folklore is a social process for creating and communicating such new adaptive strategies. Simon Bronner has written that "[f]olklore changes as people adapt it to different situations and needs. [It] becomes manipulated knowledge" (2). Similarly, W. F. H. Nicolaisen notes that folk performers often consciously select, rearrange, and modify traditional materials for new performances, and that such variation sustains tradition: "Far from being at odds with each other, creativity and tradition, individual and community, together produce vital variability thus keeping alive the very items that their integrated forces help to shape" (Bronner 11).

Similarly, Brown wrote about the continued evolution and utility of African-American traditions, examining folklore as a creative process and a source for useful social strategies. For instance, he tried to understand the process by which individual performers selected or adapted inherited materials, as with the composition of spirituals:

> It is unlikely that any group of worshipers and singers, as a group, composed spirituals. Single individuals with poetic ingenuity, a rhyming gift, or a good memory "composed" or "remembered" lines, couplets, or even quatrains out of a common storehouse. The group would join in with the refrain or the longer chorus. When one leader's ingenuity or memory was exhausted, another might take up the "composition."
>
> (**"Folk Literature"** 414)

Additionally, Brown described how tales and songs were orally transmitted and often extemporaneously composed, with narrators or singers freely drawing upon a common stockpile of rhymes, images, themes, and expressions (413-14). Yet audiences and succeeding generations of performers selected those variations that helped people address environmental and social needs, as well as satisfy individual preferences. Folklore remained functional, performing a wide variety of needed tasks in rural communities, such as socializing children, spreading news, voicing protest, pacing and timing work, defining individual identity, and reaffirming group loyalty. For instance, African-American parents used animal folktales before and after slavery to instruct children to overcome their social powerlessness. These stories presented seemingly weak heroes who learned to trick stronger opponents:

> Outsmarting was one of the few devices left [slaves]. So they made heroes out of the physically powerless [creatures such as Brer Rabbit or Brer Squirrel] who by good sense and quick wit overcame animals of brute strength who were not right bright. "You ain't go no cause to be bigger in de body, but you sho' is got cause to be bigger in de brain."
>
> (**"Negro Folk Expression"** 323)[3]

Spirituals, as another example, could profess faith, protest treatment, even spread important news (**"Negro Folk Expression: Spirituals, Seculars, Ballads and Work Songs"** 46-48).

Besides describing folklore as a process of *cultural* selection, Brown also described folklore as a process of *artistic* selection, in which the interaction between artists and audiences ensures songs' or stories' social usefulness, realism, concreteness of imagery, and emotional impact. Brown noted that some blues singers "must still sing for the jealous creators of the Blues," so that audiences influenced performance, subject matter, and group portrayal (**"The Blues as Folk Poetry"** 324). Rural audiences expected a blues performer to have first-hand knowledge of rural hardships: "As Negro musicians put it: 'You can't play the blues until you have paid your dues'" (Brown, **"The Blues"** 291). Consequently, "The true blues were sung by people close to the folk such as Ma Rainey, Mamie, Bessie, and Clara Smith, Victoria Spivey . . ." (286). Repeated performances within such tightly knit communities reaffirmed cultural identities and values, and reinforced artistic conventions. For instance, Brown was arguing that audiences were touched by Ma Rainey's performance of "Backwater Blues" partly because they influenced the song's creation and performance.

Accordingly, folklore for Brown was an exemplary poetics because it united literary and cultural evolution. Folk artists shaped their performances in response to environmental and social pressures, which in turn honed folklore's aesthetic quality and social usefulness. African-American audiences demanded and received art that was concrete, representative, and useful—more so than art over which they had little social or economic influence, such as commercial imitations of the blues. Brown demonstrated this artistic difference by contrasting "Backwater Blues" to "Mississippi Flood Song," a commercial ballad also composed after the 1927 floods:

> I am dreaming to-night in the moonlight
> Of the friends it has taken from me.
> All the world seemed so happy and gay.
> The waters rose quickly above us
> And it swept my beloved ones away-ay-ay-ay.
>
> (**"The Blues as Folk Poetry"** 330)

By insisting upon "bitter honesty" and "frankness of revelation and language," rural audiences encouraged a style which, to Brown's mind, was more concrete, realistic, and sympathetic (**"The Blues"** 288). "The gain in vividness [in "Backwater Blues" over "Mississippi Flood Song"], in feeling, in substituting the thing seen for the bookish dressing up and sentimentalizing," Brown argues, "is an obvious one" (**"The Blues as Folk Poetry"** 331).

Brown's comments about "Mississippi Flood Song" reflect his concerns that economic pressures from the Great Migration would sever the symbiotic relationship between African-American artists and audiences. He specifically feared that African-American culture would cease to be determined by the needs and interests of the community, but would be dictated increasingly by the marketplace, especially by the demand and interests of any economically dominant group. Linking economic and cultural autonomy, Brown warned:

> One of the by-products of exploitation is the development in literature of a stereotyped character of the exploited, which guards the equanimity of the "superiors" and influences even the "inferiors" when they are unwary.
>
> (**"A Literary Parallel"** 152)

For instance, he argued that Tin Pan Alley and minstrel-show performers were not interested in rendering the complexity of human behavior from within a tight focus, but in selling ready-made sentiment. Racism for Brown was a cultural industry, and falsified history a commodity:

> America, since [Stephen] Foster, has been set clamoring for idyllic content beneath Carolina skies, in the sleepy hills of Tennessee, where one may tuck oneself to sleep in his old Tucky home while the Mississippi—that lazy river—rolls on and Dandy Jim strums chords to Lucinda in the canebrake.
>
> (**"Weep Some More My Lady"** 87)

Brown regularly denounced the "imbecilities of the lyrics ground out in Tin Pan Alley," such as those for the song "That's Why Darkies Were Born":

> *Someone had to pick the cotton*
> *Someone had to hoe the corn*
> *Someone had to slave and be able to sing*
> *That's why Darkies were born.*
> *'Someone had to laugh at trouble,*
> *Someone had to be contented with any old thing,*

FROM THE AUTHOR

BROWN ON BLACK ART

Negro artists have enough to contend with in getting a hearing, in isolation, in the peculiar problems that beset all artists, in the mastery of form and in the understanding of life. It would be no less disastrous to demand of them that they shall evade truth, that they shall present us a Pollyanna philosophy of life, that, to suit our prejudices, they shall lie. It would mean that as self-respecting artists they could no longer exist.

SOURCE: Sterling Allen Brown, excerpt from "Our Literary Audience," in *Opportunity* 8, 1930.

So sing! sing! . . .
That why Darkies were born.'

(87)

By demanding and paying for such perspectives on black life, audiences reinforced extant prejudices and stereotypes: "What does the mob-mind care that it is bald-faced lying? The mob-mind wishes it, will have it so" (87). Yet black audiences, who had wielded tremendous social power during folkloric performances, wielded little economic power in the mass market, and accordingly could not exert enough economic pressure to shape their own portrayal, or to influence the artistic agenda. Worse yet, African-American artists were often co-opted by market forces into producing stereotypes themselves: "One can do no more than register a horse-laugh at the obvious Americanism of setting up sham in place of unpleasant truth, and at the Negro's easy complaisance in accepting a stereotype, and reaping his own shekels by perpetuating it" (87).

Brown illustrated such artistic exploitation in **"Cabaret,"** in which black performers are no longer offering criticism and models to the black community, but are perpetuating stereotypes of black rural life to a segregated white audience. The poem constantly cuts between images of black peonage in the Deep South in 1927 and images of black chorines, waiters, and musicians performing for an all-white audience at a Chicago speakeasy. While we are presented with images of forced labor on the levees of Arkansas (***Collected Poems*** 111-13.37-42), and communities in Mississippi destroyed by some of the worst flooding in the century (ll. 53-56, 64-67, 70-73, 84-86), scantily clad chorines wearing bandannas sing a tribute to the river and the plantation South that bears little resemblance to the living conditions of African Americans in that region:

There's peace and happiness there
I declare

. . . . .

I've got my toes turned Dixie ways
Round that Delta let me laze

. . . . .

My heart cries out for
MUDDY WATER

(ll. 35-36, 74-75, 82-83)

While **"Cabaret"** portrays the market's influence on African-American artistic production, **"Children's Children"** portrays a new generation of urban dwellers who have ceased producing their own culture, and who instead passively consume the products of the dominant culture. The effects of this change from producer to consumer are three-fold. First, these African Americans are portrayed as alienated from their history and culture, not only failing to understand spirituals, but greeting them with derision: "They laugh," "They sigh / And look goggle-eyed / At one another," "They have forgotten / What had to be endured" (***Collected Poems*** 104.5, 10-12, 20-21). Secondly, because they do not create for themselves the meaning of their heritage and experiences, they become frozen in an intellectual and sexual adolescence, "babbling young ones" who can only "Giggle / And nudge each other's satin clad / Sleek sides" in a preening, sneering immaturity (ll. 22, 28-30). Worse still, they define themselves using the dominant culture's shallow standards of beauty, applying bleaching creme to have "paled faces" (l. 23), and "cajol[ing]" their hair to "Caucasian straightness" (l. 24).

Given the threat that commercialism poses to African-American artistic production and cultural evolution, Brown proposed that black writers seek some way to *internalize* the kinds of environmental influences that folk artists experienced in their lives and during their performances. Accordingly, Brown valued literary regionalism, because he wanted "to relate the American artist to his environment, which is founded upon a direct return to the folk."[4] Brown hoped that cultural knowledge can act as both a creative source and constraint, encouraging African-American writers to shape their portrayals in accordance with black people's material conditions and social concerns. As he argued in his essay **"Local Color or Inter-**

pretation," the statement that an artist "knows 'the Negro' is of course a patent absurdity. 'The Negro' does not exist; and he never did" (223). Instead, "It would be more accurate to say that she has carefully studied a certain section of Negro life, restricted in scope and in character, and that she has revealed skillfully and beautifully and from a single point of view the results of her study" (223). Brown believed that dialect poetry from the previous generation of black poets was often rife with stereotypes precisely because these writers lacked the cultural knowledge needed to exercise artistic self-constraint:

> Dialect, or the speech of the people, is capable of expressing whatever the people are. . . . Poets more intent upon learning the ways of the folk, their speech, and their character, that is to say better poets, could have smashed the mold [of stereotyping].
>
> (***Negro Poetry and Drama*** 43)

Additionally, Brown called upon poetry to perform the same kinds of social roles performed by folklore in rural areas. For instance, **"Children's Children"** is a didactic poem aimed at a young, urban black audience, providing the socio-historical contexts needed to appreciate the romantic ideals expressed in slave songs, but also warning readers about the price paid by those who ignore or reject their cultural heritage. In the first two stanzas, the speaker challenges readers to drop their negative preconceptions of the songs by contrasting their elevated diction to the blunt, immature derision of young, urban African Americans:

> When they hear
> These songs, born of the travail of their sires,
> Diamonds of song, deep buried beneath the
> weight
> Of dark and heavy years;
> They laugh.
>
> When they hear
> Saccharine melodies of loving and its fevers,
> Soft-flowing lies of love everlasting;
> Conjuring divinity out of gross flesh itch;
> They sigh
> And look goggle-eyed
> At one another.
>
> (***Collected Poems*** 104.1-12)

By associating self-consciously inflated diction ("Diamonds of song," "travails of their sires," "Conjuring divinity") with the "Saccharine melodies" and lyrics of the slave songs, the speaker seemingly invites ridicule, but the utter viciousness with which the young people deride the songs ("They laugh," "They sigh / And look goggle-eyed / At one another") is quickly characterized as ignorant and inappropriate. The speaker explains that such derision results from a lack of knowledge and experience:

> They have forgotten, they have never known,
> Long days beneath the torrid Dixie sun
> In miasma'd riceswamps;
> The chopping of dried grass, on the third go
> round
> In strangling cotton;
> Wintry nights in mud-daubed makeshift huts,
> With these songs, sole comfort.
>
> They have forgotten
> What had to be endured—
>
> (ll. 13-21)

Within its proper historical context, the romantic idealizing of love and sex ceases to be old-fashioned prudery, but becomes acts of self-empowerment and transcendence amidst the quotidian squalor of slavery—that is, group insistence on the *humanity* rather than the animality of their sexual drives, and consequently the dignity of their existence and aspirations. Readers are cautioned, even shamed about reacting too hastily or negatively to these folksongs, and encouraged to bring the same knowledge and maturity to listening that the original singers and listeners brought to their construction.

By placing such didactic poems as **"Children's Children"** throughout ***Southern Road,*** and by allowing his "Vestiges" poems to trail portraits of urban alienation and degradation, Brown was stressing the interdependence of art and culture, and the need for African-American poets to sustain this symbiotic relationship in ways similar to folklore. He calls attention to his own attempt at cultural sustenance with "Vestiges"'s epigraph from A. E. Housman: "When I was one-and-twenty / I heard a wise man say—" (***Collected Poems*** 115). The wise man, by contrast, is the voice from a spiritual quoted on the frontispiece of ***Southern Road***: "O de ole sheep dey knows de road, / Young lambs gotta find de way."

Notes

1. Subsequent references to Brown's *Collected Poems* will appear parenthetically in the text, followed by page and line numbers separated by a period.
2. I wish to thank Robert O'Meally for suggesting that I complicate Brown's ideas about cultural evolution, particularly by noting that Brown does not stress progress so much as adaptation and survival in most of his poems—hence the many poems portraying storms and natural disasters.
3. For a fuller discussion about the relationship between hero formation in folktales and building cultures, see Roberts' *From Trickster to Badman,* pages 1-64.

4. Brown quotes this phrase from an unknown writer in his January 1931 essay, "The Literary Scene: Chronicle and Comment" (20).

Works Cited

Baker, Houston A., Jr. *Modernism and the Harlem Renaissance.* Chicago: University of Chicago Press, 1987.

Bronner, Simon J. "Introduction." *Creativity and Tradition in Folklore: New Directions.* Ed. Simon J. Bronner. Logan, UT: Utah State University Press, 1992. 1-38.

Brown, Sterling A. "The Blues." *Phylon* 13 (1952): 286-92.

———. "The Blues as Folk Poetry." *Folk Say: A Regional Miscellany, 1930.* Ed. B. A. Botkin. Vol. 1. Norman: University of Oklahoma Press, 1930. 324-39.

———. *The Collected Poems of Sterling A. Brown.* The National Poetry Series. New York: Harper, 1980.

———. "Folk Literature." *The Negro Caravan* (1941). Ed. Sterling A. Brown, Arthur P. Davis, and Ulysses Lee. New York: Arno Press and *The New York Times,* 1969. 413-34.

———. "A Literary Parallel." *Opportunity* (May 1932): 152-53.

———. "The Literary Scene: Chronicle and Comment." *Opportunity* (January 1931): 20.

———. "Local Color or Interpretation." *Opportunity* (July 1932): 223.

———. "Negro Folk Expression." *Phylon* 11 (1950): 318-27.

———. "Negro Folk Expression: Spirituals, Seculars, Ballads and Work Songs." *Phylon* 14 (1953): 45-61.

———. *Negro Poetry and Drama* (1937). *The Negro in American Fiction* and *Negro Poetry and Drama.* Afro-American Culture Series. New York: Arno Press, 1969.

———. "Our Literary Audience." *Opportunity* (February 1930): 42-46, 61.

———. *Southern Road.* New York: Harcourt, 1932.

———. "Weep Some More My Lady." *Opportunity* (March 1932): 87.

Gabbin, Joanne V. *Sterling A. Brown: Building the Black Aesthetic Tradition.* Contributions in Afro-American and African Studies, 86. Westport, CT: Greenwood Press, 1985.

Harris, Marvin. *Cultural Materialism: The Struggle for a Science of Culture.* New York: Vintage, 1979.

Henderson, Stephen. *Understanding the New Black Poetry: Black Speech and Black Music as Poetic References.* New York: Morrow, 1973.

Honey, Maureen, ed. "Introduction." *Shadowed Dreams: Women's Poetry of the Harlem Renaissance.* New Brunswick: Rutgers University Press, 1989. 1-41.

Radano, Ronald. "Soul Texts and the Blackness of Folk." *Modernism/Modernity* 2 (1995): 71-95.

Roberts, John W. *From Trickster to Badman: The Black Folk Hero in Slavery and Freedom.* Philadelphia: University of Pennsylvania Press, 1989.

Rowell, Charles H. "Sterling A. Brown and the Afro-American Folk Tradition." *Studies in the Literary Imagination* 7 (1974): 131-52. Rpt. in *The Harlem Renaissance Re-examined.* Ed. Victor Kramer. Georgia State Literary Studies 2. New York: AMS Press, 1987. 315-37.

Williams, Sherley A. "The Blues Roots of Contemporary Afro-American Poetry." *Chant of Saints: A Gathering of Afro-American Literature, Art, and Scholarship.* Ed. Michael S. Harper and Robert B. Stepto. Urbana: University of Illinois Press, 1979. 123-35.

Wright, John S. "The New Negro Poet and the Nachal Man: Sterling Brown's Folk Odyssey." *Black American Literature Forum* 23 (1989): 95-105.

The Last Ride of Wild Bill

MARK A. SANDERS (ESSAY DATE 1999)

SOURCE: Sanders, Mark A. "The Ballad, the Hero, and the Ride: A Reading of Sterling Brown's *The Last Ride of Wild Bill.*" In *The Furious Flowering of African American Poetry,* edited by Joanne V. Gabbin, pp. 118-34. Charlottesville, Va.: University Press of Virginia, 1999.

In the following essay, Sanders argues that Brown's The Last Ride of Wild Bill and Eleven Narrative Poems *is a book of and about ballads. The critic uses the folk hero to examine the fundamental nature of heroism and the hero's innate rebelliousness.*

In 1975 one of the most aggressive proponents of the Black Arts Movement, Broadside Press, published ***The Last Ride of Wild Bill and Eleven Narrative Poems,*** Sterling A. Brown's final collection. As he points out in his preface, Dudley Randall had been requesting, for some time, permission from Brown to reissue much of his poetry; Randall was especially concerned that ***Southern Road*** was out of print and therefore largely unavailable to a new generation of highly politicized readers. But Brown's eye was on a new configuration of older works—most of them not found in ***Southern Road***—and a new poem to introduce the collection.

Broadside, a press very much involved in the heated racial politics of the late sixties and early seventies, by definition sought out writers who directly engaged the various ideologies of Black Power and Black Arts. It serves as testament to Brown's longevity and insight that such a press would aggressively pursue a figure much less preoccupied with the immediate polemic than with the continuum of cultural aesthetics. But Brown's enduring applicability is not inconsistent with the times, for throughout the civil rights movement and the subsequent Black Power movement, Brown was lionized for his strident defense of grassroots folk and for his astute appraisal of African American culture. As an immensely popular teacher at Howard University, he served as mentor to a number of future political leaders—Stokely Carmichael (Kwame Ture) being one of the most prominent—and worked as advisor to NAG, the Nonviolent Action Group. In fact, the more radical students at Howard agitated to rename the institution "Sterling Brown University."[1] And as James G. Spady, a devoted Brown admirer, aptly illustrates, Brown's poetry and politics fostered a conceptual and cultural continuum from New Negro to Black Power activist. Recalling a "magnifying reading at Howard University," featuring luminaries such as Sonia Sanchez and LeRoi Jones (Amiri Baraka), Spady reflects:

> Despite the many light bombs dropped that night it was Sterling who completely detonated the audience, old and young alike. Remember this was doing [*sic*] the seething sixties when some considered anyone over thirty to be an uncle tom. As a matter of fact some of Howard University's finest professors had been burned in effigy. Why were Sterling Brown's poems so enthusiastically applauded? . . . They have simplicity, they are vivid, they are often humorous, sometimes sad, more often heroic but always capable of moving the listener. They have sense and sound. Most important they are timeless. That is the reason "Old Lem" could move both my grandparents and me. And everybody knows that Jim Fox ain't easily moved.[2]

In short, both the political activists of the Black Power movement and the aestheticians of the Black Arts Movement fully embraced Brown as mentor and progenitor; in him they found a viable antecedent for their political and cultural agendas; and as such, Brown was celebrated as a Black Arts activist far ahead of his time.

Yet given the accolades and attention produced in the late sixties and early seventies, Brown's poetics stood apart from, if not in direct opposition to, the dominant aesthetics of the day. Although ***Last Ride*** occupies the same historical moment as BAM poets such as Nikki Giovanni and Don L. Lee, Brown continues a much older tradition focused on rural and southern idioms. By presenting the dynamics of African American culture as its own liberating agent, the poem, for Brown, does not become the polemic but an aesthetic means of celebrating essential strengths and potential. In a sense ***Last Ride*** is largely anachronistic: Black Arts aesthetics notwithstanding, Brown rejects the encroaching dissonance of postmodern poetics and its emphasis upon language's chronic instability. Instead, Brown harkens back to the forms and traditions that shaped his first collection. Indeed, completing a continuum beginning with ***Southern Road*** and advanced in ***No Hiding Place, Last Ride*** reconceptualizes African American culture in modal process. Like his previous collections, ***Last Ride*** explores the means by which the culture itself actualizes its own progression and propels itself toward its own visions. In this particular collection Brown cites heroism and the omnipresent heroic spirit as the catalytic agents animating African American culture. Brown's cultural heroes—figures produced by the folk and embodying their essential strengths and aspirations—singularly confront the multiple forms of white authority and its stifling influences. Through defiance, and often martyrdom, these figures reveal a vital impulse toward autonomy and self-realization. Be they perpetually rebellious or only occasionally so, all reflect a cultural will that continues to inspire defiant acts commensurate with heroism.

With Brown's emphasis on heroism in mind, understanding ***Last Ride*** as a book of and about ballads becomes vitally important. Brown takes the ballad, an essential medium of folk culture (a "communal art form"), and reconstructs it in a search for essential cultural strengths.[3] In this collection of ballads the process of narrating itself holds center stage; the tradition of exaggeration and tall tales fuels the collection and points to its metaphoric focus. Both the folk ballad and Brown's literary ballads take up the figure of the folk hero, but where the folk ballad validates the hero's mythic stature, ***Last Ride*** seeks to examine the fundamental nature of heroism—how and why it exists, and what broader meaning it imports. Brown presents an extended address of the cultural hero, invoking the conventions of lies and toasts, but goes beyond the mere appropriation of folk idioms in order to examine the essential motivations behind the hero's perpetual rebelliousness.

If heroism is predicated upon the physical act of rebellion, so too are the various iconographic forms Brown's heroes take. The badman, the renegade, the humble worker trying to do right all combine to provide an array of personas destabilizing social conventions. By creating a diversified or multidimensional face for the heroic impulse, Brown eventually makes a strong case for its ubiquitousness. Moving beyond the stasis of a single cultural image, Brown attempts to portray the cultural dynamic, the specific catalyst that prompts the culture as a whole to confront imposed limitations. In short, ***Last Ride,*** moving through various avatars of the heroic spirit, asserts the ubiquitous yet often hidden heroic impulse—an impulse anterior to the heroic act yet gesturing toward numerous possibilities. Thus Brown's ballads seek to locate power and potential implicit yet dormant within the culture.

This gesture toward hidden potential fixes the hero in the broadest metaphoric spheres; here the hero is an ultimately transformational figure, one alluding to liberation through reformulation of self, community, and relations with white authority. ***Last Ride*** begins with an examination of the hero's power to transform confining surroundings, then embarks upon a linear progression in two modes—comic and tragic—toward ever-expansive implications in transformation. Each specific face of the cultural hero reveals new possibilities, both individual and collective, culminating in Joe Meek's encompassing gesture toward the transcendent nature of heroism itself. Brown enriches the metaphoric development of heroism and its transformational potential with an intricate dialogue between comic and tragic modes. Beginning with the comic, Brown establishes the resonant folk voice. Invoking the tradition of the toast, tall tales, and hyperbole, Wild Bill, Slim Greer, and John Bias offer various forms of the exaggerated and the burlesque, but gradually acquire undertones of tragic implications. Brown effectively blurs the distinctions between the two modes, achieving a final unity in Joe Meek—a product of the tall tale yet a tragic hero of epic proportions. Thus by reformulating the mode of their representation, Brown underscores the overt transformational qualities of his heroes. On yet a more fundamental level, Brown critiques traditional balladry through his experimentation with new narrative forms. As we will see in **"The Last Ride of Wild Bill,"** the ballad form itself serves as yet another site for Brown's invocation of liberating and rejuvenating potential in heroic resistance.

Brown achieves both formal and thematic unity through his central metaphor, "the ride." In practical terms the trope refers to narrative itself, both the episodic progression toward resolution and the formal transformation that underscores such a progression. As a central metaphor, the trope invokes the liberating possibilities inherent in the heroic act. The superlative romantic gesture of freedom and autonomy, the ride signals the broadest symbolic movement from the palpability of the physical act itself to its expansive metaphoric implications.

Thus Brown introduces this collection of ballads and heroes with a signature poem, largely defining the tenor and import of the book. In **"The Last Ride of Wild Bill"** Brown concerns himself primarily with transformation itself; in terms of form, theme, action, and final metaphor, **"Last Ride"** points toward the power and agency of change, toward the potential in reordering and redefining oppressive circumstances, and ultimately toward the fundamental value systems that create them.

Furthermore, **"Last Ride"** establishes the expansive implications of the central trope—and by extension those of the entire collection—by laying claim to epic stature. As the embodiment of collective cultural aspirations and as one willing to battle forces threatening the community, Wild Bill serves as epic hero in folk form. From Wild Bill's extended and detailed journey to his descent into the underworld, the poem takes on the trappings of high epic and thus a depth and breadth in metaphoric resonance.

But even with its epic scope, **"Last Ride"** announces itself as a ballad in the traditional sense—"verse narratives that tell dramatic stories in conventionalized ways."[4] Yet immediately evident are the reordered conventions. Brown replaces the standard quatrain structure and its regular meter with a new form that self-consciously calls attention to its own unconventionality. In fact, Brown holds true to only the most basic tenets of balladry, often constructing for the reader a set of expectations, then systematically violating them, thereby instituting the concept of flux within the very matrix of the poem. Brown's lines range broadly in length. And though most lines consist of two or three stresses, the stresses themselves constantly move; so too, quasi-conventional lines seldom succeed each other for more than two or three lines, again breaking a regularity that is tenuous at best. For example, "Challenge" begins the poem with a six-line stanza proclaiming volatility and flux as major organizing principles for the poem:

> The new chief of police
> Banged his desk
> Called in the force, and swore
> That the number-running game was done
> And Wild Bill
> Would ride no more.
>
> (121)[5]

Here Brown demonstrates his range in length of line and his perpetually mobile stresses. That he consistently uses masculine endings and rhymes "swore" and "more" serves to create some sense of regularity. Throughout the poem these nearly sporadic reminders of regularity (hard stops, masculine endings, and occasional rhymes) strain to harness the potentially discursive energies of the poem, strain, in effect, to hold the poem back from free verse, and thus from a full departure from folk oral and musical traditions. Yet all the while Brown utilizes short lines, enjambment, and irregular stresses in order to sustain a sense of rapid movement, almost a sense of tumbling.

As a result of this perpetual tension between regularity and irregularity, between conformity and freedom, the larger metaphoric implications of poetic form come into focus. Here Brown's self-conscious denial of formal expectations stresses the palpable and symbolic importance of transformation. By consistently breaking convention, and thus refusing to meet standard expectations, Brown underscores Wild Bill's significance beyond the immediate poem. As motion and progression emerge from the very matrix of the poem, they contribute directly to the effect of the narrative and the symbolism of the ride. Perhaps this symbolism goes so far as to suggest Brown's own transformational powers in his revision of Western balladry in order to create new conceptual space for black agency.

As the narrative structure begins to give itself over to metaphor, it gives rise to the progression of the ride—the physical movement across the city and the symbolic agitation against confinement. In both senses the ride serves as transformative act with Wild Bill looming as the symbolic figure embodying potential in transformation. As a folk form of the epic hero, the badman, Wild Bill possesses special qualities in subverting and transforming the status quo. Stressing such abilities, Brown devotes a conspicuously large section of the poem to the reaction of the community rather than focusing strictly on the dramatic events of the chase. The wit and humor with which the various communities respond to the central conflict reveal the essential power behind Wild Bill and his ride:

> These were the people
> That the bug had bit,
> Betting now
> On a sure-fire hit:
> Kiwanians, and Rotarians
> Daughters, Sons, Cousins
> Of Confederate Veterans,
> The Kleagle of the Ku Klux Klan,
> The Knights of the Pantry
> And Dames of the Pan,
> The aristocrats, the landed gentry,
> The cracker, and the jigaboo
> Hoi-polloi
> All seemed to think well
> Of their boy,
> Were eager to lay
> Their bucks on Bill.
>
> On Druid Hill
> An old-stock cavalier tried to bet
> His yard-boy part of his back-pay due
> But Mose he believed in Wild Bill too.
>
> (123-24)

Here, with much ironic humor, Brown allies groups that ordinarily would be diametrically opposed by class and racial divisions. White/black, rich/poor, powerful/powerless, Wild Bill effectively dismantles these oppositions fundamental to the very meaning of the community. In subverting the status quo, he creates new conceptual ground where the rudimentary potential for redefinition lies.

Much of this potential rests on Wild Bill's symbolic meaning, assigned by the newly united community. Even beyond the prospect of making money from his triumph, the community at large embraces Wild Bill as a repository of values far more significant than monetary gain. As "their boy," he implicates an expansive iconographic field incorporating the American badman, renegade, and hero. Defining himself on his own terms and thus occupying conceptual space outside of cultural conventions, Wild Bill invokes fundamental American myths celebrating the frontiersman, independence, and unbridled individuality; and it is precisely his ability to embody these mythic precepts that draws the admiration of the community.

Wild Bill states:

> "Ride my route
> Again today;
> Start at noon,
> End at three.
> Guess it will have
> To be you and me."
>
> (125)

He here sets conformity and self-reliance in practical and symbolic opposition. In doing so, he does not so much threaten the community as uphold its fundamental beliefs. Here Wild Bill as outlaw is not simply a metaphor for disruption, the trickster destabilizing the oppressive rhetoric of authority;[6] to the contrary, he looms as a sanctioned representative of agency. More than checking the forces of authority, he agitates for space within the community for both freedom and independence.

Brown completes this notion of liberating transformation through an apotheosis redefining a highly symbolic space. Although Wild Bill lands in hell, the final site and evidence of his transformational abilities, his hell is a reconstructed one that reverses the assumed value of temporal and permanent life:

> The devils rushed at him
> In a swarm,
> And the cool
> Wild Bill
> Grew awful warm.
> It looked like he'd
> Broke up a meeting;
> But this was the Convocation's
> Greeting:
> They climbed all over
> His running board,
> "Wild Bill, Wild Bill!"
> Their shouting roared
> And rang through all the streets of Hell:
>
> "Give us the number,
> Wild Bill,
> Tell us
> What fell!"
>
> (135)

Underestimating his own prowess, Wild Bill expects the Judeo-Christian notion of hell, one in which he will pay for a life of sin through eternal torment. But instead he finds a transformed hell that ultimately affirms the qualities for which he was killed. Here the final reversal relies on the juxtaposition of earth and hell. As the devils embrace Wild Bill as hero, earth and temporal reality become the site of perpetual persecution; conversely, Wild Bill's reconstructed hell then becomes the final site of resolution. In this apotheosis he expands as metaphor to represent a myriad of regenerative transformations. By subverting traditional and confining oppositions, by militating against oppressive authority, by living and dying according to self-defined principles, Wild Bill points toward a range of possibilities that lie beyond stasis and conventionality.

Thus by creating conceptual space for himself, he also points toward the possibilities suggested by the ensuing heroes and ballads. In response to this potential suggested through comedy, **"He Was a Man"** pursues potential in tragic representation. Returning to conventional balladry, Brown addresses the sobering brutality of folk life and the exorbitant costs of self-assertion. The poem, like **"Last Ride,"** works through ironic inconsistencies that conspire to defeat heroism; yet Brown meticulously constructs Will as the embodiment of social stability, one firmly grounded within the community, and one defined by stabilizing notions of work and family. As such, Brown affirms the fundamental ties that supposedly hold cultures together. In order to add pathos to Wild Bill's stature, the speaker declares that these attributes disqualify Will as hero:

> He wasn't nobody's great man,
> He wasn't nobody's good,
> Was a po'boy tried to get from life
> What happiness he could,
> He was a man, and they laid him down.
>
> (136)

Brown pits Will's agency against that of the community; in these tragic circumstances Will's act of self-assertion in self-defense is met with a greater act of assertion. Killing a man in self-defense, he willfully accepts the truth of his actions—"Didn't catch him in no manhunt." But even more boldly the whites "Didn't hide themselves, didn't have no masks, / Didn't wear no Ku Klux hoods." And with a final ironic twist, at the site of social justice they destroy his claim to autonomy. Clearly, here Brown calls into question the concept of justice and ultimately deems the term void of meaning as the sheriff and coroner decline to pursue it. Thus irony becomes tragic as allegedly just officials turn murderous, killing one wholly in support of the community they vow to protect.

Brown's elliptical style also contributes to the cathartic force of the poem. As opposed to **"Last Ride,"** which provides an abundance of detail and celebrates the process of telling the tale, **"He Was a Man"** gains much of its force through omission. Simply the facts of the lynching speak for themselves; and only the one-line incremental refrain allows for much editorial comment. As the refrain connotes a fatigued and tragic inevitability, it also identifies the essential vitality of the hero, a vitality that exists beyond physical life, a vitality that in fact emerges through martyrdom. That Will was a man, a black man no less, in the scheme of this poem, and within the broader politics of the South, demands his destruction; yet his destruction validates his agency. For both Will and Wild Bill, much of their heroism derives from the willingness to die for their convictions and from the culture's compulsion to curtail such rebellious assertions of self. Although the individual impulse toward self-assertion and the societal impulse to deny black selfhood collide to destroy the physical hero, they also conspire to create the symbol and thus the sustenance of the omnipresent spirit. Therefore the poem laments Will's loss but implicitly validates an immortality that will manifest itself in ensuing poems.

As this second poem inaugurates the theme of tragic representation, it looks forward to **"Sam Yancey"** and the further extension of the tragic mode. **"Sam Yancey," "Crispus Attucks McKoy,"** and **"Break of Day"** all represent the hero as liberating potential tragically cut short. In each poem the hero embodies essential strengths common to the culture yet threatening to white authority. In each instance, in the classic mode of the hero, he asserts these strengths, strives to defend them, and ultimately dies as a result of his agency. Martyrdom serves as the supreme affirmation of heroism, where superlative sacrifice in defense of self and culture ostensibly points toward an irrepressible continuity in heroic spirit. Each time the physical avatar is struck down another manifestation of the spirit appears, insuring sustained agitation for freedom and independence.

Having established this strident sense of agency, in both comic and tragic modes, Brown presents the Slim Greer series, which examines both the strengths and limitations of the comic hero. Following **"Sam Yancey,"** Brown moved away from the high price of heroism to complete the Slim Greer series and to explore humor's potential. In 1932 Brown first presented Slim Greer in ***Southern Road,*** with only the first three poems—**"Slim Greer," "Slim Lands a Job?,"** and **"Slim in Atlanta."** With this configuration Greer clearly conforms to the standard definition of the trickster, consistently subverting white authority through wit and humor. His introductory poem, **"Slim Greer,"** sketches his persona and demonstrates both his ability to circumvent social restrictions and his ability to use them for his own gain. Beyond the immediate action of the drama, though, Slim's ability as comic figure reveals his superlative gifts in absurdity and burlesque. His outlandishness and the circumstances in which he finds himself acquire dramatic force, as Greer uses his rhetorical skills to diffuse oppressive situations, transforming them into moments of celebration.

It is within this context that the first three Slim Greer poems add a humorous dimension to the master trope, "the road" in ***Southern Road.*** But by completing the series and placing all five poems in ***Last Ride,*** Brown implies critically different connotations. First, by moving away from high burlesque, the later two poems incorporate more ominous implications for both Greer's character and his ability to affect his surroundings. Furthermore, in relation to the broader signifying field of ***Last Ride,*** the Slim Greer series exposes the limitations of comic representation and thereby alludes to its final subsumption in **"The Ballad of Joe Meek."**

Following **"Slim in Atlanta," "Slim Hears 'The Call'"** continues the mode of burlesque, but raises serious questions concerning Slim's use of his transformative powers. Simply the title stressing "the call" questions its ultimate meaning, anticipating an ironic call to make money rather than to serve God. Furthermore, **"Slim Hears 'The Call'"** deviates from Brown's standard presentation in that it is Greer's own narrative. Rather than a third-person narrative celebrating Greer's ability to outwit whites and to undermine potentially oppressive circumstances, Greer tells his own story of victimizing the powerless. The poem begins by invoking the tradition of exaggeration and hyperbole; and much of its amusing quality stems from Greer's mastery of style and form. In the first two stanzas Greer recreates his adversity in order to elicit laughter, not pity; rather than illustrating the severity of his condition, he better demonstrates his rhetorical skills and mastery of form, a mastery implicitly asserting control over much more than oratorical tropes:

> Down at the barbershop
> Slim had the floor,
> "Ain't never been so
> Far down before.
>
> "So ragged, I make a jaybird
> About to moult,
> Look like he got on gloves
> An'a overcoat.
>
> "Got to walk backwards
> All de time
> Jes' a-puttin' on front
> Wid a bare behime.

Indeed, Greer's display of rhetorical expertise serves as prelude to his mastery of a cultural form, "de bishopric"; thus his tale is one of apprenticeship in preparation for his next money-making scheme. Greer retells, with humorous irony, the mercenary practices of a fraudulent clergyman; that his friend misrepresents himself, steals from his congregation, and ultimately undermines the religious imperative of his position, for Greer constitutes the epitome of cunning and shrewdness. Greer's admiration ultimately is for the ability to control, manipulate, and make money with the least amount of effort:

> So here he was de head man
> Of de whole heap—
> Wid dis solemn charge dat
> He had to keep:
>
> "A passel of Niggers
> From near an' far
> Bringin' in de sacred bucks
> Regular."

And Greer ends his apprenticeship and his amusing tale with a resounding endorsement of this enterprise, and with an embracing call for everyone, so inclined, to do as he does. On the one hand, Greer successfully promotes the same persona celebrated in the previous three poems; he is witty, resourceful, and above all farcically entertaining. But as he shifts the focus of his talents away from the empowered to the dispossessed, he begins to work against the iconography previously assigned him. He no longer ridicules and dismantles figures and forces of oppression; he now reinforces them. Clearly, Brown pokes fun at the disreputable figures in the African American clergy; clear enough too is the attempt to add levity to the sobering reality of African American exploitation in one of its most important institutions. But in terms of Greer's development, and in terms of his broader implications within the collection, **"Slim Hears 'The Call'"** constitutes a serious departure from the established metaphoric development.

Greer's willful exultation of his own ability to exploit begins to indicate the limitations of burlesque. At this point the mode of the tale subsumes the overt politics of the content; humor begins to serve its own ends—pure entertainment—and thus divorces itself from a broader political context.

This implication, that the very form Greer represents necessarily embodies severe limitations in terms of historical vision, receives further treatment in the last poem of the series. More so than **"Slim Hears 'The Call,'" "Slim in Hell"** entertains a number of potentially sobering ironies, while sustaining the tradition of the burlesque. The premise of the poem—Greer in an odd situation—automatically advances the comic mode of the series. But given the comic conventions, that Greer finds hell to be in truth the South strikes a poignantly accurate note. As St. Peter corroborates Greer's encroaching suspicions, comedy quickly becomes satire:

> Then Pete say, "You must
> Be crazy, I vow,
> Where'n hell dja think Hell *was,*
> Anyhow?

This acerbic indictment of the South and its racial politics works in and of itself to darken the implications of the poem. But that the poem ends, not with the realization of such a harsh reality but with Greer's expulsion from heaven due to his limited vision, shifts the focus from the injustice of the South to Greer's misunderstanding of its ramifications:

> "Git on back to de yearth,
> Cause I got de fear
> You'se a leetle too dumb,
> Fo' to stay up here."

As a product of the South, and as one having resisted many of its stifling forces, Greer fails to perceive the literally cosmic implications of racial oppression. In the broadest of religious schemes, hell and Dixie hold the same literal meaning that its victims are expected to understand. That Greer fails calls into question his understanding of his own gifts and the implications of their application. Although he perceives and fights the oppression directed specifically at him, he does not or cannot read beyond his own circumstances, nor does he invoke an appreciation for a continuum of oppressive forces. Simply put, Greer exists in a historical vacuum, employing only ad hoc measures of resistance. That Brown ends the series with Greer's expulsion from heaven due to his misreading implicates the entirety of his progression and finally raises the issue of his limitations. As the trickster fails to see or act beyond his own self-interest—thus he perpetually assumes a defensive rather than offensive political position—Brown begins to circumscribe the comic mode of the hero within a limited metaphoric and political sphere, limited at least relative to the final expansion of the tragic hero and his import.

Brown responds to the subtle but serious encroachment upon Slim Greer's levity with an unequivocal canonization of a figure fully aware of the political imperatives of his circumstances. **"Crispus Attucks McKoy"** explores the transcendent heroic spirit, a spirit completely dedicated to both individual and collective liberation. As in **"Last Ride,"** Brown creates a dramatically new ballad form in order to stress the monumental precedent McKoy represents. Yet in contrast to the continual changes in **"Last Ride,"** the form of **"Crispus Attucks McKoy"** is uniform and immediately self-evident. Brown's regimented eight-line stanzas, complete with regular rhyme and meter, first create a strident sense of regularity and clarity. As the speaker asserts an uncompromising vision of heroism, so too does the form affirm a sense of strength and assurance. Equally as important, but somewhat less obvious, Brown borders on formal rigidity in order to emphasize a consistent historical progression linking past, present, and future. Just as each stanza succeeds the previous one in a predictable fashion—almost marching toward the inevitable apotheosis in martyrdom—that "The soul of our hero / Goes marching on" ultimately affirms the inevitable progression of the heroic spirit.

Following the profundity of martyrdom, Brown advances the exchange between comic and tragic, presenting John Bias in **"A Bad, Bad Man."** Setting **"A Bad, Bad Man"** against **"Break of Day,"** John Bias serves as the farcical antithesis to the self-determined tragic hero, while Big Jess epitomizes the tragic martyr. Where Big Jess completes the tragic lineage begun with Sam Yancey, Joe Meek picks up both strands of representation in order to provide the broadest array of transformational possibilities for both kinds of heroes.

As the first and last stanzas indicate, Brown frames Joe Meek's ballad within two illustrations suggesting a wealth of meanings residing just below surface appearances. **"The Ballad of Joe Meek,"** as Brown's final representation of the hero, affirms the ubiquitous nature of the heroic spirit and thus completes Wild Bill's transformational ride. Joe Meek becomes "Joe Hero"—a compelling combination of ordinariness and extraordinariness—championing the cause of the downtrodden and illustrating the heroic potential lurking in the most unlikely individuals.

Stressing the intrinsic meaning hidden behind deceptive surfaces, Brown constructs the poem around the tension between the external and internal, between superficial illusion and permanent meaning—"You cain't never tell / How far a frog will jump, / When you jes' see him planted / On his big broad rump." In a conversation with Clark White, Brown comments: "The Joe Meek piece is an ideal peace and it's [*sic*] meaning is: don't believe the appearance of my people by the way they look . . . with Joe Meek the dramatic turn was the injustice. . . . we can take so much and then take no more."[7] Initially the form itself invokes and advances the absurdity developed in the Slim Greer series. The short lines and regular quatrains convey a light homespun folk voice that seems to indicate yet another tall tale in the burlesque. Yet the form and its comic implications belie the intrinsically political ramifications of Joe Meek's narrative. In sharp contrast to its form, the poem's content follows the basic pattern of hero construction initiated in **"Last Ride."** The solitary figure, stridently committed to his own principles, dares to combat the established order bent on compromising those principles. Of course, this battle ends in martyrdom; thus in terms of fundamental patterns, Joe Meek echoes Wild Bill's implications and completes a lineage including Will, Sam Yancey, Crispus McKoy, and Big Jess.

Thus we find that beneath the surface of the comic voice and form lie both the tragedy of potential destroyed and the promise of transformation. In this sense **"The Ballad of Joe Meek"** culminates the exploration of the heroic nature and finds its potential omnipresent. The title itself constructs Joe as the most unlikely candidate for martyrdom. Mild mannered and conciliatory to a fault, his fundamental disposition would usually allow the status quo to exist undisturbed and unchallenged. Yet given a catalyst for transformation, Meek becomes the epitome of the cultural hero. The catalyst here, heat, promotes aberrant behavior in beetles, pet bunnies, and babies, but exposes in Meek an essential and permanent nature. That "Joe didn't feel / So agreeable" is certainly a direct result of the heat, but after "The sun had gone down" and "The air it was cool," Joe continues his defiant behavior. In both cases, Joe's actions serve as manifestations of a latent heroic nature. In a typically mild manner he asks the officers if they had done "just right," and asks at his death for "one kindness / Fo' I die." These gestures and his willingness to battle an entire police department transform his "meekness" into strength and conviction, and finally reveal his heroic essence.

Finally affirming his heroism, Brown places Meek in direct reference to John Henry:

> "Won't be here much longer
> To bother you so,
> Would you bring me a drink of water
> Fo' I go?"
>
> (151)

Just as John Henry asks for a "Cool drink of water 'fore I die," Joe Meek asks for the same practical and symbolic solace. In a mode similar to Big Boy Davis, of **"Odyssey of Big Boy"** fame, Joe Meek invokes the tradition that holds the permanent meaning for both his life and death. Where Big Boy Davis invokes the rhetorical form of his idol John Henry, Joe Meek quotes him directly, attempting to achieve a similar affinity. Furthermore, Brown assigns Joe a greater degree of metaphoric weight by linking his martyrdom, and the vision of justice his martyrdom represents, to that of John Henry, perhaps the broadest symbol of black cultural agency.

In addition, Brown lends even greater resonance to his encompassing notion of transformation through the conversion of comic into tragic. **"The Ballad of Joe Meek"** serves as an apt conclusion to a collection of ballads and heroes in that it combines the two dominant modes of portrayal in order to utilize the most expressive traits of each. This ballad reinvokes the tradition of tall tales, but as we have already seen, Brown calls into question the broader scope of the comic hero's abilities. As Slim Greer makes explicit, neither he nor Wild Bill sees or acts beyond his own self-interest. Moving beyond the confines of self-concern is the tragic hero's task, particularly Joe Meek's, to exercise agency in a public sphere, to act on behalf of the surrounding community; in doing so, the tragic hero extends the nearly limitless potential of transformation to incorporate acts of liberation. Thus, both in mode and metaphor, Joe Meek successfully subsumes the comic hero and reconstructs him as a public agent for the greater community.

Returning to the framing notion of deceptive appearance, Joe Meek's tale ends alluding to the heroic possibilities lying dormant in unlikely places, thus ending a collection that celebrates the folk hero by ultimately democratizing the figure. Here, finally, Brown's notion of heroic transformation achieves its broadest scope. With Joe Meek as central metaphor for the collection, Brown creates conceptual space for the reader. Joe the commoner validates the patently unromantic, yet he stresses that we all are heir to the legacy John Henry and Wild Bill represent. As the collection ends, "The soul of our hero / Goes marching on"; unimpeded by the murders of specific figures, the idea and symbol of the hero remain immortal and continue to point toward future incarnations.

Indeed, by employing a number of cultural icons—the badman, the renegade, the humble worker trying to do right—and various ballad forms, the collection creates a diversified or multidimensional face for the heroic impulse, one perpetually agitating against social conventions and white authority. The ride, formally and metaphorically, invokes progression, movement from specific to general, from renegade (and therefore aberration) to commoner, symbolically embracing all. Through this movement beyond the stasis of a singular cultural image, Brown attempts to portray a dynamic that prompts the culture as a whole to confront imposed limitations. In short, Brown's ballads seek to locate power and potential latent within the culture. Having done so, the collection has discovered and affirmed an essential means by which African American culture attempts to realize its own liberation.

Notes

1. Gabbin, 59.
2. Spady, 35.
3. Smith, 396.
4. Laws, xi.
5. These poems, first published in Brown's *The Last Ride of Wild Bill and Eleven Narrative Poems,* are, with the exception of "Slim Hears 'The Call,'" available in *The Collected Poems of Sterling A. Brown.* When citing from this collection only the page numbers in text will be used hereafter.
6. Jackson suggests that the prototypical badman serves as a "challenge to hegemony," 31.
7. White, 114-15.

Works Cited

Brown, Sterling A. *The Collected Poems of Sterling A. Brown.* Sel. Michael S. Harper. New York: Harper, 1980.

———. *The Last Ride of Wild Bill and Eleven Narrative Poems.* Detroit: Broadside, 1975.

Gabbin, Joanne V. *Sterling A. Brown: Building the Black Aesthetic Tradition.* Westport: Greenwood, 1985.

Jackson, Bruce. *"Get Your Ass in the Water and Swim like Me": Poetry from Black Oral Tradition.* Cambridge: Harvard University Press, 1974.

Laws, Malcolm, Jr. *The British Literary Ballad: A Study in Poetic Imagination.* Carbondale: Southern Illinois University Press, 1972.

Smith, Gary. "The Literary Ballads of Sterling A. Brown." *CLA Journal* 32 (1989): 393-409.

Spady, James G. "Ah! To Have Lived in the Days of That 'Senegambian,' Sterling Brown." *Sterling A. Brown: A UMUM Tribute.* Ed. Black History Month Museum Committee. Philadelphia: Black History Museum UMUM Publishers, 1982.

White, Clark. "Sterling Brown, 'The ole sheep, they know the road . . . Young lambs gotta find the way': An Essay Dedicated to ole 'skeeta Brown." Sterling A. Brown UMUM Tribute. Ed. Black History Month Museum Committee. Philadelphia: Black History Museum UMUM Publishers, 1982. Black History Month Museum Committee.

The Collected Poems of Sterling A. Brown

SAMUEL W. ALLEN (ESSAY DATE 1983)

SOURCE: Allen, Samuel W. "Sterling Brown: Poems to Endure." *The Massachusetts Review* 24, no. 3 (autumn 1983): 649-57.

In the following essay, Allen surveys a number of Brown's poems that are collected in the 1980 anthology The Collected Poems of Sterling A. Brown.

The publication in 1980 of Sterling Brown's collected poems as the first in the National Poetry Series was a signal event in American letters.[1] From the vantage of a hundred years hence, when the nation will have moved beyond its *chauvin,* that truth will doubtlessly be recognized. Stepping back for a moment however, and looking in the opposite direction, we find that in the early decades of the century it was James Weldon Johnson more so probably than any other whose voice held *ex cathedra* authority in assessing the state of Afro-American poetry, in identifying the lame and the halt as well as the prodigies among its practitioners. Reacting against the plantation stereotypes of a genial but fettered Paul Laurence Dunbar, Johnson had become critical of the use of dialect, finding it to be a limited and limiting mode of expression, capable of only two stops on the keyboard, pathos and humor. His opinion was widely shared, becoming part of the critical canon of the day. Understandably so. The air had been redolent with a corrupted ante-bellum speech, conjuring forth an array of dark and ghostly figures, bowing contentedly and scraping, who never truly lived on the cotton festooned land or bluest sea but who seemed, at least in the stereotypes of the printed page and the popular imagination, to love to serve their masters and to do so joyously. The provocation was clear but the response was excessive. As with other critical maxims, Johnson's too, as he himself in effect conceded, fell before the contradicting fact, in this case the inspired pen of a younger poet who was to fashion his own singular way.

Sterling Brown would not confine himself to the standard English which Johnson approved, the prescribed lexicon of "high art," but ventured beyond the measured tropes of the Euro-American muse to explore and celebrate in their own idiomatic speech the range of experiences of black folk of the American South. It was a language, however, notably different from the dialect Dunbar and others had employed to perpetuate a romanticized plantation tradition. It was rather the speech one actually heard from the lips of black folk, as Brown had heard it, in the homes and work places and the cabarets, in the fields and bayous and on the chain gangs of the American South. It should be added, in regard to Johnson, that although he reacted against the older plantation stereotypes, he, too, in his own work, had sought to find a black poetic voice more authentic than the conventional literary language of his time.

The South has historically been central to the black experience in America, and it has been central to the vision of Brown's poetry. As a young man, he had won a Phi Beta Kappa key at Williams College and a Master's degree in English from Harvard University. He then, however, contrary to the more conventional choice, forsook the urban north, turning south to the blues and the spirituals of the black folk heritage to fashion a poetry which, as this volume confirms, has won an enduring place in the national literature.

Published herein are Brown's three collections: ***Southern Road*** (1932), ***The Last Ride of Wild Bill*** (1975) and ***No Hiding Place*** (hitherto unpublished). We see again the superb poems of ***Southern Road,*** ranging from the irrepressible exuberance of **"Sporting Beasley"** to the heroic strictures of the magnificent "symphonic poem," **"Strong Men,"** Brown's signature piece, a consummately crafted rallying cry for a cause and a people. It was this poem which the young men of SNCC during the sixties would ask Brown to read at meetings in the nation's capital. ***The Last Ride of Wild Bill*** is a series of tall tales which, with varying success on the inflectionless printed page, illustrate Brown's resourceful use of the folk tradition and the fertile imagination of the true storyteller. Appearing for the first time in its entirety is ***No Hiding Place,*** Brown's second collection of poetry, dating from the middle thirties, for which he could not find a publisher. It is a comment upon the industry and the cultural acumen of the country that the manuscript for this collection, which included such magnificent pieces as **"Old Lem," "Remembering Nat Turner," "Crossing," "Long Track Blues"** and others, was, in ironic rebuttal of its title, to remain under a bushed for almost half a century.

With the poems from these three groups, the present publication reveals itself to be a veritable Brownian cornucopia, a storehouse of richly varied mode, of pastoral meditation, of militant *appel,* of loveliest lyric, of withering satire, distinguished especially by its superb and transforming rendition of the black folk consciousness. Brown's enormous range demonstrates both proclivity and talent in a number of areas, some of which are fully developed, while others appear never to have engaged his fullest concern. **"Idyll,"** a pastoral meditation in "Remembrances," the last group of poems in ***No Hiding Place,*** triggers speculation. For a poet of another time and place, the stream-side setting of the Virginia countryside might have become at once a Wye River and a Tintern Abbey, but Brown's is a consciousness beset by other urgencies. The pastoral setting is persuasive, but the tranquil scene is sharply interrupted as the predatory hawk suddenly descends and the blood of a small bird spatters the rustic stream. Perhaps an Afro-American poet, especially one whose consciousness was shaped in the bleak despairing years of the early twentieth century, would be too aware of both nature and society red in tooth and claw to incline toward contemplation of the former's benevolence.

The body of Brown's work examines with unblinking stare the historic oppression of black humanity in this country. It is an uncompromising portrayal, and, unlike that of some of his contemporaries, without the consolation of an underlying sense of religious purpose. "God may be the owner, but he's rich and forgetful and far away." His poetic universe is implacable in its portrayal of suffering and injustice. Misery and racial exploitation are as certain as the seasons; both man and nature conspire to bring catastrophe. Flood and famine and unrestrained terror at the hands of whites is the lot of the black rural population in the South. Through both the more conventional Western forms and the black folk tradition—the ballad, the sonnet, blank verse, free verse, work songs, and the blues—Brown looks steadily at disaster. It is a sophisticated intelligence at work here; of the major Afro-American poets of the early part of the century, it is in Brown's work that a strong element of satire appears, often with devastating effect. The black victim of police brutality is excoriated for "bruising white knuckles." The problem of Johnny Thomas, murdered on a chain gang, is stupidity: he should have "had mo' sense than to git born." Lynching is a frequent subject of Brown's pen and the South has more than its share of "Barnums" who exploit its possibilities as spectacle. It is not only entertainment worthy of thousands: "it'll be right educational . . . bring the kiddies." The "truth and honor" of the Confederacy are poised against "eight cowering Negroes" in a Scottsboro jail "still receiving the benefactions of Noblesse Oblige." We must pity Ty Hendricks, the white cop who shot and killed a black man, for he must "hear the widow moan." As though with the comment of a satirical Greek chorus, Brown builds with cumulative force the picture of a people whose lot is victimization and grief.

This portrayal is the gravamen of much of ***Southern Road,*** but it achieves a special intensity in the aptly named ***No Hiding Place.*** In Part II **"The Cotton South,"** Part III **"Down in Atlanta,"** and Part IV "Rocks Cried Out," the story is unflinchingly told. The archetypal figure of Southern terror, the Southern sheriff, the only worthy rival of his twentieth-century twin, the Gestapo officer, is evoked in **"Arkansas Chant"**: "the devil is a rider in slouch hat and boots Gun by his side, Bull whip in his hand." In **"Old Lem"** we realize that a live, proud black man is a contradiction in terms: "They don't come by ones They don't come by twos / But they come by tens." There is no refuge; even "the rocks cried out." We begin, perhaps, to understand, at least in part, why prospects for publication of these poems in the thirties and long thereafter, were less than remote. The melancholy plight of a people forty years times ten in the wilderness is probably nowhere more tellingly expressed than in that litany of desolation, **"Crossing"**:

We have won through
to bloodred clay
to gravel and rock
to the baked lands
to the scorched barrens.

And we grow footsore
And muscle weary
Our faces grow sullen
And our hearts numb

We do not know . . .

We know only
That there lies not Canaan
That this is no River Jordan.

In its terse, laconic lines, the poem is an extraordinarily fine example of the manner in which in the hands of a gifted artist, the particular explodes into the universal, with meaning in this case for everyone who has been too long on the journey.

It is no doubt from the same sympathetic awareness that the deep sense of commitment informing Brown's work derives, a determination to confront all the ills man and a maleficent nature in a perverted generosity may proffer, and to endure, never fully acquiescing but continuing the struggle as do his **"Strong Men"** and the old couple in Red River Bottom (**"Strange Legacies"**): "Guess we'll give it one mo' try. / Guess we'll give it one mo' try." "Vestiges," the last section of ***Southern Road,*** opens with a summons for renewed effort in the form, curiously enough, of a Petrarchan sonnet, **"Salutamus,"** a moving statement of commitment to the struggle of a people for freedom:

It is a gloomy path that we must go
And yet we know relief will come someday
For these seared breasts;
These are the becons to blaze out the way
We must plunge onward, onward, gentlemen.

The poem has a hortatory quality to which the contemporary ear may be little accustomed; but here, as in numerous instances, skill and passion join forces to prevail.

Not unrelated to the sense of moral outrage so eloquently present in Brown's work is the note of compassion for ordinary men, women and children, the little people of his poetic world. For all of its sensitivity, it is not sentimental; it is a genuine and authentic sentiment, a dimension of the sympathies which seems to be an attribute of certain Black American poets, but which also recalls a similar quality, perhaps for decipherable reasons, in the writing of the Irish and the Russians, in James Stephen's account of the demented old woman wandering, muttering, down the road, in William Butler Yeats' Crazy Jane, in Dostoevsky's compassion for all the hapless wretches who comprise the human condition. When that condition finally plays itself out, none could desire finer treatment than that Brown has arranged for Sister Lou:

Jesus will find yo' bed fo' you
Won't no servant evah bother wid you' room.
Jesus will lead you

To a room wid windows
Openin' on cherry trees an' plum trees
Bloomin' everlastin'.

An' dat will be yours
Fo' keeps.

Den take yo' time
Honey, take yo' bressed time.

The folkloric tradition which so richly grounds Brown's poetic world is nowhere more evident than in its exuberant and incomparable humor. It is more than laughing to keep from crying; it is a positive and creative force which, in a manner similar to the blues, achieves a triumph of the spirit over a bleak and unsparing landscape. The tall tales of Slim Greer are classic. (One of the few editorial lapses, especially for any devotee of these stories, is the omission of **"Slim in Hell"**: "Each devil was busy / wid a devilish broad, An' Slim cried 'Lawdy, / Lawd, Lawd, Lawd.'") To hear Brown read to a Boston audience **"Crispus Attucks McCoy,"** the choleric champion of his people with a threshold for racial slurs of absolute zero, is fully to witness the poem's uproarious humor. Readily evident here, as in his other poems, especially the folk poetry, is the intensely oral quality of a genuine voice, convincingly communicating itself not only in public recitation but also eloquently in silent reading from the printed page. One of the true gems, less well-known than others, is **"The Temple,"** in which the staunch West Indian admirer of Marcus Garvey rejects every great historical figure named as a far lesser person than his hero, losing a bit of his certainty only when asked directly to compare him to Jesus Christ:

"Well . . . Oi, mohn, give de faller little chance
He de very young mohn yet . . ."

The redemptive elan of Brown's humor is probably nowhere more infectiously present than in the royal personage of **"Sporting Beasley"** (James Weldon Johnson a half century ago appropriately called him "gorgeous") who struts down the opera aisle in Prince Albert coat, "top hat cocked one side his bulldog head," to pull out his opera glasses from Row A, "Mr. Missionary" to the "drab barnfowl of the world." Brown carries him imaginatively up to the "jasper gates." It would be fitting if, through some time warp, the legion of Sporting Beasley's admirers could be present when he paces in, "knees moving like well-oiled pistons" on through the ranks of Heaven, which would doubtlessly be in a roar. It is a soaring, life sustaining, revisionist humor, a refusal to be quelled so strongly present in the black folk tradition in which Brown's poetry is rooted.

In a time of transient affections in which personal commitment is perceived by many as a curious throwback, we are brought to realize that Brown's poetic world is an expression of love, love for a person and a people. This volume, ***The Collected Poems,*** is dedicated to the woman who "bewitched" him and who for over fifty years until her death in 1979 was his wife. To her he also dedicated **"Vestiges,"** the concluding section of ***Southern Road,*** and much of **"Remembrances,"** the last section of ***No Hiding Place.*** In **"Vestiges"** especially are lines of exquisite lyric beauty extolling her loveliness and affording intermittent glimpses of a rare, shared idyll. Language is again in issue. We begin to be aware of the diversity of energies at work within the creative psyche as the poetic elan breaks through to utterance of that which is most cherished. *Chose curieuse,* it emerges in two languages. All of **"Vestiges"** is in literary English, the standard poetic idiom of the language. In the best Romantic tradition (though he disclaims it), he muses on the death of the beloved:

Death comes to some
Like a grizzled gangster
Clubbing in the night;

. . . . .

To some like a brown adder
Lurking in violet-speckled underbrush;
To some
Like a gentle nurse
Taking their toys and stroking their hot brows.

Death will come to you, I think
Like an old shrewd gardener
Culling his rarest blossom . . .

"Honey Mah Love" is a fusion of language forms, but **"Conjured"** and **"Long Track Blues"** are in the medium which is the lexical hallmark of the poet, the idiom of the folk. In World War II, the Allies employed whistles of such high frequency they could not without special apparatus be detected by the human ear. Some of Brown's poems exemplify this phenomenon. **"Long Track Blues"** is such a communication. It foresees the death of the beloved; it is a message uttered at such intense frequency, at first we do not hear it. It is at once a prophecy and the expression of the loss, a silent shout, the scream of the bereaved, uttered in the formal accents of the blues. Her departure, even as the conclusion of the lifework of the poet, sounds "wid a mighty roar." "Then the red taillight, and the place gets dark once more."

Here, as elsewhere, past and present form a circle, the end foretold in the beginning. **"Long Track Blues,"** the concluding poem, is posed against the dedication prefacing the volume, "To Rose Anne, as ever." The circularity is the more remarkable when we note in the bibliography that Brown's first published poem is **"Challenge"** (later appearing in the **"Vestiges"** section of ***Southern Road***) in which, again in the vein of the Romantics, he asserts the sustaining power of love against death itself: "My hymns (shall) float in praise undauntedly." In a reversed sequence, **"Long Track Blues,"** though written decades earlier, is a prescient cry of loss. The dedication which prefaces the volume but which was written last is the poet's stubborn reaffirmation of his challenge. The end of the journey is, again, in the setting out.

A related facet in the composition of his canvas extends even further our understanding of the poet and his purpose. Although **"Vestiges"** is dedicated to "Rose Anne" and most of the poems concern her, the lead poem in the group, **"Salutamus,"** has no ostensible relevance to their relationship. The poem is, rather, as we have seen, a "hail and farewell" to those who share with him "the searing brand" of oppression, a salute to those who will come after to pick up and advance, in turn, the struggle. It is this confluence of affections, the life long love for a woman and the love for and commitment to a people which offers possibly the deepest insight into the wellsprings of the poet's creativity and affords a measure of his heroic stature.

A brace of Harpers, editor and publisher, collaborated in bringing this long overdue volume to fruition. In providing for the first time in one place the full range of his work, this Harper and Row edition, ably edited by Michael Harper, himself a prize winning poet and Brown University professor, will hasten measurably the tardy but now swelling awareness that in Sterling Brown the country has not only a poet of the very first rank but a brilliant example, as the nation still gropes toward its meaning, of that rare, inexplicable and valued genus, an original. The century draws to a close and features will begin to fade, but we hear the voice even more clearly, still spacious, still uncomplaining, still on target:

> If man's life goes
> Beyond the bone
> Man must go lonely
> And alone,
> Unhelped, unhindered
> On his own . . .

Michael Harper as editor and Harper and Row as publisher have fashioned a craft worthy of the rich yield of Brown's historic career, and with its happy and appropriate designation as the first in the National Poetry Series, succeeded admirably in bringing it to shore.

Note

1. *The Collected Poems of Sterling A. Brown.* Edited by Michael S. Harper. New York: Harper and Row. 1980. 257 pp.

EUGENIA COLLIER (ESSAY DATE 1999)

SOURCE: Collier, Eugenia. "Message to the Generations: The Mythic Hero in Sterling Brown's Poetry." In *The Furious Flowering of African American Poetry,* edited by Joanne V. Gabbin, pp. 25-37. Charlottesville, Va.: University Press of Virginia, 1999.

In the following essay, Collier examines Brown's Collected Poems *for his use of archetype, ritual, and seriousness of effect, and gauges her own response to determine the extent to which Brown employs both local and universal mythic elements.*

* * *

> *Great poetry draws its strength from the life of mankind. . . . Whenever the collective unconscious becomes a living experience and is brought to bear upon the conscious outlook of an age, this event is a creative act which is of importance for a whole epoch. A work of art is produced that may truthfully be called a message to the generations.*
>
> —*Carl Jung*

A measure of the greatness of any artistic form is the extent to which the artist is able to reach beyond the context of the age and to address the wider concerns of mankind. In assessing the poetry of Sterling Brown, we need to include in our examination the extent to which he delves into the area of these concerns—the realm of myth.

Myth encompasses our deepest truths, tested by the ages, as fresh to us now as to our earliest ancestors. It is "the embodiment of human aspiration and its appropriate imaginative form."[1] Thus myth makes tangible our human potential. Philosopher Joseph Campbell defines mythologies as "poetic expressions of transcendental seeing." Myth transcends time itself, linking us with our forebears and with future generations. Campbell points out that "if we may take as evidence the antiquity of certain basic mythic forms . . . the beginnings of what we may take today to be mystical revelation must have been known to at least a few, even of the primitive teachers of our race, from the very start."[2] Jane Campbell, in her study *Mythic Black Fiction,* defines African American myth as "a dramatic embodiment of cultural values, of ideal states of being found in Afro-American history and experience."[3]

I speak, of course, of two levels of myth: the local and the universal. Each culture has its own ethos wrought from historical experience. The myths of the Arabian Bedouins, for example, would differ in detail from those of the Eskimos. Yet undergirding the parochial level is the level of universal response. Joseph Campbell's *The Hero with a Thousand Faces* explains that despite the numberless conceptions of the hero arising from the different cultures of mankind, there are nevertheless discernible patterns that apply to the concept of the hero in all known cultures. Local myths, then, despite certain differences, draw from a pool of universal truths. "Mythology is the study of mankind's one great story . . . our search to find our place in the drama of the universe."[4]

Who, then, are the mythmakers? Who are the people charged with making tangible these sacred truths and setting them into place in this great, eternal drama? The artists are the mythmakers, for only they can plumb the depths of human experience and elicit from it the words, the sounds, the images to clothe in a particular culture's experiences the truths that are eternal. In the past, before the recent advances in technology, the artists remained unknown, and the songs of brilliant poets and musicians were honed and perpetuated by the people to whom they were meaningful. This, perhaps, was the ultimate test, for had the songs and narratives not contained the values of the people, they would never have lasted.

Individual experience is a vehicle by which the artist moves into the area of myth. "The poet," Carl Jung has written, "has plunged into the healing and redeeming depths of the collective psyche, where man is not lost in the isolation of consciousness and its errors and sufferings, but where all men are caught in a common rhythm which allows the individual to communicate his feelings and strivings to mankind as a whole." Jung further explains that "this re-immersion in the state of participation mystique" is what causes our profound response to great art, for "at that level of experience it is no longer the weal or woe of the individual that counts but the life of the collective."[5] "It is only from the insight of its own creative seers and artists that any people has ever derived its appropriate life-supporting and maturing myths."[6]

The poet is the ultimate seer; the art of poetry is the tangible form of the forces that support the life of a people. In the case of Sterling Brown, we don't just *read* his poetry; we *experience* it. We respond on a far more profound level than enjoyment or even—for us jaded old critics—appreciation of its "literary" value. Brown's poetry "jes' gits hold of us dataway." In his brilliant essay "The Forms of Things Unseen," Stephen Henderson attributes our response to the presence of "mascon" words and images in Sterling Brown's poems. By "mascon" Henderson means "a massive concentration of Black experiential energy which powerfully affects the meaning of Black speech, Black song, and Black poetry—if one, indeed, has to make such distinctions."[7] Our response, then, arises from an area of the self that is beyond the individual self, that dips into what we call, for convenience, the black experience. Beyond even that area is the realm of universal myth.

I do not assume any deliberate attempt on Brown's part to utilize myth in his poems. Certainly his criticism does not call for mythic proportions in anyone's poetry. He does devote important scholarship to folk forms, revealing his reverence for and indebtedness to the black folk, contributing mightily to our understanding of this vital layer of our collective self. I do assume that we—writers included—are shaped by forces beyond our consciousness and that a writer, then, may call upon these hidden depths without conscious volition. One dips into myth instinctively, because only the most profound level of humanity can meet the most profound human need and thus create great art.

Much of Brown's poetry is obviously not mythic. Among these poems are the sonnets and many of the poems written in standard English. These are the personal poems, valued for other reasons. But it is in the public voice, the voice of the spokesman, that Brown's work becomes myth.

FROM THE AUTHOR

WHY BROWN BECAME A POET

I wanted to understand my people. I wanted to understand what it meant to be a Negro. What the qualities of life were. With their imagination, they combine two great loves: the love of words and the love of life.

SOURCE: Sterling Allen Brown, *New York Times Book Review,* January 11, 1981.

In examining Brown's ***Collected Poems*** to ascertain which could be said to be mythic, I used four guidelines: the presence of archetype, the use of ritual, the seriousness of effect, and the depth of my own subjective response. By *archetype* I mean an image that appears repeatedly in the historical experience and thus in the art of a particular culture and can be identified, although in different guises, in the art of other cultures. By *ritual* I mean the tangible, physical acting-out of myth. Joseph Campbell defines ritual as "the enactment of a myth." In another work he states, "Myths are the mental supports of rites; rites, the physical enactments of myths."[8] By *seriousness of effect* I mean that the effect of the work moves beyond entertainment or titillation or even accepted concepts of beauty. It addresses the reader on a deeper level; through symbols and mascon words and images it evokes deeply embedded memories of significant shared experience; it fosters a desire to read it or hear it again; it imparts wisdom or strength. The criterion is the depth of subjective response—which is, of course, unmeasurable but real. I am a black person. How does this poem move *me*? "Wherever [the tyrant monster] sets his hand there is . . . a cry for the redeeming hero, the carrier of the shining blade, whose blow, whose torch, whose existence, will liberate the land."[9]

A culture is defined—in part, at least—by its concept of the heroic, as embodied in the archetypal hero, by myths of all systems that have emerged from each culture's historical experience. Stephen Henderson has pointed out that certain folk forms "take us outside the dimension of history into the universal realm of the mythical. In the oral tradition," he continues, "the dogged determination of the work songs, the tough-minded power of the blues, the inventive energy of jazz, and the transcendent vision of God in the spirituals and the sermons, all energize the idea of Liberation, which is itself liberated from the temporal, the societal, and the political—not with the narcotic obsession to remain above the world of struggle and change and death, but with full realization of a return to that world both strengthened and renewed."[10]

I have discerned at least three faces of mythic heroism in Sterling Brown's poetry. The first is the quiet, law-abiding person who has tried for a lifetime to live within the boundaries set by an essentially violent and racist society. Something happens, some unendurable thing, or perhaps some final insult is added to a lifetime of insults, and the quiet person snaps. The perilous journey begins, out of the safety of passivity into the hell of direct resistance. It is the way of destruction, as the hero makes his choice, but he emerges transformed—though physically dead—into a hero, whose story, as the existence of the poem attests, is a beacon to his people. The second heroic archetype is the one who meets life with defiance and—yes—with style. Despite the dehumanizing force of racism, this hero has such a sense of himself, such a wholeness of spirit, that he remains unbroken. The third heroic archetype is the person whose heroism lies not in one magnificent gesture but in the lifelong struggle to Be, the struggle to maintain life and dignity and wholeness of self through the most arduous day-to-day effort, despite terrible losses. Life itself is the perilous journey, and the one who survives intact is the boon to other travelers along the "road so rocky." Here the wise elder is the archetype, known to every culture, carrying the seed of wisdom to succeeding generations. In African American culture, the wise-elder archetype merges with the hero archetype, because to survive to old age with wisdom and dignity is itself, in a system of total oppression, an act of heroism. "Invariably Brown's poetry reveals an exploration of self-hood, a celebration of the strength and stoicism of Black people, and an abiding faith in the possibilities of their lives. Brown becomes myth-maker, keeper of the images, preserver of values and definitions."[11]

The most obvious hero in Brown's poetry is a quiet, law-abiding (sometimes downright meek) person who has endured racial cruelties until finally he has simply *had* it. One final bitter drop causes the dam to burst, and the heroic journey begins. The hero ventures forth from the tenuous security of passivity and strikes out at the monster racism. He makes the choice deliberately, knowing the dreadful consequences but finding courageous death preferable to unendurable life. He becomes more than his individual self; he becomes the personification of resistance to overwhelming forces; he is the standard-bearer for black people from the first enslaved Africans to our last enslaved descendants and thus for all the heroic wretched of the earth.

A quintessential example of this hero is Crispus Attucks McKoy. With tight-lipped irony Brown recreates a modern version of the historical Crispus Attucks, the escaped slave who confronted the British on the Boston Common. Armed with only his conviction, Attucks became the first American to die in the Revolution and thus sacrificed his life for a freedom denied to him and to his progeny. **"Crispus Attucks McKoy"** is written in the form of a ballad. The irony is intensified by the mock-heroic language in which the ballad is rendered.

> I sing of a hero,
> Unsung, unrecorded,
> Known by the name
> Of Crispus Attucks McKoy.[12]

The balladeer evokes the names of others who have resisted oppression: Garvey, Trotter, Du Bois. These three men are among the giants of our culture: each had a lifelong commitment to resistance; each made immeasurable sacrifices; each took us a step closer to ultimate victory over oppression. By evoking their names the balladeer links McKoy to a heroic line.

McKoy works as a servant, hating every minute.

> No monastic hairshirt
> Stung flesh more bitterly
> Than the white coat
> In which he was arrayed.
>
> (141)

Again the irony is effective—the ancient monks wore hairshirts as a sign of willingness to suffer for religious ideals. McKoy's white coat symbolizes imposed subservience and inferiority—which he accepted unwillingly as a result of limited choices.

We encounter McKoy at the moment of extreme tension, when he has endured as much as is humanly possible. The balladeer need not enumerate the incidents that have brought him to this point: a black audience knows. The bitter humor of the next incident is based upon double entendres, as McKoy's mindset requires him to react with strong emotion to words uttered in an entirely different context. These are mascon words, uttered generations before Steve Henderson coined the term. Here Brown gives flesh to a dynamic as old as oppression and as complex as language: certain words evoke responses in the oppressed that are far different from those of the oppressor. Words can cut. And words can empower.

McKoy quits his job when a white woman at a bridge party bids one spade. For a moment he is free, but then a bootblack calls out, "Shine?" and McKoy lets loose a "blue streak" of curses. So it goes as McKoy, like an exposed nerve, is excruciatingly sensitive to the words that carry generations of insults. McKoy smashes a window of a bakery that advertises "brown Betties" (141). On the subway McKoy "could have committed murder / Mayhem and cannibalism" when a maid admonishes her little charge, "Come over here, darling / Here's a little shade" (142). Finally he goes to the boxing arena, "his refuge, / Recompense for insults, / Solace for grief" (142), where a black boxer, Slugging Joe Johnson, is fighting an Irishman, Battling Dan O'Keefe. At first McKoy expects to find solace as Joe is slugging it out with the white man, pounding him to a pulp, making recompense to all black people. Here, too, is the mythic battle of the leaders of contending armies. This arena is crowded with white people of various European backgrounds as "Crispus strode in / Regally, boldly" (142)—the only black person there.

Herein lies the tragic choice: McKoy invests great feeling into the battle—his pride, his raison d'être, assuagement for his pain are all riding on Slugging Joe. When Joe is momentarily getting the worst of the fight, someone right behind McKoy yells, "Kill the Nigger!" (143) and all the agony of all the years falls upon McKoy. The ballad endows him with the spiritual power and tragic dignity of classical heroes:

> Crispus got up
> In all his fury;
> Lightning bolts zigzagged
> Out of his eyes.
> With a voice like thunder
> He blurted his challenge,
> "Will the bastard who said that
> Please arise."
>
> (143)

All rise—3,500 strong, Irish, Polish, Bohemian, Jew, gentile, and whatever, their differences unimportant, against this black man—"our hero /

Armed with his noble cause / Armed with righteousness / To battle goes." McKoy perishes. The next three stanzas grimly catalog the various locales in the Boston area—the very seat of democracy—where parts of McKoy's body are found. But the ballad ends with the assertion that all over this nation "the soul of our hero / *Goes marching on.*"

The effectiveness of the poem is due partly to Brown's masterful use of the ballad form.[13] Here Brown recreates the traditional language of old English balladeers, serious-faced but tongue in cheek. The contrast of the orderly (or apparently orderly) world of jolly old England with the chaotic, irrational, oppressive world forced upon black people, points out poignantly the horror of McKoy's life. Gabbin says, "As a poet, Brown's most significant achievement is his subtle adaptation of song forms, especially the blues, to the literature. Experimenting with the blues, spirituals, work songs, and ballads, he invents combinations that, at their best, retain the ethos of folk forms and intensify the literary quality of poetry. Like his fellow traveler Langston Hughes, Brown discovers how to enable one form to release the power of another."[14]

"Crispus Attucks McKoy" is presented in a folkloric form, the ballad, to portray an archetype in African American culture and indeed in virtually all cultures—the tragic hero who chooses death over continued degradation. Each step along the way, as McKoy moves inevitably toward the moment of the final terrible choice, like Hector, and John Henry, McKoy's steps lead to the ultimate ritual of physical destruction, a ritual enacted repeatedly in our history—recall Denmark Vesey, Nat Turner, Medgar Evers, and myriad nameless folk whose sacrifice will ever remain unnoted and unrecorded. The ritual of gratuitous suffering and death for a principle is, in fact, a cornerstone on which Christianity itself is founded.

Other Brown heroes also choose death over continued oppression. Most fully drawn is Joe Meek, "soft as pie," who reaches the limit of forbearance when two policemen "throw a po' girl down" and then when Joe politely inquires "ef they thought / They had done *just right,*" they beat him into unconsciousness—a symbolic rebirth—a changed man, his assertiveness released by raw injustice. He buys a gun and precipitates a shootout with the cops, the reserves, and the national guard—all the representatives of law and order arrayed against meek Joe Meek. Only through the treachery of the sheriff is Joe brought down, his last words reaffirming his rage.

Joe's story, too, is a ballad, this one sung by a black balladeer utilizing the black vernacular, who leaves us with this bit of folk wisdom:

> So you cain't never tell
>   How fas' a dog can run
> When you see him a-sleepin'
>   In the sun.
>
> (152)

Crispus Attucks McKoy and Joe Meek are both little people who tried to adjust to the system and to fit white America's historic definition of good, law-abiding black people. Our culture and our literature are replete with them. In their tragic choices, however, they become larger than ordinary life; they become heroes for the world's downtrodden little people to admire and perhaps even to emulate.

Old Lem tells of another hero who makes a choice. The poem uses spare, bare-boned language that is more effective than volumes of words. The narrator says simply, "I talked to Old Lem / And Old Lem said . . ." (170). We do not know why the apparently uneducated narrator sought out Old Lem. But we can infer that he went to this unlettered man who has lived and survived for so many years because in him there is life-sustaining wisdom. Old Lem's terse, bitter words capture the awful rituals of racism, the refrain reiterating the message:

> They don't come by ones
> They don't come by twos
> But they come by tens.
>
> (170)

Old Lem tells about his buddy, "Six foot of man / Muscled up perfect / Game to the heart" who "spoke out of turn / At the commissary." Unlike the ballads of Crispus Attucks McKoy and Joe Meek, this poem does not provide a full-blown scenario. Old Lem tells us only the essentials:

> They gave him a day
> To git out of the county.
> He didn't take it.
>
> (171)

Here the hero makes a deliberate choice. He has left the relative security of anonymity not by leaving home but by *staying* home and shedding the role white society has forced upon him. He "spoke out of turn." That is all we need to know. That is the start of the heroic journey—a swift, brief journey:

> He said, "Come and get me!"
> And they came and got him.
> . . . . .
> He stayed in the county—
> He lays there dead.
>
> (171)

The simplicity of Old Lem's words intensifies the horror of the ritual—a ritual so often repeated that it is indelibly stamped on our racial memory.

Look at old Scrappy puttin' on dog,
Puttin' on dog, puttin' on dog,
Look at old Scrappy puttin' on dog,
Steppin' like nobody's business.

(227-28)

Heroism is easy to identify in tragic protagonists like Crispus Attucks McKoy, Joe Meek, and Old Lem's buddy. However, there is another type of heroism that is less obvious but just as real: here the hero repudiates the definition of the oppressed self and dares to live not meanly but flamboyantly. Unlike Joe Meek and Crispus Attucks McKoy, this hero has never played the role assigned to him by white racism. From the start he has refused to accept the role that white America imposes upon him and has dared to maintain his vision of himself.

Sterling Brown's poetry is peopled with vivid, vertical characters who maintain their selfhood in the face of ego-destroying forces. Joanne Gabbin's conversations with Brown reveal that these heroes are not paper dolls cut from the poet's imagination: they are real-life people whom Brown knew during his travels into America's black heartland—the South with its bloody, ineradicable history, its terrible testing of America's promise, its role as nucleus of African American culture in this sad land. In form as well as in content, these portrayals emanate from the blood-soaked soil from which our ancestors sprang.

It is, I think, very important that the first poem in Brown's classic ***Southern Road*** is **"The Odyssey of Big Boy."** This poem sets the tone for the rest of the volume and establishes the strength and dignity of the folk. The poem is based upon an itinerate guitar-playing roustabout, Calvin "Big Boy" Davis, whom Brown knew in that significant period when Brown taught at Virginia Seminary. Big Boy inspired two other poems, **"Long Gone"** and **"When de Saints Go Ma'ching Home,"** with the latter dedicated to Big Boy Davis "in memory of the times before he was chased out of town for vagrancy." The three poems are a trilogy that reveals a hero of mythic proportions.

"The Odyssey of Big Boy" begins and ends, as Gabbin has pointed out, with Big Boy's claim of immortality along with folk heroes Casey Jones, Stagolee, John Henry, Jazzbo, and "such like men." By evoking this lexicon of heroes, Brown has lifted Big Boy from the category of the colorful individual and made him the voice of the African American worker, whose labor has built this land. The poem, a ballad sung by Big Boy himself, is a catalog of the work Big Boy has done and the places he has traveled, as well as the listing of his sexual exploits along the way. Gabbin has written: "Big Boy represents the strong, resourceful Black worker who, denied the adventure of vertical movement in American businesses and industry, has wandered from job to job, from state to state, earning his wages with sweat and grit. . . . As Big Boy tells of his exploits in love and life, he assures his place in legend. Here, Brown is myth-maker. As the title helps to suggest a relationship between Big Boy and other heroes who had made their odysseys (Homer's Odysseus, Virgil's Aeneas, Dante's Pilgrim), Big Boy is raised to the level of mythic hero who embodies the values, attitude, *Weltshaung* of his people."[15]

Big Boy's heroic journey, then, as reiterated in **"Long Gone"** and **"When de Saints Go Ma'ching Home,"** is the long and dangerous journey not only from place to place but also through life, a battle in which he is undefeated, from which he has clearly emerged as victor.

Slim Greer is another such hero: Slim Greer, the trickster figure cut from the same cloth as Bre'r Rabbit and Anansi the Spider. The real Slim Greer was a waiter in Jefferson City—

Talkinges' guy
An' biggest liar,[16]
With always a new lie
On the fire

(77)

In a series of poems Slim Greer travels to "Arkansaw," Atlanta, and even Hell itself, where he slays the dragon of racism, escapes destruction, and returns to tell the tale. Slim not only survives but prevails to tell the story of his adventures and thus to teach and inspire.

O you rascal, puttin' on dog,
Puttin' on dog, puttin' on dog,
O you rascal, puttin' on dog,
Great Gawd, but you was a man!

(228)

Big Boy, Long Gone, Slim Greer, Sporting Beasley, and Scrappy are flamboyant heroes who have confronted the system and triumphed. There is a third type of mythic hero in Brown's poetry—the wise elder, whose life has been a journey into chaos and back. It is a chaos well-known to African Americans, not needful of description because, in various ways, we have all been there. Brown's wise elder, in the manner of the Greek seer Tiresias, teaches us survival and more than survival, not only by overt statement but more by the force of *Being.* The wise elder shows us through his or her life the strength and wisdom we are all capable of.

Perhaps the strongest "wise elder" may be immortalized in **"Sister Lou"** and **"Virginia Portrait,"** both portraits of Mrs. Bibby, the mother of one of Brown's students at Virginia Seminary. She was, as Brown told Joanne Gabbin, a "small, spry Indian-looking woman" who embodied the strength and wisdom that can emerge only from suffering. Gabbin writes, "On the many occasions that Brown was in her home, he became aware of her 'quiet nonchalance,' her 'courtly dignity of speech and carriage,' her 'strength and steadfast hardihood,' and her grief-tempered faith. Her disappointment when the crops were ruined by drought or by unexpected frost, her grief over her children who predeceased her, her simple joys are all captured in a pair of remarkably drawn portraits of a woman who was 'illiterate and somehow very wise.'"[17]

Ma Rainey, the great blues singer, was not really old enough to be an elder, but her designation as "Ma" reveals the nature of her image in the eyes of her listeners. She had seen so much, suffered so much, and emerged strong as steel tempered by fire. In her songs she told her heroic story and showed her listeners the way. In his poem **"Ma Rainey,"** Sterling Brown the poet-mythmaker tells how Ma Rainey, the carrier of the culture, is needed, how folks from miles around "flocks to hear / Ma do her stuff." Her art heals. She signs "Backwater Blues," which arose from the deepest sorrows of folks ravished not only by the cruelties of racism but also by the cruelty of nature. But the people rose from destruction, their humanity intact.

Ma's songs have had a profound impact on the audience, whose lives she has sung:

> An' den de folks, dey naturally bowed dey heads
> an' cried,
> Bowed dey heavy heads, shet dey moufs up tight
> an' cried,
> An' Ma lef' de stage, an' followed some de folks
> outside.
>
> (63)

Thus the artist merges with the people, and they become one.

Sterling Brown, too, like Ma Rainey and Mrs. Bibby, like Crispus Attucks McKoy and Joe Meek and Old Lem's buddy, like Old Lem himself and Big Boy Davis and Scrappy, like all the other heroes he has given us, all have melted into one another and added their strength and wisdom to a pool from which all of humanity can draw—now and into the unfathomable future. Thus Brown emerges as poet-hero, one who seized the sacred fire and offers its light to generations yet unborn.

Notes

1. Righter, 3.
2. Joseph Campbell, *Myths to Live By,* 30.
3. Jane Campbell, *Mythic Black Fiction,* x.
4. Joseph Campbell and Bill Moyers, *Power of Myth,* 54-55.
5. Jung, 104-5.
6. Joseph Campbell, *Myths to Live By,* 50.
7. Henderson, 44.
8. Joseph Campbell, *Myths to Live By,* 82.
9. Joseph Campbell, *Hero with a Thousand Faces,* 15-16.
10. Henderson, 20-21.
11. Gabbin, 4-5.
12. Brown, 141. Hereafter only page numbers will be cited for those poems appearing in this collection.
13. See Gabbin's analysis of the ballad in Brown's poetry, 161-69.
14. Ibid., 4.
15. Ibid., 162-63.
16. "Liar" here means teller of tall tales. Sterling Brown claimed to be "the best liar at Howard University."
17. Gabbin, 34-35.

Works Cited

Brown, Sterling A. *The Collected Poems of Sterling Brown.* Sel. Michael S. Harper. New York: Harper, 1980.

Campbell, Jane. *Mythic Black Fiction: The Transformation of History.* Knoxville: University of Tennessee Press, 1986.

Campbell, Joseph. *The Hero with a Thousand Faces.* Princeton: Princeton University Press, 1949.

———. *Myths to Live By.* New York: Bantam, 1972.

Campbell, Joseph, and Bill Moyers. *The Power of Myth.* New York: Doubleday, 1987.

Gabbin, Joanne V. *Sterling A. Brown: Building the Black Aesthetic Tradition.* Westport: Greenwood, 1985.

Gould, Eric. *Mythical Intentions in Modern Literature.* Princeton: Princeton University Press, 1981.

Henderson, Stephen. *Understanding the New Black Poetry: Black Speech and Black Music as Poetic References.* New York: Morrow, 1975.

Jung, Carl G. *Collected Works.* Princeton: Princeton University Press, 1953-79. Vol. 15.

Righter, William. *Myth and Literature.* Boston: Routledge, 1975.

FURTHER READING

Criticism

Barnes, Deborah H. "'The Elephant and the Race Problem': Sterling A. Brown and Arthur P. Davis as Cultural Conservators." *Callaloo* 21, no. 4 (fall 1998): 985-997.

Compares the use of the elephant parable by Brown and Arthur P. Davis, theorizing that it is employed as a means to record and interpret African American cultural experiences.

Benston, Kimberly W. "Listen Br'er Sterling: The Critic as Liar [A Pre(r)amble to Essays on Sterling Brown]." *Callaloo* 21, no. 4 (fall 1998): 837-45.

Considers the importance of recordings of Brown's oral presentations, lectures, and tutorials to understanding his larger body of work.

Callahan, John F. "'A Brown Study': Sterling Brown's Legacy of Compassionate Connections." *Callaloo* 21, no. 4 (fall 1998): 896-910.

Compares Brown's poetry and criticism with William Butler Yeats's Irish folklore in order to examine thematic similarities.

Collins, Michael. "Risk, Envy and Fear in Sterling Brown's Georgics." *Callaloo* 21, no. 4 (fall 1998): 950-67.

Explores Brown's portrayal of risk in his Georgic poems and considers the many links to economics in his work.

Gates, Jr., Henry Louis. "Songs of a Racial Self." *The New York Times Book Review* (11 January 1981): 11, 16.

Reviews The Collected Poems of Sterling A. Brown.

Hirsch, Edward. "Reverberations of a Work Song." *The American Poetry Review* 28, no. 2 (March-April 1999): 43-47.

Examines Brown's use of the work song and its lyrical structure.

Kutzinski, Vera M. "The Distant Closeness of Dancing Doubles: Sterling Brown and William Carlos Williams." *Black American Literature Forum* 16, no. 1 (spring 1982): 19-25.

Examines Brown's Southern Road *and William Carlos Williams's* Paterson *to demonstrate the relationship between Anglo-American and African American poetics.*

O'Meally, Robert G. "Reconsideration: Sterling A. Brown." *The New Republic* 178, no. 6 (11 February 1978): 33-36.

Briefly considers Brown's use of folk ballads, focusing on the humor and pathos in Brown's work.

Pinckney, Darryl. "The Last New Negro." *The New York Review of Books* 36, no. 4 (16 March 1989): 14-16.

Discusses Brown's rejection of the Harlem Renaissance as a "publisher's gimmick" and his position as the "Last of the New Negros."

Sanders, Mark A. "Sterling A. Brown and the Afro-Modern Moment." *African American Review* 31, no. 3 (fall 1997): 393-98.

Considers Brown's Afro-Modernism through his use of a poetic vocabulary as well as Black idiomatic expressions and rituals that articulate African American modernity.

Sanders, Mark A. "Sterling A. Brown's Master Metaphor: *Southern Road* and the Sign of Black Modernity." *Callaloo* 21, no. 4 (fall 1998): 917-930.

Reads Brown's Southern Road *and its central image—the road—for its Afro-Modernism.*

Skinner, Beverly Lanier. "Sterling Brown: An Ethnographic Perspective." *African American Review* 31, no. 3 (fall 1997): 417-23.

Examines Brown's effort to invalidate the exploitative ethnographic enterprise of white academicians of his era, a push that paved the way for ethnographers and anthropologists to write more sensitively and accurately about other cultures.

Skinner, Beverly. "Sterling Brown's Poetic Ethnography: A Black and Blues Ontology." *Callaloo* 21, no. 4 (fall 1998): 998-1011.

Considers Brown's poetry and scholarship as an ethnography of Southern African American culture and examines the "Black and blues ontology" of his work.

Stepto, Robert. "'When De Saint Go Ma'chin' Home': Sterling Brown's Blueprint for a New Negro Poetry." *Callaloo* 21, no. 4 (fall 1998): 940-49.

Examines Brown's Big Boy Davis poem "When De Saint Go Ma'chin' Home" as a blueprint for a new kind of folk poetry.

Thomas, Lorenzo. "Authenticity and Elevation: Sterling Brown's Theory of the Blues." *African American Review* 31, no. 3 (fall 1997): 409-17.

Examines Brown's early poetry for his integration of the musicality of blues and folk ballads with the complexity of poetic expression in order to discuss the originality of this artistry and for the ways it encouraged African American self-determination.

Tidwell, John Edgar. "Double Conscious Brother in the Veil: Toward an Intellectual Biography of Sterling Brown." *Callaloo* 21, no. 4 (fall 1998): 931-39.

Theorizes that Brown's intellectual evolution results from his "paradoxical existence" as an African American, an American, and an intellectual.

———. "Two Writers Sharing: Sterling A. Brown, Robert Frost, and 'In Dives' Dive.'" *African American Review* 31, no. 3 (fall 1997): 399-409.

Examines Brown's assertion that he shared rather than was influenced by Robert Frost's notion of poetic tradition, using the poem "In Dive's Dive" to demonstrate this poetic tradition in both Black and white poetry.

Traylor, Eleanor W. "'Runnin' Space': The Continuing Legacy of Sterling Allen Brown." *African American Review* 31, no. 3 (fall 1997): 389-93.

Assesses Brown's literary work as it sought to improve the plight of African Americans by validating their intellect and morality, and examines Brown's legacy to institutions of higher learning.

Wright, John S. "The New Negro Poet and the Nachal Man: Sterling Brown's Folk Odyssey." *Black American Literature Forum* 23, no. 1 (spring 1989): 95-105.

Examines Brown's role in the New Negro movement of the 1920s and the surge of interest in African American folklore at that time.

OTHER SOURCES FROM GALE:

Additional coverage of Brown's life and career is contained in the following sources published by the Gale Group: *Black Literature Criticism,* Vol. 1; *Black Writers,* Eds. 1, 3; *Contemporary Authors,* Vol. 85-88; *Contemporary Authors New Revision Series,* Vol. 26; *Contemporary Literary Criticism,* Vols. 1, 23, 59; *Dictionary of Literary Biography,* Vols. 48, 51, 63; *DISCovering Authors Modules: Multicultural Authors,* and *Poets; DISCovering Authors 3.0*; and *Major 20th-Century Writers,* Eds. 1, 2.

COUNTEE CULLEN

(1903 - 1946)

American poet, novelist, editor, and children's writer.

One of the preeminent figures of the Harlem Renaissance, Countee Cullen attained literary fame at a young age with his critically acclaimed collection of poetry *Color* (1925). Reluctant to be labeled primarily as an African American poet, Cullen strove to create poetry that transcended race. However, it is often his verses on the African American experience that capture the greatest critical and popular attention. Cullen's brilliant early works illuminated 1920s America, and many consider his earliest accomplishments to be his best. In the 1930s his poetic output dwindled steadily both in quality and quantity, and with his premature death at the age of 43, the promise of his youth was cut short. Nevertheless, Cullen sits alongside Langston Hughes and Claude McKay as one of the most honored and significant figures of the Harlem Renaissance.

BIOGRAPHICAL INFORMATION

There is considerable uncertainty surrounding the early years of Cullen's life. It is now believed that Cullen's birth date was May 30, 1903. Cullen maintained that he was born in New York, while his second wife Ida Mae Roberson Cullen claimed it was Baltimore. Langston Hughes and Harold Jackman, however, claim Cullen was born in Louisville, Kentucky. His mother, Elizabeth Lucas, left Cullen—whom she named Countee LeRoy—when he was still an infant with an older woman named Mrs. Porter, possibly his paternal grandmother. Little is known about Cullen's father. Young Countee took Mrs. Porter's last name, and when he was nine they moved to New York City. When she died in 1918, Reverend and Mrs. Frederick Cullen of the local Salem Methodist Episcopal Church informally adopted Countee, who was to be their only child. Reverend Cullen's church was the largest in Harlem and its socially progressive tenor and exuberant services influenced the younger Cullen. Settled happily with his new family, Cullen attended DeWitt Clinton High School, where he began making a name for himself. While he had started writing poetry in elementary school, the predominantly white high school's literary magazine *The Magpie* gave Cullen his first experiences with editing and publishing. His poem "I Have a Rendezvous with Life," initially published in that magazine, went on to win both literary prizes and general acclaim. Cullen was also a member of the high school scholastic honor society and served as vice-president of the senior class and treasurer of the Inter-High School Poetry Society. In 1922 Cullen graduated from high school and entered New York University, where he wrote and published with great success in a variety of literary journals reaching Black and white audiences alike. Cullen won awards in the Witter Bynner undergraduate poetry contest in 1923, 1924, and 1925. While still in college, Cullen won several poetry awards and established himself in the literary community as a promising new voice. In 1925 Cullen was elected to the prestigious Phi Beta Kappa honor society and won an award from *Poetry* magazine for his poem "Threnody for a Brown Girl," and awards from literary magazines *Crisis, Opportunity,* and *Palms.* He graduated from New York University the same year and published his first collection of poetry, *Color,* which met with great success. From here he went to Harvard University, where he continued to write and study literature, receiving his MA in 1926. That same year he became assistant editor to Charles S. Johnson at *Opportunity.* Cullen continued to write poetry that expressed anger and outrage for injustices against the African American community, but unlike his contemporaries Langston Hughes and Claude McKay—who upheld the poetic medium as a vehicle for social protest—Cullen's primary intent was to produce poetry and be, above all, a poet. *Copper Sun,* Cullen's second volume of poetry, appeared in 1927 to only slightly less enthusiastic reviews than for *Color.* At the same time Cullen launched a column in *Opportunity* called "The Dark Tower," where he regularly commented on the arts, culture, and literature. The next few years saw Cullen firmly entrenched in his editorial duties. As an offshoot of a project for *Palms,* wherein Cullen edited the first issue devoted entirely to African American poets, Cullen edited and contributed to a new anthology of African American poetry, *Caroling Dusk,* in 1927. This volume contains contributions by most of the young writers of the Harlem Renaissance and is considered an invaluable collection of African American writing of the 1920s.

In 1928, before leaving for a Guggenheim Fellowship tour abroad, Cullen married Nina Yolande Du Bois, daughter of the luminary W. E. B. Du Bois. It was the literary equivalent of a royal wedding, drawing attention from across the Harlem community. Shortly after the wedding Cullen and his adoptive father traveled to France and then to the Middle East, with Yolande meeting up with them back in France in July 1928. The marriage, however, was ill-fated and soon ended, with Yolande returning to New York and resuming her career. While in France, Cullen wrote poetry, some of which centers on the bitterness of lost love—perhaps resulting from the failed marriage, about which neither he nor his friends and family ever spoke—but his poetry from this time also explores Christian themes as well as the Black experience. He published much of this work in *The Black Christ and Other Poems* (1929) upon returning to New York. While Cullen loved France, and would return there regularly on vacations once his Guggenheim Fellowship had expired, his volume of poetry from that time was among the least successful of all his work.

While continuing to write poetry, Cullen recognized the need for a more stable income, and he decided to try his hand at prose, publishing his first and only novel, *One Way to Heaven,* in 1932. The novel employs two distinct plots that have seemingly little to do with one another, and for this reason met with little popular or critical interest. Harder economic times also made publishing a riskier enterprise and Cullen decided to turn his attention elsewhere. By this time his poetic output had slowed considerably and he became a junior-high school French and literature teacher, a career he believed his influence on young African American minds would do the most good. In the fall of 1940 Cullen married his second wife Ida Mae Roberson, whom he had known for ten years, and the two began a happy life together. Between his teaching career, his new wife, lecturing, and vacations in France, there was less time for poetry. Some critics argue that Cullen's poetic genius was waning, while others point to his other obligations as reason for the lull. In 1940 Cullen published a book of poetry for children called *The Lost Zoo,* which he followed in 1942 with a book of stories for children entitled *My Lives and How I Lost Them.* In 1945 Cullen collaborated with Arna Bontemps on the play *St. Louis Woman,* an adaptation of Bontemps's novel *God Sends Sunday.* It was set to open on Broadway and to follow with a Hollywood film adaptation, but accusations of being degrading to the Black community led to delays, nervousness on the part of sponsors and potential stars, and disagreement with Bontemps. Then, on January 9, 1946, Cullen died of uremic poisoning in New York City. He died just a few months before *St. Louis Woman* was performed at the Martin Beck Theater in New York. Prior to his death, Cullen had gathered and organized his poetry for what he felt would be the definitive anthology of his work. The result, the aptly named *On These I Stand: An Anthology of the Best Poems of Countee Cullen,* appeared in 1947, nearly a year after his death. The loss of such an influential figure both in the literary world and for the African American community was met with considerable attention and public mourning.

MAJOR WORKS

In Cullen's first collection of verse, *Color,* he blends a sense of musicality with his protest against the injustices felt by African Americans. "Heritage," which many consider to be amongst the very best of Cullen's verse, explores tensions, between the past and present, and between Africa and America. Hearkening back to a pastoral, idealized image of Africa, the poem presents a struggle between an intellectualized, Westernized, and yet degraded self with a persistent bond to a lost African past. In it the bonds of racial unity are called upon as a means to easing the tension. In his next collection of verse, *Copper Sun,* Cullen's sonnet "From the Dark Tower" captures what has been called by some critics the spirit of Harlem Renaissance poetry. Influenced by nineteenth-century Romantic poetry, the Dark Tower is actually a place on 136th street in Harlem where literary figures would gather. "From the Dark Tower" employs the symbol of planting and reaping to ask how long must African Americans continue to plant only to see others take the fruit of their labor. *The Medea and Some Poems* (1935) includes Cullen's treatment of the classical drama *Medea* as well as a selection of new poems, including "The Cat," "Medusa," and "Only the Polished Skeleton."

One Way to Heaven, Cullen's only novel, focuses on two different storylines occurring within the Harlem community. In the major plot, a Harlem maid, Mattie Johnson, becomes involved with a one-armed gambler and trickster from Texas named Sam Lucas. The characters are stereotypical, with con-man Sam convincing Mattie to marry him by pretending to find religion on Christmas Eve. Once the couple is married, the plot falls deeper into the melodramatic with Sam having an affair and the death of Mattie's baby only hours after it is born. When Sam is dying, he overhears Maggie lament that her husband will be damned for all the terrible things he's done, and in an attempt to put his wife's fears to rest, Sam again pretends an epiphany and a religious conversion. In the secondary plot, wealthy Constancia Brandon is hostess to a group of superficial Harlem intellectuals, satirizing actual experiences Cullen had at salons in the 1920s. The two plots interconnect only tenuously, and it is this discord that most critics and readers take issue with. In Cullen's other works he explores Christian and Classical themes, often borrowing in style and form from traditional writers like Keats and Shelley.

CRITICAL RECEPTION

When he burst onto the scene of what would later be known as the Harlem Renaissance, Cullen was heralded as one of the most significant poetic voices of the burgeoning movement. With his first publication as a high school student, through his numerous poetic awards during his college years and his first two collections of poetry, Cullen enjoyed great critical and popular success. His use of traditional literary forms, themes, and devices made his work recognizable to white critics and readers, while his emotional evocation of African American experience and his presentation of Blacks as real and beautiful earned him respect and acclaim from the Black community. Meanwhile, the natural musicality of his verse spoke to both critical and popular tastes. His was not an easy position to take, and he was often criticized for not being ardent enough in his protest against the social injustices faced by African Americans. Likewise, there was resistance from both Blacks and whites to his desire to be considered as a poet uncategorized by race. At the same time, he was among the most recognizable African American literary figures, with an influence that was not bound exclusively to the largely African American journals *Crisis* and *Opportunity,* but that saw favor in wider circulation publications such as *Poetry* and *Palms. Color* and *Copper Sun* were widely reviewed—and praised—in publications such as the *New York Times,* and his work was frequently anthologized. But the seemingly limitless potential of the young poet in his twenties met with increasingly cooler critical reception as he aged. The steady decline in the quantity and quality of his work has been a widely debated mystery. Some fear the muse had left the once vibrant poet, but others suggest that his work as an editor and then as a teacher used up his free time to the detriment of his creative impulse. Many critics have commented on the extent to which John Keats influenced Cullen's work, both on a technical and a more abstract thematic level, with some critics also considering the influence of William Blake, and Edna St. Vincent Millay—the subject of Cullen's senior honors thesis at New York University. A small contingent of critics speculate about Cullen's sexuality and the extent to which it is possible that homosexuality may have influenced his work. Despite disappointment in Cullen's later work, the brilliance of his early poetry and the personal political line he walked between being an African American poet and simply a poet offer a great deal for future students and critics to consider. His preeminence as a Harlem Renaissance figure demonstrates that his contribution was artistically and culturally significant not simply to Black literature but to American literature.

PRINCIPAL WORKS

Color (poetry) 1925

The Ballad of the Brown Girl: An Old Ballad Retold (poetry) 1927

Caroling Dusk: An Anthology of Verse by Negro Poets [editor and contributor] (poetry) 1927

Copper Sun (poetry) 1927

The Black Christ and Other Poems (poetry) 1929

One Way to Heaven (novel) 1932

The Medea and Some Poems (drama and poetry) 1935

The Lost Zoo (A Rhyme for the Young, But Not Too Young) (juvenilia) 1940

My Lives and How I Lost Them (juvenilia) 1942

St. Louis Woman [with Arna Bontemps] (play) 1946

On These I Stand: An Anthology of the Best Poems of Countee Cullen (poetry) 1947

My Soul's High Song: The Collected Writings of Countee Cullen, Voice of the Harlem Renaissance (poetry) 1991

PRIMARY SOURCES

COUNTEE CULLEN (POEMS DATE 1927)

SOURCE: Cullen, Countee. "From the Dark Tower" and "Sonnet to a Scornful Lady." In his *Copper Sun,* pp. 3, 35. New York: Harper & Brothers, 1927.

Taken from Cullen's second collection of poetry, these poems highlight the author's skill in utilizing evocative language to describe both the wonders of nature and sentiments of love.

"FROM THE DARK TOWER"

We shall not always plant while others reap
The golden increment of bursting fruit,
Not always countenance, abject and mute,
That lesser men should hold their brothers
    cheap;
Not everlastingly while others sleep
Shall we beguile their limbs with mellow flute,
Not always bend to some more subtle brute;
We were not made eternally to weep.

The night whose sable breast relieves the stark,
White stars is no less lovely, being dark,
And there are buds that cannot bloom at all
In light, but crumple, piteous, and fall;
So in the dark we hide the heart that bleeds,
And wait, and tend our agonizing seeds.

"SONNET TO A SCORNFUL LADY"

Some for a little while do love, and some for
    long;
And some rare few forever and for aye;
Some for the measure of a poet's song,
And some the ribbon width of a summer's day.

Some on a golden crucifix do swear,
And some in blood do plight a fickle troth;
Some struck divinely mad may only stare,
And out of silence weave an iron oath.

So many ways love has none may appear
The bitter best, and none the sweetest worst;
Strange food the hungry have been known to
    bear,
And brackish water slakes an utter thirst.

It is a rare and tantalizing fruit
Our hands reach for, but nothing absolute.

GENERAL COMMENTARY

BEULAH REIMHERR (ESSAY DATE 1963)

SOURCE: Reimherr, Beulah. "Race Consciousness in Countee Cullen's Poetry." *Susquehanna University Studies* 7, no. 2 (June 1963): 65-82.

In the following excerpt, Reimherr considers race as thematically central to Cullen's poetry.

The theme of race consciousness is one of several themes that run through the poetry of Countee Cullen. Nature, classical mythology, love, death, religion, the animals that failed to reach Noah's ark, even cats, captured his pen. Although Cullen stoutly defended his right to deal with any subject that interested him, James Weldon Johnson felt that the best of Cullen's poetry was motivated by race. . . .

In Cullen's poetry, the themes of love and religion hold a place of equal importance with the theme of race consciousness. Cullen was essentially a lyric poet; however, an awareness of color and the difference it made in America influenced his early poetry and ran as an undercurrent of frustration and depression in his later writing. There was a much greater consciousness of race in ***Color*** than in his subsequent books. One-third of the poems in ***Color*** have some reference to race, but only one-seventh of the poem in ***Copper Sun*** and ***The Black Christ*** have any racial overtones, and only two poems in ***The Medea.***

There was a tension between Cullen's desire to be purely a lyric poet and his feelings of race-consciousness. Cullen stated: "Most things I write, I do for the sheer love of the music in them. Somehow or other, however, I find my poetry of itself treating of the Negro, of his joys and his sorrows—mostly of the latter, and of the heights and the depths of emotion which I feel as a Negro."

This was especially true of ***Color,*** which was impregnated with race consciousness. A reviewer of ***Color*** stated: "Every bright glancing line abounds in color," the designation used by Cullen for his racial poems [*Crisis,* March, 1926]. This critic pointed out that there are a few poems with no mention of color which any genuine poet, black or white, could have written. These are best exemplified by such poems a **"To John Keats, Poet At Spring Time,"** the numerous epitaphs, and the shorter poems on love, death, and the swift passing of life. A second group of poems have the adjectives "black," "brown" or "ebony" deliberately introduced to show that the author had color in mind. Such poems include **"To a Brown Girl," "To a Brown Boy," "Black Magadalens," "A Brown Girl Dead," "Bread and Wine," "Wisdom Cometh with the Years,"** and **"Threnody for a Brown Girl."** Others arise with full race consciousness. These include the many poems describing the prejudice of America toward the Negro and his reactions to discrimination. As stated by Owen Dodson, if one were to ask any Negro what he found in Cullen's poetry, he would say "All my dilemmas are written here—the hurt pride, the indignation, the satirical thrust the agony of being black in America ["Countee Cullen," *Phylon,* First Quarter, 1946]

Cullen's first important poem to contain feelings of race consciousness is **"The Shroud of Color."** Before condemning it for its echoes of Milton and Edna St. Vincent Millay, it should be noted that the poem was written when Cullen was barely twenty. Yet Laurence Stallings considered it the most distinguished poem to appear in *American Mercury* for 1924.

Cullen introduced the poem by describing his joy in the beauty of the world and his idealism that saw in man "a high-perfected glass where loveliness could lie reflected. However, truth taught him that because of his color, man would kill his dreams. His color was "a shroud" that was strangling him, for it prevented others from seeing him as an individual.

> "Lord, being dark," I said, "I cannot bear
> The further touch of earth, the scented air;
> Lord, being dark, forewilled to that despair
> My color shrouds me in, I am as dirt
> Beneath my brother's heel. . . .

In a series of four visions God showed him that struggle, not suicide is the law of life In the first vision, the struggle of the plant kingdom toward fulfillment was described Some seeds thrust eager tentacles to sun and rain, climb, yet die; but others burst into triumphant bloom. The second vision revealed the struggle within the animal kingdom for life. In beautiful lines Cullen stated:

> And no thing died that did not give
> A testimony that it longed to live.
> Man, strange composite blend of brute and god,
> Pushed on, nor backward glanced where last he
> trod.
> He seemed to mount a misty ladder flung
> Pendant from a cloud, yet never gained a rung
> But at his feet another tugged and clung.

But still, his conclusion was that, "those whose flesh is fair" can fight on. The scene shifted to heaven where even God had to struggle to preserve his mastery against the forces of Lucifer. The last scene was a vision of his own people, of their flourishing life of freedom in Africa followed by the dark days of slavery. In spite of having been enslaved, the Negro maintained faith in man. His grief now seemed "puny" in light of the suffering that his people had lived through. The poem thus ended on a note of racial pride, a salient feature of the Negro Renaissance.

> With music all their hopes and hates
> Were changed, not to be downed by all the fates.
> And somehow it was borne upon my brain
> How being dark, and living through the pain
> Of it, is courage more than angels have . . .
> The cries of all dark people near or far
> Were billowed over me, a mighty surge
> Of suffering in which my puny grief must merge
> And lose itself; I had no further claim to urge
> For death. . . .

Some of Cullen's best expressions of race consciousness appear in his sonnets. In an early sonnet, **"Yet Do I Marvel,"** he presented four paradoxes and then "gathering up an infinity of irony, pathos and tragedy in the final couplet" stated the problem that most vitally concerned him. According to James Weldon Johnson, these are "the two most poignant lines in American literature [*The Book of American Negro Poetry,* 1931]. When one is oppressed for a difference beyond his control, how can he sing?

I doubt not God is good, well-meaning, kind,
And did He stoop to quibble could tell why
The little buried mole continues blind,
Why flesh that mirrors Him must some day die,
Make plain the reason tortured Tantalus
Is baited by the fickle fruit, declare
If merely brute caprice dooms Sisyphus
To struggle up a never-ending stair.
Inscrutable His ways are, and immune
To catechism by a mind too strewn
With petty cares to slightly understand
What awful brain compels His awful hand.
Yet do I marvel at this curious thing:
To make a poet black, and bid him sing!

Sorrow at the restrictions excluding Negroes from the mainstream of American life deepened in **"Hunger"** and **"The Dark Tower"** to a contemplation of suicide in **"Mood."** In **"Hunger"** Cullen expressed restlessness with the limited measure allotted him in a world that is "a pageant permeate with bliss". In **"The Dark Tower,"** Cullen cried out against the inferior position accorded Negroes. There was a place for both black and white in creation; surely then God did not intend subjection and sorrow to be the Negroes' eternal lot.

We shall not always plant while others reap
The golden increment of bursting fruit,
Not always countenance, abject and mute,
That lesser men should hold their brothers
    cheap;
Not everlastingly while others sleep
Shall we beguile their limbs with mellow flute,
We were not made eternally to weep.
The night whose sable breast relieves the stark,
White stars is no less lovely being dark,
And there are buds that cannot bloom at all
In light, but crumple, piteous, and fall;
So in the dark we hide the heart that bleeds,
And wait, and tend our agonizing seeds.

In **"A Thorn Forever in The Breast,"** he continued the thought of how far short the actual world was from the ideal world, or for the Negro, the black world from the white. Should he through his writing struggle to bring the actual closer to the ideal? He implied futility when he noted that Christ, the world's greatest idealist, died on a cross.

A hungry cancer will not let him rest
Whose heart is loyal to the least of dreams;
There is a thorn forever in his breast
Who cannot take his world for what it seems;
Aloof and lonely must he ever walk,
Plying a strange and unaccustomed tongue,
An alien to the daily round of talk,
Mute when the sordid songs of earth are sung.
This is the certain end his dream achieves:
He sweats his blood and prayers while others
    sleep,
And shoulders his own coffin up a steep
Immortal mountain, there to meet his doom
Between two wretched dying men, of whom
One doubts, and one for pity's sake believes.

All was not sorrow in Cullen's racial poems for some joy and racial pride are expressed. According to Sterling Brown, the complete picture of the Negro in America is not all tragedy. In his words: "I have heard laughter, high spirited enjoyment of living and not always—or mainly, among the lucky few—but rather among the harassed many. The Negro has ability to take it, to endure, and to wring out of life something of joy" [*The Quarterly Review of Higher Education Among Negroes,* July, 1941]. **"Harlem Wine,"** according to Arthur Davis, glorified the "uncontrollable strength of black living, contrasting it by implication with the 'watery' life of the other group" [*Phylon,* Fourth Quarter, 1953].

This is not water running here,
    These thick rebellious streams
That hurtle flesh and bone past fear
    Down alleyways of dreams.
This is a wine that must flow on
    Not caring how not where,
So it has ways to flow upon
    Where song is in the air. . . .

An equal picture of joy appeared in **"She of the Dancing Feet Sings,"** in which a girl felt her singing and dancing were out of place in heaven; she would rather join the "wistful angels down in hell."

And what would I do in heaven, pray,
    Me with my dancing feet,
And limbs like apple boughs that sway
    When the gusty rain winds beat?
And how would I thrive in a perfect place
    Where dancing would be sin,
With not a man to love my face
    Nor an arm to hold me in?

Racial pride characterized the Negro Renaissance. Instead of trying to submerge their differences, Negro writers gloried in them. In **"A Song of Praise"** Cullen pictured dark girls as being lovelier and more passionate than white girls.

You have not heard my love's dark throats,
    Slow-fluting like a reed,
Release the perfect golden note
    She caged there for my need.
Her walk is like the replica
    Of some barbaric dance
Wherein the soul of Africa
    Is Winged with arrogance. . . .

My love is dark as yours is fair,
Yet lovelier I hold her
Than listless maids with pallid hair,
And blood that's thin and colder . . .

Africa was a source of racial pride. In the Negro's search for a heritage to which he could look with pride, Africa became his dream world. The discovery of ancient Negro sculpture revealed Africa as once the possessor of an advanced civilization. America was discovered as an alien country and Africa pictured as a land of beauty and peace in **"Brown Boy to Brown Girl."**

. . . in no least wise
Am I uncertain that these alien skies
Do not our whole life measure and confine.
No less, once in a land of scarlet suns
And brooding winds, before the hurricane
Bore down upon us, long before this pain,
We found a place where quiet waters run;
I felt your hand this way upon a hill,
And felt my heart forebear, my pulse grow still.

In this distant heritage there were Negroes who were kings and queens. Thus, Jim the handsome hero of **"The Black Christ"** was of "imperial breed." The heroine of **"The Ballad of The Brown Girl"** "comes of kings" and her dagger had once been used by "a dusky queen, in a dusky, dream-lit land." One of Cullen's best sonnets [**"Black Majesty"**] described the heroic rulers of Haiti who fought for their independence against Napoleon. . . .

Cullen's treatment of Africa was influenced by the twin concepts of primitivism and atavism. For the primitivists, the Negro according to Robert Bone, had an especial appeal as "he represented the unspoiled child of nature, the noble savage—carefree, spontaneous, and sexually uninhibited" [*The Negro Novel in America*]. Atavism, in this context, was the persistence in present civilization of "old remembered ways" from Africa, a concept employed by Vachel Lindsay in "The Congo." A yearning for the African jungles, a desire to dance naked under palm trees, the imagined throbbing of tom-toms, and the feeling of savages were the expressions of atavism.

Several writers exposed the falsity of associating primitivism and atavism with the Negro. Although Wallace Thurman in his novel *Infants of the Spring* suggested that Alain Locke, Carl Van Vechten, and Countee Cullen favored atavism, he showed its falseness in his satiric description of a literary meeting at which the main writers of the Negro Renaissance debated whether African origins still persist in the American Negro. In this debate (quite the best thing in the entire book) Claude McKay, a poet and novelist of Jamaican background, proved conclusively that African origins do no persist in the American Negro, but that he is a perfect product of the melting pot. Hugh Gloster, in criticizing Van Vechten's novel *Nigger Heaven,* stated that "Van Vechten knows, or should know, that the Negro is no more primitivistic and atavistic than any other racial group that has been transplanted to America. He was merely a literary faddist capitalizing upon a current vogue and a popular demand" [*Infants of the Spring,* 1932]. Yet while the fad lasted, echoes of its appeared in Cullen's writing, especially in ***Color.*** In **"The Shroud of Color"** Cullen described the awakening of a chord long impotent in him.

Now suddenly a strange wild music smote
A chord long impotent in me; a note
Of jungles, primitive and subtle, throbbed
Against my echoing breast, and tom-toms
sobbed
In every pulse-beat of my frame. The din
A hollow log bound with a python's skin
Can make wrought every nerve to ecstasy,
And I was wind and sky again, and sea,
And all sweet things that flourish, being free.

Here the poet looked with longing to Africa because of the imagined freedom enjoyed there. A fuller statement of atavism is given in Cullen's famous poem, **"Heritage."** He introduced the poem by asking just what Africa could mean to one three centuries removed. Although the sights and sounds of Africa were forgotten, within the Negro's blood beat the savage rhythm of his "heritage". . . .

In **"Atlantic City Waiter,"** Cullen indulged in the fantasy of a waiter being more dexterous in his footwork because of a heritage of "ten thousand years on jungle clues." The spirit of the jungle flamed through his acquiescent mask.

Sheer through his acquiescent mask
Of bland gentility,
The jungle flames like a copper cask
Set where the sun strikes free.

To conclude, Cullen knew nothing about Africa save what he had gleaned in the course of his considerable reading. In the words of Arthur Davis, "Africa in his poem is not a place but a symbol; it is an idealized land in which the Negro had once been happy, kingly, and free."

Only five of Cullen's poems of love and friendship possess race consciousness, and in these five, his treatment was stereotyped rather than factual. **"Tableau"** pictures the absence of prejudice in children, but its presence in adults who have been conditioned by society.

Locked arm in arm they cross the way,
The black boy and the white,
The golden splendor of the day,
The sable pride of night.
From lowered blinds the dark folk stare,
And here the fair folk talk,
Indignant that these two should dare
In unison to walk. . . .

A more subtle picture of interracial friendship appears in **"Uncle Jim"** from ***Copper Sun.*** It is a puzzling but interesting poem. Because of the disagreement between the young man and his bitter uncle about white people, one can assume that the young man's friend was white. When he was with his friend, his mind reverted to Uncle Jim. Does this suggest that he was wondering whether there was any truth in his uncle's attitude that white folks were different, not to be trusted?

"White folks is white," says Uncle Jim;
"A platitude," I sneer;
And then I tell him so is milk,
And the froth upon his beer.
His heart walled up with bitterness,
He smokes his pungent pipe,
And nods at me as if to say,
"Young fool, you'll soon be ripe!"
I have a friend who eats his heart
Away with grief of mine,
Who drinks my joy as tipplers drain
Deep goblets filled with wine.
I wonder why here at his side,
Face-in-the-grass with him,
My mind should stray the Grecian urn
To muse on Uncle Jim.

Cullen's attitude towards God and the church was frequently interwoven with race consciousness. In **"Simon the Cyrenian Speaks"** he assumed that the man who carried the cross of Christ was a Negro because be came from Cyrene, a country of North Africa. Cullen somewhat falsely attributed to the Cyrenian his own sensitivity about color.

He never spoke a word to me,
And yet He called my name;
He never gave a sign to me,
And yet I knew and came.
At first I said, "I will not bear
His cross upon my back;
He only seeks to place it there
Because my skin is black" . . .
It was Himself my pity brought;
I did for Christ alone
What all of Rome could not have wrought
With bruise of lash or stone.

In **"Pagan Prayer,"** Cullen made his own acceptance of Christ contingent upon his people being fully accepted by society, especially by the church whose doors seemed barred from within. In this poem, he stated that his people are religious, but as for himself, he will not yield his heart until he sees more evidence that God is a God of both white and black people.

Not for myself I make this prayer,
But for this race of mine
That stretches forth from shadowed places
Dark hands for bread and wine.
For me, my heart is pagan mad,
My feet are never still,
But give them hearths to keep them warm
In homes high on a hill. . . .
Our Father, God; or Brother, Christ,
Or are we bastard kin,
That to our plaints your ears are closed,
Your doors barred from within?
Our Father, God; our Brother, Christ,
Retrieve my race again;
So shall you compass this black sheep,
This pagan heart. Amen.

He went so far in **"Heritage"** as to wish for a God who was dark, feeling then that "this flesh would know Yours had borne a kindred woe."

"The Black Christ" is Cullen's fullest synthesis of the racial with the religious theme. In this poem, as the title suggests, he came to the realization that Christ was also the God of the black people. It is both the story of a boy who was lynched and the journey from agnosticism to religious faith on the part of one who finds it hard to reconcile injustice with the rule of God. Cullen, through the description of the mother, presented the unquestioning faith of the older generation; through the speech of Jim and his brother, the doubts and agnosticism of the younger.

In the prologue, Cullen stated that the purpose of the poem was to restore the brother's faith. He also foreshadowed his conclusion that Christ is crucified afresh with every lynching and act of violence.

How God, who needs no man's applause,
For love of my stark soul, of flaws
Composed, seeing it slip, did stoop
And in the hollow of His hand
Enact again at my command
The world's supremest tragedy,
Until I die my burthen be:
How Calvary in Palestine,
Extending down to me and mine
Was but the first leaf in a line
Of trees on which a Man should swing,
World without end, in suffering
For all men's healing, let me sing.

The parallel between lynching victims and the crucified Christ interested Cullen for he had already suggested the idea in a brief poem in ***Copper Sun.***

The play is done, the crowds depart; and see
That twisted tortured thing hung from a tree,
Swart victim of a newer Calvary.

[**"Colors"**]

Could a God, who permitted lynchings to take place, actually exist?

"A man was lynched last night."
"Why?" Jim would ask, his eyes star-bright.
"A white man struck him; he showed fight.
Maybe God thinks such things are right."
"Maybe God never thinks at all—
Of us," and Jim would clench his small,
Hard fingers tight into a ball.
"Likely there ain't no God at all,"

Although the mother expressed the belief that God, who made them, would guide and protect them, Jim and his brother felt God was too far away to be concerned about them. . . .

The brother's faith in God was restored as a result of a miracle. Jim was reincarnated.

The very door he once came through
To death, now framed for us anew
His vital self, his and no other's
Live body of the dead, my brother's.

He hurried in amazement to the lynching tree, but Jim's body was not there. Throughout the poem, Cullen parallels the crucifixion suggesting that Christ substituted himself for the doomed Negro. Although the handling of the miracle is ambiguous, the thought which Cullen wished to express, that God is not worlds away but present and concerned about the pains of his people, comes out clearly.

O lovely Head to dust brought low
More times than we can ever know
Whose small regard, dust-ridden eye,
Behold Your doom, yet doubt You die;
O Form immaculately born,
Betrayed a thousand times each morn,
As many times each night denied,
Surrendered, tortured, crucified!
Nor have we seen beyond degree!
That love which has no boundary;
Our eyes have looked on Calvary". . . .

In **"The Black Christ,"** the white girl and black boy forgot hue and race in their common appreciation of the beauty of spring. Cullen did not look "to a fusion of the races as the true end, but to a cooperation in which each would share with the other, in best gifts." In a speech just before his lynching, Jim expressed the common humanity uniting black and white.

This is the song that dead men sing:
One spark of spirit Godhead gave
To all alike, to sire and slave,
From earth's red core to each white pole,
This one identity of soul;

Cullen's poems possessing race consciousness steadily declined after ***Color.*** **"The Black Christ"** was a *tour de force* which he wrote to aid his people. Witter Bynner, a close friend of Cullen's, did not like the poem; he told Cullen not to let himself be crucified on a Guggenheim cross. There were only two poems possessing race consciousness in ***The Medea***: the two sonnets expressing his abiding love for France. In Europe, he found no discrimination, and as a result spent twelve summers there. In the first sonnet, he stated that life in France brought him warmth and completeness, and in the second sonnet, he stated his desire to die in France.

As he whose eyes are gouged craves light to see,
As he whose limbs are broken strength to run,
So have I sought in you that alchemy
That knits my bones and turns me to the sun;
And found across a continent of foam
What was denied my hungry heart at home.

[**"To France"**]

Cullen bid farewell to the racial theme in a poem in ***The Black Christ.***

Then call me traitor if you must,
Shout treason and default!
Say I betray a sacred trust
Aching beyond this vault.
I'll bear your censure as your praise,
For never shall the clan
Confine my singing to its ways
Beyond the ways of man.

[**"To Certain Critics"**]

Thus, race consciousness has influenced Countee Cullen's poetry. It has added a mood of sorrow and protest to his poetry and influenced his choice of subject matter. Cullen's poems will live, for in the words of Arthur Davis, "They have made articulate the agony of racial oppression during a dark period in our continuing struggle for democracy."

More important, his poetry will live because of his lyrical beauty, manifested in such poems as **"Threnody for a Brown Girl"** and **"To John Keats, Poet at Spring Time."**

JAMES W. TUTTLETON (ESSAY DATE 1989)

SOURCE: Tuttleton, James W. "Countee Cullen At 'The Heights.'" In *The Harlem Renaissance: Revaluations,* pp. 101-37. New York: Garland Publishing, Inc., 1989.

In the following excerpt, Tuttleton examines the influence Cullen's college experience has on his poetry, and considers the significance of Cullen's study of Edna St. Vincent Millay.

The present work undertakes to describe the undergraduate career of Countee Cullen New York University between 1922 and 1925 and to present an edited text of his most significant surviving piece of undergraduate critical prose, the senior honors thesis he presented to the Department of English on May 1, 1925: **"The Poetry of Edna St. Vincent Millay: An Appreciation."** In both biographical and critical treatments of Cullen, these years have received scant attention, although they were immensely formative in his experience as a poet. In fact, the thesis that is presented here has never been published and is largely unknown to Cullen's readers or to students of the Harlem Renaissance.

The mind of a poet, the poetic influences to which he is exposed at an impressionable moment in his life, the critical context in which these influences are received, and the personalities of those having a decisive effect on the shaping of his perceptions and values—all of these are essential in understanding his originality, his development, and his reception. In the case of Countee Cullen, and adequate account of these influences—including the impact of Millay's love lyrics and ballad forms—would require a full-length biography, one devoted with greater rigor to the facts and their critical meaning moreover, than is evident in Blanche E. Ferguson's *Countee Cullen and the Negro Renaissance* (1966). In the space available here, no such full account is possible. But something of a start may be made by presenting his essay on Millay and by bringing to light some of the facts—hitherto unknown or forgotten—of this remarkable poet's education at New York University.

As will be evident to anyone reading this thesis, Countee Cullen, though only twenty-one years old when he wrote the work, was an accomplished and subtle student of poetry. The essay reflects a sensitive understanding of the varied generic and metrical gifts of Millay. And it is passionately responsive to her sense of the fragility and transience of beauty and love in a world where all must change and die. Students of Cullen's poetry have sometimes noted, without demonstrating at any length, the impact on him of Millay's lyric verse. (An exception is Margaret Perry's suggestive comparison, in the work cited below, of **"The Shroud of Color"** with Millay's "Renascence.") The present thesis offers, I believe, the critical ground on which a fuller influence study and a more informed comparative evaluation can be based. For here, in Cullen's "appreciation," will be found a description of the thematic and technical features of Millay's art that Cullen most admired, as well as a commentary on those defects of her performance of which he was most critical.

I am not of course the first to note the relation of Cullen's art to that of Millay. Walter White, for example, linked Cullen to a poetic tradition "of which A. E. Housman and Edna St. Vincent Millay are the bright stars" (quoted in Margaret Perry, *A Bio-Bibliography of Countee P. Cullen, 1903-1946,* 1971). Perry herself has remarked that "Countee Cullen's poetry also bears a close resemblance to both the poetry of Edward Arlington Robinson (whom Cullen considered to be America's finest poet) and of Edna St. Vincent Millay." But Perry was apparently not aware that Cullen had written this thesis—it is not listed among the "Unpublished Works" in her bibliography—so that the ground for a more extensive comparison was not available to her. . . .

[If] in 1930 Cullen gave to Robinson the laurel as the best American poet, in 1925—when he wrote his thesis and published ***Color***—Millay was foremost in his mind. Further, while granting that some of the following themes may also be found in Houseman and Keats, I . . . argue that common to both Cullen and Millay are these thematic elements: 1) A profound recognition of the transience of life; 2) a sense of the world as the vale of inexplicable agony and suffering; 3) an awareness of the inadequacy of the usual Christian explanation of why God permits, if he does not authorize, human suffering; 4) the impulse, therefore, to seize the day, to indulge in and celebrate poetically the pleasures of life—especially love in its erotic character an sensuous beauty in all of its forms. I would call this a frank aesthetic and sexual paganism, typical of the disillusioned youth of the 1920s; 5) nevertheless, a recognition that love is transient and sexual pleasure is fleeting—a recognition conveyed in both poets in wry, flip, cynical, and anguished tones; 6) yet the implied wish that it might be otherwise, that the order of existence might fulfill the heart's desire, especially in relation to love and sexuality, together with an occasional affirmation, sometimes like resignation, that there *is* a providential ordering, somehow, of human affairs. All this is just perhaps another way of saying what Countee Cullen himself said in a headnote in ***Caroling Dusk,*** namely, that one of his chief difficulties had always been "reconciling a Christian upbringing with a pagan inclination." This aesthetic and sexual hedonism, or paganism, in Millay was one of the chief appeals of her work. To these six thematic elements that link Millay and Cullen I would add a seventh, technical parallel: both poets' preference for the conventional forms of the poetic tradition—in relation to rhythms, rhyme schemes, stanzaic structures, and genres—especially the sonnet and the ballad.

Cullen matriculated at University College of Arts and Pure Science [New York University] in February of 1922 and was graduated on June 10, 1925, with a B.A. degree. This college, familiarly called "The Heights," was one of two undergraduate liberal arts colleges of New York University at that time; it was located at University Heights, overlooking the Harlem River in the Bronx. There Cullen majored in English and took a First Minor in French and a Second Minor in Philosophy. Since there has been, as yet, no detailed account of Cullen's educational development, and since he was a poet, it will perhaps be of value to future students of his life and art if I discuss his coursework at The Heights. . . .

Cullen's program of studies and his manifest distinction as a student . . . indicate that he received a solid liberal arts education with a strong emphasis on languages and literature, history and philosophy. He was well-prepared for graduate study at Harvard in either English or French, both of which he later taught in New York City. But ever more importantly, for our purposes, this undergraduate education—although just the foundation of his career as a poet—made him acquainted with a wide range of literary forms, styles, and techniques; it educated him about the culture of writers in several national traditions; and it helped him to understand the literary heritage in its historical and philosophical contexts. This much, of course, can be inferred from the poems alone, for his engagement with the literary heritage is implicit in all his characteristic themes and subjects, in his literary allusions, and in his strategies of versification and language use.

When one studies the transcript information against the college bulletins for the years 1922-1925, one particular facet of Cullen's program appears remarkable. Although the English Department boasted a faculty of between fifteen and twenty professors during these years—including local eminences like Dean Archibald L. Bouton, Francis Henry Stoddard, Vernon Loggins, Arthur Huntington Nason, and Homer Watt—almost all [Illegible Text] Cullen's English coursework was taken with one man, Professor Hyder E. Rollins. . . .

I shall later return to the influence of Rollins on Countee Cullen's development. But it should be noted that Cullen's apprenticeship as a poet was not limited to the classrooms at The Heights. For he was deeply involved in the extra-curricular literary life of the university—in ways that are not evident in the published biographies and bibliographies of his work.

For one thing, Cullen was published in the university literary magazines as early as 1922; and in his junior and senior years, Cullen was in fact the poetry editor of *The Arch: The Literary Magazine of New York University.* The issues of November 1924, and January, March, and May 1925 list him on the masthead. In this role, Cullen corresponded and conferred with other student writers, selected verse for publication, and oversaw the printing of this department of the magazine, which incidentally served students of every college of the university. Even more important, Cullen's own verse appeared in *The Arch.* Neither his poetry editorship nor his publications in *The Arch* have been noted in previous bibliographies of his work. This is worth stressing because critical treatments of volumes like ***Color*** (1925) and ***Copper Sun*** (1927) sometimes suggest that the poems in these volumes appeared only in national publications like *Harper's, The Nation, Poetry, Vanity Fair,* etc. However, some verses in these volumes first appeared in *The Arch.* For the sake of clarifying the record, therefore, some attention to his extracurricular work in *The Arch* and its relation to other sites of publication seems warranted.

In Volume I, Number 8 of *The Arch* (June, 1922), p. 13, there appears a **"Triolet"** beginning "I did not know she'd take it so"; this **"Triolet"** had first appeared in *The Magpie* (Christmas, 1921), the literary magazine of the De Witt Clinton High School It was renamed **"Under the Mistletoe"** and republished in ***Copper Sun.***

In Volume II (misprinted Volume I), Number 1 of *The Arch* (November, 1923), p. 8, appear two poems. The first is **"To—,"** beginning "Whatever I have loved has wounded me"; this poem is retitled **"A Poem Once Significant, Now Happily Not,"** and is reprinted in ***Copper Sun.*** The second is **"Triolet,"** beginning "I have wrapped my dreams in a silken cloth"; this poem, retitled **"For a Poet,"** was dedicated to John Gaston Edgar and was republished in *Harper's* (December, 1924) and in ***Color.***

In Volume II, Number 2 of *The Arch* (January, 1924), pp. 40-42, appears one of Cullen's most well-known poems, **"The Ballad of the Brown Girl."** This was of course the Second Prize poem in the Witter Bynner Intercollegiate Poetry Contest. Bynner thought it should have won, and advised Cullen to send it for republication to

Palms, where it appeared in the Early Summer Issue of 1924. Finally, it was republished in book form by Harper and Brothers in 1927.

In Volume II, Number 3 of *The Arch* (March, 1924), p. 88, appeared **"The Love Tree,"** which was reprinted in ***Copper Sun.*** And in Volume II, Number 4 (May, 1924), p. 122, appeared **"Sacrament,"** which was reprinted in ***Color.***

Finally, in Volume III, Number 1 of *The Arch* (November, 1924), p. 17, appeared **"Variations on a Theme,"** which was reprinted in ***Copper Sun***; and in the March 1925 issue appeared **"The Poet,"** also reprinted in ***Copper Sun.*** (This very early poem first appeared in *The Magpie* in November of 1920.)

This record of Cullen's student publications in *The Arch* suggests several things: first, that some of the poems appearing in national periodicals were first tried out in *The Arch*; second, that a number of his other poems in the published volumes first appeared in the NYU student literary magazine; and third, that some of the poems reprinted in ***Copper Sun*** as "juvenilia" were indeed the work of either his high school or undergraduate years, poems that he had not deemed worth including in ***Color.*** The pressure to publish his second volume led him to recycle them in order to expand ***Copper Sun*** to a proper book length.

[A course on Keats] had a permanent influence on Rollins's future career—as on Cullen's as well. For Rollins became enchanted with Keats and devoted to his life and work. Out of this ardor came, after Cullen's graduation, several of Rollins's major publications: *Keats' Reputation in America to 1848* (1946), the two-volume *The Keats Circle: Letters and Papers, 1816-1878* (1948), *Keats and the Bostonians* (1951), *More Letters and Poems of the Keats Circle* (1955), and the magisterial two-volume edition of *The Letters of John Keats, 1814-1821* (1958). In my judgment, the many Keatsian thematic and technical characteristics of Cullen's verse—not to speak of the encomia in **"To John Keats, Poet. At Springtime"** and **"To Endymion"**—are directly attributable to Rollins's impassioned lectures on Keats in *English Poets of the Nineteenth Century* during Cullen's junior year, 1923-1924. . . .

Setting aside Keats for the moment, Rollins's mind was also profoundly oriented toward the Renaissance, where his research involved the compilation of an immense collection of popular broadside ballads. On these ballads he worked assiduously during Cullen's undergraduate years. . . .

But if Rollins communicated enthusiasm for ballads to Countee Cullen, behind Rollins—forming a link with Cullen—was Rollins's own mentor, George Lyman Kittredge, who lectured on the ballad form at Harvard and inspired students like Rollins to carry on the work. Kittredge was a man of formidable erudition whose knowledge of the English ballad was founded on the work of *his* Harvard master, F. J. Child. The five-volume *The English and Scottish Popular Ballads,* edited by Francis James Child (to which the young Kittredge had supplied notes and annotations), was the groundwork upon which the work of Kittredge and thereafter Rollins was based. Ultimately, it was also the source of Cullen's ballad poems. Kittredge's one-volume edition of *The English and Scottish Popular Ballads* (1904) also served as the introduction to these poems for generations of Harvard students such as Rollins. But Rollins went even beyond his mentor Kittredge and rivalled Child's monumental work in preparing the original collections I have already named, as well as others published after Cullen's graduation.

Is it any wonder, then, that Cullen's first three volumes, ***Color*** (1925), ***Copper Sun*** (1927), and ***The Ballad of the Brown Girl*** (1927), are full of ballad settings, characters, and stylistic features? Or that he wrote his thesis on a woman poet who, in "The Ballad of the Harp Weaver," had established her claim to eminence with a Pulitzer Prize? Such lines as Cullen's "He rode across like a cavalier, / Spurs clicking hard and loud" (**"Two Who Crossed a Line"**), are unimaginable except under the influence of Rollins's *Cavalier and Puritan: Ballads and Broadsides*. . . . Cullen's portrait of his parents in **"Fruit of the Flower"** is a reflection of Rollins's influence: "My mother's life is puritan, / No hint of cavalier. . . ." Such narrative poems as **"Judas Iscariot,"** as well as Cullen's recurrent use of the *abcb* quatrain, culminate in **"The Ballad of the Brown Girl,"** published in *The Arch* in 1924. This is not the place to offer a full critique of that remarkable poem, which grew directly out of Millay's experiments and out of Rollins's lectures on the ballad tradition and his editing of four volumes of ballads during Cullen's undergraduate years. Yet some observations and clarifications of fact may perhaps be offered here. First, it is very unlikely that Cullen found the source for the ballad in *The Oxford Book of Ballads* or *The Ballad Book,* as Alan R. Shucard has suggested in *Countee Cullen.* In view of Rollins's intimate involvement with Kittredge, with whom he continually corresponded about his ballad work, and in view of Kittredge's connection to F. J. Child, it is more likely that Rollins steered Cullen to the source in Child's edition of "Lord Thomas and Fair Annet" and its variants like "The Nut-Brown Bride," "The Brown Bride and Lord Thomas," "Lone Thomas and Fair Elinor," or "Sweet Willie and Fair Annie." These Child versions of the ballad give the full dramatis personae of Cullen's poem, as the abbreviated version in the *Oxford* and *The Ballad Book* collections do not. Further, it is beside the point to criticize Cullen for verboseness in expanding the ballad from ten (*Oxford* version) or fifteen (*Ballad Book*) stanzas to fifty. Cullen's poem is only slightly longer than the "E" version of the ballad ("Sweet Willie and Fair Annie"), which runs to forty-two stanzas. Nor is there any point in faulting Cullen, as Houston A. Baker, Jr., does in *A Many-Colored Coat of Dreams: The Poetry of Countee Cullen,* for making Lord Thomas dependent on his mother, since this aspect of Lord Thomas is found in the originals. . . .

Was [Cullen's] individualism, as a black, "eradicated" by the program of English studies he undertook with Rollins and others? Was it inhibited by his turning to the wrong models—to Keats, Millay, Housman, Robinson, the ballad, the white English literary tradition—rather than to the literature of rising black consciousness, represented by Dunbar, McKay, Hughes, and others in Harlem? Or should his models have been the literary modernists then bursting on the scene—Pound, Eliot, cummings, and Hart Crane? Whatever the case, Dean Munn improbably remarked that "If the poetry of youth be ardently sincere, its promise frequently makes its very imperfections insignificant. Let the young poet not fear the critic who, Jeffrey-like, says 'This will never do'" [Introduction to *Some Recent New York University Verse,* edited by David L. Blum, 1926].

One New York University critic who was not afraid to say what would not do was Professor Eda Lou Walton, who taught English at the Washington Square Campus. (I have found no information on whether Cullen knew the playwright and future novelist Thomas Wolfe, who also taught at the Square.) She and Cullen sometimes read or listened to other poets. In *The Critical Review* issue in which Martin Russak fondly remembered his freshman awe of Cullen, Professor Walton undertook to criticize the negative effects on individualism of the "Teasdale-Millay school" then so popular in colleges. In view of the defensive tone of Cullen's thesis on Millay, Walton's comments in "The Undergraduate Poet" deserve serious attention. Speaking of the impact of Teasdale and Millay on youthful writers, Walton remarked: "These young poets upon first falling in love begin to sing sweetly and tritely of their hearts and souls, of longing and yearning, and burning. If they confuse their hearts and souls with trees and stars, with moons and seas, so much the better. They lift and fall with the tides; they are swept by storms, they are lonely as clouds. They are safe in the uniqueness of their emotion and blind, for the most part, to its amusing commonplaceness. Then comes the first disillusionment. They begin 'burning the candle at both ends' and pretending that 'it makes a lovely light,' although often they do not believe a word of it. They turn a bit cleverly cynical and can never end a lyric without some ironical fillip. They announce stridently the uselessness and stupidity of the opposite sex. They try to pick out figs, but are more intent on thistles." For Walton the "Teasdale-Millays" had little to say, in contrast to another camp of undergraduate poets, whom she identified as the "Cerebrals," whose masters were T. S. Eliot, Hart Crane, e.e. cummings, and Marianne Moore. In characterizing these two camps, Walton was of course implicitly highlighting—and condemning—the conventional academic romanticism of the kind of poetry Cullen was writing, although she never mentions Cullen by name. Cullen's indifference to those currents of poetic modernism developing on the campus as well as in the international literary culture, has indeed been a constant factor in the definition of his work as "minor."

Whatever one may claim to have been the proper model for Cullen's art, there is no doubt that for Hyder Rollins the English tradition from the Middle Ages onward was the right foundation for a poet. . . .

This overview of Countee Cullen's undergraduate years at "The Heights" suggests several conclusions. First, Cullen was a highly popular and academically successful student who attained an impressive celebrity with his classmates and professors. Trained in a conventional academic program that emphasized the classic writers of the white English tradition, Cullen naturally gravitated to the work of Keats, Robinson, Millay, Masters, and the old ballad writers. Essentially shaped by Hyder E. Rollins, a international scholar with a deep affinity for Keats and the ballad forms, Cullen supplemented his studies by extracurricular activities like publishing in the student literary periodical, *The Arch,* even editing the magazine in his last two years, and by attending and giving readings of poetry on campus and throughout the country. His achievement was thus an inspiration to other young poets. Some have suggested that Harvard, with its erudition, may have "ruined" Cullen for the task of elevating the quality of down-home, right-on black poetry in the twentieth century. But for better or for worse, Cullen's direction was set well before he got to Harvard: the route was fixed at The Heights.

There is no doubt that his work would have benefited from deeper immersion in the modernist poets then attaining fame—writers like Eliot, Pound, Stevens, and Williams And it is highly probable that the application of modernist techniques to problems of racial identity and experience would have deepened the impact of poems like **"Heritage," "The Black Christ,"** and others that express his sense of the meaning of blackness in white America, thereby allying him more intimately with the poetic projects of Claude McKay, Langston Hughes, and other figures of the Harlem Renaissance. But Cullen was the product of the forces that shaped him and of the choices and models that he elected. Within those terms and limits, he attained exceptional distinction as a lyric poet with an impassioned romantic sensibility. If he failed to scale the highest point of Parnassus, he did reach the lesser heights.

GERALD EARLY (ESSAY DATE 1991)

SOURCE: Early, Gerald. Introduction to his *My Soul's High Song,* pp. 3-24, 55-65. New York: Doubleday, 1991.

In the following excerpt, Early examines Cullen's life and works, paying particular attention to his relationship with his adoptive father and the strong Christian imagery in his poetry.

I. Boy Wonder, Mysterious Child

I am borne darkly, fearfully, afar
—Shelley, "Adonais"

Till all the world was sea, and I a boat
Unmoored, on what strange quest I willed to float
—Countee Cullen, ***"The Shroud of Color"***

There is not much to say about these earlier years
of Cullen—unless he himself should say it.
—James Weldon Johnson, The Book of American Negro Poetry

The Harlem Renaissance—that storied era principally occurring during the 1920s, when black letters in America reached their first real flowering—produced several significant writers whose works are now essential to the American literary canon. Poet, novelist, translator, journalist Langston Hughes; novelist, anthropologist, and playwright Zora Neale Hurston; and novelist, anthologist, historian, and poet James Weldon Johnson come to mind immediately as major stars associated with the era. Jamaican novelist and poet Claude McKay stands, perhaps, only slightly below Hughes, Hurston, Johnson, and, doubtless, Jean Toomer, who in 1923 gave the world the era's most distinguished novel, *Cane.* Even lesser-known writers of the period whose work is not as stellar—novelists Wallace Thurman, Nella Larsen, and Jessie Fauset, and poet Georgia Douglas Johnson—have been subjects of a revived critical, scholarly, and even popular interest. Yet the one who was once felt to have the most promise and whose name was on everyone's lips has been strangely and sadly neglected in recent years, when the Harlem Renaissance has otherwise enjoyed a kind of intellectual vogue in the classroom and a romantic vogue with the public. In 1925 Countee Cullen, at the age of twenty-two, was the most celebrated and probably the most famous black writer in America.[1] The 1924 publication of his poem **"The Shroud of Color"** in H. L. Mencken's *American Mercury* was the talk of the intellectual and artistic black community. Few books by a black writer were more eagerly anticipated by the white and black public than Cullen's first collection of poems, ***Color,*** in 1925. Few writers had won as many literary prizes at such a young age as Cullen. He was, indeed, a boy wonder, a young handsome black Ariel ascending, a boyish, bronze-skinned titan who, in the early and mid-twenties, embodied many of the hopes, aspirations, and maturing expressive possibilities of his people. It was once a commonplace for all educated black people to have memorized lines from Countee Cullen's work or even whole works themselves. Once everyone knew such lines as:

What is Africa to me:
Copper sun or scarlet sea,
Jungle star or jungle track,
Strong bronzed men, or regal black
Women from whose loins I sprang
When the birds of Eden sang.
One three centuries removed
From the scenes his fathers loved,
Spicy grove, cinnamon tree,
What is Africa to me?

Or this closing couplet:

Yet do I marvel at this curious thing:
To make a poet black, and bid him sing.

Or this well-known poem:

Once riding in old Baltimore,
Heart-filled, head-filled with glee,
I saw a Baltimorean
Keep looking straight at me.

Now I was eight and very small,
And he was no whit bigger,
And so I smiled, but he poked out
His tongue, and called me, "Nigger."

I saw the whole of Baltimore
From May until December;
Of all the things that happened there
That's all that I remember.[2]

On September 12, 1951, five years after his death, Cullen was still highly esteemed enough to have the 135th Street Branch of the New York Public Library named in his honor. Few black writers can claim the eminence of having a public building named for them. In this regard, only Paul Laurence Dunbar exceeds Cullen. So what happened to this extraordinarily gifted young man? What diminished the astonishing start of what seemed a fabulous career? Or did Cullen really fall off as much as critics claim he did as he grew older? He certainly wrote less after the age of twenty-six and one is forced again to ask why? Why has his work been neglected and his books out of print for so many years? To be sure, Cullen's most famous poems continue to be anthologized and this perhaps has become the problem. He remains, in many senses, a mere school-house poet who is not conceptualized holistically as a working artist but as a remote figure in a mist—like Longfellow or Lanier or Bryant—whom one knows through a few overly familiar works disembodied from a corpus. Cullen has ceased to be real and so has his work which, aside from often being complex and troubling, has the added burden of being written in strict metrical forms like the ballad, the Spenserian stanza, the Shakespearean sonnet, and the Petrarchan sonnet (Longfellow's favorite form). All of this, to many modern readers and, alas, modern free-verse poets, seems quaint and old-fashioned. We no longer desire poetic diction but only poorly conceived prose bizarrely spread out on a page. In answering questions about Cullen hangs a profound tale of the dynamics and politics of the making of a black literary reputation.

Perhaps Countee Cullen was never fully understood as a poet or a writer because he has never been understood fully as a man. There is, and always has been, a quality of unknowableness, sheer inscrutability, that surrounds Cullen and is no more better symbolized, in a small yet telling way, than by the official, but varied accounts of his height. His passport of both 1934 and 1938 gives his height as 5' 3", his selective service registrant card of 1942 lists him as 5' 10" and his war ration book number 3, issued when Cullen was forty years old, gives his height as 5' 7".

FROM THE AUTHOR

CULLEN ON THE PERCEPTIONS OF BLACK CULTURE

We have always resented the natural inclination of most white people to demand spirituals the moment it is known that a Negro is about to sing. So often the request has seemed to savor the feeling that we could do this and this alone.

SOURCE: Countee Cullen, from the "The Dark Tower," in *Opportunity,* June 1927.

We still do not know where Cullen was born. In James W. Tuttleton's extremely useful essay "Countee Cullen at 'The Heights,'" which provides a detailed account of Cullen's undergraduate years at New York University, we learn that Cullen's college transcript, for which he himself provided the information, lists his place of birth as Louisville, Kentucky.[3] This transcript was dated 1922. In the biographical headnote which Cullen wrote for his selections of poetry—contained in his own anthology of black poetry, ***Caroling Dusk***—Cullen says he was born in New York City. This anthology appeared in 1927, three years after the publication of **"The Shroud of Color"** in the *American Mercury,* two years after the critically and commercially successful publication of his first book of poems, ***Color,*** two years after having won first prize in the Witter Bynner Poetry contest, the *Poetry* magazine John Reed Memorial Prize for **"Threnody for a Brown Girl,"** the Amy Spingarn Award of *The Crisis* magazine for **"Two Moods of Love,"** second prize in *Opportunity* magazine's first poetry contest for **"To One Who Said Me Nay,"** after having been elected to Phi Beta Kappa, and second-prize winner in the poetry contest of *Palms* for **"Wisdom Cometh with the Years."** Cullen was to continue to state publicly that New York City was his place of birth for the rest of his life, as did his 1934 and 1938 passports, his 1928 French Identity Card, and James Weldon Johnson's headnote about Cullen in the 1931 edition of his anthology *The Book of American Negro Poetry.* Whatever the reasons for Cullen changing the place of his birth, one inescapable fact is that in 1922 he was a relatively obscure but well-regarded black student with some poetic inclination and ability. By 1927 only Edna St. Vincent Millay surpassed him in American poetry circles in critical and press attention. Here with the whole business of birthplaces, we have the difference between the public and private Cullen. Ida Mae Roberson Cullen, Countee Cullen's second wife (they married in 1940 and remained happily so until Cullen's death in 1946)[4], insisted to various biographers and scholars that Cullen was indeed born in Louisville. Langston Hughes and Harold Jackman, both of whom Cullen knew well, particularly Jackman, also voiced the opinion that he was born in Louisville. Around the time of Cullen's death, stories began to circulate that he was born in Baltimore (one writer even says that Mrs. Cullen confirms this). But there is little evidence for this—except, one supposes, the famous Cullen poem "Incident," which uses Baltimore as a setting. Also, Cullen's foster father was reared in Baltimore and that fact may have contributed to this new confusion. Oddly Beulah Reimherr, who had done the most extensive research into Cullen's childhood and young life, finds no record of anything about him in either the Louisville or Baltimore Bureau of Vital Statistics.[5] There is, moreover, no birth record for Cullen in New York City. The mystery remains unsolved.

And what of Cullen's assertion, in his anthology ***Caroling Dusk,*** that he was "reared in the conservative atmosphere of a Methodist parsonage." The implication here is that his adoptive parents, the Reverend Dr. Frederick A. and Carolyn Belle (Mitchell) Cullen of the Salem Methodist Episcopal Church in Harlem, were, in fact, his real parents. But Cullen supposedly was not "adopted" until 1918, when he was fifteen years old; and it would certainly over-state the case to claim that he was reared by a conservative Methodist pastor when, in fact, he lived with someone else for the first fifteen years of his life. In the somewhat unreliable biography *Countee Cullen and the Negro Renaissance,* Blanche E. Ferguson states that "Countee Cullen, eleven years, began a new life in the Salem personage.[6] This would mean that he was adopted in 1914. Harold Jackman, Cullen's closest friend, said that the adoption of Cullen was never made official. So it could have occurred in 1918, as is most commonly believed, or as early as 1914, or even as early as Cullen's infancy, which was what the second Mrs. Cullen told French scholar Jean Wagner.[7] Yet Cullen wrote an epitaph, **"For My Grandmother,"** which appeared in ***Color*** and is generally considered not to be about the mother of either of his adoptive parents. If that is so, it would indicate that someone else, perhaps the grandmother, played a significant role in rearing Cullen and that, probably, at least the first ten or eleven years of his childhood were spent outside the influence of the Salem parsonage. Or perhaps it was an obese woman relative who died, leaving Cullen an orphan, according to accounts by Wagner and Reimherr.[8] Or as another account goes, Cullen's mother, Elizabeth Lucas, reappeared in his life in the 1920s, when Cullen had achieved his fame, and Cullen helped her financially for the rest of her life and even attended her funeral in Kentucky in 1940. Or was Cullen reared by a Mrs. Porter, his grandmother, who brought him to New York City at the age of nine.[9]

In the end we do not know where Countee Cullen was born; we do not know who his natural parents were; we do not know when he was adopted or when he started living with the Reverend and Mrs. Cullen; we do not know the source in his childhood of his intense Christian consciousness: it may have been his mother, his grandmother, the Reverend and Mrs. Cullen, or someone else—or some combination of influences. We also do not know from all of this exactly how or why, what complex of biological or environmental elements made him want to be a writer generally, and, in particular, a great lyric poet. The shifts in identity are indicated by the changes in his name: he signed his earliest published works in 1918 as "Countee L. Porter," although by the time he was writing for his high school literary magazine, *The Magpie,* in 1920 and 1921, he had become "Countee P. Cullen." (This would give credence to the assumption that he was adopted by the Cullens in some sort of formal manner around 1918 and that gradually he began to use their name as his own.)[10] By the time of his first book, ***Color,*** he was known simply as Countee Cullen.

Ample evidence exists that Cullen enjoyed a close relationship with his foster parents. The Shakespearean sonnet **"Tribute (To My Mother),"** which appeared in ***The Black Christ and Other Poems*** (1929) and was written while Cullen was in France on a Guggenheim Fellowship in 1928 and 1929, suggests the influence of his mother's moral presence:

> Because man is not virtuous in himself,
> Not kind, nor given to sweet charities,
> Save goaded by the little kindling elf
> Of some dear face it pleasures him to please;
> Some men who else were humbled to the dust,
> Have marveled that the chastening hand should
> stay,
> And never dreamed they held their lives in trust
> To one the victor loved a world away.

The phrase "a world away" not only implies that Cullen is writing this poem abroad, far from his mother, but also that he and his mother are, not surprisingly, different, of separate worlds, if you will. Despite this, she continues to be conjured up by the poet; her image haunts him in a way that is conventional yet not sentimental, perhaps somewhat to his own surprise. Cullen's mother seems to have inspired the poet in another way besides being the subject of a poem. He once said: "My mother sings . . . It is wonderful . . . But I . . . I cannot sing. I do not know one note from another. My poetry, I should think, has become the way of my giving out what music is within me."[11] Carolyn Cullen was, for many years, a leading soprano in her husband's church choir. Cullen, who loved music, heard her every week for many years. Also, he probably heard some of the choir rehearsals and his mother singing around the house. She was an able pianist as well. In this sense Cullen saw his poetry as songs of singing, and we might say that his mother exercised some influence over him in his becoming a poet or at least provided significant inspiration.

But it was apparently with his foster father, Frederick A. Cullen, that the poet enjoyed his closest relationship. [. . .]

That Cullen was closer to his father than his mother is undeniable. For twelve summers, from 1926 to 1938, Dr. Cullen traveled abroad to Europe and the Middle East with his adopted son as a companion on all the trips save one. Dr. Cullen's wife, who died in 1932, never accompanied her husband and son on any of the trips. On March 13, 1926, Countee Cullen enjoyed one of his greatest triumphs when he heard a chamber orchestra conducted by Alexander Smallens play *Saturday's Child,* a song cycle of his poems **"Saturday's Child," "To One Said Me Nay,"** and **"A Song of Praise,"** set to music by Emerson Whithorne, whose compositions had been featured as part of Vincent Lopez's Carnegie Hall symphonic jazz concert in November 1924. Cullen's father was present but not his mother. In the summer of 1945, while Cullen was in Los Angeles working with cowriter Arna Bontemps and others on the production of ***St. Louis Woman,*** his father fell extremely ill. Cullen's letters to his wife often contain touching and anxious displays of concern for his father. His wife's response to one of his letters reveals the closeness between father and son to be of such magnitude that even Cullen's wife was deeply moved by it:

> Countee, your father is the most amazing person that anyone could ever know. It is indeed a privilege to have the fortune and honor to know and be with him at a time like this. His courage and faith is just something one does not have the fortune to see very much in this life. And do you know that through all of this, this week he has been in the hospital, every thought of his has been for you. Just wanting everything to be right for you. Oh, he is wonderful.[12]

Cullen also wrote three poems for his father during the course of his career—**"Dad,"** which first appeared in *The Magpie* in 1922; **"Fruit of the Flower,"** (also containing stanzas about his mother), which was first published in *Harper's* in 1924 and is included in ***Color***; and **"Lines for My Father,"** which appeared in ***Copper Sun,*** Cullen's second collection of poetry, published in 1927. Comparing the earliest with the last published poem is instructive in understanding how Cullen saw his father:

> His ways are circumspect and bound
> With trite simplicities;
> His is the grace of comforts found
> In homely hearthside ease.
> His words are sage and fall with care,
> Because he loves me so;
> And being his, he knows, I fear,
> The dizzy path I go.
> For he was once as young as I,
> As prone to take the trail,
> To find delight in the sea's low cry,
> And a lone wind's lonely wail.
> *It is his eyes that tell me most*
> *How full his life has been;*
> *There lingers there the faintest ghost*
> *Of some still sacred sin.*
> So I must quaff Life's crazy wine,
> And taste the gall and dregs;
> And I must follow, follow, follow
> The lure of a silver horn,
> That echoes from a leafy hollow,
> Where the dreams of youth are born.
> Then when the star has shed its gleam,
> The rose its crimson coat;
> When Beauty flees the hidden dream,
> And Pan's pipes blow no note;
> When both my shoes are worn too thin,
> My weight of fire to bear,
> I'll turn like dad, and like him win
> The peace of a snug arm-chair.[13]

We see here clearly that Cullen has begun the process of obscuring his origins by suggesting in this poem that Frederick Cullen is his natural father; for the poem is meant to say, to declare really, that Cullen is indeed his father's son, that the "sacred sin," the oxymoron which for Cullen was always sensuality and an obsession with the delights of the carnal, has its origins in his father. (That a theological and metaphorical reading of this as the relation of human—Christian God—original sin would be problematical is obvious.) The rest of the poem is nothing more than a kind of standard *carpe diem* theme that youth must be served in the end, and, thus, the father becomes in this way much the same figure as the old man in William Wordsworth's "Animal Tranquility and Decay." **"Lines for My Father"** is a more mature assessment of the father:

> Now ushered regally into your own,
> Look where you will, as far as eye can see,
> Your little seeds are to a fullness grown,
> And golden fruit is ripe on every tree.
>
> Yours is no fairy gift, no heritage
> Without travail, to which weak wills aspire;
> This is a merited and grief-earned wage
> From One Who holds His servants worth their
> hire.

This is a much more theologically considered (and dogmatically sound) evaluation of his father, an evaluation from which Cullen has removed himself so that, ultimately, his assessment of his father does not become, in some respects, merely a complexly dimensioned way to examine himself. Nonetheless, because Cullen was an orphan, to think about his character in relation to his foster father, for whom he bore much respect, is not surprising. Yet there must have been some tension between the two men; the father was a strict fundamentalist while Cullen experienced intellectual doubts and often expressed a kind of ongoing quarrel with Christianity in many of his poems. The father had a certain Puritan demeanor and Cullen, even as an adult, kept the occasional episodes of wild carousing with drink, dancing, and gambling away from him. In many inescapable ways, Cullen had to realize that he was not his father's son or at least not all the time *that* particular father's son. But the bond between Cullen and his adoptive parents was a very strong one, perhaps because he was adopted and so grateful to be in a loving home with a couple who had no children of their own (this fact too made it easier for Cullen to be devoted to his parents; there was no rivalry with any other children, especially any other children to whom the Cullens could have been natural parents); perhaps this made him want to be worthy of that love. As Arna Bontemps so perceptively wrote:

> He paid his adopted parents a devotion, one is almost inclined to say a submission, only rarely rendered by natural sons. But it was all a part of his choice. He did not stand in fear of his foster parents. He simply preferred pleasing them to having his own way.[14]

Countee Cullen excelled at every school he ever attended. And if excelling in school is a way for a child, particularly an orphan, to win a parent's favor, then surely Cullen played the role of an overachiever to his best advantage. On February 4, 1918, he enrolled in DeWitt Clinton High School. It was then located at Fifty-ninth Street and Tenth Avenue, which was a considerable distance from his home, but it was, and continued to be after Cullen's graduation, a highly regarded boys' school.[15] At the time Cullen attended, the school was almost exclusively white. (Ironically, considering the racial composition of the student body, it should be noted that it was while Cullen was at DeWitt Clinton that he made the most important and enduring friendship of his life, with a handsome West Indian boy named Harold Jackman, to whom he would eventually dedicate a number of his works, give his handwritten copy of **"The Ballad of the Brown Girl"** as a Christmas gift in 1923, travel to Europe several times in the 1930s, and leave a good portion of his papers when he died.[16]) Cullen was an active student serving as vice president of the senior class; associate editor of the 1921 *Magpie,* the school's literary magazine; and editor of the *Clinton News.* He also won the Douglas Fairbanks Oratorical Contest and the Magpie Cup. It was in high school that Cullen received significant recognition as a poet by winning first prize in a citywide poetry contest sponsored by the Empire Federation of Women's Clubs. His winning entry was entitled "I Have a Rendezvous with Life."[17] This acclaim had many people talking about Cullen as having a future as a major poet and was fraught with significance, suggesting things to come.

In some real sense, it was this initial success by Cullen and not the September 1923 publication of Jean Toomer's *Cane* that really kicked off the literary movement called the Harlem Renaissance; for if anyone was being groomed, being intellectually and culturally conditioned and bred, first by whites and then by blacks, to be a major black crossover literary figure, it was this thin, shy black boy. America has always loved precocious children and Cullen's was the race's first honest-to-goodness child literary star. Perhaps much of what happened to Cullen in his subsequent career might be better understood if we see him precisely in the light of being a child star, understanding as we do the inability of young gifted performers to sustain themselves over the long stretch of an adult career when the bloom and wonder of early achievement has rather lost its hypnotic, charismatic tint.

Cullen continued to "knock them in the aisles," when he went to New York University, which he attended on a New York State Regents Scholarship. He attended NYU from 1922 to 1925 and while there forged his substance and style as a poet. As James W. Tuttleton informs us, he took the traditional courses in English, French, Latin, math, physics, geology, philosophy, Greek, and physical science while writing most of the poems for which he was to become famous when ***Color*** and ***Copper Sun*** appeared.[18] Cullen took most of his English courses with Hyder E. Rollins, who wrote several treatises on the ballad during Cullen's stay at NYU. Rollins also fell in love with Keats at this time, a love that was to become an undying passion as he eventually became a leading Keats scholar. That Rollins was a big influence on Cullen's development, as Professor Tuttleton argues, can scarcely be gainsaid: Cullen took most of his English from Rollins, wrote his undergraduate thesis on Edna St. Vincent Millay for him, and, finally, had him write in support of his successful 1928 application for a Guggenheim. "Is it any wonder, then," writes Professor Tuttleton, "that Cullen's first three volumes—***Color*** (1925). ***Copper Sun*** (1927), and ***The Ballad of the Brown Girl*** (1927)—were full of ballad settings, characters, and stylistic features?"[19] Is it any wonder too that the first two books show the strong influence of Keats and Millay? Many of the poems Cullen wrote as an undergraduate appeared in the university literary magazine *The Arch,* including two major ones, **"Spirit Birth,"** which became **"The Shroud of Color"** and **"The Ballad of the Brown Girl."** (Cullen also wrote **"Heritage"** while he was an undergraduate.) Generally he was very highly regarded and apparently well liked by other undergraduates. When ***Color*** was published in 1925, Cullen's senior year, he was heartily congratulated by both faculty and students, including a handwritten note of appreciation from the chancellor.[20] Tuttleton assesses Cullen's undergraduate education as particularly well rounded and rigorous:

> Cullen's program of studies and his manifest distinction as a student, then, indicate that he received a solid liberal arts education with a strong emphasis on languages and literature, history, and philosophy. He was well prepared for graduate study at Harvard in either English or French, both of which he later taught in New York City.[21]

Cullen went to Harvard after graduating Phi Beta Kappa from NYU. It seemed the proper place to bring one phase of his education to an end. He received his Master of Arts from Harvard in 1926 and in December of that year began to write a column entitled "The Dark Tower" for *Opportunity,* the magazine the National Urban League had started just a few years earlier. Perhaps it was so that Cullen was not the leader of the Harlem Renaissance; he had neither the personality nor the vision to lead. (Among the younger writers, Wallace Thurman served that role, and James Weldon Johnson of the NAACP was the overall drum major, with Charles S. Johnson of the Urban League and W. E. B. DuBois serving as chiefs of staff.) But Cullen had left his stamp on the era more than anyone else. The title of his column, "The Dark Tower," became the name of the literary salon that A'Lelia Walker, daughter of Madame C. J. Walker and heiress of the Walker "beauty culture" fortune, started in 1928 in her fashionable townhouse at 108 West 136th Street in Harlem. It was the place for the black intelligentsia and slumming whites who sought something exotic, a place where on the walls one could read Cullen's poetry as well as the poetry of Langston Hughes. In the era of Marcus Garvey, Cullen, in his poem **"Heritage,"** had posed the central question: "What is Africa to me?" And finally in his **"Yet Do I Marvel"** he produced, according to James Weldon Johnson, "the two most poignant lines in American literature"[22]:

> Yet do I marvel at this curious thing:
> To make a poet black, and bid him sing!

As Owen Dodson wrote so appropriately in his eulogy for Cullen:

> If you asked any Negro what he found in Cullen's poetry, he would say: all my dilemmas are written here. . . .[23]

More than any other presence of the time, including Langston Hughes, Cullen defined his age and, in that sense, dominated it as much as a man of Cullen's temperament could dominate anything. Alas, what he defined was not the triumphs of being black and not even its anguish but the conundrum of blackness which, shaped as it is centrally in the black mind, ought to, in some ways, be centrally poised in the wider cultural discourse itself. When Cullen wrote the line, "Let it be allowed," he meant exactly what he said—that the divided black psyche was the single most riveting riddle of the twentieth-century Western world and it was time for the white Western world to recognize it as such. Cullen said in 1924:

> If I am going to be a poet at all, I am going to be POET and not NEGRO POET. That is what has hindered the development of artists among us. Their one note has been the concern with their race. That is all very well, none of us can get away from it. I cannot at times. You will see it in my verse. The consciousness of this is too poignant at times. I cannot escape it. But what I mean is this: I shall not write of negro subjects for the purpose of propaganda. That is not what a poet is concerned with. Of course, when the emotion rising out of the fact that I am a negro is strong, I express it. But that is another matter.[24]

But the other matter really is the whole of the point: how to express one's blackness without being trapped by it or merely seeing it as a convenient pose. This is the black writer's inviolate anxiety: to be free to be yourself and to be free to be anything but yourself. It must always be kept in mind that Cullen was a great poet. To paraphrase T. S. Eliot's sentence on Keats and Shelley, Cullen would not have been as great as he was but for the limitations which prevented him from being greater than he was. That sums up the paradoxical weight of his blackness as well as anything and comes close enough to explicating the last two lines of **"Yet Do I Marvel."**[25] In his review of ***Color*** that appeared in the March 31, 1926 issue of *The New Republic,* Eric Walrond wrote that "Countee Cullen is a fulfilment of one of the pregnant promises of the New World." Walrond was partly wrong and absolutely right. Childe Countee to the Dark Tower Came . . . .

III. Christian Heritage

I want to hear the chanting
Around a heathen fire
Of a strange black race.

—*Gwendolyn Bennett, "Heritage"*

Poetry is a potent and dangerous vehicle just because it is always and inevitably religious in its ultimate nature.

—*Amos N. Wilder,* The Christian Tradition: A Study in the Relation of Christianity to Culture

It is unjust to Christianity to call our civilization Christian; it is unjust to our civilization to call it unchristian. It is semi-Christian.

—*Walter Rauschenbush,* Christianizing the Social Order

"I find you this time writing a book which almost any one might have written. Temporarily, something has happened to you. You have fallen into other people's language, you have lapsed from your own swift simplicities. . . . Kick out hard, whatever influence is impeding. Don't let yourself be crucified on a Guggenheim cross, . . ." wrote Witter Bynner, one of Cullen's biggest boosters just a few years earlier, in a letter dated November 22, 1929. He was responding to Cullen's new collection ***The Black Christ and Other Poems.*** This was the way the thirties were to greet Cullen, with the unwavering and brutal intention of waking him from a dream. The new decade started with a bang and a whimper. With the publication of ***The Black Christ and Other Poems*** in 1929, a phase of Countee Cullen's literary career was over. In the thirties Cullen was to experience life differently; he was no longer the black literary wonder boy. He divorced Yolande in 1930, surely a kind of disillusioning and uncomfortable experience, even if not bitter or acrimonious. His novel, ***One Way to Heaven,*** was not to be reviewed in *The Crisis* and was treated with about fifteen other books by and about blacks in Alain Locke's round-up review in *Opportunity,* January 1933. These leading black magazines had previously been lavish in the attention and care they paid to Cullen's works. By the end of the decade, while working with Arna Bontemps on ***St. Louis Woman,*** he was to be attacked by the black literary establishment that had once so staunchly supported him on the very tenets of his own critical creed: producing a literary work that was degrading to blacks. In the thirties and through to the end of his life in 1946, he was to write much less.

Many have speculated on Cullen's reduced output. Part of it may have been writer's block, lack of inspiration, or sheer laziness, but a part of it must have been that after 1929, when Cullen's Guggenheim Fellowship ended, he no longer quite had the time to write that he had before. This was especially true after publication of ***One Way to Heaven*** in 1932. Shortly after that he was to become a certified public school teacher, a job he was to keep until his death. In the 1920s, Cullen had been a student and, although he worked hard, a rather indulged one. He had time, even as a hard-working student, to write, especially when one considers the fact that several of the poems he produced in the 1920s were written for classes in lieu of paper assignments. If today professors at major research institutions who spend only six hours a week in the classroom feel justified in complaining about the amount of time class preparation and grading take away from their scholarly pursuits, how much more so was Cullen, who had to teach for six hours a day.

By the age of twenty-six, virtually all of his major poems, all the poems for which he was to be known to posterity, were published. In the 1930s, Cullen explored avenues other than *tour de force* lyric poetry: namely, the novel, translation, drama, song lyrics for musical comedy, and children's literature in both poetry and prose. It was not that Countee Cullen was no longer interested in writing or could not write, it seems more likely that he was no longer interested or could not write lyric poetry of the sort that made him famous, so he cast about for some other form. This is not unusual as lyric poets often do their greatest work when quite young. Drama seems to have held a particular fascination for him; not only did he translate ***The Medea,*** but he also wrote at least two dramatic adaptations of his novel and worked with Arna Bontemps on a musical adaption of Bontemps's novel *God Sends Sunday,* the aforementioned ***St. Louis Woman.*** He also coauthored with Owen Dodson a choreo-musical called ***The Third Fourth of July,*** his only published play. He seemed to have found his niche in children's literature and had he lived may have gone on to write considerably more in this genre. At the time of his death he had already completed a manuscript called **"The Monkey Baboon"** and a prose version of his earlier **"The Lost Zoo,"** called **"The Little Lost Zoo."**[26]

There are two related things that must be understood about Cullen's major poetry: first, most of it is racial and, second, all of it is Christian or could only have been produced by a Christian consciousness. This is his dilemma, which, of course, became his pose: to wit, as he wrote, his "chief problem has been that of reconciling a Christian upbringing with a pagan inclination."[27] In poems such as **"Heritage," "The Black Christ," "The Shroud of Color," "The Litany of the Dark People,"** and **"Pagan Prayer,"** this is manifested by understanding that the poetry is the product of a black Christian who cannot reconcile two things. First, he cannot reconcile his blackness, which he refers to as his paganism, and his Christianity. However, this fact has little to do exclusively with a race consciousness and a great deal to do with an over-bearing and overburdened Christian one. What Cullen finds attractive as a writer is the basic ambiguity that exists in the meaning of his being a black Christian. That ambiguity is there, to borrow an idea from Clifford Geertz,[28] because being a black Christian has both religious and political significance, a kind of uneasy meshing of the sacred and secular. To be a black Christian is to be caught always between ideology and theology, to be unsure whether one's major concern is eschatology or a power struggle.

That disjuncture is for Cullen something that he must, in truth, have had no real interest in wanting to reconcile as it was the resulting fictive tension, the resulting dramatic functionalism, that enabled Cullen to write so well. The threat on every page that his personality would simply break apart, would absolutely defy integration was a rich, though not necessarily singular, vein for a black writer to work. But this is only one disjuncture; the other theme that preoccupies Cullen is the inherent rationalization with theodicy that every black Christian must make. The Jew, as another long-suffering former slave, knew better than to devise a religion that would tell him that the only way he can transcend his tragedy is to remain a tragic figure. But Cullen, as an intellectual black, easily saw that black Christianity must ultimately accept that the Negro's humanity must forever be his tragic suffering: this is precisely what his greatest religious poems—**"The Litany of the Dark People," "The Shroud of Color," "The Black Christ"**—say. He is constantly condemned to be entrapped by the myth of his victimization, and whether he rages against it or submits to it, he ultimately confesses that he is helpless before it. This is precisely what the poems **"Pagan Prayer"** and **"Mood"** question.

Pearl Bailey in a production of *St. Louis Woman.*

It is a curious observation that in **"Heritage,"** considered by everyone to be Cullen's finest poem, his masterpiece, he uses the phrase "So I lie . . ." five times. It seems there is a great deal of lying going on in the poem, not only lying as in the sense of reposing, à la some of the narrators of Poe and Browning, but also lying in the sense of dishonesty and duplicity. Cullen was very taken with the art of lying or why else did he have his cat tell tall tales in ***The Lost Zoo*** and in ***My Lives and How I Lost Them,*** or why else did he translate ***The Medea,*** which is all about the lying of two lovers, or why write a novel where the central character lies about his conversion? The entire scope of Cullen's 1930s career seems a long philosophical and aesthetic examination of the many creative and nefarious dimensions of lying, deception, and hypocrisy. Also the interest in lying as art explains the character Sam Lucas in ***One Way to Heaven.*** Many critics have felt that Cullen named the character Lucas because his own real name may have been Lucas. What makes a great deal more sense is that the con man character of Cullen's novel is named after the great black stage minstrel of the same name who was very popular in the early 1900s. As the novel turns on Lucas's ability to act, to play out a conversion that he does not feel convincingly, both in the beginning of the novel and at the novel's end, we see instantly that the book centers on the art of lying, and what black person was a better professional liar than a minstrel with his degrading, low, stereotypical comedy? In fact, the connection between the novel's character and the minstrel is made even more explicit by the symbols of the playing cards and razor, which Sam tosses away at every conversion. These are of course the props of the stereotypical black minstrel.

Some readers have criticized **"Heritage"** for not offering more realistic images of Africa, decrying Cullen's ignorance but that is one of the levels on which the poem, the narrator is lying. These images of Africa are lies; certainly Cullen knew that. But is the poem also lying when it suggests that Africa means nothing to the narrator? Or is the poem lying when it suggests that Africa means anything to the narrator? Or is this very interiorized speech-act, speech-event poem nothing more than the system of lies that the impotent black intellectual uses to heal his own sickness of alienation and despair? The poem deals with the black narrator's own trinity: body ("the dark blood dammed within" and the word "dammed" of course is a pun), mind ("Africa? A book one thumbs / listlessly, till slumber comes"), and heart/spirit ("Lord, forgive me if my need / Sometimes shapes a human creed"), which has been thoroughly "civilized" or acculturated, trapped in language and reflection, a room of nothing but sound. But that whole business might be lies as well. The poem does not solve anything as the speaker can neither experience true conversion—the only act that can save him—nor deny it.

In typical romantic terms, Cullen is not simply concerned with the perfectability of the black Christian but the perfectability of the black Christian's God. **"The Black Christ"** is the only Cullen poem that is centrally concerned with conversion. In fact, the poem is about precisely the absolute politicization of conversion, for in the poem Cullen wishes to reverse the tradition of liberal Christian redemption. Evil is removed from the providential history of the self and deposited into the providential history of mankind. What the atheistic narrator of the poem demands is recognition from God that blacks do indeed exist in His sight. The recognition comes in the form of a miracle—the resurrection of his lynched brother, Jim. And it is this resurrection that makes Jim the Black Christ, not simply the fact that he is lynched. Indeed, in reworking the entire Christ idea, we find Cullen has totally politicized the crucifixion or made the political significance of Christ for a black believer completely *explicit.* Jim, a militant handsome black boy, kills a white man who insults him and his white girlfriend while they are enjoying the coming of spring. The white man is accused of threatening to harm spring:

> His vile and puny fingers churned
> Our world about that sang and burned
> A while as never world before.
> He had unlatched an icy door,
> And let the winter in once more.
> To kill a man is a woeful thing,
> But he who lays a hand on spring
> Clutches the first bird by its throat
> And throttles it in the midst of a note;
> Whose breath upon the leaf-proud tree
> Turns all that wealth to penury. . . .

Here, as has been pointed out, Cullen combines his standard romantic/poetic conceit (spring and nature) with the American politics of race and sex. Note how Jim the rebel kills the white man not for any violent acts on his part, but merely for his speech:

> I had gone on unheeding but
> He struck me down, he called her slut,
> And black man's mistress, bawdy whore,
> And such like names, and many more,
> . . . My right
> I knew could not outweigh his might
> Who had the law for satellite—
> Only I turned to look at her,
> The early spring's first worshipper,
> (Spring, what have you to answer for?)
> The blood had fled from either cheek
> And from her lips; she could not speak,
> But she could only stand and stare
> And let her pain stab through the air.
> I think a blow to heart or head
> Had hurt her less than what he said.
> A blow can be so quick and kind,
> But words will feast upon the mind
> And gnaw the heart down to a shred,
> And leave you living, yet leave you dead.

This is an absolute reversal of Christ, for it was Christ himself who died for his speech, his blasphemous claims of being the Messiah and being able to forgive sins. Here it is not the Christ figure who dies for his speech but rather who kills because he has been victimized by the speech of his oppressor, defined, trapped, degraded, and belittled by it. Since Jim represents the spirit of the New Negro, the little drama played out is surprisingly like the life of the archetypal New Negro, Jack Johnson, insulted and taunted by white men because of his white wives and girlfriends (and they themselves insulted as well, as we know that Johnson's first wife committed suicide because she found being a black man's wife a hard lot) and who takes revenge by calmly beating white men in the ring, the white opponents who have come to restore the order of things, the proper political balance (the equivalent of the poetic threat "to murder spring"). Thus **"The Black Christ"** is not simply a case of making a sacrificial black lamb into a Christ figure but rather of reinventing the entire myth of disobedience to authority, which is the cornerstone of Christian theology, so that it is *that* disobedience which is understood as the expression, the assertion of political and moral right. That disobedience to the white man's authority which is so central to the poem goes counter to the prevailing social myth of blacks and Christianity—namely, that the religion made them passive and, indeed, obedient. Certainly that element is represented in the poem by Jim and the narrator's mother, but it is not ultimately what the poem is suggesting that being a black Christian means, although in poems like **"Litany of the Dark People," "Shroud of Color,"** and **"Judas Iscariot,"** where Judas's burden is clearly akin to the accursedness of color, Cullen seems attracted to Christianity as the mystification of black suffering and trial, a reworking of the Uncle Tom, blacks-as-natural-Christian idea. In a poem like **"The Black Christ,"** Cullen is obviously looking for the liberationist and nationalistic impulses inherent in this cultural stereotype.

I have said earlier that all of Cullen's poems are Christian, and this statement might puzzle some readers, who think of the many love poems, frankly sensual poems, and *carpe diem* poems that Cullen wrote as indicative that Cullen was just as attracted to something pagan as to something Christian. But paganism as an attraction (and all of those "pagan" poems finally assert that paganism is just that, an attraction) is not possible in a pagan mind but only in a Christian mind that has been taught to see paganism as an attractive alternative to the rigors of Christianity. Kierkegaard expresses this compellingly and convincingly in his *Either/Or*:

> To assert that Christianity has brought sensuousness into the world may seem boldly daring. But as we say that a bold venture is half the battle, so also here; and my proposition may be better understood if we consider that in positing one thing, we also indirectly posit the other which we exclude. Since the sensuous generally is that which should be negatived, it is clearly evident that it is posited first through the act which excludes it, in that it posits the opposite positive principle. As principle, as power, as a self-contained system, sensuousness is first posited in Christianity; and in that sense it is true that Christianity brought sensuousness into the world. Rightly to understand this proposition, that Christianity has brought sensuousness into the world, one must apprehend it as identical with the contrary proposition, that it is Christianity which has driven sensuousness out, has excluded it from the world. As principle, as power, as a self-contained system, sensuousness was first posited by Christianity. . . . This is quite natural for Christianity is spirit, and spirit is the positive principle which Christianity has brought into the world. But when sensuousness is understood in its relationship to spirit [i.e., as its contrary], it is clearly known as a thing that must be excluded, it is determined as a principle, as a power; for that which spirit—itself a principle—would exclude must be something which is also a principle, although it first reveals itself as a principle in the moment of its exclusion.[29]

So Christianity has, in effect, created its own antithesis which makes possible both sin and guilt (both of which are located in Christianity but generated by the realization or actualization of paganism), but which is, in truth, a reflection of a unitary mind. This unitary mind in terms of understanding the Christian's thinking about paganism is quite true of Cullen. But Cullen has particularized the case of the black Christian in another way. In effect, from the point of view of theodicy, God did not invent evil but rather made available the consciousness that realized, through its own demented necessity, the existence of evil as an attraction. Cullen's own version of racial theodicy is this: Why did God make a racist world—which for Cullen, as for James Baldwin, was the absolute degeneracy and debasement of paganism and sensualism, the absolute repression of it as **"The Black Christ"** clearly show—for blacks to suffer in? The answer must exceed the simplistic: so that they might suffer exquisitely according to His will. That might be, to some degree, the belief of his father, but it was not Cullen's. Once again like Baldwin, Cullen was not a Calvinist and the central quarrel he has with Christianity is why there is an elect or a consciousness—racism—which demands that there must be an elect. So, on one level, Cullen surely has the pagan/Christian split-in-unity of which Kierkegaard speaks, but what has been posited as a principle and a power in opposition to Christianity, while having reached its highest expression of perfection through Christianity, for Cullen, is the idea of the elect. Therefore, Cullen must be understood as a Christian poet.

Notes

1. Headlines such as "Countee Cullen, Young Negro Poet Aids Understanding of His Race," "'Black Pan' Sings Again," "A Young Poet of Death and African Beauty," "Young Negro Poet Guest of Woman's Club," "Harvard Negro Poet Wins Another Prize," and "A Negro Shropshire Lad" were common both in the black and white press. Indeed, Cullen was sufficiently famous that when his poem "Black Majesty," inspired by a book on Africa of the same title by John Vandercook, appeared in *The Black Christ and Other Poems* (it had first been published in the May 1928 issue of *The Crisis*), Vandercook's grandmother wrote Cullen a gushing letter requesting a copy of the poem. Letter from Mrs. Vandercook to Cullen, April 10, 1929.

2. In an open letter in *Opportunity* magazine in July 1927, Carl Van Vechten remarked about Cullen's quotability: "I might say a word or two apropos of the quotableness of Countee Cullen. Suffice to say that the fact is that he is quoted more frequently, with two or three exceptions, than any other American poet. . . . I think the concluding lines of his beautiful sonnet, 'Yet Do I Marvel,' I have seen printed more often (in periodicals in other languages than English, moreover) than any other two lines by any contemporary poet." Bruce Kellner, *"Keep A-Inchin' Along": Selected Writings of Carl Van Vechten About Black Art and Letters* (Westport, Conn.: Greenwood Press, 1979), p. 237.

3. Tuttleton, "Countee Cullen at 'The Heights,'" in Amrijit Singh, William S. Shiver, and Stanley Brodwin, eds., *The Harlem Renaissance: Revalutions* (New York: Garland Publishing, 1989), p. 117.

4. "Countee's wife Ida is quite lovely: petite, dainty, very friendly, very devoted to Countee. . . ." letter from Langston Hughes to Arna Bontemps, dated November 5, 1941, in Charles H. Nichols, ed., *Arna Bontemps-Langston Hughes Letters, 1925-1967* (New York: Dodd, Mead and Company, 1980), p. 95.

5. It is Beulah Reimherr who says that Mrs. Cullen told her that her husband was born in Baltimore. See Beulah Reimherr, "Countee Cullen: A Biographical and Critical Study" (M.A. thesis, University of Maryland, 1960), p. 20. Jean Wagner, in his *Black Poets of the United States: From Paul Lawrence Dunbar to Langston Hughes,* trans. by Kenneth Douglas (Champaign-Urbana: University of Illinois Press, 1973), states that "according to the poet's widow . . . Countee Cullen was born in Louisville, Kentucky," p. 285. In Alan Shucard's *Countee Cullen* (Boston: Twayne Publishers, 1984), Mrs. Cullen is quoted in this way: "I have never been under the impression that Countee Cullen was born in Baltimore. In 1940 shortly after Countee and I married, I was told by him that he was born in Louisville, Kentucky," p. 6. Blanche E. Ferguson in her juvenile *Countee Cullen and the Negro Renaissance* (New York: Dodd, Mead and Co., 1966) avoids the issue of Cullen's birth entirely. For her, Cullen's life begins neither with conception nor birth, but with his "adoption" by the Reverend and Mrs. Cullen at, according to her, the age of eleven. Ferguson, on the whole, suggests some connections between Cullen and Kentucky, p. 11. The connection between Cullen and Baltimore is actually a curious one. On May 4, 1926, he was scheduled to address the Baltimore Civic Club at the Emerson Hotel. When the management learned that the speaker was black, it refused to allow the meeting to be held there. Unable to reach him before Cullen left Harvard, the club's treasurer met him at the train station and explained the situation which so deeply upset Cullen that despite the fact that he had two other commitments in Baltimore he simply returned to Boston. When the affair was reported in the New York *Daily News,* "Incident" was quoted as if what happened in the poem had actually occurred. In the June 3, 1926 issue of *The Advocate,* Cullen said, "That incident [referring to the poem] has been outstanding in my memory all these years. But once I had given expression to it—once I had put it into verse—it seemed to lose its sting." But in 1939 Cullen described "Incident" as poetry, as an account of a child's reaction, and not as a biographical fact. Cullen also suggests validation of his origins through another poem, "The Ballad of the Brown Girl," which he said he first heard while growing up in Kentucky. A poem that serves as an interesting gloss of Cullen's view of his natural parents and his birth is "Saturday's Child." Cullen, apparently, was born on a Saturday.

6. Ferguson, p. 12.

7. Wagner, p. 285.

8. Wagner, p. 285, suggests it is Cullen's mother; Reimherr, p. 22, insists it is not his mother but probably his grandmother.

9. See Shucard, p. 6; Reimherr, p. 21; Wagner p. 285; and Shirley Lumpkin, the "Countee Cullen" entry in the *Dictionary of Literary Biography, Vol. 48: American Poets, 1880-1945, Second Series,* Peter Quartermain, ed. (Detroit: Gale Research Co., 1986), p. 110.

10. One of Cullen's earliest poems, "To the Swimmer," published in *The Modern School: A Monthly Magazine Devoted to Libertarian Ideas in Education* in May 1918, was signed "Countee L. Porter" (p. 142). This would seem to call into question Blanche Ferguson's assertion that Cullen received a writing certificate on May 15, 1915, which said in part, "issued to Countee Porter Cullen" (p. 17). As Ferguson provides no citations in her book, it is impossible to check her sources.

11. *The Christian Science Monitor,* October 23, 1925, p. 6.

12. Letter from Ida Cullen to Countee Cullen, July 24, 1945.

13. The four italicized lines are used verbatim in Cullen's second poem about his father, "Fruit of the Flower."

14. Arna Bontemps, "The Harlem Renaissance," *The Saturday Review of Literature,* March 22, 1947, p. 12.

15. Among some of DeWitt Clinton's outstanding graduates are Cullen, Richard Rodgers, Louis Untermeyer. Waldo Frank, Paul Gallico, Richard Avedon, James Baldwin, George Sokolsky, and Paddy Chayefsky.

16. It is appropriate to address here the issue of homosexuality as at least three major scholars have asserted that Cullen was homosexual. David Lewis in *When*

Harlem Was in Vogue [New York: Knopf, 1981], Jean Wagner in *Black Poets of the United States* [Urbana: University of Illinois Press, 1973], and Arnold Rampersad in *The Life of Langston Hughes, Vol. 1: 1902-1941* [New York: Oxford University Press, 1986-1988]. There is, however, no evidence that Cullen and Jackman were lovers. There is no evidence that Cullen was engaged in any homosexual relations with any other figures of the Renaissance. Some scholars have read letters and poems that seem suggestive in this regard but have offered nothing conclusive.

17. There are two versions of this poem, both included in this volume. The shorter version is a revision of the longer, more wordy one. The wordy version is the one for which Cullen won the award. The poem was inspired or suggested by Alan Seeger's "I Have a Rendezvous With Death," which was published in 1916.
18. Tuttleton, "Countee Cullen at 'The Heights,'" p. 118.
19. Tuttleton, p. 119, 123, 124, 125, 127.
20. Tuttleton, p. 120, 121, 129.
21. Tuttleton, p. 119.
22. James Weldon Johnson, *Black Manhattan* (Salem, N.H.: Ayer Co., 1988), p. 267.
23. Owen Dodson, "Countee Cullen (1903-1946)," *Phylon* (First Quarter, 1946), p. 20.
24. Margaret Sperry, "Countee P. Cullen, Negro Boy Poet, Tells His Story," *Brooklyn Daily Eagle,* February 10, 1924.
25. T. S. Eliot, *The Use of Poetry and the Use of Criticism* (London: Faber and Faber, 1933), p. 100.
26. Cullen received letters dated February 18, 1943, and March 6, 1943, from Eugene F. Saxton of Harper and Brothers, the first stating that because of material shortages, undoubtedly caused by the Second World War, the company was not likely to publish either "The Monkey Baboon" or a prose version of "The Lost Zoo;" the second, however, is an acceptance of the prose version of "The Lost Zoo." However, Saxton died on June 26, 1943 and his death may have affected publication, for no prose version of "The Lost Zoo" was ever published.
27. Cullen, *Caroling Dusk,* p. 179.
28. Clifford Geertz, *The Interpretation of Cultures* (New York: Basic Books, 1973), pp. 165ff.
29. Søren Kierkegaard, "The Immediate Stages of the Erotic or the Musical Erotic" in *Either/Or,* Vol. 1, translated by David F. Swenson and Lillian Marvin Swenson (Princeton: Princeton University Press, 1959), pp. 59-60.

DEBORAH TURNER (ESSAY DATE 1998)

SOURCE: Turner, Deborah. "Countee P. Cullen: Overview." In *Gay and Lesbian Literature,* Vol. 2, edited by Tom Pendergast and Sara Pendergast. Farmington Hills, Mich.: St. James Press, 1998.

In the following excerpt, Turner evaluates Cullen's poetry for the interplay between homosexual and racial themes.

Countée Cullen was nicknamed the "Poet Laureate" of the Harlem Renaissance. Although his body of works include articles, plays, and reviews, he is famous for his poetry, especially those poems from early in his career. Cullen is also known for adhering to a nineteenth-century, English romantic writing style. Of the British poets, Keats seemed to have influenced Cullen the most. Some common themes found in Cullen's works concern universal human experiences such as love, death, nature, and beauty. His earnest efforts to be acknowledged simply as a poet, not a black poet, leads one to believe he would have shunned being referred to as a black gay poet. Nonetheless, a re-examination of Cullen's traditional writing style reveals poetic references to homosexual as well as racial homosexual relations.

Most critics of Cullen seem to agree that it is essential to understand aspects of the cultural and historical context during his lifetime in order to comprehend his works. During the 1920s and early 1930s, New York City's Harlem burgeoned with great numbers of blacks who migrated from the rural South to the urban North. As a result of this migratory phenomena, as well as other political and economical dynamics, black arts blossomed. This period is widely known as the Harlem Renaissance. Many efforts were made to showcase the richness of and eradicate stereotypes associated with black culture. In "A Spectacle in Color" Eric Garber depicts a thriving Harlem gay and lesbian subculture, yet clearly indicates the frequent, dire consequences of being openly or publicly "out" during this period.

Cullen is best known for highly structured, lyric poetry—though his poems include ballads, children's verse, epitaphs, and sonnets—and his universally accessible subject matter, including disillusionment with and loss of love, images of nature, conflicts with religion, and experiences surrounding friendships. Darryl Pinckney of the *New York Review of Books* states that Cullen's adherence to this structure sometimes compromises the content of his poems. Cullen's use of traditional British aesthetics and universal themes exemplify, in part, his attempts to be known for his humanity, rather than his race. Ironically, he was more often than not remembered as a famous black poet. Perhaps the most cited example of this paradox can be found in the poem **"Yet Do I Marvel"** in ***Color,*** Cullen's first—and arguably best—book. "Yet do I marvel at this curious thing / To make a poet black, and bid him sing!" Moreover, this contradiction is also exemplified in many of Cullen's works in which he depicts the social conditions of blacks. In an essay on Cullen, Alden Reimonenq claims that Cullen's conservative style not only contains depictions of the racial climate, but also masks themes prominent in same sex relationships.

Cullen's most concrete reference to homosexuality occurs in the epic poem **"The Black Christ."** It is poem set in the rural, southern United States and narrated by the brother of the main character, Jim. Jim is wrongfully accused of and lynched for the rape of a white woman, also a friend. In spite of this familial relationship, Gregory Woods notes the narrator's homo-erotic description of his brother in "Gay Re-Readings of the Harlem Renaissance Poets." Upon Jim's death, he is referred to as Lycidas, the beloved college friend of John Milton; Jonathan, the lover of David; and, Patrocles, or Patroclus, the lover of Achilles. Woods further adds that each of these characters had died prematurely and was mourned by the men who loved them. By comparing Jim to other gay characters in history, the narrator invites readers to assume that Jim might also be gay.

In re-reading works for gay content, Woods explicates the relevance Cullen's body of works has to gay literature. By viewing themes of racial oppression under the more general topic of oppression, Woods argues that one can begin to associate, at least on the surface, the similarities it has to topics of sexual oppression. For instance, in **"Tableau"** from ***Color,*** local townspeople react to a friendship between two boys; one black, the other white. "From lowered blinds the dark folk stare / And here the fair for talk / Indignant that these two should dare / In unison to walk." In an associative, gay re-reading of the poem, the homosexual relationship becomes as apparent as the interracial relationship. Reimonenq adds that common interpretations of this poem are as much filled with heterosexism as racism. That is, readers too quickly assume that the two boys are not romantically inclined towards one another. Gays and lesbians who choose to remain abreast of both heterosexual and gay cultures also experience this sort of dual allegiance.

"Heritage," from ***Color,*** is heralded for its exploration of what Africa means to African-Americans. It is also an exploration of having an allegiance to more than one culture. At one point, the speaker in **"Heritage"** poignantly addresses Jesus, "With my mouth thus, in my heart / Do I play a double part."

Many of Cullen's poems lament the rejection of those who are considered inferior or different. Consider **"Uncle Jim"** and **"From the Dark Tower,"** both in ***Copper Sun.*** Note here the invitation for the reader to consider equality: "The night whose sable breast relieves the stark / White stars is no less lovely being dark." Additionally, Woods remarks that the night time and day light imagery in the later poem can be read as a metaphor for being "closeted," or in the dark, and "coming out," or coming into the light.

Many of Cullen's verses with love themes lack a designation of gender. Examples of these can be found in **"At a Parting," "Song in Spite of Myself,"** and **"Therefore, Adieu,"** each from ***The Black Christ and Other Poems,*** and **"Although I Name You Not . . ."** in ***The Medea and Some Poems.*** The lack of clearly identified gender lines is consistent with Cullen's attempt to portray universal human experiences. It may seem over-zealous to analyze this seemingly superficial evidence. However, if one coupled reexamination of Cullen's entire body of works as a whole together with the "closeted" social context in which he wrote, these gender-neutral love poems can be viewed as a significant codification of issues often encountered in homosexual relationships.

Much has been written on Countée Cullen. Most would agree that he wrote his best works at the start of his writing career. Many critics note that Cullen never wrote one great work, even though he personally selected the poems for inclusion in the posthumous volume, ***On These I Stand.*** Still, given the climate of the effervescent Harlem Renaissance, a gay re-reading of Cullen's works provides an opportunity to venture into parts of the gay and lesbian subculture of that time period. To re-read Cullen's works for gay content neither diminishes his references to black culture, nor fully explains those to gay culture. Instead, it aids one in beginning to appreciate the intricate, multifaceted richness of Cullen's writings.

TITLE COMMENTARY

Color

MARK VAN DOREN (REVIEW DATE 1926)

SOURCE: Van Doren, Mark. "Countee Cullen Commences." *New York Herald Tribune Books* (10 January 1926): 3.

In the following review, Pulitzer Prize-winning poet Van Doren considers Cullen's Color.

There are numerous things which Mr. Cullen as a poet has not yet begun to do, and there are some which he will never do, but in this first volume he makes it clear that he has mastered a tune. Few recent books of poems have been so tuneful—at least so tuneful in the execution of significant themes. Probably that accounts for the almost instantaneous success of Mr. Cullen when he began not long ago to appear in the magazines. He had something to say, and he sang it.

What he had to say was nothing new even in his own generation. Edna Millay had said as much and more, and she had employed something like the same melodies. Mr. Cullen's **"The Shroud of Color"** could be referred back, if one wished to treat it that way, to **"Renascence"**; **"Saturday's Child"** and **"Fruit of the Flower"** have also their counterpart in Miss Millay's most piquant and interesting pieces—those sketching a spiritual heritage. But Mr. Cullen is not seriously damaged by the reference; first, because he obviously means what he sings and, second, because he has an accent of his own.

Mr. Cullen's skill appears in the clarity and the certainty of his song. Those who have tried to do a similar thing will be in the best position to appreciate the success of the following lines from the poem which prefaces the volume:

> Soon every sprinter,
> However fleet,
> Comes to a winter
>
> Of sure defeat:
> Though he may race
> Like the hunted doe,
> Time has a pace
> To lay him low.
>
> Soon we who sing,
> However high,
> Must face the Thing
> We cannot fly.
> Yea, though we fling
> Our notes to the sun,
> Time will outsing
> Us every one.

The theme of this poem is the shortness of life—a sacred theme for lyric poets always and Mr. Cullen is so full of it that there is actually something joyous in the cadences with which he pays it his respects. The paradox is not surprising, perhaps, but it is attractive—the paradox of youth declaring that Time is a terrible enemy, and yet declaring this gayly, as if there were something delicious in the terror which the thought of death had inspired. The theme appears again and again in ***Color,*** in forming the love poems with that doctrine which we know best through the two words *carpe diem,* and imparting vitality to whatever pieces assert the preciousness of the present moment.

> Now I am young and a fool for love,
> My blood goes mad to see
> A brown girl pass me like a dove
> That flies melodiously.
>
> Let me be lavish of my tears.
> And dream that false is true;
> Though wisdom cometh with the years,
> The barren days come, too.

The prefatory poem, from which the first quotation was taken, is too long; ten further stanzas do little more than repeat the thought and beat it thin. If Mr. Cullen faces any danger it is this—that he shall call facility a virtue rather than the aspect of a virtue. Other poems here are too long for their content, and certain poems should not be here at all. It seems important both for Mr. Cullen and for the race which he so admirably represents that he should not hurry his next book into the world.

ALAIN LOCKE (REVIEW DATE 1926)

SOURCE: Locke, Alain. *"Color*—A Review." *Opportunity* 4, no. 37 (January 1926): 14-15.

In the following review, Locke examines Cullen's Color, *proclaiming the poet a rare talent whose verse is rooted both in poetic tradition and African American experience.*

Ladies and gentlemen! A genius! Posterity will laugh at us if we do not proclaim him now. ***Color*** transcends all the limiting qualifications that might be brought forward if were merely a work of talent. It is a first book, but it would be treasurable if it were the last; it is a work of extreme youth and youthfulness over which the author later may care to write the apology of "juvenilia," but it has already the integration of a distinctive and matured style; it is the work of a Negro poet writing for the most part out of the intimate emotional experience of race, but the adjective is for the first time made irrelevant, so thoroughly has he poetized the substance and fused it with the universally human moods of life. Cullen's own Villonesque poetic preface to the contrary, time will not outsing these lyrics.

The authentic lyric gift is rare today for another reason than the rarity of poetic genius and especially so in contemporary American poetry—for the substance of modern life brings a heavy sediment not easy to filter out in the poetic process. Only a few can distill a clear flowing product, Housman, de la Mare, Sara Teasdale, Edna St. Vincent Millay, one or two more perhaps. Countee Cullen's affinity with these has been instantly recognized. But he has grown in sandier soil and taken up a murkier substance; it has taken a longer tap-root to reach down to the deep tradition upon which great English poetry is nourished, and the achievement is notable. More than a personal temperament flowers, a race experience blooms; more than a reminiscent crop is gathered, a new stalk has sprouted and within the flower are, we believe, the seeds of a new stock, richly parented by two cultures. It is no disparagement to our earlier Negro poets to say this: men do not choose their time, and time is the gardener.

Why argue? Why analyze? The poet himself tells us

Drink while my blood
Colors the wine.

But it is that strange bouquet of the verses themselves that must be mulled to be right appreciated. Pour into the vat all the Tennyson, Swinburne, Housman, Patmore, Teasdale you want, and add a dash of Pope for this strange modern skill of sparkling couplets,—and all these I daresay have been intellectually culled and added to the brew and still there is another evident ingredient, fruit of the Negro inheritance and experience, that has stored up the tropic sun and ripened under the storm and stress of the American transplanting. Out of this clash and final blend of the pagan with the Christian, the sensual with the Puritanically religious, the pariah with the prodigal, has come this strange new thing. The paradoxes of Negro life and feeling that have been sad and plaintive and whimsical in the age of Dunbar and that were rhetorical and troubled, vibrant and accusatory with the Johnsons and MacKay now glow and shine and sing in this poetry of the youngest generation.

This maturing of an ancestral heritage is a constant note in Cullen's poetry. **"Fruit of the Flower"** states it as a personal experience:

My father is a quiet man
  With sober, steady ways;
For simile, a folded fan;
  His nights are like his days.
My mother's life is puritan,
  No hint of cavalier,
A pool so calm you're sure it can
  Have little depth to fear.
And yet my father's eyes can boast
  How full his life has been;
There haunts them yet the languid ghost
  Of some still sacred sin.
And though my mother chants of God,
  And of the mystic river,
I've seen a bit of checkered sod
  Set all her flesh aquiver.
Why should he deem it pure mischance
  A son of his is fain
To do a naked tribal dance
  Each time he hears the rain?
Why should she think it devil's art
  That all my songs should be
Of love and lovers, broken heart,
  And wild sweet agony?
Who plants a seed begets a bud,
  Extract of that same root;
Why marvel at the hectic blood
  That flushes this wild fruit?

Better than syllogisms, **"Gods"** states the same thing racially:

I fast and pray and go to church,
  And put my penny in,
But God's not fooled by such slight tricks,
  And I'm not saved from sin.
I cannot hide from Him the gods
  That revel in my heart,
Nor can I find an easy word
  To tell them to depart:
God's alabaster turrets gleam
  Too high for me to win,
Unless He turns His face and lets
  Me bring my own gods in.

Here as indubitably as in Petrarch or Cellini or Stella, there is the renaissance note. What body of culture would not gladly let it in! In still more conscious conviction we have this message in the **"Shroud of Color"**:

Lord, not for what I saw in flesh or bone
Of fairer men; not raised on faith alone;
Lord, I will live persuaded by mine own.
I cannot play the recreant to these;
My spirit has come home, that sailed the
  doubtful seas.

The latter is from one of the two long poems in the volume; both it and **"Heritage"** are unusual achievements. They prove Mr. Cullen capable of an unusually sustained message. There is in them perhaps a too exuberant or at least too swiftly changing imagery, but nevertheless they have a power and promise unusual in this day of the short poem and the sketchy theme. They suggest the sources of our most classic tradition, and like so much that is most moving in English style seem bred from the Bible. Occasionally one is impressed with the fault of too great verbal facility, as though words were married on the lips rather than mated in the heart and mind, but never is there pathos or sentimentality, and the poetic idea always has taste and significance.

Classic as are the fundamentals of this verse, the overtones are most modernly enlightened:

The earth that writhes eternally with pain
Of birth, and woe of taking back her slain
Laid bare her teeming bosom to my sight,
And all was struggle, gasping breath, and fight.

A blind worm here dug tunnels to the light,
And there a seed, tacked with heroic pain,
Thrust eager tentacles to sun and rain.

Still more scientifically motivated, is:

Who shall declare
  My whereabouts;
Say if in the air
  My being shouts
Along light ways,
  Or if in the sea
Or deep earth stays
  The germ of me?

The lilt is that of youth, but the body of thought is most mature. Few lyric poets carry so sane and sober a philosophy. I would sum it up as a beautiful and not too optimistic pantheism, a rare gift to a disillusioned age. Let me quote at the end my favorite poem one of its best expressions:

Dead men are wisest, for they know
How far the roots of flowers go,
How long a seed must rot to grow.
Dead men alone bear frost and rain
On throbless heart and heatless brain,
And feel no stir of joy or pain.
Dead men alone are satiate;
They sleep and dream and have no weight,
To curb their rest, of love or hate.
Strange, men should flee their company,
Or think me strange who long to be
Wrapped in their cool immunity.

"The Wise"

ROBERT T. KERLIN (REVIEW DATE 1926)

SOURCE: Kerlin, Robert T. "Singer of New Songs." *Opportunity* 4, no. 41 (May 1926): 162-64.

In the following excerpt, Kerlin reviews Cullen's volume of poetry Color, *and argues that it contains particular insights and wisdom absent from the works of Caucasian poets.*

In 1923 a Negro student in New York University won second place among the seven hundred undergraduates of American colleges who competed for the Witter Bynner prize in poetry. The next year he was still second, and in 1925 he was first. This was Countee Cullen, aged 23. On the publication of **"The Ballad of the Brown Girl"** I wrote, in *The Southern Workman,* that it placed Mr. Cullen by the side of the best modern masters of the ballad—Morris, Rossetti, and any others that may be named. Of course it is imitative—all modern ballads are, and are successful just in degree as they are imitative of the old folk ballads. But there is a felicity possible in imitation, and a creativeness, which are capable of producing the thrill we expect of supreme art. I still think, **"The Ballad of the Brown Girl"** worthy of the praise I gave it.

But now appears Mr. Cullen's first book [***Color***] and this ballad is nowhere in it! My first thought is, What must be the severity of self-criticism, and the audacity, of a poet of twenty-three who will exclude from his book a poem of such merit? It was a most conceited thing to do. But I have no sooner read his ballad entitled **"Judas Iscariot"** than I am able to guess the reason of the exclusion. Like the author, I am willing to read his case upon this ballad without the assistance of **"The Brown Girl."**

I return to his apologia, as it were, **"To You Who Read My Book"**:

Juice of the first
  Grapes of my vine,
I proffer your thirst
  My own heart's wine.
Here of my growing
  A red rose sways,
Seed of my sowing,
  And work of my days.

It is in an altogether manly strain, albeit with an undertone of melancholy—Mr. Cullen did well to entitle his book ***Color.*** It is impregnated with color. Something exotic to the Caucasian, call it *color,* call it *Africanism,* call it what you will, impregnates the fabric of Cullen's verse as the murex dye impregnated the cloth of the Tyrian looms, and made the purples worn by kings. A brown girl is thus brought before you:

Her walk is like the replica
  Of some barbaric dance
Wherein the soul of Africa
  Is winged with arrogance.

An Atlantic City waiter whose subtle poise as with his tray aloft he carves dexterous avenues, as it were through a jungle, on his way to serve choice viands to ladies who pause and gaze, is thus presented:

Sheer through his acquiescent mask
  Of bland gentility,
The jungle flames like a copper cask
  Set where the sun strikes free.

In such imagery we have a poet who is going on his own. We have here a Negro poet who is as sure of himself as Keats was. [I particularly esteem the two poems **"Black Magdalens"** and **"Simon the Cyrenian Speaks,"** primarily for] their merits as poems, and incidentally because they exemplify, as the **"Judas Iscariot"** already mentioned does, the Negro's easy penetration to the meanings we of the occidental and white mind so easily miss in "our" gospel narratives. . . .

These two poems, which are quite typical of Mr. Cullen's quality as a poet, suggest something in the way of spiritual discernment and wisdom which is the Negro's peculiar possession. It is the same quality which appears in Mr. Roland Hayes' singing—a quality that so gets hold of your heart. It surely omens a new element in our literature, art and life. Will the Negro be duly impressed with the idea that he has this contribution to make? And, a more important question, will the Caucasian, proud of his "supreme Caucasian mind," be humbly or otherwise receptive?

MICHAEL L. LOMAX (ESSAY DATE 1974)

SOURCE: Lomax, Michael L. "Countee Cullen: A Key to the Puzzle." *Studies in the Literary Imagination* 7, no. 2 (fall 1974): 39-48.

In the following essay, Lomax examines the critical reception of Cullen's Color, *as well as the poet's struggle between being an African American with a strong sense of racial identity and a culturally assimilated poet and artist. Lomax also discusses Cullen's poetic decline.*

> The early poems are as good as one remembers them, the later ones inferior. The puzzle is why Cullen did not merely stop growing, but was thrown back.
>
> Helen Wolfert, *PM,* March 16, 1947

"Ladies and gentlemen!" black critic Alain Locke announced in 1926, a peak year of the Harlem Renaissance, "A genius! Posterity will laugh at us if we do not proclaim him now."[1] Much of Locke's time and energy, guidance and concern had been focused on the New Negro artists of the era, and now his efforts in their behalf were being rewarded amply with what he considered the unquestionably high literary standard achieved in ***Color,*** a first volume by the young black poet Countee Cullen. With this volume, the New Negro had taken a significant step forward, according to Locke, and, as if to prove that point, his hosannas were picked up only a little less enthusiastically by other critics not so personally involved in Cullen's career.

White reviewers were impressed and willingly admitted that Cullen's volume heralded a new and higher epoch in black American literature. "With Countee Cullen's ***Color,***" wrote Clement Wood in the *Yale Review,* "we have the first volume of the most promising of the younger negro poets. There is no point in measuring him merely beside Dunbar . . . and other negro poets of the past and present: he must stand or fail beside Shakespeare and Keats and Masefield, Whitman and Poe and Robinson."[2] Most other white reviewers were not quite so unqualified as Wood and did not presume to place Cullen among such an auspicious group of English and American poets. While they did invoke Cullen's obvious and admitted literary influences, they still compared the young black poet favorably. "Much of his work is reminiscent of Miss Edna St. Vincent Millay and of A. E. Housman," wrote one reviewer in *The Independent,* "but always it is informed with something personal to him, some quality of his own. It is never purely imitative."[3]

The reviewers noted that the volume betrayed certain youthful weaknesses, but they were quick to point out that ***Color*** suggested a potentially powerful literary talent—a fact which they felt far overshadowed any incidental weaknesses. "There are numerous things which Mr. Cullen as a poet has not yet begun to do . . . , but in this first volume he makes it clear that he has mastered a tune," wrote poet Mark Van Doren. "Few recent books have been so tuneful—at least so tuneful in the execution of significant themes."[4]

Color and Cullen did not entirely escape negative criticism though and, significantly, it was white reviewers who pointed to Cullen's arch traditionalism and lack of stylistic originality as major flaws in his work. Locke's review had mentioned Cullen's rhyming, but glossed over it by invoking Pope as the model for what he euphemistically termed "this strange modern skill of sparkling couplets."[5] The white reviewers were not, however, so quick to justify Cullen's old-fashioned style. "Perhaps the only protest to Mr. Cullen that one cares to insist on is against his frequent use of rhetorical style which is surely neither instinctive in origin nor agreeable in effect," wrote *Poetry*'s reviewer. "Lofty diction in poetry when it is unwarranted by feeling . . . is liable to seem only stilted and prosy."[6] The general silence of black reviewers on this point seems to suggest their own agreement with Cullen. The majority black critical view was that New Negro artists should express themselves in time-honored forms and thus give stature to their racial themes. By performing well, within the confines of established literary traditions, black artists would demonstrate their capabilities in a way that could not be disputed.

White reviews of ***Color*** included one uniform and rather predictable response. They all stated that Cullen's real importance was not merely as a black poet writing of his people's experiences but as a poet expressing the universal human experience. "But though one may recognize that certain of Mr. Cullen's verses owe their being to the fact that he shares the tragedy of his people," wrote

Babette Deutsch in *The Nation,* "it must be owned that the real virtue of his work lies in his personal response to an experience which, however conditioned by his race, is not so much racial as profoundly human. The color of his mind is more important than the color of his skin."[7]

Ironically, though, it was this specifically racial element in his work which most forcefully appealed to black reviewers. "His race and its sufferings," wrote Walter White, "give him depth and an understanding of pain and sorrow."[8] White's emphasis was echoed in other black reviews which praised Cullen as the first real spokesman for sensitive and educated blacks who daily suffered through the pressures and hardships of the American racial experience. "The poems which arise out of the consciousness of being a 'Negro in a day like this' in America," wrote Jessie Fauset in *The Crisis,* ". . . are not only the most beautifully done but they are by far the most significant group in the book. . . . Here I am convinced is Mr. Cullen's forte; he has the feelings and the gift to express colored-ness in a world of whiteness. I hope he will not be deflected from continuing to do that of which he has made such a brave and beautiful beginning."[9]

Certainly the "colored-ness" which Jessie Fauset praised as an essential feature of Cullen's first volume was a quality which she sensed rather than a sentiment which she found expressed in clear and forthright statements. There were too many non-racial poems for that; and too many poems in which, as she herself pointed out, "the adjectives 'black' or 'brown' or 'ebony' are deliberately introduced to show that the type which the author had in mind was not white."[10] At least in part, though, this inclusion of non-racial and peripherally black poems did suggest Cullen's own particular brand of "colored-ness." For within the context of ***Color*** as a whole, they implied the tentativeness of Cullen's assertions of a strong sense of his own black identity. These poems, appearing along side verse dealing with specifically racial themes, point to the DuBoisean "double-consciousness" as the central contradiction in Cullen's appraisal of his own racial identity. Neither black nor white, Cullen saw himself somewhere in between, an undefined individual consciousness for whom "colored" became as good a label as any. Thus, the volume as a whole and several poems in particular are haunted by the unresolved conflict in Cullen's perception of himself as simultaneously a black man and a culturally assimilated though, admittedly, socially ostracized Westerner. This central tension became the source of dramatic conflict in Cullen's and ***Color***'s best known poem, **"Heritage."** In it, Cullen confronted the contradictions within his own identity and, though finally incapable of resolving them, he articulated his emotional and intellectual struggle with honesty and a rarely-achieved eloquence.

The opening lines of **"Heritage"** introduce Cullen's conflict in terms of tensions between past and present. Africa and America:

> What is Africa to me:
> Copper sun or scarlet sea,
> Jungle star or jungle track,
> Strong bronzed men, or regal black
> Women from whose loins I sprang
> When the birds of Eden sang?
> *One three centuries removed*
> *From the scenes his fathers loved,*
> *Spicy grove, cinnamon tree,*
> *What is Africa to me?*[11]

Africa was a frequent symbol in New Negro poetry for a pristine black identity which had not been confused by the values, "progress" and materialism of Western society. Ironically, this pastoral image bore little actual relation to contemporary colonial Africa or even to Africa three centuries before, but was instead the product of a long tradition of popular literary stereotypes. Cullen's Africa, peopled with wild animals and "young forest lovers . . . / Plighting troth beneath the sky," was just another literary conception—part Edgar Rice Burroughs, part courtly romance. Yet, in spite of Cullen's historical naivete, the essential personal problem still emerges, the conflict between a conscious and intellectualized Western self and a self which intuitively senses a bond with a lost past as well as elements of a degraded present:

> So I lie, who always hear,
> Though I cram against my ear
> Both my thumbs, and keep them there,
> Great drums throbbing through the air.
> So I lie, whose fount of pride,
> Dear distress, and joy allied,
> Is my somber flesh and skin,
> With the dark blood damned within
> Like great pulsing tides of wine
> That, I fear, must burst the fine
> Channels of the chafing net
> Where they surge and foam and fret.[12]

Elsewhere in ***Color*** Cullen had attempted to establish bonds with elements of the racial present, elements which he usually excluded from the limited range of his sensitive and, admittedly, bourgeois outlook. In **"Black Magdalens"** and **"Atlantic City Waiter"** he tried to capture the meaning of experiences toward which he responded ambivalently, feeling simultaneously a sense of separation and a kind of bond as well. The results were forced and shallow, without the compassion achieved, for example, by McKay in "Harlem Shadows" and "Harlem Dancer"—poems in which the Jamaican poet establishes himself as an observer of those within the race who have been degraded, but in which he also affirms the essential humanity of those who have been thus debased. Cullen, on the other hand, though he may have chosen to observe such elements in black life, could not resolve his own tensions of disassociation and thus could not really affirm what he saw. He remained uncomfortable in the face of such elements and thus could only ineptly describe them. The Cullen who was later to chafe under the title "Negro poet" and who saw validity only in established European modes of expression could not accept as valuable the totality of black experience, as did Langston Hughes in "The Negro Speaks of Rivers." Still, at least the conclusion of **"Heritage"** suggests that in 1925 Cullen was not quite ready to accept a totally Western identity:

All day long and all night through,
One thing only must I do:
Quench my pride and cool my blood,
Lest I perish in the flood.
Lest a hidden ember set
Timber that I thought was wet
Burning like the dryest flax,
Melting like the merest wax,
Lest the grave restore its dead.
Not yet has my heart or head
In the least way realized
They and I are civilized.[13]

"Heritage" leans towards bonds of racial unity. So does ***Color*** as a whole, and so do Cullen's works of the early twenties. In light of Cullen's later shift to the opposite pole of assimilation, and his easier acceptance of a more catholic and eclectic Western identity, one wonders why his first volume bore this black stamp. The answer lies in the *milieu* of the 1920's. ***Color*** is the product of personal struggle in an atmosphere which reinforced all that was racially distinctive. Sophisticated whites were Negrophiles who wanted to see blacks as essentially different from their own boringly Western selves. Cullen, in spite of strong misgivings, was willing to do as many other New Negroes did, and thus he bowed to white desires. So, much of his later writing became a retraction of the position taken during the twenties. But whatever Cullen did and said later, ***Color*** remains an impressive and landmark volume, one which quickly established its author as the New Negro poet *par excellence.* To many critics, it also suggested a promise and future which Cullen did not fulfill.

Countee Cullen's sudden and premature death in 1946 at the age of forty-two shocked those who remembered him as he had been at the time of ***Color***'s publication, just two brief decades before, then a youthful poet with an auspicious future. At the time of his death, he was still a relatively young man and certainly, in terms of sheer talent, a gifted one as well. And in spite of what had appeared to be a too lengthy hiatus, there were those close to him who felt that his future might have been more productive. "Creative writers sometimes have long periods of silence," mused Langston Hughes, "Had he lived he might have written brilliantly and beautifully again."[14] But Cullen's untimely death certainly put an end to such speculations. Neither his youthful promise nor his more matured talent were to be fulfilled. And when Cullen's career is viewed in a more dispassionate and, perhaps, somewhat less generous light than Hughes' affords, such sanguine prognostications of what might have been had Cullen only lived hardly seem realistic. In fact, there is a real sense in which Cullen's death, rather than cutting short a still potentially productive career, instead marked a final coda to the poet's bitter period of decline. At forty-two, Cullen had not been a progressively maturing artist confidently expressing his own vision of life—in this case, his vision of black life in America. Rather, with his original gifts atrophying from disuse, Cullen remained a forced-black man who never adjusted comfortably to his racial identity.

During the bleak years which followed the Harlem Renaissance, Cullen continued to publish but without his earlier success. The Depression cut short white interest in black art, and Cullen barely survived the loss of his white audience. Without their interest he rejected entirely the racial themes of the 1920's, limiting himself to the more conventional poetic concerns of love and death. By the 1940's, he had exhausted these and, except for occasional forays into children's literature, wrote practically nothing at all.

Fittingly enough, Cullen made plans before his death to take a final bow in the role of poet. In 1945, he compiled a collection of his published poems and appropriately titled it ***On These I Stand.*** The volume was to be "an anthology of the best poems of Countee Cullen."[15] He clearly intended the collection to be a final monument to his poetic career and thus, whatever else he might do in the future, it could serve as a basis for evaluating that favored part of his literary life. The volume appeared in 1947, almost exactly one year after his death, and, as he had anticipated, critics used ***On These I Stand*** as a scale for measuring his entire career. Unfortunately, the final evaluations were not so impressive as Cullen had apparently anticipated.

John Ciardi pointed out that the key word for Cullen's early career had been "promise." But with his death, "this edition of his selected poems is total. And . . . the total disappoints the large claims that have been made for him."[16] Looking through the volume, Ciardi and other critics reviewed Cullen's chronologically arranged poems and discerned a pattern of slow but unquestionable decline. His career was a "descending curve," wrote *Poetry*'s reviewer, as he traced the lines of deterioration from Cullen's best serious verse of the 1920's through the mediocre and poorer products of later years.[17] Everyone seemed to agree that at the time of his death Cullen had reached a literary low point. Still the question remained: Why? The answers were not so uniform.

Some critics answered that the problem lay in Cullen's conservative response to literary traditions:

> Cullen was singularly unaware of what was going on in the world of poetry. In the age of Pound and Eliot, he tortured syntax and used such words as "aught" and "albeit." He nowhere shows any evidence of studying the styles of any modern poets other than Millay, Wylie, and Housman, although, according to Robert Hillyer, he wrote imitations of most of the older poets in the days at Harvard that preceded the publication of ***Color.*** Perhaps because of his failure to absorb the technical discoveries of his contemporaries, he was singularly unself-critical and could allow such monstrosities . . . to be printed. Certainly his failure to study carefully what other poets did is in part responsible for his never developing a style peculiarly his own. Even the good poems in ***On These I Stand*** could have been written by any other craftsman, they bear no stylistic signature.[18]

Yet, while one of Cullen's deficiencies was obviously a problem of technique, such stylistic considerations do not satisfactorily resolve the issue. For Cullen could at times, through content, overcome his largely self-imposed limitations. "When the observation contained in the poem is directed and personal, dealing immediately with people seen and events that really occurred," Ciardi pointed out, "the poem emerges movingly."[19] That, however, occurred only rarely. Generally, Cullen substituted literary sentiments for sense and feeling and real, intimate response. In later poems, he seemed to have lost whatever original ability he had had to discern between artificial feelings and personal perceptions. He lost the ability to capture essential experiences, as he had done in **"Heritage."** The result for his later poetry was a bland mixture: trite sentimentality expressed in the most outmoded style.

Most white critics thought that Cullen had lapsed into clichés because the demands of race had driven him away from the sincere, personal introspection which was his true concern. According to them, Cullen's natural impulse led toward intimate expression in such pristine forms as the sonnet and "the neat, sensitive, and immediate lyric."[20] Yet, "Increasingly, Cullen's poetry . . . evidences a triumph of conscience over his particular gift, as if he told himself, 'Don't you play now. Just do your work.'"[21] To work, according to this view, was to write of racial matters—a necessary subject because he was black, an unfortunate one since he was a poet. In this view, the moral and the aesthetic responsibilities were incompatible, irreconcilable. In spite of personal inclinations to do otherwise, Cullen tragically chose race above art. "Somehow or other . . . ," Cullen had admitted, as if to substantiate this argument, "I find my poetry of itself treating of the Negro, of his joys and sorrows—mostly of the latter, and of the heights and depths of emotion which I feel as a Negro."[22] The result of such a decision was that Cullen lost his personal roots and in the process his basis for an individual vision. Without the direction he might have achieved as an integrated individual, this argument went, Cullen's only refuge was in the expression of worn and meaningless sentiments.

Race does indeed appear to be at the root of Cullen's problem, but not for those reasons suggested by white critics. Cullen had once said that he viewed poetry ideally as "a lofty thought beautifully expressed."[23] The issues of race in America constrained this ideal and trespassed upon Cullen's separate pristine world of poetry and art. For race meant harshness, violence and ugliness, all directly opposite to the delicate beauties which he envisioned as the true concerns of poetry. During the 1920's, when whites were enthusiastic Negrophiles, Cullen joined with other New Negroes in, to quote Langston Hughes, expressing their "individual dark-skinned selves without fear or shame."[24] The result for Cullen was a vital and often electric poetry, full of the tensions produced by an unresolved sense of his own racial identity in direct conflict with his desire to gain recognition from an enthusiastic white audience which demanded that blacks be different. With the waning white enthusiasm of the Depression, however, Cullen reasserted his intention to be a poet, not a black poet, and accordingly moved away from racial themes. His rejection of race as a thematic priority is nowhere more strongly expressed than in his short poem, **"To Certain Critics,"** in which Cullen defiantly asserted: "I'll bear your censure as your praise, / For never shall the clan / Confine my singing to its ways / Beyond the ways of man."[25] With his rejection of race, Cullen concentrated on the essentially fatuous literary artificialities which were, according to him, the poet's true concern.

DuBois recognized this shift, labelled it a shortcoming, and pointed to it as the reason why Cullen's career "did not culminate":

> His career was never completed. In a sense it was halted in mid-flight and becomes at once inspiration and warning to the American Negro group. First inspiration: the group needs expression. Its development toward self-revelation may become one of the greatest gifts of any group of people to modern civilization. The burning experience through which it has come is unique and precious. No one else can give voice and body to it but Negroes.
>
> It is sheer nonsense to put before Negro writers the ideal of being just writers and not Negroes. There is no such possibility. Englishmen are English from birth to death and in that fact lies most of the value of their contribution. The ideal of pure art divorced from actual life is nothing but an ideal and of questionable value in any day or time. Least of all is it of value today when the whirling tragedy, bitterness, blood and sweat of our intricate and puzzling life on this earth calls and even shrieks for that knowledge of each other's soul which only the soul itself in its own individual experience can furnish.
>
> The opportunity then for literary expression upon which American Negroes have so often turned their backs is their opportunity and not their handicap. That Countee Cullen was born with the Twentieth Century as a black boy to live in Harlem was a priceless experience. . . .
>
> Yet, as I have said, Cullen's career was not finished. It did not culminate. It laid [a] fine, beautiful foundation, but the shape of the building never emerged. . . .[26]

DuBois' evaluation does indeed strike home. Cullen's refusal to accept race as a basic and valuable segment of his total identity was an evasion which prevented him from further straightforward and clear development. Race did not have to be a circumscribing point of view. Nor was Cullen compelled to do as Langston Hughes did and make it the conscious subject of all he wrote. Race was an inescapable aspect of his identity which, in spite of all he said to the contrary, did affect him. What DuBois failed to point out was that Cullen's racial equivocations were rooted deeply in the Harlem Renaissance itself. For the decade of the 1920's was a period of racial confusion and contradiction. Blacks were in vogue, but the values the New Negroes lived by and the goals they sought were white. Blacks were forced to play racial roles they did not find comfortable in order to achieve recognition from whites. Few New Negroes overcame the limitations of the period and were able to assert and maintain their own more solid racial and personal integrity. Langston Hughes was one of those few. Countee Cullen was not.

Notes

1. *Opportunity,* 4, No. 1 (January 1926), 14.
2. "The Negro Sings," *The Yale Review,* 15 (July 1926), 824.
3. 115 (November 7, 1925), 539.
4. *New York Herald Tribune,* January 10, 1926.
5. *Opportunity,* p. 14.
6. George H. Dillon, *Poetry,* 28 (April 1926), 51.
7. "Let It Be Allowed," *The Nation,* 121 (December 30, 1925), 763.
8. "A Negro Poet," *Saturday Review of Literature,* 2 (February 13, 1926), 556.
9. "Our Book Shelf," *The Crisis,* 31, No. 3 (March 1926), 239.
10. "Our Book Shelf," p. 238.
11. Countee Cullen, "Heritage," *Color* (New York: Harper and Brothers, 1925), p. 36.
12. "Heritage," pp. 36-37.
13. "Heritage," pp. 40-41.
14. "Here to Yonder," *Chicago Defender,* February 2, 1946.
15. *On These I Stand* (New York: Harper and Row, 1947), p. iii.
16. *Atlantic Monthly,* 179 (March 1947), 144.
17. Harvey Curtis Webster, "A Difficult Career," *Poetry,* 70 (July 1947), 224.
18. "A Difficult Career," pp. 224-25. Webster was, of course, wrong in saying that Cullen's work at Harvard preceded *Color. Color* was already off the press when Cullen arrived in Cambridge in September of 1925. The poems written at Harvard are found in *Copper Sun.*
19. Ciardi, p. 145.
20. Ciardi, p. 145.
21. Helen Wolfert, *PM,* March 16, 1947, p. 7.
22. *On These I Stand.*
23. Winifred Rothermel, "Countee Cullen Sees Future for the Race," *St. Louis Argus.* February 3, 1928.
24. Langston Hughes, "The Negro Artist and the Racial Mountain," *The Nation,* 122, No. 3181 (June 23, 1926), 694.

25. *The Black Christ* (New York: Harper, 1929), p. 63.

26. W. E. B. DuBois, "The Winds of Time," *Chicago Defender,* January, 1946.

Caroling Dusk

VILMA POTTER (ESSAY DATE 1980)

SOURCE: Potter, Vilma. "Countée Cullen: The Making of a Poet-Editor." *Pacific Coast Philology* 15, no. 2 (December 1980): 19-27.

In the following essay, Potter argues that the time and effort it took for Cullen to edit a special African American poet edition of the magazine Palms*—and later his anthology* Caroling Dusk*—kept him from poetic endeavors.*

The career of Countée Cullen is a fireworks show. After the quick, separate spurts, the crackling brightness rises higher and higher out of seemingly endless internal bursts until the feeding energy diminishes, the explosions spread outward and fall into a trail of individual sparks in the onrushing dark. And those who had only a moment before been wild with pleasure and astonishment, are disappointed.

The visible Cullen burn began in 1923 when the twenty-year old college student won honorable mention in the Witter Bynner Undergraduate Poetry Contest under the auspices of the Poetry Society of America. Rapidly he earned recognition for his lyric gift and his ironic spirit. In 1925 Harper published his first volume of poetry, ***Color.*** In 1926 he earned his M.A. at Harvard, and that fall he went to work as a literary editor for the National Urban League's journal, *Opportunity*. In 1927 Harper brought out three Cullen works: a second collection of his poems, ***Copper Sun,*** a single poem, ***The Ballad of the Brown Girl,*** and his anthology of Negro poets, ***Caroling Dusk.*** It was as though there was no end to the Cullen energy. In 1927 he won the N.A.A.C.P. Harmon gold medal "for distinguished achievement in Literature by a Negro" for ***Color.*** In 1928 he won a Guggenheim Fellowship, and he married the elegant daughter of W. E. B. DuBois.

The dazzle, the brilliance, was all in a fall. In 1929 ***The Black Christ and Other Poems*** disappointed his earliest enthusiasts. Six years later came ***The Medea and Some Poems. On These I Stand,*** Cullen's own selection published in 1947, a year after his death, contained only six new poems. Between ***The Black Christ*** and ***On These I Stand*** are a play, a novel, and two works for young readers. The shrinking volume of his poetry has been the subject of both his contemporary and his posthumous critics who offer explanations which range between the psychoanalytical and the political.[1] But there is a different explanation. Recent evidence—the correspondence among Countée Cullen, Witter Bynner, Spud Johnson and Idella Purnell—suggests a different explanation for this exhaustion of Cullen's poetry.

Between 1925 and 1928 Cullen had divided his creative energy between poetry and editing. The one task is personal, the other, public. To attempt both tasks at the same time is immensely difficult, and especially so for a young poet. It is well known that Cullen began his editorial work at *Opportunity* in the late fall of 1926, after the success of his first volume of poetry. In fact, while he was working at what eventually became ***Copper Sun*** (1927), he began that subtle shift of concentration and attention which was to have such a draining effect upon his own creative work. In the fall of 1925, Idella Purnell, the young poet-editor of *PALMS,* a small poetry magazine she was publishing in Guadalajara, invited Countée Cullen to edit a Negro Poets issue for *PALMS.*

For nine months, while he was yet a graduate student at Harvard, Cullen worked enthusiastically at the job of editing that issue. His correspondence with Purnell and Bynner shows how eagerly he embraced the task, and with what self-awareness he distinguished the reasons that his own contribution to the issue was so slight. The months he gave to this issue of *PALMS* were a dress rehearsal for the 1927 anthology, ***Caroling Dusk.***

Editor Purnell was not calling upon a figure unknown to the readers of the poetry magazine she had started in 1923. Witter Bynner had brought Cullen's work to her attention in 1923. Purnell had been his poetry student at Berkeley in 1919.[2] Cullen had won an award in the Witter Bynner Undergraduate Poetry Contest in 1923. On November 5, 1923, Bynner wrote to Cullen, "In my own personal choice, you were at the head of the entire list. As an associate editor of *PALMS,* which seems to me in many respects the best verse magazine being issued in English. I have ventured to suggest to the editor, Miss Idella Purnell, that she ask you to let her see your ballad and other work as well."[3]

There was some difficulty with international postal service, but in March of 1924, Cullen wrote to Purnell, enclosing the manuscript of **"The Ballad of the Brown Girl."** On April 14, he sent her two more poems, **"Blues Singer"** and **"Timid Lover,"** and a modest vita: "There is very little biography to give. I am twenty years old, a junior at New York University, won second place in the *Witter Bynner Poetry Contest for 1923,* have had poems in the *Bookman* and in *Poetry: A Magazine of Verse.*" She accepted his work for *PALMS,* and the tone of his May 6, 1924 response is full of youthful exuberance. He doesn't expect to be paid; "what poet is ever concerned about money?" He agrees—with reservation—to Purnell's changing a title from *En Passant* to ***In Passing.***[4]

PALMS published **"The Ballad of the Brown Girl"** in 2, No. 1 (Early Summer, 1924), and the three poems, **"Blues Singer," "Timid Lover,"** and **"In Passing,"** in 2, No. 3 (Early Fall, 1924). In the Early Summer issue, Purnell also reprinted from *Poetry* (May, 1924), **"For a Virgin Lady" "For my Grandmother,"** and **"A Lady I Know."** Thus, the readers of *PALMS* had been introduced to a significant young poet more than a year before she invited him to develop the Negro Poets' issue. They admired his work. In the early volumes of *PALMS,* Idella Purnell had accepted the Bynner method of judging the work of his Berkeley poetry class: anonymous submission and reader ballot. In 1924, Purnell's readers voted for Cullen's **"The Ballad of the Brown Girl."** In *PALMS* 3, No. 2 (November 1925), she announced that the judges had chosen **"The Ballad of the Brown Girl"** as the second best poem in the entire volume of six issues, and further, that the readers of *PALMS* 3, No. 1 (Summer 1926) had chosen Cullen's **"Wisdom Cometh with the Years"** as second best poem in that single issue.

Bynner, meanwhile, had shown Cullen's poetry to Willard (Spud) Johnson, another young poet-editor who was to contribute eleven poems to *PALMS* between 1923 and 1928. Johnson sent Cullen a copy of his verse magazine, *The Laughing Horse* (Santa Fe, N.M.). Cullen sent by way of thanks, two poems, **"On Going,"** and **"A Brown Girl Dead."** This exchange illustrates how Cullen's reputation was expanding within Bynner's circle. When Johnson received a copy of ***Color,*** he sent Cullen a long letter of praise. He found the book "fittingly bound and as beautiful in appearance as in content—a lovely book. . . . A week or two ago I had a hectic week of guests—and all of them saw your book and read at least a part of it. Arthur Davison Ficke was among them" (December 7, 1925). Idella Purnell published an appreciative review of ***Color*** in *PALMS* 3, No. 4 (January 1926) in which she quoted **"Yet do I marvel"** in its entirety. The review concludes, "Countée Cullen is one of the greatest of the younger American poets. At twenty-two, after one year of publication, he finds it necessary to acknowledge his indebtedness to seventeen magazines for permission to reprint a part of the poems in his book. There are enough *good* poems in this 'little collection' for five ordinary books of verse. Countée Cullen: Twenty-two. Watch him."[5]

FROM THE AUTHOR

LEAGUE OF YOUTH ADDRESS

For we must be one thing or the other, an asset or a liability, the sinew in your wing to help you soar, or the chain to bind you to earth.

SOURCE: Countee Cullen, excerpt from the "League of Youth Address," in *Crisis,* August 1923.

As 1925 came to its end, Idella Purnell sent Cullen the invitation which was to draw him in a new direction. She announced in the January 1926 issue that "Countée Cullen has consented to act as Editor for a Negro Poets' Number of the magazine," and that his associate editors would be Witter Bynner, Haniel Long, and Idella Purnell.

At once Cullen began gathering poems and mailing them on to Purnell in Guadalajara. Given the responsibility for which he had no experience, he had to improvise, select, stay with it, despite the burden of graduate school studies. He had to commit his imagination to the project. He had to see that this effort was part of his own career as a man of letters. At the beginning, we see, he had no real idea of the work that goes into the making of even a small anthology. He wrote to Purnell in December, 1925, "I don't suppose my issue can appear before February." As Purnell had learned from Bynner, had improvised and run her own risks, Cullen was learning from the opportunity Purnell had given him. January 16, 1926 he wrote from Cambridge, "I have been waiting for certain book reviews that were promised me for my number. Only one has come and I send it along to you now. I am expecting another any minute—a review of Alain Locke's *The New Negro,* a very significant anthology. You speak of an introduction to the work; I had not thought of that but of allowing the work to speak for itself. If, however you think such an introduction very necessary, telegraph me at my expense and I will get to work at it. The machinery for this number hasn't moved along as smoothly as I expected,—I am sorry."

He did not have to be taught how to stand up for his editorial judgment. He understood that three editors would pass on his choices, but he meant to be respected. The January 16 letter makes this clear: "In those rare cases in which I have submitted only one poem by a given poet, I wish you would try to include that poet (for instance the *Lines to a Nasturtium* is by a representative poet, and I should like to have that included as well as one of the two poems by W. E. Burghardt DuBois—in brief, I should not care, if it can be avoided, to have any poet whose work I accepted absolutely ruled out."

This letter ends on a rueful note, unexpected for a young poet of whom so much is expected. His own small contribution (the poem **"A Song of Sour Grapes"**) is not due to the editorial modesty Purnell attributes to him,[6] but "is really due to lack of material." He asks whether she wants short biographies, and concludes, deprecating himself, "I feel that I am making a very poor editor, and I hope that you will forgive me."

On January 24 he forwarded Purnell the Walter White essay, "The Negro Renaissance," that opens the issue. In February his tone with Purnell is cooler: "I suppose by now the issue must be set up. I hope you will oblige me by the use of at least one poem from each of the poets represented in the material I sent you."

Purnell did not hurry the project. Her subscribers were largely college and university students and young faculty. She was tuning these readers to a fine reception for the unusual issue. In March (*PALMS* 3, No. 6), before *PALMS* closed down over the summer, she printed an expanded notice: "Countée Cullen will be the editor of the first number of Vol. IV in the fall, and the editors are pleased to announce that it will be an unusually good issue, with the added interest of being entirely written by Negro poets, from the leading article on 'The Negro Renaissance' by Walter White, to the last poem and the notes on contributors."

Although Cullen had rushed the bulk of his selections to Purnell almost at once, he continued to look for more poems for the Negro Poets' issue. Before leaving for his first trip to Europe on July 3, he sent forward from Cambridge poems by Helen Johnson and W. S. Braithwaite together with careful biographical information for both. An efficient editor, even if inexperienced, he sent Purnell the poets' addresses and asked Langston Hughes to forward to Mexico those he did not have (letters of June 4 and June 19, 1926 to Idella Purnell).

In September he was home, elated and gracefully contrite. He sent Purnell an excited note on September 18, together with small photographs of Waring Cuney and Lucy Williams. The photographs were more a link between Purnell and her new poets than a contribution for the issue. "I am glad," he wrote, "things look bright for the Negro Poets' number, and I am also much ashamed of the last minute way in which I had to shift the entire makeup over to you. Much interest has already been aroused in the number and I hope it has a record sale."

The thirty-two page issue was in his hands on October 5 when he returned from a speaking engagement with Langston Hughes in Columbus, Ohio.[7]

The unidentified poems in the table of contents are the following:

Alexander: "A Group of Japanese Hokku," "Dream Song"

Fauset: "Dead Fires," "Words! Words!" "The Return"

DuBois: "The Song of America," "O Star-kissed drifting from above"

Bennett: "Song," "Dear Things," "Dirge"

Hughes: "Fog," "Picture to the Wall"

He was very pleased. Still the editor, he sent Purnell a list of both black and white newspapers and magazines for review copies, identifying those he considered most important. He assured her that "All who have seen the issue have liked it" (October 5). Cullen sensed a wider possibility for their joint enterprise. "I hope," he continued, "that it will be so well received that you will want to repeat it sometime."

It was a success. The December *PALMS* contains Purnell's happy notice: "*The Negro Poets' number of PALMS* is exhausted. *PALMS* is in daily receipt of letters and cards requesting copies of its special issue devoted to the work of Negro Poets. This issue was exhausted soon after its appearance, and the latecomers are disappointed" (4, No. 3).

Despite the difficulties of geography and of working with editors whom he had never even met, young Cullen found himself stimulated by the *PALMS* project. The rewards of poet-editor seemed as great as the poet's rewards. On November 4, 1926, he wrote to Purnell from his desk at *Opportunity,* "The Negro Poets' issue of *PALMS* has met with such a fine reception that I am going to undertake the editing of an anthology of Negro verse which Harper's has promised to publish for me. I shall probably want to use all the material which appeared in *PALMS,* of course, with due acknowledgement."

On November 24, Purnell gladly gave permission. She noted that "daily there are requests coming in for copies of that number. And I find myself being credited with a thousand noble motives that never entered my mind. It certainly did not occur to me before that a Negro Poets' issue *could* be so extraordinary! But it seems that most people find the idea breathtaking—and, when they recover from their surprise, like it."

Caroling Dusk (1927) is the direct sequence to *PALMS* 4 No. 1 (1926). It was the first new anthology of Negro poets created by a Negro poet since James Weldon Johnson's *The Book of American Negro Poetry of 1922.* ***Caroling Dusk*** was a year in the making. His letters show that being an editor had become such an authentic experience that he could contemplate two anthologies at the same time. On December 4, 1926, his note to Purnell indicates that he was quite serious about a second *PALMS* issue. "I am glad that the Negro Poets' issue leaves you with no regrets. And I hope you can survive all the good intentions you are credited with having in mind when you published such an issue. Perhaps we can have a similar issue next year, and maybe I can get someone to donate a special prize for the number; I have my eye on several approachable persons. I'll see what I can do toward getting some guarantors for *PALMS.*"

For ***Caroling Dusk,*** Cullen expanded on his experience with *PALMS.* He had learned to take seriously his authority in taste, to see the anthology as an effort involving unique tasks. He had learned to survive the exasperations of delay. He had learned to see himself in the service of others. The details of ***Caroling Dusk*** show how he built on the foundation of *PALMS.* The book opens with his own thoughtful introduction. He had talked about this as a possibility for *PALMS.* The biographical information which is so modest in *PALMS* is expanded for ***Caroling Dusk.*** Cullen asked each contributor to submit this material; he notes the few vitas he has contributed. Although he acknowledged six, he actually carried forward twelve poems from *PALMS* into ***Caroling Dusk***:

Arna Bontemps "A Tree Design"
Albert Rice "Black Madonna"
Clarissa Scott (Delany) "The Mask"
Anne Spencer "Lines to a Nasturtium"
Jessie Fauset "Words! Words!", "The Return"
Lewis Alexander four hokkus
Gwendolyn Bennett "Dear Things" (Sonnet II)
Helene Johnson "Magula"

Four poets Cullen chose for both *PALMS* and ***Caroling Dusk*** had been represented in James Weldon Johnson's *The Book of American Negro Poetry* (1922): Braithwaite, Fauset, Spencer and Georgia Johnson. Cuney's "Grave" and Alexander's "Dream Song" were reprinted in *Poetry of the Negro,* edited in 1949 by Langston Hughes and Arna Bontemps. Fauset's "Dead Fires" appeared again in the W.P.A. collection, *Anthology of Negro Poetry,* and also in the later editions of *The Book of American Negro Poetry.*

The two poems by Langston Hughes in Cullen's *PALMS* issue he did not use again in ***Caroling Dusk.*** (These two poems have not been reported published elsewhere.) Cullen did include Hughes' four part poem, "A House in Taos" in ***Caroling Dusk*** without crediting *PALMS.* This poem was in a group for which Hughes won the Bynner Undergraduate Poetry Prize for 1926. The announcement of the prize appears in Cullen's Negro Poets' issue; the poems themselves were printed in *PALMS* 4, No. 2, one month later.

There was no second Negro Poets' issue of *PALMS,* but Cullen and Purnell maintained their friendly links. In *PALMS* 5 No. 1 (October 1927), Purnell reprinted Cullen's **"Scandal and Gossip"** and **"An Epitaph for Amy Lowell"** and wrote a loyal review of ***Copper Sun,*** his second volume of poetry, which "in every way maintains the high standard set by ***Color,*** his first book. In the first group of poems in his new volume, the flame of Cullen's genius burns most intensely and brilliantly. . . . The inclusion of Juvenilia in this volume we regret. The decorations and the wrapper, by Charles Cullen, and materially to ***Copper Sun,*** they are of more than passing note."

Her comment on the Juvenilia recognizes the dwindling output of his new poetry as more and more of his time was given over to his role as editor. By the time ***Caroling Dusk*** was published, Cullen was chiefly an editor. He moved from his editorial months for *PALMS* into his job at *Opportunity* where the editor, Charles S. Johnson, expected him to bring "rare gifts and a magnificent capacity for usefulness to the whole cause."[8] Johnson's editorial identifies Cullen's new responsibilities. He chose the young poet-editor, but not chiefly for his poetry. "Mr. Cullen," he wrote, "will select the poetry and, in his office as assistant to the editor, counsel with that large and growing group of young writers of verse whose work is gradually breaking into light. His opinion on books and events of literary significance will appear regularly as a special new department, and there will be occasional articles and poetry from his pen." At *Opportunity,* Cullen's chief output became his monthly article, **"The Dark Tower,"** which he produced with few omissions from December 1926 through September 1928.

Late in 1927, Cullen invited Purnell to review ***Caroling Dusk*** for *Opportunity*'s December issue. She never mentioned the "House in Taos" omission. What she admired in ***Caroling Dusk,*** she wrote, is simplicity, sincerity, and "sufficient depth of thought and intellectual quality to give weight and meaning to their verse." She praised Claude McKay, Sterling Brown and Langston Hughes.[9] Above all, she was true to Countée Cullen, stating, "There is no doubt that the poems by Countée Cullen constitute the finest group in the anthology; 'To Lovers of Earth: Fair Warning' reaches as high level as any short poem we have seen this year. If Countée Cullen continues writing with the maturity shown in his poems in the present year, he will be one of the great poets of America."[10]

It was a big "if," and Cullen knew it. His letters to Purnell at this time carry a melancholy self-consciousness. On November 30, 1927, he thanked her for the review of ***Caroling Dusk*** and for what he called "your unwarranted appraisal of me." She planned a special issue for March, 1928, but Cullen did not contribute to it. Instead, he wrote, "You have no idea how little time the daily stint leaves for creative work" (January 5, 1928). In the January 19th letter we hear the young poet winding down: "During the past three or four months, I have done only three poems that I feel like having published, and they were all given as an appreciative gesture to the special issue of *Opportunity* published last month.[11] But I promise you that the next two poems I write, and which I feel have any merit at all, shall go to *PALMS.*"

From Paris in 1929, he sent Purnell **"Foolish Heart,"** and **"The Law that Changeth Not"** (*PALMS* 6, No. 6). His short accompanying note sounds like a slow, and closing down of doors. "Yes I am married and quite happy. I am out of touch with literary events myself. . . . I have done very little work recently, but I send along a few poems, none of which you may like. If none suits you, just hustle it back. If any appeals to you, keep it, or them."

Certainly his personal confusions at this time may be in some part responsible for the diminishing poetic strength. But it is more likely that he was distracted by the peripheral enterprise, editing, which rapidly became central to his career. It was not the experience at *Opportunity* which sent him along a new route, but the challenge of a young editor of an obscure poetry magazine. She passed him a baton and he ran with it.

Notes

1. See Houston A. Baker, Jr., *A Many Colored Coat of Dreams: The Poetry of Countée Cullen* (Detroit: Broadside Press, 1974); Stephen H. Bronz, *Roots of Negro Racial Consciousness* (New York: Libra, 1964); Darwin T. Turner, "Countée Cullen: The Lost Ariel," in *In A Minor Chord* (Carbondale: Southern Illinois University Press, 1971).
2. "On Teaching the Young Laurel to Shoot," *The New Republic* 37 (December 5, 1923), 5-7.
3. The letters from Witter Bynner, Willard (Spud) Johnson and Idella Purnell are quoted through the courtesy of the Amistad Research Center, Dillard University, New Orleans, Louisiana.
4. The letters of Countée Cullen are quoted through the courtesy of The Humanities Research Center, University of Texas, Austin, and Mrs. Ida Mae Cullen. This correspondence is in the Idella Purnell Stone collection.
5. John M. Weatherwax is the author of the review.
6. Purnell never published her own poems in *PALMS.*
7. The table of contents page of this issue is reproduced through the courtesy of Idella Purnell Stone.
8. "Editorials," *Opportunity* 4 (November, 1926), 337.
9. Hughes had published "Young Sailor" and "Song to a Dark Virgin" in *PALMS* 3, No. 4 (1926). Brown published "Kentucky Blues" in *PALMS* 7, No. 4 (1930). See Vilma Potter and Elizabeth Zall. *Index to Palms 1923-1930,* Idella Purnell Stone Collection, Humanities Research Center, University of Texas, Austin.
10. Carbon typescript quoted through the courtesy of Idella Purnell Stone. This review is mistakenly attributed to Gwendolyn Bennett by Margaret Perry in *A Bio-Bibliography of Countée P. Cullen, 1903-1946* (Westport, Conn.: Greenwood, 1971).
11. *Ebony and Topaz* was announced as a separate publication by *Opportunity* 5 (December 1927), 349. Cullen's name is not listed among the poet contributors.

Copper Sun

HERBERT S. GORMAN (ESSAY DATE 1927)

SOURCE: Gorman, Herbert S. "Countee Cullen Is a Poet First and a Negro Afterward." *The New York Times Book Review* (21 August 1927): 5, 17.

In the following excerpt, Gorman argues that Cullen's poetry transcends racial boundaries.

Countee Cullen's ***Copper Sun*** is his second volume and it is encouraging to observe that it reveals a profounder depth than ***Color.*** Any exploration of his substance of being will immediately reveal inborn negro impulses disciplined by culture and an awareness of restraint and the more delicate nuances of emotionalized intellect. A primitive naïveté underlies his work, yet, curiously enough, the surface values are sophisticated enough. There are times when he is the more obvious negro poet sentimentalizing about himself and his people, but the admirable aspect of his work is the direct evidence in ***Copper Sun*** that he transcends this limitation time and again and becomes sheer poet. What is meant here is that his best work does not suggest the descriptive "negro poet" any more than the work of Mark Van Doren, for instance, suggests the "white poet." He is unlike Langston Hughes, who is nearly always the "negro poet." It is surely no disparagement to assert that a writer is the poet of a race, for Walt Whitman was one and so is William Butler Yeats; but there is a cul-de-sac into which the free mind of the poet should not be driven. That cul-de-sac does not contain the universal gestures of a groping humanity, but the peculiar emanations of a specific people. The great national poets transcended it. Homer for instance, being as universal as he was Greek. Countee Cullen, because he escapes this cul-de-sac so often, speaks as much for the younger era of poets in America as he does for the negro.

E. MERRILL ROOT (REVIEW DATE 1927)

SOURCE: Root, E. Merrill. "Keats in Labrador." *Opportunity* 5, no. 9 (September 1927): 270-71.

In the following excerpted review, Root examines Cullen's Copper Sun, *arguing that it demonstrates a vitality that sets it apart from the generally intellectual and lifeless poetry of the time.*

Modern American poetry has had two chief faults: a hard clear technique; a hard objective content. With brilliant exceptions, like Edna Millay (that tiger, tiger burning bright), or like the grace notes of Robert Frost (that eagle-sized lark), it has seldom been poetry that sings and that shines. If it shone—as in Amy Lowell's scissor-blades and patchwork, it did not sing; if it sang—as in the jazz records to be played on the Victrola of Vachel, it did not shine. Much of the rest of it has not been Christian enough to escape the hard intellectuality of Puritanism: like the bleak Pilgrim Fathers it wears black: it knows little of the Lilies of the Field and the Many Mansions. It has been "just a plate of current fashion" with "not a softness anywhere about it," like the formal lady in "Patterns"; it has seldom been "Eve with her body white, supple and smooth to her slim fingertips."

Therefore I, for one, welcome poetry that sings and that shines; poetry that is no plumed hearse, but a dancing star.

> I who adore exotic things
> Would shape a sound
> To be your name, a word that sings
> Until the head goes round.

So sings Countee Cullen, unashamed. And it is no boasting: it is a literal description of his sensuous rhythms, his translation of heart's blood into words, his imagery that is not the decorative cameos of the Imagists, but the suns that roar through heaven and the scarlet flowers that grow mystically from the black and humorous earth. Here is poetry that is not written with phosphorescent brains, but with the soul's blood. Here is poetry that soars on deep-damasked wings.

Countee Cullen's title is ***Copper Sun.*** And in the book we are transported into a fresher world, where the sun is a blazing copper drum sounding reveille over the morning hills, and the trees are heavy with the "golden increment of bursting fruit," and the delicate reeds quiver under the feet of the wind, that angel of the unknown color.

Technically considered, the book is a delight and a triumph. Whether we stir to the rolling echoes and the dying fall of its music, as in that haunting and perfect poem, **"Threnody"**; or thrill to the subtlety of emotion incarnated in the simplicity of art—the tears, idle tears of **"Pity the Deep in Love"**; or marvel at imagery as inevitable as the green hills haloed with the copper sun of morning, we acknowledge Countee Cullen a master of living magic.

> One to her are flame and frost;
> Silence is her singing lark;
> We alone are children, lost,
> Crying in the dark.
> Varied feature now, and form,
> Change has bred upon her;
> Crush no bug nor nauseous worm
> Lest you tread upon her.
> Pluck no flower lest she scream;
> Bruise no slender reed,
> Lest it prove more than it seem,
> Lest she groan and bleed.
> More than ever trust your brother,
> Read him golden, pure;
> It may be she finds no other
> House so safe and sure.
>
> . . . . .
>
> Lay upon her no white stone
> From a foreign quarry;
> Earth and sky be these alone
> Her obituary.

Such lines seem the earth's own green hieroglyphs. To paraphrase the poet: Earth and sky be these alone Poetry's commentary!

And (as always) it is only out of the fullness of the blood that the mouth chants. These are no Arrows of Scorning shot by an impotent brain, no acrobatics of a honeyless wasp, no finger-exercises by the Precocious Child trying to see how different he can be from Mr. Longfellow. These are pulses translated into poetry. Here is the revolt, fierce but forgiving, of **"From the Dark Tower"**; the grief wound up to a mysteriousness of **"Threnody,"** where personal anguish merges into pantheistic mysticism; the ache and ecstasy of love, sung with a simple inevitability that equals A. E. Housman, and a breadth of range that surpasses Edna Millay; the fear of all flesh (as in **"Protest"**) forms the dark halo . . . Here are magic casements opening on many seas: and Countee Cullen has himself stood at every casement and looked from each with his own eyes. His is no poetry at second brain: no tinsel of words, but a tissue of experience. He is no mirror but a face; no phonograph but a voice.

In lyricism more musical and rich, in a subtle sensuousness which shows that the years have brought him more philosophic eyes, ***Copper Sun*** surpasses ***Color.*** If I find any luck and lapse, I miss those great poems, those longer epics of philosophy, **"Heritage"** and **"Shroud of Color."** I want to see Countee Cullen again fight a campaign and not merely a battle, and with full pomp and circumstance justify man's ways to God. Yet tho he perhaps shows a relapse in scope of attack, he shows an advance in the quality of his philosophy. He is still death-shadowed; he still feels the "little room" which fifty—or fifty times fifty—Springs give to our immortal longings; but he wanders less resolutely in the Valley of the Shadow. In **"Threnody,"** in **"Epilogue,"** he shows a philosophic advance: he steps out of the dark halo that hover over us as from an eagle's wings: he sees death as it is—an accident and not an essence—a relapse of the mortal body, but a return to the immortal energy: he may yet say, with Whitman, "To die is different from what we expect—and luckier." Also, in the **"Litany of the Dark Peoples,"** he has written one of the finest manifestoes of generosity that has been written in modern years: in serenity of vision and triumph it transcends even those great poems (which belong to our common race of Adam) **"Heritage"** and **"Shroud of Color."**

And if we hunger now and thirst,
Grant our witholders may,
When heaven's constellations burst
Upon Thy crowning day,
Be fed by us and given to see
Thy mercy in our eyes,
When Bethlehem and Calvary
Are merged in Paradise.

And Countee Cullen has developed, too, a new suggestion of fighting faith, a gay insouciance of Yea-saying, that is an advance. Thus the poet is one whose

Ears are tuned to all sharp cries
Of travail and complaining,
His vision stalks a new moon's rise
In every old moon's waning.
And in his heart pride's red flag flies
Too high for sorrow's gaining.

Hegelian paradox set to gay music (**"More than a Fool's Song"**), banter with the superstition called Fate (**"Ultimatum"**), the Higher Scepticism of Epilogue, show that he is, more than most of our modern American poets, a singer after sunset—and before sunrise. Whether he knows it or not, the best in him is shaking itself loose of Disillusionment and Decay and Fallen-petal Pessimism and all our resolute, dreary Apostles of the Unholy Catholic Church of Death Everlasting, from Masters to Mencken.

I am presumptuous, but if a critic has any worth, he must be conscious of the artist's unconscious: he must translate into idea the urge and ultimatum of the blood which the artist translates into image. What, then, is the *elan vital* back of Countee Cullen's blood?—An emphasis on color and on copper suns, on the subjective and the lyric, on the heart as well as the head, on poetry that shines and that sings: in short, on Romance. That is his peculiar worth: that makes him rare and radiant. And, in future, what should be his further path and destiny? It seems to me that, having done all he can do to give immortal poignance to the ache and transience of flesh, he should go beyond good and evil, above life and death, into spirit. In denial of negation and in acceptance of affirmation, in the victorious synthesis of animal and angel, in instincts made rhythmic with intellect, in spirit defeated yet superb like Spartacus . . . there, with Shelley, he will find "life, empire, and victory." My wish for him is that he leap to the forefront of the battle; that he become the first poet in modern America to accept the universe like a master-spirit. And my wish is not merely a love and a hope, but (thanks to the tocsin that already sounds in his poetry) a faith.

Countee Cullen belongs to a great race that, because of American savagery, stupidity and jealousy, has had to walk the Valley of the Shadow. If he will rise above tragic circumstance, as we poor dwellers on Waste Lands and Main Streets are not strong enough to do, if he will (to quote Carlyle) "seek within himself for that consistency and sequence which external events will always refuse him (and us)," he can be the first American poet to become Nietzsche's child—"Innocence is the child, and forgetfulness, a new beginning, a game, a self-rolling wheel, a first movement, a Holy Yea."

Meanwhile, tho he is not yet the spiritual leader of a new day, he is one of the few poets of our generation. He sings and shines like Edna Millay, and has more wholesome life in his blood; his blood (if not always his brain) is world-accepting and life-affirming like Frost's grey elfin mysticism, and he has richer color, tho not an idiom as unique and great as Frost's tang and accent.

Countee Cullen loves Keats; therefore he will know what I mean—and how much I mean—when I say that in his sensuous richness of phrase, in his sweetness of heart, in his death-shadowed joy, he reminds me of Keats. The great tree has fallen: but from the mystic root comes up this shoot and sapling with the same rich leaves. Countee Cullen, it seems to me, is much what the young Keats would be if he wore flesh again in this minor and maddening age, this fever and fret of a fiercer Capitalism, this welted thru which war has plunged like a dinosaur trampling daffodils, this fox-fire age of cerebral realism, this Labrador of the soul which we call America.

The Black Christ

BERTHA TEN EYCK JAMES (REVIEW DATE 1930)

SOURCE: James, Bertha Ten Eyck. "On the Danger Line." *Poetry* 24, no. 5 (February 1930): 286-89.

In the following excerpted review, James explores the poetic style in Cullen's The Black Christ, and Other Poems.

[***The Black Christ, and Other Poems***] proves again that Countee Cullen is an accomplished poet, but it shows also the danger in being an accomplished poet. He writes well, he uses the proper subjects, the strong verbs, rare adjectives and inverted order of modern verse, but the polished results seem to lack that lyric freshness that makes this type of verse worth while. To give an example, here is **"Nothing Endures"**:

Nothing endures,
Not even love,
Though the warm heart purrs
Of the length thereof.
Though beauty wax,
Yet shall it wane;
Time lays a tax
On the subtlest brain.
Let the blood riot,
Give it its will;
It shall grow quiet.
It shall grow still.
Nirvana gapes
For all things given;
Nothing escapes,
Love not even.

In this poem one may see charm and skill, and a complete unimportance. Too many of the lyrics here are of this type, even the more serious, such as **"The Foolish Heart"**:

"Be still, heart, cease those measured strokes;
Lie quiet in your hollow bed;
This moving frame is but a hoax
To make you think you are not dead."
Thus spake I to my body's slave,
With beats still to be answered;
Poor foolish heart that needs a grave
To prove to it that it is dead.

That is very skilful and quotable, but it shares the common lot of too much modern verse: it has nothing new to say and it says that in a fresh form, perhaps, but without a fresh feeling. The newness of a phrase does not lend life to an old idea; there must be a new point of view. When Andrew Marvell said, "Time's winged chariot hurrying near he gave a fresh idea with his new image.

With us the time-honored emotions of love and decay are given intricate sentence-patterns, but one usually feels a lack of vitality in the resultant poem. Is it because we do not feel deeply? It may be that love and death seem less powerful, that man seems less important, but we still have trouble with us. Even though our verse suggests the Cavalier lyricists rather than the poets of a more deep-rooted emotional life, there are modern tragedies.

And the proof of this lies in the title-poem of this book, which comes last, **"The Black Christ."** It is an episode that must be associated with the deepest emotion, dedicated "hopefully" to white America. Reading it, one wishes to feel to the full the sorrow an triumph of the author, but there are barriers to that sympathy.

There are several ways of writing down such an event as the lynching of a brother for forgetting himself so far as to share love in springtime with a white girl. It could be done with violence and bitterness, or with simple realism. Countee Cullen has visualized this episode as the mirror of the death of Christ, and of the eternal Fair Young God; he makes a religious experience of it, told to further brotherhood and faith. Yet he writes it in very "poetic" language.

One has no right, perhaps, to criticize an artist's style; that is his own affair. But if it blur the force of the experience, one is inevitably disappointed.

This poem is written in an involved way, with free use of image and comparison. Such sentences as these from the speech of Jim seem to me too fanciful to be convincing:

> But when I answer I'll pay back
> The late revenge long overdue
> A thousand of my kind and hue,
> A thousand black men long since gone
> Will guide my hand, stiffen the brawn,
> And speed one life-divesting blow
> Into some granite face of snow.
> And I may swing, but not before
> I send some pale ambassador
> Hot-footing it to hell to say
> A proud black man is on his way.

The same practice of poetic law and manner that makes the briefer poems in this volume pleasant and musical and slight prevents this long poem from seeming to have a style as simple, devout and important as its theme.

Medea

LILLIAN CORTI (ESSAY DATE 1998)

SOURCE: Corti, Lillian. "Countée Cullen's *Medea.*" *African American Review* 32, no. 4 (winter 1998): 621-34.

In the following essay, Corti argues that Cullen's Medea, *despite receiving little critical or popular attention, is an impassioned and subversive drama centered significantly in the history of African American literature and scholarship.*

Among modern versions of ancient classics, Countée Cullen's ***Medea*** is a particularly interesting case, partly because of fluctuations in the critical response to Cullen's work, partly because of the author's personal investment in the myth of Medea, and partly because of his essential role in the history of the Harlem Renaissance. Although critical references to Cullen's experiment with tragic form are rare, and late-twentieth-century scholars tend to regard the work as a curious anomaly, the actual significance of the play has yet to be assessed. I will argue that Cullen's ***Medea,*** though seldom performed, little discussed, and often dismissed as an academic tribute to ancient aesthetics, is actually an impassioned and subversive drama which reflects an essential moment in the history of African American letters.

The choice of a classical motif by an African American poet of the 1930s is in itself remarkable, and contemporary reviews of the printed text, first published in ***The Medea and Some Poems*** in 1935, are instructive. Philip Blair Rice praised the poem extravagantly in *The Nation,* exulting that "Mr. Cullen has rendered Euripides' best known tragedy into living and utterable English. . . . if there is to be a popular revival of interest in the Greek drama it appears that this is more likely to originate in Harlem than in the universities" (336). But Peter Monro Jack, writing for *The New York Times,* described the play as "an interesting experiment in reducing a Greek tragedy to the content and colloquialism of a folk tale, with characteristic Negro sentiment and rhythm" (15). Whereas the contemporary critical response varied from liberal enthusiasm to racist condescension, recent considerations of the play tend to damn it with faint praise. For Houston Baker, it is an "interesting" work which "possesses little of the grandeur of the original" (50); for Gerald Early, it is a "creative racial misreading" which "simply authenticated" Cullen's "own traditionalist and classical credentials" (67). The charge that the play falls short of the ancient standard seems particularly perplexing. Euripides is, after all, a hard act to follow. Yet twentieth-century writers from T. Sturge Moore to Jean Anouilh and Heiner Müller have been tempted to create modern versions of the myth of Medea, and treatments of the motif by both Maxwell Anderson and Robinson Jeffers were successfully produced on Broadway in the early half of this century. It seems unlikely, moreover, that either Anderson or Jeffers would ever have been accused of merely authenticating his "traditional and classical credentials."

Whereas a version of an ancient myth by a white author may be presumed, for the most part, to succeed or fail on the basis of its own merits, the appreciation of Cullen's drama has been impeded by various misfortunes, not least of which was the death of Rose McClendon in 1936. A distinguished actress who had been acclaimed for her work in such plays as Paul Green's *In Abraham's Bosom* and Langston Hughes's *Mulatto,* McClendon was greatly admired by Cullen, who wrote his ***Medea*** with her in mind for the leading role (Perry 13). In view of Judith Anderson's contribution to the sensational success of Robinson Jeffers's *Medea* in the late forties, it is worth considering that, had she lived, McClendon might well have attracted favorable attention to this play. The reception of Cullen's ***Medea*** has also been plagued by racial bias, not only from white critics such as the reviewer for the *Times* cited above, for whom the idea of a black Medea was evidently a tiresome curiosity, but also from black critics who assume that Greek myths cannot possibly be relevant to African American experience. An example this kind of thinking is evident in Barksdale and Kinnamon's entry on the poet in *Black Writers of America: A Comprehensive Anthology*: "*The Medea* speaks of the rise and fall of a great woman whose story had nothing to do with race or social doctrines but instead was concerned with the consuming passions of woman as she emerged in the Græco-Roman world" (530). This judgment is problematic, first of all, because of its insistence on categorizing and separating various cultural experiences as if there were no possibility of any common ground between them. In assuming, furthermore that tragic myth is primarily concerned with the peculiarities of individual psychology, Barksdale and Kinnamon seem to disregard the fact that drama is the most social of literary forms.

Performed since antiquity in the context of public celebrations, tragedy is a dramatic structure in which psychological particulars are never separable from communal perspectives. Though several millennia have passed since Aristotle observed that "tragedy is an imitation of action and not of character" (13), his judgment is arguably as relevant to Cullen's ***Medea*** as to the Euripidean masterpiece on which it is based. The critical question posed by Cullen's treatment of Euripidean drama is not How does it compare with the ancient model? but, rather, Why would a celebrated African American poet of the 1930s suddenly decide to write a tragedy in which a mother kills her children so as to avenge herself on their arrogant, irresponsible father? I would like to begin by suggesting that the importance of this play inheres not in its psychological portraiture, which is essentially faithful to that of the ancient model, but rather in Cullen's complex and significant synthesis of ancient Greek, contemporary American, and African nationalist elements.

No mere tribute to the art of Euripides, Cullen's ***Medea*** is an expression of fundamental autobiographical, aesthetic, and communal concerns. Dealing with the most obvious of these first, we may note that, as an abandoned child who was initially raised by his grandmother and later adopted by the Reverend Frederick Asbury Cullen (Perry 3-4), the poet may well have found in Euripides' forlorn protagonist an objective correlative for his peculiarly personal experiences and anxieties. The character Medea may represent Cullen's own abandoned mother, the son she deserted when his father disappeared, or the troubled adult inheritor of a childhood haunted by crises of desertion and abandonment. Reputed to have been more interested in the company of men than of women (Lewis 76-77), Cullen may actually have identified with Medea as the spurned object of a male lover. Whereas Alan Shucard underscores the poet's insistence on "the danger and perfidy of female lovers" in this text (42), the possibility of a sympathetic identification between the author and his female character is worthy of consideration, especially in the light of Amitai F. Avi Ram's discussion of the way Cullen's gay sexual identity manifests itself in his poetry (42). In any case, Cullen's interest in the story of the black woman disastrously involved with a white lover was no casual matter.

The similarities between ***Medea*** and another of Cullen's experiments with traditional form have prompted Gerald Early to speculate that the poet was attracted to the Euripidean tragedy "for much the same reason he was drawn to ***The Ballad of the Brown Girl***; once again, his creative misreading made him think of *The Medea* in racial terms, a woman of color betrayed" (67). It is also worth noting that Cullen's fascination with this myth was not conspicuously diminished by the disappointment of his hope that ***Medea*** would bring him the theatrical success he longed for. In addition to dramatizing the conflict between Jason and Medea in Corinth, he later returned to the same material, writing an original "Prologue," which deals with Medea and Jason as young lovers in Colchis, and an "Epilogue" set in Athens at the court of Aegeus twenty years after the tragic events in Corinth. The expanded work, entitled *Byword for Evil* (Early 76), sheds light on aspects of Cullen's enterprise which may not be evident to casual readers of his ***Medea.*** For example, the "Epilogue" focuses on an invented character named Pandion, who is supposed to be the grown son of Medea by Aegeus, a child born soon after the notorious sorceress arrived in Athens after escaping from Corinth. In the dénouement, when Pandion is killed by a vengeful old sailor who turns out to be Jason himself, Medea reveals that this child was actually conceived while she was still living with Jason. Thus, Jason has actually killed his own son, and the "Epilogue" of the expanded work has the effect of changing a play about a mistreated black woman desperate for revenge into a play about a promising young man of mixed parentage who is killed by a vicious white father. Whatever the personal implications of Cullen's evident fascination with this biracial drama of generational catastrophe might have been, the essential importance of his text inheres in its insistence on the patriarchal brutality of a racially ambiguous society.

Whereas the centrality of racial concerns in Cullen's work is apparent, his youthful insistence on being "a poet and not a Negro poet" (Early 23) and poems such as **"To Certain Critics"** have been used in arguments deploring "his rejection of race" and dedication to "the essentially fatuous artificialities which were, according to him, the poet's true concern" (Lomax 220). The possibility, however, that Cullen's insistence on traditional forms might imply something other than a devotion to "fatuous artificialities" is suggested by Gary Smith in an essay on "The Black Protest Sonnet." While acknowledging that "the central paradox" of the Harlem Renaissance as a literary phenomenon "is the discrepancy between theory and practice" or the difference between "what the poets proposed in theory and what they actually accomplished in their poetry," Smith nevertheless insists on the radical import of poems such as Claude McKay's "If We Must Die" and Cullen's own **"From the Dark Tower,"** both of which are cast in the "genteel literary form" of the sonnet (2). Smith's observations on the subversive uses of traditional form seem all the more relevant to Cullen's experiment with tragic structure, since ***Medea*** was written during a period when Cullen was conspicuously concerned with contemporary racial problems.

In the year that ***Medea and Some Poems*** was published, Cullen served as a member of the commission appointed to investigate the New York race riot (Lumpkin 114). Furthermore, the volume in which his version of ***Medea*** appears also contains an emphatic articulation of his exasperation with American racism, the short poem entitled **"Scottsboro Too Is Worth Its Song."** Inspired by the notorious Scottsboro case, in which nine black men falsely accused of raping two white women were convicted and sentenced by an all-white jury (Tindall and Shi 668), the poem is remarkable for its bitter irony. In it, Cullen reproaches contemporary American writers who responded passionately to the trial of Sacco and Vanzetti for giving short shrift to the Scottsboro case. The poignant intensity of this complaint underscores the problematic nature of the claim that ***Medea*** has nothing to do with race relations.

To be sure, the mythical plot of this tragedy presents formidable difficulties in whatever version it appears. Focusing on the suffering of an emigrant woman who has been abandoned by the hero Jason, for whom she has given up everything, the play culminates in Medea's bloody revenge: In order to punish Jason, she kills the two children she has borne him. The spectacular denouement of this astonishing drama has, understandably enough troubled many critics. In an essay on the Euripidean text, the classicist Denys Lionel page observes, for example, that "the murder of the children . . . is mere brutality; if it moves us at all, it does so towards incredulity and horror. Such an act is outside our experience; we—and the fifth century Athenian—know nothing of it" (xiv). Though recent references to Page's judgment express either respectful disagreement (McDermott 25) or frank amazement (Simon 87), the fact remains that it was not until 1977 that E. P. Easterling argued that the psychology of abuse might actually have some bearing on the tragic scenario. In retrospect, the denial of significance in the act of child murder seems particularly unconvincing. Not only does the murder of children figure prominently in a great number of ancient myths, such as those of Cronos, Uranus, Thyestes, Tereus, Ino, Agave, and Erechtheus, it is also a persistent theme in dreadful current events such as the comparatively recent trials of Hedda Nussbaum and Susan Smith. It is worth noting, moreover, that Page's perspective on Medea's murder of her children is analogous to that of Barksdale and Kinnamon on Cullen's ***Medea.*** In either case, the critical argument depends on the assumption that tragic effect depends on character rather than action. For Barksdale and Kinnamon, as well as for Page, Aristotle's view of action as the soul of tragedy would seem to be a superfluity. Indeed, it is quite possible that the difficulty in evaluating dramatic versions of ***Medea*** inheres precisely in the nature of the tragic action involved.

Although the evidence of infanticidal practices and customs is abundantly and minutely documented in various sources (Langer, Radbill), McDermott's description of Medea's crime as "literally unspeakable" (26) seems justified by the feeling of horror which the very mention of the act of child-murder inspires in most people. Unspeakable in the precise degree to which it is unthinkable, the act has been cast, in the words of Maria Piers, "into the twilight of semi-consciousness, both by those who fail to see it and by those who commit it, and by the rest of us who permit it" (16). This emphasis on the role of the subconscious in the perception of violence against children suggests the operation of something very like a taboo. In fact, Barbara Johnson has observed that, "when a woman speaks about the death of children in any sense other than that of pure loss, a powerful taboo is being violated," and I have argued elsewhere (*The Myth of Medea and the Murder of Children*) that the persistent emphasis on character in discussions of *The Medea* may derive, at least in part, from the painfully repellent nature of the central act on which the drama depends. Rather than regard Medea's revenge as a response to brutal conditions with which we are uncomfortably familiar, we may distance ourselves from the gruesome implications of her act by dismissing the agent as an insane foreigner or a demonic sorceress. She is not like us. She is an eccentric savage from an uncivilized wilderness. If Medea's revenge is an emanation of deranged psychology rather than the necessary outcome of a particular conjunction of circumstance and character, we may safely dispense with any consideration of a possible link between social pathology and human suffering. A noteworthy element in the general literature on the tragic myth of Medea, the denial of significance in the act of child murder is particularly problematic in the context of American literature.

The themes of racism and infanticide regularly complement each other in the annals of slavery. Linda Brent, a woman who escaped from captivity and wrote a narrative account of her experiences, observed that colored children of white mothers were liable to be smothered at birth (52). She repeatedly wished that her own children might die in infancy or be killed rather than brought up to live as slaves (63, 81). In *Uncle Tom's Cabin,* Harriet Beecher Stowe presents the character Cassie, who actually does kill a child rather than abandon him to a life of bondage. In a short story called "Désirée's Baby," Kate Chopin tells the tale of a colored baby born to a young white woman who is so distraught that she suffocates the child. More recently, Toni Morrison has demonstrated the connection between cultural context and literary nightmare in *Beloved,* a novel based on the actual case of a young woman who escaped with her children from slavery and later, upon the point of being recaptured, killed her baby daughter in order to save her from a fate worse than death. To be sure, the idea that institutional racism kills children was widely discussed in the nineteen sixties and seventies, when black militants such as Angela Davis, Eldridge Cleaver, and Huey Newton accused the government of systematically killing black people, defining as murder the neglect of treatable illness, malnourishment in a land of abundance, and lead poisoning among children hungry enough to eat the paint off the walls of tenement apartments (Law and Clift 181-83). But the works of Brent, Stowe, Chopin, and Cullen himself suggest that the relationship between racism and child murder was well known to various writers well before the dissemination of militant ideology in the second half of this century.

Far from being a banal exercise in imitation, Cullen's ***Medea*** is a passionate critique of contemporary culture. The very choice of the myth of Medea may be regarded as subversive, not only because of the theme of child murder, but also because it is the story of a stranger in a strange land, an alien dispossessed by arrogant imperialists. Like Morrison's *Beloved,* ***Medea*** deals with the betrayal of trust, the necessity of choosing between vile enslavement and dreadful freedom, and the ferocious character of an individual incapable of voluntary self-debasement. The essential theme of this play is, in short, the question of violence as an instrument of policy. In his concern with this painful issue, Cullen found a startling congruence between ancient dramatic structure and modern political discourse.

The subversive quality of the Euripidean model is immediately evident in the fact that the first person who speaks as the play begins is a female slave. That Cullen adheres to ancient precedent by introducing the action of his own play with an expository speech by Medea's loyal servant is a significant endorsement of an inherently irreverent view of established order. Although his Nurse differs from that of the classical tragedian in that she speaks in prose, not poetry, the substance of her complaint is essentially the same as that of her ancient prototype. Regretting all the events leading up to the present moment, she wishes the Greeks had never landed in Colchis, laments the loss of an earlier period of comparative happiness, and blames her master, Jason, for "all of our troubles" The man has broken his vows, betrayed his wife and children, left Medea prostrate and fasting. The mistress spends her time grieving and weeping; she is ashamed and debased, calling to mind "all she gave up for this sad fate: home, father, country." But Medea, "brooding on her dark designs," is still a force to be reckoned with, for "she is proud, and not one to be hurt without vengeance" (264). Thus, Cullen's Nurse, like that of Euripides, is a servant who sympathizes with Medea as a woman with whom she shares a common ethnic origin as well as the state of exile. She describes her mistress as one who has been lured away from her native land and called upon to make great sacrifices by an arrogant adventurer who has left her in a wretched state.

Like the children of Africans forcibly recruited into the project of building a nation from whose promise they and their progeny would be systematically excluded, Medea is miserable and dejected, but not entirely defeated. The Nurse's reference to the lost homeland as "our country" and her insistence on Medea's characteristic pride suggest a possible analogy with Cullen's contemporary, Marcus Garvey, who advocated the establishment of an African Homeland for Black Americans. Medea's own nostalgic longing for her lost home may register as an impassioned echo of the Back to Africa movement: "O my native land, where there is peace and quiet, I wish I had never left you" (271). The choral description of her flight from Colchis contains, moreover, a possible reminder of other infamous ocean voyages: "In her anguish, she calls on the gods, who take note of every broken pledge, who led her across the sea with Jason, over the pathless waters" (269). Although the captive Africans who were forced to endure the Middle Passage did not, like Medea, embark willingly "over the pathless waters," their journey is comparable to hers in several ways. First, the Colchian sorceress was a plaything of the gods who inspired her with love for Jason, and the Greeks did not regard her decision to leave her native land as having anything to do with free will. Second, Medea cannot go home again.

If Medea echoes the lament of the chorus, describing herself as "a stranger among you, wronged by my husband, far from my native land" (269), she also concedes, in a furious exchange with Jason, that going back is not an option:

> You say you come as a friend? Give me a friend's counsel then Advise me. Where shall I go? Where can I go? Back to my father's house? Will he kill the fatted calf for the daughter who betrayed him and brought his gray hairs to shame?
>
> (275)

Though Medea's alienation from her homeland is clearly a consequence of her alliance with Jason, a partnership which he instigated and from which he has benefitted, he is prepared to take just about as much responsibility for her present predicament as certain inheritors of white American slave society are willing to assume for the social problems of African Americans today. In effect, Jason tells Medea to stop whining and pull herself up by her bootstraps. For Medea, however, the return to the land of origin is no more an option than it is for the average African American. Her lamentation for the land she left behind is less a realistic consideration of options than a nostalgic articulation of sorrow.

While Cullen's portrait of the bereaved exile underscores the analogy between mythical characters and contemporary injustice, the theme of alienation is only one of the Euripidean elements of his characterization which correspond to modern cultural expressions. To begin with a seemingly obvious consideration, Medea is a woman with the blues. She moans inconsolably from within the house before she ever sets foot on stage: "O misery and shame! To be so despised and fallen! Would that I were dead and gone and laid in my grave" (266). Thus, she expresses the abject misery of the woman abandoned, a favorite theme of such celebrated artists as Cullen's friend Alberta Hunter, who crooned:

> My man mistreated me
> And he drove me from his door
> Lord he mistreated me
> And he drove me from his door
> But the good book says
> You've got to reap just what you sow.

Like the singer who complains of "those down-hearted blues," Medea is described by the Nurse as unable "to lift her eyes from the ground" (264). Just as the singer comforts herself by the thought that her faithless lover will "reap just what he sows," Medea eventually consoles herself by plotting revenge, so that the drama actually accomplishes the reversal of fortunes which the singer patiently anticipates:

> Lord it may be a week
> And it may be a month or two
> I said it may be a week
> And it may be a month or two
> All the things you're doing to me
> Sure coming back to you.

If the lady who sings the blues seems on the whole more philosophically resigned to her fate than Medea, it is also true that her complaint is primarily directed at a man whose essential fault is that he has hurt her feelings. For Medea, however, Jason is not merely the man who "done her wrong"—he is also a deadbeat dad.

Like his Euripidean prototype, Cullen's Jason pays lip service to the concept of paternal love, piously telling his boys that their "father has never neglected or forgotten them" (287), and he assures Medea that he has "acted for [her] own good and that of [their] children" (276). But his record of broken promises does not contribute to his credibility when he tells the mother of his children, "Trust me, Medea, I'll take care of them" (288). On the other hand, Medea's simple assertion that "Jason has prepared nothing for them" (272) is corroborated by the Nurse, who describes her master as "a man who betrays his own children" (266). The possibility that, in Jason's case, neglect of parental responsibilities is linked to actual hostility toward his sons is suggested by the wording of his self-serving rationale for abandoning his wife and children:

> I did not seek this chance as you accuse me of doing, either because I was tired of you or not for new embraces. Nor God knows, because I wanted to make more brats.
>
> (276)

Not only is Jason's reference to his ostensibly esteemed progeny as "brats" disconcerting, but it also tends to undermine his argument that he is only marrying the princess in order to secure a prosperous future for his children. Since the royal family with which he plans to ally himself clearly has no interest in nurturing rival contenders for succession to the throne, Jason seems absurdly oblivious to the possible consequences of his actions. In fact, his argument suggests that the children's lives are endangered, not because their mother is a monster, but because their father regards them as something of a nuisance, and nobody else really wants to have them around. Thus, Cullen's ***Medea*** not only dramatizes the lament of the female blues singer, but also hints at the general sense of emotional deprivation and abandonment implicit in B. B. King's plaintive classic "Nobody loves me but my mother and she could be jivin', too."

Whereas Cullen's faithless husband and improvident father reflects the figure of the sexually exploitive and blatantly hypocritic white master, his abandoned wife and mother outsmarts him with an offensive ploy which is really a kind of ritualized groveling. Confiding in advance to the women of the chorus that she will cajole Jason with feigned humility, she says she "will receive him meekly" and "beg his pardon." She will "see nothing but honesty and decency in his every word and move." In short, she will humble herself before him and beg him to let her sons stay on in Corinth (284). When Jason responds to her summons, Medea is the soul of compliance:

> Forgive me, Jason, and let us bury the past if you will. I am weary of beating against the wind Forgive my bitter words in memory of the sweeter ones we once spoke together. I have wrestled with myself and I have come to my senses at last "Why," I reasoned, "why rage against the one man in all the world who has your interests at heart?" I was a fool. . . . But I am only a woman, and it takes us time to see these things.
>
> (286)

Although this delicious deception is essentially faithful to the Euripidean text, it takes on new meaning when spoken by a dispossessed black woman to a smug white master. Medea's repeated plea for forgiveness and her self-disparaging admission that she has "finally come to her senses at last" are not only outrageously out of character; they are also entirely consistent with the stereotype of the mealy-mouthed step'n'fetchit. Medea is putting the master on. Her self-deprecating "I am only a woman," which might as well read "I am only a nigger," is a wily concession to the master's characteristic prejudices. Just as the Euripidean "hero" underestimates the intelligence of the benighted female barbarian, so Cullen's Jason confuses the privileges of race and gender with the actual dimensions of human possibility. In both works, the ostracized individual, dismissed as the less-than-human Other, responds with a calculated and calculating intrigue designed to establish a tragic "equality" between subject and ruler. Cullen's perception of this scene as a study in stylized passive aggression with a peculiarly African American resonance is a brilliant dramatization of the congruence between sexist and racist assumptions of superiority.

Even in the ancient tragedy, the opposition between Jason as arrogant imperialist and Medea as royal barbarian may suggest the dimensions of a strangely familiar American struggle. In fact, the degree to which Cullen's text depends on the peculiar relevance of ancient passions to modern controversy is conspicuously evident in his version of the speech in which Jason holds forth about Medea's good fortune in having found a benefactor such as himself.

> Instead of leaving you to waste your days in your own wild country I brought you here to Greece, the queen of all the nations of the world. Here you have learned what justice is, and law and order, you who had seen nothing but violence and brute force.
>
> (276)

The language of this passage is remarkable, not only for its fidelity to the spirit of the Euripidean model (see ***Medea*** ll. 536-38), but also because such a phrase as "your own wild country" might just as easily suggest an American view of "the dark continent" as a Greek description of the land of Colchis. In fact, Jason's argument bears a noteworthy resemblance to that of certain nineteenth-century American apologists for slavery. George Fitzhugh's response to the abolitionist debate is a good example of the proslavery position:

> We would remind those who deprecate and sympathize with negro slavery, that his slavery here relieves him from a far more cruel slavery in Africa, or from idolatry and cannibalism, and every brutal vice and crime that can disgrace humanity; and that it christianizes, protects, supports and civilizes him . . .
>
> (89)

Like the apologists for slavery, Jason is in the absurd position of suggesting that his exploitive aggression is actually a demonstration of altruism and generosity for which his antagonist should thank him. On the other hand, Cullen's Nurse, the ostensible voice of slavery in this play, speaks in a style which vaguely resembles that of slave narrators such as Equiano, Frederick Douglass, and Linda Brent. The Nurse complains, for instance, that "our masters are violent and uncurbed in their passions. We who live humbly are better off than they. It is better to live contented than to be famous" (267).

Finally, the despair of Cullen's protagonist is best understood in light of the fact that the rank of a Greek woman deprived of all connections to family, husband, and country was virtually equivalent to that of a slave (Vellacott 104).

Although the dichotomy between Greek and barbarian is as deeply embedded in the ancient text as is the assumption of male superiority, Cullen's articulation of the tensions implicit in the tragedy tends to suggest the operation of essentially modern chauvinisms. Whereas the Euripidean Jason displays notable misogyny when he distinguishes between "human beings" and "the female race" (***Medea*** ll. 573-74), Cullen's Jason intensifies the insult by saying that women are nothing but animals, complaining that "the gods should have made some other animal for men to couple with and to get children by, instead of women" (277). Elsewhere, Cullen's tainted hero expresses a physical disgust for Medea which does not appear in the original. Finally vanquished, Jason fumes angrily, cursing both Medea and "the day that ever I thrust into your vile body the seed" from which their children came (303). His loathing for her "vile body" has the excessive quality of racist contempt.

Whereas Jason's physical revulsion evokes the insult of racial bigotry, Aegeus's sympathetic support recalls the solace which Cullen and other African Americans of his generation sought and found abroad, especially in Paris, during the period between the two World Wars. Listening patiently as Medea pleads for help on bended knees, the Athenian king lifts her up with an invitation and a promise:

> I'll help you, Medea. If once you come to my country, I will receive you in all friendliness. I cannot raise a finger to help you here in Corinth where Creon is king, you understand that. . . . But in my own country I do as I please! Come there of your own free will, and I promise you shelter and safety, and no man shall drive you out, or come in and take you.
>
> (282)

Although he is no more willing to tangle with the Corinthian establishment than a modern French government would be to intervene in the internal affairs of the United States, the Athenian king promises to welcome Medea if she can manage the journey on her own, thus extending to her just such comfort as individual Americans of all colors regularly found in France during Cullen's lifetime. With this offer of hospitality and protection, Aegeus opens up an avenue of escape from exploitation and injury such as the one that Paris offered to Cullen himself. In a notebook of the period, he wrote:

> . . . Paris is a peerless city. Liberty, equality, fraternity are not only words. They express the spirit of which Paris is made. . . . In Paris I find everything that appeals to me: lights, noises in the night, places where one has fun according to one's liking, a sympathetic and tolerant world, in sum, a true civilization.
>
> (qtd. in Fabre 81-82)

In fact, the genesis of Cullen's ***Medea*** may be traced to the cosmopolitan spirit and cultural ferment which repeatedly drew Cullen back to Paris during the 1930s.

A francophile who received a Guggenheim grant in 1928 which allowed him to live for several years in France, Cullen sojourned in Paris for part of every year from 1926 until 1938, earning his living by teaching French at Frederick Douglass Junior High School in New York City from 1934 until his death in 1946. An enthusiast of such popular diversions as the "Bal Colonial," a Parisian gathering place for Martiniquans which he described in an article published in *Opportunity* in 1928 (Fabre 78-79), Cullen also cultivated a wide circle of French-speaking acquaintances. Among these were the four Nardal sisters, whose literary and artistic salon was frequented by such figures as Alain Locke, René Maran, and the Haitian Dr. Sajour. Along with Paulette Nardal, Sajour organized the *Revue du monde noire,* which published the work of various artists of the African diaspora, including such writers of the Harlem Renaissance as James Weldon Johnson, Jean Toomer, Claude McKay, Langston Hughes, and Alain Locke. Described by Michel Fabre as "an important first step toward the Negritude movement," the Nardal group was a lively center of cosmopolitan black culture, and it welcomed Cullen with unreserved enthusiasm, admiring "his polish, refinement and discreet tastes," seeing in him "a fine example of Negro genius, a luminary of the Negro race" (Fabre 90). Cullen's participation in the social and intellectual ferment which anticipated the beginnings of Négritude is particularly interesting in view of the curious affinity between his dramatic heroine and the African Mother, who would loom large as a symbol of the African homeland in Négritude poetry.

Although nearly forty years would elapse between the publication of ***Medea*** and that of David Diop's "A une Danseuse noire" ("To a Black Dancer") in 1973, the kinship between the two figures is striking, and it is interesting to consider "A une Danseuse noire" as a portrait of the charms which might have beguiled Jason when he first encountered his exotic sorceress:

> Négresse; ma chaude rumeur d'Afrique
> Ma terre d'enigme et mon fruit de raison
> Tu es danse par la joie nue de ton sourire
> Par l'offrande de tes seins et tes secrets pouvoirs
>
> (14)
>
> Negress, my warm rumor of Africa
> My land of mystery and my fruit of reason
> You are the dance by the naked joy of your smile
> By the offering of your breasts and your secret powers.

While insisting on a specifically African context with such phrases as "ma chaude rumeur d'Afrique," this poem emphasizes the connection between the sensual allure of the African woman and her reproductive power—"Par l'offrande de tes seins et tes secrets pouvoirs."

The link between sexuality and generativity is also implicit in ancient tragedy, which was celebrated in the context of the festival of Dionysos, the Greek god of wine, harvests, and fecundity. A priestess of the goddess Hecate, Medea herself was associated with the magic of fertility. Thus, in the manner of her Euripidean prototype, Cullen's Medea promises King Aegeus that she will cure him of the plight of childlessness: "I know charms and magic words to give life even to your seed. Believe me, Aegeus, I can raise up children to you" (282). The "charms and magic" with which she tempts him are as redolent of Diop's "Danseuse noire" as they are faithful to her ancient model, so that, in retrospect, Cullen's Medea may seem like an ancestress of the African Mother who would be celebrated by a later generation of black poets. Yet the Négritude movement was little more than a glimmering on the horizon when Cullen sojourned in France, and his tragedy has every appearance of being the child of a cosmopolitan community in which the articulation of African identity was only a single aspect of the larger question of colonial conflict. Of particular importance in the case of a literary treatment of Medea written by an American who spent a good deal of time in France during the thirties is the fact that an important modern version of the myth was produced in Paris just four years before the publication of Cullen's ***Medea.***

Asie (*Asia*) by Henri-René Lenormand articulates the ancient plot in the context of the French colonial empire. Even in the absence of precise information as to whether this play was known to Cullen, the possibility that it might have been is worth considering, first of all because Lenormand was an important French dramatist of the period, and the wide range of Cullen's intellectual interests might well have prompted him to attend a performance of the play. Secondly, *Asie* is, like Cullen's ***Medea,*** a drama which emphasizes the racial aspect of the hostility between colonizer and colonized. In Lenormand's treatment of the myth, "Jason" is an enterprising French adventurer named De Mezzana, married to the Indochinese Princess Katha Naham Moun, by whom he has two sons. After persuading his wife to leave her home and settle down with him and their children in France, De Mezzana decides to abandon the Princess and take up with an attractive young French woman. Hoping to make "white boys" out of progeny he describes as "two little lost monkeys whimpering on the edge of the forest," De Mezzana enrolls them in a French school where the racist schoolteacher holds them up to ridicule, entertaining the class with remarks about "exotic fauna" (Lenormand 41). In short, the brutality of the colonial order is so vividly depicted in this play that the mother's fierce resolve to save her sons from becoming "the lackeys of monsters" augments the credibility of her decision to kill them along with herself. Although Lenormand's tragedy is an intriguing synthesis of ancient plot and colonial context which is likely to have attracted Cullen's interest, it is only one of many contemporary articulations of the essential problems dramatized by his ***Medea.***

Whereas *Asie* might have suggested the link between ancient tragedy and modern experience, René Maran's *Batouala* is certain to have fueled Cullen's interest in the context of colonial Africa. A novel which won Maran the Goncourt prize for literature in 1921, *Batouala* was further distinguished by being banned in all of the French African colonies. Described by Senghor as a precursor of the Négritude movement (Irele 142) and generally credited as "the first to make Africa a living presence in an imaginative work in the French language" (Irele 147), Maran attracted Cullen's attention as early as 1922, when the American read *Batouala* with considerable enthusiasm (Fabre 77). Though the action of *Batouala* has little in common with that of ***Medea,*** the novel and the play do share certain thematic concerns. Both texts insist on the destructive jealousy of women, on the inevitability of revenge, on the intervention of sorcerers, on the abuses of colonial regimes, and on the general antipathy between black and white cultures. In addition to such major concerns, Maran's novel anticipates the texture of Cullen's drama in his allusion to white men who desert the children born to them by black women (Maran 90), in his insistence on the burden of child rearing (176), and in symbolic references to lions (176-78) which recall the ancient description of Medea as a ranging lion (Euripides 190). The thematic and textual elements shared by *Batouala* and ***Medea*** suggest that Cullen's articulation of the tragic myth anticipates the drama of Wole Soyinka in its synthesis of ancient Greek and traditional African elements. To the extent that Cullen's treatment of the conflict between Jason and Medea may be read as a discreet externalization of his own frustration with the project of effecting a harmonious marriage between white and black cultures, his drama constitutes a metapoetic deployment of the demons with which he struggled throughout his creative life. Yet the claim that Cullen's ***Medea*** articulates the author's own intensely experienced grief must ultimately depend on the degree to which his most essential concerns coincide with those of Euripides.

The barbarian protagonist presented by Euripides in 431 B.C.E. personifies all too well the sensibility of the "pagan mad," "black sheep," "pagan heart" described in "Pagan Prayer" (92-93) by the poet who elsewhere rejected the concept of "civilization" outright: "Not yet has my heart or head / In the least way realized / That they and I are civilized" (**"Heritage"** 108). The very fact that Euripides' *Medea* ultimately mocks every so-called civilized pretension might sufficiently explain its appeal for Cullen, who insisted, in ***Caroling Dusk,*** on the difficulty of "reconciling a Christian upbringing with a pagan inclination" (Early 57-58), and often enough celebrated the concept of "barbarism" as a beneficent antidote to smug declarations of "civilizing" intent. In fact, Cullen's depiction of Medea's spectacular pride and passionate vengeance is not likely to be dismissed as a formal exercise by any reader of the familiar lines from **"Heritage"**: "One thing only I must do: / Quench my pride and cool my blood, / Lest I perish in the flood" (107). Although such texts demonstrate the importance of Cullen's focus on his barbarian protagonist, they are far from clarifying the basic interpretive problem posed by his tragic drama. Needless to say, the poet is not presenting Medea as a role model, or the story of her conflict with Jason as a paradigm for conflict resolution. The play is, however, a meditation on the generation and expression of violent anger. As such, it represents an essential moment in the history of the Harlem Renaissance.

At first identified with an unprecedented upsurge of optimistic belief in the possibility of peaceful, steady improvement in the lives of African Americans, the Harlem Renaissance was described by Arna Bontemps as a period of expansive hope within the Black community. He cites the poem **"I Have a Rendezvous with Life,"** written by Cullen when he was still in high school, and published in the DeWitt Clinton literary magazine in 1921, as "the first clear signal" of a period which would be distinguished by flourishing artistic and intellectual activity within the African American community (2). The tone of moderation and conciliation in the up and coming generation of black writers was especially praised by influential white scholars. Carl Van Doren observed that "being . . . a race not given to self-destroying bitterness," African Americans would "strike a happy balance between rage and complacency—that balance in which passion and humor are somehow united in the best of all possible amalgams for the creative artist" (qtd. in Bontemps 13). Speeches such as this one, published in *Opportunity* in 1924, describe a mood of relative optimism, and also contain a discreet promise: "If you behave yourselves, you will be rewarded."

Ten years later, after the eruption of the Scottsboro affair, after the intensification of activity by the Ku Klux Klan and the scourge of the Great Depression, the general disappointment would be all the more bitter, precisely because the initial promise of the "Renaissance" had been so seductive and glowing. Van Doren's complacent expectation that African Americans would achieve "a happy balance between rage and complacency" would be mocked by Cullen in such poems as **"Mood"**—

> I think an impulse stronger than my
> mind
> May some day grasp a knife, unloose a
> vial,
> Or with a little leaden ball unbind
> The cords that tie me to the rank and
> file.
>
> (187)

If he never actually did "unbind the cords that tied" him to all others, he does suggest, in this poem, that he was nevertheless familiar with the desperate and overwhelming passions which animate his tragic protagonist.

At this point, we may return to the question with which we began: Why focus on this particularly grim form of action? Why speak of the murder of children? The answer may be that Cullen deliberately wished to explore the question of violence as an instrument of political action. Fully aware that any recourse to violence inevitably entails the death not only of children but of many other defenseless human beings, the bitterly disappointed black poet chose to dramatize the agony of a tormented soul torn between the desire to spare the innocent and the passion for revolution. If, in his everyday life, Cullen rejected violence, he nevertheless permitted himself to imagine a grandly ferocious character trapped between misery and revolt, who unapologetically chooses revolt.

Works Cited

Anderson, Maxwell. *The Wingless Victory.* Washington: Anderson House, 1936.

Aristotle. *On Poetry and Style.* Trans. G. M. A. Grube. New York: Bobbs Merrill, 1958.

Baker, Houston A., Jr. *A Many-Colored Coat of Dreams: The Poetry of Countee Cullen.* Detroit: Broadside, 1974.

Barksdale, Richard, and Keneth Kinnamon, eds. *Black Writers of America: A Comprehensive Anthology.* New York: Macmillan, 1972.

Bontemps, Arna. *The Harlem Renaissance Remembered: Essays Edited with a Memoir.* New York: Dodd Mead, 1972.

Brent, Linda. *Incidents in the Life of a Slave Girl.* New York: Harcourt, 1973.

Chopin, Kate. *The Awakening and Selected Stories.* New York: Penguin, 1986.

Corti, Lillian. *The Myth of Medea and the Murder of Children.* Westport: Greenwood, forthcoming.

Cullen, Countée. *My Soul's High Song: The Collected Writings of Countee Cullen, Voice of the Harlem Renaissance.* Ed. Gerald Early. New York: Anchor, 1991.

Diop, David. *Coups de Pilon.* Paris: Présence Africaine, 1973.

Early, Gerald, ed. "Introduction." Cullen 3-76.

Easterling, P. E. "The Infanticide in Euripides' *Medea.*" *Yale Classical Studies* 25 (1977): 177-91.

Euripides. *Euripides.* Trans. Arthur S. Way. Vol. 4. Loeb Classical Library. 4 vols. Cambridge: Harvard UP, 1971.

Fabre, Michel. *From Harlem to Paris: Black Writers in Paris, 1840-1980.* Urbana: U of Illinois P, 1991.

Fitzhugh, George. *Ante-Bellum Writings of George Fitzhugh and Hinton Rowan Helper on Slavery.* Ed. Harvey Wish. New York: Capricorn, 1960.

Irele, Abiola. *The African Experience of Literature & Ideology.* London: Heinemann, 1981.

Jack, Peter Monro. Review of *Medea and Some Poems,* by Countée Cullen *New York Times* 12 Jan. 1936, sec. 6: 15.

Johnson, Barbara. "Apostrophe, Animation and Abortion." *Diacritics* 16.1 (1986): 32-39.

Langer, William. "Infanticide: A Historical Survey." *History of Childhood Quarterly: The Journal of Psychohistory* 1 (1974): 353-65.

Law, W. Augustus, and Virgil A. Clift, eds. *Encyclopedia of Black America.* New York: McGraw Hill, 1981.

Lenormand, Henri-René. *Thé tre Complet.* Paris: Albin Michel, 1938. 7-147.

Lewis, David Levering. *When Harlem Was in Vogue.* New York: Knopf, 1981.

Lomax, Michael L. "Countee Cullen: A Key to the Puzzle." *The Harlem Renaissance Re-Examined.* Ed. Victor A. Kramer. New York: AMS P, 1987. 213-22.

Lumpkin, Shirley. "Countee Cullen." *Dictionary of Literary Biography* Vol. 48. Ed. Peter Quartermain. Detroit: Bruccoli Clark, 1986. 109-16.

Maran, René. *Batouala.* Port Washington: Kennikat P, 1969.

McDermott, Emily A. *Euripides'* Medea: *The Incarnation of Disorder.* University Park: Pennsylvania State UP, 1989.

Morrison, Toni. *Beloved.* New York: NAL, 1987.

Page, Denys Lionel. "Introduction." *Medea.* By Euripides. Oxford: Clarendon, 1955.

Perry, Margaret. *A Bio-Bibliography of Countee P. Cullen, 1903-1946.* Westport: Greenwood, 1971.

Piers, Maria. *Infanticide: Past and Present.* New York: Norton, 1978.

Radbill, Samuel X. "A History of Child Abuse and Infanticide." *The Battered Child.* Ed. Ray E. Helfer and C. Henry Kempe. Chicago: U of Chicago P, 1968. 3-17.

Ram, Amitai Avi. "The Unreadable Black Body: 'Conventional' Poetic Form in the Harlem Renaissance." *Genders* 7 (1990): 32-46.

Rice, Philip Blair. "Euripides in Harlem." *Nation* 141 (1935): 336.

Shucard, Alan. "Countee Cullen." *Dictionary of Literary Biography.* Vol. 51. Ed. Trudier Harris and Thadious M. Davis. Detroit: Bruccoli Clark, 1987. 35-46.

Simon, Bennett. *Tragic Drama and the Family Psychoanalytic Studies from Aeschylus to Beckett.* New Haven: Yale UP, 1988.

Smith, Gary. "The Black Protest Sonnet." *American Poetry* 2.1 (1984): 2-12.

Stowe, Harriet Beecher. *Uncle Tom's Cabin.* New York: Bantam, 1981.

Tindall, George Brown, and David E. Shi. *America: A Narrative History.* New York: Norton, 1989.

Vellacott. Philip. *Ironic Drama: A Study of Euripides' Method and Meaning.* London: Cambridge UP, 1975.

Discography

Hunter, Alberta. *Complete Recorded Works in Chronological Order.* Vol. 4, 1927-1946. Document Records, 1996.

King. B. B. *The Best of B. B. King.* MCA Records, 1987.

FURTHER READING

Biographies

Baker, Jr., Houston A. *A Many-Colored Coat of Dreams: The Poetry of Countee Cullen.* Detroit: Broadside Press, 1974.

Explores and defends Cullen's place in the Black literary tradition.

Ferguson, Blanche E. *Countee Cullen and the Negro Renaissance.* New York: Dodd, Mead, 1966.

Biography of Cullen's life and works.

Perry, Margaret. *A Bio-Bibliography of Countee P. Cullen, 1903-1946.* Westport, CT: Greenwood Press, 1971.

Biography of Cullen's life and work, with bibliography.

Criticism

Boie, Mildred. "The Proof of the Poet." *Opportunity* 13, no. 12 (December 1935): 381-82.

Considers Cullen's The Medea, and Some Poems.

Collier, Eugenia W. "I Do Not Marvel, Countee Cullen." *CLA Journal* 11, no. 1 (September 1967): 73-87.

Examines poetry of the Harlem Renaissance, including works by McKay and Brown, and posits that Cullen's poem "From the Dark Tower" effectively expresses the spirit of the poetic movement.

Copeland, Catherine H. "The Unifying Effect of Coupling in Countee Cullen's 'Yet Do I Marvel.'" *CLA Journal* 18, no. 2 (December 1974): 258-61.

Takes a linguistic approach towards Cullen's poem "Yet Do I Marvel," focusing on his systematic use of poetic coupling.

Daniel, Walter C. "Countee Cullen as Literary Critic." *CLA Journal* 14, no. 3 (March 1971): 281-90.

Discusses Cullen's editorship of the journal Opportunity *and his monthly column "The Dark Tower" in order to examine the ways the poet and editor influenced the publication of African American authors.*

Dillon, George H. "Mr. Cullen's First Book." *Poetry* 28, no. 1 (April 1926): 50-53.

Considers Cullen's Colors, *noting a tendency towards "stilted and prosy" verse and finding the poet most successful when his language is "spare and direct."*

Dorsey, Jr., David F. "Countee Cullen's Use of Greek Mythology." *CLA Journal* 13, no. 1 (September 1969): 68-77.

Examines Cullen's use of Greek mythology to create irony and originality.

Fabre, Michael. "Countee Cullen: 'The Greatest Francophile.'" In his *From Harlem to Paris: Black American Writers in France, 1840-1980,* pp. 76-91. Urbana: University of Illinois Press, 1991.

Considers Cullen's love of France, the time he spent in Paris and the compositions written there, and his attempt to translate his own poetry into French.

Fetrow, Fred M. "Cullen's 'Yet Do I Marvel.'" *Explicator* 56, no. 1 (fall 1997): 103-5.

Through a close reading, briefly reconsiders Cullen's poem "Yet Do I Marvel."

Goldweber, David E. "Cullen, Keats, and the Privileged Liar." *Papers on Language and Literature* 38, no. 1 (winter 2002): 29-48.

Characterizes Cullen's use of illusions and humanity as being inspired by John Keats.

Jackson, Blyden. "Largo for Adonais." *The Waiting Years: Essays on American Negro Literature,* pp. 42-62. Baton Rouge: Louisiana State University Press, 1976.

Originally published in 1946, considers Cullen's aestheticism in his poetic depiction of Africa and his presentation of racial themes.

Larson, Charles R. "Three Harlem Novels of the Jazz Age." *Critique* 11, no. 3 (1969): 66-78.

Examines Claude McKay's Home to Harlem, *Carl Van Vechten's* Nigger Heaven, *and Cullen's only novel* One Way to Heaven *as collectively representing the cultural birth of the "New Negro," offering a panoramic view of 1920s Harlem.*

Powers, Peter. "'The Singing Man Who Must be Reckoned With': Private Desire and Public Responsibility in the Poetry of Countee Cullen." *African American Review* 34, no. 4 (winter 2000): 661-78.

Considers the critical perception of Cullen's masculinity and the tensions and contradictions in his poetry as reflective of the larger 1920s cultural tensions in the conception of masculinity, race, and religion.

Primeau, Ronald. "Countee Cullen and Keats's 'Vale of Soul-Making.'" *Papers on Language & Literature* 12, no. 1 (winter 1976): 73-86.

Explores Cullen's appreciation of Keats both for the self-conscious comparisons to the Romantic poet and for the subtle ways Cullen's attempts to free himself from Keats' influence.

Sheasby, Ronald E. "Dual Reality: Echoes of Blake's Tiger in Cullen's Heritage." *CLA Journal* 39, no. 2 (December 1995): 219-27.

Explores the possible influence of William Blake's poem "The Tiger" on Cullen's "Heritage" as evidenced by the identical use of meter and rhyme scheme and the repetition of thematically significant questions.

Smith, Gray. "The Black Protest Sonnet." *American Poetry* 2, no. 41 (fall 1984): 2-12.

Examines Cullen's use of the sonnet as a vehicle for protest.

Smylie, James H. "Countee Cullen's 'The Black Christ.'" *Theology Today* 38, no. 2 (July 1981): 160-73.

Provides a close reading of Cullen's poem "The Black Christ."

OTHER SOURCES FROM GALE:

Additional coverage of Cullen's life and career is contained in the following sources published by the Gale Group: *Black Literature Criticism,* Vol. 1; *Black Writers,* Ed. 1; *Concise Dictionary of American Literary Biography, 1917-1929; Contemporary Authors,* Vols. 108, 124; *Dictionary of Literary Biography,* Vols. 4, 48, 51; *DISCovering Authors; DISCovering Authors: Canadian Edition; DISCovering Authors Modules: Most-studied Authors, Multicultural,* and *Poets; DISCovering Authors 3.0; Major 20th-Century Writers,* Eds. 1, 2; *Poetry Criticism,* Vol. 20; *Poetry for Students,* Vol. 3; *Something about the Author,* Vol. 18; *Twentieth-Century Literary Criticism,* Vols. 4 , 37; and *World Literature Criticism Supplement.*

W. E. B. DU BOIS

(1868 - 1963)

(Full name William Edward Burghardt Du Bois) American social scientist, autobiographer, essayist, novelist, and poet.

Considered one of the premier African American intellectuals of the twentieth century, W. E. B. Du Bois was a co-founder of the National Association for the Advancement of Colored People (NAACP) and edited the organization's chief publication, the *Crisis,* giving him an important platform for leading the Black community from 1910 into the 1930s. Even after leaving the NAACP over ideological differences, Du Bois remained influential in the African American community throughout his long life, though he came to doubt he would ever achieve his goals for racial advancement. His contributions to the sociology of race are immense, as is the legacy of his efforts toward racial integration. Du Bois was also a very strong advocate of Black arts, both in his role as editor of the *Crisis,* a launching pad for many writers of the Harlem Renaissance, and in his own writings aimed at encouraging the development of a "Negro Aesthetic." While Du Bois never achieved the artistic heights in his own creative efforts that such peers as Langston Hughes, Zora Neale Hurston, or Claude McKay did—in part with his assistance—his influence on African American writing was considerable in his own era and beyond.

BIOGRAPHICAL INFORMATION

Du Bois had some Dutch and French ancestry, though he insisted he had no "Anglo-Saxon" blood. Somewhat embarrassed by his mixed heritage, Du Bois was often ambiguous or misleading in discussing his genealogy, including his immediate parentage. He was born William Edward Burghardt Du Bois in Great Barrington, Massachusetts, in 1868, to a bigamist father who deserted him when Du Bois was only two years old. He attended college at Fisk University in Nashville; his experiences there gave him his first taste of the bitter legacy of slavery in the South. He next attended Harvard University, starting a second bachelor's degree in 1890. When he earned his doctorate in 1895 he became the first African American to receive the PhD from Harvard. At Harvard, Du Bois worked with major American thinkers, including William James and George Santayana, whose instruction in philosophy and psychology would be highly influential in Du Bois's intellectual development. He also studied for two years at the University of Berlin. After leaving Harvard, Du Bois began teaching, first at the Black school Wilberforce University, then at the University of Pennsylvania. While in Philadelphia, Du Bois began work on the first of his major sociological studies, *The Philadelphia Negro* (1899). He moved to the South again to teach at Atlanta University from 1897 to 1910, encouraging sociological study of African Americans and promoting racial advancement through higher education. During this time he published *The Souls of Black Folk* (1903)—a collection of writings on African American history, sociology, education, and culture—and *John Brown* (1909), a biography of a white abolitionist who became a hero to African Americans. In 1910 Du Bois left teaching to co-found the NAACP and become editor of its magazine, *The Crisis,* a position he held until 1934. He began experimenting with more creative forms of expression, and published the mythological novels *The Quest of the Silver Fleece* (1911) and *Dark Princess* (1928). During this period he also became active in the Pan-African Movement, calling for solidarity of African people everywhere and linking the oppression of Blacks in America to the domination of European colonizers in Africa. Du Bois's extensive research in African history resulted in the publication of his studies *The Negro* (1915), *Darkwater* (1920), *The Gift of Black Folk* (1924), *Africa: Its Geography, People, and Products* (1930), and *Africa: Its Place in Modern History* (1930). Du Bois also wrote and spoke widely on the need for African economic independence, a belief that eventually influenced his break with the NAACP. While he supported the Pan-African movement, Du Bois feuded publicly and bitterly with Marcus Garvey and the ideas of his "Back to Africa" movement, criticizing the excesses of Garvey's rhetoric and "Garveysim" in general. Although Du Bois was an integrationist, he felt that separate economic and educational institutions for African Americans were nonetheless the surest route to equality with whites. As he developed this position further, he was no longer able to remain in the NAACP. After leaving the organization he had launched, Du Bois returned to teaching at Atlanta University. Du Bois did some research for the NAACP beginning in 1944, but by 1948 he again left in dissent. Du Bois had developed an increasingly Marxist bent to his philosophy and had begun working on peace projects that drew the attention of the U.S. government. An early indication of his growing Marxist perspective was his study *Black Reconstruction* (1935). He further developed his vision of socialism as a solution to racial oppression in *Dusk of Dawn* (1940). Du Bois and others involved with the Stockholm Appeal, a move to ban atomic weapons, were asked to register with the United States as agents of the Soviet Union; when Du Bois refused, he was served with criminal charges in 1951. Du Bois was never convicted, but the incident led him to believe that his work in America would come to nothing; he discussed the disappointment springing from his arrest in a memoir, *In Battle for Peace* (1952). Though he had been outspokenly critical of the Communist Party for decades, Du Bois came to admire the ability of the Soviet Union and Communist China to effect revolutionary change, and he joined the Communist Party in 1961, when he was ninety-three. That same year Du Bois moved to Ghana, which had recently achieved independence. He died in 1963, one day before Martin Luther King Jr. would lead the famous March on Washington.

MAJOR WORKS

Du Bois was an innovative and prolific writer. Much of what he wrote was the first of its kind and was highly influential for decades to come. His earliest contributions were as a social scientist; his study *The Philadelphia Negro* was the first sociological study of an urban Black population. Du Bois's sociological works quickly expanded to embrace autobiography, psychology, and cultural studies, as seen in his seminal masterpiece, *The Souls of Black Folk.* In that work Du Bois combined economic analysis with the study of Negro spirituals, reflections on his own life as an African American, and several other topics to present a wide-ranging view of African American culture in America. Du Bois also introduced two key concepts whose influence would extend well beyond his own philosophy and into the fabric of American studies generally: "double consciousness," a permanent sense of two-ness born of being both Black and American, and "The Veil," Du Bois's metaphor for any of the barriers separating Blacks from whites. "The Veil" was an image taken directly from the New Testament, reflective of Du Bois's tendency to adapt religious diction to his own arguments. Just as the rending of the temple veil upon the death of Christ destroyed the false distinctions between high priests and the masses, so Du Bois hoped that African Americans would not merely move past racial barriers, but fully destroy them. The motif of the veil is echoed in the title of *Darkwater,* a collection that highlights key trends in Du Bois's political opinions, including his increasing admiration for socialist ideology, his growing concern for all peoples of African descent, and his correlations between racial prejudice in America and colonial oppression in Africa. *Darkwater* also developed further Du Bois's technique of blending autobiography with sociological analysis, a demonstration of Du Bois's belief that his own biography was that of the larger Black community, and that he had an important role to play as a savior or messianic leader of African peoples everywhere.

Dusk of Dawn, published twenty years after *Darkwater,* shows Du Bois reshaping his former ideas from a stronger Marxist perspective and narrating them in a stronger thread of autobiographical writing. Du Bois later wrote two memoirs that he actually termed "autobiographies," both of which reflect his loss of faith in America and his sense that capitalism had failed. Even before Du Bois had fully embraced socialism, he felt strongly that art, particularly Black art, should have a positive function as racial propaganda. He wrote of this frequently in the *Crisis,* particularly during the Harlem Renaissance. In 1921 he published the essay "Negro Art," urging African American authors to refrain from focusing solely on the debased elements of Black society, but also stressing the importance of truth. He developed these views further in the *Crisis* essay "Criteria of Negro Art" (1926), where he also called for Black authors to avoid pandering to white tastes or standards, even though that was the most likely route to publication. In *Crisis* reviews of such works as Claude McKay's *Home to Harlem,* Wallace Thurman's *The Blacker the Berry,* and Nella Larsen's *Quicksand,* Du Bois regularly had the opportunity to measure the progress of Black art toward true Black aesthetic standards. Du Bois also wrote his own poetry and fiction to help fill the need for effective African American art. His first novel, *The Quest of the Silver Fleece,* possibly the first coming-of-age novel in African American fiction, combined economic analysis with mythical tales of witchcraft and voodoo. *Dark Princess,* Du Bois's second novel and his personal favorite, is a fictional reflection of his pan-African beliefs. His *Black Flame* trilogy—*The Ordeal of Mansart* (1957), *Mansart Builds a School* (1959), and *The Worlds of Color* (1961)—was written during his time of disillusionment and tells the story of a Black leader who comes to feel that his efforts were largely in vain.

CRITICAL RECEPTION

The value and uniqueness of Du Bois's work was recognized almost immediately. *The Souls of Black Folk,* in particular, was regarded from the beginning as a watershed work for Black consciousness. The book was deeply influential for several writers of the Harlem Renaissance and beyond, and is often considered his best and most important work. Many African American readers wrote Du Bois to tell him that his book had initiated their sense of Black consciousness, and its admirers included the sociologist Max Weber and the novelist Henry James. As Du Bois became more politically active, assessments of his works were correspondingly more politically charged. His views on integration and prejudice were, not surprisingly, troubling to many white Americans, while his appreciation for socialism, his feuds with Marcus Garvey and Booker T. Washington, and his split with the NAACP made him a sometimes controversial figure in the African American community as well. Critics have also observed the paradoxical nature of Du Bois's work: though he labored for the cause of integration, he also strongly advocated separatist policies, particularly in economics. These opposing aims led his contemporaries as well as later scholars to suggest that Du Bois's philosophy of racial advancement was not fully coherent. Modern scholarship on Du Bois falls into several categories, focusing variously on his contributions to social science, his role in racial politics and integration, and his personal transformations throughout his career. Criticism on Du Bois's writing has a similarly wide scope, though the themes of self and autobiography appear frequently, given Du Bois's tendency to weave his life writing throughout his nonfiction and his fiction. Generally speaking, Du Bois's fiction has not met with strong critical acclaim: as both Arnold Rampersad and Moses Wilson have observed, in the genres of fiction and poetry, Du Bois's work was average to mediocre. To some extent, the standard Du Bois proposed for Black art often comes into play in evaluations and analyses of his own works. Du Bois insisted that African American literature should somehow support the cause of racial advancement, and in that respect Du Bois succeeded more often than not, despite his doubts toward the end of his life. One of Du Bois's later editors, Eric J. Sundquist, has argued that much of what has been written by and about African Americans since the early twentieth century could not have existed without Du Bois's immense contributions.

PRINCIPAL WORKS

The Suppression of the African Slave-Trade to the United States of America, 1638-1870 (history) 1896

The Philadelphia Negro: A Social Study (nonfiction) 1899

The Souls of Black Folk: Essays and Sketches (fiction, nonfiction, and folklore) 1903

John Brown (biography) 1909

The Quest of the Silver Fleece (novel) 1911

The Negro (nonfiction) 1915

Darkwater: Voices from within the Veil (poetry, nonfiction, and autobiography) 1920

The Gift of Black Folk: The Negros in the Making of America (nonfiction) 1924

Dark Princess: A Romance (novel) 1928

Africa: Its Geography, People, and Products (nonfiction) 1930

Africa: Its Place in Modern History (nonfiction) 1930

Black Reconstruction: An Essay Toward a History of the Part Which Black Folk Played in the Attempt to Reconstruct Democracy in America, 1860-1880 (nonfiction) 1935

Black Folk, Then and Now: An Essay in the History and Sociology of the Negro Race (nonfiction) 1939

Color and Democracy: Colonies and Peace (nonfiction) 1940

Dusk of Dawn: An Essay Toward an Autobiography of a Race Concept (nonfiction and autobiography) 1940

The World and Africa: An Inquiry into the Part Which Africa Has Played in World History (nonfiction) 1947

In Battle for Peace: The Story of My 83rd Birthday (memoir) 1952

The Ordeal of Mansart (novel) 1957

Mansart Builds a School (novel) 1959

The Worlds of Color (novel) 1961

The Autobiography of W. E. B. Du Bois: A Soliloquy on Viewing My Life from the Last Decade of its First Century (autobiography) 1968

PRIMARY SOURCES

W. E. B. DU BOIS (ESSAY DATE 1901)

SOURCE: Du Bois, W. E. B. "The Black North: A Social Study." New York: 1901.

One of many social essays written by Du Bois, this piece addresses the issue of the "negro problem" and how it affected the northern migration of African Americans.

The negro problem is not the sole property of the South. To be sure, it is there most complicated and pressing. Yet north of Mason and Dixon's line there live to-day three-quarters of a million men of negro lineage. Nearly 400,000 of these live in New England and the Middle-Atlantic States, and it is this population that I wish especially to study in a series of papers.

The growth of this body of negroes has been rapid since the war. There were 150,000 in 1800, 225,000 in 1880, and about 385,000 to-day. It is usually assumed that this group of persons has not formed to any extent a "problem" in the North, that during a century of freedom they have had an assured social status and the same chance for rise and development as the native white American, or at least as the foreign immigrant.

This is not true. It can be safely asserted that since early Colonial times the North has had a distinct race problem. Every one of these States had slaves, and at the beginning of Washington's Administration there were 40,000 black slaves and 17,000 black freemen in this section. The economic failure of slavery as an investment here gave the better conscience of Puritan and Quaker a chance to be heard, and processes of gradual emancipation were began early in the nineteenth century.

Some of the slaves were sold South and eagerly welcomed there. Most of them staid in the North and became a free negro population.

They were not, however, really free. Socially they were ostracized. Strict laws were enacted against intermarriage. They were granted rights of suffrage with some limitations, but these limitations were either increased or the right summarily denied afterward.

North as well as South the negroes have emerged from slavery into a serfdom of poverty and restricted rights. Their history since has been the history of the gradual but by no means complete breaking down of remaining barriers.

To-day there are many contrasts between Northern and Southern negroes. Three-fourths of the Southern negroes live in the country districts. Nine-tenths of the Northern negroes live in cities and towns. The Southern negro were in nearly all cases born South and of slave parentage.

About a third of the Northern negroes were born North, partly of free negro parentage, while the rest are Southern immigrants. Thus in the North there is a sharper division of the negroes into classes and a greater difference in attainment and training than one finds in the South.

From the beginning the Northern slaves lived in towns more generally than the Southern slaves, being used largely as house servants and artisans. As town life increased, the urban negro population increased. Here and there little villages of free negroes were to be found in the country districts of the North tilling the soil, but the competition of the great West soon sent them to town along with their white brothers, and now only here and there is there a negro family left in the country districts and villages of New England and of the Middle States.

From the earliest settlement of Manhattan, when the Dutch West India Company was pledging itself to furnish the new settlers with plenty of negroes, down to 1900, when the greater city contained 60,000 black folk, New York has had a negro problem. This problem has greatly changed from time to time. Two centuries ago it was a question of obtaining "hands" to labor. Then came questions of curbing barbarians and baptizing heathen. Long before the nineteenth century citizens were puzzled about the education of the negroes, and then came negro riots and negro crime and the baffling windings of the color line.

At the beginning of the eighteenth century there were 1,500 negroes in New York City. They were house servants and laborers, and often were hired out by their masters, taking their stand for this purpose at the foot of Wall Street. By the middle of the century the population had doubled, and by the beginning of the nineteenth century it was about 9,000, five-sixths of whom were free by the act of gradual emancipation.

In 1840 the population was over 16,000, but it fell off to 12,500 in 1860 on account of the competition of foreign workmen and race riots. Since the war it has increased rapidly to 20,000 in 1880 and to 36,000 on Manhattan Island in 1900. The annexed districts raise this total to 60,000 for the whole city.

The distribution of this population presents many curious features. Conceive a large rectangle through which Seventh Avenue runs lengthwise. Let this be bounded on the south by a line near Sixteenth Street and on the north by Sixty-four or Sixty-fifth Street. On the east let the boundary be a wavering line between Fourth and Seventh Avenues and on the west the river.

In this quadrangle live over 20,000 negroes, a third of the total population. Ten thousand others live around the north end of the Park and further north, while 18,000 live in Brooklyn. The remaining 10,000 are scattered here and there in other parts of the city.

The migration of the black population to its present abode in New York has followed the growth of the city. Early in the eighteenth century the negroes lived and congregated in the hovels along the wharves and of course in the families of the masters. The centre of black population then moved slowly north, principally on the east side, until it reached Mulberry Street, about 1820. Crossing Broadway, a generation later the negroes clustered about Sullivan and Thompson Streets until after the war, when they moved northward along Seventh Avenue.

From 1870 to 1890, the population was more and more crowded and congested in the negro districts between Twenty-sixth and Sixty-third Streets. Since then there has been considerable dispersion to Brooklyn and Harlem districts, although the old centres are still full.

The migration to Brooklyn began about 1820 and received its greatest impetus from the refugees at the time of the draft riots. In 1870 there were 5,000 negroes in Brooklyn. Since then the population has increased very rapidly, and it has consisted largely of the better class of negroes in search of homes and seeking to escape the contamination of the Tenderloin.

In 1890 the Brooklyn negroes had settled chiefly in the Eleventh, Twentieth, and Seventh Wards. Since then they have increased in those wards and have moved to the east in the Twenty-third, Twenty-fourth, and Twenty-fifth Wards and in the vicinity of Coney Island.

Let us now examine any peculiarities in the colored population of New York. The first noticeable fact is the excess of women. In Philadelphia the women exceed the men six to five. In New York the excess is still larger—five to four—and this means that here even more than in Philadelphia the demand for negro housemaids is unbalanced by a corresponding demand for negro men.

This disproportion acts disastrously today on the women and the men. The excess of young people from eighteen to thirty years of age points again to large and rapid immigration. The Wilmington riot alone sent North thousands of emigrants, and as the black masses of the South awaken or as they are disturbed by violence this migration will continue and perhaps increase.

The North, therefore, and especially great cities like New York, has much more than an academic interest in the Southern negro problem. Unless the race conflict there is so adjusted as to leave the negroes a contented, industrious people, they are going to migrate here and there. And into the large cities will pour in increasing numbers the competent and the incompetent, the industrious and the lazy, the law abiding and the criminal.

Moreover, the conditions under which these new immigrants are now received are of such a nature that very frequently the good are made bad and the bad made professional criminals. One has but to read Dunbar's "Sport of the Gods" to get an idea of the temptations that surround the young immigrant. In the most thickly settled negro portion of the Nineteenth Assembly District, where 5,000 negroes live, the parents of half of the heads families were country bred. Among these families the strain of city life is immediately seen when we find that 24 per cent of the mothers are widows—a percentage only exceeded by the Irish, and far above the Americans (16.3).

In these figures lie untold tales of struggle, self-denial, despair, and crime. In the country districts of the South, as in all rural regions, early marriage and large families are the rule. These young immigrants to New York cannot afford to marry early. Two-thirds of the young men twenty to twenty-four years of age are unmarried, and five-eighths of the young women.

When they do marry it is a hard struggle to earn a living. As a race the negroes are not lazy. The canvass of the Federation of Churches in typical New York tenement districts has shown that while nearly 90 per cent of the black men were wage earners, only 92 per cent of the Americans and 90 per cent of the Germans were at work.

At the same time the work of the negroes was the least remunerative, they receiving a third less per week than the other nationalities. Nor can the disabilities of the negroes be laid altogether at the door of ignorance. Probably they are even less acquainted with city life and organized industry than most of the foreign laborers. In illiteracy, however, negroes and foreigners are about equal—five-sixths being able to read and write.

The crucial question, then, is: What does the black immigrant find to do? Some persons deem the answer to this question unnecessary to a real understanding of the negro. They say either that the case of the negro is that of the replacing of a poor workman by better ones in the neutral competition of trade or that a mass of people like the American negroes ought to furnish employment for themselves without asking others for work.

There is just enough truth in such superficial statements to make them peculiarly misleading and unfair. Before the civil war the negro was certainly as efficient a workman as the raw immigrant from Ireland or Germany. But, whereas the Irishmen found economic opportunity wide and daily growing wider, the negro found public opinion determined to "keep him in his place."

As early as 1824 Lafayette, on his second visit to New York, remarked "wish astonishment the aggravation of the prejudice against the blacks," and stated that in the Revolutionary War "the black and white soldiers meshed together without hesitation." In 1836 a well-to-do negro was refused a license as drayman in New York City, and mob violence was frequent against black men who pushed forward beyond their customary sphere.

Nor could the negro resent this by his vote. The Constitution of 1777 had given him full rights of suffrage, but in 1821 the ballot, so far as blacks were concerned, was restricted to holders of $250 worth of realty—a restriction which lasted until the war, in spite of efforts to change it, and which restricted black laborers but left white laborers with full rights of suffrage.

So, too, the draft riots of 1863 were far more than passing ebullitions of wrath and violence, but were used as a means of excluding negroes all over the city from lines of work in which they had been long employed. The relief committee pleaded in vain to have various positions restored to negroes. In numerous cases the exclusion was permanent and remains so to this day.

Thus the candid observer easily sees that the negro's economic position in New York has not been determined simply by efficiency in open competition, but that race prejudice has played a large and decisive part. Probably in free competition ex-slaves would have suffered some disadvantages in entering mechanical industries. When race feeling was added to this they were almost totally excluded.

Again, it is impossible for a group of men to maintain and employ itself while in open competition with a larger and stronger group. Only by co-operation with the industrial organization of the Nation can negroes earn a living. And this cooperation is difficult to effect. One can easily trace the struggle in a city like New York. Seventy-four per cent of the working negro population are common laborers and servants.

From this dead level they have striven long to rise. In this striving they have made many mistakes, have had some failures and some successes. They voluntarily withdrew from bootblacking, barbering, table waiting, and menial service whenever they saw a chance to climb higher, and their places were quickly filled by foreign whites.

Some of the negroes succeeded in their efforts to rise, some did not. Thus every obstacle placed in the way of their progress meant increased competition at the bottom. Twenty-six per cent of the negroes have risen to a degree and gained a firmer economic foothold. Twelve per cent of these have gone but a step higher: these are the porters, packers, messengers, draymen, and the like—a select class of laborers, often well paid and more independent than the old class of upper house servants before the war, to which they in some respect correspond.

Some of this class occupy responsible positions, others have some capital invested, and nearly all have good homes.

Ten per cent of the colored people are skilled laborers—cigarmakers, barbers, tailors and dressmakers, builders, stationary engineers, & c. Five and one-half per cent are in business enterprises, chiefly real estate, the catering business, undertaking, drug stores, hotels and restaurants, express teaming, & c. In the sixty-nine leading establishments $800,000 is invested—$13,000 in sums from $500 to $1,000 and $200,000 in sums from $1,000 to $25,000.

Forty-four of the sixty-nine businesses were established since 1885, and seventeen others since the war. Co-operative holders of real estate—i.e., hall associations, building and loan associations, and one large church, which has considerable sums in productive real estate—have over half a million dollars invested. Five leading caterers have $30,000, seven undertakers have $32,000, two saloons have over $50,000, and four small machine shops have $27,500 invested.

These are the most promising enterprises in which New York negroes have embarked. Serious obstacles are encountered. Great ingenuity is often required in finding gaps in business service where the man of small capital may use his skill or experience.

One negro has organized the cleaning of houses to a remarkable extent and has an establishment representing at least $30,000 of invested capital, some ten or twelve employees, and a large circle of clients.

Again, it is very difficult for negroes to get experience and training in modern business methods. Young colored men can seldom get positions above menial grade, and the training of the older men unfits them for competitive business. Then always the uncertain but ever present factor of racial prejudice is present to hinder or at least make more difficult the advance of the colored merchant or business man, in new or unaccustomed lines.

In clerical and professional work there are about ten negro lawyers in New York, twenty physicians, and at least ninety in the civil service as clerks, mail carriers, public school teachers, and the like. The competitive civil service has proved a great boon to young aspiring negroes, and they are being attracted to it increasing numbers. Already in the public schools there are one Principal, two special teachers, and about thirty-five classroom teachers of negro blood. So far no complaint of the work and very little objection to their presence have been heard.

In some such way as this black New York seeks to earn its daily bread, and it remains for us to ask of the homes and the public institutions just what kind of success these efforts are having.

W. E. B. DU BOIS (ESSAY DATE 1903)

SOURCE: Du Bois, W. E. B. "Forethought." In *The Souls of Black Folk,* pp. xxxi-xxxii. New York: Bantam Books, 1989.

Considered a landmark of African American thought, Du Bois's The Souls of Black Folk *first appeared in 1903. In this preface to the work, the author outlines his intentions for describing "the spiritual world in which ten thousand thousand Americans live and strive."*

Herein lie buried many things which if read with patience may show the strange meaning of being black here at the dawning of the Twentieth Century. This meaning is not without interest to you, Gentle Reader; for the problem of the Twentieth Century is the problem of the color line. I pray you, then, receive my little book in all charity, studying my words with me, forgiving mistake and foible for sake of the faith and passion that is in me, and seeking the grain of truth hidden there.

I have sought here to sketch, in vague, uncertain outline, the spiritual world in which ten thousand thousand Americans live and strive. First, in two chapters I have tried to show what Emancipation meant to them, and what was its aftermath. In a third chapter I have pointed out the slow rise of personal leadership, and criticized candidly the leader who bears the chief burden of his race to-day. Then, in two other chapters I have sketched in swift outline the two worlds within and without the Veil, and thus have come to the central problem of training men for life. Venturing now into deeper detail, I have in two chapters studied the struggles of the massed millions of the black peasantry, and in another have sought to make clear the present relations of the sons of master and man. Leaving, then, the white world, I have stepped within the Veil, raising it that you may view faintly its deeper recesses,—the meaning of its religion, the passion of its human sorrow, and the struggle of its greater souls. All this I have ended with a tale twice told but seldom written, and a chapter of song.

Some of these thoughts of mine have seen the light before in other guise. For kindly consenting to their republication here, in altered and extended form, I must thank the publishers of the *Atlantic Monthly, The World's Work, The Dial, The New World,* and the *Annals of the American Academy of Political and Social Science.* Before each chapter, as now printed, stands a bar of the Sorrow Songs,—some echo of haunting melody from the only American music which welled up from black souls in the dark past. And, finally, need I add that I who speak here am bone of the bone and flesh of the flesh of them that live within the Veil?

W. E. B. DU BOIS (ESSAY DATE 1904)

SOURCE: Du Bois, W. E. B. "Credo." The *Independent,* no. 57 (6 October 1904): 787.

Du Bois wrote this piece to outline his beliefs and publicly establish the ethics by which he strove to live his life.

I believe in God who made of one blood all races that dwell on earth. I believe that all men, black and brown and white, are brothers, varying, through Time and Opportunity, in form and gift and feature, but differing in no essential particular, and alike in soul and in the possibility of infinite development.

Especially do I believe in the Negro Race; in the beauty of its genius, the sweetness of its soul, and its strength in that meekness which shall yet inherit this turbulent earth.

I believe in pride of race and lineage and self; in pride of self so deep as to scorn injustice to other selves; in pride of lineage so great as to despise no man's father; in pride of race so chivalrous as neither to offer bastardy to the weak nor beg wedlock of the strong, knowing that men may be brothers in Christ, even tho they be not brothers-in-law.

I believe in Service—humble reverent service, from the blackening of boots to the whitening of souls; for Work is Heaven, Idleness Hell, and Wage is the "Well done!" of the Master who summoned all them that labor and are heavy laden, making no distinction between the black sweating cotton-hands of Georgia and the First Families of Virginia, since all distinction not based on deed is devilish and not divine.

I believe in the Devil and his angels, who wantonly work to narrow the opportunity of struggling human beings, especially if they be black; who spit in the faces of the fallen, strike them that cannot strike again, believe the worst and work to prove it, hating the image which their Maker stamped on a brother's soul.

I believe in the Prince of Peace. I believe that War is Murder. I believe that armies and navies are at bottom the tinsel and braggadocio of oppression and wrong; and I believe that the wicked conquest of weaker and darker nations by nations whiter and stronger but foreshadows the death of that strength.

I believe in Liberty for all men; the space to stretch their arms and their souls; the right to breathe and the right to vote, the freedom to choose their friends, enjoy the sunshine and ride on the railroads, uncursed by color; thinking, dreaming, working as they will in a kingdom of God and love.

I believe in the training of children black even as white; the leading out of little souls into the green pastures and beside the still waters, not for pelf or peace, but for Life lit by some large vision of beauty and goodness and truth; lest we forget, and the sons of the fathers, like Esau, for mere meat barter their birthright in a mighty nation.

Finally, I believe in Patience—patience with the weakness of the Weak and the strength of the Strong, the prejudice of the Ignorant and the ignorance of the Blind; patience with the tardy triumph of Joy and the mad chastening of Sorrow—patience with God.

W. E. B. DU BOIS (ESSAY DATE 1912)

SOURCE: Du Bois, W. E. B. "Votes for Women." *The Crisis* IV (September 1912): 234.

An early proponent of women's suffrage, Du Bois published this editorial seven years before the passage of the nineteenth amendment granting women the right to vote; it is also considered a typical representation of the type of socially conscious material published in The Crisis.

Why should the colored voter be interested in woman's suffrage? There are three cogent reasons. First, it is a great human question. Nothing human, must be foreign, uninteresting or unimportant to colored citizens of the world. Whatever concerns half mankind concerns us. Secondly, any agitation, discussion or reopening of the problem of voting must inevitably be a discussion of the right of black folk to vote in America and Africa. Essentially the arguments for and against are the same in the case of all groups of human beings. The world with its tendencies and temptations to caste must ever be asking itself how far may the governed govern? How far can the responsibility of directing, curbing and encouraging mankind be put upon mankind? When we face this vastest of human problems frankly, most of us, despite ourselves and half unconsciously, find ourselves strangely undemocratic, strangely tempted to exclude from participation in government larger and larger numbers of our neighbors. Only at one point, with disconcerting unanimity, do we pause, and that it with ourselves. That we should vote we cannot for a moment doubt even if we are willing to acknowledge, as most of us are, that we are neither all wise nor infinitely good.

This fact should give us pause; if we in our potent weakness and shortcomings see the vast necessity for the ballot not only for our own selfish ends, but for the larger good of all our neighbors, do not our neighbors see the same necessity? And is not the unanswerable cogency of the argument for universal suffrage regardless of race or sex merely a matter of the point of view? Merely a matter of honestly putting yourself in the position of the disfranchised, and seeing the world through their eyes? The same arguments and facts that are slowly but surely opening the ballot box to women in England and America must open it to black men in America and Africa. It only remains for us to help the movement and spread the argument wherever we may. Finally, votes for women mean votes for black women. There are in the Unites States three and a third million adult women of Negro descent. Except in the rural South, these women have larger economic opportunity than their husbands and brothers and are rapidly becoming better educated. One has only to remember the recent biennial convention of colored women's clubs with its 400 delegates to realize how the women are moving quietly but forcibly toward the intellectual leadership of the race. The enfranchisement of these women will not be a mere doubling of our vote and voice in the nation; it will tend to stronger and more normal political life, the rapid dethronement of the "heeler" and "grafter" and the making of politics a method of broadest philanthropic race betterment, rather than a disreputable means of private gain. We sincerely trust that the entire Negro vote will be cast for women suffrage in the coming elections in Ohio, Kansas, Wisconsin and Michigan.

W. E. B. DU BOIS (ESSAY DATE 1926)

SOURCE: Du Bois, W. E. B. "Criteria of Negro Art." *The Crisis* (October 1926): 290-297.

In the following essay, Du Bois outlines his ideals for Black art, stating that the concepts of beauty, truth, and justice are inseparable.

The question comes next as to the interpretation of these new stirrings, of this new spirit: Of what is the colored artist capable? We have had on the part of both colored and white people singular unanimity of judgment in the past. Colored people have said, "This work must be inferior because it comes from colored people." White people have said: "It is inferior because it is done by colored people." But today there is coming to both the realization that the work of the black man is not always inferior. Interesting stories come to us. A professor in the University of Chicago read to a class that had studied literature a passage of poetry and asked them to guess the author. They suggested a goodly company from Shelley and Robert Browning down to Tennyson and Masefield. The author was Countee Cullen. Or again the English critic John Drinkwater went down to a Southern seminary, one of the sort which finishes young white women of the South. The students sat with their wooden faces while he tried to get some response out of them. Finally he said, "Name me some of your Southern poets." They hesitated. He said finally, "I'll start out with your best: Paul Laurence Dunbar!"

With the growing recognition of Negro artists in spite of the severe handicaps, one comforting thing is occurring to both white and black. They are whispering, "Here is a way out. Here is the real solution of the color problem. The recognition accorded Cullen, Hughes, Fauset, White and others shows there is no real color line. Keep quiet! Don't complain! Work! All will be well!"

I will not say that already this chorus amounts to a conspiracy. Perhaps I am naturally too suspicious. But I will say that there are today a surprising number of white people who are getting great satisfaction out of these younger Negro writers because they think it is going to stop agitation of the Negro question. They say, "What is the use of your fighting and complaining; do the great thing and the reward is there." And many colored people are all too eager to follow this advice; especially those who weary of the eternal struggle along the color line, who are afraid to fight and to whom the money of philanthropists and the alluring publicity are subtle and deadly bribes. They say, "What is the use of fighting? Why not show simply what we deserve and let the reward come to us?"

And it is right here that the National Association for the Advancement of Colored People comes upon the field, comes with its great call to a new battle, a new fight and new things to fight before the old things are wholly won; and to say that the beauty of truth and freedom which shall some day be our heritage and the heritage of all civilized men is not in our hands yet and that we ourselves must not fail to realize.

There is in New York tonight a black woman molding clay by herself in a little bare room, because there is not a single school of sculpture in New York where she is welcome. Surely there are doors she might burst through, but when God makes a sculptor He does not always make the pushing sort of person who beats his way through doors thrust in his face. This girl is working her hands off to get out of this country so that she can get some sort of training.

There was Richard Brown. If he had been white he would have been alive today instead of dead of neglect. Many helped him when he asked but he was not the kind of boy that always asks. He was simply one who made colors sing.

There is a colored woman in Chicago who is a great musician. She thought she would like to study at Fontainebleau this summer where Walter Damrosch and a score of leaders of art have an American school of music. But the application blank of this school says: "I am a white American and I apply for admission to the school."

We can go on the stage; we can be just as funny as white Americans wish us to be; we can play all the sordid parts that America likes to assign to Negroes; but for anything else there is still small place for us.

And so I might go on. But let me sum up with this: Suppose the only Negro who survived some centuries hence was the Negro painted by white Americans in the novels and essays they have written. What would people in a hundred years say of black Americans? Now turn it around. Suppose you were to write a story and put in it the kind of people you know and like and imagine. You might get it published and you might not. And the "might not" is still far bigger than the "might." The white publishers catering to white folk would say, "It is not interesting"—to white folk, naturally not. They want Uncle Toms, Topsies, good "darkies" and clowns. I have in my office a story with all the earmarks of truth. A young man says that he started out to write and had his stories accepted. Then he began to write about the things he knew best about, that is, about his own people. He submitted a story to a magazine which said, "We are sorry, but we cannot take it." "I sat down and revised my story, changing the color of the characters and the locale and sent it under an assumed name with a change of address and it was accepted by the same magazine that had refused it, the editor promising to take anything else I might send in providing it was good enough."

We have, to be sure, a few recognized and successful Negro artists; but they are not all those fit to survive or even a good minority. They are but the remnants of that ability and genius among us whom the accidents of education and opportunity have raised on the tidal waves of chance. We black folk are not altogether peculiar in this. After all, in the world at large, it is only the accident, the remnant, that gets the chance to make the most of itself; but if this is true of the white world it is infinitely more true of the colored world. It is not simply the great clear tenor of Roland Hayes that opened the ears of America. We have had many voices of all kinds as fine as his and America was and is as deaf as she was for years to him. Then a foreign land heard Hayes and put its imprint on him and immediately America with all its imitative snobbery woke up. We approved Hayes because London, Paris, and Berlin approved him and not simply because he was a great singer.

Thus is it the bounden duty of black America to begin this great work of the creation of beauty, of the preservation of beauty, of the realization of beauty, and we must use in this work all the methods that men have used before. And what have been the tools of the artist in times gone by? First of all, he has used the truth—not for the sake of truth, not as a scientist seeking truth, but as one upon whom truth eternally thrusts itself as the highest handmaid of imagination, as the one great vehicle of universal understanding. Again artists have used goodness—goodness in all its aspects of justice, honor, and right—not for sake of an ethical sanction but as the one true method of gaining sympathy and human interest.

The apostle of beauty thus becomes the apostle of truth and right not by choice but by inner and outer compulsion. Free he is but his freedom is ever bounded by truth and justice; and slavery only dogs him when he is denied the right to tell the truth or recognize an ideal of justice.

Thus all art is propaganda and ever must be, despite the wailing of the purists. I stand in utter shamelessness and say that whatever art I have for writing has been used always for propaganda for gaining the right of black folk to love and enjoy. I do not care a damn for any art that is not used for propaganda. But I do care when propaganda is confined to one side while the other is stripped and silent.

In New York we have two plays: *White Cargo* and *Congo*. In *White Cargo* there is a fallen woman. She is black. In *Congo* the fallen woman is white. In *White Cargo* the black woman goes down further and further and in *Congo* the white woman begins with degradation but in the end is one of the angels of the Lord.

You know the current magazine story: a young white man goes down to Central America and the most beautiful colored woman there falls in love with him. She crawls across the whole isthmus to get to him. The white man says nobly, "No." He goes back to his white sweetheart in New York.

In such cases, it is not the positive propaganda of people who believe white blood divine, infallible, and holy to which I object. It is the denial of a similar right to propaganda to those who believe black blood human, lovable, and inspired with new ideals for the world. White artists themselves suffer from this narrowing of their field. They cry for freedom in dealing with Negroes because they have so little freedom in dealing with whites. DuBose Heywood writes *Porgy* and writes beautifully of the black Charleston underworld. But why does he do this? Because he cannot do a similar thing for the white people of Charleston, or they would drum him out of town. The only chance he had to tell the truth of pitiful human degradation was to tell it of colored people. I should not be surprised if Octavius Roy Cohen had approached the Saturday Evening Post and asked permission to write about a different kind of colored folk than the monstrosities he has created; but if he has, the Post has replied, "No. You are getting paid to write about the kind of colored people you are writing about."

In other words, the white public today demands from its artists, literary and pictorial, racial pre-judgment which deliberately distorts truth and justice, as far as colored races are concerned and it will pay for no other.

On the other hand, the young and slowly growing black public still wants its prophets almost equally unfree. We are bound by all sorts of customs that have come down as second-hand soul clothes of white patrons. We are ashamed of sex and we lower our eyes when people will talk of it. Our religion holds us in superstition. Our worst side has been so shamelessly emphasized that we are denying we have or ever had a worst side. In all sorts of ways we are hemmed in and our new young artists have got to fight their way to freedom.

The ultimate judge has got to be you and you have got to build yourselves up into that wide judgment, that catholicity of temper which is going to enable the artist to have his widest chance for freedom. We can afford the truth. White folk today cannot. As it is now we are handing everything over to a white jury. If a colored man wants to publish a book, he has got to get a white publisher and a white newspaper to say it is great; and then you and I say so. We must come to the place where the work of art when it appears is reviewed and acclaimed by our own free and unfettered judgment. And we are going to have a real and valuable and eternal judgment only as we make ourselves free of mind, proud of body and just of soul to all men.

And then do you know what will be said? It is already saying. Just as soon as true art emerges; just as soon as the black artist appears, someone touches the race on the shoulder and says, "He, he was born here; he was trained here; he is not a Negro—what is a Negro anyhow? He is just human; it is the kind of thing you ought to expect."

I do not doubt that the ultimate art coming from black folk is going to be just as beautiful, and beautiful largely in the same ways, as the art that comes from white folk, or yellow, or red; but the point today is that until the art of the black folk compels recognition they will not be rated as human. And when through art they compel recognition then let the world discover if it will that their art is as new as it is old and as old as new.

I have a classmate once who did three beautiful things and died. One of them was a story of a folk who found fire and then went wandering in the gloom of night seeking again the stars they had once known and lost; suddenly out of blackness they looked up and there loomed the heavens; and what was it that they said? They raised a mighty cry: "It is the stars, it is the ancient stars, it is the young and everlasting stars!"

GENERAL COMMENTARY

DARWIN T. TURNER (ESSAY DATE 1974)

SOURCE: Turner, Darwin T. "W. E. B. Du Bois and the Theory of a Black Aesthetic." *Studies in the Literary Imagination* VII, no. 2 (fall 1974): 1-21.

In this essay, Turner examines Du Bois's struggles to define and institute a Black aesthetic and his frustration with the tendency of African American authors to emphasize the seamier side of the Black community and culture. According to Turner, Du Bois maintained that Black writers should use their art to advance the interests of their race as a whole.

During the past decade many black artists and critics began to insist that work by Afro-Americans must be created and evaluated according to a Black Aesthetic. That is, the work must be appropriate to Afro-American culture and people, and its excellence must be defined according to black people's concepts of beauty. In *The Crisis of the Negro Intellectual* (1967), Harold Cruse pointed to the need for a Black Aesthetic when he castigated Negro critics for failing to establish an appropriate perspective of the relationship of Negro art to Negro culture. Cruse accused critics of rejecting their own folk culture in order to adopt models and ideas devised and approved by whites. Thus, Cruse charged, most Negro critics ignored what should have been their major responsibility: to encourage and to determine standards for original ideas, methods, materials and styles derived from the unique character of black American culture. In even sharper tones today, such critics as Imamu Amiri Baraka, Larry Neal, Don L. Lee, Hoyt Fuller, and Addison Gayle, Jr.—to name only a few of the most prominent—insist that black artists must seek subjects, themes and styles within the culture of black folk, that they must use these materials for the benefit of black Americans, and that the resulting art must be evaluated according to criteria determined by black people.

Of course it is not new for a nation, race, or ethnic group to devise an individual aesthetic. To the contrary, a cursory view of the history of European, English, and American literature reveals such a kaleidoscope that one wonders how anyone could argue that only one aesthetic can exist or could deny that any group has a right to define its own aesthetic. An aesthetic, after all, is merely a judgment of what is beautiful according to the tastes of the judge. After determining what kinds of drama were preferred by cultivated Greeks, Aristotle propounded a standard for drama. If William Shakespeare had followed that aesthetic, he might have written excellent imitations of Greek drama, but he would not have created the melodramatic shatterings of unity that dismayed Augustan critics and delighted the Romantics. Dante and Chaucer taught readers to respect the beauty of their native languages. With scant regard for the beliefs of the subjects in question. Rudyard Kipling and James Fenimore Cooper prescribed criteria for determining the beauty in the character of a "good" native. Many people have found beauty in the political theories of Machiavelli or of John Locke, but few would argue that both theories derive from the same aesthetic. When Emerson, Melville and Whitman pronounced the need for an American literature, they were arguing for an American aesthetic for literature. Equally diversified standards of beauty could be revealed in a history of painting, music, philosophy, or any of the humanistic pursuits. The fact is that any group of people which feels its identity as a group shapes and defines its own aesthetic, which it is free to change in a subsequent generation or century.

It should not be surprising, therefore, that black Americans should insist upon a need of a Black Aesthetic; for, if their African ancestry has not always bound them together, they have nevertheless found identity as a group in their exclusion from certain prerogatives of American citizenship. What is surprising then is not the concept of a Black Aesthetic in literature but that, even before the Harlem "Renaissance," it was articulated distinctly by W. E. B. Du Bois, who has been identified disparagingly with the conservative literary practices of The Genteel Tradition and with the efforts of Negroes to become assimilated by separating themselves from the folk culture. Nevertheless, before the New Negro movement had been labeled, years before Langston Hughes insisted upon the right of new artists to express their individual dark-skinned selves without caring whether they pleased white or black audiences, W. E. B. Du Bois proposed a Black Aesthetic or—as I prefer to designate it in relation to Du Bois—a theory of art from the perspective of black Americans.

Du Bois did not clearly define or delimit his theory. Despite his sustained interest in art, Du Bois was a social scientist and a political leader who considered art—especially literature—to be a vehicle for enunciating and effecting social, political, and economic ideas. Therefore, he sketched literary theory rather than constructing it with the total concentration characteristic of one whose major concern is the art itself. Moreover, like other theorists, Du Bois sometimes experienced difficulty with the practical applications of his theories. For instance, although he first urged black writers to present life exactly as they saw it, he later feared that the writers were overemphasizing lurid aspects. Consequently, to correct what he considered an imbalance, he began to urge more conservative pictures of Negro life. One must admit also that Du Bois, unlike Wordsworth or T. S. Eliot, never created in his fiction, drama, and poetry the great work which would both illustrate and justify his literary theory.

Despite whatever weaknesses he may have revealed in definition or application, there is value in examining Du Bois' theory of black art—not only because it was of extreme importance to his efforts to create a strong and respected black population, but also because he was able to pronounce it from a prominent public platform during the Harlem "Renaissance," a significant moment in the development of literature by Afro-Americans. A more complete study should examine the relationships between Du Bois' theories and his own writing. And certainly a study should analyze the relationships between his theories and the work of black writers of the Renaissance. This paper, however, is restricted to an examination of Du Bois' theory of black art as he shaped it and applied it as editor of *The Crisis* through the height of the Renaissance to the mid-Depression moment at which his insistence on the importance of independent black institutions became one of the wedges to separate him from the National Association for the Advancement of Colored People.

In 1921, the dawning of a literary Renaissance might have been viewed in the historical research of Carter G. Woodson and the cultural history of Benjamin Brawley. Its rays may have been glimpsed in the popularity of the musical *Shuffle Along,* written by Miller, Lyles, Sissle and Blake or in the interest in black people displayed by such white writers as Ridgely Torrence and Eugene O'Neill.

By 1921, however, W. E. B. Du Bois had been working for many years as editor of *The Crisis* to promote literary activity and to foster racial pride through literature. As early as 1912 he had solicited manuscripts from and had published work by such previously unknown writers as Georgia Johnson, Fenton Johnson, and Jessie Fauset. In an editorial in 1920 he had recited his pride in the accomplishments of *The Crisis* and the need for a "renaissance of American Negro literature":

> Since its founding, THE CRISIS has been eager to discover ability among Negroes, especially in literature and art. It remembers with no little pride its covers by Richard Brown, William Scott, William Farrow, and Laura Wheeler; and its cartoons by Lorenzo Harris and Albert Smith; it helped to discover the poetry of Roscoe Jamison, Georgia Johnson, Fenton Johnson, Lucian Watkins, and Otto Bohanan; and the prose of Jessie Fauset and Mary Eflie Lee. Indeed, THE CRISIS has always preferred the strong matter of unknown names, to the platitudes of well-known writers; and by its Education and Children numbers, it has shown faith in the young.
>
> One colored writer, Claude McKay, asserts that we rejected one of his poems and then quoted it from Pearson's; and intimates that colored editors, in general, defer to white editors' opinions. This is of course, arrogant nonsense. But it does call our attention to the need of encouraging Negro writers. We have today all too few, for the reason that there is small market for their ideas among whites, and their energies are being called to other and more lucrative ways of earning a living. Nevertheless, we have literary ability and the race needs it. A renaissance of American Negro literature is due; the material about us in the strange, heart-rending race tangle is rich beyond dream and only we can tell the tale and sing the song from the heart.[1]

By 1921, Du Bois was inculcating pride in Afro-American children through his publication of *The Brownies' Book,* in which—writing as "The Crow"—he taught respect for the blackness of the crow.[2]

In a more characteristic manner, writing with the confidence which Alain Locke later identified with the "New Negro," Du Bois admonished Negroes to accept artistic presentations of the truth of Negro life. In **"Criteria of Negro Art,"** he wrote:

> We are so used to seeing the truth distorted to our despite, that whenever we are portrayed on canvas, in story or on the stage, as simple humans with human frailties, we rebel. We want everything said about us to tell of the best and highest and noblest in us. We insist that our Art and Propoganda be one.
>
> This is wrong and the end is harmful. We have a right, in our effort to get just treatment, to insist that we produce something of the best in human character and that it is unfair to judge us by our criminals and prostitutes. This is justifiable propaganda.
>
> On the other hand we face the truth of Art. We have criminals and prostitutes, ignorant and debased elements, just as all folks have. When the artist paints us he has a right to paint us whole and not ignore everything which is not as perfect as we would wish it to be. The black Shakespeare must portray his black Iago as well as his white Othello.
>
> We shrink from this. We fear that evil in us will be called racial, while in others it is viewed as individual. We fear that our shortcomings are not merely human but foreshadowing and threatenings of disaster and failure. The more highly trained we become the less we can laugh at Negro comedy—we will have it all tragedy and the triumph of dark Right over pale Villainy.
>
> The results are not merely negative—they are positively bad. With a vast wealth of human material about us, our own writers and artists fear to

> paint the truth lest they criticize their own and be in turn criticized for it. They fail to see the Eternal Beauty that shines through all Truth, and try to portray a world of stilted artificial black folk such as never were on land or sea.
>
> Thus, the white artist, looking in on the colored world, if he be wise and discerning, may often see the beauty, tragedy and comedy more truly than we dare.[3]

Admitting that some white writers, such as Thomas Dixon, might see only exaggerated evil in Negroes, Du Bois nevertheless insisted that blacks would survive any honest treatment of Afro-American life:

> We stand today secure enough in our accomplishment and self-confidence to lend the whole stern human truth about ourselves to the transforming hand and seeing eye of the Artist, white and black, and Sheldon, Torrence and O'Neill are our great benefactors—forerunners of artists who will yet arise in Ethiopia of the Outstretched Arm.[4]

Within the next two years the Renaissance of the New Negro produced its first literary works: *Shuffle Along* (1921) was enthusiastically received by a Broadway audience; Claude McKay and Jean Toomer created *Harlem Shadows* (1922) and *Cane* (1923); Willis Richardson's *The Chip Woman's Fortune* (1923) became the first serious play by an Afro-American to be staged on Broadway. Even during these early triumphs, however, Du Bois worried about a barrier which might obstruct the creation of honest black art—the prejudice of American audiences, who expected blacks to be "*bizarre* and unusual and funny for whites."[5]

In the same essay, written for a predominantly white audience rather than the more mixed audience of *The Crisis,* Du Bois' exploration of the possibilities for Negroes in the contemporary theater led him to more optimistic conclusions. If they could escape from the prejudiced expectations of white audiences, they could create strong Negro drama by emphasizing their blackness.

As evidence, Du Bois cited The Ethiopian Art Theatre's successful performances of *Salome, The Chip Woman's Fortune,* and *The Comedy of Errors a la Jazz.* Published statements by the company explained that Director Raymond O'Neill restrained the black performers from attempting to imitate the more inhibited white actors. Instead, he encouraged them "to develop their peculiar racial characteristics—the freshness and vigor of their emotional responses, their spontaneity and intensity of mood, their freedom from intellectual and artistic obsession."

Du Bois was even more pleased by the Ethiopian Players' selection of black subjects. Unintentionally paraphrasing William Dean Howell's earliest praise of Paul Laurence Dunbar, Du Bois insisted that blacks could make a distinctive contribution to American drama by interpreting black subjects. He did not oppose black actors who wished to demonstrate their ability to perform "white" roles for white audiences. Nor did he deny the usefulness of expanding the cultural awareness of black audiences by staging "white" plays for them. Of greatest importance, however, was the opportunity for black actors and writers to examine "their own terrible history of experience."

Black writers, he admitted, would develop slowly. The race needed to gain "something of that leisure and detachment for artistic work which every artist must have." As evidence that serious black dramatists were emerging despite their lack of leisure, he called attention to his own ***The Star of Ethiopia,*** a pageant commemorating blackness.

Wise men believe, Du Bois concluded, "that the great gift of the Negro to the world is going to be a gift to Art." The Ethiopian Players were significantly promoting awareness of this talent by beginning to peel from drama critics "the scales that blinded them for years to the beauty of Negro folk songs, that make them still deaf to the song of Negro singers and but half-alive to the growing Negro drama and the ringing Negro actor."

Even in less laudatory reviews, Du Bois thrilled to Negro writers who truthfully and seriously probed into problems of Afro-American life. Although he complained that Jean Toomer weakened *Cane* by too little knowledge of Georgia, excessive striving for artistic effect, dearth of feeling, and "much that is difficult or even impossible to understand," Du Bois boasted:

> The world of black folk will some day arise and point to Jean Toomer as a writer who first dared to emancipate the colored world from the conventions of sex. It is quite impossible for most Americans to realize how straight-laced and conventional thought is within the Negro World, despite the very unconventional acts of the group. Yet this contradiction is true. And Jean Toomer is the first of our writers to hurl his pen across the very face of our sex conventionality. . . . [His women are] painted with a frankness that is going to make his black readers shrink and criticize; and yet they are done with a certain splendid, careless truth.[6]

In 1925, writing for a predominantly white audience, Du Bois became the first significant critic to probe issues not fully resolved today, even though they are fundamental to the establishment of a Black Aesthetic: what is the difference between art by a Negro and Negro art? Or, what are the unique characteristics of Negro art?

Although he praised Henry O. Tanner, Charles W. Chesnutt, and William Stanley Braithwaite as artists, Du Bois denied that they had contributed significantly to American Negro art. American Negro art, he explained, was a group expression consisting of biographies written by slaves and by free blacks who had achieved

> . . . poetry portraying Negro life and aspirations, and activities, of essays on the "Negro Problem" and novels about the "Color Line" . . . pictures and sculptures meant to portray Negro features and characteristics, plays to dramatize the tremendous situation of the Negro in America, and, of course, . . . music.[7]

American Negro art "was built on the sorrow and strain inherent in American slavery, on the difficulties that sprang from Emancipation, on the feelings of revenge, despair, aspirations, and hatred which arose as the Negro struggled and fought his way upward" (53-54).

Whenever a mass of millions having such common memories and experiences are granted intellectual freedom and economic wealth, Du Bois explained, they will establish a school of art which, whether using new methods of art, will inevitably bring new content—a truth which is different from anything else in the world: "If this truth . . . is beautifully expressed and transformed from sordid fact into art it becomes, from its very origin, new, unusual, splendid" (54).

The uniqueness of Afro-American artistic expression had been revealed and discovered in "new music, new rhythm, new melody and poignant, even terrible, expressions of joy, sorrow, and despair." This new music was earning respect. Next to win recognition would be Negro literature, which presented "new phrases, new uses of words, experiences unthought of and unknown to the average white person." Creating "a distinct norm and a new set of human problems" (55), the new writers were impeded only by white readers' inability to understand the work and by black readers' stubborn demands for favorable propaganda. As the new artists matured, they would improve in thought and style. In the process of maturing, they would move from the wild music, laughter, and dancing of slavery into a more deliberate, purposeful, restrained, but true artistic expression.

The conclusion of Du Bois' magnificent effort to define Afro-American art betrays a weakness which gives a curious ambivalence to his criticism. He could identify the substance of that art but not the spirit. Whenever the spirit manifested itself in an exuberance which offended his temperament—his personal preference for decorum—Du Bois, wincing, felt compelled to excuse or denounce the work. Because he did not believe such wildness to be a characteristic inherent in the Afro-American psyche, he identified it, if genuine, as evidence of the manner in which slavery had distorted or repressed the psychological development of blacks. Just as often, he feared that the wildness was not a sincere expression of the artist but an effort to attract popularity from white critics by repeating the clichés about the character of black people. Unable to resolve this dilemma, which he failed to perceive as a dilemma, Du Bois at times seems a genteel anachronism as a critic during an era characterized by wildness of whites, as well as blacks. This was the gay Jazz Age of sheiks and flappers, raccoon coats and skirts that bared the knees, bootleg gin and speakeasies where one Charlestoned in shooting distance of well-known racketeers, "new" morality and trial marriages, free love and lurid front page headlines about the latest love-nest scandal. It was an era of youth, in which many whites, Freuding themselves from their Puritan inhibitions, enviously projected upon blacks the image of the primitive untroubled by the inhibitions of society. In such an era, it is not surprising that even a relatively sedate but young Countee Cullen atavistically boasted that his heart was "pagan-mad" and that the blood of blacks was hotter than that of whites. Not so for New-England-born, Harvard-trained W. E. B. Du Bois, who was fifty-seven-years old before Cullen published his first volume of poems. Quite simply, Du Bois knew that he was not pagan-mad; but he was Negro. Therefore, Negroes were not inherently pagan-mad. Therefore such wildness was not essential to, or desirable in, Negro life and art.

Instead one sought Beauty and Truth. In *The Crisis* of May 1925, Du Bois proclaimed a new editorial policy:

> We shall stress Beauty—all Beauty, but especially the beauty of Negro life and character; its music, its dancing, its drawing and painting and the new birth of its literature. This growth which *The Crisis* long since predicted is sprouting and coming to flower. We shall encourage it in every way . . . keeping the while a high standard of merit and never stooping to cheap flattery and misspent kindliness.

At the same time, Du Bois continued his demands that black readers accept realistic portraits:

> We are seriously crippling Negro art and literature by refusing to contemplate any but handsome heroes, unblemished heroines and flawless defenders, we insist on being always and everywhere

all right and often we ruin our cause by claiming too much and admitting no faults.[8]

As early as 1926, however, Du Bois' statements reveal the ambivalent sentiments or the inherent contradictions which have deceived critics who unsuspectingly have fixed Du Bois at one or another of his positions. In a complimentary review of *The New Negro* (1925), Du Bois wrote:

> With one point alone do I differ. . . . Mr. Locke has newly been seized with the idea that Beauty rather than Propaganda should be the object of Negro literature and art. His book proves the falseness of this thesis. This is a book filled and bursting with propaganda, but it is a propaganda for the most part beautiful and painstakingly done. . . .
>
> . . . If Mr. Locke's thesis is insisted upon too much it is going to turn the Negro Renaissance into decadence. It is the fight for Life and Liberty that is giving birth to Negro literature and art today and when, turning from this fight or ignoring it, the young Negro tries to do pretty things or things that catch the passing fancy of the really unimportant critics and publishers about him, he will find that he has killed the soul of Beauty in art.[9]

In the same issue of *The Crisis,* Du Bois, announcing the second annual Krigwa awards competition in literature and art, emphasized both his belief that Negro art must act as propaganda and his willingness to accept reflections of all avenues of Afro-American life:

> We want especially to stress the fact that while we believe in Negro art we do not believe in any art simply for art's sake. . . . We want Negro writers to produce beautiful things but we stress the things rather than the beauty. It is Life and Truth that are important and Beauty comes to make their importance visible and tolerable. . . .
>
> Write then about things as you know them. . . . In *The Crisis,* at least, you do not have to confine your writings to the portrayal of beggars, scoundrels and prostitutes; you can write about ordinary decent colored people if you want. On the other hand do not fear the Truth. . . . If you want to paint Crime and Destitution and Evil paint it. . . . Use propaganda if you want. Discard it and laugh if you will. But be true, be sincere, be thorough, and do a beautiful job.
>
> (115)

Undoubtedly, Du Bois remembered the dictum of John Keats that Beauty is Truth and Truth is Beauty. With whatever license is granted to a poet, however, Keats ignored any responsibility for explaining his meaning. More lucidity is generally required of a literary critic.

If one extracts the essence of Du Bois' instruction to black readers, his rebuttal of Locke's doctrine, and his exhortation to prospective contestants, one recognizes a general pronouncement that literature by blacks must be unflinchingly true to Afro-American life even in its pictures of the ugly and the unheroic. It also must be didactic and beautiful. Even viewed superficially, the proposition seems difficult to use as a touchstone for any single work of art.

The critical process is further complicated by Du Bois' failure to clarify his abstractions. Although he occasionally perceived the need, he never successfully defined Beauty in relation to material, thought, or method—perhaps because he presumed his taste to be characteristic of all people. In **"Criteria of Negro Art,"** a speech prepared for the 1926 Chicago Conference of the NAACP, Du Bois made his most detailed effort to resolve the question of the relation of beauty to Afro-American art; yet, in his initial premise, he reflected his assumption that his standards were the standards for all blacks—at least for all cultivated blacks. "Pushed aside as we have been in America," he wrote, "there has come to us not only a certain distaste for the tawdry and flamboyant but a vision of what the world could be if it were really a beautiful world." Du Bois continued:

> After all, who shall describe Beauty? What is it? I remember tonight four beautiful things: The Cathedral at Cologne, a forest in stone, set in light and changing shadow, echoing with sunlight and solemn song; a village of the Veys in West Africa, a little thing of mauve and purple, quiet, lying content and shining in the sun; a black and velvet room where on a throne rests, in old and yellowing marble, the broken curves of the Venus of Milo; a single phrase of music in the Southern South—utter melody, haunting and appealing, suddenly arising out of night and eternity, beneath the moon.[10]

Du Bois' rhetoric is persuasive. His emphasis is upon apparent catholicity of taste. Yet a question obtrudes. Does the beauty of the scene at Cologne depend upon the viewer's reaction to a particular style of architecture and a particular quality of song? Would Du Bois' sense of ultimate beauty in the scene have been marred if the music had not been "solemn song" but jazz?

Even if Du Bois had resolved questions about Beauty, he still would have failed to appreciate the complexity of Pilate's question. Du Bois perceived a difference between a black man's and a white man's awareness of the Truth of Negro life. But he failed to comprehend that black men themselves may differ in their visions of the Truth of Afro-American life. In consequence, whereas he rejected obviously idealized portraits as untrue, he often admitted bewilderment that young authors never wrote about the decent, hard working Negroes in their own families. Moreover, although he graciously urged young writers to describe the sordid if they wished, he soon suspected them of rejecting authentic pictures of low black life in favor of derogatory stereotypes.

I do not intend to demean Du Bois by suggesting that his definitions, criteria, and perceptions are inferior to those of other artists and critics still esteemed by many literary scholars. To the contrary, compared with others of his century—or any century—he fares well. His concept of Beauty certainly is as valid and as meaningful as Edgar Allan Poe's definition of poetry. Du Bois' assumption that his visions of Beauty and Truth were universally accepted is no more arrogant than Matthew Arnold's presumption that, from his preferences in poetry, he had acquired touchstones with which to measure the excellence of the poetry of any country. Instead of wishing to demean Du Bois, I merely suggest that, because he based his critical judgment on abstractions which were concrete to him but not necessarily to all other black contemporaries, the application of his theory to particular works of black writers sometimes resulted in appraisals significantly different from those of younger black artists, who shared their own perceptions of Beauty and Truth.

Significantly, although his interest in Beauty and Truth suggests a concern for "universal" values—a concept too often used to minimize the work of a black writer on a theme of black life, Du Bois' discussions of Beauty and Truth in literature always led him to a position strikingly comparable in spirit, if not always in detail, to that adopted by many current exponents of Black Arts: literature must serve a function for the good of black people, and its worth must be judged by black people.

He concluded his discussion of Beauty in **"Criteria of Negro Art"**:

> Thus it is the bounden duty of black America to begin this great work of the creation of Beauty, of the preservation of Beauty, of the realization of Beauty, and we must use in this work all the methods that men have used before. And what have been the tools of the artist in times gone by? First of all, he has used the Truth—not for the sake of truth, not as a scientist seeking truth, but as one upon whom Truth eternally thrusts itself as the highest handmaid of imagination, as the one great vehicle of universal understanding. Again artists have used Goodness—goodness in all its aspects of justice, honor and right—not for sake of an ethical sanction but as the one true method of gaining sympathy and human interest.
>
> The apostle of Beauty thus becomes the apostle of Truth and Right not by choice but by inner and outer compulsion. Free he is but his freedom is ever bounded by Truth and Justice; and slavery only dogs him when he is denied the right to tell the Truth or recognize an ideal of Justice.
>
> Thus all Art is propaganda and ever must be, despite the wailing of the purists. I stand in utter shamelessness and say that whatever art I have for writing has been used always for propaganda for gaining the right of black folk to love and enjoy. I do not care a damn for any art that is not used for propaganda.

And in rhetoric prophetic of a Black Aesthetic, he surged to a climax:

> . . . the young and slowly growing black public still wants its prophets almost equally unfree. We are bound by all sorts of customs that have come down as second-hand soul clothes of white patrons. We are ashamed of sex and we lower our eyes when people will talk of it. Our religion holds us in superstition. Our worst side has been so shamelessly emphasized that we are denying we have or ever had a worst side. In all sorts of ways we are hemmed in and our new young artists have got to fight their way to freedom.
>
> The ultimate judge has got to be you and you have got to build yourselves up into that wide judgment, that catholicity of temper which is going to enable the artist to have his widest chance for freedom. We can afford the Truth. White folk today cannot. As it is now we are handing everything over to a white jury. If a colored man wants to publish a book, he has got to get a white publisher and a white newspaper to say it is great; and then you and I say so. We must come to the place where the work of art when it appears is reviewed and acclaimed by our own free and unfettered judgment.[11]

Du Bois argued that young black writers were being diverted from their artistic responsibilities especially by the popularity of Carl Van Vechten's *Nigger Heaven,* which he denounced as "an affront to the hospitality of black folk (who admitted Van Vechten to their circles) and to the intelligence of white." In Du Bois' opinion the book was pernicious, not only because its commercial success persuaded blacks to pandel to white stereotypes of their life but also because it destroyed both Beauty and Truth:

> It is a caricature. It is worse than untruth because it is a mass of half-truths. . . . [To Van Vechten] the black cabaret is Harlem; around it all his characters gravitate. . . . Such a theory of Harlem is nonsense. The overwhelming majority of black folk there never go to cabarets. . . .
>
> Something they have which is racial, something distinctly Negroid can be found; but it is expressed by subtle, almost delicate nuance, and not by the wildly, [sic] barbaric drunken orgy in whose details Van Vechten revels. . . .
>
> Van Vechten is not the great artist who with remorseless scalpel probes the awful depths of life.

> To him there are no depths. It is the surface mud he slops about in. . . . Life to him is just one damned orgy after another, with hate, hurt, gin and sadism.
>
> Both Langston Hughes and Carl Van Vechten know Harlem cabarets; but it is Hughes who whispers,
>
> "One said he heard the jazz band sob
> When the little dawn was grey."
>
> Van Vechten never heard a sob in a cabaret. All he hears is noise and brawling.[12]

Earlier Du Bois had lamented the limitations of Dubose Heyward's *Porgy* because, by excluding educated Afro-American Charlestonians, it implied that the waterfront world was a total picture of black life in that city. Nevertheless, Du Bois now insisted that Porgy himself had a human and interesting quality absent from Van Vechten's characters.

How does one determine that a writer has created characters who are human as well as interesting? Can any reader truly determine whether an author has delineated degraded characters with compassion or has exploited them?

Du Bois could not find answers to these questions. Perhaps his orientation to scientific research persuaded him that sincerity can be measured. Or perhaps, more concerned with other matters, he did not even consider the questions fully; the theory was clear to him at least. A black should write honestly about the Afro-Americans he knew. So created, a work would sparkle with Truth and Beauty. It would be useful black literature. If, however, the writer seemed excessively absorbed with cabaret life, Du Bois was prepared to impale him with the pen reserved for those who dished up black humanity piping hot to a slobbering white public.

Even if he did not fully examine questions needed to clarify his own criteria of art, Du Bois nevertheless quickly sensed a possible weakness in his efforts to propagandize for the race by encouraging young blacks to write about themselves. What if, for the sake of publication, they all began to imitate Van Vechten?

Earlier in 1926, Du Bois had initiated a symposium on **"The Negro in Art."** He asked various authors and publishers to consider several questions:

> Are writers under obligations or limitations as to the kinds of characters they portray? Should authors be criticized for painting the best or the worst characters of a group? Can publishers be criticized for failing to publish works about educated Negroes? What can Negroes do if they are continually painted at their worst? Should Negroes be portrayed sincerely and sympathetically? Isn't the literary emphasis upon sordid, foolish and criminal Negroes persuading readers that this is the truth and preventing authors from writing otherwise? Is there danger that young colored writers will follow the popular trend?[13]

The overlapping questions reveal Du Bois' basic concern: is the literary world conspiring to typify Negroes by sordid, foolish, and criminal characters? And if so, what can be done to prevent that?

Some of the responses by whites must have confirmed Du Bois' worst fears. Carl Van Vechten bluntly stated that the squalor and vice of Negro life *would* be overdone "for a very excellent reason." Such squalor and vice offer "a wealth of novel, exotic, picturesque material." He discounted pictures of wealthy, cultured Negroes as uninteresting because they were virtually identical with those of whites, a pronouncement which validates Du Bois' convictions about Van Vechten's superficiality. The only thing for the black writer to do, Van Vechten concluded, was to exploit the vice and squalor before the white authors did.[14]

Henry Mencken chided blacks for failing to see the humor in the derogatory caricatures created by Octavius Cohen. Instead of applying scientific criteria to art, he added, blacks should write works ridiculing whites.[15] Mencken did not explain who would publish the caricatures of whites.

Another white author, John Farrar, shrugged off the stories of Octavius Cohen with the admission that they amused him immensely and seemed not to libel Negroes. In contrast, although he confessed scant knowledge of the South, he thought Walter White's novel *The Fire in the Flint* "a trifle onesided."[16] William Lyons Phelps mildly admonished Negroes to correct false impressions by setting good examples in their lives.[17] Having no answers but more questions, Sinclair Lewis proposed a conference to consider the issues. He also suggested establishing a club for blacks—at a small hotel in Paris.[18]

Sherwood Anderson reminded *The Crisis* that he had lived among Negro laborers, whom he had found to be "about the sweetest people I know," as he had said sometimes in his books. In short, he wrote, Negroes were worrying too much and being too sensitive; they had no more reason to complain about their portraits in literature than whites would have.[19] Julia Peterkin asserted that Irish and Jewish people were not offended by caricatures, so Negroes should not be. She used the occasion to praise the "Black Negro Mammy" and to chastize Negroes for protesting against a proposal in Congress to erect a monument to the Mammy.[20]

Such responses probably did not surprise Du Bois, but they strengthened his conviction that black writers must fight for their race. Even the sympathetic white writers revealed flaws. For example, Paul Green's Pulitzer Prize winning play, *In Abraham's Bosom,* impressed Du Bois as an example of "the defeatist genre of Negro art which is so common. . . . The more honestly and sincerely a white artist looks at the situation of the Negro in America the less is he able to consider it in any way bearable and therefore his stories and plays must end in lynching, suicide or degeneracy."[21] Du Bois added that, even if such a writer learned differently by observing black people's refusal to accept failure, the publisher or producer would prohibit a portrayal of triumphant blacks. Pathetic, inevitable defeat or exotic degeneracy—these would be the dominant images of black life unless black writers corrected the images.

In April, 1927, while announcing the annual competition in literature and art, Du Bois reminded his readers of the impressive black heritage revealed in the fine arts of Ethiopia, Egypt, and the rest of Africa. In contemporary America, he insisted, that heritage must be continued in the art of spoken and written word. It must not be restrained by the white person's desire for silly and lewd entertainment; it must not be blocked by the black person's revulsion from unfavorable images. "The Negro artist must have freedom to wander where he will, portray what he will, interpret whatever he may see according to the great canons of beauty which the world through long experience has laid down."[22] Du Bois was beginning to sound like his future son-in-law Countee Cullen. He would now accept anything black writers wanted to do if only they did it beautifully, but he was no more specific about his concept of Beauty.

When James Weldon Johnson published *God's Trombones* (1927), Du Bois rejoiced at Johnson's preservation of the Negro idiom in art, Johnson's beautiful poetry, and Aaron Douglass' wild, beautiful, unconventional, daring drawings, which were stylized to emphasize Negroid rather than Caucasian features of the black figures.[23]

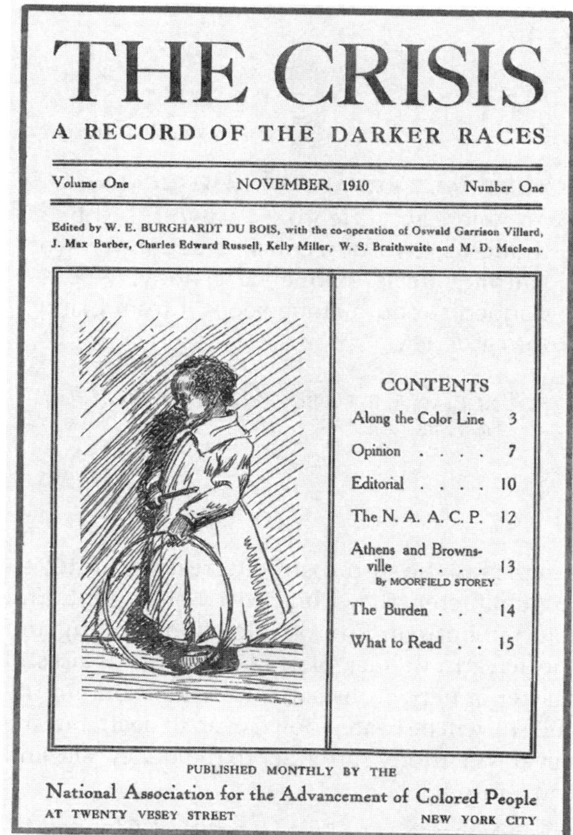

THE CRISIS

A RECORD OF THE DARKER RACES

Volume One — NOVEMBER, 1910 — Number One

Edited by W. E. BURGHARDT DU BOIS, with the co-operation of Oswald Garrison Villard, J. Max Barber, Charles Edward Russell, Kelly Miller, W. S. Braithwaite and M. D. Maclean.

CONTENTS

PUBLISHED MONTHLY BY THE
National Association for the Advancement of Colored People
AT TWENTY VESEY STREET — NEW YORK CITY

The Crisis: A Record of the Darker Races, edited by W. E. B. Du Bois.

But works by whites continued to disappoint him even when they were sufficiently good to be recommended to his readers. His praise of *Congaree Sketches* by E. C. L. Adams was dampened by what he felt to be a significant omission:

> even to the lowest black swamp peasant there are the three worlds ever present to his imagination: his own, the world of the risen black man and the world of white folks. No current folk lore can omit any one of these and be true, complete and, therefore . . . artistic.[24]

In the entire collection, Du Bois complained, he found not one allusion to the rising black man characterized by ambition, education, and aspiration to better earthly things.

In 1928, black writers provided Du Bois with examples which he used to illustrate his concept of the difference between praiseworthy black literature and atrocious black literature. He hailed Nella Larsen's *Quicksand* as a "fine, thoughtful and courageous novel," the best by any black writer since Chesnutt.[25] Subtly comprehending the curious cross currents swirling about black

FROM THE AUTHOR

THE DUALITY OF AFRICAN AMERICANS

An American, a Negro . . . two souls, two thoughts, two unreconciled strivings; two warring ideals in one dark body, whose dogged strength alone keeps it from being torn asunder.

SOURCE: W. E. B. Du Bois, from *The Souls of Black Folk,* McClurg, 1903.

Americans, the author, he felt, created an interesting character, fitted her into a close plot, and rejected both an improbable happy ending and the defeatist theme: "Helga Crane sinks at last still master of her whimsical, unsatisfied soul. In the end she will be beaten down even to death but she never will utterly surrender to hypocricy [sic] and convention."

In contrast, Du Bois stated that Claude McKay's *Home to Harlem* was a shameful novel, redeemed only by the fact that the author was "too great a poet to make any complete failure in writing." Du Bois noted virtues in the work: the beautiful, fascinating changes on themes of the beauty of colored skins; McKay's emphasis upon the fact that Negroes are physically and emotionally attracted to other Negroes rather than to whites; and the creation of Jake and Ray, interesting and appealing characters. Despite these commendably perceptive insights into black life, Du Bois argued, *Home to Harlem* pandered to white people's enjoyment of Negroes portrayed in

> that utter licentiousness which conventional civilization holds white folk back from enjoying—if enjoyment it can be called. That which a certain decadent section of the white American world, centered particularly in New York, longs for with fierce and unrestrained passions, it wants to see written out in black and white and saddled on black Harlem. . . . [McKay] has used every art and emphasis to paint drunkenness, fighting, lascivious sexual promiscuity and utter absence of restraint in as bold and as bright colors as he can. . . . Whole chapters . . . are inserted with no connection to the main plot, except that they are on the same dirty subject. As a picture of Harlem life or of Negro life anywhere, it is, of course, nonsense. Untrue, not so much on account of its facts but on account of its emphasis and glaring colors.

Between the levels of *Quicksand* and *Home to Harlem,* Du Bois placed Rudolph Fisher's *The Walls of Jericho.* Fearful that casual readers would draw from it only echoes of Van Vechten and McKay, Du Bois stressed the psychological validity of the two working-class black people who are the focus of the major plot. The book's weaknesses were the excessive sophistication and unreality of the background and such minor characters as Jinx and Bubber, who speak authentically but do not seem as human as the major figures. But, Du Bois continued in bewilderment, Fisher "has not depicted Negroes like his mother, his sister, his wife, his real Harlem friends. He has not even depicted his own soul. The glimpses of better class Negroes are ineffective make-believes."[26] Why, Du Bois asked. Hearing no answer, he concluded with the hope that Fisher's novel was an indication of black novelists' movement upward from Van Vechten and McKay.

Despite his frequent attacks upon white authors' distortions of black life and black people, Du Bois did not contend that white Americans could never portray blacks successfully. Exceptions occurred: Paul Green wrote sincerely even though he belabored the defeatist theme; the E. C. L. Adams book, *Nigger to Nigger,* was a sincere attempt to collect and present the philosophy of black peasants. Nevertheless, such exceptions did not relieve his skepticism:

> I assume that the white stranger cannot write about black people. In nine cases out of ten I am right. In the tenth case, and Du Bose Heywood [sic] is the tenth case, the stranger can write about the colored people whom he knows; but those very people whom he knows are sometimes so strange to me, that I cannot for the life of me make them authentic.[27]

In the waning moments of the Renaissance, Du Bois seemed increasingly reluctant to castigate an Afro-American writer except when that writer rejected his blackness. For example, although he had previously objected to Wallace Thurman for glib, superficial comments on black life and culture, Du Bois, when reviewing *The Blacker the Berry,* merely remonstrated with Thurman for not believing his thesis:

> The story of Emma Lou calls for genius to develop it. It needs deep psychological knowledge and pulsing sympathy. And above all, the author must believe in black folk, and in the beauty of black as a color of human skin. I may be wrong, but it does not seem to me that this is true of Wallace Thurman. He seems to me himself to deride blackness. . . .

> It seems that this inner self-despising of the very thing that he is defending, makes the author's defense less complete and sincere.[28]

Du Bois' review of Marc Connelly's *Green Pastures* (1930) was a peroration of what he had tried to teach to readers, writers, and critics during the decade:

> All art is propaganda, and without propaganda there is no true art. But, on the other hand, all propaganda is not art. . . . If a person portrays ideal Negro life, the sole judgment of its success is whether the picture is a beautiful thing. . . . If he caricatures Negro life, and makes it sordid and despicable, the critic's criterion is . . . solely, is the idea well presented? . . . The difficulty with the Negro on the American stage, is that the white audience . . . demands caricatures, and the Negro, on the other hand, either cringes to the demand because he needs the pay, or bitterly condemns every Negro book or show that does not paint colored folk at their best. Their criticisms should be aimed at the incompleteness of art expression—at the embargo which white wealth lays on full Negro expression—and a full picturing of the Negro soul.[29]

In the early years of the 1930's, while America floundered in an economic depression, it was clear that night had fallen on the heyday of the Harlem Renaissance. If Afro-Americans—intelligentsia, artists, and workers alike—were not cast out, they were at least ignored by a huge republic trying to pull itself erect. As Du Bois re-examined the position of blacks in America during those troubled times, he re-evaluated his own ideas about the appropriate course for his people. For a decade, from a platform within an integrated and pro-integrationist NAACP, he had argued that black writers must do things for black people and must be judged by black people. Now he extended that concept of black independence and black control to the entire spectrum of black existence in America: black people must develop and control strong black institutions for the good of black people. Coming as it did from the pages of the voice of the NAACP, and from a man whom white supremacists had vilified as the chief advocate of integration, the idea probably was even more startling when Du Bois expressed it in the 1930's than when, a quarter of a century later, Stokely Carmichael re-introduced it tersely as "Black Power."

Although Du Bois seemed unable to convert those who immediately attacked his position, he tried repeatedly to explain the logic which guided him to a seemingly inescapable conclusion. Personally, he still believed the best society to be an integrated one—a fact which should be obvious to anyone who remembered that, for more than twenty-five years, he had dedicated himself to effecting the full integration of blacks into American society. Despite his private desires, however, he was compelled to admit a bitter truth:

> . . . that we are segregated, apart, hammered into a separate unity by spiritual intolerance and legal sanction backed by mob law, . . . that this separation is growing in strength and fixation; that it is worse today than a half-century ago and that no character, address, culture, or desert is going to change it in one day or for centuries to come.[30]

In such a deplorable circumstance, it is futile to pretend that one is simply an American: one must recognize that he is a Negro. It is pointless to argue that there is no such creature as an American Negro when twelve million human beings are identified and treated as Negroes. It is senseless to continue to debate whether or not segregation is desirable; segregation is a fact. In such a circumstance, the only matter for American Negroes to debate is what they can do to prevent their genocide. The solution, he explained, was to "carefully plan and guide our segregated life, organize in industry and politics to protect it and expand it and above all to give it unhampered spiritual expression in art and literature." (177)

A step which blacks could take immediately was to make their institutions more serviceable by concentrating on their true purpose. That is, as one could no longer deny the fact of being Negro, so it was absurd to pretend that a Negro college was just another American college. It must be recognized as a Negro institution:

> A Negro university in the United States of America begins with Negroes. It uses that variety of English idiom which they understand; and above all, it is founded on a knowledge of the history of their people in Africa and in the United States, and their present condition . . . then it asks how shall these young men and women be trained to earn a living and live a life under the circumstances in which they find themselves.
>
> (175)

Beginning with such a premise, he explained, the Negro university would expand from the examination of black life, history, social development, science, and humanities into a study of all life and matter in the universe. The study must begin with a focus on black people, and it must continue from the perspective of black people. This is not merely the best route, it is the only route to universality.

In the antithesis of this theory, Du Bois found reasons for his failure to bring about the kind of literary Renaissance of which he had dreamed—one in which honest, artistic literary works about blacks by blacks would be bought and read by blacks. Such a Renaissance never took root, he now argued; the so-called "Renaissance" failed

> because it was a transplanted and exotic thing. It was a literature written for the benefit of white people and at the behest of white readers, and starting out privately from the white point of view. It never had a real Negro constituency and it did not grow out of the inmost heart and frank experience of Negroes; on such an artificial basis no real literature can grow.
>
> (176)

By the time he published ***Dusk of Dawn*** seven years later, Du Bois had practiced his theory. After severing connections with the NAACP, Du Bois had returned to Atlanta University to help develop a strong black institution. Although he was less interested in explaining artistic theory than he had been earlier, his brief summation in ***Dusk of Dawn*** roots him firmly in a Black Aesthetic and identifies him, more clearly than any previous statement, as a progenitor of a Black Arts movement. Creative art, he stated, was essential to the development and transmission of new ideas among blacks:

> The communalism of the African clan can be transferred to the Negro American group. . . . The emotional wealth of the American Negro, the nascent art in song, dance and drama can all be applied, not to amuse the white audience, but to inspire and direct the acting Negro group itself. I can conceive no more magnificent or promising crusade in modern times.[31]

To achieve this end, black people must be re-educated in educational institutions oriented to black people:

> There has been a larger movement on the part of the Negro intelligentsia toward racial grouping for the advancement of art and literature. There has been a distinct plan for reviving ancient African art through an American Negro art movement, and more specially a thought to use the extremely rich and colorful life of the Negro in America and elsewhere as a basis for painting, sculpture, and literature. This has been partly nullified by the fact that if these new artists expect support for their art from the Negro group itself, that group must be deliberately trained and schooled in art appreciation and in willingness to accept new canons of art and in refusal to follow the herd instinct of the nation.
>
> (202)

In two decades of conscious and unconscious questing for a Black Aesthetic, W. E. B. Du Bois experienced many difficulties in shaping and applying an idea which, he sensed, was sound. Some of the difficulties resulted from his personal limitations: his failure to clarify criteria, his dependence upon undefined abstractions, his inability to harmonize his awareness of the utilitarian value of literature for a specific group with his concern for the creation of Truth and Beauty, his fallacious assumption that his aesthetic was necessarily the aesthetic of most black people. Perhaps the major reason for his lack of success, however, is that, with this idea as with many others, Du Bois was twenty-five to fifty years ahead of those twelve million blacks he wanted to lead from self-respect to pride to achievement.

Today, a Black Arts movement exists; and, many black writers and educators are seriously defining the dimensions of a Black Aesthetic. Even today, however, when one considers the work of some self-identified Black Arts dramatists and poets who picture only the vice, squalor, contemptibility, and failure of black communities, one imagines Du Bois, in some afterworld he could not envision, muttering unhappily, "No. No. No! Will they never understand? To be black is to be beautiful and strong and proud."

Notes

1. Du Bois, "Negro Writers," *The Crisis,* 19 (April 1920), 298-99.
2. Elinor D. Sinette, "The Brownies' Book," *Freedomways,* 5 (Winter 1965), 138-39.
3. Du Bois, "Negro Art," *The Crisis,* 21 (June 1921), 55-56.
4. "Negro Art," p. 56.
5. Du Bois, "Can the Negro Serve the Drama?" *Theatre* (July 1923), pp. 16-22.
6. Du Bois, "The Younger Literary Movement," *The Crisis,* 27 (February 1924), 161-62. Du Bois probably did not know that Toomer had spent less than a month in Georgia.
7. "The Social Origins of American Negro Art," *Modern Quarterly,* 3 (Autumn 1925), 53ff. Subsequent references will appear parenthetically in the text. It is easy to understand Du Bois' exclusion of Tanner, who did not paint Negro subjects, and Braithwaite, who consciously avoided poetic themes which would identify him as Negro. It is more difficult to explain Du Bois' rejection of Chestnutt. In *The Marrow of Tradition* ([Boston: Houghton, Mifflin,] 1901), at least, Chesnutt wrote about discrimination with a violence which provoked screams of anguish from Southern white reviewers. Perhaps Du Bois' judgment was influenced by the fact that for many years Chesnutt's racial identity was concealed by the editors of *The Atlantic,* in which his stories were printed. The matter seems especially ironic when one recalls that Chesnutt's daughter, in a biography, stated that her father began writing fiction because he believed that there was a need for Negroes to interpret the lives and problems of Negroes.
8. *The Crisis,* 30 (May 1925), 8.
9. *The Crisis,* 31 (January 1926), 141.

10. "Criteria of Negro Art," *The Crisis,* 32 (October 1926), 292.

11. "Criteria of Negro Art," pp. 296-97.

12. "Books," *The Crisis,* 32 (December 1926), 81-82.

13. *The Crisis,* 31 (February 1926), 165.

14. "The Negro in Art," *The Crisis,* 31 (March 1926), 219.

15. "The Negro in Art," pp. 219-20.

16. *The Crisis,* 32 (April 1926), 280.

17. *The Crisis,* 32 (April 1926) 280.

18. *The Crisis,* 32 (May 1926), 36.

19. *The Crisis,* 32 (May 1926), 36.

20. *The Crisis,* 32 (September 1926), 238-39.

21. *The Crisis,* 34 (March 1927), 12.

22. *The Crisis,* 34 (April 1927), 70.

23. *The Crisis,* 34 (July 1927), 159.

24. *The Crisis,* 34 (September 1927), 227.

25. *The Crisis,* 35 (June 1928), 202.

26. *The Crisis,* 35 (November 1928), 374.

27. *The Crisis,* 36 (April 1929), 125.

28. *The Crisis,* 36 (July 1929), 249-50.

29. *The Crisis,* 37 (May 1930), 162.

30. "The Negro College," *The Crisis,* 40 (August 1933), 177. Subsequent references will appear parenthetically.

31. *The Dusk of Dawn, an essay toward an autobiography of a race concept* (New York: Harcourt, 1940), p. 219. Subsequent references will appear parenthetically.

WILSON J. MOSES (ESSAY DATE 1975)

SOURCE: Moses, Wilson J. "The Poetics of Ethiopianism: W. E. B. Du Bois and Literary Black Nationalism." *American Literature* XLVII, no. 3 (November 1975): 411-26.

In the essay below, Moses traces the themes of Ethiopianism—the belief in the eventual decline of the West and the rise of Africa—in Du Bois's writing, particularly his poetry. Moses suggests that Du Bois attempted to use the power of myth to fulfill the promise of racial advancement that social science had failed to achieve.

Du Bois's position with respect to Black Nationalism has been described as ambivalent, reflecting his admitted double-consciousness as both a black man and an American, his "two souls, two thoughts, two unreconciled strivings; two warring ideals in one dark body."[1] This often-quoted line registers the double-consciousness manifested in the thought of many Afro-Americans, and, indeed, many Western intellectuals who have attempted to be at once culturally nationalistic, and yet loyal to a more broadly conceived "Western Civilization." Du Bois's early work struggles to fuse two complementary but substantially different mythological traditions. The first of these is "Ethiopianism," a literary-religious tradition common to English-speaking Africans, regardless of nationality.[2] The other is the European tradition of interpretive mythology, transplanted to America by its European colonizers.

The "Ethiopian" tradition sprang organically out of certain shared political and religious experiences of English-speaking Africans during the late eighteenth and early nineteenth centuries. It found expression in the slave narratives, in the exhortations of conspiratorial slave preachers, and in the songs and folklore of the slaves of the Old and the peasants of the New South.[3] On a more literary level, it appeared in the sermons and political tracts of the sophisticated urban elite. The name "Ethiopianism" is assigned to this tradition because early black writers and even some of their white allies often referred to an inspiring Biblical passage, "Princes shall come out of Egypt; Ethiopia shall soon stretch out her hands unto God" (Psalms, 68:31). The verse was seen by some as a prophecy that Africa would "soon" be saved from the darkness of heathenism, and it came to be interpreted as a promise that Africa would "soon" experience a dramatic political, industrial, and economic renaissance. Others have insisted that the real meaning of the scripture is that some day the black man will rule the world. Such a belief is still common among older black folk today.

The "Ethiopian" prophecy seems to have been commonly known among free black people before the Civil War. In 1858, the African Civilization Society quoted the full verse in its constitution, along with an interpretation by Henry Highland Garnet. According to Garnet Ethiopia would "soon stretch forth her hands,"—"soon" meaning shortly after the work was taken up. The responsibility for seeing to it that the prophecy was fulfilled rested upon the Africans themselves. The signers of the constitution included the leading black nationalists of the day, among them, Daniel Alexander Payne, a bishop of the African Methodist Episcopal Church, and Robert Hamilton, who was later to found *The Anglo-African Magazine.*[4] The quotation appeared in any number of documents published by free Africans in the northern states, and it seems unlikely that many literate free Africans were unfamiliar with it.[5]

At times the verse was directly quoted; at times it was referred to thematically. An early eloquent articulation of the Ethiopian theme was made by Alexander Crummell, an Episcopal priest, who eventually inspired Du Bois.[6] Crummell often used the direct quotation in sermons; but sometimes, as in his 1846 *Eulogium on the Life and Character of Thomas Clarkson,* the reference was indirect:

> Amid the decay of nations a rekindled light starts up in us. Burdens under which others expire, seem to have lost their influence upon us; and while *they* are "driven to the wall" destruction keeps far from us its blasting hand. We live in the region of death, yet seem hardly mortal. We cling to life in the midst of all reverses; and our nerveful grasp thereon cannot easily be relaxed. History reverses its mandates in our behalf—our dotage is in the past. "Time writes not its wrinkles on our brow."[7]

Another example of this indirect "Ethiopianism" was Daniel Alexander Payne's oration "To the Colored People of the United States," delivered in 1862 as the Civil War approached what seemed to Payne a climax of apocalyptic proportions.

> It is said that he is the God of the white man, and not of the black. This is horrible blasphemy—a *lie* from the pit that is bottomless—believe it not—no—never. Murmur not against the Lord on account of the cruelty and injustice of man. His almighty arm is already stretched out against slavery—against every man, every constitution, and every union that upholds it. His avenging chariot is now moving over the bloody fields of the doomed south, crushing beneath its massive wheels the very foundations of the blasphemous system. Soon slavery shall sink like Pharaoh—even like the brazen-hearted tyrant, it shall sink to rise no more forever.[8]

The theme also appeared in verse, as in Francis Ellen Watkins Harper's "Ethiopia,"

> Yes, Ethiopia yet shall stretch
>   Her bleeding hands abroad;
> Her cry of agony shall reach
>   Up to the throne of God.[9]

Paul Laurence Dunbar's "Ode to Ethiopia," addressed not to Ethiopia the nation but to the "Mother Race," recounted the past and present struggles of the Afro-Americans and predicted their future triumph:

> Go on and up! Our souls and eyes
> Shall follow thy continuous rise;
>   Our ears shall list thy story
> From bards who from thy root shall spring
> And proudly tune their lyres to sing
>   Of Ethiopia's glory.[10]

Thus the Rising Africa Theme became a tradition of reinterpreting the Biblical passage to speak to the experiences of the Anglo-African peoples. But "Rising Africa" is only one aspect of "Ethiopianism"; the balancing theme looks to the Decline of the West. The rise in the fortunes of Africa and all her scattered children would be accompanied by God's judgment upon the Europeans. A powerful expression of this belief occurred in *David Walker's Appeal,* published in 1829. In this volume, one of those forgotten American classics nonetheless well known in its time, and a book of importance to the legal and intellectual history of the United States, Walker warned of the impending doom of Western civilization. It would come as a judgment upon Christian sin in enslaving the Africans.[11] "I tell you Americans! that unless you speedily alter your course, *you* and your Country are gone!!!"[12]

"Ethiopianism," with its two thematic components, Rising Africa and Decline of the West, provided one element of Anglo-African literary tradition on which Du Bois mythmaking is based. Here is a typical example of a poem in the Ethiopian tradition. It was published in the tenth Atlanta University Publication in 1905, over a pseudonym, "The Moon."[13] Probably Du Bois, who edited the Atlanta publications and also edited a periodical called *The Moon* was the author:

> "Ethiopia, my little daughter, why hast thou lingered and loitered in the Sun? See thy tall sisters, pale and blue of eye—see thy strong brothers, shrewd and slippery haried—see what they have done! Behold their gardens and their magic, their halls and wonder wheels! Behold their Gold, Gold, Gold!"
>
> "Flowers, O Mother Earth, I bring flowers, and the echo of a Song's song. Aye and the blue violet Humility, the mystic image flower of Heaven. And Mother, sweet Mother, in these great and misty years, I have seen Sights and heard Voices; Stories and Songs are quick within me—If I have loitered, sun-kissed, O forgive me, Mother yet chide me not bitterly—I too have lived."

The typically "Ethiopian" element of this poem is its assumption that Caucasians and Ethiopians are separate varieties of humanity with distinct destinies competing for honor in the eyes of history and the world. The characters of this poem represent historical forces, not real human beings. The argument is that Africans are a special people with special gifts and that blacks are in some ways superior to whites. To the African genius are attributed such traits as tropical dreaminess, feminine aestheticism, and a childlike love of nature. The Europeans of the first stanza are assigned their own traditional qualities by the use of such words as "pale," "strong," "shrewd," and "slippery."

The dreamy little Ethiopia is a minor avatar of the sleeping titaness who looms in "The Riddle of the Sphinx":[14]

> Dark Daughter of the lotus leaves that watch the
> Southern Sea!
> Wan spirit of a prisoned soul a-panting to be
> free!
> The muttered music of thy streams, the
> whisper of the deep,
> Have kissed each other in God's name and
> kissed a world to sleep.

This woman is a personification of Africa, a sleeping world, a giantess, raped by pygmies while she sleeps. "The burden of white men bore her back and the white world stifled her sighs." The poet describes the ascendancy of the West, based upon Mediterranean culture, and predicts its eventual going under:

> down
> down
> deep down,
> Till the devil's strength be shorn,
> Till some dim, darker David, a-hoeing of his
> corn,
> And married maiden, mother of God,
> Bid the black Christ be born!

In summary, Ethiopianism may be defined as the effort of the English-speaking Black or African person to view his past enslavement and present cultural dependency in terms of the broader history of civilization. It serves to remind him that this present scientific technological civilization, dominated by Western Europe for a scant four hundred years, will go under certainly—like all the empires of the past. It expresses the belief that the tragic racial experience has profound historical value, that it has endowed the African with moral superiority and made him a seer. Du Bois's poetry, while highly original, is nonetheless a product of this tradition, and therefore traditional. T. S. Eliot's poetry, by way of comparison, works within the European tradition of interpretive mythology although it is clearly innovative.

European interpretive mythology is the second of the two traditions basic to Du Bois's mythmaking. In *The Survival of the Pagan Gods,* a study of classical mythology in the Renaissance, Jean Seznec discusses the medieval practice of examining Greco-Roman mythology with the intention of either discovering within it, or assigning to it, Christian meaning.[15] He discusses the ancient origins of this practice among the pre-Christian Greeks and Romans, who, attempting to understand the meanings of stories that were already very old, developed theories of interpretation in order to render myths intelligible. This tradition, once revived in the Middle Ages, endured throughout the Renaissance, and as Douglas Bush has shown, became a mode functional to English and American poetry.[16]

How can it be known that Du Bois was aware of the tradition of interpretive mythology and that he consciously wrote in this tradition? In Chapter VIII of ***The Souls of Black Folk,*** in the section titled **"Of the Quest of the Golden Fleece,"** Du Bois demonstrated his awareness of this kind of writing and his desire to experiment with it:

> Have you ever seen a cotton-field white with harvest,—its golden fleece hovering above the black earth like a silvery cloud edged with dark green, its bold white signals waving like foam of billows from Carolina to Texas across that Black and human Sea? I have sometimes half-suspected that here the winged ram Chrysomallus left that Fleece after which Jason and his Argonauts went vaguely wandering into the shadowy East three thousand years ago; and certainly one might frame a pretty and not far-fetched analogy of witchery and dragon's teeth, and blood and armed men, between the ancient and the modern Quest of the Golden Fleece in the Black Sea.[17]

In an earlier chapter of the same book, **"Of the Wings of Atalanta,"** Du Bois had demonstrated his skill at updating mythology and adapting it to the needs of his times. ***The Quest of the Silver Fleece,*** in 1911, brought to maturity the ideas briefly outlined in the parent essay.[18] In this novel he created a universe in which the ideology of progressive socialism and the traditionalism of Christian black nationalism work harmoniously within the framework of a Greek myth.

The Quest of the Silver Fleece is a story of witchcraft and voodoo magic. Zora, the heroine of the tale, makes her first appearance as an elfin child, personifying the supposedly preternatural traits of the primitive mind. "We black folks is got the *spirit,*" she says. White folk may think they rule, but, "We'se lighter and cunninger; we fly right through them; we go and come again just as we wants to."[19] Elspeth, the mother of Zora, is a malevolent black witch, who sows a wondrous cotton crop in a scene reminiscent of Cadmus's planting the dragon's teeth.[20] The cotton crop is first stolen by the aristocratic Cresswell family, then woven into a wedding dress, and perhaps it is the magic of Medea (Elspeth-Zora) that begins to eat away at the vitality of Cresswell's bride.[21] By the end of the story, Zora matures from elf-child to Ethiopian queen, who appears as a haunting "mirage of other days," ensconced in a "setting of rich, barbaric splendor."[22]

A good clue to the meaning of any obscure poetic system may sometimes be found by examining its employment of traditional devices, and this method is useful in dealing with a poet like Du Bois. So typical was Ethiopianism of Du Bois's rhetoric that George Schuyler's satirization of his speaking style, while grotesque, was apt nonetheless. "I want to tell you that our destiny lies in the stars. Ethiopia's fate is in the balance. The Goddess of the Nile weeps bitter tears at the feet of the Sphinx. The lowering clouds gather over the Congo and the lightning flashes o'er Togoland. To your tents, O Israel! The hour is at hand."[23] Among Du Bois's longer and more difficult poems is **"Children of the Moon,"** which blends the Ethiopian and Western mythological traditions.[24] It tells the story of a despairing woman who finds a "highway to the moon," at the end of which lies

> a twilight land,
> Where, hardly-hid, the sun
> Sent softly-saddened rays of
> Red and brown to burn the iron soil
> And bathe the snow-white peaks
> In mighty splendor.

There she discovers a race of black men but no women:

> Black were the men,
> Hard-haired and silent-slow,
> Moving as shadows,
> Bending with face of fear to earthward;
> And women there were none.

Under her guidance the men build a tower which she climbs to "stand beneath the burning shadow of [a] peak, Beneath the whirring of almighty wings," where she hears a voice from "near-far" saying:

> "I am Freedom—
> Who sees my face is free—
> He and his."

The god reveals his name, but "who shall look and live?" Not daring, at first, to look, the goddess is persuaded in the end by "the sobbing of small voices—down, down far into the night," to climb:

> Up! Up! to the blazing blackness
> Of one veiled face.
> And endless folding and unfolding,
> Rolling and unrolling of almighty wings.

And then the poem moves to its climax:

> I rose upon the Mountain of the Moon
> I felt the blazing glory of the Sun;
> I heard the Song of Children crying, "Free!"
> I saw the face of Freedom—
> And I died.

The poem calls to mind the Egyptian myth in which Isis, the Nile goddess, ascends the heavens to do battle with Ra, the sun god, to force him to reveal his name.[25]

In order to create the world of **"Children of the Moon,"** Du Bois drew not only upon his knowledge of black Christian nationalism but also upon Greek and Egyptian mythology. The narrator is reminiscent of Isis, the moon goddess, patroness and teacher, Magna Mater of ancient Egypt, and Isis represents the Nilotic Africans whom Du Bois believed to have brought the Egyptians the civilizing arts. She was conceived by Du Bois as a black woman.[26] Born a woman, Isis was later elevated, according to the mythographers, to divine status. The goddess is an appropriate symbol of the spirit of black civilization within Du Bois's poetic system. She becomes the Great Mother of Men in the Moon—black people—as Isis was the nourishing mother of ancient Egypt. "Isis, the mother," said Du Bois, "is still titular goddess, in thought if not in name, of the dark continent."[27]

Du Bois provided one clue to the mythology of **"Children of the Moon"** when he spoke, in a later essay, of Ethiopian history as "the main current of Negro culture, from the Mountains of the Moon to the Mediterranean, blossoming on the lower Nile, but never severed from the Great Lakes of Inner Africa." The Children of the Moon are described as "moving shadows." They live in a twilight land," and they labor beneath the "burning shadow" of a peak. One suspects that this land in which they live is to be associated with Ethiopia, the land of shadows, mentioned in Isaiah and referred to as "Ethiopia, the shadowy," in ***The Souls of Black Folk.***[28] Throughout the tradition references to Ethiopia were meant to include all African peoples, of course.

Du Bois's interest in Ethiopian rhetoric made itself felt in much of his writing, as for example, in the herald's oration in the lost pageant ***Star of Ethiopia***:

> Hear ye, hear ye! All them that come to know the truth and listen to the tale of the Wisest and Gentlest of the Races of Men whose faces be Black. Hear ye, hear ye! And learn the ancient Glory of Ethiopia, All-Mother of men, whose wonders men forgot. See how beneath the Mountains of the Moon, alike in the Valley of Father Nile and in ancient Negro-land and Atlantis the Black Race ruled and strove and fought and sought the Star of Faith and Freedom even as other races did and do. Fathers of Men and Sires of Children golden, black and brown, keep silence and hear this mighty word.[29]

The Mountains of the Moon referred to in the above passage and in **"Children of the Moon"** are a semi-fictitious range, first mentioned in Ptolemy's *Geographica.* Recent scholarship associates them with the Ruwenzori Range. The Children of the Moon are blacks from central Africa, the area of the Nile-Congo watershed. They can be seen either as Congolese or Nilotics, therefore, which makes them symbolic of two of the great branches of African people: not only those who went down the Nile to Egypt but also those who followed the Congo, which "passed and rose red and reeking in the sunlight—thundered to the sea—thundered through the sea in one long line of blood, with tossing limbs and echoing cries of pain."[30] The Children of the Moon symbolized not only the ancient Ethiopians but twentieth-century Afro-Americans as well. And the moon goddess is no more Isis than she is the afflicted womanhood of Harlem.

The tedious tower building in **"Children of the Moon"** parallels the tower building in **"Star of Ethiopia."** "Hear ye, hear ye! All them that dwell by the Rivers of Waters and in the beautiful, the Valley of Shadows, and listen to the ending of this tale. Learn Sisters and Brothers, how above the Fear of God, Labor doth build on Knowledge; how Justice tempers Science and how Beauty shall be crowned in Love beneath the Cross. Listen, O Isles, for all the pageant returns in dance and song to build this Tower of Eternal Light beneath the Star."[31] The Tower of Eternal Light, built in "Star of Ethiopia," like the tower that the Children of the Moon build is reminiscent of Obelisk, which the Egyptians saw as representing a petrified sun's ray. It leads upward towards the sun, for which the Egyptians used the symbol of a winged disk. In 1911, an adaption of the symbol, in which the solar disk is replaced by the face of a black man, was printed on the cover of the *Crisis,* the official organ of the National Association for the Advancement of Colored People, edited by Du Bois. The black face surrounded by wings is, of course, the terrible vision that the goddess finally approaches in **"Children of the Moon."**[32] The wings are the wings of Ethiopia, mentioned by Isaiah in one of Du Bois's favorite Biblical passages:

> Ah! Land of the buzzing wings
> Which lies beyond the rivers of Ethiopia,
> That sends ambassadors by sea,
> In papyrus vessels on the face of the waters:
> To a nation tall and sleek,
> To a nation dreaded near and far,
> To a nation strong and triumphant.[33]

The narrator climbs the Tower up to the sun in much the same way that Isis ascended the heavens, when only a woman, to force the Sun God to unveil his secrets. To lift the veil of Isis is to read the meaning of some obscure riddle. Proclus, the Greek Neoplatonic philosopher, describes a statute of Isis bearing the following inscription: "I am that which is, has been, and shall be. My veil no one has lifted. The fruit I bore was the Sun."[34] What lies behind the veil of this poem? What does the woman see when the wings unveil the face? Perhaps she sees the face of blazing blackness, the eclipse of the West. Perhaps she sees her own reflection, the face of Isis, the African, "Star of Ethiopia, All-Mother of Men, who gave the world the Iron Gift and Gift of Faith, the Pain of Humility and Sorrow Song of Pain, and Freedom, Eternal Freedom, underneath the Star."[35] Du Bois's poetry often unveils the face of a black god as in the story of the King in the land of the Heavy Laden, who summons his only loyal servant, a woman, to go forth in battle against "the heathen." Smiling, the King commands:

> "Go smite me mine enemies, that they cease to do evil in my sight. . . ."
>
> "Oh King," she cried, "I am but a woman."
>
> And the King answered: "Go, then, Mother of Men."
>
> And the woman said, "Nay, King, but I am still a maid."
>
> Whereat the King cried: "O maid, made Man, thou shalt be Bride of God."
>
> And yet the third time the woman shrank at the thunder in her ears, and whispered: "Dear God, I am black!"
>
> The king spake not, but swept the veiling of his face aside and lifted up the light of his countenance upon her and lo! it was black.
>
> So the woman went forth on the hills of God to do battle for the King, on that drear day in the land of the Heavy Laden, when the heathen raged and imagined a vain thing.[36]

The King is a personification of God, it seems clear; like the "Thing of Wings," he is a veiled godhead. The "Thing of Wings," finally seen as "the blazing blackness / Of one veiled Face," is also a black God.[37] The veil is not only a barrier; it is a symbol of the challenge that this barrier provides. Blackness, or the veil, stands between black folk and the full promise of America, but the veil will be put aside for those who are brave enough to see what lies beyond it. In other words, as Ralph Ellison put it, "Black will make you, or black will unmake you."[38]

The veil is often but not always symbolic of black skin. It represents the limits within which the souls of black folk are confined, but veils also represent the limitations that white folk have placed upon their own vision. Possibly Du Bois borrowed the image from Thomas Jefferson, who spoke of "that immovable veil of black which covers all the emotions of the [black] race." But Du Bois gives things an ironic twist by persistently insisting that the veil is a gift that, like an infant's caul, endows its bearer with second sight.[39]

Du Bois was fascinated by mystic symbolism. As Kelly Miller observed, he was poetic, "his mind being cast in a weird and fantastic mold." He enjoyed ritual, as he tells us himself, in describing his solitary twenty-fifth birthday celebration: "The night before I had heard Schubert's beautiful *Unfinished Symphony,* planned my celebration and written to Grandma and Mabel and had a curious little ceremony with candles, Greek wine, oil, and song and prayer."[40] The mysticism of the Sphinx seems to have had real meaning for him as it has had, not only for Garveyites, but for the middle-class Africans and Afro-Americans who have pledged secret societies. Charles Wesley's official *History of Alpha Phi Alpha* recognizes the tendency of middle-class blacks to experiment with the Ethiopian tradition in poetry.

> Ask not culture for self alone;
> Let thy brother share thy gain.
> Perfect self is not our aim, but
> Homage to God, love for brother
> And high o'er all, the Ethiopian.
>
> J. H. Boags and R. H. Ogle, 1909

> Mighty Sphinx in Egypt standing
> Facing Eastward toward the sun.
> Glorified and e'er commanding
> Your children bravely on.
> Be to us a bond of union
> Held fast by Peace and Right.
>
> . . . . .
>
> Ethiopia Home of Sages
> Thou art still our noblest pride
> We, thy sons, through future ages
> Will take thee for our guide
> Trusting through thy bondless wisdom
> To reach virtue's supernal heights.
>
> W. A. Scott, 1915

Such poetry allows an identification with symbols of stability, permanency, and high culture. English-speaking, middle-class Afro-Americans during the late Victorian and Edwardian periods needed an opportunity to be proud of their Africanness, just as Garveyites would a decade later.[41]

Du Bois's Ethiopianism was really typical of the thinking of black middle-class intellectuals during the first two decades of the twentieth-century. Of course, Du Bois was in a position to encourage Ethiopianism by publishing the verse of young poets who were interested in the tradition. Langston Hughes's poem, "The Negro Speaks of Rivers," often reprinted with the dedication, "To W. E. B. Du Bois," first appeared in the *Crisis* of June, 1921, and was possibly inspired by Du Bois's **"The Story of Africa,"** which appeared in that same journal some seven years earlier. The similarities are, in any case, striking.[42]

Thus is it possible to speak of at least one black literary tradition in the "Ethiopian," borrowing a term from Afro-Atlantic political studies and adding it to American literary history. This tradition is manifested in the work of major poets, minor poets, and unsophisticated versifiers. It rested upon a view of history as outlined in Walker's *Appeal* and stated more calmly in such essays as Alexander Crummell's "The Destined Superiority of the Negro." W. E. B. Du Bois is the central figure in this tradition. The most traditional of Afro-American poets, he was yet the most innovative within the tradition. There is a difference in degree of sophistication—but not in sentiment expressed—between Du Bois's **"Riddle of the Sphinx"** and the following lines by Marcus Garvey:

> Out of cold old Europe these white men came,
> From caves, dens and holes, without any fame,
> Eating their dead's flesh and sucking their blood,
> Relics of the Mediterranean flood.[43]

Whether there are other Afro-American literary traditions and what, if any, effects the content of Afro-American literature may have had upon the forms employed must be the subject of future studies.[44]

Can Du Bois the social scientist be reconciled with Du Bois the poet and prophet of race? How could a man so well trained in social science have allowed the Ethiopian tradition, rooted in nineteenth-century *Volksgeist* mythologies, to dominate his thought?[45]

As a youth Du Bois was romantically involved with the idea of social science, which he naively believed might yield a science of racial advancement. He was infatuated, like many other young men of his generation with the notion of a "science of man." But Du Bois's theories of social change were not always consistent. Sociology became relatively less important with the passage of years until by 1910 it was no longer Du Bois's chief concern. Though he was capable of writing perfectly good sociology, it does not appear that he wanted to. He turned—and it would seem with more satisfactory results—to the power of imagination as his chief instrument for changing public morality. He became a crusading journalist, a novelist, and a poet of Ethiopianism, dedicated to embodying his view of history in mythical form.

Notes

1. W. E. B. Du Bois, *The Souls of Black Folk* (Chicago, 1903), p. 3.
2. I am indebted to a number of social and political historians for the term "Ethiopianism," notably George Shepperson; see his "Ethiopianism and African Nationalism," *Phylon,* No. 1, 1953. Also see St. Clair Drake, *The Redemption of Africa and Black Religion* (Chicago, 1970), Jomo Kenyatta, *Facing Mt. Kenya* (London, 1938), and Daniel Thwaite, *The Seething African Pot* (London, 1936). Unfortunately none of these authors has been concerned with the implications of Ethiopianism for literary traditions in either Africa or the New World. F. Nnabuenzi Ugonna makes some brief but incisive observations on the tradition in his introduction to the London 1969 reprint edition of J. E. Casely Hayford's *Ethiopia Unbound* (London, 1911), and this novel is the outstanding example of Ethiopianism by a West African author in the early twentieth century. I prefer to distinguish between English-speaking Ethiopianism and Francophonic *Negritude,* although Leopold Senghor ridicules the substitution of "Ethiopianism" for that term. Ethiopianism is not, as Senghor supposes, a recent development, but a centuries-old tradition.
3. For a description of the conspiratorial tradition see Vincent Harding, "Religion and Resistance Among Antebellum Negroes, 1800-1860," in August Meier and Elliott Rudwick, *The Making of Black America,* Volume I, pp. 179-197 (New York, 1971), and for more subtle forms of resistance with more clear-cut implications for literary traditionalism see Miles Mark Fisher, *Negro Slave Songs in the United States* (Ithaca, N.Y., 1953).
4. *Constitution of the African Civilization Society* (New Haven, Conn., 1861).
5. For some of the more famous examples see: Richard Allen and Absolom Jones, *A Narrative of the Proceedings of the Black People during the Late Awful Calamity in Philadelphia, in the Year 1793 and a Refutation of Some Censures Thrown upon Them in Some Late Publications* (Philadelphia, 1794), p. 23. Also see Peter Williams in Carter G. Woodson, *Negro Orators and Their Orations* (Washington, D.C., 1925), p. 41. Examples from the writings of Martin R. Delaney, Henry Highland Garnet, Edward Wilmot Blyden, James T. Holly, and Alexander Crummell can be found in Howard Brotz, *Negro Social and Political Thought, 1850-1920* (New York, 1966).
6. W. E. B. Du Bois, *The Souls of Black Folk,* p. 216, viz, "Instinctively I bowed before this man, as one bows before the prophets of the world."
7. Alexander Crummell, *Africa and America: Addresses and Discourses* (Springfield, Mass., 1891), p. 265.
8. In William Wells Brown, *The Black Man, His Antecedents, His Genius, and His Achievements* (New York, 1863), pp. 209-210.
9. Reprinted in Benjamin Brawley, *Early American Negro Writers* (Chapel Hill, N.C., 1935).
10. *The Complete Poems of Paul Laurence Dunbar* (New York, 1913), p. 16.
11. David Walker, *Walker's Appeal in Four Articles. . . .* [and] Henry Highland Garnet, *An Address to the Slaves of the United States of America* (Troy, N.Y., 1848), especially pp. 13, 15. For the importance of *Walker's Appeal* to U.S. legal history see Clement Eaton *The Freedom-of-Thought Struggle in the Old South* (New York, 1964), pp. 121-126.
12. Walker, p. 51.
13. The poem appears on the inside back cover of the original edition.
14. This poem appeared under at least three titles during Du Bois's lifetime. The text here is that of "The Riddle of the Sphinx" in *Darkwater: Voices from Within the Veil,* the Schocken reprint edition (New York, 1969). There are no substantial textual variations except that the "Hebrew Children of Morning" in the 1914 *Crisis* version become Arabian Children of Morning in the *Darkwater* version and the change is retained in the 1963 edition, "The White Man's Burden," which appears in *An ABC of Color* (Berlin, 1964).
15. *The Survival of the Pagan Gods* (New York, 1961).
16. Bush, *Mythology and the Romantic Tradition in English Poetry* (New York, 1963).
17. *The Souls of Black Folk,* pp. 135-136.
18. Du Bois, *The Quest of the Silver Fleece* (Chicago, 1911).
19. *Quest of the Silver Fleece,* p. 46.
20. Ibid., p. 100, "They heard the whispering *'swish-swish'* of falling seed: they felt the heavy tread of a great coming body."
21. Ibid., pp. 337-339.
22. Ibid., p. 326.
23. Schuyler, *Black No More* (New York, 1931), p. 91.
24. Printed in *Darkwater,* pp. 187-192.
25. E. A. Wallis Budge, *The Gods of the Egyptians, or Studies in Egyptian Mythology* (London, 1904), I, 360-363.
26. *Darkwater,* p. 166; Du Bois, *The World and Africa,* p. 103.
27. *Darkwater,* p. 166.
28. *The Souls of Black Folk,* p. 4.
29. Quoted from the excerpt in *An ABC of Color,* p. 90.
30. See "The Story of Africa," *Crisis,* Sept., 1914.
31. *An ABC of Color,* p. 93.
32. The winged solar disk is a fairly common symbol in Egyptian art and architecture. It appears on the stela erected before the Great Sphinx by Thothmes IV. For some illustrations see *The Larousse Encyclopedia of Mythology* (London, 1966), pp. 19, 34, 46. Also see Budge, p. 471. The *Crisis* cover adaptation of 1911 appeared with the November issue.
33. Isaiah, 25: 6-8. Du Bois quoted the passage in *The World and Africa,* p. 132, using the translation of Smith and Goodspeed, *The Complete Bible* (Chicago, 1944).

34. William Rose Benet, *The Reader's Encyclopedia,* 2nd ed. (New York, 1965), p. 506.

35. *An ABC of Color,* p. 94.

36. Darkwater, p. 161. Also, *Crisis* (May, 1911), p. 19, under the title "The Woman."

37. For other black gods in Du Bois see the following sketches in *Darkwater*: "The Second Coming," "A Litany of Atlanta," and "Jesus Christ in Texas," which appeared in the *Crisis,* December, 1911, under the title "Jesus Christ in Georgia." Another Darkwater poem in which a black god appears is "The Prayers of God," in which a white racist is unaware that the god he addresses is a personification of Black Folk, an exceptionally ironic poem, even for Du Bois.

38. Ralph Ellison, *Invisible Man* (New York, 1952), pp. 12-13.

39. Du Bois was aware, no doubt, of the folk belief that a child born with a veil (or caul) has preternatural powers. See *The Souls of Black Folk,* p. 3, in which he speaks of the Negro as "a seventh son, born with a veil, and gifted with second-sight in this American world." For Jefferson's complaint see his *Notes on the State of Virginia,* 2nd ed. (London, 1787), pp. 228-240. Du Bois was familiar with this work as early as 1897, and refers to it in a paper read that year before the American Academy of Political and Social Science. See his *The Study of the Negro Problems* in Julius Lester, ed., *The Seventh Son: The Thought and Writings* of W. E. B. Du Bois (New York, 1971), I, 235.

40. See Kelly Miller, *Race Adjustment,* reprinted under the title *Radicals and Conservatives* (New York, 1968), pp. 28-31. For the birthday celebration, see *Autobiography,* p. 170.

41. The Garveyites, officially called the Universal Negro Improvement Association, were a stridently militaristic organization of black fascists flourishing in Harlem and Chicago during the 1920's and drawing upon the dissatisfaction of returning black soldiers from the fields France. Garvey and Du Bois were bitter enemies. The author refers the reader to his interpretation of Garveyism in *The Black Scholar* (Nov.-Dec., 1971). The selections from [Illegible Text] *History of Alpha Phi Alpha,* 9th ed. (Chicago, 1959), are on pages 92 and 143. [Illegible Text] Kilson and Adelaide Cromwell Hill have provided a documentary history of middle-class black nationalism in *Apropos of Africa* (New York, 1971). Du Bois was a member of Alpha Phi Alpha, having become its first honorary member in 1909. One of the fraternity's founders, Henry Arthur Callis, says the founders were inspired by Du Bois's "talented tenth" philosophy. For Du Bois's participation in fraternity activities, see Wesley. Along with Eugene Kinckle Jones, a spokesman for the Urban League, and a number of other members [Illegible Text] proposed establishing an alumni chapter in New York (p. 114). Du Bois was principal banquet speaker at the convention of 1944, speaking on Haiti and "the necessity of taking time to live." The distinguished historian and pioneer Pan-Africanist, Rayford W. Logan, presided over the convention that year (p. 393).

42. "The Story of Africa," appeared in the *Crisis* (Sept., 1914). The river imagery this sketch should be compared with that in "Star of Ethiopia" as reprinted in *An ABC Color,* p. 93.

43. Quoted from Edmund David Cronon, *Black Moses: The Story of Marcus Garvey and the Universal Negro Improvement Association* (Madison, Wisc., 1966), p. 176.

44. Two pioneering works of the 1930's should aid the reader in pursuing the question of a black literary tradition: Benjamin Mays, *The Negro's God, as Reflected in His Literature* (Boston, 1938), and Benjamin Brawley, *The Negro Genius* (New York, 1937).

45. For discussions of Germanic influences on Du Bois see Vincent Harding, "W. E. B. Du Bois and the Black Messianic Vision," *Freedomways,* IX (First Quarter, 1969), 44-58. Francis L. Broderick, "German Influence on the Scholarship of W. E. B. Du Bois," XIX *Phylon* (Fourth Quarter, 1958), 367-371, and Wilson J. Moses, "The Evolution of Black National Socialist Thought: A Study of W. E. B. Du Bois," in Henry J. Richards, ed., *Topics in Black Studies* (Buffalo, 1971).

ARNOLD RAMPERSAD (ESSAY DATE 1979)

SOURCE: Rampersad, Arnold. "W. E. B. Du Bois as a Man of Literature." *American Literature* 51, no. 1 (March 1979): 50-68.

In this essay, Rampersad assesses the aesthetic and political value of Du Bois's creative efforts, maintaining that while Du Bois's literary works were not much above average, the importance of his efforts to create and sustain a Black literary movement cannot be underestimated. Rampersad suggests that Du Bois's aspirations for a Black aesthetic included optimism and positive portrayals of African American characters but did not rule out realism—if that realism avoided pessimism and a defeatist tone.

What Henry James wrote of Nathaniel Hawthorne is equally true of W. E. B. Du Bois: "our author," James wrote, "must accept the awkward as well as the graceful side of his fame; for he has the advantage of pointing a valuable moral." Hawthorne's moral was that "the flower of art blooms only where the soil is deep, that it takes a great deal of history to produce a little literature, that it needs a complex social machinery to set a writer in motion."[1] Du Bois's reputation as a man of literature is surely the "awkward" side of such fame as he possesses, and one meaning of his awkward side is essentially the same as Hawthorne's (as James saw it), with an important difference. The flower of art will bloom only where there is liberty or the memory of liberty. Du Bois understood the need for justice in the growth of the flower of art: "The time has not yet come," he wrote in 1913, "for the great development of American Negro literature. The economic stress is too great and the racial persecution too bitter to allow the leisure and the poise for which literature calls."[2] Or, as James went on in the famous passage about Hawthorne, "American civilization has hitherto had other things to do than to produce flowers. . . ."

The other, more graceful sides of Du Bois's reputation vary with the attitude of each observer but rest somewhere in his pioneering and persisting works of history and sociology and his decades of crusading journalism against neoslavery in the South and in some respects similar oppression in the North. Trained at Fisk, Harvard, and the University of Berlin, he produced essays, monographs, and books of history and sociology that gave him by themselves the most prominent place among black American thinkers, so that the NAACP could write with justification in 1934 that "he created, what never existed before, a Negro intelligentsia, and many who have not read a word of his writings are his spiritual disciples and descendants."[3] Certainly of Afro-American writers and the Afro-American theme one may claim of Du Bois what has been written of the English sociologists Sidney and Beatrice Webb—that every creative writer who has touched on the field of sociology has, directly or indirectly, been influenced by them.

But Du Bois ventured into the field of belles-lettres. And not by accident but as part of the plan of his life. On his twenty-fifth birth-night (1893) he confided solemnly to his journal that "these are my plans: to make a name in science, to make a name in art and thus to raise my race." A bibliography of his writings runs to some two thousand entries, out of which it is difficult to separate those completely untouched by his love of art. But there are poems enough for a slender volume, a multitude of partly personal, impressionistic essays, some verse drama, autobiographies, five novels—including a trilogy composed near his ninetieth birthday. Great reputations have been made of a smaller volume of writing, but most of this work has contributed little to Du Bois's fame. Indeed, his basic competence as a man of literature has been challenged. An angry Claude McKay, singed by a Du Bois review of his first novel, informed him that "nowhere in your writings do you reveal any comprehension of aesthetics." The poet, novelist, and critic Arna Bontemps thought Du Bois unimaginative in that he leaned toward "the tidy, the well-mannered, the Victorian" in his choice of literature. His first biographer Francis Broderick barely mentioned this belletristic writing and declared that Du Bois wanted "a literature of uplift in the genteel tradition." His second biographer, Elliott M. Rudwick, mentions the creative work not at all. And though Du Bois called his second novel "my favorite book" among the two dozen or more he published, a major historian of the black novel in America dismissed him as a "Philistine."[4]

Du Bois himself did not show great pride in this aspect of his work; he was apologetic on the very few occasions he wrote of his efforts in literature. His first novel was "really an economic study of some merit"—the sum total of his commentary on the work; he was hesitant to write "mere" autobiography; ***Dark Princess*** was his favorite book but that remark is all he ever ventured about the novel; his poems were "tributes to Beauty, unworthy to stand alone."[5] Nor was he always complimentary about actual achievement in black literature. In 1913 he saw the body as "large and creditable [though] only here and there work that could be called first-class." In 1915 a five-point plan for the future of the race included "a revival of art and literature," presumably moribund. In 1926, surveying the field for the *Encyclopaedia Brittanica* he judged that "all these things are beginnings rather than fulfillments," though they were certainly significant beginnings. In 1933 he mourned that the so-called "Harlem Renaissance" had "never taken real and lasting root" and that "on such an artificial basis no real literature can grow." Somewhere around 1960 one of his fictional characters looked in vain for recent work of major artistic quality: "In the last decade we have not produced a poem or a novel, a history or play of stature—nothing but gamblers, prizefighters and jazz. . . . Once we could hear Shakespeare in Harlem."[6]

But with these splashings of cold water there was an equally cool and lucid sense of the potential of black writing, so that Du Bois could write in April 1920 that "a renaissance of American Negro literature is due," and observe in the decade that followed, almost from the day of his prediction, the accuracy of his insight. Nor is there any lack of evidence that Du Bois was highly regarded as a man of literature, from the early praise of William and Henry James and the reverence in which he was held by black poets such as James Weldon Johnson and Langston Hughes, to the radical socialist magazine *The Messenger,* which in 1919 damned Du Bois with praise of him as "the leading litterateur of the race." But more important than testimonies is a survey of his somewhat motley collection of essays, poems, novels, and other work for the ways in which he helped to shape modern Afro-American writing. For Du Bois, maturing in the most repressive period of black American history, took unto himself the primary responsibility of the would-be mythmaker, applying a luminous imagination and intelligence to "Adam's task, of giving names to things." It is only slight exaggeration to say that wherever the Afro-American subsequently went as a writer, Du Bois had been there before him, anticipating both the most vital ideas of later currency and the very tropes of their expression. Some of these anticipations are slighter than others, but none is trivial to anyone who knows black literature. Collectively they underscore Du Bois's significance and raise challenging questions about the relationship of politics, art, and the individual imagination.[7]

If free verse became the basic medium of black poetry—and it did—Du Bois was, as far as I know, the first black poet publicly to break with rhyme and blank verse in **"A Litany of Atlanta."** The theme of Africa as a proper and necessary object of black celebration was introduced into black verse by Du Bois in his **"Day in Africa."** He was the first to celebrate the beauty of human blackness in his **"Song of the Smoke." "The Burden of Black Women"** is the first published poem to dwell on hatred as the consequence of the white destruction of crucial institutions, particularly marriage and motherhood, in black culture. Du Bois was the first black poet simultaneously to love trees and turn his back on what Nikki Giovanni called "tree poems"—the first, in other words, to resist the concept of poetry as escape from social and political realty. If *Native Son* dramatized the black capacity for violent protest and in so doing, as Irving Howe claimed, changed American culture "forever," Du Bois's John Jones in 1903 and Matthew Towns in 1928 had struck earlier blows against white Americans long before Bigger rebelled. Arthur P. Davis has noted that in ***The Quest of the Silver Fleece*** Du Bois ended the poisonous reign of near-white heroines in black fiction with his characterization of Zora; the novel is the first *Bildungsroman* in Afro-American fiction, as Addison Gayle points out, and the first black novel to present and analyze economics as a significant factor in American culture in the significant manner of Cable, Dreiser, and Dos Passos.[8] In its portrait of the manipulative Carolyn Wynn Du Bois published in 1911 the first truly psychological study of a character in black fiction—not, as Robert Bone argues, the hero of Johnson's *The Autobiography of an Ex-Colored Man* (1912). ***Dark Princess*** (1928) is the first work of art, as far as I know, to identify and promulgate the doctrine of the third world.

And when Du Bois wrote in the *Atlantic Monthly* in 1897 of the **"Strivings of the Negro People"** and declared the irrevocable twoness of the black American, he laid the foundation of all future literary renditions of the subject. True to his gift he both analyzed and simultaneously provided the metaphor appropriate to his analysis. The metaphor was the Veil, anticipatory of the central image of Ellison's *Invisible Man,* for "the Negro is a sort of seventh son, born with a veil, and gifted with second sight in this American world—a world which yields him no true self-consciousness, but only lets him see himself through the revelation of the other world." The crucial analysis followed: "It is a peculiar sensation, this double-consciousness, this sense of always looking at one's self through the eyes of others, of measuring one's soul by the tape of a world that looks on in amused contempt and pity. One ever feels his twoness,—an American, a Negro; two souls, two thoughts, two unreconciled strivings; two warring ideals in one dark body, whose dogged strength alone keeps it from being torn asunder."[9]

If one excludes from consideration a personal desire for fame, there are perhaps four important aspects to Du Bois's enormous concern with the development of black literature in America—and his own part in it (he understood by the middle of his teenage years that—as he told Barrett Wendell at Harvard in 1890,—he had "something to say to the world" and was determined to prepare himself "in order to say it well"). First, Du Bois believed that the production of a body of great literature and other art was the necessary basis for the entrance of Afro-America into the polity of civilized peoples, a notion based on the concept of distinct racial "gifts" then accepted by a host of scientists and social observers attempting to understand the meaning of race. He argued in 1926 that "until the art of the black folk compels recognition they will not be rated as human" (he might have argued instead that until they were rated as human, their art would not be appreciated). He believed, following the line of the more liberal sociologists and anthropologists (but using, nevertheless, the concepts of the same highly suspect racial science) that "the Negro is primarily an artist," though he knew that "the usual way of putting this is to speak disdainfully of his sensuous nature."[10]

Secondly, Du Bois unquestionably saw the art of literature as important in the almost one-sided war of propaganda waged against the black at the turn of the century in books such as Charles Carroll's *The Negro a Beast* (1900), Shufeldt's *The Negro: A Menace to American Civilization* (1907), and Thomas Dixon, Jr.'s *The Leopard's Spots* (1902) and *The Clansman* (1905), the latter filmed eventually by D. W. Griffith as *Birth of a Nation.* But if he declared in 1926 that "all art is propaganda and ever must be, despite the wailing of the purists," he also repeatedly defended the need for candor and artistic freedom. Any mention of black life in America, he noted, had caused for a hundred years "an ugly picture, a dirty allusion, a nasty comment or a pessimistic forecast. The result is that the Negro today," he wrote in 1924 in defence of Eugene O'Neill, "fears any attempt of the artist to paint Negroes. He is not satisfied unless everything is perfect and proper and beautiful and joyful and hopeful . . . lest his human foibles and shortcomings be seized by his enemies for the purposes of the ancient and hateful propaganda." Du Bois knew of black folk, as he wrote two years later, that "we can afford the Truth. White folk today cannot." The black should be set before the world, he wrote in 1915, "as both a creative artist and a strong subject for artistic treatment." But it is important to insist that Du Bois was no part of the clamor by certain middle-class and aristocratic members of the black intelligentsia for a literature set in the middle-class, to show whites that some blacks, at least, were capable of refinement—although it was a call in which his sometime (1919-1926) literary editor on *The Crisis,* Jessie Fauset, was partly complicitous, and with which he appeared to some observers to be in agreement.[11]

Thirdly, Du Bois sought out the power of art because of an increasing sense of the limitation of empirical social science and academic historiography. In 1896 he could congratulate himself on complying with "the general principles laid down in German universities" when he prepared his first book, on the African slave trade; in ***The Philadelphia Negro*** (1899) he intoned that the social scientist "must ever tremble lest some personal bias, some moral conviction or some unconscious trend of thought due to previous training, has to a degree distorted the picture in his view." But under the pressure of grave social forces he had already begun to doubt—as he stated in 1898—that empirical research into society would "eventually lead to a systematic body of knowledge deserving the name of science." In 1903 he deplored the tendency of inferior sociology to lapse into "bad metaphysics and false psychology"; the next year he declared that sociologists were "still only groping after a science." The goals of social research, and his methods and approaches, became less scholarly, more political, more imaginative. A volume of social study published by him in 1906 did not seek "definite conclusions. Its object is rather to blaze the way and point out a few general truths."[12]

And fourthly, Du Bois's turn toward art was empowered by perhaps the central factor of his overall career—his perception of the need for action, not subservience or contemplation, in the face of American racism. The growth of Du Bois's practice of art coincided with the growth of his political activism, beginning with his return to the South as an adult in 1897 and reaching its first decisive point with his 1903 challenge to the authority of Booker T. Washington, the most powerful black leader of the age. From this step eventually came Du Bois's founding of the radical Niagara Movement (radical in its demands of civil rights and other basic freedoms), and his leadership of the movement in the years between 1905 and 1910, when he felt professionally the weight of Booker T. Washington's antagonism. This period ended with his departure from the university for the fledgling NAACP in 1910, to become editor of its crusading monthly magazine *The Crisis.* His turn to art in the course of these thirteen or so years was not for relief from the hurly-burly of political action but was an aspect of political action itself. And such achievements in form and theme as he accomplished are testimony, in the context of black American literature, to the acuteness of Lukács's observation that "new styles, new ways of representing reality, though always linked to old forms and styles, never arise from any immanent dialectic within artistic forms. Every new style is socially and historically determined and is the product of a social development."[13]

For it is clear that Du Bois showed no great potential for achievement in art much beyond skilled mediocrity and imitativeness until he experienced the goad of Southern racism. He showed very little interest in the discussion of theoretical issues pertaining to art and the process of imagination and literary creation. His pronouncements on literature are generally negligible in depth and scope; one must recover, from

FROM THE AUTHOR

THE MEASUREMENT OF ONE'S SOUL

It is a peculiar sensation, this double-consciousness, this sense of always looking at one's self through the eyes of others, of measuring one's soul by the tape of a world that looks on in amused contempt and pity.

SOURCE: W. E. B. Du Bois, from *The Souls of Black Folk,* McClurg, 1903.

observation of his literary practice, the factors that pertained to his performance as a man of literature. And what empowered Du Bois as an Afro-American mythmaker and distinguished him from more superficially gifted and involved artists was a combination of great intellect, greater energy, and—above all—a capacity for feeling the political experience so intensely that its purposes were subsumed, as it were, into every fibre of his intellectual being at least as intensely as the famous poet contemplating the sparrow in the gravel; and allowing that intensity to inspire art and scholarship out of imitation and mediocrity and into the world of action.

Du Bois himself dated the time of his turn toward action. The year was 1897. With his doctoral thesis published as the first volume in the Harvard Historical Studies and the research completed for perhaps his greatest work of scholarship, ***The Philadelphia Negro,*** he set out to create the mechanism for a one-hundred-year empirical study of black life divided into ten great subjects, each subject the focus of study for one year, every ten years the cycle repeating itself. His base was the classroom and his study at Atlanta University. Du Bois recollected how he came to change the basic course of his life:

> At the very time when my studies were most successful, there cut across this plan which I had as a scientist, a red ray which could not be ignored. I remember when it first, as it were, startled me to my feet: a poor Negro in central Georgia, Sam Hose, had killed his landlord's wife. I wrote out a careful and reasoned statement concerning the evident facts and started down to the Atlanta *Constitution* office, carrying in my pocket a letter of introduction to Joel Chandler Harris. I did not get there. On the way news met me: Sam Hose had been lynched, and they said that his knuckles were on exhibition at a grocery store farther down on Mitchell Street, along which I was walking. I turned back to the University. I began to turn aside from my work. I did not meet Joel Chandler Harris nor the editor of the *Constitution.*[14]

The impact on his art of this heightened degree of Du Bois's understanding of the meaning of action, power, and the political was firm and accruing, but also gradual and sometimes wayward. For he embarked on this radical passage without any congeries of beliefs that might be called ideology in any strict sense of the term; indeed, he proceeded with two biases that on one level appeared to contradict each other as well as ideology itself, but which were, on another, more functional level, its surrogates. First, he retained his respect for empirical sociology and academic historiography; secondly, he deepened his racial or nationalistic commitment to the black folk of America, laying the foundation and developing the basic dialectical superstructure for all subsequent black nationalist pleading. Simultaneously he suppressed the socialist methodology he had learned as a student in Germany, though by the end of the first decade of the century he would identify himself as a quasi-socialist, and then briefly join the American Socialist Party. Socialist analysis—socialist fervor—was resisted both by scholarship as he understood its demands and by the exclusive tendencies of black nationalism. But Du Bois's black nationalism was further tempered by the fact that the essence of his politics was his demand for the *integration* of blacks into American society, a demand that took precedence as an idea and as a shaper of myth and image over the insistent nationalism that formed the basis of his argument that blacks should enjoy all the rights of the typical American citizen.

The absence of an ideologically consistent core of beliefs—the presence of this noble confusion—encouraged Du Bois to develop, especially in his essays between 1897 and 1903 (when ***The Souls of Black Folk*** appeared) a dazzling variety of metaphoric, ironic, pietistic, and sentimental rhetorical strategies appropriate to liberal intellection and liberal discourse. Much later in life, essentially a communist without a party card, Du Bois regretted that too much sentiment and moralizing, too little Marx and Freud, had informed his early work. The evidence is there, though, that he was aware of a problem even as he wrote. In 1904, writing about ***The Souls of Black Folk,*** he innocently admitted that "the style and workmanship" of his book did not make its meaning altogether clear, that the collection conveyed "a clear message" but that around this center floated "a penumbra" of subjectivity, vagueness, and half-veiled allusions. "In its larger aspects," he said, groping to understand what he had wrought, "the style is tropical—African."[15]

The aching ideological contradictions—in other words, the *charm* of these moving and important early essays—gave way to more rigid ideas and forms. The next collection of essays, ***Darkwater: Voices from Within the Veil*** (1920), would draw the wish from one reviewer, a longtime acquaintance of Du Bois, that the author would walk "more in the manner of the Nazarene." Here and in ***The Negro*** (1915), a survey of the African peoples on the continent and elsewhere, there is a disjunction between analysis and art, as there is in the many dramatized editorials that gave bite to the *Crisis* magazine. Du Bois had consciously become, as he admitted, a propagandist. While it is partly true that with the publication of ***The Negro*** Du Bois became, as Wilson Moses put it, "a poet of Ethiopianism, dedicated to embodying his view of history in mythical form," no significant formal poetry emerged from this aspect of his writing; he essentially preserved the approach to historiography of writers like Macaulay and Carlyle, for whom the writing of history was a dramatic art. In Du Bois's grand study of the postbellum South, ***Black Reconstruction in America*** (1935), most of the "artistic" passages can be excised from the text without the slightest modification of the argument and spirit of the work. As a historian Du Bois was showing a certain imaginative and stylistic range; as a poet, however, despite the clear passion he brought to both tasks, he seems to have been relatively uninspired.[16]

The poetry and fiction that Du Bois wrote during his first years of radical commitment are another matter. The bulk of his significant poetry was composed during his leadership of the Niagara Movement, after his decision to join the radical ranks and before the NAACP rescued him from the wilderness of deepening alienation and confusion. The art of this period—1905 to 1910—reflects an intellectual and spiritual turmoil distinctly different from that of ***The Souls of Black Folk.*** The emblem of this period might well show Du Bois in anguish on a train returning to Atlanta in the last week of September 1906, uncertain of the fate of his wife and daughter, as well as of his work and the university, in the worst race riot in the South in the first decade of the century. On this train journey Du Bois wrote **"A Litany of Atlanta."**

> We raise our shackled hands and charge thee,
> God
> by the bones of our stolen fathers, by the tears
> of our dead mothers, by the very blood of Thy
> crucified Christ: What meaneth this? Tell us the
> plan; give us the sign!

"Surely," the poet asks, "thou, too, art not white, O Lord, a pale, bloodless, heartless thing!" Or is God dead? But the poet recoils from "these wild, blasphemous words":

> Thou art still the God of our black fathers and in
> Thy Soul's Soul sit some soft darkenings, some
> shadowing of the velvet night.
> But whisper—speak—call, great God, for Thy
> silence is white terror to our heart! The way, O
> God, show us the way and point us the path![17]

The thou's and thy's and art's should not obscure the importance of the poem, or its power, for in the fire of the political moment so replete with personal meaning Du Bois severed the ancient link between black poetry and rhyme or blank verse, as well as to the three dominant modes of Afro-American verse of the age—the poetry of social uplift by writers such as Frances E. W. Harper, the Afro-Georgian lyricism of Braithwaite, Dunbar, and others, and the immensely popular dialect tradition, with its poles of maudlin pathos, on one hand, and low comedy, on the other—"the range between appetite and emotion, with certain lifts far beyond and above it," that William Dean Howells told us is the range of the black race.[18]

With **"A Litany of Atlanta"** Du Bois opened the way for a black poetry of secularism, scepticism, and cultural authenticity, a poetry that surfaced swiftly and importantly again in his own works with **"Song of the Smoke,"** where for the first time an Afro-American poet unambiguously praised blackness of skin and the potential of the race compared to the white overlords:

> I will be black as blackness can—
> The blacker the mantle, the mightier the man!
> For blackness was ancient ere whiteness began.

And in **"The Burden of Black Women,"** later retitled **"The Riddle of the Sphinx,"** the hatred authentic to the black experience of life in America but anathema to the tropes of liberal discourse surfaced for the first time in published verse:

> The white world's vermin and filth:
> All the dirt of London,
> All the scum of New York
> Valiant spoilers of women
>
> . . . . .
>
> Bearing the white man's burden
> Of Liquor and Lust and Lies.
>
> . . . . .
>
> I hate them, Oh!
> I hate them well,
> I hate them, Christ!
> As I hate Hell,
> If I were God
> I'd sound their knell
> This day![19]

Not all the verse of this period, no matter how politically charged the theme, marked a significant achievement in Du Bois's efforts to poeticize the black experience and predicament. **"A Day in Africa"** introduces a new element into black poetical consciousness—Africa as an object of veneration for black Americans—but its ideas are confused and its language reflects this confusion:

> I leaped and danced, and found
> My breakfast poised aloft,

All served in living gold.
In purple flowered fields I wandered
Wreathed in crimson, blue and green.
My noon-tide meal did fawn about my feet
In striped sleekness.
I kissed it ere I killed it.[20]

A "wild new creature" threatens the persona, who poises his spear in defiance. But the black warrior sees fear in the eyes of the animal (the white interloper in Africa) and refuses to kill it. Africa is color, freedom, sensual ease, courage, mercy. Yet the poem is an almost total failure; its form is overburdened by Du Bois's nearly absolute ignorance of his subject, Africa, whose history he had just begun to study after being awakened to its complexity by Franz Boas in 1906, when the anthropologist spoke at Atlanta University. Du Bois would not see Africa until 1923. Unlike the other three quoted poems, **"A Day in Africa"** is comparatively unmotivated except in the most abstract of ways. One is reminded again, first, that the apprehension of the need for action is hardly in itself ideology, and that still less is it automatically art when applied to the forms of art. The process and the difficulty of art are not abbreviated by the call to action. The firing of the radical imagination only further complicates the task of persuasion that the radical literateur undertakes. The problem of accommodating political thought within the scope of the imagination is still further subsumed into the creative writer's ultimate problem, at once commonplace and yet urgent—the problem of rhetoric.

Unable to achieve a consistent and credible equipoise between ideology and form, Du Bois found his final achievement as a poet in his position as pioneer, as bridge between often inspired imitation and later poetical authenticity in black literature. One clue to Du Bois's problems of equipoise lies in the fact that the dominant formal referent in his poetry is religion—and Du Bois, once his Congregationalist faith died, was never born again. A list of some of his titles shows his concern: A Litany of Atlanta, The Prayer of the Bantu, The Prayers of God, Hymn to the Peoples, Christ of the Andes; in addition to which he wrote parables featuring a black Christ and in other ways relied on religious constructs for intellectual deliverance. Religion in Du Bois's work has distinctly earthly correspondences; "the impenetrable meaning of human suffering matches the inscrutability of God; Christ is the incarnation of all human hope; Heaven is the world beyond the Veil; and life is Hell."[21] And yet the use of religion is symptomatic of the poet's problems in representing ideas often in conflict with each other but striving for integration. The justification for the use of religion in this way did not come from the place of religion in Du Bois's life, or in the culture of the black folk, but from the historic role of religion in white culture. Thus Du Bois was attempting to fuse political passion within the traditional vehicles of a white spirituality whose effectiveness, indeed, whose very existence he was simultaneously calling into question. The use of the traditional vehicles gives a superficial monumentality to the tenor of his message, but a full union is not possible.

The change in Du Bois's art between the earlier essays of ***The Souls of Black Folk*** and the poems is reflected significantly in the distance between Du Bois's first important piece of published fiction, the short story **"Of the Coming of John"** in ***Souls*** and the later novels—but especially so in the case of his first novel ***The Quest of the Silver Fleece.*** In the short story a young black man leaves his small Southern town and becomes educated—and alienated from his fellow blacks, the whites, and himself; he returns home, is ostracized as a remote and possibly radical man, reacts blindly when he finds his sister struggling with a playful would-be white seducer, kills the man, and then possibly kills himself as a lynch mob closes in. In ***The Quest of the Silver Fleece*** a young black man discovers education, goes North to work and becomes involved in politics, almost succumbs to corruption, but returns home to rally his people in their struggle for education and a better life, prepared at the end to fight physically for their rights. In ***Dark Princess*** a young black man, embittered by racism, goes to Europe and becomes involved in a plot for an uprising of the darker people against white colonialism. He returns to the United States to report on the state of black culture, becomes involved in politics, almost succumbs to corruption, but is rescued in time; he atones for his sins by hard work and at the end of the novel is a changed man, dedicated to duty and willing to fight for his beliefs. In the ***Black Flame*** trilogy (1957, 1959, 1961) a young black man embarks on a life of service to his race as a teacher. Intellectually ungifted but patient and honorable, he is shaped in his life and career by the major events of black American history and by the culture of the South, where he lives almost all his life. He dies in the 1950's in his eighty-eighth year, witness to the first cracks in the wall of segregation but tragically uncertain of the value of his life of service. The trilogy also consistently dramatizes the major personalities and passages of his lifetime—

Southern, national, international—with capitalism as the formidable villain of this complementary story, and rising socialism as its struggling hero.

The ideological shifting in the works and its effect upon form are noteworthy. In the first story, **"Of the Coming of John,"** the central drama is the struggle between the divided souls of the young black aspirant to culture in a racist world; and in spite of the violence of murder and possible suicide, pathos—not tragedy—marks the dramatic depth of the tale. The black folk is defined by its ignorance, the white folk by its reaction. The drama takes place in a world of political stasis that immobilizes time and history; society is essentially indecipherable, and the logical inference is an encompassing pessimism. The warring souls of the black, the story seems to say, must forever war, the contradictions therein are both endemic and permanent. Black alienation follows directly from education in racist America, and is worse than inevitable or pathological—black alienation is useless. The only way out of the gloom is perhaps through the wisdom and humanity of the narrator, a nameless professor at the college attended by John; but he or she, who might well be white, is baffled and quite concerned, but impotent. The black man must endure; the world prevails.

This depiction presented Du Bois with few formal problems. But he was never again to make pathos the focus of his art or to accept pessimism as the resolution of a black fiction—not because the situation of blacks never seemed rather hopeless to him or because blacks themselves were never pessimistic, but because he developed a different sense of the functioning of the world and history and a different sense of the potential of blacks and humanity in general. From this sense derived a different sense of the moral and political function of art and a different attitude toward form. The heroes of ***Quest of the Silver Fleece*** and ***Dark Princess*** are at first baffled and confused, as John was in the first story; but the burden of their stories is the resolution of bafflement and confusion, with the end of the stories presenting morally and politically earnest heroes and heroines preparing to swim boldly in a world that is still deep but now fathomable. The process shifts from one work to another but the basic pattern is the same. The baffled, divided hero is, in a sense, *reborn* into psychological monism or harmony, which is tantamount to moral and political zeal. This rebirth comes through education both from learned books and from manual labor, reuniting body and mind, intellect and muscle, as the souls are reunited. The hero discovers the way and atones for his sins, accepting duty and work as first principles of life, with love as its crowning glory. The immoral stasis of the world in **"Of the Coming of John"** gives way to the exposition of culture as process, and history and the world as both scrutable and stimulant to optimism. And the formal simplicity of the short story gives way to a formal complication that Du Bois strove with only limited success to manage.

Writing in ***The World and Africa*** just after World War II about the decline of western culture in the late nineteenth century, Du Bois deplored the fact that "art, in building, painting and literature, became cynical and decadent. Literature became realistic and therefore pessimistic." Though this was written when he was very close to communism, it is consistent with his attitudes toward fiction during the greater part of his life, or once he had become politically alert and committed to action. Art and pessimism were, for him, incompatible if art were to succeed. All art, he said in 1926, attacking the "art for art's sake" movement among certain black writers, is propaganda—and black art must be propaganda "for gaining the right of black folk to love and enjoy." But his purpose was broader than is apparent in such a crude statement. It was "the bounden duty of black America" to create, preserve, and realize "Beauty" for America, for the aim of art and political struggle was not black power in isolation but a philosophically reconstructed universe. The tools in the creation of beauty had always been and must be, he said, truth—"the highest hand-maid of imagination . . . the one great vehicle of universal understanding"; and goodness, "in all its aspects of justice, honor and right—not for sake of an ethical sanction but as the one true method of gaining sympathy and human interest." Thus, Du Bois went on, "the apostle of Beauty . . . becomes the apostle of Truth and Right not by choice but by inner and outer compulsion."[22]

These terms such as Truth and Beauty and Right are vague enough for us to miss the order of the process Du Bois is describing, but they are significant; indeed, they also suggest quaint ways in which he would, as a practicing writer, oppose realism. In both ***Quest of the Silver Fleece*** and ***Dark Princess*** (but *not* in ***The Black Flame*** decades after) the most terribly stilted language surfaces during decisive emotional or philosophical moments, and appears in the midst of otherwise conventionally mimetic dialogue and narration that show Du Bois to have some definite ability—not mere potential—as a novelist. But the failings of his work are there; though one finds depth of characterization in both novels, many more of the performers are types of humanity rather than creations credible outside of their ideological burden in the particular piece. There is, too, a fair amount of what one must regard as melodramatic and unsatisfying effects, notably in the end of ***Dark Princess,*** where a typical masque-like scene, replete with symbolism, supplants the otherwise sober auditing of the account. Such effects represent Du Bois's conscious choices as an artist, and it would be a mistake to consider them other than bad choices. They were, however, generated by his philosophy of art and by the fact that there was but one genre into which his story could fit. That genre was not finally the novel, which is what he called ***Quest of the Silver Fleece,*** or the romance, which is the way he identified ***Dark Princess,*** but the epic.

Epic in more than one sense—but literally so, in that the mature Du Bois fiction is the gravely serious story, recited in at times too lofty a tone and language, of a young (black) man of quality embarking on the most perilous of journeys within a grand landscape, on the success of which depends the future salvation of his race or nation—salvation on a relatively small scale in ***Quest of the Silver Fleece,*** on a worldwide scale in ***Dark Princess.*** What drove Du Bois to the epic form was that ecstatic optimism with which both novels end, an optimism that was the richest dividend of his awakened political consciousness. Applied to his writing, this optimism was compounded by his nostalgia for a vanished innocence within both a mythic Africa and humanity as a whole, by his sense of the potential of Africans and all humanity, and finally by his sense of the history of the world as the history of process. This sense enabled Du Bois to share vicariously in the intellectual and social homogeneity out of which the epic first sprang.

The realism to which Du Bois objected was close to that of such writers as Zola, the earlier Dreiser, and Frank Norris—and the difference between his sense of the epic and theirs is considerable. Their pessimism is formally exemplified in their worship of the fact, the detail, the superficial information of "that harsh, blunt, colorless tool called realism," as Norris himself put it in attempting to transcend its limitations. Du Bois had not turned his back on statistical sociology in order to create art based on accepting the surface as the substance of things; his politics did not allow him to be pessimistic; and his understanding of history and society diverted him—though not always—from those fallacies of naturalism and supernaturalism by which other writers complicated their art but betrayed their philosophical helplessness. Nor could he develop a highly symbolic art which would reflect a contemplative attitude to a mysterious universe and thus deflect the epic thrust of his socially centered narrative. There are two looming symbols in his first novel—cotton (the silver fleece of the title) and a great swamp. The swamp stands for the immoral past of the preliterate black; the best cotton grows where the swamp has been cleared, a task that requires unity and character on the part of the black folk. Thus literally one symbol is a transcendence of the other, and because the cotton is stripped of its monetary and inhuman significance and reidentified with human work and thought and character, it carries within itself as a symbol the force of its own self-transcendence, since its power as a symbol derives from its part in the world of human action.

The major formal tension in Du Bois's fiction, and the source of its major shortcomings, arises from the crucial relationship of the narration to history on one hand and to the particular, chosen moment on the other; between the depiction of historical process and the depiction of its immediate product; between—if you will—life, and the chosen slice of life. Characters fail as art when they take their total essence from history; they tend to succeed when they take their essence more from the historical moment, which is itself governed—but distantly—by history. In ***The Black Flame,*** hastily written as Du Bois neared death, Du Bois tried to show his understanding at last of this division. The trilogy tells two stories—the epic of history, and the counterepic or antiepic of the black hero as epiphenomenon; counterepic, because the black hero no longer triumphs in his own lifetime, but ends his life apparently inconclusively. The great achievement of this flawed work comes from the ironic interplay between the march of dialectic, crudely related, and the crawling and stumbling of humans defined by their failures as well as their modest virtues.

Du Bois claimed that his life had its significance only because he was part of the great problem of race, and that he had done little to change his day. Perhaps. Within black America, though, his achievement was incomparable. Though he never attained competence as a great poet or novelist, his efforts in those roles combine with his other works to extend our understanding of the history and character of his people and, indeed, of humanism itself. In spite of his failures as a formal artist there lingers about him more than a trace of what Lukács found in a far greater nineteenth-century writer—glimpses still of "the gloomy magnificence of primary accumulation in the field of culture."[23]

Notes

1. Henry James, *Hawthorne* (New York, 1879), pp. 2-3.
2. Du Bois, "The Negro in Literature and Art," *Annals of the American Academy of Political and Social Science,* XLIX (Sept., 1913), 236-237.
3. *Crisis,* XLI (Aug., 1934), 246.
4. For 1893: Francis L. Broderick, *W. E. B. Du Bois* (Stanford, Calif., 1959), p. 29; McKay to Du Bois, June 18, 1928, *The Correspondence of W. E. B. Du Bois, Selections, 1877-1934,* ed. Herbert Aptheker (Amherst, Mass., 1973), pp. 374-375; Arna Bontemps, *100 Years of Negro Freedom* (New York, 1961), p. 221; Broderick, p. 160; Robert A. Bone, *The Negro Novel in America* (New Haven, Conn., 1965), p. 101.
5. On *Quest of the Silver Fleece* see Du Bois, *Dusk of Dawn* (New York, 1940), p. 269; on autobiography, see *Dusk of Dawn,* p. vii; on *Dark Princess, Dusk of Dawn,* p. 270; on poems, Du Bois, *Darkwater: Voices from Within the Veil* (New York, 1920), p. vii.
6. In 1913: "The Negro in Literature and Art," p. 236; in 1915: *Crisis,* IX (April, 1915), 312; in 1926: *Encyclopaedia Brittanica,* 13th ed., *Supplement* (1926), pp. 110-111; in 1960: Du Bois, *Worlds of Color* (New York, 1961), pp. 345-346.
7. In 1920: *Crisis,* XIX (April, 1920), 299; *Messenger,* II (July, 1918), 27-28.
8. Nikki Giovanni, "For Saundra," *Black Feeling, Black Talk, Black Judgement* (New York, 1970), pp. 88-89; Irving Howe, *A World More Attractive* (New York, 1963), p. 100; Arthur P. Davis, *From the Dark Tower* (Washington, D.C., 1974), pp. 22-23; Addison Gayle, *The Way of the New World* (New York, 1976), p. 86.
9. Du Bois, "Strivings of the Negro People," *Atlantic Monthly,* LXXX (Aug., 1897), 197.
10. In 1890: *The Autobiography of W. E. B. Du Bois* (New York, 1968), p. 145; in 1926, Du Bois, "Criteria of Negro Art," *Crisis,* XXXII (Oct., 1926), 297; in 1915: *Crisis,* IX (April, 1915), 312.
11. In 1926: "Criteria of Negro Art," pp. 296, 297; in 1924: *Crisis,* XXVIII (June, 1924), 56-57; in 1915: *Crisis,* IX (April, 1915), 312.
12. In 1896: Du Bois, *The Suppression of the African Slave-Trade to the United States of America, 1638-1870* (New York, 1896), p. vi; Du Bois, *The Philadelphia Negro* (Philadelphia, 1899), p. 3; Du Bois, "The Study of the Negro Problems," *Annals of the American Academy of Political and Social Science,* XI (Jan., 1898), 1; in 1903: Du Bois, "The Laboratory in Sociology at Atlanta University," *Annals of the American Academy of Political and Social Science,* XXI (May, 1903), 160; in 1904, Du Bois, "The Atlanta Conferences," *Voice of the Negro,* I (March, 1904), 89; in 1906: Du Bois, *Health and Physique of the Negro American* (Atlanta, 1906), p. 36.
13. Georg Lukács, *Writer & Critic* (New York, 1970), p. 119.
14. *Autobiography,* pp. 221-222.
15. Du Bois, "The Souls of Black Folk," *Independent,* LVII (May 17, 1904), 1152.
16. Oswald Garrison Villard, "Darkwater," *Nation,* CX (May, 1920), 727; Wilson J. Moses, "The Poetics of Ethiopianism: W. E. B. Du Bois and Literary Black Nationalism," *American Literature,* XLVII (Nov., 1975), 426.
17. *Independent,* LXI (Oct. 11, 1906), 856-858.
18. William Dean Howells in *The Complete Poems of Paul Laurence Dunbar* (New York, 1913), p. ix.
19. *Horizon,* II (Nov., 1907), 3-5.
20. *Horizon,* III (Jan., 1908), 5-6.
21. Arnold Rampersad, *The Art and Imagination of W. E. B. Du Bois* (Cambridge, Mass., 1976), p. 104.
22. Du Bois, *The World and Africa* (New York, 1965), p. 24; in 1926: Du Bois, "Criteria of Negro Art," pp. 290-297.
23. Luk cs, p. 119.

SHAMOON ZAMIR (ESSAY DATE 1995)

SOURCE: Zamir, Shamoon. "'Double-Consciousness': Locating the Self." In *Dark Voices: W. E. B. Du Bois and American Thought, 1888-1903,* pp. 113-36. Chicago: University of Chicago Press, 1995.

In the following essay, Zamir explores the relationship between Du Bois's notion of self-consciousness, especially as developed in The Souls of Black Folk *and Georg Wilhelm Friedrich Hegel's* Phenomenology of Mind, *which Du Bois likely studied at Harvard with George Santayana. In this portion of a larger study of the intellectual context of Du Bois's development, Zamir discusses the varied applications of Hegelian philosophy in American thought, particularly the master-and-slave dialectic influential in Marxism. In this context, Zamir argues that Du Bois mediates between materialism and idealism, sidestepping a full critique of American capitalism and its role in racial oppression.*

This chapter examines Du Bois's dramatization of a divided self-consciousness in comparison with other nineteenth-century American accounts of consciousness. The discussion is anchored in a description of the ways in which Du Bois radically adapts Hegel's *Phenomenology of Mind* in order to describe the historical problematic that preoccupies him in the first chapter of [***The Souls of Black Folk***].[1] This problematic is the crisis of the black bourgeois leadership and intelligentsia generated by the clash between their political idealism and the history of race in the last two decades of the century.

Du Bois studied Hegel with George Santayana during 1889-90 in a course on modern French and German philosophy, at the same time that he was taking a course in psychology with William James, and during a period when European Romantic

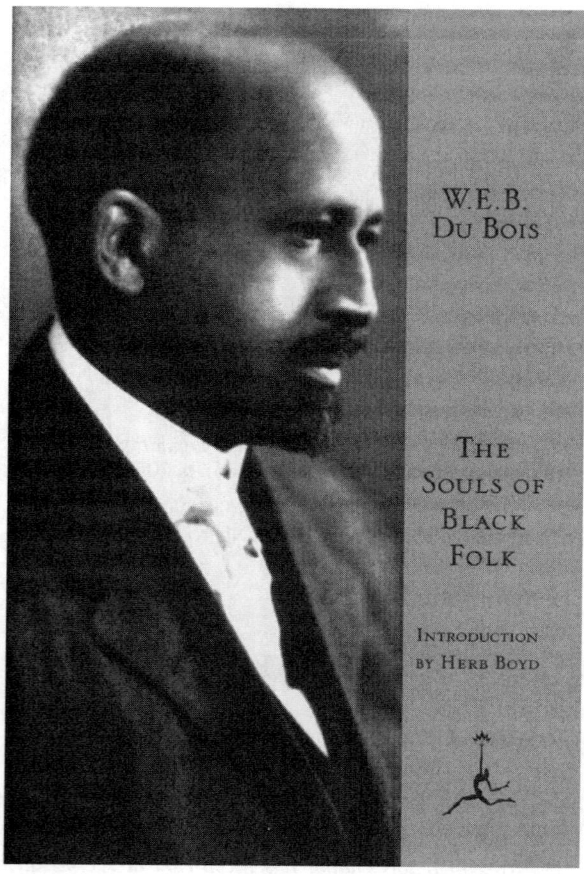

Cover of *The Souls of Black Folk,* by W. E. B. Du Bois.

and idealist philosophy was widely taught at Harvard and when Hegelianism was widespread in American philosophy and social thought. The young Santayana was excited by his reading of the *Phenomenology*. It, in combination with his reading of Greek philosophy, had set him to planning his own literary psychology of consciousness, *The Life of Reason* (1905-6). All available evidence suggests that the Hegel text studied in Santayana's course was the *Phenomenology*.[2]

"Of Our Spiritual Strivings" constitutes itself as a narrative structure by reference to key sections of the narrative that dominates the central part of Hegel's *Phenomenology,* from the differentiation of self-consciousness from consciousness to the vision of the ethical state, or *Sittlichkeit.* The parallels between the narratives of the two texts are close and can be mapped quite precisely, although, as subsequent discussion will demonstrate, Du Bois's departures from the Hegelian narrative are crucial. What is referred to here as the central section of the *Phenomenology* begins at the moment when self-consciousness discovers its own self behind the world of appearance (the moment when Hegel uses the biblical conceit of the lifting of the curtain or veil). Self-consciousness goes on to greater self-realization through a struggle with another self-consciousness (the famous "Master and Slave" dialectic), and then to an internalization of this struggle in the form of the "unhappy consciousness." The first proper resolution of this divided self is achieved in the freedom promised by national culture, what Hegel calls *Sittlichkeit.*[3]

The opening scene of ***Souls,*** where the child Du Bois realizes the separations of the "color-line" for the first time in the rejecting "glance" (***SBF*** 364) of a white playmate (the moment in Du Bois when the biblical veil *descends*), corresponds to the first stage of the Hegelian narrative outlined above. The meditation that follows on the struggle of blacks against racism in "the shades of the prison-house" (***SBF*** 364) corresponds to the conflict between Master and Slave. The passage on "double-consciousness" corresponds to Hegel's commentary on the "unhappy consciousness." And Du Bois's recognition that "double-consciousness" can be overcome only when the black American can become "a co-worker in the kingdom of culture" (***SBF*** 365) mirrors the state of *Sittlichkeit.*

An awareness of the parallels between **"Strivings"** and the *Phenomenology* aids a fuller understanding of the narrative structure of Du Bois's chapter. In doing so it also suggests that the description of "double-consciousness," which has so often been extracted from the chapter, can be properly understood only if it is read as part of the larger psychological and historical process narrated in **"Strivings."** Textual parallels are, of course, deceptive. There is not an identity of meaning between Hegel and Du Bois's critical reading of Hegel. Du Bois does not *adopt* Hegel but *adapts* him to his own ends. To understand Du Bois's investigation of historical consciousness out of Hegel it is as important to see how his reading differs from Hegel as it is to note the parallels.

By focusing on the middle chapters of the *Phenomenology* Du Bois cuts away the Hegelian concern with the development of consciousness toward the first stages of self-consciousness and also with the all-synthesizing idealistic monism of Absolute Spirit at the end of the *Phenomenology.* Du Bois's emphasis is not on the singular *Geist* but on souls. Du Bois's own projection of a possible resolution of historical division in a "kingdom of culture" may seem like a utopian negation of the tragic substance of historical particularity and multiplicity. But ***Souls,*** like *The Suppression of the African Slave Trade,* undermines exceptionalist and progressive versions of American history. Du Bois's reworking of Hegel includes a careful historical location of his own drama of alterity and entails precisely the critical testing of this cultural idealism, and so of Du Bois's own cultural and political programs of progressive reform, against the terrible facts of African-American history. Therefore, in using Hegel as a resource Du Bois neither psychologizes history nor reproduces a progressive and optimistic teleology of enlightenment. He moves instead toward a complex historicization of psychology.

Robert Gooding-Williams has argued that ***Souls*** is a kind of Hegelian philosophy of history and that Du Bois's turn to social science challenges his Hegelian idealism.[4] This may be true of the relationship of **"The Conservation of Races"** and Du Bois's work in sociology, but it is not true of ***Souls. Souls*** does not reproduce the grand idealist historical schema of the *Phenomenology*; instead it adapts to its own ends the micro-level sense of the negativity of historical experience that is embodied in Hegel's account of the "unhappy consciousness." As such ***Souls*** is a challenge not only to the idealism of **"The Conservation of Races"** but also to the positivism of Du Bois's sociology. The very sections of the *Phenomenology* that Du Bois takes as the platform for his psychological explorations (the sections narrating the development of consciousness into self-consciousness) were in fact intended by Hegel as a critique of positivism or commonsense philosophy. As Herbert Marcuse puts it in his examination of the relation of Hegel's thought to the development of social science, truth for Hegel resides not in "objective facts" but in "the living subject":

> The world is an estranged and untrue world so long as man does not destroy its dead objectivity and recognize himself and his own life "behind" the fixed form of things and laws. When he finally wins this *self-consciousness,* he is on his way not only to the truth of himself but also of his world. And with the recognition goes the doing. He will try to put this truth into action and *make* the world what it *essentially* is, namely, the fulfillment of man's self-consciousness.[5]

Hegel's critique of positivism provides a link back to the discussions of the previous chapter (Gillian Rose's critique of positivist paradigms of validity works directly out of Hegel) and also an entrance into the examination of Du Bois's account of consciousness and of the critical function of this account in the present chapter.

Ideas of fragmented consciousness and the divided self were ubiquitous in the 1880s and 1890s not only in psychology but also in literature.[6] In his autobiography Henry Adams noted that in turn-of-the-century psychology "dualism seemed to have become as common as binary stars. Alternating personalities turned up constantly, even among one's friends" (*EHA* 433). It is this very omnipresence that makes it difficult to offer anything other than a generalized account of any particular deployment of the trope of double consciousness. Du Bois's own use of this figure remains one of the most frequently cited and quoted passages in African-American letters, yet the famous passage on the "two-ness" of the African-American has received little detailed commentary. Ironically it is precisely the wide currency of Du Bois's account of "double-consciousness" in African-American cultural discourse that indicates a fundamental misunderstanding of the specificity of that account.

The frequency with which Du Bois's description is used suggests that it is commonly accepted as a universally and transhistorically true analysis of a tragic aspect of African-American self-consciousness. But Du Bois's dramatization of "double-consciousness" is a historically specific and class-specific psychology. The account of "double-consciousness" in the first chapter of ***Souls*** represents the black middle-class elite facing the failure of its own progressive ideals in the late nineteenth century, in the aftermath of failed Reconstruction and under the gaze of a white America. **"Of Our Spiritual Strivings"** is intended as a psychology of the Talented Tenth in crisis, not of the "black folk" as a homogenized collectivity.[7]

The new psychology and American Romanticism, particularly the work of James and Emerson, have been cited as possible sources or contexts for Du Bois's psychology of "double-consciousness."[8] These comparisons are useful only inasmuch as they help map out a discursive field in which Du Bois's work can be critically differentiated. Unlike Du Bois, both James and Emerson tend to offer largely ahistorical and apolitical accounts of the self. James's discussions of double consciousness or of the divided self in the realms of hysteria or religious experience favor medicalized diagnoses and remedial strategies that naturalize society in their stress on the return to healthy equilibrium. Emerson too proposes to conquer double consciousness through a transcendence of the alienation of the divided self toward a spiritual union of the "Me" and the "Not-Me." Du Bois's psychology, by contrast, is committed to a political understanding of alienation and a social and historical location of the self.[9] Its sense of the self, therefore, is radically different from James's favoring presentist experience over consciousness and its relation to the past, his optimistic celebrations of future-oriented, heroic ethical activity, and his relative lack of interest in the political contexts of psychology.

The radical nature of Du Bois's reworking of the *Phenomenology* can be understood only if it is read against other nineteenth-century American interpretations of Hegel. With very few exceptions, when Hegel is used in nineteenth-century America he is used as a prophet of American exceptionalism. The American Hegel tends to be an upbeat Hegel, a theorist of an organic nation populated by wholistic selves. This was the Hegel that James dismissed as the metaphysical absolutist. But Du Bois's Hegel is much closer to the one that emerges from Marx's or Sartre's critical readings of the *Phenomenology*. At the same time it must understood that Du Bois's psychology of alterity works within idealist frameworks. Its primary concern is with recognition. Du Bois does not offer an adequately materialist critique of the failure of Reconstruction or his own program for the "Talented Tenth" until the publication of his Marxist historiography, ***Black Reconstruction in America*** (1935). What Hegel's idealist philosophy makes available to Du Bois is a complex model for thinking about the relationship of consciousness and history. Through Hegel Du Bois can conceptualize more clearly than before a sense of history and inheritance, of the pressure of the past on present action, though without any fatalistic submission to history as necessity. How is it then that Du Bois can read Hegel quite so critically, before he has begun to read Marx, without (as far as is known) a knowledge of Kierkegaard, well before Alexandre Kojève's and Sartre's commentaries on the *Phenomenology,* and very much against the grain of the readings of Hegel common in nineteenth-century America?

It is impossible to provide a fully comprehensive answer, either intentionalist or discursive, to this question, but it is possible to point to some enabling factors. The most important of these is Du Bois's historical and cultural position as a black intellectual, well trained in speculative thought, testing available philosophical models against the political realities of late-nineteenth-century America. To this must be added Du Bois's studies with James and Santayana. As already noted, Du Bois studied psychology with James and modern French and German philosophy, including Hegel, with Santayana simultaneously during the academic year 1889-90. *The Principles of Psychology* appeared in 1890 and, according to Santayana, James was teaching portions of his book in his classes during 1889, reading out sections and offering them for discussion.[10] At the same time it is relevant for the present discussion that the reading of Hegel had set Santayana to planning his own *Life of Reason* (1905-6),[11] itself a literary psychology that attempted a history of consciousness, of the imaginative life and its responses to the material conditions of its existence. James and Santayana would have made available to Du Bois both mutually supportive and also radically opposed conceptual models with which to think about consciousness and psychology in complex ways.

The foregrounding of the political and ideological context in the reading of **"Strivings"** in this chapter is meant as a reminder that the issue here is not, to adapt Louis Althusser's commentary on the young Marx's reading of German philosophy, one of an "ideal debate" between "characters" called Du Bois, Hegel, James, and so forth. It is more a matter of debate between "*concrete* ideological characters on whom the ideological context imposed *determinate features* which do not necessarily coincide with their literal historical identities." So "the Hegel who was the opponent of the Young Marx from the time of his doctoral dissertation was not the library Hegel we can meditate on in the solitude of 1960; it was *the Hegel of the neo-Hegelian movement,* a Hegel already summoned to provide German intellectuals of the 1840s with the means to think their own history and their own hopes." And at the same time the "literal historical identities" of Hegel and his followers were "much more extensive than the explicit representations Marx gave of them" in his critiques.[12] Similarly, Du Bois's dialogue with Hegel must be seen in the context of the nationalist invocations of Hegel in nineteenth-century America, of James's dismissals of Hegel's monistic system, and also of Santayana's more sympathetic and critical reading of Hegel. And the Hegel that emerges dialectically from Du Bois's own reading of the *Phenomenology* in the context of these other available readings must be differentiated from these Hegels and also the "literal" Hegel of 1807.

The precondition of such a rupture or differentiation is, as Althusser also notes, "the rediscovery of real history."[13] The transformation of the young, Hegelian Marx into the "Marxist" Marx is dependent upon "the discovery beneath the ideology which had deformed it of *the reality it had referred to*—and the discovery beyond contemporary ideology, *which knew it not,* of *a new reality.* Marx became himself by thinking this double reality in a rigorous theory, by changing elements—and by thinking the unity and reality of this new element."[14] The causality of such a transformation in thought cannot be posited, then, as simply a matter of "*ideological immanence*" (a logic of *ideas* alone), but must be stated as a moment of "*the irruption of real history in ideology itself.*"[15] Du Bois's critical Hegelian insights are also made possible by his becoming aware of the disjuncture between dominant ideology and the reality beneath. The gradual rise of this awareness in the thought of Du Bois is what is charted in this study. It is true that in the early part of his career Du Bois does not manage to think an alternative "rigorous theory." But *Souls* does represent a critical response complex in its exploration both of the implications of "the irruption of history" into Du Bois's ideological field and of a consciousness that can actively resist the threat of passivity and the abandonment of critical thought within such a rupture.

United Selves and United States: Hegel in America

As Henry Pochmann has commented, "it is noteworthy that at precisely the time when [the] process of winning intellectual maturity was at its height [in American thought], the acculturation of German philosophy was strongest."[16] The last twenty years of the nineteenth century marked "the highest point of Germanic influence in American philosophy. As idealism became dominant, even its opponents—including pragmatists, personalists, and realists—were profoundly influenced by the German classical and post-Hegelian philosophies."[17] Hegelianism became widespread in American philosophy and social thought in the 1870s, in large part a symptom of the resurgence of nationalist sentiment during and after the Civil War. Where the common sense school and Transcendentalism had prioritized the individual, Hegelianism stressed the group. "As a system of ethics it supplemented the individualism of Locke, and prepared the ground for collectivistic theories in politics, sociology, and economics." This trend was strengthened by and combined with the prevalence of Darwin's influence in American social thought.[18]

John Dewey's adoption of Hegelianism early in his career provides an exemplary instance of an optimistic reading of Hegel in which an idealist psychology is transformed into an organic doctrine of self and the nation-state.[19] The political context in which Dewey's organicism takes shape is important for understanding the thrust of his ideas. As Dorothy Ross stresses, Dewey "felt his 'disinheritance,' the strain between inherited dogmas and the world around him, as a profound separation of self and other, ideal and reality, which set him on a lifelong effort to abolish dualism. His early essays show clearly that the threat to the American political tradition in the Gilded Age [from Civil War, Reconstruction, and rapid industrialization] was one source of his unease and a principal dimension of his reconstructive efforts."[20]

The essays from the 1880s provide key statements. The heart of Dewey's defense of Hegelianism is a rejection of all formalistic logic that separates subject and object. In "Kant and Philosophic Method" (1884), Dewey argues that the logic of difference in analytic reason is transcended by the higher unity of synthetic reason. "Reason must be that which separates itself, which differentiates, goes forth into differences, that it may then grasp these differences into a unity of its own."[21] Both British empiricism and Kant are rejected as exemplars of analytic logic in favor of Hegel, since Hegel "offers us Reason affirmative *and* negative, and affirmative only in and through its own negations, as the solution."[22] Dialectic and negation are understood as affirmations of ultimate unity.

"The New Psychology" (1884) extends the critique of formal logic to psychology, aligning "the old psychology" with formalism and defining the new through an organic conceptualization of the self in which Hegel and biology, as well as the insights of the social and historical sciences, are joined together.[23] Dewey is trying to combine the scientific emphasis of the new psychology with a focus on the relation of the human mind and behavior to cultural life.[24] He can, therefore, in "The Psychological Standpoint" (1886), propose a synthesis of idealism and empiricism via psychology, just as Du Bois was to attempt to combine the two into a "science of Mind" in **"The Renaissance of Ethics"** only two years later.[25] It is understandable then that psychology becomes for Dewey the "philosophic method," and the denial of self-consciousness signals a denial of "the possibility of philosophy."[26]

What is potentially creative and radical in Dewey's Hegelian psychology, and what could align it to Du Bois's psychology, is its stress on difference, relationality, and self-consciousness, and its sense of the individual as a "transition" or "a process of becoming."[27] But unlike Du Bois, Dewey always subsumes his particularist understandings into higher syntheses, his Hegelian sense of negativity into a Hegelian optimism of a unifying teleology. So finally "the individual consciousness is but the process of realization of the universal consciousness through itself. Looked at as process, as realizing, it is individual consciousness; looked at as produced or realized, as conscious of the process, that is, of itself, it is universal consciousness."[28]

Dewey's argument for a universal consciousness may be philosophically vague, but its social and political import becomes quite clear when Dewey transforms his psychology and his critique of formalistic logic into a defense of the American political system. In "The Ethics of Democracy" (1888) Dewey follows the arguments of George Sylvester Morris's *Hegel's Philosophy of the State and of History* (1887) and pits an organic theorization of democracy against those who see democracy as nothing but "a numerical aggregate, a conglomeration of units."[29] Dewey emphasizes that his organic conception of democracy "is as much an account of the individual as it is of the whole. One who has really adopted the notion can say not less, but more than anyone else, that society exists for and by individuals. But it is because he has given up the fiction of isolated unsocial units, and has realized that the individual embodies and realizes within himself the spirit and will of the whole organism."[30] The psycho-philosophical relation of the individual and the universal is here stated socially, and in this shift not Germany but America is made the Hegelian end of history. His organicism is for Dewey "the American theory, a doctrine which in grandeur has but one equal in history, and that its fellow, namely, that every man is a priest of God."[31] The radical puritan "priesthood of all believers" now legitimates the American state.

While Dewey's critique of atomistic social doctrine is valuable, his own Hegelian account of democracy drifts toward a centrist acceptance of the social process. As A. R. Buss has argued, the integrative nature of dialectical thought as it has developed from Hegel through Marx has been of central importance in the development of a humanistic psychology. But where Marx theorizes a transformation of the world and foregrounds the function of critique in this process, Hegel's philosophy can involve an incorporation of history "into the story of Reason's unfolding, hence a justification of everything that happens and an alibi for the status quo."[32] Dewey's subsuming of particularity within Reason's higher syntheses produces similar results. So, for example, Dewey sees the growth of industrialization and the consequent spread of wealth as adequate safeguards against the spread of socialism and communism. And while Dewey's theory of democracy lays great emphasis on individual choice and freedom, it also "admits that the full significance of personality can be learned by the individual only as it is already presented to him in objective form in society."[33] Society is for Dewey the sole criterion of the organic good. As Neil Coughlan notes, "the definition of virtue that seems eventually to have most satisfied [Dewey] was conduct that served society's end."[34]

Du Bois may or may not have known of the early work of Dewey, but a version of Hegel very close to Dewey's was available to him at Harvard in the work of Royce. Du Bois studied forensics with Royce in his junior year and met and talked with him at the Philosophical Club (*A* 143). He also studied Hegel with Santayana just a year after Santayana had read the *Phenomenology* with Royce as part of his graduate studies and during a year in which Royce was once again offering his graduate course on Hegel's system, focusing on the *Phenomenology,* in the philosophy department.[35]

Royce's interpretation of Hegel is available in his book *The Spirit of Modern Philosophy* (1892), published while Du Bois was still enrolled as a graduate student at Harvard. Like Dewey, Royce stresses that dialectical negativity is the process by which a higher harmonization and unity are achieved. "Consciousness . . . differentiates itself into various, into contrasted, forms and lives in their relationships, their conflicts, their contradictions, and in the triumph over these. . . . So, in short, everywhere in conscious life, consciousness is a union, an organization, of conflicting aims, purposes, thoughts, strivings." This is what Hegel calls "the law of universal *Negativität* of self-conscious life."[36] And like Dewey, Royce foregrounds relationality and organic collectivity in his reading of Hegel. So the self is seen as a "knot of relationships to other moments and to other people." In such an intersection, "I know myself only so far as I am known or may be known by another than my present or momentary self" and "I become myself by forsaking my isolation and by entering into community."[37]

The politics that are only implicit or half-visible in Dewey's and Royce's uses of Hegel are made more explicit in the writings of the St. Louis Hegelians, certainly the most important proponents of an American Hegelianism in the second half of the nineteenth century. Though largely forgotten now in considerations of thought in nineteenth-century America, the St. Louis movement was "the chief vehicle by which Hegel's ideas and those of virtually every other major post-Kantian German philosopher entered the mainstream of American thought."[38] The movement existed from about 1865 to the mid-1880s, during which time its members were unmatched in their publication record and the energetic dissemination of their ideas.[39] In 1867 William Torrey Harris, the leading light of the movement, founded the *Journal of Speculative Philosophy,* the first definitive and significant philosophical journal in the English language and unquestionably the most important philosophical publication in America at the time. It outlasted the group and continued publication until 1893 (past Du Bois's undergraduate work in philosophy), providing detailed and continuous coverage of German philosophy, particularly that of Kant and Hegel.[40] The uniqueness of the *Journal* made it an essential forum for both students and practitioners of philosophy, and rising American thinkers such as Royce and Dewey, as well as James, wrote for the *Journal.* As a recent assessment of the group's contribution to nineteenth-century American culture stresses, it "gave philosophy such a fresh sense of power and historicity that it was moved out of the genteel world of clerics and colleges into the realm of public affairs."[41]

Though centered in the Midwest, the movement had strong roots in New England Transcendentalism. Emerson had been an early and significant influence on Henry Brokmeyer, the leading theoretician and philosophic authority of the group. And Amos Bronson Alcott inspired Harris, who also maintained a long and continuous contact with Emerson. Both Alcott and Emerson visited the group in St. Louis, lectured there, and were auxiliary members.[42] After the breakup of the group in St. Louis, Harris and some of the other members moved to Concord around 1878 and joined Dean Alcott's Concord School. There, Harris was popular and Plato apparently was soon eclipsed by Hegel until the school closed in 1887, just a year before Du Bois entered Harvard.

Du Bois cannot have been ignorant of the history and ideas of the St. Louis Hegelians, given that the *Journal* was the major forum for philosophical debate at the time, that James and other philosophers known to Du Bois published therein, that a good part of James's animosity toward Hegelianism was, in fact, aimed at the St. Louis group,[43] and that members of the group had strong associations with the intellectual culture of New England and were active within this culture in the years just prior to Du Bois's arrival in Boston.[44] He may even have encountered the ideas of the group at Fisk through his New Englandized teachers from the Midwest. (Education was perhaps the area in which the St. Louis group was most influential.)[45]

The St. Louis movement applied Hegel's idea of Teutonic destiny and his theory of state to the conditions of contemporary America. The initial attraction was political more than metaphysical. The group, turning to Hegel as a reaction against what it saw as the flood of materialism and political chaos, was inspired by frontier expansion and saw St. Louis as the city of the future, playing its role in the fulfillment of the Teutonic destiny in America.[46] Hegel's political philosophy had itself grown as a response to a Germany in social and political disarray under Frederick William III. The volatile context of St. Louis provided "an urgent social *milieu*" in which Hegel could easily take root.[47] During the decades from 1858 to 1878, filled with the turmoil of the Civil War and its aftermath, "in a political, though not in a military sense, Missouri was at the center of the storm and St. Louis was at the center of Missouri." In the late 1850s, as the gateway to the West and Northwest, the city was also "the epitome of American frontier civilization."[48]

In *Lectures on the Philosophy of History,* Hegel himself had prophesied that America was "the land of the future, where, in the ages that lie before us, the burden of the World's History shall reveal itself." It was up to America "to abandon the ground on which hitherto the History of the World has developed itself."[49] Hegel provided the St. Louis Movement with a suitable postwar theory of the state, and the group elaborated its interpretation of Hegel's political philosophy in the pages of the *Journal* and in Denton J. Snider's *The American State.*[50] As early as 1848, Johan B. Stallo, in his *Principles of the Philosophy of Nature,* had outlined a Hegelian theory of organic, progressive, and rational society and had seen this as the true and inevitable fulfillment of the American Constitution.[51] So, despite the fact that many of the St. Louisans had fled from Prussian tyranny, they interpreted Hegel as the philosopher of liberty, not the theorist of the absolute state (a Hegel popularized by Heinrich von Treitschke's *History of Germany in the Nineteenth Century*), or the philosopher responsible for the events of 1848.[52] The faith in the destiny of American civilization was, of course, by no means confined to the St. Louis

Hegelians, but was widespread in American philosophical and historical thought.[53] Snider, among the most prolific of the St. Louis group, was perfectly aware of the parallels between the group's and Emerson's American exceptionalism.[54]

The paradoxical use of Hegel as a legitimation of American exceptionalism was not unique to the St. Louis group. In 1881, dismissing Carlyle as "quite the legitimate European product to be expected," Walt Whitman proclaimed that the "formulas of Hegel are an essential and crowning justification of New World democracy in the creative realms of time and space." And in an unpublished lecture on Hegel the American poet insisted that "only Hegel is fit for America—is large enough and free enough." At the time that *Leave of Grass* first appeared (1855), Whitman had access to Hegel and Hegelian ideas through several anthologies, translations, summaries, and adaptations, but he also corresponded with Harris, met him (and probably the other Hegelians) in St. Louis, and seems to have read, perhaps even subscribed to, their *Journal.*[55]

When the Civil War erupted, neither the St. Louis Hegelians nor Whitman abandoned the reassurances of an Americanized Hegel, though Whitman registered the shock-waves of doubt more clearly. The Hegelian historicism of both Whitman and the St. Louis Hegelians was also a flight from history, since it sought to reduce the concrete facts of history to an abstract schema of thesis, antithesis, and synthesis, an essentially static conceptualization of dialectic that Hegel himself had in fact rejected.[56] This schematization is nowhere more apparent than in the group's interpretation of the Civil War as a necessary part of the dialectic process of history in which America would assume its rightful and leading place in the onward movement of thought and culture. Hegel "was the prophet of a reunited nation after it had suffered the terrible 'dialectic' of civil war. The Southern position, Brokmeyer explained, was what Hegel termed 'abstract right'; the Northern, that of an equally 'abstract morality'; while the Union represented what Hegel called the 'ethical state.'"[57] So too the author of "Drum Taps" "can read or revise the Civil War symbolically and ahistorically as a negative moment in the destined arc of the Union."[58]

Snider wrote years later, in terms that, like Du Bois's **"Renaissance of Ethics,"** appear to combine Hegel with Spencer, "the time was calling loudly for *First Principles.* The Civil War had just concluded, in which we all had in some way participated, and we were still overwhelmed, even dazed partially by the grand historic appearance. What does it all mean? was quite the universal question. . . . Naturally our set sought in philosophy the solution, that is, in Hegel as taught by our leaders."[59] This is much of a sameness with Du Bois's turn to Bismarck or to Spencerian theodicy in the context of the postwar and post-Reconstruction South, and confirms Adams's sense of the seductiveness of a predictable and uniform system in the aftermath of the war. But it is also likely that Du Bois's satires of Teutonic nationalism in **"A Vacation Unique"** and the **"Jefferson Davis"** commencement speech were aimed in part at the St. Louis group. It will be remembered that Du Bois's experiences of racism in the Midwest, the home ground of the St. Louis group, provide the stage upon which the satire of Teutonic nationalism and of metaphysical historicism is dramatized in **"A Vacation Unique."** Similarly, the focus on Teutonism and on the Civil War as the latest manifestation of its destiny in **"Jefferson Davis,"** and Du Bois's choice of the Confederate president as its representative, not only look toward Emerson but neatly invert the St. Louisans' support for the Union and so foreground the racist potentials of their metaphysical alibis for manifest destiny. The connection between the St. Louis group and Emerson would, of course, have been suggested to Du Bois by the Concord residence of Harris and others as well as by the philosophical links between Transcendentalism and St. Louis idealism. However, Du Bois's own continued attraction to heroic vitalism meant that he was to an important extent committed to the ideological form of this nationalism. Du Bois's dilemma, then, was somehow to critique a particular instance of the political deployment of historicism while still keeping the redemptive teleologies available for black Americans. The awkward attempt to synthesize Jamesian pragmatism, Hegelian historicism, and Spencerian evolutionism in **"Renaissance of Ethics"** was Du Bois's attempt to get himself out of this double bind. Where Hegelian historicism had, in America, become a powerful ideological support for both an expansionist and racist nationalism and an idealist exceptionalism inadequately aware of its own politics, Spencer's evolutionism offered a historicism anchored in alibis of scientific neutrality and objectivity and so free from the interference of political intentionalities and human volition. The "great laws" Du Bois dreamed of were guarantors of a universal teleology that unfolded without regard for the color line. "Renaissance of Ethics" sought, in effect, to rescue history from history itself, whereas **"A Vacation Unique"** insistently tethered these metaphysical flights of fancy to the contemporary social ground.

Nowhere does Du Bois refuse to subsume the negative particularity of African-American experience into historicist teleologies so clearly as he does in *Souls,* and it is this refusal that separates him from other American Hegelians. Whitman's Hegel, like the Hegel championed by the St. Louisans or by Dewey or Royce, "was an optimist" whose system "solved contradictions and enlarged the democratic self" rather than offering "the full logical and existential negativity of the dialectic" at the heart of the *Phenomenology.*[60] The American evasion of the "existential negativity" of Hegel's *Phenomenology,* and the political consequences of this evasion, are most startlingly apparent in the accounts of the master-and-slave dialectic given by the American Hegelians in the 1890s. These accounts consistently misrepresent Hegel's account of the struggle between master and slave by falsely attributing the myth of cowardly contract to Hegel, thereby providing philosophical alibis for the proslavery arguments of the 1890s whose prevalence in historiography and social commentary has already been noted in the previous chapter.

The St. Louis group's reading of the master-and-slave dialectic is outlined in *The Rebel's Daughter: A Story of Love, Politics and War* (1899), a historical romance about the Civil War published two years after the publication of **"Strivings."** The novel was written by John Gabriel Woerner, a judge, journalist, philosopher, legal scholar, and founding member of the St. Louis Hegelians. In the novel Professor Rauhenfels, a representation of Henry Brokmeyer, another founding member of the St. Louis group and one of their leading ideologues, explains, on the eve of the Civil War, the necessity for maintaining southern slavery in order to safeguard the freedom embodied in the constitutionally elected American government:

> Under the present condition of things it is of far greater importance to humanity—to the cause of freedom—that our government remain intact, than the normal condition of the slaves be changed. As Doctor Taylor [a cipher for Denton Snider, another member of the group] once neatly expressed it—
>
> "'Tis not the outward bond that makes the slave—but the base craven thought within the man."
>
> Slaves are such upon their own compliance. No freeman, loving liberty above life or ease, was yet ever made a slave. To the slave, then, manumission is of no benefit.[61]

In the *Phenomenology* Hegel himself never says that "slaves are such upon their own compliance." His theorization of the master-and-slave relationship stresses the interdependence of two self-consciousnesses caught in "a life-and-death struggle" (*PM* 232). Hegel is concerned with the exercise and experienced mediations of power, not the justification of mastery through a theory of innate acquiescence. The *Phenomenology* in fact describes a complex dialectical process whereby the master is ultimately forced to recognize his dependence on the slave and the slave is able to realize his independence through his own labor. The cowardly contract theory of slavery simplifies this complexity and makes the servitude and subjection of the slave a means toward the absolute freedom of the master, a freedom that Hegel sees as an empty form of independence.

Royce outstrips the St. Louis Hegelians here. In *The Spirit of Modern Philosophy* he understands the master-and-slave dialectic not philogenetically but ontogenetically. That is to say, he takes Hegel's account to be a description not of actual slavery but of inner struggles of self-consciousness with its own contradictions. But Royce's reading of Hegel nevertheless presents the logic of mastery in its purest form.

> The more of a self I am, the more contradictions there are in my nature and the completer my conquest over these contradictions. The absolute self with which I am seeking to raise my soul, and which erelong I find to be a genuine self, yes, the only self, exists by the very might of its control over all these contradictions, whose infinite variety furnishes the very heart and content of its life.
>
> Hegel, as we see, makes his Absolute, the Lord, most decidedly a man of war. Consciousness is paradoxical, restless, struggling. Weak souls get weary of the fight, and give up trying to get wisdom, skill, virtue, because all these are won only in the presence of the enemy. But the absolute self is simply the absolutely strong spirit who bears the contradictions of life, and wins the eternal victory.[62]

This is not an accurate account of Hegel. It is rather an imposition onto a distorted Hegel of an ethics of self-realization that is identical to the conceptualization of ethical means and ends as a matter of the "victorious" and the "vanquished" by James, Royce's colleague at Harvard.

Woerner's dramatization of the St. Louisans' Hegelian interpretation of slavery is a little less absolute in its celebration of mastery. While insisting on the willingness of the slave to be made a slave, Rauhenfels (Brokmeyer) also paradoxically acknowledges the humanity of the slave, but does so only to temporarily trouble the master's ethics. Immediately after arguing that manumission is of no use to the slave, he goes on to say that

> the vice of slavery consists in the degradation of the master, because slavery is incompatible with his own freedom. Its recognition in the constitution is a monstrous contradiction of the principle of our government, and of the solemn declaration upon which we achieved independence. In depriving a human being of his liberty (for though this cannot be done without the slave's consent, neither can it be done without the master's act) he destroys the divine quality wherein man is the image of God. This is the sin that will bring upon us retributive punishment as surely as effect follows cause.
>
> (*RD* 332)

But if this sounds like the resounding declamation of an abolitionist (despite the troubling parenthesis), an immediate change of direction follows as Rauhenfels goes on to argue, according to a "higher" logic, that some nevertheless have the right to be more equal than others. He insists that "the forcible abolition of slavery would be no remedy" for the possibility of imminent "retributive punishment": "It would be a new crime. Not only sinning against the constitutional rights of the slave-owner, but adding the base perfidy of violating our own solemn covenant" (*RD* 333). It does not matter if one abhors slavery or not; it is more important that one abhor "the treachery involved in robbing the South of the property solemnly guaranteed to them by the constitution" (*RD* 333). When someone points out to Rauhenfels that his position implies "that under the constitution human freedom is at a discount,—good only for one class, wicked in another," he replies that such sentiments reflect only the "nursery-room morality" inculcated in the American public by Stowe's *Uncle Tom's Cabin.* This sentimental morality seeks to impose "conscience as law," to falsely violate "the law of the land" in the name of "a higher law of God" (*RD* 333; 334). "Romantic sentiment [Rauhenfels argues] makes short work of problems . . . that sorely try the wit of the anxious statemen, philanthropists and philosophers. It is so easy to follow the dictates of the heart if you can only stifle the skeptical protests of the head,—most easy to those who are least oppressed with brains" (*RD* 333).

The triumph of "the head" over "the dictates of the heart" in Rauhenfels's speech negates any sense that the meaning of history resides above all in the lived experience of human beings, and not in the sacrificing of this experience to the abstracted idols of so-called historical and institutional "laws" and "principles." The (albeit momentary and indirect) acknowledgment of the humanity of the slave is also evasive, since its implied notion of recognition is moralistic and idealist. The master is degraded because his act of conquest is an act against the divinity in Man. This suggests that the supremacy of the master can be destabilized if the humanness of the slave is recognized. But this is, once again, a gross distortion of Hegel's account of recognition, and it is a distortion perpetuated by modern critics of Hegel's theorization of the master-and-slave relationship.

Frantz Fanon, for example, insists that "the black man has no ontological resistance in the eyes of the white man."[63] For Fanon, unlike for Hegel, the master "laughs at the consciousness of the slave. What he wants from the slave is not recognition but work."[64] Orlando Patterson reinforces Fanon's conclusion in his study *Slavery and Social Death* when he argues against Hegel that slavery did *not* create "an existential impasse for the master" since "the master could and usually did achieve the recognition he needed from other free persons, including other masters."[65]

Others have repeated these criticisms, but neither Fanon nor Patterson does justice to Hegel's model of recognition in the *Phenomenology*.[66] In the *Phenomenology* the master does not seek recognition *from* the slave. Rather, he comes to recognize that his own freedom is dependent *on* the slave *and his labor* and is therefore a determined freedom and not an absolute and indeterminate one as he had thought: "for, just where the master has effectively achieved lordship, he really finds that something has come about quite different from an independent consciousness. It is not an independent, but rather a dependent consciousness that he has achieved. He is thus not assured of self-existence as his truth; he finds that his truth is rather the unessential consciousness [of the dependent slave], and the fortuitous unessential action of that consciousness" (*PM* 236-37). The master is brought to "an existential impasse" not by acknowledging the humanity of the slave and then seeking mutual recognition, but by recognizing that he himself is materialized through the property made by the slave. And just as the master comes to discover his dependency through the labor of the slave, so the slave discovers therein the possibility of his own consciousness passing "into real and true independence" (*PM* 237). Hegel is quite clear that "for recognition proper there is needed the moment that what the master does to the other he should also do to himself, and what the bondsman does to himself, he should do to the other also." Without this mutual labor, recognition remains "one sided and unequal" (*PM* 236). It is something like this mutuality that Du Bois will imagine in the first chapter of ***Souls*** when he writes that "the end" of the "striving" of the divided African-American is "to be a co-worker in the kingdom of culture" (*SBF* 365).

It was Marx who realized that "the outstanding achievement of Hegel's *Phänomenologie* and of its final outcome, the dialectic of negativity as the moving and generating principle, is thus first that Hegel conceives the self-creation of man as a process, conceives objectification as loss of the object, as alienation and transcendence of this alienation; that he thus grasps the essence of *labour* and comprehends objective man—true, because real man—as the outcome of man's *own labour.*"[67] The 1890s interpretations of Hegel in America acknowledge neither the process by which the positions of the master and slave are made interdependent and reversed, nor the centrality of the concept of labor in the *Phenomenology.* As a consequence these interpretations either ignore the political meaning of mastery and slavery, reducing self-realization to the imperial assertion of will rather than a process of alienation and transcendence through work (Royce), or they justify actual slavery (Brokmeyer). They also equate wage labor with slavery as an alibi for industrial capitalism's exploitation of workers.

In *Hegel's Logic* (1890), William Torrey Harris, the leading figure of the St. Louis Group, repeats the myth of the cowardly contract and uses Hegel as a justificatory masking for the alienation of labor within the capitalist mode of production and so for the economic status quo in the rapidly expanding industrial and commercial culture of contemporary America, the very opposite of what Marx had done with Hegel's master-and-slave dialectic almost fifty years earlier in *The Economic and Philosophic Manuscripts of 1844.* Harris argues that if self-consciousness "prefers life to independence, then it becomes a slave":

> One reflects on the fact that in savage tribes this is the characteristic condition. This is the lowest stadium of human history, but it has its uses in preparation for further developments. Hegel makes some interesting and valuable suggestions on this head, showing how the fact that the slave does not gratify his wants immediately from what is before him, but receives his food, clothing, and shelter as gifts from his master, although he, by his own labor, produces those things, develops ethical insight. The slave mediates his will through another, and begins the discipline which may lift him above a worse servitude to his passions and appetites. Even in modern civilization this discipline is retained as essential, and the system of industry demands of each man that he labor at some occupation which produces an article for the market of the world and not for his own consumption. He shall receive for his own consumption, for the most part, the products of the labor of his fellow-men. This mediation is necessary. But there can be a higher freedom attained in stoicism, and the slave who withdraws into the depths of his soul away from the actual, and renounces his finite interests, realizes this higher freedom.[68]

The extraordinary transition from the legitimated enslavement of "savage tribes" to the necessity of a slavish working class within a capitalist economy projects a seamless continuity between the antebellum agrarian South and the turn-of-the-century industrialized North and industrializing South. Across this seamless and social Darwinist transition each half of the proposition acts as an alibi for the other half, with freedom for the slave relegated to a "higher" realm "away from the actual." Harris's argument here reproduces in essential ways the ubiquitous nineteenth-century defense of the paternalism of plantation slavery projected against an alarmist vision of northern capitalism's urban poor turned into unruly masses (perhaps best known through George Fitzhugh's much earlier conflation of black slaves and the industrial working class in his *Cannibals All! or, Slaves without Masters* [1857]).

Du Bois's sense in ***Souls*** that the encroachments of northern capitalism into the South after the War have only instituted a system of peonage in place of plantation slavery also explores the intersections of plantation and industrial economies, but from a position of critical denunciation, not legitimation. But neither this denunciation nor Du Bois's vision of blacks and whites laboring together as "co-workers" should be taken as a suggestion that ***Souls*** presents a full materialist or Marxist account of alienation. Marx, who understood the radical achievement of the *Phenomenology,* also argued for the limitations of its radicalism. "For Hegel," Marx writes, "the *human being—man*—equals *self-consciousness.* All estrangement of the human being is therefore *nothing* but *estrangement of self-consciousness.* The estrangement of self-consciousness is not regarded as an *expression*—reflected in the realm of knowledge and thought—of the *real* estrangement of the human being. Instead, the *actual* estrangement—that which appears real—is according to its *innermost,* hidden nature (which is only brought to light by philosophy) nothing but the *manifestation* of the estrangement of the real human essence, of *self-consciousness.*"[69] Du Bois's own psychology of the crisis of self-consciousness works somewhere between idealist and materialist critique. The awareness of the economic and political contexts of "double-consciousness" in ***Souls*** does not translate itself into a radical critique of capitalist political economy. By focusing on the relationship of the black middle-class intelligentsia to the black "folk," ***Souls*** also tends to evade the issue of this group's relationship to the black urban working class. By appealing to white liberal sympathetic understanding, Du Bois also circles back to an idealist conception of recognition. But ***Souls*** does offer a highly politicized account of "double-consciousness." It is an account in which the class bases of Du Bois's own progressive idealist political programs and the evasions of historical reality in liberal American exceptionalism are simultaneously exposed to critical dramatizations. It is on the ground cleared by this critique that Du Bois goes on, in the final chapter of ***Souls,*** to offer a politicized account of black folk culture and to extend the insights of his psychology of alienation toward a fuller dramatization of creative self-realization.

Notes

1. Only Robert Gooding-Williams has previously noted a possible connection between *Souls* and Hegel's *Phenomenology* ("Philosophy of History and Social Critique in *The Souls of Black Folk," Social Science Information* 26, no. 1 [1987]: 99-106). Gooding-Williams reads *Souls* as a philosophy of history that embodies a "vision of unified historical process" (p. 103). He also argues that Josiah Royce's account of the *Phenomenology,* rather than the *Phenomenology* itself, is the more likely source for Du Bois. The reading of the first chapter of *Souls* that follows in the present chapter argues that the negativity of Du Bois's psychology dramatizes the failure of a unified philosophy of history, and that it cannot be aligned with Royce's reading of Hegel, but must be seen to be in direct and close dialogue with the *Phenomenology.*

   Apart from one or two other scholars who have referred in general terms to the Hegelianism of Du Bois's thought, nothing has been written on Du Bois and Hegel. There is a brief discussion of the Hegelianism of Du Bois in Joel Williamson's *The Crucible of Race: Black-White Relations in the American South since Emancipation* (New York: Oxford University Press, 1984), pp. 399-413. Williamson draws some general parallels between *The Philosophy of History* and Du Bois's ideas. While noting echoes of Hegelian vocabulary, Williamson concludes that the first chapter of *Souls* is vague and emotive and that there are no one-to-one parallels between Du Bois's work and Hegel's (p. 403). This is not so. And while Williamson is right to point out the Hegelian resonances of the *volk* ideology of *Souls* and of Du Bois's theories of racial progress, these ideas were common currency at the time and came to Du Bois through multiple sources, one of which may have been a direct or indirect knowledge of *The Philosophy of History.* In his "The Veil Transcended: Form and Meaning in W. E. B. Du Bois' *The Souls of Black Folk*" (*Journal of Black Studies* 2 [March 1972]: 303-21), Stanley Brodwin refers in passing to the "Neo-Hegelian" form of the book, but he is more concerned with a crude reduction of *Souls* to a mechanical "dialectical" structure of thesis-antithesis-synthesis (pp. 306, 310). Kendall Thomas refers to Du Bois's passage on "double-consciousness" at the end of a discussion of Hegel's master-slave dialectic, but only as an unconnected verification of Hegel's idea of the inverted world ("A House Divided against Itself: A Comment on 'Mastery, Slavery, and Emancipation,'" *Cardozo Law Review* 10, nos. 5-6 [March-April 1989], part 2: 1513-14). There is also a very brief and undeveloped suggestion of a connection between Du Bois and Hegel in Robert C. Williams, "W. E. B. Du Bois: Afro-American Philosopher of Social Reality," in Leonard Harris, ed., *Philosophy Born of Struggle: An Anthology of Afro-American Philosophy from 1917* (Dubuque: Kendall-Hunt, 1983), pp. 11-19. The title of Jesse N. McDade's "The Significance of Hegel's *das unglückliche Bewußtsein* and Du Bois' 'Double Consciousness'" [(1976) *A Luta Continua*] suggests that its concerns are closely related to those of the present study, but I have not been able to obtain a copy of this piece. The article is cited by Gooding-Williams (p. 114), though he too has been unable to obtain it.

2. According to Du Bois's course transcripts in the Harvard University archives and the course catalog for 1889-90, Du Bois that year took an introductory course in logic and psychology with James (Philosophy 2) and at the same time an advanced course on modern German and French philosophy with Santayana. Santayana's course (Philosophy 6) covered "French Philosophy from Descartes to Leibnitz, and German Philosophy, from Kant to Hegel" (see the Harvard College Course Catalogue, 1889-90, p. 118). The course had been taught by Professor Bowen the previous year. Although the catalog for 1888-89 states that Bowen's course was omitted for that year, an annotation inserted in handwriting on August 26, 1980, indicates that the course was in fact given (p. 112). The fact is confirmed by Santayana's autobiography (see below). The course catalog for 1889-90 does not list the Hegel text studied, but all available evidence points in the direction of the *Phenomenology.* The latter year, 1889-90, was Santayana's first year as instructor. The previous academic year he had taken a graduate course on Hegel's system, concentrating on the *Phenomenology,* with Josiah Royce (while also taking graduate seminars in psychology with James). Santayana was very excited by the *Phenomenology* and disliked the abstracted sophistry of Hegel's other works. The *Phenomenology* proved much more interesting than the work of Lotze, on which Santayana was writing his dissertation, and the reading of the *Phenomenology* in fact set Santayana to planning his own *Life of Reason* (see George Santayana, *Persons and Places: Fragments of an Autobiography,* ed. William G. Holzenberger and Herman J. Saatkamp [1944-53; Cambridge: MIT Press, 1986], pp. 389-90. The relationship of *The Life of Reason* to Hegel's text is discussed in more detail later). It is also worth noting that Royce was again teaching his course on Hegel during the year that Du Bois studied with Santayana. The description in the Harvard course catalog for 1889-90 reads: "The Development of the Hegelian System—Hegel's *Phaenomenologie des Geistes*" (p. 119). Santayana preferred teaching texts in the original language (*Persons and Places,* pp. 389-94), and Du Bois's German was good enough for him to do

extensive graduate work in Berlin. Du Bois received extensive training in both French and German at Fisk (see *AR,* pp. 6 and 10).

3. The key points of reference in the *Phenomenology* are the closing pages of chapter 3, titled "Force and Understanding; Appearance and the Supersensible World"; the sections titled "Independence and Dependence of Self-Consciousness: Lordship and Bondage" and "Freedom of Self-Consciousness: Stoicism, Scepticism, and the Unhappy Consciousness" in chapter 4 ("The True Nature of Self-Certainty"); and the opening section of chapter 6 ("Spirit"), titled "Objective Spirit: The Ethical Order." See G. W. F. Hegel, *The Phenomenology of Mind,* trans. J. B. Baillie (1807, trans. 1910; New York: Harper Torchbooks, 1967), pp. 212-506.
4. Gooding-Williams, "Philosophy of History and Social Critique in *The Souls of Black Folk,*" pp. 99, 101, 113.
5. Herbert Marcuse, *Reason and Revolution: Hegel and the Rise of Social Theory* (2d ed. 1954; Atlantic Highlands, N.J.: Humanities Press, 1983), p. 113.
6. Numerous discussions of this area in literature and intellectual history are available. A useful recent example is Judith Ryan, *The Vanishing Subject: Early Psychology and Literary Modernism* (Chicago: University of Chicago Press, 1991).
7. For a passing acknowledgment of the class specificity of Du Bois's psychology, see Ernest Allen, Jr., "Ever Feeling One's Twoness: 'Double Ideals' and 'Double Consciousness' in *The Souls of Black Folk,*" *Critique of Anthropology* 12, no. 3 (1992): 267.
8. See Arnold Rampersad, *The Art and Imagination of W. E. B. Du Bois* (Cambridge: Harvard University Press, 1976), p. 74; Dickson D. Bruce, Jr., "W. E. B. Du Bois and the Idea of Double Consciousness," *American Literature* 64, no. 2 (1992): 299-304; and Eric Sundquist, *To Wake the Nations: Race in the Making of American Literature* (Cambridge, Mass.: Harvard University Press, 1993), p. 571.
9. For Du Bois's sense of the political understanding that can be derived from the experience of alienation, see Thomas C. Holt, "The Political Uses of Alienation: W. E. B. Du Bois on Politics, Race, and Culture, 1903-1940," *American Quarterly* 42, no. 2 (1990): 301-23. Frank M. Kirkland, "Modernity and Intellectual Life in Black," *Philosophical Forum* 24, nos. 1-3 (1992-93): 151, also provides a brief reading of the positive and negative meaning of "double-consciousness" in the first chapter of *Souls.*
10. George Santayana, "A General Confession," in Paul Arthur Schilpp, ed., *The Philosophy of George Santayana* (New York: Tudor, 1951), p. 15. Originally published as "A Brief History of My Opinions" (1930). According to a catalog of books in Du Bois's library in the Du Bois archives at the University of Massachusetts at Amherst, Du Bois owned a copy of the two-volume, complete edition of the *Principles of Psychology.* The catalog, however, lists neither the date of publication nor the date of acquisition. The library is housed in Ghana and it has not been possible to examine its contents.
11. See note 2.
12. Louis Althusser, "On the Young Marx: Theoretical Questions" (1960), in Althusser, *For Marx,* trans. Ben Brewster (1965; London: Verso, 1990), p. 65.
13. Ibid., p. 76.
14. Ibid., p. 81.
15. Ibid., p. 82.
16. Henry A. Pochmann, *German Culture in America, 1600-1900: Philosophical and Literary Influences* (Madison: University of Wisconsin Press, 1957), p. 321. See also p. 302 on the increased influence of Hegel in American philosophy departments.
17. Ibid., p. 313.
18. Jurgen Herbst, *The German Historical School in American Scholarship: A Study in the Transfer of Culture* (New York: Cornell University Press, 1965), pp. 66-67.
19. Dewey's attempt to combine Hegelianism with the new psychology and the transformation of his Hegelianism into instrumentalism via Darwin have been well documented in two studies: Morton White's *The Origin of Dewey's Instrumentalism* (1943; New York: Octagon Press, 1964) and Neil Coughlan's *Young John Dewey: An Essay in American Intellectual History* (Chicago: University of Chicago Press, 1975).
20. Dorothy Ross, *The Origins of American Social Science* (Cambridge: Cambridge University Press, 1991), p. 163.
21. John Dewey, "Kant and Philosophic Method," in Dewey, *The Early Works of John Dewey, 1882-1898,* vol. 1 (Carbondale: Southern Illinois University Press, 1969), p. 44.
22. Ibid., p. 45.
23. Dewey, "The New Psychology," in Dewey, *The Early Works,* vol. 1, pp. 55-58.
24. On the development of the cultural emphasis in nineteenth-century psychology, see Emily D. Cahan and Sheldon H. White, "Proposals for a Second Psychology," *American Psychologist* 47, no. 2 (1992): 224-35.
25. Dewey, "The Psychological Standpoint," in Dewey, *The Early Works,* vol. 1, p. 123.
26. Dewey, "Psychology as Philosophic Method" (1886), in Dewey, *The Early Works,* vol. 1, p. 152.
27. Dewey, "The Psychological Standpoint," p. 142.
28. Ibid., p. 142.
29. Dewey, "The Ethics of Democracy," in Dewey, *The Early Works,* vol. 1, p. 229. On the relationship between Dewey and Morris (who was Dewey's Hegelian teacher and colleague), see the second chapters of White's *Origins of Dewey's Instrumentalism* and Coughlan's *Young John Dewey* (esp. pp. 29-30).
30. Dewey, "The Ethics of Democracy," p. 236.
31. Ibid., p. 237.
32. A. R. Buss, "Development of Dialectics and Development of Humanistic Psychology," *Human Development* 19, no. 4 (1976): 253.
33. Dewey, "The Ethics of Democracy," pp. 246, 244.
34. Coughlan, *Young John Dewey,* p. 85. Compare the discussion of conduct in James's thought in chapter 2.
35. For details, see note 2 above on Du Bois's studies with Santayana.

36. Josiah Royce, *The Spirit of Modern Philosophy* (Boston: Houghton Mifflin, 1892), pp. 212, 213.

37. Ibid., pp. 210, 207, 210.

38. William H. Goetzmann, "Introduction," in Goetzmann, ed., *The American Hegelians: An Intellectual Episode in the History of Western America* (New York: Alfred Knopf, 1973), p. 4. In the same volume, see Dewey's concurring assessment (p. 383). And Jacques Denton Snider, one of the leading members of the movement, recalls that the movement was remembered and talked about as late as 1920 (p. 24).

39. Pochmann, *German Culture in America,* pp. 257-94, provides a general history of the St. Louis movement. For a more lengthy history by one of the actual group members, see Denton J. Snider's *The St. Louis Movement in Philosophy, Literature, Education, Psychology, with Chapters of Autobiography* (St. Louis: Sigma, 1920). For a more up-to-date history of the group see Elizabeth Flower and Murray G. Murphey, *A History of Philosophy in America* (New York: Capricorn Books & G. P. Putnam & Sons, 1977), chap. 8. See also Herbert W. Schneider, *A History of American Philosophy* (1946; 2d ed., New York: Columbia University Press, 1963), pp. 161-68.

40. On the importance of the *Journal* in both America and Europe, see Edward L. Schaub, "Harris and the Journal of Speculative Philosophy," in Shaub, ed., *William Torrey Harris,* 1835-1935 (Chicago: Open Court, 1936), pp. 51-55.

41. Flower and Murphey, *History of Philosophy in America,* p. 463.

42. See Henry A. Pochmann, *New England Transcendentalism and St. Louis Hegelianism: Phases in the History of American Idealism* (Philadelphia: Carl Schurz Memorial Foundation, 1948), pp. 8-11, 15, 34-63, 112-13; and Goetzmann, ed., *The American Hegelians,* pp. 6-7, 9, 32, 71-75, 118-28, 149-53.

43. When, in 1882, James attacked the growing trend toward "Hegelism" in American thought, he seems, in part, to have had the St. Louis group in mind. In December 1880, James had written to Renouvier that he had spent the winter "resisting the inroads of Hegelism in our University." In a letter of February 1880, addressed to Royce, James had made it clear that his target was the St. Louis group of Hegelians. He was angry at Harris for rejecting an essay he had submitted to the *Journal* and was apprehensive about Harris's plans to move to the East Coast. "My ignorant prejudice against all Hegelians, except Hegel himself," he explained to Royce, "grows wusser and wusser. Their sacerdotal airs! and their sterility! Contemplating their navels and the syllable *oum!*" For the 1882 attack, see "On Some Hegelisms," in *The Will to Believe and Other Essays in Popular Philosophy* (1897; New York: Dover, 1956), pp. 263-98 (hereafter cited in the text as OSH). James also believed that, in 1882, Hegelianism could "be reckoned one of the most powerful influences of the time in the higher walks of thought" (263). See also note 16 above. For the letters, see Elizabeth Hardwick, ed., *The Selected Letters of William James* (New York: Farrar, Straus, and Cudahy, 1961), pp. 110-13.

44. The programs and lectures of the Concord school were regularly published in the *Journal.* James and Royce, as mentioned above, had lectured at the school, and James had even studied and discussed the manuscript of Brokmeyer's translation of Hegel's *Logic,* the unpublished bible of the St. Louis Movement, when Samuel H. Emery, a Hegelian from Quincy, Indiana, had brought a copy to Boston in 1879. See Pochmann, *New England Transcendentalism,* pp. 112-13, 104, 76-77, 72-73.

45. The St. Louis group had a significant impact on educational theory and administration throughout the country. Harris made major contributions to educational theory and administration. He was head of the Bureau of Education for seventeen years and Commissioner of Education of the United States from 1889 to 1906 and internationally recognized. See Henry Ridgely Evans, "William Torrey Harris: An Appreciation," in Schaub, ed., *William Torrey Harris,* pp. 1, 7. See also Goetzmann, ed., *American Hegelians,* section 6, "Education and Democracy," pp. 269-324. As far as the issue of Du Bois's possible knowledge of the St. Louis Hegelians is concerned, it is also worth noting that after the stay at the hotel the group traveled to Minneapolis, St. Paul, Madison, Milwaukee, and Chicago. Du Bois remembers meeting many "ministers, heads of Christian associations, and literary groups" (*A* 129). It was through this trip that he "received an impression of American civilization in the Middle West at the age of 20" (*A* 128).

46. Pochmann, *German Culture in America,* pp. 259-60.

47. Henry Gates Townsend, "The Political Philosophy of Hegel in a Frontier Society," in Shaub, ed., *William Torrey Harris,* pp. 70-72. Townsend also points out that "in 1860 one in every seven persons in the entire Missouri population was foreign born and one in fourteen was German born" (p. 71).

48. Ibid., p. 69.

49. In Goetzmann, ed., *The American Hegelians,* p. 20. The quotation is from Hegel's *Lectures on the Philosophy of History.*

50. Pochmann, *German Culture in America,* pp. 268, 282.

51. In Goetzmann, ed., *The American Hegelians,* pp. 160-61. See also pp. 184ff.

52. See Pochmann, *German Culture,* pp. 267, 643. As Townsend points out, Treitschke's interpretation of Hegel was not the one necessarily accepted at all times in America. Hegel was also seen as a liberal thinker ("Hegel in a Frontier Society," pp. 73-75).

53. "[George] Bancroft's ten-volume *History of the United States,* begun in 1834, was animated by this spirit, and the philosophical writings of [James] Marsh, [Frederic Henry] Hedge, [Carl] Follen, [Francis] Lieber, [James] Murdock, Emerson, [Freidrich Augustus] Rauch, [Francis] Bowen, H[enry] B[oynton] Smith, Phillip Schaff, G[eorge] S[ylvester] Morris, and especially the St. Louisians [Henry Conrad] Brokmeyer, Harris, [Denton Jacques] Snider, and [Adolf Ernst] Kroeger are imbued by the same principle." Pochmann, *German Culture in America,* p. 676.

54. See Goetzmann, *The American Hegelians,* pp. 29-30.

55. The quotations from and information on Whitman are drawn from Kathryne V. Lindberg, "Whitman's 'Convertible Terms': America, Self, Ideology," in Bainard Cowen and Joseph A. Kronick, eds., *Theorizing American Literature: Hegel, the Sign, and History* (Baton Rouge: Louisiana State University Press, 1991), pp. 247, 256, 252. My thanks to Prof. Lindberg for allow-

ing me to consult the manuscript draft of her essay prior to its publication. She has located Whitman's unpublished lectures on Kant, Hegel, Schelling, and Fichte in the archives of the Humanities Research Center at the University of Texas, Austin.

56. As Walter Kaufmann has pointed out, "Fichte introduced into German philosophy the three steps of thesis, antithesis, and synthesis, using these three terms. Schelling took up this terminology; Hegel did not. He never once used these three terms together to designate three stages in an argument or account in any of his books. And they do not help us understand his *Phenomenology,* his *Logic,* or his philosophy of history; they impede any open-minded comprehension of what he does by forcing it into a schema which was available to him and which he deliberately spurned" (W. Kaufmann, *Hegel: A Reinterpretation* [N. Y.: Anchor, 1966], p. 154). And as R. J. Bernstein explains, not only do the concepts of thesis, antithesis, and synthesis "play an insignificant role in Hegel's philosophy, they are essentially static concepts and completely misrepresent what Hegel means by 'dialectic.' The dialectic . . . is essentially a dynamic and organic process. One 'moment' of a dialectic process, when it is fully developed or understood, gives rise to its own negation; it is not mechanically confronted by an antithesis" (Bernstein, *Praxis and Action* [Philadelphia: University of Pennsylvania Press, 1971], p. 20).

57. Pochmann, *German Culture in America,* p. 268. See also Townsend, "Hegel in a Frontier Society," p. 76; and Goetzmann, ed., *The American Hegelians,* pp. 28-29, 30-31, 160-61. Many of the members of the St. Louis Movement were German exiles, trained not only in the philosophy of Kant and Hegel but also in the arts of war. During the war they fought on the side of the Union.

58. Lindberg, "Whitman's 'Convertible Terms,'" p. 256.

59. Snider, *The St. Louis Movement* (1921), quoted in Pochmann, *German Culture in America,* p. 258, my emphasis. Pochmann also comments on the group's adaptation of Emersonian Transcendentalism along with Hegelian idealism.

60. Lindberg, "Whitman's 'Convertible Terms,'" p. 245. On Whitman, nationalism, and Hegel, see also Schneider, *History of American Philosophy,* pp. 146-49, 162-63.

61. John Gabriel Woerner, "An American War and Peace," an extract from *The Rebel's Daughter,* in William H. Goetzman, ed., *The American Hegelians: An Intellectual Episode in the History of Western America* (New York: Alfred A. Knopf, 1973), p. 332. Hereafter abbreviated *RD.*

62. Royce, *Spirit of Modern Philosophy,* pp. 213-14.

63. Frantz Fanon, *Black Skin, White Masks,* trans. Charles Lam Markmann (Fr. ed. 1952; New York: Grove Weidenfeld, 1967), p. 110.

64. Ibid., p. 220, n. 8.

65. Orlando Patterson, *Slavery and Social Death: A Comparative Study* (Cambridge: Harvard University Press, 1982), p. 99.

66. For further commentary on the usefulness or nonusefulness of Hegel's master-and-slave dialectic for thinking about actual slavery, see the *Cardozo Law Review* 10, nos. 5-6, part 2 (March-April 1989), a special issue devoted to "Hegel and Legal Theory." Four articles discuss whether Hegel can be helpfully used to think about American slavery. Guyora Binder, "Mastery, Slavery, and Emancipation" (pp. 1435-80), deals briefly with Woerner's *The Rebel's Daughter* and repeats the equation of Hegel's account with the myth of the cowardly contract. There are three articles qualifying and criticizing some of Binder's premises: Kendall Thomas, "A House Divided against Itself: A Comment on 'Mastery, Slavery, and Emancipation'" (pp. 1481-1515); Jonathan Bush, "Hegelian Slaves and the Antebellum South" (pp. 1517-63); and Merold Westphal, "Hegel on Slavery, Independence, and Liberalism" (pp. 1565-73). Though Thomas's argument is rather crude in its literalism, his focus on the "inverted world" section of the *Phenomenology* (wherein Hegel writes of the "curtain" hanging before the world of appearances) and on the "unhappy consciousness" as more fruitful areas for exploration than the master-slave dialectic parallel as the focus of "Of Our Spiritual Strivings." Thomas mentions Du Bois's idea of "double-consciousness" at the very end of his article, though he does not pursue any possible comparisons or connections with Hegel. Nevertheless, this article, like the others mentioned here, has been helpful in clarifying some of the ideas in the present discussion. My thanks to Guillaume Balan-Gaubert for pointing me to this issue of the *Cardozo Law Review* and for all our conversations in Chicago about Hegel, Du Bois, and slavery. In the epilogue of his *The Problem of Slavery in the Age of Revolution: 1770-1823* (Ithaca: Cornell University Press, 1975), David Brion Davis argues for the utility of Hegel in thinking about the multifaceted nature of slavery.

67. Marx, *The Economic and Philosophic Manuscripts of 1844* (1959; Moscow: Progress Publishers, 1977), p. 132.

68. William T. Harris, *Hegel's Logic: A Book on the Genesis of the Categories of the Mind: A Critical Exposition* (Chicago: S. C. Griggs and Co., 1890), pp. 87-88.

69. Marx, *Economic and Philosophic Manuscripts,* pp. 133-34.

ERIC J. SUNDQUIST (ESSAY DATE 1996)

SOURCE: Sundquist, Eric J. Introduction to *The Oxford W. E. B. Du Bois Reader,* pp. 3-36. Oxford: Oxford University Press, 1996.

In the following excerpt, Sundquist reviews the development of Du Bois's political thought, focusing especially on The Souls of Black Folk *and* Dusk of Dawn *as crucial landmarks in Du Bois's corpus. Sundquist observes Du Bois's increasing tendency toward Marxism, and discusses the role of autobiography in his writings.*

At the outset of his last sustained autobiographical writing, a work undertaken in the late 1950s but published posthumously in 1968, W. E. B. Du Bois, having just provided a capsule summary of his recent invigorating trip to the Soviet Union and China, offers the following reflection on his work:

> I mention this trip in some detail because it was one of the most important trips that I had ever taken, and had wide influence on my thought. To

> explain this influence, my Soliloquy becomes an autobiography. Autobiographies do not form indisputable authorities. They are always incomplete, and often unreliable. Eager as I am to put down the truth, there are difficulties; memory fails especially in small details, so that it becomes finally but a theory of my life, with much forgotten and misconceived, with valuable testimony but often less than absolutely true, despite my intention to be frank and fair.
>
> Who and what is this I, which in the last year looked on a torn world and tried to judge it? Prejudiced I certainly am by my twisted life; by the way in which I have been treated by my fellows; by what I myself have thought and done. I have passed through changes by reason of my growth and willing; by my surroundings without; by knowledge and ignorance. What I think of myself, now and in the past, furnishes no certain document proving what I really am. Mostly my life today is a mass of memories with vast omissions, matters which are forgotten accidentally or by deep design.

Taking note of the remarkable ideological gulf between the views presented in his most recent autobiography, ***Dusk of Dawn,*** some twenty years earlier and those of the ***Autobiography,*** conceived at the height of the cold war and Du Bois's estrangement from the United States, he adds: "One must then see these varying views as contradictions to truth, and not as final and complete authority. This book then is the Soliloquy of an old man on what he dreams his life has been as he sees it slowly drifting away; and what he would like others to believe" (Du Bois, ***Autobiography,*** 12-13).

One justifiably wonders if this is not the introduction to a work of postmodern antiteleology, a radical empowerment of black subjectivity in the African diaspora, cut loose from any national identity or historical matrix. Or perhaps—as one might deduce from the volume's hyperbolic praise of communist regimes—it is intended to forecast some future state of social totality in which liberal individualism has been all but annihilated. In either event, the assumption that autobiography is premised on some notion of authenticity, even if it turns out to be self-serving or distorted by the writer, has here been swiftly undercut.

No one imagines that autobiography is transparent. At the least, any autobiography is a narrative, a single story selected from a set of possible lives to cast the protagonist in a particular light. In the instance of a more self-conscious or devious autobiographer, his text might be likened to a map wherein manifold routes are evident even as many others remain concealed. In the end, no doubt, each autobiography calls up its own set of metaphors—confession, trial and triumph, messianic personification, or some combination of like narrative modes. What stands out in the case of Du Bois—for whom all of these figures of self-dramatization are apt—is not the number of autobiographical works with which he may be credited. Nor is it simply the astonishing fact that, living to the age of ninety-five and writing to the bitter end, the span of his narrated life begins during the presidency of Andrew Johnson and ends just short of the presidency of Lyndon Johnson. As the passage cited above indicates, what is notable about Du Bois is the fundamental mutability of his conception of the represented life itself. Insofar as it initiates a final life story the burden of which is intellectual (soon to be actual) exile from the United States and a tragic defense of totalitarianism, the passage from the ***Autobiography*** has obvious political and moral implications. His final ideological choice, needless to say, brought to sudden intensity Du Bois's long-evolving view that all language—all art, as he usually put it—is a form of propaganda. From this perspective, the ***Autobiography,*** an ultimate confession of dissent from the very membership in American democracy that Du Bois had passionately sought throughout his life, illustrates the theory that it endorses. But Du Bois's political apostasy—he at long last joined the Communist Party in 1961 and immediately moved to Ghana, where he died in 1963—could hardly have been predicted, even a decade earlier; and the plaintive, even mournful quality of this late prose surely springs from the author's deep disappointment and anger that his many decades of struggle for black civil and political equality had seemed to produce so little result. That he was mistaken—his contribution to African American freedom had been immense—does little to mitigate the pain of his final soliloquy.

Despite its inherent contradiction of the ideology espoused in the ***Autobiography,*** Du Bois's choice of the term "soliloquy" is especially appropriate, for his whole writing life had, in fact, been a dramatic performance in which the first person, the often grandiloquent "I," was at center stage. Although the motives had shifted over time, irrevocably during the cold war, the underlying significance of Du Bois's typically self-centered writing remained constant. In writing his own life, however, Du Bois was at all times writing the story of his people—all those people belonging to the "race" or "nation" he grouped under the amorphous category of "Negro." Had he himself never contended that he was writing not just his own life but the "autobiography of a race," he fact would have been nonetheless evident as early as ***The Souls of Black Folk,*** which preceded the ***Autobiography*** by sixty years. Not least because he was a man in whom various paradoxes of marginality were combined, he attempted to make his life and his racial advocacy representative of all African Americans, indeed of all Africans in the diaspora. The course of his variegated public life as a historian, a sociologist, a teacher, a confounder of the National Association for the Advancement of Colored People (NAACP), a magazine editor, a novelist, a governmental envoy, a Pan-Africanist, a spokesman for socialism, and an opponent of anticommunism underscored Du Bois's claim to incarnate in himself the biography of his race. If the ***Autobiography*** is in one sense a characteristic Du Boisian performance—grandiose, almost martial in the rectitude and sweep of its judgments—the subordination of race as the defining category of Du Bois's argumentation marks a divergence, not unprecedented but nonetheless abrupt, from the evident motives of his theory of himself, of Africans in the diaspora, and of the global economic structure from his nineteenth-century writings on.

Race is a concept of great ambiguity and power in Du Bois's thought—the power, one could say, deriving precisely from the ambiguity. Both are at their highest pitch in his most complete and theoretically sophisticated autobiography, ***Dusk of Dawn,*** published in 1940. Although Du Bois at this time was enamoured of the Russian Revolution, a view dating from his initial trip to the Soviet Union in 1926, and of Marxist doctrine, up to that point most clearly articulated in his massive 1935 study ***Black Reconstruction in America,*** he could nonetheless forthrightly proclaim: "I was not and am not a communist. I do not believe in the dogma of inevitable revolution in order to right economic wrong" (Du Bois, ***Dusk,*** 302). In ***Dusk of Dawn*** race, not class, remains the driving force in Du Bois's theory of world colonialism, but not because race itself functions for him in any commonplace or predictable way. It is already apparent, for instance, that the first-person presence guiding the drama of ***The Souls of Black Folk*** and ***Darkwater,*** however chaotic is the generic identity of those cases, has been partially overtaken by conceptualized ideological forces such as "science," "empire," "propaganda," and the "colored world." To be sure, ***Dusk of Dawn*** remains organized, in both its autobiographical narrative line and its diachronic argument for the continuity of African culture, according to an abiding racialist substratum, but the close relationship between "race" and the speaking "I" of Du Bois has clearly begun to decay.

What is one to make, for instance, of the volume's enigmatic subtitle: *An Essay Toward the Autobiography of a Race Concept?* This strange phrase is, in fact, a fit summary of the wealth of Du Bois's thinking and writing over the half century preceding World War II. A passage deeper in the text demonstrates why. Following a series of chapters devoted to theories of race and racial superiority, the history of colonialism, and the potential economic and cultural benefits of African American self-segregation in the face of the realities of Jim Crow, Du Bois writes:

> My discussions of the concept of race, and of the white and colored worlds, are to be regarded as digressions from the history of my life; rather my autobiography is a digressive illustration and exemplification of what race has meant in the world of the nineteenth and twentieth centuries. It is for this reason that I have named and tried to make this book an autobiography of race rather than merely a personal reminiscence, with the idea that [the] peculiar racial situation and problems could best be explained in the life history of one who has lived them. My living gains its importance from the problems and not the problems from me.
>
> (Du Bois, ***Dusk,*** 221)

Here the life lived and the voice speaking in the autobiographical soliloquy are subordinated not to some hypothesized redemptive power of the state, as in the ***Autobiography,*** but to the commanding figure that Du Bois said time and again governed the history of the twentieth century and inscribed into a well-known aphorism, "the problem of the twentieth century is the problem of the color line," which first achieved prominence in ***The Souls of Black Folk*** in 1903. Du Bois had already employed the figure in **"The Present Outlook for the Dark Races of Mankind"** (1900), where he directed his audience at the third annual meeting of the American Negro Academy to recognize that "the color line belts the world and that the social problem of the twentieth century is to be the relation of the civilized world to the darker races of mankind" (Du Bois, *[The Oxford W. E. B. Du Bois] Reader,* 48). He would repeat it again in **"Worlds of Color,"** an essay on colonialism first published in *Foreign Affairs* in 1925 and reprinted the same year in Alain Locke's famous anthology *The New Negro*; in ***Black Folk Then and Now*** (1939), a Marxist updating of his landmark 1915 study ***The Negro,*** his reconceptu-

FROM THE AUTHOR

OF THE TRAINING OF BLACK MEN

I sit with Shakespeare and he winces not. Across the color line I move arm in arm with Balzac and Dumas, where smiling men and welcoming women glide in gilded halls. From out the caves of evening that swing between the strong-limbed earth and the tracery of the stars, I summon Aristotle and Aurelius and what soul I will, and they come all graciously with no scorn nor condescension. So, wed with Truth, I dwell above the Veil. Is this the life you grudge us, O knightly America? Is this the life you long to change into the dull red hideousness of Georgia? Are you so afraid lest peering from this high Pisgah, between Philistine and Amalekite, we sight the Promised Land?

SOURCE: W. E. B. Du Bois, closing paragraph to Chapter VI of *The Souls of Black Folk,* McClurg, 1903.

alization of the color line as a vertical rather than horizontal marking would be complete: "The proletariat of the world consists . . . overwhelmingly of the dark workers of Asia, Africa, the islands of the sea, and South and Central America. These are the ones who support a superstructure of wealth, luxury, and extravagance. . . . The problem of the twentieth century is the problem of the color line" (Du Bois, ***Black Folk,*** 283). Less a boundary or legal barrier in Du Bois's mind than a figure with temporal and geographical dimensionality, a figure that segregates and grounds at the same time, the color line at length became a means to account for the unorthodox character of his autobiography in the preface to ***Dusk of Dawn***: "My life [has] had its significance and its only deep significance because it was part of a Problem; but that problem was, as I continue to think, the central problem of the greatest of the world's democracies and so the Problem of the future world" (Du Bois, ***Dusk,*** vii-viii).

With the requisite appearance of self-abnegation, a rhetorical strategy at which the stubborn and rather egotistical Du Bois was adept, he organizes a grand theory of modern history around the experiences of his own life. Yet there is nothing at all false about this claim. To understand the various meanings that the "autobiography of race" held for Du Bois is to understand who he is and why he is a central figure in American literary and intellectual history. In his encompassing forecast of the cross-cultural studies of literature and historical events that would become commonplace by the end of the twentieth century, Du Bois himself is a central figure in the black Atlantic diaspora that Paul Gilroy has designated a "counterculture of modernity" (Gilroy, 34-40), and his exceptional range of writing summarizes the modern exile of African Americans, at once figurative and historically actual, in which the legacy of slavery and reiterated migrations from bondage to freedom form the substance of a nation's story.

From the very beginning of his public life Du Bois modeled himself on powerful public figures, at once to imitate their personal strength (and not a little of their glory) and to find in them a vehicle for his own racial leadership. His first exemplar was the German chancellor Otto von Bismarck, whose leadership he celebrated in his 1888 commencement address at Fisk University: "He had made a nation out of a mass of bickering peoples. He had dominated the whole development with his strength until he crowned an emperor at Versailles. This foreshadowed in my mind the kind of thing that American Negroes must do, marching forth with strength and determination under trained leadership" (Du Bois, ***Dusk,*** 32). To speak for American blacks required that Du Bois adopt the mantle of no less a figure than Frederick Douglass and compete with powerful men such as Booker T. Washington and Marcus Garvey. And it required that he negotiate a number of clashing positions within a racial community torn apart by prejudice without and bickering within. In finding the voice of his own leadership, Du Bois had to balance his northern birth against his desire to speak also for the black South; his elite intellectual tastes against his commitment to the equal importance of folk art; his immersion in a political tradition of liberal individualism against his evolving belief that socialism promised a more just world; his hope to link African America's liberation to anticolonial movements in Africa against the view of some Africans that he had little to offer them; and his own mixed-race heritage against the suspicions of those American blacks who considered him, by reason of his birth and his privileged education, inherently a traitor to the racial cause. In such a maelstrom of competing interests, all exacerbated by the fact that Du Bois came of age at the height of white America's denial of equality to blacks through segregation and vigilante violence, it is no surprise, perhaps, that he quickly took on something of a prophetic voice and determined to make the narrative of his own life a virtual saga of the march toward freedom. Du Bois's contemporary, the black historian William Ferris, was not far from the mark when he referred to ***The Souls of Black Folk*** as "the political Bible of the Negro race" and Du Bois himself as "the long-looked-for political Messiah, the Moses that will lead them out of the Egypt of peonage, across the Red Sea of Jim Crow legislation, through the wilderness of disfranchisement and restricted opportunity and into the promised land of liberty of opportunity and equality of rights" (Ferris, I, 274-76). Between Frederick Douglass and Martin Luther King, Jr., no black American was more suited, or more wanted, to lead the Exodus. . . .

Ernest Hemingway once remarked that all modern American literature comes from Mark Twain's *Adventures of Huckleberry Finn.* Just as plausibly, one could claim that modern African American literature and intellectual history descend from ***The Souls of Black Folk.*** Central themes and episodes of Du Bois's book are echoed in James Weldon Johnson's *Autobiography of an Ex-Coloured Man* (1912), Jean Toomer's *Cane* (1923), Richard Wright's *Black Boy* (1945), J. Saunders Redding's *Stranger and Alone* (1950), Ralph Ellison's *Invisible Man* (1952), and Alice Walker's *Meridian* (1976), to name only a few works. Johnson remarked that the book "had a greater effect upon and within the Negro race in America than any other single book published in this country since *Uncle Tom's Cabin,*" and Claude McKay reported that it "shook me like an earthquake. Dr. Du Bois stands on a pedestal illuminated in my mind. And the light that shines there comes from my first reading of ***The Souls of Black Folk.***" In 1956, Langston Hughes wrote to Du Bois: "I have just read again your ***The Souls of Black Folk***—for perhaps the tenth time—the first time having been some forty years ago when I was a child in Kansas. Its beauty and power are as moving and as meaningful as ever" (Du Bois, ***Correspondence,*** 3: 401; Johnson, 203; McKay, 110). More recently, Gerald Early has gathered twenty contemporary African American responses to the legacy of ***The Souls of Black Folk*** in a volume entitled *Lure and Loathing: Essays on Race, Identity, and the Ambivalence of Assimilation* (1993). Even though its roots lie in sources as diverse as Phillis Wheatley, Ralph Waldo Emerson, and William James, Du Bois's famous theory of "double consciousness" became a defining trope of multicultural study. One finds it adopted explicitly, for instance, in Richard Wright's remarks at the 1956 Congress of Negro Writers and Artists in Paris when he spoke of the "contradiction of being both Western and a man of color" (Legum, 99), and one hears its themes echoed as well in works springing from other traditions such as Vine Deloria, Jr.'s, *Custer Died for Your Sins* (1969) or Gloria Anzaldúa's *Borderlands/La Frontera: The New Mestiza* (1987). Like Twain and his great book, Du Bois and his are touchstones of such importance that American writing is difficult to imagine in their absence.

To a group of previously published and then revised essays on various aspects of black life from slavery through the post-Reconstruction era, Du Bois added several new chapters on life "within the veil" of African America when he came to compose ***The Souls of Black Folk.*** The resulting volume is a peculiar generic mix whose unity of argument is sometimes as perplexing as it is powerful. A masterwork of many dimensions—a first-rate history of post-Civil War race relations in the South; a pathbreaking essay in sociological and economic analysis; a brief for black education; and a study in comparative European American and African American cultures—***The Souls of Black Folk*** is the preeminent modern text of African American cultural consciousness. In his commentary on the transforming power of black music, from slave culture through post-Reconstruction modernity, Du Bois discovered a deep spiritual foundation for his social and economic analysis, one that would for many years to come make his work unique in its blending of poetics and politics—what he later argued was the necessary union of art and propaganda. As in ***Darkwater,*** Du Bois includes coherent fragments of autobiography in ***The Souls of Black Folk***; but here as elsewhere in his major writings, the life is primarily an occasion for theorizing about the relationship between biography and culture, for making the representative experience a means to recover a people's spiritual roots and erect the temple of their nationhood.

The educated Du Bois sought an ideal of culture beyond the color line where, as a famous passage puts it, "wed with Truth," he could "dwell above the Veil . . . sit with Shakespeare, move arm in arm with Balzac and Dumas, and summon Aristotle and Aurelius, all to meet him "graciously with no scorn or condescension" (Du Bois, *Reader,*

156-57). In placing the spirituals at the center of ***The Souls of Black Folk,*** however, he did not contradict this vision but instead brought it to life. The unreconciled tension between the African American songs and the epigraphic texts from the Western tradition illustrate the trap of divided identity in which Du Bois himself was caught: How could he balance the cultivation of white, European cultural forms against the preserved beliefs and cultural patterns of black America that had originated in slavery? Interwoven with his argument against Booker T. Washington, his tribute to Alexander Crummel, his moving story of his infant son's death, and his multifaceted recitation of the transition in African American life from slavery to Reconstruction to the modern age of segregation, the black spirituals anchored the written saga of ***The Souls of Black Folk*** in the true history of the African diaspora even as they illuminated its resistance to full recovery.

In a brief commentary published a year after ***The Souls of Black Folk,*** Du Bois characterized the book's style as "tropical—African," and he explained the "intimate tone of self-revelation" that runs throughout the book, in contrast to a more traditional impersonality and judiciousness, as a function of the fact that "the blood of my fathers spoke through me and cast off the English restraint of my training and surroundings" (Du Bois, *Reader,* 305). Combined with his assertion that even as a child he knew that these "weird old songs in which the soul of the black slave spoke to men" were something personal, something he recognized as being "of me and mine," such a claim suggests that one of the first things Du Bois imbibed from the sorrow songs was their combined historical and prophetic structure (Du Bois, *Reader,* 231). In the theoretical use to which he put the enigmatic bars of music, and in tying himself to the bardic role that he found to have descended from the African priest to the African American preacher, Du Bois infused his volume's rich experiment in autobiography, political history, and social essay with a power comparable to that of the African *griots,* the communal genealogists and historians who sang of their people's historical events, and of their kings and rulers, in a repertoire of song that was constantly subject to innovation. Like the anonymous collective composers of the slave spirituals in James Weldon Johnson's famous poem "O Black and Unknown Bards" (1908) or the archetype of the bardic preacher, "Singing Johnson," whose talents Johnson described first in fictional form in *The Autobiography of an Ex-Coloured Man* and then in biographical form in *The Book of American Negro Spirituals* (1925), Du Bois moved in the direction of a lived scriptural story that had sources in the African chants of tribal law, historical narrative, and folk story.

What might be called the book's crisis point of cultural recovery appears in Du Bois's reproduction of the African song first sung in his family, he says, by his grandfather's grandmother, who was stolen from Africa by a Dutch trader. Her song ("Do bana coba gene me, gene me . . .") had traveled down the generations for 200 years, "and we sing it to our children, knowing as little as our fathers what its words may mean, but knowing well the meaning of its music" (Du Bois, *Reader,* 233). The story of his great-great-grandmother reappears throughout Du Bois's autobiographical writings, its telling mutable and its accuracy questionable. Especially in ***The Souls of Black Folk,*** though, it grounds Du Bois's bardic history of black American life in a symbolic, if not a demonstrably actual, African world—a world of hypothesized ancestral memory reached, in Du Bois's case, by a reenacted typological escape from what he calls the "Egypt of the Confederacy" (Du Bois, *Reader,* 165). Because it cannot be translated, the African song evokes the coded language of the slave spirituals, thus joining Du Bois's work as a cultural critic to the anonymous lives of those unknown bards and common folk from whose toil have sprung the present generations and the beginnings of African American culture. Founding both modern African American literature and Du Bois's own writing career, ***The Souls of Black Folk*** established the coherence of African American culture as a set of values and expressions that were not annihilated by slavery but nurtured by its "voice of exile" (Du Bois, *Reader,* 233). . . .

As I have already indicated, ***Dusk of Dawn*** represents something of a way station in the course of Du Bois's written representations of himself. Taken as a whole, it is his most comprehensive autobiographical statement and the capstone to his displacement of liberalism by Marxism. At the same time, it is a work in which the very idea of race has become deracinated. Du Bois's tilt toward Marxism in the late 1920s resulted in a pathbreaking work of revisionist history, ***Black Reconstruction,*** and a series of essays devoted to black education and self-segregated economic development that are one of the strongest twentieth-century briefs for racial separatism. His prevailing trope of this period, the idea of a "nation within a nation," is, among other things, a structural reinterpretation of double consciousness: what previously belonged abstractly to the realm of personal psychology or an internalized matrix of culture is now superimposed on an economic and political geography. Whether as an *imperium in imperio* (to cite the common phrase adopted by Sutton Griggs as the title of his 1899 nationalist novel about the creation of a secret black state hidden within Texas) or as a catch phrase promoting black buying from black storeowners, the concept of a nation within resonated in the case of Du Bois with his ambiguous notion of the African identity as a "hidden self" within, or constituting, the soul of African Americans (Sundquist, 570-75).

In an age of strict segregation, the economic and political preservation of the black community lay in harnessing its powers and holding them in reserve for the future. For Du Bois, however, the cultivation of separatist strategies was no contradiction to his ultimate goal of integration. His adaptation of his theory of the Talented Tenth to a socialist and separatist model, in which educated blacks would provide the leadership of a new industrial organization, was not intended to negate his long-standing commitment to integration and cultural pluralism. Nor was his contention that a "Negro university" in the United States is justified in using "that variety of the English idiom which [African Americans] understand" and founding its curriculum "on a knowledge of the history of their people in Africa and in the United States"—a view in harmony with the last generation of moderate thought about Afrocentric education—inherently contradictory to social and economic assimilation (Du Bois, *Reader,* 416).

In his writing of the 1930s, when racial and economic separatism functioned as a prelude to collectivist political activism, Du Bois's personification of messianic leadership likewise waned. In ***Black Reconstruction,*** for instance, the place of the magnified black or abolitionist hero seems to have been usurped by the black masses; lacking a revolutionary figure comparable to Toussaint, Du Bois depicted the slaves themselves as a proletarian collective rising up in defiance of slave masters and world economic oppressors alike. Because it incorporates many traditional aspects of autobiography, ***Dusk of Dawn*** returns us to the commanding and directive life of the hero—that is, Du Bois himself—but the effects of the Depression and stirrings of the coming world war against fascism are now interwoven into Du Bois's narrative staging of his ongoing "autobiography of a race concept." A summary reinterpretation of the transformation of Du Bois's thought over the course of the 1930s, specifically its accommodation of Marxism to his goals of integration and pluralism, ***Dusk of Dawn*** recomposes the autobiographical dimensions of ***The Souls of Black Folk*** and ***Darkwater*** in large blocks of polemic, to a great degree replacing the searching lyricism of the earlier works with a Du Boisian version of scientific materialism, an odd wedding of Marxist doctrine and poetic cadence. ***Dusk of Dawn*** ends not with a beautiful tribute to slave culture (as in ***The Souls of Black Folk***) or an apocalyptic meditation on segregation (as in ***Darkwater***) but with Du Bois's announcement of the "Basic American Creed," an eleven-part program that somewhat awkwardly ties a philosophy of the Talented Tenth to belief in "the ultimate triumph of some form of Socialism the world over" (Du Bois, ***Dusk,*** 321).

In keeping with the book's scrutiny of his earlier life and beliefs in light of his mature Marxist perspective, Du Bois recapitulates and analyzes the development of his own racial philosophy in the sequential argument of the chapter entitled **"The Concept of Race."** After a brief critique of scientific views of race, he begins by sketching his own genealogical history, complete with family tree. Repeating the anecdote about the inherited song "Do bana coba," but noting that there was almost nothing African in the speech or customs of his immediate family, Du Bois now attributes his sense of Africanity to his "later learning and reaction" to the racial assumptions of whites and to his time in the South: "I felt myself African by 'race,'" he says, "and by that token was African and an integral member of the group of dark Americans who were called Negroes." Here Du Bois depicts himself wavering on the border of the kind of essentialist definition that animated, without finally determining, the early arguments of **"The Conservation of Races"** and ***The Souls of Black Folk.*** Quickly, however, the privileged power of "reaction" to racism in the formation of racial identity is now brought to the fore. Du Bois recalls that when he applied in 1908 for membership in the Massachusetts Society of the Sons of the American Revolution on the basis of his great-great-grandfather's war record, his application was denied because he could not produce a birth certificate of the man who had, of course, been a slave stolen from Africa. He then glibly remarks, "my membership was, therefore, suspended," and proceeds to quote Countee Cullen's refrain, "What is Africa to me?" as a searching counterpoint to the denationalization he has just described (Du Bois, *Reader,* 86). Africa, which Du Bois admits affords "a tie which I can feel better than I can explain," becomes a means to provide "membership" in a nation that has been denied in the United States. And one could as well say "citizenship," for the clear burden of this anecdote is to remind his readers that the evisceration of the Fourteenth and Fifteenth amendments, culminating in *Plessy* v. *Ferguson* (1896), returned blacks in many ways to the stateless condition described for them in the infamous pre-Civil War ruling of Justice Roger Taney in *Dred Scott* v. *Sandford* (1857), which declared that African Americans had no rights that whites were bound to respect.

Whether or not he intended the further word play, Du Bois's choice of "suspended" is more than appropriate. The paradox of double consciousness is not so much that it describes two (or more) potential modes of identity at war with one another, but that it describes a suspension between them—a condition of statelessness or *homelessness,* as it is often called in contemporary writing on the cultures of exile, which Du Bois anticipated with telling accuracy, as he did more recent conceptions of a nation or a people as ideological constructions or rhetorical strategies (Bhabha, 145). It is no mistake, then, that the argument of this key chapter in ***Dusk of Dawn*** hinges on a combination of tenuous ethnographic evidence—Du Bois proceeds to contend, in a passage already cited, that the Christmas singing in Monrovia echoed the sorrow songs he had heard forty years earlier in Tennessee—and autobiographical longing reconceived as political theory. Africa is "my fatherland," Du Bois asserts; but he dismisses the mere physical characteristics of race, the "badge of color," as having little meaning either to accurate science or to Negroes. Instead, he argues that what unites blacks and ties them to Africa is the fact that they "have suffered a common disaster and have one long memory" (Du Bois, *Reader,* 87). Or, as James Baldwin would later put it in an essay devoted to the 1956 Conference of Negro Writers and Artists at the Sorbonne: "What they held in common was their precarious, their unutterably painful relation to the white world . . . their ache to come into the world as men" (Baldwin, 35). Baldwin was skeptical that this was equivalent to a cultural bond. Perhaps because he was close enough to the experience of slavery, however, or because he was temporally proximate to the colonial devastation of African culture through the artificial creation of new political and economic nations, Du Bois, unlike Baldwin, often made Africa the cultural as well as the emotional centerpiece of racial identity.

And yet, such a common bond was not for Du Bois "African" or "black" alone, and he maintained that the world color line "binds together not simply the children of Africa, but extends through yellow Asia and into the South Seas. It is this unity that draws me to Africa" (Du Bois, *Reader,* 87). His willingness to extend this vague "nationhood" to virtually all people of color, as well as his corollary that precolonized Africa provided a condition of communal harmony, raises unavoidable problems. It may be, as Martin Luther King, Jr., argued, that Du Bois "did not make a mystique out of blackness," that he "was proud of his people, not because their color endowed them with some vague greatness but because their concrete achievements in struggle had advanced humanity . . . in all its hues, black, white, yellow, red and brown" (King, 18). As Kwame Anthony Appiah has argued, however, Du Bois's Pan-Colored hypothesis nearly evacuates his claim of black race solidarity of any meaning; and the appeal to "a common disaster" and "one long memory" hides a lingering biological conception of race beneath the surface of the sociohistorical explanation (Appiah, 41). Against more ardent proponents of *negritude,* Du Bois stood forth as a dissenter from racial determinism; but against those who would construct race purely of cultural predispositions and habits, Du Bois legitimated an irrational faith in African "memory" by dissolving historical differences among the world's nonwhite groups. Even after fifty years, it might seem, Du Bois had neither found a way to avoid the temptation of racial essentialism nor devised a solution to the puzzle of nationalism.

It was his 1923 visit to Africa as an official envoy to Liberia that afforded Du Bois the realization, as he now recalls it, that the "income-bearing value of race prejudice was the cause and not the result of theories of race inferiority" both in the colonized world and in America during the decades since the collapse of the cotton kingdom (Du Bois, *Reader,* 94). Having determined that slavery created racism, not the reverse, Du Bois recasts his most ethereal earlier conceptions of Africa into a form of economic, rather than racial, primitivism. All his previous romantic idealizations of Africa—from his first poems of Pan-African *negritude,* **"The Song of the Smoke"** (1907) and **"A Day in Africa"** (1908), to his arguments in **"What Is Civilization?"** (1925), ***The Gift of Black Folk,*** and ***Black Folk Then and Now,*** where the utopian socialism of the African village appears as an antidote to the destructive, capitalized industrialism of modernity—are refashioned in ***Dusk of Dawn*** as though to illustrate his progress from nineteenth-century racialism to modern Marxism. In a famous expression of his Victorian sensibilities, Du Bois had stated in **"The Primitive Black Man"** (1924) that during two months in West Africa, when he routinely saw "children quite naked and women usually naked to the waist," he witnessed "less of sex dalliance and appeal than I see daily on Fifth Avenue" (Du Bois, *Writings in Periodicals,* II, 231). This passage reappears more or less verbatim in ***Dusk of Dawn,*** but joined to it are further speculations about the pleasure of unindustrialized, uncapitalized work in Africa, the whole creating a luminous, strangely naive proof that the "communalism of the African clan can be transferred to the Negro American group" (Du Bois, ***Dusk,*** 219).

Surprisingly, the autobiographical presence is not erased but, if anything, more pronounced in ***Dusk of Dawn,*** for Du Bois's own pedagogy becomes that of black America. His unequivocal commitment to an art of overt ideology was first announced in 1926, following his first trip to Africa and his increasing admiration for the Soviet Union, when he delivered an address on the **"Criteria of Negro Art"** in which he claimed, against the "wailing of the purists," that "all Art is propaganda and ever must be" (Du Bois, *Reader,* 328). The Russian Revolution, he would write in ***Dusk of Dawn,*** "was the foundation stone of my fight for black folk; it explained me" (Du Bois, ***Dusk,*** 285). This formulation is a succinct index of the way in which the whole of the volume functions as a rewriting of previous self-conceptions. In **"The Concept of Race,"** the idealization in both economic and cultural terms allows Du Bois to create of Africa an imaginary homeland (to borrow a phrase from Salman Rushdie) against which the colonizing world in general and the United States in particular can be set for comparison. ***Dusk of Dawn*** represents the conjunction of Du Bois's propagandistic theory of culture and his desperate belief that a philosophy of separatism—a cultivation of what is referred to in this case as "The Colored World Within"—can find sustenance in Africa's anticolonial recovery of its own cultural unity. So long as discriminatory racial laws and economic practices exist, he suggests, so long as African Americans are excluded from American nationhood, they will be drawn toward Africa—most of all, perhaps, toward an inaccurately idealized Africa—by pure force of reaction to political and economic racism.

The chapter culminates in one of the most haunting passages in all of Du Bois's work, a portrait of the pain of segregation that underlies double consciousness:

> It is difficult to let others see the full psychological meaning of caste segregation. It is as though one, looking out from a dark cave in a side of an impending mountain, sees the world passing and speaks to it; speaks courteously and persuasively, showing them how these entombed souls are hindered in their natural movement, expression, and development; and how their loosening from prison would be a matter not simply of courtesy, sympathy, and help to them, but aid to all the world. One talks on evenly and logically in this way, but notices that the passing throng does not even turn its head, or if it does, glances curiously and walks on. It gradually penetrates the minds of the prisoners that the people passing do not hear; that some thick sheet of invisible but horribly tangible plate glass is between them and the world. They get excited; they talk louder; they gesticulate. Some of the passing stop in curiosity; these gesticulations seem so pointless; they laugh and pass on. They still either do not hear at all, or hear but dimly, and even what they hear, they do not understand. Then the people within may become hysterical. They may scream and hurl themselves against the barriers, hardly realizing in their bewilderment that they are screaming in a vacuum unheard and that their antics may actually seem funny to those outside looking in. They may even, here and there, break through in blood and disfigurement, and find themselves faced by a horrified, implacable, and quite overwhelming mob of people frightened for their own very existence.
>
> (Du Bois, *Reader,* 95)

The effect of this tragic incarceration, this "group imprisonment," is to make an individual provincial; he "neglects the wider aspects of national life and human existence" and focuses on "his inner group"; he "thinks of himself not as an individual but as a group man, a 'race' man." Having at best partial citizenship in the United States, black Americans in the age of Jim Crow had good reason to seek their national identity, as well as their racial consciousness, elsewhere than in America. Over the course of the chapter, Du Bois not only creates a forceful cyclical argument that enfolds his own representative life into the history of the African diaspora and the literal and emotional violence of contemporary American segregation; he also displays the crucial but ephemeral nature of the transgeographical "nation," a world of exile in his case synonymous with the autobiographical self, in which African Americans are forced to seek their only hope of justice.

Bibliography

Du Bois, W. E. B. *The Autobiography of W. E. B. Du Bois: A Soliloquy on Viewing My Life from the Last Decades of Its First Century.* New York: International, 1968.

——— *Black Folk Then and Now,* ed. Herbert Aptheker. 1924; rpt. Millwood, N.Y.: Kraus-Thomson, 1975.

——— *Black Reconstruction in America, 1860-1880.* New York: Harcourt, Brace, 1935.

——— *Correspondence of W. E. B. Du Bois,* 3 vols., ed. Herbert Aptheker. Amherst: University of Massachusetts Press, 1973.

——— *Darkwater: Voices from Within the Veil.* New York: Harcourt, Brace, 1920.

——— *Dusk to Dawn: An Essay Toward an Autobiography of a Race Concept.* 1940; rpt. New York: Schocken, 1968.

——— *The Gift of Black Folk: The Negroes in the Making of America.* Boston: Stratford, 1924.

——— *The Negro.* 1915; rpt. New York: Oxford University Press, 1970.

——— *The Souls of Black Folk.* Chicago: A. C. McClurg, 1903.

——— *Writings by W. E. B. Du Bois in Periodicals Edited by Others,* 4 vols., ed. Herbert Aptheker. Millwood, N.Y.: Kraus-Thomson, 1982.

Early, Gerald, ed. *Lure and Loathing: Essays on Race, Identity, and the Ambivalence of Assimilation.* New York: Penguin, 1993.

Ferris, William H. *The African Abroad, Or His Evolution in Western Civilization,* 2 vols. New Haven, Conn.: Tuttle, Morehouse, and Taylor, 1913.

Gilroy, Paul. *The Black Atlantic: Modernity and Double-Consciousness.* Cambridge, Mass.: Harvard University Press, 1993.

Johnson, James Weldon. *Along This Way: The Autobiography of James Weldon Johnson.* 1933; rpt. New York: Viking, 1968.

King, Martin Luther, Jr. "Honoring Dr. Du Bois." In *W. E. B. Du Bois Speaks: Speeches and Addresses, 1890-1919,* ed. Philip S. Foner. New York: Pathfinder Press, 1970, 12-20.

Legum, Colin. *Pan-Africanism: A Short Political Guide.* London: Pall Mall Press, 1962.

McKay, Claude. *A Long Way from Home: An Autobiography.* 1937; rpt. New York: Harcourt, Brace and World, 1970.

Sundquist, Eric J. *To Wake the Nations: Race in the Making of American Literature.* Cambridge, Mass.: Harvard University Press, 1993.

FURTHER READING

Biographies

Broderick, Francis L. *W. E. B. Du Bois, Negro Leader in a Time of Crisis.* Stanford, Calif.: Stanford University Press, 1959, 259 p.

Traces the evolution of Du Bois's philosophy; valuable presentation of Du Bois while he was still politically active.

Du Bois, Shirley Graham. *His Day is Marching On.* Philadelphia: J. B. Lippincott, 1971, 384 p.

Offers the perspective of Du Bois's second wife; focuses more on his personal life than his career.

Moore, Jack B. *W. E. B. Du Bois.* Boston: Twayne Publishers, 1981, 185 p.

Categorizes Du Bois's life and career by his work in social science, literature, and politics; includes a substantial bibliography.

Rudwick, Elliott M. *W. E. B. Du Bois: Propagandist of the Negro Protest.* New York: Atheneum, 1969, 390 p.

Focuses on Du Bois's role as an African American leader, up to his break with the NAACP; one of the earliest evaluations of Du Bois's lifework.

Criticism

Appiah, Anthony. "The Uncompleted Argument: Du Bois and the Illusion of Race." *Critical Inquiry* 12, no. 1 (1985): 21-37.

Considers the role of racial biology in Du Bois's work and attempts to uncover implicit or unspoken conclusions from Du Bois regarding the scientific concept of race.

Aptheker, Bettina. "W. E. B. Du Bois and the Struggle for Women's Rights: 1910-1920." *San Jose Studies* 1, no. 2 (1975): 7-15.

Looks at Du Bois's understanding of the connection between race- and gender-based oppression, focusing on the right to vote.

Byerman, Keith E. *Seizing the Word: History, Art, and Self in the Work of W. E. B. Du Bois.* Athens: University of Georgia Press, 1994, 249 p.

Interprets Du Bois's autobiographical writing as a battle for control of the Word. Byerman applies some insights from psychoanalysis and Du Bois's anxiety over his parentage.

Cain, William E. "Violence, Revolution, and the Cost of Freedom: John Brown and W. E. B. Du Bois." *boundary 2* 17, no. 1 (1990): 305-30.

Counters the negative opinion of Du Bois's biography of Brown held by most scholars and suggests that Du Bois makes the achievement of a white hero into an example of Black success.

Chandler, Nahum Dimitri. "The Economy of Desedimentation: W. E. B. Du Bois and the Discourses of the Negro." *Callaloo* 19, no. 1 (1996): 78-93.

Considers Du Bois's work on race as a struggle against an entrenched economy of racial purity or essence and calls for a continuation of the work done by Du Bois.

DeMarco, Joseph P. *The Social Thought of W. E. B. Du Bois.* New York: Lanham, 1987, 203 p.

Focuses on Du Bois's career as a sociologist, giving special attention to Du Bois's various adaptations of Marxism and socialism.

Elder, Arlene A. "Swamp Versus Plantation: Symbolic Structure in W. E. B. Du Bois' *The Quest of the Silver Fleece.*" *Phylon* 34, no. 4 (1973): 358-67.

Analyzes Du Bois's first novel from a formal perspective and considers characters and settings as metaphors for North and South, and Black and white.

Ferris, William H. "The Emerging Leader—A Contemporary View." In *W. E. B. Du Bois, A Profile,* edited by Rayford W. Logan, pp. 86-121. New York: Hill and Wang, 1971.

Study, originally written in 1913, of early assessments of Du Bois's leadership.

Green, Dan S., and Earl Smith. "W. E. B. Du Bois and the Concepts of Race and Class." *Phylon* 44, no. 4 (1983): 262-72.

Asserts the importance of Du Bois's understanding of the inherent connection between racial oppression and class tension and points to Black Reconstruction as an essential study of race and class issues.

Ijere, Martin O. "W. E. B. Du Bois and Marcus Garvey as Pan-Africanists: A Study in Contrast." *Présence Africaine* 89, no. 1 (1974): 188-207.

Compares the work and philosophy of rivals Du Bois and Garvey, without preferring either.

Johnson, Donald. "W. E. B. Du Bois, Thomas Jesse Jones, and the Struggle for Social Education, 1900-1930." *Journal of Negro History* (2000): 71-95.

Reviews the Jones-Du Bois debate in terms of the broader debate between social Darwinism—more common in Du Bois's era—and the idea that culture was learned behavior dependent on environment.

Katz, Michael B., and Thomas J. Sugrue, eds. *W. E. B. Du Bois, Race, and the City:* The Philadelphia Negro *and Its Legacy.* Philadelphia: University of Pennsylvania Press, 1998. 299 p.

Contains several essays exploring the influence and continuing relevance of Du Bois's early sociological study of urban Blacks.

Lange, Werner J. "W. E. B. Du Bois and the First Scientific Study of Afro-America." *Phylon* 44, no. 2 (1983): 135-46.

Argues for the importance of Du Bois's role in the development of American anthropology, suggesting that, in addition to his race, Du Bois's Marxism and his interdisciplinary approach have obscured the magnitude of his contributions.

Lively, Adam. "Continuity and Radicalism in American Black Nationalist Thought, 1914-29." *Journal of American Studies* 18 (1984): 207-35.

Compares the role of nationalism for Du Bois, Garvey, and Claude McKay; proposes that Du Bois achieved the most realistic connection between his political thought and activism.

Marable, Manning. "The Black Faith of W. E. B. Du Bois: Sociocultural and Political Dimensions of Black Religion." *Southern Quarterly* 23, no. 3 (1985): 15-33.

Explores the role of religion in Du Bois's work, including his rhetoric, his connections with religious leaders, and his critique of white Christianity.

Oliver, Lawrence J. "Writing from the Right During the 'Red Decade': Thomas Dixon's Attack on W. E. B. Du Bois and James Weldon Johnson in *The Flaming Sword.*" *American Literature* 70, no. 1 (1998): 131-52.

Details Dixon's representations of Du Bois and his works in this intended sequel to Birth of a Nation, *and highlights how Du Bois's Marxism heightened his threat to white society in Dixon's novel.*

Price-Spratlen, Townsand. "Negotiating Legacies: Audre Lorde, W. E. B. Du Bois, Marlon Riggs, and Me." *Harvard Educational Review* 66, no. 2 (1996): 216-30.

Recounts the role Du Bois's Souls of Black Folk *played in Price-Spratlen's intellectual development as an African American sociologist.*

Roof, Maria. "W. E. B. Du Bois, Isabel Allende, and the Empowerment of Third World Women." *CLA Journal* 39, no. 4 (1996): 401-16.

Suggests that Du Bois's concept of "double consciousness" transcends African American consciousness, acting as a useful paradigm for understanding the experiences of other minorities, including women.

Savory, Jerold J. "The Rending of the Veil in W. E. B. Du Bois's *The Souls of Black Folk.*" *CLA Journal* 15, no. 3 (1972): 334-37.

Observes the motif of the veil in Du Bois's masterwork, stressing the religious connotations.

OTHER SOURCES FROM GALE:

Additional coverage of W. E. B. Du Bois's life and career is contained in the following sources published by the Gale Group: *African American Writers,* Eds. 1, 2; *American Writers Supplement,* Vol. 2; *Authors and Artists for Young Adults,* Vol. 40; *Black Literature Criticism,* Vol. 1; *Black Writers,* Eds. 1, 3; *Concise Dictionary of American Literary Biography, 1865-1917; Contemporary Authors,* Vols. 85-88; *Contemporary Authors New Revision Series,* Vols. 34, 82; *Contemporary Literary Criticism,* Vols. 1, 2, 13, 64, 96; *Dictionary of Literary Biography,* Vols. 47, 50, 91; *DISCovering Authors; DISCovering Authors: Canadian Edition; DISCovering Authors: Modules, Most-studied Authors, Multicultural Authors,* and *Novelists; Exploring Poetry; Literature and Its Times,* Vol. 2; *Literature Resource Center; Major 20th-Century Writers,* Eds. 1, 2; *Nonfiction Classics for Students,* Vol. 1; *Poetry for Students,* Vol. 13; *Reference Guide to American Literature,* Ed. 4; *Something about the Author,* Vol. 42; and *World Literature Criticism.*

ALICE DUNBAR-NELSON

(1875 - 1935)

(Full name Alice Ruth Moore Dunbar-Nelson) American poet, fiction writer, journalist, and playwright.

The 1935 obituary for Dunbar-Nelson refers to her only as the wife of poet Paul Laurence Dunbar and later of newsman Robert J. Nelson. Though the accomplishments of her first husband may have overshadowed her own literary and political activities, over time Dunbar-Nelson's talent and importance came to be acknowledged by critics. Her poetry was widely published throughout the Harlem Renaissance and her short stories and observations on Creole identity have attracted the interest of readers and critics alike.

BIOGRAPHICAL INFORMATION

Alice Ruth Moore was born in New Orleans, Louisiana, on July 19, 1875, into a middle-class family. Her mother was of combined African and Native American heritage, while her father—about whom little is known—had some Caucasian background. Dunbar-Nelson had light skin and auburn hair, which made it possible for her to "pass" as white at times. She attended Straight University (now Dillard University) and became a teacher in New Orleans. She later attended prestigious northeastern schools including Cornell, Columbia, and the University of Pennsylvania. Her first book, entitled *Violets and Other Tales* (1895), was published when she was only twenty; her second collection of stories, *The Goodness of St. Rocque and Other Stories* (1899), followed shortly afterwards. She married Paul Laurence Dunbar on March 8, 1898; they were married for eight years but lived together for only four. Dunbar died in 1906. Though in the early part of their courtship and marriage they were considered an exemplary couple and part of the African American literary elite, Dunbar's alcohol addiction and violence, and strained relations with their extended family, eventually drove them apart. After leaving Dunbar, Dunbar-Nelson moved with her family to Wilmington, Delaware, teaching high school there until 1920, when she lost her job because of her political activism. In 1916 she married the journalist Robert J. Nelson. In 1920 they began to jointly publish the *Wilmington Advocate,* a Black newspaper. She began keeping a diary in 1921, which was eventually discovered by her niece, Pauline A. Young, and published in 1984. Her diary reveals that despite her success, she was never particularly well off. She struggled to keep her name before the public in order to keep finding work. It also documents a handful of romantic or sexual relationships with women, even during what appeared to be a very happy marriage with Nelson. Throughout the 1920s she also wrote columns for the *Pittsburgh Courier* and *Washington Eagle*. Dunbar-Nelson died on September 18, 1935, of heart failure.

MAJOR WORKS

Dunbar-Nelson read widely and excelled in a variety of genres. Her early success with short stories—*Violets* and *The Goodness of St. Rocque*—was followed by a string of nonfiction works on literature and politics. She often stressed that she wrote from a feminine perspective: her first column in the *Pittsburgh Courier* was titled "From the Woman's Point of View" and later "Une Femme Dit." Perhaps in part because of her own difficulty in finding meaningful work, she often wrote about the roles available to women in education and politics. For example, in the *Long Island Review* she wrote about "Some of the Work of the National Association of Colored Women" (1899); in Emmett J. Scott's anthology *The American Negro in the World War*, she contributed an article on "Negro Women in War Work" (1919); and in the *Messenger*, she discussed "Textbooks in Public Schools: A Job for the Negro Woman" (1927). Her poetry appeared in some of the leading journals of the Harlem Renaissance, including *Opportunity* and *Harlem: A Forum of Negro Life*. One of her poems, "Snow in October," is included in Countee Cullen's 1927 anthology *Caroling Dusk*. As a teacher, Dunbar-Nelson produced two anthologies of her own: *Masterpieces of Negro Eloquence* (1914) and *The Dunbar Speaker and Entertainer* (1920). The former includes Dunbar-Nelson's essay on "The Life of Social Service as Exemplified in David Livingston," while the latter includes a play she wrote for her students, *Mine Eyes Have Seen*, and the poems "Chalmette," "The Lights at Carney's Point," and "To the Negro Farmers of the United States." Since her death, some of her unpublished works have also come to light and have been published in a 1988 three-volume set of collected works. Among these are short stories that critics have found somewhat bolder than Dunbar-Nelson's previously published works, including "Ellen Fenton," a narrative of marital strife and redemption, and a tragedy of mixed-racial identity, entitled "The Stones of the Village." Her editor, Gloria Hull, has suggested that Dunbar-Nelson's own ambivalence about her mixed-race background, coupled with a squeamish literary marketplace, likely kept such stories out of print during her lifetime.

CRITICAL RECEPTION

Dunbar-Nelson perceived that her opportunities and her reputation were negatively affected by the fact that she was a woman. Though she was well-known as an African American woman author and activist, she was relegated to a secondary place alongside the men of her generation. She was also somewhat ashamed, as suggested by her private correspondence, of having Caucasian ancestry. More recent scholarship on Dunbar-Nelson, however, has celebrated her unique perspective on the experience of African American women during the Harlem Renaissance. Gloria Hull, perhaps the foremost Dunbar-Nelson scholar, Alisa Johnson, and Kristina Brooks have each focused on Dunbar-Nelson's unpublished stories to cull her insights into race and identity, as well as relationships. As Brooks and Hull maintain, Dunbar-Nelson's writing is also very centered on place, especially in her early writings from New Orleans. Though some scholars have suggested that her regionalism reflects her status as a minor writer, Brooks in particular has argued that her use of "local color" speaks directly to the larger issues of racial boundaries. Hull, Johnson, and Claire M. Tylee have also proposed Dunbar-Nelson as one of the earliest advocates of a unique brand of African American feminism.

PRINCIPAL WORKS

Violets and Other Tales (short stories, essays, poetry) 1895

The Goodness of St. Rocque and Other Stories (short stories) 1899

Masterpieces of Negro Eloquence (essays, speeches, poetry) 1914

The Dunbar Speaker and Entertainer (essays, speeches, poetry, drama) 1920

Give Us Each Day: The Diary of Alice Dunbar-Nelson (diary) 1984

The Works of Alice Dunbar-Nelson. 3 vols. (short stories, essays, poetry, drama) 1988

PRIMARY SOURCES

ALICE DUNBAR-NELSON (SHORT STORY DATE 1914)

SOURCE: Dunbar-Nelson, Alice. "Hope Deferred." *The Crisis* 8 (September 1914): 238-44.

Dunbar-Nelson originally published this short story under the name Mrs. Paul Laurence Dunbar. The story deals with themes of belonging and ideals.

The direct rays of the August sun smote on the pavements of the city and made the soda-water signs in front of the drug stores alluringly suggestive of relief. Women in scant garments, displaying a maximum of form and a minimum of taste, crept along the pavements, their mussy light frocks suggesting a futile disposition on the part of the wearers to keep cool. Traditional looking fat men mopped their faces, and dived frantically into screened doors to emerge redder and more perspiring. The presence of small boys, scantily clad and of dusky hue and languid steps marked the city, if not distinctively southern, at least one on the borderland between the North and the South.

Edwards joined the perspiring mob on the hot streets and mopped his face with the rest. His shoes were dusty, his collar wilted. As he caught a glimpse of himself in a mirror of a shop window, he smiled grimly. "Hardly a man to present himself before one of the Lords of Creation to ask a favor," he muttered to himself.

Edwards was young; so young that he had not outgrown his ideals. Rather than allow that to happen, he had chosen one to share them with him, and the man who can find a woman willing to face poverty for her husband's ideals has a treasure far above rubies, and more precious than one with a thorough understanding of domestic science. But ideals do not always supply the immediate wants of the body, and it was the need of the wholly material that drove Edwards wilted, worn and discouraged into the August sunshine.

The man in the office to which the elevator boy directed him looked up impatiently from his desk. The windows of the room were open on a court-yard where green tree tops waved in a humid breeze; an electric fan whirred, and sent forth flashes of coolness; cool looking leather chairs invited the dusty traveler to sink into their depths.

Edwards was not invited to rest, however. Cold gray eyes in an impassive pallid face fixed him with a sneering stare, and a thin icy voice cut in on his half spoken words with a curt dismissal in its tone.

"Sorry, Mr. Er—, but I shan't be able to grant your request."

His "Good Morning" in response to Edward's reply as he turned out of the room was of the curtest, and left the impression of decided relief at an unpleasant duty discharged.

"Now where?" He had exhausted every avenue, and this last closed the door of hope with a finality that left no doubt in his mind. He dragged himself down the little side street, which led home, instinctively, as a child draws near to its mother in its trouble.

Margaret met him at the door, and their faces lighted up with the glow that always irradiated them in each other's presence. She drew him into the green shade of the little room, and her eyes asked, though her lips did not frame the question.

"No hope," he made reply to her unspoken words.

She sat down suddenly as one grown weak.

"If I could only just stick it out, little girl," he said, "but we need food, clothes, and only money buys them, you know."

"Perhaps it would have been better if we hadn't married—" she suggested timidly. That thought had been uppermost in her mind for some days lately.

"Because you are tired of poverty?" he queried, the smile on his lips belying his words.

She rose and put her arms about his neck. "You know better than that; but because if you did not have me, you could live on less, and thus have a better chance to hold out until they see your worth."

"I'm afraid they never will." He tried to keep his tones even, but in spite of himself a tremor shook his words. "The man I saw to-day is my last hope; he is the chief clerk, and what he says controls the opinions of others. If I could have influenced the senior member of the firm, but he is a man who leaves details to his subordinates, and Mr. Hanan was suspicious of me from the first. He isn't sure," he continued with a little laugh, which he tried to make sound spontaneous, "whether I am a stupendous fraud, or an escaped lunatic."

"We can wait; your chance will come," she soothed him with a rare smile.

"But in the meanwhile—" he finished for her and paused himself.

A sheaf of unpaid bills in the afternoon mail, with the curt and wholly unnecessary "Please Remit" in boldly impertinent characters across the bottom of every one drove Edwards out into the wilting sun. He knew the main street from end to end; he could tell how many trolley poles were on its corners; he felt that he almost knew the stones in the buildings, and that the pavements were worn with the constant passing of his feet, so often in the past four months had he walked, at first buoyantly, then hopefully, at last wearily up and down its length.

The usual idle crowd jostled around the baseball bulletins. Edwards joined them mechanically. "I can be a side-walk fan, even if I am impecurious." He smiled to himself as he said the words, and then listened idly to a voice at his side, "We are getting metropolitan, see that!"

The "That" was an item above the baseball score. Edwards looked and the letters burned themselves like white fire into his consciousness.

Strike Spreads to Our City.

Waiters at Adams' Walk Out After Breakfast This Morning.

"Good!" he said aloud. The man at his side smiled appreciatively at him; the home team had scored another run, but unheeding that Edwards walked down the street with a lighter step than he had known for days.

The proprietor of Adams' restaurant belied both his name and his vocation. He should have been rubicund, corpulent, American; instead he was wiry, lank, foreign in appearance. His teeth projected over a full lower lip, his eyes set far back in his head and were concealed by wrinkles that seemed to have been acquired by years of squinting into men's motives.

"Of course I want waiters,' he replied to Edwards' question, "any fool knows that." He paused, drew in his lower lip within the safe confines of his long teeth, squinted his eye intently on Edwards. "But do I want colored waiters? Now, do I?"

"It seems to me there's no choice for you in the matter," said Edwards good-humoredly.

The reply seemed to amuse the restaurant keeper immensely; he slapped the younger man on the back with a familiarity that made him wince both physically and spiritually.

"I guess I'll take you for head waiter." He was inclined to be jocular, even in the face of the disaster which the morning's strike had brought him. "Peel off and go to work. Say, stop!" as Edwards looked around to take his bearings, "What's your name?"

"Louis Edwards."

"Uh huh, had any experience?"

"Yes, some years ago, when I was in school."

"Uh huh, then waiting ain't your general work."

"No."

"Uh huh, what do you do for a living?"

"I'm a civil engineer."

One eye-brow of the saturnine Adams shot up, and he withdrew his lower lip entirely under his teeth.

"Well, say man, if you're an engineer, what you want to be strike-breaking here in a waiter's coat for, eh?"

Edwards' face darkened, and he shrugged his shoulders. "They don't need me, I guess," he replied briefly. It was an effort, and the restaurant keeper saw it, but his wonder overcame his sympathy.

"Don't need you with all that going on at the Monarch works? Why, man, I'd a thought every engineer this side o' hell would be needed out there."

"So did I; that's why I came here, but—"

"Say, kid, I'm sorry for you, I surely am; you go on to work."

"And so," narrated Edwards to Margaret, after midnight, when he had gotten in from his first day's work, "I became at once head waiter, first assistant, all the other waiters, chief boss, steward, and high-muck-a-muck, with all the emoluments and perquisites thereof."

Margaret was silent; with her ready sympathy she knew that no words of hers were needed then, they would only add to the burdens he had to bear. Nothing could be more bitter than this apparent blasting of his lifelong hopes, this seeming lowering of his standard. She said nothing, but the pressure of her slim brown hand in his meant more than words to them both.

"It's hard to keep the vision true," he groaned.

If it was hard that night, it grew doubly so within the next few weeks. Not lightly were the deposed waiters to take their own self-dismissal and supplanting. Daily they menaced the restaurant with their surly attentions, ugly and ominous. Adams shot out his lower lip from the confines of his long teeth and swore in a various language that he'd run his own place if he had to get every nigger in Africa to help him. The three of four men whom he was able to induce to stay with him in the face of missiles of every nature, threatened every day to give up the battle. Edwards was the force that held them together. He used every argument from the purely material one of holding on to the job now that they had it, through the negative one of loyalty to the man in his hour of need, to the altruistic one of keeping the place open for colored men for all time. There were none of them of such value as his own personality, and the fact that he stuck through all the turmoil. He wiped the mud from his face, picked up the putrid vegetables that often strewed the floor, barricaded the doors at night, replaced orders that were destroyed by well-aimed stones, and stood by Adams' side when the fight threatened to grow serious.

Adams was appreciative. "Say, kid, I don't know what I'd a done without you, now that's honest. Take it from me, when you need a friend anywhere on earth, and you can send me a wireless, I'm right there with the goods in answer to your S.O.S."

This was on the afternoon when the patrol, lined up in front of the restaurant, gathered in a few of the most disturbing ones, none of whom, by the way, had ever been employed in the place. "Sympathy" had pervaded the town.

The humid August days melted into the sultry ones of September. The self-dismissed waiters had quieted down, and save for an occasional missile, annoyed Adams and his corps of dark-skinned helpers no longer. Edwards had resigned himself to his temporary discomforts. He felt, with the optimism of the idealist, that it was only for a little while; the fact that he had sought work at his profession for nearly a year had not yet discouraged him. He would explain carefully to Margaret when the day's work was over, that it was only for a little while; he would earn enough at this to enable them to get away, and then in some other place he would be able to stand up with the proud consciousness that all his training had not been in vain.

He was revolving all these plans in his mind one Saturday night. It was at the hour when business was dull, and he leaned against the window and sought entertainment from the crowd on the street. Saturday night, with all the blare and glare and garishness dear to the heart of the middle-class provincial of the smaller cities, was holding court on the city streets. The hot September sun had left humidity and closeness in its wake, and the evening mists had scarce had time to cast coolness over the town. Shop windows glared wares through popular tunes from open store doors to attract unwary passersby. Half-grown boys and girls, happy in the license of Saturday night on the crowded streets, jostled one another and pushed in long lines, shouted familiar epithets at other pedestrians with all the abandon of the ill-breeding common to the class. One crowd, in particular, attracted Edwards' attention. The girls were brave in semi-decollete waists, scant short skirts and exaggerated heads, built up in fanciful designs; the boys with flamboyant red neckties, striking hat-bands, and white trousers. They made a snake line, boys and girls, hands on each other's shoulders, and rushed shouting through the press of shoppers, scattering the inattentive right and left. Edwards' lip curled, "Now, if those were colored boys and girls—"

His reflections were never finished, for a patron moved towards his table, and the critic of human life became once more the deferential waiter.

He did not move a muscle of his face as he placed the glass of water on the table, handed the menu card, and stood at attention waiting for the order, although he had recognized at first glance the half-sneering face of his old hope—Hanan, of the great concern which had no need of him. To Hanan, the man who brought his order was but one of the horde of menials who satisfied his daily wants and soothed his vanity when the cares of the day had ceased pressing on his shoulders. He had not even looked at the man's face, and for this Edwards was grateful.

A new note had crept into the noise on the streets; there was in it now, not so much mirth and ribaldry as menace and anger. Edwards looked outside in slight alarm; he had grown used to that note in the clamor of the streets, particularly on Saturday nights; it meant that the whole restaurant must be prepared to quell a disturbance. The snake line had changed; there were only flamboyant hat-bands in it now, the decollete shirt waists and scant skirts had taken refuge on another corner. Something in the shouting attracted Hanan's attention, and he looked up wonderingly.

"What are they saying?" he inquired. Edwards did not answer; he was so familiar with the old cry that he thought it unnecessary.

"Yah! Yah! Old Adams hires niggers! Hires niggers!"

"Why, that is so," Hanan looked up at Edwards' dark face for the first time. "This is quite an innovation for Adams' place. How did it happen?"

"We are strike-breakers," replied the waiter quietly, then he grew hot, for a gleam of recognition came into Hanan's eyes.

"Oh, yes, I see. Aren't you the young man who asked me for employment as an engineer at the Monarch works?"

Edwards bowed, he could not answer; hurt pride surged up within him and made his eyes hot and his hands clammy.

"Well, er—I'm glad you've found a place to work; very sensible of you, I'm sure. I should think, too, that it is work for which you would be more fitted than engineering."

Edwards started to reply, but the hot words were checked on his lips. The shouting had reached a shrillness which boded immediate results, and with the precision of a missile from a warship's gun, a stone hurtled through the glass of the long window. It struck Edwards' hand, glanced through the dishes on the tray which he was in the act of setting on the table, and tipped half its contents over Hanan's knee. He sprang to his feet angrily, striving to brush the debris of his dinner from his immaculate clothing, and turned angrily upon Edwards.

"That is criminally careless of you!" he flared, his eyes blazing in his pallid face. "You could have prevented that; you're not even a good waiter, much less an engineer."

And then something snapped in the darker man's head. The long strain of the fruitless summer; the struggle of keeping together the men who worked under him in the restaurant; the heat, and the task of enduring what was to him the humiliation of serving, and this last injustice, all culminated in a blinding flash in his brain. Reason, intelligence, all was obscured, save a man hated, and a desire to wreak his wrongs on the man, who, for the time being, represented the author of them. He sprang at the white man's throat and bore him to the floor. They wrestled and fought together, struggling, biting, snarling, like brutes in the debris of food and the clutter of overturned chairs and tables.

The telephone rang insistently. Adams wiped his hands on a towel, and carefully moved a paint brush out of the way, as he picked up the receiver.

"Hello!" he called. "Yes, this is Adams, the restaurant keeper. Who? Uh huh. Wants to know if I'll go his bail? Say, that nigger's got softening of the brain. Course not, let him serve his time, making all that row in my place; never had no row here before. No, I don't never want to see him again."

He hung up the receiver with a bang, and went back to his painting. He had almost finished his sign, and he smiled as he ended it with a flourish:

WAITERS WANTED. NONE BUT WHITE MEN NEED APPLY.

Out in the county work-house, Edwards sat on his cot, his head buried in his hands. He wondered what Margaret was doing all this long hot Sunday, if the tears were blinding her sight as they did his; then he started to his feet, as the warden called his name. Margaret stood before him, her arms outstretched, her mouth quivering with tenderness and sympathy, her whole form yearning towards him with a passion of maternal love.

"Margaret! You here, in this place?"

"Aren't you here?" she smiled bravely, and drew his head towards the refuge of her bosom. "Did you think I wouldn't come to see you?"

"To think I should have brought you to this," he moaned.

She stilled his reproaches and heard the story from his lips. Then she murmured with bloodless mouth, "How long will it be?"

"A long time, dearest—and you?"

"I can go home, and work," she answered briefly, "and wait for you, be it ten months or ten years—and then—?"

"And then—" they stared into each other's eyes like frightened children. Suddenly his form straightened up, and the vision of his ideal irradiated his face with hope and happiness.

"And then, Beloved," he cried, "then we will start all over again. Somewhere, I am needed; somewhere in this world there are wanted dark-skinned men like me to dig and blast and build bridges and make straight the roads of the world, and I am going to find that place—with you."

She smiled back trustfully at him. "Only keep true to your ideal, dearest," she whispered, "and you will find the place. Your window faces the south, Louis. Look up and out of it all the while you are here, for it is there, in our own southland, that you will find the realization of your dream."

GENERAL COMMENTARY

GLORIA T. HULL (ESSAY DATE 1984)

SOURCE: Hull, Gloria T. Introduction. In *Give Us Each Day: The Diary of Alice Dunbar-Nelson,* pp. 13-32. New York: W. W. Norton, 1984.

In this essay, Hull gives a biography of Dunbar-Nelson, focusing on her personal life and relationships. Hull notes Dunbar-Nelson's observations on being a woman and on being light-skinned, suggesting that her diary offers a unique window into the daily life of a Black woman in the early twentieth century.

This diary of Alice Dunbar-Nelson [***Give Us Each Day***] is only the second one by a Black woman that we have had the good fortune to see. Charlotte Forten's *Journal*—kept during the middle years of the nineteenth century and first published in 1953—has been the only book-length one available. It is the record of an aware and sensitive young Black woman during her schooldays in Salem, Massachusetts, and her adventures teaching with the Civil War Port Royal experiment. However, Forten, a proper, self-effacing New Englander, had a different life and personality, moved in a different world, and consequently produced a very different document than did Dunbar-Nelson, her later counterpart.

One wonders how many other publishable diaries by Black women have been written, but have not come to light. It is impossible, of course, to answer this intriguing question. It is not impossible, though, to understand why, until now, we have been able to lay hands on only these two. Alice Walker, in her essay "In Search of Our Mothers' Gardens," feelingly sets the perspective by explaining "the agony of the lives of [Black] women who might have been Poets, Novelists, Essayists, [Diarists] and Short Story writers . . . who died with their real gifts stifled within them" because of slavery, racism, sexism, sexual abuse, overwork, child-bearing and -rearing, prohibitions against reading and writing, and exclusion from every other recognized outlet for creative expression.[1]

Even those few Black women who have somehow managed to occupy positions where diary keeping might have been a possibility have been as hampered as their less fortunate sisters by subtler forms of prejudice. Bearing the burden of their relatively privileged status, they have thrown their energies into social reform and racial uplift, and, I suspect, they have also regarded the journal as an alien and uncongenial tradition in which to package their experiences. Clearly, then, diary keeping has not been compatible with the conditions of the lives of the vast majority of Black women. Furthermore, Black women and their writings have not been so valued that life documents by them have been preserved, sought, or published. It is, therefore, also not surprising that printed collections of letters by Black women do not exist.

However, Black women have chronicled their lives in other autobiographical forms; and it is to these that we must turn for a tradition-making body of work. This tradition includes the slave narratives of such figures as Harriet Brent Jacobs, Nancy Prince, Sojourner Truth, and Elizabeth Keckley. It also comprises the relatively large number of autobiographies that have been published by diverse Black women, such as Susie King Taylor, Daisy Bates, Billie Holiday, Mary Church Terrell, Ossie Guffy, and Ann Moody. (Note though that, among writers, only Zora Neale Hurston, Pauli Murray, Gwendolyn Brooks, Nikki Giovanni, and Maya Angelou have set down versions of their lives.) It is more than interesting that Black women prefer to show themselves in the form of traditional autobiography. Of course, the autobiographical impulse in Black writing is extremely strong (some would say dominant), but it almost appears as if Black women could not assume the luxury or run the risk of the spontaneous self-disclosure of diary writing. And, finally, there is the countervailing influence of the oral tradition that suffuses all of Black culture.

What was it, then, about Dunbar-Nelson and her life that impelled her to this strange form of self-expression? Perhaps looking at her background and her circumstances when she wrote the diary will provide some clues.

Dunbar-Nelson was born Alice Ruth Moore in New Orleans, Louisiana, July 19, 1875, her father a merchant marine and mother a seamstress. After attending public school and then graduating from Straight University in 1892, she began teaching in New Orleans and assumed a prominent place in its Black and Creole society, especially in musical and literary circles. She was president of the Whittier Club of her A.M.E. church and acted in dramas that it presented. Generally, she was considered a beautiful and talented young woman from whom much was expected. In 1896, she came northeast for further schooling, subsequently matriculating at Cornell, Columbia, and the University of Pennsylvania. Her areas of study included English literature, English educational measurements, and psychology. At Cornell in 1908, she produced a thesis on the influence of Milton on Wordsworth that was so insightful that scholars such as Professor Lane Cooper wrote to her for information and an article based upon it was published in *Modern Language Notes* (April 1909).

Shortly after she began teaching at the White Rose Mission in New York City in 1897 (which later became the White Rose Home for Girls in Harlem), Alice began a storybook courtship with Paul Laurence Dunbar, America's first famous Black poet. He had seen a picture and poem of hers in a Boston magazine and initiated a decorous and romantic correspondence. After marrying on March 8, 1898, they set up house in Washington, D.C. Even though they sincerely, it seems, encouraged each other's writing ambitions, their marriage was tempestuous. Accusations of selfishness, infidelity, and cruelty cropped up between them, aggravated by gossip, the frequent separations necessitated by Paul's career, and his medically induced drinking. (Because of his tuberculosis, doctors had prescribed alcohol for him, to which he became addicted.) Moreover, Paul had always been extremely close to his protective mother, and Alice's family had exhibited some misgivings about his very dark skin color and his work with minstrel shows and musicals. After Alice left Paul in 1902, she refused to be reconciled with him. Therefore, they were estranged when he died at his home in Dayton, Ohio, on February 6, 1906. Yet the world gave respect to her as his wife, sending her numerous condolences, requests for information and souvenirs, and commercial propositions.

After the separation, Dunbar-Nelson (and her family) moved to Wilmington, Delaware, the place that remained her base for the next thirty years. From 1902 to 1920, she taught at Howard High School (then the only secondary school for Blacks in the state) and served as head of the English department. She executed her often tiresome duties well—teaching, supervising, procuring funds, directing class-night plays, writing the history of the school, assisting the administration, and so on. Though her quick tongue and near-white complexion sometimes inspired animosity, she maintained working friendships with her colleagues. For seven of these years at Howard, she also directed the summer sessions for in-service teachers at State College for Colored Students (later Delaware State College), Dover, and taught two years in the summer session at Hampton Institute.

On April 20, 1916, Dunbar-Nelson made another marriage, to Robert J. Nelson (1873-1949), whom she called Bobo, Bob O, or Bobbo (pronounced Bob-O). A journalist and widower from Harrisburg, Pennsylvania, he had two children whose mother had died of tuberculosis. Because Dunbar-Nelson and Robert were both involved in politics and racial activities, theirs was a good professional union. They cooperated when that was in order and pursued their separate activities when that was necessary. Together, they edited and published a progressive Black newspaper, *The Wilmington Advocate,* from 1920 to 1922.

During this period, Dunbar-Nelson was also active in many civic, racial, and women's causes. She was an organizer for the Middle Atlantic states in the women's suffrage campaign (1915), a field representative in the South for the Woman's Committee of the Council of National Defense (1918), and the first Black woman to serve on the State Republican Committee of Delaware (1920). She was a working member of such groups as the National Federation of Colored Women's Clubs, the National Association of Colored Women, the League of Independent Political Action, and the Delta Sigma Theta Sorority. Furthermore, Dunbar-Nelson had already achieved some renown as a writer.

When she was only twenty years old, she had published ***Violets and Other Tales*** (1895), a collection of poems, tales, sketches, essays, and stories. Being a juvenile work, the book—with its diverse inclusions—evidences a beginning writer's experimentation with various tones and genres. The pieces are usually brief, slight, impressionistic—but some of them possess charm and interest. ***Violets*** was followed in 1898 by a volume of short stories, ***The Goodness of St. Rocque,*** published by Dodd, Mead, and Company. The stories here are longer, better developed, more polished. They are all set firmly in New Orleans and fully utilize the Creole history and distinctive culture of the city, usually in conjunction with themes of love. In addition to some earlier writing and editing for the *A.M.E. Church Review,* by the time she began her diary, Dunbar-Nelson had compiled two volumes of works suitable for platform and program delivery, ***Masterpieces of Negro Eloquence*** (1913) and ***The Dunbar Speaker and Entertainer*** (1920). Articles by her were appearing in print—such as her two part **"People of Color in Louisiana"** in *The Journal of Negro History* (1916-17)—and her poetry was being regularly published and anthologized.

Throughout her life, Dunbar-Nelson was regarded as the temperamental family genius, always having to be calmed down from one emotional peak or another. She was forceful, strong-willed, inquisitive, imaginative, and stubborn. Yet, in her own way, she was very much a "lady." She liked pretty things (and even luxury), flowers, dogs, and children. There was a romantic side to her nature, and she took art, piano, and cello lessons, did lacework, and frequented the theatre. Furthermore, she had a high regard for reputation, manners, and the proprieties. A tall, attractive, auburn-haired woman, she presented an imposing appearance. In her dress, she was elegant and fashionable.

This background, then, reveals Dunbar-Nelson to be an educated, culturally sophisticated Black woman writer. Being such, she was familiar with the form and tradition of English diary keeping. She did not find it alien, was, in fact, favorably predisposed toward it, and recognized its possibilities for herself. Ever so often within the diary, she reveals her knowledge of the tradition and sense of forming a part of it, as when she begins her July 19, 1929 birthday entry with "Does one have to record thoughts?" thus showing her awareness that it was almost *de rigueur* to do so in a journal. Yet Dunbar-Nelson's background and literary bent do not sufficiently explain why she kept a diary, while other Black women similar to her in education, discretionary leisure, and sense of personal importance and destiny did not. The question remains a puzzling one, especially on a group level; and even when answers are attempted on an individual basis, they too prove tentative and inconclusive.

During the periods when she kept the diary, Dunbar-Nelson's life was in flux or crisis. This supports the axiom that diaries are most often and most interestingly written in times of change and turmoil, or, as it is often put, in times of mobility—most often thought of as geographic, but just as plausibly psychic as well. When she first began her diary on July 29, 1921, Dunbar-Nelson was undergoing agonies of soul and spirit trying to adjust to the traumas of the previous year; and the work ends after 1931, just when Robert is given the appointment that frees them from debt and worry.

During these years of upheaval and personal change, Dunbar-Nelson used the diary as a place to vent her thoughts and emotions. There was not a person in her life with whom she could openly be all of the things that she was and with whom she could be totally unguarded (a classic case of female schizophrenia and isolation). Her good friend Bowse expressed horror at her socializing with boxer Jack Johnson and his wife; her sister Leila could not share her outgoing political and social enthusiasms; her husband Robert was unable to accept her romantic and physical interest in other women—to cite only three major unmeshings. And there were many times when Dunbar-Nelson's contemplations would have frightened and alienated those around her. A husband who could not stand to be told of her anxiety about money and a sister who became alarmed at an outburst of ranting certainly would not have known how to deal with her suicidal yearnings. Such things as these she confined to the pages of her diary. As with all frank diaries, one feels that the impulse for a full, true revelation of self (perhaps for posterity) was a strong operational motivation.

However, Dunbar-Nelson never directly indicates that she is conscious of employing the journal for venting purposes. When she started the diary, she wrote in its preface, "Had I had sense enough to keep a diary all these years that I have been traveling around, . . . there would be less confusion in my mind about lots of things." And even though she had an extremely good memory and naturally retained vivid impressions of long-ago events, Dunbar-Nelson persisted throughout in referring to the diary as a mnemonic device. What she does not make clear, though, is whether she intended for it to help her recall simple events or discern the more complex patterns of her life. Thus, many of her entries are mechanical or journalistic, while introspective thinking and deeper revelations break through in others. There are only two recorded instances of her rereading what she has earlier written (her 1931 birthday, and the anniversary of her 1930 trip to California). But, based on the fact that these are significant dates, and also considering the diary's general importance to her, one can probably assume that she read it over on other occasions as well.

It seems that Dunbar-Nelson also saw the diary as a self-imposed disciplinary task and a private test of her constancy and character. She frequently voiced irritation and resentment at it (even once calling it a weight on her heart), but continued to keep it up in varying degrees. Clearly, the diary became for her a given, an unchanging focus in the midst of change and uncertainty. These attitudes accord well with her personality because she was basically orderly and precise and had very high expectations for herself, which prompted her to be self-disparaging about laziness. Finally, as is usually the case, the keeping of the diary became for her its own reward, a kind of end sufficient unto itself.

For some years, a day-by-day type of memorandum book served as the basic diary. Usually Dunbar-Nelson limited her entries to the one page per day allotted, even when she had to cramp her handwriting and disregard the lines to squeeze in everything that she wished to say. Sometimes she wrote or typed on other sheets too and pasted them in. These supplementary sheets often reflect her activities and whereabouts—for example, the letterhead of the Paramount Syndicate Company (her own, it seems) and the reverse side of programs from the National Negro Music Festival, one of her Inter-Racial Peace Committee projects. (A more detailed discussion of the original manuscript can be found in the Editorial Preface.)

Dunbar-Nelson wrote her diary, like most diarists, when the spirit moved her, and like most women diarists, when she could find the time. One pleasant morning she is sitting by the open kitchen window drinking a cup of tea and writing in the diary. Another time, she is upstairs, in bed, plugging away at 2:00 A.M. During the first years of the journal, she constantly vowed to write daily, but was never able to keep her resolves. Some lapses were five to ten days long; others lasted three or four weeks; and once she stopped writing altogether for two months. On this last occasion, she resumed by saying that she did not know why she stopped, suggesting, for one thing, that she did not clearly know why she kept it up. Finally, in 1930, she stopped making resolutions and simply let the words fall as they would.

Actually, Dunbar-Nelson's "blanket" entries are, in at least one way, preferable to her diurnal jottings because they are usually more discursive. The kinds of entries that she made also varied from year to year—ranging from the leisurely sentenced ones of 1921, to the choppy ones of 1926-27, to the intense and briefly reflective entries of 1930. Likewise, she writes in every one of her many moods, only confessing once, in 1931, that she deliberately refrained "when the misery and wretchedness and disappointment and worry were so close to me that to write it out was impossible, and not to write it out, foolish."

As fascinating as are the issues raised thus far, the heart of the diary lies in what it reveals, through Dunbar-Nelson's life, about the meaning of being a Black woman in twentieth-century America. These revelations include both the commonplace and the startling and add up to a picture whose cumulative impact is staggering.

First, one notices that during her entire career, Dunbar-Nelson received attention for being Paul Laurence Dunbar's wife and widow and not necessarily for her own individual achievement. When he was alive, she was thought of as his wife who incidentally "wrote a little herself," a secondary status that she sometimes buttressed by her deferent poses and feminine role-playing. She also chose to continue carrying his name, thus ensuring the linkage. However, upon reflection it becomes clear that Dunbar-Nelson did this partly because of her awareness that, in a racist, sexist society, it could be helpful and because of the certainly galling knowledge that, as a Black woman, she needed as much help as she could get. Ironically, sexism cuts both ways. When she died—after twenty-nine years of widowhood, a second husband, and many illustrious accomplishments of her own—the Philadelphia *Afro-American* ran a banner story with this headline: "Alice Ruth Moore's 2 Husbands / First, a Volatile Genius; Second, a Calm Newsman / Washingtonians Recall Romance of the Dunbars / Mrs. [Mary Church] Terrell Recalls When Wife of Poet Borrowed / an Ice Cream Freezer."[2]

At the outset, it is apparent that Dunbar-Nelson's basic living situation is that of a female-centered household and strong woman-to-woman family relationships. The core consisted of Alice, her sister Leila, their mother Patricia, and Leila's four children, three of whom were girls. They added on husbands and other children as their life choices dictated, but always remained together. Dunbar-Nelson never bore any children herself, but she acquired two—an elder daughter, Elizabeth, and younger son, Bobby—when she married the widowed Robert and helped to raise them as well as her sister's four. As different as these women were, their personalities seem to have complemented each other more often than they clashed, and they constituted an inhouse support system for one another. They often had fun together, too, as when Dunbar-Nelson and Leila, a very exclusive, self-styled club of two, treated Leila's daughter Pauline to a night out in Philadelphia.

Still, there were stresses between them in the home. Probably the most acute ones were generated by mother Patricia's long, difficult illness and lingering death. During this time, Dunbar-Nelson wrote things in her diary like "home—to a muddling sort of kitchen full of nervous overwrought Leila and Pauline, a diddling Miss Waters [the nurse] and a glum Robert. I sometimes wonder why I come home at all" (January 5, 1931). Money, being a scarce commodity, was also a potential sore point and leads to the even more serious observation that the household was an economic unit—albeit a marginal and precarious one, especially because its members were predominantly Black women. They all worked—very hard—when they could find jobs and until they could no longer do so because of age and health. To paraphrase Toni Morrison in *Sula,* these women had nobody/nothing "either white or male" to fall back on;[3] hence they had to rely on themselves. It was a constant struggle.

One might ask, "What about Dunbar-Nelson's husband?" His position as a *Black* man was far from the secure sufficiency that would have allowed her the luxury of leisure. He was making his way in the world as best he could, hanging on to teetering enterprises like the Black Elks' (the Improved Benevolent and Protective Order of Elks) Washington *Eagle* newspaper and hoping for political preferment. Page after page of the diary is filled with Dunbar-Nelson's financial plight. She helped to found organizations—such as the Industrial School for Colored Girls in Marshalltown, Delaware—to create employment, even if low-paying, for herself and grabbed at flimsy schemes that promised reward. Some of her most harrowing passages concern bounced checks, unpaid mortgages, humiliating inquisitions with finance companies, and the like. At her lowest point, during the height of the Depression, she seriously entertained the idea of selling encyclopedias and Spencer undergarments door-to-door.

Dunbar-Nelson's helping relationships with the women of her family were also part of a larger system of Black female support. She knew practically all of the active and prominent Black women of her time—Nannie Burroughs, Charlotte Hawkins Brown, Jessie Fauset, Laura Wheeler, Bessye Bearden, to name a few—and associated with them. As with her family, these associations were not without their jealousies and pettinesses. But, in a world that contrived to devalue them, these Black women were essential to each other's well-being.

Many of these leading women of the day were a part of the flourishing Black women's club movement, which became especially visible and effective with the 1896 founding of the National Association of Colored Women. Working first on a local level and then confederating in regional and national efforts, Black women of all classes united to combat negative stereotypes about themselves and to materially and spiritually aid in the overall betterment of the race. For a woman like Dunbar-Nelson, this work entailed such time-consuming activities as attending local executive and full membership meetings; cooperating with other clubwomen and the public to carry out official duties, tasks, and projects; planning and participating in state, regional, and national conventions. What they accomplished in housing, education, civil rights, women's suffrage, travel accomodations, health, cultural affairs, and so forth was impressive.

The beauty of the club movement was the opportunity it provided for like-minded Black women to work together. Dunbar-Nelson's relationships with three particular women in the diary reflect this kind of racial and sororal camaraderie. One is Edwina B. Kruse, founding principal of Howard High School, who gave her emotional sustenance and encouragement. Dunbar-Nelson's esteem for "Krusie" or "Ned" (as she was called) is best documented by the fact that she wrote an unpublished novel based on Kruse's life, entitled ***This Lofty Oak.*** Truly a labor of love, the original manuscript runs to 565 typewritten pages. Even after Kruse retired and became senile, Dunbar-Nelson continued to be dutifully attentive. The second is Georgia Douglas Johnson, the most popular Black woman poet of the 1920s. They shared womanly interactions (Dunbar-Nelson teaching her how to wear hats) and related to each other as sister artists. Johnson invited Dunbar-Nelson to be a special guest at one of her Washington, D.C. literary gatherings, and Dunbar-Nelson, in turn, kept up with what Johnson was producing and reviewed her work. They both benefited as women and as writers from their contact with one another.

Finally, there is Mary McLeod Bethune, who was not a close personal friend. It seems that she served certain role-model functions for Dunbar-Nelson. The diary presents a few scenes that are so pricelessly suggestive that a reader is moved to wish, "If only I could have been there." One of these is a picture of Dunbar-Nelson doing her hair while Bethune gets a pedicure at Bethune-Cookman College. It should be mentioned that Dunbar-Nelson spread her strength outward—for example, to the young women at the Industrial School. She bought them watches when they excelled in their studies, counseled abortions for them, and helped to see them through college.

The next issue of Dunbar-Nelson's life illuminated by the diary is the question of class, which becomes problematical when related to the ambiguous status of Black women. Even educated, "middle-class," professional Black women like Dunbar-Nelson almost always come from and/or have firsthand knowledge of working-class or poorer-class situations. In addition, being Black, they have no entrenched and comfortable security in even this achieved class status—and being women, their position is rendered doubly marginal and complicated. These facts foster many contradictions that the diary reveals, sometimes unwittingly. For instance, on March 28, 1927, Dunbar-Nelson writes very grimly about having to go to the pawnshop to raise twenty-five dollars on her rings and earrings to pay the water bill and then in the next paragraph details a "palatial" and "very fine" gathering of the Philadelphia Professional Woman's Club at which she spoke.

The white women ("*wives* of professional men") at this affair had no idea that they were being addressed by and were socializing with a woman who had just visited a pawnshop in order to pay her water bill. Nor was this anywhere uppermost in Dunbar-Nelson's consciousness. Undoubtedly, she was dressed to look like "a certified check" (her phrase) and was comporting herself likewise. Dunbar-Nelson had the breeding, education, culture, looks, and manners of the "higher classes" (and thought of herself in this way)—but, as we have seen, none of the money to back it up. This is and was very often the case.

Related to this class issue is the notion of the "genteel tradition" in Black life and literature, with its special ramifications for Black women. When scholars of this period talk about cultural strains, they frequently identify two—the "genteel" and the "bohemian/realistic." Dunbar-Nelson—together with W. E. B. Du Bois, novelist Jessie Fauset, scholar Alain Locke, and others—is put in the first group and considered to be "bourgie," conservative, stiff, uptight, and accomodationist. Of course, this stance was basically a part of the attempt to counter negative racial stereotypes and put the best racial foot forward. For Black *women,* extra burdens were added. They were always mindful of their need to be living refutations of the sexual slurs to which Black women were subjected and, at the same time, as much as white women, were also tyrannized by the still-prevalent Victorian cult of true womanhood.

Recalling facts like these aids in the understanding of why Dunbar-Nelson carried herself in a manner that one New York newspaper called "distinctively aristocratic."[4] It also provides perspective for some of her less flattering utterances and attitudes—her refusing to ride in a car with the printer's wife and "Taylor Street friends," her describing a poor Black high school graduation ceremony as "very monkey," and this November 6, 1929 characterization of the president of the National Federation of Colored Women:

> Sallie Stewart is a fine women. But she offends my aesthetics. Fine woman in the sense of achievement—but hopelessly, frightfully, commonplace, provincial, middle class.

The truth of the matter (that is, the other truth of the matter) is that Dunbar-Nelson was a genuine, down-to-earth person who, when she allowed herself, enjoyed all types of activities and people. She drank blackmarket Italian red wine and bootleg whiskey, played the numbers, bought "hot" clothes, had friends whom she dubbed "rough-necky," went to Harlem dives and cabarets, and indulged what she called a "low taste" for underworld films and S. S. Van Dine novels. However, one would not have guessed any of this by her appearance.

The same kind of complex duality also marks Dunbar-Nelson's life in the areas of love and sexuality. Her relationship with Robert seems to have been characterized by a strong sense of mutual self-respect and sober practicality typical of many Black heterosexual liaisons. Clearly, they were friends and partners in life. Robert's attitudes were conventionally male (he liked her to be at home when he ran in, and he scolded her for looking like a charwoman—even while she was scrubbing the house), and he was jealous and somewhat possessive (causing Dunbar-Nelson to write on one occasion that he "was cross, of course, as he always is, when I show any interest in any male or female . . ."—September 21, 1928). Nonetheless, he admired, respected, and encouraged her, and even once surprised her by giving support instead of an expected "snort of disgust" when she casually mentioned that she should study law (October 13, 1921). Regardless of whatever other people she may have involved herself with, Dunbar-Nelson appeared to always value their relationship, saying on Thanksgiving 1930: "And yet I have a lot to be thankful for. Bobbo, first, last and always, the best of all."

Before uniting with Robert, Dunbar-Nelson made a secret, short-lived marriage in 1910 with one Arthur Callis, a young Black man twelve years her junior who came fresh from Cornell to teach at Howard High School. She never publicly revealed it, clearly intended that it remain undisclosed, and spoke about it mysteriously even in the diary. Some imperatives of her position—perhaps her thinking about the differences in their age and/or social standing—bade her keep it secret. (Of course, for a man, this circumstance would not have been a problem.) Callis provides the occasion in the diary for Dunbar-Nelson to muse about her lifetime loves:

> [Leaving him] . . . I walked slowly home through the beautiful streets thinking after all, love and beautiful love has been mine from many men, but the great passion of at least four or five whose love for me transcended that for other women—and what more can any woman want?
>
> (June 4, 1931)

Apparently, she did want more. The woman-identification revealed in the diary encompassed at least two or three—and probably more—emotionally and physically intimate relationships with women. They were very important aspects of her inner life. But, of course, for her—given her personality, place, and time—it was absolutely essential that they remain hidden. Of the two such lesbian relationships explicitly recorded in the diary, the weightier was obviously with Fay Jackson Robinson. Dunbar-Nelson was ecstatic about their touching, recording that she wrote a sonnet that began with the marvelously apt, female imagery of this first line: "I had not thought to ope that secret room." And, despite misunderstandings, miscommunications, and disappointments, Dunbar-Nelson could yet sigh in her diary on March 18, 1931: "Anniversary of My One Perfect Day . . . And still we cannot meet again."

Despite the cryptic and hesitant allusions, Dunbar-Nelson clearly reveals the existence and operation of an active Black lesbian network. Dunbar-Nelson mentions that a friend of hers tells her to "look over" a Betty Linford, and that a "heavy flirtation" between two clubwomen friends of hers puts her "nose sadly out of joint" (July 25, August 1, 1928). All of these women were prominent and professional, and most had husbands and/or children. Somehow, they contrived to be themselves and carry on these relationships in what most surely must have been an extremely repressive context—with even more layers of oppression piled on by the stringencies of their roles as Black women.

In the diary, Dunbar-Nelson refers to other affairs and flirtations. Generally speaking, she was a sensuous woman whose passion could not always find expression. Its strength is often revealed, however, as in this excerpt from a sexually charged description of a midnight swim that she enjoyed with a mixed company of friends shortly after her fifty-fourth birthday:

> . . . racing in under the pulsing water to the solitary light on shore. An experience worth having—a glorious, wonderful climax. Only equalled by the velvety luxuriousness of the times when swimming far out—we slipped off our bathing suits . . . and let the water caress our naked forms.
> (July 27, 1929)

Equally as crucial for Dunbar-Nelson were the conditions and struggles of the workplace. The first year of the diary dramatizes such *Advocate*-related traumas as her being coldly dismissed from magnate Irénée du Pont's office when she tried to sell him stock in the paper and her having to endure the patronizing attitude of a Wilmington political figure who helped to finance it. Perhaps the most graphic revelation of what it meant to be a Black woman on the job emerges from her work with the Inter-Racial Peace Committee. Here, her white male boss questioned her executive ability and even stooped to complain about her lipstick. The Quaker (Society of Friends) board that controlled her committee also gave her a hard time, receiving her reports in silence, failing to attend her functions, and begrudging the two thousand dollars it would have cost to keep her Black-oriented program in operation while squandering large sums of money on other projects (see February 26, 1931). And, of course, there were inescapable annoyances like the Quaker lady who came into the office and inveighed against Blacks in her presence (not knowing her race because of her light complexion), and the member of an audience of Black ministers who, when she "railed at them" for not answering her letters, "piped up" from the back of the room, "Sister, we didn't know how you look!" (February 16, 1931).

How work outside the home and work within it interface shows up clearly in the diary through such matter-of-fact statements as "Home by seven . . . Get some dinner. Tired as I am, have *that* to do" (June 11, 1927). Dunbar-Nelson's not so matter-of-fact consciousness about the sexual politics of domestic life likewise surfaces, as in this May 25, 1929 entry, written after attending the National Negro Music Festival, an event that she planned, arranged, carried out, and worked on day and night just before its occurrence:

> Nearly cracked when I got home a wreck, and Bobbo asked me if there was anything to eat in the ice-box. It was too cruel. But when I got off my shoes, into nightie and bathrobe, and went down into the kitchen to eat the sandwiches he had cooked (fried egg) and a high ball, did not feel so near to tears. I might have bawled him out a plenty.

Like Frances E. W. Harper, a nineteenth-century Black woman writer, Dunbar-Nelson was engaged throughout her life in multifaceted social activism—showing, yet again, that aware Black women felt that they could not forego such involvement. During the time of the diary, most of this work was with the state and national organizations of the National Federation of Colored Women's Clubs. Seen against the general backdrop of the women's club movement, it helps to round out the picture of American feminism and also adds details to the record of Black activism for the period. For instance, in September 1928, Dunbar-Nelson writes about a conference sponsored by women of the Inter-Racial Council of the Federal Council of Churches where, in her words,

> It was the colored women . . . who kept the discussions on a frank and open plane; who struggled hardest to prevent the conference from degenerating into a sentimental mutual admiration society, and who insisted that all is not right and perfect in this country of ours, and that there is a deal to be done by the right thinking church women of both races.

Dunbar-Nelson's work with the Inter-Racial Peace Committee tied in, too, with her racial and political views. Following the pattern of many

FROM THE AUTHOR

RIGHTING THE WRONGS

In every race, in every nation, and in every clime in every period of history there is always an eager-eyed group of youthful patriots who seriously set themselves to right the wrongs done to their race or nation or . . . art or self-expression.

SOURCE: Alice Dunbar-Nelson, excerpt from an essay in *The Messenger,* March 1927.

Americans, she supported World War I but was strongly pacifist when sabers again began rattling in the late 1920s. At a 1929 peace conference, she notes the incongruity of their agenda being taken up with talk of tonnage, cruisers, battleships, etc., summing it up by writing: "Seems to me everyone is preparing for war and temporizing with the thought of it" (October 24, 1929). But her radical stance did not go so far as to encompass socialism-communism.

About race, Dunbar-Nelson's diary reveals a not-uncommon dual set of values. Looking at the Black race *sui generis* from within it, she often made critical and disparaging remarks. These even include some class-related aspersions against dark-complexioned Blacks and some comments that suggest personal alienation on her part. However, when she was mindful of the larger, social contexts, she was militantly pro-Black. One of the journal's longest narratives is the story of Theodore Russ, a young Black Delaware man who was tried, convicted, and hung on a trumped-up charge of raping a white woman. Dunbar-Nelson helped to mobilize for his defense and worked hard to try to save him. Once, after a piece of unusually dirty trickery, she wrote, "All day I hated white people"; and on the day he was killed she felt depressed and wished that "all those who sent him to his fate could swing alongside him" (August 19 and 22, 1930).

In addition to her work and civic activities, Dunbar-Nelson maintained a considerable social life. Much of it took place in New York City, Washington, D.C., and Philadelphia, but even in her hometown Wilmington, where old factional feuds and antipathies affected her popularity, there were many visits, parties, and other get-togethers. This added up to an existence that was full and hectic. Her days started early (some years with exercises and prayers) and usually ended at one or two in the morning, often with as many as four or five meetings (not to mention anything else) sandwiched in between. Dunbar-Nelson's energy was astounding, but even she sometimes flagged and, as she once wrote, "fairly fell in bed."

Her stamina becomes even more incredible when one thinks about her health—which was far from perfect. Here is a chronological list of the ailments and medical conditions that beset her during the years of the diary: "overheated, apoplectic spell"; high blood pressure and kidney albumen; "neuritis in knee and sciatica"; "suffer[ing] from what tries to be a stroke"; "lightness and vertigo"; "getting fat and dumpy"; "fatigue, blues and leucorrhea"; "a bad attack of heart and insomnia and nerves last night and indigestion this a.m."; "stomach, liver, intestines—misbehaving"; decayed teeth; "hay fever, bronchitis and prickly heat all at one and the same time"; "viciously bilious . . . recalcitrant stomach, gall bladder, and liver"; "hyper-acidity due to liver . . . jaundice threatened"; "another severe gas attack. Thoroughly frightened at pressure on heart. Thought I'd croak once."

The treatment was worse. Dunbar-Nelson took "hormotones" [*sic*], pituitrin, and calomel, and douched with permanganate of potash. Beginning in 1929, she regularly subjected herself to a horrific process of "draining" designed to clean out her "congested" liver (see September 25, 1929). And her doctor communicated that he knew nothing about her menopausal symptoms. However, the operation of patriarchal medicine is best illustrated by the examination that she went through when she tried to secure a Washington, D.C. public school teaching job in 1927. When the health department doctor failed her for a fluctuating blood pressure and an amount of albumen in her urine that another doctor thought was normal for women her age, Dunbar-Nelson, because she desperately wanted the position, tried to persuade him to reconsider. She ate spinach and hot water attempting to change her test results, took hot lysol douches, worried herself sick, and ran around to offices getting school officials and congressmen to aid her—all the while, of course, having to discuss the intimate particulars of her case. The control of her life and Black female body by the male/white medical establishment and white/male decision-makers is clearly revealed in her pithy understatement: "Never had my piddy-widdy so discussed before in my life, and by all kinds of gentlemen, from Senators and school superintendents down" (February 3, 1927).

Too much of the time, Dunbar-Nelson's mental health was also, as she put it, "profoundly in the D's—discouraged, depressed, disheartened, disgusted" (August 2, 1930). From the beginning of the diary, she occasionally falls prey to normal attacks of "the blues." During the last two years, her mental state was extraordinarily turbulent. She was worried about being "unestablished middle-aged" (March 9, 1931), bored to distraction, and besieged with fears about her worth and continued usefulness.

Undoubtedly, qualities that enabled her to survive were her strength of mind, spirituality, and psychic power, resources that have always served Black women well. Even though she sometimes went to church and so forth, Dunbar-Nelson was not solely a conventionally religious person. She had a freethinking and occult mind. One summer she wrote in the diary:

> Lay on the roof in the moonlight and evolved a new cosmogony—each planet with its own particular God. Too huge a task for one God to look after both the spiral nebula in Orion and the plant lice that infested my poor little ivy plant that I brought home.
>
> (June 17, 1929)

She used Unity and the Master Key (unorthodox spiritual systems that focus on the individual's mind), had a lifelong interest in psychology, believed in "bad-mouthing" (speaking curses on deserving people), read her fortune in cards, heeded dreams, and relied heavily on her subconscious mind. Interestingly enough, it appears that despite all this—or because of it—she was not a very good judge of people when she approached them in an analytical, rational manner.

The final area of discussion here is what the diary reveals about Dunbar-Nelson as a Black woman writer and public figure. Fortunately for her posthumous reputation, she flourished throughout the Harlem Renaissance, that important period from roughly 1915 to 1930 when Black American artistic and literary creativity reached a new collective zenith. During the height of the Renaissance, her poetry (some of which had been written earlier) was consistently published—even though Dunbar-Nelson, strictly speaking, did not belong to the group of bold, young, experimental poets and did not achieve new popularity or refurbish her basically traditional style. As an older, credentialed contemporary, she enjoyed the respect of the younger writers and was sent copies of their books and asked to judge contests. However, like many of the women writers of the period, her position as author was adversely affected by her themes and style and certainly by her sex, which automatically excluded her from male avenues and circles of prestige and power.

Journalism took most of Dunbar-Nelson's time; but none of her attempts at film scenarios, short stories, and a novel was successful. For example, the screenplays—which she appeared to write too fast and too opportunistically—did not suit the film companies, and the novel, a satirical one entitled ***Uplift,*** was damned by herself as "inane, sophomoric, amateurish puerility" (June 16, 1930). In addition, the realities of her status and the literary marketplace are graphically illustrated by the career of **"Harlem John Henry Views the Airmada,"** an intellectually demanding, blank verse poem that she wrote in June 1931, which featured a Black protagonist who questions war against an ironic counterpoint of Black spirituals and folk songs. She mailed it out to white magazines, which speedily and repeatedly rejected it, until it was finally spotlighted in the January 1932 issue of *Crisis,* the multipurpose official organ of the NAACP, which served as a major outlet for Black writers.

Dunbar-Nelson strove to keep up her reputation and visibility. She plotted to get invited to Fisk University, valued her 1921 Iowa trip for its prestige even though it cost her money, and continued to do her *Eagle* columns solely for the publicity. Even so, this did not pay off when she needed it most—that is, when her Friends Committee work ended and she sought other employment. One cannot help but believe that, given Dunbar-Nelson's qualifications, had it not been for sexual bias, she would certainly have found something to do, say, with *Crisis* or NAACP, or the Black newspapers and press service, places where she applied. Generally, her glum November 4, 1928 prognostication unfortunately contained a measure of truth: "It shall always be my luck, it seems, to miss the Big occasions and be starred at the tiny, bum, back yard affairs."

One of the principal means that she used to keep her name before the public was platform speaking and lecturing. Interestingly, for a woman of her ability and usual confidence, she was unnerved by speaking after male celebrities like James Weldon Johnson and R. Russa Moton, president of Tuskegee Institute, or to predominantly male audiences like the one that she characterized thus: "Too many self-satisfied males—

get my goat" (July 25, 1928). She also wanted to be more of a "fire and brimstone" orator. One very striking paragraph in the diary is taken up with her attempted analysis of her inability to arouse frenzied audience emotion:

> Now why can't I do that? Because I can't feel? But I do. Because I am cold? But I am not. I sympathize with the least of them. Too intellectual? Too cynical? Too scornful of bunk-hokum? Must be that. Now there's Nannie Burroughs, for instance, and Mrs. Bethune. But I've got more brains than either—or have I? Probably not—if I had, I'd be where they are instead of wondering at 55 where in God's name I'm going to turn next?
>
> (March 1, 1931)

Eventually, she developed a new anecdotal style that pleased both herself and her listeners.

The background against which Dunbar-Nelson stands revealed as a Black woman writer and public figure is also illuminated by the diary in a special and fascinating way—private glimpses of public figures and inside reports of major events, all of which provide even more information for Black Studies students and scholars. There is a 1927 view of Dunbar-Nelson and the great scholar W. E. B. Du Bois cooking breakfast for themselves and poet Georgia Douglas Johnson, and one of Du Bois and Dr. Virginia Alexander—a pioneering Black female Philadelphia physician—being "horribly obvious" at the Bryn Mawr (Pennsylvania college) Liberal Club Conference in the spring of 1931. And when Dunbar-Nelson tells about the famous Langston Hughes being the only *litterateur* that Bobbo ever took a liking to, Hughes's image as a "man and poet of the people" is further burnished.

The diary gives a nuts-and-bolts view of numerous national Black conventions, such as the research conference held in Durham, North Carolina, in December 1927 and the annual gatherings of the NAACP. From its pages, we also learn that, at one point, Dunbar-Nelson and Carter G. Woodson, founder of the Association for the Study of Negro Life and History, were collaborating on researching and writing a book. These are only a few of the many such facts found in the journal.

Seen in relation to her other literary work, Dunbar-Nelson's diary may be the most significant and enduring piece of writing that she produced. Unquestionably, it is a unique one that only she and she alone could have added to the body of literature. However, until such noncanonical forms as the diary are reappraised and appropriately valued, her status (and that of the many other women who write in them) will not be appreciably changed. It is also unfortunate that journalism, another form that claimed a great deal of her attention, is rendered inaccessible and ephemeral to posterity by its predominantly topical nature.

Dunbar-Nelson's diary is not like the self-consciously and/or laboriously written documents of Virginia Woolf and Anaïs Nin. Kept in the ordinary way, it has the expected virtues and limitations of the prototypical—not to say classic—diary form. Dunbar-Nelson never regarded the journal as a vehicle for creative, literary expression. Yet its style has both interest and merit. Formal British diction and latinate syntax stand side by side with Black folksay and the latest street-corner slang. There is also a great deal of tonal variety—humor, hyperbole, wit, parody, and sarcasm ("Addie Hunton comes in looking more like Death eating a cracker than ever"), brief character portraiture, high-blown purple passages, and imagistic writing:

> For my affairs are in a most parlous state. I have come to the center of a stagnant pool where I drift aimlessly around a slow oozy backwash of putrid nothingness. And Bobbo's appointment is the only thing that can wash me out of the slimy mess.
>
> (June 26, 1931)

Another noticeable feature of the diary's style is how it betrays Dunbar-Nelson's ego and her bent toward self-centering and aggrandizement. She awkwardly twists sentences to interpolate phrases like "as did by me," "as I knew," "with me." These constructions show her—a proud woman—giving to herself, in her private chronicle, the credit that may not have been accorded to her in the outside world. And, of course, there is Dunbar-Nelson's more direct self-disclosure: playing with dolls, differentiating between herself and other women who act silly, and thinking to buy a handkerchief *before* she goes into a public bathroom to cry. This kind of thing is only matched by the indelibility of a few cameos that are scattered throughout the work—for example, her bounding out of a car to break off Christmas tree branches, and her clinging to the side of a train that had unexpectedly started up.

Enough has already been said about the diary's background and content to indicate how important a document it is. Its revelations about Black culture and about women's existence are priceless. It should force a radical reassessment of the generalities we were almost becoming accustomed to accepting as truth about Black women's/writers' lives during the period. Ultimately, this diary is a singular work that has the power both of *lived* life and moving literature. As a Black woman, reading it from the beginning through to the hopefully muted end, I feel as if I have washed my face in an icy spring and my spirit in a lava bed. Every reader's response may not be this profound. However, I daresay that many will experience something of the strange mixture of depression and exaltation that always overtakes me whenever I finally come to put it down.

Notes

1. Alice Walker, "In Search of Our Mothers' Gardens: The Creativity of Black Women in the South," *Ms.* (May 1974), 66-67.
2. The Philadelphia *Afro-American,* September 28, 1935.
3. Toni Morrison, *Sula* (New York, 1973; rpt. New York: Bantam Books, 1975), p. 44.
4. The New York *Inter-State Tattler,* December [?] 1928.

GLORIA T. HULL (ESSAY DATE 1989)

SOURCE: Hull, Gloria T. "Shaping Contradictions: Alice Dunbar-Nelson and the Black Creole Experience." *New Orleans Review* 15, no. 1 (1989): 34-37.

In this essay, Hull relates Dunbar-Nelson's difficulties as a mixed-race woman to her stories, including "The Pearl in the Oyster" and "The Stones of the Village." Hull acknowledges that most of Dunbar-Nelson's major fiction does not address the issue of racial identity, suggesting that Dunbar-Nelson preferred to steer clear of too much autobiography in her writing.

Ensconced with her family in West Medford, Massachusetts, Alice wrote Paul Laurence Dunbar, her husband, in Washington, D.C., a 7 March 1899 letter recounting some remarkable personal history which she had recently learned from her mother:

> Another thing I didn't know. She [Mama], nor any of our family didn't know of the emancipation proclamation for two years! The owners fled with their slaves [from Opelousas, Louisiana] to a wild district in Texas and there held out against the law. Finally the old Judge was threatened with arrest, so he called the slaves together one morning and read the proclamation, and then like a man told them how long he had withheld the news. It must have been a dramatic scene the way mama puts it, the inflexible Yankee soldiers on each side of the white-haired old man, his sobbing daughters and wife, the open-mouthed, indignant and unforgiving slaves, for most of them were of mixed Indian blood. She says he broke down and sobbing like a child threw out his hands and begged them too if they would return to Louisiana with them he would try to pay them back wages.[1]

This plantation melodrama continued with some of the ex-slaves remaining in Texas, while others—including Alice's mother, Patricia—made the three-month journey back to Opelousas in "big covered wagons, swimming the Sabine and Red Rivers," "where the Judge tried to make amends by giving them cabins and starting them in life."

At this point, either Mother Patricia tired of talking, or Alice tired of writing. Alice probably told this tale to Paul as an attempt to match the famed southern narratives of his mother (which often served as the basis for his writing) with some "roots" lore of her own. She never referred to or used the story in any public context, for—unlike Dunbar who was Negroid in color and features—slave ancestry was not the kind of personal data which she would choose to emphasize. Dunbar-Nelson would much rather have been taken as a descendant of Louisiana's (preferably free) *gens de couleur,* those mixed-blood, "colored" people who considered themselves superior to pure Negroes, especially those who had been slaves. Throughout her life, ambiguities regarding race and color are apparent in her behavior, comments and writings. Of course, these ambiguities never reached "tragic mulatto" proportions, but they were crucial on both personal and artistic levels.

Alice was born with reddish-blonde curls which darkened to red to auburn, and was fair enough to "pass" for white. Given her mother's Black and American Indian blood, she seems to have received considerably more Caucasian influence from her father, who was always cryptically referred to as a "seaman" or "merchant marine." The specifics are shrouded in history, but there was something irregular, something shameful about her birth which Alice alluded to years later, again in a private letter to Paul. Remonstrating with him about "deriding" her and inflicting "bitterness and hurts," she wells up:

> Dearest,—dearest—I hate to write this—How often, oh how pitifully often, when scarce meaning it, perhaps, you have thrust my parentage in my face.[2]

What there was to thrust in her face could have been white ancestry, illegitimacy, or perhaps a combination of the two. At any rate, with this background, she assumed a prominent place in the racially-mixed Creole society of post-bellum New Orleans.

There she shone as a beautiful and talented young woman, starring in dramatic productions, writing the "Woman's Column" of a local newspaper, working as a stenographer and elementary school teacher, participating actively in social and literary circles, publishing her first book, ***Violets and Other Tales,*** in 1895 when she was only twenty years old. This early promise blossomed further when she came North, married Paul Laurence Dunbar, and established herself as a leading Afro-American educator, clubwoman, racial and feminist activist, poet, writer, journalist, and public speaker. Though her reputation has been shadowed by her more famous husband, she is now becoming more well-known for her own considerable accomplishments.

A good deal of her fame springs from her authorship of the Creole sketches and stories contained in ***Violets*** and in her second volume, ***The Goodness of St. Rocque*** (1898). Replete with local color, these pieces are correctly described as charming and well-written. They are also devoid of any significant references to the murkier aspects of racial identity and prejudice, even though history and sociology confirm that color, caste and race were deadly, daily realities for the mixed blood inhabitants of southern Louisiana who people her stories. A few isolated allusions can be found—to Black longshoremen during a strike, to the blond versus dark attractions of two rival heroines, to an orphan girl obliquely described as a little "brown scrap of French and American civilization" whose "glorious tropical beauty" makes her so vulnerable to racial-sexual exploitation that she consigns herself to the convent.[3]

In contrast to this work, other of Dunbar-Nelson's lesser-known writings present a more complex picture of race and the Creole, especially the Creole with immediate or identifiable Negro ancestry. Published in *The Southern Workman*, **"The Pearl in the Oyster"** chronicles the rise and fall of Auguste Picou, a Creole fair enough to live as white, but whose grandfather was a free Black. He comes to grief because, racially, he tries to have it both ways. He rejects the Negro side gallery and his brown-skinned childhood friend in favor of white uptown life, then seeks to reenter the now-closed Creole fold in order to play corrupt ward politics. His ironically shallow solution is to take his wife and child and "go away somewhere where we are not known, and we will start life again, but whether we decide to be white or black, we will stick to it." Here Dunbar-Nelson has moved beyond the safe, predominantly love themes of ***The Goodness of St. Rocque*** to an overt treatment of race and passing.

An unpublished typescript, **"The Stones of the Village,"** is even more telling. Young Victor Grabert's childhood has been blighted by his ambiguous racial identity. His loving, but stern, old West Indian grandmother forbids him social interaction with the youngsters on his street. One of his most painful memories is of himself "toddling out the side gate after a merry group of little black and yellow boys of his own age."

> When Grandmere Grabert, missing him from his accustomed garden corner, came to look for him, she found him sitting contentedly in the center of the group in the dusty street, all of them gravely scooping up handsful of the gravelly dirt and trickling it down their chubby bare legs. Grandmere snatched at him fiercely, and he whimpered, for he was learning for the first time what fear was.
>
> "What you mean?" she hissed at him, "What you mean playin' in de strit wid dose niggers?" And she struck at him wildly with her open hand.
>
> He looked up into her brown face surmounted by a wealth of curly black hair faintly streaked with gray, but he was too frightened to question.
>
> It had been loneliness ever since. For the parents of the little black and yellow boys resenting the insult Grandmere had offered their offspring, sternly bade them have nothing more to do with Victor. Then when he toddled after some other little boys, whose faces were white like his own, they ran him away with derisive hoots of "Nigger! Nigger!" And again, he could not understand . . . all the boys, white and black and yellow hooted at him and called him "White nigger! White nigger!"

Furthermore, Grandmere forced him to cease speaking "the soft, Creole patois that they chattered together" and learn English, the result being "a confused jumble which was no language at all." This "confused jumble," this silence—linguistic, racial, psychic, and emotional—determines his entire life.

Eventually, his grandmother sends Victor to New Orleans. Providence favors him, and he becomes a highly-respected lawyer and judge, marries into a leading family and fathers a fine son. Time and death have obscured his past, so that no one knows of his mixed ancestry. However, Grabert's fear of exposure torments him. To try and protect himself from showing sympathy towards Blacks or arousing suspicion, he becomes a die-hard Negro-hater, firing Black men who work for him, refusing to have a Black mammy for his son, persecuting Black defendants in his courtroom, and so on. Still, his existence is hell. He discovers that a brilliant Negro lawyer named Pavageau, whom he has taunted and unjustly treated, knows of his grandmother and his early background. Pavageau is too principled, though, to expose Grabert and only asks that he judge his cases fairly when they come before him.

Nothing, however, can halt Grabert's descent into psychosis and madness. Rising to speak at an important banquet after a "tumult of applause," he muses to himself:

> "What a sensation I could make now," he thought. He had but to open his mouth and cry out, "Fools! Fools! I whom you are honoring, I am one of the despised ones. Yes, I am a nigger—do you hear, a nigger!" What a temptation it was to end the whole miserable farce. If he were alone in the world, if it were not for Elise and the boy, he would, just to see their horror and wonder. How they would shrink from him! But what could they do? They could take away his office; but his wealth, and his former successes, and his learning, they could not touch. Well, he must speak, and he must remember Elise and the boy.

What actually happens is that his mind completely snaps. Instead of the chairman, he sees his dead grandmother at the head of the table, begins to address her, and then falls into a fit:

> When the men crowded around him with water and hastily improvised fans, he fought them away wildly and desperately with furious curses that came from his blackened lips. For were they not all boys with stones to pelt him because he wanted to play with them? He would run away to Grandmere who would soothe him and comfort him. So he arose, stumbling, shrieking and beating them back from him, ran the length of the hall, and fell across the threshold of the door.
>
> The secret died with him, for Pavageau's lips were ever sealed.

In this story, Dunbar-Nelson handles complexities she never touched any place else. Clearly, she is treating the popular Afro-American literary themes of the "color line"—that is, passing—and the tragic mulatto from the particular and unique vantage of the Louisiana Black Creole. Her general tendency as a writer was always scrupulously to separate her life and real experience from her "high" art—to the detriment, I think, of her art. For instance, in stories about women, her female characters are usually correct, conventional heroines who exhibit none of the verve and bravado that characterized her own life on both public and private levels. Regarding race, she was a pro-Black activist (despite some personal ambivalences that she harbored), but kept race as a controversial subject out of most of her traditional literary work (though she treated it unflinchingly in her essays and journalism). Looking at **"The Stones of the Village,"** this story about Victor Grabert, one is struck, first, by the fact that she is handling this troubled subject, and, second, by the possible autobiographical implications of the work.

That this story does have autobiographical resonance is made clear when it is compared with an essay which Dunbar-Nelson wrote around 1929, toward the end of her career. Entitled **"Brass Ankles Speaks,"** it is an outspoken denunciation of darker-skinned Black people's prejudice against light-skinned Blacks told by a "Brass Ankles," that is a Black person "white enough to pass for white, but with a darker family back-ground, a real love for the mother race, and no desire to be numbered among the white race." This "Brass Ankles" recalls her "miserable" childhood in "a far southern city" (read New Orleans) where other schoolchildren taunted and plagued her because she was a "light nigger, with straight hair!" This kind of rebuff and persecution continues into a Northern College and her first teaching job:

> Small wonder, then, that the few lighter persons in the community drew together; we were literally thrown upon each other, whether we liked or not. But when we began going about together and spending time in each other's society, a howl went up. We were organizing a "blue vein" society. We were mistresses of white men. We were Lesbians. We hated black folk and plotted against them. As a matter of fact, we had no other recourse but to cling together.

And she states further that "To complain would be only to bring upon themselves another storm of abuse and fury."

This essay was as close as Dunbar-Nelson ever came to revealing feelings about her own racial status as a "yaller nigger." She tried to publish it, but would not, could not do so under her own name, and the magazine editor refused to print it pseudonymously. **"The Stones of the Village"** is, likewise, as close as she ever got to turning this kind of personal and cultural confusion into art. One notes, though, that in the story, she uses a male rather than a female protagonist, thereby making it easier to write while keeping herself at a safer distance.

Finally, it must be said that Dunbar-Nelson's shying away from race as a literary theme can be partially explained by market conditions, by what agents, readers and publishers wanted. They bought her slight and charming stories, but backed away from serious explorations of the color line. Given the constraints of Dunbar-Nelson's own personal ambivalence and authorial credo, plus the limitations of the marketplace, we must be grateful that any stories like **"The Pearl in the Oyster"** and **"The Stones of the Village"** exist. They help us to understand the psycho-racial-social forces which shaped—both negatively and positively—Dunbar-Nelson as a writer, and enlarged the field of her art. She is no longer simply a female regionalist producing safe, run-of-the-mill local color stories, but a Black Creole woman writer who also tried to bring these hidden complexities into literary light.

Notes

1. Letter from Alice Dunbar-Nelson to Paul Laurence Dunbar, 7 March 1899 (unprocessed Alice Dunbar-Nelson materials, Special Collections, Morris Library, University of Delaware, Newark, Del.). All letters and unpublished materials cited come from this source.
2. Undated letter from Alice Dunbar-Nelson to Paul L. Dunbar, probably ca. Dec. 1898.
3. These stories are, respectively, "Mr. Baptiste," "The Goodness of St. Rocque" and "Sister Josepha."

ALISA JOHNSON (ESSAY DATE 1991)

SOURCE: Johnson, Alisa. "Writing within the Script: Alice Dunbar-Nelson's 'Ellen Fenton.'" *Studies in American Fiction* 19, no. 2 (1991): 165-74.

In this essay, Johnson interprets Dunbar-Nelson's short story "Ellen Fenton" in light of the author's effort to imagine better domestic and romantic possibilities for women. Johnson argues that although Dunbar-Nelson appears to stay within the confines of conventional expectations for women in the story, she redefines marriage to allow greater self-expression for both husband and wife.

In *Writing Beyond The Ending,* Rachel DuPlessis suggests a critical strategy for approaching nineteenth- and early twentieth-century texts that take romance as the narrative framework. In the work of women like Kate Chopin, the standard romance plot inhibits its female protagonists, suppressing all movement towards personal and artistic fulfillment on the part of the female characters as it incorporates them into a heterosexual union. For DuPlessis, "as a narrative pattern, the romance plot muffles the main female character, represses quest, valorizes heterosexual as opposed to homosexual ties, incorporates individuals within couples as a sign of their personal and narrative success."[1] DuPlessis argues that, rather than passively submitting to the repression inherent in this structure, many of these female writers used the plot as a means of questioning the social and sexual constriction of women. This strategy she deems "writing beyond the ending." According to DuPlessis:

> Writing beyond the ending means the transgressive invention of narrative strategies, strategies that express critical dissent from dominant narrative. These tactics . . . take issue with the mainstays of the social and ideological organization of gender, as these appear in fiction. Writing beyond the ending, "not repeating your words and following your methods but . . . finding new words and creating new methods," produces a narrative that denies or reconstructs seductive patterns of feeling that are culturally mandated, internally policed, hegemonically poised.[2]

The romance plot (as DuPlessis identifies it) that maintains that a woman's existence be relegated to the domestic sphere is one generated primarily by Euro-American ideology. This ideology historically has privileged males politically, socially, and economically, granting them almost complete ownership over their wives, and rigidly divided occupations along gender and class lines. This ideological framework, with its stringently delineated male and female roles, does not encompass the experience of the majority of women of color, particularly African-Americans. And just as there are other "American" ideologies that must exist to incorporate these different experiences—ideologies which challenge the many presuppositions of the dominant one (African-American and Native American, for example)—so must there be "other" narrative scripts generated by them.

When Alice Dunbar-Nelson, then Alice Moore, published her first volume of short stories entitled ***Violets and Other Tales*** in 1895, she had few if any literary predecessors. Published when she was just twenty years old, Dunbar-Nelson's little "potpourri" of poetry, short stories, essays, and reviews was only one in a small handful of printed works then in existence by African-American women. She completed ***The Goodness of St. Rocque and Other Stories,*** a second volume of short stories, four years later, after her marriage to celebrated poet Paul Laurence Dunbar. Although Dunbar-Nelson wrote prolifically—newspaper columns, essays, articles, and reviews identified her as a writer in her own right—these two were the only collections of her work published in her lifetime. They are particularly important, as Gloria T. Hull suggests in her introduction to ***The Works of Alice Dunbar-Nelson,*** because they helped, in their way, to "create a black short story tradition for a reading public conditioned to expect only plantation and minstrel stereotypes."[3]

Featured prominently among the narrative structures Dunbar-Nelson employed in both her published and unpublished fiction was the romance plot. In the published stories in which this plot was utilized, it was formulated in much the same way as it was in the works of her white counterparts. In **"The Goodness of St. Rocque,"** from which the second book takes its title, the female protagonist's ultimate concern is securing the affections of her wandering lover, and she turns to the mystic arts to do so. In **"Little Miss Sophie,"** the heroine is a poor creole who, despite the fact that her wealthy lover has jilted her, continues to wear his ring. The ring turns out to be a family heirloom, and at the end of the tale Miss Sophie dies (conveniently) so that the ring may be returned to him, saving him from financial ruin. These stories, aimed at an integrated audience, are not racially specific (creole is the only racial characterization offered; in many stories the race of the characters is never mentioned or alluded to), and they seem primarily to reflect the concerns of the wider culture.

It is with some of the later, unpublished works that Dunbar-Nelson begins to depart from the prevalent formula to express a narrative vision generated by other sources. In particular, her short story **"Ellen Fenton"** stands out as a marked departure both from her earlier works and many of those of her white contemporaries.[4] Written for inclusion in ***Women and Men,*** projected around 1902 (the same year she separated from her husband) but never published, **"Ellen Fenton"** is noteworthy for the way in which it handles the romance plot, combining, rather than separating, the feminine quest with the heterosexual love motif.

The tale begins where, by rights, the romance narrative would usually end, with the goals of the plot firmly, successfully, and gracefully achieved. It is the birthday of Ellen's youngest son, Eugene, and, twenty-two years after her marriage, Ellen Fenton has found her happy ending. She is everything that society could want her to be. She had achieved the prescribed goal of her life, having become a successful wife and mother as well as a productive member of her community. First and foremost, she excels as a mother.

> She had reared four sons; tall, strong manly fellows; the youngest of them already in high school. . . . She had mothered them as few women do nowadays; loving them without spoiling them, exacting obedience and obtaining love, devotion and chivalrous regard from all of them.[5]

As a wife and partner, she is outstanding, highly capable, incredibly efficient.

> She kept in touch with her husband's business, and knew every detail almost as well as he himself, so that she could have stood at the helm at any time in his absence. She had ruled and ordered a large household of servants, and overlooked a summer home with a farm attached.
>
> (p. 34)

If that were not enough, she maintains an important, active life outside of her household:

> She had served on every committee of any account in public matters in her town; had been a loyal and hard working church member; an enthusiastic club woman; a practical charity worker, and an ardent spirit in local politics as far as was compatible with womanly dignity. She had been foremost in every public movement and had never neglected home or husband or children.
>
> (p. 34)

The type of woman Ellen Fenton represents is not a fantasy figure but one with real-life counterparts in both white and African-American worlds. She could have easily been patterned after activists Mary Church Terrell or Josephine St. Pierre Ruffin. Ellen Fenton represents the successful merger of the public and private spheres of a woman's life, an achievement to be admired in both communities. Readers would have no doubt been inclined to view her as her contemporaries did: "She was looked up to by every one in town; was pointed out as the model woman, . . . the worthy and progressive twentieth-century woman with a large field, who was unspoiled by semi-public life, and unnarrowed by a large family" (p. 34).

Yet, at the height of her success, the author suggests, something is missing. The role, with all of its rewards, is not enough. It takes only a relatively minor incident to destabilize Ellen's entire world. Ellen learns that her artistic son Eugene wants an etching by Whistler for his birthday. When she inquires as to who the man is, her son is "pained at first, then indifferent." This response, unexpected, completely unsettles her: "It was not the words so much as the tone that stung her. It seemed to place her outside the pale of his life. She winced a little, then flushed, then said no more" (p. 34).

Eugene's response, and her sense that there is something more to his life than she had heretofore grasped, sends Ellen into a new mood of introspection. She begins to review her life in a way she had not previously done. And she comes to the realization that all is not perfect in her world:

> Yet, Ellen was conscious this morning for the first time that something had eluded her, and that that something, or rather the lack of it, was responsible for the new feeling of discontent, even unhappiness that assailed her.
>
> (p. 35)

This new awareness of something missing disrupts Ellen's entire schedule. Her normal tasks have little meaning for her, and she sits pondering. In an interesting and significant detail, Ellen's introspections are exemplified by her "reading" of the wallpaper in her study. Her son finds "the unwonted sight" of his mother "sitting idle at the desk, staring hard as if the roses on the wall were actors in a strange drama, and she the sole spectator" (p. 35).

It is not clear whether this use of "the drama within the wallpaper" is a conscious reference on Dunbar-Nelson's part to Charlotte Perkins Gilman's "The Yellow Wallpaper," written in 1892, or merely an interesting coincidence. Nonetheless, it is while reading the wallpaper that Ellen, albeit conveniently, discovers the source of her problem. As she terms it, "she had not become acquainted with herself" (p. 35). Armed with this conveniently provided insight, Ellen sees her life in a different, harsher light:

> She suddenly realized this morning that even her best and most well-meant efforts must have seemed cold and heartless from the viewpoint of those whose souls are attuned to sympathy by virtue of their own experience of sorrow and misery.
>
> (p. 36)

Having been unable to "know" herself, Ellen discovers that she has been unable to know others and has been in some ways a stranger to the human experience. Acting by rote, rather than by genuine desire to serve, she has been more automaton than woman, a human doing rather than a human being:

> She began to understand why she had sometimes heard herself referred to as a cold woman, whose bright smile awed, rather than reassured those who approached with petitions. She had always laughed away such suggestions before, and had been wont to assert that with some people mere dignity and reserve were so foreign to their natures that they could not understand it when they met it in others. She confessed now lamely enough, to herself, that in reality her heart had remained untouched and unswayed.
>
> (pp. 36-37)

With this new perspective on herself comes the slow disintegration of the life Ellen Fenton has built for herself. Her elegant, perfectly furnished home, a symbolic representation of her life, is suddenly shown to be as forced and pretentious as her former self. Ellen walks aimlessly through it, her actions a harsh mirroring of her previous patterns of unexamined behavior. The rest of the story becomes a sort of *Bildungsroman* in miniature, with the new, insecure Ellen Fenton attempting to shake off the trappings of her former life and discover the self she has never known. In this pattern, Dunbar-Nelson echoes the strategy of countless other female writers of her era.

But it is in the relationship of Ellen Fenton to her role as wife and to her husband Herbert that Dunbar-Nelson employs a different approach to the romance pattern. While it is clear that Ellen has been imprisoned in the domestic sphere, with her role as wife and mother subsuming her drive for a more personal development, Dunbar-Nelson's text does not blame the domestic sphere *per se* for that imprisonment. Nor does it blame the institution of marriage for the emotional estrangement that exists between Ellen and Herbert. Dunbar-Nelson's text does not engage in a critique of the social institutions in which her hero is entangled. Rather, she focuses all her attention on Ellen's quest to find herself within the confines of those institutions.

Dunbar-Nelson's reticence to criticize marriage or the woman's role in the household reflects, more than anything, her own experience as an African-American woman. While her white counterparts were indeed subsumed within their stifling socially prescribed roles as wife and mother, Dunbar-Nelson and other women of color were confronted with entirely different sets of obstacles. The majority of women of color worked outside of their homes by necessity: it is estimated that in the 1890s, of the four million women in the labor force, almost one million were African-American.[6] The African-American woman whose sphere at this time was confined solely to her own household was a rarity and highly envied within her community. Even African-American women of wealth and privilege for whom such lifestyles were possible were often too aware of the differing conditions of the rest of their race to constrict themselves solely to their own homes. Therefore, it is easy to see why Dunbar-Nelson did not place the blame for Ellen's lack of fulfillment on a specific set of circumstances. The problem, her text implies, is in Ellen herself, and so, too, is the solution. Once Ellen recognizes this—and she seems to almost immediately—she is able to begin her search for self-awareness, a search that does not necessitate terminating all of the trappings of her former life.

Interestingly enough, Dunbar-Nelson's text never questions, nor allows its protagonist to question, the validity of Ellen's new situation nor her inherent ability to cope with it. Even in the midst of her spiritual and emotional crisis, Ellen is posited as magnificently self-sufficient, brilliantly strong of spirit. As she tells her companions at a local Women's Club meeting, "while she could not tell just what there was lacking in all her past life, she knew the lack was there, and she would find it, and remedy it if possible" (p. 45).

In the remainder of the story, Ellen slowly transforms herself from the perfect woman into what can best be described as a functioning, though imperfect, human being. The most significant example of her change can be seen in her newfound awareness of the difference between acting out of duty and acting out of desire. She allows her son Eugene to forego college in order to study art abroad—an act unthinkable for the old Ellen Fenton—because she realizes that "we are happiest doing what we are best fitted for" (p. 41). And, more significantly, Ellen declines the role of delegate at her Club because she realizes that such activities are no longer meaningful to her. In a very moving scene, Ellen confronts the consequences of her awakening needs for her old life:

> She knew if she spoke conscientiously that her career in the town as a public-spirited woman was at an end, and the long-striven-for, hard-won honors were dear to her after all, even in the light of her recent mental experiences. Like the proverbial flash of life's vision before the eyes of a drowning man, she saw all her career as club-woman, public speaker, trustee, office-holder pass before her. Not lightly was all this to be relinquished, and relinquished for an idea, a quixotic, visionary thought, which after all, might prove untenable.
>
> (pp. 43-44)

In spite of her uncertainty, Ellen "confesses" the "mental shocks" which have so changed her world even though she realizes that such declarations will lower her illustrious standing in her community. And even though she is misunderstood, her act of self-revelation (the first in her life and one that takes place, significantly, among women) launches her formally on her quest.

That Ellen never doubts the validity of her quest—her "right" to find fulfillment whatever the cost—or her ability to fulfill that quest, marks her as a very modern hero and gives the otherwise dated tale a very contemporary spirit. Even in the midst of her spiritual crisis, Ellen Fenton is posited as a surprisingly strong character, powerful in her own right and fundamentally independent in her modes and actions. That she is moving, however uncomfortably, towards a more positive stage in her existence is never in doubt:

> She felt herself changing, developing. Now that she was taking time to grow, she remembered that she had a soul, apart from the religious conception of the idea, and it interested her to see it expand, like the wings of a butterfly creeping from its chrysalis. The one regret she had was that perhaps she was not as interesting to those about her as she was to herself.
>
> (p. 46)

That Alice Dunbar-Nelson, at the outset of this century, could posit a female character who believed that her primary duty was to herself was an audacious act, as indicative as anything else of the author's own independence of spirit. What her character comes to understand about her life readily applies to that of the author. Towards the end of her journey, Ellen realizes that "the average woman, she found, who 'lives her own life,' in reality, lives others, and has no life of her own" (p. 46). Once she has seen this fact clearly, "in all the richfulness of the real meaning, did Ellen now enter" (p. 46).

What Ellen finds, in striving for the "richfulness of real meaning," is a freedom from the confines of duty. The woman who emerges towards the end of her quest turns out to be much more introverted than the old self, finding more satisfaction in the private domain of her spirit. Having relinquished her semi-public life and many though not all of her household duties, Ellen fills her life with pursuits all her own: reading (an activity she had never had time for in the past), long walks, and quiet reposes in nature. And the person she becomes through these enterprises is markedly different than the one she was:

> She was happy in a dreamy, self-sufficient way. She had found herself, and henceforth she knew the world was nothing to her, be it harsh or gentle in its opinion, it could not touch her real self again.
>
> (p. 47)

Yet it cannot be emphasized enough that Ellen's newfound serenity comes to her while she is still firmly established in her roles as wife and mother. It is evident that, rather than having eliminated (with the exception of the semi-public one) the roles that previously defined her, Ellen has rather revised them to suit her new self. The way Ellen views herself in relationship to her sons at the end of the story exemplifies the flexibility and elasticity of her role: "She knew that her sons' lives had branched from hers like independent streams from a common lake-source, and that each would go adown its own way, regardless of any interference on her part" (p. 47). That Ellen is able to confer on the members of her household the freedom she claims for herself is a significant testament to her transformation.

Modern readers, conditioned to the paradigm of the solitary hero, be it male or female, would expect the story to end here, with Ellen Fenton, alone, at the height of her independence. Such a conclusion requires no writing beyond the ending, since the goals of the narrative are satisfied without such designs. And yet, Dunbar-Nelson's tale does not end here. Her story moves onward, in a surprising direction that on the surface seems to re-evoke the romance plot and give it ascendency within the text.

FROM THE AUTHOR

SITTING AND SEWING

The little useless seam, the idle patch;
Why dream I here beneath my homely thatch,
When there they lie in sodden mud and rain,
Pitifully calling me, the quick ones and the slain?
You need me, Christ! It is no roseate dream
That beckons me—this pretty futile seam,
It stifles me—God, must I sit and sew?

SOURCE: Alice Dunbar-Nelson, excerpt from "I Sit and Sew," in *Negro Poets and Their Poems,* edited by Robert T. Kerlin, Associated Publishers, 1923.

The final scene of the story takes place in a small, picturesque café, described as "Bohemian" by the author. There, Ellen, now drawn to a place where her old self would have dreaded going, savors her newfound serenity over a reasonably priced lunch and a book of modern "forbidden" poetry. But having become complete in herself, Ellen discovers that she has one strong remaining desire. At the height of her happiness, she discovers her one wish is for her husband to join her:

> Self-sufficient as she knew herself to be now, she loved Herbert Fenton, and she longed for his companionship in spirit, and longed, too, that he could attain the peace she knew. They had spent many years together, and though she knew now, that theirs had been a mere superficial intercourse, she felt that her happiness would be complete if their lives could be rounded out together in actual comradeship.
>
> (p. 48)

Miraculously, Herbert appears at Ellen's elbow, and the two discover that they have the café—and other things heretofore unknown—in common. Their "surprise" encounter, thick with the trappings of the happy romantic ending, turns out to be full of revelations. Ellen sees her husband as he is for the first time since she began her quest, older, more tired, and then discovers to her surprise that he has been on a quest—though less obviously—of his own. Ellen learns that Herbert has chosen to retire from public life in order to "live," and it is clear from the amount of feeling remaining between the two that they will "live" together.

By choosing to end her tale in such a way, with the re-introduction of the heterosexual union, the author seems to be undercutting her hero. Ellen seems to be re-inscribed within the confines of the romantic paradigm just as it appears that she has completely transcended it. Yet one of the final surprises of the tale is found in its reconception of marriage. The union the text posits between Ellen and Herbert is markedly different from the one inherent in the traditional romance narrative. This concept of marriage, rather than demanding complete self-sacrifice on the part of either partner in order to be maintained, is somehow capable of maintaining itself almost organically. What becomes clear in Ellen's dialogue with Herbert is that their marriage has been very much alive during Ellen's quest, even though neither one of them has done much to sustain it. Herbert tells Ellen "whimsically" that "we have lived together so long, I suppose, that unknowing, we have become really one, although we have both been lamenting the fact that we were distant, one self from the other" (p. 50). This kind of union, rather than being static and stifling, is completely porous, expansive enough to endure the growth and change on the part of both partners. Thus, neither Ellen nor Herbert must sacrifice any part of themselves in order to maintain it. And while Ellen and Herbert anticipate that their "new" marriage will not resemble what they have experienced for the past twenty-two years, it is they themselves who demand the change: "Now that we know and understand," Ellen tells Herbert, "henceforth, we will know each other, and be real companions and comrades such as we never dreamed possible in other days" (p. 50). Marriage as it is here conceived is capable of supporting its participants regardless; they change to satisfy their inner demands and not the demands of the marriage. Thus Ellen Fenton does not need to separate from her marriage in order to be her own woman, and this particular social script does not need to be rewritten.

Rather than to isolation and separation, the quest for self-actualization in **"Ellen Fenton"** brings the hero to a new sense of connection with her community. Even though Ellen does not occupy the position she once held in her town, she is clearly more connected to the people around her, particularly Herbert. No longer cold, she is capable of feeling things deeply and genuinely.

And because her real self is inviolate, she can assume any number of roles—even those which are constrictive and limiting to others—without losing herself. The quest, as Dunbar-Nelson offers it, is circular in nature, eventually bringing the questor back into the community she was forced to leave in order to find herself. And because the result of the quest is a codified and clearly identifiable self, relationships (whether heterosexual or homosexual) prove no threat to her independence. Indeed, one of the pleasant surprises of Dunbar-Nelson's treatment of the quest is that it seems to encourage the union of the hero with an equally self-sufficient companion at the end. Happiness can be found with another person, even one's long-term spouse, resulting in an enhancement of, rather than a diminishment of, the self. The "good and useful" life of the fulfilled person in Dunbar-Nelson's paradigm includes reaching out to others, whether in love or friendship. It is from their union with one another, Ellen tells her husband at the conclusion of the tale, that they will be better able to connect with the community: "And where we reach our lives out to touch others, how much broader will be our sympathies and understandings" (p. 50).

Dunbar-Nelson concludes her tale on what would seem, by modern standards, to be a naively optimistic note. The sentiment expressed could belong to the most standard romantic narrative.

> Ellen was happy, supremely so, for in finding herself, she had also found Herbert, and he had found himself and her. But how many lives were wasted, how many went out into the Great Unknown, all unconscious of themselves or their fellow-men, she mused sorrowfully, as they sat there with clasped hands, while the quick winter twilight settled over the distant blue hills.
>
> (p. 50)

And yet, that Dunbar-Nelson, herself in the midst of bitter separation from the husband she had once adored, could nonetheless envision such an ending for a hero so like herself, makes the notion of a naive ending impossible. That her mind and heart could imagine for another what she herself had not known is the ultimate testament to her spirit and to the grandeur of her imagination. **"Ellen Fenton"** stands as touchstone for the modern reader, one of the many examples of the ways women artists, white and African-American, envisioned change for one another and for future generations.

Notes

1. Rachel DuPlessis, *Writing Beyond the Ending: Narrative Strategies of Twentieth-Century Women Writers* (Bloomington: Indiana Univ. Press, 1985), p. 5.
2. DuPlessis, p. 5.
3. Gloria T. Hull, introduction, *The Works of Alice Dunbar-Nelson,* ed. Gloria T. Hull, Vol. 3 (New York: Oxford Univ. Press, 1988), pp. xxxi-xxxii. All factual information concerning "Ellen Fenton" is taken from Hull's introduction.
4. The depiction of marriage and its effect on women in "Ellen Fenton" is quite different from that found in Harriet Prescott Spofford's "Her Story" (1872), Mary E. Wilkins Freeman's "A New England Nun" (1891), and Kate Chopin's "The Story of an Hour" (1894), "A Pair of Silk Stockings" (1896), and *The Awakening* (1899).
5. Hull, ed., *The Works of Alice Dunbar-Nelson,* Vol. 3, p. 34. All parenthetical references will refer to this edition.
6. Barbara Wertheimer, *We Were There: The Story of Working Women in America* (New York: Pantheon Books, 1977), p. 195.

KRISTINA BROOKS (ESSAY DATE 1998)

SOURCE: Brooks, Kristina. "Alice Dunbar-Nelson's Local Colors of Ethnicity, Class, and Place." *MELUS* 23, no. 2 (1998): 3-26.

In this essay, Brooks discusses the issue of Creole identity in Dunbar-Nelson's fiction. She provides historical context for the complicated boundaries of Creole ethnicity in Louisiana after the Civil War, drawing in part from Dunbar-Nelson's essay "People of Color in Louisiana" and suggesting that her manner of using local elements in her writing calls attention to her own identity.

Pass Christian, the Bayou St. John, the Bayou Teche, Mandeville, and New Orleans's Third District are just a few of the particular locales in which Alice Dunbar-Nelson anchors her fictional characters' ethnic identities. Through direct addresses to the reader and notations of specific streets, neighborhoods, and local landmarks, Dunbar-Nelson continually puts the reader in his or her place, a place which may or may not be within the ethnic and geographical boundaries of Dunbar-Nelson's fiction. In the dynamic interactions among reader, author, and characters, such methods of reader and character placement simultaneously draw the reader's attention to his or her position inside or outside of the fictional milieu and delineate the social and economic position of the characters. "[N]ot being a Mandevillian," Dunbar-Nelson addresses the reader in **"La Juanita,"** "you would not understand" (***Works*** [***The Works of Alice Dunbar-Nelson***] 1, 199). In this example, the author calls the ethnic and cultural differences between her Mandevillian characters and the reader unbridgeable, throwing into higher relief the story's plot about a Creole community's resistance to accepting an American member through intermarriage. Weaving together narrative style and thematic content as mutual reinforcers, Dunbar-Nelson critiques oppressive social categories—such as "Mandevillian," "Creole," and "American"—based on ethnically, racially, or geographically unified group identities. The individual reader of and the individual character in Dunbar-Nelson's fiction are "put in (a) place" which may or may not allow the expression of his or her unique identity. Pitting the individual against the mob, the ethnic orphan against the social requirement for a family name, or the non-local reader against complex and ambiguous local codes, Dunbar-Nelson dramatizes the conflict that flares along fault lines between individual and group identities. By forcing the reader to recognize his or her complicity with maintaining or respecting boundaries based on ethnic, racial, class, and regional identity, Dunbar-Nelson points the way toward demythologizing the natural status of any such identity category.

Outside readers, those whom Dunbar-Nelson directly addresses in her short fiction, are those who do not make their homes in New Orleans, the setting for Dunbar-Nelson's stories in two published volumes, or the Upper East side New York neighborhood that serves as a setting for an unpublished volume of her short fiction.[1] In these locales, characters' street addresses are a strong indicator of their class position and ethnicity, but their racial identity remains ambiguous; however, her Southern characters' racial indeterminacy is not a sign of Dunbar-Nelson's own racial ambivalence, as critics Violet Harrington Bryan and Gloria Hull have asserted, but is a function of her fiction's well-defined local boundaries. Outside readers' tendency to view Dunbar-Nelson's characters as racially indeterminate is partially a function of their own unfamiliarity with Dunbar-Nelson's native city and its singular history of tripartite social stratification.

Like most New World slave societies, but unique in the United States, New Orleans (and Louisiana more generally) had a third social class distinct from the black and white social classes which made up other American communities in the nineteenth century.[2] Beginning in the eighteenth century, under both French and Spanish rule, Louisiana had a class of *gens de couleur libres,* or free people of color, whose legal and social status was wholly different from blacks in the colony. Virginia Domínguez notes that the 1808 project of the Louisiana Civil Code acknowledged the existence of three social sectors—whites, free people of color, and black slaves—and legislated against marriages between free citizens and slaves and between whites and free people of color (25). As Dunbar-Nelson writes in her two-part historical essay, **"People of Color in Louisiana,"**

> Following the War of 1812 [when Britain tried to recapture Louisiana from the United States] the free people of color occupied a peculiar position in Louisiana, especially in New Orleans. There were distinct grades of society. The caste system [in New Orleans] was almost as strong as that of India. Free people of color from other states poured into Louisiana in a steady stream. It was a haven of refuge.
>
> (II, 161)

After the Civil War, however, with the distinction between free and slave legally erased, the *gens de couleur libres* found themselves squeezed out of their tertiary social position into one or the other of the remaining racial classifications: white or black. This racial polarization of New Orleans brought the community into line with the rest of the country, but an important distinction remained. A self-identified Creole population, which included many of the *gens de couleur libre,* endured at this time as a viable non-American (and historically anti-American) ethnic classification in New Orleans.[3]

The genesis of the social definition of "Creole" sheds further light on the interwoven nature of race, class, and ethnicity in Dunbar-Nelson's characterizations. In colonial Louisiana, the adjective "creole" meant native-born or locally produced; thus, creole horses, creole slaves and the creole offspring of French or Spanish parents were those born within the colony. Only after the Louisiana Purchase of 1803 did the term "creole" take on political significance, when older residents sought to base their land rights on their creole, or native, identity (Tregle 138). In the early nineteenth century, Creole identity formed itself defensively against American and European immigrants and the "foreign French" who flooded into New Orleans from St. Domingue (now Haiti) after the revolution there. Although outsiders often associated Creole identity with racial mixture, Creoles themselves were primarily concerned with differentiating themselves from Americans—up until the Civil War. "Nativity was all" to white Creoles, Joseph Tregle explains (172), because local birth signified superior civic power; white supremacy was such an ingrained belief among whites that they gave little thought to differentiating between white and black Creoles for the benefit of the outside world. However, in the wake of the Civil War, white supremacy was definitively challenged by Southern blacks and some Northerners, and Creoles' political and economic downslide accelerated as they were increasingly outnumbered by Anglo-Americans, and Irish and German immigrants (Domínguez 132). A manifestation of the shift from a tripartite to binary social structure in New Orleans was the formation of a *Parti Blanc,* or White League, in 1873 and a deadly riot in 1874 between this white supremacist organization and the Metropolitan Police, many of whom were black, in which thirty-two were killed and civic buildings were occupied (137). Beginning in this period and continuing to the present, Creole identity, which had always implied a favored class status in Louisiana, has been a site for racial conflict.

Depicting the Creole for non-local readers of **"People of Color in Louisiana,"** Dunbar-Nelson explains the efforts of white Louisianians to police the borders of this identity. Her own definition celebrates the truly indefinable, heterogeneous qualities of the Creole:

> The native white Louisianian will tell you that a Creole is a white man, whose ancestors contain some French or Spanish blood in their veins. . . . The Caucasian will shudder with horror at the idea of including a person of color in the definition, and the person of color will retort with his definition that a Creole is a native of Louisiana, in whose blood runs mixed strains of everything un-American, with the African strain slightly apparent. The true Creole is like the famous gumbo of the state, a little bit of everything, making a whole, delightfully flavored, quite distinctive, and wholly unique.
>
> (I, 143-44)

Opposing "white" and "French or Spanish blood" with "native of Louisiana," "mixed [blood]," "everything un-American," "a little bit of everything," and "wholly unique," Dunbar-Nelson discounts the attribution of a fixed race or ethnicity to Creole identity. She proposes, instead, that Creole-ness inheres in Louisiana nativity, which was historically opposed to American-ness, and in an uncategorizable racial and ethnic mixture, "with the African strain slightly apparent." As an ethnic identity, Creole is and was a category of indeterminate race, and Dunbar-Nelson provocatively emphasizes the probability—but not the certainty—of African influence. In the nineteenth century, Dunbar-Nelson writes, "[t]he free people of color . . . kept on amassing wealth and educating their children as ever in spite of opposition, for it is difficult to enforce laws against a race when you cannot find that race" (II, 165). This notion of a problem of identification clearly intrigues Dunbar-Nelson, for she often treats in fiction the causes and consequences of the unknown or hidden racial identity of Creole characters. The flip side of this issue—the inability to find people of color within the Creole class—is the struggle faced by the many Creoles of color who legally challenged the Louisiana Civil Code to prove their legitimacy and gain an inheritance from the white side of their families (Domínguez 61ff). Metaphorically hidden within the Creole class, the *gens de couleur libres* caused immense anxiety for those Creoles drawn to the *Parti Blanc* and to the newly politicized position of white supremacy at the end of the century.

To Dunbar-Nelson's evident delight, New Orleans society was like Alice's Looking Glass when it came to Creole identity, with its specific and yet unverifiable qualifications: one could change from black to white, African to French, simply by passing through the boundaries of this Creole social class. Attempting to regulate an invisible, topsy-turvy Looking Glass realm, white-identified Creoles went to extreme lengths in their efforts to create a racially pure, culturally superior Creole mythology. A respected and influential post-bellum historian whom Dunbar-Nelson herself uses as a source for her historical essay, Charles Gayarré is an exemplary hysteric on the topic of Creole racial identity. Enraged by George Washington Cable's fictional portraits of Creoles of color, Gayarré delivered a lecture "before a large and enthusiastic audience" at Tulane University in 1885, in which he insisted that "[i]t has become high time to demonstrate that the Creoles of Louisiana, whose number to-day may approximately be established at 250,000 souls, have not, because of the names they bear, a particle of African blood in their veins" (Gayarré 3). Gayarré's extreme language here—the denial of even "a particle of African blood"—is nothing compared to the language he uses to discuss Cable's influential novel about Creole life, *The Grandissimes* (1880):

> the monstrous absurdities that form the tissue of a composition in which the audacious mutilation of what is truth in a matter of fact world, and the distortion of what could possibly be supposed by a sound mind to exist at all in the world of probabilities, exceeds all precedents.
>
> (18)

His language slips into the realms of nightmare and pathology—not to mention Alice's Looking Glass world—as he attempts to grapple with the straightforward historical fact that Creoles had always been a mixed race in Louisiana; he notes himself that "[t]he negroes born within her [Louisiana] limits were *creoles* [in the seventeenth century] to distinguish them from the imported Africans, and from those who, long after, were brought from the United States" (3). Yet, when it comes to the question of contemporary Creole identity, Gayarré unleashes a stream of delirious terms—"monstrous," "mutilation," and "distortion"—to describe the concept of a Creole with a particle of African blood.

In Dunbar-Nelson's fiction, the racial crisis inherent in Creole identity is only rarely alluded to, a fact that has frustrated her critics. Gloria Hull, Dunbar-Nelson's foremost literary critic, sets the tone: "Unfortunately, though she describes two women characters as having 'small brown hands,' . . . her stories are also separated from her black experience" (*Color* 52). Violet Harrington Bryan follows Hull's lead in criticizing the absence of racial themes in Dunbar-Nelson's fiction and labeling her fictional treatment of race "ambivalen[t]" because her characters' racial identities are not always clear (71).[4] While Hull finds Dunbar-Nelson's stories **"The Stones of the Village"** and **"The Pearl in the Oyster"** (***Works*** 3), with explicit themes of passing and color prejudice within the Creole community, to be "interesting" and "daring," she also records that in 1900 Bliss Perry, an editor at *The Atlantic Monthly,* warned Dunbar-Nelson that the American public disliked fictional treatments of "the color-line" (*Color* 54, 57). Given both the exigencies of the publishing world and Dunbar-Nelson's own background as a woman of mixed race and ethnicity in a community where racial mixture yielded a wider array of options for one's social position, contemporary critical dictates which attribute psychological motivations to Dunbar-Nelson's choice of "aracial" (Hull, Introduction xxxii) characterizations appear unwarranted. The ambivalence associated with Dunbar-Nelson's Creole characters is more likely located in the reader's response to characters whose race does not verifiably adhere to one side of the black-white binary but is positioned instead in the confusing realm of the Looking Glass.

Affirming the existence of this realm where things and people are not what they seem, a repeated theme in Dunbar-Nelson's *œuvre* is that of hidden or coded local knowledge of the interconnected relationship between race and ethnicity in Creole identity. Several of her tragic Creole stories are based on real-life prototypes that she narrates elsewhere, in her non-fiction essays, or that have been uncovered by later scholars of her work; while the prototypes feature racialized conflicts, Dunbar-Nelson's fictionalizations nearly or fully obscure their racial overtones. Thus, a local audience, privy to the well-known prototypes, will experience a racialized reading of the same stories that a non-local audience will find racially unmarked. Thus, encoding racial identity within Creole ethnicity is a means by which Dunbar-Nelson inserts a regional boundary in the reading experiences of her audience. This "hidden" boundary signifies on the free people of color who found themselves hidden within the identity of Creole and thus able to live and prosper under cover of a favored social status. Just as countless Creoles of color successfully passed for white in New Orleans at the turn of the century, several of Dunbar-Nelson's Creole characters are able to pass in their encounters with non-local readers. Choosing not to attribute a fixed racial identity to these characters, Dunbar-Nelson defines the Creole as uniquely and distinctly indefinable.

Dunbar-Nelson's use of local knowledge to racially code her stories of Creole life can be analyzed in the context of local color literature, which often opposes "a marginal, local, alternative knowledge . . . to unifying translocal disciplines" (Donovan 227). Recent criticism of local color, or regional, literature has fastened on "the regional-versus-federal dialectic" to describe this literature's resistance to national union and cultural homogenization (226). This theory holds that local color writers' attention to regional dialects and mores lodges an implicit critique against the ongoing processes of national unification at the levels of language and culture. William Dean Howells, who led the critical charge of local colorists—and, more generally, realist literature—upon the prevailing tradition of romance literature in America, believed that the diversity and decentralized culture(s) of America necessitated the production of literature that could faithfully capture a small portion of the American mosaic rather than reveal a blurred reproduction of the whole canvas. "To put it paradoxically," Howells wrote in 1901,

> our life is too large for our art to be broad. In despair at the immense scope and variety of the material offered it by American civilization, American fiction must specialize, and, turning distracted from the superabundance of character, it must burrow far down in a soul or two.
>
> (qtd. in Ziff 48)

Convinced that the universal was not only visible in the local, but was *best* discerned there, local colorists rendered up portraits of specific communities, families, and individuals as a means to capture American culture in literature.[5] This motive suggests that local-color literature is thus not inherently anti-federalist, but *is* inherently opposed to homogenization of the national character. Dunbar-Nelson shares this antipathy to a representative American, for she admired literature's capability for conveying "an individual, not a type."[6]

In Dunbar-Nelson's stories, as in local color literature generally, local practices simultaneously lend an air of exoticism and authenticate the stories' status as regional literature. She narrates such observances as cleaning the doorstep with a yellow wash to protect against evil *gris gris,* giving *lagniappe* when making a sale, or coloring glass amber by immersing it in a stream containing sulfur and iron.[7] Josephine Donovan notes that emphasizing "regional particularities and eccentricities, . . . local differences in setting, clothing, manners, and dialect" constitutes an insurrectionary act in terms of its resistance to totalizing disciplines and a unified national culture (233). Dunbar-Nelson resists totalizing forms of identity through a different kind of local knowledge, one which cannot easily be translated by the non-regional reader, much less opposed to normative practices, because it presupposes familiarity with local events. By encoding locally known traditions and locally renowned figures within her fiction, Dunbar-Nelson attempts to avert identification of her Creole characters as types such as the tragic mulatta and to present them, instead, as distinct individuals.

For example, the institutionalized mistress-keeping, or *plaçage,* arrangement, peculiar to New Orleans, covertly underlies **"Sister Josepha"** (***Works*** 1), Dunbar-Nelson's story of a Creole orphan girl who finds herself unwillingly trapped within a convent. Violet Harrington Bryan points out that there may well be a real-life precedent for several Creole tales (by Dunbar-Nelson, George Washington Cable, and Grace King) that feature a young girl finding refuge in a convent: New Orleansian Henriette Delille, a Creole woman of color, fled to a convent in order to escape the *plaçage* arrangement, in which many quadroon women were selected by wealthy white men at quadroon balls, set up in houses of their own, and often deserted later when the men married white women (Bryan 72). Delille's story was well known in New Orleans because, in 1842, she was one of the founders of an order for women of color, the Sisters of the Holy Family. These women of color were of various ethnicities, for, as Grace King wrote in 1907, members of the convent "represent every possible admixture of French, Spanish, English, Indian, and African blood. There are few pure Africans among them" (King 351).[8] In Dunbar-Nelson's **"Sister Josepha,"** the convent girl has an unknown past, and her lack of family name or of certain racial identity forces her withdrawal from the outside world. In confronting the ways of this world, which threaten (in different ways) the single woman and the woman of color, Sister Josepha is particularly vulnerable, given her ambiguous identity. She must consequently quash her individuality under cover of the veil if she wishes to avoid the institutionalized sexual victimization of *plaçage.*

With a fleeting reference to Sister Josepha's "small brown hands" (156), Dunbar-Nelson indicates to the perceptive—and mainly local—reader that the protagonist of her story is a Creole of color. Other details of her physical appearance all point to her Creole identity: her black eyes; the fact that she speaks only French as an infant; her birth name of Camille; her "tropical beauty" (158); her "silky black hair" (160); and the "quick, vivacious . . . [qualities] which belonged to her blood" (159). While this accumulation of French-Creole characteristics conveys to the non-regional reader that the orphan girl is an ethnic other, a contemporary review in the New York *Ecclesiastical Review* (February 1900) confirms that she was not read as a woman of color: "[the volume ***The Goodness of St. Rocque and Other Stories***] has no characteristics peculiar to [Dunbar-Nelson's] race" (qtd. in Hull, *Color* 52). In the context of the story, Sister Josepha's conflict is understandable solely in terms of gender; being female is enough to make the wider world a dangerous place for an orphan girl.[9] She resists adoption by a couple because she intuits a sexual threat: "Untutored in worldly knowledge, she could not divine the meaning of the pronounced leers and admiration of her physical charms which gleamed in the man's face, but she knew it made her feel creepy, and stoutly refused to go" (159).

However, a New Orleansian familiar with *plaçage* arrangements in general, and Henriette Delille's story in particular, would easily draw a parallel between Sister Josepha's predicament and that of many beautiful but socially conscripted quadroon women. Like Delille, Sister Josepha does not freely choose convent life, but is compelled to seek refuge there. She has

> no nationality, for she could never tell from whom or whence she came; no friends, and a beauty that not even an ungainly bonnet and shaven head could hide. In a flash she realized the deception of the life she would lead, and the cruel self-torture of wonder at her own identity. Already, as if in anticipation of the world's questionings, she was asking herself, "Who am I? What am I?"
>
> (170-71)

Through this identity crisis, Dunbar-Nelson portrays the complex strands of gender, race, and class which firmly bind Sister Josepha to a life "behind the heavy door" of the convent (172). Coding the young Sister's racial identity such that only local readers will be certain to read her color into her character, Dunbar-Nelson avoids typecasting her heroine in the only tragic literary role open to the racially mixed woman, the tragic mulatta.

Another story that covertly deals with the same theme of *plaçage,* **"Little Miss Sophie"** (***Works*** 1), underscores the tragic implications of an unverifiable identity in a society that relies on the categorization of individuals into discrete groups. Dunbar-Nelson codes this protagonist's racial identity even more obscurely under a Creole surface, but the story's plot hinges precisely on a problem of identification. Miss Sophie is "a poor little Creole old maid," one of the many "frail, little black-robed women with big, black bundles" who ride the streetcar to deliver the sewing they have done to their employers (142, 145). Dunbar-Nelson notes that these women are "one of the city's most pitiful sights" (145), but she does not explain to the non-regional reader the peculiar condition of Creole class status that underlies these women's labors. Domínguez claims that Creoles strictly avoided the appearance of doing manual labor for wages because of its association with working class or lower class status, so "that white Creole women impoverished by the Civil War refused even to sew for others, unless it was in the privacy of their own homes where they would not be seen by others" (227). Miss Sophie's private labors, however, are performed for the benefit of another. The melodramatic tragedy of the story, in short, is that Miss Sophie works herself to death in an effort to repurchase a ring given her by a faithless lover in order that he might gain an inheritance and support the white woman whom he has married. Miss Sophie learns of her former lover's predicament through an overheard conversation on the streetcar:

> 'the firm failed first; he didn't mind that much, he was so sure of his uncle's inheritance repairing his lost fortunes but suddenly *this difficulty of identification* springs up and he is literally on the verge of ruin.' . . . '. . . the absurd will expressly stipulates that he shall be known only by a certain quaint Roman ring. . . .' . . . '. . . It seems that Neale had some little Creole love-affair some years ago and gave this ring to his dusky-eyed fiancée'.
>
> (146-47, emphasis added)

Bryan claims that "[t]o any reader knowledgeable about New Orleans culture, the phrase 'dusky-eyed' would signify that Sophie was a quadroon" (71). In addition, the reference to a "little Creole love-affair" that is succeeded by the white man's marriage to a white woman is an allusion to the usual course of *plaçage.* The fact that it is the white man in the story who has a "difficulty of identification" places a neat twist on the racialized problem of identification typically experienced by the light-skinned African American citizen and illustrated so clearly by the characters of Sister Josepha and Miss Sophie, whose unknown or hidden racial heritage is the source of their tragedies.

Although the melodramatic tragedy of **"Little Miss Sophie"** might seem excessive, the hidden racial theme lends itself to a more politicized reading. Exploring color oppression through a consistent motif of dark/white oppositions, Dunbar-Nelson constructs a covert narrative that registers its political import only on those predisposed by their racial or their local identity to decode a black/white binary in terms of race.[10] True to her belief in the superiority of "art" to "propaganda," Dunbar-Nelson disdains the use of "a bludgeon, none too cleverly concealed within the narrative, hitting the Nordic and exalting the Negro." Instead, she conveys the hidden racial theme "without an eye for the probable effect of the story on the consciousness of the white man."[11] As Werner Sollors has observed in the fiction of Charles Chesnutt and Abraham Cahan, gendered ethnic polarizations can have a specific ideological and historical connotation in opposing "a dark-hued reminder of an ethnic past, with the refined bright women of America" (156). In **"Little Miss Sophie,"** we are introduced to the protagonist in the form of "a little, forsaken, black heap at the altar of the Virgin. . . . [T]he white-robed Madonna seemed to whisper comfort" (140). Further descriptions reinforce the color opposition between the dark Sophie and both the white mother of Christ and the white bride of Sophie's former lover. Sophie, often referred to as a "black-robed figure" (143, 150), with "black locks" (144), encounters both "the white-robed bride" and "the sweet, white-robed Virgin" (149) in the church where Neale is wed.[12] When Sophie dies of exhaustion on Christmas day, Dunbar-Nelson implicates both her white-robed religion and the white woman who has usurped her place in the white man's life. As in **"Sister Josepha,"** the Catholic religion is more oppressive than comforting, and, through this series of dark/white oppositions, Dunbar-Nelson points to pervasive color prejudice that leaves the dark woman metaphorically alone at the altar and literally excluded from the laws of inheritance. By polarizing the discarded lover and the beloved wife in terms of color, Dunbar-Nelson offers a covert, locally understood, narrative that non-regional readers would read in terms of "local color" without ever recognizing its racial overtones.

In a story with an overt black/white conflict, Dunbar-Nelson explores how the individual is destroyed when groups focus on color as a unifying force. Racial conflict in **"Mr. Baptiste"** (***Works*** 1) is deadly, for the story's conflict is based on the New Orleans labor riots of 1892, when British shippers attempted to substitute African American workers for white workers who loaded cotton bales onto ocean-going ships. C. Vann Woodward reports that several men were killed in these riots and property damage reached $750,000 (267). Assuming her readers' familiarity with these events, Dunbar-Nelson writes, "You remember, of course, how long the strike lasted, and how many battles were fought and lives lost before the final adjustment of affairs" (123-24). Her story, though, centers on a Creole character who is not known to the reader, but whose ethnicity is visible to the narrator: "He was small: most Creole men are small when they are old. . . . It must be that age withers them sooner and more effectually than those of un-Latinised extraction" (111). From Mr. Baptiste's point of view, the strike means the loss of his livelihood: picking up free baskets of imperfect fruit from the docks. He worriedly asks "a big brawny Irishman" (117), who turns out to be one Finnegan, the leader of the striking workers, what will happen to the fruit. Finnegan and his mates cheerfully greet Mr. Baptiste as the "little fruit-eater" (118), but their moods turn ugly when they see "sweat rolling from glossy black skins, the Negro stevedores were at work" (120). Although Mr. Baptiste follows the mob of white men as they approach the stevedores, his "mournful protest . . . was lost in the roar of men" (119). Dunbar-Nelson's depiction of the racial mob illustrates how the individual, in his or her particularity, is erased by the either/or and for/against dynamics of group identity.

In the heat of the ensuing riot, based on fixed racial divisions, Mr. Baptiste's ethnicity emerges as a salient and dangerous fact. When the Irish crowd shouts "'Niggers! niggers! Kill 'em, scabs!'" and the riot breaks out (120), Mr. Baptiste hides behind a bread-stall and "weakly cheer[s] the Negroes on" (122). Although Dunbar-Nelson does not explain why Mr. Baptiste supports the stevedores, the class-based Creole antipathy to Irish immigrants may lie behind the character's actions. In any case, Mr. Baptiste's partisan cheering causes the fighting Irish worker, McMahon, to draw attention for the first time to Mr. Baptiste's ethnicity: "'Will yez look at that damned fruit-eatin' Frinchman!' . . . and he let fly a brickbat in the direction of the bread-stall" (122). The Frenchman, sympathizing with the Negroes, now exists on their side, the side of the Irish enemy. As Dunbar-Nelson writes, however, for the other bystanders who rush to Mr. Baptiste's aid, "The individual, the concrete bit of helpless humanity, had more interest for them than the vast, vague fighting mob beyond" (123). Though clearly defined by their participants, ethnic mobs are "vague," based on divisions which Dunbar-Nelson indicates are only seemingly stable—the Frenchman ends up behind enemy lines with the Negro workers—while the individual is "concrete," with an identity as a member of "humanity." In the story's closing line, Dunbar-Nelson corrects the historical record of this labor conflict by saying, "It was a fearsome war, and many forgot afterwards whose was the first life lost in the struggle,—poor little Mr. Baptiste's" (124). Her story thus rewrites history by foregrounding the plight of the little man who is forgotten in ethnic wars, for his is the concrete life, the life worth saving.

A less deadly culture clash occurs in **"La Juanita,"** in which Dunbar-Nelson uses dark/white oppositions to contrast Creole and American lovers and illustrate how these cultures can be bridged, if never fully merged. The narrator of this story often uses a direct address to call attention to the American reader's cultural and geographical distance from the Creole milieu, in which the narrator herself is clearly at home. Beginning "[i]f you never lived in Mandeville, you cannot appreciate the thrill of wholesome, satisfied joy which sweeps over its inhabitants every evening at five o'clock" (195), the story goes on to explain that, "not being a Mandevillian, you could not understand" why La Juanita Alvarez's Grandpère Colomés is so ashamed of his granddaughter's American boyfriend (199). The narrator thus pointedly possesses what the reader does not: local presence and knowledge. The narrator goes on to contrast La Juanita's "petite, half-Spanish, half-French beauty" and her "black curls" (197) with the attributes of her Anglo-named boyfriend, Mercer, who has a "big and blond and brawny" physique (198) and "pale-eye[s]" (200). The community's attitude toward La Juanita's romantic choice is clear: "'Un Américain, pah!' said the little mother of the black eyes. And Mandeville sighed sadly, and shook its head, and was sorry for

Grandpère Colomés" (198-99). In the story's resolution, however, Mercer "was no longer 'un Américain' now, he was a hero" after winning a storm-wracked regatta (207). His heroic deed enables him to rise above the category of American, but only through a process described by Grandpère Colomés as earning honorary membership in a different ethnic category: "'some time dose Americain can mos' be lak one Frenchman'" (208). While the "pale" Mercer manages to bridge ethnic categories, he is now neither American nor Creole, but located in a liminal position somewhere between the two. Significantly, this position of being neither here nor there corresponds with that of the reader, who is clearly addressed as an outsider to the ethnic milieu of the story's characters and narrator but who is also invited to be a vicarious participant through asides such as "[y]ou should have seen . . ." and "now you could see . . ." (204).

Although subtly deployed, Dunbar-Nelson's direct addresses to her readers—"you must admit" (**"Tony's Wife"** ***Works*** 1, 22) or "you could not understand" (**"La Juanita"** 199)—create a particular mediated relationship among narrator, characters, and readers. At times placing the reader within the *mise en scéne,* and at times disavowing the reader's membership in the ethnic community she describes, the narrator controls the metaphoric gate which alternately allows or bars entry into a very specifically delineated geographical-cultural milieu. Dunbar-Nelson uses direct addresses in her second published volume of stories, ***The Goodness of St. Rocque*** (1899) and in a manuscript volume, ***The Annals of 'Steenth Street,*** that she probably wrote between 1900 and 1910.[13] Due to their self-identified geographical-cultural setting, New York City's Upper East Side near 87th Street and 2nd Avenue, all of the stories in the latter collection inherently serve as sites where the reader confronts an alien community. The reader's position vis à vis this community is correspondingly more often problematized by Dunbar-Nelson's addresses than it is throughout her published volume, ***The Goodness of St. Rocque,*** which consists of stories with varying degrees of foreignness in terms of class, ethnicity, and its Louisiana locales. Dunbar-Nelson's use of direct addresses has been described by Hull as "an attempt to achieve intimacy and immediacy. . . . But today's readers dislike being grabbed from behind the fictional veil of illusion" (*Color* 53). Hull's comment is typical of her chiding critical tone toward Dunbar-Nelson in *Color, Sex, and Poetry: Three Women Writers of the Harlem Renaissance* (1987). My point in regard to Dunbar-Nelson's narrative voice is quite different: while her addresses to the reader may at times promote intimacy, they also often point up the reader's problematic relationship (as a geographical and cultural outsider) to both the narrator and her characters. This effect of being literally and metaphorically put in one's place may indeed feel like an uncomfortable "grab," coming from behind the seemingly safe fictional surface of Dunbar-Nelson's stories. However, I would argue that this stylistic device, which was also deployed by Dunbar-Nelson's fellow New Orleansian George Washington Cable, is a particularly effective way to mediate across the lines of ethnicity, race, and region which make the experience of reading Dunbar-Nelson's stories an explicitly cross-cultural one.

The New Orleans story **"Tony's Wife,"** for example, opens by focusing the reader's attention on ethnic identity: "'Gimme fi' cents worth o' candy, please.' It was the little Jew girl who spoke, and Tony's wife roused herself from her knitting . . ." (19). This story depicts an ethnically mixed neighborhood where the Jewish customer buys from the Italian shopkeeper and his German wife, as well as from the grocer, Mrs. Murphy, who is no doubt Irish. Tony's "little queer old shop" and the other "tumble-down shop" of Mrs. Murphy, however, are out of place in the "semi-fashionable locality, far up-town, away from the old-time French quarter" (21). Describing the class positions of the neighborhood's occupants, Dunbar-Nelson delineates "the sort of neighbourhood where millionaires live before their fortunes are made and fashionable, high-priced private schools flourish, where the small cottages are occupied by aspiring school-teachers and choir-singers" (21-22). Having been presented with these details of the residents' class aspirations and the shopkeepers' ethnicities, the reader is addressed: "Such was this locality, and you must admit that it was indeed a condescension to tolerate Tony and Mrs. Murphy" (22). With double-edged irony, Dunbar-Nelson pushes the reader into alignment with the class-conscious neighbors who "tolerate" the ethnic merchants in their midst. By inserting the reader into the narrative in this place and in this way, Dunbar-Nelson does "grab" the reader from his or her position of complacency and thrusts him or her into a location, a particular street, where the ethnic dividing lines are clearly drawn, either one side or the other must be chosen, and neither option is a very comfortable one.

Like the stories in ***The Annals of 'Steenth Street,*** **"Tony's Wife"** records the harmful existence of an ethnic line in the sand. Atypical in ***The Goodness of St. Rocque*** collection for its naturalistic rather than romantic treatment of ethnic difference, this story's dramatic situation may be drawn from Dunbar-Nelson's experience as a settlement worker and teacher in Brooklyn, New York's Upper East Side, and Harlem.[14] Neither Tony nor his nameless German wife (a "wild theory [held] that her name was Mary" [22]) is portrayed sympathetically, although the wife is pitiful because she is brutalized. Tony's attitude towards his wife is based on his sense of superiority to her: "He hated her in a lusty, roaring fashion, as a healthy beefy boy hates a sick cat and torments it to madness. When she displeased him, he beat her, and knocked her frail form on the floor" (25). The foundation for Tony's abusive domination, though, is his sense of ethnic superiority:

> John was Tony's brother, huge and bluff, too, but fair and blond, with the beauty of Northern Italy. With the same *lack of race pride* which Tony had displayed in selecting his German spouse, John had taken unto himself Betty, a daughter of Erin, aggressive, powerful, and cross-eyed.
>
> (29, emphasis added).

When Tony falls fatally ill—"'he is completely burned out inside. Empty as a shell, madam, empty as a shell'" (28)—the reader learns that Tony has not in fact wed the German woman, and, upon his deathbed, he refuses to do so. Now, more than ever, Tony holds tight to the laws of inheritance, which he feels should preserve ethnic purity: "'You want my money,' said Tony, slowly, 'and you sha'n't have it, not a cent; John shall have it'" (31-2). Tony's stance, a rigid yet hypocritical insistence on preserving an ethnic boundary, results in his being buried "with many honours by the Society of Italia's Sons," his brother inheriting all of his property, and his common-law wife being "sent . . . forth in the world penniless" (33). Ethnic mixing, then, is represented as a tragedy in **"Tony's Wife."** Yet, the real source of misfortune and suffering is Tony's refusal to give up "race pride" and truly cross the line separating one ethnic group from another.

While a majority of the stories in ***The Goodness of St. Rocque*** at least flirt with a romanticized exoticism, centered around the narratives' Louisiana locales, those in the ***'Steenth Street*** collection are naturalistic sketches about a group of poor and uneducated residents of the 'Steenth Street "tenements and alleys" that are the very antithesis of romantic (**"Revenge,"** ***Works*** 3, 136). Dunbar-Nelson's addresses to the readers in these stories do not strive for intimacy, as they sometimes do in her Creole stories, but function as a slamming gate, bringing the reader up short at the threshold of a community about which he or she is ignorant and where he or she is not welcome. The omnipresent poverty of 'Steenth Street is never characterized as exotic, and the sharp edges of violence and alcoholism which protrude in these stories are consonant with the narrator's more aggressive stance toward the reader. As in **"Tony's Wife,"** the clear boundary of class and ethnicity which exists between characters and reader cannot be comfortably navigated; if the reader wishes to remain aloof, or, inversely, wishes to pretend a false neighborliness with those who in fact metaphorically live on the opposite side of the tracks, those wishes will be denied by Dunbar-Nelson's direct addresses. The reader is thus put in his or her place, a place far from the despised shop, the smelly tenement, or the filthy alley.

For example, in **"The Revenge of James Brown,"** a story about the crisis in 'Steenth Street caused by the opening of the Pure in Heart Mission, the reader is introduced to the neighborhood and then put on notice that his or her presence there is as intrusive as the presence of the dreaded missionaries. Beginning "[i]t was a great day in 'Steenth Street" (136), the story initiates a series of reversals of the reader's expectations. We are told that what makes the day "great" is not a fight, nor a drunken spree by Banjo Liz, nor the ambulance, police, or fire engine:

> It was a new sound, the soft rumble of rubber tires and the high-stepping of pampered horses. There was nothing familiar to the denizens of 'Steenth Street. Aristocracy had invaded its sacred precincts and was trying to establish a precedent down near Third Avenue. Aristocracy in silk-lined gowns was walking in and out among the babies and dirty little folks swarming on the curbstones. 'Steenth Street felt itself disgraced and intruded upon. It gave a sniff of contempt and pretended not to be interested, the while its eyes and ears were agog with curiosity and its lips awry with inquiry.
>
> (137)

The greatness of the day is thus called into question, ironized by the narrator's juxtaposition here of the aristocrats who are involved in "a great rejoicing" (138) over their new position in the neighborhood and the "disgraced and intruded upon" residents of the neighborhood who are cast into the discomfiting position of onlookers. To accept the greatness of the day is to accept the aristocrats' own evaluation of their great position and their great mission amongst the less fortunate. However, since the narrator asserts that, in fact, the poor residents feel disgraced by this intrusion, the reader might feel obliged to identify with the anti-aristocrat position, that of a neighborhood insider. If so, the reader is in for another reversal when told that

> Mrs. McMahon spoke not too loudly, for Mrs. Brown stood near and Mrs. Brown, in addition to being one of the despised class, was—well, she was Jimmy Brown's mother, and if that means nothing to you, why, you'll have to visit 'Steenth Street and there make inquires [sic].
>
> (137-38)

Since the status of being Jimmy Brown's mother most certainly means nothing to the reader, this direct address necessarily disabuses the reader of any false notions that he or she could ever be a neighborhood insider. The idea that one's inquiries will meet with anything but hostility is firmly denied by the residents' comments about the upper class interlopers in their midst:

> "Now, dey t'inks dey's doin' some'p'n," contemptuously remarked Jimmy Brown, "I wonder who dey s'pose is a going' ter be foolin' roun' here wid dey bible talk?" . . . "Well, dey gotter start mighty soon, er I'll brick-bat 'em onct, an' let 'em see, we ain't stuck on em."
>
> (138)

In directly addressing the reader's lack of knowledge about the 'Steenth Street residents, Dunbar-Nelson draws attention to the false postures available to the ethnic and economic outsider and flatly denies their availability within her narrative. On 'Steenth Street there is no comfortable position between the rich and the poor, and to deny this is to deny what a difference one's street address can make in defining one's class position.

In the 'Steenth Street stories, **"Tony's Wife,"** and several other Creole stories, Dunbar-Nelson thematizes the relation between non-WASP ethnicity and poverty. Hull believes that, in her 'Steenth Street stories, Dunbar-Nelson writes about "class difference. This she uses, I am sure, as a signifier for race" (Introduction xxxix). While the economic and social boundaries created by ethnic differences do signify on those created by racial difference, Dunbar-Nelson's particular concern with the inter-relations between ethnicity and poverty need not be translated into racial dramas in order to be meaningful. The 'Steenth Street stories, set as they are in a white ghetto, demonstrate how the ethnic identities of various characters—such as Dago Joe, Mrs. McMahon, and the other poor Irish residents—are both a cause and a consequence of their class position. As in several of her Creole stories, these tales are predicated on Protestant oppression of Catholics as an ethnic minority. For example, in **"The Locket"** (***Works*** 3), Sister Angela's Protestant, Louisianian family greatly disapproves of her conversion to Catholicism because they associate "Catholicism . . . with emigrants and Irish, cheap labor and Sunday picnics" (77). Dunbar-Nelson's fiction reveals how the ethnicization of Catholicism sets in motion the oppression of groups as diverse as Irish and Italian immigrants and Cajuns.

One marker of Dunbar-Nelson's concern with ethnic oppression is the high incidence of violence and deaths in her stories centered on poor ethnic characters. In **"Titee"** (***Works*** 1), the dark-skinned, Catholic, Creole boy of the title is considered an "[i]dle, lazy, dirty, troublesome boy" by his teacher, whose ethnic prejudices blind her to the fact that "there was nothing in natural history that Titee didn't know" (45). The narrator's recognition of Titee's worth thus contrasts with the view expressed by the story's authority figure, and, at the story's conclusion, the narrator includes herself in the community of Titee's mourners: "we scattered winter roses on his little grave down in old St. Rocque's cemetery" (55).[15] The reader is thus led to sympathize with the child who, before his death, is "always hungry" (45), lives in a "part of the city, [where] there was neither gas nor electricity" (52), and is beaten by his mother for returning home late (47). Titee's short and fairly brutal life ends when he breaks his leg and dies of exposure while trying to help feed and shelter a homeless man. Dunbar-Nelson implicates poverty and the oppressive stereotypes that accompany it in the death of Titee, just as the Catholic Cajun protagonist in **"When the Bayou Overflows"** (***Works*** 1) dies from the effort to support himself and family through manual labor. "[T]all and slim and agile," Sylves' is "a true 'cajan" (96), who, like all the other men in the Bayou Teche area, must perform seasonal labor like fieldwork and cigar-making. Disparaged by Creoles and considered peasants, Cajuns, reputed to be the exiled descendants of French Canadian colonists, are traditionally rural inhabitants who perform agricultural labor (Ancelet xv). Due to his ethnically constricted economic and social position, Sylves' goes to Chicago for cigar-making work but dies there because "'[i]t was too cold for him,' . . . 'and he took the consumption'" (106). Economic and cultural displacement consumes Sylves's very nature; he cannot survive outside his native environment, and

Dunbar-Nelson raises the question of why he should have to. Attributing the deaths of Titee and Sylves', at least in part, to their status as members of ethnic minority groups, Dunbar-Nelson indicates that such hierarchical group relations can indeed be lethal.

The most brutal of Dunbar-Nelson's 'Steenth Street stories, **"Witness for the Defense"** (***Works*** 3), delineates how an oppressive environment produces violent actions, even comes to encourage the valorization of violence, while never completely suppressing the community's moral standards. Noting the reader's inability to judge the effect of a murder on 'Steenth Street, the narrator says, "[i]t was good beyond the comprehension of the mere outsider. One must have been an inmate of 'Steenth Street, and have had all the natural pride of locality to have felt and understood" (108). Translating the local value system for the "mere outsider," she explains,

> [i]t was not that someone had been murdered; that was not the awful thing. Life was not so valuable in 'Steenth Street, nor so sweet a possession that it should be held in reverence. 'Steenth Street held its breath and compressed its lips in awe-struck joy that someone had actually committed a murder; that within its precincts had been found one unreformed, unregenerate and bold enough to take a human life.
>
> (109)

Local pride is based on one of their own acting boldly against all outsiders' efforts to reform the neighborhood: "At last, they could refute the dire charge brought against them that the [Pure in Heart] Mission had 'reformed them'" (108). Murder, in this context, is an act of both resistance and self-definition. Furthermore, this particular murder of Randolph Williams by his wife Belle adheres to the 'Steenth Street "code of honor," according to which "the man who maltreats his fragile stepdaughter as Randolph Williams did Lizzie steps outside the pale, and is henceforth and forever an ostracized being" (111). In presenting this murder case in its local interpretive framework, Dunbar-Nelson induces the reader to step out of the safe position as the "mere outsider" to 'Steenth Street and to consider the options held by its oppressed residents, who are considered by the police to have such a "bad reputation" that their neighborhood "must suffer for its former misdemeanors" (113). Neither Belle Williams nor her neighbors are treated as individuals by the police, who, "roughly conscious of their authority," "suppressed [the residents] with rude words" (109, 110) or by the state, which decides "to make an example of the case" (112). Portraying the ineradicably horrible consequences of the murder on Belle and her daughter, Dunbar-Nelson juxtaposes the misery of those living in an economically oppressed environment with those who coldly view 'Steenth Street from the outside as "an eyesore to law-lovers" (112). The reader must sympathetically cross the economic-cultural boundary into this environment or accept being grouped with those "law-lovers" who see 'Steenth Street residents as a monolithic and entirely unregenerate group.

Boundary-crossing, however, can as easily lead to greater violence as it can achieve revolutionary changes. As in **"Mr. Baptiste,"** Dunbar-Nelson's fictionalization of race riots on the New Orleans docks, mob encounters in the Creole sketches **"A Carnival Jangle"** and **"Anarchy Alley"** (***Works*** 1) appear to warn of the dangers of transgressing the usual boundaries between different categories of human identities. In **"A Carnival Jangle,"** Dunbar-Nelson describes the New Orleans Carnival crowd as a melting pot in microcosm:

> the streets swarm with humanity,—humanity in all shapes, manners, forms,—. . . a mass of men and women and children, as varied and as assorted in their several individual peculiarities as ever a crowd that gathered in one locality since the days of Babel.
>
> (76)

Although Dunbar-Nelson celebrates this unfettered mixing of peoples in her prose—with "merry," "intensely exhilirating" [sic], and "effervescent" qualities (76, 77)—it is also the mixed-up world of Carnival that enables a young woman, dressed as a man, to be mistakenly murdered. Hiding one's identity in the crowd, "never know[ing] who were your companions, and be[ing] yourself unknown" (80), is exciting up to a point. But completely losing one's identity in that crowd, becoming indistinguishable from the mass, is lethal. For, when "[t]wo crowds meet and laugh and shout and mingle almost inextricably, . . . if one should stagger and fall bleeding to the ground, who can tell who has given the blow?" (82). **"A Carnival Jangle"** celebrates the potential for anarchic mixing, and simultaneously warns against losing one's particular identity in the amorphous composition of the crowd.

In **"Anarchy Alley,"** the revolutionary potential of breaking the unwritten rules of ethnic and class positions is less ambiguous. This plotless sketch introduces the reader to a "quaint, narrow, little alley that lies in the heart of the city . . . [where] the restless, chafing, anarchistic Europe of to-day, [exists] in the midst of the quieter democratic institution of our republic" (56). Although associated with Europe, Dunbar-Nelson asserts that this "Latinized portion of America" is a true democracy: "Idleness and labor, poverty and opulence, the honest, law-abiding workingman, and the reckless, restless anarchist, jostle side by side, and brush each other's elbows in terms of equality as they do nowhere else" (57). This small alley is not just a physical democracy, but a space for conceptual democracy as well. With irony, Dunbar-Nelson notes the distinction between the American republic and "this stamping ground for anarchy" (62); in Anarchy Alley the atmosphere "seems impregnated with a sort of mental freedom, conducive to dangerous theorizing and broody reflections on the inequality of the classes" (59). The "danger" of theorizing about economic inequality outside this alley merely serves to point up the necessity of some anarchy in the very heart of the republic.[16] Locating this small but exceptional space in a particular neighborhood, Dunbar-Nelson names Exchange Alley as a place where the well-maintained social boundaries evident in the "calmly-thinking, quietly-laboring, cool and conservative world" evaporate (58). Celebrating the anarchy implicit in equality, Dunbar-Nelson invites the reader to become an "idle wanderer" in this physical and conceptual street.

Dunbar-Nelson does not so much draw boundary lines within her fiction as she points up the ones that already exist: boundaries demarcated by street signs, by names that give away their owners' ethnic identities, and by the class positions that are so influenced by both one's street address and one's name and ethnicity. It is no accident that place names play such an important role in her stories, such as the careful delineation of the neighborhood where Tony and his "wife" live or the exact location of the Bohemian Anarchy Alley, for this information acts as coding for her characters' races, classes, and ethnicities. The title of the volume in which **"Tony's Wife"** appears, for example, ***The Goodness of St. Rocque,*** references a specific location: St. Rocque's is a small, eccentric chapel in New Orleans which is associated with mixed Catholic and voodoo, or hoodoo, practices.[17] The manuscript volume ***The Annals of 'Steenth Street,*** of course, also situates the stories in a particular geographical-cultural setting. By particularizing the streets, neighborhoods, and communities where her characters attempt to cross ethnic boundaries or are destroyed by their fixed ethnic positions, Dunbar-Nelson denaturalizes ethnicity itself by highlighting its determinants: geographical and class position. She also avoids overromanticizing the "foreign" elements in the economic and ethnic communities she portrays by directly addressing the reader's position outside of them. Putting the reader in his or her place, typically outside of the community she depicts, Dunbar-Nelson does not just describe the divisive effects of rigidly maintained group identities. She makes the reader feel "out of place" and thus forced to recognize just what economic, ethnic, and social place he or she is in. From such a self-conscious position, the reader can see not only quaintness, but can also recognize his or her relationship to Dunbar-Nelson's palette of local colors.

Notes

1. Published under her maiden name, Alice Ruth Moore, *Violets and Other Tales* (1895) contains poetry, sketches, and short stories set in New Orleans and its environs. *The Goodness of St. Rocque and Other Stories* (1899) contains short stories set in and around New Orleans, some of which are reprinted from her first volume; this was published under the name Alice Dunbar. An unpublished manuscript volume written between 1900 and 1910, *Women and Men* contains stories set in New Orleans, some with explicit racial themes. *The Annals of 'Steenth Street* (1900-1910) also exists only as a manuscript volume and contains stories set in a white ghetto in New York city's Upper East side. All of these volumes have been collected in *The Works of Alice Dunbar-Nelson.* vol. 1–3, Gloria T. Hull, ed, and the first reference to a story will note in which reprinted volume it can be found.

2. In *Creole New Orleans,* Arnold Hirsch and Joseph Logsdon note that Charleston, SC is often held to have a similarly unique three-tiered social structure. However, Charleston's population of free people of color was 3,200 at its peak, and New Orleans' was 20,000. The former city's "third tier" was more a fringe element and was rooted in color or legal status, while New Orleans' was a more vital element of the community which defined itself by its ethnocultural differences from both whites and blacks (191).

3. Domínguez notes that, "[i]n general, though not universally, persons identified as Creoles spoke French and identified with French culture. . . . Cultural attributes of the descendants of French and Spanish colonial settlers who had been calling themselves Creole for a number of generations became criteria of Creole identity," resulting in a Creole/American polarization and the inclusion of *gens de couleur libre* and Cajuns in this Creole category (125).

4. Bryan also casts a negative light on the absence of racial themes in Dunbar-Nelson's fiction: "Unlike [Charles] Chesnutt, unfortunately, Dunbar-Nelson thought it inappropriate, in her earlier stories, either for publishing purposes or because of her own ambivalences about race, even to mention color or race" (77).

5. This belief in the universal inhering in the particular or local was not universally shared. Hamlin Garland staked his faith on the value of the particular as a good in itself, while local color writers like George Washington Cable and Kate Chopin stressed the necessity of depicting universal themes and truths in literature (Spencer 240-42).

6. This quote is from Dunbar-Nelson's newspaper column, "Une Femme Dit," which began as "From A Woman's Point of View" and appeared in the Pittsburgh *Courier* from January to September, 1926 (rpt. in *Works* 3). In this particular column of 20 February 1926, Dunbar-Nelson praises the play *Lulu Belle* for its aim "to present a cross-section of metropolitan life" (134) despite widespread criticism in the black community that the characterizations show "'[t]he worst side'" of the race and "'will hurt us with the white people'" (131). In these newspaper columns, Dunbar-Nelson is more forthright about her views on the role racial representations play in race relations.

7. Dunbar-Nelson's stories recording the practice of washing the doorstep include "The Goodness of St. Rocque" (*Works* 1) and "Cupid and the Phonograph" (*Works* 3). Dunbar-Nelson notes only that the custom stems from a superstition, but Robert Tallant explains that the most common protection from evil *gris gris* (hoodoo charms) in New Orleans was to scrub the front stoop with brick dust (199). References to *lagniappe* appear in Dunbar-Nelson's "The Praline Woman" and "Tony's Wife" (*Works* 1). Edward Larocque Tinker explains this custom: "[w]ith every purchase there is *lagniappe*—a little something, unpaid for, to promote good feeling" (278). In "Natalie," the Cajun title character explains the glass-coloring process to her Anglo-American friend, Olivia (*Works* 1).

8. In her racist account of *plaçage,* King blames quadroon women for "their relaxation and deviation from, if not their complete denial of, the code of morality accepted by white women, and their consequent adoption of a separate standard of morals for themselves, and the forcing it upon the community and upon the men of their own colour" (347-48).

9. The story clearly shows the suppression of the orphan girl's feminine nature, including her sexual longings, through her cloistering. Her feminine name, Camille, is exchanged for the masculine Sister Josepha, and "the wickedness in her heart," aroused by the sight of a handsome boy in the outside world, is not allowed to flourish in her "home of self-repression and retrospection" (168).

10. Other Dunbar-Nelson stories, which I will not discuss here, which feature a dark/white opposition are "The Goodness of St. Rocque" and "Natalie."

11. Dunbar-Nelson, "A Woman's Point of View," 6 February 1926 (rpt. in *Works* 3). Dunbar-Nelson writes, "We are forced by cruel challenges to explain, show our wares, tell our story, excuse our shortcomings, defend our positions. And we insist that every Negro be a propagandist. . . . We forget that didacticism is the death of art" (124).

12. In her newspaper column of 13 February 1926, Dunbar-Nelson denounces the type of color propaganda her story recapitulates: "For centuries the white man has built up a propaganda about that very word *white* that has driven into countless millions of minds a connotation that is about as complete and as subtle a mass of propaganda as can be found anywhere on this globe—or any other, I fancy. . . . [W]hite robes, white-winged angels, white mansions, and a white-faced God with white hair have been thrust upon the world by the subtle propagandists as the only true and possible heaven" (rpt. in *Works* 3, 127-28).

13. Hull, *Works* 3, 101. The only story in *Violets and Other Tales* to use direct address, "A Carnival Jangle," is reprinted in *The Goodness of St. Rocque.* This technique thus seems to be one Dunbar-Nelson developed during her career as a fiction writer.

14. The story's concern with a debased inter ethnic (or, inter-racial, in the story's terminology) marriage seems to echo Dunbar-Nelson's description of the home of one of her students. In a letter to her fiancé, Paul Laurence Dunbar, dated January 23, 1898, Dunbar-Nelson wrote about a visit to a student's home, with a German mother and "shiftless, dirty Negro" father who drank and beat his wife and children. Hull notes that this scene appears in one of the 'Steenth Street stories, without the reference to the father's race (Introduction, xl), but the brutal Italian husband and his German wife in "Tony's Wife" may also be a narrativization of this real-life experience.

15. In reprinting "Titee" in her second published collection, Dunbar-Nelson revised the ending so that Titee does not die. It would be interesting to know whether this change was instigated by an editor or publisher.

16. Dunbar-Nelson does give a non-ironic cast to this "dangerous theorizing" when she describes the labor union headquarters: "Behind its doors, swinging as easily between the street and the liquor-fumed halls as the soul swings between right and wrong, the disturbed minds of the working-men become clouded, heated, and wrothily ready for deeds of violence" (60-1). Recall the race riots in New Orleans between Irish union laborers and non-union African American dock workers and also note that labor unions practiced racial exclusion and separation from the 1890s well into the twentieth century, and Dunbar-Nelson's condemnation of labor union violence can be understood in the particular context of race relations. For more information on racial practices among New Orleans' labor unions see Woodward 361-66.

17. Zora Neale Hurston uses the terms "hoodoo," "conjure," and "folk magic" interchangeably in *Mules and Men* to describe various African- or Caribbean-inspired rituals and practices (193-256), while she claims that "voodoo" is the term "pronounced by whites" to describe the same (193). Lyle Saxon gives some history of St. Roch's Chapel (which Dunbar-Nelson spells St. Rocque's) in the Campo Santo, or Holy Field, cemetery (289-90). Erected in 1871 by Father Thevis, in gratitude that all of his parishioners survived the epidemic of 1866-67, St. Roch's Chapel is very small (seating only 24), with a high ceiling and walls made of tombs. Botht the chapel and the cemetery are associated with mixed hoodoo and Catholic practices.

Works Cited

Ancelet, Barry Jean, Jay D. Edwards, and Glen Pitre. *Cajun Country.* Folklife in the South Series. Gen. ed. Lynwood Montell. Jackson: UP of Mississippi, 1991.

Bryan, Violet Harrington. *The Myth of New Orleans in Literature: Dialogues of Race and Gender.* Knoxville: The U of Tennessee P, 1993.

Domínguez, Virginia R. *White by Definition: Social Classification in Creole Louisiana.* New Brunswick: Rutgers UP, 1986.

Donovan, Josephine. "Breaking the Sentence: Local-Color Literature and Subjugated Knowledges." *The (Other) American Traditions: Nineteenth-Century Women Writers.* Ed. Joyce W. Warren. New Brunswick: Rutgers UP, 1993. 226-43.

Dunbar-Nelson, Alice. "People of Color in Louisiana, Parts I and II." 1916, 1917. Rpt. in *An Alice Dunbar-Nelson Reader.* Ed. R. Ora Williams. Washington, D.C.: UP of America, 1979. 138-76.

———. *The Works of Alice Dunbar-Nelson.* Vol. 1-3. Ed. Gloria T. Hull. New York: Oxford UP, 1988.

Gayarré, Charles. "The Creoles of History and the Creoles of Romance: A Lecture Delivered in the Hall of the Tulane University, New Orleans by Hon. Charles Gayarré on the 25th of April, 1885." New Orleans, C. E. Hopkins Publisher, 1885.

Hirsch, Arnold and Joseph Logsdon, eds. Introduction to Part 3. *Creole New Orleans: Race and Americanization.* Baton Rouge: Louisiana State UP, 1992. 189-200.

Hull, Gloria T. *Color, Sex, and Poetry: Three Women Writers of the Harlem Renaissance.* Bloomington: Indiana UP, 1987.

———. Introduction. *The Works of Alice Dunbar-Nelson.* Vol. 1-3. Ed. Hull. New York: Oxford UP, 1988. xxix-liv.

Hurston, Zora Neale. *Mules and Men.* Bloomington: Indiana UP, 1935.

King, Grace. *New Orleans: The Place and the People.* New York: MacMillan, 1907.

Saxon, Lyle. *Fabulous New Orleans.* New York: D. Appleton-Century, 1935.

Sollors, Werner. *Beyond Ethnicity: Consent and Descent in American Culture.* New York: Oxford UP, 1986.

Spencer, Benjamin T. "Regionalism in American Literature." *Regionalism in America.* Ed. Merrill Jensen. Madison: U of Wisconsin P, 1952. 219-60.

Tallant, Robert. *Voodoo in New Orleans.* New York: MacMillan, 1946.

Tinker, Edward Larocque. *Creole City: Its Past and Its People.* New York: Longmans, Green, 1953.

Tregle, Joseph G., Jr. "Creoles and Americans." *Creole New Orleans: Race and Americanization.* Eds. Arnold Hirsch and Joseph Logsdon. Baton Rouge: Louisiana State UP, 1992. 131-85.

Woodward, C. Vann. *Origins of the New South: 1877-1913.* Baton Rouge: Louisiana State UP, 1951.

Ziff, Larzer. *The American 1890s: Life and Times of a Lost Generation.* New York: Viking, 1966.

FURTHER READING

Bibliographies

Lutes, Jean Marie. "Alice Dunbar-Nelson." In *Nineteenth-Century American Woman Writers: A Bio-Bibliographical Critical Sourcebook,* edited by Emmanuel S. Nelson, pp. 111-17. Westport, Conn.: Greenwood Press, 1997.

Provides a brief biography in addition to a bibliography of sources on Dunbar-Nelson.

Single, Lori Leathers. "Alice Dunbar-Nelson." In *African American Authors, 1745-1945: A Bio-Bibliographical Critical Sourcebook,* edited by Emmanuel S. Nelson, pp. 139-46. Westport, Conn.: Greenwood Press, 2000.

Cites reviews, scholarship, and other documents relating to Dunbar-Nelson's life and works.

Williams, Ora. "Works by and about Alice Ruth (Moore) Dunbar-Nelson: A Bibliography." *College Language Association Journal* 19 (1976): 322-26.

Lists the original publications in which Dunbar-Nelson's works appeared, along with a short list of secondary sources.

Biographies

Alexander, Eleanor. *Lyrics of Sunshine and Shadow: The Tragic Courtship and Marriage of Paul Laurence Dunbar and Alice Ruth Moore, A History of Love and Violence Among the African American Elite.* New York: New York University Press, 2001, 241 p.

Considers the Dunbars' relationship as a reflection of the culture in which they lived; discusses the marginalized status of women and homosexuality.

Ijeoma, Charmaine N. "Alice Dunbar-Nelson: A Biography." *Collections* 10 (2000): 25-54.

Draws from recently discovered documents that illuminate Dunbar-Nelson's life.

Criticism

Bauer, Margaret D. "When a Convent Seems the Only Viable Choice: Questionable Callings in Stories by Alice Dunbar-Nelson, Alice Walker, and Louise Erdrich." In *Critical Essays on Alice Walker,* edited by Ikenna Dieke, pp. 45-54. Westport, Conn.: Greenwood Press, 1999.

Compares Dunbar-Nelson's "Sister Josepha" to other stories about the self-fulfillment of women of color.

Bryan, Violet Harrington. "Creating and Re-Creating the Myth of New Orleans: Grace King and Alice Dunbar-Nelson." *Publications of the Mississippi Philological Association* (1987): 185-96.

Considers Dunbar-Nelson as both a regional and a feminist author.

———. "Race and Gender in the Early Works of Alice Dunbar-Nelson." In *Louisiana Women Writers: New Essays and a Comprehensive Bibliography,* edited by Dorothy H. Brown and Barbara C. Ewell, pp. 122-38. Baton Rouge: Louisiana State University Press, 1992.

Surveys the stories from Violets *and* The Goodness of St. Rocque *with an emphasis on the author's approach to issues of race and gender.*

Diggs, Marylynne. "Surveying the Intersection: Pathology, Secrecy, and the Discourses of Racial and Sexual Identity." In *Critical Essays: Gay and Lesbian Writers of Color,* edited by Emmanuel S. Nelson, pp. 1-19. New York: Haworth, 1993.

Looks at the treatment of homosexuality and race in Frances Ellen Harper's Iola Leroy *in comparison to Dunbar-Nelson's story "The Stones of the Village."*

Hull, Gloria T. "Researching Alice Dunbar-Nelson: A Personal and Literary Perspective." *Feminist Studies* 6, no. 2 (1980): 314-20.

Recounts her experience reviewing and preparing Dunbar-Nelson's unpublished documents for publication and discusses the significance of Dunbar-Nelson's life and works.

———. "'Two-Facing Life': The Duality of Alice Dunbar-Nelson." *Collections* 4 (1989): 19-35.

Reviews Dunbar-Nelson's treatment of race, drawing from both her fiction and nonfiction works.

Ijeoma, Charmaine N. "Alice Dunbar-Nelson: A Regional Approach." In *Teaching Women's Literature from a Regional Perspective,* edited by Leonore Hoffman and Deborah Rosenfelt, pp. 64-68. New York: Modern Language Association, 1982.

Examines Dunbar-Nelson's works as an example of regional literature.

———. *Color, Sex, and Poetry: Three Women Writers of the Harlem Renaissance*. Bloomington: Indiana University Press, 1987, 240 p.

Discusses Dunbar-Nelson as one of the major women poets of the movement, along with Angelina Weld Grimké and Georgia Douglas Johnson.

Johnson, Pamela. "Caressed by the Word: The Lives and Love of Paul Laurence Dunbar and Alice Dunbar-Nelson." *Black Issues Book Review* 4, no. 2 (2002): 71-74.

Tribute to the authors that focuses on Dunbar-Nelson's early career.

Tylee, Claire M. "Womanist Propaganda, African-American Great War Experience, and Cultural Strategies of the Harlem Renaissance: Plays by Alice Dunbar-Nelson and Mary P. Burill." *Women's Studies International Forum* 20, no. 1 (1997): 153-64.

Argues that their plays provided these authors with a vehicle for expressing political ideas not usually possible for Black women.

Whitlow, Roger. "Alice Dunbar-Nelson: New Orleans Writer." In *Regionalism and the Female Imagination: A Collection of Essays,* edited by Emily Toth, pp. 109-25. New York: Human Sciences, 1985.

Explores the themes of love, heroism, and feminism in the early stories of Dunbar-Nelson set in New Orleans.

OTHER SOURCES FROM GALE:

Additional coverage of Dunbar-Nelson's life and career is contained in the following sources published by the Gale Group: *Black Writers,* Eds. 1, 3; *Contemporary Authors,* Vol. 124; *Contemporary Authors-Brief Entry,* Vol. 122; *Contemporary Authors New Revision Series,* Vol. 82; *Dictionary of Literary Biography,* Vol. 50; *Feminist Writers; Major 20th-Century Writers,* Ed. 1.

JESSIE REDMON FAUSET

(1882 - 1961)

American editor, novelist, poet, and essayist.

Langston Hughes called Jessie Fauset one of "three people who midwifed the so-called New Negro Literature into being." As the literary editor of the NAACP magazine the *Crisis,* Fauset nurtured and launched the careers of several names now much better known than hers. She also edited and wrote most of the material for the *Brownie's Book,* a groundbreaking magazine for Black children overseen by her mentor, W. E. B. Du Bois. Fauset was also one of the most prolific women novelists of the Harlem Renaissance, penning four novels of Black middle-class life, and it is for her novels that she is most remembered by modern scholars.

BIOGRAPHICAL INFORMATION

Fauset was the daughter of an African Methodist Episcopal minister, Redmon Fauset, and his wife, Annie Seamon Fauset, who died when Jessie was still a child. She was born April 27, 1882, in Camden County, New Jersey, part of suburban Philadelphia. The Fausets were a large family: after Annie's death, Redmon Fauset married a widow with three children, then had three more children in the marriage. The size of the family kept them fairly poor, despite their father's middle-class profession.

Fauset attended high school in Philadelphia, where she was likely the only Black student. After graduating with honors, she applied to nearby Bryn Mawr College, which had never accepted a Black student. In order to avoid the controversy of either rejecting or accepting her, the school supported her acceptance at Cornell University, in upstate New York. She graduated from Cornell in 1905, possibly the first Black woman Phi Beta Kappa. According to some sources she also studied at the Sorbonne in Paris. After graduation, Fauset taught high school in Baltimore and Washington, D.C., then enrolled at the University of Pennsylvania to earn her master's degree.

She began contributing writings to the *Crisis* in 1912. In 1919, she moved to New York and began working with W. E. B. Du Bois as the literary editor of the *Crisis*; in 1920 they started *Brownie's Book,* which ran for only one year. Fauset was an editor at *Crisis* from 1919 to 1926, a short but crucial period. Through her reviews, her editorial critiques, and her choice of poetry, fiction, and essays for the magazine, Fauset introduced and guided the writing of Jean Toomer, Countee Cullen, Langston Hughes, Claude McKay, and others. She became interested in the pan-African movement, contributing articles on the subject to *Crisis,* and representing the NAACP at the Second Pan-African Congress in 1921. She published her first novel, *There Is Confusion,* in 1924, and her last, *Comedy, American Style,* in 1933, after which she wrote little.

The Depression changed the landscape of the Black community in Harlem and elsewhere, and Fauset, then in her fifties, was no longer in the forefront of the New Negro movement. She had married Herbert Harris in 1929, eventually moving with him to New Jersey, where she lived until 1958. She struggled to find work after leaving the *Crisis*: her race prevented her from getting employment in white publishing houses, even after she volunteered to work from home, nor could she find a place as a social secretary. For a time she returned to teaching high school. After the death of her husband, she moved back to Philadelphia to live with her family. She died there, from heart disease, on April 20, 1961.

MAJOR WORKS

Though perhaps her most important work, in the context of the Harlem Renaissance, was as an editor, Fauset's four novels are the chief works upon which her reputation is based. Her novels focus on young women and their middle-class families; often the women are light-skinned Blacks who struggle with the dilemma of "passing" for white. Her first novel, *There Is Confusion,* tells the story of Joanna Marshall, who comes from a relatively wealthy family but struggles with the realization that her race is an obstacle to achieving her dream of being a dancer. It is also a love story, as Joanna falls for the medical student Peter Bye. Among her novels, *There Is Confusion* is the most like a straightforward romance, with the lovers finally overcoming their obstacles and living happily every after. Later novels are more complex. *Plum Bun* (1928), one of Fauset's most-studied novels, also features a young woman who dreams of becoming an artist, but the heroine, Angela Murray, decides to achieve her goals by "passing," and rejecting her family and friends. Angela eventually reveals her Black identity and finds love with a light-skinned Black man, but not before her attempts to enjoy the fruits of "whiteness" demonstrate the impossibility of finding happiness as a Black woman. Her third novel, *The Chinaberry Tree* (1931), also follows a romance pattern, but delves still more deeply into the issue of "bad blood," a condition of being of mixed race, but also of being poor or illegitimate. *The Chinaberry Tree* draws from Greek tragedy, a reflection of Fauset's love of the theater, in its portrayal of an incestuous romance that nearly leads to an abominable marriage. *Comedy, American Style* is Fauset's final novel, and the darkest in tone. The love story of Christopher Cary and Phebe Grant is overshadowed by the cruelty and self-loathing of the central character, Olivia Cary, Christopher's mother. Olivia prefers to pass for white and encourages her first two children to do so as well. Her third child, Oliver, is too dark to pass, however. Her abusive behavior finally drives him to suicide. Her daughter, who marries a Frenchman and tries to live "white" in Toulouse, lives in oppressive misery. Olivia finally abandons her family to live miserably, but "white," in Paris, leaving Chris, Phebe, and old Mr. Cary to live in relative happiness, muted by prejudice, as Blacks.

CRITICAL RECEPTION

When first published, Fauset's novels were generally well received. Though some critics felt that Fauset's perspective and characters were not "Negro" enough, many in the New Negro movement praised Fauset for depicting Blacks in a positive light, as educated, cultured, and even modestly economically successful. In 1934, William Stanley Braithwaite wrote in *Opportunity* that Fauset was "the potential Jane Austen of Negro Literature," a comment that encapsulated both the praise and the criticisms. Scholarship on Fauset has followed the same pattern ever since. One of the earliest assessments of Fauset as a Black novelist came from Robert Bone, in *The Negro Novel in America* (1958), who called Fauset conservative and "Old Guard." This has been a consistent thread in Fauset scholarship, described by Vashti Crutcher Lewis as "mulatto hegemony." Critics who have considered Fauset's work more broadly, particularly her work with *Crisis,* found fault with these criticisms. In an early article on Fauset and her role as "literary midwife" of the Harlem Renaissance, Abby Arthur Johnson observed that Fauset was in fact a great champion of Blackness, suggesting that while Fauset was no radical, she did offer trenchant critiques of color-consciousness and the status of Blacks in America. Fauset was eventually discovered by feminist scholars, who maintained that important facets of Fauset's politics were overlooked because they related to women. A significant study in this vein is Carolyn Wedin Sylvander's *Jessie Redmon Fauset, Black American Writer* (1981), as well as Deborah McDowell's essay "The Neglected Dimension of Jessie Redmon Fauset" (1985). Such scholarship revitalized the study of Fauset's work, and several scholars between 1990 and 2002 considered her among the first Black women intellectuals. Both Carol J. Batker and Carol Allen argue that Fauset's depiction of women and the domestic sphere presents a significant critique of American values. Such scholars as Kathleen Pfeiffer have also re-evaluated the theme of "passing" in Fauset's fiction, suggesting that in linking "passing" to the motif of the marketplace, Fauset offers a sharper critique of color-consciousness in America than earlier critics realized.

PRINCIPAL WORKS

There Is Confusion (novel) 1924

Plum Bun (novel) 1928

The Chinaberry Tree: A Novel of American Life (novel) 1931

Comedy, American Style (novel) 1933

PRIMARY SOURCES

JESSIE R. FAUSET (ESSAY DATE 1922)

SOURCE: Fauset, Jessie R. "Some Notes on Color." *The World Tomorrow* (March 1922): 76-77.

Fauset discusses the nature of color in art, focusing on how the simple fact of being Black affects the art and literature of African Americans.

A distinguished novelist said to me not long ago: "I think you colored people make a great mistake in dragging the race problem into your books and novels. It isn't art."

"But good heavens," I told him, "it's life, it's colored life. Being colored is being a problem."

That attitude and the sort of attitude instanced by a journalist the other day who thought colored people ought to be willing to permit the term "nigger" because it carries with it so much picturesqueness defines pretty well, I think, our position in the eyes of the white world. Either we are inartistic or we are picturesque and always the inference is implied that we live objectively with one eye on the attitude of the white world as though it were the audience and we the players whose hope and design is to please.

Of course we do not think about the white world, we have to. But not at all in the sense in which that white world thinks it. For the curious thing about white people is that they expect us to judge them by their statute-books and not by their actions. But we colored people have learned better, so much so that when we prepare for a journey, when we enter on a new undertaking, when we decide on where to go to school, if we want to shop, to move, to go to the theatre, to eat (outside of our own houses) we think quite consciously, "If we can pull it through without some white person interfering."

I have hesitated more than once about writing this article because my life has been spent in the localities which are considered favorable to colored people and in the class which least meets the grossest forms of prejudice. And yet—I do not say I would if I could—but I must say I cannot if I will forget the fact of color in almost everything I do or say in the sense in which I forget the shape of my face or the size of my hands and feet.

Being colored in America at any rate means: Facing the ordinary difficulties of life, getting education, work, in fine getting a living plus fighting everyday against some inhibition of natural liberties.

Let me see if I can give you some ideas. I am a colored woman, neither white nor black, neither pretty nor ugly, neither specially graced nor at all deformed. I am fairly well educated, of fair manners and deportment. In brief, the average American done over in brown. In the morning I go to work by means of the subway, which is crowded. Presently somebody gets up. The man standing in front of the vacant place looks around meaning to point it out to a women. I am the nearest one, "But oh," says his glance, "you're colored. I'm not expected to give it to you." And down he plumps. According to my reflexes that morning, I think to myself "hypocrite" or "pig." And make a conscious effort to shake the unpleasantness of it off, for I don't want my day spoiled.

At noon I go for lunch. But I always go to the same place because I an not sure of my reception in other places. If I go to another place I must fight it through. But usually I am hungry. I want food, not a lawsuit. And, too, how long am I to wait before I am sure of the slight? Shall I march up to the proprietor and say "Do you serve colored people?" or shall I sit and drum on the table for 15 or 20 minutes, feel my anger rising, prepare to explode only to have the attendant come at that moment and nonchalantly arrange the table? I eat but I go out still not knowing whether the delay was intentional or not. The white patron would be annoyed at the delay. I am, too, but ought I to be annoyed at something in addition to that? I can't tell. The uncertainty beclouds my afternoon.

An acquaintance—a white woman—phones me that she can accept a long-standing invitation of mine for luncheon. We meet and I suggest my old standby. "Let's go somewhere else," she urges. "I don't like that place."

Ruefully but frankly I stammer, "Well you see—I'm not quite sure—that is—"

"Oh, yes," she rejoins in quick pity. "I forgot that. I'm so sorry."

But I hate to be pitied even so sincerely. I hate to have this position thrust upon me.

All of us are passionately interested in the education of our children, our younger brothers and sisters. And just as deliberately, as earnestly as white people discuss tuition, relative ability of professors, expenses, etc., so we in addition discuss the question of prejudice. "Of course he'll meet someone. But would they let it interfere with his deserts? I don't know. I guess I'd better send him to A. instead of B. They don't cater as much to the South as at B."

I think the thing that irks us most is the teasing uncertainty of it all. Did the man at the box-office give us the seat behind the post on purpose? Is the shop-girl impudent or merely nervous? Had the position really been filled before we applied for it? What actuates the teacher who tells Alice—oh, so kindly—that the college preparatory course is really very difficult. Even remarkably clever pupils have been known to fail. Now if she were Alice—

Other things cut deeper, undermine the very roots of our belief in mankind. In school we sing "America," we learn the Declaration of Independence, we read and even memorize some of the passages in the Constitution. Chivalry, kindness, consideration are the ideals held up before us—

Honor and faith and good intent,
But it wasn't at all what the lady meant.

the lady in this case being the white world. The good things of life, the true, the beautiful, the just, these are not meant for us.

So much is this difference impressed on us, "this for you but that quite other thing for me," that finally we come to take all expressions of a white man's justice with cynical disbelief, our standard of measure being a provident "How does he stand on the color question?"

I am constantly amazed as I grow older at the network of misunderstanding—to speak mildly—at the misrepresentation of things as they really are which is so persistently cast around us. Sometimes it is by implication, sometimes by open statement. Thus we grow up thinking that they are no colored heroes. The foreign student does hear of Garibaldi, of Cromwell, of Napoleon, of Marco Bozzaris. But neither he nor we hear of Crispus Attucks. There are no pictures of colored fairies in the story-books or even of colored boys and girls. "Sweetness and light" are of the white world.

Native Americans are "savages" owing their little knowledge of civilization to the kindly European traveler who is represented as half philanthropist, half savant. How much do we learn of indigenous African art, culture, morals? We are told of the horrors of polygamy without a word of the accompanying fact that prostitution in Africa was comparatively unknown—until the whites introduced it.

We are given the impression that we are the last in the scale of all races, that even other dark peoples will have none of us. I shall never forget how astonished I was to see in London at the second Pan-African Congress the very real willingness of Hindu leaders to cast in their lot with ours.

More serious still, we are constantly being confronted with a choice between expediency and intellectual dishonesty, intangible, indefinable and yet sometimes I think the greatest danger of all. If persisted in it is bound to touch the very core of our racial naturalness. And that is the tendency of the white world to judge us always at our worst and our own realization of that fact. The result is a stilled art and a lack of frank expression on our part. We find *The Emperor Jones* wonderful, but why couldn't O'Neill have portrayed a colored gentleman? We wish he had. *Batouala* [a prize-winning novel by the African, Rene Maran] is a marvellous piece of artistry, but we are half glad it is written in French so that the average white American won't insist that here is the true African prototype.

Some one will say: "These are trifles." What have I to complain of as compared with the condition of Negroes in South Africa, in Georgia, in the Portuguese possessions? I do not have to fear lynching, or burning, or dispossession.

No, only the reflex of those things. Perhaps it is mere nervousness, perhaps it is something more justifiable. Often when I am sitting in a crowded assembly I think, "I wish I had taken a seat near the door. If there should be an accident, a fire, none of these men around here would help me." Place aux dames was not meant for colored women.

I have not been dispossessed, but I have had to leave Philadelphia—the city of my birth and preference, because I was educated to do high school work and it was impossible for a colored woman to get that kind of work in that town. So I, too, have assisted in the Negro Exodus which the student of Sociology considers in class-room and seminary.

And so the puzzling, tangling, nerve-wracking consciousness of color envelops and swathes us. Some of us, it smothers.

GENERAL COMMENTARY

ABBY ARTHUR JOHNSON (ESSAY DATE 1978)

SOURCE: Johnson, Abby Arthur. "Literary Midwife: Jessie Redmon Fauset and the Harlem Renaissance." *Phylon* 39, no. 2 (June 1978): 143-53.

In this essay, Johnson contrasts the middle-class world of Fauset's novels with the more radical literature she fostered through her work at Crisis, *suggesting that past evaluations of Fauset's politics have been inaccurate. Johnson suggests that in her fiction, Fauset struggles against stereotypes of urban Blacks, while in her nonfiction essays and her editorial work, she reveals support for nationalism and pan-Africanism.*

The career of Jessie R. Fauset (1885-1961) illustrates changing responses to the black middle class, as expressed by twentieth-century literary figures. Praised in the 1920s, she was essentially ignored in the 1930s and censured in the postwar years. Each generation of critics based its evaluation of Fauset primarily on her novels, all studies of the Negro middle class—***There Is Confusion*** (1932), ***Plum Bun*** (1929), ***The Chinaberry Tree*** (1931), and ***Comedy, American Style*** (1933). Most of the writers said nothing about her literary editorship of *Crisis,* from 1919 to 1926.

During the Harlem Renaissance, established black critics endorsed Fauset for the milieu recreated in her novels. All three major black periodicals heralded her initial book as a literary landmark. W. E. B. Du Bois and Alain Locke, in the February, 1924 issue of *Crisis,* agreed that the work would "mark an epoch." Locke elaborated, calling ***There Is Confusion*** "the novel that the Negro intelligentsia have been clamoring for." He thought educated readers wanted literature portraying "the race life higher up the social pyramid and further from the base-line of the peasant and the soil than is usually taken." Montgomery Gregory, Howard University professor and colleague of Locke, wrote much the same. In *Opportunity,* June, 1924, he congratulated Fauset for "interpreting the better elements of our life to those who know us only as domestic servants, 'uncles,' or criminals."[1]

George Schuyler applauded the novel in *Messenger,* also in 1924. "I started reading this book on a Sunday morning," he recalled, "and finished its 297 pages before I went to bed. I was never bored for an instant. Not once did I yawn." The novel revived his own past: "I was like a traveler returning to familiar scenes, nodding with satisfaction and approval at the recognition of familiar landmarks." Schuyler liked to read about successful blacks: "Here for the first time we are presented with a novel built around our own 'best' people who, after all is said, are the inspiration of the rising generation."[2]

Similar remarks introduced each of Fauset's novels, including the last one. ***Comedy: American Style*** appeared at the onset of a new period in Afro-American literature. As younger voices began to be heard, writers prominent in the 1920s defended their own earlier judgments and supported Fauset. In *Opportunity,* January, 1934, Locke commended her efforts, even though he saw weaknesses in her style: "Negro fiction would be infinitely poorer without the persevering and slowly maturing art of Miss Fauset, and her almost single-handed championship of upper and middle class Negro life as an important subject for fiction."[3]

Even as Locke wrote, the literary scene was changing considerably. The demands of those days, first with the Depression and then with the Second World War, drowned out the voice of Fauset and others. Some twenty years passed before critics turned again to her work. And when they did write of her, they showed that times had changed once more, and that other militant leaders were emerging. Robert Bone was not one of those leaders, but he did, in *The Negro Novel in America* (1958), discuss Fauset in a way that would influence later authors. He found her middle-class and old-fashioned and dismissed her with labels, calling her "Victorian," "Old Guard" and "Rear Guard." In the following years, readers remembered the labels but not, unfortunately, the complexity Bone sensed in Fauset. He found her "something of a paradox," largely because of her editorial work on *Crisis.* She had repeatedly, he noted, encouraged novels and poems by black radicals, such as Claude McKay. He did not explore this paradox, seemingly because Fauset fit sufficiently well into the "Old Guard."[4]

The reaction against the Negro middle class became more vocal in the 1960s, as Leroi Jones became a spokesman for young black artists and intellectuals. In an influential essay, "The Myth of a 'Negro Literature'" (1962), he claimed that writers identified with the black middle class had impeded the emergence of an American Negro literature. Wanting to be white, they had tried to express themselves as Anglo-Saxons and had failed to be either black or white. "In most cases," he asserted,

> the Negroes who found themselves in a position to pursue some art, especially the art of literature, have been members of the Negro middle class, a group that has always gone out of its way to cultivate *any* mediocrity, as long as that mediocrity was guaranteed to prove to America, and recently to the world at large, that they were not really who they were, i.e., Negroes.[5]

He thought black writers should celebrate the richness of their own traditions and experiences.

Jones never mentioned Fauset in his essay, but others applied his ideas to her. In recent years, the most specific of such discussion has appeared in an article written by Hiroko Sato and published in *The Harlem Renaissance Remembered* (1972), edited by Arna Bontemps. Sato, a student of Bontemps, essentially reaffirmed postwar estimates of Fauset. She criticized Fauset for her middle-class outlook, shaped by her early experiences among old Philadelphians and her education at Cornell, the University of Pennsylvania and at the Sorbonne. Quoting from Jones' essay, she claimed that Fauset "does not have anything to do with 'the investigation of the human soul'." Quoting from Bone's book, she concluded that "the only thing she could do as an artist was to produce 'uniformly sophomoric, trivial and dull' novels. . . ."[6] Like other of her contemporaries, Sato considered only part of Fauset's effort. She never studied her work as literary editor, and she failed to see her as an individual, viewing her instead as an extension of a class. Fauset makes more sense when examined as an editor as well as a novelist and when discussed in relation to her particular environment.

Fauset had a long association with *Crisis.* From 1912, she contributed reviews, essays, poems and short stories to the journal. She served as literary editor from November, 1919 until May, 1926. Within that period, during 1920 and 1921, she acted as literary editor of the *Brownie's Book,* a magazine edited by Du Bois and directed towards black children. While on the staff of *Crisis,* she helped establish a literary climate favorable to black writers of varying persuasions, even to those who would never have come to her for assistance. In her reviews, which appeared regularly in the magazine, she seemed more open than was Du Bois, who said that "all Art is propaganda and ever must be" and that "whatever art I have for writing has been used always for propaganda for gaining the right of black folk to love and enjoy."[7] Fauset repeatedly claimed that literature should not overtly serve special interests. She sometimes acted upon other premises, however, and advanced propagandistic work.

One of her review essays, done early in her editorship, indicates much about her critical understanding and her sense of the 1920s. **"New Literature on the Negro,"** a review of several books, followed a pattern Fauset would use frequently. It opened with a general statement on the role of Afro-Americans in contemporary matters:

> That the Negro has come into Literature to stay is evidenced by the increasing number of books issued each year in which the Negro, or his condition, forms the main discussion. It is impossible adequately to take up the great matters of the day—economics, social welfare, labor, the whole question of national readjustment of post-war times,—without including his shadowed but persistent figure.

The review continued by distinguishing between politics and literature. Fauset commended *The Sword of Nemesis,* by R. Archer Tracy, because it was in "the realm of pure romantic fiction." The novel gave her "relief," primarily because "nearly" all the other literature "on the part of colored Americans seeks to set forth propaganda."

Fauset considered the more significant pieces towards the end of her review. She concluded with *Darkwater,* by Du Bois. As she warmed to her topic, she became emotional, as often happened in her essays. In such a mood, she adopted a rhetoric which does not square with the latest estimates of her opinions. This woman who was supposedly pandering to white society praised Du Bois for his depiction of the "terrible, grasping, raging white world." This woman who reputedly turned her back on her black culture urged readers to find satisfaction in their own heritage:

> In this darker world . . . there is ignorance and poverty and misery, but at least there are not hands dripping with another people's blood, hearts filled with hypocrisy, homes gorgeously outfitted but reared over the graves of helpless slaves. And so though they dare not become complacent, these dark folk are suddenly content to be black.[8]

Such statements suggest the complexity of Fauset. As a critic, she wanted to use objective literary standards, to judge novels as works of art. As a Negro writer, she felt the need to evaluate books in their relationship to black culture.

In subsequent reviews, Fauset gave special recognition to those who appeared to convey the heritage of black Americans honestly and artistically. She found much value in *Harlem Shadows,* by Claude McKay: "He has dwelt in fiery, impassioned language on the sufferings of his race. Yet there is no touch of propaganda. This is the truest mark of genius." As an educated woman, she knew the importance of black scholarship. Among the studies she praised were *The History of the Negro Church,* by Carter Godwin Woodson, and the *Social History of the American Negro,* by Benjamin Brawley. The later particularly pleased her because "it presents American history as it must have appeared to black men." With many of her contemporaries, she recognized the importance of African history and culture to Afro-Americans. Natalie Curtis received her support for *Songs and Tales From the Dark Continent*: "Here then are evidences that a very real, backward reaching, finely developed civilization, one that is native and endemic, has been existing over a large part of Africa."[9]

While literary editor, Fauset also contributed informative essays to *Crisis.* She especially favored biographical sketches of blacks prominent in her day and in the past. Among others, she wrote about Jose Do Patrocinio, who fought for the "abolition of slavery in Brazil"; Robert Brown Elliott, who represented a South Carolina district in the forty-second and forty-third Congresses of the United States; and Henry Ossawa Tanner, prominent artist. She found Bert Williams an appealing subject because he, as a comedian, "symbolized that deep, ineluctable strain of melancholy, which no Negro in a mixed civilization ever lacks." She regretted the "eternal black make-up" Williams wore. "Why," she questioned, "should he and we obscure our talents forever under the bushel of prejudice, jealousy, stupidity—whatever it is that makes the white world say: 'No genuine colored artist; coons, clowns, end-men, clap-trap, but no undisguisedly beautiful presentation of Negro ability'."[10]

In an interview published in the *Southern Workman,* May, 1932, Fauset discussed biography. As she explained her theories, she talked about educating young blacks, not about impressing biased whites. "No part of Negro literature needs more building up than biography," she insisted. "It is urgent that ambitious Negro youth be able to read of the achievements of their race." She remembered the bewilderment of her own girlhood:

> When I was a child I used to puzzle my head ruefully over the fact that in school we studied the lives of only great white people. I took it that there simply have been no great Negroes, and I was amazed when, as I grew older, I found that there were. It is a pity that Negro children should be permitted to suffer from that delusion at all. There should be a sort of 'Plutarch's Lives' of the Negro race. Some day, perhaps, I shall get around to writing it.[11]

She never accomplished such a project, although her brother, Arthur Huff Fauset, did write *For Freedom,* a compendium on old and New Negroes.

In other of her essays, Fauset informed *Crisis* readers about important happenings in the black world. She sometimes suggested that an apocalypse was at hand, an ultimate struggle between black and white peoples. With such a feeling, she studied British colonialism. At the end of a detailed article on **"Nationalism and Egypt,"** she considered a dawning world: "Who doubts that Egypt is really speaking for the whole dark world? Thus is the scene being staged for the greatest and most lasting conflict of peoples."[12]

She became a fervent supporter of Pan-Africanism, representing Delta Sigma Theta Sorority at the second Pan-African Congress in 1921. At the meetings in Brussels, she spoke to the delegates about Negro women in America as a significant power in the struggle for emancipation. After all the speeches and meetings were over, she returned to *Crisis* and wrote her **"Impressions of the Second Pan-African Congress,"** which was published in the journal. As explained, she had gone to the meetings thinking that "the main thing, the great thing, was that Ethiopia's sons through delegates were stretching out their hands from all over the black and yearning world." At the conclusion of the London sessions, she had much hope: "We clasped hands with our newly found brethren and departed, feeling that it was good to be alive and most wonderful to be colored. Not one of us but envisaged in his heart the dawn of a day of new and perfect African brotherhood." Upon leaving Paris, she thought of the challenge ahead: "All the possibilities of all black men are needed to weld together the black men of the world against the day when black and white meet to do battle. God grant that when that day comes we shall be so powerful that the enemy will say, 'But behold! these men are our brothers'."[13] She ended her article with these resounding assertions.

Fauset had, admittedly, been caught up in the heat of the moment. As the months passed, her diction cooled. Never again would she write so passionately about African unity. She did not, though, forget the camaraderie she had felt with other Negroes. In succeeding essays, she explored ground common to all American blacks. She reported on a YWCA conference at Talladega College in 1923 but spoke more movingly about the institution than the sessions. Talledega seemed a promised land to this woman educated at Cornell: "Imagine leaving the hot Jim-Crow Car which brings one from Anniston to spin along the rust-red roads of Talladega and suddenly to stop short before a stretch—an 880 acre stretch—of green campus and trees and fields, dotted with beautiful and picturesque buildings, an ivy covered chapel, residence halls, a Carnegie Library, lecture halls, and know that all this peace and quiet and beauty are yours!" Most memorable was Swayne Hall, "*built by slaves for white boys* in 1852." She made a symbol of that building: "What I like most to remember . . . was that troop of merry, efficient, striking girls filing in and out of Swayne Hall, built over a half century ago by slaves for the children of—free men."[14]

Other buildings occupied permanent places in her memory. One article, **"My House and a Glimpse of My Life Therein,"** showed readers a picture of Fauset's imaginary home, of life as she would have it. Searching for pleasant thoughts, Fauset sometimes occupied herself with dreams, using them as motifs in her literature. In most of her compositions, though, she varied the mood and returned to a consideration of the environment she knew, as a Negro in America. She best captured the bond she sensed with all Afro-Americans in a piece called **"Nostalgia."** American Negroes suffered, she wrote, from "spiritual nostalgia," which "arises from the lack of things of the spirit, a difference in ideals." They had given to the country and were of the land but had not been accorded full citizenship. For such people, the ideals of the American Constitution were "not here—just beyond, always beyond." "The black American is something entirely new under the sun," concluded Fauset. "Shall he ever realize the land where he would be?"[15]

Fauset did not limit her *Crisis* publications to essays. Before and during her term as literary editor, she contributed poems and short stories as well, extending many of the stories over several installments. In such pieces, she experimented with the themes and characters she would later use in her novels. She dealt with "passing" in the two parts of **"Emmy"** and the three sections of **"The Sleeper Wakes."** In the latter, Amy, with cheeks of "pearl and pink," establishes herself as Caucasian and marries a wealthy white man much her senior. When she later reveals her heritage, she loses her husband and gains her identity. "She wanted to be colored," she discovered.[16] With the two installments of **"Double Trouble,"** Fauset penned a first draft of ***The Chinaberry Tree.*** She developed the plot and characters, changing only a few of the names in the novel—Malory Fordham becomes Malory Forten and Angelique appears as Melissa. With the addition of the chinaberry tree, as unifying symbol, the novel became a more sophisticated rendition of **"Double Trouble."**

In all the stories, she portrayed black professionals, as she would in her novels. Her main characters were industrious physicians, teachers, engineers and business men and women. With the fiction published in *Crisis* and with the novels which followed, Fauset seemed preoccupied with matters far different from the concerns of her essays. She wrote of people who lived on the borderline of two races and who flirted with the idea of passing. She pictured structured and elite black communities, modeled after old Philadelphia. At times, she showed distinctions among Negro socialites living in Philadelphia, Washington and Baltimore. With such interests, she wrote to a small segment of the black population. Her essays, however, appealed to a wider audience. She discussed issues and events germane to the black community, such as Pan-Africanism. She applauded novels and poems written about ghetto life and Afro-Americans who were not formally educated. She used a rhetoric which modulated from enthusiasm to anger and which attracted the more militant young Negroes.

Robert Bone thought Fauset a "paradox" because he could not see a connecting link between her work as editor and as novelist. Fauset's work does, nevertheless, mesh into a comprehensible unit. As an educated woman, open to many interests, she could appreciate the changes and new expressions in the Negro community. She tried, while on the staff of *Crisis,* to encourage diversified interests and to attract large numbers of readers. When composing fiction, however, she could only write from herself, of the life she knew best. And that life merits brief examination, since it helps explain her literary record.

Fauset identified herself as the daughter of a Presbyterian minister. Raised in a parsonage in old Philadelphia, she learned to be a lady, in the conventional sense. As such, she naturally felt certain restraints. She could never have written in the vernacular about Harlem night clubs. Nor could she have frequented such establishments. As might be expected, her social diversions raised few eyebrows. She suggested her extracurriculars in an autobiographical statement included in *Caroling Dusk,* edited by Countee Cullen: "Like the French I am fond of dancing, and adore cards and the theatre probably because I am a minister's daughter."[17]

The atmosphere of the parsonage remained with her. She contributed an essay on **"Sunday Afternoon"** to *Crisis,* during the tenure of her editorship. "Always Sunday afternoon has made me sad," she recalled. "But it is a sweet sadness. It must have been connected at first, I think, with the inhibitions which Sunday in a very conservative, not to say very religious household, placed upon the small child." In varied situations, she would recall lines from favorite hymns. While in a *pension* in Paris, she examined the "shabby" dining room and remembered "a line from a melancholy hymn of my Presbyterian childhood . . . 'Change and decay in all around I see.'"[18]

Writing from her memories, Fauset recreated Sunday afternoons and evenings in her stories and novels. Gwendolyn Bennett, of *Opportunity,* commended such portrayals in ***Plum Bun***: "I found particular pleasure in her apt, yet subdued, picture of Sunday afternoon in a middle-class Negro home." Fauset described quiet Sundays in most of her fiction. She knew another side to religious life, however. She understood a type of desperate humor evolving from Afro-Americans' dependence upon their religious institutions. In "Mary Elizabeth," a story included in *Crisis,* the maid mentions a friend of her sister—"gal she was riz up with. That gal married well, too, lemme tell you; her husband's a Sunday School sup'rintender."[19]

Fauset wrote about people positioned between two races because she often found herself in that situation. With many of her characters, she knew what it was like to be black in an environment primarily white. As a young girl, she went to school with white children, as Benjamin Brawley noted in *The Negro Genius*: "In school she was for several terms the only student in her class identified with the Negro, and this fact may partly account for the self-conscious air in her work."[20] She was the first Negro woman to attend Cornell University and to win Phi Beta Kappa honors. Undoubtedly, she felt proud of her accomplishments. She had no illusions, though, about the broader white society and its understanding of her. Just before leaving *Crisis,* she sent a letter to Arthur Spingarn, asking for his assistance in locating another position. She wanted to be a publisher's reader but comprehended the difficulty in finding such employment: "In the case of publisher's reader, if the question of color should come up I could of course work at home."[21]

She knew persons who had passed and considered such action wrong, as emphasized over and again in her novels and stories. She realized where her loyalty lay, and she understood the beauty of color. Sato has claimed that Fauset could not make a "positive affirmation" of blackness.[22] Fauset did in fact make many such affirmations in her essays and fiction. Joanna Marshall, of ***There Is Confusion,*** first recognizes Peter Bye for his "dark arresting beauty which first drew Joanna's glance to him across the other white and pink faces in the crowded schoolroom." Phebe Grant, in ***Comedy: American Style,*** loves the blackness of Nicholas Campbell: "His dark face with that Apollo-like look, which the sculptured waviness of his hair bestowed upon him, was finely silhouetted against the moonlight with the softness of the black night for an immediate background."[23]

Fauset had always wanted to recreate life from her vantage point in novels. The catalyst for her career came in *Birthright* (1922), a supposedly well-intentioned novel about Negro life written by T. S. Stribling. In a *Crisis* review, Fauset criticized the white author, saying "he does not care how many fallacies he introduces."[24] And the fallacies did abound. Stribling used the old formulas, alluding repeatedly to "the peculiar, penetrating odor of dark, sweating skins" and the "indolence inherent" in "negro blood." He thought mulattoes in a strange situation, ambitious and lazy by turns, dependent upon the predominance of either their white or their black blood. When they succeeded—got an education or a good job—the explanation was easy, to Stribling: "It was the Caucasian in them . . ."[25]

It was pride in her own Negro heritage that caused Fauset to protest over *Birthright* once again. In a 1924 book review, she criticized whites who tried to write about blacks. A novel like Stribling's made her wonder "whether or not white people will ever be able to write evenly on this racial situation in America." She saw Negro life as the province of Negro artists: "the portrayal of black people calls increasingly for black writers."[26] Fauset issued her first novel, ***There Is Confusion,*** shortly thereafter. In the 1932 interview, she recalled the emotions that had led to that novel. "Here is an audience waiting to hear the truth about us," she remembered feeling. "Let us who are better qualified to present that truth than any white writer, try to do so." She mentioned others who had experienced a similar response:

FROM THE AUTHOR

THERE IS CONFUSION

The complex of color. . . . every colored man feels it sooner or later. It gets in the way of his dreams, of his education, of his marriage, of the rearing of his children. The time comes when he thinks, "I might just as well fall back; there's no use pushing on. A colored man just can't make any headway in this awful country." Of course, it's a fallacy. And if a fellow sticks it out he finally gets past it, but not before it has worked considerable confusion in his life. To have the ordinary job of living is bad enough, but to add to it all the thousand and one difficulties which follow simply in the train of being colored—well, all I've got to say, Sylvia, is we're some wonderful people to live through it all and keep our sanity.

SOURCE: Jessie Redmon Fauset, excerpt from *There is Confusion,* Boni & Liveright, 1924.

"A number of us started writing at that time. Nella Larson and Walter White, for instance, were affected just as I was."

It took courage to write in the manner of Fauset. In her fiction, she was countering established ideas about Afro-Americans and about the nature of Afro-American literature. She was expending her energies on books which might never receive a fair hearing. As explained in 1932, the first publisher to see ***There Is Confusion*** exclaimed—"White readers just don't expect Negroes to be like this"—and rejected the manuscript. Publishers did not improve significantly as the decade went on. In considering ***The Chinaberry Tree,*** they repeated the same objection. Before the novel could be accepted, Zona Gale had to append a preface explaining the nature of her friend's art and affirming the existence of cultured blacks.[27]

Fauset commented on the bias of such readers when answering the seven questions Du Bois asked of many artists in the 1920s. Among the queries was: "Can publishers be criticized for refusing to handle novels that portray Negroes of education and accomplishment, on the ground that these characters are no different from white folk and therefore not interesting?" With no hesitation Fauset replied: "I should think so. And what is more, it seems to me that white people should be the first to voice this criticism. Aren't *they* supposed to be interesting?" She elaborated in another answer: "I blame the publisher for not being a 'better sport'. Most of them seem to have an *idee fixe.* They, even more than the public, I do believe, persist in considering only certain types of Negroes interesting and if an author presents a variant they fear that the public either won't believe in it or won't 'stand for it'."[28]

As literary editor of *Crisis* and as a novelist, Fauset performed a valuable service in the Negro Renaissance. She was appreciated for such by her contemporaries, and not only those often believed conservative in matters of art. In *A Long Way From Home,* Claude McKay noted that "all the radicals liked her, although in her social viewpoint she was away over on the other side of the fence." He and others respected her freedom of expression: "Miss Fauset has written many novels about the people in her circle. Some white and some black critics consider these people not interesting enough to write about. I think all people are interesting to write about."[29]

Fauset was eased from the literary scene in the 1930s, along with many of her associates. The Depression changed the shape of the world she knew, as did the large migration of Southern blacks to Northern cities and the resultant instability in black communities. Newer Negroes appeared calling for a newer art. In "Blueprint For Negro Writing," published in *New Challenge,* Richard Wright deplored the chasm he saw between the Negro intelligentsia and the "Negro masses." "The Negro writer who seeks to function within his race as a purposeful agent has a serious responsibility," he admonished. "In order to do justice to his subject matter, in order to depict Negro life in all of its manifold and intricate relationships, a deep, informed, and complex consciousness is necessary; a consciousness which draws for its strength upon the fluid lore of a great people, and moulds this lore with the concepts that move and direct the forces of history today."[30]

The times had changed and Fauset had neither the energy nor the will to change with them. She was forty-eight years old when her last novel was published, in 1933, and she felt an identity with a black community which was no longer fashionable. For some twenty years, she had worked diligently at her art. In the years to follow, she would write no more novels, nor would she edit any other magazines. Her retirement became just one more sign that the Harlem Renaissance, with all its diversity, was indeed over.

One can feel mixed emotions over the passing of a period and the end of a career. In the case of Jessie Fauset, a certain pathos emerges, a sympathy for an idealistic woman who was bewildered and discouraged by the turbulence and demands of a new day. On the other hand, one can feel respect and admiration for the literary editor and novelist who helped shape black literature of the 1920s. Langston Hughes recognized the importance of Fauset. In his autobiography, *The Big Sea,* he advanced her as a significant figure in the renaissance: "Jessie Fauset at the *Crisis,* Charles Johnson at *Opportunity,* and Alaine Locke in Washington, were the three people who midwifed the so-called New Negro Literature into being."[31] Fauset was not a radical, by most estimates, but she did help to raise black consciousness, particularly through her work on *Crisis.* By choosing unpopular topics for her fiction, she challenged the preconceptions of the publishing industry and opened the way for literature which would appear in succeeding decades.

Notes

1. "The Younger Literary Movement," *Crisis,* XXVII (February, 1924), 161-62; "The Spirit of Phyllis Wheatley," *Opportunity,* II (June, 1924), 181.

2. "New Books," VI (May, 1924), 146.

3. "The Saving Grace of Realism," XII (January, 1934), 9.

4. (New Haven, 1958), pp. 99, 101.

5. *On Being Black: Writings By Afro-Americans from Frederick Douglass to the President,* ed. Charles T. Davis and Daniel Walden (New York, 1970), p. 294.

   For discussions of the black aesthetic see Larry Neal, "The Black Arts Movement," *The Drama Review,* XII (Summer, 1968), 29-39; Don L. Lee, "Directions for Black Writers," *The Black Scholar,* I (December, 1969), 53-7; Addison Gayle, Jr., ed., *Black Expression* and *The Black Aesthetic* (New York, 1969, 1971); Cecil M. Brown, "Black Literature and Leroi Jones," *Black World,* XIX (June, 1970), 24-31; Francis and Val Gray Ward, "The Black Artist—His Role in the Struggle," *The Black Scholar,* II (January, 1971), 23-32.

6. "Under the Harlem Shadow: A Study of Jessie Fauset and Nella Larsen," *Harlem Renaissance* (New York, 1972), p. 80.

7. "Criteria of Negro Art," *Crisis,* XXXII (October, 1926), 296.

8. XX (June, 1920), 78, 80, 83.

9. "As To Books," XXIV (June, 1922), 66; "Brawley's 'Social History of the American Negro'," XXIII (April, 1922), 160; "On The Bookshelf," XXII (June, 1921), 64.

10. Jessie Fauset and Cezar Pinto, "The Emancipator of Brazil," XXI (March, 1921), 208-09; "Looking Backward," XXIII (January, 1922), 125-26; "Henry Ossawa Tanner," XXVII (April, 1924), 255-58; "The Symbolism of Bert Williams," XXIV (May, 1922), 12, 14.

11. Marion L. Starkey, "Jessie Fauset," *The Southern Workman,* LXI (May, 1932), 220.

    In the characters of her novels, Fauset recaptured the bewilderment she had experienced as a schoolgirl. Young Joanna Marshall, of *There Is Confusion,* asks her father, "Didn't colored people ever do anything?" Joel Marshall provides the answer Fauset herself would give: "He told her . . . of Douglass and Vesey and Turner. There were great women, too. Harriet Tubman, Phillis Wheatley, Sojourner Truth, women who had been slaves . . . but had won their way to fame and freedom through their own efforts"—(New York, 1924), p. 14.

12. XIX (April, 1920), 316.

13. "What Europe Thought of the Pan-African Congress," XXIII (December, 1921), 66; XXIII (December, 1921), 12-13, 17-18.

14. "The 'Y' Conference at Talladega," XXVI (September, 1923), 215.

15. VIII (July, 1914), 143-45; XXII (August, 1921), 155, 157-58.

16. XX (October, 1920), 273.

17. (New York, 1927), p. 65.

18. XXIII (February, 1922), 162; "'Yarrow Revisited'," *Crisis,* XXIX (January, 1925), 108.

19. "Our Book Shelf," *Opportunity,* VII (September, 1929), 287; *Crisis,* XIX (December, 1919), 55.

20. (New York, 1937), p. 222.

    The Moorland-Spingarn Research Center of Howard University holds Brawley's unpublished comments on Fauset's novels. See Jessie Fauset, General Clipping File.

21. Arthur B. Spingarn Papers, Moorland-Spingarn Research Center, Howard University.

22. *The Harlem Renaissance, op. cit.,* p. 79.

23. *Confusion, op. cit.,* p. 21; *Comedy* (New York, 1933), p. 62.

24. XXIV (June, 1922), 67.

25. (New York, 1922), pp. 4, 128, 98.

26. "The New Books," *Crisis,* XXVII (February, 1924), 177.

27. Marion L. Starkey, "Jessie Fauset," *Southern Workman, op. cit.,* 218-19.

28. "The Negro in Art: How Shall He Be Portrayed," *Crisis,* XXXII (June, 1926), 71-2.

29. (New York, 1937), p. 112.

30. II (Fall, 1937), 59.

31. (New York, 1940), p. 218.

    Hughes mentioned that Fauset, as literary editor of *Crisis,* accepted "The Negro Speaks of Rivers," the first of his poems "to be published outside Central High School" (p. 72).

JOSEPH J. FEENEY (ESSAY DATE 1983)

SOURCE: Feeney, Joseph J. "Jessie Fauset of *The Crisis*: Novelist, Feminist, Centenarian." *Crisis* 90, no. 6 (June/July 1983): 20-22.

In this essay, Feeney gives an overview of Fauset's literary achievements, focusing on her work with the Crisis. *Feeney defends Fauset against earlier critics who called the author conservative, adding that many critics overlooked Fauset's pointed observations because she set them in the feminine, domestic sphere.*

In many ways Jessie Fauset belongs to *The Crisis,* since she wrote for it, helped edit it, and saw her novels reviewed in it. She first came to its pages in March, 1912, when the journal was sixteen months old and she was seven years out of Cornell and not quite thirty.

Arriving with a short column called **"What to Read,"** she showed herself restrained, angry, and practical as she praised a new novel: "At last a dispassionate presentation of color-prejudice—its baselessness and its shamefulness—has found its way into modern literature. And, behold! the book sells."

The poem **"Rondeau"** followed in April, and then for seventeen years she gave *The Crisis* poems, essays, stories, book reviews, and even a novelette all the way to 1929.

From Volume 3 to Volume 36 much of her life was devoted to *The Crisis,* and from 1919 to 1926 she served as Literary Editor under W. E. B. Du Bois. Fifty-eight of her 77 published works appeared in its pages, and the births of her novels were celebrated in its reviews and advertisements. And even in her fiction, in the novel ***Plum Bun,*** she had various characters avidly reading *The Crisis* each month. She was dedicated to writing, to her people, and to the Harlem Renaissance.

She had come to Harlem and Manhattan after early days in New Jersey and Philadelphia. Born, according to the Fauset family Bible, on April 26, 1882, in what is now Lawnside, New Jersey, she grew up across the Delaware among the integrated rowhouses of North Philadelphia. Her family, cultured though not wealthy, considered themselves "old Philadelphians," and a younger brother, Arthur Huff Fauset, later earned a Ph.D. in anthropology at the University of Pennsylvania.

Jessie Fauset, after graduating from Girls' High School, went to Cornell (the first black woman there, according to her brother) and won both an A.B. in 1905 and membership in Phi Beta Kappa. She taught high school for a while in Washington, D.C., and in 1919 completed her A.M. degree at the University of Pennsylvania. She then went to *The Crisis* for seven years as Literary Editor and, in 1921, attended the Second Pan-African Congress as an NAACP delegate.

In her desire to teach black children their heritage she also served from 1921-22 as literary editor of a children's magazine called *The Brownies' Book.* During these years, too, she lectured in America and traveled extensively in Europe; her knowledge of French (she had studied at the Sorbonne) also led to an interest in French-speaking black poets, and she translated their poems for the pages of *The Crisis* and *The Brownies' Book.*

After 1926 she returned to high-school teaching, this time in New York City, where she married Herbert Harris in 1929. The couple lived in Harlem and, later, in Montclair, N.J., where Harris was in real estate. After her husband's death, illness brought Miss Fauset back to her family in Philadelphia, and there she died on April 30, 1961, a few days after her seventy-ninth birthday.

Jessie Fauset is, of course, best known as the novelist who wrote ***There Is Confusion*** (1924), ***Plum Bun*** (1928), ***The Chinaberry Tree*** (1931), and ***Comedy: American Style*** (1933). With Nella Larsen she ranks as the major novelist of the middle class during the Harlem Renaissance, and—except for ***The Chinaberry Tree,*** which takes place in a small New Jersey town—she writes about black urban life in Philadelphia and New York from 1900 to 1930.

In her novels happy families enjoy Sunday morning in turn-of-the-century Philadelphia, and sophisticated artists and intellectuals talk and drink together in the Greenwich Village of the twenties. There are lively street cries in Harlem, successful doctors in West Philadelphia, trips to City Island in the Bronx. Bronze dancers cavort on a Broadway stage while black theatregoers have to sit in the balcony. Light-skinned young blacks "pass" but have to reject their families. A Du Bois-like leader speaks out for justice.

In short, Miss Fauset's novels picture a mixed world of romance and prejudice, success and humiliation. Sometimes the romance ends happily, other times prejudice stunts a career or drives a young black to suicide. In these novels one finds racial pride, proper middle-class English, Ivy-League educations, cultured "old Philadelphians"—but Miss Fauset's picture of her race's middle class hardly indicates unmixed optimism.

There is also a strong, underlying social purpose: to portray the educated black middle class and thereby uncover American racial prejudice.

The critics of Miss Fauset's novels generally dismiss her as a conventional middle-class novelist. Although in 1934 W. S. Braithwaite called her "the potential Jane Austen of Negro literature," most current critics—both black and white—consider her books as, at best, good examples of the conservative middle-class novel. At worst they consider her romantic, melodramatic, and excessively genteel.

Robert Bone's *The Negro Novel in America* even calls her a dull "novelist of the Rear Guard" whose "literary aspirations were circumscribed by her desire to convey a flattering image of respectable Negro society." Only the rare commentator recognizes her social criticism and notes how her talent ranges from comedy of manners through romance to tragedy.

Yet—as I have argued in an article in *The CLA Journal*—her novels are not simply romances but have a twofold structure and a complex tone. What appears on the surface to be a conventional romance stands also as a novel of betrayed hope or near-tragedy or sardonic "comedy." And her allegedly pleasant pictures of the comfortable middle class mask a world of pain, prejudice, suicide, unfair choices, and stunted careers.

Miss Fauset is angry and disillusioned, as well as fastidious and cultured. "To be a Negro in America posits a dramatic situation," she wrote in the preface to ***The Chinaberry Tree,*** and her novels dramatize black anguish and indict White America. She does love romance and feel racial pride, but she also feels a "bitter peace" since blacks in America are not free to aspire.

"If you're black in America," says one character, "you have to renounce." Her fiction portrays this conflict between a black's just hopes and limited possibilities and, as a result, Miss Fauset's four novels are both angrier and more interesting than critics have recognized.

Miss Fauset is also interesting as an early black feminist—an aspect unnoticed by critics. Her principal characters are generally women, and either the narrator or her characters often discuss the role of women in America.

Speaking with the post-war freedom of the twenties, they indict the double standard of morality, criticizing the "typical male defense" of this standard and noting the black male habit of arrogantly demanding a ridiculously careful virtue of their women. Men have a much easier life, they argue, and Miss Fauset ironically describes a woman whom "her husband considered a perfect woman, sweet, industrious, affectionate, and illogical. But to her he was God."

Some men simply do not like a capable woman; others want a woman to surrender herself completely in marriage. A woman in the novel ***Plum Bun*** summarizes the female dilemma: "If we don't give enough we lose them. If we give too much we lose ourselves."

To cope with such prejudice and such demands, various solutions are offered: do not marry at all; have a profession which will offer a woman shelter in a storm; or simply refuse to let femininity stand in the way of what a woman wants. And in these novels women want much and accomplish much.

There are female dancers, singers, painters, teachers, even successful planners of a peace conference. Granted, some of Miss Fauset's women are quite happy and satisfied with motherhood and family life, and Miss Fauset and her characters enjoy clothes and beauty and the great diversity of skin shades among blacks.

But if a black woman wants to be different, she should not be limited to conventional feminine roles and tastes. She should not be subordinated to men. And in ***Plum Bun*** Miss Fauset expressly recognized the terrible parallel: being a woman is like being black, for opportunities and choices are grossly limited by prejudice.

Her novels spoke for the freedom of women as well as for the freedom of blacks.

It is surely time, on her hundredth birthday, to celebrate Jessie Fauset: her life, her work for *The Crisis,* her novels, her passion for the freedom of blacks and of women. This passion was usually expressed in a low-keyed voice in both her novels of romance and her smoothly crafted prose. But below the calm surface was genuine passion as well as breadth of vision.

Her *Crisis* articles indicate the breadth: Montessori education, Egyptian nationalism, the Pan-African Congress, H. O. Tanner, the Sorbonne. Her novels, when read carefully, show the passion. And her life, gently understated as it was, itself conveys the pain of being a black woman in America.

One example suffices: Ready to leave *The Crisis* in 1926, she wrote Joel Spingarn for advice on a new job. She would prefer, she wrote, to be a publisher's reader, a woman's social secretary, or a staff member of a New York foundation. Her qualifications: she can type, speak French well, and do magazine layout. She prefers not to teach.

The letter closes: "In the case of publisher's reader, if the question of color should come up I could of course work at home."

She ended up teaching high school.

VASHTI CRUTCHER LEWIS (ESSAY DATE 1992)

SOURCE: Lewis, Vashti Crutcher. "Mulatto Hegemony in the Novels of Jessie Redmon Fauset." *College Language Association Journal* 35, no. 4 (June 1992): 375-86.

In this essay, Lewis focuses on the issue of racial hierarchy in Fauset's novels. Lewis is gently critical of Fauset's depiction of color-consciousness among light-skinned Blacks, noting that while Fauset naturally wrote about the class from which she came, her novels fail to break down the divisions between light- and dark- skinned Blacks.

The repressive nature of slavery spawned and supported a hegemonic color/caste hierarchy within African-American culture—one in which light-skinned mulatto slaves were often considered more intelligent and, certainly, more attractive than those of unmixed African ancestry. This racist social dynamic permeates nineteenth-century and most of twentieth-century African fiction, both black and white. The near-white female was depicted as beautiful and culturally superior to the racially pure but less attractive obese and passive mammy, the sexually promiscuous exotic primitive, and the cosmic Topsy. Images of Harriet Beecher Stowe's Eliza of *Uncle Tom's Cabin* (1852) and William Wells Brown's Clotel, of *Clotel; Or, The President's Daughter* (1853) were copied and repeated so often that the near-white female had become a tragic archetype by the turn of the twentieth century.[1] It has proven to be an unfortunate archetype, since near-white women of African descent have never been representative of the majority of black women in this country in numbers or, perhaps, lifestyle. It was from this nonrepresentative class of black women that Jessie Redmon Fauset selected major female characters for four novels. She was, however, following a tradition set by black women novelists in 1859, with the publication of Harriet Wilson's recently discovered *Our Nig.* Without exception, Wilson, Frances Ellen Harper, Pauline Hopkins, and Nella Larsen (a contemporary of Fauset) chose to fictionalize experiences of women who could, and very often did, pass for white.[2]

At the height of the Harlem Renaissance—when most African-American writers were metaphorically affirming their African heritage with dark images that informed a black aesthetic, and when they were making a valiant, albeit sometimes vain, attempt to capture the idiom and lifestyle of a wise but illiterate rural folk caught in the milieu of urban culture, Jessie Fauset was writing novels of gentility and class, and although it is not now popular to portray a genteel world in black fiction, Fauset's novels received much critical acclaim during her lifetime, from both white and black critics.[3]

Fauset was a popular and prolific writer; in less than ten years, she wrote ***There Is Confusion*** (1924), ***Plum Bun*** (1929), ***The Chinaberry Tree*** (1931), and ***Comedy, American Style*** (1933). During this same decade, she worked with W. E. B. Du Bois as literary editor of *Crisis* magazine and edited the *Brownies Book,* a monthly publication for children. Born into a very literary "old guard" Philadelphia family in 1886, she received a B.A. degree from Cornell and an M.A. degree from the University of Pennsylvania. She also studied at the Sorbonne and is the first black female novelist who was a college graduate.[4] Because her primary concern was to indicate the absurdity of an American caste system based upon race, she selected for her major female characters women who are ideally beautiful, by Western standards, and whose grooming and manners are impeccable but who, nevertheless, are denied social, economic, and educational access to opportunities taken for granted by white women. Fauset's novels inform white America that except for superficial differences of color, middle-class blacks are not unlike middle- and upper-class whites, and therefore deserve fair treatment. Resenting T. S. Stribling's notion of an African-American middle class portrayed in his critically acclaimed *Birthright,* she began her career as a novelist in response to it.[5]

Fauset's heroines and major female characters are variations of the popular tragic mulatto archetype of antebellum, antislavery fiction depicted by Wilson, Harper, and Hopkins. A significant difference in her presentations is in her more plausible portrayals of women who, although light in skin color, are not the children of mixed parentage; although they are not always light enough to pass for white, they are never more than "amber colored,"[6] and straight or wavy hair, aquiline noses, curly lashes, and highly arched feet are evidence of their Anglo Saxon heritage. Fauset subordinates skin color to the extent that an amber-colored heroine is not always presented less favorably than one with lighter skin; however, none of her major female characters are dark-skinned. More importantly, minor dark-skinned characters are servants to the light-skinned women, and they speak a dialect that is more a caricature of black speech than it is authentic. Although a color/class hierarchy is prominent in all of Fauset's novels, she does, on occasion, recognize the precarious nature of color/class hegemony in the black community. In ***Comedy, American Style,*** her most provocative work, she evokes a devastating and pitiable image of a near-white female obsessed with maintaining mulatto hegemony in her family. While her earlier novels are written in the popular romance tradition of the late nineteenth century, ***Comedy, American Style*** is the first sustained and effective satirical novel authored by an African-American woman.

Class tensions in Fauset's first novel, ***There Is Confusion,*** is a result of Joanna Marshall's intrusion into the life of every other major character in order to maintain and protect her families' old-guard, Eastern-seaboard status. Maggie Ellersly, a "yellow calla lily," is pitted against Joanna, whose "unobtrusive nose," "hair that holds glints of light," "long curling eyelashes," and "exquisite feet" compensate for her "luminous brown skin."[7] The daughter of a reputable New York caterer whose wife has been a school teacher, Joanna detests lower-class blacks and is enraged that Maggie, an aspiring hair dresser, whose mother is a laundress, is involved in a love affair with her brother.

Jessie Redmon Fauset, Langston Hughes, and Zora Neale Hurston in front of a statue of Booker T. Washington.

Because Maggie is not college educated, Joanna considers her unworthy of her brother, who intends to marry Maggie. She insults Maggie by sending her a letter which states emphatically that he "can not marry a hair-dresser"—to do so would hinder his career as a physician (p. 87). Maggie, not unlike popular romantic heroines of the period, looked to men as her economic saviors, and when denied the opportunity to marry into Joanna's family, she, like Theodore Drieser's Maggie, succumbs to the attention of a man of shady character.

Despite Maggie's fall, our sympathies are always with her—when she is stabbed by her gambler husband, after she divorces him, and then jilted by an upper-class, near-white Philadelphian whom Joanna loves. Ultimately, Fauset redeems Joanna, who experiences "a little private purgatory of remorse and guilt" (p. 286) over Maggie's tragedies.

Vera Manning, although a minor character, is in many respects one of Fauset's most compelling portrayals in ***There Is Confusion.*** She is a light-skinned African American who temporarily passes for white. Vera's parents are upper middle-class blacks. Her mother is Negrophobic in reference to her children marrying anyone darker that they, and she aborts Vera's marriage to a dark-skinned man. Out of spite, Vera leaves home to live and work exclusively in white communities. While doing so, she learns of the intense personal racism of whites. Stunned by the insidious contempt that whites hold for blacks, Vera becomes an undercover agent investigating lynchings and the Ku Klux Klan; in this respect, she is reminiscent of Walter White's protagonist in the *Fire in the Flint* (1924).

Recognizing the dramatic possibilities of the passing theme examined in Vera Manning's characterization, which was not essential to Joanna's and Maggie's story, Fauset's second novel, ***Plum Bun,*** is a complex study of the passing phenomenon and its effects on both the near-white female who leaves home and the family whom she deserts.

Set in Philadelphia and New Jersey during the 1920s, the novel offers insights into racist America through its light-skinned protagonist, Angela Murray, who, unlike heroines of Harper and Hopkins, severs all ties to the black community in an attempt to live permanently as a white woman. Angela's experiences, like Vera Manning's, make the reader aware of the fierce racism that informs the personal conversations of whites—conversations to which only an African American passing for white would be privy. Neither of Angela's parents is white. Her mother is a "mixed blood" whom whites often refer to as a "white nigger," and her father is very dark-skinned.[8] Angela discovers at a very early age that looking white has many advantages. When she shops with her mother in downtown Philadelphia, the two dine in white-only restaurants, and on one occasion they pass within arm's length of Angela's father and sister, but her mother makes no effort to acknowledge them. This occasion leaves a lasting impression on Angela, and after the death of both parents, she leaves her sister, Virginia, and the city of African-American elitism, to pass for white in New York.

Angela is obsessed with passing, and her sister is appalled by her calculated decision to completely disappear from her life. Fauset, herself light-skinned and solidly middle class, evokes her own voice in Virginia's condemnation of Angela. Virginia admonishes Angela to reconsider and contends that upper- and middle-class blacks are deserving of all benefits of American culture but should not abandon their families and communities to gain them.

A substantial element of Fauset's verisimilitude lies in her portrayal of women who in passing inform the readers of the depth of the personal animosity of whites toward blacks. Angela is involved romantically with a white male and learns that he detests black people and has "blackballed negroes [sic] in Harlem, aspirants for literary or honorary societies," and he has "successfully 'spoked the wheel' of various colored people" (p. 133). He supports the Garvey movement but for racist reasons. Ironically, his arguments in support of Garvey echo the sentiment of W. E. B. Du Bois, Fauset's mentor, whose integrationist philosophy was diametrically opposed to Garvey's nationalism.

Through the depiction of Angela's romance with a wealthy, Eastern-seaboard white male, Faucet examines class distinctions in white America. Angela's lover is not aware that she is of African descent, but because she has no social/class standing among the Eastern-seaboard noveau riche, he can accept her only as his clandestine mistress. Being white has not increased Angela's worth in the class of whites which she covets. It is ironic that she, as a refined white woman, qualifies only to assume the status of mistress, a role historically assigned to black women in white/black liaisons.

After several experiences that test Angela's racial pride and also expose her racial naiveté, Fauset completes Angela's metamorphosis from white to black and returns her to her sister and her Philadelphia roots. Implicit in Angela's return to the black community is Fauset's assumption that near-white African-American women should accept their own uniqueness and should not be concerned when whites discover their African heritage.

Later, in her depiction of Angela leaving the country to study in Europe (just as the author herself would do in the 1930s), Fauset offers the talented middle-class black woman, especially the marginal mulatto, an alternative to living under an American caste system that stereotypes and labels the best of the black middle class. In Europe, Angela decides to be whatever race people take her for. But again, Fauset creates color/class hegemony with the arrival in Europe of a star-crossed, near-white mulatto male of Angela's own "old guard" background who has joined her in anticipation of their marriage.

Heritage in ***The Chinaberry Tree*** is clearly defined as a product of miscegenation. Here, once again, the major female characters are fair or gold-skinned and, once again, one is used as a foil for the other. The lives of Laurentine Strange and Melissa Paul are always in a state of disaster. Laurentine, a 1920s variant of the archetypal tragic mulatto, has a "slightly foreign look"[9] and is the daughter of an African-American house servant and a wealthy white landowner. Melissa's mother is an unwed exotic primitive type, and her father is the mulatto husband of her mother's best friend. She is a "faithful reproduction" (p. 251) of her father's legitimate white daughters, while Melissa is a "high yellow" (p. 233) who just misses being "mariny"; unfortunately, her dark-red hair is crinkly, even nappy, "in its natural state" (p. 127). Fauset does not portray Laurentine's father married to her mother, although he provides well for them and visits regularly. She therefore differs from the archetype presented by earlier black women novelists in that the tragedy of her life does not result from the jarring revelation of her African ancestry after she is an adult. Because of her mother's clandestine relationship with her father, she experiences repeated rejections from both the black elite and whites in a small New Jersey town. Although upper-and middle-class black society does not initially accept Laurentine, Fauset gives her attributes of chastity, refinement, and beauty, all of which are a result of correct breeding.

Laurentine, a seamstress, refuses to sew for African-American women, but her reputation as a designer for wealthy whites finally earns her social acceptance among them. By depicting Laurentine as a seamstress during the 1920s, Fauset historically represents a goodly number, but yet a select group, of black women during the first half of the twentieth century who earned a comfortable living designing clothes for white patrons; however, most women of African descent who engaged in making clothing along the Eastern seaboard during the decade of the twenties were employed in the notorious garment industry.[10]

Fauset does not give Laurentine much racial consciousness; however, she is the vehicle through which the reader experiences culture of the Harlem Renaissance. Fauset, a 1920s resident of Harlem, allows Laurentine and the reader to become acquainted with the famed Lafayette Theater, notable restaurants, and nightclubs of the era. Laurentine's uneasiness with an animated black folk culture in Harlem cabarets indicates Fauset's own rejection of it, as well as that of Du Bois, her mentor. Fauset provides Laurentine with thoughts that mirror some of the reasons why Du Bois was critical of Harlem Renaissance writers who depicted what he considered the exotic in African-American culture. Laurentine is puzzled over reasons why anyone would frequent clubs where a "drunken black woman . . . slapped a handsome yellow girl," and "where a dark, sinuous dancer, singing . . . making movements . . . postured . . ." (p. 181).

Although Fauset never implies that white is superior to black, she is cautious in her praise of mulattoes who do not represent the "best" of their race. This caution is seen in her characterization of Melissa, who is sympathetically portrayed but never completely measures up to the standards of the Eastern-seaboard black elite and what seems to be the author's image of the ideal mulatto woman. Her mother has been married three times, and none of those times to a man who is aristocratic, wealthy, or white. The elegant, proud, and beautiful Laurentine resents Melissa's intrusion into her cloistered life when Melissa comes to live with her mother and her. Laurentine takes great pride in the fact that she has inherited her white father's aristocratic bloodline, and, ironically, Melissa resents and chides Laurentine for her illegitimacy. Both have tangled love affairs because they are constantly maneuvering to marry the best in color, character, and family among black people.

A light-skinned black male who is even more class-conscious than Laurentine rejects her, and Melissa, ignorant of her own heritage, almost marries her half brother. Disaster is circumvented when both Laurentine and Melissa eventually marry men of their same class and skin color. Laurentine, with the good Holloway blood, is rescued by a mulatto, fair-skinned Harvard physician, and "mariny" Melissa with the "crinkly hair" finds contentment with a dark-skinned graduate of Booker T. Washington's Tuskegee Institute—the prototype for black industrial arts colleges which did not conform to Du Bois's, Fauset's mentor's, ideal for higher education for blacks. Again, there are no dark-skinned major female characters, and the yellow one, whose heritage is tainted, marries her cultural equal.

Although Fauset consistently supports mulatto hegemony, she does suggest in her fourth novel that obsession with color and class can, and does, lead to absurdity. This is the most salient comment of her novels, and it is revealed through the remarkable characterization of Olivia Carey, a Negrophobic near-white female, in ***Comedy, American Style.*** Although all major female characters in this novel are of practically the same physiognomy as Olivia, none is as obsessed with color as she. In this work, Fauset alerts the reader to the tragedy that results from complete denial of one's African ancestry and to the cruel nature of color/class hegemony that can exist in black families.

Physically, Olivia is a carbon copy of her mother, but her father is dark-skinned. Neither parent can understand Olivia's early ruthlessness fused by her desire to dissociate herself from them. With her father's death and her mother's remarriage to a near-white mulatto, and after the birth of her twin brothers, who are even lighter in skin color than she, Olivia discovers a solution to her racial dilemma: she vows to marry a light-skinned mulatto to assure that she will have children who will eventually pass for white and allow her the opportunity to enter their white world.

After her marriage to a light-skinned physician and the birth of her children, Olivia's ruthlessness intensifies. When she is shopping with her white friends, she ignores her youngest son because of his brown skin. She also passes him off as her colored butler when white women visit. Because of her many rejections of him, he commits suicide. Olivia's fair-skinned daughter is not allowed to play with girls of obvious African-American descent or to date boys who are not very light-skinned. She tells her daughter that she would rather see her "dead" than married to her "bronze-skinned lover."[11] Ultimately, Olivia forces the daughter to pass for white and to marry a Frenchman, who mistreats her, and she denounces the oldest son's friendship with a young lady who does not meet her requirements of color and class. Olivia's color obsession is ultimately her undoing. By the end of the novel, she is psychologically broken and spends her days sitting by the window of her lonely Paris room, watching and waiting for an Anglo Saxon woman and her son, who sit in a courtyard reading and laughing together. This scene reminds the reader, if not Olivia, of the past—of the lost years when Olivia's dark-skinned son had sought-out his mother to confide in, and when he desperately needed her attention.

The image of Olivia is devastating, but the author does not deviate from the central premise of her previous novels—that mulatto hegemony must be maintained. Even those women who pull at the heartstrings of the reader because of Olivia's interference marry men no darker than themselves after her power over them is dissipated. Again, in ***Comedy, American Style*** there is that notion that wanting to be white is wrong and unnatural, although pride in color and class assuredly does not mean that one must "surrender a white aesthetic"[12] whose basic historical tenet has been "black, get back."

Fauset's portrayals of African-American women who are overly class- and color-conscious must be assessed against the stereotypical images that bordered on the caricature that white writers were using to depict men and women of African descent at the turn of the twentieth century and later. It is not difficult to understand her desire to reverse those images and to write with sympathy and understanding about an educated African-American middle/upper class to which she belonged. The real paradox of so much interest in class-conscious mulattoes is, as suggested earlier, that they depict a select group who have never been representative in number or lifestyle of African-American women. And just as important, the highly class-conscious mulatto has served to perpetuate a divisiveness within African-American culture since the genesis of a mulatto caste in the era of American slavery. Certainly the very images of black female arrogance so often depicted in Fauset's novels are ones that have caused "other Blacks to look at mulattoes as Greeks whose gifts should always bear watching."[13]

Notes

1. Catherine Stark, *Black Portraiture in American Fiction* (New York: Basic Books, 1974), p. 89.
2. For an examination of the treatment of the mulatto female in the novels of Harper, Hopkins, Larsen, and Hurston, see Vashti Crutcher Lewis, "The Mulatto as Major Female Character in Novels by Black Women: 1892-1937," diss., Univ. of Iowa, 1981. The term mulatto in this manuscript is not used with biological precision but refers to individuals who would also be categorized as quadroon or octoroon. For a popular definition of mulatto, quadroon, and octoroon, see Judith Berzon, *Neither Black nor White* (New York: New York Univ. Press, 1978), p. 54.
3. For an indication of Fauset's popularity among both black and white critics, see Amirit Singh, *The Novels of the Harlem Renaissance* (University Park: Pennsylvania State Univ. Press, 1976), p. 93.
4. Marion L. Starkey, "Jessie Fauset," *The Southern Workman,* May 1932, p. 219.
5. Ibid., p. 218.
6. Gerald Sykes, "Amber-Tinted Elegance," *The Nation,* 27 July 1932, p. 86.
7. Jessie Redmon Fauset, *There Is Confusion* (New York: AMS Press, 1924), pp. 20, 200. Hereafter cited parenthetically in the text by page number(s) only.
8. Jessie Redmon Fauset, *Plum Bun* (New York: Frederick A. Stokes, 1919), p. 29. Hereafter cited parenthetically in the text by page number(s) only.
9. Jessie Redmon Fauset, *The Chinaberry Tree* (1931; rpt. New York: Negro Universities Press, 1969), p. 11. Hereafter cited parenthetically in the text by page number(s) only.
10. Lorenzo J. Greene and Carter G. Woodson, *The Negro Wage Earner* (Washington, D.C.: Association for the Study of Negro Life and History), p. 41.
11. Jessie Redmon Fauset, *Comedy, American Style* (1933; rpt. New York: Negro Universities Press, 1969), p. 143. Hereafter cited parenthetically in the text by page number(s) only.
12. Addison Gayle, *The Way of the New World* (Garden City, New York: Anchor, 1975), p. 121.
13. Arde Coombs, "Mulatto Pride," *New York,* 26 June 1978, p. 37.

TITLE COMMENTARY

Plum Bun

KATHLEEN PFEIFFER (ESSAY DATE 2001)

SOURCE: Pfeiffer, Kathleen. "The Limits of Identity in Jessie Fauset's *Plum Bun.*" *Legacy: A Journal of American Women Writers* 18, no. 1 (2001): 79-93.

In this essay, Pfeiffer explores racial, national, and cultural identity in Fauset's Plum Bun, *linking Angela Murray's efforts at "passing" to the artificial values of the marketplace. Pfeiffer also discusses the significance of the title, taken from a nursery rhyme.*

Jessie Fauset, the Harlem Renaissance's most prolific woman novelist, believed that good literature conveys "the universality of experience." In a 1922 letter to then fledgling writer Jean Toomer, she encourages him to read the classics in order to find "the same reaction to beauty, to love, to freedom. It gives you a tremendous sense of fulness [sic], and completeness, a linking up of your life with others like yours" (Fauset to Toomer). She insists that literature crosses boundaries of space and time and creates communities of like-minded artists. But the cultural and social changes of the 1920s curtailed the possibility for the meaningful connection that Fauset advocates. Jessie Fauset wrote to Jean Toomer with optimism and conviction, believing, like her mentor W. E. B. DuBois, in art's potential for bridging political divides. Yet she encourages Jean Toomer to find community in a world that was fast becoming a place of alienation and estrangement. Fauset sent Toomer straight into the arms of that isolating world. "You've got personality and no prejudicing appearances," she noted. "Why not try to break into the newspaper game in one of the big cities?" As Fauset's fiction illustrates, the cutthroat competition and cynicism fostered by "the newspaper game" both caused and reflected the fragmented nature of urban communities.

Art's potential to link lives and form a common ground informs Fauset's most highly regarded novel, the 1929 bildungsroman ***Plum Bun.*** Critics have viewed the work as a novel of manners, as an investigation of racial liminality, as an analysis of gender roles that subvert or restrict female sexuality, and most often, as a pointed critique of protagonist Angela Murray's attempt to pass for white.[1] Yet many, if not all, of these analyses turn on presumptions about boundaries that the novel explicitly seeks to undermine. Of course, ***Plum Bun*** is shaped by the particularities of Angela Murray's identity and therefore grapples with the construction of race, class, and gender. But the novel also raises some of the broader philosophical questions that underlie Fauset's advice to Jean Toomer. Does absolute freedom aid or obstruct the development of meaningful identity? Do the values of a clearly defined community inform or limit individuality? The grandson of black Reconstruction politician P. B. S. Pinchback, Toomer was light enough to pass as white, and his racial complexity clearly shaped his own approach to writing. His lyrical treatment of African American culture accounts for much of the beauty of *Cane,* yet his steadfast rejection of racial categories was the subject of much of his autobiographical writing.[2] Acknowledging that the light-skinned Toomer had no "prejudicing appearances," Fauset knew well the conflicts he would face in finding employment and, more important, social and intellectual comradery when he relocated to New York. Can someone like Jean Toomer or Angela Murray—both of whom struggled to negotiate an organic sense of self apart from the (arbitrary) social categories assigned them—ever find a sense of "fullness" or "completeness"?

Plum Bun extends and complicates the analysis of identity, citizenship, and community life taking place in the public discourse of the 1920s and therefore represents a "linking up" of the Harlem Renaissance's concerns with those of American intellectual culture generally. Such a reading ventures to answer the challenge posed by Ann duCille, who insists, "Critics and theorists of African American literature must conceptualize race, class, culture, and experience, as well as tradition*s* and canon*s,* in terms far less natural, absolute, linear, and homogeneous than we have in the past" (148). To read Fauset in the context of her contemporary intellectual culture is to see that she was neither anachronistic nor marginal, as previous critics have charged. In ***Plum Bun,*** the trope of passing for white raises many of the same issues about the individual and society debated publicly by prominent intellectuals in this time period. More pointedly, Fauset's novel *racializes* those discussions and thereby reveals the role of race and gender in the debate. Angela Murray's passing reflects the multivalent transformations in which white American culture at large was then participating. Her particular movement from a black identity to a white identity invokes the larger movements—from Victorian morals to modernist ethos, from family to city, from community to individuality, from tradition to self-generation—that characterized the broader American culture.

This is not to diminish the degree to which ***Plum Bun*** conscientiously participates in an African American literary tradition in which a light skinned heroine negotiates the competing demands of race and gender. Fauset's literary predecessors made excellent use of such a protagonist to critique American racial hypocrisy. In William Wells Brown's 1853 *Clotel* and Frances E. W. Harper's 1892 *Iola Leroy,* both title characters literally embody the contradictions of characters whose light skin misrepresents their black identity. In *Iola Leroy,* passing for white is dismissed as moral weakness which would be "treason, not only to the race, but to humanity" and which makes one into "a moral cripple" (203, 266). Likewise, many of Fauset's contemporaries made use of passing and, like Fauset, they manipulated its meaning to far more nuanced and complicated ends than were possible for earlier writers. Charles

Chesnutt's 1900 *The House Behind the Cedars* and James Weldon Johnson's 1912 *The Autobiography of an Ex-Colored Man,* for example, depict the psychological complexity of passing even as both novels offer pointedly ironic critiques of the very *need* to pass, of the segregated society's tendency to overdetermine race. Fauset's contemporary Nella Larsen examines such issues as well, as her treatment of passing in *Quicksand* (1928) and *Passing* (1929) is particularly attentive to women's experience. Larsen's treatment of passing, like Fauset's in ***Plum Bun,*** questions the possibilities for sisterhood in a modern world that increasingly values individual accomplishment.

Plum Bun focuses on Angela Murray, a light-skinned young painter who tries to pass for white. To do this, she leaves her darker, younger sister Virginia and moves to New York as the white Angèle Mory, ostensibly to study drawing. In New York, she meets two men: Anthony Cross (a quiet, passionate, and poor artist who loves her) and Roger Fielding (a rich white man whom she sees as her ticket to wealth and freedom). Eventually Virginia decides to move to New York as well, agreeing to keep Angela's racial secret, but on the day she arrives in the city, Roger Fielding unexpectedly appears at the train station and Angela pretends not to know Virginia, thereby abandoning her sister to protect her racial reputation and maintain Roger's affection. The sisters ultimately reunite, and in a show of support for a fellow art student, a black woman, Angela ends her passing by announcing her so-called true racial identity to a roomful of newspaper reporters. In the end, Angela travels to Paris to study art and in the very last line of the novel is reunited with Anthony, whose own multiracial identity has been revealed and who has long been understood to be her true love.

Even before Angela passes for white, numerous references encourage the readers of ***Plum Bun*** to view her as a quintessentially American individualist. She is born in Philadelphia at the turn of the century into a family whose sentimental relations are directly influenced by such encroaching industrial developments as washing machines and automobiles. Indeed, her problems of self-definition are exacerbated by the cultural transformations following the Great War, transformations which influence her status as black and as a woman. Thus, when Angela moves to New York as the white Angèle Mory, she cannot distinguish between her perceived absolute freedom and a more elusive meaningful liberty; and when Angela betrays and abandons her sister at the train station, Fauset explores the consequences of her protagonist's radical individualism. The implications for citizenship are clear; Angela discovers that a meaningful personal identity depends upon connecting to a sympathetic community. Clear, too, are the implications for literary production. Ann duCille has noted the instability of form in Fauset's novels, arguing that "Fauset is indeed writing neither realism nor naturalism; nor is she falling back on pure romanticism. She is interrogating old forms and inventing something new" (100). In ***Plum Bun,*** Angela's rejection of her sister and her race analogizes generic transition because she has left a home that vividly evokes nineteenth-century domestic fiction. In this evocation, Fauset simultaneously engages and critiques the racial dimensions of American literature's mythology and of its presentation of the American dream.

Even before the Great War destroyed white Americans' faith in their own inviolability, Walter Lippman's 1914 *Drift and Mastery* gave voice to the same sense of cultural ennui Angela experiences. "We have changed our environment more quickly than we know how to change ourselves" (92), he writes in a chapter whose very title, "A Big World and Little Men," anticipates Angela's entrance to New York, where "Fifth Avenue is a canyon; its towering buildings dwarf the importance of the people hurrying through its narrow confines" (87). This is a world in which the "newspaper game" determines public opinion and mediates all communication. Lippman argues that religious authority has been undermined by the advent of scientific thought, that big business has rendered political systems inefficient, and that community has become increasingly fragmented. As a result, Lippman concludes, life's "impersonal quality is intolerable: people don't like to deal with abstractions" (93). For Americans in all regions—but most especially for those in urban centers like New York—the war exacerbated this alienation. Fauset privately encouraged Toomer to discover "the universality of experience" in a world where the sheer enormity of "the war to end all wars" demanded that nations recognize their membership in a global community. John Dewey's postwar analysis of *The Public and Its Problems* likened the war's spread to "an uncontrolled natural catastrophe. The consolidation of peoples in enclosed, nominally independent, national states has its counterpart in the fact that their acts affect groups and individuals in other states all over the world" (128). In shattering the boundaries through which countries defined themselves, the first World War also ruptured the boundaries through which individual identities acquired clarity and stability.

The two decades following the Great War saw dramatic alterations in white American concepts of personal identity. Ann Douglas has recently demonstrated that the war created "the culture of momentum." Profound material, political, philosophical, and epistemological changes wrought by the war irrevocably quickened the pace of modern life. "As Gertrude Stein pointed out," Douglas notes, "in a period of immense change like that of the Great War, fast assimilation is a prerequisite for power; the country least hampered by past conventions and traditions, least subject to cultural lag, most oriented toward the future, most alert to incentives to modernize, will dominate" (186-87). The appeal of Herbert Hoover, elected just before ***Plum Bun*** was published, lay in his being an engineer and in his presentation of himself as a modern man who could control the technological forces at work. Modern technology affected not only the production of Henry Ford automobiles, but also the transmission of information and the reproduction of images. The increasing availability of telephones, telegraphs, newspapers, movies, and radios made communication cheap and easy. Likewise, the mass production of food, clothing, toiletries, household appliances, and entertainment made the material conditions of life less demanding. But at what cost, asked intellectuals and cultural critics. To what end? These unsettling development in material culture and religious belief converged in the Scopes trial of 1925, where science and religion battled for legal primacy. In the first jury trial publicly broadcast live on the radio, the drama of Clarence Darrow examining William Jennings Bryan demonstrated not only the power and the limits of rhetoric, but also the market appeal of philosophical debate. Such transition—from familiarity to uncertainty, from religious conviction to scientific skepticism, from community to individualism, from nineteenth-century values to twentieth-century promise—is metonymized in Angela Murray's passing for white.

In ***Plum Bun***'s opening section, "Home," home, race, and sisterhood have already lost their coherence. Angela finds herself disenchanted with her hometown, the city where the U.S. Constitution was ratified. Twenty-seven years old at the end of the 1929 novel, Angela's birth corresponds closely with that of the twentieth century. This motif of transition figures into her character, as Angela finds herself wholly disillusioned with the small, closed, rigidly restricted domestic sphere which represented, just one generation earlier, the epitome of comfort and success. But her sense of rebellion is determined by her innate character and not her chronological age, as we see in the contrast between Angela and her younger sister. Virginia's character is fully grounded in her acceptance of a black racial identity, and she identifies wholly with her parents' old-fashioned, sentimental, and parochial traditions. Her characterization recalls heroines like Clotel and Iola Leroy and connects her to earlier African American fiction. Her name evokes more than just her virginal innocence, though that evocation certainly resonates. Virginia's values derive from slave culture of the old South: her ostensibly sweet and gentle demeanor belies her deeper strength, and ultimately she reveals herself to be shrewdly cunning.

Different skin colors—Angela's whiteness and Virginia's "rosy bronzeness" (14)—may have predisposed the sisters to their different characters, or they may have simply reinforced what already existed. In ***Plum Bun,*** the racial significance of *why* the two sisters are so different is further complicated because Angela, the older sister, shuns the ideology of domesticity that Virginia, the younger sister, embraces. Their distinct character differences reject positivism, suggesting that some generational upheaval has ruptured the flow of progress. Older and introspective, Angela craves independence and looks forward; young and vivacious, Virginia craves domesticity and looks backward. Religious devotion binds Virginia to her family, and Christian faith binds the family to its community.

Allusions to literary traditions frame references to social traditions in the novel's first half, where it becomes clear that Virginia's belief in the power of family is deepened and sustained by her religious devotion. The hyperbolic language with which Fauset describes this attachment establishes Virginia's sensibilities as deeply entrenched in the sentimental tradition: "She loved the atmosphere of golden sanctity which seemed to hover with a sweet glory about the stodgy, shabby little dwelling" (20). This "sweet glory" calls Virginia to a life of domestic service rendered noble by devotion to God and family. The first page of the "Home" section describes how, by twelve years of age, Virginia had discovered the pleasures of house-keeping. She "had already developed a singular aptitude and liking for the care of the house" and she had fulfilled "all the duties of

Sunday morning"—housecleaning, cooking breakfast, waking and serving the family, entertaining them by playing the piano as they dress for church. In these chores she "found a nameless and sweet satisfaction" (20). Virginia is so deeply and continually affected by this ritual of servitude that when, following breakfast, she plays religious hymns which her parents join her in singing, the "little girl" experiences "a sensation of happiness which lay perilously near tears" (21).

Religious services conjure a reaction in Virginia so intense as to evoke sexuality. Virginia experiences communion services as spiritually sensual; the description of these services resembles orgasm:

> In the exquisite diction of the sacramental service there were certain words, certain phrases that almost made the child faint; the minister had a faint burr in his voice and somehow this lent a peculiar underlying resonance to his intonation; he half spoke, half chanted and when, picking up the wafer he began "For in the night" and then broke it, Virginia could have cried out with the ecstasy which filled her.
>
> (23)

Significantly, Virginia is too young to participate in this ritual of consummation, here rendered multifaceted and multiply suggestive, but she senses its importance. Taking communion seems to "transfigure" people; her parents, it seems, "wore an expression of ineffable content as they returned to their seats" (23). In this interconnection of religious fervor, displaced sexuality, and consumption, Fauset not only draws together the most powerful themes of her literary ancestors; she also delineates the cultural transition in which the authority of religion will give way to the emerging complexity and prominence of modernity.

Such an analogy problematizes literature's role in writing race and in creating ideological stereotypes by which we order the world. Certainly Virginia evokes the literary heroines of black women's fiction, the so-called "tragic mulattas," like Iola Leroy, who maintain race-conscious fidelity to "their people." But many of Virginia's literary ancestors are also white heroines of nineteenth-century romances and domestic fictions; therefore, ***Plum Bun*** cannot easily be located generically or in terms of its racial ideology.[3] While the narrative explicitly draws our attention toward Angela, the obvious protagonist, Virginia operates as a background foil who recalls, critiques, and at times deconstructs the literary tradition and social history against which Angela defines herself.

It is not only the black women's convention which operates in this polarity, but the canonical tradition as well. One could argue that Nathaniel Hawthorne's echo also sounds in Virginia's characterization. The romanticization of domestic labor by which Fauset defines Virginia was a strategy deployed in *The House of the Seven Gables* to reconstitute women's work as pleasure, not labor. In fact, Carolyn Wedin Sylvander sees Hawthorne's influence in the novel's form, which incorporates the nursery rhyme motif. "The pattern of the romance as Nathaniel Hawthorne developed it in *The House of the Seven Gables,* departure and return, or isolation to communion, is thus put into child's verse," Sylvander argues. "By adopting the freedoms of the American romance for formal structure, Fauset is able to accomplish a whole series of aims in ***Plum Bun***" (184). As a figure redolent of nineteenth-century ideology, Virginia also evokes the literary tradition in which, as Michael T. Gilmore has argued, the middle class emerged in all of its potential and confusion. "Nathaniel Hawthorne," he notes, "maps the emergence of middle-class identity and simultaneously reveals the self-contradictory and unsettled nature of the new configuration" (216). Through Virginia's traditional femininity, Fauset folds this class-consciousness into a gendered role: her middle-class virtue defines the community against which Angela rebels. In ***Plum Bun***'s opening "Home" section, then, Virginia's characterization locates several nebulous historical, cultural, and literary transitions. It evokes the middle class's formulation and simultaneous instability; it subsumes personal identity into a vacuous romantic stereotype (a critique of which will become evident in her move to New York and eventual cosmopolitanism); and it establishes—in order to critique—a dialectic of opposition as the paradigm through which Angela must assert her own identity.

The sentimental trope that Virginia seems to personify was often used by the generation of black women writers preceding Fauset; these women presented the domestic ideal to affirm community and family as sites where women have social and civic presence. Claudia Tate has argued persuasively that "the idealized domesticity in these novels . . . [functioned] as a fundamental cultural symbol of the Victorian era for representing civil ambition and prosperity as a nineteenth-century 'metonym for proper social order,' a symbol that black women writers in particular used to promote the social advancement of African Americans" (5). But for all of its apparent and romanticized appeal, the ideology of domesticity, as it is incorporated into Virginia's young self, contains the elements of its own undoing. This "blessed 'Sunday feeling'" (20), which affects Virginia so deeply, has resounding political implications, for her sensibility portends cultural stagnation:

> She envied no one the incident of finer clothes or a larger home; this unity was the core of happiness, all other satisfactions must radiate from this one; greater happiness could be only a matter of degree but never of essence. When she grew up she meant to . . . marry a man exactly like her father and she would conduct her home exactly as did her mother.
>
> (22)

The incestuous undertones in Virginia's wish to marry her father hint at her desire to thwart social evolution by replicating her parents' lives rather than surpassing them. Notwithstanding her ambition "to invent a marvellous method for teaching the pianoforte" (13), Virginia feels none of the desire to succeed that fuels social change or political progress.

In ***Plum Bun*** explicit invocations of literary genre frame Angela's decision to pass for white, aligning her rejection of blackness with a rejection of the sentimental tradition of domestic fiction. Angela has little regard for the sentiments that define Virginia's world. "She did not like going to church, at least not to their church, but she did care about her appearance and she liked the luxuriousness of being 'dressed up' on two successive days" (21). In fact, being "dressed up" and attending to her appearance is Angela's single greatest pleasure. The narrator tells us that "Saturday came to be the day of the week for Angela" because on this day "Angela learned the possibilities for joy and freedom which seemed to her inherent in mere whiteness" (20, 14). Angela associates the white world with a particular kind of freedom, however; she is happiest when idle and on display. Her most satisfied Saturdays consist of shopping, lunching, and attending orchestra concerts.

To Angela and her mother Mattie, "a successful and interesting afternoon" consists of making a virtue of their uselessness and of continual self-objectification: "They had browsed among the contents of the small exclusive shops in Walnut Street; they had had soda at Adams' on Broad Street and they were standing finally in the portico of the Walton Hotel deciding with fashionable and idle elegance what they should do next" (18). For Mattie, these afternoons offer an escape from class as much as race, and they teach Angela to embrace the luxuries of consumer culture. A romantic and an idealist, Mattie wants her daughters to become great artists; her sensible husband Junius overrides that wish and insists upon giving them "a good, plain education." But Junius also indulges Mattie's love for material culture. The demands of Mattie's work-week create the pleasure of her Saturdays: "[A]ll innocent, childish pleasures pursued without malice or envy contrived to cast a glamour over Monday's washing and Tuesday's ironing, the scrubbing of the kitchen and bathroom and the fashioning of children's clothes" (16). Angela experiences the public pleasures of the marketplace's gratification individually and selfishly, but she fails to see its broader communal effects; at the same time, she inadvertently learns to conflate an artistic sensibility with material comfort.

Angela's predisposition to view Fate, rather than God, as primarily responsible for her life's path most clearly distinguishes her as representative of nascent twentieth-century thought. By arguing that "merit is not always rewarded" (12), ***Plum Bun*** racializes the nineteenth-century mythology that popularized Horatio Alger's fiction. Angela frames her desire for independence—"Freedom! That was the note which Angela heard oftenest in the melody of living which was to be hers" (13)—wholly in terms of race. The family ties that Virginia treasures mean little to Angela. Her outright rejection of Virginia, the sharpest consequence of passing, is precipitated by "a faint pity" she feels "for her unfortunate relatives" with dark skin (18). Likewise, Angela finds nothing appealing in the company of neighbors and friends who make an essential community for Virginia. Angela finds Matthew Henson, a potential beau, to be "insufferably boresome and [she] made no effort to hide her ennui" (24). She responds to Virginia's piano playing "in sheer self-defense"—she leaves the room to eat supper alone rather than experience the emotions her sister's religious music might evoke.

Significantly, Angela experiences both her greatest satisfaction and her most painful racial rejection in her beloved art class. Even though her teachers assure her that she will "find artistic folk the broadest, most liberal people in the world" (65), they cut her coldly when they learn of her racial lineage. The novel conjoins this rebuff with a similar, more public humiliation at a movie theater, and Angela's bitterness about these rejections grows more cynical in the face of her sister's calm acceptance. Angela's decision to pass emerges from such moments of pointed confusion.

FROM THE AUTHOR

PLUM BUN

She thought then of black people. . . . And she saw them as a people powerfully, almost overwhelmingly endowed with the essence of life. They had to persist, had to survive, because they did not know how to die.

SOURCE: Jessie Redmon Fauset, excerpt from *Plum Bun,* Matthews & Marrot, 1928.

How can Fauset's personal advice to Toomer and her public advocation of an "Art" that serves racial justice be reconciled with these fictional depictions? In Philadelphia, Angela's development as an artist is continually circumscribed by the fact of her race—by her invisible "blood"—and not, importantly, by the appearance of racial difference. Angela utterly rejects the community-oriented, racially loyal, and sentimentally genteel realm wholly embraced by her sister. When a friend suggests that racial experience enhances artistic growth, she responds with brutal frankness: "'Oh, don't drag me into your old discussion,' Angela answered crossly. 'I'm sick of this whole race business if you ask me. . . . No, I don't think being coloured in America is a beautiful thing. I think it's nothing short of a curse'" (53). Angela's cynical realism countermands her sister's domesticity. Sharing more attributes with fictional contemporaries like Jay Gatsby and Lily Bart than the likes of Iola Leroy or Clotel, Angela strives to become the fully individualized product of her own imagination.

The racialized contrast between (dark) Virginia's embrace of tradition and (light) Angela's desire for freedom illustrates the impossibility of "linking up" the sisters' lives with each other. The "completeness" that Fauset's letter encourages Toomer to find proves elusive in a world specifically inscribed in America's postwar cultural transitions. The Murray household has been influenced—and its familial relationships altered—by the same encroaching tensions and technologically induced displacements that many intellectuals were then lamenting. More than just the "newspaper game" reshapes communication and communities; domestic traditions are altered as well. Washing day—once a ritual that reinforced the connections between home and work life, wherein Junius tried to work uptown "so that he could run in and help Mattie"—disappears as the girls grow up. When they were young, their father "used to dart in and out two or three time [sic] in the course of a morning to lend a hand." But this ceremony has been irrevocably altered by "the advent of the washing machine" (33). The workload, to be sure, has been reduced, but the communal chore has also been dissolved and reduced to a "pleasant fiction" (33). Leisurely Saturday afternoons also disappear. During the girls' childhoods, these were days of enormous pleasure when Mattie and Angela would go shopping while Junius and Virginia toured the city, but by their adulthood, the "Saturday excursions were long since a thing of the past; Henry Ford had changed that" (56). As the sisters grow older and begin working as teachers, the family becomes increasingly fragmented and communal time dissipates; eventually, not even church services bring them together.

Plum Bun thus records cultural instability and writes race into its account. The novel's structure underscores this dissonance through its unlikely juxtaposition of nursery rhyme and marketplace. ***Plum Bun*** the novel critiques the white bias in "Plum Bun" the nursery rhyme by removing it from the nursery and projecting it into an adult, market-driven sphere. Its five sections, "Home," "Market," "Plum Bun," "Home Again," and "Market is Done," reveal transactions not anticipated in the nursery rhyme.[4] By positing a nursery rhyme motif, Fauset critiques the literary form through which cultural indoctrination into class and race-consciousness occurs. Her use of "Plum Bun" highlights the nursery rhyme's assumption that selfhood finds expression—and, indeed, children find happiness—through acquisition and consumption. "Plum Bun" the nursery rhyme simplifies its manifestations of value and exchange; ***Plum Bun*** the novel complicates them. "Plum Bun" celebrates the movement linking homes and marketplaces; ***Plum Bun*** critiques it.

In the twentieth-century marketplace of values, Angela sells her family home in order to buy her freedom: "Her plan was to sell the house and divide the proceeds. With her share of this and her half of the insurance she would go to New York or Chicago, certainly to some place where she could by no chance be known, and launch out 'into a freer, fuller life'" (80). But with Angela's sale of real estate, Fauset invests in what duCille terms "unreal estate," a fantastic fictional realm that combines the historically specific and the sentimental. In this "ideologically charged space" black writers ranging from William Wells Brown to Ann Petry have fictionally embroidered historical facts, duCille argues, "usually for decidedly political purposes" (18). Thus, even as Angela ostensibly rejects her African American *racial* heritage, Fauset arguably claims her African American *literary* heritage. ***Plum Bun***'s opening section, aptly titled "Home," concludes by depicting the real estate transaction in which Virginia purchases sole custody of the family's home and history from Angela, who gives up her name, her race, and her past. But in the second, equally well-titled "Market" section, Angela enters into a world of "unreal estate" where sculptor Augusta Savage appears in the disguise of Miss Powell and W. E. B. DuBois seems embodied in the fictional Van Meier.

When Angela moves to New York, she also encounters the pseudo-environment created by an increasingly volatile and mechanized mass society. New York is a city where, as Walter Lippmann argues, "what each man does is based not on direct and certain knowledge, but on pictures made by himself or given to him" (*Opinion* 25). Indeed, New York is a marketplace rather than a home, and Angela's familial irresponsibility translates into financial irresponsibility. The translation appears most evident in her housing decisions. Her new friend Paulette marvels at Angela's naive choice of lodging. "In a hotel?" she exclaims, as Angela blushes in embarrassment. "In Union Square? Child, are you a millionaire? Where did you come from? Don't you care anything about the delights of home?" (99). From the start, Fauset makes it clear that Angela's inability to negotiate the exchange rate of white skin parallels her bad miscalculation of the meaning of home.

In New York, Angela mistakes alienation for independence; moreover, she discovers that while whiteness imparts the kind of social freedom that comes from her newfound anonymity, such freedom does not guarantee a meaningful identity. Instead, because she views freedom as an end in itself rather than the means to an end—that is, as a means to establishing a rewarding identity—her experience of freedom is characterized by estrangement, drift, and alienation. Her aimless wandering—"she was being unconscionably idle" (91)—evinces this loss of subjectivity, and her idleness reinforces her lack of social connections. Angela's arrival in New York and her simultaneous passing for white thus reflect a transition from an identifiable community to an undifferentiated mass society, and thereby illustrates the consequences Dewey described in 1927 of a world in which "no amount of aggregated collective action of itself constitutes a community" (151). Angela's removal to New York also depicts the tensions identified by German sociologist Ferdinand Tonnies, whose 1887 work on community and society demonstrates how communities grow from acts of will, rather than from organic, inherent conditions. Tonnies raises questions that Fauset engages through Angela, and both demonstrate that community, an extension of family, faces difficult challenges in a world where family life is decaying.

In New York, Angèle Mory wants to recreate herself by associating with a sympathetic and like-minded community. But first, she finds pleasant distraction at the movies, where she now "found herself studying the screen with a strained and ardent intensity" (91). Her attraction to performative entertainment reinforces both her new name and her claim to New York, for as Douglas observes, "Constructed identity is at bottom an affair of masks and role playing, part of the politics of theatricality" (344). Angela's easy access to movies and theaters reflects white New York's desire to be entertained and its lack of interest in politics. These readily available mass-produced movies sought profit over artistic merit, and genre pictures employed assembly-line strategies to keep audiences enthralled. The easy success of Angela's own performance—her passing for white—predisposes her to accept the cinema's formulaic fictions without question, and she loses "the slight patronizing scepticism [sic]" that characterized her previous critical judgment (91). But her loss of discriminating individuality is exacerbated by a terrible loneliness, and in her favorite theater, Angela often watches the audience more than the play, noting the intimate groups that create it. In this way, her experience demonstrates an emerging truth about mass culture: Angela can be a member simply by attending the performance, but as a member of the audience, she merely watches the show in the dark. Alienated and unconnected, her membership has no significant value.

But if Angela's experience as an anonymous spectator at the theater undermines her critical perceptions, her parallel experience as a spectator in the world explicitly nourishes her artistic growth. As a spectator in the world, an observer of human behavior and of the human face, Angela becomes an artist. Fauset thus offers her protagonist the same opportunity for connection toward which she encouraged Toomer—"a linking up of your life with others like yours." Once independent, Angela finds herself drawn to the same sort of intimacy and security she rejected at home. Her expectation that whiteness and freedom would bring rewards gives way to the ironic realization that they only bring expense. Her initial weeks of residence in New York are marked both by her sense of adventure and by that adventure's cost: "[S]he had been in New York eight months and she had already spent a thousand dollars. At this rate her little fortune which had seemed at first inexhaustible would last her less than two years" (110). Friendships involve expenditure in New York: she is beholden to her comrades for lunches, teas, and gifts. Though the price of these socials adds up, the emotive rewards are less congruous: Miss Powell responds to her with an "attitude of dignified reserve" (108); Paulette "lived in a state of constant defiance" (112); and Martha Burden "was cool and slightly aloof" (112). These ostensible sisters share an understanding of the world, insights which are alien to Angela. Human interaction is regulated and commodified in this artificially constructed community, and the synthetic nature of Angela's friendships underscores the alienation of urban life.

Still, a clear sense does emerge that Angela is gifted with painterly insights. In Harlem, she sees aesthetic possibilities in a world shaped by art. "A man's sharp, high-bred face etched itself on her memory," Fauset notes, "—the face of a professional man, perhaps,—it might be an artist" (96). The language here—a formulation in which the man's face is the subject performing the action, rather than Angela's artistic eye beholding or perceiving the face—is language that posits the man's face as the agent of artistic etching, not Angela. The intimation that blackness inscribes itself as artistic vision onto Angela is underscored when Fauset tells us that Angela sees Harlem as "fuller, richer, not finer but richer with the difference in quality that there is between velvet and silk" (98). But still, she rejects the intense devotion and potential happiness in Anthony's love because it involves commitment: she "wanted none of Anthony's poverty and privation and secret vows . . . to REAL ART" (143).

The contrast between Roger and Anthony further underscores Angela's misunderstanding of the meaning of freedom. She believes that Anthony's poverty will restrict her, when in fact Roger's prosperity and the obligations to his father that accompany it bring the greatest demands. Contrary to Angela's belief that Roger represents freedom, his presence in her life proves far more inhibiting than liberating. In ironic juxtaposition to his wealth, she amasses "a little heap" of bills in the process of their affair because "she had had to dress to keep herself dainty and desirable" for him (151). Martha Burden advises Angela to manipulate Roger in order to extract a marriage proposal. Thereafter, the majority of her actions toward him are contrived; she views the relationship as a game in which she "decided to follow all the rules as laid down by Martha Burden and to add any workable ideas of her own" (146). Rather than allowing her to develop a full and meaningful identity, Angela's relationship with Roger only limits her growth. Roger's financial independence cannot even help him establish a meaningful identity for himself—for all of his advantages, he proves to be shallow, small-minded, and intimidated. His behavior in orchestrating the eviction of black patrons from a restaurant disproves Angela's belief that he "had no fears, no restraints, no worries" (129). He defers so wholly to his father's wishes that he has no independent character: "I'm not entirely my own master," he explains (185). Echoing the terms of Lippmann's *Drift and Mastery* (1914), Roger articulates the sense of dislocation characterizing much early-twentieth-century discourse.

Angela's sense of liberty is continually limited because she has accepted the restrictive classifications that govern society. Thus while her passing rejects narrow categories for herself, she easily and unself-consciously places taxonomic restrictions on others, paying a great deal of attention to social, ethnic, and national groups. In her effort to negotiate the urban community, she defines her colleagues through ethnic contrasts. This is evident, significantly, in her first art class. "She glanced about at the newcomers," Fauset writes, "a beautiful Jewess with pearly skin and a head positively foaming with curls, a tall Scandinavian, an obvious German, several more Americans" (95). Throughout the novel she sees very few Americans as "just Americans" (to employ the phrase later coined by Toomer). John Banky, the most sympathetic of the newspaper reporters, is described as "the young Hungarian" (352). Angela's heightened attention to ethnic or racial categories, in fact, misrepresents these people. As a result she misses the point about their identities: they are artists, journalists, intellectuals, and sociologists. Angela's belief that passing for white will reconstitute her racial identity similarly misunderstands the nature of identity itself. Like the society of which she is a part, she embraces only one aspect of identity and overdetermines its significance. She participates in the very same cultural predisposition to stereotype that her passing wants to dissolve. Lippmann explains the consequences: "Real space, real time, real numbers, real connections, real weights are lost. The perspective and the background and the dimensions of action are clipped and frozen in the stereotype" (*Opinion* 156).

Angela's elaborately constructed white identity is doomed to fail precisely because, like the very racial distinctions it seeks to avoid, it depends on the sort of arbitrary distinctions her passing explicitly rejects. Her desire to maintain distinct personal spheres—to keep her romantic, professional and artistic selves separate—predisposes her to catastrophe. In a brief but foreboding scene, Angela shirks Miss Powell's friendly approach for fear that Roger might witness their comradery. This rejection of Miss Powell reflects her desire to keep Roger separate from the small community of art students constituting her only circle of friends. Nor was it only Miss Powell whose familiarity she sought to hide from Roger—she separates him from all her classmates, white and black: "[S]he did not want any of the three, Martha, Paulette, nor Anthony to see whom she was meeting" (148). Miss Powell had, in fact, become part of a meaningful community for Angela. Breaking out of her habitual reserve on that day, she hailed Angela, "pleased and excited. She laid her hand on Angela's arm but the latter shook her off" (148). These manipulations and elaborate orchestrations—maneuverings that anticipate her furtive meeting with Virginia—reflect the impossibility of establishing a meaningful identity without first establishing meaningful connections. The flaws in Angela's reasoning become increasingly and painfully clear: she mistakenly views Roger's money as the end that will secure her happiness and believes that only dependence will yield independence. She fails to recognize that her own love of art (and the company of others who share that love) is the means through which she can independently establish herself.

Angela's passing for white is doomed, too, because it demands that she separate herself from others on the arbitrary basis of race rather than the organic basis of sympathy; it renounces the "universality of experience" and thereby prevents Angela from discovering the sense of "ful- ness [sic] and completeness" that Fauset encouraged Toomer to discover. In a chapter significantly titled "Search for the Great Community," Dewey distinguishes between absolute freedom (the sort which demands Angela's elaborate manipulations and misrepresents her values) and meaningful liberty. Dewey's analysis summarizes the lesson of ***Plum Bun.*** "Liberty," he writes, "is that secure release and fulfillment of personal potentialities which take place only in rich and manifold association with others: the power to be an individualized self making a distinctive contribution and enjoying in its own way the fruits of association" (150). Even before Roger's ugly racism becomes evident, Angela realizes that "[t]here had been no touching point for their minds" (129). She admits to Virginia, "I'm not in love with him at all" (172). In pursuit of this single connection—which proves meaningless—she renounces the potentially rewarding intimacies of her classmates and cruelly rejects and endangers her sister.

Yet the scene in which Angela abandons Virginia at the train station not only demonstrates the negative side of Angela's individualism, it also illustrates the limits of Virginia's world. "I'm twenty-three years old," Virginia thinks, "and I'm really all alone in the world" (167). Her embrace of family, tradition, and race has left her no better able to establish a meaningful identity than Angela's rejection of those same values. The culture that alienates Angela also shapes Virginia's world. Likewise, when the closed self-contained romanticized sphere of domestic fiction fails to sustain her as an adult, Virginia decides to sell the family home. "There is such a shortage of houses in Philadelphia just now," she comments, "Mr. Hallowell says I can get at least twice as much as father paid for it" (169). Virginia changes too: when confronted with Angela's betrayal, "[s]omething hardened, grew cold within her" (167). While Virginia becomes "almost swamped by friendships, pleasant intimacies, a thousand charming interests" in New York (241), she also becomes cunning. "I'm trying to look at things without sentiment," she tells Angela (171).

Sentiment, however, is precisely what motivates Angela to announce her "true" racial identity to a room full of newspaper reporters. And because she makes this announcement in support of Miss Powell's right to study art—her right to "the universality of experience"—the scene at last aligns newspapers and art, the two cultural forces that have long interfered with Angela's ability to establish a genuine and meaningful identity. Newspapers testify to the subsumption of distinctive communities by mass society. They illustrate the sheer vastness of life: what was once gossip and conversation is now commodified and mass-marketed. By "coming out" to a group of reporters, Angela contends with New York on her own terms for the first time, rather than shaping her decisions to suit its demands. In this transition, her renunciation of whiteness effects the goal she sought by passing into it, as she discovers that the true meaning of freedom lies not in unequivocal liberty, but in meaningful connection with others. As noted, white New York in the 1920s was much more interested in entertainment than in politics, but it is equally important to note that black New York believed that it could achieve political goals through artistic success. Angela's experience draws together both of these dynamics, celebrates their potential, and demonstrates their limits.

Once Angela allows art to become the one constant and stable factor in her life, she finds her truest and best self. Art structures her life economically: after Roger's rejection, she accepts a design job, and though the work "was a trifle narrow, a bit stultifying . . . it opened up possibilities" (235). Her attention to art gives her increasing purpose precisely because it creates a sphere of meaning where she can establish her identity:

> In the evenings she worked at the idea of a picture which she intended for a masterpiece. . . . But the urge to wander was no longer in the ascendent. The prospect of Europe did not seem as alluring now as the prospect of New York had appeared when she lived in Philadelphia. It would be nice to stay put, rooted; to have friends, experiences, memories.
>
> (240)

When Angela structures her life's decisions around her artistic goals, her actions become more consistent with her values. Roger returns to propose marriage and "she found herself hoping that he would not stay long. She wanted to think and she would like to paint" (317). Eventually, she realizes how strong the connection is between her art and her identity: "It both amused and saddened her to realize that her talent which she had once used as a blind to shield her real motives for breaking loose and coming to New York had now become the greatest, most real force in her life" (332). Angela's life is ordered by her art; in turn, her greatest work depicts "Life." Because Angela's art depends on images and not language, it affords her a means of expression free from the language of race but attentive to race's presence. Anthony cannot detect Mattie's race, for instance, based on Angela's sketch, but sees her instead as "a beautiful woman;—all woman" (280). Rather than generating a new self, painting permits her to uncover and enhance the self that already existed. By focusing thus on Angela's art as the key to her identity, ***Plum Bun*** celebrates an aspect of selfhood that neither ignores race nor depends on it.

At the novel's end, Angela explicitly articulates ***Plum Bun***'s central assertion. "Yet when I begin to delve into it," she explains to Virginia, "the matter of blood seems nothing compared with individuality, character, living" (354). Indeed, Angela and Virginia emerge at the novel's end as women who have incorporated the best of both black and white worlds. Moreover, because they ultimately define themselves wholly and individually, without regard for arbitrary or artificial barriers, they establish meaningful and successful identities. As Angela departs for Europe, the circle of friends who surrounds her at the dock testifies the quality of her character and offers a model for a genuinely multi-racial and multicultural society. Martha and Ladislas Starr, introduced specifically as "strong individualists" (113), are the liberal intellectual couple whose egalitarian marriage defies the expectations of their aristocratic families; they drive Angela to the dock. There she is embraced by Ralph Ashley, who had earlier demonstrated his open-mindedness, saying, "[I]f I met a coloured woman of my own nationality, well-bred, beautiful, sympathetic, I wouldn't let the fact of her mixed blood stand in my way" (325). Mrs. Denver, "a wealthy woman from Butte, Montana" (249), appears at the dock as well. "'I couldn't stand having you go,' she said pitifully, 'without seeing you for one last time.' And, folding the girl in a close embrace, she broke down and murmured sadly of a lost daughter who would have been 'perhaps like you, dear, had she lived'" (371-72). Walter and Elizabeth Sandberg are there also, and the latter "clung to her, weeping" (372). This circle of friends who, as Ralph Ashley explains, all love her, represents a blend of generations, classes, ethnicities, political ideologies, and sympathies. They depict as well the complexion of a multidimensional, nuanced, and complex sense of self, for their friendship incorporates the universality of experience.

By the end, Fauset has offered ostensible closure—Angela has embraced her Art, she has been reunited with Virginia, and she has renounced marriage to Roger as a path to happiness. Yet while we have the illusion of clear resolution, too many of the novel's troubling complexities remain unresolved, and Fauset never renounces the implication that they are unresolvable. Anthony's arrival in Paris indicates that marriage will shape Angela's future. Angela's celebrated portrait of her mother defines her artistic development, yet this is a deracialized celebration of the woman who taught her to reject her sister. Similarly disconcerting is the fact that Angela declares her connection to Miss Powell by depriving her "sister" of those very things she held so dear throughout the novel—her privacy and her dignity. When Angela is finally reunited with Virginia, her sister tells her that she knew all along how Angela was suffering in her isolation. Virginia giggles at Angela's apology, admitting, "I'm a hard hearted little wretch. . . . I was just putting you through" (257). Virginia's admission offers one strategy for understanding Fauset's own intentions. For instance, it is worth noting that the novel's closure depends on Angela's expatriation. Her multicultural circle of friends notwithstanding, Angela and Anthony are the only two individual characters who embody—literally—the contradictions of arbitrary racial classification.

Has Fauset, in the end, been "putting Angela through"? Or rather, has she been putting *us* through, putting her culture through? In delineating the limits of racial experience, Jessie Fauset reveals much about the racial dimensions of postwar modernism. In this depiction, she shares the company of many Harlem Renaissance writers who use the trope of passing for white to interrogate the illusion of racial progress and the limits of segregation. Yet the bleak endings in both of Nella Larsen's novels, where the independent protagonist dies or nearly sinks beneath the impossibility of locating the individuality Angela finally achieves, suggests that Angela's ending is an optimistic one. So, too, do Charles Chesnutt's passing characters end in circumstances far less promising than Angela's. While James Weldon Johnson's Ex-Colored Man, by the end of his narrative, is materially and socially comfortable, the note of regret with which his tale ends suggests a psychological discomfort that will undo his peace of mind. Rather than maintaining a segregated fictional space where race circumscribes intellectual discourse, Fauset engages in her world fully and directly, in a pointed and precise analysis of the racial dimensions of early-twentieth-century American culture. In doing so, she offers a model of identity that recognizes the limits created by race, but also resists being curtailed by them.

Notes

1. See, for instance, Ammons; Wall, 73-79; McDowell; and duCille.
2. Toomer's most complex analyses of race have only recently been made available in Robert B. Jones's edition, *Jean Toomer: Selected Essays and Literary Criticism*. In "The Crock of Problems," included in the collection, Toomer argues, for instance, "It is evident that in point of fact none of the standard color labels fit me. I am not white. I am not black. . . . I have never lived within the 'color line,' and my life has never been cut off from the general course and conduct of American white life" (56).
3. Even among theoretically and ideologically like-minded critics, disagreement reigns. Hazel Carby argues that "ultimately the conservatism of Fauset's ideology dominates her texts" (167), whereas duCille finds criticism that dismisses Fauset for her ostensible celebration of light skin and interracial marriage to be "ahistorical in the degree to which [such critics] chide early African American writers for not being 100 to 150 years ahead of their times . . . [and condemn writers like Fauset] for writing through and against the dominant racial and sexual ideologies of their times, rather than out of the enlightened, feminist vision of ours" (18).
4. Numerous critics have noted the nursery-rhyme motif through which *Plum Bun* is titled and ordered, though they have read that motif to different ends. Joseph J. Feeney argues that the nursery rhyme offers an ironic counter-structure through which Fauset exposes "the anger, the tragedy, the sardonic comedy, the disillusioned hopes, the bitterness against white Americans" felt by black Americans ("Sardonic" 367). The "Plum Bun" nursery rhyme in particular, Feeney notes, resonates with the reminder that "only whites go to market, only whites enjoy a plum bun" ("Black Childhood" 69). In addition, Deborah McDowell's feminist reading of the fairy tale motif in Fauset's 1924 novel *There is Confusion* and her story "The Sleeper Wakes" offers a useful perspective. McDowell argues that "Fauset was aware of how folk literature—particularly fairy tales—served to initiate the acculturation of children to traditional social roles, expectations and behaviors, based on their sex" (35). Thus, enacting the fairy tale critiques the fairy tale. In McDowell's reading, Fauset summarily undermines the fairy tale's implicit ideology: "'Happily-ever-after' is not marriage to a handsome, wealthy prince but realization and acceptance of the virtues of the black cultural experience as well as a realization and rejection of conventional social relationships that are injurious to the growth of selfhood" (38).

Works Cited

Ammons, Elizabeth. "New Literary History: Edith Wharton and Jessie Redmon Fauset." *College Literature* 14 (1987): 207-18.

Brown, William Wells. *Clotel, or, The President's Daughter: A Narrative of Slave Life in the United States.* New York: Carol, 1995.

Carby, Hazel. *Reconstructing Womanhood: The Emergence of the Afro-American Woman Novelist.* New York: Oxford UP, 1987.

Chesnutt, Charles. *The House Behind the Cedars.* New York: Penguin, 1993.

Dewey, John. *The Public and Its Problems.* 1927. Athens: Swallow, 1988.

Douglas, Ann. *Terrible Honesty: Mongrel Manhattan in the 1920's.* New York: Noonday, 1995.

duCille, Ann. *The Coupling Convention.* New York: Oxford UP, 1993.

Fauset, Jessie. Letter to Jean Toomer. 24 Feb. 1922.

James Weldon Johnson Collection. Beinecke Rare Book and Manuscript Library. Yale University.

———. *Plum Bun.* 1929. Boston: Beacon, 1990.

Feeney, Joseph J., S. J. "Black Childhood as Ironic: A Nursery Rhyme Transformed in Jessie Fauset's Novel *Plum Bun.*" *Minority Voices* 4.2 (1980): 65-69.

———. "A Sardonic, Unconventional Jessie Fauset: The Double Structure and Double Vision of Her Novels." *College Language Association Journal* 22 (1979): 365-82.

Gilmore, Michael T. "Hawthorne and the Making of the Middle Class." *Rethinking Class.* Ed. Wai Chee Dimock and Michael T. Gilmore. New York: Columbia UP, 1994. 215-38.

Harper, Frances E. W. *Iola Leroy.* 1892. Boston: Beacon, 1987.

Johnson, James Weldon. *The Autobiography of an Ex-Colored Man.* 1912. New York: Penguin, 1990.

Jones, Robert B., ed. *Jean Toomer: Selected Essays and Literary Criticism.* Knoxville: U of Tennessee P, 1996.

Larsen, Nella. Quicksand *and* Passing. Ed. Deborah McDowell. New Brunswick: Rutgers UP, 1986.

Lippmann, Walter. *Drift and Mastery.* New York: Mitchell Kennerley, 1914.

———. *Public Opinion.* New York: Harcourt Brace and Co., 1922.

McDowell, Deborah. "The Neglected Dimensions of Jessie Redmon Fauset." *Afro-Americans in New York Life and History* 5.2 (1981): 33-49.

Sylvander, Carolyn Wedin. *Jessie Redmon Fauset: Black American Writer.* Troy: Whitston, 1981.

Tate, Claudia. *Domestic Allegories of Political Desire.* New York: Oxford UP, 1992.

Wall, Cheryl. *Women of the Harlem Renaissance.* Bloomington: Indiana UP, 1995.

The Chinaberry Tree

GERALD SYKES (ESSAY DATE 1932)

SOURCE: Sykes, Gerald. "Amber-Tinted Elegance." *The Nation* (27 July 1932): 88.

In this essay, Sykes reviews Fauset's The Chinaberry Tree. *Although Sykes criticizes Fauset's novel for not reflecting a true Black experience, but rather mimicking white aesthetics, he also praises Fauset for her insight into the unusual status of light-skinned Blacks.*

Though faulty, [***The Chinaberry Tree***] is the work of a remarkable psychologist who can be congratulated not simply because her material is interesting but because she has understood so well the human factors involved in it . . .

The book attempts to idealize [the] polite colored world in terms of the white standards that it has adopted. And here lies the root of Miss Fauset's artistic errors. When she parades the possessions of her upper classes and when she puts her lovers through their Fauntleroy courtesies, she is not only stressing the white standards that they have adopted; she is definitely minimizing the colored blood in them. This is a decided weakness, for it steals truth and life from the book. Is not the most precious part of a Negro work of art that which is specifically Negroid, which none but a Negro could contribute?

We need not look far for the reason for Miss Fauset's idealization. It is pride, the pride of a genuine aristocrat. And it is pride also that makes her such a remarkable psychologist. However many her artistic errors, Miss Fauset has a rare understanding of people and their motives . . . Inspired by the religious motive which so many Negro writers seem to feel, she has simply been trying to justify her world to the world at large. Her mistake has consisted in trying to do this in terms of the white standard.

"To be a Negro in America posits a dramatic situation." Yes, and to be one of Miss Fauset's amber-tinted, well-to-do, refined Negroes—not having to deal much with whites, but surrounded on all sides by the white standard—posits a delicate psychological situation. It is for this reason that few white novels have anything like the shades of feeling to be found in ***The Chinaberry Tree.*** Every moment speaks of yearning. That is why, once it is seen as a whole, even its faults are charming, for the story they tell is poignant and beautiful, too.

FURTHER READING

Bibliography

Austin, Rhonda. "Jessie Redmon Fauset." In *American Women Writers, 1900-1945: A Bio-Bibliographical Critical Sourcebook,* edited by Laurie Champion, pp. 100-06. Westport, Conn.: Greenwood Press, 2000.

Provides a brief biography in addition to a bibliography of sources on Fauset.

Biographies

Davis, Thadious M. Foreword to *There Is Confusion,* pp. v-xxv. Boston: Northeaster University Press, 1989.

Relates Fauset's biography to her first novel; reviews critical evaluations of There Is Confusion.

"Jessie Fauset: Midwife to the Harlem Renaissance." *The New Crisis* 107, no. 4 (2000): 24-35.

Focuses on Fauset's connection with Du Bois and Crisis.

Sylvander, Carolyn Wedin. *Jessie Redmon Fauset: Black American Writer.* Troy, N.Y.: Whitson, 1981, 275 p.

Gives an overview of Fauset's life and career from a feminist perspective.

Criticism

Allen, Carol. "Migration through Mirrors and Memories: The Family, Home, and Creativity in the Work of Jessie Redmon Fauset." In *Black Women Intellectuals: Strategies of Nation, Family, and Neighborhood in the Works of Pauline Hopkins, Jessie Fauset, and Marita Bonner,* pp. 47-76. New York: Garland Publishing, 1998.

Argues that Fauset's observations of women and the domestic sphere reveal sharper social criticism than previous critics have found in her writing.

Ammons, Elizabeth. "New Literary History: Edith Wharton and Jessie Redmon Fauset." *College Literature* 14, no. 3 (1987): 207-18.

Argues for the influence of Edith Wharton on Fauset and the similarity between their works, especially relating to depictions of class.

Batker, Carol J. "An 'Honest-to-God' American: Patriotism, Foreignness, and Domesticity in Jessie Fauset's Fiction." *Reforming Fictions: Native, African, and Jewish American Women's Literature and Journalism in the Progressive Era,* pp. 71-88. New York: Columbia University Press, 2000.

Maintains that Fauset's patriotic Black characters were part of a larger argument for civil rights; notes the negative aspects of integration and middle-class domestic life.

Braithwaite, William Stanley. "The Novels of Jessie Fauset." *Opportunity* 12 (1934): 24-28.

Describes Fauset as the "Jane Austen" of Black novelists.

Condé, Mary. "Passing in the Fiction of Jessie Redmon Fauset and Nella Larsen." *Yearbook of English Studies* 24 (1994): 94-104.

Discusses the generally sympathetic take on "passing" in the novels of Jessie Fauset and Nella Larsen.

Feeney, Joseph J. "Greek Tragic Patters in a Black Novel: Jessie Fauset's *The Chinaberry Tree.*" *College Language Association Journal* 18, no. 2 (1974): 211-15.

Explores the incest theme in The Chinaberry Tree, *concluding that Fauset mixes Greek tragedy with conventional sentimentality.*

———. "A Sardonic, Unconventional Jessie Fauset: The Double Structure and Double Vision of her Novels." *College Language Association Journal* 22, no. 4 (1979): 365-82.

Attempts to revise critical evaluations of Fauset's novels as conservative and overly genteel; emphasizes the painful instances of prejudice in Fauset's life and work.

Griffin, Erica L. "The 'Invisible Woman' Abroad: Jessie Fauset's New Horizon." In *Recovered Writers/Recovered Texts,* edited by Dolan Hubbard, pp. 1-19. Knoxville: University of Tennessee Press, 1997.

Examines the theme of travel in Fauset's novels, as well as some of her essays; argues for the importance of Fauset's global travels to her developing consciousness.

Jones, Sharon L. "Reclaiming a Legacy: The Dialectic of Race, Class, and Gender in Jessie Fauset, Zora Neale Hurston, and Dorothy West." *Hecate* 24, no. 1 (1998): 155-64.

Suggests that Fauset, Hurston, and West are better seen as celebrating the ordinary, common traditions of African Americans, rather than bourgeois or "folk."

Kaye, Campbell D. Review of *The Chinaberry Tree and Selected Writings,* by Jesse Redmon Faucet. *MELUS* 23, no. 1 (1998): 197.

Reviews the 1995 edition of Fauset's third novel; finds that Fauset made observations about race, class, and gender that were radical for her era.

Lupton, Mary Jane. "Bad Blood in Jersey: Jessie Fauset's *The Chinaberry Tree.*" *College Language Association Journal* 27, no. 4 (1984): 383-92.

Finds that The Chinaberry Tree *has suffered unjust criticism by being judged from a purely masculinist perspective.*

———. "Clothes and Closure in Three Novels by Black Women." *Black American Literature Forum* 20, no. 4 (1986): 409-21.

Compares Fauset's Comedy, American Style *to Alice Walker's* The Color Purple *(1982) and Toni Morrison's* Tar Baby *(1981).*

McCoy, Beth. "'Is This Really What You Wanted Me to Be?': The Daughter's Disintegration in Jessie Redmon Fauset's *There Is Confusion.*" *Modern Fiction Studies* 40, no. 1 (1994): 101-18.

Suggests that Fauset's first novel has been misread by critics insisting that Fauset adhere to specific formal or ideological rules.

McDowell, Deborah E. "The Neglected Dimension of Jessie Redmon Fauset." In *Conjuring: Black Women, Fiction, and Literary Tradition,* edited by Marjorie Pryse and Hortense J. Spillers, pp. 86-104. Bloomington: Indiana University Press, 1985.

Considers Fauset among the earliest Black feminists; maintains that earlier critics focused on her portrayal of the middle class while ignoring her rendering of Black female life.

McLendon, Jacquelyn. *The Politics of Color in the Fiction of Jessie Fauset and Nella Larsen.* Charlottesville: University of Virginia Press, 1995, 142 p.

Proposes that both Fauset and Larsen parody the conventional mulatto tale rather than merely repeat it; suggests that Fauset uses the mulatto character as a "political tool."

Miller, Nina. "Femininity, Publicity, and the Class Division of Cultural Labor: Jessie Redmon Fauset's *There Is Confusion.*" *African American Review* 20, no. 2 (1996): 205-20.

Uses the idea of performance to explore the issue of identity in Fauset's first novel.

Starkey, Marion. "Jessie Fauset." *Southern Workman* (May 1932): 217-20.

Includes an interview with Fauset explaining the importance of writing about the achievements of Blacks.

OTHER SOURCES FROM GALE:

Additional coverage of Fauset's life and career is contained in the following sources published by the Gale Group: *African American Writers,* Ed. 2; *Black Literature Criticism,* Vol. 2; *Black Writers,* Ed. 1; *Contemporary Authors,* Vol. 109; *Contemporary Authors New Revision Series,* Vol. 83; *Contemporary Literary Criticism,* Vols. 19, 54; *Dictionary of Literary Biography,* Vol. 51; *DISCovering Authors Modules: Multicultural Authors*; *Feminist Writers*; *Literature Resource Center*; and *Modern American Women Writers.*

RUDOLPH FISHER

(1897 - 1934)

(Full name Rudolph John Chauncey Fisher) American novelist, short story writer, and essayist.

Fisher was a medical student whose unexpected publishing success brought him into the inner circle of the Harlem Renaissance. The first in the New Negro movement to publish in the venerable *Atlantic Monthly,* Fisher also excelled in scholarship, winning honors in public speaking and biology. He moved from Washington, D.C., to New York not to partake of the burgeoning culture of Harlem, but to train further in medicine at Columbia University before opening his own medical practice. His sense of belonging to two different worlds is reflected in fiction that strongly captures the flavor of Harlem during the 1920s, yet reveals the difficulty Harlem transplants found in adapting to urban life. Fisher also distinguished himself as the author of the first Black American detective novel, a genre that suited his dual interests in the mystery of Harlem and the details of medicine. Among friends, including Langston Hughes and Alain Locke, Fisher was known as a witty intellectual and a living embodiment of the New Negro.

BIOGRAPHICAL INFORMATION

Fisher was born May 9, 1897, in Washington, D.C. His mother was Glendora Williamson Fisher, and his father was John Wesley Fisher, a minister. In 1915, he graduated with honors from Classical High School in Providence, Rhode Island. He attended Brown University, graduating in 1919 with honors in English and biology and serving as Class Orator at the commencement ceremony. He also pursued a master's degree in English at Brown while working as a graduate assistant in biology. In his years at Brown, Fisher earned honors with Phi Beta Kappa, Delta Sigma Rho, and Sigma Xi, in addition to multiple awards for oratory. Fisher attended Howard University Medical School, where he also acted as an instructor in embryology before graduating with highest honors in 1924. That same year he married Jane Ryder and began an internship at Freedman's Hospital in Washington, D.C. In 1925, Fisher moved to New York, taking a position as a fellow with the National Research Council at Columbia University's College of Physicians and Surgeons, and studying bacteriology, pathology, and roentgenology (a subdiscipline of radiology). Also in 1925, he published four stories, two of which appeared in the *Atlantic Monthly*; that accomplishment brought him the immediate attention of Harlem writers such as Hughes and Countee Cullen. His first story, "The City of Refuge," was also chosen for the anthology *The Best Short Stories of 1925.* Fisher and his wife had their only child, Hugh, in 1926, and he opened his own practice in 1927, specializing in roentgenology, then opening an x-ray lab. Throughout this time he continued writing and publishing, with two more stories appearing in *Atlantic Monthly;* he also produced a nonfiction essay titled "The Caucasian Storms Harlem" on white curiosity about Harlem culture. In that essay he describes the Hayne Café, where he met the actor Paul Robeson, with whom he sang on more than one occasion. Fisher published his first novel in 1928, *The Walls of Jericho,* to general praise, but he continued in his medical career as well. From 1929 to 1932, Fisher worked at the International Hospital, and in 1930 he also took a position as a roentgenologist with the New York City Health Department. From 1931 to 1934, Fisher served as an Army medic, in addition to his other positions. Active in the Harlem community, Fisher held a position on the literature commission of the Harlem neighborhood YMCA and lectured at the Harlem branch of the New York Public Library. He published a handful of short stories in the early 1930s, including the start of a series for young readers, based on the twelve-year-old character Ezekiel. In 1932, he published his second novel, *The Conjure-Man Dies,* the first American detective novel to feature a Black hero. Fisher's detective, Dr. John Archer, appeared in his last published story, "John Archer's Nose" (1935). Fisher had planned to continue using both Ezekiel and Dr. Archer as characters in later fiction, but was prevented by a severe abdominal illness that finally resulted in his death on December 26, 1934.

MAJOR WORKS

Fisher's work can be divided into two general categories: his short fiction and his novels. His first story, "The City of Refuge," is among his most significant. The story of King Solomon Gillis, a North Carolina native making a new life in Harlem, "The City of Refuge" exposes some of the harsh realities of Harlem life through the perspective of an eager, naïve outsider. "The City of Refuge" depicts Harlem as a melange of types, classes, and degrees of Blackness, a theme common to Fisher's short stories, including the award-winning "High Yaller" (published 1925 in *Crisis*), "Ringtail" (1925, *Atlantic Monthly*), and "Blades of Steel" (1927, *Atlantic Monthly*). A particular concern of Fisher's is the transformation of people and culture that inevitably follows the move from the rural South to the urban Northeast. Beginning with "The South Lingers On" (1925, *Survey Graphic*) through such stories as "The Promised Land" (1927, *Atlantic Monthly*), "Guardian of the Law" (1933, *Opportunity*), and "Miss Cynthie" (1933, *Story*), Fisher examined the influence of southern folkways on new arrivals in Harlem. Many of these stories feature a wise, and wise-cracking, grandmother who represents the traditions and values of an earlier time to a protagonist losing his way in the big city. Fisher's first novel, *The Walls of Jericho,* addresses some of these themes as well. Fisher once claimed that he wrote the book on a bet, challenged with the task of representing every class of Black life in Harlem in one coherent story. The novel brings together the Black working class, the "rats," or lower classes, and the "dickties," generally light-skinned, educated professionals, and highlights the silent distinctions between the groups as well as the opportunities for solidarity. *The Conjure-Man Dies,* Fisher's second novel, brings back two working-class characters from *The Walls of Jericho,* Jinx Jenkins and Bubber Brown, who become mixed up in the death of a mysterious "conjure man," N'Gana Frimbo. When the corpse of Frimbo comes back to life, Dr. John Archer gets involved in the case. Archer and Frimbo are educated Black men of the upper classes, while Jinx and Bubber are part of Harlem's street and club life, a further reflection of Fisher's interest in the variety and duality of Black culture.

CRITICAL RECEPTION

Fisher's peers were generally enthusiastic about his talents. Langston Hughes believed Fisher to be the wittiest of his Harlem Renaissance circle. Alain Locke, in his famous work on *The New Negro* (1925), claimed the up-and-coming Fisher represented the new generation of Blacks "not because of years only, but because of a new aesthetic and a new philosophy of life." Fisher's success in placing four stories with *Atlantic Monthly,* with the first anthologized as one of the best of 1925, reflects the immediate acceptance he found in literary circles. Like many authors of the Harlem Renaissance, Fisher faced questions about his portrayal of class. Some readers felt that his realism was generally positive, compared to the more sordid depictions of Black culture coming from such authors as Claude McKay and Carl Van Vechten. Others, however, thought his portrayal of the lower classes too positive, suggesting that middle-class writers such as Fisher ought to give voice to the perspective of his own people. Later scholarship on Fisher has largely focused on his depictions of Harlem life; most have heralded his realism and authenticity, as well as his intelligence. Much of the first scholarship on Fisher worked simply to bring his writing back into the canon of African American literature, beginning with Eleanor Q. Tignor's series of articles on Fisher's short stories and novels. Later work would be more specific, addressing particular themes or works. Many critics have identified important influences: John McCluskey (1982) observes the role of Fisher's interest in music, Adrienne Johnson Gosselin (1998) focuses on the motif of liminality, and Jon Woodson (1999) notes the presence of G. I. Gurdjieff in Fisher's writing. Editions of Fisher's collected works appearing in the late 1980s have allowed critics to become more familiar with his writing and with his contributions to the Harlem Renaissance.

PRINCIPAL WORKS

The Walls of Jericho (novel) 1928

The Conjure-Man Dies: A Mystery Tale of Dark Harlem (novel) 1932

The City of Refuge: The Collected Stories (short stories) 1987

The Short Fiction of Rudolph Fisher (short stories) 1987

PRIMARY SOURCES

RUDOLPH FISHER (ESSAY DATE 1925)

SOURCE: Fisher, Rudolph. "The South Lingers on." *Survey Graphic* (Harlem Number) VI, no. 6 (March 1925): 644-47.

In this short story, Fisher notes how southern traditions continue to permeate northern Black culture.

Ezekiel Taylor, preacher of the gospel of Jesus Christ, walked slowly along One Hundred and Thirty-Third Street, conspicuously alien. He was little and old and bent. A short, bushy white beard framed his shiny black face and his tieless celluloid collar. A long, greasy, green-black Prince Albert, with lapels frayed and buttons worn through to, their metal hung loosely from his shoulders. His trousers were big and baggy and limp, yet not enough so to hide the dejected bend of his knees.

A little boy noted the beard and gibed, "Hey, Santa Claus! 'Tain't Chris'mas yet!" And the little boy's playmates chorused, "Haw, hew! Lookit the colored Santa Claus!"

"For of such is the kingdom of heaven," mused Ezekiel Taylor. No. The kingdom of Harlem. Children turned into mockers. Satan in the hearts of infants. Harlem—city of the devil—outpost of hell.

Darkness settled, like the gloom in the old preacher's heart; darkness an hour late, for these sinners even tinkered with God's time, substituting their "daylight-saving." Wicked, yes. But sad too, as though they were desperately warding off the inescapable night of sorrow in which they must suffer for their sins. Harlem. What a field! What numberless souls to save!—These very taunting children who knew not even the simplest of the commandments—

But he was old and alone and defeated. The world had called to his best. It had offered money, and they had gone; first the young men whom he had fathered, whom he had brought up from infancy in his little Southern church; then their wives and children whom they eventually sent for; and finally their parents, loath to leave their shepherd and their dear, decrepit shacks, but dependent and without choice.

"Whynit y' come to New York?" old Deacon Gassoway had insisted. "Martin and Eli and Jim Lee and his fambly's all up da' now an' doin' fine. We'll all git together an' start a chutch of our own, an' you'll still be pastor an' it'll be jes' same as 'twas hyeh." Full of that hope, he had come. But where were they? He had captained his little ship till it sank; he had clung to a splint and been tossed ashore; but the shore was cold, gray, hard and rock-strewn.

He had been in barren places before but God had been there too. Was Harlem then past hope? Was the connection between this place and heaven broken, so that the servant of God went hungry while little children ridiculed? Into his mind, like a reply, crept an old familiar hymn, and he found himself humming it softly:

> The Lord will provide,
> The Lord will provide,
> In some way or 'nother,
> The Lord will provide.
> It may not be in your way,
> It may not be in mine
> But yet in His own way
> The Lord will provide.

Then suddenly, astonished, he stopped, listening. He had not been singing alone—a chorus of voices somewhere near had caught up his hymn. Its volume was gradually increasing. He looked about for a church. There was none. He covered his deaf ear so that it might not handicap his good one. The song seemed to issue from one of the private houses a little way down the street.

He approached with eager apprehension and stood wonderingly before a long flight of brownstone steps leading to an open entrance. The high first floor of the house, that to which the steps led, was brightly lighted, and the three front windows had their panes covered with colored tissuepaper designed to resemble church windows. Strongly, cheeringly the song came out to the listener:

The Lord will provide
The Lord will provide,
In some way or 'nother,
The Lord will provide.

Ezekiel Taylor hesitated an incredulous moment, then smiling, he mounted the steps and went in.

The Reverend Shackleton Ealey had been inspired to preach the gospel by the draft laws of 1917. He remained in the profession not out of gratitude to its having kept him out of war, but because he found it a far less precarious mode of living than that devoted to poker, blackjack and dice. He was stocky and flat-faced and yellow, with many black freckles and the eyes of a dogfish. And he was clever enough not to conceal his origin, but to make capital out of his conversion from gambler to preacher and to confine himself to those less enlightened groups that thoroughly believed in the possibility of so sudden and complete a transformation.

The inflow of rural folk from the South was therefore fortune, and Reverend Shackleton Ealey spent hours in Pennsylvania station greeting newly arrived migrants, urging them to visit his meeting-place and promising them the satisfaction of "that old-time religion." Many had come—and contributed.

This was prayer-meeting night. Reverend Ealey had his seat on a low platform at the distant end of the double room originally designed for a "parlor." From behind a pulpitstand improvised out of soap-boxes and covered with calico he counted his congregation and estimated his profit.

A stranger entered uncertainly, looked about a moment, and took a seat near the door. Reverend Shackleton Ealey appraised him: a little bent-over old man with a bushy white beard and a long Prince Albert coat. Perfect type—fertile soil. He must greet this stranger at the close of the meeting and effusively make him welcome.

But Sister Gassoway was already by the stranger's side, shaking his hand vigorously and with unmistakable joy; and during the next hymn she came over to old man Gassoway and whispered in his ear, whereupon he jumped up wide-eyed, looked around, and made broadly smiling toward the newcomer. Others turned to see, and many, on seeing, began to whisper excitedly into their neighbor's ear and turnf d to see again. The stranger was occasioning altogether too great a stir. Reverend Ealey decided to pray.

His prayer was a masterpiece. It besought of God protection for His people in a strange and wicked land; it called down His damnation upon those dens of iniquity, the dance halls, the theatres, the cabarets; it berated the poker-sharp, the blackjack player, the dice-roller; it denounced the drunkard, the bootlegger, the dope-peddler; and it ended in a sweeping tirade against the wolf-in-sheep's-clothing, whatever his motive might be.

Another hymn and the meeting came to a close.

The stranger was surrounded before Reverend Ealey could reach him. When finally he approached the old preacher with extended hand and hollow-hearted smile, old man Gassoway was saying:

"Yes, suh, Rev'n Taylor, dass jes' whut we goin' do. Start makin' 'rangements tomorrer. Martin an' Jim Lee's over to Ebeneezer, but dey doan like it 'tall. Says hit's too hifalutin for 'em, de way dese Harlem cullud folks wushup; Ain' got no Holy Ghos' in 'em, dass whut. Jes' come in an' set down an' git up an' go out. Never moans, never shouts, never even says 'amen.' Most of us is hyeh, an' we gonna git together an' start us a ch'ch of our own, wid you f' pastor, like we said. Yas, suh. Hyeh's Brother Ealey now. Brother Ealey, dis hyeh's our old preacher Rev'n Taylor. We was jes' tellin him—"

The Reverend Shackleton Ealey had at last a genuine revelation—that the better-yielding half of his flock was on the wing. An old oath of frustration leaped to his lips—"God—" but he managed to bite it in the middle—"bless you, my brother," he growled.

II

"What makes you think you can cook?"

"Why, brother, I been in the neighborhood o' grub all my life!"

"Humph! Fly bird, you are."

"Pretty near all birds fly, friend."

"Yes—even black birds."

The applicant for the cook's job lost his joviality. "All right. I'm a black bird. You're a half-yeller hound. Step out in the air an' I'll fly down your dam' throat, so I can see if your insides is yeller, too!"

The clerk grinned. "You must do your cooking on the top of your head. Turn around and fly out that door there and see if the Hundred and Thirty-Fifth Street breeze won't cool you off some. We want a fireless cooker."

With an unmistakable suggestion as to how the clerk might dispose of his job the applicant rolled cloudily out of the employment office. The clerk called "Next!" and Jake Crinshaw, still convulsed with astonishment, nearly lost his turn.

"What kind of work are you looking for, buddy?"

"No purtickler kin', suh. Jes' work, dass all."

"Well, what can you do?"

"Mos' anything, I reckon."

"Drive a car?"

"No suh. Never done dat."

"Wait table?"

"Well, I never is."

"Run elevator?"

"No, suh."

"What have you been doing?"

"Farmin'."

"Farming? Where?"

"Tennin's Landin', Virginia. 'At's wha' all my folks is."

"How long you been here?"

"Sin' been hyeh a week yit. Still huntin' work." Jake answered rather apologetically. The question had been almost "Oh—migrant." In the clerk's tone were patronization, some contempt, a little cynical amusement and complete comprehension. "Migrant" meant nothing to Jake; to the clerk it explained everything.

"M-hm. Did you try the office up above—between here and Seventh Avenue? They wanted two dozen laborers for a railroad camp upstate—pay your transportation, board and everything."

"Yes, suh—up there yestiddy, but de man say dey had all dey need. Tole me to try y'all down hyeh."

"M-hm. Well, I'm sorry, but we haven't anything for you this morning. Come in later in the week. Something may turn up."

"Yes, suh. Thank y' suh."

Jake made his discouraged way to the sidewalk and stood contemplating. Eli's blue jumpers were clean and spotless—they had been his Sunday-go-to-meeting ones at home. He wore big, broad, yellow shoes and a shapeless tan felt hat, beneath whose brim the hair was close cut, the neck shaved bare. He was very much dressed up.

The applicant who had preceded him approached. "What'd that yeller dog tell you, bud?"

"Tole me come in later."

"Huh! That's what they all say. Only way for a guy with guts to get anything in this town is to be a bigger crook 'n the next one." He pointed to two well-dressed young men idling on the curb. "See them two? They used to wait on a job where I was chef. Now look at 'em—prosperous! An' how 'd they get that way? Hmph! That one's a pimp an' th' other's a pickpocket. Take your choice." And the cynic departed.

But Jake had greater faith in Harlem. Its praises had been sounded too highly—there must be something.

He turned and looked at the signboard that had led him to enter the employment office. It was a wooden blackboard, on which was written in chalk: "Help wanted. All sorts of jobs. If we haven't it, leave your name and we'll find it." The clerk hadn't asked Jake *his* name.

A clanging, shrieking fire engine appeared from nowhere and swept terrifyingly past. It frightened Jake like the first locomotive he had seen as a child. He shrank back against the building. Another engine passed. No more. He felt better. No one minded the engines. No one noticed that he did. Harlem itself was a fire engine.

Jake could read the signs on the buildings across the street: "Harlem Commercial and Savings Bank"—"Hale and Clark, Real Estate"—"Restaurant and Delicatessen, J. W. Jackson, proprietor"—"The Music Shop"—"John Gilmore, Tonsorial Parlor." He looked up at the buildings. They were menacingly big and tall and close. There were no trees. No ground for trees to grow from. Sidewalks overflowing with children. Streets crammed full of street-cars and automobiles. Noise, hurry, bustle—fire engines.

Jake looked again at the signboard. Help wanted—all sorts. After a while he heaved a great sigh, turned slowly, and slouched wearily on, hoping to catch sight of another employment office with a signboard out front.

III

It was eleven o'clock at night. Majutah knew that Harry would be waiting on the doorstep downstairs. He knew better than to ring the bell so late—she had warned him. And there was no telephone. Grandmother wouldn't consent to having a telephone in the flat—she thought it would draw lightning. As if every other flat in the house didn't have one, as if lightning would strike all the others and leave theirs unharmed! Grandmother was such a nuisance with her old fogeyisms. If it weren't for her down-home ideas there'd be no trouble getting out now to go to the cabaret with Harry. As it was, Majutah would have to steal down the hall past Grandmother's room in the hope that she would be asleep.

Majutah looked to her attire. The bright red sandals and scarlet stockings, she fancied, made her feet look smaller and her legs bigger. This was desirable, since her black crepe dress, losing in width what style had added to its length, would not permit her to sit comfortably and cross her knees without occasioning ample display of everything below them. Her vanity-case mirror revealed how exactly the long pendant earrings matched her red coral beads and how perfectly becoming the new close bob was, and assured her for the tenth time that Egyptian rouge made her skin look lighter. She was ready.

Into the narrow hallways she tipped, steadying herself against the wallsr and slowly approached the outside door at the end. Grandmother's room was the last off the hallway. Majutah reached it, slipped successfully past, and started silently to open the door to freedom.

"Jutie?"

How she hated to be called Jutie! Why couldn't the meddlesome old thing say Madge like everyone else?

"Ma'am?"

"Wha' you goin' dis time o' night?"

"Just downstairs to mail a letter."

"You Basin' out mighty quiet, if dat's all you goin' do. Come 'eh. Lemme look at you."

Majutah slipped off her pendants and beads and laid them on the floor. She entered her grandmother's room, standing where the foot of the bed would hide her gay shoes and stockings. Useless precautions. The shrewd old woman inspected her grandaughter a minute in disapproving silence, then asked:

"Well, wha's de letter?"

"Hello, Madge," said Harry. "What held you up? You look mad enough to bite bricks."

"I am. Grandmother, of course. She's a pest. Always nosing and meddling. I'm grown, and the money I make supports both of us, and I'm sick of acting like a kid just to please her."

"How'd you manage?"

"I didn't manage. I just gave her a piece of my mind and came on out."

"Mustn't hurt the old lady's feelings. It's just her way of looking out for you."

"I don't need any looking out for—or advice either!"

"Excuse me. Which way—Happy's or Edmonds'?"

"Edmonds'—darn it!"

"Right."

It was two o'clock in the morning. Majutah's grandmother closed her Bible and turned down the oil lamp by which she preferred to read it. For a long time she sat thinking of Jutie—and of Harlem, this city of Satan. It was Harlem that had changed Jutie—this great, noisy, heartless, crowded place where you lived under the same roof with a hundred people you never knew; where night was alive and morning dead. It was Harlem—those brazen women with whom Jutie sewed, who swore and shimmied and laughed at the suggestion of going to church. Jutie wore red stockings. Jutie wore dresses that looked like nightgowns. Jutie painted her face and straightened her hair, instead of leaving it as God intended. Jutie—lied—often.

And while Madge laughed at a wanton song, her grandmother knelt by her bed and through the sinful babel of the airshaft, through her own silent tears, prayed to God in heaven for Jutie's lost soul.

IV

"Too much learnin' ain' good f' nobody. When I was her age I couldn' write my own name."

"You can't write much mo' 'n that now. Too much learnin'! Whoever heard o' sich a thing!"

Anna's father, disregarding experience in arguing with his wife, pressed his point. "Sho they's sich a thing as too much learnin'! 'At gal's gittin' so she don't b'lieve nuthin'!"

"Hmph! Didn't she jes' tell me las' night she didn' b'lieve they ever was any Adam an' Eve?"

"Well, I ain' so sho they ever was any myself! An' one thing is certain: If that gal o' mine wants to keep on studyin' an' go up there to that City College an' learn how to teach school an' be somebody, I'll work my fingers to the bone to help her do it! Now!"

"That ain' what I'm takin' 'bout. You ain' worked no harder 'n I is to help her git this far. Hyeh she is ready to graduate from high school. Think of it—high school! When we come along they didn' even *have* no high schools. Fus' thing y' know she be so far above us we can't reach her with a fence-rail. Then you'll wish you'd a listened to me. What I says is, she done gone far enough."

"Ain' no sich thing as far enough when you wants to go farther. 'Tain' as if it was gonna cost a whole lot. That's the trouble with you cullud folks now. Git so far an' stop—set down—through—don't want no mo'." Her disgust was boundless. "Y' got too much cotton field in you, that's what!"

The father grinned. "They sho' ain' no cotton field in yo' mouth, honey."

"No they ain't. An' they ain' no need o' all this arguin' either, 'cause all that gal's got to do is come in hyeh right now an' put her arms 'roun' yo' neck, an' you'd send her to Europe if she wanted to go!"

"Well, all I says is, when dey gits to denyin' de Bible hit's time to stop 'em."

"Well all I says is, if Cousin Sukie an' yo' no 'count brother, Jonathan, can send their gal all the way from Athens to them Howard's an' pay car-fare an' boa'd an' ev'ything, we can send our gal—"

She broke off as a door slammed. There was a rush, a delightful squeal, and both parents were being smothered in a cyclone of embraces by a wildly jubilant daughter.

"Mummy! Daddy! I won it! I won it!"

"What under the sun—?"

"The scholarship, Mummy! The scholarship!"

"No!"

"Yes I did! I can go to Columbia! I can go to Teacher's College! Isn't it great?"

Anna's mother turned triumphantly to her husband; but he was beaming at his daughter.

"You sho' is yo' daddy's chile. Teacher's College! Why that's wha' I been wantin' you to go all along!"

V

Rare sight in a close-built, topheavy city—space. A wide open lot, extending along One Hundred and Thirty-Eighth Street almost from Lenox to Seventh Avenue; baring the mangy backs of a long row of One Hundred and Thirty-Ninth Street houses; disclosing their gaping, gasping windows, their shameless strings of half-laundered rags, which gulp up what little air the windows seek to inhale. Occupying the Lenox Avenue end of the lot, the so-called Garvey tabernacle, wide, low, squat, with its stingy little entrance; occupying the other, the church tent where summer camp meetings are held.

Pete and his buddy, Lucky, left their head-to-head game of coon-can as darkness came on. Time to go out—had to save gas. Pete went to the window and looked down at the tent across the street.

"Looks like the side show of a circus. Ever been in?"

"Not me. I'm a preacher's son—got enough o' that stuff when I was a kid and couldn't protect myself."

"Ought to be a pretty good show when some o' them old-time sisters get happy. Too early for the cabarets; let's go in a while, just for the hell of it."

"You sure are hard up for somethin' to do."

"Aw, come on. Somethin' funny's bound to happen. You might even get religion, you dam' bootlegger."

Luck grinned. "Might meet some o' my customers, you mean."

Through the thick, musty heat imprisoned by the canvas shelter a man's voice rose, leading a spiritual. Other voices chimed eagerly in, some high, clear, sweet; some low, mellow, full,—all swelling, rounding out the refrain till it filled the place, so that it seemed the flimsy walls and roof must soon be torn from their moorings and swept aloft with the song:

Where you running, sinner?
Where you running, I say?
Running from the fire—
You can't cross here!

The preacher stood waiting for the song to melt away. There was a moment of abysmal silence, into which the thousand blasphemies filtering in from outside dropped unheeded.

The preacher was talking in deep, impressive tones. One old patriarch was already supplementing each statement with a matter-of-fact "amen!" of approval.

The preacher was describing hell. He was enumerating without exception the horrors that befall the damned: maddening thirst for the drunkard; for the gambler, insatiable flame, his own greed devouring his soul. The preacher's voice no longer talked—it sang; mournfully at first, monotonously up and down, up and down—a chant in minor mode; then more intensely, more excitedly; now fairly strident.

The amens of approval were no longer matter-of-fact, perfunctory. They were quick, spontaneous, escaping the lips of their own accord; they were frequent and loud and began to come from the edges of the assembly instead of just the front rows. The old men cried, "Help him, Lord!" "Preach the word!" "Glory!" taking no apparent heed of the awfulness of the description, and the old women continuously moaned aloud, nodding their bonneted heads, or swaying rhythmically forward and back in their seats.

Suddenly the preacher stopped, leaving the old men and old women still noisy with spiritual momentum. He stood motionless till the last echo of approbation subsided, then repeated the text from which his discourse had taken origin; repeated it in a whisper, lugubrious, hoarse, almost inaudible; "'In—hell—'"—paused, then without warning wildly shrieked, "'*In hell—*'" stopped—returned to his hoarse whisper—"'he lifted up his eyes. . . .'"

"What the hell you want to leave for?" Pete complained when he and Lucky reached the sidewalk. That old bird would 'a' coughed up his gizzard in two more minutes. What's the idea?"

"Aw hell—I don't know.—You think that stuff's funny. You laugh at it. I don't, that's all." Lucky hesitated. The urge to speak outweighed the fear of being ridiculed. "Darn' 'f I know what it is—maybe because it makes me think of the old folks or somethin'—but—hell—it just sorter—gets me—"

Lucky turned abruptly away and started off. Pete watched him for a moment with a look that should have been astonished, outraged, incredulous—but wasn't. He overtook him, put an arm about his shoulders, and because he had to say something as they walked on, muttered reassuringly:

"Well—if you ain't the damnedest fool—"

GENERAL COMMENTARY

OLIVER LOUIS HENRY (ESSAY DATE 1971)

SOURCE: Henry, Oliver Louis. "Rudolph Fisher: An Evaluation." *Crisis* 78, no. 5 (July 1971): 149-54.

In the following essay, Henry emphasizes the theme of class in Fisher's short fiction. Although Henry finds some of Fisher's plots and characters somewhat contrived, he concludes that Fisher strove to depict all different classes and cultures of Blacks in a sympathetic, but still realistic, light.

Class consciousness is perhaps the single most consistent theme found in Fisher's work. He was extremely aware of the class and color distinctions present in the black community, especially the Harlem community, the locale of most of his stories. And almost the entire body of his material deals with the interaction of the various social types and groups present in that community. What makes Fisher so appealing is that he writes about black people in a manner which expresses their kinship with other peoples. He underscores and highlights the fundamental human condition of black Americans. And, through a close observation of their pursuits and concerns, shows that black men and women laugh and cry, sing and dance, work and build, hate and destroy. He captures the historically induced unique qualities of black people; but, and perhaps even more importantly, he writes of them basically as people.

Fisher authored two full-length novels and a host of short stories. The latter represent his major contribution to the literature of the black community. He ranks as a major black writer in the short story form. Of his novels, ***The Walls of Jericho*** (1928) ranks as one of the best written during the heyday of the Negro Renaissance. In *Anger and Beyond,* Herbert Hill indicates that this book gave a lift to the New Negro Movement ***The Conjure Man Dies*** (1932) represents the first detective or mystery novel written by a black American; and, according to Arthur P. Davis who reviewed the novel for *Opportunity* (October, 1932), it represents "not merely a good Negro detective story," but rather "is a good detective story."

Fisher's short stories and sketches reveal the same range and variety of human experience that he captured in his full-length novels. Criticism and evaluation of this writer should be based primarily upon his short stories rather than upon his novels because he was first and foremost a writer in that genre. In no way should this sentiment downgrade his novels; rather it maintains that the principal form in which an author writes provides a more suitable basis for criticism and evaluation. Though Fisher's full-length novels would appear more than adequate to establish him as a major contributor to the Negro Renaissance, his reputation must inevitably rise or fall on the basis of the respect accorded his short stories.

In 1925 **"High Yaller"** won the Amy Spingarn Short Story Contest sponsored by *The Crisis* magazine. The story is very much in the "tragic mulatto" tradition, a theme formerly pursued assiduously by black writers. In this case, Evelyn Brown, a mulatto is accused by Mayme Jackson, a darksome woman, of being "color struck." The accusation takes place at a dance which followed a basketball game at the Manhattan Casino:

> The air was vile—hot, full of breath and choking perfume. You were forever avoiding, colliding, making time on the same spot. So insulating was the crash that you might sway for several minutes near a familiar couple, even recognize their voices, yet catch only the merest glimpse of their vanishing faces.

Concerned about the grain of truth contained in Mayme's comment, Evelyn convinces Jay Martin, her unmistakably black dance partner, to give her the rush. Evelyn does not want the Jim Crow tag foisted upon her by the Mayme Jacksons of the world. But in assessing the reason for her attraction to Jay, she says, "'he's so—white'." (In manner and attitudes.)

Jay agrees to her plan and they make the Harlem scene. During the period of their relationship, each member of the doomed couple experiences some embarrassment and hostility. Many persons, both Negro and white, thought they were an interracial couple. Taboo. Crossing the color line was frowned upon on both sides. At one point Jay says:

> "Well, I'll tell you, Ev. This place, like some you already know about, has a mixed patronage, see? Part jigs, part ofays. That's perfectly all right as long as the jigs keep to their own parties and the ofays to theirs. But as soon as they begin to come mixed, trouble starts. . . . So the management avoids it."

Evelyn calls herself a misfit. And Fisher uses dream sequences to reveal the inner attitudes of both Evelyn and Jay regarding their relationship. Evelyn's mother, an obviously black woman, restrained any impulse Evelyn may have had to leave the race, to cross over the color line. Eventually, the mother dies, Evelyn disappears, and the police arrest and beat Jay. Formally charged with "resisting arrest," but in actuality detained for "messing" with a "white" woman. And Fisher, writing of the episode from Jay's perspective, says:

> What an enormity, blackness. . . . White, the standard of goodness and perfection. . . . An instinctive shrinking from the dark? He'd seen a little white child run in terror from his father once. . . . Instinctive. . . . Unbearable.

Writing in *The Crisis* (August, 1928), Allison Davis accused Fisher of sensationalism in **"High Yaller."** He criticized Fisher along with Langston Hughes, George Schuyler, Eugene Gordon, Claude McKay, and Countee Cullen as Negro writers who, "'confessing' the distinctive sordidness and triviality of Negro life, [make] an exhibition of their own unhealthy imagination, in the name of frankness and sincerity," The criticism is caustic, but Fisher finds himself in rather good company.

"Ringtail" (1925) did not evoke the same critical response, but it might have if some critics had displayed the same concern for the intraracial conflict which provides its motif as they showed for the rather realistic presentation Fisher made of the color consciousness pervading the black community to this very day. **"Ringtail"** involves the intraracial relationships which exist between native black Americans and other blacks, in this story, principally West Indians.

Cyril Sebastian Best is a West Indian who made his way to New York by swimming from a ship in New York harbor shortly after he was taken to task by the ship's cook. appears that Cyril sometimes had difficulty getting along with people: he had a rather large ego. "From those who picked him up exhausted and restored him to bodily comfort," Cyril stole "what he could get and made his way into New York." Fisher describes Cyril in the following manner:

> To him self-improvement meant nothing but increasing these virtues (self-esteem, craftiness, contentiousness, and acquisitiveness), certainly not eliminating or modifying them. He became fond of denying that he was "colored," insisting that he was "a British subject," hence by implication unquestionably superior to any merely American Negro.

The hostility was more than returned. One bright Sunday afternoon as Cyril promenaded down Harlem's Seventh Avenue, he was roughed up a bit by some native black Americans who were led in this sport by Punch Anderson and Meg Minor. Resisting, Cyril was punched in the nose by Anderson who told him, "Now get the hell out o' here, you ringtail monkey-chaser!"

"Monkey-chaser" was a derisive Harlem term for West Indians, and Cyril, offended, vowed revenge. Later, Punch, Meg, and some of their friends discussed the event:

> "There ain't no such thing as a harmless monkey-chaser. . . . If you've done anything to him, he'll get you sooner or later. He can't help it—he's made that way, like a spring."

> "I ain't got a thing for a monk to do, anyhow. . . . Hope Marcus Garvey takes 'em all back to Africa with him. He'll sure have a shipload."

> "You jigs are worse'n ofays. . . . You raise hell about prejudice, and look at you—doin' what you're raising' hell over yourselves."

Though intraracial animosity provides the basic theme for the story, Fisher indicates the basic unity of black people. In describing a card game attended by Punch, Meg, and some other characters he writes: "One player was startlingly white, with a heavy rash of brown freckles and short kinky red hair. Another was almost black, the hair of an Indian and the features of a Moor. The rest ranged between."

Intraracial discord plays a less significant role in **"The City of Refuge"** (1925). For in this story the theme is simply the cruelty of one man toward another, how one man can take advantage of another's friendship. King Solomon Gillis came to New York, to Harlem from his native North Carolina because he had shot a white man. He reached Washington, D.C., where a bootlegger aided his escape with $100 and directions to the place where he longed to come. Concerning the reasons for which Gillis decided that Harlem was the place for him, Fisher writes, "That was the point. In Harlem, black was white. You had rights that could not be denied you; you had privileges, money. It was a land of plenty. . . . The land of plenty was more than that now; it was also the city of refuge."

When "Gillis set down his tan cardboard extension case and wiped his black, shining brow," [he] slowly, spreadingly, grinned at what he saw: Negroes at every turn; up and down Lenox Avenue, up and down 135th Street; big, lanky Negroes, short, squat Negroes; black ones, brown ones, yellow ones . . . here and there a white face drifting along, but Negroes predominantly, overwhelmingly everywhere. . . . This was Negro Harlem."

Early recognized as a new recruit to the Harlem community, Gillis asked a stranger for directions and, immediately, trusted him. Mouse Uggam, the stranger, is in fact from Gillis' hometown, and he helps Gillis get settled in Harlem. In reality Uggam is a dope peddler who wants to transfer his dope business to Gillis because there is some danger that the dope ring may be crashed by the police. Uggam works himself into Gillis' confidence by getting him a job and, later, offering him an opportunity to earn extra money by selling "French Medicine." Gillis, the gullible newcomer to Harlem, the type Harlem treats hard, falls for it all: "'Sure y' get the idea?' Uggam carefully explained it all again. By the time he had finished, King Solomon was wallowing in gratitude."

> "'Mouse, you sho' is been a friend to me. Why, 'f't hadn't been fo' you—'"

Gillis is in business; he learns much about Harlem life. But the ways of the city are hard on those who take it at face value. And "Mouse Uggam," his friend. "Harlem. Land of plenty. City of refuge—city of refuge. If you live long enough—." Fisher writes about life as it is to those who believe, those who dream. It is a harsh reality, but there can be good times along the way. Even Gillis was exultant in his own way, for his own reasons.

In **"The Promised Land"** Fisher explores the impact of the community on an ordinary Harlem family. This theme is similar to **"The City of Refuge"** in that Fisher in both stories reveals the smiling ruthlessness, almost diffidence, and seeming impersonality with which the metropolis, Harlem, favors or disfavors those who view her as either refuge or promise.

Mammy came North to keep house for her two grandsons Wesley and Sam. Together the cousins left Virginia "to find their fortunes in Harlem." Wesley became a window washer while Sam earned more money as a mechanic. The competition of city life rewarded the cousins differently; it poisoned their relationship. Harlem broke the bond between Wesley and Sam, and "fashioned them a bludgeon with which to shatter their common life." The cousins utilized their new weapon. The hostilities caused by the differences in the rewards the city offered Wesley and Sam were accentuated by a dispute over the affection of a city woman who would not choose between them. Ellie wanted to "play the boobs off against each other, let them strut their stuff." And they did. Mammy just wondered how a girl in "the spring of her life" could subject romance to utility. But Mammy was from a different generation, another lifestyle, school of behavior. As she watched the new generation, a city generation, she pondered:

> But such a dance! The camel walk. Everybody "cameling." Had God wanted man to move like a camel He'd have put a hump in his back. Yet was there any sign of what God wanted in that scene. . . . Skins that he had made black bleached brown, brown ones bleached cream-color; hair that He had made long and kinky bobbed short and ironed dead straight. . . . Where was God in that?

He was somewhere, and perhaps for that reason Mammy attempted to make Ellie choose between Wesley and Sam. The bond broken by the metropolis might somehow be healed by human intervention. But, while Mammy talked of God and sin, Ellie responded, "'Say, what's the idea'?" She refuses to have anything to do with either cousin, and Sam blames Wesley who merely laughs.

> To Sam it was galling, derisive, contemptuous laughter, laughter of victory. Anger, epithets, blows he could have exchanged, but laughter found him defenseless. In a hot flush of rage he drew back a foot and kicked viciously at Wesley's legs.

Still, though the city worked its will on her family, Mammy realizes that in fact it is a promised land: "'New York. Harlem. Thought all along 'twas d' las stop 'fo' Heaven. Canaan hitself. Reg'lar promis' lan'. Well, dat's jus what 'tis—a promis' lan'. All hit do is promise'." And she wonders in the words of the old Negro spiritual:

> Bow low!—How low mus' I bow
> To enter in de promis' land?

"Blades of Steel" (1927) must be regarded as one of Fisher's less satisfying short stories. It contains all the elements and displays, as usual, the tremendous range of knowledge the author possessed concerning the black community. Still, the plot is rather too contrived, almost phoney.

The initial setting of the story is a barbershop on 135th Street just prior to the "Barbers' Annual Ball." The street represents the heart and soul of Negro Harlem. "It is common ground, the natural scene of unusual contacts, a region that disregards class. It neutralizes, equilibrates, binds, rescues union out of diversity." At times 135th Street does serve this function, but in **"Blades of Steel"** it serves as a setting for conflict. Eightball-Eddy Boyd and Dirty Cozzens argue as to whom is next in line for a tonsorial job. The actual reason for their dispute is the fact that Eightball Eddy dealt himself consecutive blackjacks in a darkjohn game. He won twenty dollars from Dirt who, of course, thought something was amiss. Dirty has a reputation as an evil man with a blade and he pursues his vendetta with Eightball-Eddy. Pop, proprietor of the barbershop, offers this commentary:

> "They's nineteen niggers 'round Harlem now totin' cuts he gives 'em. They through pullin' knives, too, what I mean. . . . He's that bad. Served time fo' it, but he don't give a damn. Trouble is, ain't nobody never carved him. Somebody ought to write shorthand on his face. That'd cure him."

Later that evening at the Barbers' Annual Ball, Dirty asks Effie, Eightball's girl, to dance; she refuses. Another confrontation between Eightball and Dirty seems inevitable. "Mercy—Lawd have Mercy!" A tune heard often on 135th Street.

The conflict which rages through and gives a dark cast to **"Blades of Steel"** transforms itself into the spirit of reconciliation in **"Miss Cynthie"** (1933) which ranks among Fisher's best works. Reconciliation between the generations is the theme of this story. At the request of David Tappen, her grandson, Miss Cynthie comes North, the first time she had been more than fifty miles away from her home town in North Carolina. As a southern matriarch, she is similar to Mammy in **"The Promised Land,"** and Miss Cynthie has something in common with King Solomon Gillis in **"The City of Refuge,"** for they both hail from the same town in North Carolina, Waxhaw. But she is different from both in her acceptance of the new generation, of the city, of Harlem. Fisher provides us with a glimpse of her basic wisdom in a conversation she has with a redcap upon her arrival in New York:

> "Always like to have sump'n in my hand when I walk. Can't never tell when you'll run across a snake."
>
> "There aren't any snakes in the city."
>
> "There's snakes everywhere, chile."

Indeed there are. And Miss Cynthie, who always wanted David to become either a preacher or a doctor, wonders what line of work the city has mandated for him. She had urged him to "always mind the house o' the Lord—whatever you do, do like a church steeple: aim high and go straight." The least she desired for him was that he become an undertaker. Miss Cynthia wanted him to have some contact with the church, no matter how minimal, no matter what form. And the first compliment she gives the city puts her stamp of approval on its churches "fo' colored folks." David does not tell her what his business is because he wants it to come as a surprise. But Ruth, his girl friend, warns him, "You can't fool old folks."

David and Ruth take Miss Cynthie to the Lafayette Theatre. She had always viewed the theatre as the antithesis of the church.

> As one was the refuge of righteousness, so the other was the stronghold of transgression. . . . And not any of the melodies, not any of the sketches, not all the comic philosophy of the tired—and the hungry duo, gave her figure a moment's relaxation or brightened the dull defeat in her staring eyes.

In Miss Cynthie's world, the theatre was the house of the "sinsick, the flesh-hungry mob of lost souls." But David remembered a tune which Miss Cynthie sang when he was young:

> Oh I danced with the gal with the hole in her
> stockin'

And her toe kep' a-kickin'
And her heel kep' a-knockin'
Come up, Jesse, and get a drink o' gin,
Cause you near to the heaven as you'll ever get
ag'in—

And she understands: "'Bless my soul! They didn't mean nothin'. . . . They jes' didn't se no harm in it'" Miss Cynthie reconciles herself to David's business while David thanked her for always urging him to "aim high."

One can "aim high" in many ways, not the least of which is a rule of the road: "aim high" in steering. This is an elementary driving rule because it decreases the chance of accident, of a mistake. Fisher uses this theme, check the facts—get the big picture—of the situation before making a decision, in **"Dust"** (1931), one of his few non-Harlem stories. The action takes place almost completely in Pard's brand new black and silver roadster. He and Billie, his girl friend, are on an afternoon outing. As they travel alone the Connecticut countryside, Pard notes the surprise of those in the automobiles alongside them at the appearance of Negroes in his fine car. Realizing that he and Billie are merely "niggers" to those around them, he says: "Now, damn it, eat niggers dust."' Easily his roadster passes others on the road. But Billie says, "'Horrible thing, prejudice; does you all up. Puffs you out of shape.'"

Pard can outhate whites and he likes it. Still, a yellow coupe with a Georgia license plate passes him:

"Lyncher. . . . Atta baby—go get 'im—Rednecked hillbilly. . . . Ought to run him off the road anyhow—every cracker less is a nigger more. . . . Listen. . . ."

He indulges himself in a race to catch and pass the Georgia plated car. At a fork in the road, suddenly, another car appeared from a side road, the racers hit their brakes, and the yellow coupe goes off the road. Pard and Billie drive back to see if they can help the driver. "No question of hatred." That driver astonished them.

Not very much astonishes Grammie in **"Guardian of the Law"** (1933), a story similar to **"Blades of Steel"** in that its plot is somewhat outrageous. And the theme, the protection a grandmother feels for her grandson, is a bit trite. On balance, however the story is more satisfying than **"Blades of Steel."** Grammie, who brought up Sam, her grandson, is proud when he passes the written exam to become a policeman. Yet, she realizes that he was chosen for the appointment over Grip Beasely. For that reason one afternoon as she watched over 133rd Street from her window-throne, Grammie becomes a bit agitated when she sees Sam go into Beasely's apartment building. As one might expect of a protective grandmother, she goes to investigate.

Gaining entry to Beasely's apartment, Grammie discovers that Judy, Sam's girl, is also there: something is amiss. And, while going through the apartment, Grammie enters like a "terrible angel of vengeance" a room where she finds Sam. Again, like a good grandmother, Grammie foils the plot concocted by Beasely to snare Sam's job. And she tells Sam:

"You jes' ain't got no sense. Hyeh you is a rookie, on your six months' probation, when the bossman can drop you fo' anything you do. . . . And you gettin' ready to up and tell 'em that yo' grandmammy—yo' grandmammy! had to come along and help you out. Humph!"

Grammie's account of the episode varies somewhat from the truth, and Judy reminds her of this. Grammie nods and says that when they get as old as she, they too, can lie, but not before; for there is a time and place for everything.

Rudolph Fisher looms large as a writer of stories dealing with life in the black community. He did not attempt to hide, camouflage or apologize for the lives of ordinary black men and women, no matter whether they were "dicties" or "rags." Fisher wrote about them all. As a writer, he was principally concerned with the presentation of Negro life in Harlem, the capital of the black world, during the Negro Renaissance. He knew Harlem through and through. Sometimes he satirizes, as in ***The Walls of Jericho,*** but at other moments he applauds the particular uniqueness of the people, black people, about whom he wrote. At all times he is honest, and true to his craft. Though basically a middle class Negro, Fisher portrayed the lives of both the classes and the masses through their hearts and languages, in their homes and cabaret through the prism of this experience. And he, just as they, will endure.

LEONARD J. DEUTSCH (ESSAY DATE 1979)

SOURCE: Deutsch, Leonard J. "'The Streets of Harlem': The Short Stories of Rudolph Fisher." *Phylon* 40, no. 2 (June 1979): 159-71.

In the following essay, Deutsch discusses Fisher's depiction of Harlem, maintaining that even when his characters are primarily cartoons or stereotypes, he maintains a strong realism of place. Deutsch suggests that Fisher creates an insider's guide to Harlem, preserving a unique time and place, and distinguishing it from the "tourist" Harlem visited by curious whites.

In his brief thirty-seven years Rudolph Fisher wrote two acclaimed novels: ***The Walls of Jericho,*** 1928, and the first black detective novel, ***The Conjure Man Dies,*** 1932. He also produced a body of outstanding short stories which, to this date, have not yet been assembled in a collected edition. This oversight is especially regrettable for two reasons: the stories represent Fisher's greatest talent as a writer and they establish him as the principal historian and social critic of the Harlem Renaissance period. The argument can be made that more fully than any other chronicler of the manners and morals of Harlem in the 1920s, Fisher captures the breadth of black experience—and American and universal human experience—during a spectacularly dynamic era.

The Harlem Renaissance was occasioned, as observers have remarked, by a "demographic shift of the Black population that is perhaps the most crucial fact of Afro-American history in the twentieth century."[1] Fisher took a lively look at this "crucial fact" and explored many of its consequences and manifestations in his short stories.

By his own admission, he saw himself as an interpreter of Harlem.[2] Just as F. Scott Fitzgerald took "East and West Egg" for his milieu, so Fisher took Harlem for his. He succeeded in charting the physical and moral topography of Harlem during the Renaissance period as no writer has ever done.

Fisher knew the black section of the city extremely well—as observer and participant. By profession he was a physician and research scientist; by avocation a popular writer. And as physician and writer he evinced his concern for both the body and the spirit of man. The good doctor had his finger on the pulse of Harlem, diagnosing accurately the weaknesses and strengths of his patient. He captured the high spirits as well as the darker currents of Harlem life in his stories, modulating his realism with a comic and humanistic touch.

Fisher's various concerns include the adjustments blacks were called upon to make after the Great Migration from the South; Harlem's complex and ambiguous meaning for black people—as mecca and hell; and Harlem's spirit of joy and competitiveness as reflected in its jazz. His concerns also include the intraracial and interracial problems and the identity crises fomented by differences in pigmentation. Serious as these themes are, all of Fisher's stories combine a characteristic balance of folk humor and ironic commentary. Taken together, they provide some of the basic documents—both historical and literary—of the period.

In terms of physical topography, Fisher reconstructs the black community block by block. Practically every story is set on a specific street or cluster of streets. And when those streets are revealed to the reader, they are presented in both graphically realistic and metaphorically imaginative terms.

Fisher's favorite figurative device is personification and his personified analogies imbue each street with a precise and appropriate life of its own, ranging from glamorous to sordid. In **"Ringtail,"** for example, "Harlem's Seventh Avenue was dressed in its Sunday clothes," for this is where the dicties paraded themselves; but Lenox Avenue, in **"Fire by Night,"** is like a corpse divested of its fine clothes. The sights and smells of each street are there: 133rd Street in **"Guardian of the Law"**; 135th Street in **"Blades of Steel"**; "a wide open lot, extending along One Hundred and Thirty-Eighth Street almost from Lenox to Seventh Avenue, sharing the mangy backs of a long row of One Hundred and Thirty-Ninth Street houses" in **"The South Lingers On." "Miss Cynthia"** provides a tour of the ritzier sections of the city-within-a-city; and so on.

Fisher virtually creates a verbal map of Harlem containing a great many of its hospitals, schools, cabarets, and apartment buildings. He even delineates the neighborhoods in **"Fire by Night"** and indicates the territorial disposition of the various classes—that "dictydom," for example, was located "west of Seventh Avenue" in the 1920s, and Harlem's middle class lived between Lenox and Seventh Avenues.

But most of all, Fisher presents Harlem's people.

His first story, **"The City of Refuge,"**[3] was published in the *Atlantic Monthly* (February, 1925) and was chosen for inclusion in Edward J. O'Brien's *The Best Short Stories of 1925.* It establishes the literary mode most characteristic of Fisher's work: irony. King Solomon Gillis is neither powerful nor rich nor wise; he is simply green around the gills and easily gulled. As another character says: he's "so dumb he thinks antebellum's an old woman." He has escaped from North Carolina and has come to entrancing Harlem, the city of refuge, which is so utopian it even has "cullud policemans." It is in Harlem (not the South), however, that Gillis is apprehended by the law and—an additional irony—he is arrested by a "cullud policeman." The arrest in Harlem is symbolic of all his dashed hopes, for while the appearance of freedom is greater in Harlem, the instruments of oppression are more subtle and frustrating, and they make justice more achingly

FROM THE AUTHOR

THE WEALTH OF HARLEM

In Harlem, black was white. You had rights that could not be denied you; you had privileges, protected by law. And you had money. Everybody in Harlem had money. It was a land of plenty.

SOURCE: Rudolph Fisher, from "City of Refuge," in *Atlantic Monthly* 135, February 1925.

elusive. Gillis falls victim to the myth of Harlem. It may seem to be a city of and for blacks, a place where "you had rights that could not be denied you; you had privileges protected by law. And you had money. Everybody in Harlem had money. It was a land of plenty." But Harlem is the locus of intraracial exploitation (a black operator named Uggam muses, "Guess you're the shine I been waitin' for"); it is a battlefield of intraracial hostility (Gillis, hardened by his exposure to city values, derisively yells "Monkey-chaser!" at a West Indian); and it is the stalking ground of undiminished interracial enmity ("They's a thousand shines in Harlem would change places with you in a minute jess f' the honor of killin' a cracker"). Harlem is a place where one can become rich quickly, if like Tom Edwards, he becomes a drug pusher and pays off the police. Finally, the land of plenty offers Gillis a room "half the size of his hencoop back home," replete with all the sights, sounds, and smells of a sewer. More a city of refuse than refuge.

In March of 1925 Fisher's second story appeared, **"The South Lingers On,"**[4] reappearing later that year under the title **"Vestiges: Harlem Sketches,"** in Alain Locke's famous volume, *The New Negro.* Just as his first story depicts a newcomer's evolving response to Harlem—his naivete, his disillusionment, his gradual hardening—here, too, Fisher presents vignettes indicating the ways "the South lingers on" in Harlem for those who have recently arrived. The South lingers on in terms of attitudes toward religion, education, and morality. Ezekiel Taylor, a down-home preacher who views Harlem as the "city of the devil—outpost of hell," finds remnants of his old congregation who reject their new city preacher with his phony ways in favor of Taylor's old-time moaning-and-shouting brand of fundamentalism. In another vignette, Jake Crinshaw discovers that his life on the farm at Jennin's Landin', Virginia, offers no preparation for employment in the city. As bewildered and intimidated as Dreiser's Sister Carrie on her first visit to Chicago, he rejects the advice to turn to crime and continues in his search for another employment office. The third vignette depicts the conflict between Majutah and her grandmother who the hip young lady considers a "nuisance with her old fogeyisms" and her "down-home ideas"; the old woman, in turn, prays for her grandchild who wears makeup and goes out unchaperoned at night with strange men. A fourth vignette explores a Harlem family's ambivalent attitude towards education in the face of expanded educational opportunities; proud ignorance and fear of the unknown finally yield to awe before learning and hope of advancement. In the last vignette, two young bootleggers decide to attend a tent-church meeting for laughs. But as Lucky listens to the preacher (who renders the prayer service with all the sense of "theater" one finds in Ralph Ellison's writing), Lucky can not laugh; the power of that old-time religion is ineluctible. The South lingers on.

Fisher had two other short stories published in 1925: **"Ringtail,"**[5] and **"High Yaller."**[6] The former returns to the theme of intraracial conflict announced in **"The City of Refuge."** Cyril Sebastian Best, a dandified black from the British West Indies, is called a "ringtail monkey-chaser" by some black Harlemites; Best, in turn, holds Negro Americans in contempt. Although a character named Eight-Ball may complain: "You jigs are worse 'n ofays. . . . You raise hell about prejudice, and look at you—doin' just what you're raisin' hell over yourselves," even Eight-Ball seems to be won over by his cronies who believe a West Indian is naturally inclined to maniacal revenge. The resolution of Fisher's story—Cyril Sebastian Best kills the Harlemite who insulted him—seems to demonstrate the veracity of the conventional saying. The plot of **"Ringtail"** represents a rare instance when Fisher countenanced stereotyping. Despite some fine writing and a number of interesting passages, the story is further weakened by Fisher's use of the romantic triangle; here it is simply too contrived.

"High Yaller," awarded the Spingarn Prize of 1925, is a more complicated tale. It tackles the dual themes of intraracial and interracial enmity. Evelyn Brown's problem is that she is colored but looks white—there is "nothing brown about her but her name." At first she is accused of having "yellow-fever," that is, favoring fair skinned individuals and choosing her friends on that basis. The charge rankles and she laments that she is not darker (an inversion of Emma Lou's obsessive desire to become white in *The Blacker the Berry* by Wallace Thurman). Her response is to throw herself more fully into the black community by dating a black youth, Jay Martin. This attempt to affirm her blackness creates new problems. Most people assume Evelyn and Jay are an interracial couple. The two are snubbed and abused at every turn. Finally, Fisher sets up a fantasized scene—a dialogue between Jay and his alter-ego, symbolizing his inner conflicts—in which his "other self" forces Jay to recognize that "when people look at you, it's just with surprise. All their look says is, 'Wonder what that nigger is doing with a white woman?' But when they look at her, it's with contempt. They say, 'Humph! What a cheap drab she must be to tag around with a nigger!'" Just as frank is the dream Evelyn has of an encounter with her alter-ego. When her dark-skinned mother dies, Evelyn decides to pass for white. Fisher shows with trenchant candor the vicious pressures that drive Evelyn to her decision to pass. It was undoubtedly this candor that led an early black critic to condemn the story for its "sensationalism."[7] For Fisher, it is an uncharacteristically sardonic story.

If Fisher did not have any stories published in 1926, he more than made up for it in 1927, his most prolific year. In January the *Atlantic Monthly* contained the ironically titled **"The Promised Land,"**[8] a story which demonstrates that terrestrial Harlem is as far from the celestial heaven as death is from life. Interwoven in the texture of the tale are the blues and the melody of a spiritual: "one was a prayer for the love of man, the other a prayer for the love of God." In the city, with its philosophy of "ruthless opportunism," the secular blues take dominance over the otherworldly hymns. Harlem is no more a promised land than it is a city of refuge; it makes promises that it does not keep. And so Mammy, a living symbol of the generation gap, succeeds in stopping one fight involving her two grandsons by flinging a Bible between them, but must watch one kill the other over a girl (who is every bit as shallow and unworthy as Fitzgerald's Daisy Buchanan). The migrants have evaded misery in the South only to find tragedy in the North. But some become so callous that they fail to recognize the tragic dimensions of their behavior.

"The Backslider"[9] and **"Blades of Steel"**[10] both appeared in August of 1927. The former is the ironically crafted story of Eben Grimes who, despite his religious upbringing back home, has taken to frequenting a cabaret and has become a "sinful backslider" in New York. Vacillating between the poles of Satanism and probity, Grimes discovers that the minister who has ostracized him is a hypocrite and that he (Eben) is basically a decent fellow, so he "backslide[s] on de Devil" and rejoins Christianity.

"Blades of Steel" is a brutal story which pits gambling-man Eight-Ball against knife-wielding Dirty Cozzens; Eight-Ball wins after his girl-friend, Effie, teaches him a trick with a "safety" razor blade. Despite the violence and occasional gore of the action, the story contains Fisher's full quota of puns and Harlemese. In a tale which plays upon the "blades of steel" motif we learn that "whoever whittles [Dirty Cozzens] down will be a hero," and that "Effie's tongue had cut like steel." The locale shifts from a barber shop to a dance hall, to a bar-and-grill, and in so doing Fisher utilizes music (jazz from a "low-down" orchestra at the dance hall, Tessie Smith's blues from a phonograph at the bar-and-grill) both as background and as commentary upon the story's action.

Later that year, in December, *McClure's* published **"Fire by Night,"**[11] a story that sets elements from Harlem's three social classes against each other. Rusty Pride, the son of a beloved and upstanding preacher, is born a member of the temperate, respectable middle class but, made "swaggering, regardless, and worldly-wise" by the first World War, he returns from the service and rejects his middle class values; he rebelliously submerges himself in the life of the lower class (the so-called rats). It is not an attractive picture that Fisher presents of this class or its milieu—the "tameless corner of Harlem." These are the tough men and their heirs who "protected the colony in its infancy by their skill with pistols and knives and fists"—a type akin to de Crevecoeur's wild and wretched woodsmen of the American frontier. When a group of them at Turpin's Club hear of a fracas at the posh *New Casino,* they waste no time in joining the melee; they jostle with members of the upper class, venting their resentment toward "dicties" at the same time they use the opportunity to pick pockets.

The so-called So-and-Sos tend to be snobbish and are not treated very sympathetically by Fisher either. They are comparable to the Blue Vein Society in Charles Chesnutt's "The Wife of his Youth," and Fisher satirizes the type again in ***The Walls of Jericho.*** Attending the dance at the *New Casino* thrown by the So-and-Sos—but standing apart from their aristocratic pretensions—is Roma Lee, the patient girlfriend of Rusty, who rescues her when he appears on the scene. Together they seek refuge in a dwelling which, all too patly, turns out to be Reverend Pride's parsonage. Symbolically, the two youths are saved when they come home to the safety and sanity of the God-fearing middle class (as Turpin's Club burns like a Satanic inferno in the background). The conclusion of the story suggests that Rusty is no longer going to wander around like a billiard ball, aimlessly ricochetting from one meaningless experience to another. Perhaps his father's prayers have been answered; perhaps Rusty has found God. At least he has found himself.

Aside from his numerous short stories published that year, Fisher co-authored a highly technical article, **"The Resistance of Different Concentrations of a Bacteriophage to Ultraviolet Rays,"** which appeared in the March, 1927, issue of *The Journal of Infectious Diseases.*[12] The authors are identified as members of the Department of Bacteriology, College of Physicians and Surgeons, at Columbia University. Dr. Fisher also found time to write an essay for *American Mercury* entitled **"The Caucasian Storms Harlem."**[13] Fisher's major point in this historical guide through Harlem is that the formerly black cabarets have begun catering to whites—almost to the exclusion of blacks. "Why, I am actually stared at, I frequently feel uncomfortable and out of place" in these cabarets, he confesses. He not only explores the phenomenon by contrasting the way cabarets used to be when he first came to Harlem with the way they were becoming later in the decade; he also tries to account for this change, this new "active and participating interest" in Negroes. While not a story itself, **"The Caucasian Storms Harlem"** serves as a useful companion piece to the fiction providing, as it does, factual background on famous clubs in Harlem and sketches of such black stars as Ethel Waters, Florence Mills, and the comedy team of Miller and Lyles (possible prototypes of Bubber and Jinx—two characters in both of Fisher's novels).

In 1928 Fisher's first novel, ***The Walls of Jericho,***[14] appeared. It was less sensational and more balanced than Claude McKay's salacious *Home to Harlem,* published that same year. But Fisher published no stories in 1928—nor in 1929.

In 1930 Fisher explored the ways of love and the techniques of jazz in **"Common Meter."**[15] At the Arcadia Ballroom Fess Baxter's Firemen and Bus William's Blue Devils vie with each other for the jazz championship and for Jean Ambrose, the contested girl. The story centers on their conflicting philosophies of jazz and sportsmanship. So far as jazz goes, Bus Williams "held tone to be merely the vehicle of rhythm"; he concentrates on rhythmic patterns. Fess Baxter, on the other hand, "considered rhythm a mere rack upon which to hang his tonal tricks"; he seeks "sudden disharmonies, unexpected twists of phrase, successive false resolutions." In his personal ethics he is a trickster too, and his tactics for winning Jean are underhanded. But to the delight of the audience, Baxter is exposed for the knave he is, and Bus wins Jean. To the delight of his readers, Fisher includes a great deal of winning badinage and felicitous phrasing—such as when Bus Williams's endeavor "to drain the girl's beauty with his eyes" is described as "a useless effort since it lessened neither her loveliness nor his thirst." In addition, Fisher makes thematic use of bird imagery. For example, Williams's baton droops "like the crest of a proud bird, beaten"; when Baxter faces defeat he must adjust "his ruffled plumage"; and when the men fight it out through their music, they look like "two roosters bearin' down on the jazz." But Williams finally beats the "buzzard" when "the unfaltering common meter of [his] blues" takes off and soars like "wild-winged birds." With this last metaphor, Fisher neatly merges his bird imagery and his allusions to music. It might be added that his motif of interwoven blues lyrics to comment on the action reminds one of the poems of Langston Hughes.

The year 1931 saw only one short story by Fisher in print, **"Dust."**[16] It is the single story by Fisher not set in Harlem. Pard and his girl Billie are driving along in the Connecticut countryside; when Pard's black-and-white roadster is passed by a spunky yellow sport coupe with a Georgia license plate, Pard curses the unseen "cracker" and makes it a point of honor to overtake him. In so doing he almost wrecks both cars only to discover—to his utter astonishment—that the other driver is a black man too. Here misplaced racial animosity produces comical results (by contrast, in ***The Walls of Jericho*** the results are tragic for Fred Merrit). Still, Billie's observation that prejudice is a horrible thing makes the serious point of the story. **"Dust"** is very short but it offers an exciting chase, inventive metaphors, and a concluding sentence which in itself would have made the rest of the story worthwhile: "A far hill covered the face of the sun, like a hand concealing a grin."

In 1932 Fisher produced ***The Conjure Man Dies***[17] and he also appeared *in* a novel by another Harlem Renaissance writer, Wallace Thurman. In Thurman's satirical *Infants of the Spring,* Dr. Man-fred Trout is obviously based on Fisher. That same year Fisher produced **"Ezekiel,"** the first of two stories about a twelve year old boy of that name. Ezekiel's maturation depends upon his growth of self-perception, a trait which aligns him more fully with Ralph Ellison's Buster and Riley than with Richard Wright's Big Boy.

"Ezekiel"[18] is a psychological study of a Southern boy's first day in "the Negro colony of New York City"; the story charts his inner struggle from self-doubt to growing self-assurance. Mindful of his uncle's admonition not to leave the "stoop," Ezekiel refuses to join his two new friends when they pursue a monstrous, shiny, clanging fire engine—"the most amazing thing he had ever seen." In this refusal he feels dejected, fearing his new friends will chide him or even accuse him of betraying their new friendship. While Ezekiel is imagining the worst, his friends do laugh upon their return but "it was not a laugh of ridicule but of admiration." They acknowledge his superior wisdom in not wasting his time traipsing after the fire engine; it proved to be only a false alarm. So had Ezekiel's fears been a false alarm. Having been sent North "so that he might attend the excellent New York schools," his education in self-knowledge has begun on the streets of Harlem. **"Ezekiel"** is a slight but pleasant performance by Fisher.

So is **"Ezekiel Learns,"**[19] which appeared the following year, 1933. Ezekiel, by this time, has acclimated himself to all the wonders of Harlem, including the "proud parade of uniformed societies" which had been Marcus Garvey's legacy, as well as the "occasional riots between oddly excited mobs and grimly determined policemen." He has also witnessed the incredible sights of the rest of the city. But the one enduring memory is of an experience which gave him a glimpse into the enigma of his own personality. Fisher proceeds to tell the story of Ezekiel's clever and judicious response to the spiteful vengefulness of a mischievous playmate. Except for a relatively few word-plays, such as "the vendor disgustedly turned from a *fruitless* search of Sam," a suspect in the theft of a plum—except for this, **"Ezekiel Learns"** presents its anecdotal tale in a straightforward manner. Thematically it is similar to the poem, "Incident," written by Fisher's friend, Countee Cullen; in both, one seemingly little incident leaves a deeper impression on the sensibility of a young boy than all of his other experiences put together.

"Guardian of the Law,"[20] also printed in 1933, tells how a grandmother's quick thinking saves the reputation, and possibly the life, of her grandson, a "young bronze giant in a policeman's uniform." In protecting the probationary status of her grandson, Grammie ironically proves to be the "guardian of the law." In this fine comic story, Grammie is as full of humor as Mammy (in **"The Promised Land"**) was full of disapproving, pious seriousness. Hobbled somewhat by a lame knee, she can still summon up the devilish energy that made her such a hellion in her youth. Her concern for Sam's welfare transforms her into "the same furious child who, fifty years ago, had bitten Zeke Logan's ear half off"; she is a "small, terrible angel of vengeance." A devilish-angel, she tells a white lie, but it is all for the good; as she explains: "When y'all get old as I is, y'all can lie too. . . . But not befo." The story ends, much like **"Blades of Steel,"** with a revelation of the "trick" which saved the day.

"Guardian of the Law" is notable for its humorous badinage; for its wry descriptions (as Sam and his adversary, Grip Beasley, fight they are described as "embracing each other with enthusiasm"); also notable is the story's use of personification ("a battered piano whose keyboard grinned evilly at her"); and the characterization of Grip Beasley as a hoodlum who had "too much Harlem in him." Also of interest is the skillful use Fisher makes near the beginning of the story of a quasi-stream-of-consciousness technique ("comment pursued comment" across Grammie's mind "like successive windflaws sweeping the surface of a pool"). In addition, there is the fascination of the recent migrants with the idea that blacks could become symbols of authority—police officers. Gillis in **"The City of Refuge"** thinks with awe of becoming a policeman, a position never open to a black "down home"; Sam simply becomes one.

Fisher's fondness for spry grandmothers is once again apparent in **"Miss Cynthie,"**[21] another amusing story published in 1933. James A. Emanuel and Theodore L. Gross believe it "represents Fisher at his most effective."[22] Surrounded by her "impedimenta"—her battered baggage and her "down home" morality—she has come to visit her grandson, Dave Tappen, who has become affluent in the big city. At first she is shocked when she discovers he is a famous entertainer, but while watching his act she becomes converted when Dave sings one of the songs she taught him as a child. The transformation of Miss Cynthie's attitude from stern disapproval to generous tolerance is explained in terms of her receptive and expansive nature; she is open to change, especially if the new mode of behavior is basically harmless. She has always been for good times and has not lost touch with her own youth. She still cherishes the wild times she had speeding on her mare, Betty. As Dave's Packard zips uptown she exclaims: "Shuh, boy, this ain' nothin' new to me." This gives plausibility to her adaptability. As Fisher puts it so aptly, "Neither her brief seventy years' journey through life nor her long two days' travel northward had dimmed the live brightness of her eyes."

If Miss Cynthie is too much the corn-ball at times, too saccharine at others, she projects a folksy charm and radiates a saving humanity. But she is not the only interesting feature of this story. Dave Tappen's Harlem figures as hero, too. The image Fisher creates of Harlem here is closer to Claude McKay's lusty Harlem in *Home to Harlem* than Gillis's meretricious Harlem in **"The City of Refuge."** Here the black colony is a colorful and "tireless carnival." The very atmosphere exudes "laughter, abandoned strong Negro laughter." It was a Harlem which, historically, it would seem, had passed from the scene by Depression-haunted 1933, and a Harlem which, even in the twenties, had been able to offer such ostentatious luxury to very few (Dave's car is "a robin's egg blue open Packard with scarlet wheels"; his apartment is stunningly furnished). Also pre-Depression in spirit is Dave Tappen, an unself-conscious and uninhibited man like Jake in McKay's novel (and wealthy besides) who seems to be one of those exceptional cases. His lifestyle certainly was not typical of Harlem's life in general.

Still, the change from life in the South to life in Harlem had appeared dramatic. When the female dancers in **"Miss Cynthie"** return to the stage of the Lafayette Theater after their cotton-fields number, they wear "scant travesties on their earlier voluminous costumes—tiny sun-bonnets perched jauntily on one side of their glistening bobs, bandanas reduced to scarlet neck-ribbons, waists mere brassieres, skirts mere gingham sashes"; the modern reader, in seeing the transformation from field-hand to flapper, might be prompted to say: "You've come a long way, baby." The bulk of Fisher's stories, however, demonstrate the change in geography did not necessarily improve one's legal standing or social condition, nor was the change in values always for the better.

A genre that Fisher introduced to Black Literature and perfected all in one stroke is the detective novel. An unusual and ingenious work, ***The Conjure Man Dies,*** appearing in 1932 to solid critical applause, is a classic with all the standard ingredients and complications of the suspenseful novel of detection. It holds up remarkably well and seems not at all dated. In this novel Fisher introduces Sergeant Perry Dart, the professional detective, and his associate, Dr. John Archer, an amateur sleuth, who is the more sagacious to the two. Fisher enjoyed writing about these two characters so much that he intended "to use them in at least two more mystery novels—we'll call it the Dart-Archer series," he said.[23] Fisher did not live to realize this goal but he did dramatize ***The Conjure Man Dies*** (which was produced posthumously) and he did finish a fine story featuring Dart and Archer. **"Dr. Archer's Nose,"**[24] the author's longest story, appeared in January, 1935, less than a month after Fisher's death. It is practically as good as the novel and it illustrates Fisher's inexhaustible fascination with police-work. In it Dr. Archer denounces the kind of superstition and backwardness which resists the benefits of modern medical technology. A father, he tells Dart, has refused X-ray treatment for his sick baby, relying instead on a charm consisting of human hair fried in snake oil supplied by a conjure woman. The baby had worn the charm but, of course, he had died—the victim of superstition. As they talk the phone rings and Dart and Archer are summoned to solve a baffling murder: a twenty year old man, Sonny, has been stabbed through the heart with his own knife. The other occupants of the apartment become immediate suspects: the boy's mother, sister, brother, sister-in-law, and a roomer. The solution of the crime turns on Archer's thesis that smells are extremely important. Odors, he says, "should be captured, classified, and numbered. . . . In a language of a quarter of a million words," he laments, "we haven't a single specific direct denotation of smell." This crime, too, has its "particular odor." In a supremely clever and witty story, Fisher shows how "superstition killed Sonny."

Complications from an operation killed Fisher at the age of thirty-seven, but not before he managed to create a remarkable fictional world. Just as William Faulkner, in his saga of Yoknapatawpha, creates an interrelating matrix of characters and places, so too does Fisher people his literary landscape with characters who recur in different stories. Spider Webb, for example, appear in both **"The Backslider"** and ***The Conjure Man Dies.*** Jinx and Bubber (based upon popular vaudeville teams of the twenties) appear in both novels. Dr. John Archer and Detective Perry Dart figure in ***The Conjure Man Dies*** and **"John Archer's Nose."** Even such a minor character as Sister Gassoway appears in **"The South Lingers On," "The Backslider,"** and ***The Conjure Man Dies;*** and Eight-Ball appears in **"Blades of Steel," "Ringtale,"** and **"Fire by Night."**

There are undeniable lapses into stock types—matriarchal grandmothers, awed country bumpkins, and Jinx and Bubber in his novels—but they never remain one-dimensional stereotypes. It is also true that some of Fisher's characters are cartoons. But in most cases his caricaturing serves the aims of penetrating satire.

If there is comic exaggeration of character in Fisher's stories, there is rigorous realism of place. As has already been noted, Fisher delineates Harlem—lovingly and accurately—street by street. **"Miss Cynthie"** presents one perspective on Harlem—Harlem as race capital and mecca. Most of the other stories, however, present a less sanguine perspective. In **"The South Lingers On,"** Majutah's grandmother sees Harlem as a "great, noisy, heartless, crowded place where you lived under the same roof with a hundred people you never knew." Much like Gillis's room in **"The City of Refuge,"** Mammy's apartment in **"The Promised Land"** is compared to "a fifth-story roost on the airshaft of a seven-story hencoop," and Lil in **"The Backslider"** likens her room to a clothespress. As people move into the flats of Harlem their prospects—at least for some of them—turn flat too, even if the pace of their lives speeds up.

The citizens of Harlem certainly have not left all of their old problems behind. In **"High Yaller,"** school for Jay "had been a succession of fist-fights with white boys who called him nigger," and he must remember never to cross Lenox Avenue or go beyond 135th Street or venture on or near Seventh Avenue because "it would have been almost suicidal for [a Negro] to appear unarmed on Irish Eighth." And where old problems have been left behind, they have often been replaced by new ones; for Harlem was a place "where there was so much more for one to quarrel about and resent"—as Sam and Wesley (who have such disparate salaries in **"The Promised Land"**) discover. If Fitzgerald's geography of East and West symbolically represents corruption and hope, respectively, Fisher's geography of North and South, more often than not, has the North representing disappointed hopes and expanding anxieties. And yet there is always the pulse of excitement and the counterbalance of new hopes and opportunities in Harlem.

Fisher's language is the medium of a rich style which informs while it entertains and elates. The author had appended a glossary of Harlemese to ***The Walls of Jericho*** but the stories burst with definitions too—some serious and helpful, others wry and ironic. If the reader does not know what a *dicty,* the *dozens,* a *rent party,* the *camel walk,* and other artifacts of black culture are, he will be enlightened by reading the stories in which they are explicitly defined. *Lodi,* the reader learns, is an urban game played by flicking bottle caps across a chalked-up sidewalk. An *airshaft* is "a horrible channel that separates one tall house from the next, a place full of unpleasant noises and odors." Fisher makes distinctions: *cabarets,* for example, are "not like theatres and concert halls. You don't just go to a cabaret and sit back and wait to be entertained. You get out on the floor and join the pow-wow and help entertain yourself." With sardonic wit, Fisher informs the reader that *trapwindows* on a door are "designed against rent-collectors and other robbers." And along with Eben in **"The Backslider,"** the reader learns that a *police raid* was a "legalized rampage upon blind pigs and gambling dens; that a blind pig was a place where you could buy bootleg liquor if you were wealthy enough; yes, that Harlem as a whole might be considered a prolific sow without eyes"—a wry definition and social commentary all rolled into one.

Always—whether he is being informative or entertaining—Fisher's language sings. His stories are filled with imaginative puns, inventive personifications, and other playful twists of language (as when he paradoxically describes Harlem apartment buildings as "mountains of flats"). In addition, the stories are a gold-mine of lines and stanzas from old hymns, blues, and popular songs. The collection, moreover, offers a compendium of Harlem idioms and dialects, the old-time preacher's sermons; the West Indian speech pattern; the people of Harlem bantering in Harlemese. It is no wonder that Langston Hughes considered Fisher "the wittiest of [the] New Negroes of Harlem." Hughes asserted that Fisher "could think of the most incisively clever things to say," and confessed, "I used to wish I could talk like Rudolph Fisher."[25]

In 1933 Fisher averred: "Outsiders know nothing of Harlem life as it really is. What one sees in a night club or a dance hall is nothing, doesn't scratch the surface—is in fact presented solely for the eyes of outsiders. . . . But what goes on behind the scenes and beneath the dark skins of Harlem folk—fiction has not found much of that yet."[26] Fisher was an insider who scratched deeply. The stories reveal his love for the people of Harlem and the diversity of talents they represent. They also help us to understand the quality of life of Harlem during the Renaissance period.

Notes

1. Richard Barksdale and Keneth Kinnamon, *Black Writers of America: A Comprehensive Anthology* (New York, 1972), p. 468.
2. John Louis Clarke, "Mystery Novel Writer Is Interviewed Over the Radio," *Pittsburgh Courier*, January 21, 1933.
3. "The City of Refuge," *Atlantic Monthly*, CXXXV (February, 1925), 178-87.
4. "The South Lingers On," *The Survey Graphic Number*, LIII (March 1, 1925), 644-47.
5. "Ringtail," *Atlantic Monthly*, CXXXV (May, 1925), 652-60.
6. "High Yaller," *Crisis*, XXX, No. 6 (October-November, 1925), 281-86.
7. Allison Davis, "Our Negro Intellectuals, *Crisis*, XXXV, No. 8 (August, 1928), 268.
8. "The Promised Land," *Atlantic Monthly*, CXXXIX (January, 1927), 37-45.
9. "The Backslider," *McClure's Magazine*, LIX (August, 1927), 16-17, 101-04.
10. "Blades of Steel," *Atlantic Monthly*, CXL (August, 1927), 183-92.
11. "Fire by Night," *McClure's Magazine*, LIX (December, 1927), 64-67, 98-102.
12. "The Resistance of Different Concentrations of a Bacteriophage to Ultraviolet Rays." *Journal of Infectious Diseases*, coauthored by Earl B. McKinley (March, 1927), 399-403.
13. "The Caucasian Storms Harlem," *American Mercury*, XI (August, 1927), 393-98.
14. *The Walls of Jericho* (New York, 1928).
15. "Common Meter," *Negro News Syndicate* (February, 1930), two installments, February 8 and February 15 in the *Baltimore Afro-American*.
16. "Dust," *Opportunity*, IX (February, 1931), 46-7.
17. *The Conjure Man Dies* (New York, 1932).
18. "Ezekiel," *Junior Red Cross News*, XIII (March, 1932), 151-53.
19. "Ezekiel," *Junior Red Cross News*, XIV (February, 1933), 123-25.
20. "Guardian of the Law," *Opportunity*, XI (March, 1933), 82-5, 90.
21. "Miss Cynthie" *Story*, III (June, 1933), 3-15.
22. *Dark Symphony: Negro Literature in America* (New York, 1968), p. 111.
23. Clarke, *op. cit.*
24. "Dr. Archer's Nose," *The Metropolitan; A Monthly Review*, (January, 1935), 10-12, 47-50, 52, 67, 69-71, 73-5, 80.
25. Langston Hughes, *The Big Seas: An Autobiography* (New York, 1940), pp. 240-41.
26. Clarke, *op. cit.*

ELEANOR Q. TIGNOR (ESSAY DATE 1982)

SOURCE: Tignor, Eleanor Q. "Rudolph Fisher: Harlem Novelist." *Langston Hughes Review* 1, no. 2 (fall 1982): 13-22.

In the following essay, Tignor focuses on Fisher's two novels, noting Fisher's depiction of different classes and subcultures of Blacks in Harlem. Tignor distinguishes the social satire of The Walls of Jericho *from the "non-racial" focus of Fisher's detective fiction.*

It was said that Rudolph Fisher wrote ***The Walls of Jericho*** (1928) "on a bet that no one short novel could successfully blend the extremes of Harlem society," of the 1920's, "into a single integral story."[1] Not only did he skillfully merge the various strata of Negro society of the day, but he also showed Black-White relationships.

The Negroes were primarily divided into two social groups, dickties and rats, with those between being referred to as ordinary Negroes.[2] In his glossary provided for the uninformed, the *dickty* Fisher defined as a "High-toned person" (p. 298) and *rat* he defined as the "Antithesis of *dickty*" (p. 304). Historically accurate, the *dickty*, though highly respectable, might not have been financially well off nor have achieved intellectually; the *rat*, a Negro of the lowest class, was characterized by his disrespectability. The first group generally wanted to imitate whites, while the latter preferred enjoying themselves in their own way. In ***The Walls of Jericho***, members of these two socially opposite groups generally hated each other. Whites, however, in one rat's opinion, did not see any difference between them.

Realistically reflecting the social stratification of Harlem—and of the broader Negro community—***The Walls of Jericho*** has no single major character but several central Black characters of different occupations and incomes, with diverse aims and motives, as well as white characters representative of the white 1920's frequenters of Harlem.

The furniture movers Bubber Brown and Jinx Jenkins, probably rats on Fisher's scale, thought not "the rattiest of the rats" (p. 70) since they do not commit crimes or physically harm others, are content with their manual labor and its accompanying status. They do not want to be upper-class Negroes, but in fact view that group as wicked and somewhat weak, unable to fight their battles alone against whites. Characterized as harmless hedonists, they frequent Henry Patmore's Pool Parlor, where they drink, play pool, play blackjack and any other illegal game. Not deep thinkers or race activists, they instead joke, argue, and fight with each other about anything imaginable, seldom anything significant. They hide their mutual regard under constant ridicule and contention, this distortion of behavior having been so completely imposed upon them by class tradition that even they do not realize they are masquerading.

Shine is a much more ambitious lower-class Black, having moved from shoe*shine* drudgery to foremanship of a moving company and a desire to own his own business. Distrustful of supposedly respectable dickties, he has his own high code of morality, which he will fight to protect, especially as it concerns attempted or alleged violations of Linda.

The first person from whom Shine protects Linda is Henry Patmore, a rattish type who has one trait of some upper-class Negroes: he is influential. His standing is such in the community that one might at any time find a policeman casually sitting in on an illegal card game in the rear room of his pool parlor. Pat always has a supply of banknotes "after the fashion of bootleggers" (p. 76), with some of his money being spent to support his excellent taste in clothes. He is deceptive, despite his flashy smile, since his manner never suggests his motive; his conquests are made and his reputation is enviable.

Fred Merrit, against whom Patmore holds a grudge, is clearly an upper-class Negro. The extremely fair-skinned mulatto (illegitimate offspring of a Negro mother and a white father) with kinky, sandy hair is the author's angriest Black through not one without a sense of humor. "Not the blackest of Negroes could have hated the dominant race more thoroughly" (p. 38). Ready to move into the white Court Avenue section of Manhattan, Attorney Merrit expresses his bitter racial feelings to some other prominent Blacks:

> "All of you know where I stand on things racial—I'm downright rabid. And even though . . . I'd enjoy this house, if they let me alone, purely as an individual, just the same I'm entering it as a Negro. I hate fays. Always have. Always will. Chief joy in life is making them uncomfortable. And if this doesn't do it—I'll quit the bar."
>
> (p. 38)

Another of Fisher's "dickties," a minor character in the novel but historically representative of upper-class Negroes, is Tod Bruce, the racially sensitive though not rabid young rector of the Episcopal church, who questions why a Negro's individuality is denied—why a *shine* can never do anything except as a *shine.* Although he recognizes the advantages of passive conquest, his view is that Merrit as an individual has the right to employ any method of conquest he desires. At a meeting of the dickty group the Litter Rats (introduced strategically following a scene with Patmore and a group of rats), the discussion of Merrit's integration plans takes precedence over the scheduled topic, "The Negro's Contribution to Art and the Lost Sciences of Ethiopia."

In sharp contrast to Merrit and Tod is the president of the Litter Rats, J. Pennington Potter, a "preposterous" character who considers Merrit's plan "preposterous." Vehemently opposed to the Black colony's extending "by violence and bloodshed" (p. 36), Potter holds the theory that only admixture engenders racial harmony, that prejudice and misunderstanding result from ignorance, and that ignorance stems from silence. Therefore, his syllogistic conclusion: racial groups must become acquainted; people become acquainted by admixture. Thus, he and Mrs. Potter are proud of their friendship with the white Mr. and Mrs. Noel Dunn.

The Dunns are used by Fisher to show unbalanced Black-White relations. Wherein the Potters frequently speak of the two couples' social admixture, the Dunns, instead, tell their friends of the "wealth of material" to be found in Negro Harlem. To Mr. Dunn, editor of an anti-Nordic journal, and his wife, everything Negro is "marvelous." (p. 100)

The very name of Fisher's most fully delineated white character suggests his satire and her *painful* response to Blacks who threaten to *cramp* her living style by moving too close. Envisioning herself as a servant of mankind, the wealthy Miss Agatha Cramp, who always employs a maid of the particular racial group toward which she is directing her humanitarianism, hires Linda when Negroes become her social interest. "Not until now has the startling possibility occurred to her that Negroes might be mankind, too" (p. 61). Having spoken only to Black porters, waiters, and house servants, "Negroes to her had been rather ugly but serviceable fixtures, devices that happened to be alive, dull instruments of drudgery, so observed, so accepted, so used, and so forgotten" (p. 61). Further, "Negroes she had accepted with horses, mules, and motors, and though they had brushed her shoulders, they had never actually entered her head" (p. 62). Fred Merrit, Fisher uses to "enter her head" through his next-door-to-her integration of Court Avenue.

Fisher's General Improvement Association's Annual Costume Ball serves as a microcosm of his diverse people and either shows or suggests their real life conflicts. The sponsoring group (obviously the NAACP satirized) is said to collect a dollar a year from everybody who joins and whenever a lynching occurs down South, to send somebody down to look at it just to be sure it happened. By that time, it is time to collect another dollar, for the next year.

At the Ball are Blacks of all the social strata, from the "rattiest rat to the dicktiest dickty" (p. 70) and three groups of whites, one whose sin is to enjoy not the Negroes but themselves, one who came "to raise up the darker brother" (p. 70), and the third who came "to see the niggers" (p. 73). Downstairs are the ordinary Negroes, upstairs the upper-class and the whites. The symbolism of intraracial conflict here is somewhat overdone. Further, the author places "a predominance of darker skins below . . . and fairer skins above" (p. 74), with these two groups "forgetting [their] differences" only on the dance floor; afterwards, everyone immediately seeks "his own level" (p. 74).

Fisher's small group of whites and Blacks who talk supposedly candidly about other Blacks and whites illustrates the attempted pretense that race can be disregarded. In contrast, the author's view is that between members of conflicting races the subject of race is difficult, almost delicate, and an individual of one race does not get to know an individual of another by discussing the topic:

> Neither party quite wholly sacrifices his illusions about his own people nor admits his ignorance about the other. The conversation, therefore, becomes a series of unwitting affronts, mutual mistrusts, and suppressed indignations . . . till at last it futilely breaks off . . . each inwardly smoldering at the other's unforgivable ignorance and tactlessness. . . . If Nordic and Negro wish truly to know each other, let them discuss not Negroes and Nordics; let them discuss Greek lyric poets of the fourth century, B.C.
>
> (p. 133)

Deeply ingrained anti-racial attitudes are illustrated through the Agatha Cramp-Fred Merrit encounter. Miss Cramp chats freely with Merrit only because she has mistaken him for white. To her question of whether or not he has worked among Negroes a great deal, he tells her that he likes Negroes even better than he likes whites—because he knows she would be opposed to any person's feeling this way. As a follow-up to her astonishment that Merrit knows how long Negroes have been in *our* country and her uninformed comments on complexion, ending with "Just imagine! A Negro with skin as fair as your own!" (p. 114), Merrit cannot resist defending and advocating the spiritual attitude of the Negro:

> "This tropic nonchalance, as Locke calls it. This acceptance of circumstance not with a shrug . . . but with a characteristic grin. Nobody laughs at the miseries of life like the Negro. He laughs at himself, at his own pains and dangers and disappointments and oppressions. He accepts things not with resignation but with amusement. That, it seems to me, should be a most alarming thing for his enemy to see."
>
> (p. 121)

So thoroughly deceived is Agatha Cramp that she invites the Black man for a neighborly visit. The scene, ending with Merrit's chuckling and chiding himself—"Damn shame to worry that poor woman like that—she'll die before the night's over. Somebody'll tell her sure" (p. 125)—is a climactic indication of Black-White distrust and division.

Intraracial class conflict is exemplified through Bubber, Jinx, and Shine's distrust of Merrit, in their shock at his cordiality and familiarity on moving day. When the lawyer shows Shine the note warning him against moving in, Shine thinks: "If this bird wasn't a dickty he'd be O.K. But they never was a dickty worth a damn" (p. 51). Bubber assumes Merrit wants to be friendly with them in case of trouble with the whites. Jinx thinks Merrit's allusions to a housekeeper and a country-place have no basis in truth.

Shine does not trust Merrit with Linda; just a stare makes him think: "Figgerin' on a jive . . . the doggone dickty hound. Why the hell dickties can't stick to their own women 'thout messin' around honest workin' girls" (p. 54). Extreme distrust is manifested after Linda becomes Merrit's maid and circumstances falsely point to his having attacked her.

The most bitter intraracial conflict is that between the low life character Henry Patmore and the dickty Merrit, whose home in the white neighborhood is wrecked not by a white but by this Black who is seeking revenge against the lawyer who once caused him to pay a $10,000 fine.

Rudolph Fisher, the satiric realist with a tendency toward a harmonious resolution when the plot will remain credible, merges the classes of Blacks as far as verisimilitude will allow—in that the tough but respectable and ambitious Shine of the lower class (though not a rat) is about to marry the middle class in values and respectability but lower class in wealth, education, and occupation

Linda. These two and Merrit (one of the dicktiest of the dickty) share a relationship of mutual respect and trust, especially illustrated through the Merrit-Shine business venture. It would not have been realistic for Fisher to conclude ***The Walls of Jericho*** with complete Black-Black or Black-White harmony—and he did not.

Detective Fiction

After his social-racial novel, Rudolph Fisher's two non-racial mysteries appeared: the novel, ***The Conjure-Man Dies: A Mystery Tale of Dark Harlem*** (1932), and the novelette, **"John Archer's Nose"** (1935).

The strangest element of ***The Conjure-Man Dies*** is the title character's claim to have been murdered and to have come back to life. N'Gana Frimbo, a brilliant black African with a Bachelor's degree from Harvard, is well-versed in biology, psychology, and deterministic philosophy, a reader of such books as Tankard's *Determination and Fatalism,* Bostwick's *The Concept of Inevitability,* and Fairclough's *The Philosophical Basis of Destiny.* He gave up his kingship of Buwongo, an independent territory northwest of Liberia, to seek adventure. In Harlem, he practices as a psychist, or as many of his visitors call him, a conjure-man. He believes there are orders other than the single cause and effect order and that this order can be escaped. Seeing himself "as free as a being of another order."[3] he believes he can help those who consult him not by upsetting their order but by acting as a catalyst. He claims to be able to tell a person's past and present and to predict his future by looking in his face. His consultations are held at night in a room of his chambers, located above the undertaker establishment of his landlord, Samuel Crouch. Frimbo sits in the dark while his visitor sits across the table with a bright light upon his face.

One night when Jinx Jenkins is consulting with Frimbo, the man sitting across from him is attacked. When Dr. Archer examines the body, he determines that a blow inflicted to the man's head was not severe enough to have been fatal. The dead man is naturally assumed to be the African psychist. Notification of the police brings Negro Detective Perry Dart on the case. The doctor and the detective begin to work together to unravel the mystery.

Fisher's is a well-constructed work, adhering to the generally accepted rules for detective stories.[4] In an inscription in a copy of the book given to Carl Van Vechten, the author refers to it as "this experiment with a technique."[5] The experiment was successful, for from a very careful reading of ***The Conjure-Man Dies*** one could solve the murder mystery, using the clues provided.

These were the major clues. Of the five men who came to visit Frimbo on the night of the murder, only one's identity was certain: "a genial stranger who had talked pleasantly to everybody, revealing himself to be one Easley Jones, a railroad man" (p. 54). It was not stated that the man actually was Easley Jones. Mrs. Snead, one of the other visitors that night, stated that she did see Jinx Jenkins' handkerchief and that she saw only one of two clubs on the mantelpiece (the alleged murder instrument) but Easley Jones—Samuel Crouch in disguise (found to be the murderer)—who had gone in to see Frimbo before Mrs. Snead arrived, to divert suspicion from himself, stated that he had definitely seen two clubs and that the handkerchief belonged to Jinx.

The reader might have suspected Crouch, considering other clues which were planted. Since his complexion was stated as being smooth and unblemished, conveniently without any identifying marks, he could easily change the appearance of his skin by adding freckles. When discussing Frimbo's murder with Dart, Crouch gave two clues: "Easier to handle a dead face than a live one.—I've found that out" (p. 91). "We can make the dark ones bright and the bright ones lighter . . . I venture to say that by the simplest imaginable changes, I could make Dr. Archer there quite unrecognizable" (pp. 91-92). Also, though Crouch was genial and cheerful, he was happy to hear that his wife had been there before the murder to collect the rent, causing Dr. Archer to remark to Dart: "I have an impression . . . that bright plumage oft adorns a bird of prey. Curious fellow, Crouch. Bright exterior . . . but underneath, hard as a pawnbroker, with an extraordinary keen awareness of his possessions" (p. 93). Further, Easley Jones told Dart that he had consulted Frimbo about his wife.

> "Well, I say I was hyer to ask 'bout my wife—was she true to me or f'ru *with* me. But he didn' say nothin' 'till he got good and ready, and then he didn' say much. Tole me I didn' have nothin' to worry 'bout—that he seen I had murder in my heart for somebody, but there wasn' no other mule in my stall sho' nough and to go on forgit it."
>
> (pp. 129-30)

A clue to Mrs. Crouch's love affair with Frimbo was that wherein she was waiting to see him at his consultation room (according to her story) to collect the rent, her husband had always waited in the hall and there collected from Frimbo's servant. Also, Martha Crouch was extremely excited when Frimbo "came back to life." It was she who told him that he was assumed dead. When she was leaving Frimbo's that Saturday night, it appeared that she would stop and speak to him, but instead she smiled and just said "Good-night" (p. 181). Frimbo himself told Dr. Archer that he had been indiscreet in his affairs of the heart, perhaps still was.

If one had recalled and taken seriously Dr. Archer's statements about Crouch's keen awareness of his possessions, one might have thought of Crouch when the murderer said to Frimbo near the end, "Why weren't you careful what you touched?" (p. 181). It was not until after Easley Jones had pulled the switch wired by Frimbo as a trap to detect "his" murderer that a clue was given to the fact that Jones was someone else (Crouch in disguise): "Easley Jones said nothing. His head remained sullenly lowered, the bushy kinks standing out like a black wool wig, the dark freckles sharply defined against pale brown skin" (p. 311).

This, too, is Fisher's scene of climax and resolution in that Crouch finally murders the real Frimbo. And Martha Crouch goes to the psychist in bewilderment and dread, puts her arm around him, and utters his name as one in torture, bringing about Dr. Archer's realization: "You mean—that you and Frimbo—?" (p. 313). She then rushes over to Easley Jones, tears at his face and says, "You—killed—the only man—" (p. 313); pulled away from the alleged Jones, she notices in her tightly closed fingers a kinkly black wig—taken from the head of her husband. The reader should have considered anyway that someone not obvious would be the murderer since Dr. Archer had said that one day he would write a murder mystery in which the murderer would be the most unlikely suspect.

Still another clue was given, related to the first murder. It was stated more than once that the dumbwaiter shaft appeared empty, but it was not said that it actually was. The original corpse, missing when the medical examiner came, was searched for in the old shaft which appeared empty except for a few old ropes and a set of pulleys. But Frimbo, in fact, had installed an electrically operated and almost undetectable lift, allowing him to hide his servant's dead body there and giving him a place to secret himself before pretending to rise from the dead.

Continuing to follow the rules of detective fiction, Fisher made neither the detective nor any other investigator the culprit. The culprit, furthermore, was a person who would not ordinarily come under suspicion, i.e., no one as obvious as a servant. Crouch's alibi had been verified by several people, and he had no complaints against Frimbo as a tenant. Acting as Easley Jones, he said he returned to the scene of the crime because he had nothing to hide. No Easley Jones had a motive, and an Easley Jones' service record with the railroad was beyond satisfaction.

The culprit was a person with whom the reader was familiar. The reader knew the physical traits and some of the habits and activities of Samuel Crouch, as well as of Crouch in disguise. There was moreover, only one culprit, as the rules demand. In addition, the murderer's motive was personal, Frimbo's affair with his wife.

The crime did not turn out to be an accident or a suicide. There was a corpse, although it did disappear after it was first seen and there was some confusion about its identity. The problem of the crime was solved by natural means; the answer was not that Frimbo and the man first declared dead were the same. Frimbo had not unnaturally outwitted death.

There was but one detective, i.e., one official detective, though Dr. Archer assisted in detecting and examining much of the evidence and in drawing conclusions. Dr. *Archer,* sounding very much like Dr. *Fisher,* is in fact the real mind in ***The Conjure-Man Dies.***

R. Austin Freeman has said that the author of a detective story must be equipped with an extensive amount of special knowledge.[6] Fisher knew medicine and made extensive use of his medical education. Considering that his characters Frimbo and Dr. Archer were learned in biology and psychology, this kind of knowledge was necessary for writing a credible story.

One instance in which Fisher the doctor comes through is when Dr. Archer is preparing to compare Frimbo's blood with that of the dead man. Archer says to Dart:

> "We may be able to prove these two specimens different without actually having to type them. We'll take this capillary pipette and remove a drop of this unknown serum and place it thus on a microscopic slide. Then we'll take a nichrome loop so, and remove a loopful of Professor Frimbo's best red cells, and stir them gently into the drop of serum, thus, spreading same smoothly into a small circular area in this manner. . . . Now then . . . a cover glass, and under the microscope it goes."
>
> (pp. 201-202)

When Frimbo tried to prove that the doctor's test was incorrect, Fisher knew what one could do to cause the reaction Frimbo got.

Medical knowledge, too, was necessary for understanding what Bubber found in the furnace. Bubber was only able to recognize the teeth, but the doctor, of course, knew much more:

> "Further, this cinder represents parts of two bones, the maxillary, in which the upper teeth are set, and the sphenoid which joins it . . . And I mean to tell you this also: that the presence of a sphenoid, or most of it, in a relatively free state like this is proof that its owner has left the world. On this bone, in life, rests a considerable part of the brain."
>
> (p. 253)

The tracing of the removable bridge was relatively simple and convincing since the author had the bridge to be made of a then recent dental product called deckalite, whose properties he clearly knew.

Information about the gonad was also incorporated into ***Conjure-Man:***

> The germplasm, of which the gonad is the only existing sample, is the unbroken heritage of the past. It is protoplasm which has been continuously maintained throughout thousands of generations. It's the only vital matter which goes back in a continuous line to the remotest origins of the organism.
>
> (p. 269)

Frimbo had told Dr. Archer that in his laboratory he performed a rite of the gonad, a family secret for many generations. This rite was what allegedly allowed him to escape the set pattern of cause and effect. Also, when a family member died, as in the case of his murdered servant N'Ogo, the sex glands were preserved, in accordance with a tribal duty and tradition.

The investigation by Detective Dart and Dr. Archer, with some assistance from Frimbo and Bubber, shows that Rudolph Fisher had the type of mind that lent itself to acute reasoning and logical analysis. The officer and the doctor weighed all of the suspects' stories, carefully examined all evidence, and followed all the necessary steps toward a logical deduction. Bits of evidence were discovered gradually as in an actual murder case. Even with the buildup of clues, the reader could not see through the solution as the story unfolded, for the organization of the mystery was intricate and Fisher's arrangement of details subtle.

For comic relief, Fisher brought Bubber Brown and Jinx Jenkins from ***The Walls of Jericho*** to ***The Conjure-Man Dies.*** Formerly movers, in this second novel, they are unemployed. As before, they are still friends who feign near enmity. Jinx, declared a suspect, is insulted and amazed when Bubber denies their friendship when questioned by Dart:

> "He's a good friend of yours, isn't he?"
>
> "Who—Jenkins? Friend o' mine? No indeed."
>
> "What do you mean?"
>
> "I mean I barely know the nigger. Up till night befo' las' we was perfect strangers."
>
> "You were pretty chummy with him tonight. You and he came here together."
>
> "Purely accidental, mistuh. Jes' happen to meet him on the street; he was on his way here; I come along too, thinkin' the man might gimme some high lowdown. Chummy? Shur! Didn' you and the doc burst in on us in the front room there where we was almost 'bout to fight? Friend o' mine! 'Deed you wrong there, brother. I don' have nothin' to do with gangsters, gunmen, killers, or no folks like that. I lives above reproach. Ask anybody."
>
> (p. 166)

All of this is talk; to free his friend from jail, Bubber assists informally in the solution of the crime.

Fisher's ***The Conjure-Man Dies*** was the first full-length detective story by an American Negro and the first to have all Black characters.[7] In 1932, it was probably surprising that a book was written by a Negro without touching upon racial problems in America.

The 1935 sequel to ***The Conjure-Man Dies,*** Fisher's novelette **"John Archer's Nose,"** was published in the only number of *The Metropolitan, A Monthly Review.*[8] Again the setting is Harlem and the detective is Perry Dart, unofficially assisted by Dr. John Archer.

The exposition is carefully plotted by Fisher. Perry Dart visits his friend John Archer at his office-apartment. For the sake of provoking a friendly argument, Dart says to Archer: "Your folks . . . are the most superstitious idiots on the face of the earth" (p. 10). The usually loquacious doctor is quiet for a while and then agrees with Dart. He tells the detective that an eighteen-month old patient of his has died because a retained thymus. This gland usually disappears after birth, but if it does not and goes untreated, convulsions occur, then death. Rather than allow him to give the child x-ray treatments, the parents had placed a packet with a charm, gotten from a conjure-woman, on a string around the baby's neck. "That packet . . . contained a wad of human hair, fried in snake oil" (p. 11). The doctor gets a call from a young woman to come to an apartment on West 134th Street because her brother has been stabbed. Dart goes along. The young man is dead in bed, the handle of a knife protruding from his chest. Dr. Archer concludes that the death occurred an hour or two earlier.

The investigation begins. The four other members of the family—Petal, the sister who called, Ben, a brother, his wife Letty, and Mother Dewey—are questioned. Meanwhile, the doctor detects an odor but cannot place it; intuitively, he thinks that it might lead to the identity of the killer. Also, as he and Dart search the apartment, he notices a newspaper open to advertisements of charms and conjures.

Questioned later is Red, a friend of the dead Sonny and a boarder in the Dewey household, who says that Sonny and Letty were having an affair, thus bringing Ben under suspicion. But the next day, the mother confesses, saying that Sonny had fallen in with the wrong crowd in Harlem, was drinking and coming home late or not at all. He had become thinner and had been told that he had tuberculosis and would die within a year if not hospitalized. Sonny, however, had refused to go to a sanitarium but had chosen to have a good time and to die at home. The mother says that neither her prayers nor her charms had worked. Hating to see him suffer, she stabbed him, but she thought the incident occurred in a dream. After this account, Mother Dewey faints.

John Archer, still following his nose, as the title of the mystery indicates, sees around her neck the same type of snake-oil packet worn by his patient, Solomon Bright's baby. The newspaper advertisement, noticed on the night of her son's death, had shown a faith charm available for purchase at the Dewey's apartment. The murderer is Solomon Bright, avenging the death of his child whom the charm did not save. Bright had entered Sonny's room by an entranceway earlier unnoticed by Archer.

About Mother Dewey's part in killing Sonny, Dart says, "I get it . . . When she made that charm, she was unwittingly killing her own son" (p. 82). Dr. Archer's final comment is: "No . . . Superstition killed Sonny. . . . But I doubt that we'll ever capture that" (p. 48).

This mystery, like ***The Conjure-Man Dies,*** had a superstitious angle, though the conjure-woman Mother Dewey was neither as sophisticated nor as learned as Frimbo the conjure-man. The author repeated his hidden passageway trick. In ***The Conjure-Man Dies*** there had been the misleading use of fingerprints, but here, fingerprinting was entirely insignificant.

In matching the novelette with the rules for mystery writing, it should be recalled that in a detective story, the murderer should not be the most obvious person but that he should be an individual with whom the reader is familiar. The murdered, too, should have a good motive.[9] Actually, the reader knew little about Solomon Bright, and he had not been introduced through questioning as a suspect. He could then be considered not obvious enough. It is granted, however, that Bright did have a good motive. Also, John Archer's means of determining that Bright killed Sonny were logical and based upon clues, the smell with which he was familiar, the packet with the charm in it, and the newspaper advertisement.

Dr. Archer was not as pedantic in this story as he was in ***The Conjure-Man Dies,*** but it was said of him: "Characteristically, the doctor indulged in wordy and somewhat irrelevant reflection during the tour of inspection" (p. 48). He continued, too, to be scientific; for instance, when trying to place the odor, he said, "Odors should be restricted . . . They should be captured, classified, and numbered like the lines of the spectrum" (p. 48). Further,

> "In a language of a quarter of a million words, we haven't a single specific direct denotation of a smell. . . . Whatever you're thinking of, it is an indirect and non-specific denotation, liking the odor in mind to something else. We are content with 'fragrant' and 'foul' or . . . at best, 'alcoholic' or 'moldy' which are obviously indirect. We haven't even such general direct terms as apply to colors."
>
> (p. 48)

"John Archer's Nose" might be called Rudolph Fisher's minor mystery, being less structurally complex than ***The Conjure-Man Dies.*** Like ***The Conjure-Man Dies*** and ***The Walls of Jericho,*** his two longer pieces of fiction, it makes for engaging reading reflecting Harlem's past, some vestiges of which are a part of its present.

Notes

1. *Afro-American Newspapers,* 4 August 1928, n.p., Rudolph Fisher microfiche card, Schomburg Center for Research in Black Culture, New York Public Library.
2. Rudolph Fisher, *The Walls of Jericho* (New York and London: Alfred A. Knopf, 1928), p. 70. Subsequent references to this source will appear in the text.
3. Rudolph Fisher, *The Conjure-Man Dies: A Mystery Tale of Dark Harlem* (New York: Covici-Friede Publishers, 1932), p. 228. Subsequent references to this source will appear in the text.

4. S. S. Van Dine, "Twenty Rules for Writing Detective Stories," in *The Art of the Mystery Story,* ed. Howard Haycraft (New York: Simon and Schuster, 1946), pp. 189-93.

5. This copy is in the Yale University Beinecke Rare Book and Manuscript Library (The James Weldon Johnson Memorial Collection of Negro Arts & Letters, Founded by Carl Van Vechten).

6. R. Austin Freeman, "The Art of the Detective Story," in *The Art of the Mystery Story,* ed. Howard Haycraft, p. 9.

7. Hugh M. Gloster, *Negro Voices in American Fiction* (Chapel Hill: The University of North Carolina Press, 1948), p. 177.

8. Rudolph Fisher, "John Archer's Nose," *The Metropolitan, A Monthly Review* (January, 1935), pp. 10-12, 47-50, 52, 67, 69-71, 73-75, 80-81, 82. Subsequent references to this source will appear in the text.

9. Van Dine, pp. 190-91.

JOHN MCCLUSKEY JR. (ESSAY DATE 1982)

SOURCE: McCluskey, John Jr. "Healing Songs: Secular Music in the Short Fiction of Rudolph Fisher." *CLA Journal* 26, no. 2 (December 1982): 191-203.

In the following essay, McCluskey details Fisher's use of music—a common theme in his fiction—as a tool for setting the mood, for stressing a theme of the narrative, and for promoting the power of popular forms of music. McCluskey argues that interpreting Fisher's work with a focus on musical themes reveals the depth and importance of his writing.

In the preface to the first edition of the *Book of American Negro Poetry,* published in 1921, James W. Johnson insisted that the black American poet find a form "that will express the racial spirit by symbols from within rather than symbols from without, such as the mere mutilation of English spelling and pronunciation."[1] Johnson proceeded to relate the stifling effects which the minstrel and Plantation School traditions had on the use of dialect. Perhaps a time would come when attitudes toward the use of dialect would mature, but that time, at least to Johnson's way of thinking, was not the decade of the twenties. Yet, Johnson continues, "There is no reason why these poets should not continue to do the beautiful things that can be done, and done best, in the dialect" (p. 42).

Johnson's statement is interesting for both the sense and the timing of it. Coming as it did in the first years of one of the most eventful decades in Afro-American cultural history, the statement both reviews past difficulties in utilizing the raw materials of Afro-American folk life in poetry and anticipates the extensive attempts of younger poets such as Langston Hughes and Sterling Brown to use folk materials honed to a sharp political cutting edge. If we can broaden Johnson's "dialect" somewhat to "vernacular" in order to include not only folk speech, but also elements of black folk life (religious sermons, sacred and secular music) articulated by that speech, we can further appreciate the implications of this statement. At the turn of the century that group of writers that appropriated black folk materials for literary uses emphasized the bizarre and the folksy, utilizing the double vision of the anthropologist and the sentimentalist longing for the "good ole days befo' de wah." Further, if we can substitute "writer" for Johnson's "poet," then the charge for a new generation of black writers, based primarily in the cities, comes clearer: how could the vernacular be rescued from the exhausted soil of rural local color and transplanted in the urban hot houses in poetry, fiction, and drama? Still further, after the transplanting, how do these writers nurture the forms that speak more broadly (and Johnson clearly insisted upon the ideal of universality in his preface and in all his critical statements) and yet retain a cultural integrity?

As suggested above, some members of a younger generation of poets responded to Johnson's call in vigorous and exciting ways. The early experiments of Langston Hughes are well known and have been commented upon fruitfully. Johnson himself would create a new form without the use of dialect in his *God's Trombones* (1927). In his *Southern Road* (1932) Sterling Brown created blues ballads which, in ways often humorous, indicated Southern racial mores and celebrated the toughness of black traditions. Johnson's challenge was met most consistently in the poetry of the period.

In fiction, however, the experimentation with vernacular beyond background and local color was rare. Jean Toomer in 1923 would burst on the scene with *Cane,* the haunting imagery of which was able to shrewdly suggest a different coloring of the Southern landscape. There were other prose writers of the period who, incidentally, were more familiar with black idioms than Toomer and attempted extensive applications of black oral expressions to creative prose. They included most prominently Langston Hughes, Zora Neale Hurston, and Rudolph Fisher. Though Hughes seemed equally at home in urban and small-town settings and though Hurston would work exclusively with the rural South, Rudolph Fisher would consistently choose the city, or, more specifically, Harlem, to work out the problems of a rhetoric of vernacular that would not limit his theme. It is the purpose of this paper to call attention to his specific uses of music in short fiction. His early attempts at involving the vernacular in direct and fresh ways, coupled with his concern for the plight of the Southern migrant in Harlem in a period of extensive urbanization of black America, mark him as a writer and chronicler far more important than critical attention has thus far suggested.

Born in Washington, D.C., and reared in Providence, Rhode Island, Rudolph Fisher (1897-1934) graduated Phi Beta Kappa from Boston University in English and biology. He received his M.A. in English from Brown and then entered Howard University Medical School, graduating in 1924 with highest honors. After a year's internship at Freedman's Hospital in Washington, D.C., Dr. Fisher left for New York, where for two years he was a Fellow of the National Research Council, specializing in biology at the College of Physicians and Surgeons of Columbia University. Dr. Fisher then entered the practice of medicine in New York in 1927, and after specialization in roentgenology, he opened an x-ray laboratory. A lover of music, he sang with Paul Robeson and arranged musical scores. He was the author of fifteen published stories (several of them for juvenile audiences) and two novels, ***The Walls of Jericho*** (1928) and ***The Conjure Man Dies*** (1936). Fisher's writing career had an auspicious beginning. His first published piece, **"The City of Refuge,"** was written while he was still in medical school and published in *The Atlantic Monthly* in February 1925. The story was selected for inclusion in *Best American Short Stories, 1925.* His last piece was published one month after his death. The piece was **"John Archer's Nose"** and was published in *Metropolitan Magazine* in its first and only number, January 1935. Between the piece on the fall of King Solomon Gillis, a newly arrived Southern migrant to Harlem, and the detective story, most of Fisher's pieces dealt with the struggle for the achievement of a humane ethic in the seemingly indifferent yet tantalizing Harlem. This struggle was informed by memory of a more tightly knit Southern community. The Southern tradition is often symbolized by lyrics from spirituals; the Northern urban tradition, by the raucous cry of blues, the siren call of jazz. The setting for the secular music was usually a cabaret, speakeasy, or ballroom.

The Harlem cabaret-dance scene seemed to be a rather stock scene in much American fiction of the twenties. Indeed such scenes were crucial as settings as early as Paul Laurence Dunbar's *The Sport of the Gods* (1902) and James Weldon Johnson's *The Autobiography of an Ex-Colored Man* (1912). Such scenes were useful as local color, plummeting the reader into the whirl of Harlem nightlife. Blues and jazz provided the theme music. At the same time, the scenes often foreshadowed a demise, if not a certain decadence. For example, a cabaret scene in Johnson's novel turns out to be one of the turning points in the life of the protagonist. A jealous lover murders his white mistress in the Club and the protagonist flees to safety.[2] Later he is found wandering by a wealthy and rather languid patron and whisked to Europe as a musician-companion.

Similarly, in the works of white American writers, jazz itself operates as an aphrodisiac or as general background for socio-cultural decay. In many short pieces by F. Scott Fitzgerald, but particularly in *Great Gatsby,* the deliciously sinful nature of jazz stirs the emotions of many of the *nouveaux riches.* In one scene of this novel the response to one Vladimir Tostoff's "Jazz History of the World" is similar to that of a strong wine.[3] In his controversial *Nigger Heaven,* Carl Van Vechten uses the musical background to demonstrate an unrestrained joy, a boundless passion, and a creeping decadence.

Thus by the time Fisher developed his pieces in the mid-twenties, there was no shortage of the cabaret-dance scenes in American fiction. How he would extend the possibilities of that stock scene, how he would attempt to incorporate music more deeply into the fabric of his short stories is what is at issue here. Throughout his brief writing career, Fisher would address the problem of the meaningful uses of vernacular. His growth in this direction was steady.

In **"City of Refuge,"** King Solomon Gillis' final betrayal and fantasy is played out against the background of jazz, for it is in a speakeasy that he sees the girl with the green stockings dancing with a white man. It is there, after a struggle with the police, that he confronts his adopted symbol of manhood, the black policeman, before he ceases his confused struggle. In **"High Yaller,"** published nine months later, a popular lyric operates as a mocking refrain which establishes the plot's ultimate irony.

"High Yaller," one of Fisher's few pieces to treat the passing theme, centers on the frustrations of the fair-skinned Evelyn. Eager to be accepted more fully into the black community, Evelyn seems embarrassed by her light skin. In the story's first scene, while dancing with her darker-skinned escort, Jay Martin, she is stung by a remark she has overhead. A lyric from the bandstand forces the pain even deeper.

> Oh Miss Pink thought she knew her stuff,
> But Miss High Brown has called her bluff.[4]

Bristling, Evelyn asks Jay, "Can you imagine what it's like to be white?" Despite her initial hurt, however, she decides Jay is quite "white" after he has forced a loud-talking ruffian from their presence. She soon insists on immersing herself in the life of Harlem—in blackness, if you will. While visiting an after-hours joint, the couple is subtly deflected to a side-room; the dinner-coated attendant has mistakenly identified Evelyn as white and the presence of mixed couples would surely bring trouble in the shady establishment. When Jay reveals this to Evelyn, she wails. Drifting from below "like a snicker" comes the fragment of the song "Yaller Gal's Gone Out o' Style."

In a later scene while visited by a phantom nightcaller, a nightcaller (her conscience?) who taunts her for her decision not to pass for white and thereby end her anguish, Evelyn pauses. The bizarre dialogue has been interrupted by the whistling of a nightwalker on the street below. Evelyn recognizes the melody fragment as "Yaller Gal's Gone Out o' Style."

Soon afterwards Evelyn's mother dies and Evelyn disappears. Jay is picked up by racist police who believe that he is publicly dating a white woman. After a beating in the police torture-chamber and a warning to leave white women alone, Jay is released. In the story's last scene, thoughts of racial friction flit through his mind as he sits in a movie theater. With a start he notices Evelyn in the audience. Her escort is white: Jay realizes that she has decided to pass for white. He rushes from the theater with the orchestra's familiar refrain "like a loud guffaw," "Yaller Gal's Gone Out o' Style" (p. 38).

Music in this early piece functions as an ironic frame about—and refrain within—the story. The pain of the passing dilemma has shifted from Evelyn to Jay in his consequent sense of loss. Indeed the "yaller gal" is no longer out of style but also out of his life. The song line cruelly mocks the tragic motions of their lives.

A similar refrain-and-frame mode is at work in **"The Promised Land,"** published in January 1927. Mammy has moved from the South to live with her two nephews in Harlem. She witnesses the decadence of Harlem street life, witnesses the developing jealousy over the attractive, though heartless, Ellie. As the piece progresses, the reader watches the conflict between the two men deepen. In a playful scuffle, one of the nephews falls from a window to his death. In shock, Mammy is helpless. The piece is framed by the raucous blues from a rent party and the triumph of the secular music over Mammy's softly hummed spiritual. In the opening scene, Mammy sits in a window, her Bible in her lap, and watches her two nephews in an apartment across an air shaft. As they prepare to fight over Ellie, Mammy hurls her Bible into the room, temporarily ending their conflict. In the final scene the laughing Ellie dances with Sam, and Mammy can only hum her tune in defeat. She can only witness and warn; she cannot direct the lives of her nephews. In this piece Mammy, the attendant to a sacred flame, to a tradition of warmth and close kinship ties, retreats in horror and in seeming resignation before the destructive forces of city life.

What is unique about this piece is the foreshadowing of an issue that Fisher would continue to inspect: the conflict between the fast-paced urban and secular life and the traditional ties with family and church in the South. The piece also introduces for the first time in his fiction the important Grannie figure, who would represent the South, memory, and humanity in the Fisher equation.

"Common Meter" (1930) and **"Blades of Steel"** (1927) develop in their separate ways concerns already established in **"High Yaller"** and **"The Promised Land."** Yet in these two pieces, Fisher utilizes secular music in ways significantly different from before. In **"Common Meter"** the business of Bus Williams, the darker-skinned protagonist, is music. Bus Williams and Fessenden "Fess" Baxter are rivals for the crowd's adulation and the affections of Miss Jean Ambrose. Again, as in **"High Yaller,"** the opening scene is a dance hall and Fisher swiftly uses the setting to introduce the conflict. While Bus's orchestra plays a rather popular **"She's Still My Baby,"** Fess first sights the attractive Miss Ambrose, who is working as a hostess. His interest soars. However, he soon learns that Bus has gotten Jean the job and that Bus has romantic designs on her. Undaunted by her possible allegiance to Bus, Fess dances with her and makes a pass. Jealous of her apparently rapt attention to Fess's whispers, Bus watches helplessly from the bandstand and sends his orchestra through two blues numbers. The sincere emotion of the blues instantly counters the earlier relatively innocuous tune and, of course, reflects Bus's hurt. Its power strikes a responsive chord, however, in the audience's collective soul.

The climax of the story is the jazz contest a few nights later, a contest in which the winner will receive the large victory cup and, presumably, the undivided attention of Jean Ambrose. The reader learns that the drum sheets on the trap and bass of Tappen, Bus's master percussionist, have been cut, rendering his drums useless. It is obvious that the devious Fess will stop at nothing to win. With poor audience response to the first two of the scheduled three numbers, Bus is desperate to find a means to catch up with and surpass Fess's score.

Sharing his desperation, Jean provides the key: play a blues and turn the blues into an old-fashioned shout in which the audience can join with claps and stomps. The stomping feet of the musicians would substitute for the pulse of the bass drum. The transformation of the audience is instantaneous. They become one with the music and, surprisingly, one with their pasts:

> They had been rocked thus before, this multitude. Two hundred years ago they had swayed to that same slow fateful measure, lifting their lamentation to heaven, pounding the earth with their feet, seeking the mercy of a new God through the medium of an old rhythm, zoom-zoom. They had rocked so a thousand years ago in a city whose walls were jungle, forfending the wrath of a terrible Black god who spoke in storm and pestilence, had swayed and wailed to that same slow period, beaten on a wild boar's skin stretched over the end of a hollow treetrunk.[5]

Bus's orchestra reconstructs that moment that profoundly ties past to present. The blues statement, "St. Louis Blues," taps a socio-historical chord which stretches to the sacred.

Needless to say, the villain Baxter in his final number cannot touch the depths that Bus's authentic blues have reached. Flashy craft without the emotional commitment cannot do the trick. Though by a final ruse Baxter manages to win the victory cup, Jean Ambrose renounces any claim he might make on her attention. Bus's group strikes up "She's Still My Baby" as a final mocking retort.

Far more than a frame and internal refrain, secular music here binds and connects an individual call of romantic distress with collective memory. Interestingly enough, he has foreshadowed such an effect on the audience in the first scene. However, at that time, the effect was specific to the pain of lost love. In the final scene the effect goes beyond the secular-romantic mode to a sacred moment suggesting a larger spiritual tie. Though thematically curative it is technically unsatisfactory here given its quickness. The attempt is notable, for it signals a gesture toward the use of music as a bridge which would not be fully developed until quite late in his brief career as a writer.

In **"Blades of Steel"** another rivalry between two young men is worked. Once again, the darker-skinned protagonist, in this case "Eight-Ball" Eddie Boyd, is countered by the much lighter-skinned Dirty Cozzens. And once again the essential conflict is suggested early. On the eve of the Barber's Annual Ball, Eight-Ball has stopped in a crowded barbershop to get the necessary trim for the dance. As he is about to climb into the barber's chair, Eight-Ball is stopped by Dirty Cozzens, who claims that it is his turn. A scuffle is averted by the pretty Effie, who runs a beauty parlor across the street from the barbershop. Later, Eight-Ball escorts Effie to the dance, where they meet Cozzens again. Rebuffed by Effie when he asks for a dance, Cozzens deftly slashes Eight-Ball's coat while the couple dances. The reader soon learns the root cause of the conflict: Cozzens is still angry at losing too much money to Eight-Ball in a crap game. A skilled veteran with the razor, Cozzens wants to push Eight-Ball into a fight. The stage for the showdown is Teddie's place. A blues, its lyrics the combination of the secular and sacred, establishes background.

> My man was comin' to me—said he'd
>   Let me know by mail,
> My man was comin' to me—said he'd
>   Let me know by mail—
> The letter come and tole me—
> They'd put my lovin' man in jail.
>
> Mercy-Lawd, have mercy!
>   How come I always get bad news?
> Mercy-Lawd, have mercy!
>   How come I always get the blues?[6]

Cozzens demands the money he has lost and the fight ensues. Eight-Ball gains the upper hand and is about to deliver the finishing blow when his arm is stopped in mid air by the lyric "Have Mercy—Lawd, Have Mercy." He spares Cozzens and sends him slinking off to the nearby hospital. The reader observes that Eight-Ball has beaten Cozzens with the aid of the street-wise Effie.

Though relatively minimal in the story, the blues-line has entered the plot and helped direct its essential action. This blues by Tessie Smith, "a curious mingling of the secular and religious," speaks to dual experiences: the anger of Eight-Ball at the hi-jinks of Dirty Cozzens and the resolution which, oddly in a blues tune, approaches prayer.

Although the tale is thoroughly secular, it is interesting that the song's final plea, seemingly out of context, is so logical for the action.

Fisher's choice of lyric is important in the way in which it demonstrates his notion of the unity of the sacred and secular modes of experience. That unity is built on a tension that characterizes Fisher's mature fiction: that struggle is between the actions and sensibilities (violence and indifference to family or ethnic loyalties) shaped by the urban context and the more traditional ethic of intragroup caring and generosity. However, the mode for bringing these actions into some constructive merger was not completely clear to Fisher when he wrote **"Blades of Steel."** As short fiction the piece remains a compact melodrama of Harlem street life. In the evolving Fisher cannon, both **"Common Meter"** and **"Blades of Steel"** introduce ways in which a music lyric can directly enter the narrative and alter the action.

The sacred-secular tension, the grandmother figure who symbolizes the Southern tradition hoping to transplant human concerns in Harlem, the lyric which drives the plot toward a wholesome resolution—all of these are brought together in one of Fisher's last published pieces, the popular **"Miss Cynthie."** The story was published in *Story* magazine in June 1933 and reprinted in *Best American Short Stories, 1934.* Since that time, the piece has been included in numerous anthologies of Afro-American literature. In the opening scene, Miss Cynthie arrives in New York to visit her grandson Dave Tappen. She has never been to New York; indeed, she has never traveled far from her hometown in North Carolina. She has learned that Dave is a success and she anticipates his achievement within a respectable profession. When he invites her to the theater to watch the musical review in which he stars, she is disappointed. A stage career is not her idea of a respectable profession. Her disappointment quickly shifts to shock as she watches Dave and her girl friend cavort on the stage much to the delight of the crowd. After a thundering ovation, Dave reappears on stage. He taps out a rhythm and sings a song taught to him years ago by Miss Cynthie. The song is instantly recognized by the audience. He then quiets the crowd to explain the true source of his success: the feisty Miss Cynthie, who has instructed him to do "like a church steeple—aim high and go straight."

As Dave sang his childhood song, Miss Cynthie has watched the lyric's effect on the crowd. The young men and women have been transformed from a loud and sin-loving crowd to children, children who share in Dave's memory and perhaps recall a similar song and caring from their pasts. The movement is from the throes of decadence to relative innocence. Miss Cynthie concludes that "they didn't mean no harm" in their fervent appreciation of the musical revue. In addition, the song seems to have unlocked a door to Miss Cynthie's secular past, for as she moves out of the theater, she pats her foot in time to the jazz rhythms of the orchestra's recessional.

The transformational and binding aspect of black music functions credibly in this place, since it operates through an agent who comprises the dual aspect in dynamic, comic, and moving ways. Miss Cynthie's thinking is not so rigid that she cannot accept an aspect of her own past. Incidentally, there were at least two other models for Miss Cynthie in two earlier, though less successful, stories. Grammie in **"Guardian of the Law"** takes matters into her own hands and rescues her nephew, a rookie policeman, from the clutches of two thugs.[7] In an alternative ending in an unpublished story, **"Lindy Hop"** (c. 1932-33), Grandma wins a dance contest in order to indirectly dissuade her granddaughter from working as a ballroom hostess.[8] She dances the traditional dances (reel, cake-walk, etc.) while her much younger partner dances the modern dances (Charleston and turkey trot). Youth is balanced by age here. For both stories, the older female figure is driven to seemingly unlikely actions through love.

It is Miss Cynthie's love that insists on forgiving both Dave for his choice of profession and simultaneously the young crowd for their seeming fixation with decadence. The snatch of children's rhyme is part of an informing tradition that can open up a different aspect of their lives, can deflect them from a headline flight to moral chaos, can summon the memory and possibility of love.

The capacity of a lyric to function in this way is far more credible and effective in **"Miss Cynthie"** than in **"Common Meter."** The sacred-secular duality only described in **"Blades of Steel"** is affectingly personified with Miss Cynthie, and as a result, the latter piece brings the duality into far better focus. The concerned Grandmother in **"The Promised Land"** has provided the key to deliverance in **"Miss Cynthie."** Interesting though rather contrived elements in the earlier stories are better integrated in the more mature work.

Fisher's development of music in his short pieces—the evolution from simple background and mood-setting to active agent—signals his consistent interest in demonstrating the importance of music and myth in the lives of ordinary folk. In this connection one thinks of Sterling Brown's moving tribute of Ma Rainey and the power of her performances:

> I talked to a fellow, an' the fellow say,
> "She jes' catch hold of us, somekindaway.
> She sagge Backwater Blues one day:
>
> And den de folks, dey natchally bowed dey heads an' cried,
> Bowed dey heavy heads, shet de moufs up tight an' cried,
> An' Ma lef' de stage, an' followed some de folks outside.
>
> Dere wasn't much more de fellow say.
> She jes gits hold of us dataway.[9]

The performance and the lyric are more than entertainment; they touch a profoundly collective chord.

The notion of blues/jazz-as-statement might be obvious enough to us today, informed as we have been by close studies of secular music forms by numerous writers.[10] However, during the Harlem Renaissance few writers and intellectuals took the evolving form of jazz and urban blues seriously. Nathan Huggins has commented on the matter in *Harlem Renaissance:*

> Of course, they [Harlem intellectuals, except Langston Hughes] all mentioned it as background, as descriptive of Harlem life. All said it was important in the definition of the new Negro. But none thought enough about it to try and figure out what was happening. They tended to view it as folk art—like the spirituals and the dance—the unrefined source for the new art. Men like James Weldon Johnson and Alain Locke expected some race genius to appear who would transform that source into *high* culture. That was, after all, the dream of Johnson's protagonist in *Autobiography of an Ex-Coloured Man* as he fancied symphonic scores based on ragtime.[11]

Notwithstanding the purpose of the protagonist in his only novel, Johnson does seem to have taken ragtime and blues more seriously as forms by the time he wrote his preface. However, the spirit of Huggins' argument is accurate when applied to both Alain Locke and W. E. B. Du Bois. In addition, Huggins singled out Langston Hughes as the only writer to take the new forms seriously. Rudolph Fisher must be credited with that same seriousness. His short fiction demonstrates an often entertaining approach to weaving the vernacular into the fabric of creative prose. Though perhaps infrequently, Johnson's challenge was nevertheless met in both prose and poetry before the lights of the Renaissance grew dim.

Notes

1. James Weldon Johnson, *Book of American Negro Poetry* (New York: Harcourt Brace, 1959), p. 41. All further references appear in the text.
2. James Weldon Johnson, *The Autobiography of an Ex-Coloured Man* (New York: Hill and Wang, 1960), Ch. viii.
3. F. Scott Fitzgerald, *The Great Gatsby* (New York: Scribner's, 1953), p. 50.
4. "High Yaller," *Crisis,* October/November 1925, p. 282. All further references appear in the text.
5. "Common Meter," in *Black Voices,* ed. Abraham Chapman (New York: New American Library, 1968), p. 85. The story was originally published in the Baltimore *Afro-American,* February 1930.
6. "Blades of Steel," *The Atlantic Monthly,* August 1927, p. 190.
7. "Guardian of the Law," *Opportunity,* March 1933.
8. The typescript of two drafts of this story is found in Rudolph Fisher's Collected Writings in Manuscript, Brown University, Providence, Rhode Island, Box 1-U, F535a.
9. Sterling Brown, *Southern Road* (Boston: Beacon Press, 1974), pp. 63-64.
10. See Ralph Ellison, *Shadow and Act* (New York: Random House, 1966), especially "Richard Wright's Blues" and his review "Blues People"; Leroi Jones, *Blues People* (New York: Morrow, 1963); Lawrence Levine, *Black Culture and Black Consciousness* (New York: Oxford, 1977); and Albert Murray, *Stompin the Blues* (New York: McGraw-Hill, 1976).
11. Nathan Huggins, *Harlem Renaissance* (New York: Oxford, 1973), p. 10.

JON WOODSON (ESSAY DATE 1999)

SOURCE: Woodson, Jon. "Rudolph Fisher: Minds of Another Order." In *To Make a New Race: Gurdjieff, Toomer, and the Harlem Renaissance,* pp. 75-95. Jackson: University of Mississippi Press, 1999.

In the following excerpt, Woodson argues for the influence of G. I. Gurdjieff—a philosopher whose work was introduced to Harlem writers through his follower Jean Toomer—on Fisher's work.

In his introduction to ***The City of Refuge: The Collected Stories of Rudolph Fisher,*** John McKluskey describes Dr. Rudolph Fisher as

> one of the Harlem Renaissance writers who attempted to affirm the complexity of black urban culture while steering clear of exotica and oversentimentality, two dangers of his moment. . . . In just less than ten years, fifteen of his short stories were published. Of these, **"The City of Refuge,"** his first, and **"Miss Cynthie"** are the

best known today. Both were included in *The Best American Short Stories* collections for their respective years of publication. Fisher was also the author of two novels, ***The Walls of Jericho*** and ***The Conjure-Man Dies.*** The first novel has been touted as one of the more successful Harlem novels of the period; the second is a successful detective novel and the earliest black detective novel published in book form.

(xii)

Fisher's short stories are allegorical treatments analogous to the "teaching stories" often used by Gurdjieff to demonstrate the "objective" view of the human condition. Fisher translated Gurdjieff's allegory of the cart, horse, and driver into his short story **"Dust"** so faithfully that Margaret Perry complains of "the insistent personification" in the story in which the roadster is compared to "a cruelly spurred horse" (8). Perry states that "The reader nearly forgets this is a car" (8). The same analogy was also used by Orage and Toomer and appeared early in the lectures on "self-observation without identification," such as the series that Fisher attended in 1926. The most detailed written version of the parable is recorded in Ouspensky's *In Search of the Miraculous:* "The driver is the mind. In order to be able to hear the master's voice, the driver, first of all, must *not be asleep,* that is, he must wake up. . . . The horse is our emotions. The carriage is our body. The mind must learn to control the emotions. The emotions always pull the body after them" (ISM 92).

Fundamentally, ***The Walls of Jericho*** (1928) is an expansion of the earlier short story **"Dust."** In **"Dust,"** as Pard discovers that the "lyncher . . . red-necked hillbilly . . . cracker" (151) who he has run off the road is in reality a black man, we witness the epiphany in which the self is revealed as nothing more than a delusion: "Man is divided into a multiplicity of small I's" (ISM 60). In ***The Walls of Jericho*** Fisher depicts the developing self beyond the single moment of revelation. In both texts the agent of revelation is a woman, although the doctrine of tolerance—only suggested by Billie's comments in **"Dust"**—is fully spelled out in ***The Walls of Jericho*** by the words of Reverend Tod Bruce's sermon and figured forth, as well, by the action of the novel. ***The Walls of Jericho*** functions as an allegorical treatment of Fisher's ideas about the illusory nature of the categories of race, color, and class.

John McKluskey describes the novel as

a Harlem panorama. We are introduced to nearly every layer of social class as Fisher knew them during the late 1920s. The passing theme and class conflict are introduced in ways often comic. Still further, it is a novel that attempts to hold together its many disparate parts through the exploration of the notion of self-delusion. However, the work centers on an evolving relationship between "Shine," a piano-mover, and Linda, an ambitious maid. Shine deludes himself about the possibilities for vengeance from a fellow black. All this is fueled by a metaphor crystallized late in the book. With Linda, Shine listens to a minister shape the story of Joshua and the walls of Jericho. . . .

Prepared for this wisdom by his involvement with Linda, who challenges him to accept his vulnerability, Shine takes the Jericho metaphor to heart in the last third of the book. He struggles to maintain his tough facade for his friends and at the same time come to terms with his underlying tenderness. This is shown not only in the love relationship but also in his inability to injure two rivals—one apparent (Merrit), the other real (Patmore)—in later action. . . . Near the novel's end he can state: "The guy that's really hard is the guy that's hard enough to be soft."

(xxviii-xxix)

By naming his protagonist Joshua Jones and having him go by the humiliating nickname of "Shine," Fisher indicates the two levels on which his novel operates. As Shine, his protagonist represents the entire black race, and the novel represents Fisher's prescription for the social advancement of the masses—what is now called the underclass. Through the Shine character, Fisher confronts the interracial and intraracial complexities of America's schizoid culture. By calling his protagonist Joshua Jones, Fisher alludes to the "Book of Exodus," providing an intertextuality that forces comparisons to the story of Moses in his conquest of Canaan and the establishment of the promised land. The intertextuality is emphasized by a twofold subtextual narration of Tod Bruce's parable, first incompetently, with the meaning of the sermon censored (by Joshua Jones), and a second time with the full meaning restored by the omniscient and "objectively conscious" narrator. Moreover, the narrator points out that the reverend's use of the fall of Jericho to represent his doctrine of the development of the self is less apt than it might seem: "Bruce spoke quietly, without show but with impassioned conviction; and though many of his hearers no more grasped his message than did Shine, there was none who felt the same when Bruce ended as when he began. His honesty and sincerity were contagious and the very defects in his imperfect analogy revealed a convincing absence of artifice, a contempt for trifling disparities, and impressive disregard for minor obstacles in conveying a major idea" (183).

Tod Bruce's "major idea" that "No man knows himself till he comes to an impasse; to some strange set of conditions that reveal to him his ignorance of the workings of his spirit; to some disrupting impact that shatters the wall of self illusion" (185-86) appropriately applies to the racial situation, for as Bruce says, "A man may think he is black when he is white" (185). In Tod Bruce's view everything is an illusion, even race: Without mental freedom there is no possibility of perceiving reality. Fisher's doctrine, inserted into ***The Walls of Jericho*** by Tod Bruce, is derived from Gurdjieff's comment about the condition of the common man: "He does not see the real world. The real world is hidden from him by the wall of imagination. He lives in sleep" (ISM 143). The metaphor of the walls of Jericho alludes to Gurdjieff's more general metaphor that equates the defensive wall of the ancient city with sleep.

Thus on the "objective" level Fisher's novel is about "sleep." However, he has compressed and distorted a complex array of ideas into a relatively simple and compact idea that does not reflect Gurdjieff's system exactly. According to Gurdjieff

> If a man throughout the whole of his life were to feel all the contradictions that are within him he could not live and act as calmly as he lives and acts now. . . . He must either destroy contradictions or cease to see and to feel them. A man cannot destroy contradictions. But if "buffers" are created in him he can cease to feel them and he will not feel the impact from the clash of contradictory views, contradictory emotions, contradictory words. . . . Awakening is possible only for those who seek it and want it, for those who are ready to struggle with themselves and work on themselves for a very long time and very persistently in order to attain it. For this it is necessary to destroy "buffers," that is, to go out to meet all those inner sufferings which are connected with the sensation of contradictions.
>
> (ISM 155-56)

Thus, what Tod Bruce calls the "wall of self illusion" is Gurdjieff's concept of "buffers." The idea of "buffers" was important in the version of the work presented in Harlem by Toomer and Orage, and the Harlem group incorporated it into their coded texts. It follows, then, that in ***The Walls of Jericho*** the central metaphor, what the narrator calls the "imperfect analogy," originates from one of the fundamental concepts in Gurdjieff's system. So important is this concept to Fisher that he completely halts the narrative progression to address the reader directly through the embedded text of Tod Bruce's sermon. The sermon concludes by foreshadowing the denouement: "I urge you therefore to besiege yourselves; to take honest counsel with the little fraction of God, of Truth, that dwells in us all. To follow the counsel of that Truth and beset the wall of self deception. So will the towering illusion tumble. So will you straightaway enter triumphant into the promised land" (187).

By generating a significant portion of his narrative from an episode centered on the General Improvement Association's (GIA) costume ball, Fisher demonstrates the illusory nature of the world as perceived by normal human consciousness and pursues the themes of artificiality and theatricality, which were so effectively explored by Wallace Thurman. In the "Uplift" section of the narrative, Fisher's satire takes aim at a broad range of targets including the personality of W. E. B. Du Bois, miscegenation, Negro characteristics, and integration, although the narrator is careful to indicate the actual nature of the proceedings. Fisher's GIA alludes to both the United Negro Improvement Association (UNIA) and the National Association for the Advancement of Colored People (NAACP). Although the GIA approximates the form of UNIA's name, as a white woman, Agatha Cramp would not have been allowed to join the ranks of Garvey's back-to-Africa movement. Fisher's GIA is patterned on the integrationism of Du Bois's NAACP. However, by fusing these organizations as he does, Fisher parodies them both. In Fisher's view, neither organization was capable of usefully bettering the structure of American society. There is also a pronounced irony in having the occasion be a costume ball; with their illusions or "buffers" in place, the characters are already wearing the costumes of their "false personalities." The Gurdjieffian view is that "Man consists of two parts: *essence* and *personality*. . . . Essence is the truth in man; personality is the false. Culture creates personality" (ISM 161-62). In contrast to the "buffering" effect of socialization, it is the intent of the Gurdjieff system to "take off all masks" (ISM 157). However, at the ball the characters are devoted to maintaining their illusions or "masks."

The most important illusion at the costume ball is that "The bars are down. This is for the Race. One great common fellowship in one great common cause" (71). However, the narrator reveals that even at the one dance where there is supposed to be intraracial unity, there are divisions of caste and class: "Out on the dance floor, everyone, dickty and rat, rubbed joyous elbows, laughing, mingling, forgetting differences. But whenever the music stopped everyone immediately sought his own level" (74). The narrator's insight into the psychosocial realities of life in Harlem is so distant from a normal view that he seems to become wholly an other, a voice belonging to another order of being. The narrator emphasizes the mechanical, unconscious, externally determined nature of the dancers: "So dense was the crowd of dancers, so close each couple to the next, that an observer from above might easily have lost the sense that these were actually people. They seemed rather some turbulent congress of bright colored, inanimate things, propelled by a force over which they had no control" (102). This passage may be compared to Thurman's description of Raymond's breakdown (actually a breakthrough) in *Infants,* when he grasps the mechanical nature of human life: "The people flabby puppets jingling at the end of strings over which a master hand has lost control" (204). Both of these passages are grounded in the conceptual origin of Gurdjieff's system, that man can do nothing, that things simply happen: "Man is a machine. All his deeds, actions, words, thoughts, feelings, convictions, opinions, and habits are the results of external influences, external impressions. Out of himself a man cannot produce a single thought, a single action. Everything he says, does, thinks, feels—all this happens. Man cannot discover anything, invent anything. It all happens" (ISM 21).

Fisher's passage is also a presentation of esoteric physics; he describes the dance as a play of forces of which "an observer from above" (102) is aware, for we are shown the dance while looking down from the terraces of the Manhattan Casino. The narrator indicates this force four times in the passage (102), labeling it variously as "stream," "undertrend," and "current." Here Fisher alludes to Gurdjieff's complicated discussion of cosmic physics: "The influence of the moon upon everything living manifests itself in all that happens on the earth. . . . All his [man's] movements and consequently all his activities are controlled by the moon" (ISM 85). The consequences of man's cosmic situation are spelled out by Gurdjieff in explicit terms: "'Progress' and 'civilization,' in the real meanings of these words, can appear only as the result of *conscious* efforts. . . . And what conscious efforts can there be in machines? . . . It is precisely in unconscious involuntary manifestations that all evil lies" (ISM 52).

The thrust of the Shine-Linda subplot is that Linda—an embodiment of the Moses archetype—is moving toward a higher level of consciousness and hoping to move Shine, the embodiment of black mass-man, along with her. This reading results from the fundamentally allegorical nature of Fisher's text. In Fisher's short story **"Dust,"** the woman, Billie, functions as Pard's conscience. Conscience or consciousness (for Gurdjieff these are the same thing) is defined as an "objective" or permanent idea of good (ISM 158) and is a faculty developed after removing the "buffers" that prevent one from seeing the truth of the human situation, or in Fisher's terms, after realizing that one is surrounded by a wall of illusion. Allegorically, Linda is Shine's conscience, for she leads him to a more conscious view of himself. By contrast, Fred Merrit has no conscience—all that he has is a portrait of his dead mother. The portrait is what is left of Merrit's conscience, now a mere projection, a symbol entirely external to his being. When he loses the portrait in the fire set by Patmore, the loss nearly destroys him. Although Merrit seems able to continue, his psyche is open to involuntary and unconscious evil impulses, and he is last seen awash in a sea of mental confusion.

Merrit plays out his most revealing attributes in an encounter with the hypocritical Agatha Cramp, his white neighbor. Agatha Cramp has joined the GIA to give herself something to do. At the costume ball she converses with Merrit, whom she believes to be white. To amuse himself and to discomfit Agatha Cramp (for he will see to it that she eventually learns that he is black), Merrit pretends to be white and drops provocative, doubly meant comments into their conversation. The description of Merrit emphasizes the contrast between his outer self (his "mask" or "costume") and his inner self: "And so beneath his pleasant manner, there was a disordered spirit which at this moment almost gleefully accepted the chance to vent itself on Miss Agatha Cramp's ignorance" (107). As we might expect, all of the characters in the novel lack an integrated self—a union of mind, body, and emotions. However, it is Merrit who demonstrates this Gurdjieffian concept in action.

In Gurdjieffian terms "Man has no individuality. He has no single, big I. Man is divided into a multiplicity of small I's" (ISM 60). In the scene where Merrit plays racial cat-and-mouse with Agatha Cramp, one of his "small I's" comes out for a while. Merrit's race-bating subpersonality is not interested in the consequences of such a devious course of action; it simply wants the fun it can have at that moment. Moreover, Merrit strikes out at Agatha Cramp because he is upset about the flirtation between a white man and a married African-American woman (Tony Nayle and Nora Byle): "That he should allow it to disturb him so profoundly meant that it went profoundly back into his own life, as it did into the lives of most people of heredity so diverse as his" (107). Merrit, himself a light-skinned mulatto, is divided against himself and cannot accept either half of his diverse heredity. Merrit represents the self divided against itself of Du Bois's double-consciousness. However, more to the point, Merrit is the victim of his own fragmentation, is immune to salvation, and is resistant to the formation of a universal, unitary man that is the blending of all races into a new American race. Here we see Merrit swayed by external events and stimuli, entirely mechanical, and lacking anything that can be termed "mental freedom." His own pain causes him to lash out at Agatha Cramp, who, although a member of the dominant race, is a woman faced with her own self-administered psychic tortures.

In his attempts to shock Agatha Cramp, Fred Merrit confronts her with opinions on the color question that are extremely threatening to her assumptions of racial superiority. Merrit predicts the inevitable conversion of America into a black nation: "Wouldn't it be amusing if the Negro let others worry their brains out devising and developing the civilized luxuries of life—while he spent his time simply living, developing nothing but his capacity for enjoyment; and then when the job was finished, stepped in and took complete possession? Suppose—just suppose, for one can never know—that this irrepressible laughter, this resiliency, is caused by the confidence that he will reap what his oppressors have sown" (123). What Merrit depicts for Agatha Cramp's contemplation is a veritable racial apocalypse, the coming to pass of every social horror that she can conceive (a theme expanded upon by Schuyler in *Black Empire;* see chapter 5). The all-black world, which Merrit conceives as his utopia, is for Fisher a racialist dystopia, because the novel discredits racialist thought whether it is harbored by blacks or whites.

However, the depiction of utopias is a matter of subtleties, and even when the results of certain processes give identical results, the meanings may not be the same. Fisher places the black monoracial utopia (really a dystopia) in the context of Merrit's nasty, ironic, verbal assault on Agatha Cramp to suggest that he does not condone Merrit's views. Fred Merrit and Agatha Cramp represent the tragic side of racialism in ***The Walls of Jericho:*** Although the novel limits their conflict to verbal aggression, the potential (and the means) for greater violence surrounds them both. The novel also maintains a suspenseful suggestion that Agatha Cramp plans to burn down Merrit's home. In the wider scheme of things, the threat of a race riot motivated by Merrit's move into a white neighborhood hangs over the novel from its opening pages: "In Patmore's the discussion concerned a possible riot in Harlem, a popular topic among those men who loved battle" (5). At the conclusion of the novel, Merrit dimly realizes that Shine and Linda are leaving him behind in the old world. However, he is unable to move beyond his racial preoccupations:

> He had preposterous feelings, far too absurd to admit: an impulse to run after the departing Bess, crying, "Wait—for God's sake—" as if she were carrying off some chance of his own; a terrifying sense of some slow crushing futility, allowing them to escape, but holding him captive, surrounding, insulating, oppressing him, like the haze of this morning's mist, beyond which he could perceive but out of which he could not emerge; as if he moved and must always move in a dismal, broad, gray cloud, outside of which were clear blue skies that he could know of but never reach.
>
> (292)

What has Fisher intended by making us think of Moses in this scene? Moses is the religious leader who cannot enter the promised land, and similarly, Merrit remains behind in the divided world. However, Merrit is no prophet. He remains behind because he is a "mechanical" man and his mental formulations are depraved. In Gurdjieff's terminology, Merrit is "already dead." The root assumption of Gurdjieff's system is that normal man is "asleep." Eventually even the possibility of awakening can expire: "It happens fairly often that essence dies in a man while his personality and his body are still alive. A considerable percentage of the people we meet in the streets of a great town are people who are empty inside, that is they are actually *already dead*" (ISM 164).

To emphasize Merrit's unfortunate condition, we are given a last look at his mind as he briefly recapitulates the psychic mileposts in his life. These instances pass before him without his being able to attach any meaning to them. As Merrit's life unrolls, ironically, the walls of Jericho, which served to awaken Shine, is reviewed uncomprehendingly by Merrit as "Tod Bruce in his pulpit drawing some remote and ridiculous analogy" (293). Merrit, confined in his race-obsessed inferno, is alone, continuing to propound race-obsessed insights—"jigs were inherently smart" (293), while Joshua Jones and Linda—awake to the possibilities that exist in their ever-expanding mental freedom—"drop abruptly out of vision, into another land" (293).

Thus far the discussion of ***The Walls of Jericho*** has been largely concerned with the narrative level of the text; however, Fisher's text contains a hermeneutic level as well. The following is a brief examination of Fisher's performance as an "objective" novelist in ***The Walls of Jericho.*** Fisher's novel is distinguished from the other texts by the Harlem group by his minimal use of devices that open his text to hermeneutic interpretation. Fisher's "attack on race" is pursued on the mimetic level of the novel, and his investment in an "attack on reading" is negligible. Although the title of Fisher's novel conducts us into the subtext, it is only by recognizing the pattern common to texts by Hurston, Thurman, Larsen, and Tolson that we are able to recognize the existence of wordplay in Fisher's title.

Given the preponderance of words that approximate "gurd" in Thurman's texts ("gingerale," "vulgar," and "Niggerati"); the occurrence of similar homophones in Larsen's *Passing,* such as "Gertrude," (196) "georgette" (196), and "manicured" (196); "gourd" in the title of Hurston's first novel, *Jonah's Gourd Vine,* and "G" near "eir" and "ere" in *Their Eyes Were Watching God,* we recognize the significance of the homophone "jer" in "Jericho." (We can add to this list the "jure" homophone in the title of Fisher's second novel, ***The Conjure-Man Dies.***) In each of these texts, the inclusions of approximations of the "gurd" homophone is intended to establish a "lexical overdetermination" (Ulmer 23), which will allow the reader to decipher the provider word as a rendition of Gurdjieff's name. Fisher's text provides this overdetermination by setting much of the activity on "Court Avenue," which approximates the sound of Gurdjieff's name more closely than does "jer." It also provides numerous repetitions of the homophone, which eventually accumulate into a recognition of "Gurdjieff." This recognition can only be made after the discovery that reading the text is contingent upon "first voiding, displacing, or repressing any established meaning" (Riffaterre 83)—in other words, by apprehending that the text is a code and setting about to decipher it. Fisher piles up homophones for "Gurd" in "giraffe" (15), "Great Gordon Gin" (89), and "regard" (15). He approximates the sound of the complete name by combining "*gar*ment" (11) and "*ges*tures" (11) in one case and "Acc*ord*ingly" (11) and "*aff*ection" (11) in another. Read hermeneutically, the passage states quite emphatically that something is hidden within it:

> Accordingly their own expression of this affection had to take an ironic turn. They themselves must deride it first, must *hide* their mutual inclination in a *garment* of constant ridicule and contention, the irritation of which rose into their consciousness as hostility. Words and *gestures* which in a different order of life would have required no suppression became with them necessarily inverted, *found issue only by assuming a precisely opposite aspect, concealed a profound attachment* by exposing an extravagant enmity. And this was a distortion of behavior so completely imposed upon them by their traditions and society that even they themselves did not know they were *masquerading.*
>
> (11; emphases added)

Instances where Fisher approximates the sound of "Gurdjieff" may be discovered throughout the text, yet compared to his colleagues, Fisher's accessible clues are rarities. Fisher generally renders names through the repetition of their component sounds, not as words. Although he continually sounds the names of Gurdjieff ("currents . . . jests" [139]), Orage ("Courage" [5], "disparage" [9]), and Ouspensky ("is . . . spinster . . . skirts" [44]), the names do not sufficiently announce their presence.

From the "objective" perspective, the entire text is a fuguelike intercourse of the importance of these significant homophones ("gurd," "chief"; "or," "age"; "us," "pen," "ski"; "too," "mer"), which cumulatively present these sounds so constantly, consistently, and emphatically that ultimately the names themselves break through and the subtext is perceptible to the reader. The collapse of the walls of Jericho after repeated blows of the ram's horn is at issue in Fisher's text: The collapse of the mimetic text that makes audible the subtext is the activity that generates the text itself. Only once does Fisher arrange a passage so that it has sound as its subject. However, what is important here is not only sound but the interpretation of sound:

> A familiar sound came from outside. Bess had been parked in the street below. Jinx and Bubber had grown impatient and were "laying" on the horn, by way of suggesting that the driver hurry and return. The sound came faint but clear through the open windows.
>
> "Know what that is?" Shine asked her.
>
> She smiled and answered, "I guess that must be the ram's horn."
>
> (261)

Fisher imagines that the walls of Jericho fall when the reader becomes aware of the subtext, and the sounds of the esoteric level are at last accessible: Jericho can then be entered by the wandering pilgrims. "Jericho" is revealed to be "Gurdjieff." The passage quoted above—which is a key to the subtext—contains the phonetic components of "Gurdjieff": "*g*rown," "sug*g*esting," "*g*uess"; "h*ur*ry," "ret*ur*n"; "*d*river," "soun*d,*" "parke*d*"; "sug*gest*ing," "*guess,*" "B*ess*"; "*f*amiliar," "*f*aint." The passage quoted above renders the sounds of Gurdjieff's name, although not in the proper sequence, and it concludes a chapter that has many, more complete homophones of "Gurdjieff." The passage thus summarizes and calls attention to the activity of sounding out Gurdjieff's name, which has been continuous throughout the chapter.

The contents of the subtext of ***The Walls of Jericho*** do not differ from what his associates have concealed in their novels. However, Fisher is more laconic and more ambiguous in his constructions. In many examples, even when it is clear that a passage contains a cipher, it is difficult to be sure of Fisher's intention because his devices are obscure. For example, Gurdjieff's *Beelzebub's Tales* was commonly referred to as "the book"; therefore, we know that when Linda says "I'll bring the book, Miss Cramp" (69) we are to take "the book" as a reference to *Beelzebub's Tales,* but this was very much the jargon of insiders. Similarly, the passing references to the "devil" (41, 51, 65) and "devil" followed by the reinforcing word "scratch" (51) in the subsequent paragraph are also allusions to *Beelzebub's Tales.* Likewise, there can be little doubt that Fisher is referring to the Gurdjieff work in his description of piano moving: "Every man who enters this work thereby invites this pursuit" (223).

Other requisite Gurdjieffian matters appear in Fisher's text with little concealment. The concept of the "mask" is present in the costume ball (71) given by the GIA. There are several mentions of the numbers three (4, 24, 61, 167), seven or eight (144, 150, 253), and allusions to the Laws of Three and Eight.

Fisher strikes a distinctive chord only at a few places in his novel. Foremost is his rendering of an idea that does not appear in other texts by members of the Harlem group, namely, the description of esoterism. Fisher depicts the esoteric project as a building in imitation of Gurdjieff's parable of the orderly house as a stage in the development of the harmonious self. ***The Walls of Jericho*** is a text in which buildings figure prominently. Fisher's description of esoterism in the figure of Patmore's Pool Parlor also originates in that parable, although with a different emphasis. In Fisher's treatment, the building is not the harmonious self but the esoteric school, specifically, Gurdjieff's institute. He states that

> Patm*ore*'s P*oo*l P*a*rl*or* occupied the remodeled ground fl*oor* of a once elegant ap*ar*tment-h*ouse:* *two* long low adjacent r*oom*s, with a smaller one in the re*ar.* You could enter either of the l*ar*ger *two* from the street, and a d*oor*way *join*ed them within. There were no pretenses about these *two rooms:* one was a p*oo*l r*oom,* its stolid, gr*een* col*or*ed tables extending from front to back in a long squat row; the other was a sal*oo*n, with a mahog*any* b*ar* counter, great wall mirr*or,* a shining f*oot* rail and br*ass spit*t*oo*ns. In the sal*oo*n you could get any drink you had c*ourage* and cash enough to *or*der; in the p*oo*l r*oom* you could play for any stake and *use* any langu*age* you had the in*genuity to* devise. The third r*oom* was off the p*oo*l *room* and behind the sal*oo*n; this *g*ave itself over to that triad of swift exchange, poker, black-jack, and dice.
>
> (4-5)

The italicized syllables in the above passage indicate components of the names of Jean Toomer, P. D. Ouspensky, A. R. Orage, and G. I. Gurdjieff (more commonly known as G. or Mr. G.). This passage has been superabundantly endowed with fourteen occurrences of the phoneme "oo," which is a device meant to attract the reader to the sound of Jean Toomer's name ("joined . . . two . . . more") as it echoes throughout the paragraph. Having attained that stage of recognition, the reader will be able to progress onward to the other names concealed in the paragraph. Moreover, with "use any language you had the ingenuity to devise" the paragraph alludes to Gurdjieff's interpretation of the biblical story of the confusion of tongues: "The *Esoteric* or innermost circle of all consisted of people who had attained the maximum development possible to man, full consciousness, unity and will. . . . The next circle to this was the *Mesoteric* or middle circle. . . . The third circle was the *Exoteric* circle. . . . Beyond these concentric circles there lay the outer region of the Confusion of Tongues, the great area in which dwelt the whole of the rest of humanity" (Walker 188-90). This reading usefully locates the esoteric project in its derivation from language and further illuminates the "objective" method through which Fisher and the other Gurdjieffians have created their texts.

The cardinal feature of esoterism in Ouspensky's interpretation of the story of the Tower of Babel was that between the members of all of the circles "what one understood, all of the others understood in the same way" (Walker 190). The Confusion of Tongues is most clearly represented in ***The Walls of Jericho*** by Agatha Cramp: "Miss Cramp sat staring about with eyes that comprehended nothing, the turbulence in her own mind confusing every perception" (139).

According to Gurdjieff, his institute was an esoteric school. However, his schools in New York were exoteric, having only beginners as members. Orage commented in the early 1920s that the school he convened was "Not esoteric, nor even mesoteric. These are very far from us. If we can start an exoteric group, we shall do well" (Nott *Teachings* 29). Thus, the description of Patmore's Pool Parlor may specifically apply to the structure of Gurdjieff's New York schools: Admission was available to the public, and the groups were openly conducted. It was only the Harlem group that set up secret meetings: Henry Patmore is an anagram for "inner room." Thus within the third room of Patmore's Pool Parlor, the "triad of swift exchange" (5) that transpired was the "line of work" that constituted Toomer's "attack on race" in addition to the two esoteric lines of evolutional work, work on oneself and work on other people (Walker 193).

Fisher has endowed his text with another clue to the nature of the Harlem group's enterprise in a passage that signals its hermeneutic content: "Joshua Jones, be it confessed, was himself no cipher among the ladies. There had been girls aplenty: Sarah Mosely, Babe Merrimac, Lottie Buttsby, Becky Katz, Maggie Mulligan, and others. An acknowledged master of men is usually attractive to women, and in his world of sinew and steel, Shine had the necessary reputation; there was no end of stories about what he could do with his hands" (80). Read hermeneutically, the passage offers itself as a "cipher" and refers to the "master of men," whom we know to be Gurdjieff ("*gir*l" "con*fess*ed"). The motivation for these contrivances is that Fisher must draw attention to the list of Shine's former girlfriends, which when decoded declares: "some harass," "be merry," "lots [of] us," "takes a million." The hidden message informed the readers that they were wanted as recruits in a struggle against the forces of racialism. Although it is clear that the narrative level of ***The Walls of Jericho*** presented a case against race and color discrimination, without Fisher's ciphered message, the reader would remain unaware of the African-American Gurdjieffians who were organizing to change the structure of American culture. Given such ambitious plans, we realize that the reader should take literally the utopian conclusion of ***The Walls of Jericho,*** which frames the truck with Linda and Shine beneath a "sunrise like a promise" (293) as it begins its voyage "into another land" (293), the promised land that waits beyond the racially divisive ethos of Miss Cramp, Fred Merrit, Patmore, and the other proponents of racialist thought.

Rudolph Fisher's ***The Conjure-Man Dies*** (1932) is a detective novel set in Harlem. The novel resurrects John Archer, the Harlem doctor who appeared in a short story in which Fisher struck a blow against the dependence of African-Americans on folk superstitions in medicine. The novel pairs Archer with Detective Perry Dart, a black, New York City police officer, and involves them in a case with a number of unusual aspects. The African conjure-man and Harlem fortune teller N'Gana Frimbo is found murdered. While assisting in solving the crime, John Archer discovers that Frimbo has only faked his death, and a strange relationship grows between them. They engage in a number of intellectual discussions in which Frimbo imparts some exotic views of African rituals and alludes to the possession of profound powers. In one of these conversations Frimbo reveals that he is a superman. Frimbo maintains that he is free and undetermined by the laws of cause and effect and the laws of accident that operate on the Earth: "Imagine, for instance, an order in which a cause followed its effect instead of preceding it—someone has already brought forward evidence of such a possibility. A creature of such an order could act upon our order in ways that would be utterly inconceivable to us" (227).

Frimbo refuses to reveal the method that he uses to exercise his free will or the source of his knowledge; however, he does give an abstraction of the principles involved: "I simply change the velocity of what is going on. I am a catalyst. I accelerate or retard a reaction without entering into it. This changes the cross currents, so that the coincidences are different from what they would otherwise be" (228).

The Conjure-Man Dies is particularly useful in demarcating the advances made in "objective" writing by the Harlem group. Although it may have been a good career move for Fisher to extend the geography of African-American literature into the realm of the detective story, that genre also proves a good vehicle for a writer who wishes his reader to look upon the text as a hermeneutic problem. By turning to the genre of the detective story, Fisher selected a form better suited to his semiotic and "objective" needs than what the satirical novel of manners could provide. This genre was not pursued by Fisher; however,

Schuyler capitalized upon it and turned out a number of popular newspaper serials based on intrigue, mystery, and conspiracy.

In ***The Conjure-Man Dies*** the plot hinges on an act of deception. The reader's attention is drawn to this central act (in which a man dies and rises from the dead) and to other, lesser acts of deception: Ultimately, Fisher designed the narrative to break down and thereby reveal itself as a deception, a text concealing a subtext. Parallel and complementary to the deceptive acts that drive the narrative is the theme of sight, which is brought to the reader's attention through every conceivable means. Characters are described according to defects of their vision (e.g., "unseeing eyes" [31], "cross-eyed" [50], "the cast in one eye" [66], "protruding eyes" [107], and "cock-eye" [133]) and are hyperbolically threatened with having their eyes poked out or are blinded by glaring lights. Characters are plunged into darkness, and they hold conversations in darkened rooms. Dr. John Archer joins the case because "This promises to be worth seeing" (22), and Frimbo's crisis is initiated by the words "Frimbo! Frimbo! Why do you not see?" (70). The culmination of the sight motif comes during Bubber Brown's narration of his case (in a self-referentially parodying subplot in which he assumes the role of a clownish private detective): "I couldn't use nothin' but my ears—couldn't see a thing" (52). Fisher thus informs the reader that "reading" by eye will not reveal the subtext—this is accomplished by using nothing but the ears.

Another route into the subtext is through the novel's intertextual relationship to the detective stories of the Sherlock Holmes corpus. This intertextuality is signaled by the stilted literary diction that John Archer adopts soon after Detective Perry Dart asks him to consult on the case. Although Archer and Dart apply professional techniques (the meticulous interrogation of witnesses and suspects, an examination of the "corpse," the comparison of fingerprints, an analysis of the evidence, and a logical examination of the facts), their efforts lead them to accuse an innocent man, Jinx Jenkins. Archer speaks ironically when he says that he has plans to write a murder mystery (155), as though he is the equal of Arthur Conan Doyle and can rival the famous Sherlock Holmes, who is, in the words of Dr. Watson, "the most perfect reasoning and observing machine the world has ever seen" (quoted in Rosenberg 110). However, when Archer is shown to be mistaken in his accusation of Jinx, the irony reflects back on him. The attentive reader cannot escape the implication that Archer is, despite his overweening certainty, altogether unequipped to solve the case by the means at his disposal.

The undermining of his detective, John Archer, is only the beginning of Fisher's "attack on reading." In contrast to the doctor and the detective, Bubber Brown is an untrained pseudodetective. Nevertheless, he cleverly subverts the investigation by planning his attack on the case several moves ahead of the detectives and throws suspicion away from himself so that he will be free to assist his accused friend, Jinx Jenkins. As Brown sets off on his own to solve the case, Jinx urges him on from his jail cell: "All I got to say is, Sherlock, do your stuff" (196). By setting up Bubber Brown to solve a case that Archer and Dart cannot solve, Fisher signals that he has not actually written a detective mystery. Not only has he descended into parody and comedy, robbing his text of every possibility of establishing a credible atmosphere of suspense, danger, and intrigue, but he has caused the reader to doubt the efficacy of the conventional tools by which Archer and Dart attempt to read the text of their mystery. The device that most seriously damages the text as a detective novel is that Fisher plays off a pair of clowns against Archer and Dart. Where clowns conventionally serve to elevate the hero, Bubber and Jinx are allowed to demote Archer and Dart. The text forces readers to question their own ability to competently penetrate into the real text, thereby bringing an awareness of the esoteric subtext.

Fisher's "attack on reading" is complex; it relentlessly assaults the reader with impasses, paradoxes, and riddles. This concerted "attack on reading" is not solely confined to the intertextual arena, for the attack at the intratextual level is equally destructive of the reader's complacency. Within the novel there are difficulties with text even beyond the convolutions presented by the murder case. The foremost example of an intratextual dilemma is Perry Dart's inability to negotiate John Archer's pseudo-Holmesian discourse. In fact, rather than imitating Holmes, Archer violates Holmes's prime directive, namely that "Whenever you have eliminated the impossible, whatever remains, however improbable, must be the truth" (quoted in Rosenberg 3). For his part, Archer's version of Holmes's modus operandi is delivered as an absurdity: "And I too am of the common persuasion which Mr. Frimbo so logically exposed, that one who comes to life was never dead. Logic to the contrary notwithstanding, I still believe the dead stay dead. And, while the corpse may be hard to produce, I still believe you have a murder on your hands" (182). As the investigation proceeds, the exchanges between Archer and Dart are increasingly marked by Dart's discomfort with Archer's language. Archer, nevertheless, behaves as though the successful solution of the case depends upon his use of a discourse of detection. Finally, Dart can bear no more. Archer issues a long speech that concludes: "But now, if these two blood specimens reposing in my bag present certain differences which I anticipate, I shall advise you to proceed with the total demolition of yonder dwelling—a vandalism which you have already contemplated, I believe?" (184). Dart's reply is telling: "Gosh, doc, it would be so much easier in French. Say it in French" (184).

The same speeches that Dart cannot comprehend repeatedly sound Gurdjieffian names syllabically. Jean Toomer's name, for example, sounds throughout the two quotes from ***The Conjure-Man Dies*** presented immediately above and is heard in "And I *too* am of the co*m*-*m*on per*s*uasion" (182). The reader is meant to realize that Fisher's text, like Archer's speech, is not decipherable by the normal methods: Like French, it is another language altogether, and unless one approaches it with the correct tools, the text remains indecipherable. Archer's reply to Dart's plea for a translation into French is an ironic depiction of an improbable action. If the reader takes Archer's witticism literally, it is a reification of the "attack on race": "And if you shouldn't find the elusive corpse there—a possibility with which I have already annoyed you tonight—you may proceed to demolish the house next to the right, then, the next to the left, and so on until all Harlem lies in ruins" (184). However, this passage also provides an "attack on reading." If we read the text hermeneutically, we indeed reduce the narrative to ruins and the "mystery" dissolves into the sham that it is. Moreover, if we read Archer's speech literally, we realize that it is a clear statement of the aims of the Harlem group, to so devastate racialism that nothing like Harlem could ever again exist.

Despite the overdetermined meanings contained in the passage, it is also possible to read it as mere banter, an implication that is to a degree supported by the text. In a similar exchange, Archer and Dart are examining blood cells with a microscope:

> "What are they doing?"
>
> "Nothing," Dart grinned. "Must be Negro blood."
>
> "Jest not, my friend. It is Sunday. All blood reposes. But keep looking."
>
> (203)

We can interpret these racialized high jinks literally, but they are equally loaded with ciphers. Closest to the surface we encounter the ever-present clue of the word "grinned" placed adjacent to the word "Negro" (one of the text's running gags). By itself, this signifies nothing; however, like other inclusions, this juxtaposition arises so often in ***The Conjure-Man Dies*** that the cumulative effect alerts the reader's suspicion that an anagram is intended—"grinned" is to be read as "nigger." The word "jest" may be combined with a previous occurrence of "god" to render "Gurdjieff." On another level, the dialogue reiterates the Gurdjieffian precept that "In order *to do* it is necessary *to be*" (ISM 22). As a spur to cast the attention in the direction of visual phenomena, the surface text provides a microscope through which the reader is urged to "keep looking" (203).

The contents of the hermeneutic level of ***The Conjure-Man Dies*** differ very little from what was created by others in the Harlem group. The twenty-four chapters that comprise the novel allude to the cosmic scheme known as the "ray of creation" or "three octaves of radiations." This subject is elaborated by a beam of light produced by an extension lamp used in the room where the mind-reader, Frimbo, held his interviews. By having Frimbo read minds, Fisher indicates yet another occurrence of subtextual reading. We first encounter this light when Jinx's consultation with the psychic is recounted by the narrator: "He sidled between the chair and table and sat down facing the figure beneath the hanging light. He was unable, because of the blinding glare, to descry any characteristic feature of the man he had come to see" (66-67). The police use the room to interrogate the assembled witnesses and suspects, thus justifying further descriptions of the powerful light. For instance, during the interrogation of Spider Webb, we read, "In the bright illumination of the horizontal beam of light, Spider's face twitched and changed just enough to convince Dart that he was on the right track" (135-36). The subtext is replete with such familiar inclusions as the number three (36, 44, 74, 137), "mask" (37, 57), the three divisions of man (171), the devil (81, 170), and the ciphered and phoneticized names of Gurdjieff, Ouspensky, Orage, and Toomer.

However, two inclusions are particularly unique to ***The Conjure-Man Dies*** and require some exposition. Fisher is meticulous in arranging his subject matter to complement the hidden level of his texts. Joshua Jones, the protagonist of ***The Walls of Jericho,*** was a piano mover; this

FROM THE AUTHOR

FISHER'S TONGUE-IN-CHEEK SELF-APPRAISAL

A distinguished literary journal made the error of accepting my first short story—just because I graduated from medical school. You can see what that did to my future. Now every time I begin to think my profession has claimed me for its own, some journal comes along and accepts another story. It's a hard life, really. The most uplifting thing I've ever written is a prescription for grippe. I've gone in for x-ray now—seeking greater penetration.

SOURCE: Rudolph Fisher, excerpt from an article in *McClure's,* December 1927.

warranted discussions of pianos, which could then be used to symbolize the Gurdjieffian cosmic scheme—three octaves of radiation. Likewise, Fisher's selection of a murder mystery allows for the presentation of a wide range of esoteric materials. Decisive among the inventions present in ***The Conjure-Man Dies*** is the murder weapon itself. While investigating the corpse of the murdered conjure-man, Dr. Archer draws from the dead man's throat "a large, blue bordered, white handkerchief" (21). Because the murder weapon is a handkerchief, the word "handkerchief" subsequently occurs in the text many times. Following its initial appearance by only a few pages, Archer makes a pun on the murder weapon: "He wouldn't do the expected thing—not if he was bright enough to think up a gag like this" (23). The word "hand*kerchief*" offers the ear "Gurdjieff," and Fisher underscores this reading by presenting the word near "gag," for Gurdjieff's initials are G. I. G. However, Fisher is not finished; he couples the handkerchief with a "club": "I'll bet the chap handled the club with the handkerchief" (91). Here Fisher's text points to the existence of a secret organization dedicated to the elimination of race.

In the novels by Wallace Thurman and in Fisher's ***The Walls of Jericho*** we encounter list of names that can be read as a coded message. Fisher not only includes such a list of names in ***The Conjure-Man Dies,*** he repeats it with small variations (80, 135, 298). The most concise rendition is: "Mrs. Arimintha Snead, Mrs. Martha Crouch, Easley Jones, Doty Hicks, Spider Webb, and Jinx Jenkins" (298). If the names are treated as anagrams, it reads: "Need men," "Tomorrow," "Sly ones," "Do it," "We spy," "Join in," confirming the message that Fisher included in ***The Walls of Jericho.*** Through the coded lists of names in ***The Conjure-Man Dies*** Fisher intended his readers to recognize that his novel announced an antiracial project that would fundamentally alter the structure of American life.

Before concluding this discussion of ***The Conjure-Man Dies,*** the appearance of Gurdjieff in the text requires some elaboration. Other members of the Harlem group have introduced Gurdjieff into their texts in unexpected disguises; yet Fisher seems not to have done so in his first novel, ***The Walls of Jericho.*** Instead Fisher gives his reader pieces of Gurdjieff distributed among the characters in the form of striking eyes and yellow skin. But with ***The Conjure-Man Dies,*** the case is quite different: It is evident that the "psychist" N'Gana Frimbo, an African chieftain, is meant to represent Gurdjieff. James Moore delineates the controversy about Gurdjieff's significance as a matter of whether "he was a charlatan" or, as Peter Brook stated, "'the most immediate, the most valid and the most totally representative figure of our times'" (1). After hearing Frimbo speak for a while, John Archer wonders, "What is he—charlatan or prophet?" (223). When Frimbo first appears, he is disguised in the headdress of his tribe. Later, on the night that John Archer visits Frimbo, we are told that his appearance is "Matter-of-fact"; in other words, Gurdjieff's disguise has been taken away and his identity revealed.

Gurdjieff's unusual eyes were one of his most distinctive features, and his eyes were mentioned by everyone who wrote about him. Fisher begins his description of Frimbo by mentioning his eyes: "But the deep-set eyes still held their peculiar glow, and the low resonant voice was the same" (213). There is, too, the matter of the name that has been given the character, N'Gana Frimbo. If N'Gana is reversed, the resulting "anagn" suggests the word "anagram." If we follow that clue and read "Frimbo" as an anagram, the letters can be rearranged into "form b i," which can be recognized as a Gurdjieffian exhortation to "form [the] Big 'I.'" Were it necessary to sum up Gurdjieffian self-development in a single phrase, we could do no better: Gurdjieff himself stated that the goal of the work is "Individuality, a single and permanent I, consciousness, will, the ability to do, a state of inner freedom" (ISM 159).

It is also noteworthy that Frimbo takes Archer "to that rear third-floor chamber," a location that indicates the esoteric nature of the subtext. The third room on the third floor alludes to both the concept of man as a "three-storied factory" and to the role of Gurdjieff as a teacher of hidden wisdom. Once they have situated themselves in the inner sanctum, Frimbo commences a series of revelations that strike at the foundations of John Archer's scientific beliefs. It is particularly interesting that Fisher has chosen to make his detective a medical doctor with an expressly scientific bent, for Gurdjieff's *Beelzebub's Tales* is, among other things, an attack on modern science. ***The Conjure-Man Dies*** makes a similar attack on science. Using the conventions of the detective story, Fisher exposes the shallowness of modern science by providing an alternative conception of the universe. Archer is amazed at the rightness of what he hears, for Frimbo's (Gurdjieff's) teachings do not contradict the evidence of science, they instead extend this evidence to unsuspected consequences. Archer is forced to reveal his enthusiasm for what he hears: "'You astonish me,' said the doctor. 'I thought you were a mystic, not a mechanist'" (214). Frimbo's reply is classic Gurdjieffian icon-breaking: "'This,' returned Frimbo, '*is* mysticism—an undemonstrable belief. Pure faith in anything is mysticism. Our very faith in reason is a kind of mysticism'" (214).

The concepts described by Frimbo are taken from some of the more abstruse parts of Gurdjieff's system. Frimbo's claim to have freedom of will is drawn directly from the Gurdjieff-Ouspensky literature; according to Gurdjieff "the possibility for man thus gradually to free himself from mechanical laws exists" (ISM 84). The vocabulary that Frimbo uses is virtually the same as that used by Gurdjieff, and the idea being expressed is the same: "The fewer laws there are in a given world, the nearer it is to the will of the Absolute; the more laws there are in a given world, the greater the mechanicalness, the further it is from the will of the Absolute. We live in a world subject to forty-eight orders of laws, that is to say, very far from the will of the Absolute and in a very remote and dark corner of the universe" (ISM 81).

Frimbo's claim that he is able to change the order of events is an allusion to one of Gurdjieff's ideas that was of extreme importance to Toomer and the Harlem group. Gurdjieff's system was based on the idea that by understanding the nature of universal laws, it is possible to gain control over historical events. Indeed, the Harlem group crafted their literature to be placed in the world in specific ways designed to alter the order of historical events. The group intended that their literary works act on their cultural moment as "additional shocks" that would correct the movement of certain events and influence outcomes in desired ways.

Given this context, it is not surprising to see Fisher create Frimbo, who speaks so authoritatively of such matters as controlling the very fabric of coincidence—of the coordination of time and space. Frimbo speaks of the "change in velocity" (CMD 228) with the power to reconfigure coincidences; this is an allusion to Gurdjieff's Law of the Octave, which describes "the discontinuity of vibration and . . . the deviation of forces" (ISM 130) in the universe. The technique that Frimbo alludes to is based on the assumption that events will not turn out as they have been planned unless certain forces are set in motion to correct the course of events; according to Gurdjieff, all events give opposite results from what was originally intended without mankind noticing what has happened. The language that Gurdjieff used to discuss this topic is ridden with jargon. However, the paragraph below comes closest to describing Frimbo's version of the means for changing the course of events:

> The right development of these octaves is based on what looks an *accident*. It sometimes happens that octaves going parallel to the given octave, intersecting it or meeting it, in some way or another *fill up its "intervals"* and make it possible for the vibrations of the given octave to develop in freedom and without checks. Observations of such rightly developing octaves establishes the fact that if at the necessary moment, that is, at the moment when the given octave passes through an "interval," there enters into it a "additional shock" which corresponds in force and character, it will develop further without hindrance along the original direction, neither losing anything nor changing its nature.
>
> (ISM 131)

The Gurdjieffian Harlem group had formulated a plan to alter the course of history, and this plan was based on their analysis of history as subject to the Law of the Octave. Thus, as a work of "objective" literature, Fisher's text exists more as a "legominism" than anything else, and his subject is the historical plan itself.

Fisher's "legominism" is presented in the form of an inserted text—Frimbo's description of his life in Africa, "twenty years past and five thousand miles away" (216). Frimbo's narration begins by establishing the proper mood: The initial paragraph contains such words as "unaware," "out of sight," "mysterious," "it must reveal itself," "invisibility," and "indeterminate." This vocabulary alerts us of hidden content; we are also told that the ritual is "completely symbolic" (218). The passage describes a ritual that takes place in a square. Looked at hermeneutically, the episode is a series of numbers, anagrams, and geometric figures: one hundred fighting men; twelve years old; a town of a thousand people; the village of Kimalu; Malindo, the feast of procreation; forty-eight tribes; a circle one hundred fifty feet in diameter; forty-eight torches; a chest; dancers; a baby; and a python.

Fisher uses the Buwongo ritual to symbolize the Gurdjieffian concept of "man as a three-storied factory." This concept is connected to a complicated system of diagrams that explain how man can better use the energy available to him, a problem that Gurdjieff poses as a question: "What then is a man to do when he begins to realize that he has not enough energy to attain the aims he has set before himself?" (ISM 179). In the word "Kimalu" we can recognize the word "aim": Fisher's Buwongo dialect can be read as Gurdjieffian terminology. Thus "timwe" is "time," and the name of the ritual, Malindo, holds "la" and "do"—two notes in the "food" octave that the "three-storied" concept describes. Alternatively, Malindo may be read as the important Gurdjieffian formula "I am." Man is a three-storied factory because "The upper story of this factory consists of a man's head; the middle floor, of the chest; and the lower, of the stomach, back, and the lower part of the body" (ISM 182). This is the "large square chest" (CMD 220), which is placed in the center of the circle. *In Search of the Miraculous,* Ouspensky's study of the Gurdjieff work, contains a detailed discussion of this entire subject. It is illustrated with fifteen diagrams that consist of squares containing circles and lines. The numbers given by Fisher may be found in these circles.

Thus, Fisher's "legominism" is a presentation of an extremely abstruse part of Gurdjieff's system. To provide some small indication of the significance of this concept, I briefly quote from Kenneth Walker's *A Study of Gurdjieff's Teachings:*

> Ouspensky then drew on the blackboard a new diagram which he said represented man as a three-storied chemical factory. The work of this factory was to convert coarser matters into finer matters, the coarser matters being the various materials we required for the maintenance of our machinery and for the fuel consumed in running it. Ouspensky said that one of the reasons we were unable to remember ourselves and why the Higher Centres [sic] in us did not function was that we possessed insufficient [amounts] of the finer fuels. Hydrogen 12 was needed by both Emotional and Higher Emotional Centres, and we were invariably short of this high-octave spirit, so that Emotional Centre in us usually had to work with Hydrogen 24. There were two ways of obviating this shortage: first by ceasing to waste Hydrogen on useless projects, and second, by producing more of it. It was about the manufacture of finer hydrogens that he now wanted to speak.
>
> (136)

Walker shows that two of the numbers in Fisher's ritual, twelve and forty-eight, can be understood as the key to the entire concept of man as a three-storied factory. Walker rapturously concludes: "And if things were seen pure and uncontaminated with associative thoughts what a resounding *doh* 48 impression would strike in the inner chambers of our minds, a note which would pass without any difficulty to *mi* 12" (148).

The Buwongo ritual symbolizes the birth of a new man, the higher type of man symbolized by "the unharmed infant at our feet" (CMD 223). The goal of Toomer and his followers was to produce as many individuals of this new type as they could in the time allotted to them. In a sense, an "objective" novel such as ***The Conjure-Man Dies*** was a device designed to apply the necessary shocks to American culture to move certain historical events (octaves) in the desired directions. The "objective" view of time and space described by Frimbo also applies to the literature of the Harlem group; and we may understand Fisher's novel as a popular work of art through which he introduced the idea of the superman and the perfection of the will to African-American culture at a particular time in history. Therefore, we find the word "time" ciphered in the Buwongo ritual as "timwe."

Gurdjieff stated that "The evolution of large masses of humanity is opposed to nature's purposes. The evolution of a certain small percentage may be in accord with nature's purposes" (ISM 57-58). In the figure of N'Gana Frimbo we see the result of human evolution to a higher will; here we must confront the gap between Frimbo, the superman (man number seven), and Dr. John Archer, the emblem of mass man (men numbers one, two, and three). Through Frimbo, Archer learns that man has more powers than he has ever imagined. Yet, Frimbo is murdered, leaving Archer without the means to reach higher levels of consciousness. Archer has seen the higher man, but he does not know the methods by which he can become the higher man. We are told by Gurdjieff that such gaps are a part of the natural order.

The process that Fisher traces in ***The Walls of Jericho*** takes Joshua Jones from being man number one (physical man—a piano mover) to man number two (emotional man). This is not a very big step, because the first three steps are on the same level; however, it is an important one, as it is the beginning of evolution. Jones's fiancée, Linda, symbolizes the faculty of conscience; as long as Jones has conscience, he will continue to evolve. By contrast the comic characters Bubber and Jinx, who are carried over from ***The Walls of Jericho*** to ***The Conjure-Man Dies,*** represent men who exists at the instinctive level and do not develop their emotional and intellectual faculties. Therefore, we may assume that in being confronted with Frimbo (Gurdjieff) John Archer is man number three being given a view of man number six or seven. In meeting this higher man, Archer learns that he, as an educated professional, does not possess certain properties that he assumed he had gained through his scientific education. Helplessly, he sees that there is a potentiality for him to develop far beyond his preset level. The esoteric reading of his name, John Archer,—"no race"—is a testimony to the possibilities that are inherent in his being.

Works Cited

Fisher, Rudolph. *The Walls of Jericho.* New York, N.Y.: Arno Press, 1969.

———. *The Conjure-Man Dies.* New York, N.Y.: Arno Press, 1971.

Gurdjieff, G. I. *All and Everything: An Objectively Impartial Criticism of the Life of Man, or Beelzebub's Tales to His Grandson.* New York, N.Y.: E. P. Dutton, 1973.

McKluskey, John, Jr. "Introduction." In *The City of Refuge: The Collected Stories of Rudolph Fisher.* Columbia: University of Missouri Press, 1987.

Nott, C. S. *Teachings of Gurdjieff: A Pupil's Journal—An Account of Some Years with G. I. Gurdjieff and A. R. Orage in New York, N.Y. and Fountainebleau-Avon.* York Beach, Maine: Samuel Weiser, Inc., 1982.

Ouspensky, P. D. *In Search of the Miraculous: Fragments of an Unknown Teaching.* New York, N.Y.: Harcourt, Brace & World, 1949.

———. *Tertium Organum.* New York, N.Y.: Vintage, 1950.

Riffaterre, Michael. *Fictional Truth.* Baltimore, Md.: Johns Hopkins University Press, 1990.

Rosenberg, Samuel. *Naked Is the Best Disguise: The Death and Resurrection of Sherlock Holmes.* New York, N.Y.: Bobbs-Merrill, 1974.

Schuyler, George. *Black Empire.* Ed. Robert A. Hill and R. Kent Rasmussen. Boston, Mass.: Northeastern University Press, 1991.

Thurman, Wallace. *The Blacker the Berry . . . : A Novel of Negro Life.* New York, N.Y.: Arno Press, 1969.

———. *Infants of the Spring.* Carbondale: Southern Illinois University Press, 1979.

Ulmer, Gregor L. *Applied Grammatology.* Baltimore, Md.: Johns Hopkins University Press, 1985.

Walker, Kenneth. *A Study of Gurdjieff's Teaching.* New York, N.Y.: Award, 1969.

TITLE COMMENTARY

The Conjure-Man Dies

ADRIENNE JOHNSON GOSSELIN (ESSAY DATE 1998)

SOURCE: Gosselin, Adrienne Johnson. "The World Would Do Better To Ask Why Is Frimbo Sherlock Holmes?: Investigating Liminality in Rudolph Fisher's *The Conjure-Man Dies.*" *African American Review* 32, no. 4 (winter 1998): 607-19.

In the following essay, Gosselin compares the character of Frimbo to Sherlock Holmes in order to demonstrate the role of rational individualism in Fisher's detective novel. Gosselin also uses Fisher to explore the connection between Modernism and the Harlem Renaissance.

> "But what on earth does it really matter who killed Frimbo—except to Frimbo?"
>
> They stood a moment in silence. Presently Frimbo added in an almost bitter murmur: "The rest of the world would be better to concern itself with why Frimbo is black."
>
> (Fisher, ***Conjure-Man*** 230)

The above exchange is generally considered to be the larger mystery of Rudolph Fisher's ***The Conjure-Man Dies,*** published in 1932 at the end of the Harlem Renaissance. Written two years before Fisher's death, ***The Conjure-Man Dies*** is the first non-serialized detective novel by an African American to use a black detective figure and the first in the genre to use multiple detectives.[1] Structured in the mode of classical detective fiction, the story begins when Dr. John Archer, a pedantic physician with a penchant for solving crimes, is summoned from his home by Bubber Johnson, an ex-sanitation worker turned private investigator, to examine the body of N'Gana Frimbo, the African conjure-man who lives above the mortuary across the street from Archer. Archer pronounces Frimbo dead and instructs Bubber and Bubber's partner Jinx Jenkins (the last person to see Frimbo alive) to carry the body downstairs to the mortuary until the police arrive. Heading the police investigation is Perry Dart, one of ten black men on the Harlem police force and the only one to be promoted to detective. Archer and Dart search Frimbo's apartment, revealing the victim to have been "no ordinary fakir" but a Harvard graduate and amateur scientist who has a fully equipped laboratory filled with jars of preserved biological specimens, including one Archer identifies as "male sex glands." The investigation proceeds with the interrogation of five suspects, one of whom is the wife of Stanley Crouch, Frimbo's landlord, whose mortuary occupies the first floor of the building. Although not a suspect, Crouch returns for some late night work, is questioned by Dart, and subsequently dismissed. Just as the crime and clues phase of the investigation seems to be ending, however, the body is discovered missing from the mortuary, prompting a second search. After Dart reassembles the suspects in the interrogation room, the room goes suddenly black. When the lights come up again, Frimbo is alive, seated in the same chair in which Archer examined the presumably missing corpse. Unable to convince police that, as the "corpse," he had been not dead, but in a state of suspended animation, Frimbo joins Archer and Dart in the search for his would-be murderer. Never convinced by Frimbo's story, Archer and Dart discover that the murdered man is N'Ogo Frimbo, N'Gana Frimbo's servant and fellow countryman, and attempt to prove the conjure-man to be the servant's murderer. In the solution phase of the investigation, Frimbo reveals the servant's murderer to be Stanley Crouch, but only as Crouch succeeds in committing the murder originally intended and kills N'Gana Frimbo for having an affair with his wife.

Certainly, as a Harlem conjure-man who is also an African king, graduate of Harvard, student of biology, psychology, and deterministic philosophy, and reader of such books as Tankard's *Determinism and Fatalism,* Bostwick's *The Concept of Inevitability,* and Fairclough's *The Philosophical Basis of Destiny,* the character of N'Gana Frimbo qualifies as a cultural enigma. Such figures are generally read in terms of binary conflict, and Frimbo is no exception. Stephen Soitos, for example, sees Frimbo as a representation of a cultural struggle among African Americans (97), while Helen Lock suggests that Frimbo's death at the end of the novel implies that the struggle his character embodies is ultimately won by the "forces . . . of Western discourse" (46). And although Soitos recognizes the ability of the Afrocentric world view to achieve synthesis of dualities, he nonetheless concludes that, while "Frimbo's positive role in solving the mystery and Archer's unreserved admiration of the man both suggest that a meld of Afrocentric and Euro-Americentric views might be possible . . . the real murder of N'Gana Frimbo in the last pages of the novel counters this speculation with cold, negative reality" (116). For Soitos and Lock, the "cold, negative reality" is the inability of an Afrocentric world view to maintain its own in the face of European culture, an inevitable conclusion when the character is read in terms of binary struggle. Binary logic, however, limits interpretation to either/or propositions and fails to reconcile what I argue to be some of the novel's more important liminal moments. On the other hand, nonbinary sleuthing can go where binary logic fears to tread, in this case to reveal the novel's ratiocinative detective to be not the pedantic Dr. Archer, but N'Gana Frimbo himself, thus exposing Rudolph Fisher as the perpetrator of one of the most dastardly crimes in popular fiction since "The Final Solution"—the murder of Sherlock Holmes.

According to Stephen Knight, the Holmesian detective has achieved universal recognition in that "no literary figure has a stronger hold on the public imagination than Sherlock Holmes. The name is a synonym for a detective; he has been parodied, imitated and recreated in all media with great success." Knight's sociological study of crime fiction locates the reason for Holmes's "embarrassing success" in the character's ability to calm the anxieties of a readership that "had faith in modern systems of scientific and rational inquiry" but felt a lack of such power themselves (67). For Knight, Doyle's achievement lies in the construction of fables about a "problem-solving hero who works in a recognizable world with essentially graspable and credible rational methods" (78). As an artistic creation, the heart of Doyle's success rests in Holmes's ability to offer a middle-class reading public a means of psychic protection in the frame of a superior ratiocination that embodied both the essential conservatism and patronizing autocracy inherent in the Victorian notion of rational individualism.

In Knight's analysis, Doyle's construct of rational individualism has two premises: "the rational scientific idea that events are really linked in an unaccidental chain, and the individualistic notion that a single inquirer can—and should—establish the links" (68). Both premises resonate in Frimbo's explanation of "applied determinism," which he alone, "as a being of another order," has the power to comprehend (Fisher 228).

As Frimbo explains to Archer, the power enables him to act upon the "events linked in an unaccidental chain" that occur in people's lives without upsetting their order:

> "It is thus I am able to be of service to those who come to me. I act upon their lives. I do not have to upset their order. I simply change the velocity of what is going on. I am a catalyst. I accelerate or retard a reaction without entering into it. This changes the cross currents. . . . A husband reaches home twenty minutes too soon. A traveler misses his train—and escapes death in a wreck. Simple, is it not?"
>
> (228)

Even the phrasing of Frimbo's final question—"'Simple, is it not?'"—reflects the Holmesian tendency to popularize rational individualism. Indeed, as Knight points out, Doyle's ability to popularize and, even more importantly, naturalize rational individualism is central to Sherlock Holmes's appeal (68). Holmes's use of comments as simple as "to put it mildly," or even the signature "elementary, my dear Watson," serve to demystify ratiocination, becoming in Knight's opinion "game language to make unethical faith in this ideology seem both pleasant and natural" (68). And while Frimbo's revelation leaves Archer speechless for the only time in the novel, the difference between Archer and Frimbo as "men of science" begins to dawn: Frimbo begins to emerge as a heightened version of Archer's own ambitions, illustrated later by the instruments in Archer's lab, which, unlike Frimbo's, are "mostly virgin" and "only a fraction of what Frimbo has" (197). In this light, Frimbo can be seen to embody the ideology of "personal achievement and personal morality" which Knight finds indigenous to the Holmesian detective (95). As the man of science who embraces rational individualism, Frimbo does indeed conduct a service by changing the velocity of events in the lives of the Harlem community, but unlike Archer, who sees only two patients during the course of the novel—"The first pleaded a bad cold and got his liquor prescription, the second pleaded hard times and borrowed three dollars" (197)—Frimbo is well paid for the services he provides. As a result, he can afford his passion for scientific research, if only because, as Dart points out, in Harlem "a racket like fortune telling" was probably a "better racket than medicine" (27).

The qualities of rational individualism were made physically recognizable by Sidney Paget's illustrations of Sherlock Holmes, so much so that Doyle altered his earlier description of Holmes to fit Paget's "authoritative version" (Knight 84). Like Holmes, Frimbo's appearance is distinctive and dramatic in appearance. He enters the novel as a "deep strong voice in the middle of the death room" (168), seated in the very chair in which he was supposed to have been murdered. Lights come up in the darkened room to reveal "a black man wearing a black robe and a black silk headband; a man with fine, almost delicate features, gleaming, deep-set black eyes, and an expression of supreme intelligence and tranquility" (169). Like Holmes, Frimbo is a "self-confessed Bohemian" (Knight 80) and, also like Holmes, a man of independent means. As a king, as a successful conjure-man, and as a gambler who consistently "hits" the numbers for five thousand dollars a week, Frimbo, again like Holmes, lives comfortably in, but will "not be enclosed by, the world of bourgeois professionalism" (Knight 79). And while Holmes surpasses the ratiocinative abilities of his predecessor by possessing a "greater variety of . . . miraculous powers" (Cawelti 82), Frimbo surpasses Holmes in that making miracles is Frimbo's occupation, as demonstrated by Lem Gassoway who, under Frimbo's psychic protection, survives an otherwise fatal knife wound to the head.

As a Holmesian detective, Frimbo shares a number of characteristics with other detectives derived from the Dupin-Holmes tradition. George Grella, for example, notes that, whatever their individual differences, detectives of this genre are recognized as "pronounced eccentrics, enjoying odd hobbies, interests, or life styles and frequently indulging in . . . 'solitary oral vices' of eating, drinking, smoking, and boasting" (36). Feminine company, Frimbo tells Archer is "'necessary to comfort, like blowing one's nose,'" but the study of biochemistry is "vital" to his existence (268). Beyond eccentricities, however, the Holmesian detective must possess a mind "blessed with penetrating observation, highly developed logical powers, wide knowledge, and a brilliantly synthetic imagination" (Cawelti 36), characteristics which Frimbo embodies. And while Lock argues that Frimbo's metaphysical abilities grant him "the vision to see the murderer's identity" (47), the impetus behind Frimbo's "vision" is actually a variation of the ratiocinative process of "deduction" perfected by Doyle in the early Holmes novellas. Frimbo's solution to the servant's "calculable" murder echoes Holmes's use of "deductive reasoning," whose methodology Doyle provided in chapters titled "The Science of Deduction," which appeared at the end of the earlier works. Although a misapplication of the term *science*—

and no more than a "set of fairly simple procedures within an aura of elaboration" (Knight 85-86)—the strategy established deduction as a scientific means of ordering the confusion required by the detection formula.

Beginning with Poe's Dupin, detachment has been another important characteristic of the ratiocinative detective, used to express what Poe termed the "ideality" that informs the "peculiar analytic ability" distinguishing the detective from the mere factual observer. Tracing the trope to differences between Poe and Samuel Coleridge on the nature of "reason," Knight explains:

> Where Coleridge based "reason" in Christian intuition, Poe rests his "analysis" on imaginative power, operating with intellect and feeling combined at full strength. Poe probably drew the term "ideality" from the new pseudo-science of phrenology, where it meant 'the imaginative faculty' or 'the poetical faculty': it conveniently expresses both the mentalism and the basically idealist unreality of the area where Poe's hero is specially gifted.
>
> (40)

Yet while Holmes embodies the analytic ability that characterizes Dupin, he never withdraws into his predecessor's idealist intellectualism. As a result, unlike Dupin, the Holmesian detective articulates a duality of the material and the ideal, the familiar with the exotic, the need for isolation with the need for normal contact—dualities Frimbo shares with Holmes. Both characters live in rooms that reflect their scientific interests, yet rooms that, for all their eccentricities, are "cosy [and] filled with masculine gadgets for comfort (Knight 80). Neither is a hermit, nor is either attached, and both share lodgings—Holmes with Watson and Frimbo with his servant. Like Holmes, Frimbo engages in disguise, posing as the servant, and like Holmes, works alone in that it is the servant who sits with clients while Frimbo remains in another room viewing clients through a television lens. As well as an aspect of character, detachment is also an element of formal structure, one which enables investigation to be narrated from a perspective that sees but does not participate in the Holmesian detective's process of reasoning. As John Cawelti notes, "If he uses the detective's point of view, the writer has trouble keeping the mystery a secret without creating unnatural and arbitrary limits on what is shown . . . of the detective's reasoning process" (83). While the device of the Watson-like figure as the narrative point of view is the usual strategy in classical detective fiction, ***The Conjure-Man Dies*** uses dual lines of inquiry, thus enabling Fisher to manipulate Frimbo as the detached detective by focusing on the false line of inquiry followed by Archer and Dart, a strategy that further supports the illusion of Dr. Archer as the ratiocinative detective with the superior mind.

In an inscription to Carl Van Vechten, Fisher describes ***The Conjure-Man Dies*** as an "experiment with technique" (Tignor 17), and while Fisher's experimentation involves a number of strategies associated with detection schemes, this reading focuses on the formal principle of mystification, whose balance with-inquiry is fundamental to the classical detective formula. In his study of genre and popular fiction, Cawelti explains that the proper balance between inquiry and mystification depends on the author's ability to invent some new type of mystification while still working within the conventional structure of classical detection. In the early short story form, Cawelti notes, the story of classical detection focused more on "inquiry," but as writers began to develop longer and more complex stories, there was a need to find ways of resolving the tension between detection and mystification. The solution was to place the detective at the center and add a range of other interests such as "character, action, setting, local color, or assorted bits of information" in order to "flesh out . . . the bare bones of the inquiry structure" (Cawelti 110). In this sense, if mystification depends on the author's ability to invent some new type of mystification without distracting from investigation, then one of the ways in which Fisher fleshes out the bare bones of inquiry is with notions of primitivism, one of the most controversial topics straddling the axis between modernism and the Harlem Renaissance.

In order to appreciate the ramifications of Fisher's experiment with primitivism and mystification, one needs to understand that, in the African American literary tradition, the modernist obsession with primitivism exemplifies what Henry Louis Gates would call a moment of literary liminality in which black America and white America face each other in a "paradox of ideological confrontation" (72). For example, while for white modernists "The Negro" was the central metaphor for the "uncorrupted remnant of preindustrial man" (Stoff 127), black modernists saw this representation as a "jazzed-up version of the 'contented slave'" (Sterling Brown, qtd. in McCluskey xviii). And while images spawned by Eurocentric theories of primitivism led to the modernist "white cult of the primitive" (Worth 470), these same theories led to distinctions between "high" and "low" culture held fast by the older Harlem Renaissance intelligentsia, advocates of black nationalism and racial uplift, the two ideologies dominating the African American intellectual community in the years between post-Reconstruction and the end of the First World War. Following the war, however, younger black intellectuals—Rudolph Fisher among them—felt that, as products of higher education, it was their responsibility to move beyond such delineations in order to depict a "truer synthesis of black culture" (McCluskey xii), one that included the forms and expressions of folk culture while steering clear of (white) exotica and (black) oversentimentality.

As George Kent observes, the educational background and "symbols of middle-class respectability" gave younger Renaissance intellectuals a "psychological poise . . . from which they could not easily be overawed by definitions of black realities provided by American and Western culture" (36).[2] Kevin Gaines concurs, noting that, unlike the older intellectuals, black modernists "were the product of a new historical conjuncture heading into the Depression era, characterized by white violence and southern intransigence, certainly, but also several forms of interracial cooperation. These included the convergence of New Negro militancy and cultural radicalism, a growing alliance between blacks and white left-wing activity" (236). As a result, while older Harlem intellectuals such as W. E. B. Du Bois used folklore as a "flight from the pejorative racial connotations of . . . the urban setting" (Gaines 185-86), younger intellectuals such as Fisher and Langston Hughes used folklore *in* urban settings to rethink race and class and arrive at a truer definition of black culture.[3]

One factor accounting for differences in their approaches to folklore can be found in differences in attitude toward academic theories of folklore, theories which viewed folk culture from a "larger nineteenth century European worldview, a worldview which favored romanticism and primitivism" (Dundes, qtd. in Tracy 13). As Steven Tracy explains, "By primarily associating folklore with the past, by seeking the oldest versions of particular works of folklore as if they were the most complete and 'authentic,' and by collecting folklore with the attitude that it must be preserved before it is gone, some folklorists have implied that folklore is at least static, if not devolutionary . . . suggesting that folklore is at least unchanging in a changing world, increasingly anachronistic and irrelevant to contemporary concerns" (14). At the same time, while academic theory held folklore as devolutionary and fragmented, urban folklorists such as Fisher and Hughes recognized that "the folklore that the (primarily white) critics labeled a survival of the primitive past was in fact being used and modified every day" (Tracy 14). Moreover, while academic theory held that the removal of folk material from its original source presented questions of perspective and authenticity, Fisher and Hughes recognized that a "Northern urban community made up of formerly Southern rural inhabitants is still a community, and what they make of their lore is still lore" (Tracy 15).

As Soitos's detailed analysis demonstrates, folk material—speech, sayings, songs, religion, superstitions, signs, and symbols—is central to ***The Conjure-Man Dies,*** used not only to flesh out the bare bones of inquiry, but to frame the plot as well. While the mystery itself centers on the murder, resurrection, and re-murder of N'Gana Frimbo, the novel's plot moves forward according to the folk sign "Death on the Moon," which foretells three deaths, each of which is witnessed by Bubber Johnson, the reader of the sign. Moreover, Fisher's use of double voice—described by Bernard Bell as an "ambivalent, laughing-to-keep-from-crying perspective toward life as expressed in the use of irony and parody in Afro-American folklore and formal art" (xvi)—demonstrates Fisher's ability as an urban folklorist. The interview with the no-nonsense Aramentha Snead, for example, signifies on the migration of black Southern immigrants by capitalizing on the psychological shift from rural disfranchisement to urban pluralism: Detective Dart says to Snead, "'You're an American, of course,'" to which the woman replies, "'I is now. But I originally come from Savannah, Georgia'" (Fisher 80).

At the same time, Fisher's decision to frame his interrogation of primitivism in a genre relegated to "entertainment" was not without risk. In fact, the novel was ignored by surveys of African American literature until 1987 (Bell), while critical articles, in keeping with the parameters of Arthur Davis's 1932 review, have focused on the work solely as "standard" detective fiction. Other critics question Fisher's strategy as catering to white primitivism (Lock 44) or claim the novel's interest to be "its overworking of Amos 'n' Andy dialogue to white (and, secretly, black) readers" (Lewis 275). And yet, Fisher's portrait of Africa not only circumvents the exotic primitive, but draws upon information from the four Pan-African Congresses convened by Du Bois between 1919 and 1927, as well as pioneer studies in African and

African American history by Du Bois and Carter G. Woodson. Such information is utilized to create a believable world, a hypothetical Africa constructed of "conceivable possibilities" in the sense that *believable* means "recognizable as world, as person, as event" (Wright 66-67). Once recognizable, these abstracted possibilities become the basis for whatever personal involvement or identification the reader may feel—a dynamic that explains why historical accounts are often more vivid when conventions of fiction are employed (Wright 67-68).

Fisher's presentation of Buwongo "makes form visible" by creating a matrix of recognizable elements in the prosperous African nation over which Frimbo reigns as king. Here is a country that functions in a recognizable hierarchy with recognizable politics and recognizable social systems. The description of the village of Kimalu reveals a society with civil laws, as well as one with a system of local and national taxation. Moreover, as king of a country with more than one million inhabitants, Frimbo cannot be reduced to "tribal leader" and, as king, assumes a privilege recognizable as behavior accorded those born to the divine right of the monarchy.

Fisher's experimentation with form, like that of his white counterparts, occurs at a point in literary history at which fiction, in particular, is "marked by a prevalent style of perception and feeling", as such—again, like his white counterparts—Fisher's modernity "consists in a revolt against this prevalent style" (Howe 13). The style against which Fisher as a black modernist is reacting is that of sentimentalism and social melodrama, the style embraced by so-called black Victorians in their attempts to disseminate images of civic and social behavior following Reconstruction (see Carby, Tate). And while the appropriation of Victorian gentility by blacks during the years of post-Reconstruction is one of the more liminal moments in African American history, as Claudia Tate points out, white America's adoption of Victorian gentility as a cultural value while violating the human rights of black people is liminal in itself (59). Understanding black modernism and its revolt against the prevalent style dominating black literature requires an understanding of Reconstruction and its deterioration, which in turn requires a concomitant awareness (1) that Victorian society was the dominant hegemony into which African Americans were emancipated and (2) that the values inherent in Victorian gentility (particularly moral rectitude and the patriarchal family structure) were used by both racial uplift and black nationalism to refute retrogressionism, the racist ideology espoused by white radical conservatives in both the North and South responsible for reversing what few political and economic gains blacks achieved under Reconstruction.[4]

The consequences of retrogressionism were extensive and far-reaching. The more obvious effects were seen in images of everyday life—calenders, pot holders, and playing cards that depicted black culture as intellectually inferior and black people as "lazy, ugly, intemperate, slothful, lascivious, and violent, indeed bestial" (Tate 10). Less obvious was its effect on academic scholarship, which, as noted above, contributed to notions of romanticism and primitivism in academic theories of folklore, and which influenced older black intellectuals in their attempts to define black culture. This impulse is best reflected in Du Bois's approach to the spirituals, which he sought to develop along the lines of the *Volkgeist* of German nationalism. For Du Bois, spirituals were representations of "high" black culture. Drawing on the African American and Judeo-Christian tradition, they became, in Du Bois's paradigm, a collective testament to a "faith in the ultimate justice of things . . . that sometime, somewhere, men will judge men by their souls and not by their skins" (186). By emphasizing spirituals as the "folkloric and musical expression of African Americans' racial soul," Du Bois equated the form with German romanticism, a strategy that served a multiple purpose by creating an international context for black culture as it strengthened claims of cultural autonomy (Gaines 185). At the same time, alignment with the *Volkgeist* of German nationalism separated the spirituals from the blues, ragtime, and other varieties of popular music, such as minstrelsy, thus reinforcing uplift's notion of "high" versus "low" art.

Another product of nineteenth-century academic theory is the trope of double-consciousness which, as Gaines observes, lends itself as a metaphor for educated blacks in that it "describes Du Bois's struggle, and that of other black elites, to transform a pejorative concept of race into an affirming vision of cultural distinctiveness" (9).[5] Tate points out that the theory of double-consciousness is the result of Du Bois's decision to turn from the "philosophic to the social sciences," and she traces the trope itself to a combination of Du Bois's interest in "the soul of different human races" and his later "racialized version of Hegelian dialectics," a decision Du Bois himself credits to

William James and Albert Bushness Hart (Tate 275-76). Du Bois coined the concept of "two-ness" in "Strivings of the Negro," an article published in *Atlantic Monthly* and one of nine eventually revised to become the five essays comprising *The Souls of Black Folk* (Gilroy 124). The now familiar quote expresses the particular alienation of Americans of African descent: "One ever feels his two-ness,—an American, a Negro; two souls, two thoughts, two unreconciled strivings; two warring ideals in one dark body, whose dogged strength alone keeps it from being torn asunder" (3).

Thus, double-consciousness as a trope becomes a moment of cultural liminality both in its intellectual dependence on white ideologies and white constructions of blackness, and in the black elite's perception of itself as middle-class while being denied that status by the very community being used to define it. From this perspective, Gaines finds the notion of double-consciousness ironic in its expression of a middle-class ideology without an actual middle class. His observation bears repeating in full:

> Occupations within the black community widely perceived by historians as middle-class, including that of teacher, minister, federal officer, businessman, and professional, cannot be regarded as equivalent with the business, managerial, and craft labor occupations among whites from which blacks were largely excluded. The same applies to the occupations that blacks held to service white clienteles throughout the late nineteenth century in the urban North and South, such as barbering, catering, and other personal service and domestic jobs. Calling these service occupations middle-class introduces a false universal standard for class formation that ignores the extent to which the very notion of the black middle class—indeed, of class itself—is built on shifting ideological sands.
>
> (14)

In ***The Conjure-Man Dies,*** Stanley Crouch becomes the locus of Fisher's interrogation of the effect of Victorian middle-class ideology on the black community. Although as a *black* community Harlem released new black professionals from dependence on white clientele, the Victorian standards for class formation were nonetheless appropriated. Crouch is described as a "genial businessman on whom it would be difficult to play tricks," while his manner indicates that it is his right as landlord "to know just what had come about and how" (85). He is a member of the Forty Club, a private establishment which is patronized by other members of Harlem's nouveau riche, including Sy Brandon, one of Harlem's racketeering bosses Crouch offers as an alibi for the time of Frimbo's death. Crouch epitomizes the direction of the black middle class by the 1920s. No longer grounded in equal marriage or moral rectitude, the new black middle class is increasingly materialist, having fully appropriated the values of the petit bourgeois. Pampered and suitably bored, Martha Crouch is depicted as Crouch's possession. As Crouch explains to Dart, "'You know how women are—if they haven't anything much to do they get restless and dissatisfied. We haven't any kids and she has a girl to do the housework'" (87). To counteract her boredom, Martha Crouch collects the rent from Crouch's tenants, a pastime that leads to the affair with Frimbo.

Archer describes Crouch as "'hard as a pawnbroker, with an extraordinarily keen awareness of his own possessions,'" (93) and in spite of the fact that Frimbo is the "'goose that laid golden eggs'" (92), it is this sense of possession that leads Crouch to murder Frimbo. Yet, with characteristic objectivity, Fisher refuses to condemn Crouch for his possessive nature. Instead, through Crouch's character, Fisher warns of the consequences of blindly adopting middle-class values in the same manner that the pathetic Doty Hicks is used to warn against drugs or the death of the numbers runner is used to reveal the dark side of "policy." In fact, Dart sees Crouch's callous reaction to Frimbo's death—"'. . . at least he didn't die in our debt'" (88)—as a matter of self-preservation. Nor does the text condemn Crouch for murder; indeed, at the novel's conclusion, Bubber comments to Jinx that Crouch "'jes' didn't mean to lose his wife and his life both. Couldn't blame him for that'" (316).

Like racial uplift ideology, black nationalist discourse, identified in organizations such as Marcus Garvey's [Universal] Negro Improvement Association (UNIA), also typified Victorian sensibility and associated urban poverty with pathology and immorality. Black nationalist intellectuals comprised what Gaines calls a "nationalistic circle of intellectuals" (103), whose membership, along with Du Bois, included such pan-African intellectuals as Duse Mohammed Ali, editor of the *African Times and Orient Review,* a London-based anti-colonial periodical; Anna J. Cooper; Archibald Grimké; Alexander Crummell; Alain Locke; Pauline Hopkins, author of *Of One Blood,* the first serialized detective novel by an African American; and John Edward Bruce, founder of the Negro Society for Historical Research and author of *The Black Sleuth,* the second serialized detective novel written by an African American. Membership also included William H. Ferris, editor of the UNIA's

Negro World from 1919 to 1923, who is of particular significance to this reading of ***The Conjure-Man Dies*** not only because his writings and career exemplify what Gaines sees as an "intersection of black nationalism and racial uplift ideology" (101-02), but because Ferris himself can be seen as a model for N'Gana Frimbo, embodying the authoritarian aspects against which the novel reacts.

Convinced that history was made by great *men,* Ferris, like other black nationalists, saw black (male) elites as the saviors of the race. Like Garvey, Ferris applied Darwinian notions of race survival to African American destiny and framed its rhetoric in all-or-nothing terms of survival and manliness. But, as Gaines points out, while Garvey "simply inverted racial hierarchies to assert black civilization, pride, and power," Ferris "associated civilization with power, mastery, manhood, and the Anglo-Saxon" (102). For Ferris, who considered himself a radical in his opposition to Booker T. Washington, assimilation signified an "indispensable environmental process of acculturation" whereupon blacks absorbed the ideals and values of Western civilization in order to achieve the goal of black statehood and master for themselves "the 'Anglo-Saxon' mysteries of military, financial, technological, and economic power" (Gaines 104).[6]

Educated at Yale and Harvard, Ferris, like the advocates of racial uplift, equated patriarchal ideals with freedom, and Ferris was equally convinced of the academic theories of urban pathology which held the conditions of poor blacks to be the result of "suspect morals" and "lack of cultural refinement." For Ferris, the injustice was in meting out "the same kind of treatment to the high Negro that should be meted out to the low" (qtd. in Gaines 104), and, in what Gaines terms a "severe case of double-consciousness," Ferris went so far as to propose the term *Negrosaxon,* with the intention of distinguishing black intellectuals from the pejoratives he perceived as being associated with "Negro" alone (104). In N'Gana Frimbo, one sees the ideals of Ferris's Negrosaxon—"disinterested black leadership, philosopher-king in ebony, unfettered by social constraints" (Gaines 104)—while in Ferris one sees Saitos's description of N'Gana Frimbo as "one of the more brilliant and confused blacks in modern detective literature" (97). Indeed, Soitos's suggestion that, with Frimbo's death, Fisher "perhaps . . . implies that the burden of the African American double-conscious dilemma can result in self-destruction due to the sheer difficulty of achieving equilibrium" (111) reflects the cultural schizophrenia inherent in Ferris's belief that "after the Negro-saxon has been made over into the likeness of the white man he can hope to be made into the image of God" (qtd. in Gaines 104).

Fisher's interrogation of white primitivism is also embodied in his parodic satire of Freud, whose theories of primitivism inform the intellectual sources of modernism. For Nathan Huggins, three factors shape the (white) modernist obsession with primitivism: the discovery of African art by European intellectuals, the disenchantment with Western civilization as a result of the First World War, and the popularization of Freud. And while each factor capitalized on the primitive and romantic, Huggins sees oversimplification of the concepts of id and super-ego as investing primitivism with the capacity to meet psychological needs of "soft rebellion." As Huggins explains,

> White Americans had identities of their own to find, and black men were too essential to them to be ignored. Men who sensed that they were slaves to moral codes, that they were cramped, and confined by guilt-producing norms which threatened to make them emotional cripples, found Harlem a tonic and a release. Harlem Negroes' lives appeared immediate and honest. Everything they did—their music, their art, their dance—uncoiled deep inner tensions. Harlem seemed a cultural enclave that had magically survived the psychic fetters of Puritanism.
>
> (89)

One of the ways in which Fisher parodies Freud is with the rite of the gonad, which satirizes theories of primitivism as the quintessential id attributed to blacks as a "race." The germplasm contained in the male sex glands Frimbo uses for the "Buwongo secret" is tantamount to such a racial id, containing "'protoplasm which has been continuously maintained through thousands of generations'" (269). Archer even reads the ritual in Freudian terms, diagnosing it as "'part of [Frimbo's] compensatory mechanism'" (291). In terms of style, the parody is in keeping with Fisher's talent for light satire and demonstrates his ability to orchestrate the vernacular of both the scientific and the black communities. When Dart asserts that he believes Frimbo to have killed the servant "'because he's a nut,'" Archer responds,

> "Please—not so bluntly. It sounds crude—robbed of its nuances and subtleties. You transform a portrait into a cartoon. Say, rather, that under the influence of certain compulsions, associated with a rather intricate psychosis, he was impelled to dispose of his servant for definite reasons."
>
> (290)

In their endorsement of Frimbo's Africanity, Soitos and Lock fail to recognize that the "unbroken heritage of the past" embodied in the rite of the gonad is available only to privileged men. As the "epitome of the past," the rite of the gonad "'goes back in a continuous line to the remotest origins of the organism.'" Moreover, as the sole authority who can bring "'into the present every influence which the past has implanted upon life'" (269), Frimbo becomes the monolithic voice of that text. From a liminal perspective, Frimbo's death, and with it that of the "Buwongo secret," becomes more complex than a symbolic defeat in a binary cultural struggle.

At the same time, as a scientist and man of modern sensibilities, Fisher recognizes valid aspects of Freudian theory, particularly in terms of the pathological effects of the binary cultural struggle. As Archer explains to Dart, Frimbo's "'intricate psychosis'" is the result of a paranoiac delusion of persecution. And while Dart, ever the voice of pragmatism, points out that part of being black in America is learning to negotiate such "persecution," it is clear that, because of his privileged status, Frimbo has had no cause to temper expectations. As Archer explains, episodes of racial discrimination produce in Frimbo a bitterness even "'more acute in one accustomed to absolute authority and domination'" (229). While Lock cites Frimbo's declaration to Archer—"'You are almost white. I am almost black. Find out why, and you will have solved a mystery'" (230)—as evidence of Archer's world view as "white" (46), Archer is the character whose education has been financed by struggle, first by his father's and then by his own. In fact, far from being the embodiment of a "white" world view (Lock 46), Archer is the character who has overcome the obstacles faced by black professionals, a fact not lost on Frimbo. Assessing the "drama" about which Archer is reticent, Frimbo concludes: "'If drama is struggle, my friend, your life is a perfect play'" (225). As one who has experienced struggle, it is Archer who is sympathetic to Frimbo, finding it both curious and understandable that Frimbo's reaction to racial prejudice is a "'flight into study . . . steeped in deterministic philosophy'" (259).

As I argue here, ***The Conjure-Man Dies*** crystallizes a moment of literary and cultural liminality, a moment made possible because Rudolph Fisher was *both* a Harlem Renaissance *and* a black modernist writer fully participating in the multicultural *Zeitgeist* of American modernism. As a modernist text, ***The Conjure-Man Dies*** demonstrates that the *Zeitgeist* shaping the Harlem Renaissance was both the same as and different from the *Zeitgeist* shaping Euro-American modernism, in that the work not only absorbs the modernist discourse of white primitivism but also critiques the ideology of racial uplift and black nationalism, the liminal constructs in the black community against which black modernists reacted. And although the larger mystery in ***The Conjure-Man Dies*** is generally acknowledged by critics as Frimbo's statement that "'the rest of the world would do better to concern itself with why Frimbo was black,'" my reading suggests that the larger mystery lies in *why Frimbo was killed.*

As a moment of cultural liminality, Frimbo's death enables Fisher symbolically to destroy the impulse toward authoritarianism and rational individualism embodied in racial uplift and black nationalism. At the same time, Frimbo's imposing character counters images of the cult of white primitivism to convey positive images of Africa as a culture, a concern fundamental to both generations of black intellectuals. As a moment of literary liminality, Frimbo's death enables Fisher to reject the monolithic voice of Eurocentric classical detection by destroying the genre's most recognizable symbol. The device of making the "calculable" mystery of lesser importance opens the Afrocentric story of detection to indeterminate mystery,[7] while the narrative strategy of giving the last words to Bubber, the street-smart detective, sets the stage for Chester Himes and the hard-boiled detective tradition. Finally, as a response to Alain Locke's challenge that younger artists explore folk material as the basis of a black art that moves toward "pure art," toward writing that was "racial . . . purely for the sake of art" (51), Fisher, in ***The Conjure-Man Dies,*** uses race as art and art as part of the "large responsibility" of shaping black American culture from an autonomous black perspective.

Notes

1. The first non-serialized detective novel by an African American is *The Haunting Hand* (1926) by Walter Adolphe Roberts, whose detective Frankie Y. Bailey calls "a spunky young white woman" who solves crimes by intuition (53). The only black character in the novel is a maid who makes "two brief, barely visible appearances" (Bailey 53). Arguably, Wilkie Collins's *The Moonstone* (1868) is the first novel to use multiple detectives in its strategy to incorporate what John Cawelti identifies as a "variety of narrators and a number of inquiring protagonists who play the role of detective at various phases of the inquiry" (134). Nonetheless, as Cawelti notes, *The Moonstone,* though one of the first novels to present a professional detec-

tive, is ultimately a gothic melodrama whose characteristics place it "between the nineteenth-century novel of sensation and the twentieth-century classical detective story" (135).

2. Of all the black modernists, Fisher's qualifications are perhaps the most impressive: A graduate of public schools in Providence, Rhode Island, Fisher attended Brown University, where he excelled in biology and English, as well as Latin, public speaking, and military engineering. By his graduation in 1919, Fisher had been elected to three honor fraternities, including Phi Beta Kappa, and as commencement speaker he delivered a paper on "The Emancipation of Science," which John McCluskey describes as painting "in broad strokes the birth pangs of modernity" (xiv). After receiving his first post-baccalaureate degree from Brown, Fisher attended Howard University Medical School, taking courses in roentgenology and graduating with highest honors in a class of twenty-seven. Awarded a National Research Council Fellowship in 1925, Fisher conducted research in bacteriology at the College of Physicians and Surgeons, Columbia University, and co-authored an article published in the *Journal of Infectious Diseases.* His research led to work at the Bronx and Mt. Sinai Hospitals in New York. In 1930, by then in private practice, Fisher was elected Head of the Department of Roentgenology at International Hospital in Jamaica.

3. Nonetheless, as Gaines points out, the black modernists' "bold foray into racial expression was not without problematic baggage of authenticity and primitivism" (249). Jean Toomer's *Cane,* for example, shares the devolutionary tendencies of academic folklore, while Claude McKay's *Home to Harlem* is generally seen as capitalizing on the market of white primitivism discovered by Van Vechten's *Nigger Heaven.* Like Hughes's success in negotiating these dangers, Fisher's is acknowledged by African American literary critics (see Huggins, Bell), while his ability to manipulate the black vernacular comprises the bulk of the criticism of his work.

4. See Charles Chesnutt's *The Marrow of Tradition* (1901) for one of the most comprehensive accounts of retrogression in African American fiction.

5. See also Adell.

6. While Gaines admits that assimilationists such as Ferris may not seem radical in comparison to black nationalists of the 1970s, he finds Ferris's "epic" chronicle *The African Abroad, or His Evolution in Western Civilization, Tracing His Development under Caucasian Milieu,* written between 1902 and 1913, valuable in its insight into the growing aversion to Washington as a spokesman for the race.

7. In an article not yet published, I apply Lock's notion of the indeterminacy inherent in the Osiris myth to *The Conjure-Man Dies* and analyze ways in which this change in mythological models alters the fundamental structure of the classical detective pattern.

Works Cited

Adell, Sandra. *Double Consciousness/Double Bind: Theoretical Issues in Twentieth-Century Black Literature.* Urbana: U of Illinois P, 1994.

Bailey, Frankie Y. *Out of the Woodpile: Black Characters in Crime and Detective Fiction.* New York: Greenwood P, 1991.

Bell, Bernard. *The Afro-American Novel and Its Tradition.* Amherst: U of Massachusetts P. 1987.

Carby, Hazel. *Reconstructing Womanhood: The Emergence of the Afro-American Woman Novelist.* New York: Oxford UP, 1987.

Cawelti, John. *Adventure, Mystery, and Romance: Formula Stories as Art and Popular Culture.* Chicago: U of Chicago P. 1976.

Davis, Arthur. "Harlem Mysterious." *Opportunity* Oct. 1932: 320.

Du Bois, W. E. B.. *The Souls of Black Folk.* 1903. New York: Bantam, 1989.

Fisher, Rudolph. *The Conjure-Man Dies.* 1932. Ann Arbor: U of Michigan P, 1992.

Gaines, Kevin. *Uplifting the Race: Black Leadership, Politics, and Culture in the Twentieth Century.* Chapel Hill: U of North Carolina P, 1996.

Gates, Henry Louis, Jr. "Authority, (White) Power, and the (Black) Critic; It's All Greek to Me." *The Nature of Minority Discourse.* Ed. Abdul R. Mohamed and David Lloyd. New York: Oxford UP, 1990. 72-101.

Gilroy, Paul. *The Black Atlantic: Modernity and Double Consciousness.* Cambridge: Harvard UP, 1993.

Grella, George. "Murder and Manners: The Formal Detective Novel." *Novel* 4 (1970): 30-48.

Howe, Irving. *The Idea of the Modern.* New York: Horizon P, 1967.

Huggins, Nathan. *Harlem Renaissance.* New York: Oxford UP, 1971.

Lewis, David Levering: *When Harlem Was In Vogue.* New York: Oxford UP, 1979.

Lock, Helen. *A Case of Mis-Taken Identity: Detective Undercurrents in Recent African-American Fiction.* New York: Peter Lang, 1994.

Locke, Alain. "The New Negro." *The New Negro.* 1925. Ed. Locke. New York: Atheneum, 1968. 3-16.

Kent, George. *Blackness and the Adventure of Western Culture.* Chicago: Third World P, 1972.

Knight, Stephen. *From and Ideology in Crime Fiction.* Bloomington: Indiana UP, 1980.

McCluskey, John, ed. *City of Refuge: The Collected Stories of Rudolph Fisher.* Columbia: U of Missouri P, 1987.

Soitos, Stephen. *The Blues Detective: A Study of African American Detective Fiction.* Amherst: U of Massachusetts P, 1996.

Stoff, Michael B. "Claude McKay and the Cult of Primitivism." *The Harlem Renaissance Remembered.* Ed. Arna Bontemps. New York: Dodd, Mead, 1972. 126-46.

Tate, Claudia. *Domestic Allegories of Political Desire: The Black Heroine's Text at the Turn of the Century.* New York: Oxford UP, 1992.

Tignor, Eleanor Q. "Rudolph Fisher: Harlem Novelist." *Langston Hughes Review* 2 (Fall 1982): 13-22

Tracy, Steven C. *Langston Hughes and the Blues.* Urbana: U of Illinois P. 1988.

Worth, Robert. "*Nigger Heaven* and the Harlem Renaissance." *African American Review* 29 (1996): 461-73.

Wright, Austin. *The Formal Principle in the Novel.* Ithaca: Cornell UP, 1982.

FURTHER READING

Bibliographies

Chander, Harish. "Rudolph Fisher." In *African American Authors, 1745-1945: A Bio-Bibliographical Critical Sourcebook,* edited by Emmanuel S. Nelson, pp. 161-69. Westport, Conn.: Greenwood Press, 2000.

Cites reviews, scholarship, and other documents relating to Fisher's life and works.

Gable, Craig. "Rudolph Fisher: An Updated Selected Bibliography." *Bulletin of Bibliography* 57, no. 1 (2000): 13-9.

Lists the original publications in which Fisher's fiction and essays appeared, Fisher's book reviews, unpublished materials, and secondary sources.

Criticism

Friedmann, Thomas. "The Good Guys in the Black Hats: Color Coding in Rudolph Fisher's 'Common Meter.'" *Studies in Black Literature* 7, no. 2 (1976): 8-9.

Cites Fisher's short story as a successful example of reversed color coding, noting Fisher's combination of optimism and realism.

McCluskey, John Jr. "'Aim High and Go Straight': The Grandmother Figure in the Short Fiction of Rudolph Fisher." *Black American Literature Forum* 15, no. 2 (1981): 55-9.

Suggests that Fisher's grandmother character reflects the author's realistic approach to creating an honest portrayal of the struggles of new urban Blacks.

———. Introduction to *The City of Refuge, The Collected Stories of Rudolph Fisher,* pp. xi-xxxix. Columbia: University of Missouri Press, 1987.

Focuses on Fisher's use of the urban setting for his stories; identifies recurring themes of city culture, transition between generations, and class tension.

Perry, Margaret. "A Fisher of Black Life: Short Stories by Rudolph Fisher." In *The Harlem Renaissance Re-Examined,* pp. 253-62. New York: AMS Press, 1987.

Considers Fisher's stories as exemplars of the American genre of the short story; discusses the formal elements of Fisher's work.

Soitos, Stephen F. "Detective of the Harlem Renaissance: Rudolph Fisher." In *The Blues Detective: A Study of African American Detective Fiction,* pp. 93-124. Amherst: University of Massachusetts Press, 1996.

Examines Fisher's role in the development of the genre of Black detective fiction; proposes that Fisher used the framework of a white genre to express specific Black concerns.

Tignor, Eleanor Q. "The Short Fiction of Rudolph Fisher." *Langston Hughes Review* 1, no. 1 (1982): 18-23.

Gives an overview of Fisher's short stories, noting common themes and character types; discusses some unpublished works.

Turpin, Waters E. "Four Short Fiction Writers of the Harlem Renaissance—Their Legacy of Achievement." *CLA Journal* 11, no. 1 (1967): 59-72.

Groups Fisher with Jean Toomer, Langston Hughes, and Claude McKay as an important and positive influence in Black literature.

OTHER SOURCES FROM GALE:

Additional coverage of Fisher's life and career is contained in the following sources published by the Gale Group: *Black Literature Criticism,* Vol. 2; *Black Writers,* Eds. 1, 3; *Contemporary Authors,*Vol. 124; *Contemporary Authors - Brief Entry,* Vol. 107; *Contemporary Authors New Revision Series,* Vol. 80; *Dictionary of Literary Biography,* Vols. 51, 102;*DISCovering Authors Modules: Multicultural Authors*; *Short Story Criticism,* Vol. 25; and *Twentieth-Century Literary Criticism,* Vol. 11.

MARCUS GARVEY

(1887 - 1940)

(Full name Marcus Moziah Garvey Jr.) Jamaican political philosopher, essayist, editor, and poet.

Garvey was not a writer of the Harlem Renaissance; he was, in fact, critical and sometimes contemptuous of what he considered an elitist movement of a small number of Black intellectuals. He was imprisoned and then deported before the Renaissance movement peaked, and was organizing Blacks in his native Jamaica during Harlem's heyday. Nonetheless, Garvey's influence on the Harlem Renaissance was substantial. As an activist and intellectual, Garvey was a key figure in defining the debate on race, not only in America, but worldwide. Garvey was a vocal proponent of Black nationalism, pan-Africanism, and racial purity. His journal *Negro World,* the voice of his political organization, included poetry, fiction, and essays by writers who would become the leading lights of the "New Negro movement," a phrase Garvey may have coined. Although even some of Garvey's followers found his aspirations somewhat extreme, none would deny his importance in the movement to develop Black pride.

BIOGRAPHICAL INFORMATION

Garvey was born August 17, 1887, in St. Anne's Bay, Jamaica, which was under British rule. His parents, Marcus and Sarah, had borne eleven children, nine of whom died in childhood. Marcus Jr. was the last. Marcus Sr. was a stonemason and a community leader known to be well read and somewhat severe; Sarah was a soft-spoken Christian. The senior Garvey's love of reading allowed his son to educate himself beyond what was then available to poor Blacks in Jamaica, and as an adolescent, young Marcus was apprenticed to his godfather, a printer. He moved to Kingston when he was sixteen and excelled in the printing trade, soon becoming a leader in the Printers' Union. Garvey also studied oratory, taking lessons from the Black politician J. Robert Love, an advocate of pan-Africanism, and attending various churches in order to observe the speaking style of the ministers. Around 1910 he started his first newspaper, the short-lived *Garvey's Watchman.* Frustration with conditions in Jamaica led Garvey to Costa Rica, where he worked on a banana plantation until sometime around 1912 when he went to London. He was employed as a manual laborer, but continued his study of public speaking and traveled throughout Europe until he began working with the Egyptian nationalist Duse Mohammed Ali. Garvey worked as the printer for Duse's magazine *African Times and Orient Review,* a reflection of Duse's pan-African and pan-Oriental beliefs, which Garvey also studied avidly. Among Garvey's reading was Booker T. Washington's *Up From Slavery,* which inspired Garvey to devote his career to Black unity.

Garvey returned to Jamaica in 1914 ready to begin leading his own Black nationalist movement. Five days after landing in Kingston, Garvey founded the Universal Negro Improvement Association (UNIA), which became the chief organ through which Garvey promoted Black unity and Black pride. Hoping to learn more about Black education, he came to America in 1916 to talk with Booker T. Washington, who died before the two could meet. He also toured as a lecturer, promoting UNIA and pan-Africanism, and returned to New York to give weekly lectures in Harlem's Lafayette Hall. By 1918, Harlem had become the worldwide headquarters for UNIA, with Garvey at the lead. William H. Ferris, a prominent Black intellectual of the 1920s, suggested in Garvey's *Negro World* that the New Negro Movement was born of Garvey's activism and the work of UNIA. Garvey began advocating the development of a Black nation, negotiating with Liberia and other nations to create a homeland for all peoples of African descent; this became known as the "Back to Africa" movement. Garvey was outspoken and controversial, particularly for his support of racial purity and separatism. Blacks active in the cause of integration, including W. E. B. Du Bois and other leaders of the National Association for the Advancement of Colored People (NAACP), generally supported the pan-African movement but took issue with these other aspects of "Garveyism"; Du Bois and Garvey feuded publicly and bitterly over the direction of Black politics. Garvey sometimes used his periodical *Negro World* as a pulpit for his attacks. The division in the Black community eventually turned sentiment against Garvey, whose political philosophy was sometimes overshadowed by his tendency toward outrageous and provocative public statements. Garvey mocked the light-skinned Blacks like Du Bois and the figures of the Harlem Renaissance, which he considered a mediocre cultural movement. For its part, the NAACP provided information to the U.S. Justice Department that helped convict Garvey of mail fraud—a conviction based far more on Garvey's use of the courtroom as a soapbox than on the evidence, which in fact suggested human error rather than deception. After his appeal was rejected, Garvey began his five-year prison sentence in 1925. He continued to write in prison while his wife Amy helped keep UNIA going. A worldwide movement for his release began instantly, leading President Calvin Coolidge to commute his sentence and deport him to Jamaica in 1927. He worked for Jamaican independence, but with little success, and eventually moved back to England. There he launched his magazine *Black Man* and founded the School of African Philosophy. By the late 1930s Garvey was ill, suffering at times from asthma and pneumonia. In 1940 he suffered two strokes: the first left him partially paralyzed and the second proved fatal. His death spurred the dissolution of UNIA, though the reawakening of Black pride during the civil rights movement of the 1950s and 1960s won Garvey a new and appreciative audience.

MAJOR WORKS

Garvey was a prolific writer, producing articles for his magazines and numerous papers for UNIA. In his lifetime he published only two substantial collections of his thought: *The Philosophy and Opinions of Marcus Garvey; or, Africa for the Africans* (1923–25), which was reprinted in the late 1960s, and *The Tragedy of White Injustice* (1927), a lengthy statement of Garvey's philosophy in verse form, written while he was in jail. In *The Philosophy and Opinions of Marcus Garvey,* Garvey espoused the virtue of separatism and the danger of racial genocide faced by Blacks throughout the world. The establishment of an African homeland, Garvey argued, would protect the interests of Blacks worldwide. In this effort, Garvey saw white separatists and supremacists as his allies, and he included the speech of a white supremacist in his *Philosophy and Opinions*—an editorial decision that was highly controversial. Garvey wrote a great deal while in prison, including his experimental poem *The Tragedy of White Injustice,* in which he tried to heighten the power of his message through the use of poetic eloquence. Though not generally considered an aesthetic success, the work reflects Garvey's broad, global view of racial inequality and the need for Black solidarity. Also while in prison, Garvey wrote the essay "African Fundamentalism," published in *Negro World* in 1925, in which he outlined the basic tenets for creating an Afrocentric culture, which would include a Black deity, Black aesthetic standards, and the elevation of Black heroes from history. Garvey's editorial work in *Negro World* also constitutes a significant contribution to the literature of the Harlem Renaissance, encouraging the work of such writers as Zora Neale Hurston and Claude McKay. Garvey's activism, however, was a larger part of his legend than his writing, which mostly documents and reflects the larger message of his life work. Collections of his papers associated with

UNIA, the School of African Philosophy, and his efforts to establish various Black institutions are also an important part of the Garvey corpus.

CRITICAL RECEPTION

The strength of Garvey's convictions ensured strong reactions to his writings and beliefs, and many of his peers openly opposed him. In a 1920 issue of the influential NAACP journal the *Crisis,* Du Bois cast doubt on Garvey's psychological fitness for leadership, and the Black educator and author Kelly Miller suggested that Garvey's ambitions were so outrageous as to be "grotesque." But Garvey's message resonated with many other Black Americans, particularly the theme of racial pride that provided the foundation for many of his writings and speeches. Garvey styled himself as a man of the common people, not the elite, and advocated economic independence, a position that appealed to many poor Blacks. Though the movement was in decline at the time of Garvey's death, Garveyism experienced a significant resurgence in the 1960s and 1970s, reflected in phrases like "Black is beautiful" and the rallying cry "I am somebody!" Modern scholarship on Garvey has generally sought to balance the controversial aspects of Garvey's personality and philosophy with his significant contributions to Black political and intellectual history. Tony Martin (1983), who has published five book-length studies of Garvey and Garveyism, has argued strongly for recognition of the activist's importance, downplaying his negative relationships with other Black leaders by emphasizing the role of figures such as Du Bois in tarnishing Garvey's reputation. Robert A. Hill (1987), one of Garvey's editors and an important Garvey scholar, has worked to make available the full corpus of his extensive writings. Hill has noted Garvey's skillful use of the writings of his literary predecessors, observing the broad range of Garvey's reading and education. Scholars have also produced more focused studies of different aspects of Garvey's life and work, including his connection to Rastafarianism in Jamaica, his poetry and aesthetics, his connections to white supremacists, and the role of women in the Garvey movement.

PRINCIPAL WORKS

The Philosophy and Opinions of Marcus Garvey; or, Africa for the Africans. 2 vols. (political philosophy) 1923-1925

The Tragedy of White Injustice (poetry, political philosophy) 1927

Garvey and Garveyism (political philosophy) 1963

Collected Papers and Documents (political philosophy, letters) 1974

Marcus Garvey and the Vision of Africa (political philosophy) 1974

More Philosophy and Opinions of Marcus Garvey (political philosophy) 1977

The Poetical Works of Marcus Garvey (poetry) 1983

The Marcus Garvey and Universal Negro Improvement Association Papers. 5 vols. (letters, documents, speeches, history, political philosophy) 1983-1987

Marcus Garvey: Life & Lessons (autobiography, political philosophy) 1987

PRIMARY SOURCES

J. EDGAR HOOVER (DOCUMENT DATE 1919)

SOURCE: Hoover, J. Edgar. "Memorandum for Mr. Ridgely." Federal Bureau of Investigation internal memo (11 October 1919).

The following memo from Hoover—then with the Department of Justice—to special FBI agent Ridgely illustrates the level of interest that Garvey's activities attracted within the law enforcement community.

I am transmitting herewith a communication which has come to my attention from the Panama Canal, Washington office, relative to the activities of Marcus Garvey. Garvey is a West-Indian negro and in addition to his activities in endeavoring to establish the Black Star Line Steamship Corporation he has also been particularly active among the radical elements in New York City in agitating the negro movement. Unfortunately, however, he has not as yet violated any federal law whereby he could be proceeded against on the grounds of being an undesirable alien, from the point of view of deportation. It occurs to me, however, from the attached clipping that there might be some proceeding against him for fraud in connection with his Black Star Line propaganda and for this reason I am transmitting the communication to you for your appropriate attention.

The following is a brief statement of Marcus Garvey and his activities:

* Subject a native of the West Indies and one of the most prominent negro agitators in New York;

* He is a founder of the Universal Negro Improvement Association and African Communities League;

* He is the promulgator of the Black Star Line and is the managing editor of the *Negro World;*

* He is an exceptionally fine orator, creating much excitement among the negroes through his steamship proposition;

* In his paper the *Negro World* the Soviet Russian Rule is upheld and there is open advocation of Bolshevism.

Respectfully,
J. E. Hoover

MARCUS GARVEY (ESSAY DATE 1922)

SOURCE: Garvey, Marcus. "Return to Africa." *Negro World* XII, no. 10 (22 April 1922).

In this editorial, originally published in Negro World *and re-published in* New York *soon after, Garvey outlines his plans for African Americans' repatriation to Africa.*

Fellow men of the Negro Race, Greeting:

For four and a half years the Universal Negro Improvement Association has been advocating the cause of Africa for the Africans—that is, that the Negro peoples of the world should concentrate upon the object of building up for themselves a great nation in Africa.

When we started our propaganda toward this end several of the so-called intellectual Negroes who have been bamboozling the race for over half a century said that we were crazy, that the Negro peoples of the western world were not interested in Africa and could not live in Africa. One editor and leader went so far as to say at his Pan-African Congress that American Negroes could not live in Africa, because the climate was too hot. All kinds of arguments have been adduced by these Negro intellectuals against the colonization of Africa by the black race. Some said that the black man would ultimately work out his existence alongside of the white man in countries founded and established by the latter. Therefore, it was not necessary for Negroes to seek an independent nationality of their own. The old time stories of "Africa fever," "African bad climate," "African mosquitoes," "African savages," have been repeated by these "brainless intellectuals" of ours as a scare against our people in America and the West Indies taking a kindly interest in the new program of building a racial empire of our own in our Motherland.

A "Program" at Last?

I trust that the Negro peoples of the world are now convinced that the work of the Universal Negro Improvement Association is not a visionary one, but very practical, and that it is not so far fetched, but can be realized in a short while if the entire race will only co-operate and work toward the desired end. Now that the work of our organization has started to bear fruit, we find that some of these 'doubting Thomases" of the three and four years ago are endeavoring to mix themselves up with the popular idea of rehabilitating Africa in the interest of the Negro. They are now advancing spurious "programs" and in a short while will endeavor to force themselves upon the public as advocates and leaders of the African idea.

It is felt that those who have followed the career of the Universals Negro Improvement Association will not allow themselves to be deceived by these Negro opportunists who have always sought to live off the ideas of other people.

The Dream of a Negro Empire

It is only a question of a few more years when Africa will be completely colonized by Negroes, as Europe is by the white race. It is for us to welcome the proffered help of such men as Senators McCullum and France. Though their methods are a little different to that of the Universal Negro Improvement Association, yet it is felt that the same object will be achieved. What we want is an independent African nationality, and if America is to help the Negro peoples of the world establish such a nationality, then we welcome the assistance.

It is hoped that when the time comes for American and West Indian Negroes to settle in Africa, they will realize their responsibility and their duty. It will not be to go to the natives, but it shall be the purpose of the Universal Negro Improvement Association to have established in Africa the brotherly co-operation which will make the interest of the African native and the American and West Indies Negro one and the same, that is to say, we shall enter into a common partnership to build up Africa in the interest of our race.

Your obedient servant,
Marcus Garvey, President General
Universal Negro Improvement Association
New York, April 18, 1922

MARCUS GARVEY (ESSAY DATE 1923)

SOURCE: Garvey, Marcus. "One God, One Aim, One Destiny." *The Philosophy and Opinions of Marcus Garvey*, edited by Amy Jacques-Garvey. New York: Scribner, 1925.

Originally published in 1923, this essay is another of Garvey's manifestos about Black life, this time focusing on religion.

The time has come for the Negro to forget and cast behind him his hero worship and adoration of other races, and to start out immediately to create and emulate heroes of his own. We must canonize our own saints, create our own martyrs, and elevate to positions of fame and honor black men and women who have made their distinct contributions to our racial history. Sojourner Truth is worthy of the place of sainthood alongside of Joan of Arc; Crispus Attucks and George William Gordon are entitled to the halo of martyrdom with no less glory than that of the martyrs of any other race. Touissant L'Ouverture's brilliancy as a soldier and statesmen outshone that of a Cromwell, Napoleon and Washington; hence he is entitled to the highest place as a hero among men. Africa has produced countless numbers of men and women, in war and in peace, whose lustre and bravery outshine that of any other people. Then why not see good and perfection in ourselves? We must inspire a literature and promulgate a doctrine of our own without any apologies to the powers that be. The right is ours and God's. Let contrary sentiment and cross opinions go to the winds. Opposition to race independence is the weapon of the enemy to defeat the hopes of an unfortunate people. We are entitled to our own opinions and not obligated to or bound by the opinions of others.

If others laugh at you return the laughter to them; if they mimic you return the compliment with equal force. They have no more right to dishonor, disrespect, and disregard your feeling and manhood than you have in dealing with them. Honor them when they honor you; disrespect and disregard them when they vilely treat you. Their arrogance is but skin deep and an assumption that has no foundation in moral or in law. They have sprung from the same family tree of obscurity as we have; their history is as rude in its primitiveness as ours; their ancestors ran wild and naked, lived in caves and in branches of trees like monkeys as ours; they made sacrifices, ate the flesh of their own dead and the raw meat of the wild beast for centuries even as they accuse us of doing; their cannibalism was more prolonged than ours; when we were embracing the arts and sciences on the banks of the Nile, their ancestors were still drinking human blood and eating out of the skulls of their conquered dead; when our civilization had reached the noon-day of progress, they were still running naked and sleeping in holes and caves with rats, bats and other insects and animals. After we had already unfathomed the mystery of the stars and reduced the heavenly constellations to minute and regular calculus they were still backwoodsmen, living in ignorance and blatant darkness.

The world today is indebted to us for the benefits of civilization. They stole our arts and sciences from Africa. Then why should we be ashamed of ourselves? Their modern improvements are but duplicates of a grander civilization that we reflected thousands of years ago, without the advantage of what is buried and still hidden, to be resurrected and re-introduced by the intelligence of our generation and our posterity. Why should we be discouraged because somebody laughs at us today? Who to tell what tomorrow will bring forth? Did they not laugh at Moses, Christ and Mohammed? Was there not a Carthage, Greece and Rome? We see and have changes every day, so pray, work, be steadfast and be not dismayed.

As the Jew is held together by his religion, the white races by the assumption and the unwritten law of superiority, and the Mongolian by the precious tie of blood, so likewise the Negro must be united in one grand racial hierarchy. Our union must know no clime, boundary or nationality. Like the Great Church of Rome Negroes the world over must practice one faith, that of Confidence in themselves, with One God: One Aim: One Destiny: Let no religious scruples, no political machination divide us, but let us hold together under all climes and in every country, making among ourselves a Racial Empire upon which "the sun shall never set."

Let no voice but your own speak to from the depths: Let no influence but your own rouse you in time of peace and time of war. Hear all, but attend only to that which concerns you. Your allegiance shall be to your God, then to your family, race and country. Remember always that the Jew in his political and economic urge is always first a Jew; the white man is first a white man under all circumstances, and you can do no less than being first and always a Negro, and then all else will take care of itself. Let no one innoculate you with evil doctrines to suit their own conveniences. There is no humanity before that which starts with yourself, "Charity begins at home." First to thyself be true, and "thou canst not then be false to any man."

God and nature first made us what we are, and then out of our own creative genius we make ourselves what we want to be. Follow always that great law. Let the sky and God be our limit, and Eternity our measurement. There is no height to which we cannot climb by using the active intelligence of our own minds. Mind creates, and as much as we desire in nature we can have through the creation of our own minds. Being at present the scientifically weaker race, you shall treat others only as they treat you; but in your homes and everywhere possible you must teach the higher development of science to your children; and be sure to develop a race of scientists par excellence for in science and religion lie our only hope to withstand the evil designs of modern materialism. Never forget your God. Remember, we live, work and pray for the establishment of a great and binding racial hierarchy, the founding of a racial empire whose only natural, spiritual and political limits shall be God and "Africa, at home and abroad."

MARCUS GARVEY (ESSAY DATE 1924)

SOURCE: Garvey, Marcus. "The Enemies at Work." *Negro World* (2 September 1924).

This editorial is an example of Garvey's efforts to make the Black community aware of the forces gathered against them in white society.

During the whole of the convention and a little prior thereto, the enemies of our cause tried to provoke and confuse our deliberation by the many unpleasant things they systematically published against the Universal Negro improvement Association. Our enemies in America, especially the Negro Republican politicians of New York, used the general time fuse to explode on our tranquility and thereby destroy the purpose for which we were met, but as is customary, the Universal Negro Improvement Association is always ready for the enemy. They had arranged among themselves to get certain individuals of the Liberian government along with Ernest Lyons, the Liberian Consul-General, in Baltimore, himself a reactionary Negro politician of the old school, to circulate through the Negro press and other agencies such unpleasant news purported to be from Liberia as to create consternation in our ranks and bring about the demoralization that they hoped and calculated for, but as usual, the idiots counted without their hosts. The Universal Negro Improvement Association cannot be destroyed that way, in that it is not only an organization, but is the expression of the spiritual desires of the four hundred million black peoples of the world.

Our Colonization Program

As everybody knows, we are preparing to carry out our Liberian colonization program during this and succeeding months. Every arrangement was practically made toward this end. . . . Unfortunately, after all arrangements had been made in this direction, our steamship secured to carry the colonists and all plans laid, these enemies of progress worked in every way to block the carrying out of the plan. For the purpose of deceiving the public and carrying out their obstruction, they tried to make out by the protest that was filed by Ernest Lyons of Baltimore, with the government of Washington, that our Association was of an incendiary character and that it was the intention of the organization to disturb the good relationship that existed between Liberia and other friendly powers. A greater nonsense could not have been advanced by any idiot. What could an organization like the Universal Negro Improvement Association do to destroy the peace of countries that are already established and recognized? It is supposed that England and France are the countries referred to when, in fact, the authors of the statement know that England and France are only waiting for an opportunity to seize more land in Liberia and to keep Liberia in a state of stagnation, so as to justify their argument that the blacks are not competent of self-government in Africa as well as elsewhere. If Edwin Barclay had any sense, he would know that the Universal Negro Improvement Association is more friendly to Liberia, because it is made up of Negroes, than England and France could be in a thousand years. Lyons' protest was camouflage.

Negroes Double-Crossing

Everybody knows that the hitch in the colonization plan of the University Negro Improvement Association in Liberia came about because of double-crossing. The Firestone Rubber and Tire Company, of Ohio, has been spending large sums of money among certain people. The offer, no doubt, was so attractive as to cause certain persons to found the argument to destroy the Universal Negro Improvement Association, so as to favor the Firestone Rubber and Tire Company who, subsequently, got one million acres of Liberian land for actually nothing, to be exploited for rubber and minerals, and in the face of the fact that

Liberia is one of the richest rubber countries in the world, an asset that should have been retained for the Liberian people and members of the black race, but now wantonly given over to a white company to be exploited in the interest of white capital, and to create another international complication, as evidenced in the subsequent subjugation of Haiti and the Haitians, after the New York City Bank established itself in Haiti in a similar way as the Firestone Rubber and Tire Company will establish itself in Liberia. Why, every Negro who is doing a little thinking, knows that after the Firestone Rubber and Tire Company gets into Liberia to exploit the one million acres of land, it is only a question of time when the government will be taken out of the hands of the Negroes who rule it, and Liberia will become a white man's country in violation of the constitution of that government as guaranteeing its soil as a home for all Negroes of all climes and nationalities who desire to return to their native land. The thing is so disgraceful that we, ourselves, are ashamed to give full publicity to it, but we do hope that the people of Liberia, who control the government of Liberia, will be speedily informed so that they, through the Senate and House of Representatives, will repudiate the concessions granted to the Firestone Rubber and Tire Company, so as to save their country from eternal spoliation. If the Firestone Rubber and Tire Company should get the concessions in Liberia of one million acres of land, which should have been granted to the Universal Negro Improvement Association for development by Negroes for the good of Negroes, it simply means that in another short while thousands of white men will be sent away from America by the Firestone Rubber and Tire Company to exploit their concessions. These white men going out to colonize, as they generally regard tropical countries, will carry with them the spirit of all other white colonists, superiority over and subjugation of native peoples; hence it will only be a question of time when these gentlemen will change the black population of Liberia into a mongrel race, as they have done in America, [the] West Indies and other tropical countries, and there create another race problem such as is confusing us now in these United States of America. These white gentlemen are not going to allow black men to rule and govern them, so, like China and other places, there will be such complications as to ultimately lead to the abrogation of all native control and government and the setting up of new authority in a country that once belonged to the natives.

The Rape of Liberia

It is the duty of every Negro in the world to protest against this rape of Liberia encouraged by those who are responsible for giving the concessions to the Firestone Rubber and Tire Company. Why, nearly one-half of the country has been given away and, when it is considered that out of the twelve million square miles of Africa, only Liberia is left as a free and independent black country, it becomes a shame and disgrace to see that men should be capable of giving away all this amount of land to the same people who have possession of over nine-tenths of the country's [continent's] area.

Bright Future for Race

We beg to advise, however, the members and friends of the Universal Negro Improvement Association all over the world, that what has happened has not obstructed much the program of the Universal Negro Improvement Association as far as our colonization plans are concerned. All that we want is that everybody get behind the Black Cross Navigation and Trading Company and send us the necessary amount of money to pay for our first ship and secure other ships so as to carry out our trade contract with the Negroes of Africa, West Indies, South and Central America and these United States. The Association is devoting its time and energy now to building up an international commerce and trade so as to stabilize Negro industry. There is much for us to do. In taking the raw materials from our people in Africa to America, as well as materials [from] the West Indies, South and Central America to the United States[,] and taking back to them our finished and manufactured products in exchange, we have a whole world of industrial conquest to make and it can be done splendidly if each Negro will give us the support that is necessary. We want not only one, two or three ships, but we want dozens of ships, so that every week our ships can be going out of the ports of New York, Philadelphia, Boston, Baltimore, New Orleans, Savannah or Mobile for Liberia, Sierre [sic] Leone, Gold Coast, Lagos, Abyssinia, Brazil, Argentina, Costa Rica, Guatemala, Nicaragua, Honduras, Jamaica, Barbados, Trinidad, British Guiana and British Honduras. Let our ship be on the seven seas, taking our commerce to England, France, Germany, Italy, Japan, China and India. The chance of making good in commerce and trade is as much ours as it is other races and so we call upon you everywhere to get behind the industrial program of the Universal Negro Improvement Association. If we can control the field of industry we can control the sentiment of the world and that is what the Universal Negro Improvement Association seeks for the four hundred millions of our race.

Move the Little Barriers

So, the little barriers that have been placed in the way by the envious and wicked of our own race can easily be removed if we will get together and work together. Now that the convention has risen, let us redouble our energy everywhere to put the program over. Let us work with our hearts, soul and minds to see that everything is accomplished for the good of the race. We must have our ship in action by next month. At least, we are calculating to have our ship sail out of New York by the 29th of October, laden with the first cargo for the tropics, and to bring back to us tropical fruits and produce, and from thence to sail for Africa, the land of our fathers. Help us make this possible. . . .

With very best wishes for your success, I have the honor to be, Your obedient servant,
Marcus Garvey
President-General
Universal Negro Improvement Association

GENERAL COMMENTARY

ROBERT M. KAHN (ESSAY DATE 1983)

SOURCE: Kahn, Robert M. "The Political Ideology of Marcus Garvey." *Midwest Quarterly* 24, no. 2 (winter 1983): 117-37.

In the following essay, Kahn examines Garvey's positions outlined in The Philosophy and Opinions of Marcus Garvey, *acknowledging the limitations of Garvey's ideology and the damaging effect his personal life had on his reputation, but concluding that his philosophy has maintained its relevance throughout the twentieth century.*

Marcus Garvey's strong advocacy of separatism for the American black community reflects his understanding of the fundamental principles which govern economic and political development. African nationalism is not an adventure for Garvey; it is a necessity. He concludes from his knowledge of history that there is literally no future for blacks in the United States: ultimately blacks face, as a minority race in a white nation, the certainty of economic displacement, starvation, and genocide. Garvey confidently forecasts the coming of black genocide—avoidable only if African nationalism is pursued—because of three interlocking principles of social survival which are operant in the world: (1) the world is increasingly subjected to population pressures; (2) human races are engaged in the Darwinian struggle for the survival of the fittest; (3) majority rule always places political power in the hands of a racially prejudiced majority.

Espousing the dismal lesson of Malthus and Ricardo, Marcus Garvey posits world overpopulation as the root cause of racial and national antagonism. Mankind is plagued with an increasingly unfavorable ratio between land mass and population: "the world is small and humanity in the many and various race groups, is growing larger every day" (***Philosophy and Opinions of Marcus Garvey***). Garvey indicates that, as increasing numbers of people depend on a fixed amount of land, food shortages are imminent; indeed, he argues that humanity has already outstripped its food supply. Moreover, the hungry victims of economic imbalances will create a Hobbesian world of disorder: "Hungry men have no respect for law, authority or human life." Not only is the world already experiencing tangible harm, but the land-rich United States will not be spared the ravages of over-population in the future. Garvey predicts that eventually the American scramble for food will result in racial competition and antagonism:

> In another one hundred years white America will have doubled its population; in another two hundred years it will have trebled itself. The keen student must realize that the centuries ahead will bring us an overcrowded country; opportunities, as the population grows larger, will be fewer; the competition for bread between the people of their own class will become keener, and so much more so will there be no room for two competitive races, the one strong, and the other weak.

For Garvey, the spectre of overpopulation has an immediate ideological significance for the black community. The preeminent concern of the black community must be physical survival.

In isolation, the problem of world overpopulation is as liable to inspire cooperation and to inspire antagonistic efforts. Yet, for Garvey, overcrowding is not an isolated principle of world reality; the convergence of other conditions forces a separatist response upon the black community. In Garvey's view, human history is firmly channeled along the path of antagonistic self-interest:

> The world is not in the disposition to divide the spoils of materialism, but on the contrary every group is seeking the aggrandizement of self at the expense of those who have lost or who ignore the trend of human effort in the direction of self-preservation.

Man is not selfish because of a defect in his character or reason; man acts selfishly because the laws of nature dictate that only the strongest races and nations will survive.

Garvey's belief in the Darwinian survival of the fittest, it must be emphasized, is a critical element in the appreciation of Garvey's ideology. Garvey's proclivity for the bumptious pose, bombastic declarations of African glory, and the chauvinistic touting of black nationhood must be viewed in the context of Garvey's overriding and most serious objective: black survival. It is not racial glory and prestige which form the proximate goals of Marcus Garvey. It is survival. Garvey's arousal of the black masses is a preparatory step; the American black community must be prepared and strengthened before the struggle for survival intensifies. The alternative is extinction. In concrete terms, Garvey asserts that the struggle for survival has already arrived on American shores. In a short essay entitled **"White Man's Solution for the Negro Problem in America,"** Garvey reveals the white man's genocidal plan for America:

> A hearty welcome is extended to white people from all parts of the world to come to and settle in America. They come in by the thousands every month. Why? The idea is to build up a vast white population in America, so as to make the white people independent of Negro labor; thereby depriving them of the means of livelihood, the wherewithal to buy bread, which means that in a short while they will die of starvation.

In effect, Garvey argues that massive white immigration represents the effort of American whites to prepare for an intense struggle of survival; as the result of such preparation, when food shortages do occur in America, the black community will succumb to mass starvation. To the skeptic who questions the genocidal capacity of the American white community, Garvey offers the example of American Indians as an unprepared weaker race which was exterminated by American whites. To the skeptic who cites years of black progress within the United States as evidence that American whites are not predisposed toward a policy of black extermination, Garvey replies that such progress is illusory and that such a liberal spirit on the part of whites is only temporary:

> What progress have we made when everything we do is done through the good will and grace of the liberal white man of the present day? But can he always afford to be liberal? Do you not realize that in another few decades he will have on his hands a problem of his own—a problem to feed his own children, to take care of his own flesh and blood? In the midst of that crisis, when he finds not even enough to feed himself, what will become of the Negro? The Negro naturally must die to give way, and make room for others who are better prepared to live.

Finally, to the skeptic who would attack this revelation of an extermination plan by attacking Garvey's personal integrity, Garvey responds by recalling that the whites whom he is attempting to thwart are the original critics of his character:

> because I love my race to the point of objecting to his secret and cunning policy of destruction and extermination, he claims that I am a "Bad Nigger." I would rather die than be good, if being good in this respect means that I must acquiesce to the extermination of my race, like the American Indian and other native peoples.

Garvey's basic point is that American whites, in light of nature's rule for choosing survivors in a teeming world, are preparing for the extermination of blacks in the long run.

However, even conceding both that whites are capable of exterminating the black community and that blacks possess few instruments of self-protection, the inevitability of black genocide within the American political system is still not a closed question. An additional ingredient must be added to this combustible mixture before it become undeniable that the American political community offers death, rather than a safe haven, to its black minority. Given that the United States has a democratic regime which boasts of constitutional protections for minorities lacking the tools of self-protection, it can be hypothesized that those whites who would exterminate blacks either constitute a minority or are effectively constrained by constitutional bulwarks. Garvey dismisses both possibilities. First, races are intrinsically prejudiced against each other: "No race in the world is so just as to give others, for the asking, a square deal in things economic, political and social." Indeed, Garvey is so certain of universal prejudice and suspicion that he is an open admirer of the Ku Klux Klan for its honest and lack of hypocrisy. Ultimately, "the strong hand of prejudice" will exterminate the black community which lacks organization and preparation. Thus, racial prejudice among whites is inescapable, universal, and, when unopposed by blacks, impelled toward extermination.

Marcus Garvey is equally convinced that a democratic constitution provides no protection against the exterminationist tendencies of a prejudiced majority:

> the majority of the people dictate the policy of governments, and if the majority are against a

> measure, a thing, or a race, then the government is impotent to protect that measure, thing or race.
>
> If the Negro were to live in this Western Hemisphere for another five hundred years he would still be outnumbered by other races who are prejudiced against him.

Garvey, in effect, identifies himself as an absolute majoritarian in his general conception of democracy and his specific description of the American political regime. Because a democratic regime expresses the will of a majority without impediment, the American regime places no obstacle before the prejudice of its white majority; government-level and regime-level protections for the black minority yield in the presence of that prejudice.

Whether persuasive to the modern reader or not, it must be acknowledged that, given Garvey's premises, his advocacy of black separatism represents a thoughtful conclusion for a man whose principal concern is the universal improvement of his race. In this context, black separatism is the denouement of a systematic political analysis and a consistent ideological position. Even if introduced with semi-mystical oratorical embellishments or flourishes of gaudy salesmanship, Garvey's proposal of separatist solution cannot be dismissed as a superficial *deus ex machina* or delusory *non sequitur.* Marcus Garvey perceives a world population explosion for which he discerns no solution. He perceives a Darwinian scramble of survival among nations and races for which he discerns no surcease. Finally, apropos the specific dilemma of the minority black community within the United States, he discerns no democratic remedy for black genocide in a regime which, by its very nature, is controlled by a prejudiced white majority.

Garvey proposes the establishment of a separate black nation—rejecting participation in the American government, regime, and political community—because, ultimately, nationhood offers the only effective protection for the black community:

> NATIONHOOD is the only means by which modern civilization can completely protect itself.
>
> Independence of nationality, independence of government, is the means of protecting not only the individual, but the group.
>
> Nationhood is the highest ideal of all peoples.

For the black people of the world, the abstract appreciation of nationhood translates into a concrete pursuit of African nationalism. Maintaining that "Africa is the legitimate, moral and righteous home of all Negroes," Garvey characterizes his effort as an attempt at "repatriation." Surrounding his program with Christian symbolism and the spirit of righteousness, Garvey also frequently characterizes his purpose as that of "African Redemption."

In the short run, African nationalism provides an escape from the genocidal intent of prejudiced majority; in the long run, however, successful nation-building can diminish that prejudice which is the engine of black destruction:

> Prejudice of the white race against the black race is not so much because of color as of condition; because as a race, to them, we have accomplished nothing; we have built no nation, no government; because we are dependent for our economic and political existence.

Thus, while color prejudice may remain relatively intractable in the relations between races, that component of prejudice which represents the snobbish contempt of the strong toward the weak can be lessened.

In order to avoid the inevitability of genocidal slaughter, Garvey proposes black nationalism as the salvation of the black community. Yet, a proposed solution to the predicament of the black community is only valuable to the extent that there is a realistic prospect of its achievement. Garvey is not utopian. The avoidance of future ravages through repatriation is possible, he reasons, because of the convergence of certain favorable circumstances which are immediately exploitable. Specifically, three existing circumstances foretell the achievement of black nationhood by American blacks: (1) the emergence of nationalism as an increasingly legitimate principle for justifying conduct within the international community; (2) a growing awareness and appreciation of the mutual advantages which are possible when blacks and whites join together in the cause of black nationalism; and, (3) the progress in preparing the black community for separatism which has been effected since the Garvey movement became the foremost organizational and planning instrument of African repatriation.

Marcus Garvey discerns abundant evidence that he is witnessing an era of triumphant nationalism, promising opportunity and hope for the black community. Garvey proclaims the validity of nationalism as both an intellectual and an historical force within the international political system. On the intellectual plane, the principle of self-determination appears as a hard-learned lesson of World War I and the only legitimate starting point for any discussion of international political evolution. For Garvey, the proper vehicle for securing liberty is the racial group as it pursues national independence:

> If liberty is good for certain sets of humanity it is good for all. Black men, Colored men, Negroes have as much right to be free as any other race that God Almighty ever created, and we desire freedom that is unfettered, freedom that is unlimited, freedom that will give us a chance and opportunity to rise to the fullest of our ambition and that we cannot get in countries where other men rule and dominate.

In effect, liberty is filtered through the territorial claim of each and every group: "The world is the property of all mankind, and each and every group is entitled to a portion Garvey's major premise becomes that the liberty of the black community will be secured when the world is properly partitioned.

Garvey's optimism on this point springs from his beliefs that the principle of self-determination permeates geopolitical thought and, more importantly, that the actual partitioning of the world has accelerated. Amid this international land rush, Garvey stakes a claim for the black community:

> Now that the world is readjusting itself and political changes and distributions are being made of the earth's surface, there is absolutely no reason why certain parts of Africa should not be set aside absolutely for the Negro race as our claim and heritage.

If pessimistic conclusions about the future of the American black community impelled Garvey toward embracing black separatism, optimistic themes now emerge which help to explain the enthusiasm with which Garvey advocates black separatism. Given that the principle of national self-determination is in vogue and that a trend toward world partitioning seems to exist, Garvey could expect a favorable reception for his oft-proclaimed doctrine of "Africa for the Africans." In this atmosphere, Garvey could conclude that the eventual success of his program for African nationalism depended only on the enlistment of sufficient white support and on the adequate preparation of the black community for its role as nation-builder; with his customary exuberance, Garvey could also conclude that there was considerable justification for the optimistic view that white support and black preparation would soon be forthcoming.

Marcus Garvey often expresses his confidence that a significant segment of the American white community will come to the assistance of Africa-bound black separatists. White allies will, above all else, recognize that African nationalists are not destructive haters of the white race, but basically benevolent in their intentions. In order to dispel the image of seething racial hatred within the black separatist movement, Garvey provides effusive disclaimers. The race as a whole is defended: "At no time within the last five hundred years can one point to a single instance of the Negro as a race of haters." Referring to himself in the third person, Garvey also defends his own equanimity:

> At no time has the President of the Universal Negro Improvement Association preached hatred of the white people. That in itself is a violation of the constitution of the organization, which teaches all its members to love and respect the rights of all races, believing that by so doing, others will in turn love and respect our rights.

Once denuded of false fears, there are, Garvey contends, myriad reasons for whites to make positive contributions to the cause of African redemption. Initially, it is possible to tap a reservoir of white sympathy for the subordinate black community:

> there is a deep feeling of human sympathy that touches the soul of white America, upon which the unfortunate and sorrowful can always depend for sympathy, help and action.

In Garvey's estimation, the sympathetic assistance of whites is readily obtainable because the black community is putting forth a just claim. Garvey argues that whites who possess a sense of justice will honor the debt which has accrued to the black community during its generations of productive labor in the service of the American economy.

If, however, white Americans falter in their commitment to justice and lose their penchant for a sympathetic response, white assistance to

FROM THE AUTHOR

GARVEY ON SELF-DETERMINATION

God and Nature first made us what we are, and then out of our own created genius we make ourselves what we want to be. Follow always that great law. Let the sky and God be our limit and Eternity our measurement.

SOURCE: Marcus Garvey, excerpt from "American Fundamentalism" (UNIA pamphlet), 1925.

black separatism will nevertheless flow from calculations of white community self-interest. Not only does Garvey hold out the prospect of a thriving trade between black-controlled Africa and white nations but he also reminds whites that a settlement of just claims through the racial partitioning of the world is a two-sided proposition. As American blacks achieve repatriation and national independence, American whites stand to gain undisputed possession of their homeland, eschewing in the process the rigors of racial competition with its attendant antagonism and insecurity.

When Garvey surveys the established record of white support for black separatism, he derives additional encouragement. Garvey recalls, in laudatory terms, the contribution of the nineteenth-century American Colonization Society in the founding of Liberia. Garvey also cites openly and without shame the ideological and political comradeship which he feels for white supremacist organizations such as the Ku Klux Klan and the Anglo-Saxon Clubs of America. Garvey not only praises white supremacist organizations, but even met with an official of the Ku Klux Klan and established friendly contacts with the Anglo-Saxon Clubs; indeed, these efforts culminated in a speech by a white supremacist to Garvey's followers in Liberty Hall and the printing that speech in both the *Negro World* and the ***Philosophy and Opinions of Marcus Garvey.*** These and similar actions were seen as outrageous by all American black leaders who did not share Garvey's brand of separatism.

Because of the manner in which Garvey's position served as a lightning rod for the anger of more moderate black leaders and because of the controversy it engendered, Garvey's willingness to associate with white supremacist organizations merits further consideration. In final analysis, to understand Garvey's exculpation of the most virulent embodiments of white supremacy is to understand the essential nature of Garvey's separatist ideology.

First, the Klan and other supremacist groups are supportive because their threats, warnings, and atrocities lend weight to Garvey's prediction of a genocidal future. Since genocide is rooted in impersonal forces (overpopulation and so forth), one's personal loathing of white supremacist organizations is a misappropriation of energy. White supremacists, following the laws of nature and survival, will only cease pressing their advantage when the black community is strong; such strength depends on national independence.

Second, Garvey argues more generally that white supremacists benefit the black community by presenting an unadulterated and unobstructed view of the indelible racial prejudice of white Americans:

> I regard the Klan, the Anglo-Saxon Clubs and White America Societies, as far as the Negro is concerned, as better friends of the race than all other groups of hypocritical whites put together. I like honesty and fair play. You may call me a Klansman if you will, but, potentially, every whiteman is a Klansman, as far as the Negro in competition with whites socially, economically and politically is concerned, and there is no use lying about it.

It bears repeating: potentially, every whiteman is a Klansman. Given that the white supremacist appears to Garvey, not as a special and different kind of white person, but as the prototypal white without disguise, the enemies of the black community are clearly identified as those whites and blacks who cling to illusions of white liberality and who are, therefore, incapable of dealing with white supremacist organizations. Garvey believes that, if blacks desire African redemption, they must be able to talk and bargain with even the most transparently prejudiced of whites.

Finally, it must be understood that Garvey's ability to ally himself with vicious extremists who are shunned by more moderate blacks and whites is intimately related to the nature of a separatist ideology. The Ku Klux Klan and other white supremacist organizations in America are acceptable partners for Garvey because he can find no evidence that these groups are seeking an international (i.e., extranational) role to play. Totally engrossed in reshaping their own political community, these supremacist organizations are ultimately of little consequence for the dedicated separatist whose rejection of the American political community for an African homeland is complete. is hardly surprising, therefore, that those black accommodationists, activists, and militants who are determined to pursue their goals within the American political community would take sharp exception to Garvey's tolerance of perennial enemies.

Ultimately Garvey places the responsibility for securing his separatist goals in the hands of the American black community. Garvey is convinced that American whites, destined to act from multiple motives of justice, sympathy, and self-interest, will provide material assistance for the cause of African nationalism. Yet, no external factor can succeed without the utmost effort and preparation of the black community. It is Garvey's dictum that the principle of self-determination only functions as a real and vital force for those groups which demonstrate the depth of their determination. Garvey trusts that his organization, the U.N.I.A., is well-suited for the important mission of instilling such determination in the black community:

> The mission of the Universal Negro Improvement Association is to arouse the sleeping consciousness of Negroes everywhere to the point where we will, as one concerted body, act for our own preservation.

As head of the U.N.I.A., Garvey himself delivers both pedagogical and prophetic messages designed to hasten the preparations of the American black community.

The activation of American blacks begins for Garvey with general appeals (i.e., appeals that are not only appropriate for the black separatist, but familiar to the black activist and the black militant as well). Reflecting his early absorption with the teachings of Booker T. Washington, Garvey prescribes heavy doses of racial self-help. Garvey proves a stalwart foe of fatalism:

> Some of us seem to accept the fatalist position, the fatalist attitude, that God accorded to us a certain position and condition, and therefore there is no need trying to be otherwise. The moment you accept such an attitude, the moment you accept such an opinion, the moment you harbor such an idea, you hurl an insult at the great God who created you.

In opposing religious fatalism, Garvey does not strike out at all religious belief; instead, he articulates a spiritually-based humanism which emphasizes God's desire for man to assume direct and personal responsibility for his own condition:

> All that authority which meant the regulation of human affairs, human society, and human happiness was given to man by the Creator, and man, therefore, became master of his own destiny, and architect of his own fate.

Claiming that the white world has always tried to rob the black community of its history, Garvey also educes black pride and determination by recalling the glories of past black civilizations and the primitiveness of early white history.

Once the enervated and impassive are energized by broad appeals to unity and racial pride, the mobilization efforts of Garvey and the U.N.I.A. channel such energies into organized separatist activities. Garvey argues that, in final analysis, the strength which allows a race or nation to survive is closely dependent on organization:

> If we must have justice, we must be strong; if we must be strong, we must come together; if we must come together, we can only do so through the system of organization.
>
> The wonderful force of organization is today making itself felt in every branch of human effort. Whether in industry, society, politics or war it is the force of organization that tells; hence, I can advise no better step toward racial salvation than organization among us.

Garvey argues, in general terms, that a group's strength is maximized through organization and that the nation represents the highest and most potent form of organization available to groups. It follows that, in the specific case of American blacks, power is maximized when the organization of a separate nation is adopted as the black community's primary purpose.

As a planner, promoter, and organizer of black separatism, Garvey exhibits two chief concerns: (1) the physical transfer of the American black community to its African homeland, and (2) the establishment of political authority for the incipient black nation.

Marcus Garvey is promoting a mass—indeed, total—colonization effort which envision the transfer of all blacks to their African homeland. His negotiations with the government of Liberia and the founding of the Black Star shipping line presuppose an interest in a massive exodus of the American black community. Yet some discussion of his advocacy of large-scale repatriation is necessary because of the controversy surrounding Garvey's designation as the leader of a "wholesale" Back-to-Africa movement. Indeed, in prefaces to the ***Philosophy and Opinions of Marcus Garvey*** written over forty years apart, two authors make the almost identical assertion that Garvey does not advocate mass colonization. In 1925, the author of the preface to the original edition of Garvey's second volume writes, "They [newspaper reporters] intentionally or unintentionally hailed him as the Moses of a wholesale 'Back-to-Africa' pilgrimage, a scheme which Mr. Garvey has never advocated nor planned." In 1968, the author of a new preface to the latest edition of Garvey's ***Philosophy*** writes, "Garvey never advocated or intended a wholesale 'repatriation.'" Both authors are quite incorrect.

Predicating his program of land acquisition and colonization on an outpouring of assistance from whites, Garvey reveals territorial aspirations of sweeping proportions:

> This plan when properly undertaken and prosecuted will solve the race problem in America in fifty years. Africa affords a wonderful opportunity

FROM THE AUTHOR

GARVEY ON SUCCESS

There is no force like success, and that is why the individual makes all effort to surround himself throughout life with the evidence of it; as of the individual, so should it be of the nation.

SOURCE: Marcus Garvey, excerpt from *The Philosophy and Opinions of Marcus Garvey,* Universal Publishing House, 1923-1925.

> at the present time for colonization by the Negroes of the Western world. There is Liberia, already established as an independent Negro government. Let white America assist Afro-Americans to go there and help develop the country. Then, there are the late German colonies; let white sentiment force England and France to turn the mover to the American and West Indian Negroes who fought for the Allies in the World's War. Then, France, England and Belgium owe America billions of dollars which they claim they cannot afford to repay immediately. Let them compromise by turning over Sierra Leone and the Ivory Coast on the West Coast of Africa and add them to Liberia and help make Liberia a state worthy of her history.

In another lengthy passage, Marcus Garvey outlines the principal reason for a fifty-year timetable:

> if a plebiscite of or a referendum to the masses of people were to be taken it would show an overwhelming majority in favor of the plan of returning the race to Africa by careful and proper arrangements and methods, whereby the somewhat settled national equilibrium industrially and generally, would not be disturbed, but by a gradual system of release, and replacement, at the same time, by assimilable duplicates, continue the migration until in the course of probably a half century the problem adjusts itself by the friendly and peaceful removal and by the return to the race of its native home, and the assimilating into the body politic of America those members of the majority race who would have replaced the Negro industrially and generally in the South and other sections of the Country that now depend on Negro labor.

In effect, Garvey attempts to strike a bargain with the white community. The whites in America will forgo monetary payments and accept African territories as settlement on the wartime debts of her allies. In return for title to these territories, the black community would promise an orderly withdrawal from the United States. Whites would gain, not only full possession of America, but the luxury of a half-century period of gradually effecting the internal migration of white labor to areas of the country where precipitous black departure would disrupt the economy. Clearly, this kind of concern for the destabilizing effects of sudden black emigration is only intelligible within the context of a plan for mass colonization.

Garvey, the separatist, evidences interest in the development of authoritative political structures which could serve the repatriated black community. However, it must be stated that Garvey only possesses rudimentary plans for the internal organization of a African political system. Garvey even fails to clarify whether he seeks a single African nation, a number of nations, or a political entity which transcends the conventional definition of nation. Thus, at various points, Garvey refers to a black republic, a black empire, a collection of "African Communities," and a "political superstate;" indeed, one statement outlining the objectives of the U.N.I.A. schizophrenically pledges that the association will develop "Independent Negro Nations and Communities" and establish "a central nation for the race."

Beyond a wealth of smaller discoveries, the student of Marcus Garvey's ideology is finally left with two general impressions. First, Garvey's specific formula for black separatism illustrates some of the pervasive problems of political separatism in general. For example, separatism is, by its very nature, incessantly and insistently provocative; the separatist movement finds itself constantly buffeted by a churning sea of controversy. In opposing all levels of the political system, separatism calls down upon itself the ire of all other ideologues. Thus, Garvey stands alone, supported only by the *bons mots* of apartheid minded whites, against the gentler spirits in the white community and the full panoply of black accommodationists, black activists, and black militants. Moreover, by staking a claim on Africa, Garvey also saddles himself with the responsibility for simultaneously securing: (1) recognition from the international community, (2) allegiance from the black political establishment of Africa, (3) political favors from the white American power-holders, (4) broad-based support from the American black community, and (5) the overthrow of European imperialism.

Garvey's relative neglect of regime-level phenomena is another characteristic problem of black separatism. Separatism, like all other types of political ideology, tends to concentrate its thought and action on that level of the political system which it identifies as critical. Separatism differs from its ideological competitors by emphasizing the importance of dissolving the existing political community; thus, separatist ideology addresses the merits of a new and separate nation, with insufficient regard for the nature of the new regime which it would establish concomitantly. Naive dissertations by Garvey on democracy and putting an end to official corruption illustrate this tendency.

There is a second general impression which remains when one completes a detailed examination of Garvey's thought: how easy it would be to underestimate the quality of Garvey's political ideology amid accounts of the legal difficulties, political indiscretions, and blustering style which characterized his life. Though all is not strength, there is remarkable ideological coherence in Garvey's analyses of why the black community suffers and how separatism is both a logical necessity and a practical possibility. If the contemporary student of black politics is sometimes distracted from the importance of political ideology. Marcus Garvey himself has no such problem; he recognizes that the continuing vitality of thought can surpass the importance of life itself. Prophesying that "the world shall hear from my principles even two thousand years hence," Garvey, the political ideologist and visionary thinker, writes:

> The time has come for those of us who have a vision of the future to inspire our people to a closer kinship, to a closer love of self, because it is only through this appreciation of self will we be able to rise to that higher life that will make us not an extinct race in the future, but a race of men fit to survive.

Though it has only been fifty years thus far, it can be reported that the black community's struggle for survival still continues and that his people are still listening (pp. 119-37).

TONY MARTIN (ESSAY DATE 1983)

SOURCE: Martin, Tony. "Garvey, Black Arts, Harlem Renaissance" and "Garveyism and Literature." In *Literary Garveyism: Garvey, Black Arts, and the Harlem Renaissance,* pp. 1-7, 25-42. Dover, Mass.: Majority Press, 1983.

In the following essays, Martin asserts the extensive influence of Garvey on Black literature and the Harlem Renaissance and works to rebuild Garvey's reputation among the Black leaders of the twentieth century, singling out his Negro World *as a publication central to the development of Black literature.*

Garvey, Black Arts, Harlem Renaissance

During the 1960s, the Civil Rights and Black Power movements gave birth to a flowering of literary activity which came to be known as the Black Arts Movement. Poets and playrights especially attracted a mass following for literary activity which astounded most observers. Large audiences, sometimes numbering in the thousands, flocked to street theatres in Harlem, poetry readings on campuses and the performances of community workshops. For a time recorded poetical works competed with soul music on the best selling charts. Black publishing houses, such as Broadside Press in Detroit and Third World Press in Chicago, were enabled to establish a toehold in an industry which, both before and since, has been among the most difficult for Black enterprise to break into.

Almost all commentators, both Black and white, considered this mass interest in Black poetry and literature to be a phenomenon without precedent. Even the Harlem Renaissance of the 1920s seemed less than an adequate precedent. For it was widely believed, and not without justification, that the Harlem Renaissance was more of an elite and less of a grassroots affair. Furthermore, the leading lights of the 1920s had often relied overwhelmingly on white patronage and largely on a white audience. The major figures of the Black Arts Movement, however, were inclined to espouse Black nationalism and tried harder to mobilize the resources of their own community.

It was during the period of the Black Arts Movement that the Black world rediscovered Marcus Garvey in a big way. He had never really been forgotten, but during the 1960s and '70s he again became an object of mass interest which threatened to rival in intensity his heyday of the 1920s. Such was inevitable, for in Garvey's Universal Negro Improvement Association (UNIA), the generation of the 1960s found a fitting precursor to its own actions. Garvey, too, had tried to mobilize the Black world's resources in its own behalf. Garvey, too, had preached race pride, community control, self-reliance and, in a word, Black nationalism. And Garvey had done so with unparallelled success. The Black Arts Movement, therefore, looked to Garvey for political inspiration. What it mostly did not know, was that Garvey could also have provided literary inspiration. For Garvey, too, half a century earlier, had demonstrated the fact which so surprised the commentators of the 1960s—the fact that the Black masses can be moved to an appreciation for literature and the arts on a scale not often equalled in other communities.

Garvey built the largest Pan-African mass organization of all time. His Universal Negro Improvement Association by the mid-1920s, boasted over eleven hundred branches in over forty countries in North, South and Central America, the Caribbean, Africa, Europe and Australia.[1]

Garvey was born in St. Ann's Bay, Jamaica, on August 17, 1887. Despite a lack of sustained formal schooling beyond his early teens, he nevertheless managed to develop a lasting taste for things literary. He read widely in his father's library (a rare privilege for a poor youth growing up in 19th century rural Jamaica) and spent all of his teenage years as first a printer's apprentice and later as a printer. These early experiences ensured him a constant supply of reading material.

By the time he moved to the capital city, Kingston, at the age of sixteen, he was ready to expand his literary interests into new directions. He took elocution lessons and entered public speaking contests. In 1910 he placed third in an islandwide oratorical competition. At the end of the first round, which consisted of a poetical reading, Garvey occupied first place. He fared less well on the prose reading which occupied the second round.[2]

It was about this time that Garvey also began his lifelong career as a journalist, first in Jamaica and later in Costa Rica, Panama, England, the United States, Jamaica again and England for a second time.[3] Many of his poems would eventually first appear in his own publications.

Garvey wandered through Central and South America from 1910 to 1912 and through Britain and Europe from 1912 to 1914. In England he worked for the *Africa Times and Orient Review,* edited by the African, Dusé Mohamed Ali, and one of the best literary and political magazines in the Black world of that time.

Four years of world travel convinced Garvey of the need for founding a racial uplift organization. The result was the UNIA, organized a few days after his return to Jamaica in the summer of 1914. Literature and the arts played an important role in the organization from the very start. Throughout 1914 and 1915 regular meetings and concerts featured debates, oratorical contests, poetry readings, dramatic productions and musical performances. The early UNIA was practically an uplift organization and literary and debating club all rolled into one. And even though Garvey had not yet begun his great North American undertaking, his Jamaican organization was already evincing an interest in Afro-American artistic endeavor. At one early UNIA meeting Amy Ashwood (later to become the first Mrs. Garvey) recited from the works of Paul Laurence Dunbar, Afro-America's most celebrated poet of the period. Garvey had met the seventeen year old Amy Ashwood, not insignificantly, at the weekly meeting of a Kingston literary and debating society.[4]

In his earliest extant pamphlet, ***A Talk With Afro-West Indians,*** published in Jamaica in 1915, Garvey again demonstrated his interest in the writings (especially historical) of the Black world's leading men of letters, among them the West Indian born West African statesman, Edward Wilmot Blyden and Afro-America's W. E. B. DuBois (later to become a bitter foe of Garvey). By this time Garvey had also read, and was in correspondence with, Booker T. Washington.[5]

It was Washington who encouraged Garvey to journey to the United States. Washington died before the trip could take place, but Garvey nevertheless arrived in New York on March 23, 1916. He hoped to go on a fundraising tour and return to Jamaica. But such was not to be. One thing led to another and he was destined, within a mere three short years, to become one of the best known Africans in the world.

In the meantime he toured the United States lecturing and establishing contacts. Some of these contacts were literary. For his earliest known Afro-American journal article, **"The West Indies in the Mirror of Truth,"** was published in January 1917 in the Chicago based *Champion* magazine, edited by Fenton Johnson. Johnson was one of Afro-America's better known literary figures. Alain Locke called him a "pioneer and pathbreaker" of the Harlem Renaissance.[6]

Two and a half years after arriving in New York, in the fall of 1918, Garvey established what was soon to become the crowning achievement of his journalistic career. This was the weekly *Negro World* newspaper, published in Harlem. The paper's circulation grew in time to about 200,000 and it enjoyed a worldwide distribution unequalled by any other contemporary Afro-American publication. Garvey himself was the paper's first editor, but his political activity kept him much too busy to serve as full time editor for long. To help him in this task he attracted a succession of Afro-America's leading journalistic and literary figures. Between 1920 and 1927 (the year of Garvey's deportation to Jamaica after conviction on a trumped up charge of mail fraud) the editors, associated editors and literary editors of the *Negro World* included the following luminaries—William H. Ferris, historian, literary critic and graduate of Harvard and Yale; Hubert H. Harrison, perhaps Harlem's best known and most respected intellectual; Eric D. Walrond, a major short story writer of the Harlem Renaissance; T. Thomas Fortune, the "dean of Afro-American journalists," veteran Republican Party activist and former aide to Booker T. Washington; and John Edward Bruce, founder in 1911 of the Negro Society for Historical Research, and a man whose journalistic and political credentials rivalled those of Fortune.

By 1920, two years after its inception, the *Negro World* was already well on its way to becoming the focal point of a mass preoccupation with the arts, especially poetry, unequalled by any of the better-known publications of the Harlem Renaissance. The *Negro World's* role in this was so great that one does not easily understand the near total silence on this subject in practically all of the works on the Harlem Renaissance. Garvey occasionally receives credit in these works for planting the political seeds of race consciousness and Pan-Africanism, both of which saw ample literary expression in the Renaissance. Almost never is it realized that he also had an important direct impact on the purely literary aspects of the Renaissance as well.

Yet, some of the leading figures of the period acknowledged Garvey's literary contribution, however grudgingly. Among these were the editors of the *Messenger* magazine, A. Philip Randolph and Chandler Owen. This socialist-oriented Black publication is often considered to have been one of the more important journalistic contributors to the Harlem Renaissance. Its editors, like much of Afro-America's integrationist establishment, led a virulent "Marcus Garvey Must Go" campaign in the early 1920s.[7] Yet, in the midst of this campaign in 1922, the *Messenger* could state that

> In spite of all this, Garvey has done much good work in putting into many Negroes a backbone where for years they have had only a wishbone. He has stimulated race pride. He has instilled a feeling into Negroes that they are as good as anybody else. He has criticized the hat-in-hand Negro leadership. He has inspired an interest in Negro traditions, Negro history, Negro literature, Negro art and culture. He has stressed the international aspect of the Negro problem.[8]

Charles S. Johnson, one of the most celebrated mentors of the Black authors and artists of the period and editor of *Opportunity* magazine, paid a similar, perhaps more hesitant, tribute to Garvey in Alain Locke's 1925 anthology, *The New Negro*. He saw Garvey as one who "merely had the clairvoyance to place himself at the head of" an "awakening black peasantry" and other segments of an Afro-American population who were tired of "a culture which has but partially (and again unevenly) digested the Negro masses—the black peasants least of all."[9]

But it was Claude McKay who came closest of the outstanding Renaissance figures to doing justice to Garvey's artistic contributions to the period. McKay carried on a love-hate relationship with the Garvey Movement for years. He wrote in 1940, the year of Garvey's death, that

> Garvey assembled an exhibition of Negro accomplishment in all the skilled crafts, and art work produced by exhibitors from all the Americas and Africa, which were revelations to Harlem of what the Negro people were capable of achieving.
>
> The vivid, albeit crude, paintings of the Black Christ and the Black Virgin of the African Orthodox Church[10] were startling omens of the Negro Renaissance movement of the nineteen twenties, which whipped up the appetite of literary and artistic America for a season. The flowering of Harlem's creative life came in the Garvey era. The anthology, THE NEW NEGRO, which oriented the debut of the Renaissance writers, was printed in 1925. If Marcus Garvey did not originate the phrase, New Negro, he at least made it popular.[11]

Even this assessment fell far short of adequately describing Garvey's contribution to the literary efflorescence of the 1920s. But it was as close as anybody came.

The artistic contribution of Garvey and the *Negro World* may have been even greater, had not the work of the UNIA been hindered from 1923 to 1927 by Garvey's trial, imprisonment and deportation. Yet some good was salvaged from these vicissitudes, for it was in prison that Garvey wrote much of his own poetry.

Garveyism and Literature

> . . . the UNIA is making a tremendous contribution to the education of the race. In every issue of the *Negro World* space is given to the aspirants of the race in the realm of literature and poetry. Of course, much of the prose they contribute is amateurish and lacking in etymology and syntax, crude in diction and utterly tawdry; and many of their sample verses are merely doggerels. But . . . if out of the hundreds that get a literary hearing in the columns of the Negro World just a dozen should make a lasting mark the effort would not have been in vain. . . .
>
> In the life of Marcus Garvey men have noted the fire of the prophet, the astuteness of the statesman, the conviction of the propagandist, the magnetism of the general, but few men have noted the erudition of the educator.[12]

The author of the above *Negro World* quotation was Arnold Hamilton Maloney, M.A., S.T.D., one time assistant chaplain general of the UNIA, a regular contributor to the paper's columns and a professor of psychology at Wilberforce University in Ohio. He accurately depicted the mass nature of the UNIA literary effort. No other publication of the time, neither *Opportunity,* nor the *Crisis,* nor anything else, came close to the *Negro World* for the sheer magnitude of its literary output. This was compounded by the fact that unlike the more vaunted literary journals of the period, the *Negro World* was a weekly, rather than a monthly publication.

Negro World literary activity peaked during the period 1920-1923, but remained a part of the paper until its demise in 1933. During the early 1920s, as many as dozens of poems, short stories, book reviews, articles of literary criticism and the like might be found in a single issue of the paper. The authors might range from major literary and intellectual figures, like William H. Ferris, Eric Walrond, Zora Neale Hurston, Arthur A. Schomburg, J. A. Rogers, Alain Locke, Hubert H. Harrison and John Edward Bruce, to unknown aspiring writers from Africa, Afro-America, Canada, Central America, the Caribbean and any of the myriad places where the UNIA was established and the paper was read. Though all submissions were not automatically accepted (their great volume made this impossible, anyway) the emphasis was clearly on fostering a mass interest in literature and the arts. And, as Maloney pointed out, one sure way of doing this was by providing a sympathetic forum for large numbers of would-be writers.

Maloney contrasted the policy of Marcus Garvey and the *Negro World* with that of W. E. B. DuBois and the *Crisis* magazine. He knew a young and aspiring short story writer, he said, whose literary efforts were much applauded in his home town. This young man desired wider recognition, and so he sent a sample of his work to "one of the great leaders of the race" (DuBois), in the hope that the leader would publish it in his magazine if it proved acceptable.

The leader's response was not only discouraging, but tactlessly and insensitively so. "This letter was like a wet blanket used to smother a fire," wrote Maloney, "it was like a frigid wave of wind congealing the blood. I read the letter and I sighed, and when I had become sufficiently composed to speak, I gave expression to this thought—"God, spare us from this type of leadership, if Thou really desirest that we shall go forward. . . ." What the race needed was the kind of leadership that Garvey provided, "leadership that has a keen and abiding interest in posterity and therefore, endeavors to bring to the fore the latent possibilities of the group."[13]

While many of the *Negro World* writers never achieved recognition outside of the UNIA, this was no necessary reflection on the standard of their writing, which was usually high. Many of the most regular contributors came to the paper with established reputations. Some (for example Eric D. Walrond and Zora Neale Hurston) found in the *Negro World* an important outlet for their apprentice writing and moved on from there to the bright lights of the Harlem Renaissance.

The UNIA and *Negro World* exhibited their literary interests in many other ways besides encouraging aspiring writers. A particularly striking manifestation of this interest lay in the large number of *Negro World* editorials devoted to literary subjects. The *Negro World* was the most highly political of newspapers. Yet it was simultaneously the most literary of newspapers. One is hard put to find another primarily politically oriented newspaper which devoted so much space, even on its editorial pages, to literary concerns. Perhaps it might be an appreciation of René Maran's prize winning novel, *Batouala;* or it might be an attack on the writings of T. S. Stribling, white author of the 1921 novel, *Birthright,* or a discussion of art and propaganda—such was the stuff that many a *Negro World* editorial was made of.

One 1923 editorial, **"Adina Revolts,"** actually took the form of a short story. The heroine, Adina, is a mulatto servant working for a white woman. Adina's sister is pregnant and asks permission for Adina to take nine days off from work immediately following the baby's birth. The mistress refuses, whereupon Adina overcomes her servile position and quits the job. Dignity prevails over economic necessity.[14]

Because the editors tended to be literary men, even their non-literary editorials and other articles were full of literary allusions and poetic quotations. Stylistically, their writing was of a consistently elegant quality. Even such a potentially routine topic as "A Look in Liberty Hall[15] Sunday Night," could not deter editor T. Thomas Fortune from a moving and eloquent composition. He noted on this occasion that the crowd was restless and kept peering towards the main entrance, even though the night's activities were in progress. He soon realized why. Garvey was not there—

Then I understood. We were having Hamlet with Hamlet left out, and the big audience was not satisfied.

The program dragged along in a humdrum way, with no enthusiasm, but with a wistful looking to the far entrance for the coming of the chief. What a tremendous thing it is to be able to inspire the love and admiration of millions of people, who are not satisfied when you are gone and overwhelm you with affection and attention when you are with them. Only a few men in history have been so blessed, marked men, who have changed the map of the world. . . .

And then, as if he had come right up out of the bottom of nowhere, Marcus Garvey appeared on the platform and faced the assembled host, clothed in the robes of his office, and the vast gathering broke into applause, which sounded like the rush of many waters.[16]

A witty and unusual 1924 editorial by associate editor Norton G. Thomas consisted of a delightful parody of a well-known passage from Shakespeare's *Julius Caesar.* Entitled "With Apologies to Shakespeare," it was in fact a reply to W. E. B. DuBois' notorious *Crisis* polemic characterizing Garvey as a "Lunatic or a Traitor." The editorial opened at "Act XCIX. Scene IX. Harlem Seventh Avenue"— Enter William Pickens, William DuBois and Weldon Johnson.[17]

DUBOIS: (Nervously)
Another general shout!
I do believe, that these applauses are
For some new Honors that are heaped on Garvey.
JOHNSON: Why, man, he doth bestride the world of Negroes
Like a Colossus; and we petty men
Walk under his huge legs, and peep about
To find ourselves dishonorable graves,
Men at some time are masters of their fates;
The fault, dear DuBois, is not in our stars,
But in ourselves, that we are underlings.
DuBois and Garvey: What should be in that Garvey?
Why should that name be sounded more than yours?
Write them together, yours is as fair a name;
Sound them, it doth become the mouth as well;
Weigh them, it is as heavy; conjure with them,
DuBois will start a spirit as soon as Garvey.
Now, in the names of all the Gods at once,
Upon what meat doth this our Garvey feed,
That he is grown so great?[18]

In late 1919 or early 1920 UNIA officials, including present and future *Negro World* editors, launched an apparently short-lived journal, the *Weekly Review.* McDonald McLean, its managing editor, was a staunch Garveyite and former editor of a Panama newspaper. Eric D. Walrond was one of the associate editors. He, too, had formerly worked in Panama, as a reporter for the *Star and Herald.* Among the contributing editors were William H. Ferris, Rev. J. W. H. Eason, UNIA chaplain general, and Professor B. C. Buck, UNIA secretary general.[19] In 1922 Garvey tried to launch a *Blackman* magazine which would have been devoted to literature as well as to political affairs.[20] It did not materialize, though he later published both a newspaper and a magazine bearing that same name. Had either of these efforts flourished it is likely that the Garvey Movement's contributions to the arts would have been better remembered. For historians and literary critics have hitherto tended to look at magazines (and mostly the "big name" ones at that), to the exclusion of the *Negro World,* in their quest for the reality of the Harlem Renaissance.

The *Negro World* also utilized the common device of giving away free books with subscriptions to the paper. Among the books so distributed were J. A. Rogers' *From Superman to Man,* René Maran's *Batouala* and South African Solomon Plaatje's *Native Life in South Africa.*[21]

Garvey's periodic International Conventions of the Negro Peoples of the World also interested themselves in literary and allied matters. These conventions were massive affairs. Between 1920 and 1924 they took place in Harlem and each lasted for the entire month of August. Delegates came from all over Garvey's far flung domain. The first, in 1920, is still unsurpassed in the history of Afro-American conventions. Some 25,000 people from all over the world filled New York's Madison Square Garden to overflowing for the opening celebration.

A *Negro World* editorial of April 1922 suggested that the forthcoming convention should consider commissioning a Black scholar to write a comprehensive history of Black literature. The editorial writer, possibly Ferris, felt that both Benjamin Brawley's *The Negro in Art and Literature* and James Weldon Johnson's *The Book of American Negro Poetry* were defective. Now, he thought, was "the psychological moment" for such a work, given the burgeoning interest in the subject.[22] This suggestion seems to have come to naught. The convention did, however, appoint a committee on the writing of Black history which suggested that the UNIA should itself reprint and distribute two nineteenth century classics—Robert Benjamin Lewis' *Light and Truth* and the Rev. Rufus L.

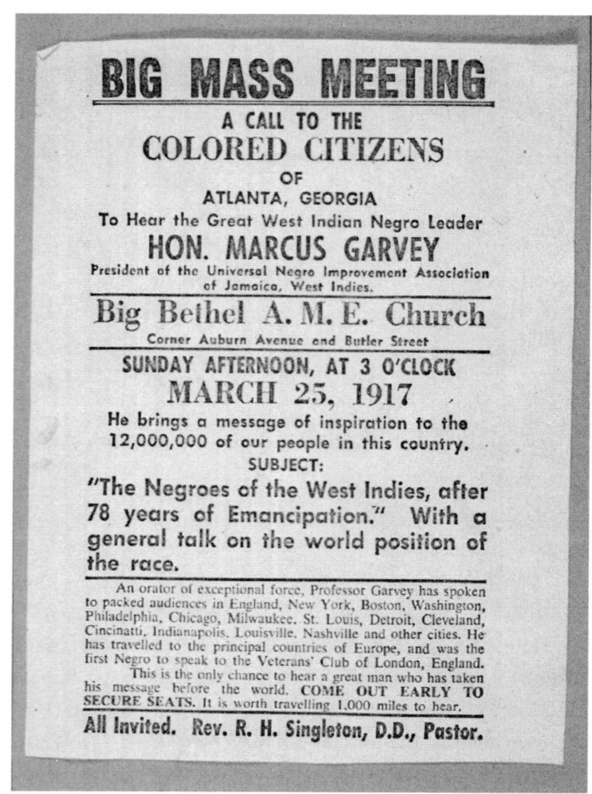

BIG MASS MEETING
A CALL TO THE
COLORED CITIZENS
OF
ATLANTA, GEORGIA
To Hear the Great West Indian Negro Leader
HON. MARCUS GARVEY
President of the Universal Negro Improvement Association of Jamaica, West Indies.
Big Bethel A. M. E. Church
Corner Auburn Avenue and Butler Street
SUNDAY AFTERNOON, AT 3 O'CLOCK
MARCH 25, 1917
He brings a message of inspiration to the 12,000,000 of our people in this country.
SUBJECT:
"The Negroes of the West Indies, after 78 years of Emancipation." With a general talk on the world position of the race.
An orator of exceptional force, Professor Garvey has spoken to packed audiences in England, New York, Boston, Washington, Philadelphia, Chicago, Milwaukee, St. Louis, Detroit, Cleveland, Cincinatti, Indianapolis, Louisville, Nashville and other cities. He has travelled to the principal countries of Europe, and was the first Negro to speak to the Veterans' Club of London, England.
This is the only chance to hear a great man who has taken his message before the world. COME OUT EARLY TO SECURE SEATS. It is worth travelling 1,000 miles to hear.
All Invited. Rev. R. H. Singleton, D.D., Pastor.

Handbill for a mass meeting lead by Marcus Garvey.

Perry's *The Cushite*. The committee also suggested approaching Daniel Murray, whose monumental *Murray's Historical and Biographical Encyclopedia of the Colored Race Throughout the World* still remained unpublished after years of effort.[23] They wanted to help him publish it. The UNIA Publishing House, significantly enough, had been established just about three months before the convention.[24] It published UNIA materials, including the two volume ***Philosophy and Opinions of Marcus Garvey.***

Women writers and artists were given special encouragement at these conventions. Women's Day at the 1921 convention featured exhibits on art, music, antiques, needle work and literature.[25]

Perhaps the most striking evidence of rank and file literary activity came from the existence of literary clubs in many UNIA branches around the world. Two of the *Negro World*'s most prolific poets, J. R. Ralph Casimir of Dominica, West Indies and Charles H. Este of Montreal, Canada, were leaders of their respective UNIA literary clubs. These clubs were following very much in the tradition, already noted, of Garvey's initial UNIA branch in Kingston, Jamaica. They arranged concerts and poetical readings, staged plays and held debates, often against non-UNIA literary clubs and debating societies.

Literary clubs and similar activity were reported also from UNIA branches in Boston, Portland (Oregon), Santiago (Cuba), Norfolk and Newport News (Virginia), Philadelphia and New York, among other places.[26]

The lack of recognition of the UNIA role in the era of the Harlem Renaissance is again made strange by the fact that the leading *Negro World* literary figures were very much a part of the wider Harlem literary community. Despite their often sharp ideological differences with the integrationist writers and the propaganda debate, there was a surprising amount of interaction among writers of differing persuasions. Perhaps this was inevitable for Harlem, after all, was not a geographically extensive area.

Furthermore, *Negro World* editors and columnists had sometimes belonged to the same organizations as non-UNIA writers in pre-Garvey days. William H. Ferris and John Edward Bruce had both been signatories to the call for W. E. B. DuBois' Niagara Movement back in 1905. DuBois in turn was a corresponding member of Bruce's Negro Society for Historical Research founded in Yonkers, New York in 1911.[27]

Robert T. Browne, a *Negro World* associate editor in the early 1920s and editor in 1933, had been president of the Negro Library Association of New York City, founded in October 1914. Its officers in 1917 included Bruce, Arthur A. Schomburg and Daniel Murray, together with A. Granville Dill, long time business manager of DuBois' *Crisis* and James Weldon Johnson of the NAACP. The Negro Library Association "aimed to collect books, acquire a library building, establish a professorship of Black history and literature, establish an endowment commission, set up libraries in several cities and publish books and a magazine."[28]

The American Negro Academy also provided a forum for the meeting of Garveyite and non-Garveyite intellectuals. It was founded by Alexander Crummell in 1897 to foster Black publications and generally raise the standard of Black intellectual activity. The academy was Afro-America's most select scholarly grouping. The presence within it of several Garveyites and Garvey sympathizers emphasizes the fallacy of the now hopefully discredited view of the UNIA as a movement lacking in intellectual substance.

In so far as it is possible to pinpoint any ideologically identifiable groupings within the American Negro Academy, the Garveyite bloc may well have been the most influential by the 1920s. It included Ferris, Bruce, A. H. Maloney and Robert T. Browne. Arthur A. Schomburg, president of the academy in the 1920s, was a frequent contributor to the *Negro World* and a supporter of Garvey against the DuBois/NAACP camp.[29]

Garveyites who did not belong to the academy also supplemented the work of Ferris, Bruce and company at its meetings. At the July 1920 meeting in New York Ferris read a paper on "The Negro in Prehistoric Times." Bruce read one entitled "Martin R. Delany, An Appreciation." Henrietta Vinton Davis, at various times international organizer and fourth assistant president general of the UNIA, also addressed the meeting.[30] For the academy's 1922 meeting in Washington, D.C., Dusé Mohamed Ali delivered a paper on "The Necessity for a Chair of Negro History in the Universities of the World."[31] This had also been a pet project of Schomburg, of Bruce's Negro Society for Historical Research (of which Schomburg was secretary) and of the Negro Library Association of New York City (of which, as has been seen, both Schomburg and Bruce were members).

Ali was the African who had employed Garvey on his *Africa Times and Orient Review* in 1913. Now he was working for Garvey, as foreign affairs specialist for the *Negro World.* An effort was made to have Garvey himself address the 1922 meeting, but this apparently did not come to pass, perhaps because of Garvey's arrest for mail fraud at about the same time that the meeting was slated to take place.[32]

At the other extreme, W. E. B. DuBois, an early president of the academy and fellow NAACP employees William Pickens and James Weldon Johnson were also members. DuBois and Pickens were leaders of the "Marcus Garvey Must Go" campaign.[33] Perhaps the ideological tensions between these camps may have contributed to the academy's demise in 1928.

The Garveyite artists were equally a part of the literary clubs, lecture series and gatherings of artists that characterized the Harlem of the 1920s. The 135th Street Harlem branch of the New York Public Library (now the Schomburg Center for Research in Black Culture) served as a focal point for much of this activity, through its "Book Lover's Club" and occasional lectures and exhibitions. The Garveyite intellectuals provided a large pool of speakers for the Book Lovers' regular meetings. Ferris addressed them in 1921 on "Negro Prose Writers." E. V. Plummer, a *Negro World* columnist, spoke in 1922 on "The New Negro Seeks Racial Unity." A month later, Hubert H. Harrison addressed the subject of "Books and How to Read Them." Harrison was followed, days later, by Robert W. Bagnall of the NAACP, a leader of the "Marcus Garvey Must Go" campaign and a man who, in 1923, described Garvey as "A Jamaican Negro of unmixed stock, fat and sleek with protruding jaws, and heavy jowls, small bright pig-like eyes and rather bulldog-like face. Boastful, egotistic, tyrannical, intolerant, cunning, shifty, smooth and suave, avaricious. . . ."[34] In 1924 Ulysses S. Poston, UNIA minister of industries and sometime associate editor of the *Negro World,* addressed the book lovers on "Nordic Culture and the Negro."[35]

In December 1922 Carl Van Doren, literary editor of *Century Magazine* and a Columbia University professor, spoke at the 135th Street library. A minor *Who's Who* of the Harlem literati turned out to hear him, among them Augustus Granville Dill of the *Crisis,* George W. Harris, editor of the *New York News* and poet Countee Cullen. A strong contingent of Garvey editors was there too, including T. Thomas Fortune (then editing Garvey's *Daily Negro Times*), William H. Ferris and Eric D. Walrond.[36] For the Garveyite editors it may have been an uncomfortable experience being in the same audience as Harris, who was yet another of the "Marcus Garvey Must Go" campaigners. But the cause of literature and scholarship continually brought the two camps together.

The 135th Street library also served as the venue in 1923 for a young writers' evening at which Countee Cullen, Gwendolyn Bennett, Langston Hughes, Sadie Peterson and Augusta Savage (whose Garveyite connections will be discussed later) all read their poems. Eric D. Walrond read a short story. Arthur A. Schomburg and 135th Street's white branch librarian, Ernestine Rose, were also present.[37]

This frequent Garveyite use of the library did not deter the *Negro World* from delivering a sharp editorial rebuke to Rose when she seemed to step out of line in 1922. The occasion was her article on "Books and the Color Line," published in *Survey* magazine. The *Negro World* explained what the problem was—"Miss Rose writes with the condescension of the Southerner. In speaking of the patrons of the 135th street branch of the library, the taxpayers who maintain it, she describes them as 'black and yellow, stately Hindoo, proud West Indian, mulatto American, little black pickaninny, turbanned mammy, porter, college professor, nurse maid, student.'" The editorial writer, in all his years as a frequenter of the library, had never seen a "little black pickaninny" or a "turbanned mammy" there. He wondered whether "in her desire to be poetical and picturesque" Miss Rose was not telling lies. Rose claimed, in defense, that she was in no way southern. "No doubt," she pleaded, "what you took to be condescension was merely a mistaken desire to be picturesque." Her explanation satisfied the paper.[38]

Negro World figures were also active in and around Harlem's Eclectic Club. Led by William Service Bell, whom Claude McKay described as "a cultivated artistic New England Negro," the Eclectic Club was a highly regarded artistic grouping, judging from the persons who addressed it. Eric D. Walrond and *Negro World* poet Lester Taylor were among its members. In January 1922 Dusé Mohamed Ali addressed the club at the Jackson School of Music at West 138th Street. His topic was "Modern Egypt."[39]

Claude McKay read selections from his then forthcoming *Harlem Shadows* for the club on April 8, 1922. Bell supplemented his reading with a talk on Black poetry. Those present included Arthur A. Schomburg, Zora Neale Hurston, J. A. Rogers and Sadie Peterson.[40] McKay recalled later that the club members turned up well dressed to hear him. He, however, did not own a dress suit and was apparently the only casually dressed person present. This did not go down well with those present, who thought that McKay had deliberately set out to offend them.[41]

There were, of course, several other salons, clubs and other venues which served as gathering places for Harlem's artistic figures. The UNIA hoped that its Phyllis [sic] Wheatley Hotel would become "one of the literary forums and social centers of Harlem."[42]

Eric Walrond has left a vivid description of one of these literary meeting places, a tea-shop ("The White Peacock") on 135th Street, near the UNIA headquarters. There, against a backdrop of "futurist paintings" and exotic furnishings, assembled nightly the "musicians and flappers, students and professional people, who sit until far into the night talking about love and death, sculpture and literature, socialism and psychoanalysis. . . . Harlem's Greenwich Village!"[43]

And just as visitors to Harlem flocked in their thousands to the UNIA offices in the hope of getting a glimpse of Garvey, so too literary visitors were attracted to the UNIA and *Negro World* offices. Fenton Johnson, who had published the unknown Garvey in 1917, was among the 1920 visitors.[44] In 1922 a white writer, Gertrude Sanborn, visited the *Negro World* editors. She had finished *Veiled Aristocrats,* a work on the light-skinned element, for publishers Boni and Liveright (later Walrond's publishers also.) Walrond, Ferris and J. A. Rogers took her to lunch at the Odds and Ends Tea Room at 145 W. 131st Street.[45]

If the *Negro World* editors could join their adversaries at library functions and take a white author to lunch, they could also be quite unselfish in their attitude to other literary efforts in general, and even to those of their adversaries. In 1920 the paper welcomed the new *Upreach Magazine,* published by Willis N. Huggins, M.A., a young Chicago scholar.[46] Huggins later became a leading Harlemite intellectual and a Garveyite.

Ferris even included DuBois in his 1922 listing of the "Twelve Greatest Negroes"—persons who had "made the deepest dent in Negro life and thought and in the life and thought of the world." The full list included Professor William S. Scarborough, Greek scholar; Dr. Francis I. Grimké, theologian; Hon. Archibald H. Grimké, author, diplomat and race leader; W. E. B. DuBois, author and founder of the Niagara Movement; Professor Kelly Miller, mathematician and sociologist; Henry O. Tanner, painter; William Monroe Trotter, agitator; Bishop Levi J. Coppin, biblical scholar and author; Dusé Mohamed Ali, editor of the *Africa and Orient Review* (a successor of the *Africa Times and Orient Review*); Robert T. Browne (of the *Negro World*), author of the *Mystery of Space;* and Marcus Garvey founder of the UNIA, "the greatest living organization."[47]

The *Negro World* was generally favorable to *Opportunity,* the contemporary magazine which, together with the *Crisis,* has received most treatment from historians and literary commentators.[48]

Despite occasional favorable references to DuBois, the paper was less apt to be kind, either to the *Crisis* editor or to his journal. Even here, though, criticisms of DuBois as literary figure were not nearly as harsh as criticisms of DuBois as political activist. In 1922, when the *Crisis* circulation had already begun to decline from its 1919-20 peak, a *Negro World* editorial, "The Passing of the Old Guard," contrasted Garvey and DuBois in terms unflattering to the latter—

> Through Marcus Garvey the Negro youth speaks out. Out on the hilltops his voice is heard. In DuBois, the leader of the old guard, is centered all the ripeness of old age, culture, skepticism, intellectual paralysis. Witness, as exhibit one, the

decadence of 'The Crisis,' once a palatable sheet, now a dry, dusty, old-fashioned vehicle of statistics, almost as senile as the 'Amsterdam News.'"[49]

Negro World editors on occasion accused DuBois of egotism, selfishness, duplicity and even plagiarism. Ferris in 1921 documented a devastating list of DuBois' tendencies to plagiarism. He had called William Monroe Trotter a fanatic, only later to produce imitations of Trotter's *Guardian* newspaper and National Equal Rights League; his short history of the Negro was nothing but an abridged version of a longer work by an author he had previously scoffed at; and he had responded discouragingly to Dusé Mohamed Ali's plans for a Pan-African magazine, only to plagiarize Ali's idea.[50] Historians Carter G. Woodson and Arthur A. Schomburg both made similar accusations against DuBois from the pages of the *Negro World*.[51]

Ferris also accused the NAACP generally of ignoring the "literary, psychic, musical and artistic achievement of men and women of color who are not in its fold. . . ." The occasion for this accusation was a 1922 NAACP press release on Black authors recently published in leading white magazines. They had ignored an Eric Walrond article in the *New Republic*.[52] Hubert H. Harrison similarly complained of having sent DuBois several hundred copies of Solomon Plaatje's *Native Life in South Africa* to no avail. DuBois refused to publicize the work.[53] Plaatje was a founder of the South African Native National Congress (later African National Congress) in 1912.

Practically all writers on the Harlem Renaissance have stressed the major role of the literary contests sponsored by the *Crisis* and *Opportunity* magazines for a few years beginning in the mid-1920s. James Weldon Johnson considered them a "decided impulse to the literary movement" of the period.[54] Yet in this as in so many other areas, the *Negro World* was earlier in the field—four years earlier.

The *Negro World* Christmas literary competition of 1921 was a grandiose affair. No less than thirty-six cash prizes were offered in several categories. These included poetry (Christmas-related) and essays and short stories on such topics as "How to Unite the West Indian and American Negroes;" "The Policy of the Hon. Marcus Garvey;" "The Negro Problem;" "Aims and Objects of the Universal Negro Improvement Association;" and "Africa Redeemed." Apart from the poetry section, the contest categories all reflected the close ties between art and struggle in the UNIA. The winning essays were clearly expected to help solve racial and organizational problems and reaffirm the goal of African redemption in addition to being technically meritorious. Yet the judges (Garvey, Ferris and Bruce) insisted on literary excellence and would not accept a favorable political perspective as a substitute, by itself, for good craftmanship. Garvey, judging the "Africa Redeemed" section, even declined to award a third prize because, he said, only two entries were well enough written to deserve prizes. He wrote—

> Among the many papers submitted, I have picked two (2) as being meritorious. The others are lacking in literary style and proper construction. The authors ought to be more careful in their writing, especially knowing that awards for prizes can only be given on the general merit of the papers submitted.[55]

Winning contest entries were all published in the *Negro World's* bumper Christmas number. One entrant, a Rev. C. Anthony Lindsay, won two prizes. The major find of the contest, however, if later success in the mainstream of the Harlem Renaissance can be used as a yardstick, was Eric D. Walrond. Walrond had immigrated to the United States by way of British Guiana, Barbados and Panama. His short story, "A Senator's Memoirs," received first prize from Garvey in the "Africa Redeemed" category. Always on the lookout for Black talent in any field, Garvey supplemented Walrond's cash prize of $100.00 with a job offer. Walrond became "assistant to the editor" and then associate editor. He remained with the paper until 1923.[56]

Walrond, as already noted, emerged in time as the only important *Negro World* voice against propaganda in art. Yet his prize-winning story on this occasion was a straightforward propaganda piece, built around the reminiscences of a Congolese senator in a future Republic of Africa. The senator mused over Africa's vast advance during a brief twenty years of freedom. A vast army, a Black Star Line shipping company, a prosperous economy—these were some of the achievements that the senator could look back upon. And all this had been accomplished in the face of dire predictions of doom from the skeptical and the malicious.[57] The story was well enough written and the message clear. Yet it was flat and structurally unexciting. His descriptions of Africans hovered at times on the brink of naïveté. Yet the effort was good enough to launch Walrond on a successful career as a short story writer.

Walrond later worked for *Opportunity* magazine, where the major financial backer for its initial literary contest was Casper Holstein. Holstein, a wealthy Harlemite (reputedly a numbers king), was in the early 1920s a frequent contributor of articles to the *Negro World* and a financial supporter of the Garvey Movement.[58] The *Negro World,* in turn, had actively supported his campaign against the United States occupation of his native Virgin Islands. So *Opportunity's* debt to the *Negro World* included not only the precedent of literary contests, but Eric Walrond and Casper Holstein as well. To this list may be added Zora Neale Hurston, whose *Negro World* connections will be discussed later.

The prize-winning essays, stories and poems did not exhaust the artistic fare presented in the *Negro World* Christmas number of 1921. Also featured were a large number of photographs of beautiful Black women from around the world. This, too, was propaganda in art. "Take Down White Pictures From Your Walls," a 1921 *Negro World* advertisement admonished, "Let Them Echo Your Racial Aspirations." This particular advertisement was for Garvey quotations artistically printed on wall cards. But the 1921 photos served at least one similar purpose—to provide an alternative to white pin-ups.

The Christmas beauties included Amy Jacques, soon to be the second Mrs. Garvey. Dr. John Wesley Cromwell, president emeritus of the American Negro Academy, was very impressed by the Christmas number in general and the Black and beautiful women in particular. The whole thing moved him to great feats of lyrical expression. He wrote, "*The Negro World* Christmas number is a delight for which to utter loud and long rejoicings, particularly for the illustrations depicting beauties of the feminine attractions of all varieties and sections of those 'who wear the shadowed livery of the burnished sun.'"[59]

There can be no doubt but that the UNIA, and more particularly the *Negro World,* was, in addition to all its other functions, a major stimulator of literary appreciation. William H. Ferris self-consciously addressed this fact in an editorial of 1922. He wrote—"While the Negro World is the organ of the Universal Negro Improvement Association and hence in some sense a propaganda paper, we endeavor also to make it a real newspaper and a literary forum."[60] Nowhere was it more successful than in its poetical work.

Notes

1. For exact location of branches see Tony Martin, *Race First: The Ideological and Organizational Struggles of Marcus Garvey and the Universal Negro Improvement Association* (Westport, Conn.: Greenwood Press, 1976), pp. 15, 16, 361-73.
2. R. N. Murray, ed., *J. J. Mills—His Own Account of His Life and Times* (Kingston: Collins and Sangster, 1969), pp. 108, 109.
3. Martin, *Race First,* pp. 91-100.
4. Tony Martin, *Amy Ashwood Garvey: Pan-Africanist, Feminist and Wife No. 1* (forthcoming).
5. Martin, *Race First,* pp. 6, 7, 280-83.
6. Alain Locke, *The New Negro* (New York: Atheneum, 1969, first published 1925), p. 49.
7. See Martin, *Race First,* pp. 314-33.
8. Quoted in *Negro World,* May 13, 1922.
9. Charles S. Johnson in Alain Locke, ed., *The New Negro* (New York: Atheneum, 1969, first published 1925), pp. 295-96.
10. The African Orthodox Church was closely connected with, though not officially a part of the UNIA. See Martin, *Race First,* pp. 71-3.
11. Claude McKay, *Harlem: Negro Metropolis* (New York: Dutton, 1940), p. 177.
12. *Negro World,* April 29, 1922.
13. Ibid. Maloney did not mention DuBois and Garvey by name, but his allusions to them were clear enough.
14. Ibid. April 7, 1923.
15. Liberty Hall was the name given to the meeting places of UNIA locals. Each branch had its Liberty Hall, whether owned or rented.
16. *Negro World,* January 19, 1924.
17. All three worked for the rival NAACP. The "Lunatic or Traitor" editorial is in the *Crisis,* May 1924, p. 8.
18. *Negro World,* May 10, 1924; Tony Martin, *Race First: The Ideological and Organizational Struggles of Marcus Garvey and the Universal Negro Improvement Association* (Westport, Conn.: Greenwood Press, 1976), pp. 302-04.
19. M. I. lc to Foreign Office on "Negro Agitation," January 7, 1920, FO 371/4567, Foreign Office files, Public Record Office, London.
20. *Negro World,* September 16, October 14, 1922.
21. Ibid, November 18, 1922, April 28, 1923.
22. Ibid, April 22, 1922.
23. On Murray see Tony Martin, "Race Men, Bibliophiles and Historians: The World of Robert M. Adger and The American Negro Historical Society of Philadelphia," in Wendy Ball and Tony Martin, *Rare Afro-Americana: A Reconstruction of the Adger Library* (Boston: G. K. Hall and Co., 1981), pp. 21-3; and Robert L. Harris, Jr., "Daniel Murray and *The Encyclopedia of the Colored Race,*" *Phylon,* XXXII, 3, Fall 1976, pp. 270-82.
24. *Negro World,* May 6, 1922.
25. Ibid, July 2, 1921.
26. Ibid, July 15, April 29, January 21, 1922; Martin, *Race First,* pp. 24, 25.
27. Martin, *Race First,* p. 285.

28. Martin, in Ball and Martin, *Rare Afro-Americana*, pp. 23, 24.

29. Tony Martin, *The Pan-African Connection* (Cambridge, Mass.: Schenkman Pub. Co., 1983), p. 106.

30. *Negro World*, July 17, 1920.

31. Ibid, January 14, 1922.

32. Garvey's invitation is discussed, somewhat unsatisfactorily, in Alfred A. Moss, Jr., *The American Negro Academy* (Baton Rouge: Louisiana State University Press, 1981), pp. 276-77. Moss is not fully aware of the extent of Garveyite involvement in the American Negro Academy, or of the depth of Schomburg's Garveyite connections.

33. Martin, *Race First*, pp. 273-333.

34. Ibid, p. 331.

35. *Negro World*, December 10, 1921, January 7 and February 11, 1922, June 17, 1924.

36. Ibid, December 22, 1922.

37. Ibid, March 31, 1923.

38. Ibid, April 22, May 22, 1922.

39. Ibid, January 14, 1922.

40. Ibid, April 15, 1922.

41. Claude McKay, *A Long Way From Home* (New York: Harcourt, Brace and World, 1970, first published 1937), pp. 114, 115.

42. *Negro World*, September 23, 1922.

43. Ibid, May 20, 1922.

44. Ibid, August 21, 1920.

45. Ibid, November 18, 1922.

46. Ibid, August 14, 1920.

47. Ibid, August 26, 1922.

48. Ibid, July 28, 1923, July 12, 1924. On the latter date the *Negro World* reprinted an *Opportunity* article.

49. Ibid, September 9, 1922.

50. Martin, *Race First*, pp. 291, 292. For plagiarisms in DuBois' *Black Reconstruction in America* see Tony Martin, "Did W. E. B. DuBois Plagiarize?" *Afro-Americans in New York Life and History*, VI, 2, January 1982, pp. 51-3.

51. Martin, *The Pan-African Connection*, p. 106.

52. *Negro World*, November 18, 1922.

53. Ibid, April 23, 1921. Plaatje sold many copies of this and other works to UNIA members throughout North America.

54. James Weldon Johnson, *Black Manhattan* (New York: Atheneum, 1968, first pub. 1930), p. 277.

55. *Negro World*, December 17, 1921.

56. A few Walrond editorials, signed simply "E. D. W." actually appeared in the *Negro World* before the contest.

57. *Negro World*, December 17, 1921.

58. Martin, *Race First*, pp. 99, 162.

59. *Negro World*, December 31, 1921.

60. Ibid, January 28, 1922.

ROBERT A. HILL (ESSAY DATE 1987)

SOURCE: Hill, Robert A. Introduction to *Marcus Garvey: Life and Lessons*, pp. xv-lxii. Berkeley: University of California Press, 1987.

In the following excerpt, Hill discusses Garvey's career as a popular hero and movement leader, and examines some of the classical and early modern influences on his philosophical and poetic writings.

What's in a name—to be precise, in the name Marcus Garvey? A century after his birth, what should we know about him and the extraordinary movement that bears his name?

The name Garvey has come to define both a discrete social phenomenon, organized under the banner of the Universal Negro Improvement Association (UNIA) and African Communities League (ACL), and an era of black renaissance, in which Garveyism and the concept of black racial pride became synonymous. Before white America fell enraptured before the spell of what Claude McKay termed "the hot syncopated fascination of Harlem" in the Jazz Age, black America had already traversed the age of Garvey and the New Negro.[1] Garveyism as an ideological movement began in black Harlem's thirty or so square blocks in the spring of 1918, and then burgeoned throughout the black world—nearly a thousand UNIA divisions were formed, and tens of thousands of members enrolled within the brief span of seven years. The reign of the Garvey movement, as Rev. Adam Clayton Powell, Sr., wrote, "awakened a race consciousness that made Harlem felt around the world."[2]

Popular Hero

Borne along on the tide of black popular culture, Garvey's memory has attained the status of a folk myth. While the 1987 centennial of Garvey's birth will be marked by formal ceremonies honoring his memory, on a more dynamic plane, Garvey is daily celebrated and re-created as a hero through the storytelling faculty of the black oral tradition.

As the embodiment of that oral tradition transmuted into musical performance, Jamaica's reggae music exhibits an amazing fixation with the memory of Garvey. Re-evoking spiritual exile and the historic experience of black dispossession, the music presents a Garvey who *speaks* from the past directly to the present:

Marcus say, Marcus say, red for the blood
that flowed like a river
Marcus say, Marcus say, green for the land,
Africa
Marcus say, Marcus say, yellow for the gold
that they stole
Marcus say, Marcus say, black for the people
they looted from . . .
—"Rally Round," Steel Pulse

In extending the legend of Garvey, the downtrodden have succeeded in rescuing his image from years of official neglect. In addition to carrying out this process of vindication, the music has succeeded in merging his name into an anthem of dispossession:

Marcus Garvey words come to pass
Marcus Garvey words come to pass
Can' get no food to eat
Can' get no money to spend
—"Marcus Garvey," Burning Spear

In the transfiguration of Garvey in popular memory, historical time has been replaced with mythical timelessness. "Garvey soul yet young / Older than Garvey / Younger than Garvey," lyrically muses Burning Spear, the Jamaican reggae songwriter and performer, venerating the ongoing importance of Garvey.

In the course of this musical apotheosis, the mythic Garvey becomes the black race's prophet, as we hear in the exhortation calling people to account:

Marcus Garvey prophesy say, Oh yeah
Man a' go find him back against the wall, yeah
It a' go bitter . . .
'Dis 'yah a' prophecy,
Hold 'dem, Marcus.
—"Right Time," Mighty Diamonds

If there is a moral in the music, it is that the memory of Garvey is a vital force—daily oral-musical performance has transformed the historic Garvey into a symbolic image that lives on in the popular imagination. Like the sacred African trickster-hero, who interprets the hidden to humans, the name Garvey serves to remind:

I'll never forget, no way
They sold Marcus Garvey for rice . . .
So don't you forget, no way
Who you are and where you stand
in the struggle
—"So Much Things to Say," Bob Marley

These lyrics are testimony to that fact that in the struggle for the ultimate regeneration of Africa, Garvey has continued to inspire succeeding generations. "While Mr. Garvey might not live to see his dream come true," prophesied one of his followers in 1924, "what he has said from the platform of Liberty Hall will be repeated in the years to come by unborn generations, and some day in the dark remote corners of Africa the Red, the Black and the Green will float."[3] This statement, with its figurative depiction of the liberation of Africa and the international influence of Garveyism in the struggle for its attainment, has proved to be an accurate prognosis of political transformation in Africa. "The question may start in America," Garvey had promised, speaking in Washington, D.C., "but [it] will not end there."[4]

The Man and the Movement

While Garvey's name has achieved legendary proportions, and his movement has had an ongoing international impact, Garvey as a mortal being was a man who embodied the contradictions of his age. He was seen by his own contemporaries in a plethora of ways, both positive and negative. "A little sawed-off and hammered down Black Man, with *determination* written all over his face, and an engaging smile that caught you and compelled you to listen to his story" was how the veteran black journalist John E. Bruce ("Bruce Grit") recalled his initial encounter with the young Jamaican in the spring of 1916. Encouraged by Booker T. Washington, Garvey had come to America hoping to gather support for a proposed school, to be built in Jamaica, patterned on the model of the famed Tuskegee Institute. By the time Garvey could get to the United States, however, Washington was dead. Garvey started with a nucleus of thirteen in a dingy Harlem lodge room. Within a few short years, he was catapulted to the front rank of black leadership, at the head of a social movement unprecedented in black history for its sheer size and scope. Writing in 1927, six months before Garvey was to be deported from America, Kelly Miller, the Afro-American educator and author, reflected upon the phenomenon:

> Marcus Garvey came to the U.S. less than ten years ago, unheralded, unfriended, without acquaintance, relationship, or means of livelihood. This Jamaican immigrant was thirty years old, partially educated, and 100 per cent black. He possessed neither comeliness of appearance nor attractive physical personality. Judged by external appraisement, there was nothing to distinguish him from thousands of West Indian blacks who flock to our seaport cities. And yet this ungainly youth by sheer indomitability of will projected a propaganda and commanded a following, within the brief space of a decade, which made the whole nation mark him and write his speeches in their books.[5]

In the world of the twenties, personalities quickly became notable and were fastened upon by admirers, detractors, and the merely curious.

But even by the standards of the day, Garvey's rise from obscurity was spectacular. Speaking to an audience at Colón, Panama, in 1921, Garvey himself noted that "two years ago in New York nobody paid any attention to us. When I used to speak, even the policeman on the beat never noticed me."[6]

Garvey voiced the marvelous nature of his own rise when he asked an audience in 1921 "how comes this New Negro? How comes this stunned awakening?"[7] The ground had been prepared for him by such outspoken voices as those of Hubert H. Harrison, A. Philip Randolph, Chandler Owen, and W. A. Domingo. These and other stepladder orators—who began speaking along Lenox Avenue with the arrival of warm weather in 1916 and whose number rapidly grew with each succeeding summer—were the persons who, along with Garvey, converted the black community of Harlem into a parliament of the people during the years of the Great War and after. The World War I era was the time of the rise of "the ebony sages," as William H. Ferris termed the New Negro intelligentsia, who laid the foundation in those years for what would eventually come to be known as the Harlem Renaissance. Garveyism was fed in an environment where "in barber shops and basements, tea shops and railroad flats," Ferris revealed, "art and education, literature and the race question were discussed with an abandon that was truly Bohemian."[8] By the middle of the decade, Ferris would go so far as to claim that "The New Negro is Garvey's own Child, whose mother is the UNIA."[9]

When the UNIA was organized in Harlem in February 1918, its Jamaican leader merged not only with representatives of the New Negro, but with another minority: from the perspective of America's polyglot of ethnic groups, Garvey was simply one more immigrant voice. The Garvey phenomenon began amidst the multiple migrations of America, and it was not unusual to find Garvey issuing pronouncements of confraternity with the causes of various immigrant groups.[10] "Just at that time," recalled Garvey, speaking in Liberty Hall in early 1920 about his start as a street orator in Harlem, "other races were engaged in seeing their cause through—the Jews through their Zionist movement and the Irish through their Irish movement—and I decided that, cost what it might, I would make this a favorable time to see the Negro's interest through."[11]

A notable feature of Garveyism as a political phenomenon was the staunch manner in which it accentuated the identity of interests among blacks all over the world. For Hodge Kirnon, this quality of internationalism essentially defined the New Negro mood. He observed:

> The Old Negro press was nationalistic to the extreme, even at times manifesting antipathy and scorn for foreign born Negroes. One widely circulated paper went as far as to cast sarcasm and slur upon the dress, dialect, etc., of the West Indian Negro, and even advised their migration and deportation back to their native lands—a people who are in every way law abiding, thrifty and industrious. The new publications have eliminated all of this narrow national sentimental stupidity. They have advanced above this. They have recognized the oneness of interests and the kindredship between all Negro peoples the world over.[12]

A special feature by Michael Gold in the 22 August 1920 Sunday supplement of the *New York World* reported upon Garvey's meteoric ascent, and registered as well his immigrant status and the international nature of his message. The headlines accompanying the story made the following announcement:

> The Moses of the Negro Race Has Come to New York
> and Heads a Universal Organization
> Already Numbering 2,000,000
> Which is About to Elect a High Potentate
> and Dreams of Reviving the Glories of Ancient Ethiopia

Gold captured a defining characteristic of the Garvey phenomenon, namely, its rapid spread throughout the world, including sub-Saharan and southern Africa. Writing from Johannesburg, South Africa, a number of years later, Enock Mazilinko echoed the messianic vision of Garvey held by many in America when he wrote that "after all is said and done, Africans have the same confidence in Marcus Garvey which the Israelites had in Moses."[13] "Marcus Garvey is now admitted as a great African leader" concurred James Stehazu, a Cape Town Garveyite; indeed, Garvey was the embodiment for tens of thousands of black South Africans in the postwar years of the myth of an Afro-American liberator.[14] "Already his name is legend, from Harlem to Zanzibar," allowed the venerable *Guardian* of Boston when it appraised the significance of his life in 1940.[15]

But not everyone shared this concept of Garvey. Detractors labeled him a madman or the greatest confidence man of the age. "We may seriously ask, is not Marcus Garvey a paranoiac?" enquired the NAACP's Robert Bagnall in his 1923 article "The Madness of Marcus Garvey."[16] An earlier psychological assessment by W. E. B. DuBois diagnosed Garvey as suffering from "very serious defects of temperament and training," and described him as "dictatorial, domineering, inordinately vain and very suspicious."[17] In the view of the organ of South Africa's African Political Organization, "the newly-created position of Provisional President of Africa [was] an empty honour which no man in the history of the world has ever held, and no sane man is likely to aspire after."[18]

It was mainly as an embarrassment to his race, however, that Garvey was dismissed. "The Garvey Movement," reported Kelly Miller in 1927, "seemed to be absurd, grotesque, and bizarre."[19] "If Gilbert and Sullivan were still collaborating," commented one African editorial writer, "what a splendid theme for a musical comic opera Garvey's pipe-dream would be."[20] W. E. B. DuBois echoed this opinion when he described UNIA pageantry as like a "dress-rehearsal of a new comic opera."[21] A West Indian resident in Panama, writing in the April 1920 issue of the *Crusader,* offered an ironic commentary on what he took to have been Garvey's assumption of the grand title of African potentate: "Pardon me," the gentleman interposed, "but this sounds like the story of 'The Count of Monte Cristo' or the 'dream of Labaudy,' or worse still, 'Carnival,' as obtains in the city of Panama, where annually they elect 'Her Gracious Majesty, Queen of the Carnival,' and other high officials."[22] White commentators were not excluded from this game of describing Garvey's conduct through the metaphor of entertainment. Borrowing from Eugene O'Neill's surrealistic play about the dramatic downfall of a self-styled black leader, Robert Morse Lovett referred to Garvey as "an Emperor Jones of Finance" to convey Garvey's financial ineptitude to highbrow readers of the *New Republic.*[23]

The wide variety of contemporary opinion about Garvey serves as a backdrop for his own eclectic descriptions of himself. He once announced that: "My garb is Scotch, my name is Irish, my blood is African, and my training is half American and half English, and I think that with that tradition I can take care of myself."[24] While Garvey told his audiences that his mind was "a complete machine," one "that thinks absolutely in the original," and, on another occasion, that his mind was "purely Negro," he also lamented that "the average Negro doesn't know much about the thought of the serious white man."[25] His own ideology encompassed these two contradictory conceptions. For him, the thought of the New Negro had to be a new thought, for it was incumbent upon the race to develop intellectual (as well as economic and political) independence as a precondition of survival in a world ruled by Darwinian ideas of the survival of the fittest. Nevertheless, the New Negro had to build this original thought on a strong foundation in the mainstream intellectual tradition, borrowing from that tradition while creating new racial imperatives. The present collection is a testimony to the diverse origins of Garvey's thought and to the ways in which he consciously embraced many of the dominant intellectual traditions of his age, reshaping them to the cause of pan-African regeneration.

The Era

Garvey's career spanned the years of the climax of the Victorian era of empire and its denouement in the period of revolution and counterrevolution. Born in 1887, just after Queen Victoria's Golden Jubilee, Garvey grew up as a black colonial during the Edwardian era. He arrived at political maturity in the era of the nationalist revolution in Ireland and the October Revolution in Russia. He died on 10 June 1940, the day that Fascist Italy declared war on the Allies and a month after Nazi Germany invaded France. He had predicted in 1937 that "the Negro's chance will come when the smoke from the fire and ashes of twentieth-century civilization has blown off."[26] His thought was of a piece with the dominant ideas of his tumultuous age, while at the same time offering a new response for blacks to the paradigm of white supremacy.

Life and Lessons

The present volume, ***Marcus Garvey: Life and Lessons,*** is a compendium of Garvey's eclectic philosophy. It is arranged in six sections. The first section, entitled **"African Fundamentalism,"** contains the 1925 creed by that name—Garvey's attempt at a modern race catechism. The second section contains his abstract vision of the ideal state. Garvey's little-known serialized autobiography supplies the third section, and the fourth features Garvey's epic poem, ***The Tragedy of White Injustice.*** A series of dramatic dialogues from the *Black Man* makes up the fifth section. The sixth, and final, section consists of the lessons in leadership from Garvey's School of African Philosophy. The whole—garnered from materials created in the last fifteen years of Garvey's life—constitutes vintage Garvey and makes possible an enriched understanding of the popular allegiance that his ideas inspired.

The Doctrine of Success

Garvey's strong belief in the success ethic, a theme that forms a constant thread throughout his speeches and writings, is reflective of the popular culture of his times. Speaking in Halifax, Nova Scotia, in 1937, Garvey summed up for his audience the principle that he claimed life had taught him. "At my age I have learnt no better lesson than that which I am going to impart to you to make a man what he ought to be—a success in life. There are two classes of men in the world, those who succeed and those who do not succeed."[27] Rejecting the class analysis being embraced by some of his black contemporaries, Garvey regularly illustrated his speeches with rags-to-riches stories, and offered examples from the fields of business and industry to his followers as models to emulate. In 1927 Joseph Lloyd, a Garveyite in Cuba, won a UNIA-sponsored "Why I am a Garveyite" contest with an essay on Garvey-inspired aspirations to become a black captain of industry or political leader. Garvey "has taught me," Lloyd wrote in the 6 January 1927 issue of the *Negro World,* "that I can be a Rockefeller, a Carnegie, a Henry Ford, a Lloyd George, or a Calvin Coolidge." Garvey himself had earlier asked readers of the *Negro World* in a 6 November 1926 editorial, "Why should not Africa give to the world its black Rockefeller, Carnegie, Schwab, and Henry Ford?" In the following year he spelled out the connection between such economic achievement and political power, informing his audience that

> there is no force like success, and that is why the individual makes all efforts to surround himself throughout life with the evidence of it. As of the individual, so should it be of the race and nation. The glittering success of Rockefeller makes him a power in the American nation; the success of Henry Ford suggests him as an object of universal respect, but no one knows and cares about the bum or hobo who is Rockefeller's or Ford's neighbor. So, also, is the world attracted by the glittering success of races and nations, and pays absolutely no attention to the bum or hobo race that lingers by the wayside.[28]

Garvey's gospel of success was distinguished from more traditional versions of the doctrine because he merged personal success with racial uplift and established a link between these twin ideals and an overarching vision of African regeneration. In Garvey's perspective, success of the individual should serve the ends of race, and vice versa. "There are people who would not think of their success," Garvey insisted, "but for the inspiration they receive from the UNIA."[29] Speaking in New York in 1924, Garvey claimed to have "already demonstrated our worth in helping others to climb the ladder of success."[30] Reciprocally, the UNIA relied for its own success on the organized support of individuals. "Help a Real Race Movement: The Way to Success Is Through Our Own Efforts" was the entreaty printed on the UNIA's contribution card in the early 1920s.

Garvey offered a doctrine of collective self-help and racial independence through competitive economic development. "As a race we want the higher success that is within humanity's grasp," Garvey was quoted in the 21 February 1931 "Garvey's Weekly Digest" column of the *Negro World:* "We must therefore reach out and get it. Don't expect others to pave the way for us towards it with a pathway of roses, go at what we want with a will and then we will be able to successfully out-do our rivals, because we will be expecting none to help us." Garvey also told his followers that the achievement of a higher class status among black people was the most direct route to obtaining opportunities and individual rights. "Be not deceived," he wrote, in the spirit of Andrew Carnegie, "wealth is strength, wealth is power, wealth is influence, wealth is justice, is liberty, is real human rights."[31]

This imperative of success was tied to what a 21 March 1922 *Negro World* article termed "a universal business consciousness" among blacks in all parts of the world. By featuring the slogan "Africa, the Land of Opportunity," emblazoned on a banner draped across a picture of the African continent, the official stationery of Garvey's Black Star Line graphically illustrated this philosophy of racial vindication and uplift through capital investment and development.

Self-Made Man

Garvey himself was frequently cited in the pages of the *Negro World* as a prime example of a self-made man, one of those "who worked their way to the top of the ladder by the long, steady climb."[32] Garvey's interest in conduct-of-life literature and the persistent echoes of it heard in his speeches and writings reflect the impact that such classic success treatises as Booker T. Washington's *Up from Slavery* and Andrew Carnegie's *Gospel of Wealth* made upon him. These works were in turn part of an older genre dating back to Emersonian treatises on self-reliance, slave narratives of personal endurance and triumph such as Frederick Douglass's *My Bondage and My Freedom,* and Benjamin Franklin's colonial guide to practical behavior and economic success. Garvey's racial ideal was built upon the concept of success, and he saw himself as a black version of the Horatio Alger myth.

New Thought

Garvey's pragmatic philosophy, with its emphasis on self-mastery, determination, and willpower, also contained elements of New Thought, which emerged during the Gilded Age out of the allied branches of the mental healing phenomenon. With its emphasis on mind mastery, New Thought offered a set of metaphysical theories that proffered to its millions of adherents a system of mental hygiene to equip them for the journey along the road to success. In 1920 Hodge Kirnon commented on the pervasiveness of ideas from the teachings of Christian Science and the New Thought movements in the black community. "The Negro has been seized by this spirit," Kirnon declared, "he has taken a real change of attitude and conduct. So great has been the change," he continued, "that he has designated himself under the name of The New Negro."[33] Another member of the New Negro phalanx, William Bridges, also alluded to the subsistence of a link between the "spirit of radicalism and new thought."[34] Garvey was assessed by one of his closest colleagues in the leadership of the UNIA, Robert L. Poston, as "the man who is truly the apostle of new thought among Negroes."[35] Indeed, what was deemed a new racial philosophy was in fact Garvey's wholesale application of the dynamics of New Thought to the black condition. "I have come to you in Jamaica," Garvey announced on his tour of the Caribbean in spring 1921, "to give new thoughts to the eight hundred thousand black people in this land."[36] Speaking before the UNIA's fourth international convention, he declared: "The Universal Negro Improvement Association is advancing a new theory and a new thought . . . ;" and in 1937 he stated that "to rise out of this racial chaos new thought must be injected into the race and it is this thought that the Universal Negro Improvement Association has been promulgating for more than twenty years."[37]

Metaphysics and politics were explicitly linked in Garvey's mind. Turning to New Thought to explain the "African vision of nationalism and imperialism," Garvey advised that "the African at home must gather a new thought. He must not only be satisfied to be a worker but he must primarily be a figure."[38] This New Thought philosophy permeated many UNIA functions and was a strong influence in the literature surrounding the movement. In 1930 the Black Cross Nurses of the Garvey Club of New York City held a medical demonstration at the facilities of the New York branch of the Field of New Thought on 94th Street.[39] The *Negro World* regularly advertised books that showed New Thought influences, including I. E. Guinn's *Twelve of the Leading Outlines of New Thought.*[40] Alonzo Potter Holly's popular book on blacks in sacred history, *God and the Negro,* was, according to Holly, inspired by Ella Wheeler Wilcox. Wilcox, whom Holly described as "an impassioned apostle of 'the New Thought,'" was in turn one of Garvey's favorite poets.[41]

Boosterism

Besides its affinity with the gospel of success and the New Thought movement, Garveyism shared the strong emphasis on boosterism that pervaded the popular culture of the Progressive period. On 28 April 1921 Garvey informed an audience in Colon, Panama, that he admired "the white man's spirit for he boosts for race and nation."[42] A few months earlier he had written that "no sensible person objects to any man boasting, booming, and advertising the work or cause that he represents. The old adage still applies: 'He who in this world would rise / Must fill his bills and advertise.'"[43] One of the *Negro World's* own advertisements read "If it is Success You Need in Business, Advertise in the Negro World"[44] and advertisements heralding various pathways to success and self-promotion regularly appeared in its pages under such titles as "Develop Your Power of Achievement," "How to Get Rich," "Key to Progress, Success, and How Attained," "Knowledge is Power: Make Your Life Yield its Greatest Good," and "Read This Book for Wealth and Health."

Victorian Sensibility

While Garvey's speeches and writings display the influence of popular success ideologies and a racial interpretation of international politics, they also reflect an adherence to a Victorian historical sensibility and literary taste. An admirer of the great and forceful men of history—statesmen, emperors, and conquerors (e.g., Alexander, Charlemagne, Hannibal, Napoleon, Genghis Khan)—Garvey called blacks to rise to a similar vision of political patriarchy and racial leadership. Likewise, while urging his readers and audiences to know and respect the works of black writers and artists, he consistently held up to blacks the work of minor and major white authors—Elbert Hubbard, William Ernest Henley, Robert Browning, Cervantes, Shakespeare—for inspiration and reference. By doing so, he upheld the tradition of schooling in "great works" common to the artisan class in the Victorian era. Indeed, Garvey's motto for the UNIA was quite likely a paraphrase of a line found in the poem of Alfred, Lord Tennyson, written for the occasion of Queen Victoria's opening of the Indian and Colonial Exhibition.

> Britain's myriad voices call,
> 'Sons, be welded each and all,
> Into one imperial whole,
> One with Britain, heart and soul!
> One life, one flag, one fleet, one Throne!'

In Garvey's hands, the triumphal exhortation of the final line is paraphrased in the well-known UNIA motto, "One God, One Aim, One Destiny." Likewise, the name given by Garvey to the general assembly hall of the UNIA in Harlem, Liberty Hall, which became the cradle of the movement, is reminiscent of Oliver Goldsmith's ever-popular *She Stoops to Conquer* (1773). In the second act of the play, the residence Liberty Hall is defined as a haven from the outer world, a place of freedom of thought and action—"pray be under no constraint in this house," Mr. Hardcastle assures his guests; "this is Liberty Hall, gentlemen. You may do just as you please here."

Vanity Fair

More deliberatively, Garvey's choice of the title for his epic poem, **"The White Man's Game, His Vanity Fair"** (later reprinted in pamphlet form under the title ***The Tragedy of White Injustice***) reflects a similar penchant for alluding to great works of English literature. But just as he endowed the gospel of success with new racial meanings, so he converted common literary allusion to his own purposes, making it a medium of a new racial politics. The incorporation of "Vanity Fair" in the poem's title alludes to the infamous marketplace by that name in John Bunyan's *Pilgrim's Progress* (1678). While William Makepeace Thackeray used the name of Bunyan's town as a metaphor for the decadence of bourgeois society in London in his 1848 novel *Vanity Fair,* Garvey employed the name of the town in his 1927 poem to encapsulate its theme of white oppression and decadence. Just as Bunyan's work is a kind of sacred picaresque in which evil is pitted against good, so Garvey's poem is a chronicle of the atrocities committed against native peoples by white colonizers. In Bunyan's allegory, Christian, the protagonist, and Faithful, his traveling companion, are waylaid on their journey toward the Celestial City at Vanity Fair, a market town ruled by Beelzebub. In this hellish town, the streets are named after Britain, France, Italy, Spain, and Germany. "Knaves and rogues" and "thefts, murders, adulteries, false swearers" are met with on these thoroughfares, and vanities bought and sold. The two travelers are taken prisoner, tortured, and ridiculed. Faithful is tried in a court presided over by Judge Hategood—with a jury made up of Mr. Blind-man, Mr. Malice, Mr. Cruelty, and others—and sentenced to death. He is whipped, stoned, and finally burned at the stake, whereupon his spiritual body is released from his ashes and carried up into the heavens by a horse-drawn chariot—a metaphor of deliverance popularly preserved in Negro spirituals.

In referring to Vanity Fair in ***The Tragedy of White Injustice,*** Garvey sought an analogy between the persecution experienced by Bunyan's travelers at the hands of the immoral townspeople and that experienced by Africans, Native Americans, and aboriginal Australians at the hands of Europeans during imperial expansion.

The Place Next to Hell

Bunyan's work was popular in the nineteenth century as a moral guide for children, and Garvey would undoubtedly have been familiar with it since his youth. Bunyan's 1678 classic was laden with social and political criticism, as was Garvey's own epic poem of the 1920s. Bunyan wrote *Pilgrim's Progress* while imprisoned for religious dissent in the county jail at Bedford, England, and gave it an autobiographical premise by having the dreamer who narrates the story sleeping in "the gaol." A vocal Nonconformist who opposed the teachings of the Church of England, he was arrested while preaching and served two six-year sentences, from 1660 to 1672, and another six-month sentence, in 1676 and 1677. Garvey wrote ***The Tragedy of White Injustice*** while imprisoned in Atlanta, where he was incarcerated in large measure for his militant racial stand, which diverged sharply from prevailing norms. In writing the poem, he translated, as Bunyan did, his excellent oratorical skills into written form and created a text intended to convert a popular audience to a new philosophy and new conduct.

Garvey's references to Bunyan's classic continued after his release from prison and his deportation to Jamaica in 1927. While campaigning for a seat in Jamaica's colonial legislature in October 1929, he was convicted of contempt of court for criticizing the judicial system on the island. He declared that many judges were influenced by bribes and suggested that some be impeached and imprisoned. The Jamaican Supreme Court did not look kindly upon such contumacy and sentenced him, as a result, to three months' imprisonment in the Spanish Town prison. The episode—a major setback in Garvey's efforts to establish a political career—contributed to his subsequent decision to make a permanent move to England in the mid-1930s. Garvey referred to Jamaica in this period as "the place next to hell."[45] In a *New Jamaican* editorial he created a Bunyanesque dialogue between two Jamaicans who referred to the country as a "Land of Agony and Tears," which was "small, small in size and small in character," and where people who spoke their minds would be imprisoned. In Bunyan's work, the City of Destruction, where Christian was born, is described as "a populous place, but possessed with a very ill conditioned, and idle sort of People." Just as Bunyan's Christian leaves the City of Destruction to its brimstone, so Garvey's two imaginary Jamaicans recommend that the only way to remedy the evils they had witnessed was "by leaving the place and make it perish by itself."[46] Garvey echoed these themes in a May 1934 speech in which he denounced the hypocrisy of the country and announced his intention to publish a book about his journey through life, called, significantly, *The Town Next to Hell.* He told his audience that he had experienced a vision of "a night in hell" in a dream and that what he had seen was an authentic reflection of life under colonial rule in the Depression.

Garvey's promise to write an allegory on the subject of Jamaica was to some extent fulfilled; in July 1934 a poem written by him and entitled **"A Night in Hell,"** was performed at a musical and poetic program at the Ward Theater in Kingston. Unfortunately, however, the text of the poem has not been preserved.

Poetry and Oral Tradition

Garvey's penchant for literary allusion and persuasion reflect his own belief that literature, particularly poetry, could be a powerful agent of personal uplift and a tool for teaching success. In the first [Illegible Text] of the School of African Philosophy course for prospective UNIA leaders, he told his students to "always select the best poets for your inspirational urge." Writing a review of a poetry reading for the *New Jamaican,* he reminded his readers that "many a man has gotten the inspiration of his career from Poetry."[47] He went on to describe the beneficial effects of poetry readings, stating that the listener "is able to enter into the spirit of the Poets who write the language of their souls," while the poets themselves, in creating poetry, are forced to contemplate their lives deeply, "and when they start to think poetic they may realize that after all life is not only an 'empty dream.'" In this perspective, poetry grants those receptive to it inspiration, and inspiration leads to ideation and action.

Garvey's writings and speeches also show the powerful legacy of his schooling in Victorian moral exhortation through elocution, as well as his genius in integrating the practice of declamation with West Indian and Afro-American traditions of verbal performance. In the dialogues created for the *Black Man* in the mid-1930s, Garvey adapted the Platonic form of didactic conversation between teacher and student, with its progression of statement, discussion, and debate, leading to the transfer and growth of knowledge. The dialogues also demonstrate his special sensitivity to communicating with an audience steeped in an oral tradition. By translating the written word into a script of two voices that was to be read as if it were spoken, Garvey created a kind of call-and-response conversational pattern designed both to uplift and to instruct. In any event, Garvey loved an argument.

Dialogues

Garvey's experimentation with the dialogue form occurred during the period of its revival following the publication of Goldsworthy Lowes Dickinson's *After Two Thousand Years: A Dialogue between Plato and a Modern Young Man* (1930). Dickinson had earlier received wide scholarly acclaim for his brilliant series of dialogues in the Socratic tradition, the most famous of which was *A Modern Symposium* (1905), a treatise that was in some ways a manual of modern politics. In 1931, while Garvey was visiting England, Dickinson broadcast a series of popular radio courses on the dialogues of Plato which were expanded for publication in *Plato and His Dialogues* (1931).

During the period of Dickinson's success, the prominent black journalist Joel A. Rogers also popularized the dialogue form as a medium for the discussion of the race question. His *From "Superman" to Man* (1919) contained debates on race issues presented under the guise of a series of conversations between the erudite Dixon, a black porter, and various passengers who traveled aboard his train, particularly a southern Senator with well-entrenched beliefs in white supremacy. What emerged was a scathing critique of the doctrine of white racial superiority. Rogers's work was widely read and acclaimed, both for its content and for what a reviewer for the *Boston Transcript* called its "fascinating style and convincing logic."[48]

Religious Influences

It might be said that Garvey's greatest achievement was his ability to change the consciousness of black people. Upon his return to New York following a month-long speaking tour of the Midwest in 1920, he likened his movement's impact upon popular consciousness to a religious conversion: "The masses of the race absorb the doctrines of the UNIA with the same eagerness with which the masses in the days of the supremacy of imperial Rome accepted Christianity. The people seem to regard the movement in the light of a new religion."[49] Garvey aimed to organize the instruction of black children according to the new "religion." He stated in a 27 June 1931 *Negro World* editorial that "the white race has a system, a method, a code of ethics laid down for the white child to go by, a philosophy, a set creed to guide its life," and that black children needed a similar code.

FROM THE AUTHOR

THE TRAGEDY OF WHITE INJUSTICE

Lying and stealing is the whiteman's
game;
For rights of God nor man he has no
shame
(A practice of his throughout the whole
world)
At all, great thunderbolts he has hurled;
He has stolen everywhere—land and sea;
A buccaneer and pirate he must be,
Killing all, as he roams from place to
place,
Leaving disease, mongrels—moral
disgrace

SOURCE: Marcus Garvey, opening stanza of *The Tragedy of White Injustice,* privately printed, 1927.

African Fundamentalism

"African Fundamentalism" was Garvey's quasi-religious manifesto of black racial pride and unity. It attained canonical status within a short time after it was first published as a front-page editorial in the *Negro World* of 6 June 1925. Written, like ***The Tragedy of White Injustice,*** while Garvey was confined in the Atlanta penitentiary, the essay proclaims ideological independence from white theories of history, makes concomitant claims of racial superiority, and articulates major themes that recur throughout Garvey's other writings and speeches. Chief among these are the ideas of racial self-confidence, self-development, and success; international black allegiance and solidarity; and the importance of acquiring a knowledge of ancient black history.

Garvey's use of the term *fundamentalism* in the title reflects this stress on the need for regaining a proud sense of selfhood by setting aside modern racist labels of inferiority and reviving the basic, fundamental beliefs in black aptitude and greatness that he saw exemplified in ancient African civilization. At the same time, the term resonated with Garvey's long-standing preoccupation with development of an original "Negro idealism." This notion was essentially grounded in religion. "I don't think that anyone who gets up to attack religion will get the sympathy of this house," Garvey declared in a speech in 1929, "for the Universal Negro Improvement Association is fundamentally a religious institution."[50]

"African Fundamentalism" was written at the peak of the fundamentalist revival that swept American following World War I. The revival was expressed both as a theological doctrine and as a conservative neopolitical movement. While the concerns of Christian fundamentalists focused on a sociocultural return to a set of principles untainted by modern rationalism and secularism, and while Populist fundamentalists called for the maintenance of an older agrarian order that would belie the impact of industrialization and urbanization—so Garvey's call heralded a recognition of the achievements of Africans in the past and a return to the principles of black dignity and self-rule, principles that had been denigrated under the impact of modern racial oppression, slavery, and imperial colonization.

As in his sardonic use of the phrase "Vanity Fair," Garvey's choice of the word *fundamentalism* reflects an intuitive understanding of the types of associations people would apply to his use of the term. He employs these associations in the context of the essay itself, wherein his references to monkeys, caves, and the process of evolution inevitably call to mind the opposing ideas of social Darwinism and the fundamentalist movement. The conflict between these two philosophies peaked symbolically in the Scopes trial, which got under way during the same summer **"African Fundamentalism"** was written. The trial, which was held in Dayton, Tennessee, in July 1925, pitted prominent attorneys William Jennings Bryan and Clarence Darrow against one another in a much-publicized courtroom battle. At issue was the acceptance of the theory of evolution and its place in the American school curriculum. Bryan argued for the creationist viewpoint (a fundamentalist perspective associated with the agrarian and southern sections of the United States and with the lower classes), while Darrow represented the modern, humanist viewpoint (a secular perspective associated with the urban and industrial areas of the North, with the growth of the social sciences, and with the educated middle classes). Bryan's side in the conflict prevailed, and teacher John T. Scopes was found guilty of breaking a law, passed by the Tennessee legislature in March 1925, prohibiting the teaching of any doctrine denying the divine creation of mankind as taught from a literal interpretation of the Bible.

In his essay, Garvey played on the social Darwinist issues that were publicly highlighted by the Scopes trial and gave them an ironic twist. He adopted elements of the evolutionary theory of the secularists and of the strong nativist strain of the fundamentalists and utilized them both as premises to support his own counterargument. He presented blacks in northern Africa as representatives of a higher form of life and culture than their white counterparts in Europe. He thus reversed the popular contemporary claims of white eugenicists, who applied evolutionary theory to the social milieu, associating people of African heritage with the slow development of the apes and offering their results as "proof" of white racial superiority.

Similar reversals of white-dictated beliefs and standards were reflected in Garvey's fervent praise for the compelling beauty of black skin and African features; in his championing of the worship of black images of the Virgin Mary, God, and Jesus Christ in the place of white conceptions of the deity; and in his call for a recognition of the heroic accomplishments of black people, such as Crispus Attucks and Sojourner Truth, whose martyrdom, selflessness, and rebelliousness qualified them for respect equal to that accorded white saints like Joan of Arc.

Classical Influences and the Ideal State

Much of Garvey's theory of education—with its emphasis on self-mastery and self-culture as precursors to good race leadership—can be traced to the classical model of education, where the training of the child is the basis of virtue, and virtue in turn is the necessary requirement of statesmanship. **"Governing the Ideal State,"** written by Garvey in Atlanta Federal Penitentiary in 1925, manifests the influence of classical philosophy on Garvey's thought and on his view of contemporary political events. The essay stands also as a propagandistic exercise in self-vindication in the wake of Garvey's recent conviction on fraud charges. It offers an indictment of the behavior of UNIA leaders and staff members whose misconduct Garvey felt had led to his imprisonment. It is also a scathing comment on the American political system at large and on the widespread corruption among government officials and leaders in the era of the Teapot Dome scandal.

Garvey enjoyed using classical allusions to convey to his audiences the concept of greatness and nobility. In his 1914 pamphlet ***A Talk with Afro-West Indians,*** he urged his readers to "arise, take on the toga of race pride, and throw off the brand of ignominy which has kept you back for so many centuries." Nearly two decades later he told readers that "the mind of Cicero" was not "purely Roman, neither were the minds of Socrates and Plato purely Greek." He went on to characterize these classical figures as members of an elite company of noble characters, "the Empire of whose minds extended around the world."[51] The title of his 1927 ***Poetic Meditations of Marcus Garvey*** parallels the title of the work of the "philosopher-emperor" of Rome, *The Meditations* of the Emperor Marcus Aurelius Antoninus (121-180). Like the work of Marcus Aurelius, Garvey's meditations included a fascination with the themes of conduct and the moral tenets of Stoicism and Platonism.

In fact, Garvey subsequently described his **"Governing the Ideal State"** as an abstract exercise to be likened to "Plato's *Republic* and *Utopia*."[52] And like Plato and the Greeks, Garvey shared a strong belief, though he applied it to Africa of antiquity, in the notion of historical decline from a golden age. Garvey believed civilizations were subject to an inevitable cyclical process of degeneration and regeneration. In one of his earliest essays, entitled **"The British West Indies in the Mirror of Civilization"** published in the October 1913 issue of the *African Times and Orient Review,* he held up the prospect of a future historical role for West Indian blacks in relation to Africa on the premise of this cyclical view. "I would point my critical friends to history and its lessons," he advised, then proceeded to draw what was to be one of his favorite historical parallels: "Would Caesar have believed that the country he was invading in 55 B.C. would be the seat of the greatest Empire of the World? Had it been suggested to him would he not have laughed at it as a huge joke? Yet it has come true."[53] The essay is important as an early example of the equation, in Garvey's mind, of history with empire building and decline.

In **"Governing the Ideal State,"** he announced the failure of modern systems of government and called for a return to the concept of the archaic state, ruled over by an "absolute authority," or what Aristotle termed an absolute kingship. The fact that Garvey was well versed in Aristotle is highlighted by his request to his wife, shortly after the beginning of his imprisonment, to send him a copy of A. E. Taylor's *Aristotle* (1919), a standard commentary. In his essay, Garvey rejected democracy in favor of a system of monarchy or oligarchy similar to the one presented in Aristotle's *Politics,* the rule of "one best man," along with an administrative aristocracy of virtuous citizens. As was the case in Aristotle's utopia—where those individuals with a disproportionate number of friends would be ostracized from society, while an individual demonstrating disproportionate virtue should be embraced and given supreme authority—in Garvey's ideal state the virtuous ruler would have no close associations other than with his family and, free from the corrupting influences that companionship might bring, would devote full attention to the responsibilities of state.

Plato's Laws

Garvey borrowed the concept that the key function of law is the maintenance of authority not only from Aristotle, but from Plato, whose *Republic* and *Laws* presented a vision of an ideal state in which virtuous behavior is encouraged through education, while conduct deemed corrupt is punished according to a harsh system of penalties. Plato's penal code was in turn partially derived from the Hammurabic code that preceded it. The crimes of embezzlement and treason to the state through political factionalization, which Garvey suggested should be punishable by death, were also crimes meriting capital punishment in Plato's ideal state (*Laws,* 9.856) (however, Garvey's call for stoning as the means of administering the death penalty is more likely derived from biblical descriptions than from Plato). Plato recommended that all public officials be subject to an audit and, should the audit reveal unjust self-aggrandizement, "be branded with public disgrace for their yielding to corruption" (*Laws,* 6.761-762). Similarly, Plato wrote that "the servants of the nation are to render their services without any taking of presents" and, if they should disobey, be convicted and "die without ceremony" (*Laws,* 12.955). If, however, leaders passed the state audit and were shown to have discharged their offices honorably, they should, as Garvey's virtuous leader would, be pronounced worthy of distinction and respect throughout the rest of their lives and be given an elaborate public funeral at their deaths (*Laws,* 12.946-947). Just as Garvey suggested that a child who identified a father's crime should be spared the penalty of death, so Plato suggested that children who "forsake their father's corrupt ways, shall have an honourable name and good report, as those that have done well and manfully in leaving evil for good" (*Laws,* 9.855).

Garvey's inclusion of kinship and property relations in consideration of the organization of his ideal state also mirrored the teachings of the Greek philosophers. He borrowed from Plato, who saw the state evolving from the family into a more communal relation and who granted free women some role in public life, in "universal education," and in the administration of the state. Garvey also borrowed from Aristotle, who, more than Plato, preserved the notion of the private household and the subordination of women as an integral part of his ideal state. Garvey centered the private life of his ideal ruler in a nuclear family and made the wife of the ruler a kind of chamberlain accountable for her husband's financial dealings. Both Aristotle and Plato based their ideal states on monogamous marriage and patriarchy, in which the household of a citizen was compared to the larger hierarchy of the state, with a wife subject to her husband as a subject is subordinate to a ruler. Garvey echoed this model in his essay, wherein the wives of leaders are deemed "responsible for their domestic households," regulated by law in the keeping of their husband's private and public accounts, and subject to capital punishment along with their husbands for financial crimes committed during their husbands' tenure in office. Garvey's recommendation that both the wife and husband should be disgraced and put to death in cases of corruption in office mirrors not only the family relations of the Greek state but archaic Mesopotamian codes governing debt slavery, in which the wives or children of a male debtor could be enslaved or put to death in payment for his financial failures.

Notes

1. Claude McKay, *A Long Way from Home* (1937; reprint New York: Lee Furman, 1970), p. 150.
2. Adam Clayton Powell, Sr., *Against the Tide: An Autobiography* (New York: Richard R. Smith, 1938), p. 71.

3. *Negro World* (hereafter *NW*), 23 November 1924.

4. *NW*, 26 January 1924.

5. Kelly Miller, "After Marcus Garvey—What?" *Contemporary Review* 131 (April 1927):492.

6. *NW*, 30 July 1921.

7. *NW*, 18 June 1921.

8. William H. Ferris, "The Negro Intellectual," *NW*, 10 June 1922.

9. *Spokesman* 1, no. 4 (March 1925): 4.

10. *New York Globe and Advertiser*, 3 August 1920.

11. *NW*, 6 March 1920.

12. Hodge Kirnon, "The New Negro and His Will to Manhood and Achievement," *Promoter*, 1 (August 1920): 7.

13. *NW*, 9 February 1929.

14. *NW*, 16 July 1932.

15. *Boston Guardian*, 18 May 1940.

16. Robert Bagnall, "The Madness of Marcus Garvey," *Messenger* 5 (March 1923): 638.

17. W. E. B. DuBois, "Marcus Garvey," *Crisis* 11 (December 1920): 58-60.

18. *NW*, 28 January 1922 (The African Political Organization was later renamed the African People's Organization).

19. Kelly Miller, "After Marcus Garvey—What?" *Spokesman*, May 1927, p. 11.

20. *Nigerian Pioneer*, 17 December 1920.

21. W. E. B. DuBois, "Back to Africa," *Century Magazine* 105, no. 4 (February 1923): 539.

22. Letter to the Editor, *Crusader*, April 1920, p. 28.

23. Robert Morse Lovett, "An Emperor Jones of Finance," *New Republic*, 11 July 1923.

24. *Daily Gleaner*, 19 January 1935.

25. *Black Man* (London) (hereafter *BM*) 3 (November 1938): 13; 4 (February 1939): 12; 3 (March 1938): 3.

26. *BM* 2 (December 1937): 3.

27. *BM* 3 (March 1938): 8.

28. *NW*, 29 January 1927.

29. *BM* 3 (July 1938): 8.

30. *NW*, 14 June 1924.

31. *BM* 1 (July 1935): 5.

32. *NW*, 23 August 1924.

33. "The New Negro and His Will to Manhood and Achievement," *Promoter* 1 (August 1920): 4.

34. *Challenge* 2, no. 5 (1919): 140.

35. *NW*, 8 September 1923.

36. *Daily Gleaner*, 4 April 1921.

37. *NW*, 9 August 1924; *BM* 2 (August 1937): 3.

38. *BM* 3 (July 1938): 5.

39. *NW*, 4 October 1930.

40. *NW*, 27 September 1930.

41. Alonzo Potter Holly, *God and the Negro* (Nashville: National Baptist Publishing Board, 1937), p. 14.

42. National Archives, RG 165, file 10218-418-18.

43. *NW*, 5 February 1921.

44. *NW*, 7 February 1925.

45. *New Jamaican*, 8 April 1933.

46. *New Jamaican*, 4 September 1933.

47. *New Jamaican*, 26 January 1933.

48. Joel A. Rogers, *From "Superman" to Man* 5th ed., 1968; reprint, Helga M. Rogers, 1982.

49. *NW*, 16 October 1920.

50. *Blackman* (Kingston), 31 August 1929.

51. "An Apostrophe to Miss Nancy Cunard," handbill, 28 July 1932.

52. *Daily Gleaner*, 21 January 1933.

53. Marcus Garvey, "The British West Indies in the Mirror of Civilization," *African Times and Orient Review* (October 1913): 160.

BERYL SATTER (ESSAY DATE 1996)

SOURCE: Satter, Beryl. "Marcus Garvey, Father Divine, and the Gender Politics of Race Difference and Race Neutrality." *American Quarterly* 48, no. 1 (March 1996): 43-76.

In the following essay, Satter examines the intersection of racial and gender politics in Garveyism and in the Peace Mission movement and finds that despite their differences, both Garvey and Father Divine advocated strict male control over women's bodies and sexuality.

C. D. Austin's 1936 letter to Marcus Garvey was not the adoring missive Garvey might have expected. After briefly recounting his years of committed support for Garvey and the Universal Negro Improvement Association (UNIA), Austin came to his main point: that Father Divine was God and that Garvey would do well to recognize this fact. "'Garveyism' was the highest grace this so-called race had. . . . But to-day a greater than Garvey is here. [Y]ou were regarded as the world's most fearless leader in this present civilization before the coming of FATHER DIVINE. . . . Please try HIM out as 23,000,000 of us did, you need HIM as all the World does," Austin exhorted.

Garvey was not about to turn to Father Divine as his personal savior. Instead, Garvey pushed through a lengthy resolution at the UNIA's 1936 convention that condemned Father Divine in no uncertain terms. Father Divine's claim to be God was "blasphemy of the worst kind." Divine was a common swindler and under the control of scheming whites. Most seriously, Garvey accused Divine of "race suicide." According to the UNIA resolution, Divinites "separate themselves sexually from the bond of matrimony" and cease to "reproduce the species of the race by having children." Such a policy, the resolution declared, would lead to the "complete extermination of the Negro race in the United States in one generation. . . ."[1]

Garvey was right to focus on race suicide in this resolution, since the valuation of racial identity was one of the key differences that separated Garvey's movement from Divine's. Marcus Garvey was the Jamaican-born head of the UNIA, an organization that reached its peak of strength in the early 1920s and whose organizing principle could be summarized in the slogan "Race First." A faith in the importance of racial solidarity underlay the three goals of Garvey's UNIA: to arouse a unified race consciousness in all peoples of African descent, whether living in the United States, the West Indies, or Africa; to strengthen this united black race by organizing black-owned and managed, large-scale business enterprises and shipping lines; and finally, to create a black-governed nation in Africa that would host the creation of a renewed black civilization and stand up for the rights of black people everywhere.[2]

Father Divine, born George Baker, was an African American of obscure origin who founded the most notorious new religion of Depression-era America—the Harlem-based Peace Mission movement. If Garvey's UNIA was premised on "Race First" and faith in national destiny, then Divine's Peace Mission was premised on a belief in race neutrality and faith in Father Divine as God. Father Divine was most well-known for his ability, during the height of the Great Depression, to feed thousands daily at his free, fifty-course Peace Mission banquets. The Peace Mission program was more clearly enacted, however, in the scores of racially integrated, sexually segregated, and celibate communes formed by Divinites in the 1930s. Within these communes, which Peace Mission members called "heavens," Divinites refused to recognize race, arguably the key social division of modern America. In a dramatic reversal of the racial segregation characteristic of the larger society, black and white Divinites worked and lived together in heavens, took care to mix the seating at Divinite banquets so as to alternate black and white diners, and refused to acknowledge verbally the existence of racial difference.[3]

Why was Marcus Garvey so enraged over Divine's success, and what role did the two men's contrasting views of race and sexuality play in this feud? When discussing the tension between Garvey and Divine, scholars of the UNIA and the Peace Mission point to the fact that large numbers of Garveyites were among the thousands[4] joining Divine's Peace Mission. Historians explain this crossover membership, and Garvey's extreme reaction to it, in terms of broad similarities between the UNIA and the Peace Mission. Both movements centered around a charismatic leader, provided concrete benefits to their members, promoted economic enterprise, and encouraged political action. Although Garvey denounced as blasphemy Divine's claims to be God, Garvey's own self-presentation as a "Black Moses" and his suggestion that blacks think of God as dark skinned may have eased the way for some black Americans to accept Father Divine as God. Finally, Garvey and Divine's shared interest in New Thought, a popular early twentieth-century religious ideology that claimed one's thoughts could literally create one's material reality, may also have facilitated the transition for those who shifted allegiances from Garvey to Divine in the mid-1930s.[5]

I would argue, however, that one cannot fully understand either the internal trajectories of the two movements or the relationships between them unless the gender politics of the two organizations are carefully examined. The need for a gender analysis is clearly suggested by the specific histories, constituencies and ideologies of the Peace Mission and the UNIA. For example, according to both contemporary and scholarly accounts, anywhere from 75 to 90 percent of Divine's followers were African American women.[6] This predominance of women suggests that the Peace Mission should be analyzed as a black women's movement and its gender politics given particular attention. In contrast, although some women held high-ranking positions, Garvey's UNIA appears to have been a predominantly male organization. Yet the very intensity of the UNIA's masculinist cast—represented in everything from its official hierarchy, which placed UNIA women's organizations under the command of male presidents, to UNIA ritual, in which black men marched in constumes of warriors, judges, and kings—suggests that a particular gender vision was at the heart of UNIA politics.[7]

In the following pages I therefore examine the gender politics of the UNIA and the Peace Mission movement. I focus particularly on the connections between the racial ideologies of the UNIA and the Peace Mission, on the one hand, and the gender ideologies, gender organizations, and experience of women within the two movements, on the other. I argue that the opposing gender politics of the two movements can help illuminate the crossover in membership between the UNIA and the Peace Mission and, more importantly, can contribute to an understanding of the relationship between racial ideologies and the choices historically available to African American women.

Scholars of Marcus Garvey and Father Divine have not analyzed the relationship between these men's racial ideologies and the roles available to their female followers. Some scholarship has explored the history of women in the two movements and (to a lesser extent) the gender politics of the two movements. While Garvey scholars agree that UNIA publications promoted public roles for men and private roles for women, more recent scholarship has added complexity to the image of a sexist UNIA. Barbara Bair points out that the UNIA's calls for active, public roles for men and passive, private roles for women overturned white images of black men as feminine and black women as masculine and challenged the white double standard, which held that white women should be sheltered in the home while black women worked. Ula Taylor suggests that the UNIA emphasis on black women as men's helpmates did not imply that black women could not also be leaders. On the contrary, she argues that black women, who have historically viewed white racism rather than black men as their oppressor, have a long tradition of both supporting their husbands (and families) and assuming community leadership roles. Finally, UNIA scholars agree that despite the official paeans to black women as wives and mothers, the UNIA in fact offered women a wide variety of participatory roles and was one of the few organizations offering leadership positions to black women in the 1920s.[8]

Unlike Garvey's UNIA, Father Divine's Peace Mission movement was a predominantly female organization. However, no scholar of the Peace Mission has considered the overwhelming numerical predominance of black women in the movement as a sign that the Peace Mission should be analyzed primarily as a black women's movement. Instead, many Peace Mission scholars have noted women's participation in the movement only to emphasize women's fanaticism, ignorance, or sensual longings for Father Divine.[9] Jill Watts, author of the most recent book on Father Divine, is one of the few scholars to discuss Divine's female followers without reducing their interest in Divine to sexual or psychological aberrations. Watts argues that the communal and celibate Peace Mission lifestyle freed women from isolated housekeeping, traditional gender roles, and the dangers of childbearing. Watts also interprets Divine's protectiveness toward his women followers (for example, his calling up a storm to punish a man who put his wife in a mental hospital) and his self-description as both mother and father to his flock as symbolic support for "women's rights."[10]

In sum, scholarship on the UNIA and the Peace Mission shows the appeal as well as the drawbacks these organizations held for their women members. This essay focuses more specifically on the connections between the racial ideologies of the two movements and the positions of women within them. By contrasting the gender politics of Garvey's Race First UNIA with those of the Peace Mission, a predominantly black movement that explicitly denied racial difference, this essay highlights the ways that ideologies of race shape the forms of activism available to women. More specifically, it addresses the following questions about the UNIA and the Peace Mission movement. What was the relationship between Garvey's Race First philosophy and the place of black women within the UNIA? Did the drastic situation faced by African Americans during the Great Depression threaten Garvey's vision of black womanhood? Why might some African American women have rejected the role of UNIA race mother for that of celibate, race-neutral Peace Mission angel? Was joining the Peace Mission simply a desperate and culturally suicidal abandonment of black racial identity, black culture, and black men? Or might the Peace Mission ideology of race and gender transcendence have enabled the creation of a new form of African American political culture, expressing the hopes of the most marginalized members of depression-era Harlem? What can the UNIA and the Peace Mission tell us about the relationship between ideas of race purity or race neutrality, on the one hand, and polarized gender oppositions, nationalism, and cultural identity, on the other?

Race and Gender in Garvey's UNIA

The contrasting gender politics of the Peace Mission and the UNIA derived most directly from their leaders' opposed understandings of the roles of black race purity and race pride in the struggle against white racism. As early as 1921, Marcus Garvey became committed to race purity as the factor distinguishing the UNIA from other black organizations. His insistence upon the importance of race purity led him to praise the race purity ideals of the Ku Klux Klan, to attack his African American opponents as "nearly all Octoroons or Quadroons," and even to suggest that lighter-skinned blacks be consciously bred out of the racial pool.[11]

As a number of scholars have observed, ideologies of race purity have, historically, led to male control of women's bodies. Southern white race purity codes, for example, entailed a double form of male control of women's bodies; relying on a gender ideology that depicted white women as pure and black women as animalistic, white race purity ideas justified both the sequestering of white women and white men's sexual terrorism against black women.[12] A race purity ideal functioned differently for the UNIA—an organization that expressed the hopes of a people struggling for dignity and self-determination—than it did for ruling whites, who used an ideology of race purity to ensure the continuation of their economic and political dominance. Garvey's brand of race purity contained none of the threats to white women that white race purity held for black women. His lauding of the beauty of dark skin was a necessary and even revolutionary counter to centuries of white maligning of the physical appearance of African Americans. In this context, Garvey's call for race unity among the dispersed peoples of African descent was a bold and politically astute effort to unite the dispossessed in a struggle for independence, as well as a courageous attempt to politicize and internationalize the awakening of black race consciousness characteristic of the 1920s.[13]

Garvey's emphasis on race consciousness and race purity inevitably molded the UNIA's proscriptions about gender. For example, race purity advocates generally value women primarily as mothers of the race. UNIA leaders clearly voiced this perspective. As one Garveyite official wrote, if "you find any woman—especially a black woman—who does not want to be a mother, you may rest assured she is not a true woman."[14] To ensure that women's offspring were of the proper race, black women needed to be maintained in the same sort of protective isolation that white men apparently secured for their women. As another UNIA official explained, black men must

> throw our protecting arms around our women . . . let us go back to the days of true manhood when women truly reverenced us . . . let us again place our women upon the pedestal from which they have been forced. . . .[15]

The UNIA was thus committed not to promoting the dignity and power of black women in general but to protecting black women from racial defilement and regaining black women's reverence and respect for the black man. Many black women supported such a policy of chivalrous protection as a welcome alternative to their position as exploited workers who were vulnerable to sexual harassment by white employers.[16] This does not, however, negate the fact that so-called protection of women by men involves control as well as benevolence.

The cultural meaning of motherhood in African American communities often had a different resonance than it did for white middle-class Americans, and it is important to note that a lauding of motherhood does not necessarily connote a limitation of women's personal autonomy or political power. Although black mothers, like white mothers, have long shouldered the primary responsibility for child raising, among African Americans this has less often meant intensive and isolated child rearing and more often meant women's willingness to engage in extradomestic, income-producing activities in order to fund their children's educations. This broader, more public and political understanding of African American motherhood is reflected in the tradition of "community mothers"—often elderly women who function as "role models, power brokers, and venerable elders" in black communities—who are respected less for the quality of their private mothering than for their activist role in holding together the broader community.[17]

In some ways, the UNIA Race Mother ideal seemed to draw upon the African American community motherhood tradition. The UNIA had a woman's page entitled "Our Women and What They Think," which was intended to give women a voice in the otherwise male-dominated journal of the U.N.I.A, *Negro World.* Edited by Garvey's wife, Amy Jacques Garvey, some "Our Women" articles asserted that black women's responsibilities were "not limited" to homemaking and childcare, but included "tackling the problems that confront the race," including working with men "in the office as well as on the platform." These articles clearly implied a vision of motherhood that entailed community activism as well as private domesticity.[18]

In many respects, however, the UNIA race mother diverged significantly from the community mother concept. While the community mother depended for her effectiveness on a base of autonomous black women's organizations, political organizations for UNIA women were not autonomous. Although each of the local UNIA divisions had both a man and a woman president, the "lady president" had authority over the women's section, while the male president had authority over the local division as a whole. In addition, a hierarchical sexual division of labor existed within the UNIA; men ran the UNIA businesses and represented the movement as statesmen and diplomats, while women provided clerical, cultural and civic support services. This system discouraged the sort of informal but powerful leadership exerted by community mothers.[19] Finally, it is clear that the term *motherhood* had a far more biological meaning for Garveyites than *community motherhood* had traditionally connoted in African American communities. (After all, the community-leading "mother" was often an elderly woman.) UNIA ideology implied that marriage and child-care held a special significance for Garveyite women. According to *Negro World* articles, while Garveyite men were to uplift the race through aggressive engagement in business and commerce, Garveyite women were literally to produce a "better and stronger race" through the quality of their childcare. *Negro World* columnists repeatedly heralded this more biological form of race-building as "the greatest privilege that can come to any woman in this age, and to the Negro woman in particular."[20]

The UNIA glorified black men as soldiers, leaders, and rulers. As Barbara Bair points out, Garvey's ritual and verbal imagery consistently invoked visions of black men as kings, emperors, and popes. Garvey called himself the Provisional President of Africa, conferred orders such as the Knight Commander of the Nile on his most devoted followers, and created a special militia, the African Legion, whose full-dress military uniforms drew large audiences at UNIA parades. The Black Cross Nurses, a UNIA women's organization that provided health counseling and services to their communities, were also a regular feature of UNIA parades, and a group of women in military uniform marched in at least one UNIA parade. This female participation does not lessen the fact that the most dramatic spectacle at UNIA parades was the uniformed male Garveyites.[21] The UNIA's identification of black men as the epitome of black humanity became even more emphatic during the Depression; in 1934 a journal entitled *Black Man* succeeded the UNIA's journal *Negro World.*

The implications of the UNIA's emphasis on martial and leadership roles for men and race motherhood roles for women were mixed for Garveyite women. On the one hand, a few prominent women achieved positions of great responsibility and influence within the UNIA despite the movement's official sanctioning of public roles for men and private roles for women. Furthermore, numerous lesser-known women learned important organizational skills by actively participating behind the scenes.[22] On the other hand, Garveyite women who tried to follow the New Negro Woman model of both creating a perfect home life and actively serving the UNIA inevitably found themselves exhausted by the multiple demands on their lives.

Amy Jacques Garvey epitomized their situation. Garvey expected her to be the perfect wife, while also serving as his secretary, legal adviser, fund-raiser, editor, and fulltime propagandist. Jacques Garvey fulfilled these multiple roles until the birth of her two children in 1930 and 1933. Their births occurred during a period when Garvey was travelling frequently, desperately strapped for money, and entirely preoccupied with reviving the UNIA. Receiving little financial or practical aid from Garvey, Jacques Garvey dropped her political work altogether in order to feed, shelter, and educate her children. Looking back over her years with Garvey and the UNIA, Jaques Garvey noted bitterly, "What did he ever give in return? The value of a wife to him was like a gold coin—expendable, to get what he wanted, and hard enough to withstand rough usage in the process."[23]

Amy Jacques Garvey's experience indicates that without considerable financial and practical support from the race father, the UNIA race mother was more likely to find herself isolated and exhausted than active and empowered. She might even begin to feel that irresponsible black men, as much as white racism, were her primary obstacles. For example, women in a Jamaican division of the UNIA complained that they were fighting the battle for race uplift alone. Angry at black men whom they called cowards for their abandonment of race and family responsibility, these women invited men to a women's meeting to remind them of their "duty towards the women of their race."[24] Maymie Leona Turpeau De Mena, a high-ranking UNIA member who later stunned Garvey by publishing the Divinite paper *World Echo,* complained in 1924 that although women formed "the backbone and sinew of the UNIA," they have been "given to understand that they must remain in their place."[25] Jacques Garvey herself wrote angry editorials in the mid-1920s in which she attacked black men for their "lack of appreciation for their noble women. . . ." She wrote, "We are tired of hearing Negro men say, 'there is a better day coming,' while they do nothing to usher in the day."[26]

By the mid-1920s, Garveyite women were not the only people with complaints about Garvey's leadership and organization. Despite its initial growth, the UNIA soon began to weaken as a result of organizational infighting, governmental harassment, and business fraud and naiveté. Garvey was eventually jailed for mail fraud in 1925, and deported to Jamaica in 1927.[27]

After Garvey's deportation the leaderless and bankrupt American branches of the UNIA gradually declined. Factional disputes within UNIA locals as well as Garvey's own growing political distance from the needs and concerns of American blacks were deeply damaging. Most detrimental of all to the UNIA, however, was the declining economic strength of black Americans. As early as 1927, private welfare agencies reported unusually high levels of suffering and unemployment in Harlem and other black communities, and conditions only became more difficult when the depression reached the rest of the nation in the 1930s. In this context of severe economic stress, the UNIA's faith in business enterprise and its push to sell stock for its shipping line became increasingly irrelevant to the working- and lower-middle-class blacks who had formerly provided the backbone of the UNIA.[28]

Marcus Garvey (center) escorted from a courtroom after being sentenced to five years in the Atlanta Penitentiary for mail fraud.

The Depression also undercut the gender strategy of the UNIA, which called for black women to cede public roles to their men in order to devote themselves to their offspring and so strengthen the race. The Depression had a particularly devastating impact on black men. In the 1920s, certain low-wage, dead-end service jobs had been reserved for African American men, but by the 1930s even these positions became scarce as desperate whites crossed the color line to complete for porter and janitorial jobs. White men were willing to take occupations formerly filled by black men, but neither black nor white men would take menial women's work, even in the worst years of the Depression. This meant that black women, like white women, could sometimes find jobs more quickly than either black or white men. The jobs were usually temporary, required grueling labor, and paid well below the minimum needed to survive.[29] Nevertheless, the fact that Depression-era black women found jobs at slightly higher rates than black men meant that by the 1930s the gender strategy of the UNIA no longer offered a viable alternative for most black Americans.

The very forces that undercut Garvey aided Divine; it is surely not coincidental that 1927—the year of Garvey's deportation and the first year in which private welfare agencies documented real suffering in Harlem—marked the year when newspapers first reported the growing popularity of a previously obscure black preacher who called himself Father Divine.[30] What were the race and gender strategies of the Peace Mission? How did these strategies fit the situation of the middle-aged, working-class African American women who constituted the vast majority of Divine's followers?[31]

Father Divine's 1930s Peace Mission Movement

One can begin to answer these questions by looking at the Peace Mission's analysis of race. From Divine's millenarian perspective, both the concept of race purity and the very existence of racial division had been transcended. In contrast to Garvey's wish to ensure Negro purity, Divine insisted that the very term *Negro* was false because it referred to no historical reality.[32] Divine claimed that race was a social construction. He explained, "there is no so-called blood of some special race. Blood is blood, Spirit is Spirit, Mind is Mind!"[33] Divine preached the unified descent of all peoples from God. He told his followers to "recognize only the lineage from whence you really came"—that is, the heavenly lineage encompassing all peoples ready to transcend their human natures. To claim this transcendent ancestry, all Divinites took new angelic names, such as Faithful Love or Glorious Illumination, upon joining the Peace Mission movement. As Divine explained, "Angelic Names . . . mean the Angelic Nature. Name means nature."[34]

Divinites stressed the importance of angelic names in part because of Divine's New Thought belief that to name something was to shape it in thought and so to create it. Calling oneself by an angelic name was therefore equivalent to becoming reborn as an angel. This belief that to speak of a thing was to create it had special application to Divine's thinking about race and racial strategy. It led to a crusade by Divinites against the use of racial and ethnic slurs; such vocabulary, Divine claimed, carried with it "the GERMS of SEGREGATION and DISCRIMINATION and the very GERM of LOWRATION by the saying of such terms unconsciously. . . ."[35] Divine carried this idea to the extreme in his preaching that the first and most significant step toward eradicating racism was avoiding words that referred to racial difference itself. As Divine explained,

> Thoughts are things! If we dwell upon them we will become to be partakers of them, automatically. Therefore we hardly use the word that is commonly known as race, creed, or color, among us.[36]

By using phrases such as the "'so-and-so' people" or "people of light complexion" in place of "Negro" or "Caucasian," Divine believed he was helping to rid the world of both racial differences and the structure of segregation and discrimination that such differences were used to justify.

Divine similarly downplayed the existence of gender difference. Divine referred to his followers as "so-called men" and "those who call themselves women."[37] When encouraging his followers to manifest in their behavior a new heavenly mind or spirit, he said, "Spirit and mind is [*sic*] the same as the principle of Mathematics, it is not confined to complexion, is it? Neither is it confined to sex, as far as male or female." He also downplayed his own gender. "GOD is your Father, your Mother, your Sister, and your Brother," he told his followers.[38] Divine's appearance seemed to suggest gender neutrality. An unusually small man who wore neat, tailored suits, Divine struck both his male and female followers as "cute" and "sweet."[39]

The resulting gender politics of the Peace Mission stood in stark contrast to those of the UNIA. The UNIA encouraged Garveyite women to see themselves primarily as mothers to the Negro race, and they had gained respect as wives and mothers at the cost of certain restrictions on their behavior. Divinite women rejected the identity of mother in favor of sister, the prefix commonly adopted by Divine's female followers. According to the Divinites, an "evangelical life" did not entail private devotion to husband and offspring in service to the race. Instead, it meant the immediate realization of an angelic—that is, communal, racially integrated, sex segregated, and celibate—lifestyle in service to God, or Father Divine.

Father Divine's insistence upon celibacy was not overtly linked to his analysis of race. It derived, first of all, from the premises of New Thought. Intrigued by the power of mind over matter, many New Thought authors advocated celibacy as the ultimate victory of the spiritual over the material. Father Divine's arguments for celibacy were indistinguishable from those offered by other New Thought leaders; like them, he insisted that sexual activity dissipated human energy, strengthened the "lower" rather than the "higher" nature, and was incompatible with the self-denial needed to achieve angelic status.[40] More crucially, however, the practice of celibacy among Divine's followers signified their millenarian perspective. Practices of sexual excess or abstinence are common in millenarian movements, whose members typically break religious or sexual taboos as a symbol of their distance from the corrupt past.[41]

Father Divine's insistence upon celibacy cannot, however, be understood entirely outside of a race context. To Garvey, the idea of a black man advocating celibacy was tantamount to race suicide; the salvation of African Americans required healthy and numerous black bodies.[42] Divine's answer to segregation and racism was to deny the body altogether—both the racialized and the sexualized body. In his millennial world of raceless and genderless angels, racial segregation could not possibly have a place.[43] It was Divine's firm belief that the human body had been transcended that enabled Divine's followers to battle segregation and to live in racially integrated groups; black and white together was the ultimate symbol that the human body itself no longer reigned.

Divine's rejection of the black sexualized body meshed perfectly with that same denial by white America. Because Divine's movement was sex segregated and celibate, it could be looked upon as a relatively nonthreatening curiosity by white outsiders.[44] The existence of large-scale, racially mixed communal living that was *not* celibate would likely have triggered white hysteria and even violence.[45] Although bound up with the claim that race difference did not exist, celibacy in Divine's movement ensured that at the most basic level race purity ideology remained unchallenged.

Divine's reasons for insisting on sex segregation and celibacy were not, however, identical to women's reasons for joining a movement with those tenets. Women's reasons for joining the Peace Mission were complex. While some joined because of severely demanding family and financial situations, others joined because of the appeal of living communally with other women.[46] The rejection of both men and conventional gender roles attracted many Divinite women.[47] Indeed, they sometimes extended that rejection farther than Divine himself intended. When encouraging his followers to disregard earthly divisions, Divine spoke almost exclusively of "races, creed and colors," rather than divisions between men and women.[48] But women heard what they wanted to hear in his words. For example, Divine told his followers, "Your bodies are pure from vice and from crime, because you have been Redeemed from all mankind." However, when arrested for voter registration disruption, Divinite women refused to ride in the same car with male prisoners, explaining that they could not because "Father has redeemed us from men."[49] This claim that God had redeemed them from men stood in stark contrast to the attitude of Garveyite women, who in the early 1920s carried banners in UNIA parades proclaiming "God Give Us Real Men!"[50]

Divinite women took new angelic names to assert publically their new status as members of a community of "sisters and brothers." While most took names like Joyous Light or Happy Flower, many chose explicitly male angelic names, such as Joshua Love, Jasper Aaron, and Jonathan Mathew.[51] This is particularly significant given Father Divine's New Thought insistence that "Name means Nature." These women were rejecting not only their status as wives, but also as women.

The sex-segregated and female-dominated Peace Mission had little hierarchy, gendered or otherwise. There was simply Father Divine; his small group of black and white, male and female "secretaries"; and the numerous, loosely organized cooperative businesses and communes of the Divinite Kingdom. This apparent lack of hierarchy was only relative, given that all Divinites saw themselves as worshipers of the movement's ultimate leader, Father Divine. Nevertheless, Peace Mission "extensions" of the 1930s were quite varied and remarkably autonomous.[52] Equally telling, the Divinite paper, *The Spoken Word,* had no women's page. Instead, reports on the doings of sisters and brothers were featured throughout.

Divinite rituals drew upon and sanctified women's experiences. At Peace Mission banquets, Divine ritually ladeled the first portion of soup, cut the first piece of meat on every platter, and poured coffee from a large silver urn. Father Divine's symbolic opening of the banquet did not overturn gender roles; indeed, a specially trained staff of Divinite women usually served the remainder of the banquet meal. Nevertheless, Divine's opening ritual must have been especially powerful for black women domestics, who probably made up the majority of Peace Mission adherents. The sight of "God himself" performing their daily service activity elevated and sanctified their labors. Moreover, women could relax and enjoy a meticulous table setting that reflected an elegance usually seen only in the homes of white employers. Now they, as domestic workers, were not serving, they were being served.[53]

What effects did Peace Mission social organization—which included no hierarchy, no heterosexuality, no private property, and no privatized home and child care—have on Divinite women? On the whole, the Peace Mission seemed to free their energy and creativity. Despite the Depression-era context, African American women formed scores of Peace Mission extensions and businesses—communal living arrangements as well as restaurants, food stores, and dressmaking and clothing shops.[54] Divinite women also collectively owned, ran and supervised the Promised Land, the nearly seven hundred Peace Mission communal farms located on over two thousand acres of land in upstate New York.[55] Observers initially doubted the feasibility of the Promised Land project. "[T]hese fanatics are hardly endowed with that stability of temperament and self-discipline required to endure the hardships of an agricultural existence," a hostile white biographer of Divine noted in 1937. However, Divine's followers—mostly middle-aged black women who had spent their younger years in the rural south—knew how to work a farm. Three years later, newspapers respectfully described the now-thriving farms and their related enterprises.[56]

Besides creating successful urban and rural cooperatives during the midst of the Great Depression, Divinite women became increasingly involved in political action. By the mid-1930s, the Divinite newspaper *Spoken Word* contained a mix of radical political reporting (often lifted from such journals as the *New Masses* and the *New Republic*) and the verbatim words of Father Divine's speeches, which combined transcendent visions with calls for political education and action. Women read the *Spoken Word* as a holy text, and soon their banquet testimonials began to reflect diverse political visions. As a *New York World-Telegraph* reporter sarcastically noted,

> followers arose to give testimonials. These took on a political hue. . . . A lean woman gave testimony to the effect that she had sat for three weeks in the spectator's gallery in the U.S. Senate and had discovered that the country was governed by a pack of noodles. Another woman told of a paradise that took on a decided Marxist tinge as she described it. Still another saw that the hope of the country lay in a benevolence reminiscent of Tammany Hall.[57]

Simultaneously, Divine introduced more practical skills to his followers. In 1935 he suggested that they attend night school to become literate and so qualify for voter registration. In response, Divinite women flooded the night schools, making up 20 percent of the students in 1935. This marked the first time in ten years that any woman had attended night school classes at Harlem's Public School 89.[58] It appears that only the radical lifestyle change involved in communal Divinite living enabled significant numbers of Harlem women to attend adult education classes—a telling indication of the depth of the problems that had hitherto made adult education virtually impossible for Harlem women.[59]

Divinite women were soon putting their new political skills into practice. They formed the overwhelming majority of the close to three hundred Harlem Divinites who attempted en masse to register to vote in 1935.[60] Women undertook other actions as well. Divinite sisters enacted peaceful resistance to segregation by entering restaurants in racially mixed groups. They also participated in joint Communist-Divinite parades (where they mixed cries of "Father Divine is God!" with slogans like "Down with Fascism!").[61] Finally, women were prominent in Divine's Righteous Government, an organization within the Peace Mission dedicated to the political implementation of Divine's vision. Of the organization's six departments, women headed at least three (politics, education, and research).[62]

Peace Mission women created a distinctive Divinite culture. Commentators, for instance, frequently noted the power of the hot swing or boogie-woogie style music at Divinite banquets. Accompanying the orchestrated music was a women's choir, which sang about social wrongs, racial injustice, or love for Divine. As one observer reported, these songs were "no orthodox hymns. They are original, colorful, completely alive outpourings. Often they attain the very heights of folk art."[63]

Peace Mission women also expressed themselves through distinctive clothing and appearance. According to the *Spoken Word,* today's woman should have "a sturdy, husky . . . physical type of beauty, as in Russia, and not the Clara Bow, Jean Harlow type of flaming youth."[64] The type of clothing favored by Divinite women can be gleaned from scattered reports. While the men of the movement wore dark, neatly pressed suits, one *New York Times* article described Divinite women as "clad chiefly in brilliant red, light blue and vivid purple garments. . . ."[65] Their dress starkly contrasted with the official costumes of some Garveyite women. As Barbara Bair points out, male members of Garvey's African Legion wore elaborate, military-style constumes, while their sister organization, the Black Cross Nurses, wore loose dresses and capes suggestive of self-sacrificing nuns and nurses.[66]

One might think that the Peace Mission's refusal even to use the word *Negro,* much less promote the physical perpetuation of African Americans as a race, would be accompanied by a devastating erasure of black culture as a whole. Again, a comparison with Garvey's UNIA proves instructive. Garvey valued black artistic expression, and his UNIA prompted a tremendous outpouring of black literary writings. UNIA poetry concentrated on the battle against racial injustice, the reawakening of Africa, and paeans to Garvey himself. The poems tended to maintain the trademark UNIA emphasis on Race Manhood, however, while depicting black women as queens, victims, virgins, or "Mothers of Men."[67] In his eagerness to promote self-respect in African Americans, Garvey encouraged the use of European poetic forms and scorned dialect poetry as degrading. He denigrated black folk culture, attacked the work of Harlem Renaissance authors, and viewed jazz and spirituals as impediments to racial progress.[68]

The cultural output of the Peace Mission similarly centered on opposition to racial injustice and hymns of praise to the movement's leader. Divinite songs and rituals did not emphasize Race Manhood, however. Instead, the 1930s Peace Mission accepted the experience of its black members as normative for the entire membership, black or white, and strongly stressed the value of black women's experience during the movement's central ritual occasions. In contrast to Garvey's contempt for jazz, Divine made an eclectic mix of popular and traditional music central to his ritual practice. He served the food and spoke the language of the black working class.[69] Divine validated the emotional testimonial style that had long been a means of expression for rural and urban African Americans and encouraged them to infuse their prayer with political content.

Later Years of the UNIA and the Peace Mission Movement

Living first in Jamaica and later in London, Garvey continued his efforts to rebuild the UNIA throughout the 1930s. His declining influence was painfully obvious, however. For example, when Garvey started his School of African Philosophy, a training course for UNIA leaders, in the mid-1930s, he published ads declaring "1,000 Students Wanted!!" The first session of the school, held in London in September 1937, attracted eleven students. By the time of Garvey's premature death in 1940, he was penniless and almost devoid of followers.[70]

During the final decade of his life, Garvey's politics became more mystical and more masculine. "*It is thought* that created the Universe. It is *thought* that will master the Universe," he wrote in 1937. Garvey had long been interested in New Thought, and in the 1920s he had drawn on New Thought rhetoric to encourage black men to persevere in business. Now he used New Thought ideas to argue that the real explanation for his movement's decline was the inner weakness of black men. "Mind is the thing that rules and the black man to-day falls below the level of a white man only because of the poverty of his mind," Garvey claimed. He also drew upon New Thought to support his arguments about the importance of racial separatism. Blacks suffered because they were captive to the denigrating thoughts and propaganda of an alien race, Garvey wrote. To be truly free, they needed to create their own thought environment or atmosphere. "Any race that accepts the thoughts of another race, automatically, becomes a slave of that other race. As men think, so they do react. . . ." he wrote in 1930.[71]

By the 1930s, Garvey increasingly spoke of a coming racial Armageddon that would bring a victory for blacks only when the "Negro makes himself a man" and forms a "great phalanx of noble fighting braves."[72] Given Garvey's commitment to the idea that mental images could make or break black people, it is not surprising that a considerable proportion of his 1930s journal *Black Man* consisted of poems he wrote with titles like **"Go And Win!"**, **"Win the Fray!"**, and **"GET UP AND DO."** These poems, replete with images of marching "He-Men," represented Garvey's final efforts to rouse a masculine, martial spirit in his readers.[73]

By the mid-1930s, Garvey apparently lost interest in the role of black women in racial uplift. His School of African Philosophy, which promised to train its students as UNIA leaders, diplomats, and entrepreneurs, included tips on how to deal with one's wife and family and seemed to assume a male audience. Yet Garvey's failure to delineate a specific role for black women seemed to allow at least some Garveyite women to assume that the UNIA leader whom the lessons promised to create could be female; of the School's initial eleven students, four were women.[74] Nevertheless, in one of Garvey's last comments on gender politics in 1934, he condemned blacks who used birth control. The resolution seemed to cast black women once again as "race mothers."[75] His attack on birth control seems of a piece with his praise of Hitler and Mussolini as self-made men and with his 1937 boast that "[w]e [in the UNIA] were the first Fascists."[76] Like the fascists, Garvey dreamed of a violent settlement of race problems. Black men would become warriors, and black women would produce the bodies needed in the coming race war.

If 1927 marked a turning point for Garvey and the UNIA, then the equivalent year for Divine's movement was 1936. That year, a number of events convinced outsiders that the Peace Mission was on the verge of becoming a radical political force: Divinites' rush to register to vote, their creation of a Righteous Government Platform to which all candidates hoping for the Divinite vote must conform, and their apparent alliance with the Communist Party. In response to this perceived political threat, U.S. government harassment of the Peace Mission intensified.[77] A series of sexual scandals, exposés, and defections further weakened Divine's movement. Finally, to escape paying reparations to a disgruntled former Divinite, Divine moved from Harlem to Philadelphia in 1942. This move left Divine, like Garvey, permanently separated from his base of support in New York City.[78]

Perhaps in response to these crises, Father Divine spent the years between 1937 and 1942 consolidating his authority over the Peace Mission movement. The *Spoken Word,* with its eclectic mix of Divine's banquet speeches; movement news; and radical local, national, and international political reporting, was replaced in late 1936 by the Divinite journal *New Day*. Typical issues of *New Day* contained approximately ninety pages of Divine's banquet speeches, ten pages of letters, and one page of world news.[79] In 1940 and 1941, Divine officially incorporated several of the movement's most active centers, began bringing all Peace Mission properties under centralized supervision, and instituted rules whereby no Peace Mission could be started without the permission of a parent church.[80]

By the mid-1940s, Peace Mission membership had declined dramatically.[81] This decline was possibly related to a number of factors, including the end of the Depression, Divine's self-imposed exile from Harlem, and Divinite dissatisfaction with the increasingly rigid nature of the movement. The Peace Mission's loss of members can also be explained in terms of the dynamics typical of millennial movements. The force driving such movements' rejection of mainstream social, political, and economic arrangements is a deeply felt protest against the injustices of mainstream society. Once these injustices are addressed directly by political movements, millennial faiths often find that their central appeal to their membership has been undercut. As Robert Weisbrot points out, the Double V campaign of the 1940s as well as the rise of the Civil Rights movement in the 1950s, both of which directly challenged segregation and other forms of deeply embedded white racism, may have severely undercut the appeal of Divine's movement.[82]

After a millenarian group begins to lose members, the message of its prophet tends to change. Instead of criticizing the evils of an oppressive social system, the prophet often begins to blame social ills on the evils of the oppressed people themselves. The prophet then preaches self-purification rather than confrontation as the means for bringing about the millennium. It is not surprising, then, that when the numbers of Divine's followers began to dwindle, he began to blame injustice on the imperfections of the oppressed.[83] African Americans "had committed the sin in setting up color in the first place," Divine now insisted. "They set it up in their consciousness and they would find it everywhere they went and *they* and no one else would be responsible."[84] This shift to self-blame echoed the attacks on black laziness leveled by Marcus Garvey in the 1930s when he too found himself the prophet of a dwindling movement.

Divine's political outlook shifted dramatically with the outbreak of World War II. He seemed to interpret the war as a contest between the racists and segregationists he abhorred, on the one hand, and the united, peaceful planet that he had long promoted, on the other. When the United States entered the war Divine therefore fiercely supported the war effort and did all he could to promote a fervent American nationalism among his followers.[85] Indeed, during the war years, the same Father Divine who had once stated that "I am none of your nationalities. You don't have to think I AM an American. . . . I AM none of them" now claimed that the only way to ensure world peace was by turning the world into a gigantic United States of America.[86] The United States, as the "amalgamation of all nations," was chosen as the site of the "Kingdom of GOD on earth," Divine insisted. Eventually all nations of the earth would fly the American flag and accept the Constitution, which Divine believed was divinely inspired, as their charter of government.[87] Instead of preaching the absence of race or gender divisions under the neutrality of African American-inflected religious practice, Divine instead preached the absence of national divisions under the neutrality of American global dominance. By the 1950s, Divine directed his most passionate tirades not against "RACISM and all MATERIALISM and every adverse and undesirable tendency," but against communists and unions, who Divine claimed were "inspired by atheism and Nazism and other isms that spell division, to undermine the foundations of our government, which we all revere!"[88]

As Divine became both increasingly nationalistic and anxious about the ideological purity of his followers, his understanding of celibacy (and with it, the position of Divinite women) changed dramatically. In the 1930s, Divine had embraced celibacy as a sign of the distance between those living as angels in Divine's millennial heavens and those who had not yet acknowledged Father Divine as God; but his comments on celibacy were few and far between. By the 1950s, celibacy as well as virginity took on increasing importance to Father Divine. He began to preach that if his followers remained celibate they would live forever.[89] His growing stress on virginity could be seen in the changing nature of three Divinite orders—the Rosebuds, the Lily-buds, and the Crusaders—first created between 1938 and 1941.

The most important of these orders was the Rosebuds, which was both a women's order and the official Divinite choir. In the mid-1940s, Divine praised the Rosebuds mainly for their skill at purchasing properties in "restricted" areas and as exemplars of economic independence.[90] By the 1950s, however, Divine seemed to value the Rosebuds primarily for their virginity. According to the Rosebuds' Creed, adopted by the early 1950s, the Rosebuds pledged to let their "every deed and action express virginity."[91]

The new emphasis on virginity had multiple meanings for the Divinites. On the one hand, Divine's insistence on virginity symbolized, as it always had, the boundaries between the elect and the unredeemed world. On the other hand, the aggressive virginity of Divine's new orders seemed linked to his belief in the millennial role of the United States. By the 1950s, Divine seemed to view the United States as a Peace Mission writ large. Just as Peace Mission members erased trouble-causing differences through both the inclusive strategy of interracial living and the exclusive strategy of repressing all potentially divisive physical desires, so too did they imagine the United States erasing difference through both the inclusive strategy of expanding to include all peoples and the exclusive strategy of battling the "ruthless ideology of Socialism and Communism." Divinites equated the words *virgin* and *virtuous*. The virgin righteousness of Divinites showed their kinship with the virgin righteousness of America itself.[92]

As the meaning of celibacy shifted under the weight of Divine's new nationalism, so too did Divine's emphasis on race neutrality take on a different meaning. Rather than stating that all race was a construction, Divine seemed particularly interested in denying the existence of the African race. Throughout the 1950s, for example, the *New Day* repeatedly published Divine's statement that "I do NOT represent races, creeds or colors. Therefore I AM NOT what you think or take me to be. *i am not* a N_____O and I AM NOT representing any such thing as the N_____O or the C_____ race. . . . I AM a REAL, TRUE AMERICAN ONE HUNDRED PERCENT ."[93]

Divine supported his One Hundred Percent Americanism by organizing his church in ways that brought it closer to mainstream white culture. Instead of challenging mainstream gender roles, for example, Divine's orders now approximated the gender norms of 1950s American culture. The Rosebuds pledged to remain "submissive, meek and sweet," while the male Crusaders pledged to be "active, effective, integral" members of Father Divine's movement.[94]

Divine also reshaped his own life and image according to more mainstream ideals. In 1946, he took a seventeen-year-old, petite and blond-haired white Canadian woman as his second wife (his first wife, Peninnah, was a heavy-set, African American woman—both marriages were "purely spiritual").[95] It appears that Divine attempted to alter his photographic image in order to downplay his dark skin. According to one observer, by the 1950s Divine's followers insisted that his complexion was not dark. The observer reported that Divine's official photographers used "every known photographic technique" to lighten the shade of Divine's skin. The result could be seen in *New Day* photographs from the mid-1950s, in which the complexions of Father and Mother Divine appear to share a similar washed out, off-white color, and in the color photographs of Divine currently on display at the Divine Tracy Hotel in Philadelphia, which give his complexion an orange cast.[96]

Divine's praise of all things American culminated in 1953 when he and his wife moved to Woodmont, an 1890s robber-baron estate located in Gladwyne, Pennsylvania. While heaven had formerly been located in a three-story Harlem collective, it was now an elegantly appointed mansion, which Divine described as "a home that is set apart for MOTHER DIVINE and MYSELF as though a private family. . . ."[97] Once installed in Woodmont, Divine seemed to believe that all was well in his own life, and so in America and in the world. "GOD IS ON THE THRONE NOW," he announced during his first week at Woodmont.[98] From this point on, Divine had little to say about the state of America or the world at large. Until his death in 1965, *New Day* editions mainly reprinted speeches by Mother Divine, along with letters and speeches written by Father Divine in the 1930s and 1940s.

Conclusion

A comparison of Divine's Peace Mission movement and Garvey's UNIA indicates that the very different racial ideologies of these movements profoundly affected their gender politics. Garvey's UNIA protested the race-caste system in America by urging blacks to unify as a race. In Garvey's view, the strength of this black race was dependent on the continued growth of a healthy and recognizably black population. The production of a healthy black population, in turn, could occur only if black women found the appropriate mates and devoted themselves to raising strong children. This left black men to provide for, defend, and rule the united black nation. Garvey's strategy ultimately put black manhood, as well as race, "first."

In contrast, Divine's 1930s Peace Mission protested the American race-caste system by denying race difference altogether and attempting to practice complete racial integration. In the context of a depression-era society predicted upon race hierarchy, however, large-scale enactments of racial transcendence would be tolerated only if accompanied by the rejection of sexuality. Divine's interest in celibacy may have had purely religious roots. Nevertheless, his choice of celibacy as the primary symbol of angelic living was crucial to his ability to create a racially integrated movement.

Both Garvey's Race First and Divine's race neutrality thus entailed control of women's sexuality. Garvey's UNIA channeled women's sexuality into the role of wife and mother, while Divine's Peace Mission forbade heterosexuality and even heterosociability. Garvey's gender strategy, however, assumed the existence of a steady male wage and was therefore a tolerable option for black women only during periods of relative economic well-being. As the UNIA crumbled during the Great Depression, thousands of African American women became followers of Father Divine and accepted his millennial race-neutral approach. They willingly accepted celibacy and sex segregation in exchange for the social, political, and economic opportunities offered by the Peace Mission movement.

Marcus Garvey felt that black culture would thrive only in the context of strong, patriarchal black families. Although he encouraged African American artistic production, Garvey nevertheless denigrated many aspects of black culture that struck him as too dreamy and undisciplined to contribute to the building of a great nation. One might assume a close tie between race pride and an assertive black culture, but the early years of the Peace Mission movement suggest that race purity ideology need not be a precondition for the assertion of a vibrant black culture. Divine's African American, working-class, female followers brought their tastes in food, music, and dress to the Peace Mission movement. These women formed the majority of Divine's followers in Harlem, and they largely shaped the purportedly race-neutral culture of the Peace Mission as a whole.

While Divine's movement peaked in the mid-1930s, these same years saw Garvey living in exile from his American base of support. Once the remaining American UNIA locals lost followers to Divine as well as to other political and religious leaders, Marcus Garvey ironically began to draw more heavily upon the same New Thought ideas that animated Divine's speeches. While Divinites used New Thought ideas about the power of words and thought to deny the existence of race as well as gender difference, Garvey articulated a New Thought philosophy that was both more political and more vindictive. He used New Thought ideas about the power of influence to shore up his calls for a renewed black art, literature, and history to counter the "thoughts of a race that has made itself by assumption superior."[99] Garvey also took to heckling his readers repeatedly about the need to become more masculine and aggressive, as if this were a realistic alternative to organized political activism. Despite the economic pressures of the Great Depression, Garvey refused to modify his vision of gender roles within the UNIA; given the fact that the only UNIA resolution of the 1930s that was directed at women condemned birth control, it appears that Garvey continued to envision black women as mothers of the race.

If Garvey's continuing emphasis on women as reproducers reflects the drawbacks of a race-purity approach, the later history of the Peace Mission suggests the extreme instability of a formula of race neutrality as a method of opposing the American race-caste system. By the 1950s, Divine's denial of race had changed into a denial of the existence of racism and a consequent lauding of the United States as a racially just (rather than simply a multiracial) society. Divine's complacency about conditions in the United States increased after he moved into the Woodmont mansion and began to live out his own version of the paterfamilias experience. Instead of a neutrality in which a form of African American culture was the norm, Divine's increasing personal comfort as well as his increasing nationalism led him to promote a neutrality that drew upon the dominant white culture. Divine's movement shows that, although the denial of race difference in some ways counters the need to control women's reproduction and can therefore allow some innovation in social and economic arrangements, such a denial is not enough to counter other forces leading to a strict policing of women's bodies—in this case the force of nationalism. Divine's movement indicates how nationalism even without anxieties over reproducing the race can be imprisoning for women, since the purity claimed for the nation is too easily symbolized by the female virgin body.

The histories of Marcus Garvey's UNIA and Father Divine's Peace Mission movement demonstrate some of the pressures faced by African American organizations that attempt to challenge the racial status quo. In addition to the usual difficulties of organizing poor or culturally marginalized people, on the one hand, and the drain of constant governmental harassment on the other, African American organizations face special stresses that result from their racialized identity in white America. Black organizations can find themselves in a double bind; while calls to race pride may unify African Americans politically, a slip from race pride to race purity can easily occur. Race purity, in turn, encourages protective attitudes toward women. These attitudes restrict women's behavior and are, in any case, extremely difficult to implement in the context of economic oppression that creates the need for antiracist organizing in the first place. At the same time, the rare black organization that attempts to claim the position of race neutrality, usually appropriated by European Americans, stands to lose the specificity of the culture it is fighting to strengthen. The gender politics of African American religious and political movements must not be overlooked; they throw into high relief the complex and confining links between nationalism, race consciousness, gender, and sexuality that continue to shape modern American politics and culture.

Notes

I would like to thank Holly Allen, Mia Bay, Jackie Goldsby, Jerma Jackson, Jody Lester, Jan Lewis, Lucy Maddox, Margaret McFadden, Barbara Melosh, Sarah Schulman, Kathryn Tanner, Deborah Gray White, and the anonymous reviewer for *American Quarterly* for their enormously helpful comments and criticism of this essay.

1. C. D. Austin's letter and the UNIA's condemnation of Father Divine are reprinted in Robert A. Hill, ed., *The Marcus Garvey and Universal Negro Improvement Association Papers,* vol. 7 (Berkeley, Calif., 1990), 707-8, 705.

2. See E. David Cronon, *Black Moses: The Story of Marcus Garvey and the Universal Negro Improvement Association* (Madison, Wis., 1974); Amy Jacques Garvey, *Garvey and Garveyism* (1963; New York, 1978); Judith Stein, *The World of Marcus Garvey: Race and Class in Modern Society* (Baton Rouge, La., 1986).

3. See Robert Weisbrot, *Father Divine and the Struggle for Racial Equality* (Urbana, Ill., 1983); Jill Watts, *God, Harlem, U.S.A.: The Father Divine Story* (Berkeley, Calif., 1992); Roma Barnes, "'Blessings Flowing Free': The Father Divine Peace Mission Movement in Harlem, New York City, 1932-1941" (Ph.D. diss., University of York, England, 1979); Charles Braden, *These Also Believe: A Study of Modern American Cults and Minority Religious Movements* (New York, 1949), 1-77.

4. Accurate membership statistics for both the UNIA and the Peace Mission are difficult to determine. In the 1920s, Garvey claimed a UNIA membership of six to eleven million, while in the 1930s Divine claimed to have twenty million followers worldwide. Historians estimate from fifty thousand to two hundred thousand active Garveyites in the mid-1920s, and from thirty thousand to fifty thousand Divinites in the 1930s. See Emory J. Tolbert, *The UNIA and Black Los Angeles: Ideology and Community in the American Garvey Movement* (Los Angeles, 1980), 7 n. 7; see Lawrence Levine, *The Unpredictable Past: Explorations in American Cultural History* (New York, 1993), 121; Watts, *God, Harlem, U.S.A.,* 142; Weisbrot, *Father Divine,* 69.

5. For comparisons of Garvey and Divine, see Weisbrot, *Father Divine,* 190-96; Watts, *God, Harlem, U.S.A.,* 115-18; Hill, *Papers,* vol. 7, 641 n. 9; Robert A. Hill and Barbara Bair, eds., *Marcus Garvey: Life and Lessons* (Berkeley, Calif., 1987), xxviii-xxx, xlix-l. Also see documents on Divine in Hill, *Papers,* vol. 7, 641, 704.

6. See Wiesbrot, *Father Divine,* 59-60; Hubert Kelly, "Heaven Incorporated," *American Century* 121 (Jan. 1936): 106; "Kingdom Sings and Registers," *New York Sun,* 4 Nov. 1935. Some west coast Divinite heavens had a majority of white followers. See Charles P. LeWarne, "Vendovi Island: Father Divine's 'Peaceful Paradise of the Pacific,'" *Pacific Northwest Quarterly* (Jan. 1984): 2-12.

7. I am indebted to the work of Barbara Bair and Tera W. Hunter on the gender politics of the UNIA. See Barbara Bair, "Women and the Garvey Movement: The Politics of Difference" (paper presented at Rockefeller Humanities-in-Residence talk, Rutgers University, 1989); Tera W. Hunter, "Feminist Consciousness and Black Nationalism: Amy Jacques-Garvey and Women in the Universal Negro Improvement Association" (paper presented at Women's History Research Seminar, Yale University, 1983). Also see Barbara Bair, "True Women, Real Men: Gender, Ideology and Social Roles in the Garvey Movement," in Dorothy O. Helly and Susan M. Reverby, eds., *Gendered Domains: Rethinking Public and Private in Women's History* (Ithaca, N.Y., 1992), 154-66.

8. See Tony Martin, "Women in the Garvey Movement," and Honor Ford-Smith, "Women and the Garvey Movement in Jamaica," in Rupert Lewis and Patrick Bryan, eds., *Garvey: His Work and Impact* (Trenton, N.J., 1991), 73, 75, 78, 81; Bair, "True Women, Real Men," 156, 160; Ula Yvette Taylor, "The Veiled

Garvey: The Life and Times of Amy Jacques Garvey" (Ph.D. diss., University of California Santa Barbara, Jan. 1992), 194, 214; Hunter, "Feminist Consciousness," 22-23.

9. For example, although Robert Weisbrot notes the preponderance of women in the Peace Mission, their gender becomes central to his analysis only when he remarks that women gazed at Divine with "sensual longing" or notes that "[s]ome of these women, black as well as white, appeared to experience sexual orgasms during their frenzied behavior at the banquets." See Weisbrot, *Father Divine,* 86. Among Divinite scholars only Sara Harris notes that male followers also gazed adoringly at Divine. See Sara Harris, *Father Divine* (New York, 1971), 339-40. Also see Barnes, "Blessings Flowing Free," 273.

10. Watts, *God, Harlem, U.S.A.,* 35, 42. Watts's sympathetic account of women in the Peace Movement still relegates their experiences to a few pages in an extensive study; she does not analyze Divine's movement as a black women's movement. Furthermore, Watts's consistently positive slant on the Peace Mission sometimes leads her to normalize what was clearly an extremely unconventional and socially challenging religious movement. For example, in addition to calling Divine an "articulate advocate of women's rights," Watts describes the typical Peace Mission heaven as a rehabilitation center that offered occupational therapy, job training, day care and support group therapy (42, 47, 106, 128). This 1980s vocabulary is misleading. Abandoning children to children's extensions where they were raised communally is not day care, absolute gender segregation and celibacy are hardly necessary in order to free women from the fear of childbirth (35), and calling up storms to avenge female mental hospital patients is not the standard definition of women's rights. Watts image of a pro-therapy, pro-women's rights Father Divine certainly makes the movement seem less alien, but at the cost of misrepresenting the less socially acceptable aspects of Divinite behavior.

    Watts's effort to portray Divine as a rational and consistent individual leads her to distort the erratic nature of Divine's political life. For example, although Father Divine joined his editorial staff in passionately attacking capitalism, encouraging his followers to be radicals, and allying himself with the Communist Party in the United States during the depression, and only turned to anti-Communism and strident American nationalism in the 1940s, Watts claims that the Father Divine of the 1930s held the same views as the Father Divine posthumously depicted by his 1970s and 1980s followers—as a man (or God) whose most passionately held political beliefs are support for capitalism and opposition to welfare. She creates this more consistent picture by attributing undated speeches by Divine that were published posthumously by his followers in the 1970s to Divine in the 1930s. For an example of Watts's anachronistic use of 1970s *New Day* reprints, see 209, nn. 50-56. For her efforts to portray Divine as a fervant procapitalist in the 1930s, see 100-101, 104-6, 119-20, 126, 128, 134-35. For an alternative view, see original *Spoken Word,* editions from 1935-36.

11. See Hill, *Papers,* vol. 1, lxxi, lxxx-lxxxi; Cronon, *Black Moses,* 111, 191-95; Jacques Garvey, *Garvey and Garveyism,* 176-78; Hill and Bair, *Marcus Garvey,* 204.

12. See Hazel Carby, *Reconstructing Womanhood: The Emergence of the Afro-American Woman Novelist* (New York, 1987), 20-39; Jacqueline Dowd Hall, "'The Mind That Burns in Each Body': Women, Rape, and Racial Violence," in Ann Snitow, Christine Stansell, and Sharon Thompson, *Powers of Desire* (New York, 1983), 328-49.

13. See Levine, *Unpredictable Past,* 107-36. In contrast, white calls for race unity functioned to convince working-class whites that nonwhites, rather than an exploitative economic system, were the source of their problems. Black race consciousness created political coalitions among the powerless internationally; white race consciousness sundered potential coalitions domestically among the powerless.

14. *Negro World,* 17 May 1924, cited in Bair, "Women and the Garvey Movement," 10. Garveyites frequently wrote of women not simply as mothers but as "Mothers of Men." See Bair, "Women and the Garvey Movement," n. 17, 28-29.

15. Percival Burrows, in *Negro World,* 9 June 1923, cited in Bair, "Women in the Garvey Movement," 10.

16. See Bair, "True Women, Real Men," 156. Articles in *Negro World* indicate that Garveyite women were angry only that UNIA men were not taking their responsibilities as chivalrous protectors seriously enough. For example, see "Ladies of Jamaica Division Lead Men in Constructive Efforts," *Negro World,* 7 Apr. 1923; "Respect and Protection of Our Women a Vital Question," *Negro World,* 23 Aug. 1924; "Listen Women!" *Negro World,* 9 Apr. 1927.

17. See Jacqueline Jones, *Labor of Love, Labor of Sorrow: Black Women, Work and the Family, from Slavery to the Present* (New York, 1986), 96-99; Cheryl Townsend Gilkes, "The Roles of Church and Community Mothers: Ambivalent American Sexism or Fragmented African Familyhood?" *Journal of Feminist Studies in Religion* 2 (spring 1986): 44; Eileen Boris, "The Power of Motherhood: Black and White Activist Women Redefine the 'Political,'" in Seth Koven and Sonya Michel, eds., *Mothers of a New World: Maternalist Politics and the Origins of the Welfare State* (New York, 1993), 213-45.

18. See "The Black Woman's Part in Race Leadership," *Negro World,* 19 Apr. 1924; "Women in the Home" and "The Kinf [*sic*] of Girl Men Like," *Negro World,* 9 Feb. 1924; "Emancipated Womanhood," *Negro World,* 15 Nov. 1924; Taylor, *The Veiled Garvey,* 222-24.

19. Bair, "Women and the Garvey Movement," 5-8; see Gilkes, "Ambivalent American Sexism."

20. See "Obligations of Motherhood," *Negro World,* 29 Mar. 1924; "Emancipated Womanhood," *Negro World,* 15 Nov. 1924. Also see Hunter, "Feminist Consciousness," 16, 18; Ford-Smith, "Jamaica," 73, 75, 78, 81.

21. See Hill, *Papers,* vol. 1, liii; Bair, "Women and the Garvey Movement," 7; photograph by James VanDerZee, "Garvey Women's Brigade, 1924," in Roger C. Birt, "For the Record: James VanDerZee, Marcus Garvey and the UNIA Photographs," *Exposure* 27 (fall 1990): 11; Martin, "Women in the Garvey Movement," 70.

22. See Bair, "True Women, Real Men," 160-66; Martin, "Women in the Garvey Movement"; Ford-Smith, "Jamaica," 67-69, 77-82. UNIA women made an un-

successful plea for more autonomy within the movement in 1922; see Bair, "True Women, Real Men," 160-61.

23. Jacques Garvey, *Garvey and Garveyism,* 169, 218-51; Taylor, "The Veiled Garvey," 301, 309, 329.

24. "Ladies of Jamaica Division Lead Men in Constructive Efforts," *Negro World,* 7 Apr. 1923.

25. M. L. T. De Mena, *Negro World,* 19 Apr. 1924, cited in Hunter, "Feminist Consciousness," 22-23.

26. "Listen Women!" *Negro World,* 9 Apr. 1927; *Negro World,* 24 Oct. 1925, cited in Gerda Lerner, ed., *Black Women in White America: A Documentary History* (New York, 1973), 579.

27. See Cronon, *Black Moses,* 75-134, 142-44; Stein, *World of Marcus Garvey,* 202, 206-7.

28. See Cheryl Lynn Greenberg, *"Or Does It Explode?" Black Harlem in the Great Depression* (New York, 1991), 13, 20-22, 28, 39-40; Levine, *Unpredictable Past,* 135; Hill, *Papers,* vol. 7, xliii-xlvii; Stein, *World of Marcus Garvey,* 255.

29. See Greenberg, *Or Does it Explode?,* 66, 74, 77, 197.

30. Watts, *God, Harlem, U.S.A.,* 62.

31. Conditions for working class African American women in 1930s Harlem were dire. During the Depression, the vast majority of African American women in Harlem were employed in domestic service. While unskilled black male workers earned between two dollars and six dollars per day, African American women employed as domestics were earning between four dollars and ten dollars per *week* for twelve- to fourteen-hour days. See Greenberg, *Or Does it Explode?,* 45, 78, 80; Jones, *Labor of Love,* 154, 179, 199. Furthermore, although most black women worked outside of the home, many of the steps taken by Harlemites to stretch their limited incomes—such as taking in boarders and preparing their own food and clothing—were performed by women and thus added considerably to African American women's already oppressive work loads. See Greenberg, *Or Does it Explode?,* 176, 180.

    The multiple stesses placed on middle-aged, African American women in Harlem helps explain why this group was particularly prepared to join a millenarian social movement like the Peace Mission. In addition, statistical evidence indicates that many of Divine's female followers had been part of the Great Migration of 1916-21. Migrants, immigrants, or colonized people are the populations most likely to join millenarian groups. See Barnes, "Blessings Flowing Free," 123-24; Yonina Talmon, "Pursuit of the Millennium: The Relation Between Religious and Social Change," *Archives Europeennes de Sociologie* 3 (1962): 133, 144-45, 149.

32. Divine explained that the term *Negro* was employed

    > for the specific purpose of bringing about a division among the people, and to belittle and lowrate those that were of a darker complexion, by calling them not AFRICAN by nature, neither an ETHIOPIAN, neither an EGYPTIAN, but by calling them something that they never were. Tell your Educators to search the Scripture, and also search the History, and see if there is a nation by the name of what they call the People in America.
    >
    > (*Spoken Word,* 30 Nov. 1935, 20)

    Also see *Spoken Word,* 4 Jan. 1936, 27.

33. See *Spoken Word,* 30 Mar. 1935, 10; *Spoken Word,* 16 Mar. 1935, 7.

34. *Spoken Word,* 26 Oct. 1935, 28; *Spoken Word,* 9 Nov. 1935, 29.

35. *New Day,* 24 Nov. 1945, 7.

36. *Spoken Word,* 4 Jan. 1936, 27. Divine's refusal to speak of (and thereby mentally create or strengthen) negative circumstances led to odd verbal practices within the group. For example, Divinites referred to Amsterdam Avenue as Amsterbliss, and used the greeting Peace instead of Hello because they did not want to speak of and so strengthen hell.

37. See Watts, *God, Harlem, U.S.A.,* 35.

38. *Spoken Word,* 30 Mar. 1935, 9; *Spoken Word,* 29 June 1935, 3; Barnes, "Blessings Flowing Free, 210 n. 82.

39. Arthur Huff Fauset, *Black Gods of the Metropolis* (1944; New York, 1970), 65, 67; Robert Allerton Parker, *The Incredible Messiah: The Deification of Father Divine* (Boston, 1937), 120. Divinite women frequently spoke of Divine's "beautiful starry baby eyes," indicating that they saw him as baby as well as father. See "A Revelation," *Spoken Word,* 23 Nov. 1935, 15; Parker, *Incredible Messiah,* 129.

40. On New Thought arguments for celibacy, see Beryl Satter, "New Thought and the Era of Woman, 1875-1895" (Ph.D. diss., Yale University, 1992), 328-96. For Father Divine's arguments in favor of celibacy, see *Spoken Word,* 6 Apr. 1935, 3; 26 Oct. 1935, 27; 2 Nov. 1935, 5. Although Divine usually spoke of celibacy as a practice of godly self-denial, he sometimes addressed the issue in terms of population control. See *Spoken Word,* 6 Apr. 1935 3; also see *Spoken Word,* 26 Oct. 1935, 18.

41. See Peter Worsley, *The Trumpet Shall Sound: A Study of "Cargo" Cults in Melanesia,* 2d augmented ed. (New York, 1968), 250-51; see *Spoken Word,* 29 Apr. 1935, 3.

42. See Marcus Garvey, "Big Conference of U.N.I.A. in Canada," in Hill, *Papers,* vol. 7, 705; Marcus Garvey, "What God Means to Us," in Hill, *Papers,* vol. 7, 107-8; Marcus Garvey, "Lessons from the School of African Philosophy," in Hill and Bair, *Marcus Garvey,* 234-37.

43. Divine's denial of the body did not extend to practices of self-mortification or to dietary restrictions. He encouraged his followers to eat heartily by making a fifty-course banquet the ritual center of his movement.

44. Even in light of the Divinite ban on sexual relations, white observers were still shocked by the level of intimacy that existed between Divine's black and white followers. For example, see John Hosher, *God in a Rolls-Royce: The Rise of Father Divine, Madman, Menace, or Messiah* (New York, 1936), 171; Braden, *These Also Believe,* 26.

45. Contemporary observers made this point. See Harris, *Father Divine* (New York, 1971), 98; Braden, *These Also Believe,* 20.

46. There is some evidence that the Peace Mission, with its insistence on sex-segregated living and repudiation of reproduction as a strategy of racial uplift, also drew lesbians seeking an alternative to the confines of family life. One 1937 denunciation of the Peace Mission movement claimed it was a lesbian haven. This exposé was highly unreliable. See Barnes, "Blessings Flowing Free," 212. On the other hand, Divine himself periodically warned his followers not to sleep in each other's rooms:

    > I do not want anyone [in] the Peace Mission movement . . . going into others' private rooms that you are not assigned to. . . . Some of you so-called sisters . . . will not stay away from others' rooms—from the other Rosebuds' rooms, other sisters' rooms. . . .
    >
    > (Harris, *Father Divine,* 338)

    A 1950s report on the movement notes that while there is no overt homosexuality in the movement, some must exist; "its practice is written all over the stances and the faces of some followers." See Harris, *Father Divine,* 338. See also Barnes, "Blessings Flowing Free," 209.

47. Divine sanctioned unconventional work roles for women by choosing a young black woman, Flying Determination, as his personal pilot, and by appointing women to serve as Peace Mission chauffeurs. See photograph of Flying Determination in scrapbook, "Father Divine," Schomburg Center for Research in Black Culture, New York; see Braden, *These Also Believe,* 27.

    The Divinites were proud of the fact that they ignored gender coded work-roles. For example, an article in the *Spoken Word* reported on a newsreel in which

    > Not only was FATHER seen digging with a pick but Faithful Mary had one too. Mother was seen expertly handling a shovel and doing other work usually considered to be a "man's" work.
    >
    > (*Spoken Word,* 14 Feb. 1925)

48. For example, see *Spoken Word,* 30 Mar. 1935, 11.

49. *Spoken Word,* 29 June 1935, 3; "29 of Divine Flock Seized in Vote Row," *New York Times,* 7 Oct. 1936. Divine sometimes came very close to this formulation, however. In a speech in October 1935, he said that the person who was redeemed from "all lust and passion" would be "Redeemed from among men. If you are in the likeness of a woman you are Redeemed from among men—that is if you live an Evangelical life. . . ." See *Spoken Word,* 19 Oct. 1935, 12. In later years, Divine explicity warned his male and female, followers not to ride together in buses. See *New Day,* 13 Aug. 1942, 110.

50. See Jacques Garvey, *Garvey and Garveyism,* 49; Bair, "Women and the Garvey Movement," 9.

51. Parker, *Incredible Messiah,* 157, 231-33; Harris, *Father Divine,* 59; *Spoken Word,* 4 Jan. 1936, 28; "Kingdom Sings and Registers," *New York Sun,* 4 Nov. 1935.

52. Although white journalists typically characterized Divine as the controlling boss of his "chain store heavens," evidence indicates that Peace Mission communes were surprisingly independent of one another. For example, see affidavits by Charles Calloway and John Lamb and a letter from John Lamb in Mother Divine, *Peace Mission Movement,* 78-81, 82-85, 110. For a detailed analysis of the economic structure of Divinite communes, see Braden, *These Also Believed,* 27-42. Also see Weisbrot, *Father Divine,* 122-31 and Kenneth E. Burnham, *God Comes to America: Father Divine and the Peace Mission Movement* (Boston, 1979), 9. On the political independence of Divinites, see Watts, *God, Harlem, U.S.A.,* 87, 125, 131; also see 111, 132.

53. See Barnes, "Blessings Flowing Free," chap. 1. One Divinite woman who identified with Divine's role as server explained, "It is a thing of infinite beauty to actually see Father Divine—God in action at the table *serving.* . . . He pours the coffee so beautifully. So much rhythm, just like music from a violin. . . ." See Parker, *Incredible Messiah,* 129. Also see Weisbrot, *Father Divine,* 180; Braden, *These Also Believe,* 3.

54. See Parker, *Incredible Messiah,* 145-50; *Spoken Word,* 9 Feb. 1935, 15; 18 May 1935, 6; 22 June 1935, 18; 4 Jan. 1936, 28. Also see "Divine's Restaurant Puzzles Magistrate," *New York Times,* 12 June 1935; Barnes, "Blessings Flowing Free," 284; Weisbrot, *Father Divine,* 123-25; and Braden, *These Also Believe,* 27-42.

55. See *Spoken Word,* 23 Nov. 1935, 7; Weisbrot, *Father Divine,* 125-31. On women as workers and managers of the Promised Land, see *Spoken Word,* 14 Feb. 1935; "Divine Pilot Arks Up 1936 Jordon," *New York Post,* 20 Aug. 1936; "Divine Scene at Olympics," *New York Sun,* 8 July 1937; and "Biggest Businessman in Harlem has Extended his Holdings to Heaven," *New York World-Telegraph,* 10 Sept. 1936.

56. Parker, *Incredible Messiah,* 285-86; see "Father Divine's Movement Expands," *New York Times,* 2 July 1939; "Strike a Balance," *New York Post,* 28 June 1939.

57. "Father Divine's 'Heaven' Favors Reapportionment," *New York World-Telegraph,* 2 Mar. 1935.

58. Weisbrot, *Father Divine,* 96; Jones, *Labor of Love,* 193; Barnes, "Blessings Flowing Free," 461-62.

59. Harlem women who had migrated from the rural south may also have spurned adult education because in their experience education did not bring mobility. See Greenberg, *Or Does It Explode?,* 18. Once they became Divinite Angels, however, previous experiences of discrimination would be discounted, since they now believed that their every desire could be fulfilled.

60. Barnes, "Blessings Flowing Free," 464; "Kingdom Sings and Registers," *New York Sun,* 4 Nov. 1935.

61. *Spoken Word,* 13 Apr. 1936; *Spoken Word,* 23 Nov. 1935, 1; Mark Naison, *Communists in Harlem During the Depression* (New York, 1983), 129.

62. Barnes, "Blessings Flowing Free," 459; *Spoken Word,* 31 Aug. 1935. As always in Peace Mission publications, no mention was made of the race of these women. It is likely, however, that at least some of the Righteous Government leaders were middle-class white women. On the effects of the Righteous Government crusade on Divinite women and men, see Barnes, "Blessings Flowing Free," 518, 521-32, 574 n. 13.

63. Harris, *Father Divine,* 328; also see Fauset, *Black Gods,* 105-6; Braden, *These Also Believed,* 72; Hosher, *God in a Rolls-Royce,* 127.

64. *Spoken Word,* 31 Aug. 1935, 7.

65. "Divine's 'Angels' Win Fight to Register," *new York Times,* 10 Oct. 1936. Also see Parker, *Incredible Messiah,* 166-67. Other observers confirmed that satiny reds, blues, and purples were the colors favored by Divinite women. One observer described Divinite Faithful Mary as "richly dressed in a white and purple satin affair. The white covered the upper part of her body and met the purple in a sharply zig-zag formation just above the waist." Hosher, *God in a Rolls-Royce,* 146. Another reporter described the dress of Divinite Sarah Moss, who wore a white straw hat; white skirt, shoes, and gloves; and a bright scarlet satin blouse. "Court Lifts Veil on Divine Garage," *New York Times,* 5 June 1936, 7. Divinite women liked to contrast firey colors with whites. This practice seemed to embody the Divinite creed of racial integration and to echo on their bodies the Peace Mission pattern of seating black and white women next to each other at Divinite banquets. See photographs accompanying "Father Divine in Harlem," *Vanity Fair,* Jan. 1936, 39; photograph of Peninnah in Weisbrot, *Father Divine,* following 90.

66. Bair, "Women and the Garvey Movement," 7. See "Notice," *Negro World,* 28 Apr. 1923; David Levering Lewis, *When Harlem Was in Vogue* (New York, 1981), 39-40.

67. Tony Martin, *Literary Garveyism* (Dover, Mass., 1983), 45-46; Bair, "Women and the Garvey Movement," n. 17, 28-29.

68. Hill, *Papers,* vol. 7, l-liv.

69. See Weisbrot, *Father Divine,* 180, on the sparerib stews and pork commonly served at Peace Mission banquets.

    Divine spoke openly of his identification with his followers. "I AM the common people," he declared. He even claimed to make grammatical errors so that his followers "might understand ME: that I might be with them in their grammatical errors, and erroneousness; that I might lift them and they might lift me." See *Spoken Word,* 18 May 1935, 5; Burnham, *God Comes to America,* 29. Peace Mission members in turn felt in Divine they had "A God Like Me." See *Spoken Word,* 23 Nov. 1935, 16.

70. See ad in *Black Man,* late Oct., 1935; Hill and Bair, *Marcus Garvey,* xlix; Stein, *World of Marcus Garvey,* 266.

71. Hill and Bair, *Marcus Garvey,* 275 (Garvey's italics), 149, 7.

72. *Black Man,* Jan. 1934, 14.

73. For example, see *Black Man,* Dec. 1933, 14; Jan. 1934, 14, 16; Mar.-Apr. 1934, front cover; Aug.-Sept. 1935, front cover; late Mar., 1936, front cover.

74. Hill and Bair, *Marcus Garvey,* xlix.

75. Amy Jacques Garvey had condemned birth control for blacks in the 1920s. She wrote that "birth control suits [white people] but not us; it is our duty to bear children, and care for those children so that our race may have good men and women through whom it can achieve honor and power." See *Negro World,* 9 Apr. 1927, 7. By the 1930s, however, Amy Jacques Garvey seemed disturbed by her observation that although "malnutrition was taking its toll" on poor Jamaicans, "the fecundity of the people was undiminished." This makes the timing of Garvey's condemnation particularly odd. See Jaques Garvey, *Garvey and Garveyism,* 217, 206. Also see "Negroes Decreasing, Whites Increasing in U.S.A.," *Black Man,* late Dec., 1935 13; see Hill, *Papers,* vol. 7, 705.

76. Hill and Bair, *Marcus Garvey,* lvii-lviii. On the relationship between pronatalism and fascism, see Claudia Koonz, *Mothers in the Fatherland: Women, the Family and Nazi Politics* (New York, 1987); Victoria De Grazia, *How Fascism Ruled Women: Italy, 1922-45* (Berkeley, Calif., 1992).

77. See Weisbrot, *Father Divine,* 165; Barnes, "Blessings Flowing Free," 286, 216; "Court Lifts Veil on Divine Garage," *New York Times,* 5 June 1936, 7; Parker, *Incredible Messiah,* 273.

78. Weisbrot, *Father Divine,* 209-10. On Peace Mission sex scandals, see Watts, *God, Harlem, U.S.A.,* 144-52, 155. Millennial movements attract rebellious and nonconformist individuals and so are inherently unstable and inclined to fissions. Thus although external harassment took its toll on the movement, the splits from within were equally damaging. As Barnes points out, the Peace Mission was in many ways a family, and "[l]ike many another . . . family, the Peace Mission Movement could be suffocating and cruel." Former members described Peace Mission Heavens as ridden with jealousy and intrigue, and told of their own terrors that Divine, as God, would find and punish them if they dared to leave the movement. See Barnes, "Blessings Flowing Free," 229; Hadley Cantril, *The Psychology of Social Movements* (New York, 1941), 136-37.

79. See *New Day,* Dec. 8, 1936. This format varied little for the next twenty years. See also Watts, *God, Harlem, U.S.A.,* 160, 144.

80. See Harris, *These Also Believe,* 215; Weisbrot, *Father Divine,* 209-10; Watts, *God, Harlem, U.S.A.,* 161-63.

81. Braden, *Father Divine,* 15, see 14-17.

82. See Weisbrot, *Father Divine,* 211; Worsley, *Trumpet Shall Sound,* xxxvii-xxxviii, xlix, 232.

83. See Worsley, *Trumpet Shall Sound,* 232-33. Although Father Divine's belief in the creative power of thought always contained the potential of self-blame, this tendency had been muted during the 1930s heydey of his movement. At that time, Divine attributed even criminal behavior to the sufferings of people under unjust laws. In one 1935 banquet speech, Divine explained that "[e]ven cultured men at times, and others that are not cultured, resort to crime because of segregation, because of the dishonesty of Politics, and the dishonesty of the Laws. . . ." See *Spoken Word,* 7 Dec. 1935, 5-6. On another occasion, Divine explicitly sanctioned rebellion against unjust laws. "God is a law-breaker and a law-violator," he said. *Spoken Word,* 26 Oct. 1935, 12.

84. *New Day,* 13 July 1974, 17, cited in Watts, *God, Harlem, U.S.A.,* 88. After Father Divine's death in 1965 the *New Day* continued to publish selected reprints of his speeches. They cite the time and place that Divine gave the speech. Because Watts gives only the date of the *New Day* issues, it is not certain whether Divine made this statement after 1936. The tone of the comment fits Divine's increasingly punitive attitude in the 1940s and 1950s, however.

85. *New Day,* 22 July 1944, 44; see *New Day,* 13 Aug. 1942, cover; Braden, *These Also Believe,* 1, 18, 21.

86. Father Divine, speech originally delivered in 1932 and published in *New Day,* 1 Mar. 1975, cited in Watts, *God, Harlem, U.S.A.,* 88.

87. See Mother Divine, *Peace Mission Movement,* 35, 144, 149-50; see Father Divine's speech of 6 Oct. 1945 in *New Day,* 18 July 1987, 7.

88. See *New Day,* 22 July 1944, 7; Divine's sermon of 6 Feb. 1951 in *New Day,* 2 Dec. 1978, cited in Weisbrot, *Father Divine,* 212.

89. See Harris, *Father Divine,* 120; Mother Divine, *Peace Mission Movement,* 52.

90. The Rosebuds, Divine said in 1944, were "making an INDEPENDENT PEOPLE in the land! And as they LIVE their INDEPENDENCE and do not depend on individuals for anything . . . they will stand INDEPENDENTLY and do any and everything for themselves. . . ." *New Day,* 22 July 1944, 8; see *New Day,* 24 Nov. 1945.

91. The Rosebuds became Divine's primary, though not exclusive, exemplars of virginity. The Crusaders, a male order, similarly pledged to "live so that every thought, word and deed is virgin pure in its righteousness." The Lily-buds, an order for older women, were not required to be literal virgins. Nevertheless, their pledge promised that they had been "redeemed from the mortal, carnal life. . . ." See *New Day* Supplement, 15 Sept. 1956, 2a, s12; Burnham, *God Comes to America,* 84-96; Mother Divine, *Peace Mission Movement,* 32. On Divine's emphasis on virginity, see Harris, *Father Divine,* 236-37.

    It is not clear exactly when the Rosebuds' Creed, with its strong emphasis on virginity, was first proposed. The earliest reference I have found is in Harris, *Father Divine,* published in 1953.

92. The Rosebuds' uniform exemplified the merging of nationalism and virginity typical of Divine's later movement. In sharp contrast to the fiery colors and satiny textures adopted by Peace Mission women of the 1930s, the Rosebuds wore blue skirts, white blouses, red jackets with large Vs on the lapels (standing for Virgin, in some accounts, and Virtue and Victory, in others), and tiny red, white, and blue neckties. The use of the famous World War II V symbol to embody not only the predestined victory of the United States but also the virginity of Divine's red-white-and-blue-clad Sweets is a near-perfect exemplification of the merging of body and community symbolism typical of religious sects. The Rosebuds' victory over lower bodily impulses symbolically merged with a hoped-for American victory over "lower" nations. See photos in *New Day,* 11 Sept. 1954; Harris, *Father Divine,* 248-49; Watts, *God, Harlem, U.S.A.,* 161; Mother Divine, *Peace Mission Movement,* 32; see Mary Douglas, *Natural Symbols: Explorations in Cosmology* (New York, 1982).

    Numerous mainstream Americans shared Divine's obsession with virginity and anti-communism in the 1950s. See Elaine Tyler May, *Homeward Bound: American Families in the Cold War Era* (New York, 1988), 92-113.

93. Letter from Father Divine to Citizens Emergency Defense Conference, 4 Aug. 1953 in *New Day,* 11 Sept. 1954, *New Day,* 30 Apr. 1955, 17, and many other *New Day* issues.

94. See Burnham, *God Comes to America,* 86-96; Watts, *God, Harlem, U.S.A.,* 161. These similarities were somewhat superficial, however, since male and female Divinites, unlike mainstream Americans, continued to live separate, celibate lives.

95. Among Peace Mission members, only Father Divine could marry. Divinites interpreted Divine's marriage as "the Marriage of CHRIST to HIS Church" and stressed that that the marriage was purely spiritual. Father Divine frequently referred to the new Mrs. Divine as his Spotless Virgin Bride. See Mother Divine, *Peace Mission Movement,* 53-58, 147.

96. See photographs of Father and Mother Divine in supplement, *New Day,* 11 Sept. 1954; see Harris, *Father Divine,* 182-83.

97. See *New Day,* 26 Sept. 1953, 6-7 and entire issue; see Mother Divine, *Peace Mission Movement,* 59, 80.

98. *New Day,* 26 Sept. 1953, 13.

99. Garvey. "African Fundamentalism," in Hill and Bair, *Marcus Garvey,* 7.

FURTHER READING

Biographies

Lewis, Rupert. *Marcus Garvey: Anti-Colonial Champion.* Trenton, N.J.: Africa World Press, 1988, 301 p.

Stresses the global nature of Garvey's life and career; gives thorough attention to Garvey's time in Jamaica.

Martin, Tony. *Marcus Garvey, Hero: A First Biography.* Dover, Mass.: Majority Press, 1983, 179 p.

Looks at the growth of Garveyism worldwide in addition to providing a chronology of Garvey's career; very sympathetic view of Garvey's controversies.

Bibliography

Ratliff, Peggy Stevenson, and Roosevelt Ratliff Jr. "Marcus Moziah Garvey, Jr. (1887-1940)." In *African American Authors, 1745-1945: A Bio-Bibliographical Critical Sourcebook,* edited by Emmanuel S. Nelson, pp. 175-83. Westport, Conn.: Greenwood Press, 2000.

Provides a brief biography and a listing of both primary and secondary sources relating to Garvey.

Criticism

Bruce, John Edward. "Marcus Garvey and the U.N.I.A." In *The Selected Writing of John Edward Bruce: Militant Black Journalist,* edited by Peter Gilbert, pp. 167-70. New York: Arno Press, 1971.

Originally written in the 1922, this essay details Bruce's initial impressions of Garvey and his conclusion that Garvey had established himself as the leader of the most signifacant movement for Black solidarity and liberation.

Cooper, Carolyn. "Unorthodox Prose: The Poetical Works of Marcus Garvey." In *Garvey: His Work and Impact,* edited by Rupert Lewis and Patrick Bryan, pp. 113-21. Trenton, N.J.: Africa World Press, 1991.

Argues that the complexity and power of Garvey's thought is often obscured by weak poetry; quotes extensively from Garvey's poetry.

Essien-Udom, E. U. Introduction to *Philosophy and Opinions of Marcus Garvey,* pp. vii-xxvii. New York: A. M. Kelly, 1967.

Asserts the continued relevance of Garvey's thought and identifies key principles; gives some biographical information about Garvey's wife and children.

Harrison, Paul Carter. "*The Black Star Line*: The De-Mystification of Marcus Garvey." *African American Review* 31, no. 4 (1997): 713-16.

Critiques the play based on Garvey's life; suggests that it focused on personal details at the expense of Garvey's standing as an African American icon.

Hill, Robert A. "'The Foremost Radical among His Race': Marcus Garvey and the Black Scare, 1918-1921." *Prologue: The Journal of the National Archives* 16, no. 4 (1984): 215-31.

Details the government's pursuit of Garvey, using extensive primary documentation from presidential and FBI records.

Jacques, Geoffrey. Review of *Marcus Garvey: Look for Me in the Whirlwind. Cinaste* 26, no. 4 (2001): 76-77.

Reviews a documentary film by Stanley Nelson based on the life of Marcus Garvey; finds that the film gives a balanced and moving portrait of Garvey.

Levine, Lawrence W. "Marcus Garvey's Moment: A Passionate and Perplexing Chapter in Black History." *New Republic* 191 (29 October 1984): 26-31.

Assesses the importance of Garvey's legacy; reviews Robert Hill's collected volumes of Garvey and UNIA documents.

Lewis, Rupert. "Marcus Garvey and the Early Rastafarians: Continuity and discontinuity." In *Chanting Down Babylon: The Rastafari Reader,* edited by Nathaniel Samuel Murrell, William David Spencer, and Adrian Anthony McFarlane, pp. 145-58. Philadelphia: Temple University Press, 1998.

Examines the intersection of Garveyism and Rastafarianism as concurrent but distinct movements in Black nationalism; observes differences in spirituality.

Martin, Tony. *Race First: The Ideological and Organizational Struggles of Marcus Garvey and the Universal Negro Improvement Association.* Westport, Conn.: Greenwood Press, 1976, 421 p.

Surveys the major controversies in Garvey's career; includes examinations of Garvey's relations with the NAACP, the Ku Klux Klan, and the Communist Party.

Smith-Irvin, Jeannette. *Footsoldiers of the Universal Negro Improvement Association.* Trenton, N.J.: Africa World Press, 1989, 93 p.

Consists chiefly of interviews with leading figures in UNIA, including Garvey's second wife.

Stein, Judith. *The World of Marcus Garvey: Race and Class in Modern Society.* Baton Rouge: Louisiana State University Press, 1986, 294 p.

Focuses on Garveyism as a movement more than Garvey the man; emphasizes the context in which the philosophy of Garveyism arose and took hold.

Watson, Elwood D. "Marcus Garvey and the Rise of Black Nationalism." *USA Today* 129 (November 2000): 64-66.

Gives an overview of Garvey and Garveyism; suggests that the major contribution of Garvey's movement was the legacy of black pride.

———. "Marcus Garvey's Garveyism: Message From a Forefather." *Journal of Religious Thought* 51, no. 2 (winter 1994-spring 1995): 77-94.

Emphasizes the self-love aspect of Garveyism; observes that the modern revival of Garvey's brand of nationalism has transcended race.

OTHER SOURCES FROM GALE:

Additional coverage of Garvey's life and career is contained in the following sources published by the Gale Group: *Black Literature Criticism,* Vol. 2; *Black Writers,* Ed. 1; *Contemporary Authors,* Vols. 120, 124; *Contemporary Authors New Revision Series,* Vol. 79; *DISCovering Authors Modules: Multicultural Authors*; and *Twentieth-Century Literary Criticism,* Vol. 41.

ANGELINA WELD GRIMKÉ

(1880 - 1958)

American poet, playwright, and short story writer.

A poet and author of the protest play *Rachel* (1916), Grimké is considered a transitional writer whose early work is grounded in the conventions of the Black Genteel School, while her later, more famous, writings are associated with the Harlem Renaissance of the 1920s.

BIOGRAPHICAL INFORMATION

Grimké was born in Boston on February 27, 1880, to Archibald Henry, an attorney, and Sarah Stanley Grimké, an author. Her paternal grandparents were Henry Grimké, a white lawyer from South Carolina, and one of his slaves, Nancy Weston. Grimké was the namesake of her great aunt Angelina Emily Grimké Weld, a prominent abolitionist and supporter of women's suffrage. Grimké's father, Archibald, was a graduate of Harvard Law School, an author, and a diplomat; he served as vice-president of the National Association for the Advancement of Colored People and devoted his life to causes associated with racial equality and social justice. Grimké's mother's family was white and opposed their daughter's marriage to Archibald because of his mixed race. In 1883 Sarah Grimké left her husband, taking young Angelina with her; four years later she returned the child to her father's custody and never saw her daughter again.

Grimké was raised by her father, to whom she was extremely close, and by her aunt, Angelina Weld. She lived a privileged existence in a family of intellectuals and activists and was shielded from the problems facing most African Americans in the late nineteenth and early twentieth centuries. Grimké was educated at a variety of private institutions for upper-class children: Fairmount School in Hyde Park, Massachusetts, Carleton Academy in Northfield, Minnesota, and Cushing Academy in Ashburnham, Massachusetts. In 1902, she graduated from the Boston Normal School of Gymnastics, and for the next several years taught English in Washington, D.C., taking classes at Harvard during the summers.

Grimké's diaries suggest that her life was characterized by unhappiness and frustration as a result of her sexual orientation. Although she apparently had a brief relationship with another woman in her youth, she suppressed her lesbianism most of her life, possibly fearing the disapproval of her father. She had always been sensitive and introspective and her father's illness and death in 1930 increased her unhappiness to the point of neurosis. She moved from Washington, D. C., to New York City and stopped writing entirely. She died on June 10, 1958.

MAJOR WORKS

Grimké began writing poetry at an early age, but with the exception of some of her tributes to famous people which appeared in periodicals and anthologies, most of it was unpublished during her lifetime. Her most famous commemorative poems include "To Theodore D. Weld on His 90th Birthday" (1893) and "To Joseph Lee" (1908). The prevailing theme of the majority of her other poems is love, most of it unfulfilled, and most of it involving women as the objects of desire. Carolivia Herron, in her introduction to the *Selected Works of Angelina Weld Grimké* (1991), the first and only collection of Grimké's writings, acknowledges that "a large percentage of the Grimké poetic canon is indeed a record of her attempt to love and be loved by another woman." Death and despair are also common features of many of Grimké's poems, including "Death" (1925) and "Where Phillis Sleeps" (1901).

On racial issues, Grimké's early work drew on the conventions of the genteel tradition, emphasizing the positive side of Black life in America. Increasingly, however, she dealt with racism and oppression more openly and more stridently, less so in her poetry than in her prose. Her most famous work is the drama *Rachel,* a protest play about lynching and its long-term effects on a Black family living in New York. The title character, Rachel Loving, and her brother, Tom, live in a tenement with their seamstress mother. Their father and older brother had been lynched ten years earlier, and the first act of the play presents Mrs. Loving's revelation of that fact to her children. The second and third acts take place four years later and involve Rachel's despair at the ongoing discrimination faced by the members of her family and by other Blacks in the neighborhood—even in the "safe" North. She vows to forgo marriage and motherhood in order to avoid bringing any more Black children into the world to be subjected to the cruelties of racism in America. The short stories "The Closing Door" (1919) and "Goldie" (1920) also deal with the subjects of lynching and the bleak future Grimké envisioned for Black children. In the first, a mother kills her infant, and in the second, a mob cuts an unborn child from its lynched mother's womb.

CRITICAL RECEPTION

Grimké's writings were not popular during her lifetime. The violence of her works on lynching was too graphic for contemporary readers, and critics claimed that her short stories, and particularly her play *Rachel,* seemed to promote a form of self-genocide for African Americans—a charge Grimké herself denied. As for her verse, Herron reports that "most of her poems were too lesbian and too sentimental for audiences during and after the Harlem Renaissance."

More recently, Grimké's work has been reexamined, particularly *Rachel* and the stories that led to charges that the author was advocating "race suicide." The success of Toni Morrison's *Beloved,* which also involves infanticide, promoted scholars to revisit Grimké's accounts of mothers who refused to bear or raise potential victims of racism and injustice. William Storm has explored the psychological complexity of *Rachel*'s title character and the early experiences that led to her decision to remain unmarried and childless. David A. Hedrich Hirsch has studied the short stories "The Closing Door" and "Blackness" (an earlier version of "Goldie"), suggesting that in her treatment of lynching victims, Grimké was attempting "to substantiate and give voice to African Americans silenced by the historical narratives of a dominant discourse." Elizabeth Brown-Guillory, in her study of minority mother-daughter relationships, has examined the controversy surrounding *Rachel* and argues that Grimké was attempting to educate white women about the meaning of motherhood for Blacks. She adds that Grimké was also offering a cautionary tale to African American mothers on the consequences of failing to prepare daughters to survive the effects of racism. According to Brown-Guillory, "Grimké suggests that black mothers must model for their daughters the various ways to reach inside to find courage to live triumphantly in a world in which they must ultimately face and overcome race and gender barriers." Rachel's failure to embrace motherhood is thus the result not only of racism, but also of Mrs. Loving's misguided attempt to shield her from the realities of it, writes Brown-Guillory.

PRINCIPAL WORKS

*"To Theodore D. Weld on His 90th Birthday" (poem) 1893

"Where Phillis Sleeps" (poem) 1901

"Beware Lest He Awakes!" (poem) 1902

"To Joseph Lee" (poem) 1908

Rachel (play) 1916

"The Closing Door" (short story) 1919

"Goldie" (short story) 1920

"The Black Finger" (poem) 1923

"Death" (poem) 1925

"Trees" (poem) 1928

Selected Works of Angelina Weld Grimké (poetry, drama, fiction, and nonfiction) 1991

* Grimké's poems and short stories were originally published in various periodicals and anthologies.

GENERAL COMMENTARY

CAROLIVIA HERRON (ESSAY DATE 1991)

SOURCE: Herron, Carolivia. Introduction to *Selected Works of Angelina Weld Grimké,* edited by Carolivia Herron, pp. 3-22. New York: Oxford University Press, 1991.

In the following introduction, Herron provides an overview of Grimké's life and career, discussing the thematic and stylistic features that characterized her writing.

The Angelina Weld Grimké Collection at the Moorland-Spingarn Research Center of Howard University includes a note in Grimké's hand that lists the titles of a projected collection of poetry. The list begins with the poem **"An Epitaph,"** which depicts the futility and despair of the narrator who longs first for joy, then for love, and is answered with pain and death. The poem is presented in three stanzas, the last of which unites the themes of death, lost love, repudiation of life, and despair. The typescript of the poem has many changes of pronoun—from *I* to *she* and from *me* to *her*—suggesting that Grimké debated between the closeness of the perspective and the participation of the narrator with the subject of the poem. The last stanza reads:

> And now I lie quite straight, and still and plain;
> Above my heart the brazen poppies flare,
> But I know naught of love, or joy, or pain;—
> Nor care, nor care.

Somewhat illegible, the list of poems moves through titles suggesting happiness and familial comfort (**"Lullaby"**) and ends with **"To Joseph Lee,"** an obituary poem that was published by the *Boston Evening Transcript* (11 Nov. 1908) and that commemorates an African-American caterer and civil rights advocate in Boston.

Grimké's projected volume thus moves from inner death to outer death, from the metaphorical death and repudiation of the love of one who loves too much to the literal death of a publicly mourned figure in a communal occasion of grief. The first poem not only records the failure of love for the narrator, but also masks the fact that the love Grimké preferred to receive, the love she missed, was probably that of a woman in a lesbian relationship. Critics such as Gloria Hull in *Color, Sex, and Poetry,* and Barbara Christian in *Black Feminist Criticism,* have discussed the hidden lesbian life of Angelina Weld Grimké as it affects her poetry. A large percentage of the Grimké poetic canon is indeed a record of her attempt to love and be loved by another woman. Many of these poems, such as **"Another Heart Is Broken," "Naughty Nan,"** and **"Caprichosa,"** are here published for the first time.

"To Joseph Lee," however, is an example of a small percentage of Grimké's poetry that was written for occasions of celebration or commemoration. Among these are **"To My Father Upon His Fifty-Fifth Birthday," "Two Pilgrims Hand in Hand,"** and **"To the Dunbar High School."** In addition, Grimké wrote and published several poems, such as **"Tenebris"** and **"Beware Lest He Awakes,"** that portray the African-American experience of racial pride, as well as reaction against and revenge for lynching and other racist acts within the United States.

Although it is an extremely powerful theme when presented in her poetry, the subject of lynching is minor in terms of the number of poetic references to it. We may say that the three major themes in Grimké's poetry are lost love, commemoration of famous people, and African-American racial concerns, but we must acknowledge that racial concerns constitute less than five percent of her total output of poetry. Most of the poems speak of love, death, and grief through narrative personae that are not explicitly identified with the interests of African Americans and that are often quite frankly white and male. **"My Shrine,"** for example, is narrated by a standard nineteenth-century (male) persona who expresses his idealized love for a woman on a pedestal.

In contrast, the entire corpus of Grimké's fiction, nonfiction, and drama focus almost exclusively on lynching and racial injustice. These works take on African-American cultural grief rather than personal grief as their thematic focus, and they express great outrage over the lynching of African Americans in the South, over the failure of Northern whites to band together and demand an end to the crimes, and over racial injustice in general. In one story, **"Jettisoned,"** Grimké also investigates the repercussions of passing for white in the African-American community.

Lynching is a particularly affecting theme in Grimké's play ***Rachel*** (1920). The play depicts the effects of lynching on the desire to live and the attraction toward genocide for members of the African-American community. The theme of lynching extends to her fiction as well, appearing in such stories as **"The Closing Door," "Goldie,"** and **"Blackness."**

Angelina Weld Grimké was named for her white great aunt, Angelina Grimké Weld. As a young woman, Weld, along with her sister, Sarah Grimké, left South Carolina in the early nineteenth century to avoid participating directly in the ownership of slaves. The two sisters settled in Hyde Park, Massachusetts, and became well-known abolitionists and advocates of women's rights. Angelina Grimké eventually married the abolitionist Theodore Weld. Several years after the Civil War, the two sisters discovered and acknowledged their mulatto nephews, Archibald and Francis, and accepted them into their home. The young men were two of the three sons born to Angelina and Sarah's brother, Henry Grimké, and his slave, Nancy Weston. Francis married Charlotte Forten. Archibald married a white woman, Sarah Stanley, and their only child was Angelina Weld Grimké.

Angelina was born on February 27, 1880, in Boston and lived most of her life with her father to whom she was extremely attached emotionally. Soon after Angelina's birth, her mother left the Grimké household. Information concerning Sarah Stanley Grimké is scant, but it appears that she was confined in some manner for mental aberration or physical incapacity. In a letter written to Angelina when she was seven years old, Sarah speaks of wanting to return to visit her daughter, of hearing her cry out "Mamma" in her dreams. "I dream about you very often. The other night—I thought—I saw you out in a large cornfield. . . . Do you ever dream of Mamma?—Some time I shall be able to come to you in my *Shadow Body* and really *see* you. How would you like that? And *some* time we will be together again."[1]

In spite of (or because of) Angelina's great affection for her father, he seems to have been the source of some restriction and oppression in her own sexual self-consciousness as a lesbian. It is clear that she decided to forgo the expression of her lesbian desires in order to please her father, and in her poem written to commemorate his fifty-fifth birthday she describes what she would have been without him in terms of a great horror and scandal avoided. Love letters to named and unnamed women appear in Grimké's papers as early as her fourteenth year, and an exchange of letters with Mamie Burrill in 1896, when Grimké was sixteen years old, makes definite reference to a prior love affair. Burrill writes to Grimké, "Angie, do you love me as you used to?" Grimké's draft letter of response answers:

> My own darling Mamie, If you will allow me to be so familiar to call you such. I hope my darling you will not be offended if your ardent lover calls you such familiar names. . . . Oh Mamie if you only knew how my heart beats when I think of you and it yearns and pants to gaze, if only for one second upon your lovely face. If there were any trouble in this wide and wicked world from which I might shield you how gladly would I do it if it were even so great a thing as to lay down my life for you. I know you are too young now to become my wife, but I hope, darling, that in a few years you will come to me and be my love, my wife! How my brain whirls how my pulse leaps with joy and madness when I think of these two words, "my wife."[2]

Grimké was educated at Fairmont Grammar School in Hyde Park (1887-1894), Carleton Academy in Northfield, Minnesota (1895), Cushing Academy in Ashburnham, Massachusetts, and Girls' Latin School in Boston, and in 1902 she took a degree in physical education at the Boston Normal School of Gymnastics (now Wellesley College). That same year she began her teaching career as a gym teacher at Armstrong Manual Training School in Washington, D.C., but in 1907, after much tension with the principal of Armstrong, she transferred to the more academic M Street High School (later Dunbar High School) where she taught English. Grimké was always more academic than vocational in her interest, and there is some question as to why she took a degree in physical education in the first place. Perhaps as a closeted lesbian she found physical education attractive because it provided sublimated contact with women.

Grimké retired from teaching and moved to New York City in 1926 where she died on June 10, 1958. Most of her works were written between 1900 and 1920. The drama ***Rachel*** is her only published book prior to this volume, but she published some of her poetry, fiction, and nonfiction (reviews and biographical sketches) in many prominent journals, particularly *Opportunity,* and in newspapers and many anthologies.

The present volume includes approximately one-third of the poetry, one-half of the short stories, and a small sampling of the nonfiction found in Grimké's papers at the Moorland-Spingarn Research Center. A republication of ***Rachel*** is also included. Almost all of the nonfiction is still in holograph, as are perhaps another two hundred poems, the incomplete play ***Mara*** (which also centers on lynching), and many unfinished short stories.

When focusing on death, women as objects of desire, lost love, motherhood, and children, the emotive import of Grimké's poems is overwhelmingly that of despair. In the poem **"The Garden Seat,"** for example, the narrator recalls a love tryst with a woman who has died:

> And then I stole up all noiseless and unseen,
> And kissed those eyes so dreamy and so sad—I
> Ah God! if I might once again see all
> Thy soul leap in their depths as then
> So hungry with long waiting and so true,
> I clasp thee close within my yearning arms
> I kiss thine eyes, thy lips, thy silky hair,
> I felt thy soft arms twining round my neck,
> Thy bashful, maiden, kisses on my cheek
> My whole heart leaping 'neath such wondrous
> joy—
> And then the vision faded and was gone
> And I was in my lonely, darkened, room,
> The old-time longing surging in my breast,
> The old-time agony within my soul
> As fresh, as new, as when I kissed thy lips
> So cold, with frenzy begging thee to speak,
> Believing not that thou wert lying dead.

Grimké's poem **"Death"** examines death abstractly as a philosophy of an afterlife and is more hopeful than her poems that describe the death of loved ones.

> When the lights blur out for thee and me,
> And the black comes in with a sweep,
> I wonder—will it mean life again,
> Or sleep?

Such philosophical investigations of death removed from expressions of lost love are rare, however. In **"Where Phillis Sleeps"** Grimké writes, "Dear one, I lie upon thy grave, my tears like rain are falling," and in **"One Little Year,"** she writes, "Quite hopeless, now, my lips refuse to pray—/ For thou art dead." The poem **"Thou Art So Far, So Far"** is one of many that depict lost love due not to death but to the unapproachable nature of the beloved:

> Thou art to me a lone, white, star,
> That I may gaze on from afar;
> But I may never, never, press
> My lips on thine in mute caress, . . .

The poem **"My Shrine"** is Grimké's prime example of poems that depict women as ideal objects of desire:

> The idol that I placed
> Within this modest shrine
> Was but a maiden small,
> But yet divinely pure,
> And there I humbly knelt
> Before those calm, grey, eyes, . . .

In this poem Grimké takes the persona of a male, "Behold the one he loves!," presumably to divert attention from the lesbian implications of the poem. **"Caprichosa"** emphasizes a sexual rather than an ideal interest in a woman, and the narrator does not take on a male persona:

> Little lady coyly shy
> With deep shadows in each eye
> Cast by lashes soft and long,
> Tender lips just bowed for song,
> And I oft have dreamed the bliss
> Of the nectar in one kiss. . . .

Grimké's most significant statement about motherhood is unconsciously embedded within her poem **"To My Father Upon His Fifty-Fifth Birthday."** While the poem purports to praise her father's help and strength, it actually focuses on diminutive images of him as an infant incapable of sustaining himself:

> . . . This day on which a new-made mother
> watched
> You lying in her arms, your little head against
> Her breast; and as you lay there, tiny wriggling
> mass, . . .

The description of her father as a "tiny wriggling mass" surely is not calculated to glorify his strength and has uncomfortable phallic implications as well. She goes on to describe her grandmother's new experience of motherhood in nursing her father. And the exclamation point is given not to a celebration of the child (her father), but to a glorification of the mother (her grandmother): "Ah, gift of Motherhood!" The poem then elaborates on the virtues of women and mothering. It is here that Grimké refers to what her life would have been like without her father (and presumably without having to restrict her lesbian inclinations):

> . . . What were I, father dear, without thy help?
> I turn my eyes away before the figure and
> Rejoice; and yet your loving hands have moul-
> ded me; . . .

Through her father's assistance, Grimké repudiates her own self-molding and takes her dependent imprint from him. Finally, after depicting the care he has given her through her life, Grimké gives her father her highest compliment, "You have been a gentle mother to your child." That is, the best she can say about her father is that he is almost a mother.

This poem gives the impression that Grimké and her father had no major disagreements in their lives, but that is belied by the opening passage in Grimké's first diary, started in July 1903 to record a lost love involvement with an unnamed person. "My father and I have been having a hard time to-night over you, dear. I guess he is right and I shall try to give you up." Earlier in this entry, she writes, "I suppose I was a fool and oh how I wish that I had a mother!" Grimké's inability to portray her father as an adult male in her poem celebrating his fatherhood reveals her ambivalent feelings toward this man whose approval she could not live without but whose moralistic dicta appear to have greatly restricted her own sexual expression.

The theme of children is almost as significant as the theme of mothers in Grimké's poetry and is usually linked, as in **"The Black Child,"** with portrayals of the ways in which African Americans suffer oppression at the hands of whites. **"The Black Child"** uses the image of a black baby playing in sunlight and then in shadow as an affecting extended metaphor of black life and external oppression. The poem opens:

I saw a little black child
Sitting in a gold circle of sunlight;
And in his little black hand,
He had a little black stick,
And he was beating, beating,
With his little black stick,
The sunlight all about him,
And laughing, laughing.

By elaborating on this scene through the passage of the day, and by refusing to explain or interpret it, Grimké increases the poignancy for the reader who alternately sees the poem as a metaphor of black life or as a realistic image of a black child playing. The image is so well formed, and the impulse to delight in it so strong, that the reader almost hopes the poem is simple realistic truth to enjoy and appreciate without confronting the psychic and sociological shadow that alters and subverts the lives of black children.

And he sat in the gold circle of sunlight
Kicking with his little feet,
And wriggling his little toes,
And beating, beating
The sunlight all about him, . . .

The shadow eases upon the black child slowly until at the end of the poem he is beating not the light but the shadows. In another poem about a black child, **"Lullaby [(2)],"** Grimké includes her only attempt to write black diction in verse. She is not, in this instance, adept in the use of black diction, but the content of the poem reveals her attitude toward the limited possibilities available to black adults in the United States:

Ain't you quit dis laffin' yet?
Don' you know de sun's done set?
Wan' me kiss dis li'l han'?
Well, well, laf de w'ile you can,
You won' laf w'en you'se a man,
Dere! Dere! Sleep! Sleep!

Grimké's fiction is more stark in portraying the horror, the accents, and the future of black children. An infant is smothered in **"The Closing Door,"** and in **"Goldie"** and **"Blackness,"** an unborn child is cut from the womb of a lynched woman, revealing the full horror of African-American life in the United States.

Grimké wrote a few poems presenting her overall world view and background philosophy. Among these are **"Life [(1)]"** and **"The Puppet-Player."** In **"Life [(1)],"** for example, human beings are out of control of the destiny of their lives and overwhelmed by the "Ocean, boundless, infinite" of life:

Thou ne'er hast known nor dead nor living
One single braggart man as master. . . .

And some are lost on rocks relentless;
And some are drowned mid storms tremendous,
. . .
The waters close again impenetrably:—
Each one must make his way alone—
And this is Life!

"The Puppet-Player" is even more pessimistic and ascribes conscious and evil intention to the power that controls the world:

Sometimes it seems as though some puppet-player
A clenchéd claw cupping a craggy chin,
Sits just beyond the border of our seeing,
Twitching the strings with slow, sardonic grin.

Other poems directly examine the value of life for the narrator. **"Epitaph on a Living Woman"** describes the annihilation of emotion and joy for the speaker: "There were tiny flames in her eyes, / Her mouth was a flame, / And her flesh. . . . / Now she is ashes." **"Life [(2)]"** is Grimké's only acknowledgment in verse that the narrator's life, in spite of its grim sadness, has at least been more dynamic than other people's:

What though I die mid racking pain,
And heart seared through and through by grief,
I still rejoice for I, at least, have lived.

By contrast, a rare poetic encounter with hope and joy is found in **"A Mood"**:

Up mocking, teasing, little, hill;
Past dancing, glancing, little, rills,
And up or down to left or right
The same compelling, wild, delight!

"The Visitor" is Grimke's only poem in which the narrator repudiates rather than longs for death:

I beg you come not near!
See! Though I am so proud
I'll fall upon my knees,
And beg, and pray, of you
To spare this little soul!

Some of Grimké's poems use such forms as the sonnet, the triolet, and the roundel. Sonnets are particularly solemn forms for Grimké, who uses them to commemorate the life of the philanthropist Mary Porter Tileston Hemenway in **"Two Sonnets to Mrs. Hemenway,"** and to represent stern authoritarian sentiments about God in **"As We Have Sowed"**:

I

As we have sowed so shall we also reap;
And it were sweet indeed if blossoms fair
Grow from the seeds to scent the sunlit air,
But oh! How sad if weeds that hide and creep
Grow in their stead to prick and sting our feet.
Too soon we'll meet the Master on our path,
And in His deep sad eyes we'll feel the wrath
Of justice or the thrill of praises sweet.
I do but pray within this humble breast,
That little flowers may blossom on my way,
But yet so pure they change the night to day,
I beg that one more fair than all the rest
So please the Master that with glad surprise
He proudly plucks it, smiling in my eyes.

II

As we have sowed so shall we also reap:—
How sweet if by our path the blossoms fair
Grow from the seeds to scent the sunlit air;
But Oh! How sad if weeds that hide and creep
Grow in their stead to prick and sting our feet.
We know not when the Master passing by
May pause, nor when from out his deep sad eye
May leap the flame of wrath or praises sweet
The sweetest flowers are those not proudly drest,
But little ones that brighten all the way,
They are so pure and white. For me I pray
That one white flower more pure than all the rest
May burst in blossom 'neath the Master's eyes,
That only He may know the sacrifice.

In the first of these sonnets, the Master plucks the narrator's most beautiful flower, and in the second the narrator's one white flower bursts into bloom as an expression of her sacrifice. The stern taskmaster in the poem is surely an extension of Grimké's own father, who often chastised her verbally for her inadequacies and demanded that she fulfill all the restraining public roles that were expected of an educated middle-class African-American woman of her time.

"A Triolet," on the other hand, with its repeated line "Molly raised shy eyes to me," is an expression of joy in lesbian affection:

Molly raised shy eyes to me,
  On an April day;
Close we stood beneath a tree;
Molly raised shy eyes to me,
Shining sweet and wistfully,
Wet and yet quite gay;
Molly raised shy eyes to me,
  On an April day.

The roundel **"Vigil"** inhabits the intersection between hope and despair. The narrator repeatedly insists that her departed loved one will return—"You will come back"—but these words are surrounded by such a strong hint of impending hopelessness—"But if it will be bright or black"—that the act of hope appears to be merely the subterfuge of holding back despair:

You will come back, sometime, somehow;
But if it will be bright or black
I cannot tell; I only know
  You will come back.

Does not the spring with fragrant pack
Return unto the orchard bough?
Do not the birds retrace their track?

All things return. Some day the glow
Of quick'ning dreams will pierce your lack;
And when you know I wait as now
  You will come back.

For the most part, Grimké uses the poetic rhythms and styles characteristic of Anglo-American poetry as a whole. The African-American distinctiveness of her work is most visible in content and plot rather than in style. In those works dealing directly with the problem of being black in the United States, she attempts to tear down the master's house by using the master's tools. That is, she calls on the moral conscience of white Americans to correct and improve their relationship with their black fellow citizens. This mode of expression is particularly evident in her play ***Rachel.*** In fact, in an essay about the play, Grimké declared that ***Rachel*** had been written to educate whites and to correct their attitudes about lynching and its effects on African Americans.

Variously called *The Pervert, The Daughter,* and *Blessed Are the Barren* before receiving the title ***Rachel,*** the play is about a young African-American woman who prefers to forgo both marriage and motherhood so as not to provide whites with more black people to destroy through lynching and other racial atrocities. Indeed, the play may be said to encourage a form of self-genocide

FROM THE AUTHOR

"THE BLACK FINGER"

I have just seen a beautiful thing
Slim and still,
Against a gold, gold sky,
A straight cypress,
Sensitive
Exquisite,
A black finger
Pointing upwards.
Why, beautiful, still finger are you black?
And why are you pointing upwards?

SOURCE: Angelina Grimké, "The Black Finger," in *Opportunity* 1, September 1923.

of African-American people. Although Grimké attempts to justify this attitude in terms of the cruelties that African Americans are forced to endure in the United States, it is probable that in this plot she is using a psychic energy that repudiates heterosexuality on a personal level to accentuate her passion for annihilating the marital and familial expectations in African-American culture. Her denial of the possibility and hopefulness of heterosexual union appears more explicitly in **"The Laughing Hand,"** a short story that does not have African-American characters. In this story, a young woman is forced to break her engagement to her fiancé because he has contracted cancer and has suffered a disfiguring and silencing operation in which his tongue is cut out. This castration of language is more than an expression of the impossibility of heterosexual union; it may also comment on Grimké's closeted sexuality. Unendurable marriage is also the subject of the short story **"The Drudge,"** whose white characters are of a lower economic class than those in **"The Laughing Hand."** Here a beaten, oppressed wife manages to get some control over her husband by refusing to accommodate herself to his adultery.

Grimké is essentially appalled at her incapacity to have a lover in this world. And she is appalled at the restricted world that the United States allows for its African-American citizens. Her inner astonishment at her failure to find sexual and romantic companionship, and her outer astonishment at finding herself in a world that denigrates her value because she is a black woman, combine to give terrifying but effective power to stories like **"The Closing Door," "Goldie," "Blackness,"** and **"Black Is, As Black Does,"** all of which, like ***Rachel,*** take lynching as their theme. Two of the stories, **"The Closing Door,"** and **"Goldie,"** were published in the *Birth Control Review* to encourage black women not to have children.

Although Grimké's consciousness of African-American culture is restricted primarily to plot, one large exception to this rule appears in **"Jettisoned,"** a story written almost entirely in African-American English. It is probably not accidental that this short story, which adopts African-American style more overtly than do her other works, is the only one with an optimistic ending, though to get to that point her characters go through hell with problems of poverty, threatened suicide, and the pain of having relatives who pass for white.

Grimké's most radical works on African-American culture, including the short stories on lynching and the poems **"Trees," "Surrender," "The Black Finger," "Tenebris,"** and **"Beware Lest He Awakes,"** all lean toward a refusal to accept the given conditions of being black in the United States. But probably because of publication restrictions, these works often stop just short of demanding unapologetic revenge for acts against African-American people.

The poem **"Beware Lest He Awakes,"** for example, has three versions, and Grimké's changes, when compared with the published text, reveal that she may have been coerced into making revisions in order for the poem to be published. The original statement of the poem, that African Americans would eventually wake up and take revenge for the actions against them, was changed from the definite statement, "Beware when he awakes" to the more suppositional, "Beware lest he awakes." Thus the final version leads us to believe that the African-American people may or may not wake up and take revenge. Further, the line "Beware lest he awakes," which in the earlier versions ("Beware when he awakes") ends the two stanzas and thereby gains greater importance than any other portion of the poem, is—in the published version—buried in the middle of the first verse. Though it still ends the poem, the line's message has nevertheless been diffused.

Similarly, the short story **"Goldie,"** which is a revised version of **"Blackness,"** ends with the statement that the African-American man who takes revenge for lynching is himself lynched as well: "And Victor Forrest died, as the other two had died, upon another tree." **"Blackness,"** however, implies that the vindicator escapes safely: "I have reason, to believe, he escaped. But I have never heard from him or seen him since." Although this unnamed vindicator must leave his position in the North to escape the retribution of Southerners who come after him, we are given to understand that, with the money he has saved and with support from friends, he is able to live a life in another country or community and is not hunted to the death. Evidently, the revised story, **"Goldie,"** was more palatable to, and therefore deemed more publishable by, the *Birth Control Review* whose subscribers were more likely to accept fiction that encouraged African Americans not to have children in order to avoid having them lynched. The same subscribers, who were primarily white, would probably not have been willing to read about African Americans successfully taking revenge for lynching. In addition, Grimké leaves the successful revenge taker unnamed, perhaps to imply that he is still at large, still among us, and therefore his name must be protected.

Finally, Angelina Weld Grimké places herself within the tradition of African-American writers who are interested in identifying what is distinctive about African-American literary works. In her **"Remarks on Literature,"** she describes the coming black literary genius in these words:

> In preparation of the coming of this black genius I believe there must be among us a stronger and a growing feeling of race consciousness, race solidarity, race pride. It means a training of the youth of to-day and of to-morrow in the recognition of the sanctity of all these things. Then perhaps, some day, somewhere black youth, will come forth, see us clearly, intelligently, sympathetically, and will write about us and then come into his own.

Grimké herself is a participant in this coming genius, which is the forerunner of contemporary and emerging African-American artistic excellence. The oppressive stance of having to assume a white male narrative persona in her poetry in order to accommodate the "freedom" to describe sexual interest and encounters with other women gave Grimké profound information about the strategies of being closeted through concerns of race, gender, and sexual preference. The two major themes of her writings, the desire for romantic and sexual companionship and the desire for social and political equity for African Americans, give her work the import, if not the discrete form, of the blues—that musical and poetic cultural form which is the repository for African-American heroic anguish over love, lost love, and political disenfranchisement. The blues, whether in form or content or both, may indeed be characterized as the African-American epic song, and Grimké sings that song as an artist creating through the triple cultural blows of being black, female, and lesbian.

Much of her work has been rigorously ignored. Most of the poems were too lesbian and too sentimental for audiences during and after the Harlem Renaissance. Her fiction, on the other hand, was too stark in its unflinching descriptions of the violence of lynching. Indeed, the directness of her scenes of violence were unknown in African-American fictional literature prior to the work of Richard Wright. Further, her short stories with their promulgation of racial self-genocide have been too politically and emotionally threatening for African Americans and others to receive and accept. As Toni Morrison writes in the conclusion to *Beloved,* a more recent tale of infanticide, "This is not a story to pass on." Thus it is a painful gift to participate in the self-investigation this work has required of me; it is an honor finally to assist in passing on this story that was not to be passed on.

Notes

1. Sarah Stanley Grimké, letter to Angelina Weld Grimké, 15 July 1887, Angelina Weld Grimké Collection, Moorland-Spingarn Research Center, Howard University, box 38-5, folder 92.

2. Angelina Weld Grimké, letter to Mamie Burrill, 1896, Angelina Weld Grimké Collection, box 38-13, folders 1 and 2.

DAVID A. HEDRICH HIRSCH (ESSAY DATE 1992)

SOURCE: Hirsch, David A. Hedrich. "Speaking Silences in Angelina Weld Grimké's 'The Closing Door' and 'Blackness.'" *African American Review* 26, no. 3 (fall 1992): 459-74.

In the following essay, Hirsch examines the relationship between silence, blackness, and narrative voice in Grimké's fiction.

In her posthumously published poem **"Life,"** Angelina Weld Grimké (1880-1958) recasts the familiar conceit of the poet as prophetic nightingale in order to contrast the privileged voice of a poet like Milton with the relative voicelessness of an African-American woman. Whereas

Milton associates himself with an Ovidian prophet whose words can "move / Harmonious numbers; as the wakeful bird / Sings darkling, and in shadiest covert hid / Tunes her nocturnal note" (*Paradise Lost* 3.37-40), Grimké's bird in "the wilds of wildernesses maiden" is noticeably silent, in opposition to the powerful ocean which the poem apostrophizes:

> Thou ne'er hast known nor dead nor living
> One single braggart man as master.
> Spirit of eternal motion
> Above whose darkling pathless depths
> There never sits the bird of silence
> Motionless, maddening, songless!
>
> (46)

Grimké's silent bird recalls the tongueless Philomela of Ovid's *Metamorphoses,* a woman mastered and disempowered of her ability to reproduce verbally the horrors of her dismemberment. By emphasizing songlessness as paradoxically central to her own song, Grimké raises a dilemma which informs much of African-American women's writing: How is one to find words expressive of the silenced lives of black women? The silence of Grimké's bird is surrounded by terms denoting absence—"pathless" darkness, "never sits," "Motionless . . . songless"—negative definitions which do not describe what is, but only what is lacking.

Yet to speak of "lack" and "absence" is to be deafened by the binarized overvaluation of one term to its purported "opposite": This is a prejudicial strategy of differentiation which underwrites the privileging of phallocentrism (men have, women have not) and of implicit racism (darkness is the absence of light). How might the silent bird, perhaps Philomela or an African-American woman in the early twentieth century, give voice to herself and thereby retrieve from the "master" her power of verbal reproduction? How can she make blackness visible? Philomela creates a silent tapestry which speaks of the cutting out of her tongue: The absence is re-presented and embodied in textile.[1] Grimké's representational texts, most forcibly her fictional reproductions of the victims of lynching in **"The Closing Door"** and **"Blackness,"** seek to substantiate and give voice to African Americans silenced by the historical narratives of a dominant discourse. Her narrative representations of lynching are efforts to repossess the traces of words in the silence which follows the black victim's death, to transform, like Philomela, that silence into an identifying "song."

By examining the silences within Grimké's work as well as her attempts to *speak* these silences, it is possible to trace the difficulties of narrative self-conception and representation with which Grimké as an African-American woman struggled in the early years of the twentieth century. Such an examination shows that Grimké's narrative repudiation of "maddening" silence connects ideas of physical and verbal reproduction with the generative defining of "blackness" as something other than a negative absence. Through such a definition and communication of silence and blackness, Grimké's narrators attempt to unify the reader and speaker by making the presence within black silence known, but this attempt at unification is made highly problematic by the differentiation required even to *define* the presence which would be known.

To define—or, even more generally, to speak—necessitates the maintenance of boundaries which *separate.* Barbara Johnson has stated that "articulate language requires the co-presence of two distinct poles, not their collapse into oneness. . . . The reduction of discourse to oneness, identity, . . . has as its necessary consequence aphasia, silence, the loss of the ability to speak" ("Metaphor" 212). Johnson's somewhat logocentric diagnosis of silence stresses the loss or absence of speech in terms of clinical disorder, but silence can also mark the achieved end of speech, a state of immediate understanding which follows articulat*ing* language.[2] "In perfect communication," writes Sumanta Chaudhury, "there is nothing but unity. . . . Thus, communication proper abolishes the very condition which makes possible communication" (126).

What can be said of Grimké's attempt to express what lies latent in black silence, an attempt which, if successful, will unify writer and reader in an understanding which makes discourse unnecessary? Just as a word or a sentence is surrounded and informed by silence, Grimké's narrative would be intermediate between two poles of silence. But would the initial and the final silences be identical? What separates the silence that signifies the loss of ability, or the refusal to speak, from the silence which negatively represents the obsolescence of speech when communi(fi)cation has been effected?

Speaking (and) Silences

To define the essence of silence has been a philosophical project of intellectuals and religious thinkers throughout world history, and recent studies recognize that the multiplicity of types of

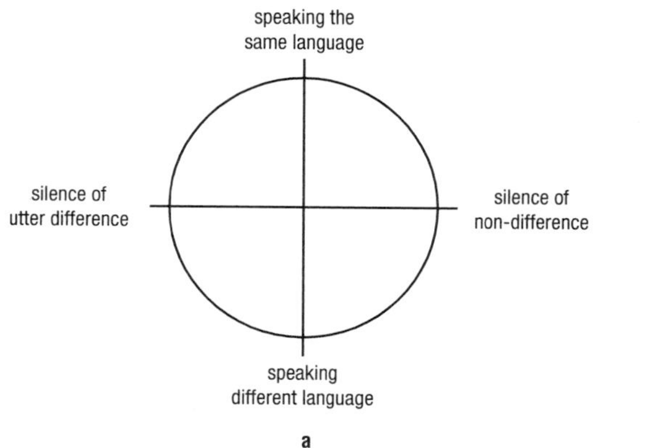

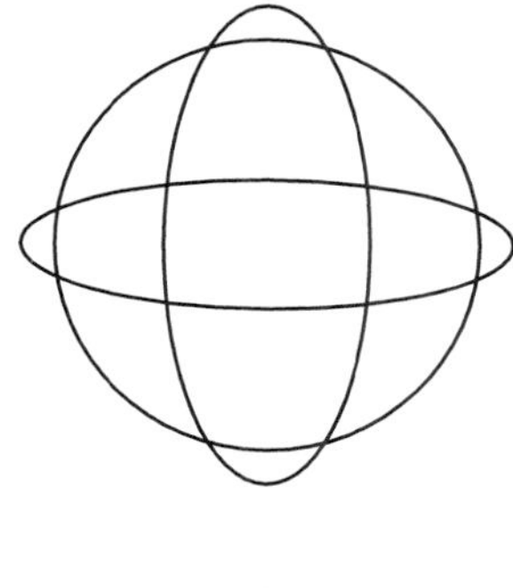

Fig. 1

silence throws into question a definition of silence as merely the absence of speech. "Persons, in fact, can be silent and keep their thought to themselves, and that is quite different from simply saying nothing. It is an active attitude," writes Max Scheler, pointing to one type of difference within the category of silence (225). Philosophical discussion of silence from Zen Buddhist thought to the work of Heidegger and Wittgenstein has concentrated on the movement toward silence as an approximation of the mystical or the Ineffable. The refusal or transcendence of speech is seen as a recognition that there exist in the world nonsensical breakings-of-rules which defy sensible reconstruction in language. If language, to paraphrase Wittgenstein, is a totalizing structure which mirrors a world made sensible by a totality of facts, then the realization that the world is more than a series of factual or rationally perceptible rules leads one to a silence which reflects the beyond-logic, the beyond-factual "nature" of reality.[3] Silence could then be viewed as the negation of the self-difference which necessitates speech, because symbolically (e.g., verbally) mediated comm*unication* is obsolete when true comm*union* has already been effected. The beyond-discursive quality of silence is, in this view, reflective of a metalinguistic comprehension of mystical reality and unity.

Yet Grimké's silence often has a different valence, a silence which, like Wittgenstein's, results from a confrontation with illogic, but this confrontation usually leads not to metaphysical understanding and communion but to a negation of meaning; it is a defeat rather than a triumph of attempted unification. Many of the silences I will examine in Grimké's work result from a very violent differentiation which prevents even the possibility of symbolic attempts to bridge or unify individuals. Perhaps this difference might be visualized using Figures 1a and 1b.

I find it useful to refer to circular diagrams for two reasons: Not only do they begin to complicate the binarity of speech and silence by suggesting divisions *within* both speech and silence, but they also question the linearity of silence → speech by marking the trajectory as a circuit (Fig. 1b) rather than an end-pointed line, positing a continuum among types of communication.

By schematizing these articulations among types of silence, speech, and communication, I mean to suggest that the silence examined by Wittgenstein and much of philosophy is predominantly the silence of non-difference beyond sensible discrimination which is seen as somehow superior to discursive attempts to communicate. Grimké refers to this state quite often in her poetry—the silent communication of lovers' eyes is a typical example. But by calling attention diagrammatically to another type of silence which occurs repeatedly in Grimké's work, the silence of utter difference through which communication is impossible, I would like to explore what I see as an effort throughout Grimké's short fiction to progress from one type of silence to the other throughout the mediation of symbolic verbal expression—to travel along the circle's circumference from difference to understanding. At the same time, however, I will show that, because the polyvalent trajectories of the symbolic word can produce communication which speaks both the "same" and a "different" language simultaneously, the attempt to achieve communion through verbal communication or to move unidirectionally along the diagrammatic circle is a double-speaking effort on the part of Grimké and her narrators both to achieve the non-difference of unity and to secure the differential state of self-possession. Is it possible through words to define an identity—an act which necessitates the structures of difference—and at the same time to communicate that identity to another, and thereby erase the differentiating boundaries? Can one attain both the differential silence of self-possession and the silence of union?

(S)Mothering the Word: "The Closing Door"

Grimké's 1919 story **"The Closing Door"** exposes the mysterious silence of Agnes Milton, a young black woman whose refusal to speak is a defensive maintenance of self-possession in a violently racist world. Although she lives in the safety of the "civilized" North, the horror of her brother's lynching in the South penetrates any illusion of security Agnes might hold for herself, or for her unborn child, whose birth may usher yet another potential victim into a world ruled by lynch mobs. The story's narrator Lucy seeks to retell the sad metamorphosis of her guardian Agnes, whose genuine happiness makes her "as rare as a white blackbird" (253), into "the poor hush" of a person "cooped up" behind a door locked from the inside (256).

On one level, the plot indicates the progression "silence of non-difference → speaking the same and/ or a different language → silence of utter difference," which would be a journey halfway around Figure 1a, from right to left. Agnes gradually passes from a state of silent communion with her husband and surrogate daughter Lucy, through a region of speech, to the ultimate silent self-containment of madness and then death. At the beginning of Lucy's narrative, Agnes and her husband Jim enact a fiction of miscommunication in which the two pretend at first not to know one another:

> "Oh, Ag!"
>
> "That you, Jim?" I can see Agnes' happy eyes and hear her eager, soft voice.
>
> And then a pause, that sad voice:
>
> "No, Ag!" . . .
>
> "Where are you, anyway?" It was the plaintive voice again.
>
> "Here!"
>
> And then he'd make believe he couldn't find her and go hunting all over that tiny flat, searching for her in every room he knew she was not. And he'd stumble over things in pretended excitement and haste and grunt and swear all in that inimitable show way of his. . . . Finally he'd appear in the door panting and disheveled and would look at her in pretended intense surprise for a second, and then he'd say in an aggrieved voice:
>
> "'S not fair, Agnes! 'S not fair!"
>
> She wouldn't say a word, just stand there smiling at him. After a little, slowly, he'd begin to smile too.
>
> (253-54)

Agnes and Jim can pretend to be unable to find one another, and can play-act verbally in mock grief ("'S not fair!'") or failed recognition, but at this early stage of the story the husband and wife share an understanding which necessitates not a word between them. They can verbally speak a language of differences, but their body language is the same. "That smile of *theirs* was one of the most beautiful things I have ever seen" (254; emphasis added), remarks Lucy of the silent bond which belongs to neither one exclusively but to both, or even to all three. In this way, the media of Agnes's and Jim's words are contradicted by the medium of their body language, and the couple reapproaches the silence of non-different union which implicitly predates the beginning of the story. The doorway in which Jim stands is an open one.

With Agnes's realization of her pregnancy, however, comes a gradual closing of the doors of communication, and verbal exchange becomes not a vehicle for game but a dangerous expression of self. Agnes attempts to tell Lucy of her pregnancy through silence and indirection, but Lucy fails to understand at first:

> "Well!" I said.
>
> "I'm trying to tell you something. Sh! not so loud."
>
> "Well, go ahead, then: and why must I sh!"
>
> "Because you must." . . .
>
> Her soft lips were kissing my ear. . . .
>
> "Agnes Milton, what is it?"
>
> "Wait, I'm just trying to think of *how* to tell you."
>
> (259)

In this exchange, even Agnes's body language ("her soft lips . . . kissing") cannot bring forth the expression she simultaneously hushes. Ultimately Agnes finds words which communicate to Lucy, but they are evasive and concealing words: Never once is pregnancy or the baby addressed directly, as if saying the words themselves is somehow dangerous. By speaking around the subject, Agnes both defines and does not define her subject. The nature of Agnes's fear of verbal self-disclosure is made slightly more apparent later in the hushed dialogue, when she stifles Lucy's inclination to "whoop" with happiness about the baby. "'No! No! No! Oh, sh!'" Agnes whispers, explaining her fear that the expression of one's internal state can lead to danger. "'. . . there's—such—a thing—as being—*too* happy,—*too* happy,'" she says, recalling a Kipling story in which the mother of a dead child advises, "'We must make no protestations of delight but go softly underneath the stars, lest God find us out.'"[4] Having said this, Agnes leaves the room and "shut[s] the door very slowly, quite noiselessly behind her. The closing was so slow, so silent that I could not tell just when it shut" (261).

Agnes has traveled a path from the silence of non-difference, through polyvalent verbal communication, and ultimately to the silence of self-containment. With the closing of the door, each room Agnes inhabits becomes a womb of protection. The story's subtle linkage of verbal and physical reproduction suggests that acts of self-representation in **"The Closing Door"**—whether the represented "self" is one's words or one's child—are exposures in which the reproducing subject places herself or selves in danger of being disempowered or seized. By the externalization of an image of her internal self, Agnes fears that a wrathful God will be able to take that expression away, much as Philomela's threatened disclosure of her story results in the excision of her tongue by the "master," Tereus.[5] Yet in Agnes's case this type of punishment does not stem from the threatened disclosure of a crime, but from the disclosure of being "*too* happy," from an expression of satisfaction with her possessions. If she expresses her happiness, it might be interpreted by a jealous God as a hubristic announcement of overabundance.[6] Once reified and transformed into a public commodity by direct identification in words, this happiness might be taken away. By closing the door behind her, by closing her mouth, Agnes attempts to contain her self-possession much as her body contains the expression of her and Jim's happiness within the womb. Through the act of containment Agnes effects the closure of differentiation, marking a closed door between inside and outside, between expression and suppression, and between privately held and publicly exposed selves.

Agnes's silence so suffuses the narrative that even the narrator Lucy becomes, in her words, "infected" (262). Lucy's narrative technique is marked by silences and indirection which duplicate Agnes's "going softly." "Just one little word" is all that Lucy dares express to explain herself, and even this description concerns not so much Lucy as the relatives who have surrounded her and "passed [her] along from one of her [dead mother's] relatives to another" (252). It is almost as if Lucy shares Agnes's fear that to make herself manifest in symbolic form is to risk losing her self. Also like Agnes, over the course of her narrative Lucy recognizes the dangers of misinterpretation endemic to verbal representation. "For fear you may not understand," Lucy asserts that Agnes was the most generous and giving person she has known, despite what Lucy's words might suggest (254).

As a writer Lucy's awareness of verbal insufficiency or duplicity recurs throughout the story, when she unsuccessfully tries to represent Jim ("I cannot tell of his face" [256]) and more provocatively in her attempt to describe Agnes: "I wish I might show you Agnes Milton of those far off happy days. She wasn't tall and she wasn't short: she wasn't stout and she wasn't thin. . . . Her hair was not very long but it was soft and silky and black. Her features were not too sharp, her eyes clear and dark. . . . This doesn't give her I find" (256-57). This failure to find words capable of describing Agnes Milton stresses the insufficiency of symbolic attempts to communicate directly. Lucy stumbles through a series of negative definitions which strive to surround Agnes, but ultimately cannot contain her. Words themselves are media which separate one's impression and expression, and in this way close a door between subjects who would understand and reach communion. Lucy generates an image but then smothers it, saying "This doesn't give her I find." Once the door is closed, Lucy says, "She seemed—*how can I express it*—blank, empty, a grey automaton, a mere shell" (256; emphasis added). How *can* Lucy express what is blank, what is silent, if she cannot even describe the external shell of a person for. whom "existence means dark, foul-smelling cages, hollow clanging doors" (256)?

Agnes's attempt to safely contain herself results not only in the transformation of her nurturing womb into the tomb of a "dark . . . cage," but it also leads Lucy, who "used to pray that in some way I might change places with her" (256), to confront the same fearful inability to express herself "directly" and to feel entrapped in the very constructions she builds for safety. Lucy's attempt to find words to capture Agnes—to define and thereby contain what is dear to her—is as frustrated as Agnes's attempt to maintain possession of her child and happiness by defining and maintaining the silent wall marking her interiority.

Yet Lucy's "inability" to describe Agnes might also be seen as a protective evasion of verbal reification, for just as her "one little word" of self-explanation describes not Lucy directly but only the family members who have surrounded her and given her away, Lucy's non-description of Agnes might be an attempt to hold on to Agnes privately. "This doesn't *give* her I find" would then be a confession that Lucy doesn't want to give Agnes away. Lucy is thus traveling between speech which would communicate to the reader and speech which would defer definition, traveling a circle by which she attempts through speech to unite with the reader in the silent understanding of non-difference, but by which she can also maintain self-possession.

If Lucy's silence is a mark of her self-possession, other silences in the text mark the utter loss of self. When a weekly letter from Agnes's brother Bob fails to come one Tuesday, the absence of his words speaks something to her, leaving her "pale and worried." In this instance, the absence of words suggests Bob's loss, rather than Agnes's or Lucy's differentiated maintenance, of self. The deadly silence which interrupts the siblings' communication is just as telling as are the words of the telegram which later comes: "'Bob died suddenly. Under no circumstances come. Father.'" Lucy as a narrator finds herself trapped, for whether she reveals the words of the telegram to Agnes or conceals the telegram "in my waist," she finds that "the rest of that day was a nightmare" to her (265). Like Agnes, Lucy finds that attempts to internalize the word result in a nightmare of differentiated non-communicativeness and the entrapment of silence. Nor is Lucy's attempt to differentiate inside and outside successful: Her silence about the telegram speaks on her face, which Agnes reads with alarm. Lucy has simultaneously contained herself and lost her self-possession, although she hasn't said a word.

Regardless of these attempts to maintain self-possession by keeping both verbal and physical reproductions of the self inside, Lucy's words and Agnes's child are eventually expressed. "I haven't spoken of this before because it wasn't necessary" (262), Lucy says, finally breaking the silence which has made the narrative to this point mysterious. The "mere shell" of the present Agnes, which contrasts strangely with Lucy's remembrances of the Agnes before, becomes more explicable once Lucy shares the significance of Bob's death. Agnes's brother, a "colored person" in the South, had refused to give the right-of-way to a white man on the sidewalk, and by this physical expression of his self-worth Bob violated an "unwritten law in the South" which denies blacks the right to manifest self-hood (271). The punishment for this expression is lynching "on a Sunday morning" (272), a non-redemptive crucifixion of one who presumed to reproduce bodily the silent word of protest.[7]

Upon hearing the news of Bob's lynching, Lucy finds herself "calling out over and over again, 'Oh, my God! Oh, my God! Oh, my God!'" (273), but this God doesn't answer, and seems to be the pitiless God Agnes has earlier spoken of.[8] Bob's lynching is paradigmatic of the entire story's awareness of the dangers of self-expression and the failure of communication to unify, for Bob's attempt to break through the barriers of discriminatory difference results not in the transcendent silence of meta-racial understanding, but in the silence of his death.

With the news of Bob's lynching, Agnes finally breaks her silence to protest "in a strange high voice" that announces she is merely "an instrument" for the continued production of African-American children to be lynched (274). Her attempt to protect her self by internalized silence is broken, and with it her conception of a protective door separating the North and the South:

> "Yes—I!—I!—An instrument!—another one of the many! a colored woman—doomed!—cursed!—put here!—willing or unwilling! for what?—to bring children here—men children—for the sport—the lust—of possible orderly mobs—who go about things—in an orderly manner—on Sunday mornings!"
>
> "Agnes," I cried out. "Agnes! Your child will be born in the North. He need never go South." . . .
>
> "Yes," she said, "In the North. In the North—And have there been no lynchings in the North?"
>
> I was silenced.
>
> "The North permits it too," she said. "The North is silent as well as the South."
>
> (274-75)

With this recognized penetrability of the "door" differentiating the womb-like North from the South comes Agnes's realization that even the interiority of self-contained silence offers no protection against dispossession. "'There is no more need for silence—in this house,'" Agnes says. "'God has found us out'" (275).

No longer willing to be an instrument in an unmerciful God's plan, and despite her avowal that there is no more need for silence, Agnes forcefully negates her reproductive capacity once more by permanently silencing her "cooing" baby. When Agnes kills the child, who was born on a Sunday, she smothers with a pillow that reproduction of self she had mothered. Lucy awakes from her sleep with an "utterly paralyzing" appreciation that there is "absolutely no sound" coming from the baby's crib (280). "I listened. It was quiet, very quiet, too quiet. But why too quiet?" Lucy wonders (281). Agnes has retracted her self-expression before the "orderly mob" of the outside world has the chance to take it from her. In a shockingly representational way, Agnes attempts to effect closure upon a generationally repetitive history of birth and lynching which is the white-written narrative of her people. The sacrifice of her son is a refusal to allow the reenactment of her brother's fate, an attempt to define the end of a cycle of death and reproduction. Yet in a cosmos structured by a God without pity, even the closure of Agnes's "revolutionary" act serves merely to effect the child's death, just as her willed silence secures not her self-possessed freedom but rather the door of her cage. She polices and silences her self; the outside "mob" has been internalized. Even while it is within her body, the baby, as a mediated representation of self, is never the same as Agnes, but is—like Lucy's words—always already in the realm of otherness.

Lucy, who says of the child, "I was its mother" (279), tries to direct herself on a different course. By reproducing Agnes's story of silence in words, the narrator attempts to regenerate both the blackness of silent despair and the blackness of her family's identity. Although the "one last word" (281) of the story is a transcription of the news Jim receives of Agnes's death (apparently in a psychiatric ward), Lucy as an "instrument" for reproducing words and silently absent lives strives to reverse Agnes's trajectory from the silence of union to the silence of ultimate difference, and thereby to unify her audience through the sympathy of the reading experience. If Agnes has traveled the diagrammatic circle halfway around from right to left, Lucy's narrative will try to reproduce this valence, and reach again the original starting point of non-different silence. Lucy as "mother" of the word publicizes her reproduction at the risk of losing it, although what the word cannot express Lucy cannot lose. By daring to repossess and express the word, regardless of the dangers of misinterpretation and her acknowledgment of the word's failure to communicate directly, Lucy's narrative effort aims to reach through the media of many closed doors and to find again the silence of unified understanding with Agnes and with her readers, even if, as a *speaker* of silences, Lucy must always remain different.

"Blackness": Translating the Word

Like the narrator of **"The Closing Door,"** Grimké would return to the circumstances surrounding lynching and the silencing of African-American voices in another attempt to achieve the non-differential understanding of her readers. Just over a year after the publication of **"The Closing Door,"** her story **"Goldie"** appeared in print, and the existence of another version of the story, entitled **"Blackness,"** suggests that within the thematic basis of these stories is a lesson Grimké felt had to be told. An undated letter of Grimké's to the editors of *The Atlantic Monthly* points to the double "lessons" in lynching as well as to the implicit connection between silence, blackness, and narrativity:

> I am sending enclosed a story. It is not a pleasant one but is based on fact. Several years ago, in Georgia, a colored woman quite naturally it would seem became wrought up because her husband had been lynched. She threatened to bring some of the leaders to justice. The mob made up of "chivalrous" and brave white men determined to teach her a lesson. She was dragged out of town to a desolate part of the woods and the lesson began. First she was strung up by her feet to the limbs of a tree, . . . and then she was set afire. While the woman shrieked and writhed in agony, one man . . . ripped her abdomen wide open. Her unborn child fell to the ground at her feet. It emitted one or two little cries but was soon silenced by brutal heels that crushed out its head. Death came at last to the poor woman. The lesson ended.[9]

Grimké's reproduction of the lesson, however, serves not to end the lesson but to repossess and redirect its significance. The words of protest and threat of "telling" which resulted in the brutal silencing of the mother and child are the same verbal expressions of self-assertion which Grimké would transcribe onto paper in an attempt to reverse the positions of lesson-teachers and lesson-learners, much as Philomela's textual weaving translates and avenges her silenced state. The black woman will be the one who speaks through the reproduced lesson, this reversal marking the con*fusion* of the difference between silence and speech, white and black voices.

In what appears to be the earlier version of the story, **"Blackness,"** Grimké begins by blurring the distinction between her projected white readers[10] and the black narrator of the tale. "I stepped from the warm and wettest blackness I ever remember into the chilling blackness of the cellar"

(218), the narrator begins, implicitly drawing a parallel between the original "blackness" from which he emerges and the warmth and wetness of a darkened womb.[11] This entrance into an Other type of blackness, "the chilling blackness of the cellar," takes the reader from the security of his or her reading environment into the hellish darkness inhabited by the black hero of the tale, whose name is never uttered. The narrator's name, quite appropriately, is Reed, and through the homophonic collapse of this name into a command, the unnamed hero addresses both his black listener (Reed the narrator, who retells the story) and Grimké's (white) readers: "'Reed,' his voice just above a whisper said almost in my ear, 'if you will wait here just where you are a moment'" (218).

As in **"The Closing Door,"** the beginning of **"Blackness"** thus dramatizes an emergence from a womb-like state, which is immediately followed by a different type of blackness. In the earlier story, Agnes's baby is born only to be smothered in an attempt to prevent his entrapment by an "orderly mob," and in **"Blackness"** the reader and narrator are borne into a black cellar which is similar to the confinement of slavery. Furthermore, the entrance into textuality is marked by both a commandment to "Reed" and the hushed whisperings of a speaker who knows the dangers of speech and the risk of self-identifying expression, a back-and-forth movement around the circles of narrative disclosure traveled by Lucy in the earlier work.

The hero of the story is in some ways representative of the epic hero who must descend into the underworld to obtain knowledge and then return to the place of his origin as a changed person. Having gone to the South on mysterious business, he returns to his home in the North marked by "a difference, a difference subtle, indefinable, true" (218), as chilling a difference as the story's entrance into the cellar blackness represents. Yet his trip to the South was itself a return to origins, for as the story progresses the reader learns not only that he was born in the South but that he has left behind there a woman with whom he was once unified, and with whom he has maintained silently telepathic communication. "'It was that way between us,'" he both describes and doesn't, "'. . . I can't explain any more than that'" (226). What he finds upon his return to the South, however, is not the silence of non-difference at the origin he had left, but instead the silence and violence of differentiation which prompts his rebirth in the North as a knowing narrator.

Before this initiation in the South, the hero was mysteriously uncommunicative to Reed about his past. Reed relates, "Ten years we had known each other, . . . but what did I actually know of him before those ten years? I was forced to acknowledge—nothing. . . . No one, surely, could accuse him of being a talker. There had always been about him an impenetrable reserve and a reticence" (222-23). The hero's reticence is reproduced by Reed's narrative, which is itself marked by interruptive pauses representing "the stillness of that oppressive gloom" (219) which like "blackness flowed about us" (226) and between them. But even this apparently "impenetrable" silence might be broken and translated, if the hero/internal narrator's attempt to reach communion with his friend and "reader" Reed is successful. In the cellar of his house in the North, the hero does "a thing I never remember doing before and, after to-night, I shall never do again. I am going to talk about myself" (231), because the lesson of a lynching in the South needs to be retold.

Like Grimké's other narrators, the hero of **"Blackness"** knows more than he can or chooses to express. Throughout his whispered narration he is constantly aware of a white detective's presence outside, like a resistant reader, who is listening for any identifying and incriminating sounds which might be generated from the hero's cage-like sanctuary. Just as the narrator of the story never dares reveal the hero's name, the hero in his own narrative never identifies the mysterious woman he had gone to visit in the South. Still another narrator within the hero's story speaks a "different" language: The white station master whom the hero confronts upon his arrival in the South suggests that, although the sleepy Southern town appears not to have changed during the hero's absence, a difference lies just below the surface of both the placid town and the station master's words:

> "Well, Well! Think of that now. Reckon mebbe you's goin' to fine a few li'l changes here."
>
> It was not so much what he said as the way he said it that gave me my first feeling of alarm.
>
> "Changes?" I asked and I was pleased to notice no difference in my voice.
>
> "Whah? You didn' reckon, did you, you could go away and come back and fine nuffin changed did you? Ten yeahs an' all?"
>
> "Is that what you meant?"
>
> "Mebbe! Mebbe!"
>
> "And maybe not," I was controlling myself with an effort.
>
> "My! Ain't he the little guesser, now. Mebbe not, he says."
>
> (237)

Despite the juxtaposition of dialects and the different valences within the speakers' words, the two seem to share a partial understanding through the duplicity of insinuation. Somehow, too, Reed can respond sympathetically when the hero recounts his journey through "'tall black trees, nothing more, line on line, row on row, deep on deep. Trees, Reed.'" And read he does: "I shuddered involuntarily and quite unaccountably" (239).

If an unaccountable understanding can be achieved even through words which speak a different language, perhaps it is necessary to reconsider the distinction made earlier between the two types of speech plotted along the diameter of my diagrammatical circle. In **"Blackness"** Grimké uses the foreshadowing of verbal insinuation to prompt in readers within the text and readers of the text a sympathetic shudder of recognition even before the readers are intellectually aware of the shudder's accountable cause. By collapsing the differences between (black) readers in the text and (white) readers of the text, a union, however temporary, is created. It would seem that the languages of difference within the text can be translated, and are then not truly divisible from the language of the same to which they were diagrammatically opposed.

Still, there seems to be a difference between the *kind* of understanding possessed by a narrator and that possessed by the reader, for if the narrator's speech can only attempt to represent something truly absent from the referential state, then it is not until the reader her- or himself has been in the presence of the referent that an unmediated equality of knowledge could possibly take place. The hero of **"Blackness"** intuitively hears the unspoken words of the woman in the South, and is alarmed by the insinuation within the station master's words, but until he witnesses the source of the referential description, he cannot rationally define his intuition's significance. Likewise, Reed does not know why he shudders listening to the hero's description of trees until he is presented with the "speech" emanating from the trees themselves and becomes able to translate their "words'" significance. Until this point, the one who narrates and withholds information possesses a power of knowledge different from that held by the silent listener.

The hero/narrator thus moves at this point to the trees' description, which attempts to reproduce their voices as directly as possible:

> "Reed," his voice went on quietly, "would you believe it, that night continued to be as genial, as gracious, as beautiful, and yes, as peaceful as ever. . . . And then I began to hear what I came to call 'the two voices and the duet.' Somewhere—from over there it came—where the blackness was—of the trees."
>
> And with the blackness of that room I shuddered involuntarily again.
>
> But he was speaking once more.
>
> "Creak! Creak! Creak!" That was the voice that was a little higher.
>
> "Creak! Creak! Creak!" And that was the voice that was a little lower.
>
> "Creak! Creak! Creak!" And that was the two together. "Stillness would follow and then it would begin all over again—and end."
>
> (241)

Like Lucy in **"The Closing Door,"** this narrator recognizes his inability to completely represent a past experience through the media of verbal reconstructions. "'Reed, I wish I could tell you of the breathtaking, poignant beauty and . . . the wonder of the bird songs here there and everywhere and with every bird well hidden, well I can't.'" Indeed, he seems to contradict his own meaning when he expresses the lack of sound in a vocalized word "'Silence!'" (241).

Nevertheless, Reed, a "little guesser" himself, predicts that the creaking duet and the silence which informs it represent the sound of a tree branch from which two lynched bodies hang. The hero's telepathic lover and her husband have been stripped naked and murdered, the woman's belly sliced open and dispossessed of "her child—unborn," which has been brutally borne into the world only to be crushed (244). Having protested the station master's Tereus-like attempt to rape her, both the wife and husband are grotesquely silenced and dismembered. Their disfigured bodies bear the violent traces of lynching's differentiation of black characters from the whiteness of the "page," the differentiation between the one privileged to write the self and the Other, who is written. Just as in **"The Closing Door,"** the narrative representation of the hanging bodies can only attempt to recall the violence at the temporal origin of such a spectacle, for the voices of those who would protest are silent, and this silence can be heard only through its narrative reproduction.

The active violence of lynching is never directly represented in Grimké's work but is always recounted in retrospect. Only the after-traces of the child's birth and death, and of the mothering and smothering of the victims' self-generative words, remain. The body language this couple speaks is not the unspoken intimacy shared by Agnes, Jim, and Lucy, or even the silently telepathic communication once shared by the hero and the woman. These bodies speak the language of difference and the silence of symbolic supplementation.

The trees, however, are double agents. On a most apparent level, they carry out the lesson and death sentence dictated by the "lynching bee" in answer to the victims' sentences of protest. But the trees, like those sentences reproduced, also embody and regenerate the voices of the silent hanging victims to one able to read the sounds' import. "'Creak! Creak! Creak!'" plus the intervening silences becomes a translation of the self-expressive speech once present, but now absent from the silent bodies. The underbrush of these same trees furthermore serves as a hidden tomb for the strangled body of the station master, whose "slavering" mouth is silenced by the hero's masterful reversal of the lesson (248). "'Trees, Reed,'" the hero has commanded in a different voice, and trees can speak this difference, as well.

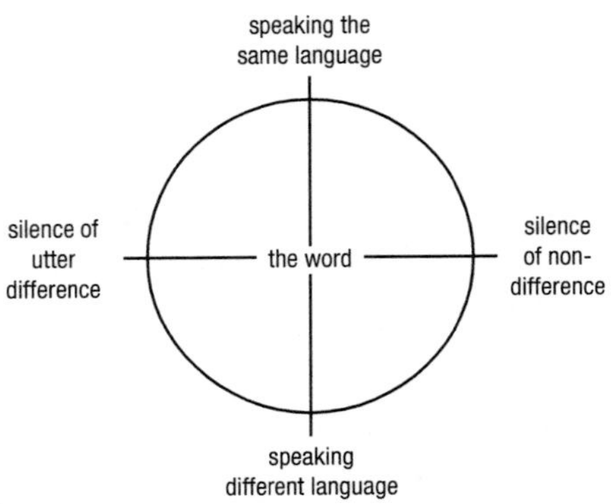

Fig. 2

By the hero's reproduction of the trees' different language to Reed, and Reed's translation of this language to the readers, the language of difference is metamorphosed into the language of the same, and the word fixed in the middle of the diagrammatically circumscribed cross becomes a vehicle for the attempted transcendence of silent difference and the aspiration to silent non-difference (see Fig. 2). The word, like the Christian Word, is a symbolic mediator, for to represent the lynching in this way is once again to point to the redemptive possibilities in the word seized by Grimké's narrators. Yet the question of the possibility of attaining this state of non-different silence by means of the word still remains to be answered. Grimké's narrators would hope finally to be understood immediately, but is this possible through representation, and must this necessitate the loss of self-possession definitive of anti-differential, anti-individualistic union? Can "blackness" (or, likewise, "whiteness") as an identity be defined without difference?

The ending of **"Blackness"** is the silence which follows the hero's departure from Reed. "Neither of us said a word and then abruptly he turned away and went down the alley. . . . He came to [a streetlight], passed through *and was lost in the blackness beyond*" (250-51; emphasis added). The unity the two had shared appears to be broken by the unnamed hero's loss, and the cessation of his narrative. It would appear that this dividing silence of absence works against the possibility for narrative attempts to reach non-difference, but through Reed's repetition of the hero's narrative he achieves some degree of identification with the hero. And if the mimetic chain is continued by Grimké's white readers' reproducing Reed's understanding of the original narrative, the silence at the end of the story would seem to be a shared one.

All the narrators in the text, however, have kept some things to themselves, and Reed is no exception. The penultimate sentence in **"Blackness"** reads, "I have reason to believe he escaped" (251), but this reason, like the hero's name, is never revealed. This reason and the disappearing hero are "lost in the blackness beyond" the illumination offering description and intellection (from *intellegere,* to perceive, choose *between*). This loss of the hero's identity into blackness posits a *lack* of differentiation which makes his presence unknowable to Reed and the reader, who can no longer discriminate a figure in the darkness. Despite his unstated reason to believe that the hero escaped, Reed must end his narration with the statement "But I have never heard from him or seen him since," a sentence which hangs almost expectantly on the brink of the narrator's closing silence, as if waiting for the hero's return or some direct sign of his presence or transcendence.

Reed's attempt to re-present the hero through narrative has ended with a recognition of the hero's absence. Can Reed, as a reteller of a tale, reach identification with the original tale-teller? Can a (white) reader reach back through these words to the silence of the lynched bodies, then to the unrecorded words of protest which these bodies once expressed, then to the unexpressed immediate presence of "blackness" which this chain of representation would define? By not speaking the reason why he believes the hero to have escaped, Reed creates a silent wall of difference which defines the "blackness" of the hero internally and marks the narrator's "blackness" as well. In the process of withholding this knowledge of what might exist in these blacknesses, Reed necessarily *defines*—puts an end to—the reader he stamps with the blank whiteness of unknowing. Yet to reinscribe polarities of metaphoric blackness and whiteness in this manner is to disregard Grimké's problematization of racial understanding: Reed, however black he may be, inhabits a separate blackness which cannot be subsumed into the "blackness" of the disappeared hero. Just as the reader of **"Blackness"** is left alone, in unknowing silence, Reed's effort to reach communion is limited by the hero's silence and distance. "A great loneliness and desolateness was upon me" (250). The differences *within* blackness are apparently as inarticulable as are the differences between white and black.

Grimké's retitling of **"Blackness"** in its published version as **"Goldie"**—a name given to the golden-brown woman whose lynching the narrator will avenge—suggests that the many colors within blackness, like the various songs within silence, point to the insufficiency of definitions which would transfix identity by stressing differences between. And as the silence at the ending of **"Blackness"** implies, it is precisely within this freedom from determinacy that a productive confusion of "black" and "white" readers might be effected, through the collapse of one type of silence into the other in a shared knowledge of undefinability.

The Silent Finale

> The obsessive cry for oneness, for sameness, always, however, meets the same fate: it cannot subsume and erase the trace of its own elaboration.
>
> (Barbara Johnson, "Gender" 105)

Can the reproduced word ever speak the language of same, or must the silence which defines its boundaries always be the silence of difference? Grimké's fiction suggests that the reader, like the epic hero, can descend to an underworld of darkness on a search for knowledge but cannot return to his or her origin unchanged. The narrating hero of **"Blackness"** learns the language of difference when he attempts to find again in the South the silent union he had left ten years before. Both the hero and the origin are changed with his return. Lucy's descent into memory is likewise an attempt to return to a lost unity, and her narrative would reproduce this return so that the reader might learn the lessons of difference, as well. But the reproduction itself is always different from the situation described, and the narrator's inability or unwillingness to duplicate the voice and experience of silence and blackness prevents the reader's complete incorporation into understanding. The words which oscillate between poles of silence never are still and never present enough to carry one unidirectionally from expression to impression or from non-understanding to understanding.

If the word does not bring transcendence in Grimké's text, the repossession and translation of the word by her narrators at least continues its trajectory around the diagrammatic circle. By returning (to) the lesson of lynching "with a vengeance," Grimké's narrators and heroes try to give voice to silenced African Americans; and at the same time, by withholding information, these narrators attempt to deprive the reader from being able to master their blackness. This repossession of the word is translated in **"Goldie"** into the repossession of the lynching trees:

> There is a country road upon either side of which grow trees even to its very edges. *Each tree has been chosen and transplanted here for a reason* and that reason is that at some time each has borne upon its boughs a creaking victim. Hundreds of these trees, there are, thousands of them. They form a forest—"Creaking Forest" it is called. And over this road many pass very, very many. And they go jauntily, joyously here—even at night. . . . If their souls were not deaf there would be many things for them to hear in "Creaking Forest." At night the trees become an ocean dark and sinister, for it is made up of all the evil in all the hearts of all the mobs that have done to death their creaking victims. It is an ocean arrested at the very edges of the road by a strange spell. But this spell may snap at any second and with that snapping this sea of evil will move, rush, hurl itself heavily and swiftly together from the two sides of the road, engulfing, grinding, crushing, blotting out all in its way.
>
> (305-06; emphasis added)

The words, like the trees, being at one point during their cycle agents of death and at another point symbols of regeneration, are carefully chosen and seized from their plots of death to be replanted as agents of revenge. Words are the roaring ocean of difference marking the boundary between the knowing self and unknowing other, and, like the path through the parting Red Sea, they point one moment to the direction of freedom and at the next to the engulfment of death. Grimké's narrators seek the path which would transplant and master the voice of this "ocean dark," for by repossessing the strange spell of the word they might cause their pursuing readers to go under, to be blotted out, to know as immediately as possible the sound, the touch, of the black water.

In this sense, the word in Grimké's texts is the w/Word of the Old Testament repeated rather than the Word of the New: The word is the creator's tool of justice and revenge, but cannot yet symbolize or effect transcendence. Moses' word is a double-edged sword or staff which Elaine Scarry likens to "the image of the weapon. It provides the human mind with something that is a singular vertical line yet so radically different at its two ends that it can in the same moment be pictured as connecting the two realms and preserving their absolute difference" (198). Unless the word can be stilled in its orbit—its meaning (cruci)fixed within the diagrammatic circle—there can only exist an alternation between the speaker and the listener, between the black and the white, master and slave, lyncher and lynched . . . the reproducing cycle of a vengeant chase which in Philomela's story never ends. The narrator of **"Goldie"** recognizes that the knowledge of absence can never fully be represented to souls deafened by difference. Because lynched victims are always witnessed in narrative after the fact, the spectacle is irretrievably distanced, and its reconstructed "voice" is always deferred and differed in time: The words can make one shudder, but they cannot make one know.

Blackness can be defined, but not understood, by whiteness. Its reproduction can be seized and contained, but blackness "itself" cannot be. Only when one passes *through* and is "lost in the blackness beyond" can its "identity" be immediately known. In this sense, to reach identification is paradoxically to destroy definition, to lose the self-possession which Grimké's narrators strive to maintain. Nevertheless, they continue to hope for transcendence of (and through) the word. The silence which ends the "Creaking Forest" passage is then one *not* of a represented absent past: It is the silence of *waiting* for "this spell to snap," of a sentence suspended but not yet closed, a silence anticipating the superfluity of words when neither the silent bird nor the roaring ocean dark will exist as differentiated identities.

Notes

1. For another indication of Grimké's use of Philomela to represent stifled but ultimately powerful creativity, see her story "The Laughing Hand," in which a painter struggles to overcome artistic disability following the surgical removal of his tongue. Alice Walker has made similar allusion to Philomela in her depiction of the de-tongued storyteller Louvinie in *Meridian.*
2. This doubleness of silence as a mark of separation and/or unification is mirrored in Johnson's use of the adjective *articulate* to describe language. According to the *American Heritage Dictionary, articulate*—from the Latin *articulare,* to divide into joints, to utter distinctly—denotes both the differentiation of parts ("Spoken in or divided into clear and distinct words or syllables") and the joining of parts ("To unite by forming a joint or joints").
3. The (in)famous ending of Wittgenstein's *Tractatus Logico-Philosophicus* (1918), "Wovon man nicht sprechen kann, dar über muß man schweigen" ('What we cannot speak about we must pass over in silence'), is the culmination of an argument which posits words as the steps of a ladder which must be thrown away once their unmeaning mediation has been transcended. Chaudhury makes a similar point regarding language: "In its fulfillment, it abolishes itself. Communication, thus, begins and ends in silence" (125). For brief explications of Wittgenstein's views on silence in the *Tractatus,* see Bindeman, 1-7, 37-42; and McDonough, 236-45. More extended philosophical treatments of silence can be found in Bernard P. Dauenhauer's *Silence* and Max Picard's *The World of Silence.*
4. Compare the beginning lines of one of Grimké's untitled poems: "Ask of life nothing, nothing. / Ask only to go greyly, grey ways / Ask only to touch grey things / With grey fingers. / Ask life for numbness only" (56). The source of Grimké's quotation is Kipling's story "Without Benefit of Clergy," which concerns the dissolution of a marriage between a British colonialist and his vain Indian wife after the death of their child.
5. Ovid's telling of the Philomela myth comes in Book 6 of the *Metamorphoses.* Also in Book 6 is the story of Niobe, whose vain praise of her fourteen children results in their execution by the gods and the silencing of Niobe's tongue. For a suggestion of Niobe's "presence" in Grimké's work, see the following note.
6. In Grimké's story "Goldie," the possibility of such an interpretation by God is made even more explicit. Like Agnes in "The Closing Door," Goldie comes to realize that the expression or, even more precisely, the *projection* of one's happiness falls dangerously under the risk of being interpreted as hubristic. Goldie tells her brother of the possessions she hopes to call *her own:* She will have children, "'all my own; and kittens and puppies and little fluffy chickens and ducks and little birds in my trees . . . near the little home all my own.'" Her brother teasingly responds, "'Look here, Goldie, isn't this an awful lot you're asking God to put over for you?'" (288). This doesn't silence Goldie as it does Agnes, but in recognition of the danger she concedes to give up the ducks, chickens, birds, kittens, etc. if only she can keep the children. Goldie's child is ultimately ripped from her womb and crushed by white lynchers, and God's silent permission of this suggests "His" complicity.
7. In her poem "Trees," Grimké makes explicit the association between a black victim of lynching and Christ: "Yet here amid the wistful sounds of leaves, / A black-hued gruesome something swings and swings; / Laughter it knew and joy in little things / Till

man's hate ended all.—And so man weaves. / And God, how slow, how very slow weaves He—/ Was Christ Himself not nailed to a tree?" (109). In one of Grimké's most powerful poems, "Beware When He Awakes" (which exists in three versions), the Christ-like resurrection of a lynched black man is anticipated as revenge on the whites who "burn him if he speaks / . . . If he should whisper 'free'" (116): "But list! There slowly nears / A day of endless fears / A day of endless tears / Beware when he awakes!" (118).

8. In Grimké's poetry, God is typically represented as a "Master" from whose mouth "May leap the flame of wrath or praises sweet" ("As We Have Sowed" 60), and God's wrath is more often evident than is his praise. Perhaps her most despairing depiction of God is as "The Puppet-Player": "Sometimes it seems as though some puppet-player / A clenched claw cupping a craggy chin, / Sits just beyond the border of our seeing, / Twitching the strings with slow, sardonic grin" (94). The similarity of a suspended puppet to a lynched body is suggested by comparing this image with the "black-hued gruesome something [which] swings and swings" from the trees made by God "to bring us to our knees" ("Trees" 109).

9. Cited in Hull 129-30. Chapter 3 of Hull's study offers the most extended analysis to date of Grimké's life and works; the recent publication of Herron's edition of the *Selected Works* will do much to bring Grimké's voice out of the silence which has obscured so many artists of the Harlem Renaissance, a period of great creativity which Hull argues has been misrepresented "by repeating the same handful of works and critical clichés" (31).

10. The published version of the story first appeared in *The Birth Control Review* 4 (Nov.-Dec. 1920), a journal which had a largely white readership. In an unpublished essay from 1990 Carolyn M. Dever explores the political implications of the publication of Grimké's stories of black infanticide in a journal written largely by white feminists, including editor Margaret Sanger. The *Review,* Dever notes, carried several slogans over the course of its publication between 1917 and 1939, and for a short time after 1921 the editors championed voluntary motherhood under the banner "Birth control: To create a race of thoroughbreds" (7n9). Although Grimké's political impulse, Dever argues, is to motivate powerful white women "to change a world that victimizes their black sisters and those sisters' children" (14), the centrality of dead infants to Grimké's stories takes on a highly vexed symbolism in the context of *The Birth Control Review*'s political agenda. Gloria Hull has remarked of "The Closing Door"'s publication in the *Review* that "it seems somehow wrong that this tale of madness and infanticide would appear in such a journal and even more peculiar that the killing societal reasons for Agnes' misfortune would be used as an argument for birth control among black people" (129). For a brief discussion of Grimké's attitude toward her work in its relation to a projected white audience, see Hull 117-18.

11. Grimké again suggests a metaphorical birth into darkness in the poem "The Black Child," in which an infant undergoes a reverse birth into blackness ("a little black hand slid into the shadows, / Into black shadows, / And a little black leg, / . . . And a little black braided head, / And a little black shoulder") as the sun moves in its course (64).

Works Cited

Bindeman, Steven L. *Heidegger and Wittgenstein: The Poetics of Silence.* Washington: UP of America, 1981.

Chaudhury, Sumanta. "Silence and Communication: An Essay on the Limits of Language." *Indian Literature* 29.4 (1986): 113-26.

Dauenhauer, Bernard P. *Silence: The Phenomenon and Its Ontological Significance.* Bloomington: Indiana UP, 1980.

Dever, Carolyn M. "Voluntary Motherhood: Angelina Weld Grimké and *The Birth Control Review.*" Unpublished essay, 1990.

Grimké, Angelina Weld. *Selected Works of Angelina Weld Grimké.* Ed. Carolivia Herron. New York: Oxford UP, 1991.

Hull, Gloria T. *Color, Sex, and Poetry: Three Women Writers of the Harlem Renaissance.* Bloomington: Indiana UP, 1987.

Johnson, Barbara. "Gender Theory and the Yale School." *Rhetoric and Form: Deconstruction at Yale.* Ed. Robert Con Davis and Robert Schleifer. Norman: U of Oklahoma P, 1985. 101-12.

———. "Metaphor, Metonymy and Voice in *Their Eyes Were Watching God.*" *Black Literature and Literary Theory.* Ed. Henry Louis Gates, Jr. New York: Methuen, 1984. 205-19.

McDonough, Richard M. *The Argument of the* Tractatus. Albany: State U of New York P, 1986.

Picard, Max. *The World of Silence.* Trans. Stanley Godman. Chicago: Gateway, 1952.

Scarry, Elaine. *The Body in Pain: The Making and Unmaking of the World.* New York: Oxford UP, 1985.

Scheler, Max. *The Nature of Sympathy.* Trans. Peter Heath. London: Routledge, 1954.

TITLE COMMENTARY

Rachel

WILLIAM STORM (ESSAY DATE 1993)

SOURCE: Storm, William. "Reactions of a 'Highly-Strung Girl': Psychology and Dramatic Representation in Angelina W. Grimké's *Rachel.*" *African American Review* 27, no. 3 (fall 1993): 461-71.

In the following essay, Storm analyzes the complex psychology of Rachel, the title character of Grimké's drama, focusing on the effects of racism on her development.

Grimké's ***Rachel*** is a play that is frequently credited with historical significance but which has rarely, since its first performances and publication, been the subject of extensive or individual critical analysis. With few exceptions, the more recent tendency has been to situate and consider the play within some larger context: the development of black playwriting in America, the tradition of dramatic writing established by a number of black female playwrights in the early century, or Grimké's literary career as seen in its overall perspective or in relation to other writing of the Harlem Renaissance. As a result, there is surprisingly little current criticism that focuses exclusively on ***Rachel***'s own particular theatrical identity or upon what Grimké has wrought in purely dramaturgical terms. Part of the reason for this may arise from the play's relative unfamiliarity, or from perceptions concerning aspects of Grimké's dramatic style, which has often been rather apologetically characterized as romantic, Victorian, or sentimental.[1] Despite the possible legitimacy of such reservations, however, what Grimké has created in this first play of hers is an extraordinarily complex title character. Rachel is a figure of considerable psychological intricacy and emotional volatility, and these are factors that continually complicate and enrich the larger drama and provide many of the play's interactions with an arresting, unusual, and highly charged dramatic tension.

Of ***Rachel***'s historical importance there can be little doubt. Produced in March of 1916 by the Drama Committee of the NAACP in Washington D.C., it was, according to Locke and Gregory, "apparently the first successful drama written by a Negro and interpreted by Negro actors" (414)—an assertion that has been qualified in certain ways by later critics.[2] Moreover, the play was a first in terms of its deliberate program and platform. The playbill for its premiere production contained the following message: "This is the first attempt to use the stage for race propaganda in order to enlighten the American people relative to the lamentable condition of the ten million of colored citizens in this free Republic" (qtd. in Hull 117). As Hatch and Shine report, the play was immediately controversial, even among members of the Drama Committee, some of whom favored a more "artistic" approach over deliberate propaganda; the play's black audience was also divided in its response (137).[3] Such controversy apparently intensified in the aftermath of subsequent productions (in 1917), and especially following the publication of the play in 1920. Kathy Perkins writes that ***Rachel***'s publication "drew a large number of reviews that were primarily favorable. However, there were those critics who charged Rachel with advocating genocide" (9).

Responding to criticisms of the play, Grimké clarified her own ambitions for the work, defined the audience she hoped to reach with it, and denied that it "preaches race suicide."[4] In an article in the January 1920 issue of *The Competitor,* the author provided significant clues about the "nature" of her title character and also about the particular "purpose" that her play would address:

> Because of environment and certain inherent qualities each of us reacts correspondingly and logically to the various forces about us. For example, if these forces be of love we react with love, and if of hate with hate. . . . Now the colored people in this country form what may be called the "submerged tenth." From morning until night, week in week out, year in year out, until death ends all, they never know what it means to draw one clean, deep breath free from the contamination of the poison of that enveloping force which we call race prejudice. . . . Now the purpose was to show how a refined, sensitive, highly-strung girl, a dreamer and an idealist, the strongest instinct in whose nature is a love for children and a desire some day to be a mother herself—how this girl would react to this force.
>
> (51-52)

Here, then, we have an indication of the central relations the play proposes between Rachel and the "force" of love (as seen, perhaps, in the Loving household), and that of hate and race prejudice. We also have a key allusion to a fundamental aspect of the play's dramatic configuration: It is to a large extent the reactions of this "highly-strung girl" that Grimké sets out to dramatize.

Let us examine the psychological nature of these reactions, the stresses they exert upon Rachel's character, and the way such reactions are evoked in Grimké's dramaturgy.

The playwright begins with a familiar *mise-en-scène* and a basic pattern of character and incident that is fairly typical of the time in which Grimké was writing and also of her gender. Perkins indicates that plays by black female writers in the early century often featured domestic situations in which mothers and children were prominent, with the husband either deceased or absent. Such plays were generally set in the home, and often began with the mother character "sewing, cooking, cleaning, or praying" (2); the event of a lynching is often significant in the play's action (9-10). True to such conventions, ***Rachel*** takes place in the living room of the Lovings' small apartment; as the play begins, Mrs. Loving—who makes her living as a seamstress—is sewing. Her husband is dead, having been lynched, along with her son, exactly ten years earlier "by Christian people—in a Christian land" (21). The action features a number of children, not only Mrs. Loving's own, who are grown, but the little neighborhood girls who look up to Rachel and the little boy Jimmy, who is adopted into the Loving household and relates to

Rachel as a mother. Much of the writing, indeed, is concerned with the issue of motherhood, not only through Mrs. Loving's (and also Mrs. Lane's) relationship to her offspring but, more importantly, through Rachel's avowed desire to be a mother herself.

In many ways, however, the play transcends its more familiar setting and configuration of character. In particular, it is Rachel's psychological and emotional constituency, and the force of her reaction to events and interactions, that elevates the play beyond its fundamental patterns and mitigates against its possible sentimentality. According to Helene Keyssar, "The response of [Rachel] to the situations and histories she encounters is anything but facile or maudlin" (227). Indeed, the intensity of ***Rachel***'s action arises not so much from its exterior plot as from an interior struggle within its central character's psyche; the primary "drama" in the play is one that is enacted, not between characters, but among severe internal stresses. The play's central conflict, in fact, is not between its people, or even between Rachel and the outside world of racial prejudice; it is rather a battle that this character wages in the arena of religious doubt and faith. ***Rachel*** is thematically preoccupied with issues of theodicy, and it is in this context that its main character approaches an authentically tragic identity, as manifested in her direct and impassioned arguments with God.

To look more closely at Rachel's personal history, and at the foundations of her psychological state, it is important to consider the information we are given, non-sequentially in the play's action, about what her early life might have been like, and to examine the implications of such clues. It is not, in fact, until the play is nearly over that we are allowed a key insight into Rachel's background. She has just told her gentleman caller, John Strong, about Jimmy's traumatic response to what happened to him after school ("They chased him through the streets calling him, 'Nigger! Nigger! Nigger!' One boy threw stones at him"), and now she correlates this with her own experience:

> . . . I have seen that look of deadly fear—in the eyes—of other children. I know what it is myself.—I was twelve—when some big boys chased me and called me names.—I never left the house afterwards—without being afraid. I was afraid, in the streets—in the school—in the church, everywhere, always, afraid of being hurt. And I—was not—afraid in vain.
>
> (94)

When we first meet Rachel, at the play's beginning, she is eighteen years old. At this point we know nothing of what happened to her when she was twelve, nor have we yet learned of the lynchings that took place ten years prior to this date—October 16. And yet, by way of constituting her psychological background, one might speculate on what the juxtaposition of these two events can suggest.

When Rachel was eight, she lost both her father and older brother, suddenly and inexplicably; she doesn't find out the reason for this loss until ten years later. At age twelve, she experiences a trauma that sends her into hiding, afraid to leave her home for fear of being tormented. And so we wonder what this household refuge may have been like during these years of childhood, adolescence, and early womanhood. Superficially, the Loving family appears to be nurturing; the mother is apparently quite able to sustain the household financially, at least with her son Tom's help, and the relationships among the three family members appear to be close and supportive. Rachel is antic and cheerful in the play's early sequences, and her interactions with Tom are lively, playful, and witty. Their mood is belied, however, by Mrs. Loving's own; she is distracted and somber, especially when Rachel introduces her to Jimmy (who reminds her of her dead son George) and in her general awareness of what this anniversary means to her family. What lies beneath the exterior behavior presented in this household is, in fact, a fearful and insecure psychological world, a realm that is characterized by absence and dread. Rachel is torn between two realities, the external behavior of the household in which she energetically participates and the darker internal world of loss and torment. It is the perpetual tension between these opposing conditions that produces in Rachel a neurotic, and finally hysterical, reaction.

She is fixated upon motherhood; ostensibly, she wants to be a mother herself. One must look, however, at the models of motherhood that provide her main points of reference. In Mrs. Loving, we have a woman who—in Rachel's view, between the ages of eight and eighteen—is simply without a husband. The image that has been presented to Rachel is that of a mother alone, apparently self-sufficient and with no need of a conjugal relationship. But are we to believe that Rachel never questioned the absence of the other parent, or never sensed that her mother was keeping a secret from her children through all of these years? Aside from Mrs. Loving, the other model of motherhood that Rachel refers to is the Blessed Virgin, pictured on the wall of the living room in a reproduction of Raphael's *Sistine Madonna.* Early in Act I, Rachel "raises her eyes" to this portrait and sings "Mighty Lak a Rose." Finishing the song, she exclaims: "I think the loveliest thing of all the lovely things in the world is just (almost a whisper) being a mother!" (11-12). Soon after this, in the company of her own mother, she reveals her strong personal identification with this second model of motherhood. She tells Mrs. Loving of the dream she had in which "a voice" told her: "Rachel, you are to be a mother to little children." Following this dream, Rachel has "known how Mary felt at the 'Annunciation.'" In a whisper, Rachel says, "God spoke to me through some one, and I believe" (12). Here is our first clue, not only to the way in which Rachel deals with a variety of models of motherhood (including a projection of herself as mother), but to her sense of the will of a God who participates directly in her life. Significantly, there is also evidence in this sequence of one of Rachel's more deep-seated "reactions": a tendency toward role-identification and self-aggrandizement that marks her behavior throughout the play.

Despite the apparently comfortable and inviting qualities of the Loving household, one quickly discerns that this is an extremely insular environment. Its inhabitants have turned in upon themselves in retreat from the hostility of the world outside. Mrs. Loving rarely goes out, as we discover in Rachel's first scene with John Strong:

> . . . when you're poor, you have to live in a top flat. There is always a compensation, though; we have bully—I mean nice air, better light, a lovely view, and nobody "thud-thudding" up and down over our heads night and day. The people below have our "thud-thudding," and it must be something *awful,* especially when Tom and I play "Ivanhoe" and have a tournament up here. We're entirely too old, but we still play. Ma dear rather dreads the climb up three flights, so Tom and I do all the errands.
>
> (7)

That Rachel and Tom have chosen *Ivanhoe* as a source of play might be seen as an effort on their part to deal with matters of prejudice—and also religion—through means of fantasy and role-playing, at once enacting and distancing themselves from the real prejudices that both of them confront. Did Rachel play the role of Rebecca, the condemned Jewess who is to be burned but is instead saved by Ivanhoe? If so, then Rebecca (whose mother's name is Rachel) might be construed as yet another model for role-identification: She ultimately decides to devote her life to God and good works, never to marry or have children.

On Rachel's choice of character in *Ivanhoe* one can only speculate. Yet her allusion to the games that she and her nineteen-year-old brother play, though "entirely too old," is critical to our understanding of this family's inward-turning retreat from a hostile exterior world. It is not only *Ivanhoe* that Rachel and Tom enact in this apartment; their ongoing interplay is a charade of safety and respectability. Their exaggerated, courtly dialogue with each other ("May T. Loving be of any service to you?" [37]) is an attempt to create a shared image of a desirable and attainable reality, an effort to offset the rejection that they continually experience outside of the household.

Rachel has, in fact, constructed a complex fantasy life which has allowed her, at least through adolescence, to maintain a degree of equilibrium. But it is a fantasy that is not at all congruent with outside realities, or with her developing womanhood. Her images of what life is supposed to be—a peculiar amalgam of her mother fixation, her own mother's lack of a husband, her relationship to the Madonna, her charades with Tom—cannot finally withstand either the social realities that she is awakening to or the energetic courtship of John Strong. The illusions that she has intricately constructed for herself within this household refuge must inevitably be shattered. Rachel seems to know this intuitively from early in the play's action, and yet she continues to struggle determinedly with a series of self-contradictory impulses.[5] She cannot reconcile a loving God with her own treatment or that of "colored" people; she cannot make her own desire for motherhood congruent with her models of fatherless conception; she cannot, finally, make peace with her life-giving instinct in the face of a stronger impulse to destroy rather than "torture." These powerful conflicts are manifest in a suppressed hysteria from the play's outset, and they lead inexorably toward Rachel's breakdown at the end of the action, and toward her hint at suicide.

Let us now examine the way in which this progression develops, and how the reactions of this "highly-strung girl" are intensified. Toward the play's end, after Rachel has crushed the roses sent to her by John Strong, and then fallen unconscious to the floor, Mrs. Loving has a scene with Strong in which she describes the way that Rachel has behaved since this event. She tells him: "Tom and I believe her soul has been hurt. The trouble isn't with her body. You'll find her highly nervous. Sometimes she is very much depressed; again she is feverishly gay, almost reckless" (84). In saying this, Mrs. Loving means to characterize Rachel's recent behavior, but the truth is that Rachel has been exactly like this throughout the play's action—and perhaps for longer than that. Her "soul has been hurt" at least since she was twelve, if not since the age of eight when she lost both her father and brother. Her behavior from the play's opening moments continually vacillates between episodes of nervousness (as she is with Strong in Act I), forced gaiety (of the sort that we see around the dinner table, in her interplay with Tom and her mother), and sudden, intense sobriety—as when she accuses Mrs. Loving of laughing at God. Rachel has just finished singing "Mighty Lak a Rose," and has confessed her feelings about motherhood, when the exchange continues:

> MRS. LOVING: (Turns and laughs) Well, of all the startling children, Rachel! I am getting to feel, when you're around as though I'm shut up with dynamite. What next? (Rachel rises, goes slowly to her mother, and kneels down beside her. She does not touch her mother.) Why so serious, chickabiddy?
>
> RACHEL: (Slowly and quietly) It is not kind to laugh at sacred things. When you laughed, it was as though you laughed—at God!
>
> MRS. LOVING: (Startled) Rachel!
>
> RACHEL: (Still quietly) It's true. It was the best in me that said that—it was God!
>
> (12)

Here Mrs. Loving has inadvertently, yet quite accurately, characterized her daughter's condition; living in this insular household with Rachel, she is indeed "shut up with dynamite." Rachel continually fluctuates between explosiveness and introspective sobriety. When she tells her mother about meeting little Jimmy, she proclaims, "I nearly hugged him to death, and it's a wonder my hat is still on my head" (5).

Moments later, when Strong comes in, Rachel is "manifestly ill at ease at being left alone with a stranger, attempting however to be the polite hostess" (6). Just before he leaves the apartment, there is a cryptic exchange which follows immediately upon her reference to *Ivanhoe:*

> RACHEL: . . . I've got to grow up it seems.
>
> STRONG: (Evidently amused) It is rather hard being a girl, isn't it?
>
> RACHEL: Oh, no! It's not hard at all. That's the trouble; they won't let me be a girl. I'd love to be.
>
> (7-8)

In the first act, Rachel is no longer the adolescent she was when she was taunted by "some big boys," nor is she the twenty-two-year-old woman we encounter in Act II. Here she can still maintain a naïveté, still be "a girl," even if her efforts seem forced at times. On the issue of racial prejudice, though, she has fewer illusions. When Mrs. Loving tells her about Strong's background, and the reasons for his work as a waiter, Rachel says: "Just because he is *colored!* (Pause.) We sing a song at school, I believe, about 'The land of the free and the home of the brave.' What an amusing nation it is" (9).

Rachel has developed a complex anxiety about growing up in this "amusing nation." Although she has yet to reach her later conclusion, that to kill black babies would be a mercy, she is still deeply ambivalent about becoming an adult. In one sense, she has a strong feeling for her own messianic mission, as revealed in the "Annunciation" dream. Yet at the same time she muses, "Wouldn't it be nice if we could keep all the babies in the world—always little babies" (10)? She has postponed her own growing up as long as possible; later on, she will deny herself the possibility of biological motherhood. In the first act, though, she is simply confused about her relationship to a complex ideal of motherhood. After accusing her mother of laughing at God, she says:

> . . . I pray God every night to give me, when I grow up, little black and brown babies—to protect and guard. (Wistfully.) Now, Ma, dear, don't you see why you must never laugh at me again? Dear, dear, Ma, dear? (Buries her face in her mother's lap and sobs.)
>
> (13)

Did her mother laugh at *her* or at God—or at God within her? There is a profound confusion in this character, arising from her relationship to her own mother, her attachment to the Madonna and her memory of the "Annunciation" dream, her aggrandized self-image, and her apparent conviction that it is up to God—not a man—to bring her babies once she "grows up." Rachel is already grown up, but since she cannot begin to untangle her filial and religious allegiances, or discern between her human self and her divine mission, or reconcile her mandate to be a mother with becoming one sexually, she can only insist on remaining a child, sobbing in her mother's lap.

The encounter between the two of them that ends the first act brings this confusion to a climax. Rachel realizes that Jimmy, when he grows up, might well meet the same fate as George, the older brother who was lynched. The nation where such things can happen is no longer "amusing":

> Why—it would be more merciful—to strangle the little things at birth. And so this nation—this white Christian nation—has deliberately set its curse upon the most holy thing in life—motherhood. Why—it—makes—you doubt—God!
>
> MRS. LOVING: Oh, hush! little girl. Hush!
>
> RACHEL: (Suddenly with a great cry): Why, Ma dear, *you know. You* were a *mother, George's mother.* So, this is what it means. Oh, Ma dear! Ma dear! (Faints in her mother's arms.)
>
> (28)

In the second act, Grimké creates the impression of a tragically fateful series of events. By a curious and highly selective visitation of smallpox upon the apartment building, little Jimmy has lost both parents and come to live with the Lovings. "Ma Rachel" is now the mother figure to the child who will be the agent in bringing back the memory of her childhood trauma. Mrs. Loving wonders if "perhaps, God—hasn't relented a little—and given me back my boy, my George" (35).

It is four years later (Rachel is now twenty-two) and the games played by Rachel and Tom have evolved into a charade of parenthood. Their relationship has an incestuous quality, hinted at in Act I when Rachel chases Tom around the dinner table trying to kiss him, and then again in Act II when it is Tom who kisses her, with exaggerated courtly formality: "May I request, humbly, that before I press my chaste, morning salute upon your forbidding lips, that you—that you—that you—er—in some way rid yourself of that—er—knife?" (37). Jimmy refers to him as "Uncle Tom," but it is clear from their play-acting and breakfast table discourse that Tom has taken over the father role with respect to the boy, complementing the mother role that dates to Rachel's first meeting with him. The game of "Ivanhoe" has developed into a game of marriage, and yet the purpose behind the play-acting hasn't substantially changed. The game is still designed to bond Rachel and Tom close together in a protected world that is their joint creation.

In spite of their achievements—Tom is an "electrical engineer" and Rachel is a "graduate in Domestic Science"—they still cannot find a place in the exterior world, and so they remain faithful to the illusions that can only be nurtured, albeit with increasing difficulty, in the insular world of the top-floor apartment. For Tom, as for Rachel, this prompts a questioning of "God's justice." Mrs. Loving urges him not to lose faith, but then she concludes: "Each one, I suppose, has to work out his own salvation" (42). As the remainder of the play's action indicates, finding her "own salvation" is precisely what Rachel can never accomplish.

The possibility for escape, if not salvation, takes the form of John Strong's courtship. He asks Rachel to the theatre, and suggests that if she had "a little more fun in [her] life, [her] point of view would be—more normal" (51). Yet "normal" is exactly what Rachel's point of view can never be. In the rhythm of the play's action here, whenever she allows herself a vision of possible happiness, such illusions are immediately frustrated or destroyed. Following Strong's departure, Rachel has a moment of reverie; she "is lost in a beautiful daydream. Presently she sighs happily, and after looking furtively around the room, lifts the palm John has kissed to her lips" (52). Such moments cannot last, and Rachel's daydream is abruptly interrupted by the arrival of Mrs. Lane and her daughter—"Little, black, crushed Ethel" (59). The experience of yet another black child is fiercely impressed upon Rachel once again, and she sinks back into despondency.

> MRS. LANE: . . . We strive and save and sacrifice to educate them—and the whole time—down underneath we know—they'll have no chance.
>
> RACHEL: (Sadly): Yes, that's true, all right.—God seems to have forgotten us.
>
> MRS. LANE: God! It's all a lie about God.
>
> (58)

The play's original title (*Blessed Are the Barren*) is echoed in what Mrs. Lane tells Rachel: "If I had another—I'd kill it. It's kinder." She adds, "Don't marry—that's my advice" (58).

By now the play's preoccupation with issues of theodicy has been considerably intensified and complicated, and Rachel's argument with God comes to a climax at the end of Act II. Rachel despairs as she equates the plight of her own family and little Ethel (59), but then the roses that have been sent to her by John Strong arrive, and once again she enjoys a brief moment of imagined happiness. As she looks at the rosebuds, her "face softens and grows beautiful" (59). She compares the flowers to happy babies, and says: "When—I look—at you—I believe—God is beautiful" (60). But once more the rhythm of the action fatefully cuts short her moment of peace. Jimmy comes home from school, having been called "Nigger" by "some big boys" (61), thereby bringing Rachel's childhood experience directly in line with another child's trauma. Rachel recalls the "Annunciation" dream, and concludes that she was betrayed by God: "Why, God, you were making a mock of me; you were laughing at me. I didn't believe God could laugh at our sufferings, but He can. We are accursed, accursed!" (62-63). The second act ends with a powerfully impassioned address to God:

> You God!—You terrible, laughing God! Listen! I swear—and may my soul be damned to all eternity, if I do break this oath—I swear—that no child of mine shall ever lie upon my breast, for I will not have it rise up, in the terrible days that are to be—and call me cursed.
>
> (63)

Rachel, too, can laugh, as she does here in a "terrible, racking" manner. Here again we see her in the act, not only of arguing with God, but in elevating herself to a god-like level. If God can laugh, then so can she; if God can destroy, then she can, too. She, like God, will assume power over life and death. She tears the rosebuds from their stems, thereby killing her imagined happy babies, and cries: "If I kill, You Mighty God, I kill at once—I do not torture" (63).

In Act III, Grimké continues to use the motif of laughter as a reflection of mockery and desperation as well as happiness. In a lengthy story, Rachel tells Jimmy of a "Land of Laughter," where it is indeed possible to find happiness, but as the act develops we see that Rachel's own pained laughter will take her to another of the story's realms—the "Land of Sacrifice."

Rachel is caught, in the third act, in a state of extreme tension that arises not only from her arguments with God but from the divergent demands of Jimmy and John Strong—forces that she can find no way of reconciling. The physical signs of her suffering are quite apparent: Mrs. Loving refers to "her face pale and haggard" with "black hollows" under the eyes (78), and she tells Tom that when Rachel comes out of Jimmy's room, after trying to still his crying, "her face is like a dead woman's" (79). Following his trauma, Jimmy cries continually at night, and Rachel is unable to console him. At the same time, she is unable to deal with Strong's courtship. When they are alone in the apartment together, Rachel attempts to fall back on the kind of charade she plays out with Tom, this time by enacting what she imagines is expected of a young lady with a "gentleman caller." He pushes his case further, refusing to be dissuaded by her evasions; she, in her role as "hostess," goes to the piano and sings. When he takes her in his arms and "kisses her many times," she "breaks suddenly into convulsive laughter" (90).

Here again we see Rachel's own confused and tortured journey to the "Land of Laughter." In this moment, when there is overt sexual contact with a man, a man who intends to marry her and who could father her children, Rachel retreats immediately into a mocking laughter which she then connects not with the sexual male but with God: "God is laughing.—We're his puppets.—He pulls the wires,—and we're so funny to Him.—I'm laughing too—because I can hear—my little children—weeping" (91). In spite of her efforts to duplicate what she feels is God's laughter, she does not, after all, have god-like power; she cannot still the cries of children that she now hears in the night, in nightmarish contrast to the "Annunciation" dream.

When Strong holds out the possibility of another insular apartment, where they could live together as man and wife, she is temporarily enchanted with the idea. Yet once again, the play's fateful pattern is enacted; her moment of imagined happiness is sharply interrupted by Jimmy's crying, and she refuses Strong's proposal. Jimmy's soul has been "bruised" (94), just as hers has been "hurt," and she has no recourse but to attend the weeping child. And yet, as the play ends, we may wonder how long Rachel will continue her role as Jimmy's mother. In the final scene with Strong, she alludes to her own death, and we are led to believe that suicide, not marriage, may well be Rachel's way out of these circumstances, the only escape possible from the cries that haunt her soul. The song she sings for Strong at the piano ends with lyrics that she hopes he will remember:

> The roses of white are sere,
> All faded the roses red,
> And one who loves me is not here
> And one that I love is dead.
>
> (90)

In light of the complexity with which Rachel's character is drawn, and considering the intensity of her expression, it is perhaps fair to consider the extent to which Grimké has brought aspects of her own experience to this portrayal. As Gloria Hull puts it, "A provocative question that Rachel's characterization raises is the degree to which she may be autobiographical." Hull points to the fact that Grimké herself "made an early decision not to marry and have children" and mentions a "disastrous love affair" that may have had a bearing on this choice (124). Grimké's own mother, who was white, separated from the family when her daughter was very young; Grimké was raised by her father, with whom she apparently had an unusually close and binding relationship. Parallels can no doubt be imagined, psychologically, between the black woman who loses her white mother at an early age and the character she creates who fervently wants to be mother to "little black and brown babies" (13). One might speculate, as well, on the relation between Grimké's lesbianism and her title character's rejection of both her male suitor and the possibility of biological motherhood.[6]

Such considerations, however, are finally subordinate to what Grimké has wrought in her portrayal of Rachel, and to the precise form that her "propaganda" takes in this play. ***Rachel*** is more than a protest against lynching, more than an outcry against prejudice, more even than a deliberately fashioned portrait of the "lamentable conditions" of "colored citizens." What takes this drama beyond the level of its overt purpose and content, and raises it well above its possibly sentimental or melodramatic qualities, is Grimké's dramatization of the progressive destruction of a "hurt soul," the disintegration of a complex and contradictory character whose outcries must ultimately be directed, not only at white society, but at God. Rachel's point of view on racial hatred is directly stated at the play's end: "We are all blighted; we are all accursed—all of us—everywhere, we whose skins are dark—our lives blasted by the white man's prejudice" (93). The way in which Grimké has chosen to dramatize such a blight, however, is neither straightforward nor easily fathomed.

Grimké's drama, at its most potent, is located in the psychological effects of racism upon the development of a single personality, from early childhood to barren womanhood, and in the impossible circumstances in which this character must inevitably find herself at the end of her fated journey. Grimké's strategy in ***Rachel*** is to create a dramatic situation with ever-narrowing possibilities, a tragic series of developments that, taken together with the particular constituency of Rachel's character, can only lead to a solitary confrontation with divine will. Rachel's belittlement at the hands of schoolmates at age twelve sends her into retreat within the family, and then into a world of fantasy where she can only act out scenarios of happiness or romance—or normalcy—with her brother. She and Tom, unable to grow up and join society, can only grow more and more insulated in this world of retreat, finally enacting the roles of mother and father to Jimmy, who, like Rachel before him, will in his own turn be "accursed."

The role of biological mother is one that Rachel cannot play. There is no place for a sexual male in her scenario of motherhood; she can only imagine motherhood in light of her own mother's solitary life, the Virgin Mary, or the message of the "Annunciation" dream, which said that she would be mother "to" instead of mother "of" the little children. Indeed, Rachel's confusion over motherhood, brought about perhaps by the secret of her father's disappearance and her own mother's inability to "protect and guard" her in the outside world, has led her to the opposite of the belittlement to which she was subjected to as a small child. What Rachel exhibits, finally, is a personal grandiosity that is her only form of compensation or retaliation for what has befallen her.

Rachel can arrive at no coherent sense of selfhood that allows for God, sexual desire, and motherhood—and racial prejudice. The equation will not work, no matter how she configures it. Her response to prejudice is at first confusion, then a suppressed hysteria, and finally an image of self that borders on megalomania. Her invented, grandiose self can not only play "Ivanhoe" and other courtly games with her "chaste" brother, but can equate itself with the Madonna and enter into argument with the deity. Rachel's is a tragic pride that is born of hatred; it emerges directly from an experience of early girlhood, only to expand its reach in doomed womanhood. It is Grimké's achievement to have fully dramatized the degradation and also the aggrandizement, and to have given birth to a character who is so tragically stranded that she can only find discourse with another child "accursed" like herself—or with God.

Notes

1. For example, Hatch and Shine refer to "a concession the modern reader must make: acceptance of the sentimental style. . . . Miss Grimké is writing with true feeling, but the four wars since the writing make her tender feelings seem Victorian and precious" (138). Brown-Guillory writes that, "A contemporary audience might find the sentimentality in *Rachel* objectionable, but one must bear in mind that Grimké was born in 1880 and grew up with Victorian influences" (6).

2. Locke and Gregory's use of the word *successful* as a modifier already qualifies their statement in certain ways. Hatch and Shine observe that, "Some critics have said that, *Rachel* is the first play to be written by a black that was publicly performed by black actors. This is true only if musicals are ignored—and if Mr. Brown's *King Shotaway* of 1823 is disregarded" (137). Kathy Perkins refers to "the first twentieth century full-length play written, performed, and produced by blacks—*Rachel*" (8).

3. On the issue of the "artistic" versus propagandistic intention, Hatch and Shine quote from Locke and Gregory: "A minority section of (the Drama Committee) dissented from this propagandist platform and were instrumental later in founding the Howard Players organization, promoting the purely artistic approach and the folk-drama idea" (414).

4. Grimké begins her article in *The Competitor* as follows: "Since it has been understood that 'Rachel' preaches race suicide, I would emphasize that that was not my intention. To the contrary, the appeal is not primarily to the colored people, but to the whites" (51).

5. For a contrasting view of what I call the "contradictory" elements in Rachel's character, see Helene Keyssar's discussion, in which she describes the character's "double existence as woman and black person," Rachel's "hybrid self," and her "polyphonous voice" (228).

6. Hull specifically relates Grimké's sexuality to her literary work, especially her poetry, noting that Grimké's "poetic themes of sadness and void, longing and frustration . . . relate directly to Grimké's convoluted life and thwarted sexuality," and drawing a "connection between [Grimké's] lesbianism and the slimness of her creative output" (145). Hull also comments on Grimké's ties to her father, with whom she had an "extremely close relationship." In Hull's words, "Lacking lovers, husband, her own family, these ties grew into an unhealthy, lifetime dependency" (149).

Works Cited

Brown-Guillory, Elizabeth. *Their Place on the Stage: Black Women Playwrights in America.* Westport: Greenwood, 1988.

Grimké, Angelina W. *Rachel.* 1920. College Park: McGrath, 1969.

———. "*Rachel:* The Play of the Month—The Reason and Synopsis by the Author." *Competitor* Jan. 1920: 51-52.

Hatch, James V., and Ted Shine, eds. *Black Theater, U.S.A.: Forty-Five Plays by Black Americans, 1847-1974.* New York: Free, 1974.

Hull, Gloria T. *Color, Sex, and Poetry: Three Women Writers of the Harlem Renaissance.* Bloomington: Indiana UP, 1987.

Keyssar, Helene. "Rites and Responsibilities: The Drama of Black American Women." *Feminine Focus: The New Women Playwrights.* Ed. Enoch Brater. New York: Oxford UP, 1989. 226-40.

Locke, Alain and Montgomery Gregory, eds. *Plays of Negro Life: A Source-Book of Native American Drama.* New York: Harper, 1927.

Perkins, Kathy A., ed. with intro. *Black Female Playwrights: An Anthology of Plays Before 1950.* Bloomington: Indiana UP, 1989.

ELIZABETH BROWN-GUILLORY (ESSAY DATE 1996)

SOURCE: Brown-Guillory, Elizabeth. "Disrupted Motherlines: Mothers and Daughters in a Genderized, Sexualized, and Racialized World." In *Women of Color: Mother-Daughter Relationships in 20th-Century Literature,* edited by Elizabeth Brown-Guillory, pp. 188-207. Austin: University of Texas Press, 1996.

In the following excerpt, Brown-Guillory discusses Grimké's play, Rachel, *as a lesson to Black mothers who must prepare their daughters for the hostility they will face in the white world.*

Angelina Weld Grimke's treatment of mother-daughter relationships is especially germane to any discussion of the writings of contemporary women of color. Grimke's 1916 play ***Rachel*** became the "first twentieth-century full-length play written, performed, and produced by blacks" (Perkins, 8). ***Rachel*** examines the devastating effects of racism on an innocent child and his surrogate mother. When the play was published in 1917, inflamed critics accused Grimke of advocating genocide. However, a counter to her critics can be found in Grimke's papers in the Moorland-Spingarn Research Center at Howard University. Grimke justifies writing ***Rachel*** by saying that the play was directed as much at whites as it was at blacks. She was particularly interested in reaching white women, who are "the worst enemies with which the colored race has to contend" (quoted in Perkins, 9). Grimke's intentions in ***Rachel*** are elucidated when she says:

> My belief was then that if I could find a vulnerable point in their armour, if I could reach their hearts, even if only a little, then perhaps instead of being active or passive enemies they might become, at least, less inimical and possibly friendly. Did they have a vulnerable point and if so what was it? I believed it to be motherhood. . . . If anything can make all women sisters underneath the skins, it is motherhood. If, then, I could make the white women of this country see, feel, understand just what [effect] their prejudice and the prejudice of their fathers, brothers, husbands, and sons were having on the souls of the colored mothers everywhere, and upon the mothers that are to be, a great power to affect public opinion would be set free and the battle would be half won.
>
> (quoted in Perkins, 9)

While Grimke notes that she was partly trying to appeal to white women, there is evidence that she was also seriously concerned with mothering practices in the black community. Grimke scholars have tended to focus on ***Rachel*** as an anti-lynching play, not an unlikely subject since Walter White in *Rope and Faggot* estimated that 3,389 blacks, including 76 women, were lynched between 1882 and 1927 (229). Grimke was, indeed, concerned that white women seemed oblivious to the plight of black women, including their pain of witnessing the lynching of their sons, husbands, and brothers. In a 1992 essay, Judith L. Stephens argues that "in ***Rachel,*** Angelina Grimke threw the image of idealized motherhood back at white women in an attempt to make them see what meaning this so-called 'revered institution' might hold for black women. . . . Grimke was attempting to make white women question the desirability of motherhood from a black woman's perspective at a time when lynchings were at an all-time high" (333-334).

A closer reading of Grimke's play, however, reveals a key issue which has not been explored in critical studies. Grimke clearly points out that Rachel's own mother, Mrs. Loving, has not adequately prepared her for mothering. Grimke suggests that Rachel's depression and feelings of alienation could have been prevented had her mother adequately prepared her for a hostile world. While Grimke certainly protests against lynching practices in America in this play, she, more importantly, makes the point that mothers must tell their daughters the truth about the obstacles in the world which they will probably face and instruct them to survive with strength and dignity. Grimke suggests that black mothers must model for their daughters the various ways to reach inside to find courage to live triumphantly in a world in which they must ultimately face and overcome race and gender barriers. Rachel, who becomes Jimmy's legal guardian when his parents die of smallpox, is ill-equipped to mother because her own mother has sheltered her from the harsh realities of the world, which, in turn, short-circuits her ability to nurture little Jimmy properly. When Jimmy comes home crying to Rachel that he has been called a "nigger" and has had stones thrown at him, Rachel's mother tries to comfort Jimmy and the distraught Rachel. Rachel is devastated because of her inability to give Jimmy a satisfactory explanation of what it means to be subaltern and to be treated with derision because of race biases. She feels powerless to protect her child and becomes overwhelmed by his confusion and pain. While Rachel never blames her own mother for not teaching her how to cope with racism, it seems clear that Grimke is leveling precisely that indictment in her development of Rachel, who becomes increasingly neurotic during the course of the play. Patricia Hill Collins in *Black Feminist Thought* underscores Grimke's view of black motherhood: "African-American mothers place a strong emphasis on protection, either by trying to shield their daughters as long as possible from the penalties attached to their race, class, and gender status or by teaching them skills of independence and self reliance so that they will be able to protect themselves" (126).

Grimke indicts Mrs. Loving for sheltering Rachel, thereby fostering her dependence. She uses her play to caution black women that too much protection can be destructive. Mrs. Loving's delayed revelation that Rachel's father and brother had been lynched in the South some ten years prior, causing the Loving family to flee to the North for refuge, backfires and traumatizes Rachel instead of helping her to understand Jimmy's dilemma. Mrs. Loving's silence about the two lynchings is held up by Grimke as unfortunate and unwise, particularly since her silence prevents Rachel from understanding her own mother's idiosyncratic behavior for so many years. While Mrs. Loving's storytelling is meant to bolster Rachel and foster courage in her because of her father's valiant attempts at staving off an angry white mob before the lynching, this revelation only serves further to erode Rachel's already low self-esteem. She is incapacitated by her mother's overprotection. Furthermore, Mrs. Loving's story does nothing to reassure Rachel that life will be any better in the North for her son, who has just experienced a violent initiation into the real world. In fact, the positioning of the story of the lynchings convinces Rachel that there is no hope for a better world for poor black children. Mrs. Loving breaks silence too late to militate against Rachel's perception of herself as a failed mother. Rachel expresses her fear at mothering other children in the future:

> Everywhere, everywhere, throughout the South, there are hundreds of dark mothers who live in fear, terrible suffocating fear, whose rest by night is broken, and whose joy by day in their babies on their hearts is three parts—pain. . . . Why—it would be more merciful—to strangle the little things at birth. And so this nation—this white Christian nation—has deliberately set its curse upon the most beautiful—the most holy thing in life—motherhood!
>
> (149)

Note Rachel's pain as she vows that she will never give birth: "You god!—You terrible, laughing God! Listen! I swear—and my soul be damned to all eternity, if I do break this oath—I swear—that no child of mine shall ever lie upon my breast, for I will not have it rise up, in the terrible days that are to be—and call me cursed" (161). Helene Keyssar in "Rites and Responsibilities: The Drama of Black American Women" views Rachel's promise never to marry and have babies as an act of abortion: "For Rachel abortion, as she conceives it, is the only act that will authenticate her double existence as woman and black person. Any other act would, for her, be a false resolution of her hybrid self" (228). Contrary to Keyssar's interpretation, Rachel's vow never to have babies has less to do with Grimke's offering abortion as a viable option and more to do with illustrating that women sometimes erroneously consider desperate and destructive measures when mothering practices are disrupted. Racist cultural practices coupled with a black mother's attempts to veil the truth, according to Grimke, prevent children, daughters in particular, from learning how to cope with racial injustices which they must inevitably face. Grimke seems to be suggesting that black mothers and daughters pay a high price when mothers shield their daughters from racial hostility. She clearly makes the point that children lose their equilibrium when they go out into the world unprepared and that naive daughters become naive mothers who have great difficulty nurturing and empowering their children. This play makes it clear that when daughters are not taught survival skills by their mothers, they are forced to learn from the world, which can be a callous teacher.

Grimke's vision is in direct opposition to those blacks who believe that it is not important to tell their children about slavery or other race-related atrocities because they are an ugly part of their past. In her play ***Rachel*** Grimke addresses the need not only for mothers to educate their daughters (i.e, tell their stories of struggle and survival), but for daughters to listen to their mothers' stories and find healing and courage. In short, Grimke's play fulfills Mary Helen Washington's call for black women writers to reach back "into their black and female past for the authority to rename their experiences" ("New Lives and New Letters: Black Women Writers at the End of the Seventies," 10). Rachel learns too late of her mother's stories of struggle, but Grimke holds Rachel up as a lesson to daughters and mothers beyond the text who do not communicate, who do not hear each other. Rachel's choice never to have babies is a sacrifice that results from a daughter not being mothered properly. Grimke's play, then, can be viewed as one which calls for mothers to prepare their daughters for a hostile world by teaching them coping strategies early in life and by reinforcing those strategies at every stage of development in a female's life. . . .

Works Cited

Collins, Patricia Hill. *Black Feminist Thought.* New York: Routledge, 1990.

Grimke, Angelina Weld. *Rachel.* In *Black Theater U.S.A.: Forty-five Plays by Black Americans, 1847-1974,* ed. James V. Hatch and Ted Shine, 139-172. New York: Free Press, 1974.

Keyssar, Helene. "Rites and Responsibilities: The Drama of Black American Women. In *Feminine Focus: The New American Playwrights,* 226-240. Oxford: Oxford University Press, 1989.

Perkins, Kathy A., ed. *Black Female Playwrights: An Anthology of Plays before 1950.* Bloomington and Indianapolis: Indiana University Press, 1989.

Stephens, Judith L. "Anti-Lynch Plays by African-American Women: Race, Gender, and Social Protest in American Drama." *African-American Review* 26 (Summer 1992): 329-339.

Washington, Mary Helen. "New Lives and New Letters: Black Women Writers at the End of the Seventies." *College English* 43 (January 1981): 1-11.

White, Walter. *Rope and Faggot: A Biography of Judge Lynch.* New York: Alfred A. Knopf, 1929.

FURTHER READING

Criticism

Gourdine, Angeletta Km. "The *Drama* of Lynching in Two Blackwomen's Drama, or Relating Grimké's *Rachel* to Hansberry's *A Raisin in the Sun.*" *Modern Drama* 41, no. 4 (winter 1998): 533-45.

Discusses the dramatic strategies employed by Grimké and Lorraine Hansberry to negotiate issues of race and gender surrounding lynching.

Keyssar, Helene. "Rites and Responsibilities: The Drama of Black American Women." In *Feminine Focus: The New Women Playwrights,* edited by Enoch Brater, pp. 226-40. New York: Oxford University Press, 1989.

Studies the necessity for playwrights like Grimké to represent on stage the sometimes conflicting world views that reflect their status as both American women and Black women.

Miller, Jeanne-Marie A. "Images of Black Women in Plays by Black Playwrights." *CLA Journal* 20, no. 4 (June 1977): 494-507.

Studies Black female characterizations that defy racial and gender stereotypes in drama, among them Grimké's Rachel.

Molette, Barbara. "They Speak: Who Listens?: Black Women Playwrights." *Black World* 25, no. 6 (April 1976): 28-34.

Examines the marginalized status of Black female playwrights, Grimké among them, whose work has been deemed too controversial for mainstream audiences.

Schroeder, Patricia R. "Remembering the Disremembered: Feminist Realists of the Harlem Renaissance." In *Realism and the American Dramatic Tradition,* edited by William W. Demastes, pp. 91-106. Tuscaloosa: University of Alabama Press, 1996.

Discusses the way Black female playwrights of the early twentieth century, beginning with Grimké, used realist conventions to expose discrimination and combat racial stereotyping.

Young, Patricia. "Shackled: Angelina Weld Grimké." *Women and Language* 15, no. 2 (fall 1992): 25-31.

Argues that Grimké's writings offer positive Black characters to offset negative stereotypes of African Americans, and participate in a larger literary protest against lynching.

OTHER SOURCES FROM GALE:

Additional coverage of Grimké's life and career is contained in the following sources published by the Gale Group: *Black Writers*, Ed. 1; *Contemporary Authors,*Vol. 124; *Dictionary of Literary Biography,* Vols. 50, 54; *Discovering Authors Modules: Poets*; and *Feminist Writers.*

DUBOSE HEYWARD

(1885 - 1940)

(Full name Edwin DuBose Heyward) American poet, novelist, playwright, and librettist.

Heyward enjoyed modest success as a poet, playwright, and novelist during his lifetime, but his reputation today rests exclusively on his novel *Porgy* (1925), which became the basis for George Gershwin's folk opera, *Porgy and Bess.* The novel tells the story of Blacks living on Catfish Row, the waterfront of Heyward's native Charleston. The protagonist Porgy, a disabled beggar, was one of the first sympathetic and complex portrayals by a white author of an African American character. Heyward also wrote several poems and the novel, *Mamba's Daughters* (1929), about African American life, and wrote the screenplay for *The Emperor Jones,* which he adapted from Eugene O'Neill's play of the same name. His writing, whether about Blacks or whites, was firmly rooted in the landscape and culture of South Carolina. Although Heyward is little read today, critics note his important contribution to American folklore with his character of Porgy and claim that his depiction of African American life had a profound influence on the writers of the Harlem Renaissance.

BIOGRAPHICAL INFORMATION

Heyward was born August 31, 1885, and although his parents were descended from Charleston aristocracy, his family lived modestly. Heyward's father worked at a rice mill, and after he was killed in an accident at work in 1888, Heyward's mother supported the family by taking in boarders, sewing, and writing advertisements for a printing company. Heyward attended private and public schools, but he was absent-minded and sickly, and so performed poorly academically. At fourteen he left school and began working in a hardware store; a few years later he was stricken with infantile paralysis and never recovered the complete use of his right arm. Around 1905 he took a job as a cotton checker for a steamship line where he observed the Black Americans who were to become the subject of his later writing. In his early twenties, Heyward, together with a friend, bought an insurance business that became quite successful. Because of his ill health, Heyward spent his summers in Hendersonville, North Carolina, in a small cottage where he painted and wrote poetry. He began writing seriously, and in he 1920 co-founded the Poetry Society of South Carolina. In 1921, Heyward met Dorothy Kuhns, an aspiring playwright, and the couple married two years later. His first book of verse, *Carolina Chansons: Legends of the Low Country,* which he co-wrote with Hervey Allen, was published in 1922. This was followed in 1924 by a volume of Heyward's own, *Skylines and Horizons.* In order to devote himself to writing and lecturing, Heyward quit the insurance business in 1924, abandoning poetry to concentrate instead on fiction and drama. In 1925 he published his most famous work, *Porgy,* which he and his wife adapted for the stage in 1927. Heyward produced another volume of poetry and a number of other successful novels and plays, and then collaborated with George and Ira Gershwin on *Porgy and Bess.* The opera, based on his novel, premiered in 1935 but was not immediately successful. Heyward died of a heart attack in the North Carolina mountains in 1940 and never witnessed the immense popularity the opera later enjoyed.

MAJOR WORKS

Carolina Chansons, Heyward's 1922 collaboration with Hervey Allen, contains eight of the young writers' poems, mostly narratives about historical figures and events. The best known of these was "Gamesters All," a lengthy account of Joe, a Black gambler gunned down by a white policeman. Heyward's solo volume of poetry, *Skylines and Horizons,* contains poems about the South Carolina low country and the North Carolina mountains, dramatically depicting the spirit of the people of these regions that Heyward knew so well. Although Heyward gave up writing poetry in the mid-1920s, he published *Jasbo Brown and Selected Poems,*which contained some of his earlier work, in 1931. The title poem is a long narrative about the musician who would give his name to jazz music, a character who is also featured in *Porgy and Bess.*

Porgy, Heyward's first foray into prose, was his most successful work. It is the story of a disabled beggar named Porgy and his lover, Bess, and their brief, passionate, and sometimes violent, relationship. In 1926 Heyward published *Angel,* a tale of the North Carolina mountains, and the following year the stage version of *Porgy* was produced, enjoying considerable success on Broadway. In 1929 Heyward published *Mamba's Daughters,* a complex story about race relations in Charleston in the early part of the twentieth century, which was adapted for the stage in 1939. Before beginning his collaboration with the Gershwin brothers, Heyward wrote the screenplay for *The Emperor Jones,* which would star the famous Black actor Paul Robeson, and the novel, *Peter Ashley* (1932), about the Civil War. Heyward collaborated with the Gershwins on every aspect of *Porgy and Bess,* composing the entire libretto. Many of the lyrics for the opera were taken directly from Heyward's novel or play, and the words of some of the most famous arias, such as "Summertime" and "I Got Plenty o' Nuttin" are entirely his. In addition to publishing essays in periodicals, in his final years Heyward wrote *Lost Morning* (1936), about an artist who "sells out" to achieve commercial success, and *Star Spangled Virgin* (1939), a novel about the New Deal era in the Virgin Islands.

CRITICAL RECEPTION

Heyward won the 1921 Contemporary Verse Prize for "Gamesters All," and by 1924, critics were calling him the most important native Southern poet writing at the time. Heyward also enjoyed immediate success with *Porgy* and its stage adaptation as well as his other novels and dramatic collaborations. However, the only work of Heyward's that is remembered today, the libretto for *Porgy and Bess,* did not garner him any critical attention during his lifetime, and most readers and theatergoers to this day do not associate his name with the American folk opera made famous by the Gershwin brothers. For some years after his death, Heyward's wife attempted to make known her husband's role in the collaboration, but his contribution has remained largely overlooked. Several critics have attempted to emphasize his part in the opera's composition, showing how the stage version evolved from the novel, and others have pointed out his unacknowledged influence on later writers of the Harlem Renaissance.

PRINCIPAL WORKS

An Artistic Triumph (play) 1913

Carolina Chansons: Legends of the Low Country [with Hervey Allen] (poetry) 1922

Skylines and Horizons (poetry) 1924

Porgy (novel) 1925

Angel (novel) 1926

"The Half Pint Flask" (short story) 1927

Porgy: A Play in Four Acts [with Dorothy Heyward] (play) 1927

Mamba's Daughters: A Novel of Charleston (novel) 1929

Brass Ankle (play) 1931

Jasbo Brown and Selected Poems (poetry) 1931

Peter Ashley (novel) 1932

Emperor Jones [adaptor; from a play by Eugene O'Neill] (screenplay) 1933

Porgy and Bess [libretto by Heyward, lyrics by Heyward and Ira Gershwin, music by George Gershwin] (opera) 1935

Lost Morning (novel) 1936

The Country Bunny and the Little Gold Shoes: As Told to Jenifer (children's story) 1939

Mamba's Daughters: A Play [with Dorothy Heyward] (play) 1939

Star Spangled Virgin (novel) 1939

GENERAL COMMENTARY

ANTHONY HARRIGAN (ESSAY DATE 1951)

SOURCE: Harrigan, Anthony. "DuBose Heyward: Memorialist and Realist." *Georgia Review* 5, no. 3 (fall 1951): 335-44.

In the following essay, Harrigan claims that Heyward's works, particularly Porgy *and* Mamba's Daughters, *are a memorial to the Blacks of the South Carolina low country and that they realistically depict the lives of Blacks in the modern world after the breakdown of the old social order.*

I

Among Southern writers of recent times whose achievements have gone largely unrecognized is DuBose Heyward, who prior to his tragically early death in 1940 had come to represent to perfection the Southern writer's image of the tradition-conscious artist.

Unlike Faulkner's work, Heyward's novels do not constitute a myth or legend of the South. Indeed the most fitting subject for a novelist is not a social abstraction but a particular people in a particular place. His great strength was that he wrote so completely and convincingly of the place in which he was born and lived and died. Heyward was born in Charleston, South Carolina, in the year 1885. His own generation, the generation which restored Charleston and the South to the nation, had in its ranks many wise and intelligent men. This generation of Southerners took a long look back into the past as it rejoined the modern world. It is significant that Heyward's fellow Charlestonian Herbert Ravenel Sass entitled one of his novels of the Old South *Look Back to Glory.* These two writers aimed at a literature in which the past comes alive in the living present.

Heyward created a lasting portion of this literature. He did it in the city of his birth, remote from New York and Paris, and in spite of all the resistance to a true understanding of the South. He was the finest expression of the Southern literary genius. Unlike his Northern contemporaries, he had no need to become an expatriate. He was at once closer to and yet more distant from European civilization. Indeed if one is to understand Heyward's work one has to comprehend the fact that his world retained an inner spiritual propriety. He was not compelled to search the face of the globe in order to discover "a way of life." Heyward was a Charlestonian; and a Charlestonian of his generation possessed a sense of tradition which enabled him to recognize where he belonged and the manner in which he should act. Consequently he did not lack a vision of the good life or a body of well-defined standards.

Not only did he possess a clear vision of the good life, as poor F. Scott Fitzgerald unfortunately lacked, but he was not prone to a fatal head-heart split. The sophisticate and the unsophisticated may share his experience as recorded in his novels. Heyward's style is clear and straightforward, and his created realm is a realm of uncomplicated hearts and minds—despite the complexity of the situation in which many of his characters find themselves.

DuBose Heyward's finest and most significant works of fiction are ***Porgy*** and ***Mamba's Daughters.*** These novels are a memorial to the Gullah Negro of the Carolina Low-Country. The memorial is constituted of affection and understanding—affection in token of the Negro's faithfulness and understanding of his struggle. Since the First World War many thousands of Negroes have left the old Rice Coast and gone to live in Harlem and the Negro quarters of the large Northern cities. The new Negro cannot understand the tragic connection between his ancestors and the Low-Country planter class. Nevertheless, ***Porgy*** and ***Mamba's Daughters*** are a testament to this lost relationship. Sterling A. Brown, the Negro social historian, has termed this relationship: "a mystical cult of mutual affection."

The relationships between people separated by race is the central issue of these novels and constitutes a major theme of Southern writing. At a time when the stability of the relationships between whites and blacks is decreasing, the question of relationships must be considered anew—the breakdown of the old social order and the consequent dislocation of the ruling and servant classes. Heyward's attitude towards the Negro and this changing relationship is the attitude typical of his class. In an essay, **"The Negro in the Low-Country,"** he wrote eloquently of the Negro in his part of the South:

> . . . we [in America] have forgotten that there can be such a thing as pride of caste among the lowly, that there could exist in a man who had been born a servant and expected to die a servant a self-respect equally as great, and as jealously guarded as that enjoyed by the master, and yet, paradoxically, this very cleavage between the ruling and the servant classes in the South which has imposed an obligation to respect the dignity of each other has constituted the bond which has held the two classes together in affection and mutual understanding through the vicissitudes of two and a half centuries.

Heyward did not find the Negro better or worse than the whites, merely different. But he was keenly alive to the differences between the races. Delving into the inmost qualities of the black race, he showed the deepest insight and grasped the essence of the black man's soul:

> . . . we must remember that the Negro probably to a greater extent than any other living race is possessed of a genius for forming happy human relationships, for inspiring affection, for instinctively divining the mood of the one with whom he comes in contact, and of accommodating his own mood to that of the other.

It is important to bear in mind, however, that Heyward was primarily concerned with the Negro of his own day—not with the Negro of antebellum times. And he was profoundly mindful of the fact that the Negro of his own lifetime was groping towards a strange new destiny in America. His awareness of the latter is most evident in ***Mamba's Daughters.*** He puts the following words into Mamba's mouth when the old Negro woman asks Mrs. Wentworth for a letter stating that she was an old family servant of the Wentworth's: "Tain't fuh me, Miss. Ah kin tek care ob Mamba. But time is changin'. Nigger gots tuh git diff'ent kind ob sense now tuh git long."

Later in the novel when Hagar decides to kill herself and is speaking to the crowd in the company store at the phosphate works, Heyward has Hagar say,

> "Time comin' when nigger goin' worry jes like white folks, an' den Gawd show 'em what to do when he trouble get too deep fur he to walk t'rough."

Yet in ***Mamba's Daughters*** the *age of anxiety* has touched but the upper levels of Charleston's Negro world. Of the great mass of the blacks, Heyward wrote:

> The corrosion of hidden sin did not mark the faces, for the consciences that might have been sitting in judgement had not yet been scourged into consciousness.

It is perfectly clear that despite his sympathy for the struggle the Negro was making to improve himself, Heyward had deep misgivings as to the future that awaited the race. He was too keen an observer of contemporary life and too acutely aware of the pitiful inadequacy of it in comparison with the old mode of life in the American republic to hold any foolish notions of automatic progress and human betterment through so over-simple a device as a change in social institutions and class structure. Nevertheless, he realized that the Low-Country Negro, the Negro in ***Porgy*** and ***Mamba's Daughters,*** was heeding the call of an illusory new modern world. He understood that certain types of change could not be resisted and that the black race was certain to be absorbed into the cruel and destructive way of life prevailing in so many portions of the country.

> We watch him [the Negro] with his family, his unquestioning belief in a personal God, his spontaneous abandonment to emotion, his faith in his simple destiny. And seeing these things, out of our own fuller and sadder knowledge, we wonder whether he will be happier when the last of the bonds are severed and finally and triumphantly he has conformed to the stereotyped pattern of American success.

However, DuBose Heyward was not exclusively concerned with the relationships between the races. He was also greatly interested in the relationship of the artist to his society and the standard of literary taste. In an essay entitled **"The New Note in Southern Literature"** which he prepared prior to publication of the first of his novels he gave a forthright exposition of his ideas:

> In spite of its lynchings, its paternity of the Klan, its evolution trials, and its legislatures that naively exclude chewing tobacco from taxation, the south is artistically, probably the most civilized section of America; and for the reason that it has a large, if reticent aristocracy which possesses a congenial feeling for beauty and a tolerant attitude towards the artist.

It is noteworthy that Heyward wrote this in 1925, exactly five years after H. L. Mencken published his essay "The Sahara of Bozart" which commenced with J. Gordon Coogler's lines:

> Alas, for the South! Her books have grown
> fewer—
> She never was much given to literature.

Mencken had eyes to see the South of the fish-fry, hysterical religious revivals, and drunken politicians. He was not wise enough to detect in process of creation a new Southern literature which was traditional in tone and contemporary in technique. He did not discover the slightest clue concerning the rise of a new generation, the generation of DuBose Heyward, Stark Young, John Crowe Ransom, Allen Tate, and the many others who filled the ranks of the most productive generation of writers the United States has ever witnessed.

Heyward noted the situation at an early date and recognized it in its full dimensions. He acknowledged that the task of Southern writers was to establish a new concept of good taste which was based upon completely honest observation of Southern life. It seemed perfectly natural to him that the standard of artistic depiction should be fundamentally different from the standard of drawing room conversation. According to his ideas, the new standard and new literature were intimately connected with the wealth of the South in the vestiges of European civilization. He cited this as the soil of American art:

> The important thing is that now, in most of the older [Southern] communities, there is an intelligent and vocal minority that does not consider Colonial architecture evidence of a retarded civilization to be razed and supplanted by the skyscraper. It realizes that by holding an older beauty before the eye, it is preserving sources from which springs the ability to appreciate all true beauty.

It is important to bear this statement in mind when one reads John Crowe Ransom's criticism of DuBose Heyward and several other Charleston writers. Ransom accepts the things Heyward postulates, but he does not consider that the past and its heritage have been appropriately handled by these writers. Ten years after Heyward published **"The New Note in Southern Literature"** Ransom wrote:

> . . . the Charleston writers . . . are less subtle, and easier to define, than some other writers; and there is another reason too. At Charleston the Southern idea of a formal society, I presume, is in a better state of preservation than anywhere else. The beautiful houses are still there, so are the ample drawing-rooms and dining rooms. But still there is, I am afraid, the old paralysis, the failure of understanding in this particular art, which used to keep the South from producing its appropriate literature. The Charleston writers are producing a literature, but it is irrelevant to what Charleston stands for and it is not Southern.

The substance of Ransom's criticism is the idea that because Charleston is a formal society it is automatically genteel. Consequently he avows it is impossible for a person bred in his mythical drawing-room atmosphere to accept the realities of life and, hence, fine art. It is evident that he misunderstands the character of Charleston; it is formal but not genteel. The tone of the old city is fundamentally eighteenth century and never Victorian. It has long demanded for itself the chief aristocratic privilege: the right to be both fastidious and bawdy. The homogeneous quality of the cultural background of a Charlestonian destines an artist reared in the traditions of the city to be a formalist but not a prude. Heyward sensed this, and his awareness is evident in what he writes of his character St. Julien de C. Wentworth in ***Mamba's Daughters:***

> The town looked with indulgent eyes upon youth in its wild oats stage. That was something rooted in tradition, understood. Good blood could be counted upon to win through in that reckless period.

Here is one of the European vestiges of which Heyward spoke, although in this case it is not a material vestige. Rather was it the old conception that permitted men to be divergent from routine morality provided they remained within the framework of tradition and the class habits. This very thing made possible Heyward's complete freedom in writing of the Negro in his imaginative literature. For Heyward departed from the customary picture of the Negro as a clown. He created, instead, a figure who, although he possessed definite racial characteristics, is a human being with human problems. He redeemed the Negro from the hands of the writers who presented the Negro as a grotesque white man. Heyward acknowledged the stature and dignity which the Negro had acquired in his bouts with adversity of every description. He was completely truthful in his analysis of the strength and weakness of the whole race as well as of the individuals. It is fitting that the man who should redeem the Negro in American literature is a scion of the Carolina Low-Country rice planters.

The truly fine works of fiction written by modern Southern writers have all been tragic and based upon the lives of passionate characters. Inasmuch as the civilization of the Southern states has not required endless action in life, it is understandable that endless motivation has not been required in its literature. Because there is a fixed code between the races and within each racial group, character interpretation does not have to be carried to the lengths to which it is carried in Northern fiction. ***Porgy*** is an excellent example of the tragic novel with a passionate character as a central figure.

Porgy is the story of a crippled beggar who lives in the ruined grandeur which is Catfish Row in the old city of Charleston. He drives his goat-cart through the streets every day, returning at night with the money he has collected. Heyward wrote of Porgy and Porgy's era in which "the profession was one with a tradition." As he explained in the opening pages of the book:

> A man begged, presumably, because he was hungry, much as a man of more energetic temperament became a stevedore from the same cause. His plea for help produced the simple reactions of a generous impulse, a movement of the hand, and a gift of a coin, instead of the elaborate and terrifying processes of organized philanthropy. His antecedents and his mental age were his own affair, and, in the majority of cases, he was as happily oblivious of one as he was of the other.

One night there is a crap game and Crown, a giant Negro stevedore, kills another Negro. Crown flees the city. Heyward gives a superb description of the dead man's room with the corpse laid out in the center and the women singing dirges until neighbors place sufficient money in a saucer to insure the murdered man a decent burial. There is a great sweeping scene which reveals the Negro's primitive passion and which comes to a fabulous end with the mourners in the dingy room bursting forth in the jubilant spiritual "Oh, I gots a little brudder in de new grabe-yard what outshine de sun." Sympathetically and compassionately Heyward describes the funeral cortege with its "odd fusion of comedy and tragedy so inextricably a part of negro life in its deepest moments." The funeral comes to an end and the crowd dashes madly from the burial ground inasmuch as there is a superstition that "De las' man in de grabe yahd goin' tuh be de nex' one tuh git buried." The story then proceeds to the incarceration of an old Negro man by the name of Peter and the confiscation of his few belongings by the dishonest merchants. Heyward's description of this constitutes one of the rare bitter moments in the novel: a moment in which he strikes at the middle class white man's injustice in his dealings with the Negro. Heyward says of the man who takes away old Peter's wagon that he exhibited "a contract, dated three years previous, by which Peter was to pay two dollars a week for an indefinite period, on an exorbitant purchase price. Failure to pay any installment would cause the property to revert to the seller. It all looked thoroughly legal." Heyward cites the irony of the situation which is that one of the few belongings left by the swindling merchants is a chromo of The Great Emancipator.

Later in the summer of the same year, Bess, who is Crown's woman, comes to live with Porgy in Catfish Row. After she has been living with Porgy a while, there takes place "the grand parade and picnic of the Sons and Daughters of Repent Ye Saith the Lord" and the trip aboard a sternwheel excursion boat to Kiawah Island, which is south of Charleston. His comment on the parade is excellent:

> Out of its fetters of civilization this people has risen suddenly, amazingly. Exotic as the Congo, and still able to abandon themselves utterly to the wild joy of fantastic play, they had taken the reticent, old Anglo-Saxon town and stamped their mood swiftly and indelibly into its heart. Then they passed, leaving behind them a wistful envy among those who watched them go—those whom the ages had rendered old and wise.

Bess encounters Crown on Kiawah and makes plans to join him after the cotton crop is sent to the city. This action is followed by the magnificent hurricane scene—the most superb piece of writing in all of Heyward's fiction. The end follows soon after with the killing of Crown by Porgy and the loss of Bess when she is taken aboard a river boat by some Negro boatmen. And in this manner the story comes to an end.

Porgy is the story of a Negro's inner life, the years of complete peace and eventually the moments of passion and extreme violence. ***Porgy*** is, after a fashion, the story of all the black men of the South. One cannot escape its symbolism and the fact that the central characters embody so many of the expectations and disappointments of the race.

Many years before Heyward published any fiction he wrote for the *Reviewer* an article which may be properly considered in relation to ***Porgy:***

> . . . Are they an aeon behind, or an aeon ahead of us? Who knows? But one thing is certain: the reformer will have them in the fullness of time. They will surely be cleaned, married, conventionalized. They will be taken from the fields, and given to machines, their instinctive feeling for the way that leads to happiness, saved as it is from selfishness, by humour and genuine kindness of heart, will be supplanted by a stifling moral straitjacket. They will languish, but they will submit, because they will be trained into a habit of thought that makes blind submission a virtue. . . . And my stevedore, there out of the window. I look at him again. I cannot see him a joke. Most certainly I cannot contort him into a menace, I can only be profoundly sorry for him, for there he sits in the sunshine unconsciously awaiting his supreme tragedy. He is about to be saved.

II

Sixteen years ago Gerald W. Johnson wrote: "The case of DuBose Heyward is peculiarly interesting because his work, like that of R. L. Stevenson, represents a triumph of acute observation." It is true that ***Mamba's Daughters*** is not the typical regional novel. Heyward carefully observes the present. His theme embraces more than the elements of *loss:* destructive family conflicts, the forced sale of an ancestral property, the breakdown of tradition. ***Mamba's Daughters*** is not a sorrowful tale about the old ruling class which is so often pictured as devoid of will power and courage with which to meet the problems of a new era. Fundamentally, it is a story of development and change on the part of both the black and white races.

This novel is exceedingly complex in comparison with ***Porgy.*** It covers a period of twenty-odd years, and the action sheds light on several utterly different worlds: everything from aristocratic white Charleston to wealthy Harlem circles. The reader has revealed to him the respective modes of living of the old Charleston families, the Negroes of the servant class, the Northern, newly rich, educated Negroes of the post First World War era, the white "crackers," and the workers in the phosphate mining camps. The bare outline of the story is built around the figure of Mamba, a sly, indomitable old Negro woman who insinuates herself into a poor but exceedingly proud Charleston family. Her purpose is to develop the habits and contacts necessary to obtain a job with a wealthy social-climbing Northern family. This job would enable her to educate Lissa, her granddaughter, who is the child of Hagar, a simple-minded giantess. Mamba's intriguing and Hagar's labour in the phosphate diggings make possible Lissa's education and training as a singer. The novel is also the story of St. Julien de C. Wentworth, only son in the poor but aristocratic family with which Mamba allies herself. Saint has a decided inclination towards the arts. His family depends upon him, however, and he has to find employment in the phosphate mining camp. Lissa's family sacrifices everything in order that she may attain a place in the world. In the case of the Wentworths, it is the young man who has to make the sacrifice. Saint assumes the family's financial obligations. Lissa eventually is an artistic success in New York and attains stardom in a Negro opera. The price of Lissa's success is, however, the suicide of Hagar and the confession of a murder the giant Negro woman did not commit. Her purpose in this was to prevent Lissa becoming involved in a situation which might be disastrous to her career. Saint's difficulties are removed with the event of a happy marriage.

The characters of Mamba and Hagar are the dual source of the novel's power. Mamba's shrewdness and Hagar's strength bring about their victory as regards Lissa. This victory is achieved in a world that is compounded of poverty, drunkenness, poor-white scoundrels, villainous Negroes, and callous policemen. These two elemental beings strive together to bring into being an utterly new creature.

In discussing Heyward's presentation of the Negro world, one must stress his realization of the existence of the educated Negro in the South. He wrote in ***Mamba's Daughters:***

> In the old city that was so strong in its class consciousness among the whites it was singular that there was so little realization of the fact, that, across the colour line, there existed much the same state of affairs. . . . Far above, in the life of the aristocracy, the new freedom was beginning to be manifest, smashing conventional usage; talking its Freud and Jung—rearranging moral standards, and explaining lapses in its pat psychological jargon. But in the Monday Night Music Club ladies were ladies, those who were pale enough blushed, a leg was still a limb—and a gentleman asked permission to smoke cigarettes.

Heyward was perfectly well aware of the fact that these Negroes were pioneers of a definite sort, fashioning standards for their less educated brethren and learning new behavior.

He described the Negro with realism. But he did not write with equal realism of the white race and the class to which he belonged. One receives the impression when reading his novels that he felt no limitations in his portrait of the black race. But his analysis of Charlestonians is deficient in the critical spirit. It is as if he were speaking to his first cousin about the manners of his second cousin. The writing is too restrained and protective. Stringfellow Barr writes that "Aristocracy exists only where there is faith in the worthwhileness of some intangible values." Perhaps these intangible values were too vivid in his thoughts when he sat down to describe his own kind of human being. One is led to think of Heyward's description of the character of Saint:

> But the past had reached dead hands after him, guiding him imperceptibly this way and that. Forces that had driven forward in grooves for generations had pulled against his amorphous longings, his only half-realized dreams—had held him true to form and tradition.

There is part of the answer to the question of the imperfectness of his characterization of Charlestonians of his class. Too many of the unpleasant facts are omitted. With that in mind, Gerald W. Johnson wrote of him:

"He can evoke Paradise, but he cannot, or will not, raise Hell; and that is both his strength and his weakness." But, nevertheless, his characterization of the Negro is superb.

Other Southern writers have dealt more completely with the aristocratic Southern white. But Heyward was at once the most eloquent memorialist of the older type Negro and the most compassionate observer of the new.

FRANK DURHAM (ESSAY DATE 1954)

SOURCE: Durham, Frank. "Maker of Folklore." In *DuBose Heyward: The Man Who Wrote "Porgy,"* pp. 140-46. Columbia: University of South Carolina Press, 1954.

In the following essay, Durham offers an assessment of Heyward's writing, claiming that his most famous works are significant for their representation of the aristocratic tradition of the past, and that Porgy *has become a part of the folklore of the American South.*

Almost fifteen years have passed since DuBose Heyward's death. During these years his name grew dim in the minds of the American public. In the anthologies his poems no longer appeared, and the histories of literature dismissed his work in a phrase or a sentence. Much of his writing, one must admit, will never again capture the interest of the reading public. But his and Gershwin's opera promises to live on as a permanent part of our national culture; and the novel ***Porgy,*** long out of print, has been issued in a new edition, with an introduction by Dorothy Heyward, for a generation of readers who know the tenants of Catfish Row only as characters in an opera.

By now all America and most of the major capitals of Europe have had a colorful glimpse of Charleston, and people of many tongues have been moved by the pathetic story of an obscure beggar, once a familiar figure on King Street. Porgy and his goat wagon have joined that immortal company of whom Paul Bunyan, Uncle Tom, Huck Finn, and John Henry are distinguished members. The Negro cripple, who in a golden summer knew love and heroism and tragedy, is already one with the figures of American folklore whose names are familiar throughout the nation.

Porgy now seems timeless—wise with the sagacity of mellow age, childlike with the innocence of a half-tamed savage, shrewd with a strategy born of the necessity to survive among an alien people, gay with the insouciance of one who lets tomorrow take care of itself, and tragic with the courage of one who knows his own impotence before the inescapable force of destiny. Huddled in the ruined ballroom while the hurricane outside rips an entire roof from a nearby building and turns it into a flapping and tearing instrument of destruction, Porgy murmurs to his beloved Bess, "You an' me, Bess, . . . we *sho* is a little somet'ing attuh all."

Porgy the novel and ***Porgy*** the play and *Porgy and Bess* the opera have assured the immortality of a little segment of Charleston life—Catfish Row teeming with vitality and drama. All the world now knows Porgy and his Charleston. But with that sly irony which Porgy's creator always saw in the scheme of things, Fate has increasingly obscured the name of the man who breathed life into Catfish Row and gave its story to posterity.

And yet who can name the creator of Paul Bunyan, of Robin Hood, of even that cherished Mademoiselle from Armentières? Students of literature can tell you who first wrote of Frankenstein's monster; some few, usually unreconstructed Southerners, can still recall the creator of Uncle Tom and Little Eva. Mark Twain is, of course, the exception that proves the rule. But the authorship of most folklore soon fades into limbo; it is the creation, not the creator, that achieves identity in the popular mind.

Such, in great measure, has been the immortality attained by DuBose Heyward of Charleston. When I was collecting material for this study I used to amuse myself with a little experiment when I ranged beyond the confines of the pluff mud and the marsh grass of the Carolina coast. I would announce that I was writing on DuBose Heyward and then watch my vis-à-vis develop a blank expression while trying to appear knowing. At last I would say, "He wrote ***Porgy,*** you know." And the response was almost always the same: a sudden smile of recognition and then, "Oh, ***Porgy***!" Soon my friend would enthusiastically recall incidents from DuBose Heyward's story of Catfish Row: the hurricane; Crown's murder of Robbins in the flickering light of a single lantern; the parade of The Sons and Daughters of "Repent Ye Saith the Lord" with its flashes of orange, emerald, and purple; Porgy's triumph over the white lawyer Archdale; his pathetic flight in his goat wagon with the police patrol in amused and clangorous pursuit. To my friends it was Porgy who was alive; Heyward was just an unfamiliar name. But Porgy and Bess, Maria and Crown, Simon Frazier and old Peter have achieved a life of their own. Once in a bookshop on Fourth Avenue I asked for one of Heyward's volumes of poetry. The proprietor regretted the lack of such a book but assured me that he had an anthology which contained selections by DuBose Heyward. The book was one confined to the works of American Negro poets.

When tourists, complete with cameras and Chamber of Commerce folders, invade Charleston in the early spring, one of the first places they ask to be shown is Catfish Row; and since there was no Catfish Row Charlestonians have been forced to create one. Now the tourists can look affectionately at some quaint modern apartments near the waterfront and conjure up familiar scenes from the idyll of Porgy and Bess. Only a few of them pause before a tiny house on Church Street and read the weathering sign which tells them that here DuBose Heyward lived for a while and worked on a portion of his famous story. And to the passer-by the green and white residence at 24 South Battery where Heyward spent the last few years of his life is just another Charleston house, not so handsome as many but comfortable looking.

In 1942 when ***Porgy and Bess*** was given its second production in New York, the billboards and the window cards proclaimed boldly that George Gershwin's ***Porgy and Bess*** was in the offing. Somewhere, hidden down among the lines of small type, appeared the name of Porgy's creator. It was not until Mrs. Heyward took the matter to the Dramatists Guild that George Gershwin's name was joined in large letters by that of DuBose Heyward. Even with the most recent and most widely acclaimed revival of the opera, it is Gershwin's name that is generally cited as that of the man responsible for the musical version of the story. But, as we have seen, DuBose Heyward played a major role in the writing of this opera, advised and often guided the composer in the creation of the music. It is undeniably true that it is Gershwin's music which has helped Porgy to achieve his place in American folklore; but it is also undeniable—if generally unrecognized—that without DuBose Heyward's sensitivity and dramatic skill the opera would probably never have become the American classic that it is.

We shall never know anything about the aboriginal North German who sat by a campfire and first sang of Beowulf and Grendel. The dark-skinned stevedore who first chanted of John Henry lies somewhere—anonymous dust in an unmarked grave. Behind every piece of folklore there lived a man, sometimes many men, who walked for a brief hour on the world's stage, sorrowed, laughed, struggled, and died unknown, unheralded, but leaving behind a progeny more alive to millions of human beings than the man across the street, the face seen every day on the bus or behind the counter.

The story of DuBose Heyward's own life has about it much of the quality of folklore: the dispossessed young aristocrat born impoverished into a world where the old values were crumbling, the grinding struggle for existence cloaked beneath a threadbare gentility, prostrating illness and the triumph over it, strange adventures and discoveries in an exotic and barbaric world hidden beneath the calm surface of his city, love for his region and devotion to art driving the young man on to a career that was to result in a happy marriage and worldwide fame. Here are details from the legend of the scullery boy who proved to be a prince—from Hans Christian Andersen to Horatio Alger.

But there is more than romance, more than the American success story, in the career of DuBose Heyward. There is the reflection of a phase of Southern thinking, still widely practiced but too rarely appearing in the literature of the region. DuBose Heyward's South is not the Tobacco Road of Erskine Caldwell nor the sometimes miasmic but compelling Yoknapatawpha County of William Faulkner; and in spite of the surface similarities, Heyward's South is a far remove from that Never-Never Land of magnolias and ol' Massas of Thomas Nelson Page.

The story of Heyward and the stories he wrote reveal the dilemma of the liberal but nonrevolutionary Southern aristocrat confronted by a world he never made. The true Charlestonian, like Heyward, never completely relinquishes his abiding love of his home city and his native region; its history is his history, its tradition is his tradition, its values are his values, and its past glory is his rightful heritage. But fame and success increasingly widened the horizon of this Charleston author, as early poverty had deepened his knowledge of the many-faceted life of his city. From the comforting security of an inherited position he makes forays into worlds where achievement, not inherited position, with the criterion of acceptance, where the color of a man's skin mattered less than his skill in the arts, where he began to question intellectually the things he still cherished in his heart—and would always cherish.

This progressive dichotomy in Heyward's thinking grows more and more apparent as one follows the development of his talent. Like many Southerners of his background, he was never to let his intellectual skepticism in regard to the ideals of his region displace his instinctive love for those ideals and for the region itself. He would never man the barricades, but neither could he blindly proclaim that God was in His Heaven and all was right with the world below the line surveyed by the Messrs. Mason and Dixon. He achieved a somewhat uncomfortable equilibrium between the head and the heart; but if it came to a crisis there is little doubt that the heart would triumph.

The story of DuBose Heyward and his writing, then, is in many respects a story of regional chauvinism, an enlightened chauvinism, not the kind that produces hooded hooligans and fiery crosses. It represents much that is fine in Southern thought: an abiding love of one's region, a sense of *noblesse oblige,* an admirable if sometimes quixotic code of honor, a sincere if limited humanitarianism, a reverence for the past that manifests itself in a productive archivism, a sensitivity to the color and beauty and strangeness of the landscape, and, finally, an attitude toward the Negro that has been widely misunderstood. If one seeks a keynote to this Southern thinking, perhaps the best word is *responsibility*.

The story of DuBose Heyward is also the story of a professional literary man who never forgot that he was an artist. In his work he came in contact with almost every phase of literary activity in America. He gained his initial recognition as a poet and as a pioneer in the Southern literary revival. His first acclaim was accorded his novel ***Porgy,*** which was to be followed by five other novels. Alone and with his wife he wrote three plays, two of them successful, for Broadway production. He was the sole author of one motion picture scenario and participated in the preparation of another. He achieved some success as a lecturer on literary subjects. And, finally, he wrote the libretto and most of the lyrics for a folk opera that has already taken its place as an American classic. So the account of DuBose Heyward's career is in miniature the narrative of literary America in the 1920's and the 1930's. He made a living by his pen—a good living, and he was constantly subjected to the pressure of publishers and the need for satisfying popular taste. But he never lost the belief that he was basically a practitioner of a demanding art, not a mere business man of letters. He scrupulously avoided repeating the formula of his successes and ever sought with each new project to strike out into fresh spheres of subject matter and technique.

But as an artist DuBose Heyward was also a Southerner. To be sure, under the influence of John Bennett and Hervey Allen he learned early that literature is more than the result of a burst of fine creative fury, that painstaking craftsmanship is important. However, as a Southerner he held to the credo of his region that art was the product more of the heart than of the intellect. Thus there was always something lyric, something vividly pictorial about his prose style; at its best it evokes the color, the rhythms, and the atmosphere of the Carolina Low Country and the North Carolina mountains. But sometimes it takes on the magniloquence of the oratory still heard on Confederate Memorial Day; sometimes the sentiment goes over into sentimentality and "fine writing." We Southerners too often have a kind of cabalistic devotion to the purple and the sesquipedalian. Heyward's delineation of the Negro, and occasionally of the mountaineer, exhibits keen observation and keener sympathy for the natural, the primitive, the barbaric; but too frequently his well-born white characters, especially the Charlestonians, emerge as mere cut-out stereotypes of departed gallantry and immaculate (if devilishly whimsical) Southern womanhood. Inherited concepts and love can produce apparently inexplicable blind spots in even the most perceptive; this was the way Heyward had been taught to see his ancestors and his compeers, and thus he saw them.

Murder, hurricanes, and suicide run like crimson threads through Heyward's stories; but he is never needlessly melodramatic, never morbid. Over all the violence and bloodshed there is a romantic sheen which not only makes them acceptable but causes them to appear right and inevitable. Only when he leaves his Negroes, his mountaineers, and his tragic defenders of the Lost Cause, and turns to the contemporary scene does his gift for melodrama seem ill used.

As he believed that literature was the product more of the heart than of the intellect, Heyward never seems a profound or strikingly original thinker. When he attempts to philosophize, he usually writes his least successful prose and interrupts his narrative with rather sententious comment. But it would be wrong to think his work devoid of ideas. To the student of the South, Heyward's ideas, both expressed and tacitly accepted, are among the most rewarding phases of his work. For he was essentially the Southern gentleman, in the best sense of the term.

Many of his poems and stories are now interesting mainly for their reflection of this Southern aristocratic tradition. Undeniably, ***Porgy,*** in its three forms, is his most significant and his most satisfying work, with ***Mamba's Daughters*** and **"The Half Pint Flask"** of next importance. In ***Porgy*** he exhibited the virtues of the old tradition successfully modified by his absorption of the artistic theories of the twentieth century and made less obvious by his careful avoidance of propaganda. It is, as he felt it to be, the work of an artist, the artist-gentleman, the enlightened but not totally Reconstructed Southerner. On ***Porgy*** largely rests Heyward's fame; it is the work always associated with him, no matter how many other novels and plays he wrote.

Porgy is memorable because it presents for the first time in our national letters a fictional treatment of the Southern Negro as a human being and not merely as a pathetically comic figure or a subject for racial and social propaganda. ***Porgy*** is also significant for its recording of a people and a way of life now fading into the past. As a play it brought something new to the theater and encouraged the recognition of the Negro as a dramatic artist. As an opera it achieved the first widespread acceptance of an American work in that field. But, most of all, ***Porgy*** has become a part of native folklore, its characters and their romantic story having gradually so imbedded themselves into the group consciousness that the name of their creator is almost forgotten. Not many authors have gained such enduring, if increasingly anonymous, immortality.

FRANK DURHAM (ESSAY DATE 1965)

SOURCE: Durham, Frank. "DuBose Heyward's 'Lost' Short Stories." *Studies in Short Fiction* 2, no. 2 (1965): 157-63.

In the following essay, Durham examines seven early short stories by Heyward, arguing that although they are clearly the work of a beginning writer, they exhibit some of the same stylistic and thematic features found in his more mature work.

Now that his and George Gershwin's ***Porgy and Bess*** is generally accepted as the outstanding American folk opera, DuBose Heyward is emerging as a figure worthy of consideration in any account of American literature. His story of Porgy, the crippled Negro beggar of Charleston, in its novelistic, dramatic, and operatic forms has become part of American folklore; his ***Mamba's Daughters*** is still remembered as both a novel and a play; and his **"Half Pint Flask"** has been reprinted frequently in anthologies of short stories.

Though he first gained national recognition in 1922 with a thin volume of verse done in collaboration with Hervey Allen, Heyward had served a hitherto unrecorded apprenticeship in prose fiction. His ***Porgy*** in 1925 was not, as many think, his first attempt at imaginative prose. Nor is Miss Emily Clark correct in stating that Heyward's first published work in prose was an article **"And Once Again—the Negro,"** which appeared in October, 1923, in her little magazine *The Reviewer.* Heyward had published at least two short stories before 1923. And five others, apparently unpublished, are extant in manuscript among the Heyward papers, now on deposit at the South Carolina Historical Society in Charleston. Most biographical sketches of Heyward omit any reference to these early stories, and Hervey Allen wrote [in his *Dubose Heyward, a Critical and Biographical Sketch*] only that "there were a few short stories," without further comment. John Bennett, Heyward's literary mentor during the early years, remembered merely that his protégé at one time tried without marked success to write commercial stories "in the manner of Octavus Roy Cōhen." Before sorting her husband's papers, Mrs. Heyward said that she had heard Heyward mention some early stories and that she believed that one of them contained the germ of ***Angel,*** his second novel. Heyward himself never publicly acknowledged these early stories.

To the reader of these apprentice efforts, Heyward's silence is understandable. Only one of them, **"The Brute,"** suggests anything other than the work of a fledgling. However, to one familiar with Heyward's maturer work, these seven stories are interesting because they show him seeking his appropriate medium and foreshadowing characteristics found in his successful novels and plays.

He was working at the short story as early as 1917, for in that year he submitted **"Making a Man of Rayburn"** (later called **"The Winning Loser"**) and **"The Quade Sense of Humor"** to the Writecrafters, an organization offering criticism and marketing suggestions. In the next year, 1918, Heyward achieved what seems to be his first appearance in print as an author of fiction. His story **"The Brute"** was published in the *Pagan, a Magazine for Eudaemonists,* edited by Joseph Kling, Hart Crane, and E. O'Neill. In 1920 *Ainslee's* carried Heyward's **"The Winning Loser,"** his only other fiction to be printed before ***Porgy.*** By 1920 he had temporarily given up prose for poetry and was for the next four years to be one of the prime movers in the so-called Southern poetic renaissance.

If quality is considered, **"The Winning Loser"** probably preceded **"The Brute"** in composition, for it is an incredibly bad story. It suggests that Heyward was a close reader of the minor works of Bret Harte, for here one finds all the trappings of the story of the West: the frontier prostitute with a heart of gold, her brutal and unscrupulous lover, her idealistic young admirer from the East, two men facing each other alone in the rugged land, a barroom with an assortment of typical habitués, and kind of misty-eyed sentiment coating the violence and crudity.

Chained to the cash register in Jerry's Place in the frontier town of Puma is a diamond necklace priced at one hundred dollars. Belle Flavant, the lady of weightless virtue, covets the bauble because it is *"real,"* in contrast to the insincerity which has been he lot. After Rayburn, the young Easterner, protests the genuineness of his affection for her, Belle delivers herself of a speech that must have made the maturer Heyward blush:

> I know, lad. Forgive me! I think it is your friendship, my first genuine possession, that has made me wish for less sham. I want to throw these cheap sparklers away. I believe I could make a better start if I knew there was one little bit of fourteen carat about me to live up to.

Later, "Brag" Calloway, Belle's less platonic friend, hears of the price she now places on her affections and, like Rayburn, determines to secure the necklace for her. Unfortunately, neither gentleman is in funds; so separately they set out to kill a marauding mountain lion on which there is a bounty of one hundred dollars.

Out in Dead Man's Ca on Rayburn tracks the beast and shoots it but hears another shot at the same time. Calloway appears and claims to be the killer. After an extended eyeing of each other, Calloway (through a low trick) knocks Rayburn unconscious and leaves him there alone.

The next day Rayburn drags himself into Jerry's Place and is given a letter left there for him. He is stunned by its contents: Belle has gone away with her "husband" (she was not really a widow), but her love for Rayburn is eternal; Rayburn must be brave, must return East to a career in his family's lumber business, and must be "a good, strong man for her sake." After blanching a bit and interlacing his fingers convulsively, Rayburn raises his head, and "like the coming of dawn, a new glad light was born in his face. 'That's her!' he breathed. 'True as steel!' Then, in a voice of incredible wonder, 'and there were those who could speak lightly of her. God!'" Then, "quite irrelevantly," he decides to marry Eileen, the girl who patiently waits for him back East.

Undeniably a fumbling effort, **"The Winning Loser"** does reveal an occasional flash of the descriptive skill that became one of Heyward's signal virtues in both his verse and his novels. He was always effective in picturing violence and a kind of primitive animal beauty, especially the rhythmic play of the muscles. Here is a hint of this skill "Presently the bushes parted, and against the background of the stars, the lean sinuous form of the lion appeared. Very delicately he advanced along the summit of the ridge now and then testing his footing with a tentative forepaw, and again standing superb, immobile as a Robin bronze—the very epitome of life."

Heyward seems most successful in describing the setting, creating an atmosphere, and depicting his favorite primitive type of action. When he attempts characterization, dialogue, and authorial comment, he falls back upon the most obvious types and upon often ludicrous and melodramatic clichés; but he does exhibit skill in handling the dramatic scene, in building up suspense—in spite of the almost complete lack of motivation, or at least of credible motivation. **"The Winning Loser"** does, however, show Heyward experimenting with the local color story, though at this early stage in his career he had not yet found the proper locality on which to exercise his talents; in the five unpublished stories Heyward is trying his hand tentatively in a variety of forms and employing different locales in the slow search for his proper field.

"The Quade Sense of Humor" is perhaps the least indicative of his later work. It is urban in setting, emphasizes a highly coincidental plot at the expense of character and atmosphere, and is written in a style remarkably prosaic for Heyward. It tells the story of a promoter who plans a fraud to escape paying taxes but is trapped and robbed as a result of his own excessive cleverness. **"The Mayfield Miracle"** is of interest because it reflects Heyward's feeling about illness (and is thus, one suspects, partly autobiographical) and again shows his admiration for physical beauty in animals and human beings. Its hero, injured in an explosion so that he must walk with a ridiculous dancing motion, vows never to walk again and invite the jeers of his fellow patients at the hospital. But when a fire breaks out, he averts a riot by putting on a "performance"—his eccentric walk amuses the audience. Here again Heyward uses rather raw melodrama, but melodrama made acceptable through its primitive and romantic setting was to pervade his most successful works.

In both **"A Man's Job"** and **"Dorothy Grumpet, Graduate Lady,"** Heyward presents an outdoor setting and shows his preference for the untouched, rather primitive life close to nature. In the first, the hero must prove himself "a man" (in the Teddy Roosevelt-Jack London tradition) in order to regain his job as superintendent of a gang of lumberjacks and to win the hand of the heroine. He does so, defeating a villain who turns "yellow" and braving a climactic forest fire. Heyward's use of a natural cataclysm anticipates the powerful hurricane scene in ***Porgy.***

"Dorothy Grumpet" satirically depicts the corrupting influence of new-found wealth and inappropriate education on old Aaron Grumpet and his child-of-nature daughter. Of young Dorothy the narrator says:

> Yes, they had taken the vital natural young creature I had known, had taken that big wholesome soul of hers, that was just throwing its windows open to the sunlight, catching its first sky glimpses of its destiny in wifehood and motherhood, and they had sent the pure gold of her to be minted into the coinage of the age. Here she was—a perfect specimen of the period. She was a graduate lady—God help her.

Heyward's persistent sentimentalizing of young girls in rustic settings is somewhat counterbalanced here by an occasional satiric thrust. As Dorothy plays the piano, her father "posted me as to the number of notes she could hit in a minute, until I half expected to see the dial of a speedometer beside the music rack." Along with its crudities, the story does suggest Heyward's later irony and does show an early treatment of one of his constant themes: the superiority of the natural, the rustic, the primitive, over the false civilization of money and the city.

The last of the unpublished stories, **"The Ghost of the *Helen of Troy,*"** is perhaps the most interesting of the group. For the first time Heyward uses the South Carolina Low Country as a setting, refers (if only briefly) to Negro spirituals, and gives a hint of his skill in treating the fear of the supernatural, a skill more fully exhibited in **"The Half Pint Flask."** The captain's daughter persuades a young investigator of psychic phenomena not to reveal that the tourist-attracting "ghost" on a small boat is really a fraud. She promises to marry him after he returns from making his report. Then he discovers her to be a retired vaudeville actress (as well as a mother) hired by the captain to protect the "ghost" from exposure. Silly as the plot is, Heyward's descriptions of the Low Country landscapes are excellent, and his passing references to Negro singing and folk ballads foreshadow his use of such material in ***Porgy*** and ***Mamba's Daughters:***

> Out of the night somewhere a row boat passed, and from it with wonderful sweetness, drifted a plaintive darkey rowing melody—the voices and the clank of the row-locks blending harmoniously as the men rowed in time to the rhythm [*sic*].
>
> . . . she drifted into song again with one of those Southern Ballads that one never finds in print, but which, in the undiscovered corners of our country, have been taught in the cradle, and from year to year have accumulated all the nameless longings that have been sung into them from countless mother hearts.

Here Heyward seems to be approaching the material which he was to make characteristically his own. Of course, in this story the Southern material appears only in embryo, but he was groping in the right direction.

The best of these early stories is **"The Brute,"** the first to be published. Here Heyward has found his subject matter and setting, his characteristic style and treatment of plot and character. Later, when pressed by his publishers to follow ***Porgy*** quickly with another novel, he turned to **"The Brute"** and his mountain poems for the characters, setting, and germ of the plot for ***Angel.*** Also, in **"The Brute"** for the first time Heyward treats the North Carolina mountain setting in his typical descriptive and symbolic manner.

Brutus Galoway comes upon his wife Sarah and young Hal Patton as the latter assists Sarah in chopping down a tree.

> Unnoticed by the two, Brutus Galoway rounded the corner of the cabin and paused; a slow, dark, [*sic*] malignity gathering in his face; while behind him, immense, sinister, Greybeard Mountain towered twenty-five hundred feet into the purple evening.

After Hal leaves, Brutus accuses Sarah of loving the young man and forbids her seeing him again. Sarah had married him, Brutus says, only after Hal had gone off to Asheville and left her. When Sarah maintains a tense silence, Brutus strikes her to the ground. Four days later he orders her to hitch up the steer and go to visit her sister, as he must work with the road gang at a spot notorious for landslides. Ignoring Sarah's plea that she senses impending danger, he watches her drive off.

On the height where the gang works, the debris of a slide blocks the road and hangs on the edge of a sheer drop. Brutus is the blaster, the one who sets off the powerful charges of dynamite. As he stands on the mountainside:

> Then Fate reached for Galoway, and he raised his eyes from his work. . . .
>
> The thunder-storm had passed down the valley, leaving the atmosphere unbelievably clear; and in the crystalline air of the altitudes, perspective and distance were set at naught. Before him the mountains, range upon range, seemed piled one on top of the other until the most distant notched the sky in a vivid saw-like line of blue, while, over a thousand feet below, his little farm stood revealed in each minute detail, as though held below a lens.

Suddenly he sees that the steer and the cart have returned, that Sarah is there. Then Hal appears and embraces her.

Brutus places three dynamite cartridges beneath the debris and seeks the shelter of a jutting ledge of rock.

> Suddenly the earth surged slightly beneath his feet, as though awaking from slumber; and a muffled boom thudded against the deathlike quiet: the great incubus shuddered from end to end, as if throwing off some distasteful, detaining hand; and lifting itself over the slight hindrance, like a great tidal wave of earth, crested high with its loot of trees and rocks, it leaped sheer off the edge and hurtled downward.

Seeing the mass falling toward them, Hal and Sarah freeze for a split second; then Hal throws his arm around Sarah as they are crushed beneath the mighty weight.

Brutus laughs in triumph, and with "So yer would, would yer?" he turns to eat the lunch Sarah had prepared for him.

In **"The Brute"** Heyward exhibits practically all the traits, both good and bad, characteristic of the plays and the novels by which he gained public recognition. Here is the full use of a colorful, exotic setting and primitive characters. Here, too, though slightly overwritten, are his vivid description of nature and his symbolic treatment of it. Here is the violence of melodrama, potentially good melodrama, that runs like a crimson thread through all his writings. Here also are the touches of sententious philosophizing and commentary and the sometimes too broad sentimentality found in even the best of his later work. By 1918 in a single story he had found his medium.

WILLIAM H. SLAVICK (ESSAY DATE 1981)

SOURCE: Slavick, William H. "The Vision and the Achievement." In *DuBose Heyward,* pp. 163-74. Boston: Twayne, 1981.

In the following essay, Slavick reviews Heyward's career and reputation, noting his importance as a figure in the "Southern Renascence," examining the social reality of his works, considering his place in the Harlem Renaissance, and evaluating the "gentlemanly" quality of his writings.

I. A Transitional Figure of Importance

When DuBose Heyward began to write in earnest, at the end of the First World War, the recognized contemporary Southern writers were long-lived nineteenth-century figures, Mark Twain, George Washington Cable, and Joel Chandler Harris, and two of these were émigrés to the North. By 1925, all of these, as well as Thomas Nelson Page, Mary Noailles Murfree, and James Lane Allen, had gone to the grave. Glasgow and the more recently published James Branch Cabell appeared almost as sports in Mr. Mencken's Sahara; he could account for them in his notorious article only by ignoring them. No middle class had developed in the hard times of Reconstruction to produce writers, and the southern mind still labored under its fealty to ideas irreconcilable with its classical-Christian heritage.[1]

Yet, a dozen years after the Great War, the Southern Renascence was in full progress; Heyward had been off only a moment ahead of the pack. Since much of the Fugitives' best work, *The Time of Man,* and *Soldier's Pay* were published within a year of ***Porgy***'s appearance, Heyward had certainly exercised no appreciable influence as a writer on this burst of new creative energy in the South. Rather, because he was a decade or more older than all in that group except Miss Roberts and because, unlike them, he was little aware, if aware at all, of new currents in thought and technique, Heyward should be viewed as a transitional figure between the propaganda and Old South myth-making of Page and the renascence that appeared in the late 1920s. To appreciate his place in that transition is largely to define his achievement as a writer.

Heyward's place and his achievement are modest, first because he was not the serious writer such contemporaries in the 1920s as Glasgow, Cabell, Ransom, Tate, Faulkner, and Roberts were. He was poorly educated. Unlike the midwesterners who gravitated to Chicago as journalists at the turn of the century or who, after World War I, went abroad and enlarged their experience, he remained largely unaffected by what lay beyond Broad Street until well after he became an established writer. Hervey Allen found that limiting, indeed: "Nobody outside the plank road gives a damn about what is thought in that strange little antipodes which thinks deity has congealed in it."[2]

Heyward wrote as if modern literature did not exist. We see no influence of the major figures whose work was appearing at about the time Heyward reached maturity. He probably read the more popular G. P. R. James, Walter Scott, Bulwer-Lytton, and Kipling. Timrod's mark on his poetry is evident, and the Harlem stage at least indirectly influenced the Heywards' plays and the libretto for ***Porgy and Bess.*** But Heyward seems to have had little interest in contemporary literature; Louis Rubin finds this true of the Charleston group in general.[3]

Certainly, as a fiction writer, he would not have understood what was meant by the claim of the modern novelist to discover the intellectual and moral implications of the subject through technique. Only the ironic fatalism in the narrative voice of ***Peter Ashley,*** so close to that of Pierre Chardon, suggests that Heyward could employ point of view as a technique to reveal the truth more fully. Rather, writing in the nineteenth-century tradition, with the omniscient narrator often front and center, too often ostentatiously, he came much closer to the decadent but popular fiction style of Joseph Hergesheimer, with its weak shifts in point of view, pretentious and decorative language, narrow and imprecise vocabulary, a high proportion of abstract and formal words, frequent adjective and adverb qualifiers, careless sentence structures, too condensed action, disconnected structure, and a tone out of character, literary, or condescending.[4] Add plot contrivances, sententious philosophy, irrelevancies, diffusion of focus, and a weakness for melodrama, and one has a fair catalog of the weaknesses of Heyward's fiction style.

As a dramatist, Heyward relies heavily on melodrama and local color, particularly crowd effects and music. Action is not sustained, nor does it lead to awareness. His poetry is too often fragmentary, ordinary, and sometimes unclear. His drama and fiction characters are often inadequately developed. And while he learns from his experience and mistakes, as evidenced by the handling of point of view in ***Peter Ashley,*** the developed conflict of ***Lost Morning,*** and the focusing of the ***Mamba's Daughters*** play on Hagar, these works are flawed, too.

Yet, Heyward cannot be dismissed. In his fiction he was capable of honest observation and was saved by it. In historical perspective, he successfully carried local color farther in poetry than anyone else in his time, without succumbing to quaintness or mere folklore. The Negro folk life, song, and crowd scenes of the Heywards' two plays assisted in opening the American stage to black music, new materials, and greater realism. ***Porgy and Bess*** is the first great American folk opera. Moreover, Heyward's realistic and sympathetic handling of the Negro, particularly the Negro community, and his Charleston aristocrat's sober and realistic view of the changing southern scene in fiction provide important new perspectives in the Negro Renaissance of the 1920s and the Southern Renascence that followed.

II. Memorialist, Stoic, Realist—and Mencken Iconoclast

Heyward's role in the Southern Renascence is a minor but special one. Ellen Glasgow argued that the South's greatest needs were "blood and irony," the one "because Southern culture had strained too far from its roots in the earth," the other because she thought irony "the safest antidote to sentimental decay."[5] Faulkner's Negroes, yeoman farmers, and tragic vision provided the blood, and Glasgow's ironic vision, as Hugh Holman observes, "lay bare the inner nature of the social order" of the South which was the subject of her novels of manners.[6] A Charlestonian, Heyward could not share the mythical vision of Faulkner's South; he belonged to that city's eighteenth-century conservative tradition to which the Civil War was not the Apocalypse; Charleston, after all, was "the city that care forgot." Heyward could see the evils of crass commercialism and feel some of Mencken's barbs hit home, but he did not, as Allen Tate, see the South as a peculiar battleground of Western values and the modern spirit. He could not distance himself enough from Charleston's decadent aristocracy to offer the ironic criticism of his world that Glasgow could of hers.

The voice frequently heard in ***Peter Ashley*** suggests that Heyward might have been an ironist. But there is as much sentimentality as irony in Heyward, and he is more often and better defined as a memorialist and as often as a realist.

Like Faulkner, Heyward sees from without and feels from within, but the ambiguous response in Heyward lacks the creative conflict; Heyward's perspective remains more discrete.[7] His feelings have more to do with manners than moral passion.

Heyward's role, then, is transitional, memorializing and criticizing, telling the truth—not all of it but enough to be called courageous for his time. He is less the Glasgow ironist, Faulkner moralist, or Stribling satirist than the mannered Charleston stoic who is largely resigned to the imperfections of the world in his gratitude for its blessings or to the hopelessness of affecting the future—but not quite always resigned. Heyward's special brew was a combination of this inborn aristocratic conservatism; the local colorist's nostalgia for the traditional, particularly the primitive qualities of the Negro; that eighteenth-century southern stoicism that hesitates to judge or strongly criticize; an honest recognition of the practical evils that follow from the doctrine of white supremacy; and a recognition of the change that was upon the region, whether it wanted such change or not, and of the inability of the aristocracy to meet such change effectively. It might be called social realism.

Central in Heyward's contribution to the Southern Renascence is his truth-telling, in the first years after it had become possible to "tell the actual truth about any phase of life in the South."[8] Latter-day readers will find Heyward's truth selective and pallid, and his style and point of view are sometimes a challenge to that truth. But **"Gamesters All,"** ***Porgy, Angel,*** and ***Mamba's Daughters*** are not lacking in a certain investment of courage. At least enough of Catfish Row, the elemental mountaineers' struggle, and the phosphate mines is there to guess the whole truth. Then, in ***Peter Ashley,*** he dares tell the less than heroic truth about how some—at least one—of the gallant heroes of the Confederate army came to be there in the first place: against his better judgment. And in ***Lost Morning*** there is no mistaking the vulgar nouveau-riche decadence that has engulfed whole communities and the frustration of the artist caught in it. Still, by viewing the reality of Negro urban life in ***Porgy*** largely apart from the moral issues involved in white exploitation and social irresponsibility—and apart from the historical context of black experience, Heyward has his truth . . . without alienating a Southern audience. The same strategy carries over into ***Mamba's Daughters*** where Saint's class, ineffectual conventional Christianity, and a stoic acceptance of the status quo obscure the burning social questions raised by the difficulties Mamba and her daughters face. It is truth within limits: the reader does not encounter anywhere an adequate image of that oppressive and brutal conformity experienced throughout the South in the early twentieth century. ***Brass Ankle*** is the nearest approximation.

Yet, Heyward's work reflects the truth of his childhood experience of poverty, of his clerkship in a hardware store, of his waterfront observation, of his summers in the mountains, of the firsthand accounts he heard of what the Sumter prelude was really like, and of the new aristocracy he as surely met in the 1930s as a defeated Felix Hollister met it in Exeter.

Assessment of Heyward's criticism of his world—and appreciation of the origin of that criticism—is assisted by returning to Donald Davidson's question about why Heyward's studies of Negro life are "so palpably tinged with latter-day abolitionism." Davidson's concern was what he saw, in certain southern works, Heyward's included, to be "a dissociation of the artist from his environment, resulting in a literature of mingled protest and escape."[9] Davidson answers his own question about Heyward extremely well: "The Southern tradition in which these writers would share has been discredited and made artistically inaccessible; and the ideas, modes, attitudes that discredited it, largely not southern, have been current and could be used."[10]

And whose ideas discredited it? Ironically, where the Nashville academics could discount H. L. Mencken as a "vulgar rhetorician," DuBose Heyward, as this study has shown, repeatedly adopts a perspective consistent with Mencken's iconoclastic stance and his campaign to "free" the Southern mind.[11] ***Angel*** is a good example. Heyward sees little of value in the backwoods life of Thunder Cove; in ridiculing Thornley's revival as an emotional orgy, he fails to acknowledge anything genuine in Fundamentalist Protestantism; he scorns the mechanical and uniformly tawdry lives of the mill folk. And, like Mencken, he has nothing to put in place of what he scorns, save the indomitable spirits of Buck and Angel. Again, in ***Mamba's Daughters,*** Heyward sees the inadequacies of the life Charleston's whites inherit but offers only a healthy mercantile career as an inferior alternative—and escape for blacks. Nor are the religious values of Mamba and Hagar duly credited as motives until the play version. ***Peter Ashley*** probes the closed Southern mind—sympathetically but without mercy. Southern provincialism in Rivertown has no redeeming features, and in Exeter the modern secular world is fully realized and dominant; Hollister at his best is part of it, too, if hostile to the commercialism. As Davidson observes, Heyward's treatment of the South—the Negro, race relations, Puritanism, or whatever—serves to confirm Mencken's narrow view of the South as reflecting "bigotry, ignorance, hatred, superstition, every sort of blackness" as opposed to "sense."[12] Heyward appears to need Mencken to begin to see meanings in what he so well observes.

Whatever prompts Heyward's insight, when he is finished, the illusion of the white aristocracy's superiority is dispelled. But Heyward also goes beyond Mencken's concerns to recognize certain primitive Negro strengths and qualities, particularly rhythm, community spirit, and a *joie de vivre,* as well as such sad realities of black life as Hagar's pathetic self-hatred and the self-deprecation of Row inhabitants who see themselves as "just niggers." Also, the relentless inroads of modern industrialism and progress are reflected in the changing economics of the aristocracy, the aspirations of the urban Negroes, the invasion of the mountains, the incorporation of Rivertown, the modernization of the city ("Chant for an Old Town"), and the bourgeois respectability that rules Exeter. The truth of Heyward's vision is primarily social, for the struggles of his characters are chiefly with society or representatives of it.

III. The Search for Life

But the social reality is not all that Heyward sees. His main characters all seek identity, self-realization, and fulfillment, and their experiences—in large part painful encounters with the social reality of Heyward's changing South—both define the requisites for human life and reveal the narrow possibilities of its realization here.

Black, crippled, and alone, Porgy finds life in Catfish Row, and his mysterious sense of expectation finds fulfillment in his love for Bess. But that personal happiness is contingent upon reconciling the primitive and the rubrics of white society, and when that reconciliation fails, Porgy is left alone with his awareness that the juices of life no longer flow for him.

Angel must meet the challenges of her father's religious fanaticism and the mountains' harshness by escaping the one, surviving the other, and facing the challenge of the future in town with Buck.

In ***Mamba's Daughters,*** Lissa discovers herself only when she fully appreciates the sacrifices that have brought her to New York and reconciles her racial spirit and her art. Hagar, particularly in the play, finds self-realization in total sacrifice—first of her daughter and then of her life. Saint discovers in Lissa's success that his fate, the achievement of creature comforts within the Charleston aristocratic mold, is to have missed the more genuine fulfillment.

Ruth Leamer looks for life in the sounds of nature and her family, Larry in the doubtful progress of moonshine profits, segregation, and incorporation. For both race becomes the destructive absolute.

In ***Peter Ashley,*** Peter's youthful dreams give way to the realization that he would sacrifice anything for his past, his place, and his people—to his participation in the southern mind of his time.

In ***Lost Morning,*** Felix Hollister learns that business and art, compromise and integrity, are incompatible, that he must honor his experience of life in sculpture and that this experience of life is necessarily a lonely one.

In ***Star Spangled Virgin,*** Rhoda and Adam Work find bliss only when they are in harmony with the land.

Southern society and social institutions invariably fail Heyward's characters: noblesse oblige and the white man's law in ***Porgy,*** religion and married respectability in ***Angel,*** the unbridgeable gulf between the races and the bondage of the aristocracy's code in ***Mamba's Daughters,*** the racist religion of Rivertown, the magnetic power of placeways in ***Peter Ashley,*** and the cultural decadence of the new moneyed aristocracy of the South in ***Lost Morning.*** The homestead in ***Star Spangled Virgin*** may appear to be a Noodeal reality, but it follows the failure of Noodeal and comes via the grace of the Nineteenth Amendment, which permits a reunion with the past. It is, in truth, a wish that answers Heyward's yearning for a traditional life of primitive rhythm, sex, and harmony with the earth.

Southern society and white social institutions are the major enemies of life, chiefly in that they command conformity. The Charleston past, which is for Heyward an inescapable part of the present, more often than not is a dead hand that kills whatever it touches and denies the possibility of life. For Peter Ashley and Saint Wentworth—but also for Felix Hollister, Angel Thornley, and the Leamers—the demand for conformity frustrates the harmony with nature, community, love, spirit of sacrifice, and dedication Heyward's blacks know as life. Those few whites who refuse to conform—Buck, Angel, and Hollister—must abandon the past and their own people, which foreshadows a poorer success for them. Ruth Leamer contemplates flight, as do Hagar and the play Porgy. Lissa does flee, and Saint and Peter should.

Catfish Row, on the other hand, has made the necessary accommodations to the urban white world. And with common values and faith that weather death and defeat, it lives—uninhibited, a real community. Only here is there the freedom to pursue and realize a meaningful personal life. Perhaps Heyward's first poem, **"Gamblers All,"** should be read in this context: the black gambler seeks freedom at any cost; the policeman who shoots him is actually enslaved by his racist role. The Ediwander blacks brook no interference with the harmony of their lives.

Unlike the major figures of the Southern Renascence who seek to recover the classical-Christian values of history, Heyward finds the meaning of life empirically, in observing the contemporary black community where man's tie to nature has not been broken, where dead social codes do not frustrate freedom, and where rhythm and religion, courage and community, give meaning to the struggle for survival and dignity in the white man's world.

The vision of life that emerges from the several searches of Heyward's characters lacks full definition. His whites are too passive about their fates, too easily compromised, or, in the Leamers' case, too uncomplicated and unintelligent for the struggle to be fully engaged. While his black characters have a sense of direction and values, in the pursuit of which they achieve identity and freedom, they are simple, elemental folk in pursuit of simple objectives—a woman, a career, a place on the land. Hagar's inner pain is seen, but she remains Heyward's simplest character.

This lack of moral engagement shows the limitations of Heyward's work more than anything else. But what we see of the pursuit of life in his work at least sketches a vision. Like Faulkner, he sees the paralyzing influence of a closed society and rigid caste system upon his characters. But his interest in his black characters is less in the conflict between the white social code and the individual, less in moral conflict, than in the individual's capacity to find life despite white supremacy and Noodeal. Life is found in harmony with the earth, in the bond of community suffering, in joy and its expression in song and dance which constitutes rhythm, and in integrity and love. All are achievable apart from white society. Heyward's whites seek life and expression in art, but they lack the depth of feeling, the rhythm, and, save Felix Hollister, Porgy's and Hagar's integrity of purpose.

All of Heyward's whites share a deep alienation from their world. Heyward's vision of life may be defined by envy both of the black rhythm of Charleston and, the crowning irony of his Charleston aristocrat's vision, of the black man's relative insularity from white society. The rhythms of Charleston are not only different; they are, Heyward sees, essentially antithetical.

In *A Certain Measure,* Ellen Glasgow observes that she was, in her "humble place and way, beginning a solitary revolt against the formal, the false, the affected, the sentimental, and the pretentious, in Southern writing," solitary because she "had no guide."[13] Heyward could have used her for a guide—or Balzac and Flaubert, who did guide her. John Bennett had other ideas, so Glasgow does not save Heyward from the occasionally affected and pretentious in style. But when Miss Glasgow goes on to say that her revolt came because "life had broken through these elegiac tones," she is striking the note of Heyward's fiction as well.[14] He, too, could recount what life had shown him. And certainly his fiction and plays facilitate the serious criticism of the South and modern man that was to follow in the Southern Renascence.

IV. "A Member of Harlem's Intellectual Colony"

Heyward's contributions to the image of the black man in the Harlem Renaissance may be more precisely defined.

As Negro writers have been saying for years—and more recently, white scholars, too—the historical image of the Negro in American literature is largely one of distortion.[15] The Harlem Renaissance occurs against a background of demeaning stereotypes and exaggerated primitivism that deny the black man's dignity. These distortions and others—fancied primitivism, exoticism, and indulgence in varying forms—continue through the 1930s. But in the early 1920s southerners Heyward, T. S. Stribling, and Julia Peterkin, as well as Jean Toomer and others, begin to see the human qualities of the black man with a truth that changes that image significantly. Heyward's special place in this group is his portrayal of southern Negroes who are relatively contemporary, urban, involved in the white man's world—the Negroes white men encounter or expect to encounter, neither historically remote as Stribling's nor geographically remote as Peterkin's rural folk, seen through the double perspective of a paternalistic white Southern aristocrat and an honest observer who satisfies even Negro critics in his fidelity to the truth of what he observes. If Heyward's paternalism is sometimes condescending, so is it sympathetic and understanding. The reader does not escape with his complacency.

Moreover, in his close observation and awareness of the complexity of what he sees within the Negro community, Heyward corrects a host of stereotypes and rescues Negro primitive qualities from the distortions of the work of his contemporaries to reveal the elements that make the Negro more responsive to life and nature than his mannered white Charleston neighbors. Specifically, the rhythm Heyward sees is neither primitive exuberance, the echo of atavistic drums, nor both but the essential element in the cultural expression of a folk close to the earth and their God and joined in suffering and misery, joy and hope. Nathan Huggins tells us that in the Harlem Renaissance, "The Negro was in the process of telling himself and the world that he was worthy, had a rich culture, and could make contributions of value."[16] Heyward was showing the Negro—and the world.

Most important of all, he shows us Porgy and Hagar performing in the intimacy of a black world, an opportunity seldom given Faulkner's Negroes. Thus Heyward won an audience for fiction that treated the Negro seriously and sympathetically as a human being that no American writer since Twain and Joel Chandler Harris had reached.

One need not argue with Ralph Ellison's contention that the Negro playwrights and musical-comedy writers of the 1920s came closer to reality than ***Porgy and Bess*** or ***Emperor Jones.***[17] One could even accept Ellison's view that ***Porgy and Bess*** is pretty much a "a negative contribution except as a vehicle for excellent singers and actors."[18] But such a judgment about ***Porgy,*** the novel, and ***Mamba's Daughters*** would be an unfortunate confusion of Heyward's fiction with the simplified opera story. Certainly Heyward's observation of the Negro is not flawless, but if it is seriously flawed he has fooled a lot of people who should know better. Shortly after the publication of *A Different Drummer,* I heard William Melvin Kelley, upon mention of ***Porgy,*** quote much of the concluding passage of the novel. Witness one university lecture program statement: "We have great pleasure in presenting this evening Mr. DuBose Heyward, who is not only a member of Harlem's intellectual colony, but who is also a Southern Negro of the old tradition."[19]

In the 1960s and after, a new surge of Negro primitivism as part of a new assertion of racial identity and aspiration occurred. Unfortunately, the same phony primitivism and claim of atavistic ties with the jungle gained ascendancy again, once more Vachel Lindsay's drums were heard, and the American Negro was seen searching for himself in African art, a tradition from which he has been separated for 300 years. Heyward served as an important moderating influence in response to the excesses of primitivism in the 1920s. Placed in an appropriate or "native" habitat in ***Porgy*** rather than the artificial night world of Harlem, primitivism was something more modest, subtle, and genuine than the white writers visiting Harlem fancied. By the time Heyward had defined it as "rhythm," it was something more positive and admirable.

Likewise, the strength, the determination, the faith that the nation recognized in the civil rights movement in the South in the 1960s Heyward had recognized in the Catfish Row community scenes and in the imposing wills of Mamba and Hagar and Lissa forty years before.

Heyward may have had nothing to say to the civil rights militants of the 1960s, but this somewhat stuffy southern gentleman of the old school could serve to call blacks to a recognition of what is genuinely positive, superior, and real in their American past. For the worn phrase of condescension, "They sho' got rhythm," takes on a different meaning in ***Porgy,*** **"Half Pint Flask,"** and ***Mamba's Daughters.*** It serves as a criticism of the creeping paralysis afflicting white Charleston and as the crucial, primary term of praise for the Low Country Negroes.

Heyward's work may be, as Hervey Allen says of Heyward's most loved characters in his poem "DuBose Heyward of Charleston," written on the occasion of Heyward's death, "of simple lives whose mouths were dumb."[20] But Heyward appreciated, as James McBride Dabbs has, so eloquently, since, that there is human value in these dumb ones that should not be lost.[21] As an ardent Low Country memorialist, the loss of that primitive "rhythm" of life was surely his greatest fear.

V. A Gentleman—But Not Hopelessly

For DuBose Heyward, whom Emily Clark called "hopelessly a gentleman," respect for the manners and rituals of his society, for the beauty and charm of his locale, and for what was genuine and living in its people was certainly an essential part of the definition of a gentleman—at least of the voice heard in Heyward's poems and stories.[22]

While exploring the Charleston of Heyward's poetry, fiction, and plays, one could not help but notice that the current events of half a century later provide a curious commentary on that now dimming time and place Heyward knew and of which he wrote and on the tension he saw between the dying aristocracy and those struggling to live as they were affected by time and circumstance. One South Carolina U.S. Senator's public complaint of starvation and dire poverty in the Low Country clearly echoes our Charleston gentleman's noblesse oblige as a response to the callous Rivertown spew of the up-country Strom Thurmond. But Senator Hollings was, in those days, an exception. The racist mouthings of Thurmond shifted hardly a decibel when state troopers massacred black students at Orangeburg. Almost daily, the late U.S. Representative Mendel Rivers of Charleston was proving himself a true heir of Secession Day and, by implication, his constituents showed themselves to be the most bellicose in the land. Again, there were echoes of Heyward's phosphate mine in a television report on worms in Beaufort Country Negro children, which gave a leading county doctor occasion to call another doctor, who had not learned to serve blacks discretely, "a liar" who was "trying to be a martyr."[23] Meanwhile, a Charleston social lion became a lioness and announced her engagement to her servant, a local Negro, "the first young man I'd never been afraid of."[24]

Our Charleston gentleman Mr. Heyward would have difficulty with the stupidity, stridency, vulgarity, inhumanity, and injustice evident in several of these events and would have understood the last. As an honest observer of his world, which included the often dubious changes taking place in all areas of southern life, he would not really be surprised. His memorialist stance looks as much to the future as to the past. It is his anxiety about the future as well as the present, his painful awareness of the difficulty of finding life in the modern South as he saw it, that quickens his observations—and makes him more than a local colorist.

Notes

1. Frances Newman, "On the State of Literature in the Late Confederacy" [*New York Herald Tribune,* Books, August 16, 1925].
2. Letter to John Bennett, May 19, 1925. Bennett Papers.
3. "The Southern Muse," Louis D. Rubin, Jr., *The Curious Death of the Novel,* 1967. p. 216.
4. See Ronald E. Martin, *The Fiction of Joseph Hergesheimer* (Philadelphia: University of Pennsylvania Press, 1965), pp. 164, 196, 230-242, 267.
5. *A Certain Measure* [New York; Harcourt, 1943], p. 28.
6. *Three Modes of Modern Southern Fiction* [Athens: University of Georgia Press, 1966], p. 19.
7. See Frank Durham, "The Southern Literary Tradition: Shadow or Substance," *South Atlantic Quarterly* 67 (Summer 1968): 467.
8. Julia Peterkin, "Southern View-Point," p. 392 [*North American Review* 244 (Winter 1937-38)].
9. Donald Davidson, "The Artist as Southerner," *Saturday Review of Literature* 2 (May 15, 1926): 782.
10. "A Mirror for Artists," pp. 58-59 [in Twelve Southerners, *I'll Take My Stand,* 1962].
11. Davidson, *Southern Writers in the Modern World,* p. 30; Fred C. Hobson, *Serpent in Eden: H. L. Mencken and the South* (Chapel Hill: University of North Carolina Press, 1973), pp. 109, 148-52.
12. The characterization of Mencken's view is his, not Davidson's. See "Aftermath," *Baltimore Evening Sun,* September 14, 1925, cited in Hobson, p. 151.
13. *A Certain Measure,* p. 8.
14. Ibid.
15. See Seymour L. Gross, "Stereotype to Archetype: The Negro in American Literary Criticism"; Theodore L. Gross, "The Negro in the Literature of the Reconstruction"; and Leslie A. Fiedler, "The Blackness of Darkness: The Negro in the Development of American Gothic," in *Images of the Negro in American Literature,* ed. Seymour L. Gross and John Edward Hardy (Chicago: University of Chicago Press, 1966).
16. Nathan Irvin Huggins, *Harlem Renaissance* (New York: Oxford, 1971), p. 59.
17. Telephone interview, October 22, 1967.
18. Ibid.
19. Brickell, "Creator and Catfish Row" [*New York Herald Tribune Books,* March 10, 1929].
20. "For DuBose Heyward of Charleston," *Saturday Review of Literature* 22 (June 29, 1940): 8.
21. *Who Speaks for the South?* (New York: Funk and Wagnalls, 1964), passim. This study is also invaluable in providing a perspective on white stoicism in the South.
22. Clark, p. 556 [DuBose Heyward, *Virginia Quarterly Review* 6 (1930) 546-56].
23. Columbia Broadcasting Company television newscast, December 23, 1968.
24. *Milwaukee Journal,* November 21, 1968.

WILLIAM H. SLAVICK (ESSAY DATE 1987)

SOURCE: Slavick, William H. "Going to School to DuBose Heyward." In *The Harlem Renaissance Re-Examined,* edited by Victor A. Kramer, pp. 65-91. New York: AMS, 1987.

In the following essay, Slavick claims that Heyward is a more important figure in the Harlem Renaissance than has been acknowledged and asserts that his works about Black Americans are marked by realism and a poetic understanding of their humanity.

DuBose Heyward's brief ascendancy among Southern regionalists in the middle 1920s—as poet, novelist, and playwright—was quickly eclipsed by the emergence of the Fugitive poets, Elizabeth Madox Roberts, Thomas Wolfe, and William Faulkner by the end of the decade. Today he is little more than mentioned in discussion of important figures in the Southern Renascence, but his social realism, which juxtaposes the sterility of the white Charleston aristocracy and the possibility of life in the Negro community, deserves recognition.

It is within the framework of the Harlem Renaissance—black writers from Kansas to the Indies and from New Orleans to New York as well as Eugene O'Neill, Sherwood Anderson, Carl Van Vechten, and Waldo Frank—that Heyward remains significant. His ***Porgy,*** with its human treatment of Catfish Row; the 1927 Broadway staging of the DuBose and Dorothy Heyward play version; and ***Mamba's Daughters,*** a second Charleston novel concerned with the relationship of black primitivism and folk culture to high art and changing times, all qualify Heyward for such consideration. Heyward has been mistakenly introduced as a "member of Harlem's intellectual colony" and "a Southern Negro of the old tradition," but he was of the Charleston white aristocracy (an ancestor signed the Declaration of Independence), and apparently did not meet any members of the Harlem "intellectual colony" until late 1926.[1] His identification with the Harlem Renaissance has continued in second-hand booksellers' catalogs and occasional identification of him as a black writer. But in assessments of the Harlem Renaissance, Heyward is given a relatively small place. This is mistaken.

Heyward's keenness of observation of the black man in Charleston and its surrounding environs—in his own community—is marked by an authority and freedom from the exotic and fake often lacking in Anderson, Van Vechten, O'Neill, and the less gifted of the black writers. His largely successful escape from stereotypes was recognized by Donald Davidson, who approved of the way Heyward's "Negro was allowed to stand forth as a human being in his own right" and by Countee Cullen, who called ***Porgy*** the "best novel by a white about Negroes he had read" and suggested that it "gives one the uncanny feeling that Negroes are human beings and that white and black southerners are brothers under the skin."[2] Cullen's remarks properly extend the measure of Heyward's realism to an understanding of white Southerners, too.

At a time when much of the interest in Harlem focused on the black man's primitive innocence and freedom from inhibitions, Heyward was painfully aware that the black man was being forced to change in Charleston and Harlem, a change that endangered those very qualities whites had come to admire. Heyward emphasized this awareness in the poem-prayer prelude to ***Porgy:***

Porgy, Maria, and Bess,
Robbins, and Peter, and Crown;
Life was a three-stringed harp
Brought from the woods to town.

Marvelous tunes you rang
From passion, and death, and birth,
You who had laughed and wept
On the warm, brown lap of the earth.

Now in your untried hands
An instrument, terrible, new,
Is thrust by a master who frowns,
Demanding strange songs of you.

God of the White and Black,
Grant us great hearts on the way
That we may understand
Until you have learned to play.[3]

Such a burden of change marks all of Heyward's fiction as well as his three plays.

Heyward's most intense interest in the black world of Charleston also parallels the post-World War I disillusionment with civilization and turn from Puritan restraint to the primitive qualities found in African art and the uninhibited night world of Harlem. Also, on his own and apart from the literary world's turn toward primitivism, Heyward's sense of the deadness of white Southern culture and study of Catfish Row led him to see in simple folk not an escape into primitive exoticism but into the possibility of life. For Heyward the primitive life he admired and envied is observed and realized rather than thinly imagined. That life is rooted in the earth, the past, and ordinary daily experience. The result is a responsibility and restraint in treatment notably missing from "The Congo," *Nigger Heaven, Dark Laughter,* and O'Neill's plays.

Finally, Heyward came to recognize, as others did not, what the essential rhythm of Negro life was. He appreciated the strength of the black man's faith, the reality of his community, and the essentiality of his race's suffering and long history of suffering. In 1959, a long-time leading Harlem writer summed up Heyward's accomplishment. Langston Hughes suggested that Negro writers could go to school to Heyward, the writer, who saw, "with his white eyes, wonderful, poetic human qualities in the inhabitants of Catfish Row that makes them come alive in his book."[4]

I

Heyward was slow to find his proper subject in the black man. In 1918, he had clipped a story of a crippled goat-cart beggar shooting at woman and noted the beggar's display of manhood. Later, he explained that before seeing that article he "had concluded that such a life could never lift above the dead level of the commonplace," while in the brief account "one could read passion, hate, despair."[5] Nevertheless the 1918 clipping went unused for several years.

Only two poems collected in his first two volumes had dealt with the black man and none of his seven apprentice stories. Those two poems look sharply into the black man's plight in a white man's world. **"Gamesters All"** is a brief drama of a fatalistic crapshooter's instinctive gamble for freedom through flight and a policeman's single "sporting"—albeit fatal—shot. The ironic tone is clear. (Heyward had witnessed such a shooting; it was this experience that made him decide to write about blacks.) **"Modern Philosopher"** balances images of black servants who lack Puritan morals but work faithfully in the white world, "undaunted by a century of strife," and a black world of carefree music and simple faith. Another poem, **"Jasbo Brown,"** published in 1925, is a flawed imitation of Vachel Lindsay and recounts the lonely life of a blues pianist. Heyward did not pursue this interest in black experience further, however, until after he had traveled north to MacDowell Colony in 1922 and 1923 where he met his wife, a budding Ohio playwright; had spent some time in New York City; and, in 1924, had sold his insurance business to give himself entirely to writing. Upon returning to MacDowell Colony in 1925 he settled down to writing ***Porgy.***

The ***Porgy*** story is simple and familiar, of a summer in a Negro quarter in Charleston at the turn of the century. It is novella length and seemingly little more than a series of vignettes in structure. But ***Porgy*** is generally considered Heyward's most accomplished work and it is, with Jean Toomer's *Cane,* the most successful piece of fiction associated with the Negro Renaissance of the 1920s.[6] It was also the first longer work of fiction with predominantly Negro characters to appeal to the whole country.

That appeal results from Porgy's heroic but doomed effort to find human dignity and happiness. The achievement is in Heyward's realization of the conflict that leads to Porgy's defeat. In Bess, Porgy finds contentment; surviving the hurricane, Porgy experiences a sense of worth: "'You an' me, Bess,' he said with conviction. 'We sho' is a little somet'ing attuh all'" (p. 148). But in the end, when Bess is gone, the Row leaves "Porgy and the goat alone in an irony of morning sunlight" (p. 196). His superstitious fear of Crown's corpse, the white world's interference, and Bess's weakness to men and drugs in Porgy's absence bring defeat.

The weaknesses of Porgy and Bess are representative of Catfish Row. The Negroes of the Row are unready for the world in which they must live. Porgy is more intelligent than most but, like Crown, Clara, and Jake, Bess and Sportin' Life, his hopes and self-discipline are insufficient. Primitive instincts, innocence, and lack of self-discipline; the forces of the white world surrounding them; and fate are formidable antagonists and their undoing. The movement of the summer toward Porgy's defeat is really a choral movement in which all move from life and hope and love toward death, resignation, and loneliness.

The one notable power the protagonists bring to the struggle is a community spirit. Catfish Row has its own inner rhythm and style; its own code, especially in dealing with the white world; and its rituals of joy and defeat. Thus, the single enveloping conflict is the almost, but not even, struggle of Catfish Row with the snares of life. Heyward's genius is his ability to explore the operation of this complexity of forces in the modest space of ***Porgy.***

The initial scene, the crap game that ends in Crown's murder of Robbins, begins the orchestration of these forces. The murder is enacted before "shadowy watchers" who "wailed eerily" (p. 20). Porgy, who "shivered violently, whimpered in the gloom, then threw himself across his threshold," is a focal witness (p. 21). Heyward's imagery turns the scene into an atavistic ritual: Crown exhibits "gleaming teeth," "thrusting jaw," "sloping brow," and the "prehensile claw" of a cotton hook, and he emits a "low snarl." "Down, down, down the centuries they slid," the narrator tells us, until "a heady, bestial stench absorbed all other odors" (pp. 19-20). Since Robbins most aspires to white ways, Crown's conquest is a victory for the jungle.

The following saucer burial is a community ritual of identification with Robbins, of resignation, of common cause in financing the burial, and, finally, of triumphant song in consignment of Robbins to heaven. The burial spirituals, one providing a catharsis of grief and the other an act of faith, are followed by the panic of superstition as all flee the graveyard: the second hymn has not quieted primitive fears of death.

The episode had begun with a growling thunderhead that left "the air hot, vitiated, and moist" and the Row irritable, as Crown's "moody silence" illustrates (p. 16). It ends with the police taking Peter away as a material witness and a creditor repossessing his things.

In Part I, the setting becomes characters, the characters a community, and the community an action, with the Row as protagonist and nature, primitivism, and the white police as antagonists. It is a recurrent pattern, as the other tragedies of love in the book demonstrate. In another powerful Row scene, the conjure-beset Clara abandons herself in the storm in a futile effort to save Jake. The separation of Porgy and Bess involves Crown's bestiality, Bess's wildness, and Porgy's "aboriginal" laugh; the jailing of Bess and then Porgy; and Porgy's superstitious fears (p. 172). The Porgy-Bess relationship is emphasized by the space given it and by its centrality. It is also marked by strong suggestions of a mythic-moral dimension: a snake-like Sportin' Life tempts the repentant Bess, and Bess, who passes a rattler in search of a fan-shaped leaf in the Kittiwar wilderness, meets a seducer, Crown, whose "small wicked eyes burned" (p. 119). But whether agents or principals, the antagonists remain the same.

The structure of the novella is itself an illustration of Heyward's subtle shifts of attention between Porgy and the Row and among the forces—the primitive, the white world, and fate—opposed to the Row's good fortune. After the wild fight and emotional outpouring of Part I, the second part is a quiet interlude between encounters with primitive power and white power. Part III involves both Porgy's conquest of Archdale with his odorous goat cart and Bess's conquest by life in the white man's jail. Apart from Bess's encounter with Crown and the consequent apprehension regarding Crown's return, the primitive parade and picnic in Part IV show the Row in command of its fate. But then, in Part V, the storm confronts the Row with Destiny personified. In Part VI, the Row saves Porgy from discovery, after his murder of Crown, but then a solitary buzzard settling on the roof of his room sends him in flight from a primitive sense of doom toward the woods of his origin and into the casual hands of white justice.

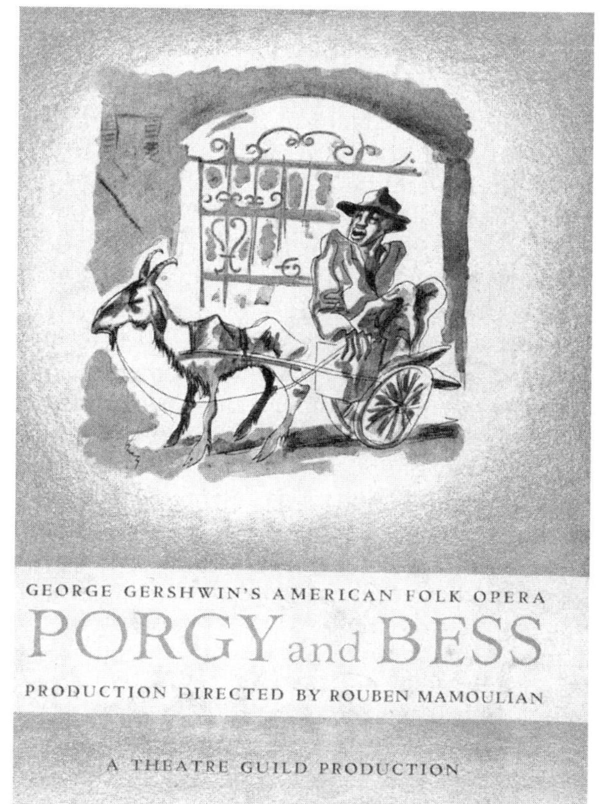

Program cover for DuBose Heyward and Ira Gershwin's libretto for *Porgy and Bess.*

Each of the major characters in the novel is, the action suggests, a distinctive battlefield of these forces. Porgy is shrewd, sensitive, hopeful, and patient. But his shriveled legs and primitive laugh upon killing Crown and his fear of Crown's corpse indicate that he remains divided. Bess recognizes Porgy's humanity and love, but her honesty and sense of values reside in a primitive mind challenged in ways it has not been disciplined to withstand. Serena's strait-laced Puritan religion leads her to reject the life of the Row and her husband to his death, just as Crown's violence exiles him from society. As an emancipated Harlem black, Sportin' Life is an example of the tragedy Heyward sees awaiting Negroes divorced from their roots and values and cast loose in the modern world. Maria, who presides over the island of humanity that is the Catfish Row chorus—as surrogate mother, moral arbiter and symbol of order, is herself caught between her dependence on conjuring and her grudging respect for Christianity while authoritatively upholding the Row's basic law of survival. The characters all tell us that the Negro's effort to "learn to play" is beset with major difficulties.

How does Heyward view these powerful antagonistic forces and assess their effects on Catfish Row?

The initial characterization of the primitive influence operative in Heyward's world is in the poem prelude reference to the journey of Row inhabitants from "woods to town." The primitive traits and acts of the Row are traceable less to atavistic memory than to the isolated, elemental, largely undisciplined life—the free natural life (real or a fancied antecedent of the Golden Age)—of Negro cabins hidden away from plantation houses and the demands of white society. In that world, the black man had his own relaxed code and way of life, Heyward posits, which help explain Crown's conduct, Porgy's violent defense of Bess, and the characters' sundry superstitions. The separation from that natural state and its simple gratifications of emotional need, rather than some African susceptibility to drugs, better explains Bess's lapses. Heyward's characters are, first of all, Americans, and their conduct is rooted in their American experience.

Heyward is not altogether unambiguous in defining the primitivism encountered in Catfish Row. The African note is struck in the initial description of Porgy's "unadulterated Congo blood" and his "pleasant atavistic calm" (pp. 13-14). The lapses into wildness are frequent. Crown turns beast in the fight with Robbins. Under the influence of dope, Bess "whirled like a dervish and called horribly upon her God, striking and clawing wildly" (p. 86). The parade strikes a "wild, barbaric chord" (p. 113). Animal imagery extends from the atavism of the crap game fight to Maria's characterization of Sportin' Life as a "yellow snake" (p. 127). However, Heyward also associates certain traits he admires—Porgy's "infinite patience" and "unrealized, but terrific, energy" and the marchers' abandon in the parade—with the Row's primitive character (p. 13). Yet, the repeated falls, which Eric Bentley sees as unrelieved, and the often violent note in the past suggest as well Heyward's somewhat condescending participation in the common Southern belief of the time that it might take centuries to civilize the Negro and that perhaps he is, after all, somehow less than man.[7] In any case, the handicap of the primitive past is so great that none surmount it.

These ambiguities remain unresolved in ***Porgy,*** but Heyward's attitude is sufficiently clear. The lapses of Porgy, Bess, Crown, even Clara and Jake, are, first of all, lapses in a learning process such as might be found following from the frustrations of virtually any simple rural folk thrust into a modern industrial society. But their frequency and seriousness indicate a level of difficulty that contributes greatly to the effect of pathos. At the same time, in such major scenes as the saucer burial, the parade and picnic, the hurricane, and the choral exchange of silences with Porgy in his loss of Bess, Heyward recognizes a primitive dimension, a culture, that he clearly admires and would not see disappear in the adjustment to "town."

The lack of atavistic motivation, the narrator's civilized view of the Row's failings, the restraint and the understatement indicate a notable movement toward genuine realism in the treatment of primitivism. Thus, Heyward's primitivism must be clearly distinguished from the pseudo-realism that Alain Locke called the "last serious majority cliché, that of blood atavism and inherited Negro primitivism."[8] Where an inhibited Van Vechten character wallows in self-pity at her lack of the primitive passions she sees in other blacks, Heyward evokes a largely indefinite sense of atavistic influences but focuses on the lack of discipline and on the depth and quality of human feeling in the Row's and Porgy's expressions. While Heyward identified such primitive traits as savagery and strange rhythms as relics of a heritage quite unlike white Anglo-Saxon Protestantism, he also saw them as expressions of the elemental life Southern blacks experienced. And he knew very well that the song and dance of Catfish Row was the simple black man's ritual response to his frustrations and suffering in a white world and in no significant sense atavistic in origin or the continuance of African tradition. Heyward's restraint in the handling of primitivism is further evidenced by contrasting it with the strongly lyrical and mystical qualities in Toomer's Georgia scenes and the haunting world of Julia Peterkin's superstitious and passionate rural folk. But the important distinction here is its distance from Van Vechten. When Van Vechten says, "She watched Lasca and Byron glide softly, dangerously, like panthers," it is something else than Heyward's big stevedore crossing the court, "his body moving easily with the panther-like flow of enormous muscular power under absolute control" (p. 44).[9] Heyward's simile is only a simile, fitting for the muscular stevedore. Van Vechten's is coupled with "dangerously" and follows the insistence that Lasca and Byron are more animal than she is or whites are in general. Heyward's blacks never forget, as does Vachel Lindsay in "The Congo," the 200 years between the jungle of his imagination and 1900. Nor does he ever, as Countee Cullen in "Heritage," have his contemporary characters hear great African drums beating.

Thus Porgy comes much closer to honesty about Negroes, closer to squaring with reality than does what Ralph Ellison calls the "Paul Robeson and silver bullet in the jungle bill of goods" of ***Emperor Jones*** and many other works of the Negro Renaissance.[10] As Harlan Hatcher observed long ago, Heyward succeeds in "giving to the primitive life the illusion of complete realism without losing the sense of awe and wonder and pathos which belong to romance."[11] It might be added that Heyward does so without sacrificing or ignoring what Alain Locke calls the disciplined, sophisticated, laconic, and fatalistic qualities of African expression[12] Porgy manifests all of these qualities in an environment of exuberance and emotional upheaval, among a people whose art is equally emotional.

Where primitive forces and nature do not bring trouble to the Row, the white man does. On the other hand, whites make no positive contribution to the Row beyond occasional partial ameliorization of the suffering other whites have caused. In this sense, the story becomes Heyward's ironic response to his prayer in the prelude poem: it is a story of the non-understanding of the Negro until he has "learned to play," for the understanding the Row receives from the white community is invariably a parody of understanding. The whites laugh as Robbins' funeral passes. The "vile-mouthed bearded Teuton" merchant leaves Peter only a chrome of "the Great Emancipator," which makes the reference to Porgy's "new emancipation" ironic (pp. 33, 48). Peter well understands the white man's readiness to start him again on his weekly furniture installments: "'De buckra sho got nigger figgered out tuh a cent'" (p. 62).

Archdale's assistance to Peter and Frasier, who sells divorces outside the law, is pure paternalism. And the whites go on laughing—at the colorful parade as well as at Porgy's futile goat-cart flight from the police. Beyond this pervasive irony, Heyward's comments on race relations are largely concentrated in a few pages where Bess appears before the magistrate and the jail and jailers' attitudes are described. The scene begins with a description of the judge:

> Behind a high desk sat a man well past middle age. His florid complexion caused his long grey mustache to appear very white. His eyes were far apart and suggested a kindness that was born of indolence, rather than of wide compassion. His hands were slender and beautifully made, and he sat with elbows on desk, and fingertips touching. When he spoke it was in a drawl that suggested weariness.
>
> (p. 87)

Turning to the jail, Heyward notices that "When life reaches a certain level of misery, it envelopes [sic] itself in a protective anesthesia which deadens the senses to extremes" (p. 92).

Frank Durham notes that there is no "conscious cruelty, no sadistic malignancy on the part of the judges or the jailers" but "merely apathy, indifference, and an occasional flash of the affection one might display while punishing a wayward child."[13] But the irony in the jailers' indifference and the judge's hands, mustache, and impatience with crime's inconvenience to him is evident: the jailers' indifference is inhumanity, and the judge's indifference is insensitivity to the consequences of his casual use of unlimited power.

This account also reveals another side of Heyward's handling of this antagonist, however: Heyward's comment about the Negro being anesthetized against further suffering, though the further suffering may be fatal, appears to be only accidentally ironic. It is also Heyward's commonplace excuse for white indolence. As Frances Newman, a contemporary Southern novelist, noted, Heyward should "leave the souls of black folks to black folks."[14]

Archdale is a white bridge to the Row, but less so than the police are an instrument and symbol of the Row's isolation from the white community. This isolation of the Row from the white world is further emphasized by the narrator's lack of omniscience. While Heyward's narrator stations himself inside the Row, no inner thoughts of the Row's inhabitants serve to contradict the white narrator's perspective.

The Row's isolation is an element in Heyward's realism and allows him to focus narrowly on the Row—more closely on an urban Negro community than had any previous white American writer. But it is also part of a narrative strategy by which Heyward finds the white community inadequate in meeting its responsibility to the Row while stopping well short of a full exploration of the realities of racism in South Carolina in the "Golden Age." There are no black-white confrontations, as Samuel Allen has noted; the crippled hero is no threat to the white community, and the one Negro of stature is kept altogether away from whites.[15] Except for that one revealing moment of attention to the courtroom and jail, the Row's difficulties are attributed not to a faulty social order but to a few unscrupulous merchants and insensitive police officers.

The Row's inhabitants are themselves largely uncomplaining and resigned to incarceration, exploitation, and the harshness of the elements. The very brevity of the quickly shifting vignette scenes cloaks the lack of interiority and allows great freedom in choice of moments to treat or ignore. Finally, the white aristocratic narrator condescends: while he respects primitive virtues and the Row's community spirit, his emphasis is on primitive failings, social immaturity, resignation, and, always, defeat. As James Southall Wilson observed, "Heyward's darkies have the distilled honey of the Old South's sweetness in their mouths."[16]

This limited perspective means that Heyward's dedication to realism is not complete. But in a deeper sense Porgy is more authentically realistic than such omissions might suggest. For Heyward is historically quite accurate—and, therefore, implicitly critical—in placing the Row squarely in that Southern order which recognizes for the Negro no past or future or real place in the present. The Row is a place apart, an enigma, and no real white communication with it is possible—despite the relaxed view of life and other qualities its citizens share with the other Charleston.

Life in the Row has a timeless quality; only Porgy seems to sense that life is passing unfulfilled. But the Row is repeatedly forced—in such experiences of terror and death as the Robbins-Crown fight, the saucer burial, the resort to conjurers, and the unnatural power of the hurricane—to contemplate the primacy of the future. After death in the Row, life reasserts itself, as in the adoption of Clara's baby. But the working of Destiny is not only another adversary; it effects a resignation and humility before life shared by all.

The storm is the central experience of fate in the novel. Porgy responds in fear and wonder and soon all turn to the "Sabior" who offers a "home in de rock" (p. 152). In such scenes, Heyward employs the spiritual, a choral folk expression, to provide a powerful articulation of the inner life of the Row. As Heyward observed in 1931: "The spiritual said everything for him that he could not say in the new language that he found here—awe in the presence of death—his racial terror of being left alone—his escape from bondage into the new heaven—everything."[17]

The events of ***Porgy*** call forth the Negro's profound response—primitive, human, Christian—to the workings of fate. Also, skillfully, Heyward employs sun imagery to indicate the movement of fate, a sun causal, indifferent, benevolent, comforting, concealing, and, finally, mockingly benevolent. Fate overwhelms all, and its ways are as whimsical, as merciless and harsh, as the weather. Nature, sun, time, the cosmos are beyond man's power, nor has Christianity, Heyward implies, reduced their awesomeness to human size for the Row. Humbled, the Row does not challenge fate.

Heyward's exploration of the array of forces confronting Catfish Row authenticates the Row's reality. The reader sees Porgy, crippled and alone, and Bess, alone and desperate, as representatives of that back-alley community, seeking to reconcile past, present, and future, at least to accept their meeting, and to survive in the face of the obstacles they afford. In accounting for so much, Heyward largely compensates for the sentimentality found in the simplifications of white supremacy, the cosmic, and primitivism.

Porgy has faults. One of the largest is a point of view that remains on the outside while conspicuously surmising what is inside. As a part of it, Heyward's unwillingness to quarrel with that complacent society mutes the irony the story demands, causes him to miss the fullness of the black man's suffering. Clearly, Heyward strikes a gentleman's bargain with Charleston.

Far overbalancing any failings are those "wonderful, poetic human qualities." Heyward's characters are sometimes dismissed as stereotypes, but they are not. None of his characters fits James Weldon Johnson's 1928 characterization:

> What is the Negro in the artistic conception of white America? In the brighter light, he is a simple, indolent, docile, improvident peasant; a singing, dancing, laughing, weeping child, picturesque beside his log cabin and in the snowy fields of cotton; naively charming with his banjo and his songs in the moonlight and along the lazy Southern rivers; a faithful, ever-smiling and genuflecting old servitor to the white folks of quality; a pathetic and pitiable figure. In a darker light, he is an impulsive, irrational, passionate savage, reluctantly wearing a thin coat of culture, sullenly hating the white man, but holding an innate and inescapable belief in the white man's superiority; an everlasting alien and irredeemable element in the nation; a menace to Southern civilization; a threat to Nordic race purity; a figure casting a sinister shadow across the future of the country.[18]

And while all of the adjectives John Hope Franklin sees characterizing the magazine and press depictions of the Negro during Heyward's formative years are in some ways applicable to Catfish Row—ignorant, lazy, improvident, clownish, irresponsible, childish, criminal—the Row is not a composite reflection of these images.[19] These elements are played down. Sportin' Life clowns, but not for white audiences. Porgy's clowning is deliberate frustration of white power. Porgy also plays Uncle Tom, but he is never servile and lives for no white master. Heyward's erotic primitive, Crown, is quickly exiled to the nearest facsimile of Africa.

Porgy represents, instead, Heyward's view of the Negro at his best. He is sensitive to rhythm and color, better attuned than whites to the elemental rhythms and mysteries of life, committed to justice, and desirous of a human life of love and peace. His weaknesses are a primitive legacy of fear he has yet to overcome, his loneliness, and the ability to kill to secure himself from that loneliness. He is, finally, only human; he would survive and escape loneliness in love. Porgy is not the complex Negro character Ellison calls for in his essay on "Twentieth Century Fiction and the Black Mask of Humanity" and offers in *Invisible Man.* But Porgy is, in his time and setting and role as central representative, the first among several representatives of a society complex and human enough to transcend the stereotypes.

Moreover, although it shackles him to fear, Porgy's primitivism provides him many good qualities. As Heywood Broun's review observed, Heyward grants Porgy's, the Negro's, superiority over the white man, at least in sensitivity, rhythm, and emotion.[20]

The book's worth is in Heyward's revelation of Porgy's humanity. In ***Porgy,*** the "instrument" of freedom requires "strange songs" from the Row, songs which the past, the white community, and an uncertainty about the future make it difficult to play. Yet, despite the irony that accompanies this freedom—for such freedom requires conformity—there is a poignancy and pathos about the Row's affirmation of life in the face of great odds.

Affirmation is made possible by the book's substantial realism. The search in ***Porgy*** is not so obtrusive, perhaps because less consciously pursued by the characters than observed as a way of life lived in the Row. What Heyward envies in the Row is that it confronts the elemental forces of life without the inhibitions and repressed feelings of the mannered white aristocracy and that it is a living community of mutual interests, affections, and cares. What Heyward sees in Porgy is a sensitive man who finds identity and dignity in a summer of love and accepts his loss as summer ends. The failure of any of Heyward's white characters to achieve as much makes ***Porgy***'s affirmation all the more notable.

II

Porgy is doubly important in the Harlem Renaissance. The novel offers a fully-realized black world and a fully-realized black hero of unmistakable humanity. The play, which Heyward adapted from the novel with his wife, Dorothy, added to that small number of plays that gave black actors their first access, in the Twenties, to the serious Broadway stage. Moreover, the changes for the stage result in a fuller appreciation of the role of Negro folk expression and a richer understanding of the inner spirit—the rhythm—of the black community. For by 1927 Heyward felt that he had identified the "unique characteristic" in Negro life that made the black's delight the white man's envy.[21] It was the "secret law" of "rhythm," which he defined as "a sort of race personality that dominated and swayed the mass, making of it a sum vastly greater than the total of its individual entities." So the dramatization of ***Porgy*** became a challenge to "give the flow of life . . . its proper place in the canvas":

> That it was bigger than the individual who moved upon it was evident, for it had driven its dark stream on under our civilization, while generations came, were swept forward by it, and vanished. As with singing, where the Negro seldom excels as a soloist and yet with three or four friends picked up almost at random creates a successful chorus, so in their work and play it is the mass rhythms, the concerted movements, the crowd laughter, the communal interrelationships of the Negro quarter that differentiate it most sharply from its white slum neighbour. We felt that the play in order to possess any degree of verisimilitude must show its people moving in response to the deep undertow of this tide. . . .
>
> (pp. xiii-xiv)

Heyward attributed their success in expressing what Stark Young called the "glow" and "rhythm of life" to the cast's involvement in the unconscious rhythms of the primitive Negro in becoming "a living representation" of Catfish Row (p. iv).[22] And to the play's techniques:

> We used the spirituals as they actually occur to express emotional stress when the limited spoken vocabulary becomes inadequate. We employed the rhythmic, spontaneous prayer with which the primitive Negro makes his supplications; the un-

> faltering rhythm of time, expressed in the ebb and flow of day and night, and the chiming of St. Michael's bells; and the crowd movements, with their shifting pattern of colour and sound.
>
> (xvii-xviii)

But the Heywards also place more emphasis upon the community, where rhythm is generated, than does the novella. There is more song and group movement. And, as Frank Durham points out, the scene structure is usually a mass effect, then a dramatic dialogue, followed by a mass effect.[23]

While the heightened dramatic effects make the play a lively folk drama, the proportion and harmony between community and main characters is sacrificed. Primitivism fades as theme but balloons as atmosphere in the pervasive Negro rhythms. The moral theme becomes central, so the race conflict is soft-pedalled, lest it now have to be faced directly in moral terms. To accomplish this obscuration, Heyward makes the Row a minstrel world and shifts the primary focus to the next world—a shift to which Heyward's use of spirituals contributes largely.

Disjointed, too, is Heyward's pursuit of life in the play. While individual characters move toward racial stereotypes of the 1920s—clown, loose woman, brute and bad (Harlem) nigger—Heyward is identifying life as the ability to experience rhythm, secular and Christian.

Judged as a play, the characters remain too simple and Porgy is too unchanging. In him there is no radical incongruity with ordinary life, no defiance of the universe. He is essentially a good fellow who corresponds to our ideals; too little of his inner life is exposed for us to identify with him. In the end, he blindly refuses the awareness the sunlight offers. The conflict is too slight and unconcentrated. Characters seldom confront one another. Important scenes cease to be functional.

Still, the play overcomes most of the major failings of the novella. The excessive primitive weakness, white patronizing, and stoic acceptance of fate largely disappear. The narrator with his pretentious and fancy words is absent, an immediate consequence of which is stronger dramatic scenes.

The most notable addition is the secret "rhythm" Heyward had discovered and expressed in music and group expression. It saves—and makes—the play and sweeps almost all objections before it. As Oliver M. Sayler observed: "No one can sit through ***Porgy,*** in the theatre and deny that his eye, ears, and mind have been played on like so many instruments by the various hands of rhythm. No one can read ***Porgy*** the novel or the play, and report half so vivid an experience."[24] The price Heyward pays in the adaptation is considerable, though, especially the sacrifice of the novel's subtle unity and some of the elements comprising it.

Ironically—and perhaps most importantly—it was the courtly and reserved white aristocrat, Heyward, along with O'Neill and Ridgely Torrence, who forced Harlem to begin to recognize and appreciate the American black folk culture and experience what it was so studiously ignoring.

Heyward also did the libretto and many of the lyrics for ***Porgy and Bess.*** The primary virtue of America's first folk opera is its transformation of the Row into an effective chorus and the agency of song to reveal theme and character more effectively than does the play. Spirituals, songs, refrains, and chants powerfully convey the Row's contentment with this world and faith in the next, and give voice to the community's heart. But song also becomes interior monologue for the characters, from Porgy to Sportin' Life, and an excellent vehicle for their expression of feeling. Although the admixture of the Gershwins' music and New York City style led to some criticism of the opera's Charleston authenticity, Heyward clearly manages, once more, to convey that rhythm and community life he so admired.

In 1926, between the ***Porgy*** novella and the play, Heyward published a novella, ***Angel,*** and a story, **"The Half Pint Flask."** The first is the somewhat strained story of a young girl who moves from an Eden-like union with life through the Calvinist judgment of her father into exile in the barren and harsh life of the mountains, finally to turn hopefully to a future in town when her old lover arrives to take her away. ***Angel*** is the first of several Heyward novels in which whites futilely seek the inner harmony with life he recognizes in Catfish Row.

"The Half Pint Flask" is the story of the encounter of an obsessed scientist who is studying "Negroid Primates" on Ediwander Island with the evil voodoo spirit Plat-eye. Here Heyward reaches behind ***Porgy*** to a *cul de sac* in the world of progress, the first of three excursions he made into the primitive life of the "woods." The others were his 1933 movie scenario for Eugene O'Neill's ***Emperor Jones,*** and a late play, **"Set My People Free,"** later entitled "Charleston, 1820," completed by his wife.[25] The movie scenario opens with an African ceremonial dance fading into an equally rhythmic church scene. The dramatization of Denmark Vesey's 1820 uprising includes a lonely island night scene which moves, as the drums beat, from primitive ecstasy and voodoo to Old Testament messianism; throughout, the drums call the conspirators back to the gods of their fathers.

"The Half Pint Flask" is seriously flawed by Heyward's narrative strategy. Still, even at a distance, Courtney, the courtier-narrator, recognizes the double world of the Ediwander Negro community, placid by day and possessed by primitive rhythms and powers at night and more than a match for the scientist's rationalism. Courtney is open to the clear evidence of Plateye's existence, a judge of Barksdale's arrogance and racial prejudice, and sensitive to the rhythmic flow of island life from night to day and sun to moon. The sense of setting, primitive beliefs, and the rhythm and color of ***Porgy*** are all here. The distinctive difference is Heyward's respect for the harmonious half-pagan life of the Ediwander blacks, a balance of order and mystery, resistant to any change or violation—however anachronistic its inscrutable ways might appear to Barksdale.

In each of these works, Heyward's handling of the primitive scene has a Poelike Gothic quality. What is interesting, though, is that the African note is not struck in an educated poet's atavistic moment in Harlem, but on an offshore Carolina island geographically and culturally as near as one could get to Africa in the United States. The blacks of **"The Half Pint Flask"** are nearest the "woods" and least involved with whites. Without individualized black characters, **"The Half Pint Flask"** remains a general commentary on Heyward's search for life: Barksdale lacks what the Ediwanders have.

III

By 1928, when ***Mamba's Daughters*** was serialized in the *Women's Home Companion,* Heyward was ready to look directly at the Negro's effort, in the 1920s, to "learn to play." Catfish Row is the point of departure, unchanged from ***Porgy*** except in its blatant amorality. One major difference, though, is that Mamba leaves the community of freedom and common cause in which she finds her being: "Nigger gots tuh git diff'ent kind ob sense now tuh git long. Ah gots daughtuh, an' she gots daughtuh, an' all-two dem female is born fuh trouble. Ah gots tuh be ready when de time come."'[26] Mamba's anxiety sets the story in motion. The near-static process of ***Porgy*** becomes dynamic and the clash between tradition and change inevitable. A second difference is that the white world is not peripheral. The story of Saint Julien de Chatigny Wentworth, the white narrator and observer who is also in search of life, only to have to admit his relative failure in celebrating Lissa's success, provides a second plot. As Mamba, Hagar, and Lissa negotiate the obstacles, they not only involve Saint's world but comment upon his life.

Generally, the struggle is again with the alien forces met in ***Porgy.*** But the concern here is not survival; it is what of the primitive past can be taken into the future, in how the black man can change without losing his identity. And in ***Mamba's Daughters,*** a greater force than the Row's united front appears to make victory possible: love.

Primitivism shows itself here as animality and a native sense of rhythm. There is the animality of the physical scene where, after leaving Gilly's corpse in the swamp, Hagar broke "savagely" through the tangle until she found high ground: "Crouched over almost on all fours, with prehensile hands tearing her way through the undergrowth, the great woman emerged like a prehistoric creature quitting its primal slime, and climbed out upon the knoll" (p. 274). Hagar is a sort of driven animal from the start, massive and powerful but lacking the intelligence to avoid trouble or to control her simple instincts. The difference with ***Porgy*** here is that the wilderness of Mamba's daughters is an unpremeditated burst of feeling, not deliberate violence, as with Porgy, or a brutal way of life, as Crown's. Moreover, strong racial feeling is important as a critical element Lissa must not lose in her transformation into a Metropolitan opera star. On the other hand, Lissa's mother, Hagar, is too simple—and goodhearted—to survive in white society: her expressions of feeling too often lead to jail.

The name of the game is accommodation. But Lissa finds such accommodation as the leading forces in the cultured Negroes' Monday Night Music Club make—aping white manners, tastes, and styles—impossibly sterile and alien. She can discipline her art, can meet the Music Club's technical standards, but no more than her mother or grandmother can Lissa abandon for their Victorian mode the "gaiety of life" or the other strong feelings of life that she recognizes as part of her racial identity and which seek expression in her song (p. 68). Hagar must accommodate her feelings for Lissa by living in exile away from her daughter.

In an **"Introduction on the American Negro in Art,"** published with the play version of ***Porgy,*** Heyward had tried to identify what he called "the secret law of rhythm." He had recognized it as a "sort of race personality that dominated and swayed the mass, making of it a scene vastly greater than the total of its individual activities" (p. x). this evasive definition and the example of Sam Smalls that follows are less helpful than Heyward's indication in ***Mamba's Daughters*** of what lies behind that faculty Lissa shares with other Negroes of "giving her whole being to an emotion" (p. 208). Passing the jail with North, who has just dismissed a revival service as "'a lot of dirty Negroes,'" Lissa finds the "night suddenly dark with the suffering of the thousands who had lain there in the cages—slaves, freemen, her own people" (p. 218). And the following Sunday, she "let herself go into the music" (p. 219). This quality is again reflected in the preference of the congregation for Rev. Whaley's God "who wanted them to pour their sorrow out in a flood of song . . ." (p. 188). As Heyward defines and illustrates it, rhythm would seem to be the Negro's unique expression, with his whole being, of the strong experience of suffering and longing and joy common to the race, an expression that communicates truth and infects those of the race who join the expression.

In ***Mamba's Daughters,*** the vehicle of expression, which may also be a vehicle of persuasion, is music—spirituals, shouts, or jazz. For Mamba and her daughters, it is primarily song, and it would appear that racial rhythm or feeling reaches its most subtle, profound expression in this verbal and physical form. So we meet song, from the doorway harmony of Maum Netta and Mamba's "longing throb" to Lissa's New York triumph (p. 12). Mamba even seals Saint's and Valerie's love by taking them on an adventure that speaks tongues of wildness and rhythm:

> Over them, like the crash of breakers, swept the terrific, cumulative intensity of the worship, now throbbing with an old terror of jungle gods, again lifting suddenly into rapt adoration of the new Christ. This, and the pounding rhythms of the spirituals, the amazing emotional release wrought by the music, so fascinated and yet frightened the white girl that she sat huddled against Saint, clinging to his hand with tense fingers, her head pressed against his shoulder.
>
> (p. 164)

Mamba and her daughters all express themselves in song, culminating in Lissa's disciplined Met performance: "The song lifted and hovered above the shadowed figures in a repressed agony of yearning and supplication" (p. 301).

The rhythm of the Row and race seen at the beginning extends from the swaying bodies singing spirituals at the mining camp to the church near the Charleston jail where the "air rocked to a deep solid chorus . . . shaving harmonies with fractional notes so fine and so spontaneous that no written page could ever capture and prison the sound" (p. 217).

As the authentic vehicle by which the essence of racial integrity is expressed and transmitted to the future, Lissa must somehow honor and reconcile rhythm with her musical training. This reconciliation is, moreover, her avenue to social and economic success in a white world. The story of Mamba and her daughters is, then, the story of three women, each a story of struggle and sacrifice toward Lissa's achievement of this goal, the consistent vehicle of which is song. Mamba leaves the Row and sings. The lonely, inarticulate, slaving Hagar finds voice only in song. Lissa's voice is to be trained.

Lissa is tempted to emulate her friend Gardinia who manages to satisfy the Monday night snobs with only the slightest sacrifice of her "sheer animal spirits," and, in New York, to give way to the "alien syncopation of laughter and song" in the lazy rhythms of Harlem (pp. 228, 300). Lissa resolves her conflict—between racial spirit and art—only when she fully appreciates the sacrifices that have brought her to New York, a resolution her final Met song reflects:

> The music caught the mood of the sky. The arresting dissonances, the sharp syncopations of the early acts, were no longer individually evident but seemed to merge into a broader irresistible current of sound. The rhythm, too, was no longer a thing separate. It became a force as indistinguishable and pervasive as the life current. It was a fundamental law that moved light, music, the sway of the crowd, the passage of time, in a concerted and inevitable progression. The artificial declamations of operatic convention were gone. The cast was reduced to two elemental forces. The crowd with its heavy mass rhythms and reiterated choruses was the body, and the single transendent mezzo-soprano that soared above it was the spirit, aspiring, daring, despairing, lifting again.
>
> (p. 306)

When Lissa sings the "National Anthem of the American Negro" for an encore, Wentworth feels something reaching back to claim "its heritage of beauty from the past" (p. 308).

Lissa's accomplishment represents the kind of victory over change—perhaps of Heyward's wishful thinking—that Heyward hoped for but had appeared to despair could come. In his first essay, **"And Once Again—the Negro,"** published in 1923, he wonders if the Negro is "an aeon behind, or an aeon ahead of us."[27] However, his main concern in this essay is that the old Negro ways that led to happiness will succumb, with urbanization, to a "stiffling moral straitjacket," because the Negro is blindly submissive. "He is about to be saved," Heyward observes with sorrow and fear. Such salvation meant the disappearance of the Negro's soul, his racial integrity, and what Heyward described in 1931 as "his spontaneous abandonment to emotion, his faith in his simple destiny."[28]

Lissa's success constitutes Heyward's response to those black voices of the Harlem Renaissance who recognized only high art as created by whites as the proper objective for black expression. But Heyward's sense of the fullness of Negro humanity directs his attention as well, perhaps more credibly, to the still stronger force that stands against an excessive and self-destructive primitivism and that conquers changes: Mamba's and Hagar's love, which becomes a testament for all their kind.

Hagar, like Mamba, is seen sketchily, but she emerges clearly as a combination of great physical strength, great simplicity, and great virtue—and as doomed in town as Billy Budd in the world. She has risked jail to save the worthless Bluton from bleeding to death so that when her efforts for Lissa are completed and her suicide is necessary to assure Lissa her chance, she deliberately ends her long loneliness. Her violence, then, is a matter of simplicity and strength, moral outrage, and maternal concern. And it is always balanced by humility. When she is gone, Lissa "imagined her as vast inarticulate power—encompassing love, possessing her all the more now because of her silence" (p. 294).

Heyward has a problem in aesthetic distance with Saint Wentworth, the pattern of whose early life largely reflects Heyward's own. The narrator is divided, until the last page, between sentimental attachment to the remnant of Charleston aristocratic tradition, including approval of Saint's success story, and criticism of the weakness and sterility, compromises and inadequacies, of that world. In short, Saint's pursuit of identity and freedom parallels Lissa's maturation. But where his intellectual curiosity, artistic sensibility, and social awareness suggest a great potentiality for freedom and a fullness of life, he succumbs to the pressures of class and meets only the challenge of a business career. Freedom, fulfillment, become participation in the rituals of the Charleston aristocracy with the means to do so. But then he recognizes that Lissa had pursued the beautiful and lonely ecstasy of her dream while he had been guided out of that delight in dreamy loneliness into social responsibility, pursued within more or less acceptable limits: economic responsibility, paternalism in race relations, marriage and family, and, perhaps, later, leisurely dabbling in art. Mamba and her daughters have transcended economics. The same quest for freedom occupies Heyward in ***Peter Ashley*** and ***Lost Morning.*** Are economic success, social conformity, and the role of gentleman compatible with life? Is Saint dead and only the creative Lissa alive? Now, almost desperately, Saint vows, "Life would still be an adventure" (p. 266).

But the narrator looks at Saint's sensitive mouth and realizes that he is no hero. He lacks the faith of Mamba and her daughters. Likewise, in his relationships with Mamba, Hagar, and Lissa, we find less than courage. He meets the demands of *noblesse oblige* but he is passive toward the black masses and accepts the white power structure at the mine.

But Heyward does not stop with parallel stories. In ***Porgy,*** black and white worlds largely avoid one another and the burden of responsibility in only once recognized. Here, as the black man's claim to dignity clashes with the white man's fear of change, Heyward's realism cannot ignore the facts. Atkinson notes how the impersonality of the race problem dies when one confronts an individual "battling with destiny, needing a leg up most terribly" (pp. 71-72). White supremacy, in its more callous forms, rules supreme at he phosphate mine where Hagar works, and Saint's silence appears to defend the status quo. Also, while Heyward scrupulously avoids overt criticism of the aristocracy and white supremacy, not only does the aristocracy emerge pale, wan, dull, racist, and perhaps irrelevant, but the inadequacy and evils of white supremacy become apparent as well. If there is no future for the black man in ***Porgy,*** neither is there here. He can be an Uncle Tom, like Whaley, a corrupt lackey, like Gilly, a slum landlord, a sterile parody of white culture, or he can gamble, like Mamba, sacrifice and die, like Hagar, or flee, like Lissa.

Notably, ***Mamba's Daughters*** is Heyward's last work treating of the Charleston Negro. But his accomplishment in that novel, if more diffuse, is as many-sided as in ***Porgy.*** The climate of change that overlays the balancing of plots produces, finally, an ironic effect. The Wentworths laugh at Mamba and Saint achieves economic success among the miners, but the last laugh is Mamba's and the miraculous economic success is Hagar's.

Aristocracy leans on racism and decadence results; out of subjugation comes the Negro's strength. Out of the Negro's primitive rhythm comes art; in the white aristocracy the "essential spark" never appears. Apparently, Heyward's last word in ***Mamba's Daughters*** is this contrapuntal statement, this overarching irony. Heyward might be called a memorialist of Low Country society in this novel, but the implications of the changes in fortune in the course of the story go beyond the memorialist's fidelity. Again, as were those elsewhere who turned to the Negro in the Twenties, Heyward is looking for life. He does not find it in Charleston manners or business success but among those who are living. And, better than in ***Porgy,*** he understands what that life is.

IV

Mamba's Daughters was Heyward's last work before the Depression hit and Harlem's hopes plunged. But Heyward's pursuit of the key to life did not end when he turned from Catfish Row in the Thirties. It is largely subdued in ***Brass Ankle,*** a play, where a too passive Ruth Leamer's participation in the beauty and rhythm of life is crushed by Race and Progress. In ***Peter Ashley,*** Peter turns from his own judgment about Secession and slavery and his own talent in the realization that he would sacrifice anything for his past, his place, and his people. In ***Lost Morning*** and ***Star Spangled Virgin,*** however, Heyward again probes the spirit's escape from the deadness of contemporary life.

In ***Lost Morning,*** Felix Hollister's compromise of his artistic talent for the security of home, marriage, and money comes unstuck under the pressures of his increasingly cold and calculating wife and the commercial-industrial values of Exeter she has adopted, and the urging of an assistant. To recover the lost morning of his art and life he must free himself from a world without heart or inner life and assert his independence. Alone in New York, he sees that good work is done by "a man who has given himself to life and let it eat him."[29]

Star Spangled Virgin, published in 1939, is located in the Virgin Islands, far from the Harlem Renaissance in time and place. But in his last work, Heyward returns to a theme that appears variously in each of his first three longer works of fiction: those who remain in harmony with the rhythms of nature in the corrupted atmosphere of civilization and progress are purer, wiser, and happier—and to be envied. In ***Lost Morning*** the civilized white man's one hope to experience the mysterious depths of life appears to be in art. Felix can recover the pulse of life—the rhythm of nature—only by an uncompromising dedication to art.

In ***Star Spangled Virgin*** this theme receives its strongest, yet least obtrusive, expression in that there is a general black victory over the evils accompanying white change. Adam Work, who has abandoned his earthy common-law Crucian wife and children, returns from Tortola and his church-wed wife, Victoria. From his boat, he smells the earth of St. Croix and would be reunited with Rhoda and the land. But that is not possible until Rhoda has led her crusade to success in saving the native matriarchy from bureaucratic meddling; a season of public relief and the consequent dissipations and white seductions ("Noodeal") passes. The novel ends with a ritual under the open sky, on Adam's and Rhoda's own land:

> He felt the old irresistible pull and sweep of her in the dark beside him. It communicated itself to the earth upon which he lay, and set it rocking. It poured into his body, and for a moment he choked with the beat of it in his throat. Then the separate elements yielded themselves to the march of a universal rhythm, and he could not have said which was the woman, which the man, and which the earth that bore their weight upon its sustaining hand.[30]

V

With the publication of ***Porgy,*** Heyward began to recognize that life eluded him and his kind, and so he pursued it into Catfish Row, Hagar's heart, and the artist's lonely garret. Initially, his work is a series of personal struggles of lonely characters to find life—in rhythm, love, art, community, freedom, or integrity—in a changing traditional society which denies life. As a Southern writer, Heyward is a transitional figure between Mencken's "Sahara of the Bozarts" and the younger Wolfe and Faulkner. His role is to memorialize the past and to criticize the present, to tell the truth—not all of it but enough to be called courageous for his time. When Heyward is done, the illusion of the white aristocracy's superiority is dispelled. Certain primitive Negro strengths and qualities, particularly rhythm, and a *joie de vivre* are seen, along with the reality and uniqueness of the Negro community, the Negro's dissembling for the white audience, and that pathetic self-hatred of Hagar and those inhabitants of the Row who deprecate themselves as "just niggers." Also, the relentless inroads of the modern industrialism and progress are seen everywhere so that the truth of his vision is primarily social: the struggles of his characters are chiefly with society or representatives of it. Southern society and social institutions invariably fail Heyward's characters, black and white. They exclude the possibility of black dignity. They require that whites conform to class and community mores. The demand for conformity frustrates the harmony with nature, community, love, spirit of sacrifice, and dedication Heyward's blacks know as life.

Catfish Row, on the other hand, has made the necessary accommodations to the urban white world. And with common values and faith that weather death and defeat, it lives, uninhibited, a real community. Only here is there the necessary freedom to pursue and realize a meaningful personal life. Perhaps Heyward's first poem, **"Gamblers All,"** should be read primarily in this context: the black gambler seeks freedom at any cost; the policeman who shoots him is actually enslaved by his racist role.

Life in Heyward's South, then, is found only in the black community where man's tie to nature has not been broken, where dead social codes do not frustrate freedom, and where rhythm and religion give meaning to the struggle for survival and dignity in the white man's world. Consequently, Porgy, Mamba, Hagar, Lissa, Adam, and Rhoda all have the energy, courage, and endurance to reach out for life until they achieve it, if only vicariously.

Heyward's additional contributions to the image of the black man in the Harlem Renaissance may be more precisely defined. The Harlem Renaissance occurs against a background of demeaning stereotypes and exaggerated primitivism that deny the black man's dignity. These distortions and others—fancied primitivism, exoticism, and indulgence in varying forms—continue through the Thirties. But in the early Twenties Southerners Heyward, T. S. Stribling, and Julia Peterkin, as well as Jean Toomer and, to a lesser degree, others, begin to examine the human qualities of the black man with a truth that changes that image significantly. Heyward's special place in this group is that his Southern Negroes are relatively contemporary, urban, involved in the white man's world, and seen through the double perspective of a paternalistic white Southern aristocrat and an honest observer who satisfies even Negro critics in his fidelity to the truth. If Heyward's paternalism is condescending, so is it sympathetic and understanding. And while he filters out the harsher truths, the reader does not escape complacent and guiltless.

More important is that honesty and understanding as Heyward moves inside the Negro community to see its passions, hopes, fears, suffering, code, community order, ties with the past, and capacity to prevail. In his close observation and awareness of the full complexity of what he sees, he rescues Negro primitive qualities from ersatz distortions to reveal the elements that make the Negro more responsive to life and nature than his mannered white Charleston neighbors. Specifically, the rhythm Heyward sees is neither primitive exuberance, the echo of atavistic drums, or both, but the essential element in the cultural expression of a folk close to the earth and their God and joined in suffering and misery, joy and hope. In the Harlem Renaissance, Nathan Huggins tells us, "The Negro was in the process of telling himself and the world that he was worthy, had a rich culture, and could make contributions of value."[31] Heyward was showing the Negro and the world.

Most important of all, he simply shows us Porgy and Hagar performing in the intimacy of a black world, an opportunity seldom given Faulkner's Negroes. Thus, Heyward won an audience for fiction that treated the Negro seriously and sympathetically as a human being that no American writer since Twain and Joel Chandler Harris had reached. The strength, the determination, the faith that the nation recognized in the Civil Rights movement in the South in the Sixties, Heyward had recognized in the Catfish Row community scenes forty years before.

Heyward's importance to the Harlem Renaissance, then, is his success in showing the black man's humanity and culture in the world of nature, his own society, primitive influences, change, white racism, and fate, as illustrated in the concluding lines of ***Porgy:***

> The keen autumn sun flooded boldly through the entrance and bathed the drooping form of the goat, the ridiculous wagon, and the bent figure of the man in hard, satirical radiance. In the revealing light, Maria saw that Porgy was an old man. The early tension that had characterized him, the mellow mood that he had known for one eventful summer, both had gone; and in their place she saw a face that sagged wearily, and the eyes of age lit only by a faint reminiscent glow from suns and moons that had looked into them, and had already dropped down the west.
>
> She looked until she could bear the sight no longer; then she stumbled into her shop and closed the door, leaving Porgy and the goat alone in an irony of morning sunlight.
>
> (p. 196)

In the spring of 1965, I had occasion to mention Heyward to the young black fiction writer, William Melvin Kelley, whose first novel, *A Different Drummer,* and collection of stories were attracting considerable interest. His response was to quote much of this passage. Apparently, we can still go to school to DuBose Heyward.

Sixty years after the appearance of ***Porgy*** and fifty after the 1935 premier of ***Porgy and Bess,*** these claims for Heyward appear more firmly established than when they were first made. ***Porgy and Bess*** reappears regularly, on stage and in recordings, recalling its fictional origin. A film of **"The Half Pint Flask"** improves upon the story. At the 1985 Heyward Centennial Conference in Charleston, that story and the fiction and theater versions of ***Porgy*** and ***Mamba's Daughters*** provided the focus of attention in papers by Theodore Rosengarten, Harlan Greene, John Crum, James Meriwether, Susan W. Walker, and Frederic Roffman, demonstrating the integrity of Heyward's work in several art forms, his kinship with the Harlem black writers, his contributions to black advances on the American stage, his delineations of black classes and subtle changes in race relations, and the humanity of his black characters. A concurrent Gibbes Art Gallery exhibition was appropriately titled "Charleston and the Age of Porgy and Bess."

Notes

1. Herschel Brickell, "Creator and Catfish Row," *New York Herald Tribune Books,* March 10, 1929.
2. "Critic's Almanac," *Nashville Tennessean,* February 3, 1929; Cullen, "Book Shelf," *Opportunity,* 3 (December 1925), 379.
3. DuBose Heyward, *Porgy* (New York: George H. Doran Co., 1925). Subsequent references are to this edition.
4. Writers: Black and White," in *The American Negro Writer and His Roots: Selected Papers from the First Conference of Negro Writers, March, 1959,* ed. John O. Killens (New York: American Society of African Culture, 1960), p. 43.
5. DuBose Heyward, "Introduction on the American Negro in Art," Dorothy Heyward and DuBose Heyward, *Porgy: A Play in Four Acts.* Theatre Guild Acting Version (Garden City, N. Y.: Doubleday, 1928), p. ix.
6. On one occasion Heyward's and Toomer's careers lightly touched. John Bennett, an editor of the South Carolina Poetry Society's *Yearbook,* anxiously wrote Heyward, the society's executive secretary, when he discovered that Toomer had become an associate member of the society. A crisis in the Charleston blueblood organization was averted by quietly listing Toomer as a member in the next *Yearbook* but omitting the usual courtesy reference to his new book, *Cane.* See John Bennett to DuBose Heyward (August 19, 1923), Bennett Papers, South Carolina Historical Society, Charleston, S.C.
7. "A Major Musical," *New Republic,* 128 (April 6, 1953), 31.
8. "The Negro in American Literature," *New World Writing,* 1 (April 1952), 28. According to Charles Glicksberg, this pseudo-realism was a form of psychological regression to nature, the spontaneous, and the decadent. Add condescension, he argues, and you have "white slumming": writers cast Negroes in the roles of child-like, emotional, and irrational creatures engaged in atavistic dances and tribal crimes without ever questioning whether blood is a creative principle or whether Negroes are truly so anti-intellectual. See "The Negro Cult of the Primitive," *Antioch Review,* 4 (March 1944), 49.
9. *Nigger Heaven* (New York: Knopf, 1926), p. 165. Subsequent references are to this edition.
10. Telephone interview with Ralph Ellison, Milwaukee, Wis., October 22, 1967.
11. *Creating the Modern American Novel* (London: Williams and Norgate, Ltd., 1936), p. 145.
12. "The Legacy of the Ancestral Arts," in *the New Negro: An Interpretation,* ed. Locke (New York: Albert and Charles Boni, 1925), p. 153.
13. *DuBose Heyward: The Man Who Wrote Porgy* (Columbia, S.C.: Univ. of South Carolina Press, 1954), p. 70.
14. "Orchestrated," *New York Herald Tribune Books,* October 18, 1925.
15. "Negritude and Its Relevance to the American Negro Writer," in *The American Negro Writer and His Roots,* p. 15.
16. "Back-Country Novels," *Virginia Quarterly Review,* 8 (July 1932), 467.
17. DuBose Heyward to Kathryn Bourne, December 21, 1931. Cited from Frank Durham, "DuBose Heyward's Use of Folklore in His Negro Fiction," *The Citadel: Monograph Series,* No. 2 (Charleston: The Citadel, 1961), pp. 18-19.
18. "The Dilemma of the Negro Author," *American Mercury,* 15 (December 1928), 478.
19. "Introduction," *Three Negro Classics,* ed. Franklin (New York: Avon, 1965), p. viii.
20. "It Seems To Me," *New York World,* October 14, 1925.
21. Heyward and Heyward, *Porgy: A Play in Four Acts,* p. xiii. Subsequent references are to this edition.
22. Stark Young, "Races," *New Republic,* 52 (Oct. 26, 1927), 261.
23. *DuBose Heyward: Southerner as Literary Artist* (Diss.: Columbia University, 1953), p. 342.
24. "The Play of the Week," *Saturday Review of Literature,* 4 (Oct. 29, 1927).
25. Eugene O'Neill, *The Emperor Jones, with a Study Guide for the Screen Version of the Play* by William Lewin and Max J. Herzberg (New York: Appleton, 1949), p. 60. Lewin and Herzberg do not identify the source for Heyward's statement.
26. DuBose Heyward, *Mamba's Daughters* (New York: Doubleday, 1929), p. 36. Subsequent references are to this edition.

27. *The Reviewer,* 4 (October 1923), cited from Emily Clark, "DuBose Heyward," *Virginia Quarterly Review,* 6 (October 1930), 551.

28. DuBose Heyward, "The Negro in the Low Country," in *the Carolina Low-Country,* ed. Augustine T. Smythe *et al.* (New York: Macmillan, 1932), pp. 186-87.

29. *Lost Morning* (New York: Farrar and Rinehart, 1936), pp. 268-69.

30. *Star Spangled Virgin* (New York: Farrar and Rinehart, 1939), p. 230.

31. *Harlem Renaissance* (New York: Oxford Univ. Press, 1971), p. 59.

TITLE COMMENTARY

Porgy

THE NEW YORK TIMES BOOK REVIEW (REVIEW DATE 1925)

SOURCE: "A Romance of Negro Life." *The New York Times Book Review* (27 September 1925): 10-11.

In the following review, the critic comments favorably on Porgy, *focusing on the quality of Heyward's characterization in the work.*

[In ***Porgy***] DuBose Heyward challenges attention and evokes a mood with his initial daring stroke: "Porgy lived in the Golden Age." It is a timeless, innocently grotesque world that Porgy knows, and the reader through Porgy. It is a Southern seaport, possibly Mr. Heyward's own Charleston, S. C., though the geography is not insisted upon. More specifically, it is Catfish Row, the glamorous retreat of the crippled darkly Porgy, and his friendly neighbors. The white world but vaguely impinges upon their absorptions, their sorrows, their tragedies and their rude but satisfying justice. The interventions of the whites are often meaningless, often disastrous, always impertinent Mr. Heyward establishes by implication an antithesis in civilization which is not wholly to the glory of the white race. He conveys an intimate and authentic sense of the dignity, the pathos, the unending minor chords of a folk-melancholy, the latent high spirits, the primitive passion, the color, the movement, the intrinsic energy, the superstitions and the religious faith, the very essence of his chosen community. It is a noteworthy achievement in the sympathetic and convincing interpretation of negro life by a member of an "outside" race.

Although it is matter for wonder that Mr. Heyward has seemed to have gotten inside his characters and their surroundings, it is cause for rejoicing that he has communicated these things he has found to the reader. Porgy is at no time an alien being: his author has magically insinuated him into the very quick of attention. He deserves to rank with the fantastic Italian puppet, Pinocchió; such a creation as bankrupts in reality the next-door neighbor. Mr. Heyward's method is diametrically opposed to that of Ronald Firbank in *Prancing Nigger,* there was a delectable, a charming, a gay spectacle. Porgy is understood and his eyes are the eyes we see through, his ears the ears we hear by. Yet, amazingly, Porgy is merely an ingredient in the larger aspects of Mr. Heyward's intention: the evocation of a curious, wistful, day dreaming mood.

Porgy is a beggar with a very subtle "line." There is an arresting look of contained power about him and an air of incessant, quiescent, yet intensified, waiting for something, some vision beyond experience, or some fulfillment transcending wish. The other beggars are envious of him, for, without apparent effort, pennies and nickels and dimes come to Porgy's unasking hands. His own kind are almost suspicious of the strong man with the wasted legs, who beseeches the dice: "Oh, little stars, roll me some light! Roll me a sun an' moon!" making his points and taking the winnings with that same calm, unquestioning silence.

It is almost a legend that grows up about Porgy. When his friend is jailed and he can no longer count on a lift in the friendly wagon, he is saved from threatened starvation by a goat and cart of his own, in which royally to make his rounds. Naturally, the penetrating qualities of the goat's smell complicate Porgy's leisure a bit and compel him to adopt the hustling tactics of an alien philosophy. In spite of himself, Porgy has become a "go-getter," and his reputation goes abroad in Catfish Row. In the casual manner of those childlike peoples, Porgy one night finds himself adopted as provider and protector to Bess, untamed, hardliving woman, who is temporarily widowed. Crown, her husband, in hiding until his last murder is forgotten, comes back for Bess one dark night. He is found with a knife in his ribs and Porgy's floor has a suspicious wetness for the early morning hours. And Bess has a shine of wonder in her eyes for the strength of Porgy's arms.

The law comes for Porgy and he runs away, racing the motor-driven patrol wagon in his absurd goat-cart, to the keen delight of the entire populace. He is wanted, it develops, merely to identify Crown for the Coroner's inquest, and is jailed for contempt of court. When he comes out

FROM THE AUTHOR

INTRODUCTORY VERSE FROM *PORGY*

Porgy, Maria, and Bess,
Robbins, and Peter, and Crown;
Life was a three-stringed harp
Brought from the woods to town.

Marvelous tunes you rang
From passion, and death, and birth,
You who had laughed and wept
On the warm, brown lap of the earth.

Now in your untried hands
An instrument, terrible, new,
Is thrust by a master who frowns,
Demanding strange songs of you

God of the White and Black,
Grant us great hearts on the way
That we may understand
Until you have learned to play

SOURCE: DuBose Heyward, title page verse from *Porgy,* George H. Doran Company, 1925.

Bess has been lured away by her all but forgotten cravings for gin and "happy dust." Porgy's Indian Summer of life is over.

Crap games, savage, moonlit fights, incongruous funerals, a terrifying hurricane sweeping over the harbor and battering at the frail houses of the darkies, a boat excursion and picnic, interventions of white man's justice and the close-mouthed loyalty of the negroes, rough-and-ready justice among the colored people, and, above all, the unforgettable character of Porgy, move through Mr. Heyward's pages in a lavish, yet reticent, magnificence of highly organized prose. Maria, the Amazonian fish-fry woman; the patient, hard-working Serena, the shifty yellow negro from New York, with his strange vices and insinuating ways, and Bess and Crown are all vividly individual. Maria's methods of adjusting matters more nearly to her liking are a delight; her effective cure of the dopepeddling New York mulatto, with the help of a well-aimed brick and a few well-chosen epithets and threats, is wholly satisfying. Even Porgy's goat is a person, a strong person, indeed, on its own account.

FRANK DURHAM (ESSAY DATE 1970)

SOURCE: Durham, Frank. "Porgy Comes Home—At Last!" *South Carolina Review* 2, no. 2 (May 1970): 5-13.

In the following essay, prompted by the performance of Porgy and Bess *at South Carolina's Tricentennial celebration, Durham discusses the history of the folk opera and its evolution to stage from Heyward's novel.*

I have been writing and talking about DuBose Heyward and ***Porgy*** and ***Porgy and Bess*** for almost twenty years. And now, with a Charleston production of the opera, as a part of the State's Tricentennial Celebration, I am prompted to write once again of my apparently threadbare subject. Naturally, I ask myself, "Is there anything new that I can say about Heyward and ***Porgy*** and ***Porgy and Bess***?"

Of course, I must first say something old, for a new generation has arisen, and for it I must again help to establish the beginnings of this story of Porgy and Bess, Maria and Crown, Serena and Sportin' Life and their summer of love and violence and tragedy.

Porgy was conceived in Charleston—born in the imagination of DuBose Heyward when he remembered many things and people and events his eyes had seen in the ancient city of his birth. Among the raw materials for the immortal story are Samuel Smalls, the crippled goat beggar in his soapbox chariot; a *News and Courier* clipping recounting the story of Smalls' attempted escape from the police, a clipping long cherished in Heyward's billfold; the memories of more than a year the young man spent as a cotton-checker on the Charleston waterfront, where he saw the swaggering Negro stevedores, the dope-peddler, and the violence and passion and laughter of a people whose dominant quality was, as he said, a powerful, innate rhythm, grown pale or lost entirely in the white man. Then, too, there was the city itself, with the spires of St. Michael's and St. Philip's soaring skyward above the cobbled streets and the fading mansions filled with treasured heirlooms from a bygone era of grandeur and elegance. There were also the teeming Negro tenements, vibrant with life and song and drama. These, then, were the ingredients of the deathless tale of love gained and love lost which has found its way into the hearts of the world—and which will, at long last, be enacted for the first time in the city of its nativity. An event long, long overdue.

Even before Porgy began his long journey in the pages of a book and then in the theatres and opera houses of five continents and on the cinema screens of the whole world, young DuBose Heyward had turned to the stage in his early, faltering efforts to become a writer. Behind him, in Charleston, lay a noteworthy theatrical tradition, commencing in 1703 when poor Anthony Aston landed in the city and later wrote of his experience: "Well, we arrived in Charles-Town, full of Lice, Shame, Poverty, Nakedness and Hunger: I turned Player and Poet, and wrote one Play on the Subject of the Country." This is the first record of a professional actor and playwright in the Colonies. And in 1735 appeared an announcement of the first opera to be done in America, *Flora, or Hob in the Well,* performed in Charleston's Courtroom. (Incidentally, *Flora* will also be done as a part of the Tricentennial Celebration.) And the Theatre on Dock Street could claim the honor of being the third regular theatre built in the Colonies. In Charleston the stage flourished until the Civil War, and even during Heyward's boyhood and young manhood traveling productions and seasonal stock companies drew local audiences.

Over a decade before he wrote the novel ***Porgy,*** Heyward made his debut as a playwright. In 1913 his one-act comedy **"An Artistic Triumph"** (which it sadly isn't) was performed at the South Carolina Society Hall, with a prologue in verse spoken by Augustine Smythe, a local cast, "a witty" curtain speech by the author, and a jolly social hour or two of dancing afterward. Ten years were to elapse before he again turned to the stage, a decade in which he tried short fiction and poetry, the latter with increasing success. In 1923, on the one hundred and fiftieth anniversary of the founding of the Charleston Museum, Heyward produced a playlet entitled **"1773, A Historical Interlude,"** dramatizing the establishment of the Museum. In it Josephine Pinckney portrayed her own ancestress; Charles Cotesworth Pinckney played Charles Cotesworth Pinckney; and Heyward, as his ancestor Thomas Heyward, made a startling entrance brandishing a very dead chicken.

This deceased fowl may be seen as prophetically symbolic, for the playlet seemed to mark the end of Heyward's local career as a dramatist. Though hereafter three of his plays were to be acted on Broadway—one of them also throughout the country and in England, and his opera was to journey all over America, Europe, Asia, Africa, Australia, and New Zealand, no Charleston stage was to echo to any lines composed by her native son.

Meanwhile, Heyward was making decisions that would bring him closer to his masterwork. In 1924 he was a successful insurance man who had published two very bad short stories, many poems, and two volumes of verse. Through his work with the Poetry Society of South Carolina, he had gained a respectable national reputation as a poet and a lecturer on poetry. But his writings brought him little in the way of income. On September 22, 1923, he had married Dorothy Kuhns, an Ohioan and a former student in George Pierce Baker's famous class in playwriting. The next year he wrote John Bennett, his mentor in Charleston, that he had decided to give up insurance and devote himself entirely to writing. And so at his cottage in North Carolina he settled in and pondered on a subject.

From his wallet he drew the crumpled clipping relating the serio-comic flight of Samuel Smalls in his goat wagon with the constabulary in hot pursuit. And suddenly it happened. As if by magic, things seemed to fall into place.

On July 28, 1924, apparently in a state of excitement, Heyward wrote Bennett: "Dorothy and I are both off: she on a new play, and your humble (very much so in this case) servant hell bent on the Negro novel." Later, possibly in November, Heyward wrote again: "John, I am almost sure that I have closed my hands about something alive in my 'PORGO.' The Spirit of God has been perched upon the studio gable for a month, and where the stuff came from else, I can't imagine." He reported that it was all done, except for the final copying and revision, and he added: "But I think the stuff's there."

It was.

The novel ***Porgy*** is local color at its best, and, at its appearance in 1925, it presented a distinctly fresh and different treatment of the Negro in fiction. Heyward was determined not to follow the old Negro stereotypes, mainly the comic ones, and he succeeded magnificently. As local color ***Porgy*** achieves a happy combination of the universal and the local, a rare blend. The local background is in reality the framework for the story, furnishing an interesting and exotic setting for the action but effectively subordinated to it. Though the story itself seems inevitably rooted in the Charleston Negro underworld, it is in reality a basic human tale. It could in its essentials be set almost anywhere and be peopled by actors of any race.

Among critics for national journals and newspapers, ***Porgy*** was greeted with acclaim. It was hailed as a significant achievement in the depiction of the Negro as a human being—and it did so without any propaganda or social protest.

Locally, in Charleston and in the rest of the state, the reception was mixed. Yates Snowden, distinguished South Carolina historian, was outraged at the very "brilliancy" of the novel and exclaimed that Heyward should use his great talents to a better purpose: he should, said Snowden, write of "Pinopolis folk . . . WHITE . . . Don't he dare write of our WHITE FOLKS . . . ?" Bennett reported that Miss Arabella Mazyck was "delighted" and that two Charleston ladies who opened the book with "apprehension and doubt" were easy converts, but a "Mrs. L . . . thinks the paper was wasted on which it was writ! Mrs. W . . . says when she laid it down she felt dirty!" Still, the consensus in Charleston and the South was that ***Porgy*** was a beautiful and significant book.

Dorothy Heyward, already with a Broadway play behind her, suggested a dramatic version, but Heyward was uncertain and his publishers were pressing him for a new novel to take advantage of ***Porgy's*** success. So he ground out ***Angel,*** a rather sentimental treatment of a North Carolina mountain girl, which did not win its predecessor's acclaim.

Dorothy persisted in her belief that ***Porgy*** would make a play and quietly wrote her own first draft of a dramatic version. When Heyward saw it, he was convinced—and thus began the collaboration which was to produce two successful plays and would lead to ***Porgy and Bess.***

"As collaborators we get along very well," said Dorothy. "It helps to talk out the scenes together. I generally write them too long, DuBose cuts them down too short, and then we work up from there." Actually, it was she who roughed out the scenarios first, and then together they wrote the dialogue.

Determined to rise or fall with a Negro cast, Heyward believed that the play was closer to the truth than the novel was, for in it the Negroes were themselves interpreting their own race, not as in the book, being seen through a white man's eyes. Then, too, the play marked an important step forward for Negro performers—an early opportunity for them to appear as serious actors rather than as mere specialty performers, song-and-dance artists, or comics.

What the New York audience saw on the opening night, October 10, 1927, was something new in the American theatre. Before eyes accustomed to the regular commercial plays, there swirled color and movement, clashing, barbaric; to ears used to the "blues" of *Shuffle Along* and the Cotton Club, there came the melody of childlike laughter, shouts of savage ecstasy, the blood-tingling beat and wail of the spiritual, the primal chant of group prayer. As a hurricane roared to its crescendo, a terrified mass of people swayed in unison, thrusting up arms and faces, chanting to a primitive God, while above them on the walls and the ceiling grotesque shadows leapt and danced. Here was primordial savagery in its essence. Here, too, was "theatre" at its most effective.

Brooks Atkinson said, "On stage, ***Porgy*** is ruder, deeper, franker, coarser than it is between book covers."

Genre picture after genre picture of Negro life and love and joy and violence and sorrow follow one another. Catfish Row, filled or empty, has a seething, turbulent life of its own. The characters of Porgy and Bess and Maria and Sportin' Life and Crown emerge gigantically for endearing or exciting moments, only to be swallowed up in the stupendous sense of the group, the mass. Reinforcing this mass effect is the constant use of songs and spirituals, more numerous—and now heard—than in the novel. One critic said that the music was more than worth the price of admission, and another wished that Heyward had, instead of a play, written "an American grand opera. Is there no composer," he asked, "who will consider this?"

As a matter of fact, there was. There had been one for some time, waiting rather impatiently.

One night in 1926 George Gershwin, exhausted from rehearsals of his latest musical, had "tumbled into bed and picked up a copy of DuBose Heyward's novel ***Porgy*** to read himself to sleep. Instead, he read himself very much awake. At 4 o'clock in the morning he was at his desk writing Mr. Heyward a letter. It all seemed very simple to Mr. Gershwin. He would make an opera of **Porgy.**" But it was not that easy. At this time Heyward was dramatizing the novel; so the opera had to wait. Apparently the two met and made plans for the future. Gershwin said that it would take him a few years to be ready to compose an opera, and finally in 1932 he wrote Heyward that he was again interested in collaborating on the work—but not until 1933. The failure of a New York bank strained Heyward's finances, and at this point Al Jolson, of "Mammy" fame, evinced an overwhelming desire to appear in a musical version of ***Porgy.*** Gershwin was not enthusiastic but agreed not to stand in the way. Fortunately, the Jolson threat subsided. Now Gershwin went abroad to study in France. Then he and Heyward decided that it would take them at least two years of intensive effort to complete the opera, and they set about finding ways to finance themselves during this period. Heyward went to Hollywood and had a hand in two movie scripts—that of O'Neill's ***The Emperor Jones,*** shot with Paul Robeson in the jungles of New Jersey, and that of *The Good Earth,* for which he was one of several writers. Gershwin undertook a weekly radio program sponsored by Feenamint, a popular laxative—and Heyward commented, ". . . we felt that the end justified the means, and that they also served who only sat and waited."

At last the two set to work, largely by correspondence, though Gershwin came to Folly Beach for seven weeks, attended a Negro religious meeting on James Island, joined in the "shouting," and listened to the singing at Negro churches. For the most part, Heyward wrote both the libretto and the lyrics before Gershwin composed the music, and Heyward helped greatly in setting the tones and the rhythms for the music itself. Of the songs for which Heyward did the lyrics, only **"I Got Plenty o' Nuttin'"** was composed before the writing of the words. Gershwin's brother Ira was called in to do some of the lyrics and to polish in New York some of Heyward's lyrics mailed from Charleston.

George Gershwin was determined to write a grand opera and insisted on the use of recitative instead of spoken dialogue; and the result was indeed full-fledged opera. The collaborators hoped for a production at the Metropolitan Opera House, but the Theatre Guild, owners of the rights to play, asserted its prerogatives and became the producer of the opera.

At last New York saw the fruits of this joint effort on October 10, 1935, and drama critics as a whole praised it, but music critics were far from unanimously enthusiastic. The production ran for 124 performances, unusual for an opera but not very good for a Broadway musical, and the authors really made little or nothing from the run. A three-month national tour—not including South Carolina—seemed to mark the end of ***Porgy and Bess.***

Heyward and Gershwin went their separate ways, talked of another collaboration for Ethel Waters, but both died before seeing ***Porgy and Bess*** really come into its own. A year after Gershwin's death and two years before that of Heyward, there was a successful revival of the piece in Los Angeles. Soon after Heyward's death in 1940 Cheryl Crawford radically cut the recitative and made other alterations for a production at her summer theatre in Maplewood, New Jersey. The result was so popular that the opera was moved to New York in January, 1942. Now the music critics changed their tune: this, they said, was an American classic, a truly native folk opera. Broadway saw ***Porgy and Bess*** for eight months, and then it went on a tour of twenty-six cities, including Columbia, South Carolina—but not Charleston, before returning to New York for two weeks.

But this was only the beginning.

Europe quickly awoke to the virtues of ***Porgy and Bess,*** treating it with all the respect due a major operatic work. During the Nazi occupation of Denmark, the opera was done in Danish at the Royal Opera in Copenhagen on March 27, 1943, and became, because it was American, a symbol of the Danes' resistance to the Nazis. The performances ceased only when the Nazis threatened to bomb the opera house, but the song "It Ain't Necessarily So" became a staple of the resistance radio, its title reflecting the popular attitude toward the pronouncements of the occupation forces. In 1948, 1949, and 1952, the opera houses of Gothenburg, Stockholm, and Malmo, Sweden, did their own productions—successfully.

In 1945 the Stanislavsky Players of Moscow performed ***Porgy and Bess,*** and the composer Shostakovich called it "magnificent" and compared it to Borodin, Rimsky-Korsakov, and Mussorgsky. In the same year at Zurich a production in German was done, with the favorite aria being "Bess, du bist meine frau jetst." An all-white cast wore blue make-up and fuzzy black-and-white wigs—triumphantly. This production was revived in 1950.

Finally ***Porgy and Bess*** was reborn in America. In 1952 a new production, restoring the recitative and even some of the material cut from the original version, opened in Dallas and made a successful tour to the Nation's Capital. Now the State Department sent it on the first of several international good-will tours. First, it went to Vienna, where tickets were at a premium. Then on to Berlin, Paris, London. In the last city it played for almost six months, and it was returned to Paris the next season by popular demand for a ten-week engagement, the record for an American production in that city.

In 1953 *Porgy and Bess* came back to New York for an extended run and then toured nineteen cities in the United States and Canada—but not Charleston. Again the State Department sent the company abroad, to Venice, to Paris again, to

Zagreb in Yugoslavia—where Communists, from the highest to the lowest street boys, were reported to be singing the songs from the opera. Cairo, Athens, Tel Aviv, Bucharest, Casablanca, Barcelona, Naples, La Scala in Milan, Florence, Rome, Marseilles, Switzerland, Belgium, the Netherlands—all greeted Porgy and company warmly. Next came a four-month tour of South America, then Mexico, and then the famous Russian tour so delightfully reported in a book by Truman Capote. Moscow, Warsaw, Leningrad, the Far East—everywhere in the world ***Porgy and Bess*** was performed and praised and loved. Everywhere, that is, but its own birthplace. Catfish Row and its inhabitants were known all over the world. Iron Curtain critics hailed it not only as opera and entertainment but as a vital means of increasing international understanding.

In New Zealand, sponsored by the New Zealand Brewing Company, ***Porgy and Bess*** was performed by a cast of native Maoris, aided by three American singers. It was a box-office sell-out all over New Zealand and moved on to a successful tour of Australia and selection as the chief cultural item of the Adelaide Festival of the Arts. New York saw it again recently in a new production at the City Center, and at present it is being performed once more in Germany.

The film version, with Catfish Row only a trifle smaller than Rockefeller Center, has played on screens all over the world and on national television. I saw the motion picture first in a theatre in Saigon, South Vietnam, with an English sound track and three sets of subtitles—French, Chinese, and Vietnamese—and the Oriental audience was quickly swept up into the story of Porgy and Bess and Maria and Crown.

All the world, then, has seen and heard ***Porgy and Bess.***

Except Charleston. Was Porgy never again to ride his goat cart along the streets of his native city?

Let us examine the distressing story.

The novel, as we have seen, was read and, on the whole, admired in Charleston, and DuBose Heyward became one of the city's most prominent and respected native sons. But no play by him was, in his lifetime, presented in that city.

Some time in the 1930's it was proposed that the play ***Porgy*** be produced in Charleston with a local cast. It was, I believe, to be a part of the annual Azalea Festival. But this project never got beyond the planning stage, and the rest seemed to be silence.

Then, in the 1940's a similar idea was proposed. The play was actually cast with local Negro actors and went into rehearsal at the Dock Street Theatre. Again there were difficulties, and the project was abandoned.

In the 1950's Jack Fracht of the Charleston Symphony Orchestra and Emmett Robinson of the Footlight Players projected a "concert" version of ***Porgy and Bess***—the opera, this time—to be presented at County Hall. But now the Gershwin Estate, ignoring European precedents, refused to allow a performance of the piece by white singers. So again Porgy was denied access to his home city.

But in South Carolina's Tricentennial year Porgy is at last coming home. As a part of the celebration of the three hundredth birthday of South Carolina the Charleston Symphony Association, in co-operation with the Chamber of Commerce and other local groups, will produce the opera at the Charleston Municipal Auditorium. Ella Gerber, who directed the New Zealand ***Porgy and Bess*** and several American stagings of the Heyward-Gershwin opera, has been brought in to guide a local Negro cast through the complexities of the production. So once more Catfish Row will stir with brilliant life. Once more Porgy will ride his goat cart to glory and tragedy. Sportin' Life will wryly tell us "It Ain't Necessarily So," and Crown will break in upon the mourners during the great lashing hurricane. All the color and vitality, the wild exuberance, the barbaric and touching harmonies, the age-old, world-entrancing drama of love gained and love lost—these will once more be where they have for so many years belonged—in that ancient and beautiful city which gave them birth.

Mamba's Daughters

DON H. DOYLE (ESSAY DATE 1995)

SOURCE: Doyle, Don H. Introduction to *Mamba's Daughters: A Novel of Charleston,* by DuBose Heyward, pp. vii-xxiii. Columbia: University of South Carolina Press, 1995.

In the following introduction, Doyle examines Mamba's Daughters *against the background of Heyward's life and the social situation in the American South during the 1920s.*

"Time is changin'," Mamba explains to her adopted white benefactors, and in these few words she summarizes a good part of DuBose Heyward's ***Mamba's Daughters.*** The novel is carefully set within a particular time and place, Charleston, South Carolina, during the two decades that bracket U.S. involvement in World War I. It is Heyward's ability to capture that moment, to reveal the interior social world of Charleston's white society, and to penetrate the lives of its black people, that makes this book worthy of our attention after all these years.

Most readers, aside from a few natives of Charleston and some literary scholars, will not have heard of this novel or even recognize its author. Neither has won the kind of enduring stature in American letters that one usually associates with a "southern classic." For a brief period in the 1920s Heyward stood among the foremost literary figures of the South, at a time when the "Sahara of the Bozart," to borrow H. L. Mencken's memorable epithet, was stirring with new life. Heyward was a founder of the Poetry Society of South Carolina, which was instrumental in the birth of the Southern Renaissance. He helped open the doors of New York publishers to southern writers. Through his work on African Americans Heyward also became identified with the Harlem Renaissance and all that it did to bring black culture into view. If reviews and commercial success were any indication, most critics would have pointed to Heyward rather than to his contemporary in Oxford, Mississippi, William Faulkner, as the more promising southern writer.

But whatever success he enjoyed during his lifetime, his poems were forgotten and his novels went out of print not long after his death in 1940. Even Heyward's most famous contribution to literature, ***Porgy,*** published in 1925, remains obscure. A successful novel and later play, Porgy's story became immortalized in 1935 in the opera ***Porgy and Bess,*** and the novel and its author have since survived in relative anonymity in the shadow of George Gershwin's classic.

Mamba's Daughters represents a piece of fiction far broader in its social and historical scope than the more focused study of Porgy and the denizens of Catfish Row. In Mamba's story, too, readers will find a much deeper, more sophisticated effort at understanding the African-American experience and the complicated relations between the races that existed in Charleston, and to some extent throughout the United States, in the early twentieth century.

Like Faulkner and other writers of the Southern Renaissance, DuBose Heyward turned to his native South—to its history, its people, their dialects and folkways—for the material out of which he fashioned his poetry and fiction. Though a far more conventional writer, Heyward shared with Faulkner an intense interest in utilizing knowledge of local society and history to work out his tales of the human condition. And if he stayed close to home and to what he knew in writing his fiction, at the same time he reached beyond the familiarity of his own people, who were the prominent white families of Charleston. More than any other white southern writer of his time, and well ahead of Faulkner, Heyward sought to transcend racial boundaries, to understand blacks, to understand how white southerners thought about blacks, and to tell their mutual story.

Mamba's Daughters is in every sense "a novel of Charleston," the city in which DuBose Heyward lived most of his life. In the "Author's Note" he prefaces his story with the usual disclaimer that his characters are "fictional creations" not "representations of actual characters either living or dead." But he also uses this occasion to affirm that this is "regional literature" and that as such it must be "unequivocal in its identification with its locale." Heyward used his knowledge of local people and events quite deliberately. Porgy's story had its original inspiration in a newspaper account of one Samuel Smalls, a crippled beggar arrested for murder. No one knows of any similar counterpart to Mamba or her progeny, but the Wentworth family is clearly a replica of the author's own, and numerous other characters in the novel had their parallels in the actual world.

Born in 1885, DuBose Heyward had an illustrious South Carolina ancestry that extended deep into the Lowcountry's colonial origins. Nathaniel Heyward had been among the founders of the colony in the late seventeenth century. He built an empire with two thousand slaves and fourteen plantations, the wealth from which placed the Heyward line among the South Carolina aristocracy for generations to come. The Heyward-Washington (the president slept there) house, visited by throngs of Charleston tourists today, was built in 1770 by Daniel Heyward. It was his son, Thomas, who signed the Declaration of Independence, continuing a dynasty of Heyward wealth and leadership that extended into the Civil War era. The author's first name, taken from his mother's side, was also redolent of old South Carolina aristocracy. Edwin DuBose, his grandfather, had been a wealthy cotton planter and slave owner with two plantations near Bonneau.

With the defeat of the Confederacy, the emancipation of the slaves, and the upheaval that came with defeat, both families slid into genteel poverty by the time of the author's birth. Heyward's father, Edwin Watkins Heyward, born to wealth as the son of a great cotton planter, was reduced to taking work at a rice mill in Charleston. His mother, Jane Screven DuBose, had come to town as a young girl after her widowed mother lost much of the family estate in bad cotton deals. There they both joined an intricate circle of old Lowcountry families living in the mansions and town houses of their ancestors. It was within this society that these two unfortunate descendants of DuBoses and Heywards met, courted, and married. Within a year their son was born, followed two years later by the birth of a daughter.

Then, at the rice mill one day Edwin Heyward got caught in the band of a machine and was killed. Jane Heyward and two small children were left to face life with little in resources beyond their family name. Like Kate Wentworth in ***Mamba's Daughters,*** Mrs. Heyward was not too proud to do what had to be done to keep her family from falling into poverty. She took in sewing, lodged boarders, accepted "paying guests" at the beach house, and wrote poems and stories to sell to magazines. In this last endeavor, and quite in contrast to the fictional Saint Wentworth who spurns his late father's artistic dream in favor of business success, it was the mother who showed the way to an artistic career for her son. Hers was art born of economic need. Her favorite subject was the local African-American culture, which she captured in Gullah dialect. Her Gullah stories were collected and published locally as *Brown Jackets* in 1923, two years before ***Porgy*** appeared. By that time Mrs. Heyward was earning money and a reputation by offering "dialect recitals" in which she told stories in simulated Gullah for the amusement of white Charlestonians.

As the mother struggled to provide for her family in its straitened circumstances, the son was thrown into the uncomfortable role of man of the family, struggling in his own way to provide income and to ease the burden on his mother. Despite the family's difficulties, his mother had seen to it that he went to the private schools deemed appropriate for boys of their social class. Heyward proved to be a miserable student—inattentive, absentminded, and altogether lacking in motivation. At the age of nine he had taken up a newspaper delivery route, and at fourteen he dropped out of high school to work full time in a hardware store. He may as well have been writing about himself when he said of Saint Wentworth that he was "a disappointment to everyone but Mamba. He had failed utterly to yield to the standardising process of . . . school. He was sensitive and took refuge from humiliating realities in a dream world of his own; . . . he spent most of his time roaming the waterfront." The demands of the working world were punishing to the boy's frail body. He fell ill repeatedly, first and most seriously with polio, which struck him in 1903 at age eighteen. Still weakened by this disease, he suffered typhoid in 1905, and the next year pleurisy. He had to be sent to Arizona for a year and half in order to make a full recovery. It was another bout of pleurisy ten years later that drove him from a business career and into the life of the artist.

In 1905 he worked as a cotton checker and time keeper for a steamship company on Charleston's old waterfront, which at that time was still located along East Battery. There he discovered a whole new world among the black stevedores, a world completely different from that of the mostly female house servants with whom he had grown up. Many of them lived in the tenements, often converted mansions and townhouses of the old elite neighborhoods. One of these tenements was Cabbage Row (the model for Catfish Row). It was from this corner of Charleston, teeming with the rough life of black refugees from the surrounding plantations, that Heyward had Mamba emerge in this tale set at about the same time that he began his labors at the docks.

For a time Heyward overcame his health problems to establish a promising business in real estate about 1906. The influx of wealthy outsiders into Charleston, to which Heyward refers in ***Mamba's Daughters,*** no doubt explains the quickening pace of business he enjoyed. In the novel, as Heyward's alter ego Saint Wentworth points out, the brutal economic necessity of earning income for one's family are sometimes at odds with the social rules that governed the life of a gentleman—even an impoverished one—in Charleston: "Unfortunately there were only certain occupations that a gentleman could follow in Charleston without sacrifice of family dignity," Saint Wentworth laments. Without professional training the choice was limited to work in a bank, as a cotton expert (the rice economy had failed by this time) or broker on East Bay, or in connection with the phosphate industry which was located outside the city. "But a gentleman seeking a livelihood in the early nineteen hundreds could not engage in any branch of the retail business without imposing upon his humiliated family the burden of incessant explanation."

In Saint Wentworth's lament Heyward is poking a bit of fun at Charleston, but he is also documenting the peculiar traits of a local subculture that had taken hold among many of Charleston's old elite families during the long decline extending through most of the nineteenth century. The chief port and capital of a thriving rice and cotton plantation economy in the Lowcountry, Charleston had been the premier city of the early South. Even as the cotton economy eclipsed the rice culture and moved into the Upcountry, the "City by the Sea" served as entrepôt for a region rich in rice and cotton plantations. But when South Carolina's soil became exhausted and the center of King Cotton's empire shifted to the lower Mississippi Valley, Charleston languished. Other eastern ports—New York, Philadelphia, Boston, and Baltimore—all competed for a share of the new western empire and began to channel capital into railroads and industry. Charleston's leaders were demoralized by the shift of tide that was draining the city of its wealth.

It was no coincidence that Charleston became the seed bed of radical secessionist sentiment that culminated in December 1860 when the streets of Charleston were the scene of delirious celebration as South Carolina seceded from the Union. Secession, the fire eaters of Charleston proclaimed, would be the path to economic independence from the North and to a rebirth of Charleston's greatness as an Atlantic port. The war that began in Charleston harbor that next April was welcomed with great festivity by the families who watched the shelling of Fort Sumter from the Battery, but it was to be the doom of their city. Charleston fell to Union forces early in 1865, following one of the longest and most damaging sieges in United States history. Union soldiers, led by the black troops, entered what journalist Sidney Andrews described in *The South Since the War* (1866) as "a city of ruins, of desolation, of vacant houses, of widowed women, of rotting wharves, of deserted warehouses, of weed-wild gardens, of miles of grass-grown streets, of acres of pitiful and voiceful barrenness."

Charleston was staggered by the destruction of war and the depressing effects of Reconstruction. The scars from the fires and shells were slowly repaired, but the city was then shattered by a massive earthquake in 1886. Many, many of Charleston's young men were killed or maimed during the war, and those who came of age in the postwar city faced bleak prospects. For a time the discovery of Lowcountry phosphates, an essential ingredient in fertilizer, promised not only to replenish the South's exhausted cotton fields but also to heal Charleston's battered economy. But the phosphate boom was short-lived, and the tide of prosperity that had brought the construction of the many mansions and splendid gardens south of Broad Street ebbed. Out of ambition or desperation young men flocked to Birmingham and Atlanta, or to the bustling cotton mills of the Carolina piedmont, leaving behind a city depleted of youthful, masculine energy. Owen Wister, who lived in Charleston just after the turn of the century while he was writing *Lady Baltimore,* described it as a "beautiful, sad place" filled with "deeply veiled ladies . . . hushed in their perpetual mourning." Henry James, who described Charleston in *The Americans,* wrote of much the same: "a city of gardens and absolutely of no men—or of so few that, save for the general sweetness, the War might still have been raging and all the manhood at the front."

Visitors to Charleston around the turn of the century were struck by the old fashioned quaintness of the city, not only in manner and custom but also, and most notably, in the architecture, most of it having originated in the golden age of antebellum splendor. During the late nineteenth century most American cities were busy tearing down and rebuilding to make room for the skyscrapers that occupied the new central business districts, while the wealthy former residents of the inner city sought refuge in the spacious green suburbs, from which they commuted to offices and stores by electric trolley. Charleston seemed equally intent on preserving its old buildings and landmarks and, with them, a more traditional way of life. "Charleston ought to be walled in and roofed over and kept for a museum!" one midwestern visitor proclaimed in the local newspaper in 1898. This was the city, as Heyward introduced it in ***Porgy,*** that "time forgot before it destroyed."

Less visible to outsiders, but equally well preserved, was the city's exclusive social hierarchy. Charleston, local observers boasted, did not pay honor to a "dollar aristocracy." Here survived an aristocracy of genealogy and manners, a group whose status was inherited by the descendants of the colonial-era planters. They defined their social circle by a constellation of societies, many of them stretching back a century or more by the time Heyward was writing. At the center of this circle was the St. Cecilia Society whose affairs become the subject of rare disclosure in ***Mamba's Daughters.*** St. Cecilia was founded early in the eighteenth century as a music society, and membership or even an invitation to its balls became the hallmark of acceptance in white society. It was a gentleman's club with representatives of each of the city's most prominent families on the Board of Directors, which guarded the privileges of membership and invitations with utmost discretion. A local reporter for the *News and Courier* noted in 1894 that St. Cecilia remained "the great bulwark of society in the quaint old city, which defends it from the onslaught and inroads of the nouveaux riches and self asserting." "Membership," one insider explained, "is not founded on birth except as a probable presumption of gentlemenlike conduct, nor because of wealth, nor success in life, nor talent, but the possession of the manners, instincts, and feelings of a gentlemen."

This closed social circle was beginning to open, a transition reflected in Heyward's novel. During the Spanish American War the navy adopted Charleston as a major port on the South Atlantic ocean. Inspired by the possibilities for revival, in 1901 the city's most energetic business leaders pushed the city into sponsoring the South Carolina Interstate and West Indian Exposition. A new crowd, described by two amazed *Atlanta Constitution* reporters in 1903 as "brainy, pushing and progressive young men," several of them from the wealthy German community in Charleston, began to agitate for "progress" through the Young Men's Business League and the new Commercial Club. Despite his Old South Carolina name, Robert Goodwin Rhett became a leading spokesman for what he proclaimed as "the new Charleston." He was elected mayor and pushed forward an ambitious agenda to modernize the economy and open the mind of Charleston.

With the quickening of the economy, new families, often from the North, began to infiltrate the city, appropriate the old mansions, and, in a variety of ways, exert influence in the city. In ***Mamba's Daughters*** Heyward captures the ascent of this new element marvelously in the amusing efforts of Mrs. Atkinson and her practical midwestern husband, George, who has come to Charleston to run a cotton seed oil manufactory. The Atkinsons are rich, and the wife wants to trade on their wealth among the women of prominent Charleston families—the "High Goddesses" of the "social Olympus." The Atkinsons have tried to imitate the lifestyle of the local elite. They have restored an old mansion on Legaré Street, bought antiques, hired antique house servants, and they attempt in every way to create the "illusion of indigenousness." Mrs. Atkinson busies herself with a constant round of luncheons, teas, and bridge parties, all aimed at ingratiating herself with the local aristocracy. But Mrs. Atkinson is the consummate monied snob. She judges people, like her neighbor Kate Wentworth, by their wealth and thinks Charlestonians will in turn judge the Atkinsons favorably by *their* wealth. Instead, as Heyward explains, her display of wealth is insulting to those old families whose "straitened circumstances" dictate "simple living" as the "criterion for good taste"; ostentation is "mere vulgarity." Mrs. Atkinson's design is to win an invitation to the St. Cecilia ball, and she is utterly mystified by the lack of response to her gracious entertainment.

Her husband George, though completely without social ambition, is eager to keep his wife happy and immediately grasps the solution. His wife has been keeping him at home to help entertain the ladies when, he somehow understands, the path to social acceptance in Charleston is through masculine camaraderie. He begins to linger after work at the Yacht Club, where he imbibes bourbon and fellowship. After Atkinson makes himself useful to the local business elite, one of the "hereditary aristocracy" casually extends an invitation to the St. Cecilia ball.

The Atkinsons are caricatures of Yankee intruders. They are wealthy products of a shallow American business culture of the kind that Sinclair Lewis sought to portray in George Babbitt. They are made to serve throughout the novel as foils by which we learn about the nature of Charleston elite society and race relations. They provide an American standard against which Heyward defines Charleston's peculiar customs and modes of thinking. In particular, the Atkinsons offer a counterpoint to the Wentworths, who have full access to the social circle Mrs. Atkinson covets but lack the wealth—their "worth" has "went" but not their social value. Saint Wentworth, Heyward's fictional alter ego, is feckless and impractical in dealing with the hard reality of getting ahead in life, at least until he meets Valerie, Atkinson's niece from New York, at the St. Cecilia ball. It is Valerie who steers Saint away from the life of the artist and awakens in him a surprising business acumen. Without forsaking his inherited destiny as a Charleston gentleman, Saint finds a way to absorb the Yankee business skills George Atkinson represents.

Heyward's stories of social ambition among the wealthy and well born of white Charleston serve as parallels to the central story of this novel, which is about Mamba, her daughter and granddaughter, and their aspirations. Mamba may seem at first just another comic caricature of the black mammy, but Heyward makes it quite clear that much of her "cajolery, flattery, clowning" is a deliberate act contrived to ingratiate herself with white folks and to manipulate them to serve her own "amazing plan." The mask is removed when she returns to Catfish Row and complains that she has had to "leabe my frien', an' de talk an' all, an' put up wid de damn' quality w'it folks." "Ah swear tuh Gawd my belly fair ache from de pure polite." She also offers a nondeferential evaluation of Judge Harkness: "Yas, Ah seen um once, a-settin' on he bench wid he long black robe on, sendin' nigger tuh jail, like he been Gawd. But don' yuh fergit, onnerneat' dat black wrapper he gots on two-leg pants same like Cook dere."

Mamba is a shrewd student of Charleston's hierarchy of class and race. She belongs to what Heyward describes as the lower mass of blacks, the rural refugees of the former slave plantations who have floated into the city to take up jobs on the waterfront or phosphate mines. These people work for white bosses but in relationships that are impersonal and uncaring, in contrast to the house servants who "had white folks" and "enjoyed a certain dolorous respectability." It is Mamba's scheme to reinvent herself, to rise from that lower mass into the more privileged and secure class of "negro quality," insuring thereby the protection of her daughter and the advancement of her granddaughter. She adroitly attaches herself to the Wentworth family, wins favor with their house servant, Maum Netta, and insinuates herself into a situation where she might trade on their social status.

It is here that the stories of the three families, each with its own ambitions, intertwine in an amusing plot whereby the Wentworth children help pass Mamba off on the Atkinsons as a "genuine" house servant to the "Charleston quality." Mamba reveals her plot to the Wentworths: "Yo' and Mauma here, yo' know Ah ain't a real house-raise' nigger, but dese new w'ite folks whut comin' tuh Chas'n now, dey ain't knows de different, an' dey is want ole-time house-raise' nigger whut use' tuh b'long tuh de quality. Ah is Axin' yuh now tuh gib me letter an' say Ah is raise' wid yo' fambly." Mrs. Atkinson, oblivious to the fraud, is indeed delighted to have "Maum Mamba," not only because of her impeccable recommendations from *the* Wentworths, but even more so because she is informed that "Mamba Atkinson" "belonged to the South Carolina branch of George's family, you know, and with that fine old-fashioned loyalty that one encounters all too seldom in these days." Mamba has deftly used Wentworth blood as a stepping stone to Atkinson money, and she has imported some bogus Charleston genealogy to the Atkinson family in the bargain. For her part, Mamba's new identification with the "Charleston quality" is eloquently expressed when she offers the Wentworths her estimate of Mrs. Atkinson: "she ain't one ob us."

Again, it is through the Atkinsons that we learn about the nature of race relations and the obligations entailed in taking on a servant such as Mamba. Just as Mamba has anticipated, her daughter, Hagar, who is "born for trouble," runs afoul of the law and is thrown at the mercy of a draconian legal system. To those unlucky blacks in the lower class (those who don't "have white folks") minor infractions of the law are punished with harsh sentences. But those who have white patrons, the courts treat with remarkable generosity. Mrs. Atkinson invokes the Charleston upper-class tradition of white paternalism, pleading with her husband to intervene on Hagar's behalf: "The right sort of people here do look after their negroes." "Their negroes!" George Atkinson scoffs; to which his wife responds: "Everybody knows that Mamba's people used to belong to the Atkinsons, and now, since the South Carolina branch of the family has died out, you are in a way the head."

Embarrassed by the pretence of this "absurd fiction" about Mamba's and his own genealogy, he goes to court to do his duty as a husband, not as a white patron of "his negroes." But in the process George Atkinson, the incarnation of rational American sensibility, discovers in the ritual of paternalism a genuine human bond between himself and a "known individual," a connection that transcends the abstract "race problem." In the courtroom, witnessing Mamba and her daughter, uncontrollably "his heart contracted with an unfamiliar spasm of pity, then expanded with a desire to protect." Through Atkinson, Heyward makes an argument he developed repeatedly in his writing about blacks; a defense of southern upper-class white paternalism as a remedy to the more abstract and unmanageable "race problem." "This negro business," Atkinson ponders; "millions and millions of them. Race problem. What to do with the whole mass." "But this old woman, now, and her ungainly daughter and that child. . . . These three were not a race problem.

They were individual entities battling with destiny, needing a leg up most terribly. The weak throwing themselves on the mercy of the strong."

Heyward was romanticizing the traditional bonds of dependence and mutual obligation, but he was also making his argument against northern liberals who wanted to uplift the masses through legal reform, education, and other efforts at social improvement. Atkinson is later quoted as saying: "the Yankee was all for the negro race, and hated him as an individual, but . . . in the South, we love the individual negro, while we hate, or at least fear, him as a race." Heyward acknowledges the harsh, unjust aspects of southern race relations, particularly in his observations of the legal system as it operates in the city and, worse, in the nearby rural phosphate district. But his characters explain the use of the law to punish and oppress blacks in terms that sound more apologetic than condemnatory. The dictatorial regime of magistrate Proc Baggart in the Charleston neck is blamed on poor whites "who fear the negro in the mass worse than they do the devil."

Whatever misery African Americans may suffer, there is no call in ***Mamba's Daughters*** to reform the structures that oppress them or to uplift them as a group. The Reverend Thomas Grayson, a mulatto from New York educated in New England, comes to the phosphate camps on a mission sponsored by northern whites. In his white robe and with his Yankee diction, he offers the Gullah miners and their families a gospel of piety and sober reverence, an alternative to the wildly emotional style of the local black preacher, the Reverend Quintus Whaley. Proc Baggart is prepared to use coercion to expel Grayson as a potentially subversive influence, but the black people themselves have already rejected him and his religion; for the same reason, horses prefer hay to spaghetti, muses Baggart.

Grayson's failed mission in South Carolina illustrates Heyward's notion of the futility of racial reform, but Grayson reappears later in the book to express the author's more optimistic message about the value of individual charity. It is Grayson, now at the head of an elite Harlem church, who provides refuge and assistance to Lissa Atkinson. Between Mamba's diligent efforts, by which she has managed to put away a handsome little nest egg for Lissa, and Grayson's Christian benevolence, Lissa is able to launch a successful singing career and fulfill the dream that Mamba had conceived two decades earlier.

Heyward is ambivalent about the new world that Lissa and others of her race are entering in the 1920s, and so is Lissa. Embraced by Charleston's refined, often northern-educated, mulatto elite and responsive to every opportunity they offer her to develop a musical career and absorb their manners, she is at the same time torn between her (and Mamba's) aspirations for success and her deep bond with the essential nature of her race. In the "copybook gentility" of this tan-skinned elite, music becomes a replica of white culture. Lissa senses the pretentiousness and falseness of the Monday Night Music Club where European classics are played by string ensembles. When she harkens to the rhythm of revival music emerging from a black church she confronts her refined companion, North, to ask: "can't you feel the difference?" "They're having fun when they sing." North, the embodiment of the new Negro, tells her "that's all right for these ignorant negroes . . . We've got to go beyond it." Lissa later reproaches her cultivated friends who speak of racial pride but "are trying their damndest to be white." Heyward ridicules this imitation of white culture because it is a denial of African culture. He often looked through a romantic haze to a rural black culture in the South Carolina Lowcountry which he imagined had been sheltered from the corruption of modern life. Since World War I and the Great Migration of blacks northward, that world was fast disappearing. His views on race seem at first glance little different from traditional southern white paternalism, which viewed slaves and their descendants as childlike and irresponsible. But if he saw in the rural blacks a simple emotional spirit given to song, and sometimes also a primitive savagery capable of violence, he did not seem to see these traits as unchangeable. On the contrary he is resigned to the notion that the cityward and northward migration of blacks will eradicate a traditional African-American culture that could only survive in rural isolation. Heyward's romantic views of African-American culture were not just southern; many northern intellectuals in the 1920s shared this fascination with African primitivism. Like Heyward, they often employed it to criticize the sterility and inhumanity of modern American civilization and the horrifying results of civilization that came with World War I. In an essay entitled **"The Negro in the Low-Country"** (published in 1931 by Charleston's Society for the Preservation of Spirituals), Heyward lamented the passing of the old plantation Negroes, their songs, religion, and simple faith.

"They will be taken from our fields, fired with ambition, and fed to the machines of our glittering new civilization." He wondered whether the Negro "will be much happier when the last of the bonds are severed and finally and triumphantly he has conformed to the stereotyped pattern of American success."

With all its romantic racial stereotypes and its ambiguous message about changing race relations, ***Mamba's Daughters*** was unsettling to many readers. It would be a mistake for contemporary readers to simply dismiss Heyward as just another white apologist for southern race relations without understanding the ways in which he challenged convention. If Heyward discouraged others from the folly of racial reform in his writing, he was involved in "patriotic work" among Charleston blacks during World War I and a member of the Interracial Committee after the war. Local readers were upset by some details in ***Mamba's Daughters,*** such as when Saint Wentworth carries Lissa's bag in New York or when Saint considers addressing a middle-class mulatto as "Mister," both serious breaches of the system of southern racial etiquette that dictated interactions between the races in the age of Jim Crow and, as such, gentle challenges to the reigning orthodoxy in southern race relations. Heyward also gave his black characters a full measure of dignity and humanity that was rare in most literature to that time. He imbued Mamba and Lissa with qualities that defied the usual racial stereotypes. Mamba acts the clown, but behind that mask is a woman of enormous will and ambition for her granddaughter, to say nothing of her calculating shrewdness in manipulating people to serve her design. Indeed, most readers will find Heyward's black characters more fully rendered, more interesting than the arid white figures whose emotions are bound by manners. To the extent that readers come to care about Mamba and her daughters, this story may have been more subversive than the author intended.

Modern readers of this novel will bring to it sensibilities and experience that Heyward never would have anticipated. The pre-World War I world of social class and race and the manners that governed it are barely recognizable to modern Americans. Visitors to Charleston still see remnants of the world Mamba, the Wentworths, and Atkinsons occupied close to a century ago—the beautifully restored old homes and gardens, St. Michael's church and the Hibernian Hall where the St. Cecilia balls still take place, the Gullah women selling baskets on the streets. But these serve largely to remind us of what Mamba understood, that for better and for worse, "time is changin'."

FURTHER READING

Biographies

Allen, Hervey. *DuBose Heyward, a Critical and Biographical Sketch, Including Contemporary Estimates of His Work.* New York: Doran, 1927, 19 p.

Biography by Heyward's friend and co-author of his first published volume of poetry.

Hutchisson, James M. *DuBose Heyward: A Charleston Gentleman and the World of Porgy and Bess.* Jackson: University Press of Mississippi, 2000, 225 p.

Comprehensive biography drawing on nearly fifty years of private papers and on previously untapped personal correspondence that sees Heyward as a southerner who overcame social restrictions to perceive humanity beyond class and color lines.

Criticism

Brown, Rosellen. "On DuBose Heyward's *Peter Ashley.*" In *Classics of Civil War Fiction,* pp. 117-30. Jackson: University Press of Mississippi, 1991.

Examines Peter Ashley, *maintaining that the novel, while engaging, fails to explore the significant social and psychological issues it raises.*

Durham, Frank. "The Rise of DuBose Heyward and the Rise and Fall of the Poetry Society of South Carolina." *Mississippi Quarterly* 19 (spring 1966): 66-78.

Traces Heyward's involvement with the South Carolina Poetry Society, discussing his resignation as president in 1927 and the society's decline thereafter.

Gaines, Clarence. "Americana." *The North American Review* 222 (1925-26): 354-61.

Negative review of Porgy *that says the story evokes sympathy but faults its poor characterization.*

Monroe, Harriet. "A Poet of the Carolinas." *Poetry: A Magazine of Verse* 25 (December 1924): 164-67.

Generally favorable review of Skylines and Horizons *that sees Heyward's poems as rooted in his country and ancestry.*

Rhodes, Chip. "Writing Up the New Negro: The Construction of Consumer Desire in the Twenties." *Journal of American Studies* 28, no. 2 (1994): 191-207.

Discusses Heyward's Porgy *as an example of a "Negrotarian" novel and compares Heyward's attitudes toward capitalism to those of Nella Larsen in her novel* Quicksand.

Shirley, Wayne D. "*Porgy and Bess.*" *Quarterly Journal of the Library of Congress* 31, no. 2 (April 1974): 97-107.

Provides a brief history of Porgy and Bess *and its development from Heyward's novel.*

———. "Reconciliation on Catfish Row: Bess, Serena, and the Short Score of Porgy and Bess." *Quarterly Journal of the Library of Congress* 38, no. 3 (summer 1981): 145-65.

Examines the "short score," or first draft, of Porgy and Bess and the new scene not found in the final, orchestral version.

Stenberg, Theodore T. Review of *Skylines and Horizons. Sewanee Review* 33 (1925): 111.

Finds Heyward's poems tentative and experimental.

Theatre Arts. "'Porgy': The Play That Set a Pattern." *Theatre Arts* 39, vol. 10 (October 1955): 33-34.

Offers a production history of Heyward's play and comments on its transformation into George Gershwin's famous folk opera.

OTHER SOURCES FROM GALE:

Additional coverage of Heyward's life and career is contained in the following sources published by the Gale Group: *Contemporary Authors,* Vol. 157; *Contemporary Authors—Brief Entry,* Vol. 108; *Dictionary of Literary Biography,* Vols. 7, 9, 45, 249; *Something about the Author,* Vol. 21; and *Twentieth-Century Literary Criticism,* Vol. 59.

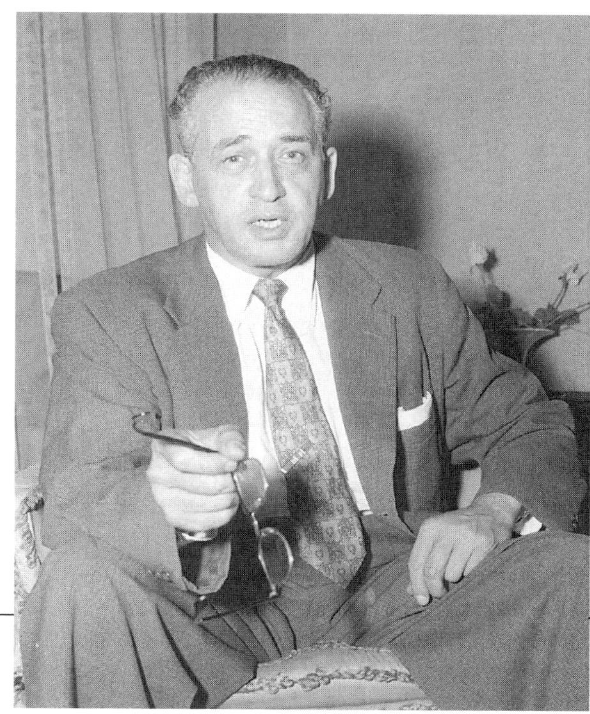

FRANK S. HORNE

(1899 - 1974)

(Full name Frank Smith Horne) American poet and essayist.

Considered one of the second echelon poets of the Harlem Renaissance, Horne is best known for his series of poems titled "Letters Found Near a Suicide" (1925). Although his body of poetry is small, usually expressing a heroic stoicism in the face of personal melancholy rather than indignation at racial oppression, it was admired by such notables of the Harlem Renaissance movement as Langston Hughes, Arna Bontemps, and Countee Cullen.

BIOGRAPHICAL INFORMATION

Little is known about Horne's early life. He was born in Brooklyn, New York, and enjoyed athletic, intellectual, and professional success as a young man. He earned a bachelor's degree at City College, where he was an outstanding track star, a master's degree from the University of Southern California, and a Doctor of Optometry degree from the Northern Illinois College of Ophthalmology and Otology in 1923. He practiced ophthalmology for several years but a paralyzing illness forced him into a wheel chair and led him to seek the warm climate of the South in 1927, when he moved to Georgia. He abandoned ophthalmology entirely and began a career as a teacher and an administrator, which would take him to Washington, D.C., to work with the National Youth Administration, the U.S. Housing Authority, and in Franklin Roosevelt's "Black Cabinet." He returned to New York City in 1938 and remained there as a public administrator in several city housing, finance, and health programs. Although he wrote throughout his life and a slim volume of his poetry, *Haverstraw,* was published in London in 1963, poetry was his avocation rather than his profession.

MAJOR WORKS

Horne is best known for a series of poems grouped together as "Letters Found Near A Suicide," published in *Crisis* magazine in 1925. Addressed to a variety of individuals in the speaker's life, the poems examine various types of suffering and doubt and the protagonist's heroic encounter with the seductive desire for death. "I Am Initiated into the Negro Race" (1928) is one of the few poems by Horne that directly treats racial experience, along with his jazzy "Harlem" (1928) and "Nigger: A Chant for Children (1928)." Many of his later poems concern his physical agonies, paralysis, and his emotional and spiritual struggle to resist despair. In addition to his poetry, Horne contributed many articles, including "Providing New Housing for Negroes" (1940), on the issues involved in administering public schooling, housing, and health programs, most published in *Opportunity* and *Crisis*. He also wrote an anti-racist children's story called "The Man Who Wanted to be Red" (1928).

CRITICAL RECEPTION

Horne's poetry was never well known to the reading public, but it was admired by such luminaries as Langston Hughes and Countee Cullen. In 1925 he was awarded second prize for "Letters Found Near a Suicide" in the Amy Spingarn Contest in Literature and Art sponsored by *Crisis* magazine. Critics continue to discuss Horne's life and work in the context of the Harlem Renaissance and its spirit of encouraging both art and public service.

PRINCIPAL WORKS

"Letters Found Near a Suicide" [published in journal *Crisis*] (poetry) 1925

"Harlem" [published in journal *Crisis*] (poem) 1928

"I Am Initiated into the Negro Race" [published in journal *Opportunity*] (poem) 1928

"The Man Who Wanted to Be Red" [published in journal *Crisis*] (short story) 1928

"More Letters Found near a Suicide" [published in journal *Crisis*] (poetry) 1929

"Henry A. Hunt: Sixteenth Spingarn Medallist" [published in journal *Crisis*] (essay) 1930

"Running Fools: Athletics in a Colored School" [published in journal *Crisis*] (essay) 1930

"Concerning White People" [published in journal *Opportunity*] (essay) 1934

"The Industrial School of the South" [published in journal *Opportunity*] (essay) 1935

"Dog House Education" [published in *Journal of Negro Education*] (essay) 1936

"Providing New Housing for Negroes" (essay) 1940

Haverstraw (poetry) 1963

"Balm in Gilead" [published in journal *Crisis*] (poem) 1965

"Mamma!" [published in journal *Crisis*] (poem) 1966

"He Won't Stay Put: A Carol for All Seasons" [published in journal *Crisis*] (poem) 1970

GENERAL COMMENTARY

FRANK S. HORNE (ESSAY DATE 1924)

SOURCE: Horne, Frank S. "Black Verse." Reprinted in *The Emergence of the Harlem Renaissance,* edited by Cary D. Wintz, pp. 54-6. New York: Garland Publishers, Inc., 1996.

In the following review originally published in Opportunity *magazine in 1924, Horne castigates the editors of an anthology of African American verse for accommodating then prevailing stereotypes of African Americans, and offers a tribute to Countee Cullen.*

". . . And do not ask the poor man not to sing, For song is all he has."—Robert Nathan.

* * *

From the Trinity College Press, Durham, North Carolina, comes an "Anthology of Verse by American Negroes," edited by Newman Ivey White, Ph.D., Professor of English at Trinity College, and Walter Clinton Jackson, Vice President of the North Carolina College of Women, with an introduction by James Hardy Dillard, Ph.D., L.L.D., President of the Jeanes Foundation and the John F. Slater Fund.

We have here something more than just another anthology. It distinguishes itself, on the one side, by coming from the heart of the Southland, by its utter impartiality, and its scholarly completeness; on the other, by its lack of direction in development, absence of personality, and faultiness of viewpoint.

The professors have been most diligent. There is evidence of concentrated application and profound probing into obscure poetical sources. The book is redolent of the South, the schoolroom, and the professorial dictum. The work is scholarly, and the treatment is both critical and sympathetic to some degree. It at least demonstrates that these two southern scholars have looked upon this definite body of literary production, and deemed it worthy of their recognition. But for all that, the anthology is sluggish; it lacks distinction and verse. It possesses neither the vigor and raciness of Professor Talley's folk lore collection, nor the poetical finesse and judgment of James Weldon Johnson's "Book of American Negro Poetry." The book lacks, in a sense, personality. To a student of the subject, the work is undeniably a worthy contribution; but to the reader of verse, it is a volume he can as well get along without.

In an effort to achieve completeness, the authors have included several worthy features. There is a more or less critical and historical general "Introduction"; brief biographies of the authors accompanying the selections; and a mass of "Bibliographical and Critical Notes" at the end. We shall consider them each in turn. The general "Introduction" is truly more historical than critical. The professors, not being poets, lack the poetical judgment and the insight that is so evident in James Weldon Johnson's "Essay on the Negro's Creative Genius" which serves so aptly as an introduction to his own admirable collection. In essence the two viewpoints stand sharply contrasted when it comes to the question of the ultimate contribution of the Negro to American poetry. The professors, after correctly stating that the constant themes of religion and race in Negro poetry contribute nothing new, go on to say: "There is, however, a kind of Negro humor that deals in a distinctively racial manner with the Negro's love of music, talk, animals, meetings, dancing, loafing and fishing, and is best exemplified in the poems of Dunbar, Allen, and Davis. In this direction, the Negro is perhaps likely to make a purely racial contribution to American poetry. Otherwise, his contribution is apt to be individual and not racial in character." And there you have it! The compilers of this volume appear to believe that the "loud guffaw and the wide grin" are the paramount expressions of Negro aesthetics. At this point, I join the company of Johnson, Braithwaite, and DuBois, and vehemently dissent. The Negro poet has long since forsaken the jester's tatterdemalion. His contribution is more subtle and pregnant; more sensitive to the adventures of his own harassed soul. And in support might be offered such examples as "Self-Determination", by Leslie Pinckney Hill; "When I Die", by Fenton Johnson; "Fifty Years", by James Weldon Johnson; "And What Shall You Say", by Joseph Cotter, Jr.,—I offer you William Stanley Braithwaite, Jessie Redmond Fauset, and Claude McKay—and I offer you the youngest voices, Countee P. Cullen, Gwendolyn B. Bennett, and Langston Hughes. With the work of such as these already significant, the dictum of the professors need not be taken too seriously.

The brief biographies of the authors accompanying the selections are adequate and interesting. The critical and bibliographical notes at the end of the volume are indispensable to the student, and add much to the value and completeness of the volume.

As for the body of the poetry included, there is little new or distinctive. The verse up to the time of Dunbar is below any real critical standard. It is to be marveled at, that in this period of sordid darkness, even voice was found to essay song. Its essence is a whimpering prayer for the Balm of Gilead to ease these mortal wounds. From Dunbar on, slowly but surely, the expression takes on form and virility, growing sophistication, and an enlivened interest in the life to be lived here and now. There comes the realization that the life of the Negro is a many sided adventure, worthy of recording.

The authors note that it was lack of education that impoverished earlier Negro poetry. They go on to say that this same lack of education perhaps accounts for the almost total absence of free verse from the mass of Negro poetry. This statement is open to considerable doubt. In the first place, the Negro is essentially lyrical. And the subtle rhythm of the best free verse, it might be urged, is not sufficient for the fullness of his song. From the mass of so-called free verse floating about that has been my lot to read, one might be inclined to express little regret if the Negro never gets educated in that direction. A decided and unmistakable progress in Negro verse, however, is graciously admitted as the compilers conclude that the quality of the poetry has depended generally upon the cultural opportunities of the poets. England took three centuries after the Norman Conquest to produce her first great poet; the Negro has been hardly that long out of Africa! Period for period, we have developed as fully and as rapidly. They see no reason, nor do we, why Negro poets will not reach as ultimate a peak of expression as has ever been or will ever be attained.

After much has been said on either side, we can conclude that the book justifies its existence for us, if only because it includes a selection by Countee P. Cullen. This man, though still very, very young, pens lyrics that already sing. Twice, successively in the last two years, his work has gained second place in the Undergraduate Poetry Contest of the Poetry Society of America; most all of the better magazines have included him in their pages; his sonnets have often topped F. P. A.'s "Conning Tower" in the New York *World:* the *American Mercury* will soon carry something like a hundred and ninety of his lines. He steps with a sure tread, and we expect him to go far.

So set to, makers of black verse. We have already shown that we can write their music, give them their dance, make their money, and play their games. Your task is definite, grand, and fine.

You are to sing the attributes of a soul. Be superbly conscious of the many tributaries to our pulsing stream of life. You must articulate what the hidden sting of the slaver's lash leaves reverberating in its train,—the subtle hates, the burnt desires, sudden hopes, and dark despairs; you must show that the sigh is mother of the laugh they know so well. Sing, so that they might know the eyes of black babes—eyes that so sadly laugh; that they might know that we, too, like Shylock, cry when we are hurt, but with a cry distinctive, and subtly pregnant with overtones, and fraught with hidden associations. Sing, O black poets, for song is all we have!

SARAH M. WASHINGTON (ESSAY DATE 1987)

SOURCE: Washington, Sarah M. "Frank S. Horne." In *Dictionary of Literary Biography,* Vol. 51: *Afro-American Writers from the Harlem Renaissance to 1940,* edited by Trudier Harris, pp. 106-11. Detroit, Mi.: Gale Research, Inc., 1987.

In the following essay, Washington provides an overview of Horne's life and work.

Frank S. Horne is an important minor voice of the Harlem Renaissance whose reputation rests primarily upon a group of award-winning poems he published in the *Crisis* in 1925. His success during this period links him to New Negro Renaissance poets, but his poems are generally more personal and traditional in concern than many of those of the other young writers of the 1920s. While several of these younger artists wrote of the New Negro, his atavistic connections to the deep South and to Africa, Horne focused on death, illness, and a crisis of faith shared by many white writers of the early twentieth century. A northerner who went against the pattern of migration by going to live in the South, Horne wrote poetry early in his life before becoming a physician and an administrator with the United States Housing Authority in Washington, D.C., and later in New York.

Horne was born in Brooklyn, New York, and grew up in that area. He attended undergraduate school at the City College of the City University of New York, where he received his bachelor's degree in 1921. He was an outstanding track star at City College, gaining experience that would serve him in good stead during his teaching career in the late 1920s. He earned a master's degree from the University of Southern California and a Doctor of Optometry degree from Northern Illinois College of Ophthalmology and Otology in 1923. While he was able to practice ophthalmology in Chicago and New York for a few years, his medical profession was cut short by what he called a "mean illness," which forced him to seek a warmer climate. Although information about Horne's life is skimpy, it may be assumed that the illness resulted in some loss of the use of his legs. Many of his later poems use images of failing to walk, of the legs being strapped into cumbersome contraptions, and of the pain associated with "reluctant" legs.

Though he developed an early interest in writing, Horne acknowledged that Charles S. Johnson, editor of *Opportunity,* and Gwendolyn Bennett, one of the younger poets, urged him to publish his work. His first prose was published while he was still a physician; **"Black Verse,"** a review of *Anthology of Verse by American Negroes,* edited by Newman Ivey White and Walter Clinton Jackson, appeared in the November 1924 issue of *Opportunity.* Horne praised the editors for their effort to mark the achievements of Afro-American poets but criticized them for their stereotypical expectations of poetry purely of a racial bent. He singled out the inclusion of work by Countee Cullen for special praise and encouraged other young poets to sound distinct notes in their creativity.

Although Horne wanted to write good prose, he was more successful as a poet. He reached his height of success in 1925, when he received second prize in the poetry category in the Amy Spingarn Contest in Literature and Art sponsored by the *Crisis* magazine. He submitted his winning entry, **"Letters Found Near a Suicide,"** under the pseudonym of Xavier I; the poems were published in the November 1925 issue of the journal. There were eleven letters in the prizewinning version of the poem; by 1930 Horne had added an additional seven poems to **"Letters,"** all of which would be published as the first section of ***Haverstraw,*** his collection brought out by Breman in 1963.

"Letters Found Near a Suicide" is characteristic of the variety of somber issues Horne treats; he describes the setting of a man's preparation for death, during which the persona directs several short poems to individuals who have had significant roles in his life. **"To All of You,"** the first letter in the series, sets the stage for the poetic flirting with suicide; the persona is curious about "the bosom of this deep, dark pool / Of oblivion" and is destined to explore "those far shores / That knew me not." **"To Mother,"** the third letter in the series, bemoans the fact that living is a painful existence beyond man's control. The speaker wonders how anybody can care, particularly his mother, whom he has caused much agony, but he knows the power of a black mother's love. If he dies she will grieve and want him back, because to her suicide is not the answer.

In **"To Chick,"** the tenth and longest letter in the series, the speaker recalls his childhood friend and their football-playing days. Together they had been awesome, charging across lines to score, universally recognized as "The Terrible Two." To offset the possibility that Chick might view his suicide as less than sporting, less than manly, the speaker couches his death in the familiar terms of the football skirmish. He has essentially "scored" in killing himself, moved on to another level of victory that Chick can at least envision vicariously. He urges Chick to remember that they had been great warriors, thereby suggesting that he view this final act from the positive perspective of fighting and winning.

When you gaze at me here
Let that same light
Of faith and admiration
Shine in your eyes
For I have battered the stark stonewall
. . . . .
I have kept faith with you
And now
I have called my signal,
Found my opening
And slipped through
Fighting and squirming
Over the line
To victory . . .

"To Chick" is perhaps the most celebratory of the poems, for others, such as **"To Jean," "To Catalina," "To Mariette,"** and **"To Wanda,"** show the speaker's disappointment in love and his inability to understand his place in the world.

In 1927 illness forced Horne to move from New York to Georgia, where he began a teaching and administrative career at Fort Valley High and Industrial School (later Fort Valley State College). Although he was light enough to pass for white, he did not choose to do so. His coming south, therefore, gave him a perspective comparable to that of Charles Chesnutt. He was especially sensitive to the changes in accommodation and treatment as he journeyed into the South. In **"I Am Initiated Into the Negro Race,"** published in *Opportunity* in 1928, he detailed the transition from privilege and comfort to the physical absence of these luxuries, connecting them to actual travel from points north to those in the South. His initial negative impressions, however, did not prevent him from doing useful work or from supporting the industrial school concept.

He continued his creative efforts in 1928 by publishing **"Harlem,"** a poem, and **"The Man Who Wanted to be Red,"** a short story, in the *Crisis* magazine. **"Harlem"** most approximates the work of other young writers of the period, especially Langston Hughes. Horne uses the background of a saxophonist's performance to conjure up images of what Harlem means. In its experimental stanzaic form and its attempt to imitate jazz rhythms, it is reminiscent of many of the folk-based poems Hughes wrote:

". . . Oh say it, brother
Say it . . ."
Pullman porters, shipping clerks an'
monkey chasers
Actors, lawyers, Black Jews an' fairies
Ofays, pimps, low-downs an' dicties
Cabarets, gin an' number tickets
All mixed in
With gangs o' churches—
Sugar-foot misters an' sun-dodgin' sisters
Don't get up
Till other folks long in bed . . .
. . . Hey! . . . Hey!
"Say it, brother
Say it . . ."

"The Man Who Wanted to be Red" is called "a fairy tale for children of the earth." The story is an allegory of the slave trade and the animosity between blacks and whites in the United States. Horne depicts the "Reds," a predatory race who enslave the "Greens," bringing them to the Kingdom of Ur to work for them. Eventually, some of the Red men notice the beautiful Green women and have children by them. These children become the "Whites," a degraded outcast group. Juda, the protagonist of the story, is a "White." From experiments initially begun by his Red father, he perfects a technique for turning Greeners into Reds. He abandons his plan, however, when he witnesses a group of Reds abusing a Green; he does not want the people with whom he identifies through his mother to turn into such brutes. As a story for children, the piece is engaging through its emphasis upon unusual colors to show how absurd racial prejudices can be.

As trainer of the track team at Fort Valley High, Horne led his runners to several championships in the late 1920s and early 1930s. In **"Running Fools: Athletics in a Colored School,"** published in the *Crisis* in 1930, he discussed the exploits of some of his famous stars (male and female) and introduced the larger world to life in an industrial school. He extended this introduction in **"The Industrial School of the South,"** the two-part series published in *Opportunity* in 1935; he shared the philosophy of training espoused by Booker T. Washington at Tuskegee and was greatly inspired by his example.

Most of Horne's poems first published in the *Crisis* were almost immediately reprinted in anthologies. In 1927 Countee Cullen published **"Letters Found Near a Suicide"** in the critically acclaimed *Caroling Dusk*. He also included **"On Seeing Two Brown Boys in a Catholic Church"** and **"To a Persistent Phantom"** in that volume. **"On Seeing Two Brown Boys in a Catholic Church"** touches on the religious theme that Horne would return to in his poetry. For him, it is initially ironic to see the black boys in a traditionally "white" church, but when he contemplates the matter further, he concludes that their presence is appropriate, for the crucifix upon which they gaze epitomizes their lives. Their existence as black human beings will be equivalent to a cross of suffering associated with their blackness.

Others of his poems from this period are political as well as didactic. For instance, in **"Nigger, A Chant for Children,"** Horne teaches history by listing names of eminent, famous black people such as Hannibal, Othello, and Crispus Attucks. He feels that the world should know these "Niggers," and black children should not be hurt by name calling but be proud of the great ones of the race.

The use of the word "nigger" in the title is a deliberate effort to transcend the negative connotations of that word. It is also a declamation against injustice. In this seven-stanza poem, Horne repeats "nigger" for dramatic emphasis and creates ironic contrasts through the juxtaposition of children's songs and the shouts of the bigot. In spite of persecution and prejudice, he was able to say to Afro-American children that blacks historically have had a great deal to be proud of, and no race-baiting epithets need cause them to lose sight of this fact.

In 1929 Horne published **"More Letters Found Near a Suicide"** in the *Crisis* magazine. The seven new poems included **"To the Poets," "To Henry," "To One Who Called Me 'Nigger,'" "To Caroline," "To Alfred," "To You,"** and **"To James,"** which has perhaps become Horne's most widely read piece of **"Letters Found Near a Suicide."** In **"To James,"** he shows that competition in racing is similar to competition in life. The speaker believes that one must give his best and live his fullest at every moment, and he envies those who are able to do that. The speaker himself feels, as Horne must have felt physically or emotionally, since he was unable to give his best in life due to the "mean illness" to which he often referred.

Live
as I have taught you
to run, Boy—
it's a short dash.
Dig your starting holes
deep and firm
lurch out of them
into the straightaway
with all the power
that is in you
look straight ahead
to the finish line
think only of the goal
run straight
run high
run hard
save nothing
and finish
with an ecstatic burst
that carries you
hurtling
through the tape
to victory . . .

The tone of the advice suggests a father speaking to his son, an imaginative role comparable to the one Horne played with his track students. The reference to victory also harks back to "To Chick" and suggests a pattern of living as well as a code for dying.

During the nine years he worked at Fort Valley High and Industrial School, Horne moved from teaching to serving as dean and acting president. He also occasionally completed prose pieces for journals. In 1930 he wrote the essay for *Crisis* in which Henry A. Hunt, the former principal of Fort Valley High and Industrial School, was recognized for receiving the Spingarn medal. In 1936 he moved out of education and into work with various housing agencies. By 1940 he was acting special assistant to the administrator of the U.S. Housing Authority, and he had turned his attention to writing about problems connected with public housing; his article **"Providing New Housing for Negroes"** appeared in the October 1940 issue of *Opportunity*. His life of public service eclipsed his poetry writing, and it was not until 1963, when the Englishman Paul Breman brought out a collection of his poems, that Horne's poetry became readily accessible to a larger audience.

Haverstraw, Horne's collected poetry, is a thin volume consisting of an expanded eighteen poems in **"Letters Found Near a Suicide,"** which comprises the first section, and eight poems in the second section, entitled **"Haverstraw."** The suicide poems are listed with the notation "(1920-1930)," indicating that their composition extended beyond the original *Crisis* publication in 1925; a section from the last poem, **"To James,"** had appeared as the epigraph for the **"Running Fools"** essay in 1930 as well as in the *Crisis* **"More Letters Found Near a Suicide"** in 1929. The **"Haverstraw"** poems are listed with the notation "(1960)," suggesting that Horne had perhaps had long intervals during which he had not written poems. Except for moving **"To Mother"** to the second position in the series and **"To . . ."** from the eighth position to the sixth, the ordering of the original poems is the same.

In **"To the Poets"** Horne comments on the traditional view of the sentimental poet by describing him as singing "raptures to the grave." Perhaps the grave is the only place the poet's singing may be appreciated. In **"To Henry,"** he suggests that only in the regions of forgetfulness will he find the answers to perplexing problems of being.

The complexities of Horne's own existence are summed up in the sixteenth letter in the collection, **"To You."** Addressing Christ, the persona recounts that he was always taught that by kneeling in church "And eating of your body / And drinking of your blood" he could be born again and saved. However, one night he "offered up / The sacrifice of body / Upon the altar / Of her breast." The speaker upon whom the world weighs heavily queries:

You
Who were conceived
Without ecstasy
Or pain
Can you understand
That I knelt last night
In your house
And ate of your body
And drank of your blood
. . . . and thought only of her?

Through the ambiguous symbol of the woman—a lover, or Mary, or even human nature itself, the poet articulates the problem of having his soul saved by one who was conceived without human feelings—ecstasy or pain. Horne's Catholic background obviously informs the poem.

FROM THE AUTHOR

"HARLEM"

". . . Oh say it, brother
Say it . . ."
Pullman porters, shipping clerks an'
monkey chasers
Actors, lawyers, Black Jews an' fairies
Ofays, pimps, low-downs an' dicties
Cabarets, gin an' number tickets
All mixed in
With gangs o' churches—
Sugar-foot misters an' sun-dodgin'
sisters
Don't get up
Till other folks long in bed . . .
. . . Hey! . . . Hey!
"Say it, brother
Say it . . ."

SOURCE: Frank Smith Horne, excerpt from "Harlem," in *Crisis* 35, June 1928.

The **"Haverstraw"** section of the volume is more personal in orientation, as the dedication reflects: "Lyrics for the halt / To Dr. Seymour Bluestone and his competent staff in token of their interest and compassion." The eight poems make recurring references to physical and spiritual illness, perhaps chronicling Horne's emotional journey through pain and suffering. In **"Walk,"** he stresses the need to walk again in spite of falling: "I know that I will walk again / into your healing / outstretched arms / in answer / to your tender command. . . . / I have been lost / and fallen / in the dark underbrush / but I will arise and walk / and find the path / at your soft command." In **"Mamma!"** he imitates the role of the child in looking for some source beyond himself to reach out and assist "this faltering leg / and this unconscious arm."

In **"Patience"** he symbolically chides those who offer such counsel by describing his pent-up emotions and his desire to have immediate release. He asks if patience will enable him to do routine things such as climb up a stair or pick up a spoon. How can he be patient when he does "not have a hundred years / nor forty / nor ten"? He beseeches the god who measures time in a different way ("To whom a thousand years / are but the wink of a languid eye") to grant him a similar ability to deal with the time that weighs so heavily upon his hands.

Religious references are also the center of **"Hubbard Tank,"** in which the ill body immersed in water is compared to "the baptismal fount / of John the Baptist," and **"Communion,"** in which the poet questions whether death is the only way to be reunited with God, whom circumstances had taught him to live without.

The volume ends with **"Symphony,"** in which the persona pictures the dancing sunlight shining into his sick room upon his "legs strapped in leather" as a variation of the rhythms of the universe.

Are prancing light
and faltering crutch
variations of the dance
of suns
and moons
and pain
and glory
point and counterpoint
to the baton
of the maestro
to whom
all rhythms
and periods
are the stuff
of the symphony
of life . . . ?

The volume is more subdued than joyful, more painful than celebratory. Yet it pictures a poet grappling with some of the central issues of life and being.

After the publication of ***Haverstraw,*** Horne published poems occasionally in the *Crisis,* including **"'Balm in Gilead': A Christmas Jingle"** in 1965, the reprinting of **"'Mamma!'"** from ***Haverstraw*** in 1966, and **"He Won't Stay Put: A Carol for All Seasons"** in 1970. In **"'Balm in Gilead'"** he likens the treatment of blacks during the 1960s, especially the deaths of the five black girls bombed in the church in Birmingham, Alabama, and the assassination of Malcolm X, to the martyrdom of Christ. In **"He Won't Stay Put"** Horne illustrates his ability to change with the times, to use the speech patterns and stanzaic forms typical of the black arts movement; his subject, however, is still the question of the place of religion in the world. "I ain't got me / no piney tree / ain't got no sparkling balls to hang / no golden cord / ain't got no silver strands / to glint delight," he asserts in suggesting that Christmas decoration and Santa Claus are foreign ideas to him. Why look to special seasons for hanging things on trees, he then asks, for every day someone has been nailed on trees, beginning with Christ and extending to Martin Luther King, Malcolm X, Medgar Evers, and others. None of them have "stayed put," which may mean that religion is just as fanciful as Santa Claus or just as likely to fail.

Haverstraw and Horne's sporadically published poems are a testament to the fact that, in spite of the pressures. of illness and public service, he cared enough about creativity to leave a little monument for posterity. When he died in 1974, he was far from being a famous poet, but those who had consistently anthologized his work over the years recognized that his poems were worthy of continued reading and discussion.

FURTHER READING

Criticism

Kerlin, Robert T. "The New Forms of Poetry: Frank Horne." In *Negro Poets and Their Poems,* pp. 206-08. Revised edition. Washington, D. C.: Associated Publishers, 1947.

Reprints several poems by Horne, terming his verse "distinctly original." This collection was first published in 1923.

Primeau, Ronald. "Frank Horne and the Second Echalon Poets of the Harlem Renaissance." In *Remembering the Harlem Renaissance,* edited by Cary D. Wintz, pp. 371–91. New York: Garland Publishers, Inc., 1996.

Examines the work of some lesser-known poets of the Harlem Renaissance, focusing on Horne.

OTHER SOURCES FROM GALE:

Additional coverage of Horne's life and career is contained in the following sources published by the Gale Group: *Black Writers,* Ed. 1; *Contemporary Authors,* Vol. 125; *Contemporary Authors - Obituary,* Vols. 53-56; *Dictionary of Literary Biography,*Vol. 51; and *World Poets.*

LANGSTON HUGHES

(1902 - 1967)

American poet, short story writer, nonfiction writer, novelist, librettist, and playwright.

Regarded among the most significant and prolific American writers of the twentieth century, Hughes was a preeminent figure of the Harlem Renaissance and, with Claude McKay and Jean Toomer, was one of the principal shapers of that movement. With his poem "The Negro Speaks of Rivers" (1921), Hughes celebrated the history, spirit, and endurance of African Americans, themes that would recur throughout his writings. In his first collection of poetry, *The Weary Blues* (1926), Hughes used innovative techniques that looked not to white culture for inspiration, but to the rhythms of African American jazz. Because of his determination to write about the authentic experience of Black America, Hughes was criticized by some of his contemporaries for what they perceived as negative portrayals of African Americans, as well as for dealing with subjects that some reviewers considered not fitting for serious literature. Hughes spent much of his career writing about the experience of Blacks in the United States, exploring issues of race and racism in his poetry, fiction, nonfiction, and plays.

BIOGRAPHICAL INFORMATION

Hughes was born in Joplin, Missouri. His parents separated shortly after his birth, and his father moved to Mexico. Hughes was raised by his grandmother in Kansas until he was thirteen, when he joined his mother in Lincoln, Illinois, after she had remarried. They subsequently settled in Cleveland. Hughes visited his father periodically and spent a year with him in Mexico after graduating from high school. In 1921 Hughes moved to New York, where he enrolled at Columbia University. That same year he published his most famous poem, "The Negro Speaks of Rivers," in the NAACP's magazine *Crisis.* When Hughes could no longer afford to attend Columbia, he moved to Harlem, where he at once became involved in the flourishing literary scene. During the early 1920s Hughes held a series of odd jobs and, working as a seaman, traveled to Africa and Europe. In late 1924, after returning from his travels abroad, he lived in Washington, D.C., then moved back to New York fourteen months later. *The Weary Blues* was published in New York in 1926, launching what was to be an extraordinary literary career. A year later, Hughes published *Fine Clothes to the Jew,* which established him as a major poet of the Harlem Renaissance. The awards he received for his early collections allowed Hughes to finance his education at Lincoln University in Pennsylvania; he finished his degree in 1929. During the late 1920s, Hughes met Charlotte Osgood Mason, an elderly white widow who served as both his literary patron and friend. Strongly committed to developing the talents of young Black artists, Mason supported Hughes while he wrote his first novel, *Not Without Laughter* (1930). Following the book's publication, however, Hughes and Mason suffered a dramatic and bitter break in their relationship. Hughes later reconstructed these events in his short story "The Blues I'm Playing." Like many writers and intellectuals of the time, Hughes sympathized with the principles of socialism. From 1932 to 1933 he lived in the Soviet Union, where he wrote his most politically radical poetry. He spent most of 1934 in California, where he wrote the short story collection *The Ways of White Folks* (1934).

When Hughes's mother fell ill in 1936, he moved to Chicago to earn money for her medical expenses. The following year he went to Spain to work as a war correspondent for a Baltimore newspaper. In the years that followed, he became increasingly well known and received frequent requests to give lectures, enabling him to support himself solely as writer. He also disassociated himself from socialist politics. In 1942 Hughes returned to Harlem and began writing a weekly column in the Chicago *Defender* in the voice of the character Jesse B. Semple, better known as "Simple." The column would run for twenty years and Simple would become the subject of five collections of short stories. By the 1950s Hughes was a well-known and prosperous writer; he continued to write plays, poetry, nonfiction, as well as numerous books for children that introduced young readers to such subjects as the history of Black Americans, Africa, and jazz. By the 1960s he was lionized, and despite the fact that his ideas were considered "old fashioned" compared with those of many militant thinkers of the decade, he continued to write about issues of race and to fight for the ideals, values, and rights of Black Americans. He died in Harlem in 1967.

MAJOR WORKS

Over the course of his forty-five year career, Hughes published more than fifty books, including volumes of poetry, novels, short story collections, books for children, translation, and autobiography. Hughes's writings from the Harlem Renaissance era are among his earliest, and they reveal a young writer exploring the theme of being an African American in the United States. Before the 1920s, race was not considered a worthy literary subject, but Hughes's 1926 essay "The Negro Artist and the Racial Mountain" urged Blacks to claim the freedom to write about racial issues from a perspective of racial pride. Hughes's first poetry collection, *The Weary Blues,* was written to be performed with musical accompaniment in the clubs of Harlem. The influence of jazz and the rhythms of African American music evident in these poems became a signature trait of Hughes's verse. In *Fine Clothes to the Jew* Hughes focuses on depicting the experience of Blacks of the lower classes. Other important works by Hughes from the Harlem Renaissance era include his novel *Not without Laughter,* the play *Mulatto* (1931), and the collections *The Dream Keeper, and Other Poems* (1932) and *Scottsboro Limited: Four Poems and a Play in Verse* (1932). *Not without Laughter* is a story about six apparently simple people from Kansas and their complex inner lives. With these characters, Hughes examines conflicts between races, between older and younger people, between faith and secularism, and between social respectability and personal authenticity. Hughes's two 1932 poetry collections reveal his socialist leanings, and his *Mulatto,* a dramatic account of race relations in the South, was performed on Broadway 373 times. Later works by Hughes of particular note include the poetry collections *Shakespeare in Harlem* (1942), *Fields of Wonder* (1947), and *Montage of a Dream Deferred* (1951); the short story collections *Simple Speaks His Mind* (1950) and *Simple Takes a Wife* (1953); the novel *Tambourines to Glory* (1958); and the autobiographies *The Big Sea* (1940) and *I Wonder as I Wander* (1956).

CRITICAL RECEPTION

When *The Weary Blues* appeared in 1926, Hughes was praised by Alain Locke as being the voice of the Black masses. Others praised the technical innovations of Hughes's poetry, although some, including Countee Cullen, found the racial subject matter inappropriate for poetry. *Fine Clothes to the Jew* received a cooler response, and again there were objections to the depiction of lower-class Black life and to the treatment of such subjects as sexuality, poverty, and violence. *Not without Laughter* also received mixed reviews. Hughes's early works nonetheless earned him a reputation as an important young Black American artist and one of the luminaries of the Harlem Renaissance. In the 1940s and 1950s Hughes's reputation continued to grow. By the time of his death he was considered one of the most significant American authors of the twentieth century. Since his death, hundreds of books and articles have been written about Hughes and his work. A scholarly journal, *The Langston Hughes Review,* established in 1982, is devoted solely to criticism of his writing.

PRINCIPAL WORKS

"The Negro Speaks of Rivers" [published in journal *Crisis*] (poem) 1921

The Weary Blues (poetry) 1926

Fine Clothes to the Jew (poetry) 1927

Not without Laughter (novel) 1930

Dear Lovely Death (poetry) 1931

Mulatto (play) 1931

Mule Bone: A Comedy of Negro Life in Three Acts [with Zora Neale Hurston] (play) 1931

The Negro Mother, and Other Dramatic Recitations (poetry) 1931

The Dream Keeper, and Other Poems (poetry) 1932

Popo and Fifina: Children of Haiti [with Arna Bontemps] (juvenilia) 1932

Scottsboro Limited: Four Poems and a Play in Verse (poetry and play) 1932

The Ways of White Folks (short stories) 1934

Little Ham (play) 1936

Troubled Island (libretto) 1936

Joy to My Soul (play) 1937

Soul Gone Home (play) 1937

Don't You Want to Be Free? (play) 1938

A New Song (poetry) 1938

The Organizer (libretto) 1939

The Big Sea: An Autobiography (autobiography) 1940

Shakespeare in Harlem (poetry) 1942

Freedom's Plow (poetry) 1943

Jim Crow's Last Stand (poetry) 1943

Lament for Dark Peoples, and Other Poems (poetry) 1944

Fields of Wonder (poetry) 1947

Street Scene (libretto) 1948

One-Way Ticket (poetry) 1949

Troubled Island (libretto) 1949

The Barrier (libretto) 1950

Simple Speaks His Mind (short stories) 1950

Montage of a Dream Deferred (poetry) 1951

The First Book of Negroes (nonfiction) 1952

Laughing to Keep from Crying (short stories) 1952

The Glory Round His Head (libretto) 1953

Simple Takes a Wife (short stories) 1953

Famous American Negroes (nonfiction) 1954

The First Book of Rhythms (nonfiction) 1954

Famous Negro Music Makers (nonfiction) 1955

The First Book of Jazz (nonfiction) 1955

The Sweet Flypaper of Life (novel) 1955

The First Book of the West Indies (nonfiction) 1956

I Wonder as I Wander: An Autobiographical Journey (autobiography) 1956

A Pictorial History of the Negro in America [with Milton Meltzer] (nonfiction) 1956

Esther (libretto) 1957

Gabriela Mistral (Lucila Godoy Alcayaga): Selected Poems [translator] (poetry) 1957

Simple Stakes a Claim (short stories) 1957

Simply Heavenly (play) 1957

Famous Negro Heroes of America (nonfiction) 1958

The Langston Hughes Reader (poetry, fiction, nonfiction, essays, plays, and translations) 1958

Tambourines to Glory (novel) 1958

Selected Poems of Langston Hughes (poetry) 1959

The Ballad of the Brown King (libretto) 1960

The First Book of Africa (nonfiction) 1960

Ask Your Mama: 12 Moods for Jazz (poetry) 1961

The Best of Simple (short stories) 1961

Black Nativity (play) 1961

Fight for Freedom: The Story of the NAACP (nonfiction) 1962

Five Plays by Langston Hughes (plays) 1963

Something in Common, and Other Stories (short stories) 1963

Simple's Uncle Sam (short stories) 1965

The Panther & The Lash (poetry) 1967

Good Morning Revolution: Uncollected Social Protest Writings by Langston Hughes (nonfiction) 1973

Arna Bontemps-Langston Hughes Letters, 1925-1967 (letters) 1980

PRIMARY SOURCES

LANGSTON HUGHES (POEM DATE 1921)

SOURCE: Hughes, Langston. "The Negro Speaks of Rivers." *Crisis* (June 1921).

In the following poem, Hughes employs descriptions of rivers to symbolize his own soul as well as the collective spirit of the African American people.

"THE NEGRO SPEAKS OF RIVERS"

I've known rivers:
I've known rivers ancient as the world and older
than the flow of human blood in human
veins.

My soul has grown deep like the rivers.

I bathed in the Euphrates when dawns were
young.
I built my hut near the Congo and it lulled me to
sleep.

I looked upon the Nile and raised the pyramids
above it.
I heard the singing of the Mississippi when Abe
Lincoln went down to New Orleans, and
I've seen its muddy bosom turn all golden in
the sunset.

I've known rivers:
Ancient, dusky rivers.

My soul has grown deep like the rivers.

LANGSTON HUGHES (ESSAY DATE 1926)

SOURCE: Hughes, Langston. "The Negro Artist and the Racial Mountain." In *African American Literary Criticism,* edited by Hazel Arnett Ervin, pp. 44-8. New York: Twayne Publishers, 1999.

In the following essay, written in 1926 in response to George Schuyler's dismissal of an African American racial and literary heritage, Hughes employs the metaphor of a "racial mountain" to describe the obstacles that face a Black writer as both an individual and as a representative of his race.

One of the most promising of the young Negro poets said to me once, "I want to be a poet—not a Negro poet," meaning, I believe, "I want to write like a white poet"; meaning subconsciously, "I would like to be a white poet"; meaning behind that, "I would like to be white." And I was sorry the young man said that, for no great poet has ever been afraid of being himself. And I doubted then that, with his desire to run away spiritually from his race, this boy would ever be a great poet. But this is the mountain standing in the way of any true Negro art in America—this urge within the race toward whiteness, the desire to pour racial individuality into the mold of American standardization, and to be as little Negro and as much American as possible.

But let us look at the immediate background of this young poet. His family is of what I suppose one would call the Negro middle class: people who are by no means rich yet never uncomfortable nor hungry—smug, contented, respectable folk, members of the Baptist church. The father goes to work every morning. He is a chief steward at a large white club. The mother sometimes does fancy sewing or supervises parties for the rich families of the town. The children go to a mixed school. In the home they read white papers and magazines. And the mother often says "Don't be like niggers" when the children are bad. A frequent phrase from the father is, "Look how well a white man does things." And so the word white comes to be unconsciously a symbol of all virtues. It holds for the children beauty, morality, and money. The whisper of "I want to be white" runs silently through their minds. This young poet's home is, I believe, a fairly typical home of the colored middle class. One sees immediately how difficult it would be for an artist born in such a home to interest himself in interpreting the beauty of his own people. He is never taught to see that beauty. He is taught rather not to see it, or if he does, to be ashamed of it when it is not according to Caucasian patterns.

For racial culture the home of a self-styled "high-class" Negro has nothing better to offer. Instead there will perhaps be more aping of things white than in a less cultured or less wealthy home. The father is perhaps a doctor, lawyer, landowner, or politician. The mother may be a social worker, or a teacher, or she may do nothing and have a maid. Father is often dark but he has usually married the lightest woman he could find. The family attend a fashionable church where few really colored faces are to be found. And they themselves draw a color line. In the North they go to white theatres and white movies. And in the South they have at least two cars and house "like white folks." Nordic manners, Nordic faces, Nordic hair, Nordic art (if any), and an Episcopal heaven. A very high mountain indeed for the would-be racial artist to climb in order to discover himself and his people.

But then there are the low-down folks, the so-called common element, and they are the majority—may the Lord be praised! The people who have their sip of gin on Saturday nights and are not too important to themselves or the community, or too well fed, or too learned to watch the lazy world go round. They live on Seventh Street in Washington or State Street in Chicago and they do not particularly care whether they are like white folks or anybody else. Their joy runs, bang! into ecstasy. Their religion soars to a shout. Work maybe a little today, rest a little tomorrow. Play awhile. Sing awhile. O, let's dance! These common people are not afraid of spirituals, as for a long time their more intellectual brethren were, and jazz is their child. They furnish a wealth of colorful, distinctive material for any artist because they still hold their own individuality in the face of American standardizations. And perhaps these common people will give to the world its truly great Negro artist, the one who is not afraid to be himself. Whereas the better-class Negro would tell the artist what to do, the people at least let him alone when he does appear. And they are not ashamed of him—if they know he exists at all. And they accept what beauty is their own without question.

Certainly there is, for the American Negro artist who can escape the restrictions the more advanced among his own group would put upon him, a great field of unused material ready for his art. Without going outside his race, and even among the better classes with their "white" culture and conscious American manners, but still Negro enough to be different, there is sufficient matter to furnish a black artist with a lifetime of creative work. And when he chooses to touch on the relations between Negroes and whites in this country with their innumerable overtones and undertones surely, and especially for literature and the drama, there is an inexhaustible supply of themes at hand. To these the Negro artist can give his racial individuality, his heritage of rhythm and warmth, and his incongruous humor that so often, as in the Blues, becomes ironic laughter mixed with tears. But let us look again at the mountain.

A prominent Negro clubwoman in Philadelphia paid eleven dollars to hear Raquel Meller sing Andalusian popular songs. But she told me a few weeks before she would not think of going to hear "that woman," Clara Smith, a great black artist, sing Negro folksongs. And many an upper-class Negro church, even now, would not dream of employing a spiritual in its services. The drab melodies in white folks' hymnbooks are much to be preferred. "We want to worship the Lord correctly and quietly. We don't believe in 'shouting.' Let's be dull like the Nordics," they say, in effect.

The road for the serious black artist, then, who would produce a racial art is most certainly rocky and the mountain is high. Until recently he received almost no encouragement for his work from either white or colored people. The fine novels of Chesnutt go out of print with neither race noticing their passing. The quaint charm and humor of Dunbar's dialect verse brought to him, in his day, largely the same kind of encouragement one would give a sideshow freak (A colored man writing poetry! How odd!) or a clown (How amusing!).

The present vogue in things Negro, although it may do as much harm as good for the budding colored artist, has at least done this: it has brought him forcibly to the attention of his own people among whom for so long, unless the other race had noticed him beforehand, he was a prophet with little honor. I understand that Charles Gilpin acted for years in Negro theatres without any special acclaim from his own, but when Broadway gave him eight curtain calls, Negroes, too, began to beat a tin pan in his honor. I know a young colored writer, a manual worker by day, who had been writing well for the colored magazines for some years, but it was not until he recently broke into the white publications and his first book was accepted by a prominent New York publisher that the "best" Negroes in his city took the trouble to discover that he lived there. Then almost immediately they decided to give a grand dinner for him. But the society ladies were careful to whisper to his mother that perhaps she'd better not come. They were not sure she would have an evening gown.

The Negro artist works against an undertow of sharp criticism and misunderstanding from his own group and unintentional bribes from the whites. "Oh, be respectable, write about nice people, show how good we are," say the Negroes. "Be stereotyped, don't go too far, don't shatter our illusions about you, don't amuse us too seriously. We will pay you," say the whites. Both would have told Jean Toomer not to write *Cane.* The colored people did not praise it. The white people did not buy it. Most of the colored people who did read *Cane* hate it. They are afraid of it. Although the critics gave it good reviews the public remained indifferent. Yet (excepting the work of DuBois) *Cane* contains the finest prose written by a Negro in America. And like the singing of Robeson, it is truly racial.

But in spite of the Nordicized Negro intelligentsia and the desires of some white editors we have an honest American Negro literature already with us. Now I await the rise of the Negro theatre. Our folk music, having achieved world-wide fame, offers itself to the genius of the great individual American composer who is to come. And within the next decade I expect to see the work of a growing school of colored artists who paint and model the beauty of dark faces and create with new technique the expressions of their own soul-world. And the Negro dancers who will dance like flame and the singers who will continue to carry our songs to all who listen—they will be with us in even greater numbers tomorrow.

Most of my own poems are racial in theme and treatment, derived from the life I know. In many of them I try to grasp and hold some of the meanings and rhythms of jazz. I am as sincere as I know how to be in these poems and yet after every reading I answer questions like these from my own people: Do you think Negroes should always write about Negroes? I wish you wouldn't read some of your poems to white folks. How do you find anything interesting in a place like a cabaret? Why do you write about black people? You aren't black. What makes you do so many jazz poems?

But jazz to me is one of the inherent expressions of Negro life in America; the eternal tom-tom beating in the Negro soul—the tom-tom of revolt against weariness in a white world, a world of subway trains, and work, work, work; the tom-tom of joy and laughter, and pain swallowed in a smile. Yet the Philadelphia clubwoman is ashamed to say that her race created it and she does not like me to write about it. The old subconscious "white is best" runs through her mind. Years of study under white teachers, a lifetime of white books, pictures, and papers, and white manners, morals, and Puritan standards made her dislike the spirituals. And now she turns up her nose at jazz and all its manifestations—likewise almost everything else distinctly racial. She doesn't care for the Winold Reiss portraits of Negroes because they are "too Negro." She does not want a true picture of herself from anybody. She wants the artist to flatter her, to make the white world believe that all Negroes are as smug and as near white in soul as she wants to be. But, to my mind, it is the duty of the younger Negro artist, if he accepts any duties at all from outsiders, to change through the force of his art that old whispering "I want to be white," hidden in the aspirations of his people, to "Why should I want to be white? I am a Negro—and beautiful!"

So I am ashamed for the black poet who says, "I want to be a poet, not a Negro poet," as though his own racial world were not as interesting as any other world. I am ashamed, too, for the colored artist who runs from the painting of Negro faces to the painting of sunsets after the manner of the academicians because he fears the strange unwhiteness of his own features. An artist must be free to choose what he does, certainly, but he must also never be afraid to do what he might choose.

Let the blare of Negro jazz bands and the bellowing voice of Bessie Smith singing Blues penetrate the closed ears of the colored near-intellectual until they listen and perhaps understand. Let Paul Robeson singing "Water Boy," and Rudolph Fisher writing about the streets of Harlem, and Jean Toomer holding the heart of Georgia in his hands, and Aaron Douglas drawing strange black fantasies cause the smug Negro middle class to turn from their white, respectable, ordinary books and papers to catch a glimmer of their own beauty. We younger Negro artists who create now intend to express our individual dark-skinned selves without fear or shame. If white people are pleased we are glad. If they are not, it doesn't matter. We know we are beautiful. And ugly too. The tom-tom cries and the tom-tom laughs. If colored people are pleased we are glad. If they are not, their displeasure doesn't matter either. We build our temples for tomorrow, strong as we know how, and we stand on top of the mountain, free within ourselves.

GENERAL COMMENTARY

R. BAXTER MILLER (ESSAY DATE 1986)

SOURCE: Miller, R. Baxter. "'Some Mark to Make': The Lyrical Imagination of Langston Hughes." In *Critical Essays on Langston Hughes,* edited by Edward J. Mullen, pp. 154-66. Boston: G. K. Hall, 1986.

In the following essay, Miller presents an assessment of Hughes's poetry.

W. R. Johnson, a superior theorist, illuminates the lyric well:

> We want the pictures, yes, but we also want the hates and loves, the blame and the praise, the sense of a living voice, of a mind and heart that are profoundly engaged by a life they live richly, eagerly. Art, then, any art, is not a reproduction of what is seen: it is a highly complex action (action both by artist and audience) in which what is outer and what is inner—things, perceptions, conceptions, actualities, emotions, and ideas—are gathered into and made manifest by emotional and intelligible forms. The artist cannot be undisciplined in searching for such forms; . . . he can no more be slovenly in his habits of feeling and thinking than he can be slovenly in his habits of looking and listening or of using the implements of his craft; but neither can he be dispassionate, emotionless, unconcerned. The lie in modern imagism is that no one snaps the picture. But the difference between a bad or mediocre photo and a good or great one is precisely who takes the photo—and the photographer, like any other artist, is defined not merely by his technique or his mastery of his instrument but also by the quality of his feeling, by the precision and vitality . . . which his composition captures and reveals . . . the thing that called his mind and heart into action. . . .[1]

The words describe well many poems by Langston Hughes, one of Black America's greatest lyricists. Over nearly sixty years one has hardly dared think so. While the Greeks believed the lyric to be a communal performance in song, the shared epiphany between the singer and the audience, the form implied the aristocratic elitism at court during the Middle Ages and the Elizabethan period. In the romantic and Victorian eras, the genre suggested privacy and isolation from the masses. Today, somewhat diminished in favor of the dramatic monologue, as poetry has possibly ebbed into esoterism, those who prefer personal lyric often disclaim the social rhetoric of direct address. Indeed, one might almost take Langston Hughes at his word and accept the distinction between the forms. But while the margins between genres are convenient, they are yet flexible and partly illusory. Literary forms really mean only variations in degree. **"The Negro Speaks of Rivers"** (*Crisis,* June 1921), Hughes's first published poem, displaces the personal reflection, or the narrative, through a sequence of shifts from ancient Egypt in 3,000 B.C. to the United States in the nineteenth century. Through the speaker's placement in history, it leads back to the present. Drawing upon the narrative and the dramatic elements, the poem celebrates Black America and humankind.

But, ironically, Black American history complicates the appreciation of Hughes as a lyricist. In a personal voice the poet revises the tradition he inherited. Where Phillis Wheatley praised George Washington, he honors the Black Everyman and, indeed, Everyperson. Though his contemporary, Countee Cullen, depended on sources in the poetry of John Keats, Hughes relied on allusions to the folk ballads of 1830-50 and on the nature and prophetic poems of Walt Whitman. Hughes drew upon the more contemplative verse of Vachel Lindsay. Where Paul Laurence Dunbar had earlier accommodated himself to the Old South, Hughes revised the pastoral for the times. But, as regards the folk integrity, Hughes was less naive.

From ***Weary Blues*** in 1926, to **"Daybreak in Alabama"** at the end of ***Panther and the Lash*** in 1967, the lyric serves to open and close Hughes's literary life and work.[2] When other genres attract his attention, this one retains particular resilience. But the impulse wanes in the fifties and sixties. For Langston Hughes the lyric illuminates the graphic and timeless. Against the backdrop of time, he invokes dynamic feeling in order to subordinate and control personal loneliness, but he never excludes the communal response. In retrospection, he downplays the narrative of miscegenation (**"Cross"**) and the allegorical tragedy (**"Pierrot"**) into precise understatement. Or he sometimes disguises the lyrics themselves as dramatic performances through the blues song and the jazz instrument. What one finds ultimately in the lyricist concerns the sensitive self who speaks to Nature and the masses. In an epiphany the solo and the chorus face each other, at the height of the performance, itself timeless through intensity and will, but the personae live within three decades (1920-40), no matter how universal the writer dreams them to be. Whether in the twenties or the forties, one ultimately redescends from **"The Negro Speaks of Rivers"** or from **"Oppression"** to the fallen world.[3] From the poetic re-creation of Black American history in particular and the American South in general, the narrator inevitably returns to a certain death in Harlem. Sequential history is fact.

For Langston Hughes the lyric highlights the human and social dream. Incarnated in the blues singer and player, it signifies the artistic performance in general. It suggests the oral teller and the cultural priest, who recount the sacred story about experience and the past. From the history of 1855-65, the lyric records the poetic remembrance of the Civil War and the presence of one poet, Walt Whitman, who wrote it down.[4] Almost indifferent to the historical context, the speaker never mentions whom Whitman met, or when, or says why so. Including the death of Abraham Lincoln, the narrator overlooks the troubled circumstances. But what he manages yet involves a frozen moment in human and self-communion. Sometimes disguised as the blues performance, Hughes's lyric first subsumes social rhetoric into epiphany (***The Weary Blues,*** 1926). Then it encourages inquiry into the technical means for the evocation of awe and wonder, for astonishment, and for the sublime.[5] Finally, the lyric demonstrates the compression and acrostic power in ***Fields of Wonder*** (1947). Over the years Langston Hughes abandons much lyricism to the use of dramatic monologue.

Largely to assess the significance of the change, it profits one to define the purpose and function of lyric.[6] The genre involves poetic emotion which, expressed in time, insists that time itself or, sequential thought, is illusion. Just as the lyric quality displaces the narrative poem on the grand scale, so it often represses from itself much analytic idea and dramatic action. Yet lyric situates itself in the dramatic context from which emotion emerges. Though drama takes place in history and time, the lyric distances itself from them. While the drama tends to move, the lyric remains still. The drama reveals the development of plot and character, but the lyric illuminates the progression of emotion. While the drama signifies the narrative and historical action, the lyric signifies the story of the self. At times Langston Hughes succeeds through the projection of the lyric personality into the narrator who speaks and feels truly. While the implicit dramatic action depends upon time and space, the particular situation, the lyric quality suspends them. And though a play such as ***Mulatto*** benefits from a precise setting, **"The Negro Speaks of Rivers"** reveals the permanency of memory and human existence.

However academic the overtones, any elitist assessment of Langston Hughes's lyrics must fail. Open to the range of human emotion, they express misanthropy, egoism, or cynicism.[7] In the display of the solo self, they reveal a concern for the choral one as well.[8] Here the individual talent speaks within cultural and racial tradition. So even Hughes's lyrics are covertly rhetorical. Where poetic images exist, as part of human language, they necessarily contribute to emotive and moral discourse. For the Black American and social poet, they intensely reconfirm the tension between the pictured world (American Dream) and the real one (racial lynching): "A totally unrhetorical poetry will be, as we have come to know all too well, a poetry void of passion, void of choosing, void of rational freedom—it will be in Paul Valery's metaphor, the rind of the orange without the pulp and the juice."[9] Even lyric distills the sublime, the humane and social spirit that informs figurative language: "In our technological societies, when the individual human began more and more to feel cut off from his fellows and from the world, when inwardness became less a matter of anger and terror, the modern choralists, in their different ways, attempted to countervail this process of alienation by reaffirming our kinship with each other and with the world that begets us and nourishes us, by denying that the exploitations of empire and the degradations worked by the machine had or would or could succeed. . . ."[10]

To recognize the covert rhetoric in lyric means to appreciate the overlap between emotive and discursive poetry.[11] Rooted in song, the lyric reestablishes the ritual of human communion. From the ancients who sang out the odyssey, to Woody Guthrie and Bob Dylan, to Roberta Flack and Lionel Richie, the flow contains an inspirational power nearly akin to religion. What one remembers, finally, concerns the double presence that allows Langston Hughes to speak at once within and without history, to participate in the dynamic story, yet inertly reflect upon it, to read as well as feel the meaning.

For Langston Hughes the lyric imagination bridges the prelapsarian and lapsarian worlds. Aware of the discrepancy between the American word and deed, he hardly mistakes the country itself for the ideal. The imagination and social mind separate only in the failure to impose the coherent vision upon the entire range of human experience. While the tragic ***Mulatto,*** or the comic ***Semple Takes a Wife*** represents the diverse sides present, the lyrics express the duality of the whole imagination. The poems convert fact into value, power into thought, and the "dualism of word and deed into an orphic unity."[12] While Hughes's speakers perform the historical rites from the Harlem Renaissance (1920-28), from the Great Depression (1930s), from World War II (1940s), and from the Civil Rights Movement (1954-68), they supersede historical sequence. They contain ideals that transcend time or, indeed, Time (human pattern): "'words' and 'silence' denote two different states of feeling, the second higher and purer than the first. Words issue from time (*tempus*) and are vitiated by the penury of our daily concerns. However, they know enough to aspire to a higher and purer state, given in Eliot's lines as 'form' and 'pattern' in which the mere contents of form are not transcended but enhanced, fulfilled, redeemed. Silence is therefore a scruple which attends upon the local satisfaction of words, the voice which says that words are often self-delusions, trivial gratifications. Silence speaks against time to redeem time. Silence therefore corresponds to the fine excess of the imagination."[13] Hughes's lyric voice clarifies his own signature to Black American history. Shaped through words themselves become symbols,[14] it mediates between antonyms which are untranslatable, at least completely, into each other, including Black and White, Harlem and Africa, war and peace. However apparently private, the lyrics ultimately implode back into the folk center implied. Where the images suggest cultural beliefs and myths, the values are Black American: "Expressions cannot save us from temporality, but thanks to symbols, we can ascend to the realm of eternity."[15] While Hughes's lyricism displaces the drama and narrative of Black American history, it nevertheless signifies the passage from the Harlem Renaissance to the Civil Rights Movement. The lyrics imply the very drama which they displace, the advance from tragedy to peace.[16] While Hughes confines racial suffering and conflict to the half-light, he clarifies the need for reconciliation. Langston Hughes reclaims from American history the right to reimagine Black humanity and, indeed, humankind.[17]

A broad overview of ***The Weary Blues*** clarifies the thematic unity and diverse technique. Grouped according to seven romantic ideas, sixty-eight poems appear under seven headings. While the emphasis goes to the collective consciousness derived from African ancestry in particular and human history in general, other concerns are personal loneliness, isolation, and loss. Still signifying the Harlem Renaissance and the jazz age, a third set presents the cabarets, infusing interracial sex within overtones of the exotic. In a deftness often overlooked, Hughes uses anaphora to narrate an imperial self so as to sustain the blues stanza as countermelody and ironic understatement. What most complements the lyric skill concerns the dramatic movement of feeling. Through the impulse, he portrays the child's maturation into the state of the lost imagination and the transmutation of suffering into art. In narrative distancing his speakers achieve a double identification. While they situate themselves in the dramatic situation implied, they share the reader's historical consciousness. The lyric hardly represents all of the range, but the formal movement does counterplay to the dramatic tragedy suggested.

Indeed, the performance in the title poem completes the ritualistic conversion from Black American suffering into epic communion. On 1 May 1925, during a banquet at an "elegant" Fifth Avenue restaurant in New York City, the poem won a prize from *Opportunity* magazine, where it subsequently appeared. The thirty-five-line lyric presents a singer who plays one night on Harlem's Lenox Avenue. Having performed well in the club, the pianist goes to bed, as the song still sounds in the mind. In the dull pallor, and beneath the old gas light, he has played his ebony hands on the ivory keys. During the "lazy sway" from the bar stool, he has patted the floor with his feet, done a few chords, and then sung some more. Finally, he sleeps "like a rock that's dead," the artistic spirit exhausted.[18]

His performance clearly implies several dramatic actions. While one sets the dynamic playing, the Black self-affirmation against what fades, a second concerns a vital remaking of the Black self-image. A third shows the transcendence through racial stereotype into lyrical style. From the dramatic situation of the player, both musical as well as performed, the poem imposes the isolation and loneliness, yet the refusal to accept them. The song marks a metonym for the human imagination.

When Hughes's speakers step back from the dramatic performance into the lyric perception, they delimit the space of dream, sometimes in covertly sexual metaphor. At the detached distance from any dramatic situation, they even remake the iconography of Black and White, often revising and neutralizing the traditional code of culture, race, and value. Written in two stanzas, **"Dream Variations"** has nine lines in the first part and eight in the second one. While the persona longs for his dream, he sees the externalization in Nature, the place and the sun. What confronts him concerns the very duality of dream, which exists only in the lyric moment of timelessness. For the player within the concealed story, on the night in 1924, the performance must be completed in time to assure the customary paycheck.

While the lyric dream may therefore seem static, it finally has a meaning in the dynamic world of social change, where it would decay. In **"Dream Variations"** the Black self impregnates the lighted world and even Time itself. While the phallic drive into the Harlem Renaissance, the advance in chronological time, is finite, the vaginal response to sentiment, as the imaginative reassertion, remains infinite. Insofar as the Western world asserts the priority of linear time over the natural frontier, the view ultimately vanishes into darkness. Survival depends upon universal harmony with the world.

whirl
Till the white day is done
Then rest at cool evening
Beneath a tall tree
. . . .

A tall, slim tree
Night coming tenderly
Black like me

Here the speaker balances the double compulsion toward reason and light (white day) with the mythic sentiment which justifies life.

While the double identification with phallic time and vaginal time-lessness appears perhaps most notably in **"The Negro Speaks of Rivers"** (*Crisis,* June 1921), a poem dedicated to the late W. E. B. Du Bois, it is more essential to the well-crafted and allegorical **"Jester." "Rivers"** presents the narrator's skill in retracting known civilization back to the source in East Africa. Within thirteen lines and five stanzas, through the evocation of wisdom and anagoge, one marks human consciousness. Then the speaker affirms the spirit distilled from human history, ranging from 3,000 B.C., through the mid-nineteenth century to the author himself at the brink of the Harlem Renaissance.[19] The powerful repetend, "I've known rivers. / Ancient, dusky rivers," closes the human narrative in nearly a circle, for the verse has subtly turned itself from an external focus to a now unified and internal one: "My soul has grown deep like the rivers." Except for the physical and spiritual dimensions, the subjective "I" and the "river" read the same.

So East Africa marks the source for both physical and spiritual humanity. When the Euphrates flows from East Turkey southeast and southwest into the Tigris, it recalls the rise as well as the fall of the Roman Empire. For over two thousand years, the water helped delimit the domain. Less so did the Congo which south of the Sahara demarcates the natural boundaries between White and Black Africa. The latter empties into the Atlantic Ocean, just as the Nile flows northward from Uganda into the Mediterranean. In the United States, the Mississippi River flows in the southeast from North Central Minnesota to the Gulf of Mexico. Whether north or south, east or west, the rivers signify in concentric half-circles the fertility as well as the dissemination of life. For the imaginative mind, the liquid externalizes the flow and depth. In suggesting the challenge to explore brave new worlds, Europe and the Americas, **"The Negro Speaks of Rivers"** reclaims the origins in Africa.

Just as the speaker in **"The Negro Speaks of Rivers"** stands outside of historical time, so the narrator in "Jester" distances himself from literary forms as well:

> In one hand
> I hold tragedy
> And in the other
> Comedy—
> Masks for the Soul

Detached from the dramatic situation, the narrator makes a choral appeal without didacticism, not excluding the epigrammatic twist, abruptly closing the lyric in understatement and rhetorical question. Here appears the invocation to chorus through recovery of the solo:

> Laugh at my sorrow's reign.
> I *am* the Black jester
> The dumb clown of the world,
> . . . .
>
> Once I was wise
> Shall I be wise again?

What some would mistake for simplistic discourse is thoughtful reflection.

While the lyric dream in Langston Hughes suggests the personal solo, the sea implies the choral response in Nature. Sometimes the parts coalesce in an epiphany. **"As I Grew Older"** tells about the persona's loss of a dream and the subsequent disillusion. The poem opens with a memory of the ideal, but the rising wall eclipses it. In color the "dark hands" resemble the shadow. What challenges the speaker concerns the need to deconstruct the negative associations and to reimage himself as positive Black light.

While the social restrictions (the wall) exist during the 1920s, they ironically imply the dream that transcends Time. In the rise, the wall demonstrates the dynamic recurrence. The social eclipse appears as "dimming" and "hiding." When dynamism leads finally to stasis, the solo self invokes Nature:

> Find my dream!
> Help me to shatter this darkness,
> To smash this night;
> To break this shadow
> Into a thousand lights of sun,
> Into a thousand whirling dreams
> Of sun!

Where color was descriptive ("my dark hands"), it becomes metaphorical, for any real "darkness" exists within.

Whatever the imminent dangers, the sea provides a means for lyric escape. Written in two stanzas, **"Water-Front Streets"** is simply a romantic ballad that shows a movement from external nature to the poetic mind. Hughes achieves the personal revision of the pastoral tradition in English. Evolved from Edmund Spenser, the genre was already decadent by the time of Alfred Lord Tennyson, but it subsisted in the lyrics of the Georgians near the turn of the century, just as it does today in confessional and neo-romantic poetry. While biographical and autobiographical sources generally note Lindsay and Lowell as the major influences on Hughes's verse, the diction and tone suggest Tennyson's "Crossing the Bar" (1889). The placement of life and death reverses itself, "But lads put out to sea / Who carry their beauties in their hearts / And dreams, like me." From Milton's "Il Penseroso" to Gray's "Elegy Written In A Country Churchyard," Gothic ascent and romantic isolation suggest the evolution of English lyricism. When the sailor (the poet) lifts anchor in "A Farewell," those on shore hardly miss him. Realists lack patience with dreamers. The gypsies and the sailors are metonyms, or the "wanderers of the hills and seas." Seeking the fortune, they leave "folk and fair." For Hughes's speakers, the invoked chorus provides only silence, for the "you" who live between the hills / And have never seen the seas." And they counterplay to the poet, the Black Odysseus. In **"Seascape"** Hughes's narrator redescends from lyric heights to sequential history. When a ship passes off the coast of Ireland, the seamen view a line of fishing ships etched against sky. Later, off the coast of England, the seamen ride ("rode") the foam where they observe an Indian merchant "coming home." Still, realism infringes upon the dreamworld. While the seascape is a revelation, the speaker rides in time as well, not merely toward his literal "home" but toward death.[20]

For Langston Hughes the lyric arrests the movement of the personal narrative toward extinction. **"Death of an Old Seaman"** portrays a persona who has returned home. Through alliteration and assonance, he appears against the background of the hill and sea. In facing the winds, he sets into relief all of the natural elements except fire, possibly because his life now ends. The musical recovery may exist as much within the narrative content as in the sentimental rhythm. Clearly a ballad more than a lyric, **"Beggar Boy"** dramatizes the mysterious performance of a black flute player. Despite the poverty, he incarnates the creativity that eludes all imagery. Distilled from Black American deprivation, the introspection tells: "And yet he plays . . . / As if Fate had not bled him. . . ." However much the final line bumps, the beggar boy remains a "shadow," but the narrator truly reads the "Fate." The story resembles the boy's "flute," the "sun." What the child feels but cannot articulate, the speaker understands well. As the signs for self-determination, the story and song oppose dark fate.

In ***Fields of Wonder*** (1947) Hughes disproves the critic's arbitrary and condescending claim: "His lyric poetry is no doubt of secondary importance in his work; yet, as usually happens with the minor work of great artists, this minor (lyric) poetry is high enough in quality and great enough in quantity to have sustained the reputation of a lesser poet."[21] Where the prescriptive critic favors the "social" verse, he accepts too readily the distinction between lyric and rhetoric.[22] But what generates the lyrical power in ***Fields*** conceals the real concern with community. While the persona feigns privacy, he addresses the men and women who would hear him, for the lyric, like the dramatic monologue, implies the respondent. Sometimes the hearer is anthromorphic Nature, almost elegiac in the counterplay and impervious to Time.

In ***Fields*** Hughes makes the external world (fields) parallel the personal sentiment (desire and tears). The language shows greater compression. Derived from the acrostic design, it displays alliteration as well as assonance. What sometimes begins as a skillful apostrophe ends in rhetorical and cryptic counterpoint.[23] Published originally in the *Christian Register* (May 1947), a twelve-line lyric, **"Birth,"** signifies the artistic credo. Without direct address to the social mission, as does the "cool poet" in **"Motto,"**[24] it images the creative calling into the metonyms of stars, moon, and sun. Just as the lyric emotion subsides into the lyric process, so the pictorial frieze fades into the surge of dramatic action. Private feeling has become public deed. Where the social revolutionary seems displaced, he still speaks in undertone. Indeed, he imposes the signature and voice upon human history: "stroke / Of lightening / In the night / Some mark to Make / Some Word / to Tell." Indirectly, the persona partially confirms: "The imagination deals with feelings preferably wayward, congenitally wild, and it wants to move them not into formulae but toward the state of value and purity for which Eliot's 'form' and 'pattern' at once moving and still. . . . The imagination makes nothing happen, but it lets things happen by removing obstacles of routine and providing a context of feeling from which they appear naturally to emerge."[25] But for Langston Hughes the lyrical imagination is dynamic and fertile.

"Carolina Cabin," a neglected poem, displaces lyricism into the dramatic situation. In twenty-two lines and four stanzas, two lovers take warm refuge near a fireplace. Viewed first as an imaginative landscape, the setting has hanging moss, holly, and "tall straight pine." The unfolding drama parallels the narrator's silent movement inward. Near the cracking fire and rare red wine, the narrator hears good laughter. When he looks then outward, the gloomy world has

> The winds of winter cold
> As down the road
> A wandering poet
> Must roam.

Still, the plot peacefully evolves itself in reinforced laughter. Where love's old story recurs, people make a home. The poem reveals the angle on post-World War II alienation in the United States. While the aesthetic world lures the narra-

FROM THE AUTHOR

"THE NEGRO MOTHER"

I have written the "The Negro Mother" with the hope that my own people will like it, and will buy it. If they do, I shall write other booklets of both verse and prose in this unpretentious fashion, to sell for as reasonable a price.

SOURCE: Langston Hughes, excerpt from a letter to William Pickens, October 13, 1931, from the William Pickens Papers, the Schomburg Center for Research in Black Culture.

tor, he must eventually return to realistic commitment. The diction has both secular and religious connotations. As a participant in the racial narrative implied, the speaker achieves the mythic dimensions of the Wandering Jew. In the way, he perceives the limits of literary myth and historical reality.

"Old Sailor," far less dramatic and well-structured, subordinates the lyric quality to greater narrative. For twenty lines, a paralyzed mariner fancies women all over the world lament his absence. Indebted to Hughes's own days as a sailor (1923-24), the tragicomic poem completes the career vicariously. The literary work closes the frame on the historical life. In the first twelve lines, the narrator has "tasted" mysteries in Oriental cities. With Bohemian joy and international sorrow, he pursues the Dionysian urge. Then, in the last eight lines, he deteriorates into a poor dreamer. Unable to perform "heroic" deeds, he remembers from youth the sexual prowess and laughter. Yet while the mind itself faces decay, it "re-minds" itself of the spiritual recovery that resists physical death. Embodied in Time, the poetic urge remains timeless.

In twenty-four lines and four stanzas, **"Sailing Date"** tells the story of old mariners who face the fading years. Here are the twist, strangeness, and "bitter rage" of the lives. The sailors have deteriorated from youthful adventure ("salt sea water") to lushness ("whiskey shore"). While the decline marks the broken dreams and the imminent aging, the men narrate the past. Experienced in a thousand storms, they have survived world wars. Since the days when submarines once threatened them, they have mastered an ironic indifference.

For the tone Hughes draws heavily upon the poetry of England and the United States, especially from the nineteenth century, though the sources still merit original consideration.[26] In "O Captain! My Captain!" Whitman alludes to Abraham Lincoln (history) and to God (eternity). For "Crossing the Bar," on the contrary, Tennyson allegorizes God (the Pilot) alone. And Hughes himself celebrates Whitman in **"Old Walt,"**[27] a poem which appropriately reappeared in a chapbook called ***The Pilot*** (26 December 1954). Whether about the president during the Civil War or the God beyond, the narrator portrays events within historical time, but imaginatively projects himself beyond them. The implicit drama of history underscores Lincoln's death and Tennyson's life, but the lyric highlights the symbolic actions of mourning and faith. Thus in the repressed rhetoric Hughes's lyrics bridge the disparate worlds of fact and value.

In **"Trumpet Player: 52nd Street,"** as in **"The Weary Blues,"** the dramatic performance completes the lyrical impulse.[28] The quality implodes in the instrumental metaphor rather than in the choral rhetoric. During the forty-four lines, the player distills jazz from old desire and hardship. Then, with the trumpet at his lips, he blows against and through the ambivalence for acculturation, the paradox of racial identity. In the "tamed down hair," the straightened "process" he demonstrates more than style, for he would resemble Whites whose hair is naturally so. But what the player has accepted socially, he rejects artistically. The inner Black light, the implicit metaphor, "glows" brilliantly through the "process" and "gleams" as "jet [Black] were yet a crown."

What gives the image dramatic power concerns the lighted frieze in the counterplay to the persona's inner light and, indeed, to the musical time in the played song as well as to Time. The light on the player moves so fast as to feign no movement. But the music, the movement of which is clearly heard, sounds rhythmically. And the music reminds the reader that the temporal lapse between 1947 and 1985, indeed the future, is hardly the static illusion by which speeding light tricks the eye. Immediate in the challenge to lyrical experience, history and time are real. Distanced from them, the narrator focuses on different angles for the trumpeter and for the performance. Partly identifying with the sound and light, he narrates the communion of the dramatic performance. In the arrestment of time, both auditory (sound) and visible (light), the player mixes "honey" with "liquid fire," an oxymoron in flowing and "burning" sweetness. The dynamic performance merely plays out the inert desire. Though the scene gives the illusion of permanence, he expresses "longing for the moon" and "longing for the sea." In the reflection of the moonlight, from earth at night, he has resolved a paradox, for if fire can flow yet appropriate to itself the quality of the contrasting element, water, so the imagination might reverse the very racial terms through which poets image human experience. Literary light, like the trumpeted song, may well be Black. And the Black light exercises the previous self-disillusion. When the repetend reinforces the dramatic performance, including the frieze, the player sports his "one-button roll" or jacket. In the convenient shift from the dramatic mode to the lyric one, the narrator wonders about the trumpeter's motivation.

While the performance obscures the lyric form itself, the latter subsides in the instrumental music. Herein modernity only appears to have displaced the pastoral world. Through rhetorical convention, the soloist delivers the song to the chorus but expects no answer. While any reaffirmations are silent from the poem, they are yet implied. Thus Langston Hughes, like Ezra Pound, "found that he loved and praised only what Pindar and Horace and Johnson and Whitman had loved and praised: perfection of good order, the kinship of earth, the earth herself in her epiphanies of fertility, Nature, and culture, the paradises of earth and the unearthly paradises that engender them, the dignity of humankind and of the universe. Like his predecessors in choral, he had also blamed what offered to harm or destroy what he loved and praised, but he had spent too much time in blaming. And the joy and celebration survived even that."[29]

Even the sensitive insight implies the illusions that Western critics impose upon human history. At least three thousand years before Pindar, the lyric in Africa must have made for the communal recitation during which the original humans listened to history from the oral teller. Today the lyric still marks the ritual through which the self and society collectively reaffirm community. Whether the song is vocal or instrumental, the writer's narrators merely displace the racial history that the speakers inevitably signify. The lyric implies both the social narrative and the dramatic event. Never completely detoured into aristocratic and private poetry, Langston Hughes helps restore the ancient form to rhetorical timelessness.

Notes

1. W. R. Johnson, *The Idea of Lyric* (Berkeley: University of California Press, 1982), 23.
2. See R. Baxter Miller, "'A Mere Poem'; 'Daybreak in Alabama,' Resolution to Langston Hughes's Commentary on Music and Art," *Obsidian* 2 (1976):30-37.
3. I am mainly concerned here with *The Weary Blues* (1926; reprint, New York: Alfred A. Knopf, 1945) and *Fields of Wonder* (New York: Alfred A. Knopf, 1947).
4. See Donald B. Gibson, "The Good Black Poet and the Good Gray Poet: The Poetry of Hughes and Whitman," in *Modern Black Poets,* ed. Donald B. Gibson (Englewood Cliffs, N.J.: Prentice-Hall, 1973), 43-56; reprinted from *Langston Hughes: Black Genius,* ed. Therman B. O'Daniel (New York: William Morrow, 1971).
5. Edmund Burke, *The Philosophy of Edmund Burke,* ed. Louis I. Bredvold and Ralph G. Ross (Ann Arbor: University of Michigan, 1967), 256-67.
6. See Felix E. Schelling, *The English Lyric* (Boston: Houghton Mifflin, 1913), 1-2; Barbara Hardy, *The Advantage of Lyric* (Bloomington: Indiana University Press, 1977), 1-3.
7. The position disagrees with Schelling's (*The English Lyric,* 5-12).
8. The distinction is Johnson's (*The Idea of Lyric*).
9. Ibid., 23.
10. Ibid.
11. Ruth Finnegan, *Oral Poetry* (London: Cambridge University Press, 1977), 25-29; Thomas R. Edwards, *Imagination and Power: A Study of Poetry on Public Themes* (New York: Oxford University Press, 1971), 6.
12. Denis Donoghue, *The Sovereign Ghost* (Berkeley: University of California Press, 1976), 221-22.
13. Ibid., 228
14. Seiichi Hatano, *Time and Eternity,* trans. Ichiro Suzuki (Tokyo: Ministry of Education, 1963), 20.
15. Ibid., 20, 148.
16. See Albert William Levi, *Literature, Philosophy, and the Imagination* (Bloomington: Indiana University Press, 1962), 274.
17. See Peter Conrad, *Imagining America* (New York: Oxford University Press, 1980), 5.
18. See Faith Berry, *Langston Hughes: Before and Beyond Harlem* (Westport: Lawrence Hill, 1983), 61.
19. See Chancellor Williams, *The Destruction of Black Civilization* (Chicago: Third World Press, 1976), 139.
20. "Home," the metaphor of death, occurs in "Soul Gone Home," in *Five Plays by Langston Hughes,* ed. Webster Smalley (Bloomington: Indiana University Press, 1963).

21. Onwuchekwa Jemie, *Langston Hughes* (New York: Columbia University Press, 1976), 139.

22. See Johnson, *The Idea of Lyric,* 1-23.

23. The groupings are Fields of Wonder, Border Line, Heart of the World, Silver Rain, Desire, and Tearless.

24. Arthur P. Davis, "Langston Hughes: Cool Poet," *CLA Journal* 11 (June 1968):276-83.

25. Donoghue, *The Sovereign Ghost,* 226-27.

26. Though Gibson ("The Good Black Poet") deals satisfactorily with the sources in Whitman, nearly everyone overlooks the Victorians.

27. "Old Walt," *Beloit Poetry Journal,* no. 5 (1954):10.

28. For a folk reading, see Richard K. Barksdale, "Langston Hughes: His Times and Humanistic Techniques," in *Black American Literature and Humanism,* ed. R. Baxter Miller (Lexington: University Press of Kentucky, 1981), 23-25.

29. See Johnson, *The Idea of Lyric,* 195.

ARNOLD RAMPERSAD (ESSAY DATE 1989)

SOURCE: Rampersad, Arnold. "Langston Hughes and Approaches to Modernism in the Harlem Renaissance." In *The Harlem Renaissance: Revaluations,* edited by Amritjit Singh, William S. Shiver, and Stanley Brodwin, pp. 49-71. New York: Garland Publishing, 1989.

In the following essay, Rampersad assesses Hughes's place in the movement toward the modern and says that his work and that of other Harlem Renaissance writers was an attempt by Black artists to understand blues values and to communicate them to the modern world.

In 1936, certainly after the end of the Harlem Renaissance, one highly literate young black student, a junior at Tuskegee Institute, saw no connection between modernism and black American verse even as he recognized a link between modernism and black culture. "Somehow in my uninstructed reading of Pound and Eliot," he later wrote, "I had recognized a relationship between modern poetry and jazz music, and this led me to wonder why I was not encountering similar devices in the work of Afro-American writers." In 1936, however, the youth came across a poem by a young black Communist based in Chicago, published in *New Masses.* Although the poem "was not a masterpiece," he would write, at last "I found in it traces of the modern poetic sensibility and techniques that I had been seeking."[1]

The student was Ralph Ellison; the Communist poet, Richard Wright. The point is that Ellison, following the Harlem Renaissance, could see nothing of literary modernism in its writing, but had to depend for a glimpse of modernism in black poetry on a writer who not only had nothing to do with either Harlem or its Renaissance, but would the following year, 1937, dismiss virtually all of black writing. "Generally speaking," Wright declared (without offering an exception), "Negro writing in the past has been confined to humble novels, poems, and plays, prim and decorous ambassadors who went a-begging to white America." Wright knew well that ambassadors speak typically in archaic, sanctioned formulae; in general, they initiate nothing, make nothing new.[2]

The writers of the Harlem Renaissance apparently had not responded to Emerson's primal dictum that "the experience of each new age requires a new confession, and the world seems always waiting for its poet." Or had they? Let us resolve modernism into a series of questions aimed at these writers. Did they sense some historic shift in the world that justified Pound's famous charge to writers to "Make it new!"?[3] Did they perceive a crisis of expression, a need to, again in Pound's words, "resuscitate the dead art / Of poetry?"[4] Had blacks made a pact with Walt Whitman, as Pound had done ("I make a pact with you, Walt Whitman— / I have detested you long enough")?[5] Did they perceive the modern dominance of science and technology as requiring a self-preserving, adaptive response by art, in order to make something, in Frost's phrase, of "a diminished thing?"[6] Did they recognize a crisis in the loss of prestige by religion? Or were the black writers of the Harlem Renaissance merely, as Ellison and Wright would have us believe, dull and uninspired imitators of mediocre white writers?

I would argue that writers such as Jean Toomer, Countee Cullen, Langston Hughes, Claude McKay, Wallace Thurman, Richard Bruce Nugent, and Zora Neale Hurston were as aware as anyone else about the pressure of the modern on their lives and their art. Of course, to be aware of a situation does not mean that one acts responsibly; to act responsibly does not guarantee success. My purpose here is to look at some of the ways in which black writers engaged or failed to engage various compelling aspects of the age in which they lived. Perhaps we can thus learn something about the Renaissance, and perhaps even about modernism itself.

The movement toward the modern in black letters began, in fact, a generation before the Harlem school, when Afro-American poetry was dominated by the work, in standard English but more popularly in dialect form, of Paul Laurence Dunbar. By 1900 (he would die six years later) Dunbar's poetry enjoyed a national vogue; as a boy, for example, William Carlos Williams read the black poet as a matter of course. To Dunbar himself, however, and to at least one other black writer, James Weldon Johnson, dialect poetry, and thus Afro-American poetry, was a dead art. In it, "darkies" most often either sang, danced, ate, and stole comically, or they mourned some minor loss pathetically. Dunbar's verse led William Dean Howells to note "a precious difference of temperament between the races which it would be a great pity to lose," and to see "the range between appetite and emotion, with certain lifts far beyond and above it," as the range of the black race.[7] Such a reaction made Dunbar despair, without showing him a way out of his dilemma. "He sang of life, serenely sweet, / With, now and then, a deeper note," he wrote once about himself. "He of love when earth was young, / And Love, itself, was in his lays. / But ah, the world, it turned to praise / A jingle in a broken tongue."[8]

The first step in the resuscitation of black poetry came late in the summer of 1900, when Dunbar's friend and admirer James Weldon Johnson at last read the work of a white writer who had died during the previous decade. "I was engulfed and submerged by the book, and set floundering again," Johnson later recalled in his autobiography, *Along This Way*:

> I got a sudden realization of the artificiality of conventionalized Negro dialect poetry: of its exaggerated geniality, childish optimism, forced comicality and mawkish sentiment. . . . I could see that the poet writing in the conventionalized dialect, no matter how sincere he might be, was dominated by his audience; that his audience was a section of the white American reading public; that when he wrote he was expressing what often bore little relation, sometime no relation at all, to actual Negro life; that he was really expressing only certain conceptions about Negro life that his audience was willing to accept and ready to enjoy; that, in fact, he wrote mainly for the delectation of an audience that was an outside group. And I could discern that it was on this line that the psychological attitude of the poets writing in the dialect and that of the folk artists faced in different directions; because the latter, although working in the dialect, sought only to express themselves for themselves, and to their *own group*.[9]

Thus Johnson laid bare the central dilemma facing not merely Dunbar but all black writers in America. The white poet was, of course, Walt Whitman, with whom Johnson made a pact more than a dozen years before Pound did. Neither Johnson nor Pound, however, would have been sensitive to Whitman had it not been for altering social and historical conditions that first gradually, then torrentially, made Whitman's insights into social meaning and poetic form shine forth. For Pound, the twin factors were, perhaps, science and technology, on one hand, and the Great War on the other. I suspect that in 1900, when Johnson first read Whitman, science meant relatively little to him as a threat, and the Great War was still more than a dozen years away. Or was it? For blacks, there was another great war, one that saw in the 1890s (the "nadir" of Afro-American history, as Rayford Logan has called it) racial segregation and black disfranchisement made law by the Supreme Court and enforced brutally by the Ku Klux Klan. In *Along This Way,* Johnson's discussion of *Leaves of Grass* follows immediately on his horrified recollection of the fourth major race riot in the history of blacks in New York, occurring in 1900 and capping a decade in which almost 1700 blacks had been lynched, "numbers of them with a savagery that was satiated with nothing short of torture, mutilation, and burning alive at the stake."[10] This was for blacks the "Great War," compared to which their involvement in the later carnage in Europe was almost a form of affirmative action—affirmative action with a vengeance, if you will. Every major American war from the Revolution to Vietnam, it must be remembered, has led to a material *advance* in the freedom of black Americans.

That this pressure had its effect on poetic form among blacks is independently demonstrated in the sometime poetry of the scholar-turned-protagonist, W. E. B. DuBois. In DuBois's verse we see rage against racism making the tropes of traditional poetic discourse impossible, and pushing his pen, willy-nilly, toward free verse and liberated rhyme in a series of poems, such as "A Litany of Atlanta," "The Burden of Black Women," "Song of the Smoke," and "Prayers of God," published in the first two decades of this century. When the war in Europe came, it only added to the pressure toward the modern. "We darker men said," DuBois wrote in his essay "The Souls of White Folk," "This is not Europe gone mad; this is not aberration nor insanity; this *is* Europe; this seeming Terrible is the real soul of white culture,—stripped and visible today. This is where the world has arrived—these dark and awful depths and not the shining and ineffable heights of which it boasted."[11]

By this time, at least one younger black writer had taken black poetry closer to the modern. In 1912 Fenton Johnson's first book of verse, *A Little Dreaming,* was conventional and included both a long poem in blank verse and Dunbaresque dialect verse. Within two or three years, however, he had completely renovated his sense of poetry. In

1 st
8/9/48

Keep together
Glick

Harlem

Good morning, Daddy!

I was born here, he said,

and I've watched Harlem grow,

colored folks

until spread

from river to river,

all across the island,

middle of the

I've watched us spread.

3 #

out of Penn Station

a new nation,

out of planes from Porto Rico

and the holds of boats

of boats from Cuba, chico,

Jamaica, Haiti, Panama,

out of busses from Georgia,

Florida, Louisiana, marked NEW YORK—

to Harlem, Brooklyn, Bronx, San Juan Hill,

but most of all to Harlem:

~~Montage of a dream defered.~~

~~Tomorrow, ain't you heard?~~

3

A dream defered

Does it dry up like a raisin

in the sun?

Or fester like a sore,

and then run?

Does it stink like rotten meat?

Or crust, and sugar over —

like a syrupy sweet?

Maybe it just sags
like a heavy load.

syrupy

Or does it explode?

over

~~Has anybody heard // what happened to a dream defered?~~

Original typewritten manuscript from *Harlem/Good Morning, Daddy,* by Langston Hughes.

Visions of Dusk (1915) and *Songs of the Soil* (1916) he not only adopted free verse but altered his ways of viewing civilization itself. Instead of glorifying white high culture, Fenton Johnson spurned it, as Pound would do in writing of Europe as "an old bitch gone in the teeth," and "a botched civilization."[12] Unlike Pound, however, Fenton Johnson did so from an unmistakably racial perspective:

> I am tired of work; I am tired of building up some
> body else's civilization.
> Let us take a rest, M'Lissy Jane.
> I will go down to the Last Chance Saloon, drink a
> gallon or two of gin, shoot a game or two of
> dice and sleep the rest of the night on one of
> Mike's barrels.
> You will let the old shanty go to rot, the white
> people's clothes turn to dust, and the
> Cavalry Baptist Church sink to the bottom-
> less pit. . . .
> Throw the children into the river; civilization
> has given us too many. It is better to die
> than it is to grow up and find out that you
> are colored.
> Pluck the stars out of the heavens. The stars mark
> our destiny. The stars marked my destiny.
> I am tired of civilization.[13]

In "The Banjo Player," the speaker wanders the land playing "the music of the peasant people." He is a favorite in saloons and with little children. "But I fear that I am a failure. Last night a woman called me a troubadour. What is a troubadour?"[14] "The Scarlet Woman," who possesses "a white girl's education and a face that enchanted the men of both races," spurns classical mythic language and enters a bordello for white men: "Now I can drink more gin than any man for miles around. Gin is better than all the water in Lethe."[15]

Fenton Johnson was so close to the center of the Chicago manifestation of modernism, which is to say the center of literary modernism except for wherever Ezra Pound happened to be at the moment, that it is unclear how much he owes to the more famous poets he resembles in his work—Carl Sandburg, whose groundbreaking *Chicago and Other Poems* appeared in 1916, and Edgar Lee Masters in his *Spoon River Anthology* (1915). Johnson published in Harriet Monroe's *Poetry* magazine and at least one other important modernist outlet, *Others.* One point must be noted, however, about the work thus far of Fenton Johnson, James Weldon Johnson, and DuBois. For all its incipient modernism, their verse betrays no sign of any specific innovative formal influence by the culture, or subculture, they championed. Indignation at the treatment of blacks moved them to change as poets; black culture itself did not. This was the crucial hurdle facing would-be black modernists.

Yet another poet to balk at the highest fence was Claude McKay, the Jamaican-born writer who first gained notice in the United States in 1917, when he published two sonnets in *Seven Arts* magazine. Subsequent publications in *Pearson's,* Max Eastman's *Liberator* (where he would serve as an associate editor), and the leading black journals, such as the radical socialist *Messenger* and DuBois's *Crisis,* as well as in prestigious English publications, such as C. K. Ogden's *Cambridge Magazine,* made him for a while the most respected of Afro-American versifiers. Two volumes of verse, *Spring in New Hampshire* (London, 1920), with an introduction by I. A. Richards, and *Harlem Shadows* (Harcourt, Brace, 1922) anchored his reputation. For black Americans, however, McKay's single most impressive publication was not one of his lyric evocations of nature but a sonnet published in 1919, following perhaps the bloodiest summer of anti-black riots since the end of the Civil War. In "If We Must Die," McKay implored his readers not to die "like hogs / Hunted and penned in an inglorious spot" but to "nobly die, / So that our precious blood may not be shed / In vain." Even if death is certain, "Like men we'll face the murderous, cowardly pack, / Pressed to the wall, dying, but fighting back."[16]

With McKay and "If We Must Die," we come not only directed to the Harlem school but also to one of its principal tensions—that between radicalism of political and racial thought, on the one hand, and, on the other, a bone-deep commitment to conservatism of form. As a poet, McKay was absolutely ensnared by the sonnet, which—for all the variety possible within its lines—is perhaps the most telling sign of formal conservatism in the writing of poetry in English. Perhaps no greater tension exists in a brief Afro-American text than that between the rage of "If We Must Die" and the sonnet form. McKay used the form again and again to write some of the most hostile verse in Afro-American letters, as in "To the White Fiends" ("Think you I am not a fiend and savage too? / Think you I could not arm me with a gun / And shoot down ten of you for every one / Of my black brothers murdered, burnt by you?"[17] and in "The White House," or "Tiger," where "The white man is a tiger at my throat, / Drinking my blood as my life ebbs away, / And muttering that his terrible striped coat / Is Freedom's."[18]

McKay was not alone in his commitment to conservative forms even in the postwar modernist heyday. If the work of Countee Cullen, a far younger writer, was more varied than McKay's, his formal conservatism was as powerful. Cullen's idols were John Keats ("I cannot hold my peace, John Keats; / There never was a spring like this"), and A. E. Housman, still alive but moribund surely when one considers the distance between his blue remembered hills and the steamy streets of Harlem.[19] And unlike McKay, who wrote of both race and "universal" topics without a sense of contradiction, Cullen resented the inspiration that came from racial outrage. In a novel, *One Way to Heaven* (1932), he satirized a black woman who insists upon teaching her students verse by Langston Hughes. "While her pupils could recite like small bronze Ciceros, 'I Too Sing America'," the narrator jibes, "they never had heard of 'Old Ironsides,' 'The Blue and the Gray,' or 'The Wreck of the Hesperides.' They could identify lines from Hughes, Dunbar, Cotter, and the multitudinous Johnsons, but were unaware of the contributions of Longfellow, Whittier, and Holmes to American literature."[20] Elsewhere he ridicules a poem by a so-called "Negro poet." "Taken in a nutshell," a character explains scornfully, "it means that niggers have a hell of a time in this God-damned country. That's all Negro poets write about."[21] In perhaps his best-known couplet, Cullen lamented "this curious thing: / To make a poet black, and bid him sing!"[22]

Exactly why McKay and Cullen stuck by conservative forms in the midst of a decade of change is too complicated a question to answer here.[23] But we might take note of one or two points. If McKay was a radical socialist and an antimodernist, he was in line with a tradition of taste among great radicals from Marx to Lenin, who fomented revolution but clung to the classics like bourgeois intellectuals. "I am unable to consider the productions of futurism, cubism, expressionism and other isms," Lenin wrote privately somewhere. "I do not understand them. I get no joy from them."[24] In addition, McKay was in line with the very philosophy of Marxism, which defines the world in a way diametrically opposed to modernism; Marxism and modernism are poles apart.

Langston Hughes, in opening his *Nation* essay in 1926, **"The Negro and the Racial Mountain,"** bluntly attacked Cullen's dilemma without naming him. He wrote about a black friend, a writer, who wished to be known not as a Negro poet, but as a poet. "Meaning subconsciously," Hughes wrote, "'I would like to be white.'"[25] Cullen might have defended himself by quoting T. S. Eliot on tradition—or, if you permit an anachronism—by quoting Ralph Ellison, who would distinguish between (on one hand) his ancestors—T. S. Eliot and Hemingway, above all, who strongly influenced him, and (on the other) his family, such as Richard Wright and Langston Hughes, who apparently influenced him not at all. But Cullen was not Eliot nor could ever be. Eliot spoke up for the power of dead poets on aesthetic grounds, but the choice of white ancestors over black relatives cannot ever be, to say the least, a purely aesthetic matter. In addition, one must be wary of the motives of anyone, of any color, who exalts his ancestors at the expense of his family.

Let us turn from the most conservative members of the Harlem school to probably the *least* conservative according to modernist standards—Jean Toomer and Richard Bruce Nugent. Toomer's *Cane,* a pastiche of fiction, poetry, drama, and hieroglyphics published in 1923, has been hailed almost invariably as the greatest single document of the Renaissance. Bruce Nugent's published work in the 1920s was scant but very striking, especially the hallucinogenic, stream-of-consciousness story "Smoke, Lilies and Jade," which was too quickly compared by at least one review of *FIRE!!* magazine, where it first appeared in 1926, to *Ulysses.* Is it significant that Toomer and Nugent, the most modernist of the black writers, were also probably the least racial either personally or in their writing? From the start, Nugent seemed to consider race a great irrelevancy. And while Jean Toomer's *Cane* is saturated with a concern for race and the complex fate of being black in America, even as his book was appearing the extremely light-skinned Toomer was vehemently denying that he was a Negro—an attitude that only intensified over the years as his writing became more modernist and purged of the racial theme. Bruce Nugent, one black modernist, says that race doesn't matter; Toomer, another, says that race doesn't matter as long as nobody calls him black. Are we to conclude, then, that modernism and black racial feeling, with its political consequences, are incompatible?

It might be useful here to look at the work of Melvin B. Tolson, who began writing at the tail end of the Renaissance with a limited sense of the modern, but grew to be acclaimed as the first authentic black modernist poet. Tolson was the author of *A Gallery of Harlem Portraits,* posthumously published but in manuscript form by 1931; the Marxist-influenced *Rendezvous with America* (1944); and a deeply modernist *Libretto for the Republic of Liberia* (1953), among other works. Beginning with the sense of the modern derived from Edwin Arlington Robinson and Carl Sandburg, Tolson repudiated their blending of free verse, highly accessible language, and folk references in order to master the most complex version of modernism. The result was poetry beyond the ability of all but a few readers to understand, let alone enjoy. This new poetry, however, tremendously excited those privileged few, including the reformed racist Allen Tate, who in 1931 refused to attend a dinner for Langston Hughes and James Weldon Johnson in Nashville because they were black, but lived to write an introduction in 1953 to *Libretto for the Republic of Liberia.* Tolson not only showed a "first rate intelligence at work from first to last," Tate marvelled, but for "the first time, it seems to me, a Negro poet has assimilated completely the full poetic language of his time, and by implication, the language of the Anglo-American tradition."[26] As if that were not praise enough, William Carlos Williams found a place of honor for Tolson, and Allen Tate, in the fourth book of *Paterson*:

—and to Tolson and to his ode
and to Liberia and to Allen Tate
(give him credit)
and to the South generally
"Selah!"[27]

Thus encouraged, Tolson deepened his commitment to modernism with *Harlem Gallery: Book I. The Curator* (1965). In his introduction to the book, however, Karl Shapiro questioned Tate's statement that Tolson was indebted to white modernist masters and their special language. "*Tolson writes in Negro,*" Shapiro declared.[28] Let me quote some lines from the first stanza of the book:

Lord of the House of Flies,
jaundiced-eyed, synapses purled,
wries before the tumultuous canvas,
The Second of May—
by Goya:
the dagger of Madrid
vs.
the scimitar of Murat.
In Africa, in Asia, on the Day
of Barricades, alarm birds bedevil the Great
White
World, a Burdian's ass—not Balaam's—between
oats
and hay.[29]

Any Negro who speaks naturally like this is probably wearing a straightjacket. In its stated themes, the poem justifies Tolson's continuing sense of himself as a champion of his fellow blacks and their history; in its full language, it repudiates that sense. A while ago, Toomer and Nugent led me to *ask* whether modernism can be compatible with strong racial feeling. Tolson leads me to *understand* that complex modernism cannot be so compatible. Racial feeling, which is spurious unless accompanied by a deep sense of political wrong, demands an accessible art; the more pervasive the political wrong, the more accessible must be the art. Melvin Tolson may be on his way to Mount Olympus, but only at the expense of his people and their common poets, washed up on the shores of oblivion while the mighty modernist river rolls by.

When we drive by the scene of an accident, we feel the pain of broken bones and flowing blood. We tremble, but we drive on, unscathed and unstained. Are all of us integral victims of the accident of modernism (which followed the accident of World War I)? Or are some of us only rubbernecking? Must we assume that what is modern for the white goose is also modern for the black gander, that the dominant quality of white life in the twentieth century, as perceived by certain great white poets, is the same as the dominant temper for black? Or that the white quality is something to which blacks should have *aspired* (a tragic attitude, but one to which Jean Toomer, I think, succumbed)? Nor is this a matter of black and white alone. Robert Frost, to my mind, achieved unquestioned greatness swimming against the tide of modernism, ridiculing free verse, gentrifying run-down forms, forging out of a mixture, in which New England regionalism played a very strong part, both a critique of modernism and a body of work beyond easy category.

The major meditative poem by a black writer of the decade, Arna Bontemps's "Nocturne at Bethesda," reveals a black poet "flying low, / I thought I saw the flicker of a wing / Above the mulberry trees; but not again. / Bethesda sleeps. This ancient pool that healed / A host of bearded Jews does not awake. . . ."[30] "Nocturne at Bethesda" is the black counterpart to Wallace Stevens's magnificent "Sunday Morning," in which Stevens dwells on the crisis of spirituality but denies transcendent religion in favor of a future of hedonism: "Supple and turbulent, a ring of men / Shall chant in orgy on a summer morn / Their boisterous devotion to the sun, / Not as a god, but as a god might be, / Naked among them, like a savage source."[31] In "Nocturne at Bethesda," Arna Bontemps, who never outgrew completely the lugubriousness of his Seventh Day Adventism, nevertheless also looks to a new day beyond religion: "Yet I hope, still I long to live. / If there can be returning after death / I shall come back. But it will not be here; / If you want me you must search for me / Beneath the palms of Africa."

The finest black poet of the decade, Langston Hughes, rejected metaphysics and superstition altogether; loyal to perhaps the essential modernist criterion, Hughes for the most part looked not before and after, but at what *is*. Hughes went in the only direction a black poet could go and still be great in the 1920s: he had to lead blacks, in at least one corner of their lives—in his case, through poetry—into the modern world. His genius lay in his uncanny ability to lead by following (one is tempted to invoke Eliot's image of the poet's mind as a platinum filament), to identify the black modern, recognize that it was not the same as the white modern, and to structure his art (not completely, to be sure, but to a sufficient extent for it to be historic) along the lines of that black modernism.

Modernism began for Hughes on January 1919, a month short of his seventeenth birthday, when the Cleveland Central High School *Monthly*, in which he had been publishing undistinguished verse for more than a year, announced a long poem "in free verse"—apparently the first in the history of the magazine. **"A Song of the Soul of Central"** ("Children of all people and all creeds / Come to you and you make them welcome") indicates that Hughes had made his individual pact with Walt Whitman.[32] With Whitman's influence came a break with the genteel tyranny of rhyme and the pieties of the Fireside poets and the majority of black versifiers. Already conscious of himself as a black, however, Hughes could not accept, much less internalize, a vision of the modern defined largely by the fate of Europe after the war. Sharing little or nothing of J. Alfred Prufrock's sense of an incurably diseased world, Hughes looked with indifference on the ruined splendors of the waste land. In practice, modernism for him would mean not Pound, Eliot, or Stevens, but Whitman, Vachel Lindsay, and, above all, Sandburg. The last became "my guiding star."[33] Hughes, however, did not remain star-struck for long; within a year or so he had emancipated himself from direct influence. In one instance, where the well-meaning Sandburg had written: "I am the nigger. / Singer of Songs, / Dancer," Hughes had responded with the more dignified (though not superior) "Negro": "I am the Negro: / Black as the night is black, / Black like the depths of my Africa."[34]

The key to his release as a poet was his discovery of the significance of race, as well as other psychological factors (beyond our scope here) that amount to a final admission of his aloneness in the world, with both factors combining to make Hughes dependent on the regard of his race as practically no other black poet has been. He responded by consciously accepting the challenge of Whitman and Sandburg but also by accepting as his own special task, within the exploration of modern democratic vistas in the United States, the search for a genuinely Afro-American poetic form. At the center of his poetic consciousness stood the black masses,

> Dream-singers all,
> Story-tellers,
> Dancers,
> Loud laughers in the hands of Fate—
> My people.[35]

Or, as he soon more calmly, and yet more passionately, would express his admiration and love:

> The night is beautiful,
> So the faces of my people.
>
> The stars are beautiful,
> So the eyes of my people.
>
> Beautiful, also, is the sun
> Beautiful, also, are the souls of my people.[36]

Before he was nineteen, Hughes had written at least three of the poems on which his revered position among black readers would rest. The most important was **"The Negro Speaks of Rivers"** ("I've known rivers: / I've known rivers ancient as the world and older than the flow of human blood in human veins. / My soul has grown deep like the rivers.")[37] **"When Sue Wears Red"** drew on the ecstatic cries of the black church to express a tribute to black woman unprecedented in the literature of the race.

> When Susanna Jones wears red
> Her face is like an ancient cameo
> Turned brown by the ages.
>
> Come with a blast of trumpets,
> Jesus! . . .[38]

The third major poem of this first phase of Hughes's adult creativity was **"Mother to Son,"** a dramatic monologue that reclaimed dialect (Dunbar's "jingle in a broken tongue") for the black poet ("Well, son, I'll tell you: / Life for me ain't been no crystal stair. / It's had tacks in it, / And splinters").[39] With this poem and the resuscitation of dialect, Hughes came closer than any of the poets before him to what I have identified as the great hurdle facing the committed black poet-how to allow the race to infuse and inspire the very form of a poem, and not merely its surface contentions. Until this step could be taken, black poetry would remain antiquarian, anti-modern.

To a degree greater than that of any other young black poet, however, Hughes trained himself to be a modern poet—I am conscious here of Pound's words on the general subject, and on Eliot in particular. His high school, dominated by the children of east European immigrants, and where he was class poet and editor of the yearbook, was a training ground in cosmopolitanism. Mainly from Jewish classmates, "who were mostly interested in more than basketball and the glee club," he was introduced to basic texts of radical socialism.[40] Although at 21 he began his first ocean voyage by dumping overboard a box of his books, the detritus of his year at Columbia (he saved only one book—*Leaves of Grass*: "That one I could not throw away"), it was not out of ignorance of what they might contain.[41] "Have you read or tried to read," he wrote in 1923 to a friend, "Joyce's much discussed 'Ulysses'?"[42] By the age of 23 he could speak both French and Spanish. In 1923 he was writing poems about Pierrot (a *black* Pierrot, to be sure), after Jules Laforgue, like Edna St. Vincent Millay in *Aria da Capo,* and another young man who would soon concede that he was a poet manqué and turn to fiction to confront the gap between lowly provincialism and modernism—William Faulkner. If Hughes went to Paris and Italy without finding the Lost Generation, at least he was able in 1932 to assure Ezra Pound (who had written to him from Rappallo to complain about the lack of instruction in African culture in America) that "Many of your poems insist on remaining in my head, not the words, but the mood and the meaning, which, after all, is the heart of a poem."[43]

Hughes also shared with white modernists, to a degree far greater than might be inferred from his most popular poems, an instinct toward existentialism in its more pessimistic form. One poem, written just before his first book of poems appeared in 1926, suggests the relative ease with which he could have taken to "raceless" modernist idioms. From **"A House in Taos"**:

Thunder of the Rain God
And we three
Smitten by beauty.
Thunder of the Rain God:
And we three
Weary, weary.
Thunder of the Rain God
And you, she and I
Waiting for the nothingness. . . .[44]

Hughes, however, had already committed himself to a very different vision of poetry and the modern world, a vision rooted in the modern black experience and expressed most powerfully and definitively in the music called blues. What is the blues? Although W. C. Handy was the first musician to popularize it, notably with *St. Louis Blues,* the form is so deeply based in the chants of Afro-American slave labor, field hollers, and sorrow songs as to be ancient and comprises perhaps the greatest art of Africans in North America. Oral and improvisational by definition, the blues nevertheless has a classical regimen. Its most consistent form finds a three-line stanza, in which the second line restates the first, and the third provides a contrasting response to both. "The blues speak to us simultaneously of the tragic and the comic aspects of the human condition," Ralph Ellison has written; they must be seen "first as poetry and as ritual," and thus as "a transcendence of those conditions created within the Negro community by the denial of social justice."[45] "It was a language," Samuel Charters asserts in *The Legacy of the Blues,* "a rich, vital, expressive language that stripped away the misconception that the black society in the United States was simply a poor, discouraged version of the white. It was impossible not to hear the differences. No one could listen to the blues without realizing that there were two Americas."[46]

A long brooding on the psychology of his people, and a Whitmanesque predisposition to make the native languages of America guide his art, led Hughes early in 1923 to begin his greatest single literary endeavor: his attempt to resuscitate the dead art of an American poetry and culture by invoking the blues (exactly as George Gershwin, the following year, would try to elevate American music in his *Rhapsody in Blue*). If Pound had looked in a similar way, at one point, to the authority of the Provencal lyric of the middle ages, Hughes could still hear the blues in night clubs and on street corners, as blacks responded in art to the modern world. At the very least, Pound and Hughes (and Whitman) shared a sense that poetry and music were intimately related. To Hughes, black music at its best was the infallible metronome of racial grace: "Like the waves of the sea coming one after another, always one after another, like the earth moving around the sun, night, day—night, day—night, day—forever, so is the undertow of black music with its rhythm that never betrays you, its rooted power."[47] In the blues, in its mixture of pain and laughter, its lean affirmation of humanity in the face of circumstance, all in a secular mode (no "shantih, shantih" here; no brand plucked from the "burning!"), he found the tone, the texture, the basic language of true black modernism. A line from the epigraphic note to the volume says it all: "The mood of the *Blues* is almost always despondency, but when they are sung people laugh."[48]

Over a period of five years, starting some time around 1922, he slowly engaged the blues as a literary poet, first describing the blues from a distance, then enclosing the blues within a traditional poem, as he did in the prize-winning **"The Weary Blues"** ("Droning a drowsy syncopated tune, / Rocking back and forth to a mellow croon, / I heard a Negro play"), until, at last, in his most important collection, ***Fine Clothes to the Jew*** (1927), he proposed the blues exclusively on its own terms by writing in the form itself, alone.[49] Thus he acknowledged at last the full dignity of the people who had invented it.

Savagely attacked in black newspapers as "about 100 pages of trash [reeking] of the gutter and sewer," containing "poems that are insanitary, insipid, and repulsing," this book nevertheless was Hughes's greatest achievement in poetry, and remarkable by almost any American standard, as the literary historian Howard Mumford Jones recognized in a 1927 review.[50] "In a sense," Jones wrote of Hughes, "he has contributed a really new verse form to the English language."[51]

More important, blues offered, in a real sense, a new mode of feeling to the world (Eudora Welty has reminded us that literature teaches us how to feel) and a new life to art. To probe this point we would have to make a fresh reading of art and culture in the 1920s, for which I do not have the time or, truly, the skills. But instead of dismissively talking about the jazz age we would have to see that 1920, when the first commercial recording of a black singer, Mamie Smith's *Crazy Blues,* appeared, was perhaps as important a year for some people (certainly the millions of blacks who bought blues records in the decade, and the millions of whites down to our day who would thereafter sing and dance to the blues and its kindred forms) as was 1922, the year of Eliot's *The Waste Land,* for other people. We would see Gershwin's *Rhapsody in Blue,* premiered at Paul Whiteman's concert "An Experiment in Modern Music" in New York in 1924, as a modern American landmark that is in fact an alternative to the spirit of European modernism. We might go further, not simply to the work of other musicians such as Stravinsky and Bartok and Aaron Copland but also to the work of writers like Faulkner, whose genius was emancipated in *The Sound and the Fury,* I would suggest, by a balance between the modernism of Joyce, which dominates the first section of the novel, and the counter-modernism of the blues, which dominates the last in spite of the religious overtones there, and in spite of Faulkner's ultimate unwillingness to take on the consciousness of a black character whose life is informed by the blues. To me, it is instructive that Joycean technique facilitates the utterance of the idiot, Benjy, but that the blues temper informs the most affirmative section of the book, that dominated by black Dilsey Gibson and her people ("they endured").[52]

Far from suggesting that only Langston Hughes in the Harlem Renaissance discovered the black modern, I see the whole Harlem movement as struggling toward its uncovering. Why? Because it was inescapable; it was what the masses lived. In one sense, reductive no doubt, the Harlem Renaissance was simply an attempt by the artists to understand blues values and to communicate them to the wider modern world.

Finally, I would suggest that this question of modernism, and Hughes's place in it, needs to be seen in the context not merely of Harlem but of international cultural change in the twentieth century. By the age of twenty-one, he belonged already to an advanced guard of writers, largely from the yet unspoken world outside Europe and North America, that would eventually include Neruda of Chile, the young Borges of Argentina (who translated **"The Negro Speaks of Rivers"** in 1931), Garcia Lorca of Spain (see his "El Rey de Harlem"), Jacques Roumain of Haiti (see his poem "Langston Hughes"), Senghor of Senegal (who would hail Hughes in 1966 as the greatest poetic influence of the *Negritude* movement), Césaire of Martinique, Damas of French Guyana, and Guillen of Cuba (who freely asserted in 1930 that his first authentically Cuban or "Negro" poems, the eight pieces of *Motivos de Son,* were inspired by Hughes's visit to Havana that year). To these names should be added painters such as Diego Rivera, following his return from Paris in 1923, and his friends Orozco and Siquieros.

The collective aim of these writers and artists was to develop, even as they composed in the languages and styles of Europe and faced the challenge of European modernism, an aesthetic tied to a sense of myth, geography, history, and culture that was truly indigenous to their countries, rather than merely reflective of European trends, whether conservative or avant-garde. Finally, let me suggest that Hughes's virtual precedence of place among them has less to do with his date of birth or his individual talent than with the fact that he was the poetic fruition of the Afro-American intellectual tradition, where these questions of race and culture and this challenge to civilization had long been debated, and under the harshest social conditions. In 1910, after all, when DuBois founded *Crisis* magazine, he gave it a challenging subtitle—but one he had already used for an even earlier publication. He called it "A Record of the Darker Races."

Notes

1. Ralph Ellison, "Remembering Richard Wright," *Delta* (April 1984), 1-2.
2. Richard Wright, "Blueprint for Negro Writing," *New Challenge* 2 (Fall 1937), 53.
3. George McMichael, ed., *Anthology of American Literature: Vol. 2: Realism to the Present* (New York: Macmillan, 1974), p. 1225.
4. Ezra Pound, "E. P. Ode pour L'Election de Son Sepulchre," *Hugh Selwyn Mauberley,* in George McMichael, p. 1233.
5. Ezra Pound, "A Pact," in George McMichael, p. 1232.
6. Robert Frost, "The Oven Bird," *Complete Poems* (New York: Holt, Rinehart, and Winston, 1964), p. 150.
7. William Dean Howells, "Introduction to Lyrics of Lowly Life," in Paul Laurence Dunbar, *Complete Poems* (New York: Dodd, Mead, 1913), p. ix.
8. Paul Laurence Dunbar, "The Poet," *Complete Poems,* p. 191.
9. James Weldon Johnson, *Along This Way* (New York: Viking, 1968), pp. 158-159.
10. *Along This Way,* p. 158.
11. W. E. B. DuBois, "The Souls of White Folk," *Darkwater: Voice from Within the Veil* (New York: Schocken, 1969), p. 39.
12. Ezra Pound, "E. P. Ode," in George McMichael, p. 1237.
13. Fenton Johnson, "Tried," in James Weldon Johnson, ed., *Book of American Negro Poetry* (New York: Harcourt, Brace & World, 1931), p. 144.
14. Fenton Johnson, "The Banjo Player," *Book of American Negro Poetry,* p. 145.
15. Fenton Johnson, "The Scarlet Woman," *Book of American Negro Poetry,* pp. 145-146.
16. Claude McKay, "If We Must Die," in Wayne Cooper, ed., *The Passion of Claude McKay* (New York: Schocken, 1973), p. 124.
17. Claude McKay, "To the White Fiends," in Cooper, p. 123.
18. Claude McKay, "Tiger," *Selected Poems* (New York: Bookman, 1953), p. 47.
19. Countee Cullen, "To John Keats, Poet. At Spring Time," *Color* (New York: Harper and Brothers, 1925), p. 102.
20. Countee Cullen, *One Way to Heaven* (New York: Harper and Brothers, 1932), p. 154.
21. Countee Cullen, *One Way to Heaven* (New York: Harper and Brother, 1932), p. 162.
22. Countee Cullen, "Yet Do I Marvel," *On These I Stand,* p. 3.
23. For a suggestive treatment of Cullen's interest in traditional forms and its sources, see James W. Tuttleton's essay, "Countee Cullen at 'The Heights,'" included in this volume.
24. David Caute, *The Illusion* (New York: Harper & Row, 1972), p. 109.
25. Langston Hughes, "The Negro Artist and the Racial Mountain," *Nation* 122 (June 23, 1926), 692.
26. Melvin B. Tolson, *Libretto for the Republic of Liberia* (London: Collier-Macmillan, 1970), pp. 10-11.
27. William Carlos Williams, *Paterson* (Norfolk, Conn.: New Directions, 1963).
28. Melvin B. Tolson, *Harlem Gallery: Book I: The Curator* (London: Collier-Macmillan, 1969), p. 12.
29. Melvin B. Tolson, *Harlem Gallery,* p. 17.
30. Arna Bontemps, "Nocturne at Bethesda," in Langston Hughes and Arna Bontemps, *The Poetry of the Negro, 1946-1970* (New York: Doubleday, 1970), p. 211.
31. Wallace Stevens, "Sunday Morning," *Complete Poems* (New York: Knopf, 1968), pp. 69-70.
32. Langston Hughes, "A Song of the Soul of Central," *Central High School Monthly* 20 (January 1919), 9-10.
33. Langston Hughes, *The Big Sea* (New York: Knopf, 1940), p. 29.
34. Carl Sandburg, "Nigger," *Complete Poems* (New York: Harcourt, Brace & Jovanovich, 1970), p. 23; Hughes, "Negro," *Selected Poems* (New York: Knopf, 1959), p. 8.
35. Hughes, "My People," *Crisis* 24 (June 1922), 72.
36. Hughes, "My People," [No. 2], *Selected Poems,* p. 13.
37. Hughes, "The Negro Speaks of Rivers," *Selected Poems,* p. 4.
38. Hughes, "When Sue Wears Red," *Selected Poems,* p. 69.
39. Hughes, "Mother to Son," *Selected Poems,* p. 187.
40. Hughes, *The Big Sea,* p. 41.
41. Hughes, "The Big Sea," ms. draft; Vivian Harsh Collection, Carter G. Woodson Regional Library, Chicago.
42. Langston Hughes to Alain Locke, n.d. [1923]; Alain Leroy Locke Papers, Moorland-Spingarn Research Center, Howard University.
43. Langston Hughes to Ezra Pound, 22 April 1932; Langston Hughes Papers, Beinecke Rare Book and Manuscript Library, Yale University.
44. Hughes, "A House in Taos," *The Big Sea,* p. 260.
45. Ralph Ellison, *Shadow and Act* (New York: New American Library, 1966), p. 249.
46. Samuel Charters, *The Legacy of the Blues* (New York: Da Capo, 1977), p. 22.

47. Hughes, *The Big Sea,* p. 209.
48. Hughes, *Fine Clothes to the Jew* (New York: Knopf, 1927), n.p.
49. Hughes, "The Weary Blues," *Selected Poems,* p. 33.
50. *New York Amsterdam News,* 5 February 1927; *Chicago Whip,* 26 February 1927.
51. *Chicago Daily News,* 29 June 1927.
52. William Faulkner, "Appendix," *The Sound and the Fury & As I Lay Dying* (New York: Modern Library, 1957), p. 22.

RICHARD K. BARKSDALE (ESSAY DATE 1989)

SOURCE: Barksdale, Richard K. "Langston Hughes and the Blues He Couldn't Lose." In *The Harlem Renaissance: Revaluations,* edited by Amritjit Singh, William S. Shiver, and Stanley Brodwin, pp. 83-90. New York: Garland Publishing, 1989.

In the following essay, Barksdale discusses Hughes's apparent preoccupation with the "tragic mulatto" theme, which was unpopular among other Harlem Renaissance artists, and argues that this interest was rooted in the author's life.

My old man's a white man
And my old mother's black.
If ever I cursed my white old man,
I take my curses back.

If ever I cursed my black old mother
And wished she were in hell,
I am sorry for that evil wish
And now I wish her well.

My old man died in a fine big house
My ma died in a shack.
I woner where I'm gonna die,
Being neither white nor black?

Langston Hughes wrote this short but emotionally powerful poem in 1925, the year in which he won his first literary prize in the competition sponsored by *Opportunity* magazine. Significantly, this poem, which he entitled **"Cross,"** was not the poem that brought him first honors; his **"The Weary Blues"** was the prizewinner. According to Faith Berry, Hughes thought that **"Cross"** had merit and submitted it for consideration in the first Amy Spingarn Contest in Literature and Art in August 1925.[1] The chief judge in that contest, William Stanley Braithwaite, however, did not think Hughes's submission was poetically meritorious and awarded it only a third prize. Countee Cullen, who apparently wrote poetry more attuned to Braithwaite's "talented tenth" sensibilities, won first prize. Undaunted, Hughes submitted his "third class" poem to *The Crisis,* where it was accepted and published in December 1925. Since that time, **"Cross"** has been one of the poet's widely reprinted poems; it was included in Hughes's first volume, ***The Weary Blues,*** and in the 1959 volume of ***Selected Poems*** and has been widely anthologized ever since.

Evidently, Hughes entitled the poem **"Cross"** because of the *double entendre* suggested by that word. One meaning is that mulattoes were "crossbred" or "little mules" in the original meaning of the Spanish term. A second meaning was that the mulatto heritage was slavery's bitterest memory and thus, in the poet's opinion, the heaviest cross that blacks had to bear. Later, in a poem entitled **"Black Seed,"** Hughes softened the mulatto image: in this poem mulattoes were likened to scattered flowers of many hues spread throughout the diaspora like "Hybrid plants / In another's garden / Flowers . . . / Cut by the shears / Of the white-faced gardeners."

However, Hughes captured the full drama of the tragic mulatto's status in a poem entitled **"Mulatto,"** which he wrote in the summer of 1926. In his autobiography ***The Big Sea,*** the poet recalls that "I worked harder on that poem than any other that I have ever written." He reports further that he felt more than amply rewarded when, at a poetry reading session at James Weldon Johnson's house, the poem received warm applause.[2] Like **"Cross," "Mulatto"** has been reprinted many times—in ***Fine Clothes to the Jew*** and in *The Saturday Review of Literature* in 1927, in ***Selected Poems*** in 1959, and in many anthologies.

In **"Mulatto,"** the ironic tone found in **"Cross"** is intensified and the generalized comment on the cultural and psychological dilemma of the mulatto described in the earlier poem is changed into a highly dramatic confrontation between a white father and his unacknowledged bastard mulatto son. Although throughout the poem the spotlight remains on "the little yellow bastard boy" who cries, "I am your son, white man!," the poet uses several lines to describe the background of a sensual South where defenseless black women were powerless to resist the raping and seduction that forced them into concubinage.

The moon over the turpentine woods
The southern night
Full of stars
Great big yellow stars.
What's a body but a toy?
  Juicy bodies
  Of nigger wenches
  Blue black
  Against black fences
  O, you little bastard boy
What's a body but a toy?
The scent of pine woods stings the soft
    night air
  What's the body of your mother?

Sharp pine scent in the evening air.
A nigger night
A nigger joy
A little yellow
Bastard boy.

This dynamically assertive poetic statement, written when Hughes was 24 years old, later became the basis of a short story, **"Father and Son,"** in the poet's first collection of short stories, ***The Ways of White Folks,*** written upon his return from the Soviet Union in 1933. And, as Arthur P. Davis has indicated, Hughes's preoccupation with the mulatto theme led him to write two more short stories on the subject (**"Passing"** in ***Ways of White Folks*** and **"African Morning"** in ***Laughing to Keep from Crying***); a play, ***Mulatto,*** which enjoyed a successful Broadway run in 1935—1936; and an opera, ***The Barrier,*** which the poet wrote in collaboration with Jan Meyerowitz.[3]

There are at least three conclusions which can be drawn from Hughes's preoccupation with the tragic mulatto theme. First, his ability to write on this subject in four different genres indicates a literary virtuosity that few of his contemporaries, white or black, could rival. Among his black literary friends, Bontemps, McKay, and Cullen had each turned from poetry to fiction; and Cullen did come out of literary retirement in the early 1940s to collaborate with Bontemps on *St. Louis Woman*; but none of Hughes's contemporaries in the Renaissance period demonstrated a comparable range and versatility. A second conclusion—that Hughes's preoccupation with the tragic mulatto theme flew in the face of Renaissance literary trends and tastes—has significant and challenging implications. Similarly challenging is a third conclusion—namely that there was something psychologically engrossing about the poet's seemingly obsessive preoccupation with the mulatto theme—that he had a deeply rooted personal involvement with the mulatto theme—a blues he could not lose, however debonairly he sought to "Play it cool / And dig all jive" in the never-ending struggle to "stay alive."

Although one cannot agree with Jean Wagner's assertion that the tragic mulatto theme in Hughes's poetry was "irrelevant" for American blacks,[4] it is true that it was by no means a popular theme with the writers of the Harlem Renaissance. Indeed, one can justifiably ask, how could a literary and cultural movement led by mulattoes concentrate its literary energies on excoriating mulattoes? For the composite "New Negro" whom Locke and others sought to define had, in searching for new literary and cultural perspectives, long since turned away from the tragic mulatto or tragic octoroon themes once so popular in Reconstruction times. Few if any of Hughes's associates remembered Harper's *Iola LeRoy* or William Wells Brown's *Clotel.* Rather, young black writers, like young white writers, of the gin-drinking 1920s, were dedicated in their struggle to counter the Establishment and shake the tree of cultural orthodoxy. If there was a concern about mulattoes and their heritage among black writers, it was positive and not negative and manifested itself in a prideful awareness of the fact that mulattoes were probably more integration worthy than other blacks because of their education and cultural attainments. At least, that seemed to be the message of Jessie Fauset's *There Is Confusion* (1924), which was hailed by literary Harlem with the first of the decade's gala literary banquets. Fauset wrote her novel in response to white author T. S. Stribling's race novel, *Birthright.* She sought to prove that the mulatto mainliners of Philadelphia lived just as well, dressed just as well, and socialized just as elegantly as Philadelphia's upper middle-class whites. Indeed, as one critic has written:

> *There Is Confusion* was Stribling's *Birthright* rewritten to the approved literary canons of the Talented Tenth, a saga of the sophisticated in which French, and occasionally German, tripped from the protagonists' tongues as readily as precise English; a novel about people with good blood lines. . . .[5]

Apparently, all literary Harlem rejoiced over the appearance of its first authentic mulatto novel, including a somewhat misanthropic George Schuyler and the elitist W. E. B. DuBois, who wanted works of fiction to be propaganda tracts first and literature only secondarily.

Fauset's 1924 novel was followed by three more novels, all with mulatto protagonists who were sometimes illegitimate but always socially proper. Undoubtedly, Fauset's success stimulated Nella Larsen to write *Quicksand,* a novel which was also enthusiastically accepted and reviewed by DuBois when it appeared in 1928, even though its mulatto heroine, Helga Crane, was, by the end of the novel, sucked into a quicksand of self-destructive eroticism, evidently caused, the novelist strongly implies, by the heroine's black genes.

So Langston Hughes's persistent involvement with the tragic mulatto theme was for the period's literary and cultural arbiters a preoccupation that appeared to deny what they fervently believed in—mainly the existence of a psychologically secure and stable mulatto-colored "talented tenth" whose members were firmly and deservedly in control of the black man's present and future cultural and literary destiny. They were not, as Hughes seemed to suggest, appalled by their illegitimate backgrounds and sometimes in-

ABOUT THE AUTHOR

ISHMAEL REED ON HUGHES

In the middle of the next century, when the literary establishment will reflect the multicultural makeup of this country and not be dominated by assimiliationists with similar tastes, from similar backgrounds, and of similar pretensions, Langston Hughes will be to the twentieth century what Walt Whitman was to the nineteenth.

SOURCE: Ishmael Reed, excerpt from his *Airing Dirty Laundry,* Addison-Wesley, 1993.

cestual family trees; nor were they traumatized by racial memories of cruel rapings and bastard beginnings.

Although Hughes was never specifically attacked for his emphasis on the tragic mulatto's dilemma, he knew that the Talented Tenth neither understood nor sympathized with his emphasis on the subject. In a sense, his response is contained in his 1926 essay, **"The Negro Artist and the Racial Mountain,"** in which he inveighs against black writers whose mulatto dispositions and "urge for whiteness" dictated a primary concern for what he termed "Nordic faces, Nordic art, and Episcopal Heaven."

Finally, there is no doubt that Langston Hughes's emphasis on the tragic mulatto theme reflected a deeply rooted personal concern about his own mulatto heritage. Both his maternal and paternal great grandparents had white male progenitors. His father, James Nathaniel Hughes, had white grandparents on both his maternal and paternal sides; and the poet's mother, Carolyn Langston Hughes, had as her paternal grandfather a wealthy Virginia planter named Ralph Quarles. The latter's three children by Lucy Langston, Quarles's half-Indian, half-Negro housekeeper, included John Mercer Langston, the first black Oberlin graduate and a distinguished Reconstruction educator and statesman. Charles Langston, the poet's maternal grandparent, did not become as famous as his younger brother John, but he did complete two years at Oberlin and was so active in the affairs of the Ohio Antislavery Society that he was jailed and fined for helping a fugitive slave escape to Canada in 1851.

Notwithstanding the achievements of some of his immediate ancestors, Hughes was apparently less than enamored with his mulatto background. An incident which he recorded in ***The Big Sea*** gives a hint about his attitude. In 1923, after a less-than-fulfilling academic year at Columbia in 1921-1922, the poet shipped out as a mess boy on a merchant ship, the S.S. *Malone,* bound for Africa. In his autobiography, he recalls his feelings as he first glimpsed the African shoreline:

> When I saw the dust-green hills in the sunlight something took hold of me inside. My Africa, Motherland of the Negro peoples! And me a Negro! Africa! The real thing to be touched and seen. . . .[6]

But his exultation about returning to his motherland was quickly tempered when he went ashore and found that African natives considered him to be a white man. "They looked at my copper-brown skin and straight black hair . . . and they said 'You white man.'" His racial status in Africa was confirmed when, desiring to attend a juju ceremony in a Nigerian village, he was told, "White man never go see JuJu."

His experiences at ports of call on Africa's West Coast reflected mere surface concerns, however. Of much deeper import were his relations with his mulatto father from whom he was estranged after 1922. The intensity of the confrontational dialogue between white father and mulatto son both in the story **"Father and Son"** and in ***Mulatto,*** the play, suggests that by the time of the composition of these two works, the poet was convinced that he was indeed a "little yellow bastard boy" who had been cruelly abandoned by an uncaring "white" father. For prior to his two-year visit with his father in Toluca, Mexico, after his high school graduation, Hughes had seen his father only twice—once when he accompanied his mother to Mexico in 1908 on her fruitless quest for a marital reconciliation and once when he spent an unhappy summer in a visit between his junior and senior years in high school. The poet relates that on all of these visits, his relations with his father were always strained. Gradually, he came to view his father as a businessman and capitalist who was, in his attitude and bearing, more white than black. Indeed, the young poet found that because of his father's success as a Yankee entrepreneur in Mexico, he had developed great scorn and disdain for his erstwhile black American brothers who, in the latter's opinion, were mired in the muck of their own racial inertia.

So, after 1922, when the poet became fully estranged from a father who, having abandoned him as an infant, now lived in another country, spoke another language, and had married another woman, it was as though a door in his life had closed, which in reality had never quite opened.

One does not sense the extent of the alienation and psychological damage wrought on the son's psyche by the image of the unopened door until one reads the scenes in **"Father and Son"** and in ***Mulatto*** in which Bert, the unacknowledged mulatto son, swept by a towering Oedipal rage, slowly chokes his white father to death. Significantly, the murder occurs just inside the closed front door of the father's plantation mansion—a door that had always been closed to the "little yellow bastard boy." It is a compelling dramatic scene that provides chilling evidence that, in his preoccupation with the mulatto theme, Langston Hughes truly had the blues he could not lose.

Notes

1. Faith Berry, *Langston Hughes: Before and Beyond Harlem* (New York: Lawrence Hill, 1983), pp. 62-63.
2. *The Big Sea* (1940; New York: Hill & Wang, 1963), p. 262.
3. Davis, "The Tragic Mulatto Theme in Six Works of Langston Hughes," *Phylon,* 15, 2 (1955), 195-204.
4. Jean Wagner, *Black Poets of the United States,* trans. Kenneth Douglas (Chicago: University of Illinois Press, 1973), p. 455.
5. David Levering Lewis, *When Harlem Was in Vogue* (New York: Knopf, 1981), p. 124.
6. *The Big Sea,* p. 107.

STEVEN C. TRACY (ESSAY DATE 1993)

SOURCE: Tracy, Steven C. "To The Tune of Those Weary Blues." In *Langston Hughes: Critical Perspectives Past and Present,* edited by Henry Louis Gates. Jr., and K. A. Appiah, pp. 69-93. New York: Amistad Press, 1993.

In the following essay, Tracy explores the folk sources of Hughes's knowledge of blues to illuminate how he used blues structure, themes, and imagery in his poetry.

Most readers of Black American literature recognize that Langston Hughes drew upon jazz and blues as resources for much of his work, particularly his poetry. In the case of the blues, however, critics often demonstrate an incomplete knowledge of the field, an inability or lack of desire to explore the blues influence, or they assume that the reader has an in-depth knowledge of the field already. What emerges from these studies is an incomplete understanding of Hughes's knowledge of the blues and of its influence on his work. By first exploring the sources for his knowledge and his attitudes toward his folk sources and their creations, a clearer picture of the way Hughes makes use of blues structure, themes, and imagery will emerge. What becomes evident is that although Hughes takes a multiplicity of traditional and literary approaches to blues in his own poems, his use of blues is limited in expression by some dominant influences.

There are many different types of blues styles, often subcategorized by blues researchers in terms of geographical location and historical time period. For example, the early Texas blues style—from about the 1880s to the 1920s—differed from the Mississippi blues style of the same era. Blues researcher Sam Charters has attributed the difference in style to the difference in environments that caused a variance in interaction of similar events.

> There was little of the oppressive plantation life of the Mississippi delta to shape the Texas blues. . . . In some Mississippi counties the Negro population is more than eighty percent of the people living in the county. . . . At its highest point, just after the Civil War, the colored population of Texas was less than thirty percent of the state's still sparse growth. . . . This has not meant that life has been easier for colored men and women in Texas. . . . But it has meant a less isolated, less confined life than the brutal colored society of Mississippi.[1]

As Charters points out, this less crowded environment produced less local competition, therefore traditional elements like slave and work songs were not displaced but were carried over wholesale into the blues performed by early Texas blues performers like Henry Thomas, "Ramblin'" Thomas, and Texas Alexander. As time went on, brilliant original performers like Blind Lemon Jefferson cast the material in a more personal style, a style less crowded, insistent, and rhythmic than the heavy Mississippi blues. In the late 1930s and early 1940s the rural style identified with Jefferson—the dominant figure of the Texas blues of the 1920s—with its single-string figures set off against a regular bass beat, combined with the recorded styles of Lonnie Johnson, Scrapper Blackwell, and some jazz guitarists. At that point Texas T-Bone Walker created his own style of playing, a more urban style performed in the company of a larger ensemble, a style today largely identified with B. B. King. Therefore, a blues style is based on the time, location, environment and the interaction of elements in that environment, the rise of a dominant local figure, and, after blues were recorded, the introduction of elements not normally associated with that area via the phonograph. As we examine the influence of the blues tradition on Langston Hughes, then, we must consider the type of blues Hughes encountered in the various environments in which he lived, keeping in mind that none of the blues environments had absolutely and exclusively one style, and that the styles were often dynamic and in transitional phases.

In his autobiography ***The Big Sea***[2] Hughes discusses his birth in 1902 in Joplin, Missouri, and his childhood in Lawrence, Kansas, recounting the fact that he heard the blues in the area where he grew up until about 1915. According to Hughes, the first blues song he heard was used in his poem **"The Weary Blues,"** written about a piano player he heard in Harlem:

I got de weary blues
And I can't be satisfied.
Got de weary blues
And can't be satisfied.
I ain't happy no mo'
And I wish that I had died.

The lyric, of course, is formulaic: the formula is repeated with many minor variations in the oral blues tradition, as by Texas songster Henry Thomas whose "Texas Worried Blues" makes the common substitution of "worried" for "weary";

The worried blues
God, I'm feelin' bad.
I've got the worried blues
God, I'm feelin' bad.
I've got the worried blues
God, I'm feelin' bad.[3]

Thomas, who was around fifty-three years old when he first recorded in 1927, represents a link to pre-war blues music, and his blues were often primitive. Hence he characteristically repeats the same three line three times, as opposed to creating a third-line resolution, as younger bluesmen have done.

The ballads, reels and crude blues of an older man like Henry Thomas, that Hughes first heard in his Lawrence childhood from 1902-15, were his earliest musical influence; therefore it is important to place that tradition in order to discern the type of the music. Lawrence is in northeast Kansas on the Kansas River, approximately sixty miles west of Kansas City, connected by highways 69 and 70 and the Santa Fe, Rock Island, and Missouri-Kansas-Texas railways to Oklahoma, Missouri, Kansas and Texas. Indeed Henry Thomas, at a 1929 recording session, recounted his experience hopping the Texas and Pacific and "Katy" (MKT) lines in his "Railroading Some," going from Texas through Kansas City and on through to Chicago, following a route that had been open to passengers, migrants and hoboes for years.[4] The blues were indeed no newcomer to the area: it was in Kansas City in 1902 (the date of Hughes's birth) that blues singer Gertrude "Ma" Rainey reportedly first heard blues music, and Kansas City blues shouter Big Joe Turner, roughly a contemporary of Hughes, recalled leading around blues singers on the streets in the late teens and early twenties, and hearing the crude banjos, gas pipes, and water jugs that were used as instruments.[5] These early blues, often sung unaccompanied, or accompanied by a guitar, piano, or crude home instruments were, in Kansas City, set in a milieu of varied musical idioms—ragtime, jazz, orchestral music—which produced the "loose, lithe, resilient orchestral jazz style to which the city gives its name." This orchestral-type blues were emerging in the teens, flowering in the era of 1925-1942, when larger ensembles touring the southwest played blues in arranged form.[6] Thus, during his childhood and visits back home, Hughes was hearing not only "pure" loosely arranged, spontaneous early blues, but most likely these other idioms and various combinations of a more arranged and sophisticated nature. What ultimately emerged in 1925-42 was the ensemble Kansas City blues style, "big city blues, but with a country, earthy feeling,"[7] that helped produce or catapult to success Big Joe Turner, Peter Johnson, Jay McShann, Mary Lou Williams, and Count Basie, among others.

But it was the early blues of itinerant musicians of the first two decades of the 20th century that influenced Hughes in his Lawrence, Kansas, days and the blues of that area were strongly influenced by slave and work songs. The Texas blues scene is more readily identifiable than that of Kansas, Missouri, or other surrounding states because more record companies held sessions in Texas,[8] whereas only the Okeh Record Company recorded sessions in Kansas City. However, the highways and train lines provided easily accessible connections to Kansas, so it is not hard to imagine someone like Texan Willard "Ramblin'" Thomas rambling in Kansas singing:

Poor Boy
Poor Boy
Poor Boy long ways from home.[9]

There is a loose-formed quality to the Texas bluesman's music, due to a reduced rhythmic emphasis, a beat that is "diffuse and idiosyncratic"[10] and the influence of the extended phrases characteristic of workshops. Even so, there was a variety of approaches, exemplified by the recordings of such Texas blues greats as Blind Lemon Jefferson, Little Hat Jones, Willie Reed, Funny Papa Smith, and "Texas" Alexander—all of whom recorded in the 1920s and '30s. These bluesmen played in the area for some time before recording: Texas Alexander, whose field holler-like qualities produced a clear link between Texas blues and work songs, was born in 1880, and performed in the region for years before recording. This type of music provided Hughes's earliest source of the blues tradition, and the strong links to slave songs and field hollers present in the performances of Henry Thomas, Texas Alexander, and others, coupled with the diversity of musical styles present in the area, were to influence the diversity of presentation in his later blues poems, particularly his old, rural-type moaning blues like "Bound No'th Blues."

The next clearly discernible blues influence occurred during his year in Harlem in 1922-23. This was two years after black singer Mamie Smith opened up the market for black singers through the success of her Okeh label releases, "That Thing Called Love," "You Can't Keep A Good Man Down," and "Crazy Blues." In ***The Big Sea,*** Hughes describes the 1920s Harlem music scene by recounting the big name, popular performers: Hall Johnson, William Brant Still, Eubie Blake, Noble Sissle, Duke Ellington, Florence Mills, Josephine Baker, Ethel Waters, Gladys Bentley, Trixie Smith, Clara Smith, Bessie Smith, and other cabaret theatre performers offered a somewhat more sophisticated style of performing. Those among this group who sang blues, particularly the last three named, often had a marked vaudeville edge to their musical performances, although they also often derived their music from the more archaic styles prevalent in rural areas. This "classic" blues style, as it is called, was established on record by Mamie Smith, and other record companies rushed to record female blues singers in this "classic" style. Indeed this more highly arranged, dramatic, stage-influenced vaudeville style made it on phonograph recordings before the older, rural blues that preceded it in development. Hughes was drawn strongly towards these vaudeville blues singers and their performances. While these vaudeville singers usually had a more sophisticated approach, delivery, and accompaniment than performers like Henry Thomas, Texas Alexander, and Blind Lemon Jefferson, they were not necessarily the slick professionals remote from the roots of the blues that folklorist Sam Charters and Leroi Jones have claimed they were. As ethnomusicologist Jeff Titon states, "the matter needs reexamination."[11] Undoubtedly some were slick professionals; others might have substituted the more sophisticated lyrics of Andry Razaf, Clarence Williams, and W. C. Handy for the lyrics of the oral tradition they knew better. Nonetheless, their performances were often smoother and less traditional than those of their rural blues counterparts. Hughes demonstrates his preference for singers of the vaudeville-type blues by naming Bessie, Clara, and Mamie Smith and Midge Williams as the finest blues singers, along with other polished but non-vaudeville blues performers like Lonnie Johnson and Jimmy Rushing, adding barrel-house pianist-vocalist Georgia White and folk-song performer Leadbelly; in the same essay he expresses a wish that Paul Robeson and Marian Anderson would have used blues in their performances.[12] This preference for a more sophisticated vaudeville-type approach fostered by the prevalence of that style in Harlem is markedly noticeable in the form and content of many of Hughes's blues poems.

Hughes also recounts in ***The Big Sea*** other sources for his knowledge of the blues: the singing of George from Kentucky aboard the *S.S. Malone* in 1923; pianist Palmer Jones in Paris, who sang "Old blues and folksongs . . . inserting off-color lyrics if the crowd was that kind of crowd;"[13] all night jam sessions in 1924 that produced earthy ensemble blues, featuring trumpet, violin, piano, clarinet, drums and vocals by blacks escaping back into the most traditional blues lyrics they could remember; folks on the streets, in pool halls and barrelhouses of Washington's Seventh Street in 1925; blues singers like Memphis Minnie, whose music he reviewed in 1943 in *The Defender;*[14] Josh White, who performed some of Hughes's lyrics; Brownie McGhee, who played Gitfiddle in "Simple Heavenly" in 1952; and many other blues performers like Meade Lux Lewis, Leadbelly, and Ray Charles, both in person and on record. The sources were diverse: rural and urban, lowdown and sophisticated, male and female.

Folklorists and aficionados were also an important source for collected material, and Hughes either knew many experts personally or could draw upon their works. Sterling Brown and Zora Neale Hurston were probably the closest to Hughes: both very likely had a broader knowledge of black folklore than Hughes, both published folklore articles. Hughes felt that Hurston was the most amusing of all Harlem Renaissance artists, due probably in no small part to her folk-knowledge and motherwit. The close contact with these people and the knowledge of the work of the Lomaxes and John Work provided additional blues material for Hughes.[15]

An artist's exposure to black folk culture does not automatically guarantee work of the calibre of Hughes's; a certain attitude towards the people and their creations is required to produce fine poetry. As early as 1925 in his **"The Negro Artist and the Racial Mountain,"** Hughes demonstrated an admiration for the ethnic distinctiveness of the "low down folks" with their heritage of rhythm and warmth, incongruous humor that so often, as in the blues, becomes ironic laughter mixed with tears."[16] As Onwuchekwa Jemie points out, the artist who wishes to express his blackness

> . . . will find a sturdy ally in the Black masses . . . with their confident humanity, their indifference to white opinion, their joie de vivre amidst depressing circumstances . . . they are the uncontaminated reservoir of the strength of the race, the body and vehicle of its traditions.[17]

Ultimately in this essay Hughes argues that black writers, sculptors, painters, and dramatists should use folklore and folk life as professional musicians have used black folk music. He is apparently thinking of more polished musicians like the "classic" blues singers or lyricist/arrangers like Razaf, Williams and Handy, who drew upon their black folk roots but had a somewhat more distanced perspective on those roots. In 1926 and the years to follow, there were many folk musicians recorded by recording companies; indeed the peak years of the "classic" blues singers (1923-26) gave over to the peak prewar years of blues recording (1927-30), when more folk artists than ever were recording—averaging nearly 500 blues and gospel records per year.[18] Thus one can speculate that, while Hughes held great admiration for the "low down folks," his artistic strategy was to attempt to impose a more sophisticated and literary scheme on the material.

Hughes's attitude toward the material itself is evident: "The real Negro blues are as fine as any folk music we have."[19] He feels that blues and spirituals are "the two great Negro gifts to American music." Generally Hughes is accurate in his statements about the oral blues tradition: the blues are, under normal circumstances, "usually sung by one man or woman alone"; they are "songs folks make up when their hearts hurt . . . sad funny songs. Too sad to be funny, and too funny to be sad;"[20] there are, in fact, "many kinds of blues . . . family blues . . . loveless blues . . . left lonesome blues . . . broke and hungry blues . . . desperate going-to-the-war blues."[21] However, the blues are to Hughes like the old hat he described finding in ***The Big Sea***: ". . . so valuable . . . quaint and folk-like . . ."[22] Since Hughes didn't intend his poetry to be simply unusual or an old-fashioned curiosity, his artistic attitude seems to revolve around the blues as a central resource for his literary art as opposed to finely wrought literary art in themselves. Hughes was much better at using the blues as a resource for his art than he was at producing a poem attempting to approximate authentic folk blues lyrics, because he tried to make those poems of his generally representative and quaintly humorous in a sad way, whereas there are startlingly original folk blues performers whose lyrics are either all sad or all funny. After all, if the blues are cathartic, and the audience laughs in response to a particularly sad lyric or experience with which they can identify, the song itself is still sad. Hughes knew that there are many different kinds of blues; thus when he calls blues "city songs rising from the crowded streets of big towns"[23] he indicates a preference for the types of blues closest to his artistic temperament: the composed, arranged, sophisticated blues of the "classic" blues singers he heard in Harlem, and of composers like W. C. Handy.

Handy, widely acclaimed "Father of the Blues," consciously took the songs of rural black musicians and worked them up into published material. Titon reports that Handy "believed he had refined black folk music by 'polishing' and publishing compositions based on the blues songs he had heard as a boy."[24] Hughes admired Handy for his part in helping disseminate and "legitimize" the blues through publishing efforts, particularly "Memphis Blues," and Handy's most famous composition, "St. Louis Blues." Hughes called the latter "one of America's best-known popular songs all over the world."[25] His letters to and from Arna Bontemps are peppered with references to Handy, especially regarding the use of "St. Louis Blues" in the play "St. Louis Woman,"[26] and as Jemie points out, Handy commented that Hughes's poem **"Hope"** said in four lines "what it would have taken Shakespeare two acts and three scenes to say."[27] Although the relationship between the two men needs to be further illuminated, it is apparent that both were concerned with "championing" the blues and with imposing some of their own ideas on the authentic folk material as well, Handy as a publishing musician/arranger and Hughes as a publishing poet.

Out of these varied sources and attitudes Hughes created his own blues-influenced poems, drawing heavily on oral tradition for his own literary ends in terms of structure, themes, and imagery. Hughes's poems, being written and not sung to accompaniment, obviously rely on carefully plotted attempts to render them in such a way as to capture the rhythm and spirit of performance on the page. Structurally, the traditional blues form is stanzaic, developing from the AAA pattern (the same thought repeated three times, as in Henry Thomas's "Texas Worried Blues") to the more common standard AAB pattern (the first thought repeated twice, the last word of which rhymes with the final word of the last line, which is a resolution). The chord structure of a standard blues, which characteristically lasts twelve bars, performed in the key of C involves three chords: C, F and G. Using numbers to indicate the beats (four beats to a bar) as the words are sung and placing the chord changes above the word where the chord changes, "Texas Worried Blues" is annotated thus:

```
      C
      1       2   3 4
The worried blues
  1  23 4          1     2 3 4     1 2 3
God I'm feelin' bad.
                 F
      4          1    2    3 4
I've got the worried blues
                        C
  1   2    3    4    1    2 3 4     1 2 3
God, I'm feelin' bad.
                   G
      4             1  2  3    4
I've got the worried blues
                        C
 1    2    3    4    1    2 3 4     1 2 3 4
God, I'm feelin' bad.
```

As shown, each bar does not begin or end with the first or last word of a line: here the first five words of lines 1, 3 and 5 are sung on pick up beats—the last beat of a bar—and the last words of lines 2, 3 and 6 end almost two bars before the words of the next line. Hughes was trying to capture the beat and rhythm of blues songs like this in his poetry, so if we were to annotate a part of his **"The Weary Blues"** like the blues lyric—not suggesting that Hughes's poems were sung or accompanied but simply that they were attempting to capture the spirit and structure of performance, the annotation would look like this:

```
          C
          1  2  3
I got de weary blues
     4          2   3 4   1    2 3 4     1 2 3
And I can't be satisfied.
         F
   4     1   2    3
Got de weary blues
                          C
4    1      2   3   4   1     2 3 4     1 2 3
And can't be satisfied.
          G
  4       1    2  3
I ain't happy no mo'
                               C
    4    1    2    3  4    1     2 3 4    1 2 3 4
And I wish that I had died.
```

A comparison of the two shows a remarkable similarity—basically it is Hughes's use of "and I" in lines 2 and 4 and 6 that accounts for the only substantial beat difference between the two.

Hughes, then, shows a strong ability to capture the beat and phrasing of blues songs. He also demonstrates a remarkable success with manipulating the formulaic quality of blues lyrics. Phrases like "I'm goin' away, babe" or "my gal mistreats me" recur frequently, but the formulas are not so fixed as to be merely memorized. They are part of a generating system that produces "a variety of rhythmic combinations that may be accommodated to a given tune."[28] Thus Hughes's

I woke up this mornin'
'Bout half past three[29]

and bluesman Furry Lewis's

Woke up this mornin'
Looked up against the wall[30]

are generated from the same song formula. Hughes generated many of his blues poems from these formulas, as a comparison between several of his blues poems and the lyrics of bluesmen reveals. Hughes's

I went down to the river
Sat down on the bank
I tried to think but couldn't
So I jumped in and sank.

(**"Life Is Fine"**)

parallels bluesman Peg Leg Howell's "Rock and Gravel Blues:"

Honey, let's go to the
River and sit down
Honey, let's go to the
River and sit down
If the blues overtakes us
Jump overboard and drown.[31]

Hughes's

I wish I had wings to
Fly like the eagle flies
Wish I had wings to
Fly like the eagle flies

I'd fly on ma man an'
I'd scratch out both his eyes.
(**"Hard Daddy"**)

is generated from the same formula as Peg Leg Howell's "Turtle Dove Blues:"

If I had wings like
Noah's turtle dove
If I had wings like
Noah's turtle dove
If I had wings like
Noah's turtle dove
I would rise and fly and
Light on the one I love.[32]

and Hughes's

I got de weary blues
And I can't be satisfied
(**"The Weary Blues"**)

derives from the same formula as Henry Thomas's "Texas Worried Blues" and Mississippi John Hurt's

Got the blues
Can't be satisfied[33]

Not only does Hughes draw upon song formulas for his lyrics, but he also presents his blues-influenced poems on the page in a manner approximating the blues singer's methods of singing his lines. Blues singers most often sing relatively short bursts of text, the pause sometimes located in off-beat places, as in Hughes's

I wish I had wings to

and Howell's

Honey, let's go to the

Thus when one transcribes these lines using Charles Olson's idea of Projective Verse, the single line of the blues singer can often be halved, creating two lines such as Hughes used in much of his twelve-bar blues poems. Therefore it is Hughes's knowledge of the blues tradition, not typographical accommodation nor the maintenance of a closer semblance to poetic form, that causes him to divide the lines as he does, rather than to render the stanza into a three-line AAB pattern. "Hard Daddy" (above), then, is in actuality a twelve-bar AAB stanza poem accommodated to the blues singer's way of rendering his material orally.

While poems like **"Morning After," "Widow Women," "Young Gal's Blues," "Midwinter Blues," "Lament Over Love,"** and **"Bound No'th Blues"** use this traditional twelve-bar AAB stanza form, other Hughes blues poems drawn on the traditional eight-bar ABCB pattern for their form. When Willie McTell sang,

C G
1 2 3 4 1 2 3
You may search the ocean
F
4 1 2 3 4 1 2 3
You might go 'cross the deep blue sea
C
4 1 2 3 4
Honey you'll never find
C
1 2 3 4 1 2 3 4 1 2 3 4
Another hot shot like me.[34]

to an eight-bar musical pattern, he was thinking in the same musical terms as Hughes in writing **"Sylvester's Dyin' Bed"**:

C G F
1 2 3 4 1 2 3 4 1
I woke up this mornin'
2 3 4 1 2 3 4
'Bout half past three.
C
4 1 2 3
All the womens in town
G C
4 1 2 3 4 1 2 3 4 1 2 3 4
Was gathered 'round me.

"Could Be," "Bad Luck Card," "Reverie on Harlem River," and **"As Befits a Man"** also follow the same pattern:

C G
1 2 3 4 1 2 3
I don't mind dyin'—
F
4 1 2 3 4 1 2 3
But I'd hate to die all alone!
C
4 1 2 3
I want a dozen pretty women
G C
4 1 2 3 4 1 2 3 4 1 2 3 4
To holler, cry and moan.
(**"As Befits a Man"**)

Thus these poems should not be seen as twelve-bar blues; the first thought is not repeated for typographical accommodation. Hughes is conceiving the above-mentioned poems in the same way as the blues singers conceived their eight-bar lyrics, as demonstrated by placing the chord changes and 32 beats applicable to the blues singers' performed eight-bar blues on Hughes's literary efforts.

"Reverie on Harlem River" is one of these eight-bar poems that uses typography for dramatic effect in its last stanza:

Down on Harlem River
Two A.M.
Midnight
By yourself

Lawd, I wish I could die—
But who would miss me if I left?

Here the second, third, and fourth lines are dramatically emphasized by division into three lines of material which actually lasts the same amount of beats as lines one, five, or six. Thus, we have here a kind of literary use of typography in a traditional blues stanza, indicating Hughes's willingness to use the resources of both the oral and written tradition to successfully deliver his work.

This is not the only eight-bar pattern in blues, and Hughes makes use of another eight-bar blues pattern, employed, for example, in Peetie Wheatstraw's "Ice and Snow Blues:"

```
                    C
                    1 2 3
I did more for you
   4              1   2 3
Than you understand
                    F
  4                 1       2   3
You can tell by the bullet holes
              4             1      2 3
Mama, now, here in my hand
                        C
     4                  1       2    3
Baby, now, you got to reap, baby
        G
  4   1    2 3
Just what,
          C
 4        1    2 3 4    1 2 3 4
what you sow.[35]
```

Hughes uses the same pattern in **"Southern Mammy Sings"**:

```
                         C
                       1          2 3
Miss Gardner's in her garden
  4                     1   2 3
Miss Yardman's in her yard
                          F
  4                     1        2 3
Miss Michaelmas is at de mass
  4              1        2 3 4
And I'm getting tired.
   C              G
   1234    123
   Lawd!
 C
 4         1         2 3 4    1 2 3 4
I'm gettin' tired!
```

In both the blues lyrics and the poems the first four lines are completed by the end of sixteen beats or four bars, and the last four bars comprise a kind of refrain that recurs in each stanza of both works. The last two lines of Hughes's poem replace the final three in Wheatstraw's stanza, which are admittedly protracted. The exclamation "Lawd" is stretched, for dramatic effect, to cover several beats—a common enough occurrence in blues music. Within this standard pattern Hughes presents a world in which people's names describe their activities or occupations, much more like a medieval order than a democracy. One each person is "in his place," typed, defined and/or limited by it, the Southern mammy—white folks' symbol of the beneficent, kind, happy, mother figure—protests her weariness of the situation. The poem goes on to complain about white folks in an unmasked way not common to traditional blues—at least as far as reflected by commercial releases, though there are black blues and non-blues traditional songs with direct anti-white statements.

Hughes's **"Same in Blues"** follows this same pattern, as demonstrated here with a comparison to Tampa Red's "It Hurts Me Too":

I said to my baby
Baby take it slow
I can't she said, I can't
I got to go!
    There's a certain
    amount of travelling
    in a dream deferred.

(**"Same in Blues"**)

I can't be happy, mama
For bein' so blue
When you keep on worryin'
The way you do
When things go wrong
Go wrong with you
It hurts me too.[36]

In **"Same in Blues,"** however, Hughes's modulation of the last three lines in each stanza—the refrain—creates a masterful effect quite unlike anything in traditional blues, as "travelling," "nothing," "importance," and "confusion" are identified as aspects of a dream deferred.

Poems like **"Life is Fine"** could fit into either one of the eight-bar patterns: the first if we consider the italicized words as interjections, the second if we consider them as a refrain:

I came up once and hollered!
I came up once and cried!
If that water hadn't a-been so cold
I might've sunk and died.

But it was
Cold in that water!
It was cold!

The former is much more likely, since Hughes doesn't use the words regularly as a refrain, and since he has used interjections in **"Ballad of the Gypsy," "Stony Lonesome,"** and his "boogie poems" in ***Montage of a Dream Deferred.***

The influences of twelve- and eight-bar stanzas are not always mutually exclusive in Hughes's poetry or traditional blues songs. Critic George Kent, in discussing **"Early Evening Quarrel"** and **"Lover's Return,"** states that "Hughes is at his best when he attempts to capture the blues spirit and varied forms of response to existence in a poem that uses non-blues devices."[37] He goes on to list free verse, free dramatizing of concrete situations, and the formal resources of literary technique as those non-blues devices applied in these poems. But these poems both use standard blues forms, not free verse, and the dramatizing in "Early Evening Quarrel" is not unlike the comedy-blues dialogues by such duos as Butterbeans and Susie, Grant and Wilson, Billy and Mary Mack, and Johy Byrd and Mae Glover. In **"Early Evening Quarrel"** the speaker alternates between male and female partners, each having one twelve-bar stanza apiece; as the poem continues, however, the stanzas switch to four lines apiece, and we need to confront the question of whether the stanza influence is eight-bar or something else. Something else seems more likely: Hughes may be resorting to a common device of comedy dialogue blues. These lines may be spoken lines, each lasting one bar, the whole three stanzas lasting twelve, but merely drawing upon a common popular device of comedy-blues dialogues.

"Lover's Return" may depend on a similar pattern, only this time the one-bar lines open the poem, which finishes with a traditional twelve-bar stanza. On the other hand, there is the possibility that the structure of the poem is based on four-line eight-bar stanzas for the first three stanzas of Hughes's poem, ending with a twelve-bar stanza. There are precedents for this mixture of stanzas in traditional blues, as in King Solomon Hill's "That Gone Dead Train":

And I'm goin' way down
Lord, I'm gonna try to leave here today
Tell me that's a mean old fireman
And that train is just that way.

Get on that train
I said I'd even brought my trunk
Boys if you had been running around this world
This train will wreck your mind.

Lord I once was a hobo
I crossed many points
But I decided I'd pull down for a fast life
And take it as it comes.

There's so many people
Have gone down today
And these fast trains north and south
Settled in . . . [?] . . . and Clay.

Mm Mm
I want to ride your train
I said look here engineer
Can I ride your train
He said look you ought to know this train ain't
mine
And you asking me in vain.[38]

These eight-bar stanzas are in actuality twelve-bar stanzas with the middle four bars removed, and from the twelve-bar stanza the song continues with two more twelve-bar stanzas, ending finally with a four-bar stanza. This modulation of stanza length is used elsewhere in traditional blues: Tommy Johnson's "Canned Heat Blues" and Furry Lewis's "Big Chief Blues" both employ twelve-bar stanzas throughout the performances, changing in the last verse to eight-bar stanzas, and Sunny Boy and His Pals in "France Blues" use all twelve-bar stanzas save for the second last verse.[39] While this practice on modulation of stanza length is not all that common, there is a precedent for Hughes to follow in his blues-influenced poems.

My old time daddy
Came back home last night.
His face was pale and
His eyes didn't look just right.
He says, "Mary, I'm
Comin' home to you—
So sick and lonesome
I don't know what to do!"

Oh, men treats women
Just like a pair o' shoes—
You kicks 'em round and
Does like you choose.

I looked at my daddy—
Lawd! And I wanted to cry.
He looked so thin—
Lawd! That I wanted to cry.
But the devil told me:

Damn a lover
Come home to die!

In this poem the first two stanzas set up the situation that causes the blues, while the third stanza, italicized, presents the woman's direct statement of her troubles. When in the last stanza the speaker reports that the devil said, "Damn a lover / come home to die!" and the words are italicized, one can identify the earlier stanza with the devil's words and motives, and realize that the female speaker is battling with herself from two points of view, personifying her bitterness and her rejection of her lover in the form of the devil, and identifying her true self with the compassion expressed in her description of his pitiful appearance and in the first four lines of the final stanza. The final stanza is lengthened to a twelve-bar stanza for an important purpose: stanza one sets the stage; stanza two gives the man's point of view; stanza three gives the "devil's"/hard line point of view; and the last stanza, the most lengthy one, combines the woman's/compassionate point of view with the devil/hard line approach. Thus Hughes uses traditional forms and typographical effect to build to his dramatic conclusion and indicate the psychological complexity of the situation.

From this more sophisticated use of the twelve- and eight-bar forms one can move to the slicker, vaudeville-type blues that seemed to attract Hughes so much. Vaudeville or "classic" blues singers often had a background in vaudeville or musical stage shows, as opposed to the traditional wandering blues singers who often played for small groups of friends or neighbors or at country dances or small, crowded bars. "Classic" blues singers were predominantly female, and were often billed as "queens" as they rather flamboyantly burlesqued opera prima donnas. As Titon points out, vaudeville blues "ordinarily began with a sung introduction, variable in form, in which the singer explained why she was blue," followed by the standard twelve-bar blues stanza, although the introduction could be, and was often, omitted. This structure owed a great deal to W. C. Handy.[40] While this is standard structure, the Tin Pan Alley tunesmiths, the often jazz or ragtime accompanists, and the "classic" blues singers often took liberties with the blues stanzas, and Hughes demonstrates a broad knowledge of those liberties.

"The Weary Blues" is a Hughes poem that seems influenced by vaudeville blues structures. Here Hughes narrates the story of a Harlem pianist, with an introduction that leads into standard twelve-bar blues stanzas and lyrics, and closes once again on the narrative role. The repeated use of rhymed couplets separated by refrains—lines 3, 6, 7, 8, 11, 14, 15, 16—lends heightened dramatization to the words after the manner of the vaudeville blues singers, and phrases like "mellow croon" and "crooned that tune" evoke a vaudeville-stage aura identifiable with the heightened drama and stagey romanticism of the vaudeville stage. However, here it is not the singer describing why he or she is blue, but the experience of a poet hearing a blues singer and understanding at bottom what the weary blues are and what they mean. While Hughes draws on the "classic" blues format, he is not a performer but an analytical, detached voice striving to identify with the "Sweet Blues! / Coming back from a black man's soul!"

THE WEARY BLUES

by

LANGSTON HUGHES

WITH AN INTRODUCTION BY
CARL VAN VECHTEN

NEW YORK
ALFRED · A · KNOPF
1926

Title page from *The Weary Blues,* by Langston Hughes.

"Blue Monday" is another type of vaudeville blues stanza, a sixteen-bar stanza:

1 2 3 4
No use in my going
1 2 3 4 1234 123
Downtown to work today,
4 1
It's eight
2 3 4 1
I'm late
2 3 4 1 234 1234
And it's marked down that-a-way
1 2 3
Saturday's and Sunday's
4 1 2 3 4
Fun to sport around
1 2 3
But no use denying—
4 1 2 3
Monday'll get you down
4 1 2 3 4
That old blue Monday
1 2 3 4 1 234 1234
Will surely get you down.

"Classic" blues singer Margaret Carter's "I Want Plenty Grease In My Frying Pan" has a similar structure:

1 2 3 4 1 2 3
I need plenty grease in my frying pan
4 1 2 3 4 1 234
'Cause I don't want my meat to burn
1 2 3 4 1 2 3
You know I asked you first to get me some lard
4 1 2 3 4 1 234
But it seems that you cannot learn.
1 2 3 4 1
You know I use plenty grease
2 3
Everyday
4 1 2 3 4
But I ain't did no frying while
1 2 3 4
You was away.
1 2 3 4 1 2 3
I need plenty grease in my frying pan
4 1 2 3 4 1 234
Cause I don't want my meat to burn.[41]

Basically the two works divide into three sections: the first five lines of the poem and the first four lines of the blues lyrics; the next four lines of each; and final two lines of each. While Carter's lyric is framed with the same two lines, and Hughes's builds to the conclusion, the two have a fairly similar vaudeville blues structure, and it is not hard to imagine a "red hot mama" singing Hughes's poem, complete with jazz-blues accompaniment and stop-time musical accompaniment to lines 6-9.

Other Hughes poems like **"Missing," "Cora," "Blues at Dawn," "Miss Blues'es Child,"** and **"Down and Out"** also draw on vaudeville blues influences, and since the vast majority of vaudeville blues singers were female, it is not surprising to find that the blues influences on Hughes's poems extend to the characterizations in that Hughes often uses female speakers in both his vaudeville and traditional blues poems. Clearly this is an influence of the Harlem environment and the prevalence of vaudeville blues singers in that locale. Hughes's blues-influenced poems **"Misery," "Cora," "Down and Out," "Widow Woman," "Young Gal Blues," "Hard Daddy," "Midwinter Blues," "Lament Over Love," "Lover's Return,"** and **"Southern Mammy Sings"** all utilize female speakers, indicating an interest not only in female vaudeville blues attitudes but also in the female point of view, as opposed to a strictly personal male point of view, as one would expect from a male traditional blues performer.

Therefore we can see in Hughes's work an attempt to represent both male and female speakers, portraying a broader spectrum of attitudes and experience. This is demonstrated clearly in Hughes's play ***Don't You Want To Be Free?*** which dramatizes a series of situations by illuminating them with blues lyrics appropriate to the situation. While Hughes's blues-influenced poems often indicate the sex of the speaker, **"Blue Monday," "The Weary Blues," "Blues at Dawn," "Miss Blues'es Child," "Bound No'th Blues"** and others sung in the play by a young man could be just as easily appropriate for a female. We cannot therefore automatically assume that a vaudeville blues poem necessarily has a female speaker, although within the blues tradition the female singer would be much more likely.

The female "blues-singers" of Hughes's blues poems are in direct contrast to the young female cabaret girls of some of his non-blues poems. Edward Waldron contends that the "blues women" are older and wiser than some of the sweet, young cabaret girls [Hughes] has whirling around much of his non-blues poetry.[42] The women of the blues poems are indeed world-wise and world-weary, alternately resolved and resigned, sometimes protesting, but these characteristics are meant to indicate advanced age. Those whirling cabaret girls function as exotic illusions to be played off against the reality of growing up fast in an overcrowded ghetto where the blues are never far off, where, as the poem goes, it "seems like trouble gonna drive me to my grave."[43] In other words, the difference in "age" is not so much chronological as it is experiential. Still, there is a poem like **"Young Gal's Blues"** that deals with the fear of the losses of looks and companionship that accompany the aging process. Ultimately, though, the vaudeville blues singers were not necessarily old women—in fact they were often young, vivacious, and extravagant—and the difference between them and the females in the non-blues poems has more to do with experience and outlook than with age.

The subject matter of Hughes's blues poems is, as Jemie points out, less varied than in the blues tradition:

> No topical or occasional blues, no prison or chain gang blues, no gambling blues, no blues about someone running his mouth . . . elaborate gun bores and weaponry of popular blues are absent . . . the popular letter motif is rare . . . there are no talking blues . . . social protest is rare in Hughes as in popular blues.[44]

In general these comments are true, though it should be pointed out that Hughes wrote an impromptu **"Goodbye Newport Blues"** for Muddy Waters and Otis Spann, commemorating the closing down of the Newport Jazz Festival due to rioting.[45] There are also brief, peripheral references to gambling in **"Ballad of the Fortune-Teller"** and **"Midnight Raffle."** The question of social protest is somewhat more difficult. The most pertinent question is whether the fact of a black man complaining of social status, situation, lifestyle, or complaining against social institutions, constitutes social protest. The powers that be certainly seem to perceive complaints—both direct and indirect—as threats, and therefore a form of protest. In this respect, the negative description of black social conditions in blues lyrics constitutes a complaint, albeit covert. Richard Wright has suggested that protest is encoded, and that unsuccessful love relationships described in blues lyrics are sublimated racial hostilities,[46] and indeed this is a possibility. Therefore the question of protest in blues lyrics is a complicated matter arguable from both sides.

Even under Jemie's definition, though, a poem like **"Southern Mammy Sings"** could be considered social protest. After stanza one puts everyone in his "proper place" and expresses a world-weariness, the southern mammy leaves her "place" by overtly criticizing the white man for wars, lynching, and slavery. In the last stanza she makes an ironic apology as precursor to her most telling comment, that white folks "just ain't got no heart." Clearly the last three stanzas express what was repressed or merely hinted at in the first stanza: a movement from covert to overt protest. This type of overt protest is, however, rare both in Hughes's poetry and in traditional blues.

Both these limitations in theme and imagery may be due in part to the influence of the urban vaudeville blues singers and their lyrics on Hughes. While both traditional and vaudeville blues took relations between lovers as primary subject matter, audiences—particularly white audiences—were much more likely to run across vaudeville blues on stage. Acknowledged attempts to "touch" up the rough, earthy, overtly sexual blues for the stage could help explain vaudeville blues' contribution to these limitations in Hughes's vaudeville-blues influenced poems. The lack of this sexual perspective in Hughes's traditional blues poems also helps explain part of the problem with the authenticity of those poems. Admittedly, sexual imagery was present in vaudeville blues, as evident from the text by Margaret Carter cited earlier, and by the recorded output of "Ma" Rainey and Bessie Smith—two of Hughes's favorites, which were often close to the direct, honest, and earthy expression of the folk roots. We need, then, to look elsewhere for further explanation of the causes of these restrictions on Hughes's work.

Hughes's vantage point seems to have caused him to aim for a quaint, clever humor with sometimes overly romantic lyrics, as in **"Miss Blues'es Child,"** as opposed to, for example, the powerful and/or double entendre lyrics of Peetie Wheatstraw's "Ice and Snow Blues," cited previously, or Robert Johnson's "Hellhound on My Trail,"

> I can tell the wind is risin'
> The leaves tremblin' on the trees
> Tremblin' on the trees.

and "Terraplane Blues,"

> I'm gonna hoist your hood, mama,
> I'm bound to check your oil.[47]

Bluesmen like Wheatstraw and Johnson were able to create stronger pure blues lyrics than Hughes because their blues were personal expressions of their own lives and experiences within the tradition; not something, as in Hughes's poems, often written about or for other people, symbolic of the souls' desires of a nation of "low down folks." In Hughes, though, those wants eliminate the sexual desires so often expressed in blues lyrics. That he was aware of the sexuality in blues lyrics is evident: in ***The Big Sea*** he quotes a blues from the rue Pigalle:

> Lawd, I looked and saw a spider
> Goin' up de wall.
> I say, I looked and saw a spider
> Goin' up de wall.
> I say where you goin', Mister Spider?
> I'm goin' to get my ashes hauled![48]

It is likely also that Hughes was not bawdy, violent, or extreme in much of his published work because publishers were not interested in so-called "objectionable" material like that published posthumously in ***Good Morning Revolution.*** Indeed Hughes himself developed a natural reticence to discuss such material. Hughes seems to have struck a compromise: a deep pride in, a deep commitment to, the blues tradition in America, tempered by a desire to present a less extreme or offensive face to the public for acceptance, and by the imposed limitations of the publishing establishment. The acceptance that Hughes sought was not only for himself, but for the black oral tradition, and it was an acceptance that provided a beat to which his poetic successors would sing more bawdy, violent, or extreme verses.

If the startling impact and poetic devices of top-drawer bluesmen like Wheatstraw and Johnson are not matched by Hughes's blues poems, Hughes's impact as a popularizer and "legitimizer" of blues and as a professional artist imposing some external intellectual constraints of the genre—in variety and violation of structure and manipulation of the benefits of a writer as opposed to oral work—more than make up for his limitations. Poems like **"The Weary Blues," "Southern Mammy Sings,"** and **"Same in Blues"** are most successful, transcending the absence of an actual musical and vocal performance by capturing the spirit in the cadence of the lines, and extending the limits of the oral tradition by altering or breaking the existing structures or themes of the blues.

The range of Langston Hughes's interest in and knowledge of the blues tradition and his attempts to employ aspects of the oral blues tradition in his work reveal his genius in recognizing the blues as a truly great folk art in itself, and a worthy resource for writers of the Harlem Renaissance and beyond. While there are some obvious limitations to Hughes's work in presenting a totally forthright picture of the blues tradition, the poems he has left, in their skillful use of a tradition whose beauty and creativity is still often only suspected, deserve to be read and remembered.

A Selection of Hughes's Poems Categorized by the Blues Stanza Form Utilized, With Identification of the Sex of the Speaker

12 Bar Blues	
Morning After	Male
Widow Woman	Female
Young Gal's Blues	Female
Hard Daddy	Female
Midwinter Blues	Female
Lament Over Love	Female
Bound No'th Blues	Undetermined
Stony Lonesome	Undetermined
8 Bar Blues	
Sylvester's Dyin' Bed	Male
Could Be	Undetermined
Bad Luck Card	Undetermined
As Befits A Man	Male
Midnight Raffle	Undetermined
Life is Fine	Undetermined
Southern Mammy Sings	Female
Same in Blues	Male and Female
Vaudeville Type Blues	
The Weary Blues	Undetermined
Blue Monday	Undetermined
Misery	Female
Cora	Female
Blues at Dawn	Undetermined
Miss Blues'es Child	Undetermined
Down and Out	Female
Stanzaic Mixtures	
Early Evening Quarrel	Male and Female
Lover's Return	Female

Notes

1. Samuel Charters, *The Bluesmen* (New York: Oak Publications, 1967), p. 166.
2. Langston Hughes, *The Big Sea* (New York: Hill and Wang, 1963), p. 215. The following lines from "The Weary Blues" are quoted from the same page.
3. Henry Thomas, "Texas Worried Blues," *Ragtime Texas,* Herwin LP 209. Throughout this work references to blues recordings will be listed not by the original 78 RPM issues, but by available 33 RPM reissues. This practice will enable the reader to procure copies of the recordings for illumination.
4. Henry Thomas, "Railroading Some," Herwin LP 209.
5. Liner notes to *Have No Fear, Big Joe Turner Is Here,* Savoy LP 2223. The following quote also occurs in these notes.
6. Charles Keil, *Urban Blues* (Chicago: University of Chicago Press, 1966), p. 61.
7. Nat Pierce, Liner Notes to *Kansas City Piano,* Decca LP 79226.
8. ARC, Columbia, Brunswick, Library of Congress, Vocalion, and Okeh, among others.
9. Ramblin' Willard Thomas, "Poor Boy Blues," *Blind Lemon Jefferson/Ramblin' Willard Thomas,* Collector's Classics LP CC5.
10. Horace Butterworth, Liner Notes to *Tex-Arkana-Louisiana Country,* Yazoo, LP 1004.
11. Jeff Titon, *Early Downhome Blues* (Urbana, Ill.: Univ. of Chicago Press, 1979), p. 104. See also Samuel Charters, *The Country Blues* (New York: Holt, Rinehart, and Winston, 1959) and Leroi Jones, *Blues People* (New York: William Morrow, 1959).
12. Langston Hughes, "Songs Called the Blues," *The Langston Hughes Reader,* ed. George Braziller (New York: George Braziller, Inc. 1958), pp. 159-61.
13. Hughes, *The Big Sea,* p. 161.
14. Langston Hughes, "Music at Year's End," *Chicago Defender,* 9 January 1943.
15. Langston Hughes, Cliff Roberts, and David Martin, *The First Book of Jazz* (New York: Franklin Watts, Inc. 1955).
16. Langston Hughes, "The Negro Artist and the Racial Mountain," The *Nation,* 23 June 1925, pp. 692-714.
17. Onwuchekwa Jemie, *Langston Hughes* (New York: Columbia University Press, 1976), pp. 77.
18. R. M. W. Dixon and John Godrich, *Recording the Blues* (New York: Stein and Day, 1970), pp. 104-5.
19. *The Langston Hughes Reader,* p. 161. The next two quotations also occur on p. 161.
20. *The Negro Renaissance,* ed. Arthur P. Davis and Michael W. Peplow (New York: Holt, Rinehart and Winston, 1975), p. 280.
21. *The Langston Hughes Reader,* p. 159.
22. Hughes, *The Big Sea,* p. 299.
23. *The Langston Hughes Reader,* p. 159.
24. Titon, p. 203.
25. Hughes, Roberts and Martin, p. 19.
26. *Arna Bontemps-Langston Hughes Letters 1925-67.* Selected and ed. by Chas. H. Nichols (New York: Dodd & Mead, 1980), p. 524.

27. Jemie, p. 77.

28. Titon, p. 179.

29. Langston Hughes, "Sylvester's Dyin' Bed," *Selected Poems of Langston Hughes,* ed. Langston Hughes (New York: Vintage Books, 1974), p. 38. Hereafter all quotations of Hughes's poems will be from this edition, and will be documented by poem titles and page numbers in parentheses within the text.

30. Furry Lewis, "Creeper's Blues," *Frank Stokes' Dream,* Yazoo LP 1008.

31. Peg Leg Howell, "Rock and Gravel Blues," *Blues From Georgia,* Roots LP RL 309.

32. Peg Leg Howell, "Turtle Dove Blues," *Blues from Georgia,* Roots LP RL 309.

33. Mississippi John Hurt, "Got the Blues, Can't Be Satisfied," *Mississippi John Hurt 1928.* Biograph LP BLP-C4.

34. Blind Willie McTell, "Searching the Desert for the Blues," *Bluebird Blues,* RCA Victor LP V-518.

35. Peetie Wheatstraw, "Ice and Snow Blues," *Kokoma Arnold/Peetie Wheatstraw,* Blues Classics, LP PC4.

36. Tampa Red, "It Hurts Me Too," *The Guitar Wizard,* Blues Classics LP BC25.

37. George Kent, "Langston Hughes and Afro American Folk and Cultural Tradition," *Langston Hughes: Black Genius,* ed. Therman B. O'Daniel (New York: William Morrow and Co., Inc., 1971), p. 202.

38. King Solomon Hill, "That Gone Dead Train," *Tex-Arkana-Louisiana Country.* Yazoo LP 1004.

39. Tommy Johnson, "Canned Heat Blues," *The Famous 1928 Tommy Johnson Ishman Bracey Session,* Roots LP RL330; Furry Lewis, "Big Chief Blues," in *The Blues Line,* ed. Eric Sackheim, (New York: Schirmer Books, 1975), p. 253; and Sunny Boy and his Pals, "France Blues," *Really! The Country Blues,* Origin LP OJL-2.

40. Titon, p. xvi (preface), referring to Handy's published blues efforts that helped to standardize structure, much as the employment of the printing press had helped to standardize language.

41. Margaret Carter, "I Want Plenty Grease In My Frying Pan," *Pot Hound Blues,* Historical LP HLP15.

42. Edward Waldron, "The Blues Poetry of Langston Hughes," *Negro American Literature Forum* 5 (1971), 144.

43. Davis, p. 282.

44. Jemie, p. 45.

45. Muddy Waters, "Goodbye Newport Blues," *Muddy Waters at Newport,* Chess LP 1449.

46. Richard Wright, Forward to Paul Oliver's *Meaning of the Blues* (New York: Collier Books, 1972), pp. 7-12. See also Paul Oliver, *The Blues Tradition* (New York: Oak Publications, 1970), pp. 258-9.

47. Robert Johnson, "Hellhound on My Trail," and "Terraplane Blues," *King of the Delta Blues Singers,* Columbia LP CL1654.

48. Hughes, *The Big Sea,* p. 162.

TITLE COMMENTARY

The Weary Blues

COUNTEE CULLEN (ESSAY DATE 1926)

SOURCE: Cullen, Countee. Review of Langston Hughes's *The Weary Blues. Opportunity* (February 2, 1926).

In the following review, Cullen admires Hughes's "traditional" lyrics but is less than enthusiastic about his jazz poems and the emphasis on "Negro themes" in The Weary Blues.

Here is a poet with whom to reckon, to experience, and here and there, with that apologetic feeling of presumption that should companion all criticism, to quarrel.

What has always struck me most forcibly in reading Mr. Hughes' poems has been their utter spontaneity and expression of a unique personality. This feeling is intensified with the appearance of his work in concert between the covers of a book. It must be acknowledged at the outset that these poems are peculiarly Mr. Hughes' and no one's else. I cannot imagine his work as that of any other poet, not even of any poet of that particular group of which Mr. Hughes is a member. Of course, a microscopic assiduity might reveal derivation and influences, but these are weak undercurrents in the flow of Mr. Hughes' own talent. This poet represents a transcendently emancipated spirit among a class of young writers whose particular battle-cry is freedom. With the enthusiasm of a zealot, he pursues his way, scornful, in subject matter, in photography, and rhythmical treatment, of whatever obstructions time and tradition have placed before him. To him it is essential that he be himself. Essential and commendable surely; yet the thought persists that some of these poems would have been better had Mr. Hughes held himself a bit in check. In his admirable introduction to the book, Carl Van Vechten says the poems have a *highly deceptive air of spontaneous improvisation.* I do not feel that the air is deceptive.

If I have the least powers of prediction, the first section of this book, "The Weary Blues," will be most admired, even if less from intrinsic poetical worth than because of its dissociation from the traditionally poetic. Never having been one to think all subjects and forms proper for poetic consideration, I regard these jazz poems as interlopers in the company of the truly beautiful poems in other sections of the book. They move along with the frenzy and electric heat of a Meth-

FROM THE AUTHOR

"THE WEARY BLUES"

Droning a drowsy syncopated tune,
Rocking back and forth to a mellow
croon,
I heard a Negro play.

Down on Lenox Avenue the other night
By the pale dull pallor of an old gas light

SOURCE: Langston Hughes, opening lines to "The Weary Blues," in *The Weary Blues,* Knopf, 1926.

odist or Baptist revival meeting, and affect me in much the same manner. The revival meeting excites me, cooling and flushing me with alternate chills and fevers of emotion; so do these poems. But when the storm is over, I wonder if the quiet way of communing is not more spiritual for the God-seeking heart; and in the light of reflection I wonder if jazz poems really belong to that dignified company, that select and austere circle of high literary expression which we call poetry. Surely, when in **"Negro Dancers"** Mr. Hughes says

Me an' ma baby's
Got two mo' ways,
Two mo' ways to do de buck!

he voices, in lyrical, thumb-at-nose fashion the happy careless attitude, akin to poetry, that is found in certain types. And certainly he achieves one of his loveliest lyrics in **"Young Singer."** Thus I find myself straddling a fence. It needs only **"The Cat and The Saxophone,"** however, to knock me over completely on the side of bewilderment, and incredulity. This creation is a *tour de force* of its kind, but is it a poem:

EVERYBODY

Half-pint,
Gin?
No, make it

LOVES MY BABY
corn. You like
don't you, honey?
BUT MY BABY. . . .

In the face of accomplished fact, I cannot say *This will never do,* but I feel that it ought never to have been done.

But Mr. Hughes can be as fine and as polished as you like, etching his work in calm, quiet lyrics that linger and repeat themselves. Witness **"Sea Calm:"**

How still,
How strangely still
The water is today.
It is not good
For water
To be so still that way.

Or take **"Suicide's Note"**:

The Calm,
Cool face of the river
Asked me for a kiss.

Then crown your admiration with **"Fantasy in Purple,"** this imperial swan-song that sounds like the requiem of a dying people:

Beat the drums of tragedy for me,
Beat the drums of tragedy and death.
And let the choir sing a stormy song
To drown the rattle of my dying breath.

Beat the drums of tragedy for me,
And let the white violins whir thin and slow,
But blow one blaring trumpet note of sun
To go with me to the darkness where I go.

Mr. Hughes is a remarkable poet of the colorful; through all his verses the rainbow riots and dazzles, yet never wearies the eye, although at times it intrigues the brain into astonishment and exaggerated admiration when reading, say something like **"Caribbean Sunset:"**

God having a hemorrhage,
Blood coughed across the sky,
Staining the dark sea red:
That is sunset in the Caribbean.

Taken as a group the selections in this book seem one-sided to me. They tend to hurl this poet into the gaping pit that lies before all Negro writers, in the confines of which they become racial artists instead of artists pure and simple. There is too much emphasis here on strictly Negro themes; and this is probably an added reason for my coldness toward the jazz poems—they seem to set a too definite limit upon an already limited field.

Dull books cause no schisms, raise no dissensions, create no parties. Much will be said of ***The Weary Blues*** because it is a definite achievement, and because Mr. Hughes, in his own way, with a first book that cannot be dismissed as merely *promising,* has arrived.

ALAIN LOCKE (ESSAY DATE 1926)

SOURCE: Locke, Alain. Review of *The Weary Blues*. In *The Critics and the Harlem Renaissance*, edited by Cary D. Wintz, pp. 151-54. New York: Garland Publishing, 1996.

In the following review, which was originally published in 1926, Locke sees Hughes as the spokesman for Black Americans and praises his poetry.

I believe there are lyrics in [***The Weary Blues***] which are such contributions to pure poetry that it makes little difference what substance of life and experience they were made of, and yet I know no other volume of verse that I should put forward as more representatively the work of a race poet than ***The Weary Blues.*** Nor would I style Langston Hughes a race poet merely because he writes in many instances of Negro life and consciously as a Negro; but because all his poetry seems to be saturated with the rhythms and moods of Negro folk life. A true 'people's poet' has their balladry in his veins; and to me many of these poems seem based on rhythms as seasoned as folk-songs and on moods as deep-seated as folk-ballads. Dunbar is supposed to have expressed the peasant heart of his people. But Dunbar was the showman of the Negro masses; here is their spokesman. The acid test is the entire absence of sentimentalism; the clean simplicity of speech the deep terseness of mood. Taking these poems too much merely as the expressions of a personality, Carl Van Vechten in his debonair introduction wonders at what he calls "their deceptive air of spontaneous improvisation". The technique of folk song and dance are instinctively there, giving to the individual talent the bardic touch and power. Especially if Hughes should turn more and more to the colloquial experiences of the common folk whom he so intimately knows and so deeply loves, we may say that the Negro masses have found a voice, and promise to add to their natural domain of music and the dance the conquest of the province of poetry. Remember—I am not speaking of Negro poets, but of Negro poetry.

Poetry of a vitally characteristic racial flow and feeling then is the next step in our cultural development. Is it to be a jazz-product? The title poem and first section of ***The Weary Blues*** seem superficially to suggest it. But let us see.

And far into the night he crooned that tune.
The stars went out and so did the moon.

Or this:

Sing your Blues song,
Pretty baby,
You want lovin'
And you don't mean maybe.

Jungle lover. . . .
Night-black boy. . . .
Two against the moon
And the moon was joy.

Here,—I suspect yet uncombined, are the two ingredients of the Negro poetry that will be truly and beautifully representative: the rhythm of the secular ballad but the imagery and diction of the Spiritual. Stranger opposites than these have fused to the fashioning of new beauty. Nor is this so doctrinaire a question as it seems, when considering a poet who has gone to the cabaret for some of his rhythms and to the Bible for others.

In the poems that are avowedly racial, Hughes has a distinctive note. Not only are these poems full of that passionate declaration and acceptance of race which is a general characteristic of present day Negro poets, but there is a mystic identification with the race experience which is, I think, instinctively deeper and broader than any of our poets has yet achieved.

"The Negro Speaks of Rivers" catches this note for us most unmistakably:

I've known rivers;
I've known rivers ancient as this world and older
    than the flow of human blood in human in
    veins.

My soul has grown deep like the rivers.

I bathed in the Euphrates when dawns were
    young.
I built my hut near the Congo and it lulled me to
    sleep.
I looked upon the Nile and raised the pyramids
    above it.
I heard the singing of the Mississippi when Abe
    Lincoln went down to New Orleans, and
    I've seen its muddy bosom turn all golden in
    the sunset.

I've known rivers;
Ancient, dusky rivers.

My soul has grown deep like the rivers.

Remembering this as the basic substratum of this poetry, we may discriminatingly know to what to attribute the epic surge underneath its lyric swing the primitive fatalism back of its nonchalance, the ancient force in its pert colloquialisms, the tropic abandon and irresistibleness of its sorrow and laughter.

No matter how whimsical or gay the poet may carry his overtones after this, or how much of a bohemian or happy troubadour he may assume to be, we will always hear a deep, tragic undertone pulsing in his verse. For the Negro experience rightly sensed even in the moods of the common folk is complex and paradoxical like the Blues which Hughes has pointed out to be so characteristic, with their nonchalant humor against a background of tragedy; there is always a double mood, mercurial to the artist's touch like an easily improvised tune. As our poet himself puts it:

In one hand
I hold tragedy
And in the other
Comedy,—
Masks for the soul.

Laugh with me.
You would laugh!
Weep with me,
Would you weep!

Tears are my laughter.
Laughter is my pain.
Cry at my grinning mouth,
If you will.
Laugh at my sorrow's reign.

Fine Clothes for the Jew

ARNOLD RAMPERSAD (ESSAY DATE 1986)

SOURCE: Rampersad, Arnold. "Langston Hughes's *Fine Clothes to the Jew.*" *Callaloo* 9, no. 1 (1986): 144-58.

In the following essay, Rampersad offers a detailed reading of the poems in Fine Clothes for the Jew, *which he considers to be Hughes's finest collection of verse and one of the most significant volumes of American poetry.*

As prolific as Langston Hughes strove to be in a variety of genres—poetry, fiction, drama, and essays notably—he saw himself from first to last primarily as a poet. Of his many collections of verse, nine must be considered major in his career by almost any accounting: ***The Weary Blues*** (1926); ***Fine Clothes to the Jew*** (1927); ***Shakespeare in Harlem*** (1942); ***Fields of Wonder*** (1947); ***One-Way Ticket*** (1949); ***Montage of a Dream Deferred*** (1951); ***Ask Your Mama*** (1961); and ***The Panther and the Lash*** (posthumously in 1967, the year of his death). To these efforts might be added the volume published by the leftist International Workers Order, ***A New Song*** (1938); although it contained no new poems, the verse in that slender pamphlet was unusually radical and had not been collected previously.

Of these volumes, the least successful both in terms of sales and of critical reception, at least among black reviewers, was unquestionably ***Fine Clothes to the Jew.*** I would like to argue that, paradoxically, this volume was by far Hughes's greatest collection of verse, that the collection marked the height of his creative originality as a poet, and that it remains one of the most significant single volumes of poetry ever published in the United States. In fact, despite its failure to gain recognition, ***Fine Clothes to the Jew*** may stand in relationship to black American poetry in a way not unlike Walt Whitman's 1855 edition of *Leaves of Grass* stands in relationship to white American poetry, or to the poetry of the nation as a whole.

Fine Clothes to the Jew appeared almost ten years after Hughes first began to write poetry. While his work in Lincoln, Illinois (where by his own account he wrote his first poem, in 1916), is lost, almost all of his poems written in high school in Cleveland and thereafter are available to scholars. They may be found in the *Central High School Monthly, Crisis, Opportunity,* and other magazines published largely by blacks, as well as in white magazines that cover the broad ideological spectrum from *Vanity Fair,* on one hand, to the communist *New Masses,* on the other. The work of these first years culminated in the appearance from Knopf of Hughes's first book of any kind, ***The Weary Blues. Fine Clothes to the Jew,*** the next, built on elements found in the previous volume and in the magazines, but with such emphases and revisions that it marked, in effect, an unparalleled rethinking by Hughes about poetry in the context of black America.

Once Hughes shed his most youthful approaches to poetry and felt the stirring influence of Walt Whitman, whose lines he echoed unmistakably in his first published free verse poem, **"A Song of the Soul of Central"** (*Central High School Monthly,* January 1919) and Carl Sandburg ("my guiding star"), his poetry fell almost inevitably into three distinct areas.[1] The first area found Hughes dwelling on isolation, despair, suicide, and the like—conventional themes for a young, romantic poet, to be sure, but notions strongly felt by Hughes personally as he struggled to overcome the effects of his father's desertion and his mother's flighty compromise of her relationship with her son. A poem such as **"Suicide's Note"** ("The calm / Cool face of the river / Asked me for a kiss") exemplifies this mode.[2] The second area, also present virtually from the start of Hughes's career as a poet and fiction writer, reveals an aggressive socialist, non-racial intelligence, as for example in the very titles of two poems written later, in 1932: **"Good Morning Revolution"** and **"Goodbye Christ."** The third area, for which

Hughes is almost certainly best known, finds him creating in direct response to the needs of black people—epitomized by **"The Negro Speaks of Rivers,"** published in 1921.

Whatever distinction as a poet Hughes possesses almost certainly derives from his work in this last, racial vein. In his poetry of race, one again notes relatively clear subdivisions. Some poems protest the social conditions of blacks specifically; some are boldly declarative of the beauty and dignity of the race; still others—perhaps the most revered—transcend both angry protest and bold declaration to affirm quietly the dignity and historicity of blacks. Hughes's best known poems, such as **"The Negro," "Dream Variations,"** and **"When Sue Wears Red,"** almost all fall into one or another of these categories.

In its most representative work, however, ***Fine Clothes to the Jew*** falls outside of these categories. Although all of the poems in the various categories naturally involve a poetic concern with the manipulation of form, ***Fine Clothes to the Jew*** is based in essence on what one might acknowledge as a separate aesthetic, a different approach to poetic art. In the other work, Hughes writes—in spite of his concern with race—as a poet impelled by the literary tradition as defined by certain major poets of the language—in particular, Walt Whitman and his epigones, notably Carl Sandburg and Vachel Lindsay. But in ***Fine Clothes*** Hughes attempted to work in a way no black or white poet had ever attempted to work: deliberately defining poetic tradition according to the standards of a group often seen as sub-poetic—the black masses.

In the interest of accuracy, it must be noted that although the two approaches are presented here as contradictory, Hughes would probably never have attempted the latter if he had not found the encouragement and the signs to do so in the former, especially in Whitman's historic vision of democratic voices and his primary search for an authentic, American language of poetry. On the other hand, in his dignifying of certain Afro-American forms, Hughes explored areas which Whitman had not conceived, and of which Whitman, with his documented biases against blacks in spite of his attractive portraits of them in a few places in *Leaves of Grass,* probably would not have approved.

Hughes himself did not suddenly become enlightened by his finest insights into Afro-American form. Until 1923, perhaps the closest he had come to letting the black masses speak through his art was in **"Mother to Son."** This apparently simple poem amounted to nothing less than a personal reclamation of black dialect (Dunbar's "jingle in a broken tongue") for the black poet; surely **"Mother to Son"** takes us beyond the poles of low comedy and pathos identified by William Dean Howells (in praising Dunbar's use of dialect) as the range of the black race.[3] In Hughes's poem, black speech is invoked in the context of the race's courage, endurance, and sense of duty. But dialect would be only incidental to the major initiative of Hughes in the question of poetic form; at the center of his effort would be the recognition of a link between poetry and black music, and in particular the music not of the dignified and Europeanized spirituals, so often lauded, but of the earthy, almost "unspeakable" blues.

For his first few years as a poet, even as he grew technically proficient, Hughes had no idea what to do with a form he had heard first as a child in Lawrence, Kansas, and in Kansas City, Missouri. Even then he had responded emotionally, as he would assert, to the deep, piercing sadness of the music; later, no doubt, he began to marvel at its curious, accompanying impulse toward laughter. But how was he to effect a link between his learned standards of formal poetry and songs created by the artist among the masses? This question masquerades as one simply of technique; however, it concerns not only the realities of political power—the social powerlessness of blacks translated into the declassification of their art—but the ability of the individual to attain a sufficiently deep identification with his people and their modes of utterance so that, on an individual initiative, he is able to affect a dignified fusion of learned poetic values with those of the despised masses.

When Hughes opened his greatest essay, **"The Negro Artist and the Racial Mountain"** (1926) by equating the desire of a certain young black poet to be seen as nothing but a poet with the desire to be white, he was (perhaps reductively) stating his understanding of the most complex problem facing the young black writer. Hughes and, no doubt, some other young black writers had no literal desire to be white. Nevertheless, the domination of white poetic standards through the many unquestionably alluring volumes of white verse, backed ultimately by the domination of white culture, effectively made their dilemma forbiddingly close to that of a racial death-wish described by Hughes at the start of the essay. Because his will to solve this conundrum was so strong, however, Langston Hughes progressed where others stagnated. But he progressed only in stages.

Not long after **"The Negro Speaks of Rivers,"** Hughes began to offer, as poetry, the barely mediated recording of the sounds and sights of black life, notably in religion. One poem, **"Prayer Meeting"** (1922-1923), may stand here as an example.

> Glory! Hallelujah!
> The dawn's a-comin'!
> Glory! Hallelujah!
> The dawn's a-comin'!
> A black old woman croons
> In the amen-corner of the
> Ebecaneezer Baptist Church—
> A black old woman croons—
> The dawn's a-comin'![4]

In his willingness to stand back and record, with minimal intervention, aspects of the drama of black religion (and, later, of music and dance), Hughes clearly showed that he had begun to see his own learned poetic art, even with his individual talent, as inferior to that of "ordinary" blacks—inferior, for example, to an old black woman in the amen corner who cries to Jesus, "Glory! Hallelujah!" At the heart of his sense of inferiority—which empowered rather than debilitated Hughes—was the knowledge that he (and other would-be poets) stood to a great extent *outside* the culture he worshipped. Perhaps Hughes stood at a greater distance from the masses than did most other black poets. Raised in relative isolation and with a haunting sense of parental abandonment, he stood outside because much of his life had been spent away from consistent involvement with the very people whose affection and regard he craved.

A more fateful step came one night in March, 1923, after a visit to a cabaret in Harlem, when he finally wrote himself and his awkward position *vis à vis* his race accurately into a poem, **"The Weary Blues."**

> Droning a drowsy syncopated tune,
> Rocking back and forth to a mellow croon,
>   I heard a Negro play.
> Down on Lenox Avenue the other night
> By the pale dull pallor of an old gas light
>   He did a lazy sway. . . .
>   He did a lazy sway. . . .
> To the tune o' those Weary Blues . . .

The distance between the persona or narrator of the poem (what is his race, for example, if he hears "a Negro" play and for whom is he writing?) and the black bluesman is the distance between the would-be black poet and his people. The poem has sprung equally from the poet's isolation and his will to admire. But Hughes, in an unprecedented step, also allowed the black bluesman a chance to sing his song, with minimal interference from conventional white poetic values.

> "Ain't got nobody in all this world,
> Ain't got nobody but ma self.
> I's gwine to quit ma frownin'
> And put ma troubles on the shelf."
> Thump, thump, thump, went his foot on the
>   floor.
> He played a few chords then he sang some
>   more . . .[5]

Within a poem based in conventional form, Hughes sets blues lyrics he had heard as a child in Kansas. The result is that, in one and the same work, the poet honors both the tradition of Europe (out of necessity, since he is writing in English) and the tradition of black America (achieved *in spite of* the English language). The latter tradition, in fact, invades the former; one must measure the opening lines of the poem against the cadences of urban black speech, derived from the South. This invasion was so unprecedented that the persona (and the poet, of course) does not know what to make of it. By his own admission, Hughes had a hard time ending the poem. For two years, he kept the poem, "whose ending I had never been able to get quite right," unpublished—at a time when he was trying to publish almost everything he wrote.[6] Rather than share this "beauty of a cabaret poem" with anyone, Hughes kept it from sight.[7] Meanwhile, he struggled to shape its ending—"I could not achieve an ending I liked, although I worked and worked on it."[8] Finally, the end confirms the persona's bewilderment and the bluesman's mystery:

> And far into the night he crooned that tune.
> The stars went out and so did the moon.
> The singer stopped playing and went to bed
> While the Weary Blues echoed through his head
> He slept like a rock or a man that's dead.

Hughes was for two years indecisive about how to end the poem. During that period, he spent a few months in a Paris nightclub in 1924, where the entertainers were black American jazz singers and musicians. He then became bolder in his incorporations of black music and dance into his poetry. One poem frames the cry of an exuberant black dancer: "Me an' ma baby's / Got two mo' ways, / Two mo' ways to do de buck!"[9] In **"To A Negro Jazz Band in a Parisian Cabaret,"** he urges the black musicians to "Play that thing" for the white lords and ladies, "whores and gigolos," and "the school teachers out on a spree. Play it!"

May I?
Mais oui.
Mein Gott!
Parece una rumba.
!Que rumba!
Play it, jazz band!
You've got seven languages to speak in
And then some.
Can I?
Sure.[10]

A year in Washington, D.C., 1925, away from Parisian nightclub glitter but closer to the more elemental art forms of the black masses, only deepened his respect for the power of black music and its "lowly" source. "Like the waves of the sea coming one after another," he would write, "like the earth moving around the sun, night, day—night, day—forever, so is the undertow of black music with its rhythm that never betrays you, its strength like the beat of the human heart, its humor, and its rooted power." More and more he let the common people, and not the poets deemed great by the master culture, guide him. "I tried to write poems like the songs they sang on Seventh Street—gay songs, because you had to be gay or die; sad songs, because you couldn't help being sad sometimes. But gay or sad, you kept on living and you kept on going."[11]

The publication of ***The Weary Blues*** (January, 1926) did not entirely reflect this commitment; the manuscript was accepted in May of the previous year, and mainly comprised poems written much earlier. Apart from the quotation of blues in the title poem, and even briefer quotations in **"Blues Fantasy"** (Hey! Hey! / That's what the / Blues singers say . . ."), the blues is not present in the book—in spite of its sonorous title.[12] For every "race poem," another exists that has nothing to do with black culture. The result is a mulatto-like text. This should not be surprising since the mulatto theme—and its transcendence—is one of the most prominent in Hughes's work. But to many readers ***The Weary Blues*** had gone much too far toward the black masses. Countee Cullen questioned in print whether the jazz poems were poems at all, and Hughes received a frightening reminder of black snobbishness when the veteran poet George M. McClellan wrote to tell him that while he liked the poems in ***The Weary Blues,*** he had scissored from the dust-jacket (designed by Covarrubias) "that hideous black 'nigger' playing the piano."[13]

While ***The Weary Blues*** was in press and in the months following its appearance, Hughes went through certain experiences that revolutionized his aesthetic. First was his sojourn, already mentioned, among the black poor in Washington. Second was his entry into black Lincon University a few days after ***The Weary Blues*** appeared, when for the first time since he was nine or ten, Hughes went to school with a majority of blacks (and all male)—an experience of incalculable effect on his sense of race. Third was the impact of the brilliant circle of young stars—the key members of the Harlem Renaissance—in Harlem at the same time: Aaron Douglass, Arna Bontemps, Wallace Thurman, Bruce Nugent, and Zora Neale Hurston, for whom Hughes's *Nation* essay of June 1926, **"The Negro Artist and the Racial Mountain,"** was manifesto; to these should be added the names of musicians Hall Johnson, Paul Robeson, Clarence Cameron White, and W. C. Handy (often called the father of the blues), with whom Hughes either worked or consulted in the summer of 1926, especially in connection with a musical, to star Robeson, called "O Blues!" (from **"The Weary Blues"**). The fourth experience was the reaction of the black press to Carl Van Vechten's Harlem novel, *Nigger Heaven,* and to the appearance of *Fire!!* magazine.

The younger writers in general enthusiastically approved of *Nigger Heaven* ("Colored people can't help but like it," Hughes had predicted; the novel read as if it were written by "an N.A.A.C.P. official or Jessie Fauset. But it's good").[14] To almost all the young black writers, Van Vechten's troubles were their own. The attack on him was an attack on what they themselves, or most of them, stood for—artistic and sexual freedom, a love of the black masses, a refusal to idealize black life, and a revolt against bourgeois hypocrisy. They decided to publish their own magazine, instead of relying on the staid *Crisis* and the like. For their pains, *Fire!!* received a withering reception in the black press. "I have just tossed the first issue of *Fire* into the fire," the reviewer in the *Baltimore Afro-American* fumed; Aaron Douglass had ruined "three perfectly good pages and a cover" with his drawings, while Langston Hughes displayed "his usual ability to say nothing in many words."[15]

These experiences prompted Hughes to go where no poet had gone before; in the summer of 1926 he wrote poems that differed sharply from the spirit of ***The Weary Blues*** and that contested the right of the middle class to criticize the mores and manners of the black masses. (The rebellious campaign continued into the fall, when Hughes wrote his first short stories since high school, the "West Illana" sequence of stories set on a ship much like the one on which he had sailed to Africa in 1923. Hughes's fiction navigated more sensual waters than ever before; whatever their limitations as art, the stories that resulted steam suggestively of miscegenation, adultery, promiscuity, and the turmoil of sexual repression—subjects all taboo to the critics who hated *Fire!!.*) During the summer he wrote almost feverishly; back in Lincoln for the fall term, he soon gathered his new poems into what he hoped would be his second book.

On Sunday, October 3, he visited New York and delivered the manuscript to Carl Van Vechten, to whom the collection was dedicated. As with Hughes's first book, they went over each of the poems; exactly what part Van Vechten played now is unclear. Three weeks later, Langston presented the revised collection to him to take to Knopf. By this time it had a name: ***Fine Clothes to the Jew,*** after a line from Hughes's **"Hard Luck"**:

When hard luck overtakes you
Nothin' for you to do
Gather up yo' fine clothes
An' sell 'em to de Jew . . .[16]

Knopf accepted "Fine Clothes to the Jew," but not without balking at the title (the firm had published *Nigger Heaven* apparently without difficulty). After Van Vechten personally defended the name, as he recorded in his journal, it was allowed to stand. Van Vechten perhaps had also chosen it, as he had chosen "The Weary Blues." Certainly, Hughes had been thinking of using "Brass Spitoons," from one of his poems. The choice was unfortunate. Apparently no one alerted Hughes to the effect his title would have on sales, which proved to be opposite to the result of Van Vechten's own crudeness. But he later regarded the title as one of the main reasons for the failure of the book: it was "a bad title, because it was confusing and many Jewish people did not like it."[17]

By mid-January, 1927, Hughes had copies of ***Fine Clothes to the Jew.*** The first reports were encouraging. Far from objecting to the title, his friend and supporter, Amy Spingarn, liked the book even more than ***The Weary Blues,*** because it seemed "more out of the core of life."[18] Her brother-in-law, Arthur Spingarn, who was also Jewish, noted the title but found the book a "splendid" work, in which "Jacob and the Negro come into their own."[19] The black conservative George Schuyler praised Hughes as "the poet of the modern Negro proletariat."[20] But after the attacks on *Nigger Heaven* and *Fire!!,* Hughes was nervous. "It's harder and more cynical," he explained defensively to Dewey Jones of the Chicago *Defender,* and "limited to an interpretation of the 'lower classes,' the ones to whom life is least kind. I try to catch the hurt of their lives, the monotony of their 'jobs,' and the veiled weariness of their songs. They are the people I know best."[21]

On February 5, just as he prepared to set out on a tour for Negro History Week, the black critics opened fire. Under a headline proclaiming Hughes a "SEWER DWELLER," William M. Kelley of the New York *Amsterdam News,* denounced ***Fine Clothes to the Jew*** as "about 100 pages of trash. . . . It reeks of the gutter and sewer." The regular reviewer of the *Philadelphia Tribune* adamantly refused to publicize it; Eustance Gay confessed that ***Fine Clothes to the Jew*** "disgusts me." In the *Pittsburgh Courier,* historian J. A. Rogers called it "piffling trash" that left him "positively sick." The Chicago *Whip* sneered at the dedication to Van Vechten, "a literary gutter-rat" who perhaps alone "will revel in the lecherous, lust-reeking characters that Hughes finds time to poeticize about. . . . These poems are unsanitary, insipid and repulsing." Hughes was the "poet 'low-rate' of Harlem." The following week, refining its position, the *Tribune* lamented Hughes's "obsession for the more degenerate elements" of black life; the book was "a study in the perversions of the Negro." It is questionable whether any book of American poetry, other than *Leaves of Grass,* had ever been greeted so contemptuously.[22]

To these and other black critics, Hughes had allowed the "secret" shame of their culture, especially its apparently unspeakable or unprintable sexual mores, to be bruited by thick-lipped black whores and roustabouts. How could he have dared to publish **"Red Silk Stockings"**?

Put on yo' red silk stockings,
Black gal.
Go out an' let de white boys
Look at yo' legs.

Ain't nothin' to do for you, nohow,
Round this town,—
You's too pretty.
Put on yo' red silk stockings, gal,
An' tomorrow's chile'll
Be a high yaller.
Go out an' let de white boys
Look at yo' legs.

Or **"Beale Street Love"**?

Love
Is a brown man's fist
With hard knuckles
Crushing the lips,
Blackening the eyes,—

Hit me again
Says Clorinda.

By pandering to the taste of whites for the sensational (the critics ignored their own sensationalism, demonstrable in the scandal-ridden sheets of most black weeklies), Hughes had betrayed his race.[23]

In spite of this hostility, ***Fine Clothes to the Jew*** marked Hughes's maturity as a poet after a decade of writing, and his most radical achievement in language. While ***The Weary Blues*** had opened with references to the blues and poems written in dialect, before presenting the sweeter, more traditional lyrics, a prefatory note ("the mood of the *Blues* is almost always despondency, but when they are sung people laugh") now indicated the far greater extent to which ***Fine Clothes to the Jew*** falls deliberately within the range of authentic blues emotion and blues culture. Gone are the conventional lyrics about nature and loneliness, or poems in which the experience of the common black folk is framed by conventional poetic language and a superior, sometimes ironic poetic diction. Here few poems are beyond range of utterance of common black folk, except in so far as any formal poetry by definition belongs to a more privileged world. ***Fine Clothes to the Jew*** was the perfect companion piece to Hughes's manifesto, **"The Negro Artist and the Racial Mountain."**

As a measure of his deeper penetration of the culture and his increased confidence as a poet, three kinds of poems are barely present in ***Fine Clothes to the Jew***—those that praise black people and culture directly, those that directly protest their condition, and those that reflect his own personal sense of desolation. For example: **"Laughers,"** which celebrates blacks as "Loud laughers in the hands of Fate," is also probably the earliest piece in the book, having been published first as **"My People"** in June, 1922. **"Mulatto"** lodges perhaps the strongest protest, but is staged dramatically:

. . . The Southern night is full of stars,
Great big yellow stars.
O, sweet as earth,
Dusk dark bodies
Give sweet birth
To little yellow bastard boys.

Git on back there in the night.
You aint white.

The bright stars scatter everywhere.
Pine wood scent in the evening air.
A nigger night,
A nigger joy.

I am your son, white man!

A little yellow
Bastard boy.

Only one poem, **"Sport,"** proposes life as an empty nothingness—as "the shivering of a great drum / Beaten with swift sticks."

Sorrow and despair dominate ***Fine Clothes to the Jew,*** but mainly through the expressive medium of the blues and its place in the lives of poor black men and women. In **"Hey!"** the blues is mysterious: "I feels de blues a comin', / Wonder what de blues'll bring?" It is also, as in **"Misery,"** soothing, or even cathartic:

Play de blues for me.
Play de blues for me.
No other music
'Ll ease ma misery . . .

Although the blues drifts in most often on the heels of lost love, the feeling can come for other reasons and still have poetic power. **"Homesick Blues"**:

De railroad bridge's
A sad song in de air.
De railroad bridge's
A sad song in de air.
Ever time de trains pass
I wants to go somewhere . . .

In ***Fine Clothes to the Jew,*** the singers and mourners are mainly women. By comparison, men are almost shallow; one man (**"Bad Man"**) beats his wife and "ma side gal too": "Don't know why I do it but / It keeps me from feelin' blue." Men may be hurt in love, like the fellow in **"Po' Boy Blues"** who met "a gal I thought was kind. / She made me lose ma money / An' almost lose ma mind." But the blues are sung most often, and most brilliantly, by black women. Sometimes they sing to warn their sisters (**"Listen Here Blues"**):

Sweet girls, sweet girls,
Listen here to me.
All you sweet girls,
Gin an' whiskey
Kin make you lose yo' 'ginity . . .

Or, as in **"Lament Over Love,"** their daughters:

I hope ma chile'll
Never love a man.
I say I hope ma chile'll
Never love a man.
Cause love can hurt you
Mo'n anything else can.

Women lament being cheated, for having been done wrong by "a yellow papa," who "took ma last thin dime" (**"Gypsy Man"**); or, as in **"Hard Daddy,"** they grieve over male coldness:

I cried on his shoulder but
He turned his back on me.
Cried on his shoulder but
He turned his back on me.
He said a woman's cryin's
Never gonna bother me.

Sometimes the sorrow is greater when loss or the prospect of loss is mixed with profound self-abnegation and despair. **"Gal's Cry For A Dying Lover"**:

. . . Hound dawg's barkin'
Means he's gonna leave this world.
Houng dawg's barkin'
Means he's gonna leave this world.
O, Lawd have mercy
On a po' black girl.

Black an' ugly
But he sho do treat me kind.
I'm black an' ugly
But he sho do treat me kind.
High-in-heaben Jesus,
Please don't take this man o' mine.

But the blues can reflect great joy as well as sorrow, as in **"Ma Man,"** where a black woman's emotional and sexual ecstasy is so overpowering it drives her into song:

When ma man looks at me
He knocks me off ma feet.
When ma man looks at me
He knocks me off ma feet
He's got those 'lectric-shockin' eyes an'
De way he shocks me sho is sweet.

He kin play a banjo.
Lordy, he kin plunk, plunk, plunk.
He kin play a banjo.
I mean plunk, plunk . . . plunk, plunk.
He plays good when he's sober
An' better, better, better when he's drunk.

Eagle-rockin',
Daddy, eagle-rock with me.
Eagle-rockin',
    Come and eagle-rock with me.
Honey baby,
Eagle-rockish as I kin be!

The last stanza of this poem, the second to last in the book (as if Hughes tried to hide it), was among the most sexually teasing in American poetry—to those who understood that "eagle-rocking" was possibly more than a popular dance step.

His critics had not howled without cause, but Hughes did not retreat. First at a Baptist church and then before an African Methodist Episcopal congregation in Philadelphia, he fulfilled engagements to read his poems. Then he coolly faced Floyd Calvin of the *Pittsburgh Courier* at the Knopf office on Fifth Avenue. In spite of the reviews, Hughes said, he declined to write about Vanderbilts and Goulds. At least two-thirds of all blacks were lower-class—"even I myself, belong to that class." In any event, "I have a right to portray any side of Negro life I wish to." He defended the blues singers Bessie Smith and Clara Smith as equal to the best of European folk singers, who were honored in America; and he declared that Carl Van Vechten had done more than anyone else for black artists.[24] To the white Cleveland *Plain Dealer,* curious about the hubbub in the black press over poetry, he explained that the black reviewers still thought that "we should display our 'higher selves'—whatever they are," missing the point "that every 'ugly' poem I write is a protest against the ugliness it pictures."[25]

When the *Pittsburgh Courier* invited Hughes to defend himself against his critics, he did not hesitate. In **"These Bad New Negros: A Critique on Critics,"** he identified four reasons for the attacks: the low self-esteem of the "best" blacks; their obsession with white opinion; their *nouveau riche* snobbery; and their lack of artistic and cultural training "from which to view either their own or the white man's books or pictures." As for the "ill-mannered onslaught" on Van Vechten: the man's "sincere, friendly, and helpful interest in things Negro" should have brought "serious, rather than vulgar, reviews of his book." A nine-point defense of his own views and practices ended in praise of the young writers, including Toomer, Fisher, Thurman, Cullen, Hurston, and the Lincoln poet Edward Silvera. And Hughes himself: "My poems are indelicate. But so is life," he pointed out. He wrote about "harlots and gin-bibers. But they are human. Solomon, Homer, Shakespeare, and Walt Whitman were not afraid or ashamed to include them."[26] (Van Vechten thought the situation easy to explain; "you and I," he joked to Hughes while making an important distinction, "are the only colored people who really love *niggers.*"[27]

Hughes was not without friends in the black press. The *New York Age* found the book evocative of the joy and pathos, beauty and ugliness of black Americans, if of the more primitive type. The poet Alice Dunbar-Nelson, once married to Paul Laurence Dunbar, compared the book to Wordsworth and Coleridge's once maligned yet celebrated venture, *Lyrical Ballads,* which used the lives and speech of the common people; Hughes was "a rare poet."[28] Theophilus Lewis praised the book in the

Messenger, and in the *Saturday Review of Literature* Alain Locke was deft about ***Fine Clothes to the Jew***: "Its open frankness will be a shock and a snare for the critic and moralist who cannot distinguish clay from mire."[29] And Claude McKay wrote privately to congratulate Hughes on having written a book superior to his first.

Among white reviewers, perhaps the most perceptive evaluation came from the young cultural historian Howard Mumford Jones. Using black dialect austerely, Hughes had scraped the blues form down to the bone, and raised the folk form to literary art. "In a sense," Jones concluded, "He has contributed a really new verse form to the English language." Although, like Wordsworth, he sometimes lapsed into "vapid simplicity." But if Hughes continued to grow, he was "dangerously near becoming a major American poet."[30] V. F. Calverton, Margaret Larkin, Arthur Davison Ficke, Hunter Stagg, Abbe Niles, Babette Deutsch, Julia Peterkin, and a wide range of reviewers praised the stark lyrical simplicity and beauty of most of the verse. More than once he was compared to Coleridge and Wordsworth's *Lyrical Ballads*; the critics understood that Hughes was trying to effect a historic change in poetry by compelling both blacks and whites to admit the power of black language. Other critics were not so sympathetic. The Boston *Transcript* flatly preferred Countee Cullen's work and called some of the Hughes verse "tawdry"; the *Nation* reviewer thought that Hughes was merely transcribing folklore, not writing poetry; the *New York Times* judged the volume "uneven and flawed."[31]

The ignorant blasts of the black press were nicely offset when Hughes accepted an invitation ("a great honor for me") from the Walt Whitman foundation to speak at the poet's home on Mickle Street in Camden, New Jersey. Stressing Whitman's humane depictions of blacks in his poetry, Hughes went on to claim that modern free verse, and his own work, descended from Whitman's great example. "I believe," Langston told the little gathering, "that poetry should be direct, comprehensible and the epitome of simplicity."[32] Suspicious of theory, Hughes had nevertheless identified one of the main ideas behind his theory of composition—the notion of an aesthetic of simplicity, sanctioned finally by democratic culture but having a discipline and standards just as the baroque or the rococo, for example, had their own. That simplicity had its dangers both extended its challenge and increased its rewards. The visit to Whitman's home left Hughes elated; to Van Vechten he mailed a postcard imprinted with an excerpt from Whitman's "Song of the Open Road": "All seems beautiful to me."[33]

Although Hughes would place the emphasis in his poetry in a different direction in the 1930s, when he wrote his most politically radical verse, he continued to write the blues even during this period. After the Depression, when Knopf published his ***Shakespeare in Harlem,*** the blues dominated the volume. When in the late 1940s and 1950s he allowed first be-bop (as in ***Montage of a Dream Deferred***) and then increasingly "progressive" jazz (as in ***Ask Your Mama***) also to shape his poetry, he was applying a basic principle he had first learned in the context of the blues. He never abandoned the form, because the blues continued as perhaps the most fertile form of black expressivity; ***Ask Your Mama,*** for example, is explicitly based on the "Hesitation Blues."

His initiative in the blues remains the only genuinely original achievement in form by any black American poet—notwithstanding the excellence of much of the work of writers such as Countee Cullen, Melvin Tolson, Gwendolyn Brooks, Robert Hayden, and even the rebel Amiri Baraka (surely the greatest names in modern black poetry). Their art is largely derivative by comparison. Afro-American poets did not rush to build on Hughes's foundation; most remained black poets who wished to be known simply as poets. But some poets followed the lead. Sterling Brown's *Southern Roads,* the most distinguished book of verse by an Afro-American in the 1930s, was certainly indebted to Hughes, although Alain Locke—anxious to be seen by Mrs. R. Osgood Mason ("Godmother") as opposed to Hughes after the ***Mule Bone*** controversy involving Hughes and Zora Hurston—used a review of *Southern Roads* to dismiss Hughes's blues and jazz writing as faddish, and to hail Brown as the authentic master of black folk poetry—a judgement without merit in spite of Brown's brilliance. Richard Wright, initially a poet, tried to write the blues, and even published one poem in collaboration with Hughes. Among whites, Elizabeth Bishop tried her hand at the form, with results certainly no worse than Wright's—the blues, they learned, is not as simple as it seems.

Black poetry, however, had to wait until the late 1960s and 1970s, with the emergence of writers such as Sherley Anne Williams, Michael S. Harper, and Raymond Patterson, to capitalize fully on Hughes's historic achievement. Ironically, because of the obscurity in which ***Fine***

Clothes to the Jew remains, and because the full extent of Hughes's artistic revolution has not been appreciated, many young black poets are unaware of the history of the form that they nevertheless understand as providing the only indisputably honorable link between their literary and cultural ambitions as blacks and the language compelled on them by history.

Notes

1. Langston Hughes, *The Big Sea* (New York: Knopf, 1940).
2. "Suicide's Note," *The Weary Blues* (New York: Knopf, 1926) 87.
3. Paul Laurence Dunbar, "The Poet," *Complete Poems* (New York: Dodd, Mead, 1913) 191.
4. Hughes, "Prayer Meeting," *Fine Clothes to the Jew* (New York: Knopf, 1927) 46.
5. "The Weary Blues," *Weary Blues,* 23-24.
6. *Big Sea,* 215.
7. LH to Countee Cullen, 7 April 1923; Countee Cullen Papers, Amistad Research Center, New Orleans.
8. *Big Sea,* 92.
9. "Negro Dancers," *Crisis* 29 (1925): 221.
10. "To a Negro Jazz Band in a Parisian Cabaret," *Crisis* 31 (1925): 67.
11. *Big Sea,* 209.
12. "Blues Fantasy," *Weary Blues,* 37.
13. George M. McClellan to LH, 14 July 1926; Langston Hughes Papers, Beinecke Rare Books and Manuscript Library, Yale University.
14. Langston Hughes to Alain Locke, 12 August [1926]; Alain Locke Papers, Moorland-Spingarn Research Center, Howard University.
15. *Big Sea,* 237.
16. "Hard Luck," *Fine Clothes to the Jew,* 18.
17. *Big Sea,* 264.
18. Amy Spingarn to Langston Hughes, [n.d.]; Langston Hughes Papers.
19. Arthur Spingarn to Langston Hughes, 3 February 1927; Langston Hughes Papers.
20. George Schuyler to Langston Hughes, 27 January 1927; Langston Hughes Papers.
21. James A. Emanuel, *Langston Hughes* (New York: Twayne, 1967), 31-32.
22. *New York Amsterdam News* February 5, 1927; *Philadelphia Tribune,* February 5, 1927; *Pittsburgh Courier,* February 5, 1927; *Chicago Whip,* February 26, 1927; *Philadelphia Tribune,* February 12, 1927.
23. "Red Silk Stockings," *Fine Clothes to the Jew,* 73; "Beale Street Love," 57; "Laughers," 77-78; "Mulatto," 71; "Sport," 40; "Hey!" 17; "Homesick Blues," 24; "Bad Man," 21; "Po' Boy Blues," 23; "Listen Here Blues," 85; "Lament Over Love," 81; "Gypsy Man," 22; "Hard Daddy," 86; "Gal's Cry For A Dying Lover," 82; "Ma Man," 88.
24. *Pittsburgh Courier,* February 26, 1927.
25. *Cleveland Plain Dealer,* March 27, 1927.
26. "Those Bad New Negroes," *Pittsburgh Courier,* April 16, 1927.
27. Carl Van Vechten to Langston Hughes, March 25 (1927); Papers.
28. *Washington Eagle,* March 11, 1927.
29. *Saturday Review of Literature* 3 (April 9, 1927): 712.
30. *Chicago Daily News,* June 29, 1927.
31. *Boston Transcript,* March 2, 1927; *New York Times Book Review,* March 27, 1927.
32. *Camden Evening Courier,* March 3, 1927.
33. Langston Hughes to Carl Van Vechten, March 1, 1927.

FURTHER READING

Bibliography

Mikolyzk, Thomas A. *Langston Hughes: A Bio-Bibliography.* Westport, Conn.: Greenwood Press, 1990, 295 p.

Comprehensive annotated bibliography of secondary sources.

Biographies

Berry, Faith. *Langston Hughes: Before and Beyond Harlem.* Westport, Conn: Lawrence Hill, 1983, 376 p.

Biography of Hughes written for a popular audience.

Rampersad, Arnold. *The Life of Langston Hughes.* 2 vols. New York: Oxford University Press, 1986-88.

The definitive biography by the foremost Hughes scholar.

Criticism

Barksdale, Richard K. *Langston Hughes: The Poet and His Critics.* Chicago: American Library Association, 1977, 155 p.

Study that assesses critics' responses to Hughes's poetry.

———. "Comic Relief in Langston Hughes' Poetry." *Black American Literature Forum* 15, no. 3 (1981): 108-11.

Analyzes Hughes's comic gift, especially in Shakespeare in Harlem, One-Way Ticket, *and* Ask Your Mama.

Berry, Faith. "Did Van Vechten Make or Take Hughes' 'Blues?'" *Black World* 25, no. 4 (1976): 22-8.

Discusses the extent of Carl Van Vechten's influence on Hughes.

Brown, Lloyd. "The Portrait of the Artist as a Black American in the Poetry of Langston Hughes." *Studies in Black Literature* 5, no. 1 (1974): 24-7.

Discusses how Hughes viewed his artistic responsibility as an African American.

Chinitz, David. "Literacy and Authenticity: The Blues Poems of Langston Hughes." *Callaloo* 19, no. 1 (1996): 177-92.

Claims that Hughes produced poems that capture the quality of genuine blues in performance while remaining effective as poetry.

Dace, Trish, ed. *Langston Hughes: The Contemporary Review.* Cambridge: Cambridge University Press, 1997, 766 p.

Collection of reviews of Hughes's works from 1926 to 1968.

Davis, Arthur P. "The Harlem of Langston Hughes's Poetry." *Phylon* 13 (1952): 276-83.

Traces Hughes's evolving depiction of Harlem, an exciting world of escape and release in The Weary Blues *and a disillusioned city in* Shakespeare in Harlem.

———. "Langston Hughes: Cool Poet." *CLA Journal* 11, no. 4 (1968): 280-96.

Discusses Hughes's growth as a poet, his unifying themes, and his "coolness."

Dickinson, Donald C. "The Harlem Renaissance 1926–1930." In *A Bio-Bibliography of Langston Hughes, 1902–1967,* pp. 32–58. Hamden, Conn.,: Archon Books, 1967.

Examines the poetry, short stories, and novel that Hughes wrote during the Harlem Renaissance period and maintains that the author built his reputation on the foundation of the works he produced in those years.

Emanuel, James. *Langston Hughes.* New York: Twayne, 1967, 192 p.

Provides a detailed examination of Hughes's works from a literary rather than a sociological perspective, the latter having previously been the dominant critical approach to the writings of African Americans.

———. "The Literary Experiments of Langston Hughes." *CLA Journal* 11, no. 4 (1968): 335-44.

Examines Hughes's literary innovations, especially in his short stories.

Farrison, W. Edward. "Langston Hughes: Poet of the Negro Renaissance." *CLA Journal* 15, no. 4 (1972): 401-10.

Discusses Hughes's early days in Harlem as described in The Big Sea *and several essays.*

Gates, Henry Louis and Appiah, K. A., eds. *Langston Hughes: Critical Perspectives Past and Present.* New York: Amistad Press, 1993, 255 p.

Collection including reviews by Hughes's contemporaries and essays by major Hughes scholars.

Hansell, William H. "Black Music in the Poetry of Langston Hughes: Roots, Race, Release." *Obsidian* 4, no. 3 (1978): 16-38.

Examines a number of Hughes's poems in which music is central.

Jemie, Onwucheckwa. *Langston Hughes: An Introduction to the Poetry.* New York: Columbia University Press, 1976, 234 p.

Delineates the major themes and techniques of Hughes's poetry especially with respect to the African American oral tradition.

Kellner, Bruce. "Langston Hughes's *Nigger Heaven Blues.*" *Langston Hughes Review* 11, no. 1 (1992): 21-7.

Examines Hughes's poems written to promote Carl Van Vechten's novel.

McLaren, Joseph. "Early Recognitions: Duke Ellington and Langston Hughes." In *The Harlem Renaissance: Revaluations,* edited by Amritjit Singh, William S. Shiver, and Stanley Brodwin, pp. 195-208. New York: Garland Publishing, 1989.

Discusses the intersection of the early careers of Hughes and Duke Ellington in Harlem during the 1920s.

Miller, R. Baxter. *The Art and Imagination of Langston Hughes.* Lexington: The University Press of Kentucky, 1989, 149 p.

Study of the complex patterns of meaning in Hughes's writings.

Mullen, Edward J., ed. *Critical Essays on Langston Hughes.* Boston: G. K. Hall, 1986, 207 p.

Collection of criticism of Hughes's works, from early reviews to critical studies of the 1980s.

O'Daniel, Therman B., ed. *Langston Hughes: Black Genius.* New York: Morrow, 1971, 246 p.

Collection of essays covering Hughes's works as a poet, novelist, short story writer, playwright, columnist, and translator.

Rampersad, Arnold. "The Origins of Poetry in Langston Hughes." *Southern Review* 21 (1985): 695-705.

Examines the influences on and development of Hughes as a poet.

Salaam, Kalamu Ya. "Langston Hughes: A Poet Supreme." In *The Furious Flowering of African American Poetry,* edited by Joanne V. Gabbin, pp. 17-24. Charlottesville: University Press of Virginia, 1999.

Examines the jazz idiom in Hughes's poetry, showing Montage of a Dream Deferred *to be the first jazz poem.*

Taylor, Patricia A. "Langston Hughes and the Harlem Renaissance, 1921–1931: Major Events and Publications." In *The Harlem Renaissance Remembered,* edited by Arna Bontemps, pp. 90–102. New York: Dodd, Mead, 1972.

Discusses Hughes's literary activities during the Harlem Renaissance.

Trotman, C. James, ed. *Langston Hughes: The Man, His Art, and His Continuing Influence.* New York: Garland Publishing, 1995, 178 p.

Proceedings from a 1992 conference on Hughes at his alma mater, Lincoln University, with essays focusing on Hughes's Harlem Renaissance years, his continuing influence, and issues of gender, race, and culture.

Turner, Darwin T. "Langston Hughes as Playwright." *CLA Journal* 11, no. 4 (1968): 297-309.

Close reading of Hughes's plays that commends Hughes's contribution to the development of African American drama but ultimately finds that Hughes is not a major American playwright.

Walker, Alice. "Turning into Love: Some Thoughts on Surviving and Meeting Langston Hughes." *Callaloo* 12, no. 4 (1989): 663-66.

Transcript of Walker's personal reminiscences on Hughes delivered at City College of New York's Langston Hughes Festival.

Wintz, Cary D. "Langston Hughes: A Kansas Poet in the Harlem Renaissance." *Kansas Quarterly* 7, no. 3 (1975): 58-71.

Contends that both Hughes's early and later poetry reflects the urban environment in which he grew up as well as the teachings inculcated by his grandmother when he lived with her in Kansas.

———, ed. *The Critics and the Harlem Renaissance, 1920-1940.* New York: Garland Publishing, 1996, 382 p.

Collection of essays and reviews that define and evaluate the literature of the Harlem Renaissance; includes numerous articles by and about Hughes.

———, ed. *The Emergence of the Harlem Renaissance.* New York: Garland Publishing, 1996, 382 p.

Collection containing essays written between 1910 and 1925 stressing the developing African American literature; includes the entire 1925 issue of the Survey Graphic, *which heralded the Harlem Renaissance, and several pieces by and about Hughes.*

OTHER SOURCES FROM GALE:

Additional coverage of Hughes's life and career is contained in the following sources published by the Gale Group: *African American Writers,* Eds. 1, 2; *American Writers Retrospective Supplement,* Vol. 1; *American Writers Supplement,* Vol. 1; *Authors and Artists for Young Adults,* Vol. 12; *Black Literature Criticism,* Vol. 2; *Black Writers,* Eds. 1, 3; *Children's Literature Review,* Vol. 17; *Concise Dictionary of American Literary Biography,* Vol. 1929-1941; *Contemporary Authors,* Vols. 1-4R, 25-28R; *Contemporary Authors New Revision Series,* Vols. 1, 34, 82; *Contemporary Literary Criticism,* Vols. 1, 5, 10, 15, 35, 44, 108; *Dictionary of Literary Biography,* Vols. 4, 7, 48, 51, 86, 228; *DISCovering Authors*; *DISCovering Authors: British Edition*; *DISCovering Authors: Canadian Edition*; *DISCovering Authors Modules: Dramatists, Most-studied Authors, Multicultural Authors,* and *Poets*; *DISCovering Authors 3.0*; *Drama Criticism,* Vol. 3; *Exploring Poetry*; *Exploring Short Stories*; *Junior DISCovering Authors*; *Literature and Its Times,* Vol. 3; *Major Authors and Illustrators for Children and Young Adults,* Vol. 1; *Major 20th-Century Writers,* Eds. 1, 2; *Poetry Criticism,* Vol. 1; *Poetry for Students,* Vols. 1, 3, 6, 10; *Poets: American and British*; *Reference Guide to American Literature,* Ed. 4; *Reference Guide to Short Fiction,* Ed. 2; *St. James Guide to Young Adult Writers*; *Short Stories for Students,* Vols. 4, 7; *Short Story Criticism,* Vol. 6; *Something about the Author,* Vols. 4, 33; *World Literature Criticism*; *World Poets*; and *Writers for Children.*

ZORA NEALE HURSTON

(1891 - 1960)

American novelist, folklorist, essayist, short story writer, and playwright.

Hurston was known during the Harlem Renaissance not only for her writing of fiction and folklore but for her vibrant personality, humor, outspokenness, and pride in her culture. She coined the term "niggerati" to describe Harlem's Black literati, and although she was an important member of the movement, she was also criticized because of the support she received from white patrons. Hurston was the first Black American to collect and publish African American folklore, and she also drew on these materials for her fiction and drama. Her most productive years were the late 1930s and the 1940s, after the Harlem Renaissance, when she produced a work of folklore, her autobiography, and three novels, the best known of which is *Their Eyes Were Watching God* (1937). Although Hurston has been criticized for her sometimes conservative ideas about race, her writing has been admired for disrupting stereotypes of Black women, developing characters that are complex studies of cultural and personal identity, and reminding her fellow Black artists about the richness in their heritage.

BIOGRAPHICAL INFORMATION

Hurston was born in Notasulga, Alabama, on January 7, 1891, although she claimed that she was born in 1901. She grew up in Eatonville, Florida, a town founded by African Americans and the first incorporated Black town in the country. When her mother died in 1904, Hurston joined a traveling theatrical company and then worked as a maid. She attended high school in Baltimore and enrolled at Howard University in Washington, D.C., from 1923 to 1924. In 1925 Hurston went to New York City, drawn to the circle of Black artists of the Harlem Renaissance, and began writing fiction. She contributed work to magazines and was involved in the production of *Fire!!,* the short-lived Black literary journal. She also studied anthropology at Barnard College and at Columbia University under the noted anthropologists Frank Boas, Ruth Benedict, and Gladys Reichard. While at Barnard she also worked as a secretary for the novelist Fannie Hurst. After graduating from college in 1927, Hurston returned to the South, married Herbert Sheen (whom she divorced in 1931), and began collecting folklore. She also continued to write fiction, publishing *Jonah's Gourd Vine* in 1934. In 1936 she received a Guggenheim Fellowship to study Obeah (or Voodoo) practices in the West Indies. She published her research in *Tell My Horse* (1938). In the late 1930s and 1940s Hurston continued a successful career writing fiction and folklore. Her most famous work, *Their Eyes Were Watching God,* was followed by *Moses, Man of the Mountain* (1939) and her autobiography, *Dust Tracks on a Road* (1942). During this period she also remarried (and later divorced) and worked as a staff writer for Paramount Studios in Hollywood. After the publication of her novel *Seraph on the Suwanee* in 1948, however, her popularity waned. She was also indicted on a morals charge involving a minor, which was dropped when Hurston cleared herself. Hurston continued to write articles for newspapers and magazines in Florida, but for the remainder of her life she lived in obscurity, occasionally employed as a librarian, teacher, or maid. She died in extreme poverty in Fort Pierce, Florida, on January 28, 1960, and was buried in an unmarked grave.

MAJOR WORKS

In her novels, autobiography, folklore, short stories, and essays, Hurston celebrates the folk heritage of African Americans, particularly in the rural South, while providing insights into larger human questions of community and identity. In the 1920s Hurston wrote numerous short pieces for magazines. Her short story "Spunk" (first published in *Opportunity* in June 1925) won second prize at the annual *Opportunity* magazine awards ceremony, and the story was published in Alain Locke's anthology *The New Negro,* a seminal work of the Harlem Renaissance. The story makes use of her special relationship to her hometown of Eatonville. Many of her stories written during the Harlem Renaissance period deal with Eatonville; the "Eatonville Anthology," a series of thirteen sketches, was published between September and November 1926 in *The Messenger.* One of her most important nonfiction works of the 1920s is the essay "How It Feels to Be Colored Me" (first published in *World Tomorrow* in 1928), in which Hurston declares that she is not "tragically colored." In the late 1920s she wrote a number of essays on anthropology, wrote more short stories (which have since been collected), and collaborated with Langston Hughes on a play, entitled *Mule Bone,* that was never published or produced during her lifetime because of a conflict between the two writers. *Jonah's Gourd Vine,* Hurston's first novel, is set in Eatonville and based on her parents' lives. It combines folklore and biblical themes. Her masterpiece, *Their Eyes Were Watching God,* is the story of Janie Crawford, a Black woman from Eatonville who has married three times and been tried for the murder of one of her husbands. The first and last chapters of the work are "framed" around two long-lost friends who meet on a back porch and converse. Readers thus "listen in" on the story of Janie's quest for identity in a racist and sexist society. Hurston's use of southern Black dialect lends a realistic quality to the novel, which also abounds in metaphoric language, myth, and folklore. Hurston's next novel, *Moses, Man of the Mountain,* is an allegorical novel of American slavery. *Seraph on the Suwanee,* her last long fiction work, focuses on working-class whites in a small town. Hurston's important nonfiction works are her two works of folklore, *Mules and Men* (1935) and *Tell My Horse,* and her 1942 autobiography. *Mules and Men* is a collection of humorous and serious sketches that reflect the customs, beliefs, and folklore of Blacks in rural Florida and Louisiana. *Tell My Horse* describes the folk practices of West Indians, particularly the Obeah.

CRITICAL RECEPTION

During the years of the Harlem Renaissance movement, Hurston was well known in Black literary circles. She published stories and essays in important Black journals and was best known for her consuming interest in folklore. Some of her contemporaries objected to the fact that Hurston was supported in her efforts by white patrons and that she was politically conservative. In the 1930s and early 1940s, Hurston's longer works received favorable reviews but were also criticized for their use of dialect and their supposed stereotypes of Blacks. Despite this criticism, Hurston was considered the most important Black female writer of her day, and in 1942 she won the Anisfield-Wolf Book Award for her autobiography. By the mid-1940s Hurston began to publish less and less, and by 1950 she was forgotten as a writer and working as a maid in Florida. It was not until the mid-1970s that her work was rediscovered and Hurston's place as a major writer was restored. Robert Hemenway published an essay on Hurston in 1972, and a year later the novelist Alice Walker traveled to Florida to find and honor Hurston's unmarked grave. After Walker's publication of the essay "In Search of Zora Neale Hurston" in *Ms.* magazine in 1975, Hurston's reputation was resurrected and numerous books and critical articles have been written about her and her writings. Scholars have focused on a number of issues, including Hurston's use of folklore, her characters' search for identity, her use of dialect, her examination of gender stereotypes, and the use of her hometown in her writings. Although many critics still note that her work could today be considered "politically incorrect" because of her attitude toward race, it has been admired for realistically and lovingly portraying rural southern Black Americans.

PRINCIPAL WORKS

Color Struck [published in the journal *Fire!!*] (play) 1926

Fast and Furious [with Clinton Fletcher and Time Moore] (musical drama) 1931

Jonah's Gourd Vine (novel) 1934

Mules and Men (folklore) 1935

Their Eyes Were Watching God (novel) 1937

Tell My Horse (folklore) 1938; also published as *Voodoo Gods: An Inquiry into Native Myths and Magic in Jamaica and Haiti,* 1939

Moses, Man of the Mountain (novel) 1939

Dust Tracks on a Road (autobiography) 1942

Stephen Kelen-d'Oxylion Presents Polk County: A Comedy of Negro Life on a Sawmill Camp with Authentic Negro Music [with Dorothy Waring] (drama) 1944

Seraph on the Suwanee (novel) 1948

I Love Myself When I Am Laughing . . . And Then again When I Am Looking Mean and Impressive: A Zora Neale Hurston Reader (collected works) 1979

The Sanctified Church (essays) 1983

Spunk: The Selected Stories of Zora Neale Hurston (short stories) 1985

**Mule Bone: A Comedy of Negro Life in Three Acts* [with Langston Hughes] (drama) 1991

The Complete Stories (short stories) 1994

Folklore, Memoirs, and Other Writings (essays) 1995

Collected Essays (essays) 1998

Every Tongue Got to Confess: Negro Folk Tales of the Gulf States (folklore) 2001

* This work was written in the early 1930s but it was not produced until 1991.

PRIMARY SOURCES

ZORA NEALE HURSTON (SHORT STORY DATE 1925)

SOURCE: Hurston, Zora Neale. "Spunk." *Opportunity,* 3, no. 30 (June 1925): 171-73.

In this short story, Hurston examines the art of storytelling.

I

A Giant of a brown-skinned man sauntered up the one street of the village and out into the palmetto thickets with a small pretty woman clinging lovingly to his arm.

"Looka theah, folkses!" cried Elijah Mosley, slapping his leg gleefully, "Theah they go, big as life an' brassy as tacks."

All the loungers in the store tried to walk to the door with an air of nonchalance but with small success.

"Now pee-eople!" Walter Thomas gasped. "Will you look at 'em!"

"But that's one thing Ah likes about Spunk Banks—he ain't skeered of nothin'on God's green footstool—*nothin'*! He rides that log down at sawmill jus' like he struts 'round wid another man's wife—jus' don't give a kitty. When Tes' Miller got cut to giblets on that circle-saw, Spunk steps right up and starts ridin'. The rest of us was skeered to go near it."

A round-shouldered figure in overalls much too large came nervously in the door and the talking ceased. The men looked at each other and winked.

"Gimme some soda-water. Sass'prilla Ah reckon," the newcomer ordered, and stood far down the counter near the open pickled pig-feet tub to drink it.

Elijah nudged Walter and turned with mock gravity to the new-comer.

"Say, Joe, how's everything up yo' way? How's yo' wife?"

Joe started and all but dropped the bottle he held in his hands. He swallowed several times painfully and his lips trembled.

"Aw 'Lige, you oughtn't to do nothin' like that," Walter grumbled. Elijah ignored him.

"She jus' passed heah a few minutes ago goin' thata way," with a wave of his hand in the direction of the woods.

Now Joe knew his wife had passed that way. He knew that the men lounging in the general store had seen her, moreover, he knew that the men knew *he* knew. He stood there silent for a long moment staring blankly, with his Adam's apple twitching nervously up and down his throat. One could actually *see* the pain he was suffering, his eyes, his face, his hands and even the dejected slump of his shoulders. He set the bottle down upon the counter. He didn't bang it, just eased it out of his hand silently and fiddled with his suspender buckle.

"Well, Ah'm goin' after her to-day. Ah'm goin' an fetch her back. Spunk's done gone too fur."

He reached deep down into his trouser pocket and drew out a hollow ground razor, large and shiny, and passed his moistened thumb back and forth over the edge.

"Talkin' like a man, Joe. 'Course that's *yo'* fambly affairs, but Ah like to see grit in anybody."

Joe Kanty laid down a nickel and stumbled out into the street.

Dusk crept in from the woods. Ike Clarke lit the swinging oil lamp that was almost immediately surrounded by candleflies. The men laughed boisterously behind Joe's back as they watched him shamble woodward.

"You oughtn't to said whut you did to him, Lige—look how it worked him up," Walter chided.

"And Ah hope it did work him up. Tain't even decent for a man to take and take like he do."

"Spunk will sho' kill him."

"Aw, Ah doan't know. You never kin tell. He might turn him up an' spank him fur gettin' in the way, but Spunk wouldn't shoot no unarmed man. Dat razor he carried outa heah ain't gonna run Spunk down an'cut him, an' Joe ain't got the nerve to go up to Spunk with it knowing he totes that Army. 45. He makes that break outa heah to bluff us. He's gonna hide that razor behind the first palmetto root an' sneak back home to bed. Don't tell me nothin' 'bout that rabbit-foot colored man. Didn't he meet Spunk an' Lena face to face one day las' week an' mumble sumthin' to Spunk 'bout lettin' his wife alone?"

"What did Spunk say?" Walter broke in—"Ah like him fine but tain't right the way he carries on wid Lena Kanty, jus' cause Joe's timid 'bout fightin'."

"You wrong theah, Walter. Tain't 'cause Joe's timid at all, it's 'cause Spunk wants Lena. If Joe was a passle of wile cats Spunk would tackle the job just the same. He'd go after anything he wanted the same way. As Ah wuz sayin' a minute ago, he tole Joe right to his face that Lena was his. 'Call her and see if she'll come. A woman knows her boss an' she answers when he calls.' 'Lena, ain't I yo' husband?' Joe sorter whines out. Lena looked at him real disgusted but she don't answer and she don't move outa her tracks. Then Spunk reaches out an' takes hold of her arm an' says: 'Lena, youse mine. From now on ah works for you an' fights for you an' Ah never wants you to look to nobody for a crumb of bread, a stitch of close or a shingle to go over yo' head, but *me* long as Ah live. Ah'll git the lumber foh owah house tomorrow. Go home an' git yo' things together!' 'Thass mah house,' Lena speaks up. 'Papa gimme that.' 'Well,' says Spunk, 'doan give up whut's yours, but when youse inside doan forgit youse mine, an' let no other man git outa his place wid you!'"

"Lena looked up at him with her eyes so full of love that they wuz runnin' over, an' Spunk seen it an' Joe seen it too, and his lip started to tremblin' and his Adam's apple was galloping up and down his neck like a race horse. Ah bet he's wore out half a dozen Adam's apples since Spunk's been on the job with Lena. That's all he'll do. He'll be back heah after while swallowin' en' workin' his lips like he wants to say somethin' an' can't."

"But didn't he do nothin' to stop 'em?"

"Nope, not a frazzlin' thing—jus' stood there. Spunk took Lena's arm and walked off jus' like nothin' ain't happened and he stood there gazin' after them till they was outa sight. Now you know a woman don't want no man like that. I'm jus' waitin' to see whut he's goin' to say when he gits back."

II

But Joe Kanty never came back, never. The men in the store heard the sharp report of a pistol somewhere distant in the palmetto thicket and soon Spunk came walking leisurely, with his big black Stetson set at the same rakish angle and Lena clinging to his arm, came walking right into the general store. Lena wept in a frightened manner.

"Well," Spunk announced calmly, "Joe come out there wid a meat axe an' made me kill him."

He sent Lena home and led the men back to Joe—crumpled and limp with his right hand still clutching his razor.

"See mah back? Mah close cut clear through. He sneaked up en' tried to kill me from the back, but Ah got him, an' got him good, first shot," Spunk said.

The men glared at Elijah, accusingly.

"Take him up an' plant him in Stony Lonesome," Spunk said in a careless voice. "Ah didn't wanna shoot him but he made me do it. He's a dirty coward, jumpin' on a man from behind."

Spunk turned on his heel and sauntered away to where he knew his love wept in fear for him and no man stopped him. At the general store later on, they all talked of locking him up until the sheriff should come from Orlando, but no one did anything but talk.

A clear case of self-defense, the trial was a short one, and Spunk walked out of the court house to freedom again. He could work again, ride the dangerous log-carriage that fed the singing, snarling, biting circle-saw; he could stroll the soft dark lanes with his guitar. He was free to roam the woods again; he was free to return to Lena. He did all of these things.

III

"Whut you reckon, Walt?" Elijah asked one night later. "Spunk's gittin' ready to marry Lena!"

"New! Why, Joe ain't had time to git cold yit . . . Nohow Ah didn't figger Spunk was the maryin' kind."

"Well, he is," rejoined Elijah. "He done moved most of Lena's things—and her along wid'em—over to the Bradley house. He's buying it. Jus' like Ah told yo' all right in heah the night Joe wuz kilt. Spunk's crazy 'bout Lena. He don't want folks to keep on takin' 'bout her—thass reason he's rushin' so. Funny thing 'bout that bob-cat, wasn't it?"

"What bob-cat, 'Lige? Ah ain't heered 'bout none."

"Ain't cher?? Well, night befo' las' was the fust night Spunk an' Lena moved together an' just then as they was goin' to bed, a big black bob-cat, black all over, you hear me, black, walked round and round that house and howled like forty, an' when Spunk got his gun an' went to the winder to shoot it, he says it stood right still an' and looked him in the eye, an' howled right at him. The thing got Spunk so nervoused up he couldn't shoot. But Spunk says twan't no bob-cat nohow. He says it was Joe done sneaked back from Hell!"

"Humph!" sniffed Walter, "he oughter be nervous after what he done. Ah reckon Joe come back to dare him to marry Lena, or to come out an' fight. Ah bet he'll be back time and again, too. Know what Ah think? Joe wuz a braver man than Spunk."

There was a general shout of derision from the group.

"Thass a fact," went on Walter. "Lookit whut he done; took a razor an' went out to fight a man he knowed toted a gun an' wuz a crack shot, too; 'nother thing Joe wuz skeered of Spunk, skeered plumb stiff! But he went jes' the same. It took him a long time to get his nerve up. Tain't nothin' for Spunk to fight when he ain't skeered of nothin'. Now, Joe's done come back to have it out wid the man that's got all he ever had. Y'all know Joe ain't never had nothin' or wanted nothin' besides Lena. It musta been a h'ant [ghost] cause ain't nobody never seen no black bob-cat."

'"Nother thing," cut in one of the men, "Spunk wuz cussin' a blue streak to-day 'cause he 'lowed dat saw wuz wobblin'—almos' got 'im once. The machinist come, looked it over an' said it wuz alright. Spunk musta been leanin' t'wards it some. Den he claimed somebody pushed 'im but twan't nobody close to 'im. Ah wuz glad when knockin' off time come. I'm skeered of dat man when he gits hot. He'd beat you full of button holes as quick as he's look etcher."

IV

The men gathered the next evening in a different mood, no laughter. No badinage this time.

"Look, 'Lige, you goin' to set up wid Spunk?"

"New, Ah reckon not, Walter. Tell yuh the truth, Ah'm a li'l bit skittish, Spunk died too wicket—died cussin' he did. You know he thought he was done outa life."

"Good Lawd, who'd he think done it?"

"Joe."

"Joe Kanty? How come?"

"Walter, Ah b'leeve Ah will walk up thata way an' set. Lena would like it Ah reckon."

"But whut did he say, 'Lige?"

Elijah did not answer until they had left the lighted store and were strolling down the dark street.

"Ah wuz loadin'a wagon wid scantlin' right near the saw when Spunk fell on the carriage but 'fore Ah could git to him the saw got him in the body—awful sight. Me an' Skint Miller got him off but it was too late. Anybody could see that. The fust thing he said wuz: 'He pushed me, 'Lige—the dirty hound pushed me in the back!'—he was spittin' blood at ev'ry breath. We laid him on the sawdust pile with his face to the east so's he could die easy. He helt mah hen' till the last, Walter, and said: 'It was Joe, 'Lige . . . the dirty sneak shoved me . . . he didn't dare to come to mah face . . . but Ah'll git the son-of-a-wood louse soon's Ah get there an' make Hell too hot for him. . . . Ah felt him shove me . . . !' Thass how he died."

"If spirits kin fight, there's a powerful tussle goin' on somewhere ovah Jordan 'cause Ah b'leeve Joe's ready for Spunk an' ain't skeered any more—yas, Ah b'leeve Joe pushed 'im mahself:'

They had arrived at the house. Lena's lamentations were deep and loud. She had filled the room with magnolia blossoms that gave off a heavy sweet odor. The keepers of the wake tipped about whispering in frightened tones. Everyone in the Village was there, even old Jeff Kanty, Joe's father, who a few hours before would have been afraid to come with ten feet of him, stood leering triumphantly down upon the fallen giant as if his fingers had been the teeth of steel that laid him low.

The cooling board consisted of three sixteen-inch boards on saw horses, a dingy sheet was his shroud.

The women ate heartily of the funeral baked meats and wondered who would be Lena's next. The men whispered coarse conjectures between guzzles of whiskey.

LANGSTON HUGHES (ESSAY DATE 1940)

SOURCE: Hughes, Langston. "Harlem Literati." In *The Big Sea,* pp. 233-40. New York: Hill and Wang, 1940.

In this short piece, Hughes offers background information on his fellow writer Hurston and notes her skill as a folklorist.

Of [the] "niggerati," Zora Neale Hurston was certainly the most amusing. Only to reach a wider audience, need she ever write books—because she is a perfect book of entertainment in herself. In her youth she was always getting scholarships and things from wealthy white people, some of whom simply paid her just to sit around and represent the Negro race for them, she did it in such a racy fashion. She was full of side-splitting anecdotes, humorous tales, and tragicomic stories, remembered out of her life in the South as a daughter of a travelling minister of God. She could make you laugh one minute and cry the next. To many of her white friends, no doubt, she was a perfect "darkie" in the nice meaning they give the term that is a naive, childlike, sweet, humorous, and highly colored Negro.

But Miss Hurston was clever, too—a student who didn't let college give her a broad *a* and who had great scorn for all pretensions, academic or otherwise. That is why she was such a fine folklore collector, able to go among the people and never act as if she had been to school at all. Almost nobody else could stop the average Harlemite on Lenox Avenue and measure his head with a strange-looking anthropological device and not get bawled out for the attempt, except Zora, who used to stop anyone whose head looked interesting, and measure it.

GENERAL COMMENTARY

ROBERT E. HEMENWAY (ESSAY DATE 1972)

SOURCE: Hemenway, Robert E. "Zora Neale Hurston and the Eatonville Anthropology." In *Harlem Renaissance Remembered,* edited by Arna Bontemps, pp. 190-214. New York: Dodd, Mead, 1972.

In the following essay, Hemenway argues that Hurston's main concern during the Harlem Renaissance was with anthropology and that she conceptualized her experience in her native Eatonville using tools she learned as a social scientist.

On January 16, 1959, Zora Neale Hurston, suffering from the effects of a stroke and writing painfully in longhand, composed a letter to the "editorial department" of Harper & Brothers inquiring if they would be interested in seeing "the book I am laboring upon at present—a life of Herod the Great."[1] One year and twelve days later, Zora Neale Hurston died without funds to provide for her burial, a resident of the St. Lucie County, Florida, Welfare Home. She lies today in an unmarked grave in a segregated cemetery in Ft. Pierce, Florida, a resting place generally symbolic of the black writer's fate in America. The letter to Harper's does not expose a publisher's rejection of an unknown masterpiece, but it does reveal how the bright promise of the Harlem Renaissance deteriorated for many of the writers who shared in its exuberance. It also indicates the personal tragedy of Zora Neale Hurston: Barnard graduate, author of four novels, two books of folklore, one volume of autobiography, the most important collector of Afro-American folklore in America, reduced by poverty and circumstance to seek a publisher by unsolicited mail. The letter makes the survival of three hundred pages of the ***Herod the Great*** manuscript all the more poignant; its posthumous destruction by county custodians was halted when a deputy sheriff extinguished its flame with a garden hose.

Herod the Great is a good beginning for understanding Hurston's role in the Harlem Renaissance, because it is unlike any of her Renaissance work. It is a straightforward, standard English, historical narrative of the ruler of Galilee from 40 to 4 B.C., the father of the Herod to whom

Christ was sent for trial by Pontius Pilate. Hurston spent most of her energy over the last seven years of her life in the attempt to write this story, and yet even the most sympathetic reader concludes that the manuscript is not a major achievement, that it lacks the force, style, and significance of her other work. I think it fails because it illustrates how far Hurston had retreated from the unique sources of her esthetic: the music and speech, energy and wisdom, dignity and humor, of the black rural South. Her achievements during the Renaissance increase or diminish in direct proportion to her use of the folk environment which she had grown up in and would later return to analyze.

I

Zora Neale Hurston was born in 1903 in Eatonville, Florida,[2] an all-black town in central Orange County which claims to be the first incorporated totally black city in America. This fact of birth makes Hurston unique among black writers, and it was the major shaping force in her life. Growing up in Eatonville meant that Zora Hurston could reach the age of ten before she would realize that she had been labeled a "Negro" and restricted from certain social possibilities by chance of race. It meant that from early childhood she would hear the "lying sessions" on Mayor Joe Clark's storefront porch, the men "straining against each other in telling folks tales. God, Devil, Brer Rabbit, Brer Fox, Sis Cat, Brer Bear, Lion, Tiger, Buzzard and all the wood folk walked and talked like natural men."[3] It meant that the Saturday night music and the Sunday morning praying, the singing, working, loving, and fighting of black rural life would become the fecund source for her adult imagination.

The strong daughter of strong parents, Hurston was graced by the evangelical Christianity of her father's preaching and the permanent truths of her mother's rustic wisdom. Her parents and their neighbors had little formal education. They lived lives of rural poverty in a society of white racism, and they contributed to that elaborate mechanism of survival which makes Afro-American folklore one of the most remarkable products of ingenuity and intelligence in the human species. Hurston left the familial environment at fifteen, after her mother had died, working variously as a maid in a traveling Gilbert and Sullivan troupe, a manicurist in a barbershop catering to congressmen, and a servant for prominent black Washingtonians. She also finished high school and managed two years of credit at Howard University (where she studied under Alain Locke), before Charles S. Johnson, the editor of *Opportunity,* solicited her fiction and suggested she come to New York sometime. She arrived in January 1925 with "$1.50, no job, no friends, and a lot of hope."[4]

If one accepts the geography in the label, Zora Hurston's physical presence during the Harlem Renaissance could be overemphasized. She did not arrive on the scene until fairly late, and in February 1927 she left for four years of more or less continuous folklore collecting. Yet she was an important contributor to the Renaissance spirit, as any survivor of the age will confirm. She very quickly became one of the most dazzling émigrés of the influx of young black artists. A brilliant raconteur, a delightful if sometimes eccentric companion, she fit in well with the "Roaring Twenties"—both black and white divisions. Shortly after her arrival she was employed as Fannie Hurst's private secretary; she quickly became a favorite of the black intelligentsia and the recipient of a scholarship specially arranged for by a Barnard trustee. Her wit was lengendary; she called Negro uplifters "Negrotarians," and Carl Van Vechten claimed she combined Negro and literati into one of the famous ironic labels of the period: "Niggerati." Much of her personal success was built around her storytelling, which more often than not emphasized the Eatonville milieu. She could become a living representative of the Southern folk-idiom and she never failed to entertain with the material. Her stories, of course, were not unknown to Harlem, for black immigrants of the "great migration" could tell similar tales from neighborhood stoops. William Wells Brown, Arthur Huff Fauset, and other blacks had reported folklore sympathetically; Joel Chandler Harris's Uncle Remus stories had been popular among whites in the late nineteenth century.

But the folk materials seldom had been dramatized for the black artists and intellectuals of Hurston's acquaintance, and almost never for the white folks so often in attendance on the "New Negro." In fact, few of the literary participants in the Renaissance knew intimately the rural South; Hughes arrived from Cleveland and Washington, Bontemps from California, Thurman from Utah and Los Angeles; Cullen was from New York City, Toomer from Washington; the list can go on, but the point is obvious. Zora Neale Hurston represented a known, but unexperienced segment of black life in America. Although it is impossible to gauge such matters, there seems little question that she helped to remind the Renaissance—

especially its more bourgeois members—of the richness in the racial heritage; she also added new dimensions to the interest in exotic primitivism that was one of the most ambiguous products of the age.

Yet the brilliance of her personality should not obscure her personal development. Hurston in New York was initially a country girl, wide-eyed, and if not altogether innocent, at least capable of being often impressed. She is still remembered at Howard by fellow students and retired faculty as merely a bright working girl, very rough about the edges. In the midst of her duties as Hurst's secretary, she could take time out to send a friend some matches shared one night by "Fannie Hurst, Stefansson (the explorer), Charles Norris and Zora Neale Hurston," adding that "Irvin S. Cobb was there also but he used another pack with Jessie Lasky and Margaret Anglin."[5] Later she would write the same friend about all there is to see in New York, admitting, "I won't try to pretend that I am not thrilled at the chance to see and do what I am. I love it!"[6] The sending of used matchbooks hardly constitutes jaded sophistication, and although Hurston could frequently hide behind masks, the youthful excitement here seems genuine. Her emotions are also the social analogs to her intellectual experience at Barnard.

Hurston came to New York in 1925 as a writer but left Barnard two years later as a serious social scientist, and although these are not incompatible vocations, they can imply different uses for personal experience. She had the relatively rare opportunity to confront her culture both emotionally and analytically, both as subject and object. She lived Afro-American folklore before she knew that such a thing existed as a scientific concept, or had special value as the product of the adaptive creativity of a unique subculture. This is extraordinary knowledge for one to learn about oneself, and Zora Hurston found it a fascinating and frustrating acquisition. Even before coming to New York there had begun to build within her a distance between the facts of her Eatonville existence and the esthetic uses she would make of it. Barnard conceptualized that distance between 1925 and 1927, the years of her most active participation in the cultural uprisings of Harlem.

The Barnard experience is seldom discussed when dealing with Hurston, but I believe it is central to understanding her role in the Renaissance and her subsequent career. She entered Barnard as a young, earnest scholar, feeling "highly privileged and determined to make the most of it." She was particularly impressed with her own admission—"not everyone who cries 'Lord! Lord!' can enter those sacred iron gates"—and with Barnard's "high scholastic standards, equipment, the quality of her student body and graduates." She quickly came under the influence of anthropologists Ruth Benedict, Gladys Reichard, and Franz Boas. By far the most important of these was Boas, one of the leading American scientists of the early twentieth century and a man of great personal magnetism. Boas recognized Hurston's genius almost immediately and urged her to begin training as a professional anthropologist. One can grasp how important Boas became to Hurston by reading her autobiography, ***Dust Tracks on a Road*** (1942).[7] Boas was "the greatest anthropologist alive," the "king of kings," and yet she was permitted to call him "Papa Franz." She admittedly "idolized" him. Perhaps the conclusive example of Hurston's serious commitment to Boas's training lies in her willingness to be equipped with a set of calipers and sent to Harlem to measure skulls—an act which many contemporaries feel only Zora Hurston could have gotten away with, and which only a dedicated student would be likely to attempt. Finally, in Febraury 1927, after she had completed the requirements for her B.A. degree, Boas arranged, through Carter Woodson's Association for the Study of Negro Life and History, to finance her on a folklore collecting trip to the South.

Going back was a difficult experience, one she describes with some anguish:

> My first six months were disappointing. I found out later that it was not because I had no talents for research, but because I did not have the right approach. The glamor of Barnard College was still upon me. I dwelt in marble halls. I knew where the material was all right. But, when I went about asking, in carefully accented Barnardese, 'Pardon me, but do you know any folk-tales or folk-songs?' The men and women who had whole treasuries of material just seeping through their pores looked at me and shook their heads. No, they had never heard of anything like that around there. Maybe it was over in the next county. Why didn't I try over there? I did, and got the selfsame answer. Oh, I got a few little items. But compared with what I did later, not enough to make a flea a waltzing jacket. Considering the mood of my going South, I went back to New York with my heart beneath my knees and my knees in some lonesome valley.
>
> I stood before Papa Franz and cried salty tears.[8]

The causes of her initial failure were varied, but at least one of them was philosophical. She was not returning to the South as a local girl home from college, but as a young, serious intellectual equipped with the analytic tools of anthropological theory and a desire to further the cause of science. In her experience with Boas she had tried to emulate what she called his "genius for pure objectivity,"[9] but her academic training did not suffice once she was in the field. The problem went beyond techniques of collecting. Hurston had acquired a conceptualization for her experience. The Eatonville folk were no longer simply good storytellers, admirable in their lifestyles, remarkable in their superstitions, the creators of profound humor, the matrix for a vital, local-color fiction. Now they were a part of cultural anthropology; scientific objects who could and should be studied for their academic values. These are not irreconcilable positions, but for one who has previously conceived of such experience esthetically, it is a definite skewing of perception. Where before Eatonville had been considered a totally unique body of material known only to Zora Hurston (even her black fellow artists in the Renaissance knew little about it), now the town and her experience in it were abstracted to the level of science—a subculture created and maintained by adaptive techniques of survival, many of which had scientific labels and theoretical significance. The altered perception created in Hurston a dual consciousness.

A tension, perhaps latent since her removal from the Eatonville scene, became manifest between the subjective folk experience and the abstract knowledge of the meaning of that experience, and it was complicated by the stress on objectivity intrinsic to the Boas training. First in New York, and then in the South as a collector, Zora Hurston sought a scientific explanation for why her own experience in the black rural South, despite all her education, remained the most vital part of her life, and further, why the black folk-experience generally was such a source of vitality in literature. Moving between art and science, fiction and anthropology, she searched for an expressive instrument, an intellectual formula, that could accommodate the poetry of Eatonville, the theories of Morningside Heights, and the esthetic ferment she had known in Harlem.

This was a unique intellectual tension complicated by the personal factors of sex, race, and nationality, that whole complex of ambiguous identifications American culture imposes on its members. Hurston struggled with it during the Renaissance, and to some extent throughout her life. It is reflected in her unsuccessful attempt to return to Columbia for a Ph.D. in 1934—she told Boas, "You don't know how I have longed for a chance to stay at Columbia and study"[10]—her handling of her collected folklore in ***Mules and Men*** (1935) and ***Tell My Horse*** (1938); the attempts at esthetic resolution in her novels of the thirties (***Jonah's Gourd Vine,*** 1934; ***Their Eyes Were Watching God,*** 1937; ***Moses, Man of the Mountain,*** 1939); and her final retreat from the issue entirely. Bitter over the rejection of her folklore's value, especially in the black community, frustrated by what she felt was her failure to convert the Afro-American world view into the forms of prose fiction, Hurston finally gave up. Her unsuccessful 1948 novel, ***Seraph on the Suwanee,*** is about white people; her later research interests were the Mayan Indian cultures of Central America; she spent the final seven years of her life writing a "nonracial" biography of Herod the Great.

II

Hurston's writing during the Renaissance years comes generally from the pre-Barnard or early Barnard period. After she became a serious Boas student, most of her energies were turned to the problems of folklore collecting. As a student at Howard she had been a striving English major, capable of such lyrics as **"O Night":**

> O Night, calm Night,
> Creep down and close my burning eyes,
> Blot out this day of heavy sighs,
> O Night.
> Dam up my tears and hide my face,
> Efface from mind this time and place,
> O Night, black Night.[11]

"John Redding Goes to Sea," in Howard's *Stylus* for 1921 (later reprinted in *Opportunity*), is a sentimental story—the account of a rustic dreamer who achieves his wish of going to sea only after a heavy rain sends an errant log downstream with his corpse. Yet Hurston also realized early the rich possibilities of the Eatonville material, even if she did not quite understand her personal relationship to it. The first story sent in response to Charles S. Johnson's request was **"Drenched in Light,"** published in *Opportunity* in December 1924, a month before her arrival in New York. It is a day in the life of Isie Watts, a "little Brown figure perched upon the gate post" in front of her Eatonville home. "Everybody in the country," knows "Isie Watts, the joyful," and how she likes to laugh and play, how she lives to the fullest every minute of her young life. Isie gets into various scrapes, including an attempt to shave her sleeping grandmother, and eventually is given a ride by a passing white motorist, despite her grandmother's disapproval. The point appears to be that Isie, poor and black, is far from tragic: rather, she is "drenched in light," a condition which endears her to everyone and presents her grandmother with a discipline problem. Isie is persistently happy, and the implication is that whites suffer from an absence of such joy; Isie's white benefactor ends the story, "I want a little of her sunshine to soak into my soul. I need it."

Hurston is probably manipulating white stereotypes of black people here, but it is not a simple matter of satire. She remembered Eatonville as a place of great happiness, and **"Drenched in Light"** is clearly autobiographical. To realize how much so, one has only to read her autobiography, or her May 1928 article in *The World Tomorrow,* **"How It Feels to be Colored Me."** In this essay Hurston admits "My favorite place was atop the gate-post. Proscenium box for a born first-nighter. Not only did I enjoy the show, but I didn't mind the actors knowing that I liked it." She, too, used to take rides from white motorists if her family was not watching, and she admits to liking to perform for the white folks:

> They liked to hear me "speak pieces" and sing and wanted to see me dance the parse-me-la, and gave me generously of their small silver for doing these things, which seemed strange to me for I wanted to do them so much that I needed bribing to stop. Only they didn't know it.

There is an element of satire in both pieces, but it seems useful to place the emphasis on the Eatonville memory. The whole point to **"How It Feels to be Colored Me"** is that

> I am not tragically colored. There is no great sorrow dammed up in my soul, nor lurking behind my eyes. I do not mind at all. I do not belong to the sobbing school of Negrohood who hold that nature somehow has given them a lowdown dirty deal and whose feelings are all hurt about it . . . No, I do not weep at the world—I am too busy sharpening my oyster knife.

This is hardly a satiric tone, and Hurston is making a serious point: she is proud to be black, proud to be the product of a culture which endows her with a special response to the jazz of the "New World Cabaret." When the band starts playing she "follows them exultingly" and is amazed that "the great blobs of purple and red emotion" have not touched her white companion.

Hurston was as vulnerable as anyone to the cult of primitivism in the twenties, and some of the vulnerability is illustrated in the *World Tomorrow* article. Still, even before coming to New York, as the autobiographical **"Drenched in Light"** indicates, Hurston was trying to define her own special relationship to Eatonville, its folklore, the pastoral idyll that she associated with her first ten years there, and the implications of all of this for her art.

Hurston's use of Eatonville is also seen in her prize-winning story in the 1925 *Opportunity* contest, **"Spunk."** Spunk takes another man's wife, kills the cuckolded husband, and then rides to his death on the log at the saw mill—apparently the victim of the dead husband's return for vengeance. Eatonville is not exactly idyllic, although the violence just below the town's surface admittedly does not appear ominous. It is a place where superstition and "conjure" are everyday facts of life, and where existence has a continuity that transcends the moment. As the story ends: "The women ate heartily of the funeral baked meats and wondered who would be Lena's next. The men whispered coarse conjectures between guzzles of whiskey."

Not all of Hurston's writing during the Renaissance years deals with Eatonville, but certainly the best of it does. Her attempt to illustrate the Eatonville novice newly arrived on the Harlem cabaret scene, **"Muttsy"** (*Opportunity,* August 1926), is poorly plotted but provides a nice ironic touch to the *Pamela* motif; the girl preserves her innocence in capturing the worldly Muttsy, but the story ends with him going back to his gambling ways: "What man can't keep one li'l wife an' two li'l bones?" Her play ***Color Struck,*** the second-prize winner in the 1926 *Opportunity* contest and later reprinted in *Fire,*[12] is sentimental, a somewhat unconvincing account of color consciousness within the black community, but its cakewalk setting has considerable vitality. Another play, **"The First One,"** also submitted to the *Opportunity* contests and later printed in Charles S. Johnson's *Ebony and Topaz,* is a biblical account of the Ham legend, comic in its presentation of Ham's curse being a product of shrewishness in Shem's and Arafat's wives; Ham is presented as a lover of dancing and music, a man of joy contrasted with his brothers' materialism.

More representative of Hurston's talent during this period is **"Sweat,"** published in *Fire*'s single issue, and the **"Eatonville Anthology,"** published serially in *The Messenger* between September and November 1926. The **"Anthology"** is a series of thirteen brief sketches told with great economy and humor. **"Sweat"** is probably Hurston's finest short story of the decade, remarkably complex at both narrative and symbolic levels. The account of a Christian woman learning how to hate in spite of herself, a story of marital cruelty, an allegory of good and evil, it illustrates the unlimited potential in the Eatonville material. The story centers on Delia and her husband Sykes. Sykes hates his wife, beats her, and lives with another woman; he finds excuses to be cruel. And yet Hurston sees through even such a distasteful character; one reason Sykes hates his wife is that she emasculates him by earning their living washing white men's clothes. His resultant behavior is perceptively analyzed by Joe Clark: "There's plenty men dat takes a wife lak dey do a joint uh sugar-cane. It's round, juicy an' sweet when dey gits it. But dey squeeze an' grind, squeeze an' grind an' wring tell dey wring every drop uh pleasure dat's in em out. When dey's satisfied dat dey is wrung dry, dey treats em jes lak de do a cane-chew. Dey throws em away. Dey knows whut dey is doin' while dey is at it, an' hates theirselves fuh it but they keeps on hangin' after huh tell she's empty. Den dey hates huh fuh bein' a cane-chew an' in de way." Sykes eventually tries to drive Delia from her own house by penning a rattlesnake near her back door, and then attempts murder by moving it to her clothes hamper. When the released rattler kills Sykes instead, even though Delia could have saved him, we understand how high Delia's "spiritual earthworks" of Old Testament vengeance have been built against Sykes; she truly hates him "like a suck-egg dog." But this makes the story Delia's tragedy, too, and when Sykes dies at Delia's feet with "his horribly swollen neck and his one open eye shining with hope," a burden is not lifted but newly imposed. Her situation testifies to the prevalence of evil in a world we shape with our own needs.

What these early Eatonville stories illustrate is that by 1925-26, Zora Hurston had taken the irrevocable step of the artist who must remove himself from his experience in order to give it form and meaning. The step was both physical—she had removed herself to Washington and New York, she had entered college—and mental: she was analyzing her experience for its esthetic possibility. When this removal was placed in an academic setting, the process of assigning meaning to her experience became transferred from the esthetic to the scientific, and the next four years of Hurston's life exhibit the ascendency of a scientific impulse toward the systematic collecting of folklore for serious academic purposes.

"Sweat" and the **"Eatonville Anthology"** were published during her last semester at Barnard, the time in which she became most closely associated with Boas and advanced anthropological study. Significantly, Hurston does not return again to Eatonville as a source for fiction until **"The Gilded Six-bits,"** published in *Story* in 1933, an account of marital infidelity that led in 1934 to a contract for her first novel, ***Jonah's Gourd Vine.*** What happened to her in the intervening period is largely an untold or misunderstood story.

FROM THE AUTHOR

"SWEAT"

It was eleven o'clock of a Spring night in Florida. It was Sunday. Any other night, Delia Jones would have been in bed for two hours by this time. But she was washwoman, and Monday morning meant a great deal to her. So she collected the soiled clothes on Saturday when she returned the clean things. Sunday night after church, she sorted them and put the white things to soak. It saved her almost half a day's start. A great hamper in the bedroom held the clothes that she brought home. It was so much neater than a number of bundles lying around.

SOURCE: Zora Neale Hurston, excerpt from "Sweat," first published in *Fire!!*, November 1926.

III

Hurston's 1927 collecting expedition lasted for six months, from February to October. Neither Woodson nor Boas was overly impressed. Woodson printed her article on Cudjo Lewis, a survivor of the last slave ship to America, in the *Journal of Negro History*,[13] but he apparently also used her as a common research hack. At one point she was copying legal documents from the Jacksonville, Florida, court records about a black-owned traction company of 1909. The folk material sent to Boas did not please, for it was similar to material collected by others, and her report to Boas on the conclusions of the expedition took only three double-spaced pages. Hurston had now, however, largely given up the writing of fiction to pursue a career as a scientist. Even though her field trip had not been a success, she is dedicated to anthropology, convinced of the need to collect her people's folklore before it is obliterated by the encroachments of modern civilization. In her report to Boas she stresses that material is slowly slipping away: "The bulk of the population now spends its leisure in the motion picture theatres or with the phonograph."[14] One cannot overemphasize the extent of her commitment. It was so great that her marriage in the spring of 1927 to Herbert Sheen was short-lived. Although divorce did not come officially until 1931, the two separated amicably after only a few months, Hurston to continue her collecting, Sheen to attend Medical School. Hurston never married again.

Hurston's return to her folklore collecting in December of 1927 was made possible by Mrs. R. Osgood Mason, an elderly white patron of the arts, who at various times also helped Langston Hughes, Alain Locke, Richmond Barthé, and Miguel Covarrubias. Hurston apparently came to her attention through the intercession of Locke, who frequently served as a kind of liaison between young black talent and Mrs. Mason. The entire relationship between this woman and the Harlem Renaissance deserves extended study, for it represents much of the ambiguity involved in white patronage of black artists. All her artists were instructed to call her "Godmother"; there was a decided emphasis on the "primitive" aspects of black culture, apparently a holdover from Mrs. Mason's interest in the Plains Indians. In Hurston's case there were special restrictions imposed by her patron: although she was to be paid a handsome salary for her folklore collecting, she was to limit her correspondence and publish nothing of her research without prior approval.

Hurston was financed by Mrs. Mason for an initial two-year period, from December 1927 to December 1929, and then was given an extension to March 31 of 1931. Although she spent time in the West Indies, most of her effort was in the South, and she collected a body of material which she would draw on for the rest of her life. Her correspondence during these years is remarkable for its enthusiasm. She feels that she is getting to the core of Afro-American culture, seeing it as an illustration of man's most basic impulses. She wants to present the material unadorned, letting it speak for itself as eloquent testimony for black creativity. She is impressed with the inherent beauty of the folklore itself, the way preaching is poetry, the way folk singing is more alive than classical music. She frequently rails against white distortions of this material, especially against Howard Odum and Guy Johnson, early white collectors in the field. In one letter she asks Boas point-blank if these men can be "serious scientists."[15] She also thought analytically about the material, formulating general principles to guide her study. She wrote Langston Hughes about theories of dialect: "Some laws in dialect. The same form is not always used. Some syllables and words are long before or after certain words and short in the same position. Example: you as subject gets full value but is shortened to yuh as an object. Him in certain positions and 'im in others depending on consonant preceding. Several laws of aspirate H."[16] In letter after letter Hurston emphasizes the uniqueness of black culture. She stresses the "basic drama" of black life, the ingenuity and wit in black dialect, the "asymmetry" of black art, the "dynamism" of black dancing, the originality of the entire Afro-American subculture.[17]

A measure of her sense of discovery and scientific commitment to it is the absence of her own creative effort between the fall of 1927 and the spring of 1930; even then she only began work with Langston Hughes on an ill-fated play, ***Mule Bone,*** itself a drama constructed out of a folktale. Hurston had previously used the Eatonville setting and its rural folklore as the stuff of fiction; now she is given to the collecting of songs, dances, games, conjure ceremonies, or anything else that can contribute to her body of information. As she told Hughes, "I am truly dedicated to the work at hand and so I am not even writing."[18] Her reports of her research are basically academic, apparently mainly by choice, although it was also a form approved by Locke and Mrs. Mason. She completed two pieces for the *Journal of American Folklore,* **"Dance Songs and Tales of the Bahamas"**[19] and the 110-page monograph, **"Hoodoo in America."**[20] She consulted with Boas and Benedict about her efforts and asked Boas's advice about the theories she was formulating—many of which were eventually published in a most unscientific volume, Nancy Cunard's *Negro* (1934). At one point she had planned seven books from her materials: "One volume of stories. One children's games. One dance and the Negro. One 'Mules and Men' a volume of work songs with guitar accompaniment. One on religion. One on words and meanings. One volume of love letters with an introduction on Negro love."[21] She was also interested in presenting on stage the true folk experience, eventually putting together a group of actors, singers, and dancers, and with Mrs. Mason's help producing an authentic folk concert at the John Golden Theatre on January 10, 1932. Extremely proud of her admission to the American Folklore Society, the American Ethnological Society, and the American Anthropological Society, she made sure that any news stories about her contained mention of these professional memberships. The Howard English major and the short-story writer of the Harlem Renaissance had apparently become a Barnard anthropologist, a folklore collector of considerable zeal and importance.

That transformation never fully took place, however, and although Hurston would continue to collect and use folklore for most of her career, establishing herself as the most important collector in the field, she grew away from the scientific view of her material. She came to doubt the efficacy of scholarly publication, pointing out to the Rosenwald Fund in 1934 that "it is almost useless to collect material to lie upon the shelves of scientific societies."[22] My own opinion is that she never became a professional, academic anthropologist, because such a vocation was alien to her exuberant sense of self, her admittedly artistic and sometimes erratic temperament. A good argument can be made for Hurston's never completely realizing this herself, but if there is a single theme which emerges from her creative effort during the thirties—her five books, her fiction, her essays—it is that eventually immediate experience takes precedence over analysis, emotion over reason, the self over society, the personal over the theoretical. She learned that scientific objectivity is not enough for a black writer in America, and she went on to expose the excessive rationality behind the materialism of American life, the inadequacy of a sterile reason to deal with the phenomena of living. She forcefully affirmed the humanistic values of black life, contrasting them to the rationalized inhumanity of white society, and she asserted early arguments for black cultural nationalism. Beginning with ***Jonah's Gourd Vine*** (1934), her writing exhibits a studied anti-scientific approach, and in her nonfiction even the most technical data is personalized. Her rejection of the scholarly bias and the scientific form was a process instead of a revelation, forming a chapter in her personal history too complex to detail here. Its cultural context is relevant, however, for Hurston's intellectual experience is in some ways a paradigm for the much debated "Crisis" of the black creative intellectual of the Harlem Renaissance.

I think Hurston was predisposed in favor of an anthropological conception of Eatonville simply because she was a creative writer. Although that sounds paradoxical, it is actually a logical product of the environment of ideas surrounding her. The black writer is especially vulnerable to the prescriptions which an idolatry of western European "high culture" imposes on American artists. He is urged to aspire toward a "raceless ideal" of literature, which technically interpreted has meant that he should not write about race, that he should not create "Negroes" but "human beings"—as if they were mutually exclusive categories. Above all, he must never stoop to "propaganda." Such prescriptions were constantly offered during the Harlem Renaissance, and many of its participants aided and abetted such dubious aims. In fact, prior to the revolution in consciousness attending the current Black Arts Revolution, all black writers were badgered with such advice, the writer's success occurring in direct proportion to his ability to reject it. The attitude which invites the act of this prescribing, as well as the substance of the prescription, is a conception of the black condition as something which must be "overcome," since it is somehow manifestly less than human—a habit of mind institutionalized as American racism. All black American writers confront in some way this attitude and its resultant phenomena: the condition of black people. Thus, the dynamics of the culture make it as natural as breathing for the black artist to confront the issue of race.

In such a context, the attraction of a scientific conception for black experience becomes considerable for the writer-intellectual, especially if he has taken part in the formal educational system. The educational process in America is essentially one of assigning and reinforcing class structures through the creation of an educated middle class. This acculturative process informed Hurston that black sharecroppers were peasants (a pejorative term, especially within the self-enterprise mythology of American agriculture), that superstition was a crutch of the ignorant, that her folk experience was quaintly interesting but hopelessly unsophisticated. It is to Hurston's credit that she resisted much of this sort of knowledge, as is illustrated in an article she wrote for the *Messenger* in 1925, **"The Hue and Cry About Howard University."** Howard's white president liked to hear his students sing, and his motives are suspect at best. When the students objected, however, they did so for the wrong reasons; they argued that the spirituals were (a) "low and degrading, being the product of slaves and slavery"; (b) "not good grammar"; (c) "they are not sung in white universities."

Hurston supported the president for the right reasons, when she should have resisted his unconscious racism. Her prospiritual argument would later become a fight to make blacks aware of how "conservatory concepts" had corrupted native Afro-American music, and her awareness of the inadequacies in the antispiritual argument is part of her larger awareness of the black condition. For she *knew* that Joe Clarke and his Eatonville cronies were human beings of complexity and dignity, no matter what their grammar, no matter how unsophisticated their manner might be, no matter how much white society distorted them. This knowledge typifies a dilemma of the black intellectual, for knowing this fact, how does one assert its truth and assign it meaning in the midst of a country whose institutions are structured to deny it? For Zora Neale Hurston, and for others, one way has been to assert black humanity by emphasizing its anthropological confirmation, a particularly effective way of accounting for human truth in a technological society, and one which mostly sidesteps the purely esthetic issue of "universality" vs. "propaganda." Blacks can be measured, studied, and charted in the interests of proving the general equality of the races. One has only to cultivate a "genius for pure objectivity" and let the evidence prove the absurdity of racial prejudice. Moreover, because anthropology also proves the existence of particular cultural differences while simultaneously positing a basic sameness in the human condition, one can maintain the integrity of black culture without sacrificing it to the mythical American melting pot. The scientific collection of the data of black life, its folklore, comes to prove black humanity as it asserts the beauty of the culture; meanwhile the artist who affirms the same thing is accused of special pleading.

What I should like to conclude with is the hypothesis that one reason Zora Neale Hurston was attracted to the scientific conceptualization of her racial experience during the late twenties and early thirties was its *prima facie* offering of a structure for black folklore. That is, it offered a pattern of meaning for material that white racism consistently distorted into "Negro" stereotypes. A folk singer was a cultural object of considerable scientific importance to the collecting anthropologist precisely because his folk experience affirms his humanity, a fact that Hurston could know subjectively as she proved it scientifically. The scientific attraction became so strong that she was led into seriously planning a career as a professional anthropologst, and it continued to affect her writing even after she had rejected such a possibility. When she used Eatonville as fiction in ***Jonah's Gourd Vine*** (1934) and folklore as personal narrative in her collection, ***Mules and Men*** (1935), she was in the process of rejecting the scientific conceptualization, but had not yet reached the esthetic resolution in fiction that characterized her two masterpieces of the late thirties, ***Their Eyes Were Watching God,*** (1937), and ***Moses, Man of the Mountain*** (1939). Hurston never denied the usefulness of the Barnard training, but she made it clear that something more was needed for the creation of art. As she once told a reporter: "I needed my Barnard education to help me see my people as they really are. But I found that it did not do to be too detached as I stepped aside to study them. I had to go back, dress as they did, talk as they did, live their life, so that I could get into my stories the world I knew as a child."[23]

In sum, then, Zora Neale Hurston was shaped by the Harlem Renaissance, but by Boas as well as by Thurman and Hughes, by Barnard as well as by Harlem. This should not necessarily suggest that the Boas experience was of a superior quality; in many ways it seriously hindered her development as an artist. Nor should it suggest that the esthetic excitement among the Harlem literati failed to influence her thought. It does mean that the attraction of scientific objectivity was something Hurston had to work through to arrive at the subjective triumphs of her later books. But the ferment of the Harlem Renaissance should also not be underestimated. Hughes, in particular, showed Hurston the poetic possibilities of the folk idiom and she was continually impressed when a reading from Hughes's poems would break the ice with dock loaders, turpentine workers, and jook singers. The mutual effort involved in the creation of *Fire,* the nights at Charles S. and James Weldon Johnson's, the *Opportunity* dinners, even the teas at Jessie Fauset's helped make Zora Hurston aware of the rich block of material which was hers by chance of birth, and they stimulated her thinking about the techniques of collecting and presenting it.

Yet, even Wallace Thurman, the chief of the "Niggerrati," tacitly acknowledged that anthropology was Hurston's primary concern during the Renaissance years. In his 1934 novel, *Infants of the Spring,* a scarcely disguised account of the Harlem Renaissance, Thurman's Sweetie May Carr is transparent reportage of Zora Neale Hurston. Sweetie May is a storyteller from an all-black Mississippi town, "too indifferent to literary creation to transfer to paper that which she told so well." In one of his better jokes Thurman transfers Hurston's area of study and probably imposes some of his own cynicism on her character, but still suggests a preoccupation with scientific study: "'It's like this,' she [Sweetie May] told Raymond. 'I have to eat. I also wish to finish my education. Being a Negro writer these days is a racket and I'm going to make the most of it while it lasts . . . I don't know a tinker's damn about art. I care less about it. My ultimate ambition, as you know, is to become a gynecologist. And the only way I can live easily until I have the requisite training is to pose as a writer of potential ability.'"

One should be careful about accepting fictional characters as biographical evidence, but I hope the previous reconstruction suggests that Thurman was at least partially right. His insight provides a context for the study of Hurston's published books of the 1930s, a period in which she *did* give a tinker's damn, and created some of the best fiction ever written by a black American.

Notes

1. ALS., Zora Neale Hurston to Harper & Brothers, in the Hurston Collection, University of Florida Library. Quoted by permission of the Hurston family, Mrs. Marjorie Silver, and the University of Florida Library.
2. Hurston variously gave her birthdate as January 7, 1900, 1901, 1902, and 1903; no contemporary records were kept, but the 1903 date is the one given in a 1936 affadavit by her brother John, and the one she most often cited.
3. Zora Neale Hurston, *Dust Tracks on a Road* (New York, 1942), p. 71.
4. *Ibid.,* p. 176.
5. ALS., Zora Neale Hurston to Constance Sheen, January 5, [1926], in the University of Florida Hurston collection. Quoted by permission of the Hurston family, the University of Florida Library, and Mrs. Marjorie Silver.
6. ALS., Zora Neale Hurston to Constance Sheen, February 2, [1926], in Florida's Hurston collection. Quoted by same permission as above.
7. All quotations in this paragraph from *Dust Tracks,* pp. 177-79.
8. *Ibid.,* pp. 182-83.
9. *Ibid.,* p. 182.
10. ALS., Zora Neale Hurston to Franz Boas, December 14, 1934. In The American Philosophical Society Library. Quoted by permission of the Hurston family and The American Philosophical Society.
11. *The Stylus* (Howard University), I, (May 1921), p. 42.
12. *Fire*'s only issue was published in either December 1926 or January 1927. Countee Cullen, writing in *Opportunity* of January 1927, welcomes it as the "outstanding birth" of the month.
13. XII (October 1927), pp. 648-63.
14. Zora Neale Hurston, "The Florida Expedition," 3 pp., typescript, signed, in The American Philosophical Society Library. Quoted by permission of the Hurston family and The American Philosophical Society.
15. ALS., Zora Neale Hurston to Franz Boas, October 20, 1929, in The American Philosophical Society Library. Quoted by permission of the Hurston family and The American Philosophical Society.
16. ALS., Zora Neale Hurston to Langston Hughes, April 12, 1928, in the James Weldon Johnson Memorial Collection of Yale University's Beinecke Library. Quoted by permission of the Hurston family and Yale.
17. *Ibid.* Quoted with same permissions as above.
18. ALS., Zora Neale Hurston to Langston Hughes, March 8, 1928, in James Weldon Johnson Memorial Collection of Yale University's Beinecke Library. Quoted by permission of the Hurston family and Yale.
19. XLIII (July-October 1930), pp. 294-312.
20. XLIV (October-December 1931), pp. 317-417.
21. ALS., Zora Neale Hurston to Langston Hughes, August 6, 1928, in James Weldon Johnson Memorial Collection at Yale University's Beinecke Library. Quoted by permission of the Hurston family and Yale.
22. Application for Rosenwald Fellowship, December 14, 1934, in Fisk University Library's Rosenwald Collection.
23. "Author Plans to Upbraid Own Race," *New York World Telegram,* February 6, 1935.

ANN RAYSON (ESSAY DATE 1974)

SOURCE: Rayson, Ann. "The Novels of Zora Neale Hurston." *Studies in Black Literature* 5, no. 3 (winter 1974): 1-10.

In the following essay, Rayson discusses some recurring patterns and themes in Hurston's four novels.

Zora Neale Hurston (1903-1960) wrote four novels during her literary career. She is best known for the collections of folklore, ***Mules and Men,*** 1935, and ***Tell My Horse,*** 1939, and her engaging autobiography, ***Dust Tracks on a Road,*** 1942. Of her novels, only one, ***Their Eyes Were Watching God,*** 1937, is relatively well-known, though a few readers know ***Jonah's Gourd Vine,*** 1934, her first novel. The novels are an odd assortment. [Biblical, Black, and White] She published a strange version of the Moses story, ***Moses, Man of the Mountain,*** 1939. In her last novel, ***Seraph on the Suwanee,*** 1948, Hurston returns to the successful female protagonist she had created in ***Their Eyes Were Watching God,*** only this time her main characters are white rather than black.

Zora Neale Hurston's novels, despite the surface differences, follow certain patterns. No matter what the novel may concern, her characters speak the Southern folk idiom and espouse a transcendent philosophy of harmony with one's own sexual role and the cosmos. Her themes suggest that one must go beyond the quest for bourgeois life to a comprehension of what is ultimately meaningful—love, fun, a full relationship with one of the opposite sex. And characters—from the embryonic Janie who comes of age or the "hysterical" Arvay to the womanizer-preacher John Buddy or the Hemingwayesque Tea Cake and Jim Meserve, "real" women and men—play similar roles and resolve similar conflicts. In her novels Zora Hurston uses just one plot formula: a protagonist finds his or her way to understanding and love. While the traditional sexual roles are proven to offer the only fulfillment, in order to attain the rather Lawrencian plateau, characters must undergo personal psychological struggles. It is on "becoming," therefore, rather than being, that Hurston focuses her novels.

Jonah's Gourd Vine, Zora Neale Hurston's first novel, sets the standard formula for the novels that are to follow. The plot of ***Jonah's Gourd Vine*** concerns the rise of a mulatto sharecropper-preacher, John Pearson, who marries the intelligent and good woman, Lucy Potts, and begins his rise from the plantation in Macon County, Georgia, to the church in Sanford, Florida. At crucial steps along the way John Pearson backslides as a result of his susceptibility to feminine charms. Lucy suffers. After John Buddy moves the family to Sanford, he becomes the controversial pastor of Zion Hope. Lucy dies after bearing John many children and John marries his no-good mistress, Hattie, who later sues him for divorce. Beaten down, having lost his church as a result of the scandal, he moves to Plant City, marries the rich widow, Sally Lovelace, and kills himself by absent-mindedly running her new car into a train on his way back from yet one more liaison (with Ora in Oviedo).

The central conflict, nevertheless, is between John and Lucy over the inequality of their love and constancy. The martyr is pitted against the profligate. Here the double standard is unabashedly upheld:

> "Lucy, is you sorry you married me instid uh some big nigger wid uh whole heap uh money and titles hung on tuh him?"
>
> "What make you ast me dat? If you tired uh me, jus' leave me. Another man over de fence waitin fuh ye' job."
>
> John stood up, ". . . lemme tell you somethin' right now, and it ain't two, don't you never tell me no mo' whut you jus' told me, 'cause if you do, Ahm goin' tuh kill yuh jes' ez she ez gun is rien. Ahm de first wid you, and Ah means tuh be de last. Ain't never no man tuh breathe in ye' face but me. You hear me?"
>
> "You done—"
>
> "Don't tell me 'bout dem trashy women Ah lusts after once in uh while. Dey's less dan leaves uh grass."[1]

More than this, the struggle is that of man against himself; John never wins the battle over his baser impulses and so dies in disgrace. His is a life of temptation and torment, of begging forgiveness and flaunting sin, of nobility and degradation. An incarnation of the double standard in sexual roles, John Pearson is, moreover, a stereotype of the Southern Negro preacher. The ambivalence of this type further emphasizes John's personal conflict with his own lust. It is after the argument over the double standard that John (raising the song, "He's a Battle-Axe in de time Uh Trouble," in church,) feels the call to preach. Thus, John is a man's man, a folk hero, and an orator—in other words, a con artist ineluctable. However, unable to resolve his sexual conflict, John has to die as a victim of his own roguery.

Character, not plot, is of primary importance in this novel. While criticism of ***Jonah's Gourd Vine*** has been sparse, there has been some comment on character archetypes. Nancy Tischler in *Black Masks: Negro Characters in Modern Southern Fiction,* 1969, discusses the preacher as a type, examples of which include John Buddy, Rinehart of *Invisible Man,* Nat Turner, and Daddy Faith of *Lie Down in Darkness.*

> The preachers were gradually to metamorphosize into aggressive race leaders, but the earlier stories showed them as mindless, selfish, over-sexed conjurmen, preaching hell fire and the golden streets of Glory Land, categorizing sin and salvation neatly and superficially, reveling in the applause of the crowds, shrewdly soliciting money from supporters, and at times seducing the females in the congregation.[2]

John Buddy has only one of these negative traits and serves as a prototype for Baldwin's more sinister Gabriel Grimes in his fleshly weakness. But, while Gabriel attempts to transfer his guilt and self-hate to the illegitimate son John and to Elizabeth, his once-fallen, now redeemed second wife, John Buddy Pearson rationalizes his actions and accepts his humanity in a folksy way that makes up for some of the pain he causes himself and others. Suffering and joy comprise the fabric of his life, not selfishness, hate, and evasion alone. John Buddy thus, becomes a transparent con artist unlike the oily Daddy Faith and a more pardonable sexual transgressor, who, unlike Gabriel, doesn't brutalize his women. John Buddy's crimes are crimes against his better nature, not against others. Never willfully and consciously taking advantage of people, he seems inadvertently to find himself in dubious situations. Lucy is hurt repeatedly by his exuberance, but she realizes that he loves her above all. They both participate in the pattern of jubilance, estrangement, and remorse. She suffers and endures; he kneels and rises to commit adultery once again.

The novel's theme arises from the presentation of character in conflict with itself, not with society. Hence, ***Jonah's Gourd Vine*** is more a folk tale than a novel of social analysis or protest. Hugh Gloster in *Negro Voices in American Fiction,* 1948, says Hurston has "an unusual capacity for appropriating folklore to the purposes of fiction,"[3] but further sees validity in Andrew Burris' comment that she uses "'her characters and the various situations created for them as mere pegs upon which to hang their dialect and folkways.'" Therefore, the critical attitude toward what Zora Hurston is doing with fiction is simultaneously laudatory and censorious. Her knowledge and implementation of the folk idiom through the speech and action of her characters, while a valuable and admirable contribution to American literature, nevertheless prevents her from tackling problems of social and racial import. This leads Gloster to praise, then criticize:

> The peculiar idiom of folk speech and the "big old lies" of folk characters are competently handled. Less convincing is the development of character and the analysis of social problems. Racial difficulties never disturb the even tenor of the novel, and the Negro peons of the story are resigned to exploitation and oppression.[4]

Here is the idea that setting, not plot, theme, or character, is Hurston's main concern. However, character appears to be the major focus in all four of Hurston's novels. The process of one's growing psychologically to maturity and reaching a comprehension of "true" values—as DuBois would say, not apples of gold, but "Truth, Beauty, Goodness"—provides the tension. John strives to be true to his Beatrice, but fails. On the other hand, Janie, having undergone her psychological and experiential baptism by fire in ***Their Eyes Were Watching God,*** emerges as the model heroine.

All fiction by black novelists does not have to dwell on serious racial conflict. Hurston, as her autobiography shows, is a flamboyant individualist. Judging her from the vantage point of what she attempts, we realize that she succeeds brilliantly. Her characters and plots are simple; her novels are extended ballads composed through incremental repetition and traditional characters and situations. It is here that she achieves universality. Her novels are meant to be evaluated according to specialized criteria. They do not form a part of the mainstream of black American protest literature, but belong to a genre of their own, probably stemming from the Uncle Remus stories. In the field of folklore, Hurston is well versed. While collecting folklore for Franz Boas at Columbia, she lived and worked among those in Florida and Georgia who carried on these traditions unconsciously. Her vision in this framework is realistic; to her, folklore is life.

On a visit to Hurston in Longwood, Florida, (she had only published ***Jonah's Gourd Vine*** at the time) Nick Aaron Ford asks her about the significance of her philosophy. She expresses it in the interview as follows:

> "Many Negroes criticise my book," she said, as the conversation drifted to literature, "because I did not make it a lecture on the race problem."
>
> "Well, why didn't you?" I asked.
>
> "Because," she replied simply, "I was writing a novel and not a treatise on sociology. There is where many Negro novelists make their mistakes. They confuse art with sociology."
>
> "But," I said, "how can you write without being forever conscious of your race and the multitude of injustices which is heaped upon it in our present social order?"
>
> She smiled a bit condescendingly. "You see," she began benignantly, "I have ceased to think in terms of race; I think only in terms of individuals. I am interested in you now, not as a *Negro* man but as a *man.* I am not interested in the *race* problem, but I am interested in the problems of *individuals,* white ones and black ones."[5]

Thus, Hurston herself substantiates the thesis that the portrayal of individual character conflict is her major concern. She deals with psychology and private philosophy rather than political, economic, or social theory. The tension between the given character and his "coming of age" makes Hurston's novels.

From reading ***Dust Tracks on a Road*** one has the unmistakable feeling that Hurston is genuine, genuinely a character. She may thrive on this kind of notoriety and do all she can to uphold it, but beyond the conscious role playing is the Zora Hurston who lives and feels the way her protagonists do. Like John Buddy and Janie, she espouses a flexible, natural morality that places human relationships above getting and spending. Problems are the basic ones between husband and wife; society furnishes a backdrop for the working out of one's private harmony with man and God's nature. Protest can grow boring and oppressive. Certainly the answers Hurston gives are pat, but her style of preaching is refreshing. Individual growth is the key.

In ***Their Eyes Were Watching God,*** which happens to be Hurston's best novel, Hurston continues her use of stereotyped characters and plots. The main character, Janie, is Hurston's psychological self-portrait. Furthermore, Hurston's depiction of the various socio-economic levels of blacks reveals her insight into class and caste and demonstrates her ability to project these levels fictionally. Her milieu here is more comprehensive as she moves her protagonist from rural West Florida, to the Negro city of Eatonville, to the Everglades. Each move involves a different man, the last of whom gives Janie her reason for being. Thus, plot, conflict, character, setting, and structure follow the basic pattern, but work together more effectively than in ***Jonah's Gourd Vine.*** Because Hurston can identify with the heroine, the outcome of Janie's conflict is positive. Janie is real while John Buddy remains a type; her plight communicates itself to the reader.

The novel's action begins with a flashback. Janie, back in Eatonville as an "odd" forty-year-old woman with long hair and muddy overalls, tells her story to a friend. Thus, we first see Janie when at sixteen she is forced by her granny to marry an old farmer with sixty acres, thus prostituting her youth and beauty for Brother Logan Killicks' wealth and position in the community. Janie learns her initial lesson: "She knew now that marriage did not make love. Janie's first dream was dead, so she became a woman."[6] Then Joe Starks, "a citified stylish dressed man,"[7] comes along, charms Janie, marries her, and takes her away with him to Eatonville. (Bigamy never becomes an issue worthy of mention.) As Jody rises from store owner to landowner and mayor, Janie grows increasingly disillusioned with her social status attained at the expense of her husband's absence from her. Jody crushes her identity, belittles her publicly. Money and position, social class, destroy the happiness of marriage. Thus, when Jody dies, Janie is ready for the remarkable Tea Cake. She burns her head rags in a gesture of defiance. Other realizations follow:

> She hated her grandmother and had hidden it from herself all these years under a cloak of pity. She had been getting ready for her great journey to the horizons in search of *people;* it was important to all the world that she should find them and they find her. But she had been whipped like a cur dog, and run off down a back road after things.[8]

Then Tea Cake, a genuine good-time man, comes along to teach her to fish, play checkers, pick beans, and make love. He takes her to Jacksonville to marry, then disappears with her secreted two hundred dollars, and inadvertently falls in with good company. He ends up staging a huge, spontaneous barbecue party and returns to Janie twenty-four hours later. She feels used and betrayed only to discover his honest intentions: partying is the staff of life—money is meaningless unless you can enjoy spending it. However, you can also do without it just as well. Consequently, Janie learns yet another lesson from Tea Cake and ceases to worry about money, manipulation, and selfishness. Espousing this philosophy, Janie and Tea Cake are the exception, not the rule. Nancy Tischler explains the significance of Janie's position in relation to its application to black aspirations:

> Her soul needs freedom and experience, not security and power and wealth. But significantly, her search for real values comes after the acquisition of material wealth proves unsatisfying. This cannot become a paradigm for Negro-centered novels until more Negroes have known and reject affluence. To the Dink Britt [industrious drudge] type of dirt farmer, money is the closest thing to heaven.[9]

After this escapade, Tea Cake takes Janie to the Everglades and they earn a living in the groves. In this section of the novel Hurston shows a consciousness of racial oppression. For example, a hurricane destroys the area and Tea Cake is forcibly recruited to dig grave pits for the dead. Whereas the dead whites are at least given pine coffins, the blacks are thrown indiscriminately into ditches. Furthermore, an intergroup racial conflict is introduced by the "color-struck" Mrs. Turner who disapproves of Janie's liaison with the dark Tea Cake. "'Ah can't stand black niggers. Ah don't blame di white folks from hatin' 'em 'cause Ah can't stand 'em mahself. Nother thing, Ah hates tuh see folks lak me and you mixed up wid 'em. Us oughta class off.'"[10] Hurston makes a strong case against this attitude:

> Mrs. Turner, like all other believers had built an altar to the unattainable—Caucasian characteristics for all. Her god would smite her, would hurl her from pinnacles and lose her in deserts. But she would not forsake his altars. Behind her crude words was a belief that somehow she and others

> through worship could attain her paradise—a heaven of straight-haired, thin-lipped, high-noseboned white seraphs.[11]

Both of these race conflicts contribute to the irony and horror of the climax. When the hurricane occurs, Tea Cake is bitten by a rabid dog in the scuffle. Crazed, he accuses Janie of sneaking out with Mrs. Turner's light-colored brother. This rage drives him in his delirium to attempt murder, but Janie kills him in self-defense first, his teeth in her arm.

Thus, Zora Neale Hurston probes into the psychology of race, which leads to self-hate based on caste insecurity. Not only do blacks bear the myth of white superiority, but also that of the standard preference for mulattos. Janie is above all such discriminations, yet there is talk of her acquital for murder being due to her good looks. The aspirations of the landowning farmer and the black bourgeoisie, as represented by Logan Killicks and Joe Starks, are severely criticized as, on the other hand, the simple values, disregard for money and position with corresponding regard for love, unselfishness, and good-timing as represented by Tea Cake, are praised, making ***Their Eyes Were Watching God*** a novel of *carpe diem,* zest for life.

Their Eyes Were Watching God is a more complex novel than ***Jonah's Gourd Vine*** and avoids the forced cuteness and sentimentality of both it and ***Seraph on the Suwanee.*** Hurston's mode is successful here. The language and emotion of the characters are realistically presented. The events have substance; the novel says something profound in its own way. Janie's experience has been positive, whereas John Buddy's ends in negative self-destruction. Even Lucy's experience, which parallels Janie's in many ways, lacks the beauty and meaning of Janie's, since Lucy dies as she lives, in pinched martyrdom. Essentially the novel's action serves to demonstrate Hurston's opening statement that "women forget all those things they don't want to remember and remember everything they don't want to forget. The dream is the truth. They act and do things accordingly."[12]

So Janie begins her story to Phoeby in response to the town's petty gossip.

> Now they got to look into me loving Tea Cake and/ see whether it was done right or not! They don't know if life is a mess of corn-meal dumplings, and if love is a bed-quilt!"
>
> "So long as they get a name to gnaw on they don't care whose it is, and what about, 'specially if they can make it sound like evil."
>
> "If they wants to see and know, why they don't come kiss and be kissed? Ah could then sit down and tell 'em things. Ah been a delegate to de big 'ssociation of life. Yessuh! De Grand Lodge, de big convention of livin' is just where Ah been dis year and a half y'all ain't seen me."[13]

As Ellison's protagonist says, "the end is the beginning."

Moses, Man of the Mountain, 1939, is a novel based upon the Old Testament account of Moses. After the manner of those in *Ol' Man Adam an' His Chillun* (1928) and *The Green Pastures* (1930), Hurston's characters speak a black dialect with colloquialisms, folk wisdom, and double negatives. They try to con each other. What Darwin Turner says about ***Jonah's Gourd Vine*** and ***Their Eyes Were Watching God,*** a standard criticism of the Harlem Renascence's exploitation of the primitive, can be applied to Moses. "Superficially considered, both novels authentically depict Negroes limited both educationally and economically. Consciously writing for a non-Negro audience, however, Miss Hurston exploits the exotic qualities of the colorful, imaginative language."[14] What Hurston tries in her first two novels, she continues here *in extremis.* The personalities of Moses, Pharoah, Aaron, Miriam, the Hebrews, and the Egyptians are fantastic distortions that verge on parody after *Ol' Man Adam.* Hurston infuses these ikons with a hearty realism. The characters only appear ridiculous because of the historical solemnity associated with them in most other depictions.

Hurston's ***Moses, Man of the Mountain*** has parallels with Roark Bradford's *Ol' Man Adam an' His Chillun,* a parody of the Old Testament in which black characters reenact the major tales and speak black dialect. The Moses story takes up seven chapters in Bradford's book and is the most extensively portrayed of the tales. While *Ol' Man Adam* is obvious parody, later dramatized as *The Green Pastures,* ***Moses, Man of the Mountain*** veers between parody and serious fiction. Hurston's introduction indicates that she is attempting a realistic portrayal of the Moses story of pagan and Christian traditions. The allusions to American Negro slavery are, of course, expressed in both treatments, but more explicitly in *Ol' Man Adam* as Pharoah wants to Jim Crow the Hebrews with a "granddaddy clause" to keep the election(!) under control. The Sheriff says nix, "De last man Jim Crowed 'em and Uncle Sam got him draggin' a ball and chain."[15] The stories follow the same plot lines, ***Moses, Man of the Mountain*** being the more detailed. Dialect is thicker in *Ol' Man Adam* and there are references to the U.S., "Uncle Sam,"

"Jay Gould" (the lawd says "my chilluns is got more land den old Jay Gould, over across Jurdin.")[16] In ***Moses, Man of the Mountain*** the Lord speaks standard English as do Moses and Pharoah, although Moses uses double negatives and other informalities.

No characters are distinguished from others in *Ol' Man Adam*—all are congenial; there is no sinister threat of evil. [The Chilluns eat beans and onions, cawn bread and turnip greens; in other words, light hearted parody is the keynote.] However, in ***Moses, Man of the Mountain*** Aaron and Miriam are suspect connivers, the Lord is a serious God and Pharoah is a smarter adversary.

Here Moses, not culturally a man of the Hebrews, is continually trying to overcome the Hebrews' greed and distrust by performing "hoodoo"—the rod changed to a budding stick (a snake in *Ol' Man Adam*), water turned to blood, and the plague of frogs put upon Egypt. Not imbued with the religious sense of his mission, Moses seems to lead the Chosen amidst reservations, clouds of self-doubt, naivete, and the brash heroism of a confidence man. A group of dimestore gangsters play the roles of the historically magnificent, making the story a parody that was probably not intended by Hurston. While the parodies of Bradford and Connelly are intentional exaggerations, that of Hurston is unconscious, since her preface underscores the cross-cultural significance of the Moses story. Zora Hurston tries, in her fiction, to make the characters act and sound what to her is natural, folksy. Folks continually try one-upmanship with each other, are careless about grammar, have an indigenous suspicion of others, particularly outsiders (Pharoah's Egypt suits this motif well), and enjoy the simple, homey pleasures of life.

A beastial sensuality and intelligence, coupled with the shrewdness of the market place, surrounds Hurston's characters in this most improbable fictional work. Their personalities manifest themselves largely through speech rather than action. How they communicate tells the reader much about their characters. Hurston uses black dialect more and more as the book progresses. As Moses escapes Egypt to Gotham after killing the overseer, marries Zipporah, and returns to lead the people, he alternates between dialect and good English, the former gaining precedence over the latter as he leaves the aristocracy and mingles with the Israelite masses.

Early in the novel the Hebrews resent Moses' interference in their slave labor and castigate him openly.

> One of the men who had been fighting turned to Moses with a sneer on his lips. "We thought this was Prince Moses, chief of the Egyptian army. We did not know that you was straw-boss of public works. In fact we didn't know that you was our bossman at all. Nobody ain't told us you was suppose to come round here acting like a overseer."
>
> "I don't want to be anybody's boss. In fact, that is the very thing I want to do away with." he said quietly.
>
> "Don't look like it," one of the men retorted. "If what you are doing ain't bossing then there ain't a crocodile in the Nile! Calling yourself our friend, and liable to get anybody in Goshen killed if ever they find—" (Moses has killed the Egyptian overseer).[17]

Later, after his flight from Egypt due to disfavor, Moses talks with Jethro, his new father-in-law, about his plans. Jethro urges Moses to take up the cause, but Moses hesitates.

> "Those people, I mean those Hebrews, need help, Moses. And besides, we could convert 'em, maybe. That really would be something—a big crowd like that coming through religion, all at one time."
>
> "I don't say it wouldn't. But I don't want to be the preacher. I'm through trying to regulate other folks' business. There ain't no future to it at all—just a whole lot of past. If you find a cow struck in the mire, and pull her out, she'll hook you sure. I just want to practice up on all this new stuff I done learned."[18]

Then, Moses, in his burning bush talk with the Lord, receives the message later discovered by Ellison's invisible man:

> "I AM WHAT I AM."[19]

Aaron and Miriam emerge as conniving double-dealers in a petty power struggle with Moses for the Hebrew following. Aaron in the Hurston American Southern black folk idiom tells Moses about Miriam's abilities as prophetess:

> "She can hit a straight like with a crooked stick, just the same as you can do."[20]

Later, his con-artistry is blatant as he tries to explain to Moses what happened among the Hebrews while Moses, atop the mountain, was receiving the Ten Commandments from the Lord:

> "Now, Moses, you know these people is always up for something that ain't no good. They don't mean nobody no good including theirselves. Know what they did? When you didn't come back right away they was going round behind your back running you down and scandalizing your

name and making out you was dead or done run off and they took and brought me all them ornaments, just because they knowed I used to work in gold, and they told me, we don't know what become of that man Moses. Make us some gods to march in front of us instead of that cloud. And they shoved all them earrings and things in my hands and naturally I didn't want to be bothered with the things, so just to get 'em out of my hands I took and threw 'em in the fire and what you reckon, boss? All I did was to fling them earrings into the fire, and out come that calf."

Moses retorts:

> "Aaron, you haven't said a thing yet and that is because you haven't thought a thing yet, nor felt anything except your own importance. Your whole body is nothing but a big bag to tote your littleness in."[21]

Pharoah's personality emerges in his confrontations with Moses. However, Moses expresses the real power of his character in his final tripartite confrontation with Pharoah. Here two charismatic leaders flaunt their egos—the men are matched. Of course, with God on his side Moses is ordained to triumph.

> "You see what power I got behind me, Pharoah. Will you let my people go?" Moses asked earnestly.
>
> "No! I got work from those Hebrews to do, and they are going to do it, too."
>
> "But the god of the mountain told me to tell you to let them go regardless."
>
> "Moses, do you think you can come back here and scare me with a jumped-up tale about a mountain god and a few tricks and make me change my plans?"
>
> "Pharoah, do you think you can holler loud enough to break into a god's arrangements? *Will you let those Hebrews go?*"
>
> "No! I won't."
>
> "I see you call yourself a hooking-bull at the landing. You don't aim to let nothing pass."[22]

The rich Egyptians of the court comment on Moses' tricks as the chorus:

> "So he is going to carry off our slaves by hoodoo, is he? . . . What would slaves want to be free for anyway? They are being fed and taken care of. What more could they want?"[23]

A clever allegory of slavery? This doesn't seem to be Hurston's intention, although the overtones are heavy. The universality of the Bible finds yet another application with a little help from the black American idiom. The idea of mean men, Killicks and Jody, versus complete men, John Buddy, in part, and Tea Cake, is reiterated. Individual stature is the one true value. Moses confounds Pharoah, his political rival, then Aaron, his internecine rival, and overcomes them in their falseness and pettiness because Moses is a MAN. In ***Moses, Man of the Mountain,*** contrary to ***Jonah's Gourd Vine*** and ***Their Eyes Were Watching God,*** the prize is a good relationship with God rather than with a woman. John Buddy fails to achieve this communion with Lucy and dies; Tea Cake achieves this Lawrencian ultimate with Janie, but dies also. Moses goes in this direction initially by marrying Zipporah. However, they become estranged as Moses is drawn towards the Lord's mission and Zipporah becomes a harping American housewife with upper-class aspirations. If Moses is a king, where are her golden robes and jewels? She and Miriam become sexual rivals—both want the adoration of the Hebrew people. Then Zipporah fades away as a viable character; she returns to her father. Moses then defeats Aaron and ends his mission as God's emissary.

Two things that Hurston does with ***Moses, Man of the Mountain*** are unique. First, she continues the character development of the Southern black preacher-womanizer with a gift for oratory and charm. Secondly, she reintroduces the theme of petty men versus real men. Thus, ***Moses*** is a natural outgrowth of ***Jonah's Gourd Vine*** just as ***Seraph on the Suwanee*** is a further development of what Hurston did in ***Their Eyes Were Watching God.*** Moses is a composite of John Buddy and Tea Cake with greater qualities than both. He is the preacher who meets his adversaries victoriously while John Buddy fails due to character weakness. Moses is the "aristocratic" (beyond monetary concerns) free liver like Tea Cake who knows where true values are to be found, but goes beyond his relationship with Zipporah to one with God while Tea Cake dies having only attained the human sexual plateau. Moses has more and greater stages to experience than John Buddy or Tea Cake, but, of course, his milieu is cosmic. The irony and humor come through in the disparity between the high Christian myth and the low dialect and character representation. Again what Hurston tries to do above all is exploit the petty meanness of the mass of people who make life difficult for the selfless, Christian few. She severely chastizes the negative human element and depicts how it interferes with or ruins the positive. Of the male characters presented thus far, only Moses overcomes these influences. John and Tea Cake are mortal, their worlds are more circumscribed. Yet, Moses is a man, but also a myth. Tea Cake can be Janie's myth (women remember only what they want to remember), but Moses is the world's, Christian and pagan.

The way in which Hurston tries to justify the theme of this novel leads us away from the suggested allegory of American slavery and away from the suggested parody in the manner of *Ol' Man Adam.* In her introduction, she emphasizes the figure of Moses as a god in many cultures of Africa, America, and the West Indies that have tales of the powers of Moses and worship him not because of the Ten Commandments, but because of his rod of power used against Pharoah. This puts a primitive, phallic stress on the story. Hurston concludes that millions of copies of *The Sixth and Seventh Books of Moses* are being read and consulted in secret. Thus, the novel is not one of social protest, but of myth and folklore. What she says in the introduction seems to underscore the seriousness of her intention, undercutting the possibilities of intentional parody.

Moses, Man of the Mountain can be related to Zora Hurston's other novels on the basis of its folk idiom, the presentation of a flashy, powerful, unconventional hero who does not esteem money and position, and the portrayal of a strong class-caste system with its concomitant racial oppression. However, the Chosen People (the oppressed) are depicted in an unfavorable light, just as the Negro masses are presented as a vindictive, jealous, backbiting lot in ***Jonah's Gourd Vine*** and ***Their Eyes Were Watching God.*** Moses, Jethro, and Pharoah, ironically, are the admirable characters, the ones with shrewd intelligence and natural dignity. Moses, in this unique interpretation, does contain the paganism of John Buddy and Tea Cake, together with the Christianity, becoming a true folk hero that supercedes religious boundaries. Again—the end is the beginning. Zora Neale Hurston has enacted the mystery of Moses with which she prefaces the novel. A strange treatment of human bondage and of the primitive god, ***Moses, Man of the Mountain*** finds applicable parallels in American slavery as portrayed via the Jewish persecution. But the *man* is all.

Zora Neale Hurston published ***Seraph on the Suwanee*** in 1949; it was her last novel, centered upon a white family and was set in Central Florida, beginning around 1905. Here, perhaps, she is following a new trend among black writers like Willard Motley, Chester Himes, and Ann Petry, who avoided concentrating on black characters. She returns to a female protagonist and initiates an analysis of race relations between the white Meserve family and the black servant family of Joe and Dessie Kelsey, subsumed later by the Portuguese family Corregio. Most importantly, Hurston develops the conflicts that Janie faced in ***Their Eyes Were Watching God*** and gives them greater psychological dimensions in her portrayal of Arvay, making ***Seraph on the Suwanee*** a Freudian study of female sexuality. As John Hughes in *The Negro Novelist* says,

> ***Seraph on the Suwanee*** places Hurston at once among the many American writers who have paid homage to Sigmund Freud.
>
> Arvay introduces the reader to a neurotic woman known to clinical psychologists as the hysterical female. This type has certain repressions which originate in the libido. Here the emphasis is upon sex.[24]

The plot is more complicated than those of the other novels mainly because Hurston does penetrate the levels of her protagonist's complicated subconscious mind. The novel begins as a stranger, Jim Meserve, comes to Sawley, Florida, and begins courting the twenty-one year old Arvay Henson, who has "turned her back on the world" for five years because her secret beau, Carl Middleton, married her older sister, Larraine. No one understands the reason for Arvay's unnatural withdrawal and tendency towards hysteria (she has secret pregnancy spasms with Larraine); thus she is thought odd and too incorrigible to court. But the Black Irish Jim "Meserve" is not to be deterred and succeeds in courting and "raping" Arvay one afternoon before actually marrying her. Against her principles she enjoys the experience and has him repeat the performance. From the onset the relationship is defined in the psycho-sexual terms that are to cause ensuing marital conflicts. A year after the marriage she gives birth to Earl, who is retarded. With the faithful black retainers Joe and Dessie, they move to five acres in Citrabelle and Jim, becoming a financial success, invests in groves. Meanwhile Arvay has a daughter, Angeline, and another son, Kenny. Her growing preoccupation with Earl prevents her from relating to the two normal children and to her husband. She begins to identify with Earl as a defense for her obsessive guilt over his deformity and attacks Joe and her husband as a substitute for and extension of her own self-punishment.

Jim lets Joe go to appease Arvay and replaces him with the Corregios, who satisfy Arvay no better. The plot's climax occurs when Earl, as a sinister sixteen-year old, sexually attacks one of the Corregio daughters and escapes to the swamp with his father's gun where he is hunted and trapped by a sheriff's citizen group and finally shot by his wounded father. Again—murder in self-defense as in ***Their Eyes Were Watching God,*** with even more Freudian overtones. The sexual rivalry between Earl and Jim for Arvay has been submerged until this drama of Earl's taking his father's shot gun to kill his father. Deprived of her identity through Earl, Arvay retreats and ignores the others in her family. Decisions are made without her. Angeline and Kenny grow up; Angeline elopes at seventeen with her father's consent and Kenny goes off to college, then leaves to become a jazz musician. Driven to his limits by Arvay's hysterical fits, Jim finally walks out on her. In the midst of a mental breakdown due to these pressures and her sense of uselessness, Arvay is called to her mother's deathbed. This trip home is the turning point in the novel. Once poor, the typical Southern cracker, now rich, a woman of prominence due to Jim's efforts, she sees herself in a new light.

The heroine, Arvay Henson Meserve, has a long way to go in her development as a woman and as a generous, accepting person, perhaps because she is white, hysterical, and sexually frustrated, unlike the easy-going, matter of fact Janie. Specifically, Arvay's shortcomings are evinced in her needless social cruelty towards both black and Portuguese families who live in the servants' house on the grounds. Her rages, however, are not directed specifically at these victimized underlings, but are paranoid bursts of frustration over her imagined lack of influence and power over her husband and children and bursts of self-castigation because her first child, Ben, is retarded and criminally dangerous. Feeling she is a failure, she blames others for her misfortunes, plays the martyr, and refuses to adjust to circumstances. Finally her successful, rakish, though loyal husband leaves her. She returns to Sawley for her mother's death and funeral, and confronts her sister's husband Carl. Seeing him for the first time as a worthless, pitiable failure, instead of her lost hero, she comes back to Citrabelle with a new personality, evidenced by her sudden generosity towards Jeff and Janie, Joe's son and daughter-in-law, involving gifts and patronizing playfulness. Here Hurston's social and racial views enter.

In the Sawley episode Hurston severely criticizes the poor whites, favoring rich whites and black pets, as evidenced in her treatment of Jim and Joe. Discussing faithful and faithless retainers, Nancy Tischler says that Hurston

> views the Southern pattern of pet Negroes as parallel to the animal-master or at best the child-father one, not a man-to-man friendship between equals (in ***Seraph on the Suwanee***). With modern emphasis on motivation and Freudian psychology, there are many new efforts to understand the truth behind the grinning Negro mask of servility and love.[25]

This interpretation of the relationship between Jim Meserve and Joe Kelsey, though, is one-sided. They do have an adult friendship—Joe is responsible for financial affairs and protecting the grove; he is a business partner—although Jim's roughhousing and favoritism with Joe give it the trappings of the child-father syndrome. Joe does have power of his own as the faithful retainer; it is not merely on the surface. Yet Hurston stresses the importance of appearance, avoiding racial conflict. Joe perhaps appears to be something other than what he is—Chesnutt's Uncle Julius grins beneath the novel's surface.

A new Arvay, out of character, goes to New Smyrna to meet Jim. Before she had viewed herself as the unwanted, ugly cracker in the midst of beautiful people (her husband, Angeline, and Kenny). (She now realizes the power of her position, loosens up and becomes generous, and acts the benevolent goddess accordingly.) Arvay is literal and naive, lacks a sense of humor, takes life too seriously, and, consequently, has to suffer and learn her lesson. Her outlook crosses from pessimism to optimism as she fears, faces challenge, and conquers. The novel ends as Jim and Arvay reunite in each other's arms in a berth aboard the shrimper "Arvay Henson." Arvay becomes the seraph on the Suwanee (the white seraph Mrs. Turner worships in ***Their Eyes Were Watching God***). She undergoes the classic rebirth as Hurston relates:

> All that had happened to her, good or bad, was a part of her own self and had come out of her. Within her own flesh were many mysteries. She lifted her left hand before her eyes and studied it in every detail with wonder. With wonder and deep awe like Moses before his burning bush. What all, Arvay asked of herself, was buried and hidden in human flesh? You toted it around with you all your life time, but you couldn't know. If you just could know, it would be all the religion that anybody needed. And what was in you was bound to come out some way or another.
>
> Then it was like the Resurrection.
>
> What she had considered her cross, she now saw as her glory.[26]

It is unfortunately easy to put ***Seraph on the Suwanee,*** as ***Moses, Man of the Mountain,*** in a ludicrous light, but the novel does have merit. Hurston succeeds in ***Jonah's Gourd Vine*** and especially in ***Their Eyes Were Watching God,*** but afterwards does not achieve the same level of artistry. Interesting character types and thematic patterns do give her fiction a unique sense of continuity. The lesser novels provide a basis for interpreting the greater ones. Thus, an examination of Hurston's complete works enables one to form a valid critical evaluation of her range.

In summary, Hurston uses the same formula in all of her novels: One protagonist who finds his or her way to understanding. "Good" women and men have the same characteristics—endurance, generosity, natural morality. John Buddy, Lucy, Janie, Tea Cake, and Jim (later Arvay) are easygoing, fun-loving folks who value sensation over reason, invention and chance over stability, and genuine Christianity over official social mores. Their sense of morality goes deep and aims not to hurt another; they are all sexual creatures. Love is based essentially on a physical passion of one being that cannot live without the other. Thus, sexual union has a primary mystique. Whether or not characters understand each other philosophically, they do understand one another in bed. The ultimate union, though, is of body and mind. Tea Cake and Janie and Jim and Arvay achieve this.

In place of tension, hatred, and violence between the races is a camaraderie between black and white characters, particularly in ***Seraph on the Suwanee.*** The two early novels treat the black milieu almost exclusively. (However, the white milieu is not too different in tone; Babbittry is decried in both. Yet there are strong religious and folk elements in the black cultures and an emphasis on economic progress and social climbing in the dominant white culture.) As shown in the novels, these cultural traits are interchangeable—Janie rejects her first two homes because of the bourgeois compulsion and the Meserves are rooted in the poor white folk culture. (Despite its redneck attributes, it still has some piquancy to it.) In both cultures, the highest value from Hurston's point of view is having a good time. It is important for characters also to grow and strive, try new things (Janie, Jim Meserve), but there is a counter-emphasis on *carpe diem* (Tea Cake and the fishermen who work for Meserve). Savers, like Jim and Janie, can also have the admired generous qualities—it is alright to get your pie if you give away some of the pieces, still leaving a lot for yourself. And the *carpe diem* philosophers lose in the end. Thus, Hurston's attitudes are based on the simple-shrewd, folksy, well-to-do few who have triumphed economically because of drive and risk-taking, yet have retained a sense of the old natural ways of doing things. Because they have experienced largesse, they are free to reject it.

Women come to change via the influence of a "real" (sensual) man. Male dominance (the right male, of course) over the female is viewed as the ultimate relationship. Women are essentially good sexual creatures who need to loosen up, suffer conflicts, and finally come around to subsuming themselves to the master. The emphasis on rape in ***Seraph on the Suwanee*** is interesting psychologically as the term is used both for the crime and for consentual copulation. Hurston perhaps uses it to add a sado-masochistic or criminal taboo leer to the book—popularized prurience. Perhaps this is imbued in the minds of the characters; the taboo excites them—forbidden fruit made more so. Women seem to want sexual brutality and men enjoy the stud role. Women live only through their men, have emotional reservations, and are obsessed with their relationships, male motivations, and the possibility of their being used by men. Thus, there is a great sense of insecurity among the women, which the men have to a lesser degree. Hurston's dominant motif involves the downgrading of women as subservient to men. Sexuality is a weapon, but a welcome, desired weapon. Hurston's more universal concerns involve sex as a fulfillment of personality and the course of nature. She aims to portray cosmic relationships and does succeed in enlarging the sexual scope of her characters.

Notes

1. *Jonah's Gourd Vine* (Philadelphia: J. B. Lippincott Company, 1971), pp. 179-180.
2. (University Park: The Pennsylvania State University Press, 1969), p. 158.
3. (New York: Russell & Russell, Inc., 1948), p. 235.
4. *Ibid.,* p. 236.
5. *Ibid.,* p. 96.
6. (Philadelphia: J. B. Lippincott Company, 1937, 1969), p. 25.
7. *Ibid.,* p. 26.
8. *Ibid.,* pp. 76-77.
9. Tischler, p. 143.
10. *Ibid.,* pp. 116-117.
11. *Ibid.,* p. 120.
12. *Their Eyes Were Watching God,* p. 5.
13. *Ibid.,* pp. 9-10.

14. Darwin T. Turner, "The Negro Novelist and the South," *Southern Humanities Review* I (1967), p. 22.
15. (New York: Harper & Row, Publishers, 1928), p. 94.
16. *Ibid.,* p. 104.
17. (Philadelphia: J. B. Lippincott Company, 1939), pp. 94-95.
18. *Ibid.,* p. 157.
19. *Ibid.,* p. 162.
20. *Ibid.,* p. 171.
21. *Ibid.,* p. 291.
22. *Ibid.,* p. 182.
23. *Ibid.,* p. 183.
24. (Freeport, N.Y.: Books for Libraries Press, Inc., 1953), pp. 172-173.
25. Tischler, p. 48.
26. (New York: Charles Scribner's Sons, 1948), pp. 309-310.

FROM THE AUTHOR

THE SUM OF LIFE

While I am still below the allotted span of time, and notwithstanding, I feel that I have lived. I have had the joy and pain of strong friendships. I have served and been served. I have made enemies of which I am not ashamed. I have been faithless, and then I have been faithful and steadfast until the blood ran down into my shoes. I have loved unselfishly with all the ardor of a strong heart, and I have hated with all the power of my soul. What waits for me in the future? I do not know. I can't even imagine, and I am glad for that. But already, I have touched the four corners of the horizon, for from hard searching it seems to me that tears and laughter, love and hate make up the sum of life.

SOURCE: Zora Neal Hurston, excerpt from her autobiography, *Dust Tracks on a Road,* Lippincott, 1942.

JAMES RAMBEAU (ESSAY DATE 1976)

SOURCE: Rambeau, James. "The Fiction of Zora Neale Hurston." *Markham Review* 5 (summer 1976): 61-64.

In the following essay, Rambeau discusses Hurston's personal background and her attempt to write fiction that did not explore the "race problem."

> I was born in a Negro town. I do not mean by that the black back-side of an average town. Eatonville, Florida, is, and was at the time of my birth, a pure Negro town—charter mayor, council, town marshal and all. It was not the first Negro community in America, but it was the first to be incorporated, the first attempt at organized self-government on the part of Negroes in America.
>
> Eatonville is what you might call hitting a straight lick with a crooked stick. The town was not in the original plan. It is a by-product of something else.[1]

This passage occurs early in the first chapter of Zora Neale Hurston's autobiography, ***Dust Tracks on a Road*** (1942), and it is worth contemplating for several reasons. The fact that Miss Hurston was brought up in a "pure Negro town," the daughter of a prominent town figure, in the American South—Eatonville is in the north-central section of Florida, and related more in history to the traditional South than to the Twentieth Century east coast of Florida—this fact perhaps explains more about her development and limitations as a writer than any other.

Moreover, the passage suggests Miss Hurston's awareness of the uniqueness of her experience, the ways in which it sets her apart from the rest of the rural Deep South as well as from the growing experience of blacks in the Northern cities—Chicago or New York City's Harlem. That awareness of the differences is apparent everywhere in her work. It is clear that she sees herself, in her fiction and in the occasional articles she wrote specifically on racial matters and the experience of the American black, as someone particularly qualified to see the truth. Further, in the self-conscious use of a "down-home" idiom—"hitting a straight lick with a crooked stick"—which she quickly explains in her next two sentences, we can recognize whom she conceives her audience to be. It is an audience not familiar with the circumstances of the South, nor with the idiom she draws from it. Her audience is white. And she is attempting to charm that audience, both with her authenticity and with her good cheer. It should not surprise us that ***Dust Tracks on a Road*** "won the Anisfield Wolf Award for its contribution to improving race relations."[2]

Zora Neale Hurston's life, as she tells it in her autobiography, and as we hear it in the few other testimonies available,[3] has several mysteries and not a few contradictions. The facts which are certain are these. She was born in and raised in Eatonville, traveling among various relatives after her mother's death in 1912, going to high school in Jacksonville and, later, in Baltimore. She then attended Howard University in Washington for a year and a half in 1923-24, and was able to transfer to Barnard College, the women's college of Columbia University, from which she graduated in 1928 at the age of twenty-five. She was drawn to New York by the writing opportunities she felt were there because of the presence of Charles Spurgeon Johnson, founder of the black-run *Opportunity Magazine*. The move was possible because of the offer of scholarship assistance to Barnard by Mrs. Annie Nathan Meyer, a trustee of the College. Mrs. Meyer was not the first white person who responded strongly to Miss Hurston's intelligence and charm, nor was she the last. The next was the popular novelist Fannie Hurst, for whom Miss Hurston was briefly a secretary and, for a much longer period, a house guest and occasional chauffeur.[4] This connection explains the introduction to ***Jonah's Gourd Vine.***

Miss Hurston went on to Columbia as a graduate student in anthropology, and became a favorite student of the anthropologist Frank Boas. She received a grant to study black folklore in the South, which was followed in the next few years by several fellowships. She went to Haiti to collect folklore in 1936-37. In 1942, she was in Hollywood apparently working on a film. Between 1934 and 1942, she published six of her seven books. The seventh came out six years later in 1948, and between that novel and her death in 1960 there is not much known. In 1950 she "reappeared in Florida working as a maid in Riva Alto. Ten years later, she died penniless in a hospital in Fort Pierce. Her funeral expenses were paid by collection and contribution."[5]

The mysteries and contradictions are many, and some of them at least can be traced to Miss Hurston's autobiography, and to private statements which were recorded. She was apparently married briefly in 1939—although the date is not certain—and her husband is unknown. There were some mysterious rumors near the time of her death, which apparently involved a court case, but again the details are unclear and unverified. In short, we know very little about Miss Hurston's life after about 1938, and this impression is verified by those who knew her and spoke of her. It is hard to pin her down, or to know, fully, why her remarkable productivity in the 1930's fell off so quickly and, finally, all but stopped.

Miss Hurston's time of great productivity falls between the burst of activity known as the Harlem Renaissance in the 1920's, and the rise of Richard Wright in *Native Son* (1940). If it is true that Miss Hurston's first novel "expresses a sensibility molded predominantly by the Negro Renaissance,"[6] it is still a sensibility based on the fact of Eatonville, Florida.

Jonah's Gourd Vine (1934) is Zora Neale Hurston's first novel, and it was published before, but written after, her first folklore collection, ***Mules and Men*** (1935). The two collections of folklore—the second is ***Tell My Horse*** (1938)—are surprising, given our knowledge of Miss Hurston's anthropological training, because they are so personal and anecdotal. They suggest, in fact, that her essential interest is in the telling of the tales. ***Mules and Men*** collects black folktales and Voodoo and Hoodoo rituals from communities in Florida and Louisiana; but they are told in a narrative which encloses Hurston herself as a character, responding to the stories and parties at which they are told. ***Tell My Horse,*** about the Caribbean, mostly Haiti, collects folktales and Voodoo rituals too, including an account of a Zombie, and, although there is a historical narrative about Haiti and various interpolations about the Haitian culture, we are still often aware of Hurston as a participant or onlooker who is engaged at the site of her gathering of materials. The chapter "Hunting the Wild Hog" is an interesting account of a custom in which we are made aware of Hurston's presence. While in both collections there is some of the apparatus of the professional anthropologist—appendices, glossaries, and the like—our overriding sense is of an amateur collector of folklore who includes those discoveries in the narrative of her experiences. To suggest this limitation is not to disparage the books; the opinion of folklorists about her work seems to be high.[7]

The novels which succeed ***Jonah's Gourd Vine*** can be discussed briefly before we turn to a detailed discussion of that novel. ***Their Eyes Were Watching God*** (1937) was written, Miss Hurston tells us, "under internal pressure in seven weeks"[8] in Haiti. Robert Bone makes a large claim for the novel: "it is Miss Hurston's best novel, and possibly the best novel of the period, excepting *Native Son.*"[9] The novel is framed by the central figure, Janie, now middle-aged, telling the story of her past to her friends of the present after a two-year absence. Her story is essentially that of her relation to men—her progression *toward* a full participation in life through her relations with three men, from an older farmer to the livelier Jody Starks to Tea-Cake, "an incarnation of the folk culture."[10] Although Janie is forced to kill Tea-

Cake, the conclusion of the novel suggests that she has learned a great wisdom in her lifetime with men, and that she accepts her losses as part of that wisdom.

Moses, Man of the Mountain (1939) is probably the sort of a novel which only a folklorist would think of—or dare to attempt. The Biblical story of Moses, in fact the sweep of the Pentateuch, is retold, with Moses accompanying his deeds with speeches in an early Twentieth Century Florida black idiom, without the dialect. The metaphorical connection, of course, is of the persecuted Jews in bondage and the black experience in America. Moses is identified with the voodoo artists of Haiti—whom Miss Hurston had recently studied—and with the heroic "trickster" of black American folklore. But certain problems arise as a result of the merging of black idiom and the Mosaic legend, as in the following exchange between Moses and Egypt's Pharoah:

> "Pharaoh, do you think you can holler loud enough to break into god's arrangements? *Will you let those Hebrews go?*"
>
> "No! I won't."
>
> "I see you call yourself a hooking-bull at the landing. You don't aim to let nothing pass."
>
> "That's right, Moses. And certainly I won't let those Hebrews go."
>
> "You're right sure about that, I take it?"
>
> "Just as sure as you snore."[11]

It is the longest of Miss Hurston's novels, and the most difficult to read because of the strain imposed upon the reader by the grafting of a modern idiom on the Mosaic legend.

Seraph on the Suwanee (1948), her last novel, is the story of the marriage of two whites, Arvay Henson and Jim Meserve, and their progress from the pine and turpentine-producing woods of upper West Florida to East Florida and to hard-won respectability. The novel is flat, partly because the Meserves are white, rising to the middle class, and the point of view is Arvay's. It seems likely, in fact, that the dialect they speak is accurately and discriminatingly white, and suggests Miss Hurston's skill at that matter. But the novel focuses sharply on the marriage and upon Arvay's various anxieties, and its sentimental domesticity seems weak and uninteresting. We might find here an explanation of Miss Hurston's failure to produce more novels; she had imagined herself out of Eatonville, out, finally, of her blackness, and what was left? But there were no more novels; at the end of her life, she was apparently working on a novel concerning Herod the Great.[12]

Jonah's Gourd Vine is in large part the story of Miss Hurston's parents, as we learn when we read her autobiography. Her father's history closely parallels that of the protagonist of ***Jonah's Gourd Vine,*** John Buddy Pearson; the account of her mother's death in the autobiography could have been taken from the novel. The plot of the novel is that of a man's full growth and failure, but it is probably fair to say that our interest is not focused on the plot, anyway. It is focused on the breathtaking recreation of a particular and specified dialect, and, through that, the particular and intensely realized life of a Southern black man, removed from the world of overt racism halfway through the novel, struggling against the weaknesses of his nature—and losing.

We define John Pearson through his marriages—to Lucy and Hattie and Sally—much as we define Janie through her husbands in ***Their Eyes Were Watching God.*** We define him further through his enterprise as a worker, from plowhand to carpenter, and through his growing skill as a preacher in the course of the latter part of the novel, which is demonstrated for us in the marvellous sermon in Chapter XXIV.[13]

But the vitality of the book comes entirely from its folkloristic reporting of a language, a dialect, of the black rural South. The plot construction, the sense of time in the novel, the acting out of imagined scenes—all these qualities are deficient, which is not surprising in a first novel. The novel still lives, through the language of the characters; for example, at the end of Chapter VI, after John fights and defeats Coon in the tie-camp (a lumber camp in the wilderness where railroad ties are cut), Coon broods:

> "Know whut," he lisped to the others, "dat boy slipped up on me, but Ahm gwine git even wid him. 'Tain't too late. Seben years ain't too long fuh uh coudar tuh wear uh ruffled bosom shirt. Ahm gwine gently chain-gang fuh dat same nigger."
>
> "Aw," Dump disparaged, "you got uh belly full uh John. You ain't wantin' no mo' uh him."
>
> "Yeah Ah wants tuh fight 'im, but not wid no fist. Ah flies hot quick but Ahm very easy cooled when de man Ahm mad wid is biggern me."

We may in fact have to look to the glossary for a definition of "coudar" and the expression "to wear a ruffled bosom shirt," but in the cadences of the dialect, in the complex form of boasting that the passage suggests is present in male conversation throughout the book, we get the full force of what is meant, and *how* it is meant. Further, we overhear verbal formulas, obviously familiar to the user and to the listener, throughout the book:

> "Ah takes mah tex' and Ah takes mah time."
>
> "She so little Ah hafta shake de sheets tuh find her in bed."
>
> "We got 'em so black 'til lightnin' bugs would follow 'em at twelve o'clock in de day—thinkin' iss midnight and us got 'em in between."
>
> "All mah switches done growed tuh trees!"
>
> "Ah means tuh prop you up on ev'y leanin' side."

What we discover in such formulas, and also in the reported burial customs, the hoodoo rituals which Hattie appeals to, and the complex of language and manners which surround the churches in the novel, is a literal recreation of a language which is already getting lost in the life of the South. We have an almost anthropological fixing of a time and place, and the life it expresses through the manifestations of a culture—its habits and customs and uses of language.

We should remember how rare this quality is, the precision of this reporting. We may find better novelists in whom it does not exist at all, and our most striking example would be Faulkner. Compare, for example, the sermon here in Chapter XXIV and the sermon in *The Sound and the Fury*. Faulkner's use of the sermon is certainly more explicitly "literary," and while it maintains the rhythms and the images of a conventional black Southern sermon, we are still aware of the composed, the literally written, quality in Faulkner's recreation. It is simply not as direct; Faulkner uses some of the sermon elements, while Miss Hurston seems to have put down, *verbatim,* one of her father's most familiar sermons.[14]

It is finally the immediacy of these details of the novel which makes ***Jonah's Gourd Vine*** worth reading; it is hard to find sources which convey more directly the particular quality of black life in the rural South in the first half of the Twentieth Century. In Chapter XIX, in fact, Miss Hurston tries to sum up black Southern experience through and beyond the First World War in about four pages of unattributed speech, which absorbs a kind of fractured French after the Armistice:

> "Ah could uh married one uh dem French women but shucks, gimme uh brown skin eve'y time. Blacker de berry sweeter de juice. Come tuh mah pick, gimme uh good black gal. De wine wuz sour, and Ah says parley vous, hell! You gimme mah right change! Comme telly vous. Nar, Ah ain't goin' back tuh no farm no mo'. Ah don't mean tuh say, 'Git up' tuh nary 'nother mule lessen he's setting down in mah lap. God made de world bu he never made no hog outa me tuh go 'round rootin' it up. Done done too much bookoo plowing already! Woman quick gimmer mah sumpin t'eat. Toot sweet."

This passage—and its significance for the South—is simply dropped into the middle of the plot of the novel, at the time of the crisis of John's marriage to Hattie and his losing battle to maintain his place in the community. Such a curiosity should suggest Miss Hurston's real interest, as she comments on the history:

> Whereas in Egypt the coming of the locust made desolation, in the farming South the departure of the Negro laid waste the agricultural industry—crops rotted, houses careened crazily in their utter desertion, and grass grew up in the streets. On to the North! The land of promise.

But that is another story, the story of the migrating black, and it is told by other novelists—Richard Wright and William Attaway, among others, and, in a non-fiction work, the implications of the migration are touchingly told in Claude Brown's *Manchild in the Promised Land* (1965). What Zora Neale Hurston has told us, in great detail, is a part of the life those migrants left behind. That is the great value of ***Jonah's Gourd Vine,*** and the strength of her first two novels.

Implied in the preceding discussion of Zora Neale Hurston's work is a standard of judgement, by which we can say that, for instance, ***Moses, Man of the Mountain*** is a failure as a novel, or that ***Jonah's Gourd Vine*** has serious structural deficiencies. It is a contemporary black argument that the conventional standards of judgement are themselves deficient, or even pointless and irrelevant, when considering work by black writers. Such standards are those of the "White Aesthetic," and we need, in order to understand adequately black creativity, a "Black Aesthetic."[15]

But the point of a "Black Aesthetic," after all the definitions by negatives and the talk of "style"—innate, soulful, "style"—is finally this: the black writer has to be granted his subject, and his mode of discussing his subject, *which will be of necessity*—in divided America—*black and in that sense peculiar and unique.* Hoyt W. Fuller, a leading proponent of the Black Aesthetic, quotes Louis Simpson reviewing a book of Gwendolyn Brooks's poetry: "On the other hand, if being a Negro is the only subject, the writing is not important."[16] One guesses Simpson's meaning—that any writing has to be full of resonances which extend beyond the particular in order to be good—but it sounds prohibitive in a tense time. And one has to grant the artist his subject, as Henry James argued long ago.

Zora Neale Hurston sounds like the "White Aesthetician" in her direct remarks on the subject. And when she discusses the writing of ***Jonah's Gourd Vine*** in her autobiography, she says:

> What I wanted to tell was a story about a man, and from what I had read and heard, Negroes were supposed to write about the Race Problem. I was and am thoroughly sick of the subject. My interest lies in what makes a man or a woman so such-and-so, regardless of his color. It seemed to me that the human beings I met reacted pretty much the same to the same stimuli. Different idioms, yes. Circumstances and conditions have power to influence, yes. Inherent difference, no.[17]

In one sense, Miss Hurston reconciled herself to this dilemma, in ***Jonah's Gourd Vine,*** by using the Eatonville strategy: remove John Pearson from the world of the Race Problem. But she nonetheless created a figure, fixed in time and place, who is—who can only be—black. Later, in her use of the Mosaic legend, and in her employment of white characters in ***Seraph on the Suwannee*** (a strategy other black writers of the 1940's used, Willard Motley and Frank Yerby in particular), we can understand that at least part of her intention is to evade this issue, or to solve it by accepting what we call here the "White Aesthetic."

This acceptance of an aesthetic which denies Miss Hurston a large part of her own experience may go a long way to explain her decline as a novelist and her later silence. But what if she had been able to say this?

> So I am ashamed for the black poet who says, "I want to be a poet, not a Negro poet," as though his own racial world were not as interesting as any other world. I am ashamed, too, for the colored artist who runs from the painting of Negro faces to the painting of sunsets after the manner of the academicians because he fears the strange un-whiteness of his own features. An artist must be free to choose what he does, certainly, but he must also never be afraid to do what he might choose. . . . We younger Negro artists who create now intend to express our individual dark-skinned selves without fear or shame. If white people are pleased we are glad. If they are not, it doesn't matter. We know we are beautiful. And ugly too. The tom-tom cries and the tom-tom laughs. If colored people are pleased we are glad. If they are not, their displeasure doesn't matter either. We build our temples for tomorrow, strong as we know how, and we stand on top of the mountain, free within ourselves.[18]

For the most part this passage sounds like it was written in the militant 1960's. It was not. Langston Hughes published it in *The Nation,* June 23, 1926.

We may well wonder what Zora Neale Hurston's writing career would have been like had she read, or responded to, those words. We can only be certain that it would have been different, and that her long silence and mysterious later career and life might have been easier for her. But we have, from her first outburst, ***Jonah's Gourd Vine*** and ***Their Eyes Were Watching God.*** In the story of John Pearson's rise and fall, we have the story of a black man in his time and place, his particular honor and dishonor.

Notes

1. Zora Neale Hurston, *Dust Tracks on a Road* (Philadelphia: J. B. Lippincott, 1942), p. 11.
2. Darwin T. Turner, *In a Minor Chord: Three Afro-American Writers and Their Search for Identity* (Carbondale and Edwardsville: Southern Illinois University Press, 1971), p. 134, n. 7. This study is at present the best and lengthiest examination of Miss Hurston's work.
3. See, besides Turner, Langston Hughes, *The Big Sea* (New York: Knopf, 1940); Fannie Hurst, "Zora Hurston: A Personality Sketch," *Yale University Library Gazette,* 35 (1961), 17-22; and Theodore Pratt, "A Memoir: Zora Neal Hurston, Florida's First Distinguished Author," *Negro Digest,* February 1962, 52-56.
4. Hurst, 17-22.
5. Turner, p. 90.
6. Robert Bone, *The Negro Novel in America* (New Haven: Yale University Press, revised edition, 1965), p. 127.
7. James W. Byrd, "Zora Neale Hurston: A Novel Folklorist," *Tennessee Folklore Society Bulletin,* 21 (1955), 37-41; Blyden Jackson, "Some Negroes in the Land of Goshen," *Tennessee Folklore Society Bulletin,* 19 (1953), 103-107; and Frank Boas, "Preface," *Mules and Men* (repr. New York: Harper & Row Perennial Library, 1970), p. 16. See also Darwin T. Turner's introduction to this edition, pp. 6-15.
8. Hurston, *Dust Tracks,* p. 220.
9. Bone, p. 128.
10. Bone, p. 130.
11. Zora Neale Hurston, *Moses, Man of the Mountain* (Philadelphia: J. B. Lippincott, 1939), p. 182.
12. Turner, p. 137, n. 40.
13. The full implications of the sermon form are studied in Bruce A. Rosenberg, *The Art of the American Folk Preacher* (New York: Oxford University Press, 1970).
14. See the way in which distinction between folk and literary forms is defined in Bruce A. Rosenberg, "The Oral Quality of Rev. Shegog's Sermon in William Faulkner's *The Sound and the Fury," Literatur in Wissenschaft und Unterricht,* 2 (1969), 73-88.

15. The formulations of this Black Aesthetic can be found in Addison Gayle, Jr., ed., *The Black Aesthetic* (Garden City: Doubleday Anchor, 1972), particularly in the articles by Hoyt W. Fuller, Larry Neal, Alain Locke, Julian Mayfield, Ron Karenga, Addison Gayle, Jr., John O'Neal, and Darwin T. Turner, pp. 3-74; and in Addison Gayle, Jr., ed. *Black Expression* (New York: Weybright and Talley, 1969), particularly in the articles by Hugh M. Gloster, Langston Hughes, Hoyt W. Fuller, Julian Mayfield, Nick Aaron Ford, Addison Gayle Jr., and William Gardner Smith, pp. 255-295. For a divergent and suggestive discussion see also LeRoi Jones, "The Myth of a 'Negro Literature,'" in *Black Expression,* pp. 190-197.
16. Hoyt W. Fuller, "Towards a Black Aesthetic," *The Black Aesthetic,* p. 4.
17. Hurston, *Dust Tracks,* p. 214.
18. Reprinted in *Amistad 1,* ed. John A. Williams and Charles F. Harris (New York: Random House-Vintage Books, 1970), pp. 304-305.

ALICE WALKER (ESSAY DATE 1979)

SOURCE: Walker, Alice. "Dedication." In *I Love Myself When I am Laughing . . . And Then Again When I am Looking Mean and Impressive: A Zora Neale Hurston Reader,* edited by Alice Walker, pp. 1-5. Old Westbury, N.Y.: The Feminist Press, 1979.

In the following essay, Walker offers a sketch of Hurston's character, creativity, and trials as an artist.

A friend of mine called one day to tell me that she and another woman had been discussing Zora Neale Hurston and had decided they wouldn't have liked her. They wouldn't have liked the way—when her play ***Color Struck!*** won second prize in a literary contest at the beginning of her career—Hurston walked into a room full of her competitors, flung her scarf dramatically over her shoulder, and yelled "COLOR . . . R. R. STRUCK . . . K. K!" at the top of her voice.

Apparently it isn't easy to like a person who is not humbled by second place.

Zora Neale Hurston was outrageous—it appears by nature. She was quite capable of saying, writing, or doing things *different* from what one might have wished. Because she recognized the contradictions and complexity of her own personality, Robert Hemenway, her biographer, writes that Hurston came to "delight" in the chaos she sometimes left behind.

Yet for all her contrariness, her "chaos," her ability to stir up dislike that is as strong today as it was fifty years ago, many of us love Zora Neale Hurston.

We do not love her for her lack of modesty (that tends to amuse us: an assertive black person during Hurston's time was considered an anomaly); we do not love her for her unpredictable and occasionally weird politics (they tend to confuse us); we do not, certainly, applaud many of the *mad* things she is alleged to have said and sometimes actually did say; we do not even claim never to dislike her. In reading through the thirty-odd-year span of her writing, most of us, I imagine, find her alternately winning and appalling, but rarely dull, which is worth a lot. We love Zora Neale Hurston for her work, first, and then again (as she and all Eatonville would say), we love her for herself. For the humor and courage with which she encountered a life she infrequently designed, for her absolute disinterest in becoming either white or bourgeois, and for her *devoted* appreciation of her own culture, which is an inspiration to us all.

Reading ***Their Eyes Were Watching God*** for perhaps the eleventh time, I am still amazed that Hurston wrote it in seven weeks; that it speaks to me as no novel, past or present, has ever done; and that the language of the characters, that "comical nigger 'dialect'" that has been laughed at, denied, ignored, or "improved" so that white folks and educated black folks can understand it, is simply beautiful. There is enough self-love in that one book—love of community, culture, traditions—to restore a world. Or create a new one.

I do not presume to judge or defend Zora Neale Hurston. I have nothing of finality to say of Hurston the person. I believe any artist's true character is seen in the work she or he does, or it is not seen. In Hurston's work, what she was is revealed. The purpose of this anthology is to present enough of that work so that the reader can make up her or his own mind.

Is ***Mules and Men*** racist? Or does it reflect the flawed but nonetheless beautifully creative insights of an oppressed people's collective mythology? Is **"The Gilded Six-Bits"** so sexist it makes us cringe to think Zora Neale Hurston wrote it? Or does it make a true statement about deep love functioning in the only pattern that at the time of its action seemed correct? Did Zora Neale Hurston never question "America" or the status-quo, as some have accused, or was she questioning it profoundly when she wrote phrases like "the arse-and-all of Democracy"? Is Janie Crawford, the main character in ***Their Eyes Were Watching God*** light-skinned and silken-haired because *Hurston* was a colorist, as a black male critic has claimed, or because Hurston was not blind and therefore saw that black men (and black women) have been, and are, colorist to an embarrassing degree?

Is Hurston the messenger who brings the bad news, or is she the bad news herself? Is Hurston a reflection of ourselves? And if so, is that not, perhaps, part of our "problem" with her?

I think we are better off if we think of Zora Neale Hurston as an artist, period—rather than as the artist/politician most black writers have been required to be. This frees us to appreciate the complexity and richness of her work in the same way we can appreciate Billie Holiday's glorious phrasing or Bessie Smith's perfect and raunchy lyrics, without the necessity of ridiculing the former's addiction to heroin or the latter's excessive love of gin.

Implicit in Hurston's determination to "make it" in a career was her need to express "the folk" and herself. Someone who knew her has said: "Zora would have been Zora even if she'd been an Eskimo." That is what it means to be yourself; it is surely what it means to be an artist.

It is instructive to consider the lives of Zora Hurston and Bessie Smith (whom no one, it seems, thought to ask what *she* thought of things like integration!) particularly in relation to the white "patrons of the Negro" they both knew. There is a wonderful story told of how Bessie Smith once attended a Carl Van Vechten party which that reigning patron of Negro Art threw in her honor. As she entered, never having seen Carl or Fania Van Vechten before (and dragging her full length, white ermine on the floor behind her, an ermine purchased with money from her best-selling records), Fania Van Vechten flung herself into Bessie's arms. Bessie knocked her flat, exclaiming over a glass of straight gin: "I never *heard* of such shit!"

Bessie Smith knew shit when she saw it, and from Zora Hurston's work, we can assume she did too. Yet she never knocked anyone flat for having the audacity to patronize her, nor does she ever complain in print about the hypocrisy she must have borne. The difference between Hurston and Smith? One's work—singing, to which one could dance or make love—supported her. The other's work—writing down the unwritten doings and sayings of a culture nobody else seemed to give a damn about, except to wish it would more speedily conform to white, middle-class standards—did not.

Financial dependency is the thread that sewed a cloud over Hurston's life, from the time she left home to work as a maid at fourteen to the day of her death. It is ironic that *this* woman, who many claimed sold her soul to record the sources of authentic, black American folk art (whereas it is apparently cool to sell your soul for a university job, say, or a new car) and who was made of some of the universe's most naturally free stuff (one would be hard pressed to find a more nonmaterialistic person), was denied even a steady pittance, free from strings that would have kept her secure enough to do her best work.

It has been pointed out that one of the reasons Zora Neale Hurston's work has suffered neglect is that her critics never considered her "sincere." Only after she died penniless, still laboring at her craft, still immersed in her work, still following *her* vision and *her* road, did it begin to seem to some that yes, perhaps this woman *was* a serious artist after all, since artists are known to live poor and die broke. But you're up against a hard game if you have to die to win it, and we must insist that dying in poverty is an unacceptable extreme.

We live in a society, as blacks, women, and artists, whose contests we do not design and with whose insistence on ranking us we are permanently at war. To know that second place, in such a society, has often required more work and innate genius than first, a longer, grimmer struggle over greater odds than first—and to be able to fling your scarf about dramatically while you demonstrate that you know—is to trust your own self-evaluation in the face of the Great White Western Commercial of white and male supremacy, which is virtually everything we see, outside and often inside our own homes. That Hurston held her own, literally, against the flood of whiteness and maleness that diluted so much other black art of the period in which she worked is a testimony to her genius and her faith.

As black women and as artists, we are prepared, I think, to keep that faith. There are other choices, but they are despicable.

Zora Neale Hurston, who went forth into the world with one dress to her name, and who was permitted, at other times in her life, only a single pair of shoes, rescued and recreated a world which she labored to hand us whole, never underestimating the value of her gift, if at times doubting the good sense of its recipients. She appreciated us, in any case, *as we fashioned ourselves.* That is something. And of all the people in the world to be, she chose to be herself, *and more and more herself.* That, too, is something.

So this book is dedicated to Zora Neale Hurston. And it is sent off to her wherever she is now in the universe with the good wishes and love of all those who have glimpsed her heart through her work, as well as those who gave joyfully of their thought and scholarship and feelings to make this collection an offering from more relatives than one: the intrepid and sharp Mary Helen Washington, the brave and brilliant Barbara Smith, the thoughtful and insistent Gloria Hull, the women of The Feminist Press, Robert Allen and Robert Hemenway, and me.

CHERYL A. WALL (ESSAY DATE 1982)

SOURCE: Wall, Cheryl A. "Zora Neale Hurston: Changing Her Own Words." In *American Novelists Revisited: Essays in Feminist Criticism,* edited by Fritz Fleischmann, pp. 371-93. Boston: G. K. Hall, 1982.

In the following essay, Wall presents an overview of Hurston's novels, noting that her poetic prose is nurtured by the folk expression of her native rural Black community.

The developing tradition of black women's writing nurtured now in the prose and poetry of such writers as Toni Morrison and Alice Walker began with the work of Zora Neale Hurston. Hurston was not the first Afro-American woman to publish a novel, but she was the first to create language and imagery that reflected the reality of black women's lives. Ignoring the stereotypes, social and literary, that her predecessors spent their energies rejecting, Hurston rooted her art in the cultural traditions of the black rural South. As a daughter of the region, she claimed these traditions by birthright. As an anthropologist, she reclaimed them through years of intense, often perilous, research. As a novelist, she summoned this legacy in her choice of setting, her delineation of character, and most devotedly in her distillation of language. Hers became the first authentic black female voice in American literature.

Despite this achievement, Hurston's work suffered years of obscurity and critical neglect. Ten years ago, outside of that small group of readers and scholars whose primary devotion is to Afro-American literature, few had even heard her name. Still fewer were able to read her work, as it had been out of print since long before her death in 1960. Today Hurston's work has been revived, her reputation restored. She is now considered one of the major writers to have emerged from the Harlem Renaissance. Moreover, hers is the preeminent achievement in Afro-American letters during the 1930s; five of her seven books were published in that decade. Two of these, the folklore collection, ***Mules and Men*** (1935), and the novel, ***Their Eyes Were Watching God*** (1937), are now recognized classics in the Afro-American canon. The novel is becoming a favorite in American literature and women's studies courses as well. Although very much of its time, ***Their Eyes Were Watching God*** is timeless. As Sherley Anne Williams has written, its heroine's "individual quest for fulfillment becomes any woman's tale."[1] Other scholars and critics have begun to analyze Hurston's fiction in numerous articles and essays. The fascinating but hitherto fragmented story of her life has been reconstructed in a meticulously researched biography. Although her work is not nearly as well known as it deserves to be, more people have read it in the last few years than in Hurston's lifetime. For general readers and scholars alike, Zora Neale Hurston has emerged as a writer who must be taken seriously.

The black consciousness and feminist movements spurred the rediscovery and reassessment of Hurston's work. Under this impetus, her work began to be reprinted in the 1960s; it garnered little attention initially, overlooked in the flood of books by black writers suddenly returned to print. More of her books became available in the 1970s, often republished with introductions by leading black scholars and critics. By this time, feminists were retrieving works by "lost" women writers, a category for which Hurston was eminently qualified. Hurston's strong, resilient female characters won further favor; the first anthology of her prose, edited by Alice Walker, carried the imprint of the Feminist Press. Walker, whose championing of Hurston has been unselfish and unstinting, surely spoke for others when she wrote, "I became aware of my need of Zora Neale Hurston some time before I knew her work existed."[2] Walker explained that she found in Hurston a conviction of "racial health"; Hurston's characters were invaluable because of their ability to accept and love themselves.

The critical perspectives inspired by the black consciousness and feminist movements allow us to see Hurston's writings in a new way. They correct distorted views of her folklore as charming and quaint, set aside misperceptions of her characters as minstrels caught, in Richard Wright's phrase, "between laughter and tears."[3] These new perspectives inform this re-evaluation of Hurston's work. She asserted that black people, while living in a racist society that denied their humanity, had created an alternative culture that validated their worth as human beings. Although that culture was in some respects sexist, black women, like black men, attained personal identity not by transcending the culture but by embracing it.

Hurston's respect for the cultural traditions of black people is the most important constant in her career. This respect threads through her entire oeuvre, linking the local-color short fiction of her youth, her ethnographic research in the rural South and the Caribbean (an account of her field-work in Jamaica and Haiti, ***Tell My Horse,*** was published in 1938), her novels, and the essays she contributed to popular journals in her later years. In all, she published more than fifty short stories and articles in addition to her book-length works. Because her focus was on black cultural traditions, she rarely explored interracial themes. The black/white conflict, which loomed paramount in the fiction of her black contemporaries, in Wright's novels especially, hardly surfaced in Hurston's. Poet and critic June Jordan has described how the absence of explicitly political protest caused Hurston's work to be devalued. Affirmation, not protest, is Hurston's hallmark. Yet, as Jordan argues, "affirmation of Black values and lifestyle within the American context is, indeed, an act of protest."[4] Hurston appreciated and approved the reluctance of blacks to reveal "that which the soul lives by" to the hostile and uncomprehending gaze of outsiders. But the interior reality was what she wished to probe. In that reality, blacks ceased to be "tongueless, earless, eyeless conveniences" whose labor whites exploited; they ceased to be mules and were men and women.

The survival of the spirit was proclaimed first and foremost through language. As a writer, Hurston was keenly sensitive to the richness of black verbal expression. Like Langston Hughes and Sterling Brown, she had no patience with theories of linguistic deficiency among blacks; she ignored racist assumptions that rural blacks spoke as they did because they were too stupid to learn standard English. Hurston, whose father was a Baptist preacher, was well acquainted with the tradition of verbal elegance among black people. From her father's example, she perceived how verbal agility conferred status within the community. His sermons had demonstrated as well the power of his language to convey the complexity of the lives of his parishioners. Early in her career, Hurston attempted to delineate "characteristics of Negro expression." She stressed the heightened sense of drama revealed in the preference for action words and the "will to adorn" reflected in the profusion of metaphor and simile, and in the use of double descriptives (*low-down*) and verbal nouns (*funeralize*). To her, the "will to adorn" bespoke a feeling "that there can never be enough of beauty, let alone too much." Zora Hurston shared that feeling, as the beautifully poetic prose of her novels attests. The collective folk expression was the soil that nourished the individual expression of her novels. After a lengthy dialogue with her homefolk, Hurston was prepared to change some words of her own.[5]

In one of her first published articles, Hurston declared:

> But I am not tragically colored. There is no great sorrow dammed up in my soul, nor lurking behind my eyes. I do not mind at all. I do not belong to the sobbing school of Negrohood who hold that nature somehow has given them a lowdown dirty deal and whose feelings are all hurt about it. . . . No, I do not weep at the world—I am to busy sharpening my oyster knife.[6]

The exuberant tone of the assertions in **"How It Feels to Be Colored Me"** suggests that they were more strongly felt than reasoned. Hurston locates the source of her feelings in her childhood experiences in Eatonville, Florida, the hometown to which she often returned in fiction and fact. Eatonville was an all-black town, the first to be incorporated in the United States. Hurston remembered it as a place of possibility and promise. She revered the wit and wisdom of the townspeople, admired the originality of their culture and their moral and aesthetic values, saw in their language drama and the "will to adorn." Having been insulated from racism in her early years, unaware of racial distinctions until she was nine, she professed herself "astonished" rather than angered by discrimination. The lingering astonishment accounts perhaps for the shortcomings of the article as self and racial definition; Hurston relied on "exotic primitive" myths popular in the twenties to round out the explanation of herself and her people.

During this time Hurston was studying anthropology at Barnard under the tutelage of Franz Boas. This study complemented by her fieldwork in Florida and Louisiana allowed her to appreciate her past intellectually as well as intuitively. No longer were her homefolk simply good storytellers, whose values were commendable, superstitions remarkable, and humor penetrating. As such, they had been well suited for local-color fiction of the kind Hurston published in the 1920s. Now however, "they became a part of cultural anthropology; scientific objects who could and should be studied for their academic value."[7] The cultural relativity of anthropology freed Hurston from the need to defend her subjects' alleged inferiority. She could discard behavioral explanations drawn from racial mythology. Eatonville blacks were neither exotic nor primitive; they had

FROM THE AUTHOR

MULES AND MEN

As I crossed the Maitland-Eatonville township line I could see a group on the store porch. I was delighted. The town had not changed. Same love of talk and song. So I drove on down there before I stopped. Yes, there was George Thomas, Calvin Daniels, Jack, and Charlie Jones, Gene Brazzle, B. Moseley and "Seaboard." Deep in a game of Florida-flip. All of those who were not actually playing were giving advice—"bet straightening" they called it.

"Hello, boys," I hailed them as I went into neutral.

They looked up from the game and for a moment it looked as if they had forgotten me. Then B. Moseley said, "Well, if it ain't Zora Hurston!" Then everybody crowded around the car to help greet me.

SOURCE: Zora Neale Hurston, opening lines to *Mules and Men,* Lippincott, 1935, p. 1.

simply selected different characteristics from what Ruth Benedict, another pioneering anthropologist trained by Boas, called the "great arc of human potentialities."

In possession of these liberating theories, Hurston set forth in 1927 on the first of a series of field expeditions. Not surprisingly her first stop was Eatonville, a site she confidently expected to yield a rich lode of material. When the results of her fieldwork were published in ***Mules and Men,*** she introduced the book by stating, "I was glad when somebody told me, 'you may go and collect Negro folk-lore.'"[8] Her attitude was not typical of a professional anthropologist and neither was her method. She immersed herself in the culture she studied. Sitting on the porch of Joe Clarke's store in Eatonville, later signing on at sawmill camps and apprenticing herself to hoodoo doctors, she became a member of each community she entered. Clearly her race and personal heritage gave her an entrée previous researchers lacked. Beyond that, Hurston felt herself part and parcel of the culture she investigated. The diligence and skill with which she pursued her studies enabled her to capitalize on these advantages.

Mules and Men holds the distinction of being the first collection of Afro-American folklore published by an Afro-American. It distinguishes itself in other ways. Alan Lomax called it "the most engaging, genuine, and skillfully written book in the field of folklore."[9] Unlike many of its predecessors, it presents the lore not to patronize or demean but to affirm and celebrate. Written for a popular audience, it is highly readable; after nearly half a century, it has lost none of its capacity to delight. ***Mules and Men*** contains seventy folktales, but it is more than a transcription of individual texts. As her biographer Robert Hemenway points out, Hurston adds an unifying narrative that provides contexts as well as texts. By showing when a story is told, how, and to what purpose, Hurston attempts to restore the original meanings of the tales. Folktales, she understood, serve a function more significant than mere entertainment; "they are profound expressions of a group's behavior."[10] They cannot be comprehended without reference to those whose values and beliefs they embody. Consequently, the tales in ***Mules and Men*** are not collected from faceless informants, but from real men and women whose lives readers are briefly invited to share. Sharing their lives more profoundly, Hurston was ultimately forced to confront the role of women in rural black life. Her response, necessarily personal and engaged, gave shape to her most successful fiction.

Hurston met the woman who most informed this response soon after she arrived in Polk County, Florida, in January 1928. The sawmill camp where Hurston settled was an even richer repository of the folktales, worksongs, blues and cries, proverbs, and sermons than Eatonville had been. And of the people who lived there, Big Sweet was the most memorable. Hurston devoted several pages of her autobiography, ***Dust Tracks on a Road*** (1942), to her friendship with this woman; the influence of Big Sweet is highly visible in characters in Hurston's novels. Although Hurston gives few details about her appearance, the woman's name, with its suggestions of physical power and sexual attractiveness, of strength and tenderness, aptly sums up her character. Significantly, Hurston hears her before she sees her, and it is her talk that attracts her attention. Big Sweet is "specifying," "playing the dozens" with an outmatched male opponent. Before a large and appreciative audience, she breaks the news to him "in one of her mildest bulletins that his pa was a double-humpted camel and his ma a grass-gut cow." This performance gives Hurston "a measure of this Big Sweet," and her judgment is soon verified by the opinions of others on the job. Though fearsome, Big Sweet is not feared as much as she is respected, because the community draws a distinction between meanness and the defense of one's integrity. Hurston sees the wisdom of acquiring her friendship and hence protection. Big Sweet becomes the author's guardian and guide. She identifies informants, awards prizes in "lying" contests, and eventually saves Hurston's life.[11]

In his article, "Negotiating Respect: Patterns of Presentation among Black Women," folklorist Roger Abrahams notes: "how women assert their image and values as women is seldom found in the folklore literature."[12] In keeping with this premise, Big Sweet contributes only two folktales to ***Mules and Men;*** neither focuses on female identity. The relative scarcity of woman-centered tales in the oral tradition must have been one of the revelations of Hurston's fieldwork. Although tales created by men about women, many of them virulently antifemale, exist in some quantity, tales about women told from a female point of view are rare.[13] Hurston's narrative strategy permits her to sustain a female perspective in her account of Big Sweet. Her presentation of the context as well as the text of the lore is crucial in this regard. In the general narrative of her experiences in Polk County and in her descriptions of the specific situations in which stories are told, Hurston shows how Big Sweet asserts and maintains her identity. From these descriptions, the reader can take her own measure of this woman.

The dramatic performance of Big Sweet's "specifying" is not recounted in ***Mules and Men;*** her entrance here is low-keyed. She tells her two tales, **"Why the Mocking Bird Is Away on Friday"** and **"How the 'Gator Got Black,"** matter-of-factly, but the second is preceded by an exchange that reveals a bit of her mettle. Someone else has recited "How Brer 'Gator Got His Tongue Worn Out" which has reminded Big Sweet of the similar tale she knows. Thus the reader sees one way the lore is transmitted. Before she gets a chance to begin her story, however, Big Sweet is interrupted and must reclaim her place in the discussion. "When Ah'm shellin' my corn, you keep out yo' nubbins" wins her readmission and the tale is told. A bit later, as the others joke and lie good-naturedly, Big Sweet injects a personal and pointed warning to her lover not to repeat his infidelity of the night before. He appeals to the other men for assistance, but they cannot beat her "specifying." Her declaration of independence cuts right to the heart of the matter: "Lemme tell *you* something, *any* time Ah shack up wid any man Ah gives myself de privilege to go wherever he might be, night or day. Ah got de law in my mouth."[14]

Big Sweet's behavior conforms to a pattern Abrahams outlines. Respect in the black community is not a permanent given; it must constantly be earned and negotiated. For women, these negotiations usually occur, as in the scenes described above, when people are "just talking." No one, whatever her reputation, is beyond challenge. "Ideally a woman has the ability to *talk sweet* with her infants and peers but *talk smart* or *cold* with anyone who might threaten her self-image."[15] Big Sweet exemplifies this ideal. She uses "Little-Bit" as a term of endearment for the narrator Zora in ***Mules and Men,*** warns her that collecting songs from one of the men has provoked his lover's jealousy, and promises to defend her. A conversation between her and Hurston quoted in ***Dust Tracks*** further evidences her ability to "talk sweet." Not understanding why Hurston wants to collect "lies" (folktales), she pledges to aid her in doing so. Such conversations are held privately; the public smart talking she does earns Big Sweet respect. A crucial incident recounted in ***Mules and Men*** pits Big Sweet against her arch rival, Ella Wall, a woman whose feats are also chronicled by Leadbelly and other country blues singers. Ella Wall enters the camp "jook" (a combination dance hall, gaming parlor and bawdy house) and sends a bold message to Big Sweet's man. The two women exchange verbal insults and then physical threats, until the conflict is halted by the arrival of the white quarters boss. While Ella Wall is disarmed and thrown off the job, Big Sweet stands up to the white man and refuses to yield her weapon. Her erstwhile lover expresses the admiration of the group in a telling compliment: "You wuz noble! You wuz uh whole woman and half uh man."[16] Big Sweet's increased respect is not earned at the cost of her femininity. Her value as a woman is in fact enhanced by her fierce conduct. After the argument, her lover proudly escorts her home.

Zora Hurston knew that approval of Big Sweet was not shared by the world outside the lumber camp. The life of this hard-living, knife-toting woman was the stuff of myriad stereotypes. And Hurston seemed all too aware of this judgment when she wrote, "I thought of all I had to live for and turned cold at the thought of dying in a violent manner in a sordid sawmill camp." A dramatic revelation follows: "But for my very life I knew I couldn't leave Big Sweet if the fight came. She had been too faithful to me."[17] Hurston vows to stand by her friend. Passages such as this have caused some critics to accuse Hurston of being condescending and self-serving in her presentation of the poor. She does seem to be playing to her audience here; *sordid* voices their opinion of the camp and its people. It does not express Hurston's view. Her problem was to legitimize Big Sweet's conduct without defending it or positing sociological explanations for it. Her solution was to identify the sources of its legitimacy within the folk culture itself. Characteristically, her approach was subtle and easily overlooked by the casual reader; it was deliberate nonetheless. Just before the fight scene, Hurston described the visit of a traveling preacher to the camp. His sermon, "Behold de Rib," is a variant of the creation myth; its text is Genesis 2:21, its subject is female equality.

"Behold de Rib" is one of the book's highlights. It captures the pithy logic of folk wisdom, the rhythmic cadence and vivid imagery of the downhome preacher, and a good measure of folk humor. The preacher begins by defining his terms: he instructs his congregants, "Behold means to look and see," and invites them to "look at dis woman God done made." Before focusing on woman, however, he pauses to consider God's previous handiwork and envisions the acts of creation. A cluster of visual images along with the repetition of the phrase "I can see" unify this section of the sermon/poem, as the preacher bears witness to what can be seen through the "eye of Faith." God emerges as regent and warrior, striding through space, wearing the elements as a helmet, blowing storms through his lips. To make a place for the world, he seizes "de mighty axe of his proving power" and opens a gash in "stubborn-standing space." To light the heavens, ". . . God shook his head / And a thousand million diamonds / Flew out from his glittering crown / And studded de evening sky and made de stars."

This last is a familiar trope in black preaching and brings to mind James Weldon Johnson's poem, "The Creation." One notes that both speakers have an anthropomorphic conception of God, but in "The Creation" He is "lonely"; in his most stirring analogy the speaker compares Him to a "mammy" bending over her baby. A masculine, even martial, God presides over the world of sexual equality. Johnson's speaker ends his story before getting to what is the central event of "Behold de Rib." Here stars are lit especially to shine on sleeping man and emerging woman:

So God put Adam into a deep sleep
And took out a bone, ah hah!
And it is said that it was a rib.
Behold de rib!
A bone out of a man's side.
He put de man to sleep and made wo-man,
And men and women been sleeping together
    ever since.
Behold de rib!
Brothers, if God
Had taken dat bone out of man's head
He would have meant for woman to rule, hah
If he had taken a bone out of his foot,
He would have meant for us to dominize and
    rule.
He could have made her out of back-bone
And then she would have been behind us.
But, no, God Amighty, he took de bone out of
    his side
So dat places de woman beside us;
Hah! God knowed his own mind.
Behold de rib!

The preacher has modulated to a comic key, deepening the humor by alluding to that most famous of folk sermons, "Dry Bones." Still, his message is a serious one, as is apparent in the conclusion when he calls on his listeners, male and female, to march to glory side by side "in step wid de host dat John saw."[18]

Its rhythm and imagery place "Behold de Rib" squarely in the tradition of black preaching, but its message is anomalous. Female equality was not, is not, a common subject in black sermons. Hurston had transcribed other sermons in her field notes, including the one that became the centerpiece of her first novel, ***Jonah's Gourd Vine.*** Her selection of "Behold de Rib" was deliberate and so was its placement in ***Mules and Men.*** It prepares the reader to accept and approve Big Sweet's actions in the conflict that follows. She is heroic, as any man who similarly defended his honor would be. Although Hurston draws no connection between the sermon and the struggle—here and throughout the book her method is presentational, not analytical—the reader's approbation of Big Sweet is won in part by the juxtaposition of the two scenes.

The portrayal of Big Sweet anticipates the process of self-discovery Hurston's fictional heroines undergo. Like her, they must learn to manipulate language. The novels disclose Hurston's awareness that women, like children, are encouraged to be seen but not heard. She knew that few women had joined the lying sessions on Joe Clarke's store porch in Eatonville; Big Sweet was one of a small number of female storytellers in the folklore collection. It was Big Sweet's talk though that first captured Hurston's attention. Her words were emblematic of her power, for they signaled her ownership of self. The ability to back up words with actions was a second indicator of an independent self. The care Hurston took to legitimize Big Sweet's behavior intimated the expected reaction to an assertive woman. Nevertheless, Hurston believed that individual black women could base their personal autonomy on communal traditions. In so doing, her characters achieved their status as heroines.

Lucy Potts Pearson is such a character. Although her husband John is its main protagonist, ***Jonah's Gourd Vine*** traces Lucy's coming of age as well as his. Loosely based on the lives of Hurston's parents, ***Jonah's Gourd Vine*** tells the story of Lucy and John's courtship and marriage, John's swift rise to prominence as a Baptist preacher, his equally swift fall resulting from his marital infidelities, Lucy's strength and perseverance, and the family's ultimate dissolution. All this takes place against a background of social and technological change occurring in the South around the turn of the century. These changes are subordinate to the cultural traditions that remain intact: the sermons and sayings, children's games and rhymes, hoodoo beliefs and practices. In the foreground are the experiences of John and Lucy. Lucy dies two thirds of the way through the novel, but her spirit hovers above it until the end.

That talk, and especially women's talk, is a major concern of the book is established on the very first page. Ned Crittenden accuses his wife, John's mother, of "always talkin' more'n yuh know."[19] Amy Crittenden is undaunted, "Ah changes jes ez many words ez Ah durn please!" (p. 17), but her ability to act on her words is limited. An ex-slave whose eldest son John is the child of her former master, Amy has been "freed" to a marriage with a ne'er-do-well sharecropper. Abused by a husband who is unable to "treasure" his children as she does, Amy must watch him hire John out to a white man, the equivalent of selling him into slavery. Amy's resistance is covert: she encourages her son to escape his stepfather's tyranny by seeking work on the plantation owned by his unacknowledged white father. John's return to the town of his birth adheres to the pattern of the young man arriving from the provinces. Every new thing, from shoes to trains, is a source of fascination. But the greatest fascination is with words. The verbal play of the plantation's children, the ribald ditties of youths, and the prayers and sermons of the elders spark John's imagination. To win Lucy's love, he must learn to speak for himself. Both lovers search for words that can express mutual affection and respect.

Their effort is complicated by class distinctions within the community. John is an "over-the-creek nigger" with no prospects. Lucy's father is a landowner, and her mother has arranged for her to marry a well-to-do farmer when she is of age. John has no education. Lucy is the star pupil in her school, famed for the long recitations she commits to memory. Though attracted to Lucy from the first, John finds her difficult to approach:

> When the opportunity presented itself he couldn't find words. Handling Big 'Oman, Lacey, Semmie, Bootsie and Mehaley merely called for action, but with Lucy he needed words and words that he did not have.
>
> [P. 63]

Recognizing that Lucy will not be swayed by the charms that capture other girls' affection, John yearns to master her language. Lucy assures him that he can learn recitations better than she, and he enrolls in school. Neither realizes that the needed words cannot be found in textbooks. They can only be learned from a deeper engagement with the folk culture. John achieves this when he spends a time in a work camp, where "next to showing muscle-power, [he] loved to tell stories." Upon his return, he is prepared to court Lucy in the traditional style. This time she is the one who must master a new tongue.

Robert Hemenway has identified the folkloric origins of the courtship ritual John employs.[20] Organized around the riddle—"are you a flying lark or a setting dove?"—the ritual allows the questioner to ascertain a woman's availability and willingness to pursue romance. A problem arises in the novel because the woman-child Lucy (she is only fourteen) does not know how to respond to the question. She had begun the conversation gaily, coyly matching wits with John. But as John broached more substantive concerns, "Lucy suddenly lost her fluency of speech." John presses this point thus:

> "Lucy, you pay much 'tention tuh birds?"
>
> "Unhunh. De Jay bird say 'Laz'ness will kill you,' and he go to hell ev'ry Friday and totes uh grain uh sand in his mouf tuh put out de fire, and den de doves say, 'Where you *been* so long?'"
>
> John cut her short. "Ah don't mean dat way, Lucy. Whut Ah wants tuh know is, which would you ruther be, if you had yo' ruthers—uh lark uh flyin', uh uh dove uh settin'?"
>
> "Ah don't know whut you talkin' 'bout, John. It mus' be uh new riddle."

"Naw 'tain't, Lucy. Po' me, Lucy. Ahm uh one wingded bird. Don't leave me lak dat, Lucy."

[Pp. 124-25]

Far from new, the riddle is ancient and is meant to elicit a formulaic response. If Lucy wants to encourage John's advances, she should identify herself as a flying lark. Her ignorance of the proper answer imperils the future of the relationship. Lucy is resourceful enough to sift through her memory for plausible replies. She does not hit upon the correct one, but she does keep the conversation going. Her references to the jaybird, for example, demonstrates her awareness that the answer is to be found in folk traditions. The reference is to a familiar folktale, a variant of which, interestingly, is recounted by Big Sweet in ***Mules and Men.*** Here it is beside the point, as John's quick rejoinder makes clear. He poses the riddle directly. Lucy's continued inability to respond calls forth a plaintive cry: "Po' me, Lucy. Ahm uh one wingded bird."

Although her book learning is commendable, Lucy is clearly not sufficiently conversant with the rituals of her own culture. This suggests an immaturity and lack of experience that would render her an unsuitable wife. The situation is saved only when Lucy helps John improvise a new ritual that can substitute for the old. The instrument is a handkerchief out of which John has crafted what Hurston calls "a love knot." The lovers hold opposite ends of it throughout the conversation, and when Lucy misses the riddle, she points John's attention to the knot. Regaining her ground, she asks John to state what is on his mind. Wary, he asks first for a kiss ("Kiss me and loose me so Ah kin talk.") The kiss unlocks the poetic power that characterizes John's speech for the rest of the novel:

"Lucy, Ah looked up intuh Heben and Ah seen you among de angels right 'round de throne, and when Ah seen *you,* mah heart swole up and put wings on mah shoulders, and Ah 'gin tuh fly 'round too, but Ah never would uh knowed yo' name if ole Gab'ull hadn't uh whispered it tuh me."

[P. 125]

Lucy has reconferred John's wings. Though not as thoroughly grounded in the folk culture as he, she is knowledgeable enough to induce him to state his proposal in terms they *both* can understand. When he does, she accepts.[21] Their acting out of the courtship ritual predicts a marriage between two active partners, both of whom are able to manipulate language and negotiate respect between themselves and with others. It does not, however, foretell a marriage between equals. The prerogatives of maleness ultimately undo the balance.

Although he continues to profess and feel love and respect for Lucy, John Pearson does not remain faithful to her. His philandering, which begins shortly after the marriage and continues until her death, not only causes her great emotional pain but frequently jeopardizes the well-being of the entire family. He struggles against his weakness, expresses remorse when he fails, yet lacks all insight into his behavior. A serious flaw in the novel is Hurston's failure to provide a compelling motivation for John's conduct. A reader may infer that John's irresponsibility is, at least in part, a legacy of slavery. The plantation owner's initial reaction to John is, "What a fine stud." He projects all of his sexual fantasies on to John, labeling him at one point "a walking orgasm. A living exultation." John's sexual misadventures never cease to enthrall this man, who aids him in escaping rather than standing up to their consequences. In a period of transition between slavery and freedom, John remains bound by the slaveholder's conception of black men.

Lucy is, by contrast, a new black woman. Whenever John is irresponsible, Lucy is prepared to compensate. What he lacks in ambition and initiative, she is more than able to supply. She had defied her family to marry him and remains steadfast in her love and loyalty. She even looks with compassion on John's struggle to conquer the "brute beast" within, a struggle that intensifies after he is called to the ministry. John's spiritual call is genuine, but his acceptance of it also permits him to design a self-image independent of the white world. His move to Eatonville has further encouraged this possibility. There he can assume his rightful role as leader, his talents can be given free rein. The canker that galls is his recognition that Lucy deserves much of the credit for his success.

John's fellows are not blind to this fact, and they enjoy baiting him with the knowledge: "Aw, 'tain't you, Pearson, . . . iss dat li'l' handful uh woman you got on de place" (p. 178). His resentment of his dependence on Lucy grows and expresses itself in his demand for her total dependence on him. A comparison of the following passage with the courtship ritual discussed above measures the damage the marriage suffers.

"Lucy, is you sorry you married me instid uh some big nigger wid uh whole heap uh money and titles hung on tuh him?"

"Whut make you ast me dat? If you tired uh me, jus' leave me. Another man over de fence waiting fuh yo' job."

[P. 179]

John's reaction to Lucy's verbal play is a violent threat; he will kill her if she ever repeats that fanciful remark. He stakes out claims of ownership, vowing to be Lucy's first and last man. Calming himself, he asks why Lucy has said such a thing. Her response is telling: "Aw, John, you know dat's jus' uh by-word. Ah hears all de women say dat." Lucy is answering John in terms sanctioned by the folk culture, terms that allow for her autonomy. She is engaging in the same kind of verbal sparring the courtship ritual required. The "by-word" would permit Lucy to negotiate respect in this exchange too, but John is no longer concerned with Lucy's ability to participate in cultural traditions. He concedes that the expression is a common one, but forbids her to use it.

Lucy continues to be supportive of John's career. Through her maneuvering, John becomes pastor of a large church, moderator of the State Baptist Association, and mayor of Eatonville. He can never accept her assistance as a complement to his gifts. He accuses: "You always tryin' tuh tell me whut tuh do. Ah wouldn't be where Ah is, if Ah didn't know more'n you think Ah do. You ain't mah guardzeen nohow" (p. 189). John's real defense against what he perceives to be Lucy's domination is other women. Of course, she cannot retaliate in kind. Words are her only defense, righteous, chastising words that strike fear in John's heart but fail to make him change his ways.

The climactic exchange takes one back to the opening pages of the novel. In his home, though not outside it, John has come to resemble Ned Crittenden, telling his wife to shut her mouth. Like Amy, Lucy refuses to be silenced. Instead she reproaches John severely and claims rights for herself and her children. "Big talk," she tells him, "ain't changin' whut you doin'. You can't clean yo' self wid yo' tongue lak uh cat." For the first time in their marriage, John strikes his wife. This action, Hurston later suggested, prompted the novel's title. Taken from Jonah 4:6-10, the title refers to the gourd vine which grew profusely and gave the prophet shade. The next morning a worm attacked the vine and it withered. Thus did God punish his disobedient servant. To Hurston the Biblical story represented: "Great and sudden growth. One act of malice and it is withered and gone."[22] Slapping Lucy marks the beginning of the end for John; his public fortunes decline, and his private life falls into disarray. Years later he has no understanding of what has happened to him. It is literally the end for Lucy, who dies of an illness soon after. Unlike John, however, she has learned something from her experiences, a lesson she passes on to her favorite daughter. "Don't you love nobody better'n you do yo'self. Do, you'll be dying befo' yo' time is out."

Though Lucy's insight is personal, she has expressed it in the manner of a folk proverb. Throughout the novel, her speech is aphoristic. Sayings like the still current "God sho' don't like ugly" and the less familiar, more ingenious "God don't eat okra" (in other words, He doesn't like crooked, slick ways) roll easily off Lucy's tongue. She has mastered the language and absorbed much of the wisdom of her culture. In the end, she apprehends some of its limitations. She hears the silence where the sayings affirming female identity should be. She espies the untaught knowledge that no one can live through someone else and begins to teach it. Without her realizing it, the folk culture through her husband had assigned Lucy Pearson a "place"; she warns her daughter to be on guard against such a fate. Loving John too much, she has acquiesced in her own suppression. At her death, she remains on the threshold of self-discovery.

Although Lucy is the character who is given insight, the novel is less hers than John's. He becomes the central character because he serves the author's purposes beyond the demands of the plot. A contemporary reviewer rightly called ***Jonah's Gourd Vine*** a "talkfest," and a recent critic describes it as "a series of linguistic moments." Both discern that language is Hurston's priority. Published before ***Mules and Men*** though written afterward, the novel was Hurston's first opportunity to share at length the discoveries of her fieldwork. She incorporated so much of her research that one reviewer objected to her characters being mere pegs on which she hung their dialect and folkways.[23] The objection is grossly overstated, but it does highlight a problem in the book. Too often the folklore overwhelms the formal narrative. The novel is enriched nonetheless by its numerous examples of the Negro's "will to adorn," many of the expressions coming directly from Hurston's notes. She believed resolutely that blacks aspired for and achieved beauty in their verbal expression. With extraordinary care, she sought to reproduce their speech exactly as it was spoken. Given these concerns, John Pearson's was necessarily the key role. As preacher, hence poet, he represented the verbal artistry of his people at its height. He became, in the words of critic Larry Neal, "the intelligence of the community, the bearer of its traditions and highest possibilities."[24] This profound engagement with his culture causes John's struggle to reconcile his physical and spiritual selves to take precedence over Lucy's effort to claim her autonomy. In Hurston's second and most compelling novel, the female quest is paramount. The heroine, through acquiring an intimate knowledge of the folk culture, gains the self-knowledge necessary for true fulfillment.

With the publication of ***Their Eyes Were Watching God,*** it was clear that Zora Neale Hurston was an artist in full command of her talent. Here the folk material complements rather than overwhelms the narrative. The sustained beauty of Hurston's prose owes much to the body of folk expression she had recorded and studied, but much more to the maturity of her individual voice. The language of this novel *sings.* Unlike Lucy, Janie, the heroine of ***Their Eyes,*** is a fully realized character. During the twenty-odd years spanned by the plot, she grows from a diffident teenager to a woman in complete possession of her self. Two recurring metaphors, the pear tree and the horizon, help unify the narrative. The first symbolizes organic union with another, the second, the individual experiences one must acquire to achieve selfhood. Early reviewers thought of the novel as a love story, but recent commentators designate Janie's search for identity as the novel's major theme. Following the pattern we have observed, Janie's self-discovery depends on her learning to manipulate language. Her success is announced in the novel's prologue when, as a friend listens in rapt attention, Janie begins to tell her own story.

The action of the novel proper begins when Janie is sixteen, beautiful, and eager to struggle with life, but unable to articulate her wishes and dreams. Her consciousness awakens as she watches bees fertilizing the blossoms of a pear tree. In the following passage, the narrative voice is not Janie's but the scene, like the novel as a whole, expresses her point of view:

> She was stretched on her back beneath the pear tree soaking in the alto chant of the visiting bees, the gold of the sun and the panting breath of the breeze when the inaudible voice of it all came to her. She saw a dust-bearing bee sink into the sanctum of a bloom; the thousand sister-calyxes arch to meet the love embrace and the ecstatic shiver of the tree from root to tiniest branch creaming in every blossom and frothing with delight. So this was a marriage! She had felt a pain remorseless sweet that left her limp and languid.[25]

The lyricism of the passage mutes somewhat its intensely sexual imagery. Still, the imagery is remarkably explicit for a woman novelist of Hurston's time. Janie's response to the scene and her acceptance of its implications for her own life are instructive: "Oh to be a pear tree—*any* tree in bloom!" Janie acknowledges sexuality as a natural part of life, a major aspect of her identity. Before she has the chance to act on this belief, however, her grandmother interposes a radically different viewpoint.

To Nanny, her granddaughter's nascent sexuality is alarming. Having been unable to protect herself and her daughter from sexual exploitation, Nanny determines to safeguard Janie. Janie must repress her sexuality in order to avoid sexual abuse; the only haven is marriage. Marriage had not been an option for Nanny, who as a slave was impregnated by her master; her mistress had forced her to flee with her newborn infant. Her daughter was raped by a black schoolteacher, convincing Nanny that male treachery knows no racial bounds. The world has thwarted her dreams of what a woman should be for herself and her daughter, "Ah wanted to preach a great sermon about colored women sittin' on high, but they wasn't no pulpit for me," but she has saved the text for Janie. She envisions her on the pedestal reserved for southern white women, far above the drudgery that has characterized Nanny's own life—the drudgery that has made the black woman "de mule uh de world." She arranges for Janie to marry Logan Killicks, an old man whose sixty acres and a mule constitute his eligibility. "The vision of Logan Killicks was desecrating the pear tree, but Janie didn't know how to tell Nanny that." So she assents to her grandmother's wish.

Joe Starks offers Janie an escape from her loveless marriage. He arrives just after Logan Killicks, despairing of his efforts to win his wife's affection by "pampering" her, has bought a second mule and ordered Janie to plow alongside him. Perceiving that Killicks's command threatens to reduce her to the status her grandmother abhorred, Janie decides to escape with Joe. Their marriage fulfills Nanny's dreams. Eventually it causes Janie to understand that the old woman's dreams are not her own. Initially though, Joe Starks cuts a fine figure. Stylishly dressed and citified, he is a man of great ambition and drive. He is like no *black* man Janie has ever seen. He reminds her vaguely of successful white men, but she cannot grasp the implications of the resemblance. She can appreciate his big plans and the élan with which he courts her. Tempering her reservations that "he did not represent sun-up and pollen and blooming trees," Janie resolves, "he spoke for far horizon. He spoke for change and chance" (p. 50).

It quickly becomes apparent that, like Nanny, Joe has borrowed his criteria for success from the white world. He takes Janie to Eatonville because there, he believes, he can be a "big ruler of things." His ambition is soon realized. He buys property and opens a store which becomes the town's meeting place. He decrees that roads be dug, a post office established, a street lamp installed, and town incorporation papers drawn. Already landlord, storekeeper, and postmaster, Joe runs for mayor to consolidate his power. After his election, he builds a large white house that is a travesty of a plantation mansion, and then furnishes it in the grand manner right down to brass spittoons. His brashness elicits equal measures of respect and resentment from the townspeople. As much as they admire his accomplishments, they take exception to his manner. One citizen's observation is widely shared: "he loves obedience out of everybody under de sound of his voice" (p. 78).

Everybody naturally includes Janie. Joe assigns her the role of "Mrs. Mayor Starks." She must hold herself apart from the townspeople, conduct herself according to the requirements of his position. Under no circumstances must she speak in public. Starks first imposes this rule during a ceremony marking the opening of the store. The ceremony has occasioned much speech-making, and toward the end, Janie is invited to say a few words. Before she can respond, her husband takes the floor to announce:

> Thank yuh fuh yo' compliments, but mah wife don't know nothin''bout no speech-makin'. Ah never married her for nothin' lak dat. She's uh woman and her place is in de home.
>
> [P. 69]

Joe's announcement takes Janie by surprise. Unsure that she even wants to speak, she strongly resents being denied the right to decide for herself. Joe's prohibitions increase. He forbids Janie to participate in the lying sessions held on the store porch; she is hustled inside when they begin. Janie loves these conversations and notes that Joe, while not deigning to join in, stays around to listen and laugh. Being forbidden to speak is a severe penalty in an oral culture. It short-circuits Janie's attempt to claim an identity of her own, robs her of the opportunity to negotiate respect from her peers. Barred from speaking to anyone but Joe, she loses the desire to say anything at all. "So gradually, she pressed her teeth together and learned to hush."

After seven years of marriage, Janie recognizes that Joe requires her total submission. She yields. As she does so however, she retains a clear perception of herself and her situation, a perception that becomes her salvation in the end. On one occasion after Joe has slapped her (for naturally, her submission has not slowed his verbal or physical abuse), she experiences the following revelation:

> Janie stood where he left her for unmeasured time and thought. She stood there until something fell off the shelf inside her. Then she went inside to see what it was. It was her image of Jody tumbled down and shattered. But looking at it she saw that it never was the flesh and blood figure of her dreams. Just something she had grabbed up to drape her dreams over. In a way she turned her back upon the image where it lay and looked further. She had no more blossomy openings dusting pollen over her man, neither any glistening young fruit where the petals used to be. She found that she had a host of thoughts she had never expressed to him, and numerous emotions she had never let Jody know about. Things packed up and put away in parts of her heart where he could never find them. She was saving up feelings for some man she had never seen. She had an inside and an outside now and suddenly she knew how not to mix them.
>
> [Pp. 112-13]

Facing the truth about Joe allows Janie to divorce him emotionally. She accepts her share of responsibility for the failure of the marriage, knowing now that if Joe has used her for his purposes, she has used him for hers. Yet she understands that her dreams have not impinged on Joe's selfhood; they have been naive but not destructive. By creating inside and outside selves, she hopes to insulate the core of her being from the destructive consequences of Joe's dreams. She cannot claim her autonomy, because she is not yet capable of imagining herself except in relationship to a man. Still, she is no longer willing to jeopardize her inner being for the sake of any such relationship.

Janie remains content to practice a kind of passive resistance against Joe's tyranny until he pushes her to the point when she must "talk smart" to salvage her self-respect. For many years, Joe has forced her to clerk in the store, taking every opportunity to ridicule her for minor mistakes. As he grows older, he adds taunts about her age to his repertoire of verbal insults. Sensing that her womanhood as well as her intelligence is under attack, she retaliates: "Humph! Talkin''bout *me* lookin' old! When you pull down yo' britches, you look lak de change uh life" (p. 123). So unaccustomed is Joe to hearing his wife "specify" that he imputes nefarious motives to her words. Ill and suspicious, he hires a hoodoo doctor to counteract the curse he believes Janie is putting on him. No curse exists, of course, but Starks is dying of kidney disease and of mortal wounds to his vanity. As he lies on his deathbed, Janie confronts him with more painful truths. Again she reveals how well she comprehends the effect of his domination: "Mah own mind had tuh be squeezed and crowded out tuh make room for yours in me" (p. 133).

The attack on her dying husband is not an act of gratuitous cruelty; it is an essential step toward self-reclamation. Moreover, in terms of the narrative, the deathbed episode posits a dramatic break with Janie's past. She is henceforth a different woman. Independent for the first time in her life, she exults in the "freedom feeling." Reflecting on her past, she realizes that her grandmother, though acting out of love, has wronged her deeply. At base, Nanny's sermon had been about things, when Janie wanted to journey to the horizons in search of people. Janie is able at last to reject her grandmother's way and resume her original quest. That quest culminates in her marriage to Tea Cake Woods with whom she builds a relationship totally unlike the others she has had.

Tea Cake is a troubadour, a traveling bluesman, whose life is dedicated to joyful pursuits. With this character, Hurston explores an alternative definition of manhood, one that does not rely on external manifestations of power, money, and position. Tea Cake has none of these. He is so thoroughly immune to the influence of white American society that he does not even desire them. Tea Cake is at ease being who and what he is. Consequently, he fosters the growth of Janie's self-acceptance. Together they achieve the ideal sought by most characters in Hurston's fiction. They trust emotion over intellect, value the spiritual over the material, preserve a sense of humor and are comfortable with their sensuality. Tea Cake confirms Janie's right to self-expression and invites her to share equally in their adventures. She sees that he "could be a bee to a blossom—a pear tree blossom in the spring" (p. 161). Over the protests of her neighbors, she marries this man several years younger than she whose only worldly possession is a guitar.

They embark on a nomadic existence which takes them to the rich farmland of the Florida Everglades where both Tea Cake and Janie work on the muck and where both share household chores. Their cabin becomes "the unauthorized center of the job," the focal point of the community like the store in Eatonville. Here, however, Janie "could listen and laugh and even talk some herself if she wanted to. She got so she could tell big stories herself from listening to the rest" (p. 200). This is an important and hard-won accomplishment. Even Tea Cake, strongly idealized character though he is, has had difficulty accepting Janie's full participation in their life together. Zora Hurston knew that Tea Cake, a son of the folk culture, would have inherited its negative attitudes toward women. She knew besides that female autonomy cannot be granted by men, it must be demanded by women. Janie gains her autonomy only when she insists upon it. Under pressure, Tea Cake occasionally falls back on the prerogatives of his sex. His one act of physical cruelty toward Janie results from his need to show someone else who is boss in his home. In the main though, Tea Cake transcends the chauvinistic attitudes of the group. He largely keeps his pledge to Janie that she "partake wid everything."

The marriage of Janie and Tea Cake ends in the wake of a fierce hurricane that is vividly evoked in the novel. In the process of saving Janie's life, Tea Cake is bitten by a rabid dog. Deranged, he tries to kill Janie, and she shoots him in self-defense. Despite these events, the conclusion of ***Their Eyes Were Watching God*** is not tragic. For, with Tea Cake as her guide, Jane has explored the soul of her culture and learned how to value herself. This fact is underscored in the prologue and epilogue of the novel, sections set after Janie's return to Eatonville following Tea Cake's death. In the former, she tells her friend Pheoby: "Ah been a delegate to de big 'ssociation of life. Yessuh! De Grand Lodge, de big convention of livin' is just where Ah been dis year and a half y'all ain't seen me" (p. 18). Having been to the horizon and back, as she puts it, she is eager to teach the crucial lesson she has learned in her travels. Everybody must do two things for themselves: "They got tuh go tuh God, and they got tuh find out about livin' fuh theyselves" (p. 285). This is Janie's text; the sermon she preaches is the novel itself. She has claimed the right to change her own words.

Hurston was never to duplicate the triumph of ***Their Eyes Were Watching God.*** In her subsequent novels, she changed the direction of her work dramatically. ***Moses: Man of the Mountain*** (1939) is a seriocomic novel which attempts to fuse Biblical narrative and folk myth. ***Seraph***

on the Suwanee (1948) is a psychological novel whose principal characters are upwardly mobile white Floridians. Although Hurston's willingness to experiment is admirable, the results are disappointing. Neither of her new settings is as compelling as the Eatonville milieu. Though the impact of black folk expression is always discernible, it is diminished and so is the power of Hurston's own voice. In these novels, the question of female autonomy recedes in importance, and when it is posed in ***Seraph,*** the answer is decidedly reactionary. What is of interest in terms of this essay is Hurston's reworking of themes identified in her earlier work.

Hurston's Moses is a combination of Biblical lawgiver and Afro-American hoodoo man. He is officially a highborn Egyptian, but according to legend, he is a Hebrew; Moses neither wholly rejects nor accepts the legend. The uncertainties about his identity complicate his quest for fulfillment. That quest conforms in part to the pattern we have outlined. Moses becomes a great manipulator of language, and much of his authority derives from the power of his words. As an educated man, he has been taught the formal language of the Egyptian elite. He later spends many years with the Midianites in spiritual preparation for his divinely appointed task; this period is somewhat comparable to John Pearson's stay in the work camp and Janie's sojourn on the muck. With the Midianites, Moses adapts to the rhythms of a rural folk culture and learns to speak more colloquial English. The Hebrews speak in the black folk idiom, and when he becomes their leader, Moses masters their tongue. Moses is of course a man of action, and as befits a leader, he fights most often for the rights of those under his stewardship. Though he knows he would be more beloved as a king and more popular as a politician, Moses rejects the accouterments of power. He has as little use for class distinctions as Janie and Tea Cake. In Moses, Hurston developed a character who was already a certified hero, not only in the Judeo-Christian tradition, but according to her introduction, also among the peoples of Asia and Africa. What she adds are new points of emphasis, and these had precedents in her earlier work. The most important is implicit in her attempt to reconcile the Biblical Moses and her conception of Moses as conjurer. Hurston had been the first scholar ever to research hoodoo in America and had studied the more systematic religion of Vodun in Haiti. In both instances, she had noted the coexistence of seemingly antithetical religious beliefs in the lives of her informants. In ***Moses: Man of the Mountain,*** one looks in vain for a synthesis of the two belief systems to which the hero is heir. Hurston simply allows them to coexist. In a novel whose protagonist seeks and achieves cosmic fulfillment, the failure to explicate the spiritual sources of that fulfillment is serious indeed.

Moses is a very ambitious novel. If it fails in some respects, it succeeds in others. It offers a very effective satire on the transition from slavery to freedom for black Americans. Hurston drew on the long-standing identification of blacks with the enslaved Hebrews, the identification that had inspired the majestic spiritual "Go Down, Moses" and countless other sacred and secular expressions. Most dwelt on the sufferings of bondage and the joys of emancipation. Hurston's concerns were the responsibilities of freedom. In the novel, the people of Goshen are hesitant to rebel against slavery and unable to fully comprehend freedom. Hurston satirizes their ready assent to the commands of their slavemasters and their reluctance to follow Moses. She mocks the vainglory of self-appointed leaders and the failure of the people to understand the need for sacrifice. Their petty bickering and constant backbiting are also objects of her ridicule. Hurston's satirical sallies are invariably good-natured and often very funny. But her novel is not the serious statement about faith and freedom she seems to have intended.

Hurston did not publish another novel for nine years. In the interim, her political instincts grew markedly conservative. World War II and its Cold War aftermath hastened the rightward drift of her thinking. At the suggestion of her publisher, she revised the manuscript of ***Dust Tracks on a Road*** to eliminate sections critical of the American system; as it was published in 1942, her autobiography seemed a celebration of the American way. Through the decade, Hurston contributed a number of articles to the *American Mercury* and the *Saturday Evening Post* which developed patriotic themes. By the 1950s, her work was welcome in the pages of the *American Legion Magazine.* Not all of Hurston's articles were reactionary. Some applauded the achievements of blacks in various endeavors. Others reaffirmed her belief in the value of black folklore, though she had ceased her research in the field. A few pieces, written for *Negro Digest,* protested racism in diplomacy, publishing, and everyday life. On the whole, however, Hurston's political views, which she expounded more often in the 1940s than at any other time in her life, supported the status quo. The same charge might be leveled at her last work of fiction, ***Seraph on the Suwanee.***

This novel restates the major themes of ***Their Eyes Were Watching God,*** perhaps in a misguided attempt to universalize them. Here the protagonist is Arvay Henson Meserve, who like Janie searches for self-identity. She is hindered in her quest by the deep-rooted inferiority she feels about her poor cracker background. For the wrong reason, she has come to the right conclusion. As Hurston depicts her, she is inferior to her husband Jim and the only identity she can attain is through accepting her subordinate role as his wife. Hurston endows Jim Meserve with a mixture of the attractive qualities found in Joe Starks and Tea Cake. He is more crudely chauvinistic than either of them, but this aspect of his character is treated with amazing tolerance. Early in the novel, Arvay reflects that if she married Jim, "her whole duty as a wife was to just love him good, be nice and kind around the house and have children for him. She could do that and be more than happy and satisfied, but it looked too simple."[26] The novel demonstrates that it is much too simple, but at the conclusion the happiness Arvay supposedly realizes is achieved on exactly these terms. The problem is Hurston's inability to grant her protagonist the resources that would permit her to claim autonomy. Although Arvay "mounts the pulpit" at the end of the novel, she has no words of her own to speak.

Ultimately, Arvay's weakness may be less a personal problem than a cultural one. Though black characters play minor roles in the novel, black cultural traditions permeate the narrative. They influence everyone's speech, so much so that at times the whites sound suspiciously like the storytellers in Eatonville. Jim relishes the company of his black employees, whom he treats in a disgustingly condescending manner; and one of his sons, after being tutored by a black neighbor, leaves home to join a jazz band. Unlike the earlier protagonists, Arvay cannot attain her identity through a profound engagement with the folk culture, because she has no culture to engage. The culture of the people Arvay despises has supplanted her own. Seen from this perspective, ***Seraph on the Suwanee*** is not as anomalous or as reactionary a work as it otherwise appears.

From any vantage point, however, it represents an artistic decline. Hurston was at her best when she drew her material directly from black folk culture; it was the source of her creative power. Throughout her career, she endeavored to negotiate respect for it, talking smart then sweet in her folklore and fiction, proclaiming its richness and complexity to all who would hear. Her most memorable characters are born of this tradition. In portraying them, she was always cognizant of the difficulties in reconciling the demands of community and the requirements of self, difficulties that were especially intense for women. The tension could not be resolved by rejecting the community or negating the self. Hurston challenged black people to dig deep into their culture to unearth the values on which it was built. Those values could restore the balance. They could give men and women words to speak. They could set their spirits free.

Notes

1. Introduction to *Their Eyes Were Watching God* (Urbana: University of Illinois Press, 1978), p. xiv.
2. *I Love Myself When I Am Laughing . . . and Then Again When I Am Looking Mean and Impressive, A Zora Hurston Reader* (Old Westbury, N.Y.: The Feminist Press, 1979); the quotation is from Walker's introduction to Robert Hemenway, *Zora Neale Hurston: A Literary Biography* (Urbana: University of Illinois Press, 1977), p. xii.
3. "Between Laughter and Tears," review of *Their Eyes Were Watching God, New Masses* 23, no. 10 (5 October 1937):25.
4. June Jordan, "On Richard Wright and Zora Neale Hurston: Notes toward a Balancing of Love and Hatred," *Black World* (August 1974):5.
5. "Characteristics of Negro Expression," [1934]; in *Voices from the Harlem Renaissance* ed. Nathan Huggins (New York: Oxford University Press, 1976), pp. 224-27. The expression "changing words" appears in several of Hurston's works. I suspect it derives from a form of the word "exchange," in which the weakly stressed syllable has been dropped. J. L. Dillard identifies the dropping of such syllables as a common characteristic of Black English. See *Black English* (New York: Random House, 1972), p. 249.
6. *I Love Myself,* p. 153.
7. Hemenway, *Zora Neale Hurston,* p. 62.
8. *Mules and Men* (1935; reprint ed., Bloomington: Indiana University Press, 1978), p. 3.
9. Quoted in Robert Hemenway, "Are You a Flying Lark or a Setting Dove," *Afro-American Literature: The Reconstruction of Instruction* (New York: Modern Language Association, 1979), p. 132.
10. Hemenway, *Zora Neale Hurston,* p. 168.
11. *Dust Tracks on a Road* (Philadelphia: J. P. Lippincott, 1942; rpt. 1971), pp. 186-91.
12. *Journal of American Folklore* 88 (Jan.-March 1975):58.
13. Hurston first noted "this scornful attitude towards black women" in "Characteristics of Negro Expression," p. 234. For examples of sexism in folktales, see Daryl C. Dance, *Shuckin' and Jivin': Folklore from Contemporary Black Americans* (Bloomington: Indiana University Press, 1978), pp. 110-42.
14. *Mules and Men,* p. 134.

15. Abrahams, "Negotiating Respect," pp. 58-62.

16. *Mules and Men,* p. 162.

17. *Mules and Men,* p. 160.

18. *Mules and Men,* pp. 148-51.

19. *Jonah's Gourd Vine* (Philadelphia: J. P. Lippincott, 1934; rpt. 1971), p. 9. All further references to this work appear in the text.

20. Hemenway, "Flying Lark or Setting Dove," pp. 134-38.

21. See Hemenway, "Flying Lark or Setting Dove," pp. 139-47, for an extended gloss on this passage. The essay as a whole has influenced my reading of the novel.

22. Hemenway, *Zora Neale Hurston,* p. 192.

23. John Chamberlain, *New York Times,* 3 May 1934, p. 7; Hemenway, *Zora Neale Hurston,* p. 192; Andrew Burris, review of *Jonah's Gourd Vine, Crisis* 41 (1934):166.

24. Introduction to *Jonah's Gourd Vine,* p. 7.

25. *Their Eyes,* p. 24. All further references to this work appear in the text.

26. *Seraph on the Suwanee* (New York: Scribner's, 1948), p. 33.

TITLE COMMENTARY

Their Eyes Were Watching God

JAMES R. GILES (ESSAY DATE 1972)

SOURCE: Giles, James R. "The Significance of Time in Zora Neale Hurston's *Their Eyes Were Watching God." Negro American Literature Forum* 6, no. 2 (summer 1972): 52-53, 60.

In the following essay, Giles examines the way Hurston uses time in Their Eyes Were Watching God *to accentuate the thematic conflict between Puritanism and hedonism.*

In *The Negro Novel in America,* Robert A. Bone has given Zora Neale Hurston's excellent novel, ***Their Eyes Were Watching God*** (1937), its only significant critical attention.[1] Bone proclaims Hurston's book as "possibly the best [black] novel of the period, excepting *Native Son*" (p. 128) and correctly describes its central tension as residing in the conflict between the ways of life personified by the heroine's husbands. He describes Janie's life with Logan Killicks and Jody Starks as an unnatural commitment to "prose" (materialism) and her life with Tea-Cake as one of loving devotion to "poetry" (the "folk culture" and sensual "intensity") (pp. 127-132). This analysis is true as far as it goes; however, it needs extension. The "prose" is closer to a Puritan sense of duty which is unnatural to Janie and her world because it more correctly belongs to white people, and the "poetry" is actually a primitive form of hedonism which Miss Hurston is associating with blacks. The concept of time is employed to sharpen the conflict between these two life styles.

Prior to a discussion of time in the novel, it is necessary to clarify a few related points. It is significant that Miss Hurston makes Nannie, Janie's grandmother, the chief spokesman for prosaic materialism. First, Nannie reached adulthood and bore an illegitimate child as a slave; then, when freed, she was taken in by a kind white lady only to see her daughter also bear an illegitimate child. Her own sexual transgreesion cannot ultimately be laid at her moral door—she was forced by her white master and, in fact, threatened with being tortured to death by her vengeful white mistress. But Nannie feels that her daughter's "sin" is her own, and she feels that it is a poor way to repay her white benefactress. Thus, since Nannie's entire moral code has developed in reaction to white pressure, she longs for that white moral respectability which she has never had. She sees Janie as the last chance to achieve this respectability. Jody Starks, Janie's second husband, is a character whose value system is an imitation of the white world; after "workin' for white folks all his life" (p. 26). Jody has saved three hundred dollars and intends to go to a newly-founded all black town in Florida and convert it to veneration of materialism. After a struggle with the easy-going inhabitants, he does just that and acquires considerable financial power for himself in the process. Thus, the two characters who most clearly represent materialism or "prose" in the novel are black characters with imitation white values. Though Bone is correct in relating this aspect of the novel to the "Harlem Renaissance" fiction which ridiculed the black middle class (p. 129), the degree of white influence needs to be stressed.

Tea-Cake, in contrast to these two characters, worries very little about money; instead he plays the banjo, hunts, plays checkers, and gives mammoth parties. It is significant that nearly all their acquaintances believe that Tea-Cake only wants to marry Janie for her money—they also bear signs of white brain-washing. Bone is right to associate Tea-Cake with the "folk culture," but specifically he represents that hedonistic element in the folk which lives only for momentary sensual pleasure. In fact, Tea-Cake can be compared to the *paisanos* in Steinbeck's *Tortilla Flat*—the "primitives" who love only for live fighting, and a glass of wine.

It is through her treatment of time, more than any other single element, that Miss Hurston brings these conflicts to a focus. There are actually three concepts of time in the novel. First, the strictly deterministic view of time as a force leading inexorably to death; the opening metaphor of the novel emphasizes this idea:

> Ships at a distance have every man's wish on board. For some they come in with the tide. For others they sail forever on the horizon, never out of sight, never landing until the Watcher turns his eyes away in resignation, *his dreams mocked to death by Time. That is the* life of men.
>
> [p. 15. Italics mine.]

When Jody is struggling with death, the doctor assures Janie of its inevitability with these words: "'Just a matter of time'" (p. 72). Interestingly, on his deathbed, Jody turns to the folk culture for aid—he hires a conjure man. It is, of course, far too late for such an abrupt change in his life; for he has ridiculed the folk throughout the novel. After the townspeople have engaged in a mock funeral for a mule, Jody ridicules them. Janie answers: "'Everybody can't be lak you, Jody. Somebody is bound tuh want tuh laugh and play.'" Jody replies, "'But it's uh time fuh all things'" (p. 55).

This is the second view of time in the novel—it is a thing to be measured, to be controlled rationally. This rational control is, to Jody, inevitably associated with work and making money. This view is the "white" view based upon materialism and rationality. It is no accident that Jody's answer has a Biblical ring; for the Bible is the book of that religion adopted by blacks from whites. His philosophy is what makes Jody so vulnerable to Janie's climactic verbal attack upon him. In a fit of desperation, she yells at him, in front of others, that "'When you pull down yo' britches, you look lak de change uh life'" (p. 69). In addition to the obvious assault on his manhood, this attack destroys Jody because it emphasizes the long-range failure of his method of ordering time. Money and respectability cannot prevent age and death. It is significant, in view of the sexuality associated with Tea-Cake, that Janie makes this point in a specifically sexual context. It is also significant that Tea-Cake, the epitome of hedonism, dies tragically and thus avoids old age and death.

The third concept of time is that folk hedonism personified by Tea-Cake. As mentioned, it is significant that Tea-Cake dies at the end of the novel; for, as always in a hedonistic code, sensual pleasure and a dramatic existence are no ultimate defense against death and the deterministic view of time. But, also as in traditional hedonism, such a life does mitigate death's victory. As Janie tells Tea-Cake: "'If you kin see de light at daybreak, you don't keer if you die at dusk'" (p. 131). "Dusk" inevitably must come, but enough "light" (sexuality, dramatic existence) lessens its power. This point explains the use of the hurricane in the novel—Janie's life contains more drama during it than in all the years before.

That Janie is ready for hedonism before she meets Tea-Cake is revealed several times in the novel. She sees her work in Jody's store as "a waste of life and time" (p. 48). During Jody's final illness, she has a vision of her husband's body "running down like candle grease as time moves on" (p. 70). Thus, when Tea-Cake appears and proposes an emotional, black philosophy of dealing with the passage of time, she is ready. Unlike her grandmother, Janie's blackness is still predominant and a rationally measured philosophy of time is "a waste of life" to her.

She experiences one false start with Tea-Cake. After their marriage, he leaves her for a day while he gives a mass celebration for his acquaintances. He doesn't ask Janie because he fears that her respectability as a store keeper will make her disapprove of the people he knows—people, like himself, who are embodiments of the folk heritage. During Tea-Cake's absence, "she worried time like a bone" (p. 99) and, upon his return, makes him realize that she plans "tuh partake wid everything" (p. 104) as she must for the hedonistic code to be meaningful. After this initial failure, Janie's life becomes one of uninterrupted sexuality and drama until Tea-Cake's death. Thus, when Tea-Cake is taken from her, Janie has stored up enough experience to withstand the loss. "She pulled in her horizon like a great fish-net . . . She called in her soul to come and see" (p. 159). The implication is that Janie will now develop a new method of coping with time—reflective hedonism. She will cultivate memories of sexuality and drama. She needs no new experience because her cup is full.

Bone is correct is describing ***Their Eyes Were Watching God*** as having "abnormally low racial tension" (p. 251) in the sense that the only direct protest is in Nannie's narrative of her slavery experiences and in the hurricane scenes. However, perhaps the major underlying theme is contained in the contrast between those characters (Nannie and Jody, especially) who are so white-oriented that they measure time in a rational, materialistic way and those whose blackness is so intact that they view time emotionally and hedonistically (Tea-Cake primarily). It is for the dominance of Janie's soul that they struggle; and Tea-Cake, or black purity, wins.

Note

1. Robert A. Bone, *The Negro Novel in America* (New Haven, 1968). Zora Neale Hurston, *Their Eyes Were Watching God* (New York, 1969).

ANITA M. VICKERS (ESSAY DATE 1994)

SOURCE: Vickers, Anita M. "The Reaffirmation of African-American Dignity through the Oral Tradition in Zora Neale Hurston's *Their Eyes Were Watching God.*" *College Language Association Journal* 37, no. 3 (March 1994): 303-15.

In the following essay, Vickers discusses the importance of community and oral transmission of stories in Their Eyes Were Watching God, *which she says affirms the dignity of an oppressed people.*

Their Eyes Were Watching God has been described as one African-American woman's quest for self-definition and self-discovery[1]—and also as "a love story."[2] Yet to interpret the novel in such rudimentary terms is to ignore the structural and thematic complexities within the work, a work fraught with multi-narrative frames, life/death imagery, and journey motifs, devices which intertwine and fold over upon themselves, creating a text rich in symbolism and powerful in theme. For instance, the polyphony of narrative voices creates a nested narrative structure, harmonizing with the imagery of nature, animals and the life/death cycle, each device repeating itself throughout the work. The folkloric tradition functions within the novel as a mode to create the illusion of reality. The self-reflexivity of the novel draws attention to the oral telling process while deemphasizing the writing process, thus giving the illusion within a fictional framework that this is an actual folk experience.[3]

Basically, ***Their Eyes Were Watching God*** is the song of Janie Crawford, a plaintive lament but, simultaneously, a joyous paean to the role that women play in the community as a whole and with men in particular. Janie's romantic dream of spiritual and physical fulfillment with a man makes her an Everywoman, for her dream is a universal one. Eventually, the dream is realized when she marries Tea Cake; however, her dream is not shattered at his death, for "he could never be dead until she herself had finished feeling and thinking."[4] The novel records Janie's progression from an isolated "porch sitter" to an integral part of her community. As Janie moves closer to the fulfillment of her dream, she becomes more articulate, ultimately adopting the role of storyteller, becoming a creator/artist. Thus, Janie is transformed from Mute to Muse. But this transformation is only part of a greater theme, that of the African-American affirmation of humanity through the oral tradition. In an introduction to Hurston's folklore anthology, ***Mules and Men,*** Robert E. Hemenway states that the oral tradition (in this case, African-American folklore) has historically promoted African-American dignity, and that the perpetuation of the oral transmission of folklore demonstrates that oppressed people cannot survive without a sense of self-worth and a sense of shared culture.[5]

Oral transmission also plays an integral role in ***Their Eyes Were Watching God,*** evincing the communal oneness of Eatonville, a community from which the silent Janie is excluded. The novel is therefore not only the story of the birth of an artist but a chronicle of the affirmation of the dignity of an oppressed people, of which Janie is a member.

The nested narrative device serves as an illustration of the oral tradition, for within her story (framed by a setting and a situation that is not her story) Janie recounts her life to the sympathetic Pheoby. She is, from the outset, the teller of the tale, the creator/artist. Janie is drawing upon the tradition of oral transmission as a means of self-affirmation. By choosing to tell her story to another woman, she is following the tradition of female bonding. According to Lorraine Bethel, American women have always withstood and resisted the dominant male society by bonding together, employing oral literature as a means of emotional support and survival information.[6] Consequently, the telling of her story to another woman is Janie's bonding with her community and a reaffirmation of her dignity.

The novel opens with the lyrical, third-person narrative, a narrative that, because it reappears at the end of the work, provides the overall cohesive structure. This narration is lyrical because it is characterized by its emotion, its melodic tone, and, most importantly, its evocation of a unified impression. For example, the lyrical narrator begins by introducing two dichotomous ways of viewing life:

> Ships at a distance have every man's wish on board. For some they come in with the tide. For others they sail forever on the horizon, never out of sight, never landing until the Watcher turns his eyes away in resignation, his dreams mocked to death by Time. That is the life of men.

> Now, women forget all those things they don't want to remember, and remember everything they don't want to forget. The dream is the truth. They act and do things accordingly.
>
> (9)

The dichotomy of both viewpoints stems from gender differences, the first paragraph giving the "male" view that "dreams [are] mocked to death by Time," the second revealing the "female" belief in dreams as representations of truth. In the paragraph that follows the aforementioned passage, the lyrical narrator tells the reader that the ensuing tale is a woman's story. The prose that follows will not be an historical representation of the events, but the lyrical invention of a "dream."[7] The lyrical narrative fades into the voice of the third person, omniscient narrator, a narrator who focuses on what *appears* to be Janie's ignominious return to Eatonville.

Within the subjective frame the reader is introduced to the first-narrative "chorus," albeit a distant one, for also watching Janie's return are the gossipy porch sitters, people who are described as having been "tongueless, earless, eyeless conveniences all day long" (10). After they cast aside their daytime roles as bests of burden (the narrator describes them as "mules and other brutes") they don their human "skins" once more, regaining the power of speech. A as community they bond together, using oral transmission to cement their unity, for although they are sharing culture and their ideas with one another, this sharing is based upon cruelty. Such cruelty strips them of their humanity causing them to become beast-like once more. Here, speech is used as the only weapon available to a people made helpless by their poverty. Articulation is not seen here as a creative force; rather, it is destructive. The porch sitters harbor the hope that Janie "might fall to their level some day" (11). In the meantime they lash out at her strength and dignity with piercing eyes and scathing words. They are entitled in their jealous and hostile voicing. Sadly, the porch sitters' futile attempts at reaffirming their own self-worth is at the expense of a member of their own community.

The narrative then moves from the scene of the porch sitters surveying their world tot he dimly lit vignette of two women on a porch at dusk. With this shift in scene comes a shift in tone, a tone which encompasses a more positive view of humanity. Both women desire the bonding that comes from self-disclosure, Pheoby "eager to feel and do through Janie" and Janie seduced into the role of storyteller by—as the narrator tells us—"that oldest human longing—self-revelation." (18). Juxtaposed against the motif of words wielded as weapons is this scene where speech serves as a balm, as a healing device. The narrative voice has now shifted to the first person. Janie is asserting her right to tell her own story to her "kissin'-friend." Words here are used to express the personal vision, the woman's dream which was first alluded to in the lyrical narrative. There is an implied understanding at this point that Phoeby will retell Janie's story to the hostile porch sitters, the *true* audience of the narrative. The porch sitters will, in turn, retell it among themselves, giving the story another life, one which is separate from the memory that lives on in Janie's mind. Her tale will then become part of the local lore, an oral art form which not only expresses the vision of a woman, but one which will teach a lesson as well.

As Phoeby's "hungry listening" (23) encourages Janie to tell her story, the narrative is reframed by the intrusion of the omniscient, third-person narrator, who becomes the speaker for the greater duration of the novel. Often this shift in voice is viewed as a flaw in the narrative.[8] It is not, I would argue, a weakness; rather, it is a consistent, symmetrical narrative device which permits Hurston to bring in events that are outside of Janie's sphere. The reframing of the narrative serves as a refocusing of subject and theme.

The omniscient, third-person narrative not only traces Janie's development and growth as a speaker but also evinces the levels of orality within the African-American community. Speech is employed within the novel to reaffirm human dignity, such as in the telling of tales; to wound and subjugate the less fortunate, as in the tongue as a weapon motif; to aggrandize one's stature in the community, as exemplified by the big talkers of Eatonville; and to rebel against the oppressive, as Janie finally does on the porch of Jody Starks's general store. Janie's tale is masterfully interwoven with such observations of orality within the community, each comparing and contrasting with the other.

Early in the novel the reader is told that Janie's definition of herself comes from others, not from within. As a child she was called "Alphabet 'cause so many people had done named me different names" (233). This unorthodox name emphasizes Janie's lack of identity; whatever name she is addressed by depends upon the perceptions of her addresser. The appellation "Alphabet" represents her muddled sense of identity. Moreover, the community's bestowal of such a name foreshadows Janie's future proclivity for linguistic creativity, the alphabet serving as the rudiments of the formation of words. It is natural that the little girl with the strange sobriquet would become the woman of powerful and eloquent speech.

Janie is not only a gifted speaker but an astute listener as well. She listens not only to other people but to the natural forces around her. Nature speaks to her and provides her with her dream of a true marriage, as demonstrated by the recounting of her observation of the pollination of the blooming pear tree: "She knew things that nobody had ever told her. For instance, the words of the trees and the wind" (44). When she answers Nature, she becomes a woman, a woman who has realized that marriage and love are not interchangeable, burying her first dream deep within her soul just as the falling seeds are buried within the ground. Both the tiny seeds and Janie's romantic dream will, nonetheless, spring forth later as mighty, leafy trees.

Janie's ensuing silence acts as a cadence in her life's song. Her dream is no longer verbally articulated but is kept within. Her leaving the inarticulate Logan Killicks for the "big voiced" Jody Starks signals the renaissance of her romantic dream. Although this dream may be composed of her old thoughts, "new words would have to be made and said to fit them" (55). These new words, however, will not be spoken. Janie's marriage to Starks isolates her from the community more so than Nanny's admonitions and Killicks's gruffness ever did. She becomes immured within herself because of Jody's edict to be silent.

While Janie has become mute during this period, the community sings with life. Central to Eatonville community life are the storytellers who pass the day sitting on the porch of Starks's store, regaling the citizenry with their tales of courtship, gossip, and Matt Bonner's old yaller mule. These tellers of tales are artists in their own right, "big picture talkers . . . using a side of the world as a canvas" (85), taking poetic license to expand upon and to emblazon their oral artistry. The artist motif is emphasized throughout the novel, the narrator commenting that when

> the people sat around on the porch and passed around the pictures of their thoughts for the others to look at and see, it was nice. The fact that the thought pictures were always crayon enlargements of life made it even nicer to listen to.
>
> (81)

One of the "crayon enlargements of life" is the "mule talk" that everyone in Eatonville engages in, that is, everyone except Mayor Starks and his silent wife. But even Jody is audience to the spinning of mule tales, punctuating the conversations with his big "heh, heh" laugh. Janie, on the other hand, is forbidden to associate with the mule talkers. (Starks hustles her off into the store when the "big picture talkers" engage in mule lore.) Janie's exclusion from the spinning of mule lore marks her isolation from the community. She enjoys the mule stories and derives great pleasure from them yet is forbidden by her husband to participate in this folkloric process, neither as a speaker nor as an audience, even though she is the most gifted storyteller of all. Her artistry is locked within since she must be content to spin mule yarns in her head.

The mule first becomes the subject of jokes, each joketeller trying to best the other. Later the jokes evolve into stories about the mule's travels, his "free-mule doings" (92). The mule has become a folk hero; new "lies" (tales) are concocted, each lie grander and more fanciful than the preceding one. He is the topic of the community and is therefore community property, just as by the end of the novel Janie's story will become community property. Finally, when the mule is found dead in an unnatural position (he is discovered on his back with his feet in the air), one of the mule talkers explains why the mule died in such a bizarre manner:

> He [the mule] had seen Death coming and had stood his ground and fought it *like a natural man.* He had fought it to the last breath. Naturally he didn't have the time to straighten himself out. Death had to take him like it found him.
>
> (93; emphasis added)

Notice that the mule has been elevated in stature: he is now a "natural man," endowed with superior "human" qualities such as fortitude and courage. Consequently, the mule stories will serve as tales of inspiration for the people of Eatonville. Like the mule they are "beasts of burden" during the daylight hours, and like the mule they can face their destinies with spirit and resolution as "natural men."

The carcass of the mule is led away in great pomp and ceremony, eulogized by Jody Starks and other "big picture talkers." Jody's eulogy evinces his own formidable powers of speech; his speech makes him "more solid than building the schoolhouse had done" (95). Starks's reputation is subsequently amplified by his skill as an artist in the oral tradition. Absent from the revelry, however, by Jody's edict, is Janie.

Although Janie was not present at the festivities, the mule funeral is retold in her story. In ad-

Playbill cover for the 1991 theatrical production of *Mule Bone,* written by Langston Hughes and Zora Neale Hurston.

dition, within the tale of the mule's funeral there is another tale, that of the fabulous buzzard feast. The unknown author of the buzzard tale has bestowed upon the vultures the gift of speech. The buzzard party consists of a "Parson" and his "flock," a flock whose choric function parallels that of the townspeople's for Mayor Starks's delivery of the eulogy. The animal story mirrors the mock funeral conducted by the humans, the birds appropriating human qualities in an emulation of the ritual performed by their human counterparts.

Obviously, Janie is repeating a tale that has been told to her, just as the omniscient narrator is retelling Janie's tale for a wider audience. A purely imaginative tale is thus told within a retelling of a parodic event that has been retold to a fictional character within the framework of a fictional work. To stretch the nested narrative device even further, this is not the first time Hurston had used the tale of the old yaller mule. The mule story first appeared in Hurston's theatrical collaboration with Langston Hughes, ***Mule Bone: A Comedy of Negro Life.***[9]

The mule has become a town legend. The narrator states that although the mule may be physically gone, he is still present in "the porch talk" and in the children's visits to his "bleaching bones now and then in the spirit of adventure" (97). He not only lives again in the oral tradition, but his story has been passed on to the next generation, as well as to the literary audience.

Ironically, the subject of the mule initiates Janie's first of three public speeches in the Eatonville episode. When Jody overhears Janie muttering to herself over the tormenting of the mule, he decides to free the poor brute. Janie can hold in her feelings no longer. Bursting with pride she praises her husband before the entire town, equating him with the Great Emancipator, Abraham Lincoln. The quality of her speech does not go unnoticed by the community: "Yo' wife is uh born orator, Starks. Us never knowe dat befor'. She put jus' de right words tuh our thoughts" (92).

Janie's second speech, on the other hand, evinces her growing frustration and subsequent rebellion against her husband's oppression. Enraged by the empty talk of the "big talkers" on the porch, she preaches a sermon on women to them, verbally articulating the thoughts that Nanny had wanted to utter but never could:[10]

> "Sometimes God gits familiar wid us womenfolks too and talks His inside business. He told me how surprised He was 'bout y'all turning out so smart after Him makin' yuh different; and how surprised y'all is goin' tuh be if you ever find out you don't know half as much 'bout us as you think you do. It's so easy to make yo'self out God Almighty when you ain't got nothin' tuh strain against but women and chickens."
>
> (117)

Janie's final speech becomes her declaration of independence. After years of silently accepting Starks's verbal abuse, she figuratively emasculates him in front of his "big talker" cronies.[11] Her verbal skills are now quite impressive; she silences the supreme big voice of Eatonville, stripping him of his power of speech and, consequently, his authority.[12] Jody's only retaliation is to strike her since he has been deprived of the "only weapon of weak folks" (275): his tongue. He has reached his nadir; his only recourse is to die.

After the death of her second husband, Jody Starks, Janie is successfully wooed by the charismatic Tea Cake Woods. During her marriage to Tea Cake, she simultaneously finds her dream and her voice. Under his tutelage Janie becomes a proficient teller of tales, encouraged by his love and understanding. Unlike Starks, who had sought to "class off" Janie by forbidding her to talk to what he had labelled "trashy people" (85), Tea Cake draws her into the center of the community, whether it is by working alongside him in the muck or by watching him shoot craps on the floor of a jook joint:

> The men held big arguments here like they used to do on the store porch. Only here, she could listen and laugh and even talk herself if she wanted to. She got so she could tell big stories herself from listening to the rest.
>
> (200)

Unfortunately, Janie's happiness is short-lived. When Tea Cake goes mad after being attacked by a rabid dog, Janie uses her powers of speech to shield herself from the fiend within his brain. Ironically, this is the only time in the novel where her eloquence fails her, leaving her no choice but to resort to violent means to defend herself. Afterwards, when she cradles her dead husband's head in her lap, the narrator tells us that she "thank[ed] him wordlessly for giving her the chance for loving service" (273). Words could not defend her, nor could they express her grief. She is promptly taken into custody and tried, not by a jury of her peers but by a white court.

The actions of the African-American courtroom observers during Janie's trial in the penultimate chapter parallel the speech as a weapon motif in Chapter One. Once more the omniscient narrator intrudes: "They were there with their tongues cocked and loaded, the only real weapon left to weak folks" (275). Unlike the porch sitters, these verbal assassins are not the masters of their world; they have been silenced by the masters of the community: the white judicial system.

Conversely, Janie uses her tongue as a defense weapon—and wins. Intuitively, she knows that she is fighting not only for her life but also for the life of her dream, a fight against "lying thoughts" (278). She becomes both barrister and witness. Yet her defense is not transcribed in the narrative; rather it is briefly summarized in one paragraph. The absence of dialogue at this point permits the reader to imagine the eloquence of her defense. To include Janie's speech here in the narrative would be redundant; her defense is the story that she has just told Pheoby (and, of course, the reader through the third-person narrative). Janie's maturation as artist/creator is now complete. The verdict serves as testimony to her powers of oral expression. She has convinced the twelve white men who have sworn to uphold the law that her shooting of Tea Cake was in self-defense. More importantly, she has defended herself against the "lying thoughts," evidenced by the reactions of the white women in the courtroom. After the trial is over, these women cry and stand around Janie, protecting her from any disparaging glances or harsh words. Janie's words have surmounted all social and racial barriers. She has appealed to them as women, and as women they have absolved her from any wrongdoing. They understand her vision, which is represented by her life with Tea Cake, for it is a vision that they, as women, share and comprehend.

As Janie's tale draws to a close, there is an abrupt reversion to the early first-person narration, allowing Janie to resume and reassert her role as creator/artist. She draws and formulates her own conclusion, calling upon Pheoby to repeat her story for the porch sitters.

The inferences made at the beginning of the novel concerning the true audience of ***Their Eyes Were Watching God***—the porch sitters—are now made explicit. Thus, the reader suspects that Janie's narrative was told somewhat self-consciously because she is still, even at the completion of her tale, very much aware of this secondary, hostile audience. Because she insists that Pheoby retell the story to the porch sitters, one may assume that Janie will become part of the Eatonville folklore; her story will be told, retold and retold once more.[13] Yet there is a certain nobility in such a gesture, for the sharing of her vision may assuage the pain and frustration of those less admirable members of her own sex—and perhaps their mates. She has selflessly relinquished the possession of her vision; it now belongs to the community, an oral art form from which to share and from which to learn.

Janie's narrative does serve a didactic purpose, which it accomplishes. Witness Pheoby's reaction to Janie's tale:

> "Lawd!" Pheoby breathed out heavily. "Ah done growed ten feet higher from jus' listenin' tuh you, Janie. Ah ain't satisfied wid mahself no mo'. Ah means tuh make Sam take me fishin' wid him after this. Nobody better not criticize yuh in mah hearin'."
>
> (284)

Thus Janie's telling of her story has served two purposes. It has rejuvenated Pheoby's feelings of self-worth and has renewed her own woman's vision, a vision of truth. She will then "act and do things accordingly."

The final three paragraphs in the novel are not expressed in the first person but in the original, lyrical narrative voice; therefore, the framing of the tale is complete. Mirroring the initial lyrical narrative, this passage reiterates the theme of a woman's vision. "Women," the lyrical narrator declares at the beginning, "remember everything they don't want to forget." And at the end this same narrator reveals that for Janie, Tea Cake "could never be dead until she herself had finished feeling and thinking. The kiss of his memory made pictures of love and light against the wall" (286). The dream is still intact despite the death of the dream object.

Janie's story will live on, then, as part of the lore of the fictional town of Eatonville, enhancing and enriching the lives of its fictional audience. On a greater scale, by using the motif of the oral tradition and transforming it into the printed word, Hurston, the artist/creator, gives yet another life to Janie's dream and broadens the scope of Janie-the-fictional-character's audience. Thus ***Their Eyes Were Watching God*** perpetuates the dream of a woman, a dream that transcends racial and social lines. By using the folkloric motif within this multi-structured work, Hurston has chronicled and reaffirmed the dignity of all audiences. It is for us, the reading audience, to call in our "soul[s] to come and see" (286).

Notes

1. Missy Dehn Kubitschek, "'Tuh de Horizon and Back': The Female Quest in *Their Eyes Were Watching God,*" *Black American Literature Forum* 17 (1983): 110.
2. Robert E. Hemenway, *Zora Neale Hurston: A Literary Biography* (1977; Urbana: U of Illinois P, 1980) 231.
3. Claire Crabtree, "The Confluence of Folklore, Feminism and Black Self-Determination in Zora Neale Hurston's *Their Eyes Were Watching God,*" *Southern Literary Journal* 17 (1985): 56.
4. Zora Neale Hurston, *Their Eyes Were Watching God* (1937; Urbana: U of Illinois P, 1978) 286. Hereafter cited parenthetically in the text.
5. Robert E. Hemenway, introduction, *Mules and Men,* by Zora Neale Hurston (1935; Bloomington: Indiana UP, 1963) xx.
6. Lorraine Bethel, "This Infinity of Conscious Pain: Zora Neale Hurston and the Black Literary Tradition," *All the Women Are White, All the Blacks Are Men, But Some of Us Are Brave: Black Women's Studies,* ed. Gloria T. Hull, Patricia Bell Scott, and Barbara Scott (Old Westbury, New York: The Feminist Press) 179.
7. Maria Tai Wolff, "Listening and Reliving: Reading:Experience in *Their Eyes Were Watching God,*" *Black American Literature Forum* 16 (1982): 29.
8. Hemenway, *Zora Neale Hurston,* 233.
9. Hemenway, *Zora Neale Hurston* 234.
10. Elizabeth A. Meese, *Crossing the Double-Cross: The Practice of Feminist Criticism* (Chapel Hill: U of North Carolina P, 1986) 48.
11. Michael G. Cooke, *Afro-American Literature in the Twentieth Century: The Achievement of Intimacy* (New Haven: Yale UP, 1984) 77.
12. Meese 48.
13. Marjorie Pryse, "Zora Neale Hurston, Alice Walker and the 'Ancient Power' of Black Women," *Conjuring: Black Women, Fiction and Literary Tradition,* ed. Marjorie Pryse and Hortense Spillers (Bloomington: Indiana UP, 1985) 15.

MARY HELEN WASHINGTON (ESSAY DATE 1987)

SOURCE: Washington, Mary Helen. "'I Love the Way Janie Crawford Left Her Husbands': Hurston's Emergent Female Hero." In *Zora Neale Hurston: Critical Perspectives Past and Present,* edited by Henry Louis Gates, Jr. and K. A. Appiah, pp. 98-109. New York: Amistad, 1993.

In the following essay, originally published in 1987, Washington rejects previous feminist interpretations of Their Eyes Were Watching God, *finding in the novel the dominant themes of exclusion and disempowerment.*

In the past few years of teaching Zora Neale Hurston's ***Their Eyes Were Watching God,***[1] I have become increasingly disturbed by this text, particularly by two problematic relationships I see in the novel: women's relationship to the community and women's relationship to language. ***Their Eyes*** has often been described as a novel about a woman in a folk community, but it might be more accurately described as a novel about a woman outside of the folk community. And while feminists have been eager to seize upon this text as an expression of female power, I think it is a novel that represents women's exclusion from power, particularly from the power of oral speech. Most contemporary critics contend that Janie is the articulate voice in the tradition, that the novel celebrates a woman coming to self-discovery and that this self-discovery leads her ultimately to a meaningful participation in black folk traditions.[2] Perhaps. But before bestowing the title of "articulate hero" on Janie, we should look to Hurston's first novel, ***Jonah's Gourd Vine,*** to its main character, Reverend John Pearson, and to the power that Hurston is able to confer on a male folk hero.[3]

From the beginning of his life, John Pearson's relationship to the community is as assured as Janie's is problematic. Living in a small Alabama town and then in Eatonville, where Janie also migrates, he discovers his preaching voice early and is encouraged to use it. His ability to control and manipulate the folk language is a source of power within the community. Even his relationships with women help him to connect to his community, leading him to literacy and to speech while Janie's relationship with men deprive her of community and of her voice. John's friendship with Hambo, his closest friend, is much more dynamic than Janie and Pheoby's because Hurston makes the male friendship a deeper and more complex one, and because the community acknowledges and comments on the men's friendship. In his Introduction to ***Jonah's Gourd Vine,*** Larry Neal describes John Pearson's exalted function in the folk community:

> John Pearson, as Zora notes in her letter to [James Weldon] Johnson is a poet. That is to say, one who manipulates words in order to convey to others the mystery of that Unknowable force which we call God. And he is more; he is the intelligence of the community, the bearer of its traditions and highest possibilities.[4]

One could hardly make such an unequivocal claim for Janie's heroic posture in ***Their Eyes.*** Singled out for her extraordinary, anglicized beauty, Janie cannot "get but so close to them [the people in Eatonville] in spirit." Her friendship with Pheoby, occurring apart from the community, encapsulates Janie and Pheoby in a private dyad that insulates Janie from the jealousy of other women. Like the other women in the town, she is barred from participation in the culture's oral tradition. When the voice of the black oral tradition is summoned in ***Their Eyes,*** it is not used to represent the collective black community, but to invoke and valorize the voice of the black *male* community.[5]

As critic Margaret Homans points out, our attentiveness to the possibility that women are excluded categorically from the language of the dominant discourse should help us to be aware of the inadequacy of language, its inability to represent female experience, its tendency not only to silence women but to make women complicitous in that silence.[6] Part of Janie's dilemma in ***Their Eyes*** is that she is both subject and object—both hero and heroine—and Hurston, apparently could not retrieve her from that paradoxical position except in the frame story, where she is talking to her friend and equal, Pheoby Watson. As object in that text, Janie is often passive when she should be active, deprived of speech when she should be in command of language, made powerless by her three husbands and by Hurston's narrative strategies. I would like to focus on several passages in ***Jonah's Gourd Vine*** and in ***Their Eyes*** to show how Janie is trapped in her status as object, as passive female, and to contrast the freedom John Pearson has as subject to aspire to an heroic posture in his community.

In both ***Their Eyes*** and in ***Jonah's Gourd Vine*** sexuality is established in the early lives of Janie and John as a symbol of their growing maturity. The symbol of Janie's emerging sexuality is the blossoming pear tree being pollinated by the dust-bearing bee. Early in the text, when Janie is about fifteen, Hurston presents her stretched out on her back beneath a pear tree, observing the activity of the bees:

> She saw a dust-bearing bee sink into the sanctum of a bloom; the thousand sister-calyxes arch to meet the love embrace and the ecstatic shiver of the tree from root to tiniest branch creaming in every blossom and frothing with delight. So this was marriage! She had been summoned to behold a revelation. Then Janie felt a pain remorseless sweet that left her limp and languid.

She leaves this scene of the pear tree looking for "an answer seeking her" and finds that answer in the person of Johnny Taylor who, in her rapturous state, looks like a golden glorious being. Janie's first sexual encounter is observed by her grandmother and she is summarily punished.[7] To introduce such a sexual scene at the age when Janie is about to enter adulthood, to turn it into romantic fantasy, and to make it end in punishment certainly limits the possibility of any growth resulting from that experience.

John's sexual encounters are never observed by any adult and thus he is spared the humiliation and the punishment Janie endures for her adolescent experimentation. In an early scene when he is playing a game called "Hide the Switch" with the girl in the quarters where he works, he is the active pursuer, and, in contrast to Janie's romantic fantasies, John's experience of sexuality is earthy and energetic and confirms his sense of power:

> . . . when he was "it" he managed to catch every girl in the quarters. The other boys were less successful but girls were screaming under John's lash behind the cowpen and under sweet-gum trees around the spring until the moon rose. John never forgot that night. Even the strong odor of their sweaty bodies was lovely to remember. He went in to bed when all of the girls had been called in by their folks. He could have romped till morning.

A recurring symbol Hurston uses to represent John's sexuality is the train, which he sees for the first time after he meets Lucy, the woman destined to become his first wife. A country boy, John is at first terrified by the "panting monster," but he is also mesmerized by this threatening machine whose sides "seemed to expand and contract like a fiery-lunged monster." It looks frightening, but it is also "uh pretty thing" and it has as many destinations as John in his philandering will have. As a symbol of male sexuality, the train suggests power, dynamism, and mobility.[8]

Janie's image of herself as a blossom waiting to be pollinated by a bee transforms her figuratively and literally into the space in which men's action may occur.[9] She waits for an answer and the answer appears in the form of two men, both of whom direct Janie's life and the action of the plot. Janie at least resists her first husband, Logan, but once Jody takes her to Eatonville, he controls her life as well as the narrative. He buys the land, builds the town, makes Janie tie up her hair, and prescribes her relationship with the rest of the town. We know that Hurston means for Janie to free herself from male domination, but Hurston's language, as much as Jody's behavior, signifies Janie's status as an object. Janie's arrival in Eatonville is described through the eyes and speech of the men on the front porch. Jody joins the men, but Janie is seen "through the bedroom window getting settled." Not only are Janie and the other women barred from participation in the ceremonies and rituals of the community, but they become the objects of the sessions on the porch, included in the men's tale-telling as the butt of their jokes, or their flattery, or their scorn. The experience of having one's body become an object to be looked at is considered so demeaning that when it happens to a man, it figuratively transforms him into a woman. When Janie launches her most devastating attack on Jody in front of all the men in the store, she tells him not to talk about her looking old because "When you pull down yo' britches you look lak de change uh life. Since the "change of life" ordinarily refers to a woman's menopause, Janie is signifying that Jody, like a woman, is subject to the humiliation of exposure. Now that he is the object of the gaze, Jody realizes that other men will "look" on him with pity: "Janie had robbed him of his illusion of irresistible maleness that all men cherish."

Eventually Janie does speak, and, interestingly, her first speech, on behalf of women, is a commentary on the limitations of a male-dominated society.

> Sometimes God gits familiar wid us womenfolks too and talks His inside business. He told me how surprised He was 'bout y'all turning out so smart after Him makin' yuh different; and how surprised y'all is goin' tuh be if you ever find out you don't know half as much 'bout us as you think you do.

Speech does not lead Janie to power, however, but to self-division and to further acquiescence in her status as object. As her marriage to Jody deteriorates she begins to observe herself: "one day she sat and watched the shadows of herself going about tending store and prostrating itself before Jody, while all the time she herself sat under a shady tree with the wind blowing through her hair and her clothes."

In contrast to Janie's psychic split in which her imagination asserts itself while her body makes a show of obedience, John Pearson, trapped in a similarly constricting marriage with his second wife, Hattie, experiences not self-division but a kind of self-unification in which the past memories he has repressed seep into his consciousness and drive him to confront his life with Hattie: "Then too his daily self seemed to be wearing thin, and the past seeped thru and mastered him for increasingly longer periods. He whose present had always been so bubbling that it crowded out past and future now found himself with a memory." In this new state John begins to remember and visit old friends. His memories prompt him to confront Hattie and even to deny that he ever married her. Of course his memory is selective and self-serving, and quite devastating to Hattie, but it does drive him to action.

Even after Janie acquires the power of speech which allows her to stand up to Jody, Hurston continues to objectify her so that she does not take action. Immediately after Jody's death she goes to the looking glass where, she tells us, she has told her girl self to wait for her, and there she discovers that a handsome woman has taken her place. She tears off the kerchief Jody has forced her to wear and lets down her plentiful hair: "The weight, the length, the glory was there. She took careful stock of herself, then combed her hair and tied it back up again." In her first moment of independence Janie is not seen as autonomous subject but again as visual object, "seeing herself seeing herself," draping before herself that "hidden mystery" which attracts men and makes her superior to women. Note that when she turns to the mirror, it is not to experience her own sensual pleasure in her hair. She does not tell us how her hair felt to her—did it tingle at the roots? Did she shiver with delight?—no, she takes stock of herself, makes an assessment of herself. What's in the mirror that she cannot experience without it: that imaginary other whom the mirror represents, looking on in judgment, recording, not her own sensations, but the way others see her.

Barbara Johnson's reading of ***Their Eyes*** suggests that once Janie is able to identify the split between her inside and outside selves, incorporating and articulating her own sense of self-division, she develops an increasing ability to speak.[10] I have come to different conclusions: that Hurston continues to subvert Janie's voice, that in crucial places where we need to hear her speak she is curiously silent, that even when Hurston sets out to explore Janie's internal consciousness, her internal speech, what we actually hear are the voices of men. Once Tea Cake enters the narrative his name and his voice are heard nearly twice as often as Janie's. He walks into Janie's life with a guitar and a grin and tells her, "Honey since you loose me and gimme privelege tuh tell yuh all about mahself. Ah'll tell yuh." And from then on it is Tea Cake's tale, the only reason for Janie's account of her life to Pheoby being to vindicate Tea Cake's name. Insisting on Tea Cake's innocence as well as his central place in her story, Janie tells Pheoby, "Teacake ain't wasted no money of mine, and he ain't left me for no young gal, neither. He give me every consolation in the world. He'd tell 'em so too, if he was here. If he wasn't gone."

As many feminist critics have pointed out, women do get silenced, even in text by women, and there are critical places in ***Their Eyes*** where Janie's voice needs to be heard and is not, places where we would expect her as the subject of the story to speak. Perhaps the most stunning silence in the text occurs after Tea Cake beats Janie. The beating is seen entirely through the eyes of the male community, while Janie's reaction is never given. Tea Cake becomes the envy of the other men for having a woman whose flesh is so tender that one can see every place she's been hit. Sop-de-Bottom declares in awe, "wouldn't Ah love tuh whip uh tender woman lak Janie!" Janie is silent, so thoroughly repressed in this section that all that remains of her is what Tea Cake and the other men desire.

Passages which are supposed to represent Janie's interior consciousness begin by marking some internal change in Janie, then gradually or abruptly shift so that a male character takes Janie's place as the subject of the discourse; at the conclusion of these passages, ostensibly devoted to the revelation of Janie's interior life, the male voice predominates. Janie's life just before and after Jody's death is a fertile period for such self-reflection, but Hurston does not focus the attention of the text on Janie even in these significant turning points in Janie's life. In the long paragraph that tells us how she has changed in the six months after Jody's death, we are told that Janie talked and laughed in the store at time and was happy except for the store. To solve the problem of the store she hires Hezikiah "who was the best imitation of Joe that his seventeen years could make." At this point, the paragraph shifts its focus from Janie and her growing sense of independence to Hezikiah and his imitation of Jody, describing Hezikiah in a way that evokes Jody's presence and obliterates Janie. We are told at the end of the paragraph, in tongue-in-cheek humor, that because "managing stores and women store-owners was trying on a man's nerves," Hezikiah "needed to take a drink of liquor now and then to keep up." Thus Janie is not only removed as the subject of this passage but is subsumed under the male-defined category of worrisome women. Even the much-celebrated description of Janie's discovery of her split selves: "She had an inside and an outside now and suddenly she knew how not to mix them" represents her internal life as divided between two men: her outside self exists for Joe and her inside self she is "saving up" for "some man she had never seen."[11]

Critic Robert Stepto was the first to raise the question about Janie's lack of voice in ***Their Eyes.*** In his critique of Afro-American narrative he claims that Hurston creates only the illusion that Janie has achieved her voice, that Hurston's strategy of having much of Janie's tale told by an omniscient third person rather than by a first person narrator undercuts the development of Janie's "voice."[12] While I was initially resistant to this criticism of ***Their Eyes,*** my reading of ***Jonah's Gourd Vine*** suggests that Hurston was indeed ambivalent about giving a powerful voice to a woman like Janie who is already in rebellion against male authority and against the roles prescribed for women in a male dominated society. As Stepto notes, Janie's lack of voice is particularly disturbing in the courtroom scene, which comes at the end of her tale and, presumably, at a point where she has developed her capacity to speak. Hurston tells us that down in the Everglades "She got so she could tell big stories herself," but in the courtroom scene the story of Janie and Tea Cake is told entirely in third person: "She had to go way back to let them know how she and Tea Cake had been with one another." We do not hear Janie speaking in her own voice until we return to the frame where she is speaking to her friend, Pheoby.[13]

There is a similar courtroom scene in ***Jonah's Gourd Vine,*** and there is also a silence, not an enforced silence, but the silence of a man who deliberately chooses not to speak. John is hauled into court by his second wife, Hattie, on the grounds of adultery. Like the court system in ***Their Eyes,*** this too is one where "de laws and de cote houses and de jail houses all b'longed tuh white folks" and, as in Janie's situation, the black community is united against John. His former friends take the stand against him, testifying on Hattie's behalf in order to spite John, but John refuses to call any witnesses for his defense. After he has lost the trial, his friend Hambo angrily asks him why he didn't allow him to testify. John's eloquent answer explains his silence in the courtroom, but more than that, it shows that he has such power over his own voice that he can choose when and where to use it, in this case to defy a hypocritical, racist system and to protect the black community:

> Ah didn't want de white folks tuh hear 'bout nothin' lak dat. Dey knows too much 'bout us as it is, but dey some things dey ain't tuh know. Dey's some strings on our harp fuh us tuh play on an sing all tuh ourselves. Dey thinks wese all ignorant as it is, and dey thinks wese all alike, and dat dey knows us inside and out, but you know better. Dey wouldn't make no great 'miration if you had uh tole 'em Hattie had all dem mens. Dey wouldn't zarn 'tween uh woman lak Hattie and one lak Lucy, uh yo' wife befo' she died. Dey thinks all colored folks is de same dat way.

John's deliberate silence is motivated by his political consciousness. In spite of the community's rejection of him, he is still their defender, especially in the face of common adversary. Hurston does not allow Janie the insight John has, nor the voice, nor the loyalty to her people. To Mrs. Turner's racial insults, Janie is nearly silent, offering only a cold shoulder to show her resistance to the woman's bigotry. In the courtroom scene Janie is divorced from the other blacks and surrounded by a "protecting wall of white women." She is vindicated, and the black community humbled. Janie is the outsider; John is the culture's hero, their "inspired artist," the traditional male hero in possession of traditional male power.

But John's power in the community and his gift for words do not always serve him well. As Robert Hemenway asserts in his critical biography of Hurston, John is "a captive of the community's need for a public giver of words."

> His language does not serve to articulate his personal problems because it is directed away from the self toward the communal celebration. John, the man of words, becomes the victim of his bardic function. He is the epic poet of the community who sacrifices himself for the group vision.[14]

For John, words mean power and status rather than the expression of feeling. When he first discovers the power of his voice, he thinks immediately of how good he sounds and how his voice can be exploited for his benefits:

> Dat sho sound good . . . If mah voice sound *dat* good de first time Ah ever prayed in, de church house, it sho won't be de las'.

John never feels the call to preach until the day on Joe Clarke's porch when the men tease John about being a "wife-made man." One of his buddies tells him that with a wife like Lucy any man could get ahead in life: "Anybody could put hisself on de ladder wid her in de house." The following Sunday in his continuing quest for manhood and power, John turns to preaching. The dramatic quality of his preaching and his showmanship easily make him the most famous preacher and the most powerful man in the area. John's inability to achieve maturity and his sudden death at the moment of his greatest insight suggest a great deal about Hurston's discomfort with the traditional male hero, with the values of the community he represents, with the culture's privileging of orality over inward development. Janie Starks is almost the complete antithesis of John Pearson, "She assumes heroic stature not by externals, but by her own struggle for self-definition, for autonomy, for liberation from the illusions that others have tried to make her live by or that she has submitted to herself."[15]

While Janie's culture honors the oral art, "this picture making with words," Janie's final speech in ***Their Eyes*** actually casts doubt on the relevance of oral speech:

> Talkin' don't amunt tuh uh hill uh beans when you can't do nothin else . . . Pheoby you got tuh *go* there tuh *know* there. Yo papa and yo' mamma and nobody else can't tell yuh and show yuh. Two things everybody's got tuh do fuh theyselves. They got tuh go tuh God, and they got tuh find out about livin' fuh theyselves.

Janie's final comment that experience is more important than words is an implicit criticism of the culture that celebrates orality to the exclusion of inner growth. The language of men in ***Their Eyes*** and in ***Jonah's Gourd Vine*** is almost always divorced from any kind of interiority. The men are rarely shown in the process of growth. Their talking is a game. Janie's life is about the experience of relationships. Logan, Jody, and Tea Cake and John Pearson are essentially static characters, whereas Pheoby and Janie allow experience to change them. John, who seems almost constitutionally unfitted for self-examination, is killed at the end of the novel by a train, that very symbol of male power he has been seduced by all of his life.[16]

Vladimir Propp, in his study of folklore and narrative, cautions us not to think that plots directly reflect a given social order but "rather emerge out of the conflict, the contradictions of different social orders as they succeed or replace one another." What is manifested in the tensions of plots is "the difficult coexistence of different orders of historical reality in the long period of transition from one to the other . . ."[17]

Hurston's plots may very well reflect such a tension in the social order, a period of transition in which the conflictual coexistence of a predominantly male and a more egalitarian culture is inscribed in these two forms of culture heroes. Both novels end in an ambiguous stance: John dies alone, so dominated by the ideals of his community that he is completely unable to understand his spiritual dilemma. And Janie, having returned to the community she once rejected, is left in a position of interiority so total it seems to represent another structure of confinement. Alone in her bedroom she watches pictures of "love and light against the walls," almost as though she is a spectator at a film. She pulls in the horizon and drapes it over her shoulder and calls in her soul to come and see. The language of this section gives us the illusion of growth and development, but the language is deceptive. The horizon represents the outside world—the world of adventure where Janie journeyed in search of people and a value system that would allow her real self to shine. If the horizon is the world of possibility, of journeys, of meeting new people and eschewing materialistic values, then Janie seems to be canceling out any further exploration of that world. In Eatonville she is a landlady with a fat bank account and a scorn for the people that ensures her alienation. Like the heroine of romantic fiction, left without a man she exists in a position of stasis with no suggestion of how she will employ her considerable energies in her now—perhaps temporarily—manless life.

Hurston was obviously comfortable with the role of the traditional male hero in ***Jonah's Gourd Vine,*** but ***Their Eyes*** presented Hurston with a problem she could not solve—the questing hero as woman. That Hurston intended Janie to be such a hero—at least on some level—is undeniable. She puts Janie on the track of autonomy, self-realization, and independence. She allows her to put on the outward trappings of male power. Janie dresses in overalls, goes on the muck, learns to shoot—even better than Tea Cake—and her rebellion changes her and potentially her friend Pheoby. If the rightful end of the romantic heroine is marriage, then Hurston has certainly resisted the script of romance by having Janie kill Tea Cake. (Though he exists in death in a far more mythical and exalted way than in life.) As Rachel Blau Du Plessis argues, when the narrative resolves itself in the repression of romance and the reassertion of quest, the result is a narrative that is critical of those patriarchal rules that govern women and deny them a role outside of the boundaries of patriarchy.[18]

While such a critique of patriarchal norms is obvious in ***Their Eyes,*** we still see Hurston's ambivalence about Janie's role as "hero" as opposed to "heroine."[19] Like all romantic *heroines,* Janie follows the dreams of men. She takes off after Jody because "he spoke for far horizon," and she takes off after Tea Cake's dream of going "on de muck." By the rules of romantic fiction, the *heroine* is extremely feminine in looks. Janie's long, heavy, Caucasianlike hair is mentioned so many times in ***Their Eyes*** that, as one of my students said, it becomes another character in the novel. A "hidden mystery," Janie's hair is one of the most powerful forces in her life, mesmerizing men and alienating the women. As a trope straight out of the turn-of-the-century "mulatto" novel, *(Clotel, Iola Leroy, The House Behind the Cedars),* the hair connects Janie inexorably to the conventional romantic heroine. Employing other standard devices of romantic fiction, Hurston creates the excitement and tension of romantic seduction. Tea Cake—a tall, dark, mysterious stranger—strides into the novel and wrenches Janie away from her prim and proper life. The age and class differences between Janie and Tea Cake, the secrecy of their affair, the town's disapproval, the sense of risk and helplessness as Janie discovers passionate love and the fear, desire, even the potential violence of becoming the possessed are all standard features of romance fiction. Janie is not the subject of these romantic episodes, she is the object of Tea Cake's quest, subsumed under his desires, and, at times so subordinate to Tea Cake that even her interior consciousness reveals more about him than it does about her.

In spite of his infidelities, his arrogance, and his incapacity for self-reflection, John Pearson is unambiguously the heroic center of ***Jonah's Gourd Vine.*** He inhabits the entire text, his voice is heard on nearly every page, he follows his own dreams, he is selected by the community to be its leader and is recognized by the community for his powers and chastised for his shortcomings. The preacher's sermon as he eulogized John at his funeral is not so much a tribute to the man as it is a recognition that the narrative exists to assert the power of the male story and its claim to our attention. Janie has, of course, reformed her community simply by her resistance to its values. The very fact of her status as outsider makes her seem heroic by contemporary standards. Unable to achieve the easy integration into the society that John Pearson assumes, she stands on the outside and calls into question her culture's dependence on externals, its lack of self-reflection, and its treatment of women. Her rebellion changes her and her friend Pheoby, and, in the words of Lee Edwards, her life becomes "a compelling model of possibility for anyone who hears her tale."[20]

Notes

1. Zora Neale Hurston, *Their Eyes Were Watching God* (Urbana: University of Illinois Press, 1978).
2. Robert Hemenway, *Zora Neale Hurston: A Literary Biography* (Urbana: University of Illinois Press, 1977), p. 239. Hemenway says that Janie's "blossoming" refers personally to "her discovery of self and ultimately to her meaningful participation in black tradition." But at the end of *Their Eyes,* Janie does not return to an accepting community. She returns to Eatonville as an outsider, and even in the Everglades she does not have an insider's role in the community as Tea Cake does.
3. Zora Neale Hurston, *Jonah's Gourd Vine* (Philadelphia: J. B. Lippincott, 1971).
4. Ibid., p. 7.
5. Henry Louis Gates, Jr., "Zora Neale Hurston and the Speakerly Text," in *The Signifying Monkey* (New York: Oxford University Press, 1987). Gates argues that *Their Eyes* resolves the implicit tension between standard English and black dialect, that Hurston's rhetorical strategies create a kind of new language in which Janie's thoughts are cast—not in black dialect per se but a colloquial form of standard English that is informed by the black idiom. By the end of the novel this language (or free indirect discourse) makes Janie's voice almost inseparable from the narrator's—a synthesis that becomes a trope for the self-knowledge Janie has achieved. While Gates sees the language of *Their Eyes* representing the collective black community's speech and thoughts in this "dialect-informed" colloquial idiom that Hurston has invented, I read the text in a much more literal way and continue to maintain that however inventive this new language might be it is still often used to invoke the thoughts, ideas, and presence of men.
6. Margaret Homans, "Her Very Own Howl," *SIGNS* 9 (Winter 1983): 186-205.
7. One of the ways women's sexuality is made to seem less dignified than men's is to have a woman's sexual experience seen or described by an unsympathetic observer. A good example of the double standard in reporting sexual behavior occurs in Ann Petry's "In Darkness and Confusion" in *Black Voices: An Anthology of Afro-American Literature,* ed. Abraham Chapman (New York: New American Library 1968), pp. 161-91. The young Annie Mae is observed by her uncle-in-law who reports that her sexual behavior is indecent. In contrast, his son's sexual adventures are alluded to respectfully as activities a father may not pry into.
8. The image of the train as fearsome and theatening occurs in Hurston's autobiography, *Dust Tracks on a Road; An Autobiography,* ed. Robert Hemenway (Urbana: University of Illinois Press, 1984). When she is a young girl on her way to Jacksonville, Zora, like John Pearson, is at first terrified of its "big, mean-looking eye" and has to be dragged on board "kicking and screaming to the huge amusement of everybody but me." Later when she is inside the coach and sees the "glamor of the plus and metal," she calms down and begins to enjoy the ride which, she says "didn't hurt a bit." In both *Dust Tracks* and *Jonah's Gourd Vine* the imagery of the train is clearly sexual, but, while Zora sees the train as something external to herself, something that is powerful but will not hurt her, John imagines the train as an extension of his own power.
9. Teresa De Lauretis, *Alice Doesn't: Feminism, Semiotics, Cinema* (Bloomington: Indiana University Press, 1984), p. 143. De Lauretis notes that the movement of narrative discourse specifies and produces the masculine position as that of mythical subject and the feminine position as mythical obstacle, or, simply "the space in which that movement occurs."
10. I am indebted to Barbara Johnson for this insight which she suggested when I presented an early version of this paper to her class of Afro-American women writers at Harvard in the fall of 1985. I was struck by her comment that Jody's vulnerability makes him like a woman and therefore subject to this kind of attack.
11. Barbara Johnson, 'Metaphor, metonymy and voice in *Their Eyes Were Watching God,*" in *Black Literature and Literary Theory,* ed. Henry-Louis Gates, (New York: Methuen, 1984), pp. 204-19. Johnson's essay probes very carefully the relation between Janie's ability to speak and her ability to recognize her own self-division. Once Janie is able "to assume and articulate the incompatible forces involved in her own division," she begins to achieve an authentic voice. Arguing for a more literal reading of *Their Eyes,* I maintain that we hear precious little of Janie's voice even after she makes this pronouncement of knowing that she has "an inside and an outside self." A great deal of the "voice" of the text is devoted to the men in the story even after Janie's discovery of self-division.
12. Robert Stepto, *From Behind the Veil: A Study of Afro-American Narrative* (Urbana: University of Illinois Press, 1979), pp. 164-67).

    When Robert Stepto raised this issue at the 1979 Modern Language Association Meeting, he set off an intense debate. While I do not totally agree with his reading of *Their Eyes* and I think he short-changes Hurston by alloting so little space to her in *From Behind the Veil,* I do think he is right about Janie's lack of voice in the courtroom scene.
13. More accurately the style of this section should be called *free indirect discourse* because both Janie's voice and the narrator's voice are evoked here. In his *Introduction to Poetics: Theory and History of Literature,* vol. I

(Minneapolis: University of Minnesota Press, 1982), Tzvetan Todorov explains Gerard Genette's definition of free indirect discourse as a grammatical form that adopts the indirect style but retains the "semantic nuances of the 'original' discourse."

14. Hemenway, *Zora Neale Hurston,* p. 198.

15. Mary Helen Washington, "Zora Neale Hurston: A Woman Half in Shadow," in *I Love Myself When I Am Laughing. . . . And Then Again When I Am Looking Mean and Impressive: A Zora Neale Hurston Reader,* ed. Alice Walker (Old Westbury, N.Y.: Feminist Press, 1979), p. 16. In the original version of this essay, I showed how Joseph Campbell's model of the hero, though it had been applied to Ralph Ellison's invisible man, could more appropriately be applied to Janie, who defies her status as the mule of the world, and, unlike Ellison's antihero, does not end up in an underground hideout.

    Following the pattern of the classic mythological hero, defined by Campbell in *The Hero with a Thousand Faces,* (Princeton, N.J.: Princeton University Press, 1968), Janie leaves her everyday world to proceed to the threshold of adventure (leaves Nanny and Logan to run off with Jody to Eatonville); she is confronted by a power that threatens her spiritual life (Jody Starks and his efforts to make her submissive to him); she goes beyond that threat to a world of unfamiliar forces some of which threaten her and some of which give aid (Tea Cake, his wild adventures, and his ability to see her as an equal); she descends into an underworld where she must undergo the supreme ordeal (the journey to the Everglades; the killing of Tea Cake and the trial); and the final work is that of the return when the hero reemerges from the kingdom of dread and brings a gift that restores the world (Janie returns to Eatonville and tells her story to her friend Pheoby who recognizes immediately her communion with Janie's experience "Ah done growed ten feet higher from jus' listenin' tuh you, Janie").

16. Anne Jones, "Pheoby's Hungry Listening: Zora Neale Hurston's *Their Eyes Were Watching God*" (Paper presented at the National Women's Studies Association, Humboldt State University, Arcata, California, June 1982).

17. De Lauretis, *Alice Doesn't,* p. 113. In the chapter, "Desire in Narrative," De Lauretis refers to Vladimir Propp's essay, "Oedipus in the Light of Folklore," which studies plot types and their diachronic or historical transformations.

18. Rachel Blau Du Plessis, *Writing Beyond the Ending: Narrative Strategies of Twentieth-Century Women Writers* (Bloomington: Indiana University Press, 1985). Du Plessis asserts that "it is the project of twentieth-century women writers to solve the contradiction between love and quest and to replace the alternate endings in marriage and death that are their cultural legacy from nineteenth-century life and letters by offering a different set of choices."

19. Du Plessis distinguishes between *hero* and *heroine* in this way: "the female hero is a central character whose activities, growth, and insight are given much narrative attention and authorial interest." By *heroine* she means "the object of male attention or rescue." (*Writing Beyond the Ending,* n. 22, p. 200), Hurston oscillates between these two positions, making Janie at one time a conventional romantic heroine, at other times a woman whose quest for independence drives the narrative.

20. Lee R. Edwards, *Psyche As Hero: Female Heroism and Fictional Form* (Middletown, Conn.: Wesleyan University Press, 1984), p. 212.

FURTHER READING

Bibliography

Davis, Rose Parkman. *Zora Neale Hurston: An Annotated Bibliography and Reference Guide.* Westport, Conn. Greenwood Press, 1997, 210 p.

Detailed bibliography of Hurston's writing and secondary literature in the following categories: books, dissertations, essays, periodical literature, reviews, bibliographies, biographical information, anthological work, juvenile literature, media resources, Internet sites, special collections, and chronological listing of works.

Biographies

Hemenway, Robert E. *Zora Neale Hurston: A Literary Biography.* Chicago: University of Illinois Press, 1977, 271 p.

In-depth study of Hurston's life and works, from the beginning of her writing career to her death in 1960.

Kaplan, Carla, editor. *Zora Neale Hurston: A Life in Letters.* New York: Doubleday, 2002, 864 p.

Includes about 600 letters by Hurston to various correspondents, including Langston Hughes, W. E. B. Du Bois, Carl Van Vechten, and her patron, Charlotte Osgood Mason.

Criticism

Awkward, Michael, ed. *New Essays on "Their Eyes Were Watching God."* New York: Cambridge University Press, 1990, 129 p.

Essays on Their Eyes Were Watching God *by Robert Hemenway, Nellie McKay, Hazel V. Carby, Rachel Blau Du Plessis, and others.*

Bloom, Harold, ed. *Modern Critical Interpretations on Zora Neale Hurston's "Their Eyes Were Watching God."* New York: Chelsea House Publishers, 1987, 130 p.

Collection of eight essays on Hurston's most famous novel written by leading critics, including Barbara Johnson, Henry Louis Gates, and Houston Baker.

Bone, Robert. *The Negro Novel in America,* revised edition. New Haven: Yale University Press, 1965, 268 p.

Offers a brief biography and critical assessments of Jonah's Gourd Vine *and* Their Eyes Were Watching God.

———. *Down Home: A History of Afro-American Short Fiction from Its Beginnings to the End of the Harlem Renaissance.* New York: G. P. Putnam's Sons, 1975, 328 p.

Places Hurston in the pastoral tradition.

Byrd, James W. "Zora Neale Hurston: A Novel Folklorist." *Tennessee Folklore Society Bulletin* 21 (1955): 37-41.

Discusses Hurston's use of folklore in her fiction.

Champion, Laurie, and Bruce A Glasrud. "Zora Neale Hurston (1891-1860)." *American Women Writers, 1900-1945: A Bio-Bibliographical Critical Sourcebook,* edited by Laurie Champion, pp. 162-72. Westport: Greenwood, 2000.

Presents a biography of Hurston, discusses her major works, and surveys the major general studies of her writings.

Ford, Sarah. "Necessary Chaos in *Their Eyes Were Watching God.*" *CLA Journal* 43, no. 4 (June 2000): 407-19.

Contends that the hurricane is central to the narrative of the novel.

Gates, Jr., Henry Louis, and K. A. Appiah, eds. *Zora Neale Hurston: Critical Perspectives Past and Present.* New York: Amistad, 1993, 330 p.

Collection of reviews by Hurston's contemporaries and essays by the leading Hurston scholars.

Grant, Alice Morgan, ed. *All about Zora: Views and Reviews by Colleagues and Scholars.* Florida: Four-G Publishers, Inc., 1991, 127 p.

Compilation of papers presented at the 1990 Academic Conference of the Zora Neale Hurston Festival of the Arts, offering insights into Hurston's life and works.

Helmick, Evelyn T. "Zora Neale Hurston." *The Carrell* 11, nos. 1-2 (June-December 1970): 1-19.

General introduction to Hurston's works.

Howard, Lillie P. "Marriage: Zora Neale Hurston's System of Values." *College Language Association Journal* 21, no. 2 (December 1977): 256-68.

Discusses the idea of marriage, which figures prominently in Hurston's works.

———. 0*Zora Neale Hurston.* Boston: Twayne Publishers, 1980, 192 p.

Provides a biography and detailed readings of the major works in the context of Hurston's life and personality.

Hurst, Fannie. "Zora Neale Hurston: A Personality Sketch." *Yale University Library Gazette* 35 (1960): 17-22.

Reminiscences from Hurston's one-time employer noting her unpredictability.

Jones, Evora. "Ascent and Immersion: Narrative Expression in *Their Eyes Were Watching God.*" *CLA Journal* 39, no. 3 (March 1996): 369-79.

Argues that Hurston's narrative expression in Their Eyes Were Watching God *is that of ascent and immersion, as the protagonist Jamie moves from a bound selfhood to a free selfhood.*

Kilson, Marion. "The Transformation of Eatonville's Ethnographer." *Phylon* 33, no. 2 (summer 1972): 112-19.

Discussion of Hurston's change from an ethnographic artist to a critical ethnographer.

Rayson, Ann. "*Dust Tracks on a Road*: Zora Neale Hurston and the Form of Black Autobiography." *Negro American Literature Forum* 7 (summer 1973): 39.

Views Hurston's work as different from that of other African American autobiographers.

Southerland, Ellease. "The Novelist-Anthropologist's Life/Works." *Black World* 23, no. 10 (August 1974): 20-30.

General introduction to Hurston and her works.

Turner, Darwin. *In a Minor Chord: Three Afro-American Writers and Their Search for Identity.* Carbondale: Southern Illinois University Press, 1971, 155 p.

Discussion of Jean Toomer, Countee Cullen, and Hurston that recognizes Hurston's value as novelist but sees many flaws in her work.

Verdelle, A. J. "The Largesse of Zora Neale Hurston." *Village Voice* XLVII, no. 16 (April 2002):17-23.

Discusses the publication of Hurston's Every Tongue Got to Confess: Negro Folk-Tales from the Gulf States *fifty years after it was written.*

Walker, Alice. "In Search of Zora Neale Hurston." *Ms. Magazine* (March 1975): 74-79, 85-89.

Chronicles Walker's trek to Florida to place a marker on Hurston's unmarked grave; interspersed with a running commentary by Robert Hemenway.

Walker, S. Jay. "Zora Neale Hurston's *Their Eyes Were Watching God*: Black Novel of Sexism." *Modern Fiction Studies* 20 (1974-5): 519-27.

Argues that the novel is all about sexism and thus anticipates the feminist movement.

OTHER SOURCES FROM GALE:

Additional coverage of Hurston' life and career is contained in the following sources published by the Gale Group: *African American Writers,* Eds. 1, 2: *American Writers Supplement,* Vol. 6; *Authors and Artists for Young Adults,* Vol. 15; *Beacham's Guide to Literature for Young Adults,* Vol. 12; *Black Literature Criticism* Vol. 2; *Black Writers,* Eds. 1, 3; *Concise Dictionary of American Literary Biography Supplement; Contemporary Authors,* Vols. 85-88; *Contemporary Authors New Revision Series,* Vol. 61; *Contemporary Literary Criticism,* Vols. 7, 30, 61; *Dictionary of Literary Biography,* Vols. 51, 86; *DISCovering Authors; DISCovering Authors: Canadian Edition; DISCovering Authors Modules: Most-studied Authors, Multicultural Authors,* and *Novelists; DISCovering Authors 3.0; Drama Criticism,* Vol. 12; *Drama for Students,* Vol. 6; *Exploring Novels; Exploring Short Stories; Feminist Writers; Literature and Its Times,* Vol. 3; *Major 20th-Century Writers,* Eds. 1, 2; *Modern American Women Writers; Novels for Students,* Vol. 3; *Reference Guide to American Literature,* Ed. 4; *Reference Guide to Short Fiction,* Ed. 2; *St. James Guide to Young Adult Writers; Short Story Criticism,* Vol. 4; *Short Stories for Students,* Vols. 1, 6, 11; and *World Literature Criticism Supplement.*

INDEXES

The main reference

Hughes, (James) Langston (1902-1967) **1:** 24, 82, 87, 91–92, 94, 124, 176, 191, 215, 253, 257, 279, 281–282, 284–285, 288, 307, 321–325, 348–363, 438–443, 442–443; **2:** 69, 171, 373, 413, **595–646,** 652; **3:** 5, 39, 144, 199, 281, 282, 290, 296, 299, 315, 347–348, 390–391, 413, 482, 593–594

lists the featured author's entry in either volume 2 or 3 of Harlem Renaissance; *it also lists commentary on the featured author in other author entries and in volume 1, which includes topics associated with the Harlem Renaissance. Page references to substantial discussions of the author appear in boldface.*

The cross-references

See also AAYA 12; AFAW 1, 2; AMWR 1; AMWS 1; BLC 2; BW 1, 3; CA 1-4R; 25-28R; CANR 1, 34, 82; CDALB 1929-1941; CLC 1, 5, 10, 15, 35, 44, 108; CLR 17; DA; DA3; DAB; DAC; DAM DRAM, MST, MULT, POET; DC 3; DLB 4, 7, 48, 51, 86, 228; EXPP; EXPS; JRDA; LAIT 3; MAICYA 1, 2; MTCW 1, 2; PAB; PC 1; PFS 1, 3, 6, 10; RGAL 4; RGSF 2; SATA 4, 33; SSC 6; SSFS 4, 7; WCH; WLC; WP; YAW

list entries on the author in the following Gale biographical and literary sources:

AAL: Asian American Literature
AAYA: Authors & Artists for Young Adults
AFAW: African American Writers
AFW: African Writers
AITN: Authors in the News
AMW: American Writers
AMWR: American Writers Retrospective Supplement
AMWS: American Writers Supplement
ANW: American Nature Writers
AW: Ancient Writers
BEST: Bestsellers (quarterly, citations appear as Year: Issue number)
BLC: Black Literature Criticism
BLCS: Black Literature Criticism Supplement
BPFB: Beacham's Encyclopedia of Popular Fiction: Biography and Resources
BRW: British Writers
BRWS: British Writers Supplement
BW: Black Writers
BYA: Beacham's Guide to Literature for Young Adults
CA: Contemporary Authors
CAAS: Contemporary Authors Autobiography Series
CABS: Contemporary Authors Bibliographical Series
CAD: Contemporary American Dramatists
CANR: Contemporary Authors New Revision Series
CAP: Contemporary Authors Permanent Series
CBD: Contemporary British Dramatists
CCA: Contemporary Canadian Authors
CD: Contemporary Dramatists
CDALB: Concise Dictionary of American Literary Biography
CDALBS: Concise Dictionary of American Literary Biography Supplement
CDBLB: Concise Dictionary of British Literary Biography
CLC: Contemporary Literary Criticism
CLR: Children's Literature Review
CMLC: Classical and Medieval Literature Criticism
CMW: St. James Guide to Crime & Mystery Writers
CN: Contemporary Novelists
CP: Contemporary Poets
CPW: Contemporary Popular Writers
CSW: Contemporary Southern Writers
CWD: Contemporary Women Dramatists
CWP: Contemporary Women Poets
CWRI: St. James Guide to Children's Writers
CWW: Contemporary World Writers
DA: DISCovering Authors
DA3: DISCovering Authors 3.0
DAB: DISCovering Authors: British Edition
DAC: DISCovering Authors: Canadian Edition
DAM: DISCovering Authors: Modules
DRAM: Dramatists Module; *MST:* Most-Studied Authors Module;
MULT: Multicultural Authors Module; *NOV:* Novelists Module;
POET: Poets Module; *POP:* Popular Fiction and Genre Authors Module
DC: Drama Criticism
DFS: Drama for Students
DLB: Dictionary of Literary Biography
DLBD: Dictionary of Literary Biography Documentary Series
DLBY: Dictionary of Literary Biography Yearbook
DNFS: Literature of Developing Nations for Students
EFS: Epics for Students
EXPN: Exploring Novels

EXPP: Exploring Poetry
EXPS: Exploring Short Stories
EW: European Writers
FANT: St. James Guide to Fantasy Writers
FW: Feminist Writers
GFL: Guide to French Literature, Beginnings to 1789, 1798 to the Present
GLL: Gay and Lesbian Literature
HGG: St. James Guide to Horror, Ghost & Gothic Writers
HLC: Hispanic Literature Criticism
HLCS: Hispanic Literature Criticism Supplement
HW: Hispanic Writers
IDFW: International Dictionary of Films and Filmmakers: Writers and Production Artists
IDTP: International Dictionary of Theatre: Playwrights
LAIT: Literature and Its Times
LAW: Latin American Writers
JRDA: Junior DISCovering Authors
LC: Literature Criticism from 1400 to 1800
MAICYA: Major Authors and Illustrators for Children and Young Adults
MAICYA: Major Authors and Illustrators for Children and Young Adults Supplement
MAWW: Modern American Women Writers
MJW: Modern Japanese Writers
MTCW: Major 20th-Century Writers
NCFS: Nonfiction Classics for Students
NCLC: Nineteenth-Century Literature Criticism
NFS: Novels for Students
NNAL: Native North American Literature
PAB: Poets: American and British
PC: Poetry Criticism
PFS: Poetry for Students
RGAL: Reference Guide to American Literature
RGEL: Reference Guide to English Literature
RGSF: Reference Guide to Short Fiction
RGWL: Reference Guide to World Literature
RHW: Twentieth-Century Romance and Historical Writers
SAAS: Something about the Author Autobiography Series
SATA: Something about the Author
SFW: St. James Guide to Science Fiction Writers
SSC: Short Story Criticism
SSFS: Short Stories for Students
TCLC: Twentieth-Century Literary Criticism
TCWW: Twentieth-Century Western Writers
WCH: Writers for Children
WLC: World Literature Criticism, 1500 to the Present
WLCS: World Literature Criticism Supplement
WLIT: World Literature and Its Times
WP: World Poets
YABC: Yesterday's Authors of Books for Children
YAW: St. James Guide to Young Adult Writers

AUTHOR INDEX

The Author Index lists all of the authors featured in the Harlem Renaissance *set. It includes references to the main author entries in volumes 2 and 3; it also lists commentary on the featured author in other author entries and in volume 1, which includes topics associated with the Harlem Renaissance. Page references to author entries appear in boldface. The Author Index also includes birth and death dates, cross references between pseudonyms or name variants and actual names, and cross references to other Gale series in which the authors have appeared. A complete list of these sources is found facing the first page of the Author Index.*

B

Bennett, Gwendolyn B. (1902-1981) **1:** 86, 262, 324; **2: 1–34; 3:** 7, 160
See also BW 1; CA 125; DLB 51; WP

Bonner, Marita (1898-1971) **1:** 122–125, 391–392; **2: 35–59**
See also BW 2; CA 142; DFS 13; DLB 51, 228

Bontemps, Arna(ud Wendell) (1902-1973) **1:** 254, 312; **2: 61–103,** 222, 613–614; **3:** 395
See also BLC 1; BW 1; CA 1-4R; 41-44R; CANR 4, 35; CLC 1, 18; CLR 6; CWRI 5; DA3; DAM MULT, NOV, POET; DLB 48, 51; JRDA; MAICYA 1, 2; MTCW 1, 2; SATA 2, 44; SATA-Obit 24; WCH; WP

Braithwaite, William Stanley (Beaumont) (1878-1962) **1:** 293; **2: 105–143; 3:** 26, 47, 49, 133–137, 187–191
See also BLC 1; BW 1; CA 125; DAM MULT; DLB 50, 54

Brown, Sterling Allen (1901-1989) **1:** 84, 85, 87, 125–126, 214; **2: 145–203; 3:** 161–162, 291
See also AFAW 1, 2; BLC 1; BW 1, 3; CA 85-88; 127; CANR 26; CLC 1, 23, 59; DA3; DAM MULT, POET; DLB 48, 51, 63; MTCW 1, 2; RGAL 4; WP

Bruce, Richard
See Nugent, Richard Bruce

C

Casey, Patrick
See Thurman, Wallace

Christopher, Mary
See West, Dorothy

Cullen, Countee (1903-1946) **1:** 67, 77–78, 258, 276–278, 280, 295–297, 321, 324; **2:** 25, **205–258,** 589–590, 612, 633–634; **3:** 4–5, 130–133, 528, 585–586, 596–598
See also AFAW 2; AMWS 4; BLC 1; BW 1; CA 108; 124; CDALB 1917-1929; DA; DA3; DAC; DAM MST, MULT, POET; DLB 4, 48, 51; EXPP; MTCW 1, 2; PC 20; PFS 3; RGAL 4; SATA 18; TCLC 4, 37; WLCS; WP

D

Du Bois, W(illiam) E(dward) B(urghardt) (1868-1963) **1:** 22, 45, 67–68, 119, 157–158, 163, 182, 192, 220, 236–239, 249–252, 305, 316–318, 319, 324, 330–334, 335–336, 337, 388–392, 456–459, 489–490, 518–519, 545–546, 552; **2:** 83, 84–85, 132–133, 238, **259–321,** 444–445, 445, 472–473, 609; **3:** 4, 19, 26, 38, 254, 315, 322, 324, 341–345, 409, 414, 482, 488, 509, 522
See also AAYA 40; AFAW 1, 2; AMWS 2; BLC 1; BW 1, 3; CA 85-88; CANR 34, 82; CDALB 1865-1917; CLC 1, 2, 13, 64, 96; DA; DA3; DAC; DAM MST, MULT, NOV; DLB 47, 50, 91,

N

O

P

R

S

T

V

W

TITLE INDEX

The Title Index alphabetically lists the titles of works written by the authors featured in volumes 2 and 3 of Harlem Renaissance *and provides page numbers or page ranges where commentary on these titles can be found. English translations of foreign titles and variations of titles are cross referenced to the title under which a work was originally published. Titles of novels, dramas, nonfiction books, and poetry, short story, or essay collections are printed in italics; individual poems, short stories, and essays are printed in body type within quotation marks.*

A

B

C

D

E

F

G

H

I

J

K

L

M

N

O

P

Q

R

S

T

U

V

W

Y

SUBJECT INDEX

The Subject Index includes the authors and titles that appear in the Author Index and the Title Index as well as the names of other authors and figures that are discussed in the Harlem Renaissance *set. The Subject Index also lists literary terms and topics covered in the criticism. The index provides page numbers or page ranges where subjects are discussed and is fully cross referenced. Page references to significant discussions of authors, titles, or subjects appear in boldface; page references to illustrations appear in italic.*

A

B

C

SUBJECT INDEX

D

E

F

G

SUBJECT INDEX

H

SUBJECT INDEX

I

J

K

L

M

SUBJECT INDEX

N

O

P

Q

R

T

U

V

W

Y

Z